Visual Guides to Nine Essential Upgrades

Dynamic visual layouts of nine essential upgrades guide you through upgrading your computer step-by-step, including installing video cards, adding computer memory, installing DVD drives, and installing hard drives.

Building the Ultimate Computer

Create the perfect computer for you. Learn what's possible and the important steps to building your own PC *from scratch*.

This Old Computer

Don't throw out your old 486! What you need to know to rejuvenate *your legacy computers and hardware* and keep them working for you.

Software Solutions

Make your computer the best it can be. Uncover the secrets of configuring the Control Panel and improving your PC's performance.

Buyer's Guide

Learn what you need to know before you buy. "A Buyer's Guide to PCs" shows you how to get more computer for your $$$.

Extensive Glossary

Written exclusively for the eleventh edition, the glossary keeps you current with the latest computer terminology and jargon.

Portable Computing

Laptops and notebook computers are the fastest growing segment of computer system purchases. Learn the important things you need to know about connecting to networks, PCMCIA cards, and preventive maintenance for screens, cases, and batteries.

Internet Resources

Put the Web to work for you. Learn how the *Internet can be an invaluable tool* in upgrading your computer.

The Complete PC Upgrade & Maintenance Guide

Praise for the Book...

A must have for all technicians. If you only own one book as a PC technician, Mark Minasi's book is the one you should own. It is a highly recommended read (cover to cover) for anyone taking their A+ exams. The writing is clear, entertaining, easy to understand, and informative. In other words, this one won't put you to sleep like most other computer books and won't give you only half the story like the "For Dummies..." books. I only wish more books were written like this. I have owned an earlier edition of this book for two years now, and it is the only reference manual that I still use and recommend to all technicians, beginners and experts alike.

Dan D, Michigan *(courtesy of Amazon.com)*

Outstanding guide to PC hardware and its maintenance and upgrade. This instruction is lucid, erudite, and all-encompassing.... If you can afford only one guide, this would be it!

Computer Book Review

Maybe you've seen Mark Minasi on CNN, talking computers. Or maybe you've taken his legendary $800 course on PC maintenance or heard him speak at Comdex. Or perhaps you took our advice...and purchased his dynamite *Expert Guide to Windows 98*. Regardless of how you first encounter Minasi's work, you're likely to become a fan pretty quick. So when it comes time to troubleshoot those miserable computer problems that seem as inevitable as death and taxes, who better to call?...The coverage is soup-to-nuts, with detailed chapters on topics that other troubleshooting books either skip altogether or surf over lightly. Notebook computers. CD-ROM drives. Laser printers. Scanners. Modems. Sound boards, video capture cards, and other PC devices notorious for devouring both your IRQs and your patience...whether you're out to fix everyone else's computer problems or you'd be thrilled to simply fix a few of your own, no other book delivers this much authoritative, practical, easy-to-understand help—period!

Cyberian Express, Barnes & Noble

Minasi is the man!!!!!!!!! I thought I was very knowledgeable in PC repair and maintenance—that was, until I read this book. I was amazed at the total amount of information packed into the book. Minasi's ability and knowledge are evident right from the first page. Minasi is able to simplify the technical talk while giving you a detailed breakdown of the subject. The read was easy and yet info-packed. The book is for all skill levels, from novice to expert. Everyone has something to learn from this book.

Michael Woznicki, Holland, MA, A+, Net+, and MCT certified technical trainer and freelance hardware reviewer *(courtesy of Amazon.com)*

I am the Technical Committee Chair for the Computer Maintenance Technology contest. This contest essentially follows the A+ Certification standard, and your book is a key reference. If it's not on the A+ test or in your book, it's not in the contest.

John Oliphant, Technical Committee Chair, Vocational-Industrial Clubs of America (VICA)

It solved my PC problem—what more can you ask? My CD-ROM drive had been gradually failing and now it wasn't reading CDs at all. The PC maker's support site talked about reinstalling drivers and checking the configuration files. Minasi said, "Clean the drive." So I bought a CD-ROM cleaning disk and a can of compressed air for about $25, used them, and in just minutes my drive was working fine. Thanks!

Edward E. Rigdon, Associate Professor, Marketing Department, Georgia State University *(courtesy of Amazon.com)*

The Complete PC Upgrade & Maintenance Guide

More Praise for the Book...

Finally, a PC maintenance book that won't end up in storage after the first two chapters! Minasi has a gift for turning dry technical concepts and jargon into something the undergrad can understand. Fantastic book!

Troy *(courtesy of Amazon.com)*

Thanks again for writing such a wonderful book. Before I read the chapter on printers, I got a 40 percent on the pretest; after reading the two chapters on printers, I was scoring 90–100 percent on the pretest for laser printers! I passed the A+ Certification with a 93 percent overall on the hardware and 91 percent on DOS and Windows 3.11. The teacher said that 93 percent was the highest anyone has ever scored on hardware at that school! :-) Thank you for helping me start my new career and getting me back into corporate life.

Kent Harris, Certified A+ Technician

I bought your book...this past Christmas as a present to myself. It was the best money I spent.... I now treat your book like the Bible; it is a source of useful information that I can depend on.... I'm a complete dummy as far as computers go, but your book has helped me tremendously. I can now partition my hard drive correctly without too much trouble because it is easy to understand the way you have it laid out and explained. Because of your book, I don't get that sick sinking feeling every time my computer crashes.

B. Wilson, Missisauga, Ontario, Canada

I read the first chapter and couldn't put it down! I read it from cover to cover. I now own three computers (two PCs and one laptop). One of the PCs (a 486), I bought ($20) from a friend that told me it was totally fried. He had taken it to the local PC shop and they told him it was useless. I took it apart, cleaned it up, and put it back together step by step with your book. When I turned on the power switch, it booted right up! It's still going with no problems today....I now have fixed several of my friends' computers (Plug and Play, my FOOT!!!) and believe that there is nothing that I can't fix on a computer....Thanks for...taking the fear out of my favorite hobby.

Sergeant Derrick Ball, Loadmaster on the C-130 aircraft in the U.S. Marine Corps

The Complete PC Upgrade & Maintenance Guide was chosen by Heathkit Educational Systems as part of their PC Servicing and A+ Certification Preparation courses. Quite frankly, we use it because it is the best book on the subject available today.

Douglas M. Bonham, Heathkit Educational Systems

Congratulations on your excellent book, *The Complete PC Upgrade & Maintenance Guide.* We pride our PC service and repair center as being one of the best in western Pennsylvania, and your book is an integral part of our success. Not only is it required reading for every PC technician that we employ, it is the most important reference tool in our shop. The advice in the hard drive chapters alone has saved us hundreds of hours of troubleshooting throughout the years.

Anthony J. Pugliese, President, PCE Computers

It is witty, easy reading, and very informative. I find most books boring and tedious..., but this book was actually fascinating to me. I read it for hours at a time and the amazing thing is it's a technical book.... I now use it as my PC bible.

Brett Havener, Computer Tech, Proprietor, Q-Point

THE COMPLETE

PC

UPGRADE &
MAINTENANCE
GUIDE

Eleventh Edition

MARK MINASI

San Francisco • Paris • Düsseldorf • Soest • London

SYBEX®

Publisher: Jordan Gold
Contracts and Licensing Manager: Kristine O'Callaghan
Director of Special Projects: Gary Masters
Acquisitions and Developmental Editor: Ellen L. Dendy
Editors: Sally Engelfried and Sharon Wilkey
Production Editor: Kylie Johnston
Associate Production Editor: Nathan Whiteside
Technical Editor: James F. Kelly
Book Designer: Mark Ong, Side by Side Studios
Graphic Illustrators: Duane Bibby, Susie Hendrickson, Tony Jonick, and Jerry Williams!
Photo Researcher: Annette Coolidge
Electronic Publishing Specialists: Mark Ong, Side by Side Studios, and Maureen Forys, Happenstance Type-O-Rama
Proofreaders: Andrea Fox and Nancy Riddiough
Indexer: Ted Laux
CD Technicians: Keith McNeil and Ginger Warner
CD Coordinator: Kara Eve Schwartz
Beta and Licensing Specialist: Heather O'Connor
Cover Designer: emdesign

Library of Congress Card Number: 00-105606
ISBN: 0-7821-2800-9

SYBEX and the SYBEX logo are trademarks of SYBEX Inc, in the USA and other countries.

Screen reproductions produced with Collage Complete.
Collage Complete is a trademark of Inner Media Inc.

The CD interface was created using Macromedia Director, COPYRIGHT 1994, 1997–1999 Macromedia Inc. For more information on Macromedia and Macromedia Director, visit http://www.macromedia.com.

All video clips © 1999 SYBEX, Inc.

QuickTime and the QuickTime logo are trademarks used under license. QuickTime is registered in the U.S. and other countries.

TRADEMARKS: SYBEX has attempted throughout this book to distinguish proprietary trademarks from descriptive terms by following the capitalization style used by the manufacturer.

The author and publisher have made their best efforts to prepare this book, and the content is based upon final release software whenever possible. Portions of the manuscript may be based upon pre-release versions supplied by software manufacturer(s). The author and the publisher make no representation or warranties of any kind with regard to the completeness or accuracy of the contents herein and accept no liability of any kind including but not limited to performance, merchantability, fitness for any particular purpose, or any losses or damages of any kind caused or alleged to be caused directly or indirectly from this book.

An earlier version of this book was published by Compute! Books under the title *Maintaining, Upgrading, and Troubleshooting IBM PCs, Compatibles, and PS/2 Computers*. Copyright © 1990 Mark Minasi.

Manufactured in the United States of America

10 9 8 7 6 5 4 3 2 1

. . . .

To the people who have helped me and continue to help me over the years, the people who gave me a chance or gave me a hand: Ludwig Braun, Andy Kydes, Nancy Denkhe, Pete Moulton, John, Doug, Julie, and the other Data-Tech folks, Maureen Quinn, all of the thousands of students who've read this book and helped make it better, Fred Langa, Steve Levy, Wayne Rash, the Sybex gang (Dianne, Rudy, Rodnay, Gary, Neil, Ellen, Guy, Barbara, and many others), Donna Cook, Stan Altman, and everyone else I've overlooked. Thank you all very much!

ACKNOWLEDGMENTS

Since this book's first incarnation in 1986, I've had help from many people. I can't thank them all here, but let me mention a few. My apologies to anyone I miss.

A hearty thanks to Faithe Wempen, Kate Chase, and Kitty Niles for their hard work on the eleventh edition. Thanks also to Fred Jones, Bob Correll, and Rima and Tyler Regas.

Big thanks for the tenth edition updates to John Heilborn.

Thanks to Joe Jorden, Bruce Jones, and David Groth for their able contributions to the ninth edition.

Thanks to Glenn Hartwig for updating this book for the eighth edition. He provided a much needed new chapter on notebook and laptop computers (Chapter 29) as well as several new and revised topics.

Thanks to Christa Anderson for updating this book for the seventh edition. Her work was tireless, and I appreciate it.

Our artist-in-residence (even though she's no longer in residence), Elizabeth Creegan, and one of our long-time Troubleshooting instructors, Terry Keaton, did the original versions of the illustrations. They both excel in a world in which I've never exceeded apprentice status—the visual arts—and they've always been patient with my sometimes muddy requests. Thanks to them both, and (how could I forget?) thanks also to Doug Zimmer, instructor emeritus, for the original versions of the SCSI cable diagrams.

My associate, Paula Longhi, wrote the initial draft of the CD-ROM chapter, and I thank her for that.

Over the years, I've gotten plenty of editorial assistance and suggestions from Sheila Walsh, the biggest, baddest Tae Kwon Do black belt to ever open up a PC; Pete Moulton, my old partner and good buddy; and Rob Oreglia and Scott Foerster, more instructors emeriti. I continue to get good feedback from the staff of Tech Teach International: Kris Ashton, Peter Brondos, Shawn Caison, Patrick Campbell, David Costow, Eric Christiansen, Bob Deyo, Ceen Dowell, Brandi Dunnegan, Paul Eve, Scot Hull, Lisa Justice, Andrew McGoff, Ellen O'Day, Nicole Price, Holliday Ridge, David Sheridan, Marc Spedden, Frederick Thornton, and Steven Wright. And you, too, can give me feedback at `help@minasi.com` on the Internet.

And speaking of my e-mail address, thanks to all of you who have taken a few minutes to tell me how much you liked the book.

These books don't get into your hands unless some publisher who thinks they're worth it puts them there. The first such person was Stephen Levy, the publisher of the first version of this book, and my thanks go to him. Dianne King at Sybex arranged for Sybex to start publishing this; Dianne's goofing off somewhere, but we miss her. Gary Masters, the Maxwell Perkins of the computer press, remains this book's guardian angel. Thanks also to this and the previous edition's Acquisitions and Developmental Editors, Ellen Dendy, Brenda Frink, and Neil Edde. Thanks go also to past and present editors Sally Engelfried, Sharon Wilkey, Linda Lambeth Orlando, Doug Robert, Peter Weverka, Vivian Perry, and Anamary Ehlen; Technical Editors Jim Kelly, Rima Regas, Mike Hanna, Aaron Kushner, Maryann Brown, and Kim Ringer; Electronic Publishing Specialists Mark Ong, Maureen Forys, Susie Hendrickson, Tony Jonick, and Bill Gibson; Production Editor Kylie Johnston; CD Technicians Kara Schwartz and Ginger Warner; Beta and Licensing Specialist Heather O'Connor; Graphic Illustrators Duane Bibby, Susie Hendrickson, Tony Jonick, and Jerry Williams; Proofreaders Andrea Fox and Nancy Riddiough; and of course, Indexer Ted Laux.

Thanks also to the folks at Adaptec and Creative Labs, Inc. who graciously allowed us to excerpt their documentation for this book. Kudos also to Dale Palovich and his team, who put together the new videos for the tenth edition.

CONTENTS AT A GLANCE

CONTENTS

Chapter 3 Inside the PC: Pieces of the Picture **73**

Chapter 4   Avoiding Service: Preventive Maintenance   243

Chapter 5   Troubleshooting PC Problems   281

Chapter 8   Semiconductor Memory   **421**

Chapter 9   Power Supplies and Power Protection   **453**

Chapter 14 How Hard Drives Organize Data   **633**

Chapter 15 An Overview of Viruses   **657**

Chapter 17 **Understanding, Installing, and Repairing Floppy Drives**   **739**

Chapter 20   **Troubleshooting Laser Printers**   **805**

Chapter 21   Communications Devices   **859**

Chapter 22   Keyboards and Mice   **895**

Chapter 23 Video Adapters and Displays   917

Chapter 30   Using the Internet and Online Services   1209

Chapter 32 Building the Ultimate Computer   1291

Chapter 33   Software Solutions: Using the Control Panel   1351

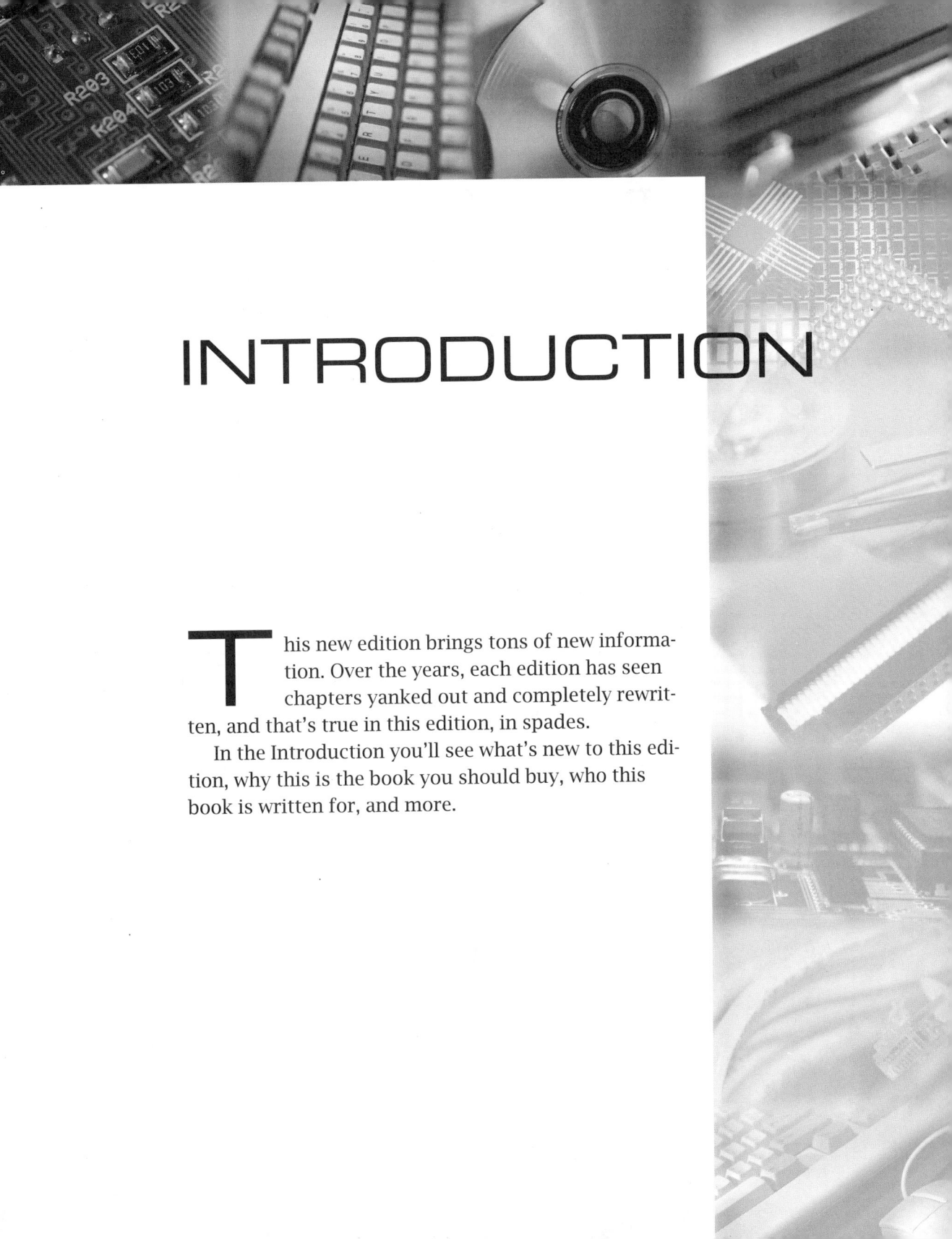

INTRODUCTION

This new edition brings tons of new information. Over the years, each edition has seen chapters yanked out and completely rewritten, and that's true in this edition, in spades.

In the Introduction you'll see what's new to this edition, why this is the book you should buy, who this book is written for, and more.

What's New in the Eleventh Edition

In some ways, the PC hardware world doesn't change much. After 12 years, VGA is still the baseline video standard and floppies still hold only 1.44MB of data. But in other ways, it's moving all the time, and that's motivated this latest overhaul of *The Complete PC Upgrade & Maintenance Guide.*

As we do each year, we've updated this edition to cover the latest technologies that affect end-users. Among the new topics included in this edition are the Athlon processor, the USB peripheral connection standard, cable modems, DSL, video capture hardware, and the MP3 audio format.

Note

Be sure to check out the bonus chapter available on the Sybex Web site (www.sybex.com) that covers storage devices. Its topics include Zip, Jaz, and tape drives.

In addition to updating the chapters to include the latest technologies, we've added handy QuickSteps sections to the beginning of many chapters—these sections get straight to the point by providing step-by-step instructions for many major upgrade and repair procedures. QuickStep sections also include a list of the items you'll need on hand, and preparations you'll need in place before you begin.

A portion of the QuickSteps sections are followed immediately by the Visual Upgrades that ran in the tenth edition, which, as their name implies, walk you through the process visually. The combination of QuickSteps, Visual Upgrades, and the videos included on the CD, will provide the confidence you need as you work through a particular procedure.

Also new to the eleventh edition are Troubleshooting sections at the end of many chapters. You'll find workarounds to many common problems concentrated in this distinct section. These sections also alert you about gotchas lurking within major hardware components and upgrading scenarios.

Why This Book?

I've been programming computers since 1973. But for years, I wasn't a "hardware guy." After moving from mainframe programming to the early PCs that came out in the mid-'70s, I watched the microcomputer market, waiting for the computer that was useful and didn't require any soldering to get it up and running.

That's why I liked the IBM PC from the very beginning. Just take it out of the box, plug some stuff together, and *voilá*! A completely usable computer—and *no soldering*.

That was, of course, until I'd had it for nine months. Then, right in the middle of doing some work, all of a sudden, the floppy drive light came on for no apparent reason, the system rebooted itself, and the number 601 appeared on the screen. Nothing else happened—the machine refused to do any more. I turned it on and off again, and it did the same thing.

"What now?" I thought. It was 1982. Replacing *everything* was expensive. Floppy drives cost $500 apiece. A PC motherboard cost $1,400. A floppy controller cost $275. Of course, all of this happened shortly *after* the warranty on my PC ran out. I had an all-IBM machine, but some of the parts came from a dealer who was not an authorized IBM dealer, so IBM wouldn't even talk to me. I went to a service department of a large computer store chain seeking help. I looked at their hourly rates and *knew* from their high prices that they must know what they're doing (I was younger and dumber), so I confidently left my machine with them. They kept the machine for two months, said they couldn't find anything wrong with it, and charged me $800.

The problem, of course, persisted. I was scared. I mean, I'd just spent some big bucks for this computer, and then add to that $800 on some non-repairs, and it still didn't work. So I figured, "What the heck, I can't make it any worse," and took the top off.

What I saw was that the drive was connected with a ribbon cable to a circuit board, a board I later found was called the "floppy controller board." The controller board was new, the drive was new (the repair shop had already replaced them)—but what about the cable? You guessed it; $35 bought a new cable from a local computer supply place, and the problem went away forever.

I found out that I wasn't the only person with PC repair needs. On average, seven out of ten PCs suffer a breakdown of some kind. It takes an average of five days to fix, and the fix costs an average of $257. (This is according to a survey from the Business Products Consulting Group. The results were based on a survey of 500 business users. Besides, it was about time to throw in a statistic.) Even if you pay a maintenance company lots of money to keep your machines in shape, you should *still* do whatever repairs you can. That's because the big cost of machine failures isn't the cost of the machine—it's the cost of lost employee time, as employees must wait in line to use machines or forgo the services of a PC altogether. You may have to wait four hours for a service person, only to find that the fix was a simple five-minute operation. The result: four hours of lost employee time. Furthermore, and perhaps more important, service bureaus don't repair hard disks; they throw them away—along with your data. It's not hard to bring dead hard drives back to life, as you'll learn in this book.

Emboldened by my success, I read what few references existed about microcomputer repair, and I tried fixing a lot of things. Some things got fixed, some got "smoked." I asked a lot of questions and made a lot of mistakes, and finally got to the point where at worst I didn't do any damage and usually met with success. I'd like to accelerate *you* to that point with this book. (But you'll still "smoke" the occasional device—everybody does.) Once I figured out how simple it was to fix PCs, I developed a series of seminars on PC repair that I conduct in the United States, Canada, and Europe. By 1994, more than 30,000 people had attended those seminars.

That's why you're reading this. (Unless you're thumbing through it in the bookstore. If you are, then *buy* the silly thing. Hundreds of thousands of people already have, so it's a good bet that you'll like it.)

This book won't teach you to fix *all* problems. Not all problems *can* be fixed—for instance, leaving your hard disk out in the rain will probably render your erstwhile data storage medium usable for little more than a paperweight. Nevertheless, even if you've never opened up a PC or installed an expansion board, this book can help you.

It will also help with terminology. Part of your job may involve talking to technical types. Some of those folks are good at talking to ordinary mortals, but there are some (and I'm sure you know a few of them) who can't seem to speak a single sentence without a liberal sprinkling of TLAs (you know, Three-Letter Acronyms). A thorough reading of this book will enable you to speak fluent "PC-ese," and the index will point you to definitions of most PC terms.

You'll also see a fair amount about installation in this book. Installation of new equipment often brings headaches: how to do it, why doesn't it work once installed, testing the new equipment, ensuring that it doesn't adversely affect already installed equipment. And I'll talk about how to take a tired old PC and soup it up to get better performance from it.

In the process of working with IBM PCs since 1981 and microcomputers since 1976, I have picked up or written a number of very useful utilities that assist in the diagnosis of PC problems. I'll discuss them in this book, and you'll find the programs on the book's CDs.

Who Is This Book For?

I'm writing this for the needy and the curious. Some of you *must* understand the machines that you depend on so much so that you can better keep them in top shape. Others may just wonder what's going on under the hood. Whoever you are, dig in and try something!

So don't let that useful little gray box on your desk control *you* when it goes down. Take control of *it*. (Remember who's supposed to be boss.) Even if you never take the machine apart (coward!), you'll still learn a lot about what goes on under the hood of your machine, and how to make it work faster and live longer.

Terminology

There are so many machines that it's hard to know how to refer generically to PCs. So here's the informal convention that I'll use in this book: when I say *PC* in this text, I include all PC-compatible machines—anything from an 8088 CPU to a Pentium II/Xeon, a laptop to a desktop, big to small, unless otherwise specified. Where necessary, I'll use *XT* to refer to XTs and XT clones—the 8088-based machines that you may still have hanging around. I'll use *AT* to refer to 286, 386, 486, Pentium, Pentium Pro/II, or Pentium III machines in general. More specifically, an *AT-type machine* is a desktop machine using a processor of 286 or later vintage. Most nowadays use a combination of expansion slots called "ISA" and "PCI" slots, but you may come across other kinds like EISA and VESA bus slots (and don't worry, I'm going to explain what those are in greater detail in Chapter 3, "Inside the PC: Pieces of the Picture"). Examples of those machines include not only the common clone, but also big names like Compaq, HP, Dell, Gateway, and Packard Bell.

Back in 1987, IBM decided to go its own way in the PC market, so I'll usually be specific about discussing IBM machines. *PS/2* refers to the Micro Channel-based (again, another Chapter 3 term) PS/2s, the ones numbered from 50 up. They're not making them any more (to my knowledge), but you'll probably come across Micro Channel machines now and then. Currently IBM's focusing on building machines pretty much like others', basically souped-up AT architectures.

My goal in developing this book is to include material of use to "techies" as well as to those who've never even opened up a PC. I'm not going to try to make an electrical engineer out of you; I'm not one myself. All it takes to do most PC maintenance is a screwdriver and some patience. I've made every effort to keep the jargon to a minimum and to define unusual PC terms when I use them. I *am* going to use jargon, however, as it will get you used to the "industry-speak"; that will equip you to read industry journals, Web sites, and other books.

Structure of This Book

First, we'll take a minute to survey the machines out on the market and look at the features that separate one type of PC from another. Then we'll look under the hood and see what's inside a PC. After that we'll step back and examine some preventive maintenance techniques and troubleshooting approaches. Next we'll look in detail at circuit boards, fixing dead machines, and PC memory. Then you'll learn all about hard disks: how they work, how to install them, how to do data recovery on them, and everything you could ever need to know about viruses and virus prevention. The book then takes a look at floppy disks, printers, and multimedia essentials (CD-ROMs, sound cards, and video capture boards). There's even a whole chapter on tapping into the vast sea of resources and information available on the Internet. Chapter 31, "This Old Computer," is designed for those of you with legacy equipment and Chapter 32, "Building the Ultimate Computer," provides step-by-step instructions for assembling a cutting-edge PC. Finally, we wrap up neatly with an extensive hardware glossary for easy reference.

Safety Notes and Cautions

Before we get started, a few words of disclaimer:

Please heed the warnings that you'll see in the text. Read *all* of a chapter before trying surgery. The reason for this is simple. If I've put something in an order that isn't clear, you could damage the computer or yourself.

I mention many products in this text. I am not endorsing these products. Where I make note of them, they have been of value to me.

However, manufacturer quality can vary, and goods can be redesigned.

In general, it's pretty hard to hurt yourself with a PC, short of dropping it on your toe. But there are a few exceptions.

▶ Power Supply: There's a silver or black box with a fan in it in the back of your machine. It's the power supply; it converts AC from the wall socket into DC for the PC's use. You can't miss the label, in five languages, that says, "If you open me, I'll kill you." Do not open it.

If you were to open the top of the power supply while the machine was plugged in, or even if the power was off, you could get a full 120 volts (220–240 for those of you on the other side of the Atlantic) through you if you touched the wrong things. Even if it's not plugged in, there are power-storing devices called *capacitors* that can give you a good shock even after the machine has been unplugged and turned off. The same, by the way, goes for monitors: don't open them up.

Warning

Let me reiterate this: do not open the power supply or the monitor. Under the wrong circumstances *it could kill you*. There's always somebody who doesn't pay attention to the important stuff, but PAY ATTENTION TO THIS WARNING.

▶ It is certainly safe to *replace* a power supply, although when doing such a replacement, again, be double sure that it is unplugged before removing the original power supply. More important, why go into the power supply in the first place? The only possible user repair I can imagine is to replace the fuse in the box, and again, don't even think of trying it unless you know how to discharge large capacitors safely.

▶ Another power supply item. Never connect a power supply to the wall socket and turn it on *when it is not connected to a PC motherboard*. Only turn on a power supply when the motherboard power connectors are in place.

Why? Back in the original PC days, some of the power supplies on the market would literally *explode* if you ran them like this (called "running it without a load"). Power supplies aren't glamorous things; no one touts the quality of their power supplies when selling PCs. Result? The cheapest power supplies possible get put into PCs. Your modern power supply is almost certainly not one of the explosive kinds, but I'd avoid the risk, myself. Besides, there isn't anything that you can test with a power supply just standing alone.

▶ Unless it's an emergency procedure, *back up* your data before doing anything drastic. What if something goes wrong and the machine never comes back?

▶ You can damage circuit boards by removing them with the power on. Don't do it. Turn the machine off before removing a circuit board.

▶ Take static electricity precautions; they're discussed in Chapter 4, "Avoiding Service: Preventive Maintenance."

The rest of the things you'll find in the PC are safe, but don't ignore these warnings.

Having said all of that, welcome! Let's get to know your PC better and have some fun in the process.

Five Easy Pieces: PC Hardware in a Nutshell

If you have any experience with buying, using, or fixing PCs, you've no doubt heard a bushel of strange terms—RAM, CPU, USB, PCI, FireWire, Pentium, Itanium, you name it. And believe me, it's not going to get any better, because this business *loves* jargon.

Since their introduction in the 1980s, PCs have continued to evolve nonstop. The most recent changes are bringing them more closely in line with consumer hardware such as video cameras, DVD players, and televisions. Standards tend to feel less chiseled in stone and more written in shifting sand. Until today, our consumer electronics and our PCs really didn't talk to one another or know the other existed. But technology is moving towards a wired home. You'll be able to turn the TV on by a click of the PC keyboard, and your PC's hard drive or recordable DVD drive will automatically record a TV show while you work on an Excel worksheet. Different companies are coming up with different ways to implement this type of technology, fueling a rapid-pace change in hardware and increasing the number of "standards."

There's also a trend to put add-on hardware boards like video and sound cards, and even modems, right on the motherboards to save a little extra money in production.

If you don't know already, the motherboard is the central board in a PC to which everything else ultimately connects. The motherboard has a socket or slot for the CPU (Central Processing Unit), expansion slots to add other hardware boards that control things like video and audio, ports to which devices like your mouse connect, sockets for adding extra RAM, and connectors called IDE channels for plugging in hard drives. You'll learn a lot more about them in Chapter 3, "Inside the PC: Pieces of the Picture."

Seriously, PC hardware *can* be confusing because there are so many parts to a PC—and some of these parts change pretty quickly. I wish I could write this book so that it completely avoids the geeky details like, "the standard keyboard port uses I/O addresses 60 hex through 64 hex and IRQ1," but ultimately you'll *have* to know that stuff or you won't really be effective as a buyer, upgrader, or fixer. (A *keyboard port*, by the way, is the connector and circuitry in the computer that makes it possible for you to attach a keyboard to your PC.) And until they get those direct neural interfaces working in the next century or two, keyboards will remain kind of essential. I'll explain that "IRQ" and "I/O" stuff in Chapter 6, "Installing New Circuit Boards (without Creating New Problems)." Jumping in at that level right now, however, would probably convince the average reader that perhaps quantum physics would be a simpler course of study.

Knowledge really *is* power where computers are concerned. What we need, then, is some structure, along with a bird's-eye view of PC hardware. It's a lot easier to understand some new term if you've got a classification system. What I'm going to explain in this chapter is the mental model that I use to understand PC hardware. It's not perfect—not *everything* will fit into this model—but I think you'll find it useful in your hardware education.

CPUs, Peripherals, and Controllers

Basically, PC hardware boils down to three kinds of devices: the *Central Processing Unit* (*CPU*) (or, as more and more machines offer multiprocessor capabilities, the CPUs), *peripherals* (the input, output, and storage devices that the CPU needs in order to do actual work), and in-between devices that I'll generically call *controllers* or *adapters.*

For example, consider what makes it possible for the PC to put images on your video monitor. Every PC has a video monitor, and every PC also has a chip inside it called the CPU, often called the *processor,* which is essentially the "engine" of the PC. When you hear people say that they have a "Pentium II computer," they're describing the particular model name of the CPU around which their computer is built. Common CPU names you might hear are Celeron, Pentium Pro, Pentium, Pentium II, or Pentium III. These are all names for CPUs made by Intel. Other processors that are commonly used today are made by AMD and Cyrix, who market CPU chips with names like M II, 686, K6, or 586 and, more recently, the Athlon.

In between the CPU and the monitor is a kind of diplomatic device—a circuit that knows how to talk to both the CPU and the video monitor—called the *video adapter* or *video controller.* If you ever see a reference to an S3 graphics adapter, a super VGA (SVGA) adapter, or a 3D adapter, then you're reading references to *video adapters.* Video adapters contain memory that they use to retain the current video image, as well as on-board electronics that know how to do many useful graphical tasks like drawing lines, circles, and polygons. In fact, one of the most important specifications today for 3D video cards is the number of polygons they can draw in a second (measured in millions of polygons per second). Companies such as 3Dfx, Diamond, Matrox, ATI, STB, Creative Laboratories, Cirrus, Trident, and S3 build video controllers as well as the components for other manufacturers' video controllers; some of these components are now actually integrated on the motherboard.

You'll see this CPU-adapter or controller-peripheral connection throughout all PC hardware, for example:

▶ Figures 1.1 and 1.2 show speaker connections on the motherboard and a Creative Labs Sound Blaster Live sound card. By the way, there are two kinds of speakers used on computers today. One is the small PC speaker that's attached directly to your motherboard. The other is attached to special stereo sound circuitry that may also be built on the motherboard or on a separate circuit board that you plug into your motherboard. Once just cheap multimedia components, PC sound systems have risen in technology and performance, rivaling consumer audio.

Figure 1.1

The PC speaker and its connection on the motherboard

Figure 1.2

A Creative Labs Sound Blaster Live sound card

▶ Most motherboards today have built-in circuitry to control EIDE (Enhanced Integrated Drive Electronics) hard drives and CD-ROMs. In fact, 80–85 percent of all drives being used in PCs today use the EIDE interface. Because of the prominence of the EIDE interface (which is discussed in more detail later in this chapter), you may have to install a special adapter if you want to connect another kind of drive to your system. For example, if you want to install a *Small Computer System Interface (SCSI)* hard drive, you'll need to install a special SCSI adapter (also called a *host adapter*) in one of the I/O slots on your motherboard.

▶ To connect a printer to the PC, you'll need a parallel port adapter.

These are just a few examples of the different types of electronic components; you'll see tons more in this book.

Buses and Interfaces

But wait, we're not done yet. We've got three parts of my PC model down—CPUs, peripherals, and controllers/adapters. I'd better explain two more pieces that I've already mentioned: *buses* and *interfaces.*

You're talking to a friend who has just bought a new computer. Lapsing into fluent computerese, your friend says, "Hey, I just got this 800 megahertz Pentium III with 128 megabytes of RAM, a 16-gig hard disk, and AGP video." Notice how your friend describes the computer—the first thing mentioned was an "800 megahertz Pentium III." As you've already read, "Pentium III" describes the central processing unit or CPU, the chip around which the entire computer is built. Some people compare it to a car's engine—not a terrible analogy, with megahertz being vaguely analogous to horsepower—but we'll take up CPUs in greater detail in Chapter 3.

The next part of the statement, "128 megabytes of RAM, 16-gig hard disk, and AGP video," refers to hardware *other than* the CPU—hardware that helps to make the computer useful. *RAM* is the computer's memory, a bunch of electronic chips that the CPU uses to store the program and data it's currently working on. (RAM, by the way, stands for *random-access memory,* and no, it's not a very useful acronym. What we ought to call it is "chips that the CPU can both store data to and read data from," but I suppose that would make for far too long an acronym.) We'll take up RAM in some detail in Chapter 3 as well as in Chapter 9, "Power Supplies and Power Protection." What about "16-gig hard disk"? Sixteen *gigs* (*gigabytes,* or billion bytes) describe the amount of data storage space the computer has on its hard drive. This is memory that will remain intact even after the computer has been shut down. Many explanations of computers show simple block diagrams that look something like Figure 1.3.

Figure 1.3

The CPU is logically connected to its memory (both RAM and hard disk), video display, and printer.

For PCs to be easily upgraded, PC manufacturers put empty electronic connectors inside each PC; most people call them *expansion slots.* The expansion slots are the easily visible part of the *bus,* which communicates with the CPU. Over the years, several bus types have become popular. The most common bus nowadays is PCI; don't worry about what "PCI" stands for—we'll take it up in detail in Chapter 3. Most motherboards today have at least two kinds of expansion slots: PCI and ISA. Figure 1.4 shows a motherboard with both of these kinds of slots. Notice which is which—you can really run into trouble if you try to plug an expansion board into the wrong kind of slot.

Figure 1.4

Notice the PCI and ISA expansion slots on this typical Pentium motherboard.

PCI

ISA

Why are there PCI and ISA bus connectors in this computer? Because it's a standard that computer system designers and computer expansion board designers can agree on. *That's* important because, just as the standard electrical sockets in your house's walls make it easy for you to buy appliances with electrical plugs and immediately use those appliances, a standard bus connector like PCI or ISA means you can buy your PC from one vendor and your sound card, display board, or internal modem (to name just a few examples) from another vendor and still be pretty sure that they'll work on your PC. (The mildly tentative tone of that last sentence reflects the fact that hardware compatibility in the PC world is sadly not a sure thing, and even the biggest names in the PC business sometimes sell hardware that just plain doesn't do what it's supposed to.) Some other bus names you may come across in addition to PCI and ISA are *Video Electronic Standards Association* (*VESA*), and *Micro Channel Architecture* (*MCA*). We'll cover the newer buses (current and upcoming) in Chapter 3, and we'll look at the older ones like VESA in Chapter 32, "This Old Computer."

One piece of trivia you may find helpful to remember: the later the PC mother-board, the fewer the number of ISA devices that will be supported by it. The most recent motherboards may have just one ISA slot that shares with PCI or no ISA connections at all. ISA has been provided all along for backward compatibility, but it's on its way out as it's replaced by faster buses.

By now you may be wondering exactly *who* sets the standards for how PCs are designed. Sadly, the answer in most cases is that there are a lot of cooks in the kitchen, and that makes standards seem less than . . . well, *standard*. One of the chief pairs of cooks is Microsoft and Intel (sometimes called "WinTel"), who, almost every year, issue a set of design guidelines that spell out the minimum requirements that a PC must have to carry the label "Microsoft Windows compatible."

While most current video boards connect to the CPU through a PCI interface, one of the main things that drives innovation in the computer business is speed: the faster the CPU and the video controller can blast pictures onto the screen, the more popular the computer is likely to be. But PCI's top speed was too slow in the eyes of some, which made PCI the bottleneck in your PC's video subsystem. Intel's answer? Add another bus for graphics boards only that the computer will use instead of a PCI. The new bus is called an *Advanced Graphics Port* (*AGP*). Thus, when you read an ad saying that a computer has "AGP video," it means there's a connector inside the PC that is designed to offer higher speed than PCI, and the system uses an AGP-compatible video controller. We've seen CPUs, peripherals, controllers, and buses; now what about interfaces?

The first AGP controllers offered a speed of 1X or 2X, but the faster 4Xs are now on the market, along with the motherboards that support them. This is important because the original AGPs weren't a lot faster than using a PCI video board, though using AGP video meant you freed up a PCI slot. The 4X refers to a much faster rate of transfer from the video to the CPU and back again, something which is finally helping to end some of the video speed bottlenecks that most people have experienced.

Just as standard buses like PCI make it easy for one vendor to offer a PC and another a disk controller, there's also a standard interface between the disk controller and the disk. For historical reasons, there is more than one way to connect a disk to a disk controller. Most PC systems nowadays use a disk interface called the *Enhanced Integrated Drive Electronics* (*EIDE*). EIDE is so popular, in fact, that virtually all new motherboards have EIDE controller circuitry built right in. Typically, you'll find two EIDE connectors, each of which can accommodate up to two EIDE drives (either hard drives or CD-ROMs). How are CPUs, buses, adapters, interfaces, and peripherals connected? Does one have to go with another? For example, will you find that SCSI adapters are available only for PCI? Not at all. As far as I know, SCSI adapters are available for every bus around, with the exception of AGP. Five easy pieces, then: CPUs, buses, controllers/adapters, interfaces, and peripherals. The CPU does the thinkin', the peripherals do the doin', and the controllers/adapters help them communicate. Buses and interfaces are just the glue that sticks them all together.

Actually, There's a Sixth Piece

Buying all of this hardware is of no value if you can't make it all work. As you probably know, computer hardware is of no value if there isn't *software* to control it. So, in a sense, there's a *sixth* piece to my five-piece model: software that's designed to control specific pieces of hardware. These pieces of software are called *drivers*.

The best hardware in the world is no good if your operating system and applications don't support it. The question of whether or not a particular piece of hardware has drivers for, say, Windows 95, Windows 98, Windows NT, Windows 2000, or Linux is of vital importance when you're buying new hardware. Many operating systems, particularly NT, offer formal or informal hardware compatibility lists—a roster of hardware directly supported by that operating system version. At the very least, they'll have notes about devices known to have problems when used with that operating system (sometimes they include suggested workarounds, too). You should find this information for your operating system before you shop for any new piece of hardware. Buying and using unsupported hardware can make for a long walk down a lonely road—such hardware may work just as well as one that's supported, but it may also require a lot more work on your part. So check with your software vendor before falling in love with some new doodad.

Note

Microsoft's hardware compatibility list for the entire family of Windows operating systems can be accessed at
`http://www.microsoft.com/hcl/default.asp`.

Typical PC Components and Issues

At this point, you may be thinking, "Yes, I've heard of Pentium III, megahertz, EIDE, and AGP, but that's not *all* I've heard of—what about BIOS, or Ethernet, or Zip drives?" The intention of this chapter is to give you a very brief introduction to almost all basic PC terms and to help you start to organize the concepts of PC hardware in your mind—but first I needed to explain the five-part model. Now that I've got you basically comfortable with the terms CPU, bus, adapter/controller, interface, and peripheral, I can round out the chapter with a five-second explanation of what I see as the most significant PC terms. (We'll take most of these on in greater detail in the rest of the book.)

What you'll see in Table 1.1 are PC features, a few common examples of the feature, and a brief bit of "why you care." Following the table, Figure 1.5 identifies some of the connectors you'll see on the back of your PC.

TABLE 1.1 PC Pieces

Feature	Typical Examples	Brief Description
CPU type	Pentium, Pentium Pro, Pentium II, Pentium III, Pentium III Xeon, Celeron, Itanium, K5, K6, Athlon, Alpha	The CPU determines how much memory the system can address, what kind of software it can run, and how fast it can go. The main difference in modern processors is speed, although newer ones add other capabilities like better graphics handling and multiprocessor support.
CPU speed	100MHz–1.1GHz	Megahertz (MHz) and gigahertz (GHz) are very rough measures of system speed. All other things being equal, a 10MHz processor would run twice as fast as a 5MHz processor. Generally, though, all things are rarely equal.
Bus type	PCI, PC Card (also known as PCMCIA), CardBus, PC bus (8-bit ISA), AT bus (16-bit ISA), Proprietary 32-bit, 16- or 32-bit Micro Channel Architecture (MCA), EISA, Local or VESA bus, AGP, FireWire	The bus determines what kind of expansion circuit boards will work in the machine. As with a CPU, a major bus characteristic is speed. Boards built for one bus generally will not work on other buses, so the second main bus characteristic is compatibility. (Having a PC with the fastest bus in the world is no good if no one makes boards that work in that bus.) PC Card and CardBus are mainly used in laptops; most current desktops use PCI or ISA, or possibly AGP. You'll find that most controllers come in versions for any kind of bus.
AGP bus	Your system either has it or it doesn't.	This is a relatively new bus designed only for use with very fast video boards.
BIOS manufacturer	American Megatrends, Inc. (AMI); IBM; Compaq; Phoenix; Award	The *basic input/output system (BIOS)* is the most basic control software for your computer. The BIOS is what makes a PC IBM-compatible. It tells the computer how to look at the bus, memory, and floppy drive, and how to read other programs. The BIOS isn't a plug-in card, it's a chip that's mounted right on the motherboard.
Plug-and-Play compatibility	PC systems are identified as being either PnP compatible or not. Unfortunately, many are *almost*.	*Plug-and-Play (PnP)* is a standard that allows a computer to automatically identify and configure devices that you want to add to the system. Trouble is, many PCs that claim to be PnP compatible are not quite because they incorporate some older

continued on next page

TABLE 1.1 PC Pieces (continued)

Feature	Typical Examples	Brief Description
		hardware (older is cheaper) that isn't PnP compatible. For fullest PnP compliance, your operating system has to support PnP (Windows 95/98/2000 do, Windows 3.x and Windows NT 4 do not), your motherboard's BIOS needs to support it (an upgrade may be available if it doesn't), and the use of only PnP-capable hardware (usually spelled out on the box or in the manual).
Hard disk/ storage adapter	ATA/IDE, EIDE, SCSI	The interface controller that allows your computer to communicate with your hard drive and CD-ROM. Most systems today use EIDE because it is inexpensive, easy to install, and fast. EIDE uses a 40-pin cable to interface with drives. IDE and EIDE are often replaced by ATA in common terminology, though they're all the same thing. An ATA-33 drive with 33MBps throughput (simply put, how fast data moves to and from the drive) is the same as an Ultra DMA 33 drive, which is the same as an Ultra ATA 33 drive. Newer still are ATA-66 drives (offering a possible 66MBps throughput), but they are only available on newer motherboards that support the new standard or with a special add-on controller card and a motherboard BIOS that recognizes this speed.
CD-ROM speed, interface	EIDE or SCSI	CD-ROMs are the basic means for distributing programs and data today. For less than $2/disc, a vendor can provide the equivalent of about 600 books' worth of text. CD-ROM drives are the peripherals that make it possible to read those discs. With a CD-ROM, speed is a relative thing. If you're using it to read text files or load software, a slower drive (around 16X by today's standards) will do. But if you're using it to play games, then you want the fastest CD drive you can get (50X plus, today).

continued on next page

TABLE 1.1 PC Pieces (continued)

Feature	Typical Examples	Brief Description
CD recorder (CD-R)/ CD rewritable (CD-RW), also called CD burner	IDE, EIDE, SCSI, USB	A drive that permits either the one-time (recorder) or multiple (rewritable) writing of a CD-ROM disk, usually used for data storage or the writing of a program or music for distribution. A CD-ROM disk can hold over 720MB, but most CD-ROM recorder/writers write no more than 650MB (and rewritable CDs even less—440–550MB). These drives can also be used like a regular CD-ROM drive to install software and play audio CDs. USB versions are external and can easily be shared between multiple PCs (so long as all have at least one USB port).
DVD (digital versatile disc)	Currently primarily used for movies, DVDs are starting to be used as a distribution medium for software as well.	Basically, the next step after CD-ROM. DVDs look like CD-ROM discs, but DVDs can store more than 26 times as much data as CD-ROMs. While current CD-ROMs can store around 650MB, DVD drives can store as much as 17GB, depending on the model drive and disc you use. Expected to come into popular use soon are DVD-RAM drives, which allow you to write data in DVD format, recording as much as 2.6–3GB per side.
Video board	Current manufacturers: 3DfX, ATI, Diamond, STB, Matrox, S3, Cirrus, Chips & Technologies Types/standards: Video Graphics Array (VGA), Super Video Graphics Array (SVGA), 8514 Adapter, Extended Graphics Array (XGA)	The video board determines how images are displayed on your monitor. This in turn affects what kind of software you can run and how quickly data can appear on the screen. Video boards vary by the number of colors and pixels (the dots on the screen) that they can display. Most important in modern video boards, however, is whether they hold video data as a simple "dumb frame buffer," which requires that the CPU do all the video work, or they contain circuitry that can help with the grunt work of graphical screens (boards like this are called "bitblitter" boards). The main issues in video nowadays are speed, resolution, and color depth (the number of colors the system can display at one time). The interface between most video boards and their monitors is called an *analog RGB interface*, where RGB stands for red, green, and blue. Although some of the newer

continued on next page

TABLE 1.1 PC Pieces (continued)

Feature	Typical Examples	Brief Description
		video boards today interface with the new flat panel displays with analog boards, more and more of the new flat panel displays use a faster digital interface. Among today's fastest video boards are those including the 256-bit graphics processing unit for optimum 3D graphics performance.
IEEE 1394	FireWire	A new external bus standard that's much faster than traditional bus options, allowing for a maximum data transfer speed of over 400Mbps. While only now beginning to appear on more PC mother-boards, IEEE 1394 was developed and implemented by Apple in the mid-1990s. Its expense and PC manufacturers' reluctance to include it—as well as, until recently, no PC operating system supporting it—slowed its arrival. Now, it can be found on more motherboards and as an interface on high-end digi-tal consumer electronics like digital video cameras. The speed makes it ideal for high-speed, real-time data storage and video use.
Parallel port	Unidirectional, bidirectional, Enhanced Parallel Port (EPP), and Enhanced Capabilities Port (ECP)	The parallel port is the basic adapter for printers and external drives (such as Zip and rewritable CD-ROMs). The interface uses a connector called a Centronics connector at the printer end and what's known as a DB-25 connector on the computer end. In its sim-plest form, the parallel port is unidirectional (data goes from the computer to the printer and not the reverse). Most current parallel ports now also sup-port bidirectional data flow (data can go back and forth between the computer and the parallel device) and higher data transmission speeds.
Serial port	COM1, 2, 3, 4, 5, 6	Serial ports are adapters that support a wide variety of low-speed peripherals including modems, serial mice, digital cameras, Personal Digital Assistants like the 3Com Palm Pilot, and some kinds of scanners. They connect to peripherals using an interface called RS-232, which most commonly uses a male DB-25 or DB-9 connector.

continued on next page

TABLE 1.1 PC Pieces (continued)

Feature	Typical Examples	Brief Description
Serial port UART	8250, 16450, 16550, 16650, 16750, 16950	The Universal Asynchronous Receiver/Transmitter (UART) is the main chip around which a serial port or internal modem is built. The 16550 UART is no longer the fastest of the lot, but it is still commonly used for high-speed communications and communications in multitasking environments. Software supports fast serial ports through a FIFO (first-in, first-out) buffer. 16550 UART offers a 16-byte FIFO, the 16650 offers 32-byte FIFO, the 16750 offers 64-byte FIFO, and the 16950 offers 128-bit FIFO.
Universal Serial Bus	Available as a built-in port or an add-on interface card	This adapter (also called USB) was first introduced in 1995. It features both speed and flexibility; one USB interface can support up to 127 devices at speeds of up to 12 million bits per second. Keyboards, mice, scanners, digital cameras, and modems are examples of devices that USB can support. Problems: only Windows 95 (later version), Windows 98, and Windows 2000 do a good job of supporting it; Windows NT, OS/2, and Linux lag behind. USB adapters use a small proprietary connector as their interface to USB-compliant peripherals. Using multiple USB devices may require the use of one or more USB hubs. USB 2 (still in development as we write) is much faster and beats out SCSI and FireWire for drive throughput.
Main memory RAM	16, 32, 48, 64, 96, 128, 256, 512MB	This is the workspace PCs use for the software they're currently processing. Newer software generally requires more RAM than older software.
Amount of L2 (level 2) static cache	256K, 512K, 1MB	Main memory is slower than most CPUs, making memory speed an important system bottleneck. Faster memory exists, but it's expensive. PCs compromise by including just a small amount of this faster memory called *cache*.
Type of RAM	DRAM, EDO, SDRAM, Rambus DRAM	While main memory *is* slower than most CPUs, memory chip vendors have been working hard to try to bridge that gap. The fastest current kind of main memory is called *synchronous dynamic random access memory (SDRAM)*. It is preferable in

continued on next page

TABLE 1.1 PC Pieces (continued)

Feature	Typical Examples	Brief Description
		new systems. While traditional RAM operates at 66MHz, newer forms operate at 100 and 133MHz to match faster motherboard clock speeds. Current forms of RAM are expected to be replaced by still-faster types, such as the Rambus DRAM (RDRAM) standard adopted by Intel and developed by Rambus Corp. Rambus is supposed to run at up to 600MHz, but its expense and developmental issues are delaying implementation. By the way, memory usually connects to the CPU through a proprietary bus, rather than PCI or some other standard.
System clock/ calendar	Built in on the motherboard or added on an expansion board	Though the time and date clock on computers was rarely considered important in the past, before the millennium there was a lot of concern about the date in computers. This was called the *Y2K bug*. The problem: Some programs in PCs and other computers use only a two-digit year format, which could cause some minor system failures. But the Y2K bug was more bark than bite. Most people were inconvenienced by a wrong date or program problem for just a short time, if at all.
Keyboard	Key layouts vary	Keyboards have a controller on the PC's main board and use either a mini-DIN (PS/2) or a full-sized DIN interface (or USB). Most new keyboards are compatible, and you've got a choice about what kind of shape, color, size, and ergonomics you prefer.
Floppy disks	5¼": 1.2MB; 3½": 1.44MB, 2.88MB (unusual), LS-120	Floppy disks (also called floppies) are low-capacity removable media used to make your data portable. Today, since files are getting larger and larger, many computers are equipped with both a floppy drive and a Zip drive or some other high-capacity drive. The most common floppy drive today holds 1.44MB (just under a million and a half) bytes of data. Zip drives, by contrast, hold 100 million bytes—about the same as 70 floppy diskettes. Floppies are driven by circuits called (not surprisingly) floppy controllers, and they interface with these controllers through a standard 40-wire connector.

continued on next page

TABLE 1.1 PC Pieces (continued)

Feature	Typical Examples	Brief Description
Cartridge storage devices	Iomega Jaz, Zip drives, Shark drive, Syquest drives, Castlewood Orb drives	These work like hard disks but are usually a bit slower. Their main feature is that they're reasonably priced backup devices. Some attach to a parallel port, some to EIDE, others to SCSI or USB.
Number of expansion slots	3–10	The more the merrier. Many big-name computers sport only three expansion slots. Look instead for the eight-slot models.
Configuration method	Changes BIOS (CMOS) configuration information for the device or component	Computers won't work until you tell them about themselves, or *configure* them. Today, virtually all computers configure themselves using built-in software in the BIOS. In some cases, you may need to set a few jumpers to configure CPU voltage levels, bus frequency, and cache memory on the motherboard.
Number of interrupts (IRQ levels) supported	8 or 16 (only very old PCs have 8)	For the computer to use its peripheral devices, it needs to know when a device has information for it. For example, if you press a key on the keyboard, the keyboard has to have a way to get that information to the computer. In the past, computers would get this information by "polling" their external devices (looking first at one device, then the next, and so on, repeating the process many times per second). Trouble is, this takes up a lot of computing time, and early microcomputers had little power to spare. So the engineers that developed the microcomputer changed instead to a new system that uses interrupts. Interrupts (also called *IRQs* or, more properly, *interrupt requests*) are associated with the external devices. When a device has information for the computer, it signals the CPU through its interrupt line. The problem is, generally no two devices can share an interrupt. This means that when you're configuring your system, you need to make sure that you don't assign the same interrupt to two or more devices. Doing so will cause the two devices to have a conflict and can make the system crash— or at least not recognize the devices.

continued on next page

TABLE 1.1 PC Pieces (continued)

Feature	Typical Examples	Brief Description
Number of direct memory access (DMA) channels supported	4 or 8 (only very old PCs have just 4)	Usually, the only thing talking to your memory is the CPU. Information stored in RAM is read by the CPU, and the CPU uses RAM to store information. Some devices, however, such as hard drives, take a (relatively) long time to move data back and forth. And if the computer needs to act as the go-between for this data, the CPU can get bogged down in the process. *DMA (direct memory access)* allows certain devices to communicate directly with RAM (main memory), allowing the CPU to attend to other processes while the hard drive, for instance, transfers data to RAM. Using DMA to handle data transfer between many of the external devices and RAM really improves the overall processing speed of your computer.
Sound card	8-bit, 16-bit, 32-bit, 64-bit, 128-bit, FM, MIDI, and/or wavetable audio interface	Sound cards support music and sound reproduction on your PC, but music and sound are represented in an 8-bit, 16-bit, 32-bit, 64-bit or 128-bit format. 32-bit is better, but it takes up more space. The sounds are recorded and reproduced either with FM synthesis, MIDI control, or wavetables. Additionally, with the right audio interface cable, a sound card in combination with a CD-ROM can play music on your PC.
LAN board	Ethernet, Token Ring, FDDI, ATM, and ARCNet	*Local area networks (LANs)* allow PCs to communicate with each other and share data and printers. To do this, each PC on a LAN needs a *network interface card (NIC)*. There are several types of NICs, including Ethernet, Token Ring, Fiber Distributed Data Interface (FDDI), and Asynchronous Transfer Mode (ATM). Ethernet is the most common. Most businesses have LANs, and more and more homes are adding LANs as they acquire two or more PCs.
Printer control language	Epson codes, HPPCL (LaserJet commands), PostScript, others	Printer control languages tell your printer how to underline words, put pictures on the page, and change typefaces.

Figure 1.5

The connectors you'll see on the back of your computer

Whew! Looks like a lot of stuff? Well, of course, it *is* a lot of stuff! If there weren't a whole bunch of things to learn in PC hardware this would be a pretty short book, right? But fear not, I promise we'll cover it all, nice and easy. First, though, let's get comfy with the inside of the PC in the next chapter.

Disassembling the PC

INTRODUCTION

In this chapter, we'll take a look at how to disassemble a PC so that it can be reassembled. Now, it might seem that I ought to spend a few chapters just *talking* about PCs and PC repair before actually taking the thing apart. But that's *not* what we're going to do. You see, in teaching PC repair to thousands of people, I've found that understanding PC repair and upgrade requires two *kinds* of knowledge.

The first kind of knowledge is a sort of "how it all fits together" knowledge—an understanding of things like how extended memory is different from conventional memory or what a superscalar CPU is. It's this knowledge of the components and interfaces—the connections between those components—that enables you to diagnose a problem or select the correct upgrade part. You'll learn about this kind of "microcomputer anatomy and physiology" throughout most of the rest of the book—in fact, the extended/expanded and superscalar stuff is in the next chapter, "Inside the PC: Pieces of the Picture."

The second sort of knowledge that you'll need is a different kind; it's a familiarity with tools and with some simple rules of disassembly. Perhaps it's my personal bias, but I prefer to teach these skills before getting into the concepts of Chapter 3. It may be that I do that because I'm kind of clumsy personally: I'm the kind of guy who forgets to put the plug in the bottom of the oil pan before I start refilling the engine with oil, so this is hard-won knowledge. That won't be true for all of you—if you're already someone who's comfortable with tools, then you probably *don't* have to be reminded that screwdrivers go "lefty loosey, righty tighty"—but us klutzes do, at least sometimes, and that's what this chapter is about. There are right ways to take a machine apart and there are wrong ways; this chapter shows you one of the right ways and talks about some of the wrong ways.

Disassembling the PC

Here's a run-down of the procedure for taking apart your PC that we will discuss in detail in this chapter, plus a list of the tools you'll need in order to get the job done right.

Be Prepared

Before you start, there are some things you'll need to perform the operation. These include:

▶ Documentation for your PC or its separate components (including warranty information)

▶ A container for placing screws between removal and reinstallation

▶ Appropriate screwdriver(s), such as a Phillips-head. (Today's machines offer a lot of diversity in the types of screws—and even the hard plastic retaining pins used in place of screws—that keep the cover in place and mount expansion cards inside the case. You may need to put a little effort into finding the right screwdriver—and it's possible that you'll need more than one size.)

▶ Chip extraction tool or L-shaped slim piece of metal for removing the CPU if it's in other than a ZIF socket

▶ Paper and pen for taking notes and diagramming, or the ability to record information on another PC until you're done with the one you're fixing

Other things you'll need are

▶ Adequate room to work (with sufficient lighting)

▶ Antistatic wrist strap

▶ Make sure the PC and externals are not only turned off, but that the power is disconnected

---

1. First determine whether your PC is still under warranty. If it is, call your vendor first—they have more experience and you may invalidate your warranty by opening it up yourself. Next, determine if you actually need to take apart your PC.

2. Find adequate, clean space on a tabletop, with good lighting in the work area.

3. Have the proper tools available, including a container in which you can store screws (or you can replace the screws in their holes in the part once it's fully removed) and other small hardware pieces. Also, be equipped with an antistatic wrist strap.

4. Back up the configuration before disassembly, noting the following regarding your hard drive(s):

   ▶ Some PCs don't permit the user to set drive type, so you don't need to worry about storing the configuration because it should reset itself next boot.

   ▶ For most PCs that do let you set drive type, record any information available on drive type and drive parameters (including cylinders, heads, and sectors per track)— you'll need this if your system can't be or isn't set to autodetect the drive(s).

   ▶ Most of the drives you're apt to see will be user-defined, or drive type 47. For these, you should record the parameter information (cylinders, heads, sectors), including the write precompensation cylinder and the drive's landing zone

   ▶ The controllers of SCSI drives have their own BIOS that stores the configuration information, so you may see that (a) the PC BIOS doesn't see a drive of that type listed at all, and/or (b) you need to tell your BIOS not to worry about the SCSI drive.

5. Turn off the PC and anything attached to it.

6. Remove the monitor and put it aside.

7. Unplug the PC and remove the cover, setting screws into the container discussed in step 3.

Warning

Be careful that you don't rip cables when removing the top.

8. Diagram the setup and internals before you begin removing anything, then rediagram as necessary to add information you couldn't see when you first began, noting in particular:

   ▶ Types and placement of different types of cables

   ▶ Location and status of DIP switches and jumpers

   ▶ Motherboard connections, including power supply, power, speaker, and keyboard (detach the battery only if it's really necessary)

9. Start detaching connections.

10. Remove the boards. Set the boards in a clean, safe location.

Warning

Don't force things. If something won't come out, stop and look again.

11. Remove the drives, along with their various drive screws (store these in a container) and cables. Set the boards in a clean, safe location.

12. Remove the power supply (see the section "The Three Basic Power Supply Types" in this chapter for information on the difference between power supplies).

13. Carefully remove the CPU by unlocking the locking lever on the ZIF socket or, if it's in a LIF socket, by using a chip extraction tool to gently pry the CPU from the socket.

14. Carefully remove the motherboard as necessary for the type of case in use, being cautious not to bend it or exert undue pressure on it. Put this aside in a clean place where it can't be jostled or knocked to the floor.

15. Evaluate the removed components, as desired.

16. Begin reassembling the PC while checking to make certain you're not making one of the common errors such as reversing the way a cable should connect, forgetting to reconnect a wire, or failing to seat a board.

Choose Your Weapons: PC Repair Tools

Most PC problems can be fixed with nothing more complex than a screwdriver. But if you do a *lot* of PC work, there are other tools that you will no doubt want to add to your toolkit.

What's the best kind of PC? Ask me at different times and I'll give you different answers. If I'm in the process of fixing a PC when you ask me, then I'll tell you, "A PC sitting on the middle of a table, which is sitting in the middle of a room on a nice, low-static wood floor." Fixing PCs is actually a lot of fun; getting at the PC to work on it, however, is usually a pain. Computers are frequently shoved into corners—dark corners—connectors, if they are labeled at all, are labeled in the smallest print possible, and the machines get more and more tightly packed inside. (You'll find that PCs get darker inside and the lettering on the connectors gets smaller every year, for some strange reason. Maybe it's like my father's claim that snow gets heavier and more difficult to shovel every year; he's always speculated that it was due to variations in gravity.)

Tip

One of the best tools to add to your toolkit is a little flashlight like the Mini-Maglite. The flexible flashlights, like the Snake Light, can be useful, too. And, for seeing those hard-to-see places, a small dental mirror is great. The flashlights are easy to find in any good hardware store, and auto supply stores and hobby stores often carry dental mirrors.

Screwdrivers

The basic tool. They come in straight-slot, Phillips, and Torx varieties. You may also occasionally need a tool called a nut driver, which is a sort of screwdriver that has a hex drive at the end instead of a blade. The most common size nut driver for computers is ¼-inch. The straight-slot screw has, as its name implies, a single metal slot across its top. Be careful with these—it's easy for the screwdriver to slip from the slot, which makes it hard to bear down on a straight-slot screw and easy to jab yourself in the hand.

That's probably why Phillips screws were invented. Phillips screws have two slots at right angles to one another that taper in toward the center of the two slots. A corresponding peak in the Phillips screwdriver's tip fits nicely into that indentation, helping the screwdriver to stay centered and not slip as easily.

Or at least that's the idea.

There are two problems with Phillips screws, at least in the PC business. First, the screws that PC makers use are often made of some kind of soft, presumably cheap steel. And to make matters worse, the slots aren't very deep, making it very easy to strip the heads of the screws. So be careful when removing Phillips screws from your computer.

The second problem is related to the first. It seems that half of the computers that I work on have previously been worked on by Ignatz the Strong Man, apparently on loan from the circus. People tighten PC case screws as if their data will leak out of the seams otherwise. It's a dumb practice for two reasons—first, it's unnecessary and second, you'll strip the heads of the screws. Tighten screws to a snug fit; don't cinch them down as if they'll be subjected to a vibration test.

Another thought along those lines: there are several sizes of Phillips screwdrivers. I'm aware of sizes 000, 00, 0, 1, 2, and 3, and I'm sure there are more. Most PC screws are size No. 1. However, you may come across a case screw (one of the screws that secures the case to the chassis) that's a No. 2. The important point is to use the correct size screwdriver for the screw you're working with. Don't try to remove a No. 2 with a No. 1 Phillips; again, you'll strip the head. By the way, if you should happen to come across a screw that *has* a stripped slot, get out the ¼-inch nut driver I mentioned earlier. You can screw it in (or out) with that, since virtually all PC screws these days also have hex heads instead of round heads. See Figure 2.1.

Figure 2.1

The typical hex-head/Phillips-head PC screw can be turned with either a Phillips screwdriver or a ¼-inch nut driver.

Personally, I like electric screwdrivers. The Black and Decker that I got for Christmas was just about the most useful present I ever received (and remember, it's made in the United States!).

Compaq computers usually use a third type of screw, called a *Torx screw*. The Torx uses a six-sided, star-shaped hole in the head of the screw. Torx screwdrivers come in at least 15 sizes, which is a major pain for support people. You'll probably use only sizes T-10 and T-15. Why do manufacturers use Torx screws? Well, it's certainly not because of convenience—whatever they are, they are not *convenient*. I think it's because until about 10 years ago, most people couldn't easily buy Torx screwdrivers. The idea was probably that a computer company that used Torx screws could keep casual users from attempting to work on their computers. This was, however, a dumb idea. Things sometimes go wrong with PCs. Also, you may want to upgrade yours or replace a battery. If you can't get inside it, it can become useless junk before its time. Fortunately, anyone who's ever had to change the headlights on a GM car already *has* a set of Torx screwdrivers.

While I'm on this topic, let me tell you a quick story. Years ago, I bought a number of PCs from a PC configuration/sales company. We'd specified on the bid that we wanted 100 percent IBM components, as this was 1983 and the clone stuff was a bit iffy on compatibility. The company delivered the PC with seals on the back of the box. When I had trouble installing software on one of the computers, I broke the seals, took the cover off, and discovered that the video board, floppy controller, and hard disk controller *weren't* IBM products. I called the vendor and explained that he had not fulfilled the contract when he sent us the non-IBM parts. His answer: that I'd violated the warranty on the computer by removing the seals. (I suppose he would have used Torx fasteners if he'd thought of it.) My answer: after I thanked him for the first really good laugh I'd had in a while, I told him to either take the PCs back or outfit them correctly. He agreed to rebuild them with IBM components. Now, the moral of the story is *not* that IBM makes the best parts (although they're often quite good). The moral *is* that you should specify what you want in your PC and then make sure that you get it. And if you buy a computer and the vendor tries to keep you out of its insides, be suspicious.

Antistatic Wrist Straps

Repairing your PC can do more harm than good if you're not careful. I'll say this again in Chapter 4, "Avoiding Service: Preventive Maintenance," but it's worthwhile mentioning it here (even if it *will* end up being a bit redundant). Remember that:

▶ Static electricity can damage chips.

▶ You generate static all the time.

▶ In order for you to *feel* a static charge, it must be in excess of 2,000 volts.

▶ You can destroy a chip with less than 35 volts!

We're all aware of static electricity on dry winter days, when walking across a carpet and touching a metal doorknob results in an annoying shock. But you're probably not aware that you generate static almost all of the time, static that you don't even feel. It's entirely possible that you can reach over and pick up a board or a chip, not feel any tingle at all, and destroy the board or chip.

The answer to this problem is an antistatic wrist strap. It's an elastic fabric band that fits over your wrist and then attaches to an electrical ground. Some antistatic wrist straps attach to ground by plugging into a wall socket; they've actually got a plug on them! Since it *is* possible that a badly wired outlet could shock you, don't plug yourself in until you've read Chapter 9, "Power Supplies and Power Protection." In it, you'll find information about an outlet-wiring tester that you can use to check an outlet before hooking yourself up to it. Other antistatic wrist straps have alligator clips on them, which you connect to a piece of unpainted metal on your computer's case.

No matter what kind of antistatic strap you get, be sure to get *something*. Or you could end up breaking more things than you fix.

Now that you know the right way to handle the possibility of static, let's discuss the most common way people ground themselves to work on a PC: touching their hands to the outer frame of the PC before beginning to work inside the case. Why shouldn't you use this method? Because it's too easy to forget to ground yourself each time you go back in. It's also not foolproof. And, quite frankly, the wrist strap reminds you that you need to focus on the task at hand. So, use it.

Tip

While we're at it, here's a tip that doesn't just apply to women doing tech: remove any jewelry from fingers or wrists. Rings can catch on objects inside the case, as can watch straps, bracelet links, and long necklaces. Scratches may result on either internal components or the jewelry itself. Better to remove such items and pocket them while you work.

If you happen to be wearing a loose bandage, rewrap it so it's snug and less likely to be caught on something. If you're not wearing a bandage yet, you might want to have one handy. The edges of some of these frames and controller cards are razor sharp.

> **Note**
>
> Interestingly, although newer computers use smaller and denser components, most current components are actually less susceptible to static damage than older ones because they are designed with buffers on the input and output lines. Although this can save you if you happen to make a mistake, don't use it as an excuse to be careless with your system and components—they can still be destroyed by static. Also, don't be fooled into thinking you'll see a big zap if this happens. You may not even feel the kind of discharge that can ruin a piece of delicate electronics.

Retrieving Tools

Here's the scenario. You're putting a PC back together, and you're mostly done. You're threading one of the last screws into the back of an expansion board, and the screw slips . . . and drops into the bowels of the PC. Arggh.

What do you do? Well, one approach is to pick up the PC, hold it upside-down, and give it a shake. C'mon, admit it—you've done it. (*I* have.) But it's not a good idea. First of all, the silly screw will end up hitting the floor and rolling under something, so you'll never find it. Second, you'll probably rearrange something inside the cabinet of the PC.

Some people have screwdrivers with magnetic tips that they use to retrieve lost screws. This method works, but I'm awfully leery of having magnets around PCs. It's far too easy to forget that the screwdriver is magnetic and to lay it on top of a floppy disk or a tape cassette. Doing any of those things might erase data on the disk or tape (and, parenthetically, that's why you shouldn't put refrigerator magnets on your PC case).

Instead, pick up a little gadget called a retrieving tool (also known as a *pickup tool* or a *multifinger tool*). They look kind of like giant hypodermic needles, with a button or a plunger at one end and a set of little spring-loaded fingers on the other end (see Figure 2.2). Push the plunger and the fingers pop out like a tiny hand; let go of the plunger and the little fingers retract, grabbing anything within their grasp. Retrieving tools come in different sizes ranging from the "too short" version, which doesn't quite reach as far as you need it to, and the "way too long" version, usable for oil refinery part retrieval, presumably. There are also versions with flexible shafts to aid with retrieval in hard-to-reach corners. You can find them in hardware stores.

Figure 2.2

Retrieving tool

Hemostats

Some people call these "forceps"; they look somewhat like a pair of skinny pliers. Their tips are narrow, allowing you to grab things in hard-to-get-to spaces (like the extractors, mentioned above). Additionally, this tool has a little clamp, so you can use it to hold things together. And, if you went to college in the early '70s as I did, then hey, you may even have one of these around from those days.

The extractor is smaller, so it can get into a wider range of places. On the other hand, hemostats can grip better, making them ideal for removing things jammed into the wrong place, like the narrow space between your internal CD-ROM and disk drives.

Pliers and Diagonal Cutters

Extractors, hemostats, and pliers make a kind of hierarchy. Pliers are not nearly as good at getting to difficult places as the other two are, but their gripping power is wonderful. Another incredibly useful tool is known to techies as *diagonal cutters* or, for reasons I've never heard explained, *dikes* (see Figure 2.3). This tool is shaped a bit like a pair of pliers, but it has diagonal cutters at the business end instead of grippers. So, when someone says that they're going to "dike that chip off the board," they're not talking about water control devices, they're just saying that they'll use the diagonal cutters to remove a chip.

Long nose pliers

Diagonal cutter (dike)

Figure 2.3

Pliers and diagonal cutters (dikes)

Chip Extractors (PLCC and PGA)

As you'll learn in Chapter 3, there are many types of integrated circuits (chips). Some are rectangular in shape, and others are square. The square chips come in two varieties. One is called a *Plastic Leadless Chip Carrier (PLCC)*, and the other is called a *Pin Grid Array (PGA)*. PLCCs are pretty tough to remove from their sockets without breaking them unless you've got the right tool; it requires a special extractor. Today, most socketed PGAs (such as Pentium processors) are in zero insertion force (ZIF) sockets and don't require a tool. All you do is lift the locking lever and lift out the chip. For the older PGAs, you'll need a different extractor than for the PLCCs.

Where do you get those tools? JDR has a PLCC extractor for around $14 (Part No. EXT-PLCC). I haven't been able to find a source of 273-pin PGA extractors; they're the type that you use to remove some of the older Pentiums. Jensen Tools does carry an any-size PGA extraction/inserter for $225, however. Fortunately, the Pentium II and III are large (and the Xeon's even larger), and they are quite easy to insert or remove without special tools—but for those with "ancient" machines, chip extractors can be wonderful. The JDR Microdevices PLCC extractor is shown in Figure 2.4; contact information for them is in the Vendor Guide on CD #2.

Figure 2.4

JDR Microdevices'
PLCC extractor

Tools to Avoid

Many PC repair types start their tool collections with one of those 10-piece sets that you can pick up at computer stores for 10 bucks or so. Some of these are better than others—some super-cheap kits may not survive their first job. Overall, however, they're not a bad start, and they usually contain a few straight-slot, Phillips, and Torx screwdrivers, as well as a multifinger retrieving tool and the "chip-mangler twins"—chip extractors and chip inserters. The manufacturers of these devices think they are useful extraction/insertion tools, but they are not. If you get them in a kit, throw them away. They do more damage than good and are to be avoided. The integrated circuit extraction/insertion kit is shown in Figure 2.5.

Figure 2.5

Integrated circuit extraction/ insertion kit

Common rectangular-shaped chips are called DIP chips, or Dual Inline Package chips. The *chip extractor* has two hooks that you snag under the DIP chip, then you pull up to remove the chip. The first problem with these tools is their inaccuracy. It's just as easy to yank a chip's socket off the motherboard as it is to yank the chip itself. The second problem is the lack of control that they offer. When removing a DIP chip with this extractor, you end up grabbing the tool as you would a pair of pliers, a hand/muscle configuration better suited to pulling *teeth* than to pulling delicate chips. You'll get the chip out, all right—or, at least, you'll get *most* of it out.

It is better to use a flat blade screwdriver to remove DIP chips. Just pry up one end of the chip a bit, then go to the other end of the chip and pry up the other end a bit, then return to the first end, and so on. Gradually work it out of the socket, and it'll come out whole and reusable.

The *chip inserter* is a small cylindrical tool with a plunger in it. The idea is that you put a chip into the slot at the end of this tool, position the tool over the chip socket, push the plunger, and the chip slides right into the socket. The reality is that the chip smashes against the socket, mashing all of the chip's legs and generally rendering the chip unusable. *Stay away from this tool.*

Now that you've got the right tools (and gotten rid of the wrong ones), let's see what to do with them.

Tip

Whatever kind of tool set you start out with, make certain you can manage it in your hands and that you can work both within and outside the case with the tools. Tools too large or too small for the job or your hands are ill advised. Check the grip, too. Some ultra-cheap kits have slippery handles—you don't want to drop a screwdriver on the card below—and tools that won't withstand much stress.

General PC Disassembly Advice

It's quite important to keep a few basics in mind when disassembling computers. Something as simple as not having enough elbow room could cause you physical discomfort, while losing all of your data because you forgot to back up your hard drive would certainly cause another type of discomfort!

Be Sure That Disassembly Is Necessary

New troubleshooters are always trigger-happy with their electric screwdrivers, but, as I'll discuss in Chapter 5, "Troubleshooting PC Problems," the vast majority of PC problems *aren't* hardware problems.

The most important thing you can do before opening the PC is to consider what else might be causing the problems aside from the hardware within the case. While going inside the PC is not a big deal, it can be a hassle, and each trip inside increases the chances that perhaps a cable can come unseated or you might short out a board. So you want to avoid opening the machine up when it's not necessary.

Here are some common things to check first:

▶ Outdated hardware drivers—particularly after upgrading your operating system, Web browser, or other major application. Updated drivers can usually be obtained from the manufacturer's Web site.

▶ Is everything plugged in and otherwise connected as it should be? Is everything plugged into a wall socket; is the socket live (test it by plugging in something that you know is working). The dumb little things we should have noticed can account for a lot of wasted time.

▶ Anything you added, removed, or modified just before the problem developed—this can be hardware, software, or drivers—try to reverse the changes you made to see if the current problem "disappears."

Even if you *do* have a hardware problem, you should stop before opening the machine and ask yourself a very important trouble-shooter's question: Is this thing still under warranty? If you can make the problem SEP (Somebody Else's Problem), then by all means do. If you're sure it's a printer that's dead out of the box, don't try to fix it—just send it back. Stuff that's dead right out of the box usually can't be fixed because it never worked to begin with. (There *are* a few exceptions to that rule, but it's true in general.) Always ask: "Is this trip necessary?"

Make Sure You Have Adequate Workspace

You will need a lot of room—most of a tabletop would be good; all of it would be better. Reduce the potential for static electricity. Raise the air humidity to 50 percent or so, use a commercial antistatic remedy, or just touch something metal before you touch any PC component. (See Chapter 4 for more ideas on handling static electricity.)

Keep the Small Parts Organized

Get a cup or a bag in which to store screws and small pieces of hardware. If you just leave the screws on the table, you'll eventually end up accidentally sweeping the screws off the table and onto the floor, where they'll roll down a floor register or under the heaviest object available. I knew a guy who kept the screws in the vent on top of the power supply—the one just above the fan. One day, he forgot they were there and turned the machine on. Power supply fans can *really* sling screws around!

Note

An important goal of good PC maintenance is to end up without any spare parts.

Since there will be at least two kinds of screws, it's not a bad idea to steal a page from car mechanics' books and use an egg carton to store them in. Screws to secure the case, for example, tend to be a different size from the rest of the screws in the system, and sometimes you'll run across hard disks or CD-ROMs that require short screws. Anyway, egg cartons have a bunch of compartments, and you can label each compartment to correspond to the screw(s) you put there. Or if you want something even more secure, many hardware and sporting good stores sell small plastic compartmentalized boxes with hinged lids. They aren't very expensive, and you can close the lid on each compartment as you fill it. That way, you'll know what goes where when you go to put the computer back together.

Or use yet another approach: Once you've removed a part, put all of the screws into the holes they came out of. You'll have to remove them again before replacing the part in its original location, so there's a bit of extra work with this method, but the chances of losing screws or getting them mixed up are much slimmer this way. This is particularly true because now and then you'll see a drive mounted in some kind of bracket in such a way that you've *got* to use the very short screws that came with the drive and bracket. If you use standard-length PC mounting screws instead, you'll end up driving the screw into the housing of the drive itself, making the drive unusable.

Remember that the plan here is to end up without any spare parts.

Back Up the Configuration

Every post-XT computer (which means virtually every modern PC) stores a small bit of vital configuration information in a special memory chip called *CMOS memory*. That memory chip can't work—to be more specific, it "forgets"—unless it's hooked up to a working battery. If you end up removing the battery, the system will complain about not being configured when you reassemble it.

Let's take a minute and be sure that you understand what I'm talking about here, because there's a pretty common error that you may see when you reassemble your PC. When your computer's CMOS memory loses its information, your computer announces that with an error message on bootup. The message will say something like, "I've lost my configuration information, so I don't know what kind of hardware I've got. Please reload the setup information in my CMOS."

On some older computers you'll see some pretty cryptic messages, ranging from "162" and two beeps (on a PS/2) to "Invalid CMOS information—run SETUP" and the like. I'll cover this later, in Chapter 6, "Installing New Circuit Boards (without Creating New Problems)," but the SETUP program is usually built into your computer and is accessed with different combinations of keystrokes. For example, on a computer with an AMI BIOS, you press the Delete key (Del) while the computer is booting. On an Award or Phoenix BIOS, you usually start up SETUP by pressing Ctrl+Alt+Esc while the system boots; it's Ctrl+Alt+Ins for some other machines. You make a Dell computer run SETUP by pressing Ctrl+Alt+Enter at any time. Some computers (such as Compaq) flash a rectangular-shaped cursor in the upper-right or upper-left corner of the screen for a brief period while booting up; the computer will enter its SETUP if you press F1 or F10 (depending on the computer model) during that time.

By the way, do you see the extreme variation in methods of accessing SETUP? That's only the first of many, many reasons why it's essential to keep your computer's documentation someplace handy, something I'll end up harping on throughout this book.

No matter how you get into SETUP, seeing this error message is pretty unsettling for first-time PC explorers. Relax; if you end up getting this message when you reassemble your system, it's probably not something that you did wrong. More than likely, your computer lost its CMOS because you disconnected the battery while disassembling, or it may just be that the battery was failing. All you've got to do is run SETUP and restore the PC's values.

In general, a PC that's lost its CMOS information can make pretty good guesses about what the correct values for the CMOS parameters should be. In many cases, it will beep at you and make you look over what it comes up with, and you'll be content with its choices. But one place where the computer might need a bit of help is in identifying your hard disk. This is more often true on earlier systems, because post-1995 PCs are pretty good at figuring out what kind of hard disk or disks they have, but even the newest PC might get confused, so it's a good idea to note the hard disk information on your PC before disassembling it. Run your PC's SETUP program and look in the "basic configuration" screen; you'll see information on up to four disks there.

Tip

In an effort to be "idiot-proof," some PCs don't let you set a drive type at all. By doing this, the designers of these PCs have severely limited the range of drives that you use in their computers—but maybe that was the idea, unfortunately. In any case, if you run across a computer that just plain won't let you examine or modify its drive information, then relax—you've got nothing to worry about. The system will configure itself automatically if you clear the CMOS while disassembling it.

It may be obvious, but I'll say it anyway: do this *before* you disassemble the PC. In the basic configuration screen on some systems, hard disk type is represented as a number between 1 and 47. Some of the newer systems are able to autodetect the hard drive type. On those systems, you may be able to just boot up, and the computer will autodetect the hard drive(s) during bootup. On others, you may need to go into the BIOS setup and select the autodetect option. Whatever your system does, it's a good idea to write down the drive type (if present) and the drive parameters (cylinders, heads, and sectors per track). Also, consider these two special conditions:

▶ SCSI hard disks are sufficiently unusual that the basic software that's built into the PC can't handle them. As a result, these unusual drives have their own built-in software (it's called a BIOS) to support themselves. However, because the basic BIOS that comes with the PC is of no use, you must tell the PC's BIOS to not worry about the hard disk. That leads to this seeming paradox: If you have a SCSI disk drive, your computer's SETUP program will probably indicate that you have no hard disks.

▶ It is likely that most of the drives you'll see will be "User-defined" (Type 47). That means you've got to write down some extra information: the number of heads, cylinders, and sectors; the write precompensation cylinder; and the landing zone of the drive. Again, we'll get into all of those things later in the book.

If you've got all of that written down, you'll be set in case you find that the CMOS data has dissolved. If you own Norton Utilities, then take a look at the utility named DISKTOOL; among other things, it will save CMOS information to a file as part of making what it calls a *rescue disk*.

Again, recording the CMOS information is important; you never know when you're going to need this information.

Turn the PC and Associated Peripherals Off

This should be a relatively straightforward step. Leave the PC plugged in, for reasons I'll get to in a minute.

Take the Monitor off the PC and Set It Aside

If you haven't got much work space, it's not a bad idea to put the monitor on the floor *with the tube facing into the room.* This might seem like exactly the wrong thing to do, since you might think that you could accidentally kick in the picture tube. In fact, just the opposite is true. It's very difficult to kick in the front of a picture tube. The glass in front is usually between ½ and ¾ of an inch thick! Kick the front and you're more likely to break your foot than the picture tube. The most vulnerable part of a monitor is the little stem that's at the rear of the picture tube. It's usually protected by only a thin wall of plastic, and the glass stem is only about 1⁄16 of an inch or so thick.

Unplug the Computer and Remove the Cover

Now, I don't know about you, but whenever I look at the back of a PC that I'm trying to disassemble for the first time, all I see are screws.

The problem then becomes knowing which screws help get the top off the computer and which screws will, when loosened, cause something in the computer to go "thunk!" (if the screw was supporting something big) or "dink!" (if the screw was supporting something small). You'll see case support screws on the back and sometimes on the side of PC cases. There are typically two to four screws on the back of a PC that don't hold the cover in place—they fasten the power supply to the inside of the PC. So look carefully, and make sound decisions when removing PC screws.

I can't detail how to get into every kind of PC case, but let's take a look at two common case types: the desktop and the tower. Let's start with a desktop case. Take a look at Figures 2.6 and 2.7.

Figure 2.6

Typical desktop case   Remove screws   Pull cover back, then up, to remove.

"Cable ripper"

Power
supply
screws

Case slides
forward

Figure 2.7

Older "cable ripper"
desktop case

Cover screws

These figures depict typical desktop PC cases. Note that on the back of the PC in Figures 2.6 and 2.7 there are four to six screws that hold the case in place and four others that hold the power supply in place. When you remove the screws, remember that you've got to keep track of them somehow, so store them in one of the ways I recommended earlier (or use your own storage method if you're feeling adventuresome). Be careful not to knock the screws over onto the floor. (If you're as clumsy as I am, you'll wait until there are more small screws and hardware and knock them all over at once.) Some models save you some trouble by using thumbscrews, which are attached to the case so they can't get lost.

If you have a case like the one shown in Figure 2.7, slide the cover carefully forward and set it aside. And I mean *carefully*—don't rip the thin ribbon cables when you remove the top. The part of the case that mates with the middle screw is often a piece of unsmoothed sheet metal, and those of us who've met it before know it as the *cable ripper.* So be careful, because it is *very easy* to scratch a cable with the ripper. Just a nick can make your floppy or hard disk (the peripherals that use these cables) misbehave. I once saw a cable that had gotten the "rip the top open and scratch the cable" treatment and although floppies could read and write fine, it caused them to refuse to format.

Now let's take a look at how to remove the cover on a tower case, like the one in Figure 2.8.

First, remove the screws holding the cover in place.

Then carefully pull the cover toward the back.

Figure 2.8

Typical tower case

This is a full-sized tower. There are also midsized towers and mini-towers. They all come apart basically the same way. You remove some screws from the back and swing the cover off. Note that the power supply screws are on the inside of the back of the computer. The case screws, in contrast, sit outside of the metal lip that runs around the outside of the back of the computer.

It's usually tougher getting the cover back onto a tower than it is removing the cover in the first place, so keep an eye on how the cover comes *off*, so that you can figure out how it goes back *on*. Expect that the worst part of reassembling the computer will be convincing the cover to fit nicely on the case.

Now that you've got the top off, take this opportunity to write your name on the inside of the case with an indelible marker, as a small extra bit of security. By the way, in desktop cases, the most important screw in the back is the top center screw—it holds the weight of the monitor. In normal usage, it is best to ensure that all five screws are in place. However, if you're going to be lazy, the one screw that *you must have* in place is the center screw. When you're reassembling, however, *don't* be lazy. Every one of those screws has a job. Look, PC companies are cheap, believe me. If they could save five cents on a screw, then they would. Those screws are in that case for a good reason.

Today's machines offer a lot of diversity in the types of screws—and even the hard plastic retaining pins used in place of screws—to keep the cover in place and to mount expansion cards inside the case. So you may need to put a little effort into finding the right screwdriver—and it's possible that you'll need more than one size. A good tip here is to set aside any tools you find to be a good match so you can use them exclusively for doing PC hardware repairs. This helps ensure not only that you have the tools ready for troubleshooting, but also that they're clean and in good condition (and didn't just come in from repairing the lawnmower).

Note

I've got five machines in my office. Two of them use hex screws (of different sizes) only at the four corners. The rest use an assortment of screw sizes and numbers (one has just one retaining screw and the side slides off). Some of the cheap clones today use hard plastic retaining pins rather than screws to hold expansion boards in place. You have to pop the pin in and out—and try really hard not to fracture the board while doing so.

Diagram!

Ensure that you have some paper and a pen so you can diagram what you disassemble. What order were the boards in? When you unplug something, it may not be simple to see how to reconnect it *unless* you have a good diagram. If there is no distinct marking on a cable, take a marker and *make* one. These machines aren't library books—it's okay to write on them. Remember that the game plan is that you should at least leave the machine the way you found it. You may not be able to fix the system, but you certainly don't want to leave it any *worse* off than you found it. If you're new in the business, pay special attention to the problem sources discussed in the following sections.

Ribbon Cables

Ribbon cables (also called *data cables*) are flat cables connected to upright pins on circuit boards. There is a definite correct way to put them on a connector. As you can see in Figure 2.9, the ribbon cables have a dark stripe on one edge (usually red). By the way, some manufacturers have begun using fine red speckles along one edge of the ribbon cables, so look carefully if you don't see the stripe at first.

Figure 2.9

Ribbon cable   Dark red stripe on this edge

The stripe on the ribbon cable corresponds to the position of pin number 1 on the connector. Trouble is, often the connector you're plugging the cable into will not be labeled. Therefore, it's a good idea to take a close look at how the cable is connected to the board/device. A few landmarks can be very useful. For example, does that dark stripe go up on the board? Down? Toward the speaker? Toward the power supply? (Note that I didn't say "left" or "right"—those can get you into trouble.) Make sure to note the current position of the cables in your diagram.

And while you're diagramming cables and cable placement, remember to not only diagram what cables are there; diagram what cables are *not* there. I know this sounds sort of like a Zen koan, but what I mean is this: Suppose there is a ribbon connector on one of your computer's circuit boards, but you're not using it. For example, many sound cards nowadays have a connector on them for a proprietary CD-ROM interface. If you're not using the interface—for instance, if you don't have a CD-ROM, or if you have a SCSI CD-ROM—then you probably won't notice the connector when you disassemble the computer. When you reassemble the computer, however, you'll say to yourself, "Hmmm . . . a connector. I wonder what goes on it . . ."—and then you'll get creative, usually with bad results. (Plugging a floppy drive into a CD-ROM interface will toast the floppy drive. It might even toast the CD-ROM interface.)

I recently removed a motherboard from a system that had two rows of 15 pins on the corner of the motherboard. Small wires connected to the pins for power control, reset, status lights, and the like, as normal. But the connectors seemed to have been put on randomly: one connector sat across three pins, then four pins were unused, then another connector covered two pins, then six pins were unused in the first row. The second row was just as bad. Now, if I hadn't written these connections down, try to imagine how many different possibilities I'd have had to try when I reinstalled the motherboard—it boggles the mind. So remember: Noting which connections are *unused* is as important as noting which connections are *used*.

Board and Cable Placement

Students often ask, "Does it matter which slot you put a board into?" Well, it depends, but in general, when you pull a board from a slot, you should replace it in that slot when you reassemble. Additionally, as you'll learn in the next chapter, there may be several different types of slots on your motherboard. You've got to put boards of type X into slots of type X. For example, one kind of slot on the motherboard is called an ISA slot, and another is called a PCI slot—again, they're both defined in the next chapter. Not only won't an ISA board work electronically in a PCI slot, but the connectors don't match.

Furthermore, more advanced bus types require that you note which slot you took a board from and restore the board to that slot. Plug a board into the wrong slot and the PC will either emit lots of error messages, or may fail to work altogether when you put it back together. In other words, if you took a board out of the second slot over from the power supply, then put the board back into the third slot over from the power supply, you may encounter problems.

Some boards require that you return them to their original slot for electronic reasons. Other boards require that you return them to their original slot for more pedestrian reasons: their slot may be the only slot that they fit in. You may not be able to get cables routed to and from the boards unless you put the boards in particular slots. Or a board may sit a mite higher than the others, and only one slot offers enough vertical clearance to accommodate that board; or some slots may be effectively truncated by memory modules, rendering them useless for longer boards.

And speaking of cables, you should be able to tuck cables out of the way when reassembling—take note of how it is done on the machine before you take it apart.

DIP Switches

Before you remove a board, look to see if the board has any DIP switches. If it does, it never hurts to make a note of the DIP switch settings (see Figure 2.10). I've spent 20 minutes setting a DIP switch bank only to find that I set the *wrong* bank! I messed up a perfectly good configuration and made my reassembly task all the more difficult. Besides, there are DIP switch gremlins who move the switches when you're not looking. (Honest, there *are*—I can think of no other explanation, and I don't have kids or cats.)

Figure 2.10

Typical DIP switches   **Rocker switch**   **Slide switch**

Jumpers

These have the same story as DIP switches. Write them down, take a picture of them, try putting the board on a copying machine, whatever works—but document the things.

Motherboard Connections

Once you've got the case open, you'll see the main circuit board (the motherboard). It'll have a bunch of things connected to it:

> **Power supply connections**   This depends on your PC. Older PCs, which use something called the AT form factor for case/motherboard design, often have two white plastic connectors labeled P8 and P9. Newer computers using the ATX form factor use only one big connector, rather than two smaller ones. If yours has two connectors, be careful. Whether they're labeled or not, mix 'em up when you reassemble the machine and poof! goes the system. Fortunately, all you need to do is remember two simple rules, and you'll never install the power plugs incorrectly: (1) Keep the black wires together. (2) Never force the plugs onto the connectors. That's it! Look at the illustration in Figure 2.11. See the piece of plastic that fits beside the plug? That's there to make it very hard to push the plugs on backward. If you don't force the plugs on,

you can't put them on backward. Now the only thing you can do incorrectly is switch the left and right plugs. But if you always keep the black wires together, you won't make that mistake either.

Figure 2.11

The dual power connectors labeled P1 and P2 (labeling may vary from vendor to vendor)

Speaker connection This connects the timer (which generates the sound signal) to the speaker. It's generally a connector with yellow and black wires.

Keylock connection On systems with front panel keylocks, a set of wires (two on some systems, four on others) connects the motherboard to the keylock. Fail to reconnect it, and the keylock feature won't work.

Power connection Some PCs have "soft power" switches to allow software to control whether the computer is powered up or not. There's a button on the front of the PC that tells the power management software that it's okay to completely power up the computer. But the button must be connected to the motherboard for that to happen. Forget to reconnect the button, and the PC will look awfully dead, and that sort of thing can panic your clients (or you, if it's your PC and it's the first time you're disassembling it).

Remove Boards Correctly

If you have never removed a circuit board, take a look at Figure 2.12.

First, detach all connectors from the board. When you do that, again, please be sure to diagram which connector went where. Don't just assume you can check the circuit board's schematic or diagram later, if needed, on the vendor's Web site. These diagrams are sometimes mislabeled or poorly displayed, so you want to be able to depend on your eyes and your diagram. Be very careful about forcing anything open or off. Remove the board's retaining screw (put the screw in the cup, remember) and grasp the board front and back with two hands. Rock the board back and forth (*not side to side!*), and it'll come out. *Don't* touch the gold edge connectors on the bottom part of the board—keep your finger gunk off the edge connectors.

1. Remove any connectors (diagramming them first).
2. Remove the board's mounting screw.
3. Grasp the board along its top edge and rock it *gently* up and out.
4. Once the board is out of its slot, avoid touching the edge connector.

Grasp here

Motherboard

Bus slot

Edge connector (obscured in bus slot connection)

Figure 2.12

Removing a circuit board

Now that you've got those boards out, you may be noticing how very similar boards are. How do you keep track of the fact that *this* green-and-black circuit board with lots of jumpers goes into the first slot, but *that* green-and-black circuit board with lots of jumpers goes into the *third* slot? Take a look at Figure 2.13 for some hints.

1. Chips with distinctive markings on circuit board

3. Unusual connections on circuit board

Duzitall Multifunction Board
Model No. GZ093421
Made in USA

2. Writing on circuit board

Duzitall Multifunction Board
Model No. GZ093421
Made in USA

4. Distinctive connectors on back of circuit board

Figure 2.13

Various identification marks on boards

When you get started in the PC disassembly business, all boards look the same. But after a while, you'll see that they have quite distinguishable characteristics.

As you know, circuit boards are covered with chips. And those chips may have a distinctive look, like a company logo or the like. It's hard, for example, to miss Intel's logo on their CPUs.

Boards may also have some kind of writing on them. Sometimes it's a copyright or patent notice or the logo of the board designer. Sometimes it's even a label on the board that actually tells you what the thing does. Use these things to distinguish various boards.

Other boards have connectors that stand out, either on the board's face or on the back of the board. Use them, chip logos, and writing on the board to differentiate boards. You don't have to know yet what a board does; you've only got to be able to document where it came from and what it was connected to.

Of course, if there's no other way to differentiate boards, you can always just put a paper label on the boards—printer-ready mailing labels are just fine.

Remove the Drives

After you've removed the boards, you may want to take a bit of a breather—you've done some real work there if it's your first time. As a matter of fact, in some classes we stop here, put the boards back in, power the system up, and verify that it still works. A gradual approach to exploration isn't a bad idea. (Remember, we *did* orbit the Earth for practice for eight years before going to the Moon . . .)

When you *are* ready to remove some drives, you'll find up to five main types of drives in your computer:

▶ Floppy disk drives

▶ Hard disk drives

▶ CD-ROM drives

▶ Tape drives

▶ Removable cartridge storage drives (Zip, Jaz, SuperDisk)

Of course, you may not have all five types. But no matter what kind of drive you've got, they all come out roughly the same way:

▶ They're secured to the chassis in some way.

▶ They get power from the power supply.

▶ They're connected to a board in the computer.

Removing Drive Screws

First, free the drives from the PC's chassis. Most drives come out something like the diagram in Figure 2.14.

Figure 2.14

Removing the
hard drive

Part of the PC chassis is usually a metal cradle with holes drilled on either side of it. Screws threaded through the holes secure the drive to the chassis. There are usually four screws holding a drive in place, two on either side (there are exceptions, but most computers work this way). Remove the screws, and you'll be able to move the drive around; that'll make removing the cables easier. Once you have removed the screws, pull out the cables from the back of the drive and remove the drive.

Notice that most modern hard drives remove from the back. The floppy drives and CD-ROMs on most machines can be removed from the front or the back. Take a look at Figure 2.15. You can remove a floppy drive from the front or the rear of the computer.

Figure 2.15

Removing a 3½-inch
floppy drive

Disconnect the Cables

Your drive will have a power cable and a data cable connected to
it. Your CD-ROM drive will probably also have an audio cable.
Remove those next. (Are you remembering to add this to your
diagram?)

    The first, and easier, cable to find and remove is the power cable.
Power cables extend, as you'd imagine, from the power supply (the
silver box with the big thick power cable on the back of it) to the
drive. You'll see one of two types of power connectors, as shown in
Figure 2.16.

Figure 2.16

Two types of power
connectors

Molex connector   Berg connector

Most drives use the larger, more common Molex connector (named for the company that makes them). It's a milky white plastic connector with four relatively thick wires extending from its back; it has one yellow, one red, and two black wires. Just work the connector from side to side to remove it. 3½-inch floppy drives use the smaller Berg connector. On some machines, the drive power cables are labeled P10, P11, or P12. Remove them from the drive's circuit board *carefully*, as the connector tends to be a bit balky about coming loose from some drives. Now and then, I see some would-be Hercules who ends up breaking the connector right off the drive altogether. Just grasp the power connector and gently rock it from side to side. It'll come loose.

Once you've got the power connector off, get the data cables off. These are usually flat ribbon cables. Floppy drives and tape drives have 34-wire cables. IDE CD-ROMs (the most common type) have 40-wire cables, as do IDE hard disks. SCSI drives have 50-wire cables. Again, diagramming is important. Replace one of these cables backward, and you could permanently damage something. In my experience, one of the top two or three mistakes that troubleshooting tyros make is to blithely remove cables without first noting where they should go upon reassembly, or in what configuration—red line up, red line down, or whatever. Every cable's layout looks obvious when it's removed, I know. But it's often *not* obvious when the time comes to replace it. (End of sermon.)

Remove the Power Supply

By now, the boards are out of the machine, and the drives are also gone. That'll make removing the power supply simple. At this point, the power supply's drive connections are detached, so you needn't worry about them. What you *haven't* yet detached, however, are the power connections to the motherboard. Some computers have two motherboard power connectors that must be detached. Others (those with advanced power management abilities) have just one big power connector.

The Three Basic Power Supply Types

How do you know whether or not you've got advanced power management? Simple. Look at the back of the computer. Is there a rocker switch for the system's power? Now look at the front of the computer. Is there a "power" button? Most computers before around 1990 had a power switch only on the back of the computer. The power switch was inconvenient there, but it was simple for the PC designers: the power supply was back there, and it was just easier to put the switch on the power supply.

Around 1990, PC designers decided that people wanted power switches on the front of their computers, so they routed a big thick cable from inside the power supply to the front of the PC, and the switch controlled that. It's a bit cumbersome for anyone building a new PC (as you'll read in a bit), but the switch was in a convenient place.

Around 1997, PCs got a whole new level of power management. If you're running Windows 98 or a late version of Windows 95, the computer can shut down your system or sort of put it into a light sleep when you're not using it. (Yes, I know, this isn't news in the laptop world, but it's sort of new for desktops.) These computers also have a power switch on their front panels—but it's not a *real* power switch. Follow the wires from the "power" switch and you'll see that it doesn't go to the power supply; it connects to the motherboard. The front power switch is a kind of "soft" power switch. You can power up your computer with it, or you can turn the computer off—but it doesn't *really* go off. It goes into a low-power suspended state. That way, when you turn on your computer, it doesn't have to go through the entire boot process; it needs only to "wake itself up" and it's ready to go. The *real* power switch is on the back of the PC.

So the quick and easy to way to figure out if you've got an advanced power management PC is to look at the power switches. If there's one on the back, it's old. If there's one on the front, it's medium-old. If there's one on the back *and* the front, it's relatively new, with advanced power management.

Note

By the way, the computers with advanced power management have only *one* connector to the motherboard, rather than two as with the older systems.

Handling Advanced Power Management PCs

If you've got a PC with two power switches, removing the power supply is actually quite like removing a power supply with a single rear switch. The power supply itself is held to the chassis with four screws. Take out the first three, and support the power supply a bit as you remove the fourth one. When you remove the last screw, the power supply just falls out of the case, which could be disastrous if it falls onto something delicate like the motherboard, so beware.

The front-panel power switch is really just a software-driven switch, and you'll notice that the wires from the motherboard to the front-panel switch are pretty small—which would be another clue to the fact that it's not a real power switch. It'll be connected to the motherboard with a Berg connector. Diagram it and remove it.

Removing the Power Supply of a Rear Power Switch PC

Once you've removed the power connectors to the motherboard, you're ready to pull the power supply. Remove the four screws in the back of the chassis that hold the power supply in place. Then, if the power supply comes free, great; if not, try pushing it forward a bit to disengage it.

Again, be sure to diagram the power connectors! They look almost exactly the same . . . but put them on the motherboard backward, and you'll smoke that motherboard. You can see the typical power supply connections in Figure 2.17. Remember, keep the black wires together as shown in the illustration.

Figure 2.17

Power supply
connectors

Removing a Power Supply of a Front Power Switch PC

If you have one of those PCs with only one power switch located in
the front, as I described earlier, you'll use a slightly different
approach. Take a look at Figure 2.18 to see how.

Figure 2.18

Removing the power
supply from a PC with
a front power switch

As before, remove any connections, and remove the power supply case. But there's a middle step that doesn't exist on the power supplies with rear switches. There's a thick, black cable that extends from inside the power supply all the way to the front switch. There are four wires inside the thick black cable: a black, a blue, a white, and a brown wire. Now, AC power doesn't include positive and negative wires—there's a *hot* wire and a *return* wire instead. Ordinarily, the black is the hot, and the white is the return; older power supplies just ran a white and black into the power supply from the wall socket, and that was all that was needed—but the needs of the new power supply's front panel switches change all that. In order to build a front-panel switch, power supply/case makers decided to drag both the hot *and* the return out to the *front* of the case, and then send the hot and return *back* into the power supply.

- The *black* wire connects the *hot* side of the wall outlet to the switch.

- The *brown* wire connects the *hot* side of the power supply's power input to the power switch. When you push the switch on, you connect white and brown, providing a *hot* AC connection for the power supply.

- The *white* wire connects the *return* side of the wall outlet to the power switch.

- The *blue* wire connects the *return* side of the power supply's power input to the power switch. When you push the switch on, you connect black and blue, providing a return AC connection for the power supply.

If you disconnect the black, blue, white, and brown wires from the front panel switch, you should be able to see from the previous discussion how important it is to diagram your connections. This is one case where if you reconnect things backward, you could end up directly connecting *hot* from the wall socket right into *return* from the wall socket. That would cause a short circuit that could make your computer catch fire!

If you look at the front panel switch, you'll see four flat connection points called *spade lugs* where you can connect or disconnect the white, black, brown, or blue wires. You'll notice a very low ridge on the connector and that there are two spade lugs on either side of the ridge. Before disconnecting the wires from the switch, notice that the black and the blue are on one side of the ridge, and the white and the brown are on the other side. The ridge is just a "reminder" about which wires go with which other wires. Just keep the white and the brown on one side, and the black and the blue on the other side, and all will be well. The way I remember it is that one side is "black and blue."

I've been beating the drum of "diagram" for the entire chapter, but there is no more important place to diagram than this. Put simply, these wires run directly from the AC line current to the power supply. Mix them up when you put them back together, and you will create a direct short circuit on your house or office wiring. If you don't diagram this, don't put it back together. (Unless, of course, you need a reason for a fire drill . . .)

Remove the CPU

Just how you remove the CPU depends to some degree on the type of motherboard, but it depends more on the type of socket the CPU is situated in. Two major CPU socket types are used: the ZIF (zero insertion force) and the LIF (low insertion force). LIF sockets are sometimes called standard sockets. As its name suggests, the ZIF makes for easier installation and removal of the CPU.

A ZIF socket features a small locking lever. Gently push up on the lever, and the CPU is freed (push down on the lever to lock the CPU back into place) and ready to be carefully removed—you can just use your fingers.

A LIF socket requires a special tool known as a chip extraction tool. This tool is sometime packaged with CPU upgrades, but it can also be found at PC fairs, computer stores, and online PC specialty shops. Many hardware veterans, however, use (with great care, please) a strong but slender L-shaped (bent to shape, if necessary) piece of metal that they slide between the CPU and the socket and gently push up to lever the CPU slowly out. Patience and care are mandatory, because damaging any of the CPU's pins can mean having to replace it. You also don't want to drop the CPU into the belly of the PC as you're prying it free.

Starting back with the Pentium II and Slot 1, when the CPU stopped looking like a slender Lego block and changed to a tiny credit card–sized component you slip into place in a slot on the motherboard, it became all but impossible to insert the CPU into the socket in any other way but the right way.

Remove the Motherboard

Finally, the motherboard comes out. (Recall that the motherboard is the circuit board lying flat on the bottom of the case.)

Before you remove it, look on the motherboard for small wires and flat rectangular connectors; they usually lead to the keylock, speaker connections, status LEDs, a reset switch, and perhaps (with a new system) the front panel power switch, if you haven't removed it already. Take these connectors off but again, be *very, very, very sure* to diagram those connections before removing them.

Drawer-Type Cases

If you have a system with the drawer-type case, look around the back of the case near the peripheral connections and see if you can find the latch that holds the drawer in place. It's usually a sheet metal tab you slide to the side that lets you then smoothly slide out the motherboard. "Smoothly," if you've remembered to disconnect everything, that is—keep a watchful eye out for wires you've forgotten; it's easy to sever them with the often-sharp edges of the sheet metal of the PC case. If you're replacing the motherboard, you unbolt it from the drawer and bolt the new one in.

You can remove the motherboard from the drawer by removing two to six screws. They attach the motherboard to the drawer with metal standoffs.

Standard Cases

With standard PC cases, you'll have to unbolt the motherboard from the bottom of the PC case to remove it (or the side, if you have a tower case). You'll see from one to five small plastic connectors, depending on the make of the case. Most systems have a speaker cable and a keylock connector with four wires on a five-pin connector. You may also find a turbo LED and switch connectors, a reset switch connector, and a hard disk activity light connector (on motherboards that have integral IDE controllers). On most motherboards these days, the connections are labeled, as are the plugs on the ends of the cables.

You could remove the battery from the motherboard (assuming it has one), but if possible, remove the motherboard with the battery attached. It saves you the trouble of reconfiguring the system when you reassemble it. In Figure 2.19, I've diagrammed a motherboard.

Figure 2.19

Pentium motherboard with detail showing connection points

PS/2 mouse connector

PS/2 keyboard connector

USB connectors

Comm2

Comm1

Parallel port connector

Different motherboards are held in place in different ways, but the most common method involves a couple of screws and some plastic spacers.

Note that the motherboard is usually held down by only two screws. Your motherboard may be held in place with more than two screws, but two is most common. Remove them and store them.

Once you've removed the screws, you still won't be able to just pull out the motherboard. It is held off the metal case with some plastic spacers. In most cases, you don't need to remove the spacers. Instead, grab the board and carefully move it away from the power supply. The motherboard should slide over and out of the case. If it doesn't, work it *gently* until it does. Applying pressure or force will damage the motherboard.

Note

Some motherboards are too wide to slide over and out of the channels that hold the plastic spacers. With these boards, you'll need to use a pair of needle-nose pliers to pinch the tips of the spacers in the motherboard. This releases them, allowing you to pull the motherboard up and off the spacers. Figure 2.20 shows how to release the spacers.

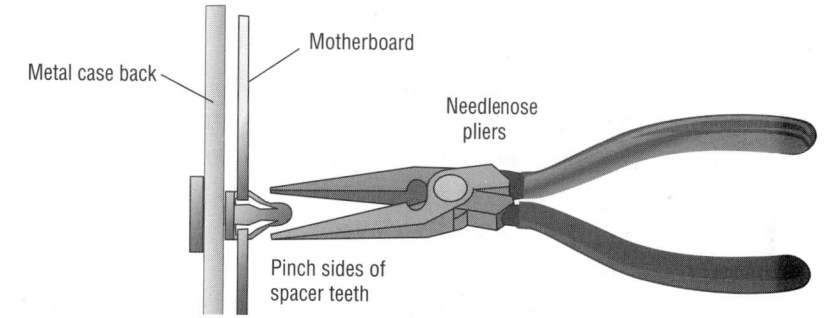

Figure 2.20

Pinching the spacers to release them from the motherboard

Some motherboards use metal standoffs instead of plastic spacers. In that case, you'll remove from three to six screws, and the motherboard will lift right out of the case.

Did you get this far? Then congratulations! You've completely disassembled a PC. (And you've remembered to diagram everything, right?)

Reassembly Hints

A rock climber friend once explained to me some of the ins and outs of rock climbing. The thing that surprised me most was the fact that people get into the most trouble when climbing *down* mountains, not *up.* I guess that shouldn't have been all that surprising, though since PC disassembly is pretty similar. It's during the reassembly that the mistakes get made.

Basically, when reassembling machines, just reverse the order of disassembly. Plan ahead. Don't be afraid to pull some things out and start over if you're in a corner. The important thing is to *take your time.* Here are a few tips on putting your computer back together.

Connecting Cables and Edge Connectors: The Pin 1 Rule

Expansion boards in the PC are often controller boards for external devices like disk drives or displays. Cables connect the boards to the displays. A common short cable type is a ribbon cable, also called a ribbon connector.

Most ribbon connectors can plug in either of two ways. Plugging in a connector upside-down will usually not damage the device or the controller board, but it will keep it from working. Many cables are "keyed"—that is, a connector is modified so that it cannot be plugged in incorrectly. However, many aren't, so the following bit of information is valuable.

A ribbon cable consists of many small wires laid out flat in parallel to form a flat cable, hence the "ribbon" name. One of the wires on the extreme outside of the cable will be colored differently than the others. For instance, ribbon cables are usually blue, white, or gray. The edge wire's color is often darker, like dark blue or red. This wire—the colored edge—connects to pin 1 of the connector. This is the Pin 1 Rule. (Some cables are multicolored, looking like small rainbows. Use the brown wire for pin 1 there.) This information has saved me more times than I care to recount. (I learned it after incinerating a hard disk. If you're going to make mistakes, you might as well learn from them.)

How do you find pin 1 on the circuit board? Many labels are stenciled right onto the board—very nice. Others label only pin 2, as pin 1 is on the back of the board. So look for a "1," and if you can't find it, look for "2." If you can't find either, turn the circuit board over.

Notice the round blobs of solder where chips are secured to the circuit board. These are called "solder pads." On some circuit boards, all of the solder pads are round except for the pin 1s—they're square. Take a look at Figure 2.21, which shows how to find pin 1 if it's not labeled.

Here, pin 1 is indicated by a stencil right on the circuit board.

Figure 2.21

How to find pin 1 on a circuit board

You'll find pin 1 on the circuit board of a hard or floppy disk, on disk controllers, or anywhere a ribbon cable connects to a circuit board.

Like most other convenient rules, there are exceptions. You may not find any indication of pin 1. Not all boards are labeled. Sadly, there is no Pin 1 Police. That's why diagrams are so important.

With ribbon cables comes one of the most common—and most dangerous—reassembly mistakes; you can see it in Figure 2.22.

Missed an entire row of pins

Missed a pair of pins

Figure 2.22

Examples of ribbon
cables installed
incorrectly

Unfortunately, it's remarkably easy to put a ribbon cable back on and accidentally offset it by one pin or a row of pins, either vertically or horizontally. On one motherboard that I worked with, offsetting the pins by one destroyed the motherboard.

The diagram in Figure 2.22 shows the missed pins as being nicely visible, but bear in mind that it's just as easy to leave the naked pins *below* the connector, where it'll take close inspection to find them. So check your pin header connections closely.

Common Reassembly Mistakes

In general, all you need for a good reassembly is patience and a good diagram. But here's what people tend to do wrong. Most of this stuff isn't fatal to your system *in the long term*, but it'll make you sweat until you figure it out. And if you take it to a repair shop to get it "fixed," the repair people will know who caused the problem (heh, heh).

Bad Motherboard Seating

Pay special attention when reseating the motherboard on its plastic spacers. Notice that the spacers are designed with a top disk and a bottom disk and a bit of space between. Then notice that the motherboard has raised metal slots with a V shape. The spacers are supposed to sit so that the V is between the upper and lower disks. Get a flashlight and check the spacers. Another way to test motherboard seating is to insert a circuit board—if it doesn't fit right, your motherboard is probably seated wrong.

In a related issue, make sure that the motherboard isn't sitting right on the metal case; there must be a bit of air space between it and the case, or you'll short-circuit the board for sure. I tend to come across a lot of cheap cases whose screw holes don't line up exactly right, and I worry that some stray piece of metal on the (cheap) case will short out the (expensive) motherboard. So I tuck a sheet of cardboard between the motherboard and the case, punching holes in the cardboard to allow the screws and plastic spacers to pass through.

Reversed Data or Control Cables

"Let's see, which side *does* this blue line go on?" Very common. If you don't diagram carefully, you may find yourself having trouble trying to figure out how a ribbon cable connects to, say, a drive. Well, if you didn't diagram carefully, use the Pin 1 Rule to help you.

Mishandled Boards

Don't stack boards. Lay them out separately. Occasionally, rough handling can scratch and remove a circuit board trace. This can be repaired by soldering a short (*as short as possible!*) wire across the cut in the trace. If you're unsure whether there's been a cut or scratch significant enough to make a difference (traces can be faint or thin to begin with), use your ohmmeter. Set to low ohms (Rx1 on the dial), then put the probes on either side of the suspected cut. The meter should read "0" if everything's okay.

Tip

When a board comes in an antistatic bag, inspect the board but then put it back in the bag until you're ready to install it. I have a miserable story about a hot new Matrox board I removed from the bag too soon: it was discovered by my cat with a queasy stomach before I had a chance to install it. Let's just say the cat christened the video adapter.

Forgetting to Attach Power

This one's good for a heart attack. You forget to attach that Molex or Berg power connector to the hard disk, and—arggh!—you get disk boot failure.

Neglecting to Plan Cabling

Novice troubleshooters stuff the cables any which way to get them in the box. Then, the next time they open the box, the cables pop up and get caught on the tab for the center screw. Cables rip and bend, teardrops flow—you get the picture. Stuffed cables also impede air-flow in the case and heat up the inside of the machine.

Put the drives part way in, then attach their cables, then look and ask: How can I route these cables so they'll be out of the way? Sometimes the best way is to move the drives around, so don't hesitate to be creative.

There's another very good reason for watching your cables: heat. Fans in your PC try to remove warmer air from the hot components and circulate the cooler air drawn in through the vents through. If a cluster of cables is allowed to block airflow within the case, you'll end up with a PC running hotter, and this makes delicate components more inclined to fail or report strange errors.

Forgetting the Speaker Connection, Keylock Connection, and Battery

The first two are minor, the last annoying. Forget to reconnect the battery, and your computer won't remember the configuration you set up. This can be very frustrating since the system will run when you set it up, but the next time you try to boot gives you the INVALID CONFIGURATION error.

Panicking When It Doesn't Power Up Immediately

I've seen students do this sometimes. They can't get the computer to boot up, so they tear it apart again, ripping cables and forcing boards out before removing their screws. Stay calm. If necessary, take a break and come back to it when you can evaluate the situation more objectively—you're more likely to catch something you've missed if you don't stare at it. No matter how important the machine is, you cannot fix it by rushing.

Tip

We've covered hardware here, but there is a pesky little operating system matter. Whenever doing anything of this nature, it's wise to have a system boot disk, also called a startup disk, updated for whatever version of the operating system you're using. This helps you to boot the system even if the operating system is having a problem that precludes it from starting normally.

Troubleshooting Tips

One of the major mistakes you can make in working with hardware is to assume. And you run the risk of assuming when you don't follow some of the suggestions I offer you in this chapter and beyond, in the rest of the book.

One suggestion I've offered is that you diagram as you work, so you know how things were when you started and how to put them back together when you're done. Don't make the mistake of assuming you can go look up the schematics for a particular motherboard or other circuit board later. Many times, you'll be able to find what you need, but sometimes you won't find the board diagram at all, or worse, it may be mislabeled. If you're new to hardware, you may not be able to spot the mislabeling.

A user recently came to me, tearing out his hair because he bought a used system in which he wanted to upgrade the old ISA video adapter with a faster, better-featured AGP video adapter. He had the new adapter in hand, but with the PC apart for hours, he still couldn't find where to plug the AGP adapter in. His motherboard's age and chipset indicated he shouldn't have AGP support onboard, but his motherboard's documentation and the diagram of the motherboard on the manufacturer's Web site showed one. Indeed, the poor guy didn't have an AGP port on the motherboard despite what he'd read, so he had to go exchange his super new AGP adapter for a PCI.

With this in mind, consider these steps when you're looking at documentation and diagrams and trying to match them against the diagram you drew of the motherboard:

▶ Try to orient any diagrams and figures in the documentation to the way you're looking at the motherboard, to reduce confusion—this means try to look at the diagram from the same perspective you're looking into the case to view the motherboard.

▶ Always locate major components like the CPU and the PCI slots in the diagrams or documentation—if your motherboard and your diagram show four PCI slots but the documentation shows three or five, you're probably not looking at an accurate diagram.

▶ When what you see and your diagram looks different from the documentation, consult the manufacturer's Web site first. Sometimes, you'll find updated and/or corrected material there that was printed incorrectly in the paper manual.

▶ If there's still a discrepancy, go out to other sources to try to find out whether you've got a different motherboard than you thought, or whether the manufacturer just provided the wrong model in the documentation. Some of the online hardware resources provided in Chapter 30, "Using the Internet and Online Services," are a good place to start for this information, since many of these resources review motherboards new to the market and provide pictures and specifics about them.

▶ When the differences between your diagram and the printed documentation are minor, note the differences on both the diagram and the documentation. That way, if you find just one (the diagram or the documentation) for a later troubleshooting session, you'll have a record of the correct information.

Now that you know how to take your PC apart, in the next chapter we'll examine the individual pieces you'll find inside the PC.

3

Inside the PC: Pieces of the Picture

Got it apart? Excellent. Now let's see what's in there. The PC is a modular device—that is, it consists of a number of standard modules such as video cards, disk drives, and so on. This modularity is convenient to users and manufacturers because it enables computer systems to be compatible with each other and (as a result of standardization) inexpensive.

For our purposes, the PC's modularity also makes troubleshooting and repair much easier for regular people without thousands of dollars' worth of test equipment. Fixing your PC is much more tractable than, say, repairing your TV. (Also, your PC lacks the large *capacitors* that make the TV dangerous to fool around with even when unplugged.) If the problem's really bad, you may have to open the machine to fix it—but remember that most PC problems involve broken software or "broken" users, not hardware. Many repairs just require finding and replacing the faulty component. (Simply being able to go to a strange machine and identify the components impresses the heck out of a skeptical audience, including those folks who question your troubleshooting abilities.) So the first step is to identify what's in the box.

But before jumping into the components found within a PC, it's important to understand that PC hardware is undergoing changes as the technology and its designs become smaller, faster, and more integrated. Although PCs have traditionally been made up of separate components, the push is toward integration, or bringing more of the work of the additional expansion cards (such as those for audio and video) onto the motherboard itself. Your PC's motherboard may already include a sound or video chip in place of the separate cards discussed in this chapter.

A PC is composed of just a few components:

- A system board or motherboard; this usually contains these:
- Central Processing Unit (CPU)
- Main memory (DRAM, EDO, SDRAM)

- Expansion slots attached to Peripheral Component Interconnect (PCI) or Industry Standard Architecture (ISA) bus connectors
- System clock/calendar
- Keyboard adapter (interface)
- Mouse adapter (interface)
- Floppy disk controller
- Primary Enhanced Integrated Drive Electronics (EIDE) interface, mainly for hard disks and CD-ROMs
- Secondary EIDE interface

- Many motherboards also contain these:
    - Heat sink unit
    - Serial port (RS-232C) or COM port
    - Parallel (printer) port
    - Static cache memory
    - Universal Serial Bus (USB) connections (usually two on a desktop PC and one on a portable PC)

- Video card adapter (sometimes built into the motherboard)
- Sound card (a few systems build this into the motherboard)
- Power supply
- Floppy disk drive(s)
- Hard disk drive(s)
- CD-ROM drive(s), including CD recordable and CD rewritable drives
- Cooling fan(s)

In this chapter, you'll take a look at each of these components.

Installing a CPU

All in all, CPUs can be one of the easier things to install and remove. The tricky part is making certain that the CPU and the motherboard you're installing it into are compatible. Try to install a PIII CPU into a Pentium motherboard—it won't fit.

Be Prepared

Before you start, there are some things you may need on hand. These include:

- Documentation related to both your new CPU and your motherboard for referencing. Diagrams (often found on the manufacturer's Web site) are also helpful for understanding orientation.

- Screwdriver(s) for opening the PC.

- Container for holding the screws.

- Antistatic wrist strap.

- Slender, flat bracket or similar tool for extracting the CPU (depending on CPU type).

1. Turn off the PC, disconnect the power, and remove any screws holding the PC cover in place.

2. Ground yourself using the antistatic wrist strap.

3. Locate your current CPU on the motherboard and remove it carefully. If still usable, it should be stored in an antistatic bag.

4. Consult the documentation for your motherboard and the new CPU (make sure they are compatible, see whether any adjustments need to be made for multipliers, etc.), and then gently seat the CPU into its place on the motherboard.

5. Replace the cover and screws, reconnect power, and turn on the PC.

6. Go into CMOS Setup (during boot, your screen will likely report `To enter Setup, press <key>`), and make certain that the new CPU is seen.

VISUAL UPGRADE

Installing a CPU

1 Black plastic guides help you slide the CPU cartridge into its slot.

2 Front view of the Pentium II. Note the fan power connector.

gold edge connectors

3 Back view of the Pentium II. Don't touch the gold edge connectors when handling or installing.

4 Insert the cartridge between the plastic guides and into the CPU slot.

5 Connect the cartridge fan's power cord to the power connector on the motherboard behind the CPU slot.

6 An installed Pentium II, with the fan power cord connected.

The System Board/Motherboard

Since their creation in 1971, microcomputers of all kinds have usually included most of their essential electronics on a single printed circuit board, called the *motherboard*. There are other ways of designing a computer, but the put-most-of-it-on-one-board approach is most popular, although even that goes through fads.

The first IBM PC in 1981 had a relatively simple motherboard and lots of expansion boards; modern computers tend to have more complex motherboards and a smaller number of expansion boards. Eventually, the majority of PCs will have no expansion boards at all, because the functions that most of us need will be completely incorporated into the motherboard. In fact, that's the case with some laptops, such as the Digital Ultra HiNote 2000, which has a motherboard that includes a 56K modem, a 10/100 megabit Ethernet card, 16-bit sound, a joystick interface, and video.

I have mixed feelings about these heavily integrated motherboards: on one hand, they're tremendously convenient, but on the other hand, there's a "take it or leave it" aspect to them. Some of the newer-style integrated motherboards have components you can't disable in order to install a separate card. For example, a colleague is having a devil of a time with hang-ups in his Web browser because of an integrated video chip set on his motherboard that refuses to be disabled so a free-standing video card can be used. Get in that situation, and when the video adapter fails, you don't toss the video card and buy a new one—you get to replace the whole motherboard.

The 1981 motherboards had room for a processor chip, 64KB of memory, a keyboard connection, and some expansion slots. The 2000 motherboards on the common clone desktop also include a clock/calendar, serial port, parallel port, hard and floppy drive interfaces, mouse port, quite a bit more memory (512MB or more on some models), and a couple of USB ports. And *that's* for a clone; proprietary models from firms such as Compaq Computer Corporation go even further by putting sound and video on the motherboard as well.

Now and then, however, the industry will decide to basically shrink the motherboard down to nothing and adopt a so-called *backplane* design. In the backplane design, the basic computer has *only* expansion slots, and the CPU sits on one of them. When vendors go through these backplane phases, they claim that it makes their PCs *modular*. By that, they mean that you'd upgrade your PC's CPU simply by removing the circuit board that contains the CPU and replacing it with a new CPU board—a five-minute bit of brain surgery that instantly transforms your PC from, say, a Pentium II to a Pentium III computer. Sounds good, yes, but the reality is less attractive: since the board that the machine's CPU is on is not built to any kind of standard, you can't just buy a faster CPU board from anyone—you've got to buy it from the original vendor. And in my experience, those vendors price their proprietary CPU upgrade boards quite high, often more expensive than just buying a whole new *faster* system!

If you want modularity, take my advice: the ultimate upgradable computer is a generic clone. It's based on a standard-sized motherboard that fits into a standard-sized case and takes standard boards and drives. When I want to upgrade it, all I do is buy a new motherboard and swap it for the old one. Motherboard prices are usually very high only when a new board is first introduced. Many Pentium II/III motherboards sell for just under $100 to just over $200, depending on make and model, and special features on the motherboard (extra slots, faster front-side bus, whether it's jumper-less for fewer hardware hassles).

Note

Now, I've been calling this board a *motherboard*, but some vendors have used different names for it; over the years, IBM has called it a *system board* or a *planar board*, so don't be surprised if you hear those terms. I've also seen clone motherboard manufacturers call their boards *mainboards*.

But enough talking about them—what do they look like? Figures 3.1, 3.2, and 3.3 show three motherboards of old and new machines.

Figure 3.1

Pentium
motherboard

Figure 3.2

Pentium II
motherboard

Figure 3.3

Pentium III
motherboard

Central Processing Unit (CPU)

There are a lot of chips on those motherboards, and they all kind of look alike, don't they? They may look equal, but some are more critical to the PC's operation than others. The big boss is the CPU. It's the part of the computer that knows how to do mathematics (and it's pretty smart; it can even do logarithms and cosines and that sort of thing) and logic, the two parts of all computer programs.

Since the first IBM PC in 1981, most PCs have been built around CPUs designed by Intel Corporation. Today, there are two other manufacturers whose microprocessors have made considerable inroads into the PCs we buy: Advanced Micro Devices (AMD) and Cyrix. But both of these manufacturers' chips were based upon the processors that Intel developed. (AMD took a turn in the road with their recent Athlon CPU, which I'll talk about later in this chapter, and Cyrix faltered, almost disappearing altogether until it was bought by Via Technologies in 1999.)

Since all these processors are able to run Microsoft Windows, they have been nicknamed *Wintel* computers. In truth, though, they are also able to run other operating systems such as DOS, Unix, and Linux (a variation of Unix that works well on PCs and has been gaining more and more popularity recently).

Intel has designed and created many microprocessors over the years, but the ones that interest us here are members of a family of chips starting with the 8086 and progressing to the Pentium III chips. Why is there a family? Why aren't people still using the 8086? In a word, performance. CPU performance determines, in large part, computer performance. A modern Pentium III is hundreds of times faster than the original 8086, and differences of speed on that order change how you use computers. Back in the early 1980s, people started using spreadsheet programs, and those programs strained the power of then-contemporary chips such as the 8088. It wasn't unusual for a complex spreadsheet to require hours to recalculate. Nowadays, even the cheapest PC is so fast that I can't remember the last time I waited for a spreadsheet to recalculate.

Intel has been improving CPU performance in two main ways. First, they improved some micro components quantitatively, by just taking an old circuit and making it run faster. Simple CPU speed, measured in *megahertz* (defined in a page or two), is an example. The second way that CPUs get snappier is through qualitative improvements, such as new manufacturing techniques that improve chip quality.

Whether improvements come quantitatively or qualitatively, CPUs vary in several ways that affect their performance. These variations are introduced in Table 3.1, which shows CPU properties. Take a minute to look over this table so that later you'll understand where a lot of PC limitations come from.

TABLE 3.1 CPU Properties

Property	Description
CPU speed	The number of operations that can be done per second
Microcode efficiency	The number of steps required to multiply two numbers (for example)
Word size	The largest number that can be operated on in one operation
Numeric coprocessor	Enables the CPU to directly perform floating-point numerical computations
Number of instruction pipelines	The number of processes that can run simultaneously on this chip
Pipeline management	Enables the CPU to "look ahead" to future instructions so as to make the best of its power
Internal cache RAM	The amount of internal, high-speed memory that the chip includes
Data path	The largest number that can be transported into the chip in one operation
Maximum memory	The largest amount of memory that the chip can use

CPU Speeds (Megahertz)

Computers are a little like clockwork devices. A clock strikes a beat, and a certain small amount of work gets done. Just like a beginning piano player plays to the beat of a metronome, computers run to the beat of a clock (although it's an electronic clock). If you set the metronome too fast for the beginning piano player, they will become confused and the music won't come out right; the player won't have enough time to find the next piano key, and the rendition will probably fall apart. Similarly, if you set the clock rate of a CPU too high, it will malfunction, but the result isn't discordant music; it's a system crash.

Normally, running a CPU too fast can damage the chip; at the very least, the computer may not function properly and the problems may not seem directly related to the CPU—for example, drive read and write errors. Part of the design of a PC entails determining a clock rate.

In some ways, the clock on a computer is like the coxswain on a rowing team. The coxswain is the person who holds up the mega-phone, exhorting the rowers "Stroke! Stroke! Stroke!" If he tells them to stroke too fast, they get out of sync and the boat slows down or stops. The coxswain is restricted to telling the team to stroke *no faster than the slowest rower.* In a PC, many chips all work to the beat of the computer's clock. That means that the computer's clock can't run any faster than the slowest computer component. CPU clocks generally "tick" millions of times per second. A clock that ticks at exactly one million times per second is said to be a one megahertz (1MHz) clock. The Apple II used a 2MHz clock. The early PCs and XTs (the first PCs with hard drives using an 8088 processor) used a 4.77MHz clock. IBM followed the PC with the AT, whose origi-nal model used a 6MHz clock, and later IBM offered a version that ran at 8MHz. Modern systems are up to 800MHz or faster.

Since the speed of a computer is used as a means of measuring how well it operates, the megahertz value of a computer is an impor-tant measure of its power. It's similar to looking at horsepower as an approximate measure of a car's power. All other things being equal, a faster clock means faster execution and better performance.

It's worth mentioning, however, that all things usually *aren't* equal. The CPU is only part of what makes a computer fast. A really fast CPU paired with an amazingly slow hard disk would turn in a mediocre performance. I once benchmarked a circa-1983 XT against a 1994 Pentium and found that the Pentium's hard disk and graphic boards were about 10 times faster than the XT's, but that the CPU was almost *300* times faster. A Pentium seems quick compared to an XT, of course, but not anywhere near 300 times faster, mostly because of the slower peripherals. If a computer were about 30 times faster than an XT in its disk, graphics board, and CPU, then it would probably feel faster than the Pentium system I benchmarked.

My advice, then—and I'll repeat it throughout this book—is this: when buying a computer on a budget, you may have to choose between a faster CPU or faster peripherals. I'd take the faster periph-erals. Having said that, however, I should also mention that Intel and other CPU manufacturers tend to stop making any but the fastest CPUs at any given time, so you probably won't have the option to buy a really out-of-date, slow CPU anyway.

Nowadays, the slowest computer you're likely to come across will be 133MHz or 166MHz. The fastest speeds you'll hear may get up to 800MHz to 1GHz or faster.

Megahertz Revisited: Hot Chips, Clock Doublers, Triplers, Quintuplers, and In-Between

For many years, the maximum possible CPU speed determined a lot about the rest of the computer. Usually a PC manufacturer would design the entire motherboard to operate at the same speed as the CPU. When CPUs rose in speed from 5MHz to 8MHz, motherboards changed in speed from 5MHz to 8MHz. All the chips on the motherboard, including complex chips such as memory chips, had to operate at 8MHz to support an 8MHz motherboard. At the time, this turned out to be pretty difficult for speeds beyond 8MHz, so since about 1984, motherboards have been designed so that their different parts could run at different speeds. Coupling slowpoke components with speed demons means that some of the speed demons' power is wasted, but it's the only way to build economical systems.

From 1984 on, the section of the motherboard that supported memory was decoupled from the rest of the motherboard, speed-wise, as were the expansion slots or *bus slots* (you'll read more about memory and bus slot speeds a bit later in this chapter). But memory and bus slots constituted only a fraction of the motherboard real estate. Most of the chips and circuits on the motherboards of the mid-to-late-'80s had to match the CPU's speed, so every time Intel came out with a faster chip, the motherboard designers had to go back to the drawing boards and design faster motherboards.

But building faster and faster motherboards is like climbing a mountain that gets steeper and steeper as you climb. Moving from 5MHz to 8MHz was easy; from 8MHz to 12MHz was harder. And 12MHz to 20MHz was even harder, as was the move around 1989 to motherboards that ran most of their components at 33MHz. In the closing months of the '80s, however, Intel started talking about producing 50MHz and 66MHz chips. Building motherboards that fast must have seemed just about impossible at the time.

Clock Doubler Chips

Intel needed to address several issues with their 50+MHz chips in 1989/1990. First was the motherboard question: what good is a 66MHz chip if no one knows how to build a motherboard that can use it? The second question came from the owners of existing systems. Weary of buying systems that seemed obsolete as soon as they were purchased, people wanted the ability to upgrade their systems without major surgery. So Intel came up with an alternative way to speed up CPUs: *clock doublers.*

The original clock doubler was a special 80486 (a processor I'll introduce later, but for the moment, understand that it was Intel's flagship processor between 1989 and 1993) that could plug right into a CPU socket on a standard 25MHz motherboard. This special processor was designed to operate at 25MHz from the motherboard's point of view, but to operate internally at *twice* that rate—50MHz. Any internal action in the CPU, such as numeric calculations or moving data from one internal area of the CPU to another, was accomplished at 50MHz. But external instructions, such as loading data from memory or storing data to memory, happened more slowly, at 25MHz.

Note

Intel has names for these two clock rates, by the way. The external speed (25MHz, in the case of the preceding example) is called the *system bus frequency,* or front-side bus. The internal clock rate (50MHz, in the preceding example) is called the *processor core frequency.*

Now, given that this chip ran at 25MHz for external instructions and 50MHz for internal instructions, what should Intel have called this chip—a 25MHz chip or a 50MHz chip? It's a bit of a conundrum, until you realize that the folks making the decision were, well, more oriented to the *marketing* side of Intel than the engineering side. So the new chip got the name 80486DX2-50—the 2 referring to the clock doubling, the *50* referring to its higher speed. They also offered an 80486DX2-66, a chip that plugged into a 33MHz motherboard but ran at 66MHz internally. DX, in those days, referred to a fuller, more capable system compared to its SX counterparts that were an interim upgrade (a 486SX was midway between a 386 and a 486).

At the time, Intel made an 80486DX-25 (a chip that ran both inside and out at 25MHz) and an 80486DX-50 (a chip that ran both inside and out at 50MHz), in addition to the 80486DX2-50. People often asked, "How fast is the DX2 *really*—is it more like the 'straight 25' or the 'straight 50'?" The answer was that it depended on what you were doing. CPU-intensive operations such as calculating spreadsheets or drawing complex graphics probably looked more like 50MHz, and input/output-oriented programs such as databases probably looked more like 25MHz. An in-between application, such as a word processor, fell somewhere in between. And, remember, Intel *also* offered the 80486DX-50, a 50MHz chip that ran 50MHz both inside and out. Many people *thought* they were buying a 50MHz DX but actually bought a "50MHz" DX2, and the difference in performance could be significant.

Clock Tripler Chips

In 1994, Intel introduced yet another variation on the 486 line, an 80486DX that was a *clock tripler.* Offered in 75MHz and 100MHz versions, these chips operated on motherboards that were 25MHz and 33MHz, respectively.

Note

Why does 33MHz tripled equal 100MHz? Why not 99MHz? Marketing reality again. After all, round up 99MHz and you get 100MHz . . . well, kind of.

Intel also took the opportunity to spruce up the internal workings of this new 486, and they added a bit more very fast internal memory (it's called *internal cache*, and I'll get to it soon), raising the amount inside the chip from 8KB (which the 80486 previously contained) to

16KB. That small amount of internal memory did indeed speed up the computer a bit in addition to the clock tripling, leading Intel to explore new realms of salesmanship by calling the new chip the *DX4*. That name is just DX4, by the way; there's no *80486* in the name. There's also a clock-tripled Pentium 200MHz chip that runs on a 66MHz motherboard.

Clock "One and a Halfers" and Some *Really* Hot Chips

We've seen clocks doubled and tripled. Are there clock-quadrupled chips? Yes, and quintupled chips: the 333MHz Pentium II runs 66MHz externally, and 333 internally, a fivefold increase. While figuring out how to build the 4*x* and 5*x* systems, Intel started playing around with noninteger multiples. Some CPUs have their clocks increased by *50 percent*, kind of a *one and a half clock*. The original Pentium models were offered in speeds of 60MHz and 66MHz. Later Pentium chips, code-named the P54C by Intel, were rated at 90 and 100MHz. They used 60MHz and 66MHz motherboards and increased their internal clock rates by half.

Before leaving megahertz behind, it's worth quickly discussing exactly why there were originally two Pentium models with two clock rates so close. Why bother offering both a 60MHz and a 66MHz model?

The Pentium was a really tough chip to design. Every Intel chip design team is extremely limited in that no matter what the new chip's able to do, the one thing that it *must* do is run old software. This demand for backward compatibility makes for complex chips. Complex means lots of little components go into the chip, or, as insiders would say, the backward compatibility "needs a lot of silicon." Now, all that silicon generates heat. Put too much silicon in too small a place, and it starts to damage itself. Make the clock run faster, and the silicon gets even hotter. The Intel folks were just plain running up against some physical design barriers.

The Pentium's heat generation standards were shown in its technical specifications. According to Intel, the 66MHz Pentium should be expected to generate heat enough to bring the chip to 85 degrees. *Centigrade.*

That's about 185 degrees Fahrenheit. Good grief, you could toast marshmallows on that thing (and as I'll discuss, heat isn't good for the electronics within a PC)! Intel tried its hardest to make a 66MHz Pentium chip work, but it was just so difficult that they ended up making Pentium chips that were mostly rejects. They *weren't* rejects, however, if they ran at a somewhat slower, *cooler*, rate, like 60MHz. So the 60MHz chips are, unfortunately, the rejects; Intel just lowered the standards to make them sellable.

Besides clock speed, however, another determining factor in chip heat is in the voltage that the chip operates on. The heat created by a chip is related to the square of the voltage. For a long time, most CPUs ran at 5 volts.

Intel decided to build the clock one-and-a-half P54C chips with 3.3-volt power supplies. Five squared is 25; 3.3 squared is about 11. A 3.3-volt chip runs a lot cooler, which is why Intel uses 3.3 volts for the DX4, the newer Pentiums, and some later chips. Pentium Pros use 1.5 volts.

The DX4's use of 3.3 volts means that, paradoxically, it was the fastest 80486 chip, but was also the coolest.

Clock "Two and a Halfers": The Pentium OverDrive

I know that all these chip speed permutations are getting a bit bizarre, but I'm not done yet. Intel marketed a Pentium OverDrive chip, a chip that upgraded some existing 486 systems to Pentium-level speed.

A couple of caveats about this: first, this wouldn't work on all 486s; you had to have a 486 system that was designed with an extra-large socket. The extra-large socket had extra pins and was designed for the Pentium OverDrive chip. Second, it was kind of dubious how much like a Pentium the Pentium OverDrive could be, because the OverDrive is a 32-bit chip, whereas the true Pentium is a 64-bit chip (meaning it has a data path advantage because it's wider).

But enough bad news. The *good* news is that the Pentium Over-Drive increased the internal speed of the OverDrive chip to two and a half times the speed of the motherboard. A Pentium OverDrive for a 25MHz 486 system runs internally at 63MHz. The OverDrive for a 33MHz system runs internally at 83MHz.

So What *Is* the Fastest Chip?

This has been a record period for chip speed development, particularly with CPUs. It began in earnest in mid-1998, when Intel released two new Pentium II systems, the 350MHz and 400MHz chips. The next year brought the Pentium III (not a faster CPU by itself but with a faster clock speed) and AMD's first significantly different chip, the Athlon, with speeds of up to 700MHz. As I write this, the 800- and 850MHz systems are at hand, and the 1- and 1.1GHz chip sets will soon debut, with 10GHz chip sets already in development. If you're feeling a bit of whiplash trying to keep up with hardware changes, you're not alone.

Intel was able to make the higher speeds work by using smaller components in a process first tested on the 333MHz chip, a design code-named *Deschutes*. (It was expensive to design, and Intel feared they were throwing all that research money down Deschutes . . . no, that's not true. Deschutes is a river in the West; that's where Intel gets its names for design projects, don't ask me why.)

Since the 300MHz and 333MHz systems both use a 66MHz system bus speed, the performance difference between a 300MHz system and a 333MHz system is quite small. The 350MHz and faster systems, however, have a system bus speed of 100 or 133MHz. The difference between a 333MHz (a 66 multiplied by 5—which actually comes out to 330, but, again, you'll see some variation like this) and a 350MHz (a 100 multiplied by 3.5) is quite significant, not so much because of the processor speed, but because the rest of the system runs at 100MHz versus 66MHz. One downside to the extra speed you get with the 100MHz bus, however, is that it runs a lot hotter than the 66MHz systems.

The heat problem is actually one reason for the newest version of the Pentium Pro, the Pentium II Xeon and the Pentium III Xeon chip. One of the Xeon's new features is a built-in thermometer that monitors the chip's temperature. If the temperature gets above a safe level, the Xeon can safely close its process and shut down the system.

Before I move along, was your curiosity piqued by the mention of the 10GHz chips above? Those won't be seen for some time, although the rapid pace at which processor speeds are increasing makes this more of a *when* than an *if*. We're already at the point where you may not appreciate a great deal of difference between 600MHz, 800MHz, and 1GHz in your usual day-to-day work at your PC. More times than not, you are more likely to get bottlenecked by your net communications speed (especially if you're using a dial-up on a traditional modem over analog phone lines) long before you feel your CPU is too slow for the task at hand.

So the power of the future may not be in overall speed of the desktop processor, but in its capability to perform *parallel instruction processing*, or sharing work among multiple processors all working together.

But back to the 10GHz: analysts predict that speed like this will finally break the barrier between PC and human interaction. Even today, we're still experiencing problems making speech recognition and other human-to-PC interactions work as they should so that we as humans can work with PCs more naturally. Voice and handwriting recognition have come a long way from where they started, but are still in very rudimentary, slow form. Heavy-duty PC performance is required for success here, and that may be one of the chief roles played by processors faster than 1GHz.

A Word on Overclocking and Matching Clock Speeds

Clock rates on chips and clock rates on motherboards are related. If the motherboard is built for 66MHz, then you should get a CPU that can handle a 66MHz clock. (Note I'm talking about the external or *system bus frequency*, not the internal rate.) Similarly, it's not a good idea to get a chip that's designed to run at a higher clock rate than the motherboard. The fit between motherboard and chip should be "just right."

Why is this true? Well, consider what happens if you get a chip that's too slow for the motherboard. For example, the Intel Pentium 150MHz chip had an external clock rate of 50MHz and was tripled. If you put it on a motherboard that is designed to provide a 66MHz clock signal to the processor, then the processor will not be able to keep up with that rate. The result is that the chip will fail and overheat, possibly permanently damaging it. In the reverse situation, suppose you had a motherboard that put out a 66MHz-clock signal, and you installed a 400MHz Xeon, which can handle an external clock rate of 100MHz. You wouldn't be driving the "400MHz" chip at 100MHz, you'd be driving it at 66MHz. It's a clock quadrupler, so the chip would dutifully quadruple that value, giving you a 266MHz Xeon. (OK, again, we have a case where 66×4 isn't quite 266, but welcome to PC hardware!) That would be a waste of money.

This underscores a general point about chips and sockets: put a chip in that's too slow, and it will overheat and fail. Install a chip that's too fast, and it will work fine, but you're throwing your money away.

That all sounds logical, but some people point out that the difference between slow chips and fast chips is often luck anyway, because chip manufacturers just build a few thousand chips and then test them to see which ones are fast and which are slow. When testing, chip makers are conservative, goes the argument, so they might rate a chip at xMHz that could actually work at $1.3x$ or the like. Modern motherboards let you dial in any clock rate you want, so people buy a middle-rated chip and dial up a high clock rate. If the system doesn't crash immediately, they figure they've gotten lucky and bought a fast chip for the price of a slow one.

This is called *overclocking*. I don't recommend it, and basically here's why: Intel gets to charge more money for faster chips, and Intel's profit ratio indicates to me that they have no aversion to a healthy ROI (return on investment, that is). Yes, I suppose a few slip through the cracks, but in general a chip rated at x is no better than x. The symptoms of overclocking can be quite subtle and masquerade as problems with a hard disk, or keyboard, or something else. In addition, overclocking by its very nature invalidates your product warranty, so you're on your own. Overclocking can also cause other problems, as you'll read later in the "PC Expansion Buses" section. One thing you should be aware of is that Intel has now locked down the ability to overclock in most of its product line, driving true overclocking fans to other makes of processor.

Microcode Efficiency and Pipelines

As you just read, one way to make a chip faster is to simply drive it faster, by running up its clock in some way. Another way is to design the chip to make better use of each clock cycle.

Microcode Improvements

Microcode was a big advancement in that it allowed the CPU's instruction set to be implemented as a series of microinstructions. It's also called microprogramming. Microcode improvements have been an important part of Intel's strategy for ever-faster chips over the years; for example, the 8088 chip was succeeded by the 80188 chip, a chip that seemed to do all the same things that the 8088 does. Where's the difference?

In the case of the 8088 versus the 80188 (and, actually, in the case of the 80386 versus the 80486), a lot of the difference lies in its *microcode efficiency*. Put simply, microcode efficiency just means: "How many clock ticks does it take a CPU to get a particular task done?" For example, an 8088 can calculate an integer division—that is, a division without any decimal places; divide 7 by 2 on an 8088 and you get 3, not 3.5. And to make matters worse, it can take the 8088 up to 70 clock cycles to get that done. The 80188, in contrast, can do it in only 25 clock cycles. Compare two machines that are identical except that one runs an 80188 and the other runs an 8088, and the 80188 will be able to do some things faster than an 8088.

The 80386 and 80486 are also similar in many ways, as you'll learn later in this chapter, but they differ in microcode efficiency. The simplest useful instruction that you can do with an 80386 is the MOV AX, BX, an assembly-language command that invokes a microcode instruction that moves data from a storage area inside the microcomputer, called BX, to another storage area inside the microcomputer, called AX. Technically, it's called a *register-to-register transfer*. All register operations on an 80386 require at least two clock cycles. The 80486 was designed so that all the two-cycle register instructions on the 80386 run in just one clock cycle on the

80486. One of the places that Intel is always looking to improve its chips is via the chip's microcode.

Pipelining Instructions

By now, the folks at Intel had squeezed a lot of the "juice" out of improving microcode efficiency. So they needed some other tricks to continue to beat better speed out of newer chips. So starting with the Pentium, Intel has designed CPUs with smarter and smarter *pipelines.*

What's a pipeline? Well, if you peek inside the workings of a CPU, you'll see that it looks somewhat like an assembly line—I'll get specific about what happens in that line in a moment, but for now just visualize an assembly line, like one that builds cars. Instead of turning out cars, however, CPUs turn out executed instructions, and they don't call it an assembly line; they call it a pipeline. With pipelining, a bit of data goes to the first station in the pipeline; then after that bit moves on to the next station, another bit takes its place at the first station. With pipelining, there's a bit along every station of the process. So instead of each bit of data having to wait for the preceding bit to go through the entire pipeline before starting off, a bit moves to each station along the way immediately after its predecessor leaves.

Now, if you wanted to assemble more cars per hour, you could approach it in two ways. The obvious way is to just try to get each of the workers to do their jobs faster, enabling you to run the assembly line faster. That would be like taking an existing CPU and increasing its clock rate, upping its megahertz. It's not a bad approach to speed, but there's another way. Instead of just trying to do the same old thing, only faster, you could reengineer the entire process, streamlining the steps along the way.

What happens along a CPU's pipeline? It varies from chip to chip, but basically you can break down the execution of any instruction into five basic steps:

Fetch Get the next instruction, either from random access memory (RAM) outside the CPU (on CPUs before the 486) or from the CPU's "instruction cache" memory (on 486 and later chips).

Decode Instructions differ in length; some are one byte long, and some are several bytes long. A given instruction, such as a MOVE command, may come in several different flavors: move from one location inside the CPU chip to a location outside the CPU chip, move from one place inside the CPU to another place inside the CPU, and so on. Even though the instruction differences are subtle, they're important. The decode section handles that.

Get the operands Most instructions require data to work on. Simply saying MOVE means nothing; the CPU must know *what* you want to move *where*. The *what* and *where* are operands. Similarly, if you tell the CPU, "Add 34 and 22," then *34* and *22* are the operands.

Execute As the Nike guys say, just do it. Whatever the instruction said to do—add, move, divide, compare, or whatever—now's the time to get it done.

Write back results After the operation has been done, the results of the operation—both the values created and any status information—get written to registers inside the computer.

By breaking up the task of executing an instruction into smaller subtasks, chip makers can divide the job of chip design into smaller chunks, and that in turn makes it possible to build these subsystems faster and faster. In other words, it's easier to build a CPU made up of five fast subpieces than it is to build a CPU out of one fast piece. This process of fetch-decode-get operands-execute-write back results is called the *CPU pipeline*. Some CPUs put multiple pipelines in a CPU, but I'll discuss that in a few pages.

Some of Intel's competitors try to outdo Intel in the speed department by changing the structure of a pipeline. Cyrix makes a chip called the M1 that uses seven substeps rather than five. AMD makes a CPU called the K5 with six substeps, and NexGen makes an Nx586 with seven substeps. Intel even outdid itself with the Pentium Pro/Pentium II/Celeron/Xeon, which divides its pipelines into 14 steps!

Intel has stated a goal that, ultimately, some future member of the *x86* family will execute each of its instructions in just one clock cycle. (Then again, world peace and funding Social Security are two goals that the government doesn't seem to be getting too far on, so don't hold your breath on the one-cycle promise either.)

Word Size

Every computer uses internal work areas, kind of like workbenches. These workbenches are called *registers.*

Any computer can be programmed to manipulate any size number, but the bigger the number, the longer it takes. The largest number that the computer can manipulate in one operation is determined by its *word size.* This is 8, 16, or 32 bits.

Think of it this way: if I ask you, "What is 5 times 6," you'd answer, "30" immediately—you did it in one operation. If I ask, "What is 55 times 66," you will do a series of steps to arrive at the answer. 55 is larger than your word size; 5 isn't. If you had a bigger "workbench," a bigger word size, then you could get complex calculations done in fewer steps and therefore more quickly. That's one reason why a 386, with 32-bit registers, is faster than a 286, with 16-bit registers.

The 8088 through 80286 chips used 16-bit words. The 80386 through Pentium Pro/II and III/Celeron/Xeon systems use 32-bit words. And future processors will most probably use 64, 128, and even larger word lengths.

Data Path

No matter how large the computer's word size, the data must be transported into the CPU. This is the width of the computer's "loading door," or the *data path.* It can also be 8, 16, 32 bits or 64 bits. Obviously, a wider door will allow more data to be transported in less time than will a narrower door.

Consider, for example, an 8MHz 8088 versus an 8MHz 8086. The *only difference* between the 8088 and the 8086 is that the 8088 has an 8-bit data path, and the 8086 has a 16-bit data path. Now, both the 8088 and the 8086 have 16-bit registers, so a programmer would issue the same command to load 16 bits into either one—the command MOV AX , 0200 will move the 16-bit value 200 hex into a

16-bit register called AX. That will take twice as long on the 8088 as it would on the 8086, because the 8086 can do it in one operation while the 8088 takes two. Note what's going on—although they're both 8MHz computers, the 8088 machine computes more slowly for some operations.

Now, you can see that the 8086 is a faster, more powerful chip than the 8088. But did you know that the 8088 was released *later* than the 8086? It's true; here's why.

When the 8086 was first released in 1977, it was one of the first microprocessors with a 16-bit data path. Almost every popular microprocessor-based computer available at the time was based on a CPU with an 8-bit data path. (*Almost* because the LSI-11 micro-processor had a 16-bit data path, and a few Heathkit computers used the LSI-11.) Because the CPUs all expected 8 bits whenever they *read* data and provided 8 bits when they *wrote* data, the mother-boards of computers in those days contained enough circuitry to transport 8 bits around.

Now, the 8086 was a neat-looking chip, because its 16 bits seemed just the stuff to build a powerful microcomputer. But con-sider the *bad* side of a 16-bit CPU: it requires a 16-bit motherboard. An 8086's motherboard must contain enough circuitry to transport *16* bits around, so it could be *twice* as expensive as an 8-bit mother-board of the same type. That put the 8086 at an economic disadvan-tage. (It may seem like a trivial matter now, but in the late '70s, hard-ware was more expensive, and an 8086-based motherboard was significantly more expensive than an 8-bit motherboard.)

So the folks at Intel said to themselves, "How can we offer the power of the 8086 and still keep motherboard prices down?" And so they built the 8088, a year after the 8086's release. Inside, the 8088 is identical to the 8086. The only difference is in the size of its "front door"—the path that the 8088 uses to transport data into and out of the chip. Because it is only 8 bits wide, motherboard design-ers could easily adapt existing designs to the new chip. As a result, the 8088 enjoyed a moderate amount of success from 1979 to 1981. Of course, after IBM released the PC in 1981 based on the 8088, moderate eventually changed to amazing.

History repeated itself in 1988 with the 80386SX. The original 80386 was introduced in 1985—Intel's next-generation chip with a 32-bit data path. The 386 did fairly well fairly quickly, but not quickly enough for Intel. The 286 sold well also, but the 286 had a problem as far as Intel was concerned: Intel didn't *own* the 286. By that, I mean that while Intel invented the 286, it had also licensed several vendors to make the 286, so many 286s being sold were lining the pockets of AMD, Fairchild, Siemens, and a number of other chip builders. Intel wanted *all* the profit from the 386, however, so they refused to license the 386 to any other company.

The 286 was not only a cheap chip, it was also a 16-bit chip, and a pure 16-bit chip at that—both word size and data path. That meant that 286 PCs could be built around 16-bit motherboards, and 32-bit motherboards were going to be just plain expensive. Therefore, 286-based PCs would be *tons* cheaper than 386 PCs, so more 286s would sell than 386s; Intel didn't like that. So they embarked on a campaign of what has to be characterized as chip infanticide. They ran a huge advertising campaign advising people to stay away from the 286 and to buy 386-based PCs. They *also* answered the manufacturer's concerns about the costs of building a 32-bit motherboard by offering the 80386SX.

The 80386SX was an 80386 with one difference: its "front door" was 16 bits, not 32 bits. Vendors liked that because they could take their old 16-bit 80286 motherboards, modify their design a bit, and voilà! They could offer "386 technology." After a year, it became clear that the original 80386 needed a real name to distinguish it from its less powerful cousin's name, so it became known as the 80386DX.

The 80486 line of chips also included an 80486SX, but was it a 16-bit chip? No. It *was* a chip with reduced functionality, but the reduction was not due to changes in data path. Instead, the 486SX was different from the 486DX in the way that it calculated arithmetic. You'll learn more about that type of processing in the upcoming section "Numeric Coprocessors."

The Pentium, MMX, Pentium Pro, Pentium II and III, Celeron, and Xeon chips actually have a data path *larger* than the word size; these chips have a 64-bit data path and 32-bit word sizes. What good is it having a front door that's twice the size of the workbench? Again,

Pentium and later chips aren't so much faster because of higher megahertz, but because of internal design—to use an old phrase, you might say that they don't work *harder*, they work *smarter*. Once Intel figured that it could only do so much with a single 32-bit system, they decided to speed up the process by essentially giving the Pentium a *second* workbench, a second pipeline, as you'll read in a few pages. That second pipeline needs feeding, hence the value of a larger data path.

As I've stated earlier, the early Pentium line of chips also included an SX-like chip called the Pentium OverDrive chip. The Pentium uses a 64-bit data path, and 486 manufacturers wanted to include Pentium compatibility on their motherboards. However, 486 motherboards are 32-bit in nature. How, then, to offer Pentium compatibility? Simple: enter the Pentium OverDrive chip, which features a 32-bit data path. Kind of a Pentium SX, you might say. Was it a good idea? Sure, if your 486 motherboard could accommodate it (a few could). But, again, that'll all make sense when you get to the discussion of instruction pipelines, coming soon in the section "Superscalar and Instruction Pipelines." But first, let's look at yet another way to speed up your computer: give it a little shot of super-fast memory, *internal cache*.

Internal Cache Memory

When people talk of RAM on a computer, they're talking about chips that the CPU uses to store its programs and data as it works, chips external to the CPU. The increasing speed of CPUs has driven a corresponding need for faster RAM.

The Memory Tradeoff: SRAM versus DRAM

RAM is commonly designed to be *dynamic* RAM, a simpler and cheaper design than its alternative, *static* RAM. I'll discuss static versus dynamic RAM in more detail in Chapter 8, "Semiconductor Memory," but for now, just understand that RAM presents a very fundamental tradeoff to system designers. Those designers can build computers to use either dynamic RAM or static RAM, and here's the tradeoff:

▶ Dynamic RAM (DRAM) is relatively cheap, but it is also relatively slow. In fact, no one makes DRAM that's fast enough to match speeds of modern CPUs.

▶ Static RAM (SRAM) is fast—it can be as fast as any of Intel's chips. But it's expensive, up to 10 to 20 times as expensive for a given amount of memory as DRAM.

At this point, the only way to build RAM that is as fast as the CPU is to populate the entire PC with static RAM, but that would be much too expensive. So PCs use a lot of dynamic RAM, which unfortunately sacrifices speed. To get back some of that speed, Intel puts a small amount of fast static RAM right into the CPU. That way, oft-used data needn't be accessed via the relatively slow DRAM; instead, the CPU can keep the most important data right by its side, in this small cache of storage. In fact, that's what it's called—*cache RAM.* It first appeared in some of the faster 386-based systems, because designers included space on the motherboards of high-performance systems for a bit of SRAM.

L1 Cache, L2 Cache, and the 80486 Family

Many computers designed since about 1987 have included cache RAM on their motherboards. The 80486 took the idea of cache a step further, however, in that the 80486 line of chips was the first in the x86 family to include cache RAM right on the CPU. With the exception of the DX4, they all contain 8KB of internal cache. The DX4 doubled that amount to 16KB. But even that small amount of extra, fast memory significantly improved CPU performance. Of course, while a few KB of cache is *nice*, it'd be nicer to have even more.

Most desktop motherboards today add from 64KB to 1024KB more static RAM cache to the motherboard. That's not *internal* cache, however, because it's not internal to the CPU. It's *external* cache and it's commonly called *L2 cache.* (The meaning of *external* when it comes to L2 cache gets a bit stretched with the Pentium II, as you'll see in a minute.) The internal cache in the 80486 and later processors is called *L1 cache*. L1 cache is built into the processor and usually runs at a speed nearly equaling or equaling the internal processor speed (the *core processor frequency* in Intel-ese).

Some Systems Are "Broke"

L2 cache is terrific for speed, but notice that I said most *desktop* PCs include cache. That's *very* important to anyone trying to compare the power of laptop computers to that of desktops. For example, right at the moment I'm writing on an "ancient" (late 1995) 166MHz clone Pentium. Sitting next to it on my desk is a 266MHz Digital Ultra HiNote 2000, a laptop. The HiNote is a wonderful machine, but put it next to the 166MHz desktop and they seem to be about the same speed; if anything, the 166 often seems faster. Why? Because the 166 has 256KB of L2 static cache on its motherboard. The HiNote, like most laptops of its era, has no L2 cache (less true today but the mechanics of a laptop still affect speed compared to desktop units with much fuller hardware). Basically, most laptop designs are "broke," by which I mean that they have less cache overall than their desktop cousins.

By the same token, many inexpensive *store clones* (clones you can buy off the shelf when you buy your garden tools at Sears or your barbecue at Price Club) of the original Pentium era also eliminated the L2 cache as a cost-saving measure. Some enabled you (for a considerable price) to add an L2 cache later, if desired, while others did not.

Tip

Removing the L2 cache temporarily (on systems that permit it) can sometimes help resolve problems. For example, on problematic installations or upgrades of Windows on PCs with an L2 cache, the short-term disabling of the L2 cache will let you install or upgrade Windows, and you can then re-enable the L2 cache to working status.

Pentium Cache

Speaking of the Pentium, by the way—part of how it turned out better-than-486 performance was through its cache. The Pentium's cache system is better than the 486's in four ways. First, the Pentium has twice as much cache, with two 8KB caches—one for data, one for program code. (A later variation of the Pentium, the MMX chip, had double that amount, a 16KB data cache and a 16KB instruction cache.) Second, the cache's method of organizing its cached data is more efficient, using a *write-back* algorithm. The opposite of a write-back algorithm, a *write-through* algorithm (used by the 486), forces data written to the SRAM cache memory to be immediately written to the slower DRAM memory. That means that memory *reads* can come out of the cache quickly, but memory *writes* must always occur at the slower DRAM time. Reasoning that not every piece of information written to memory *stays* in memory very long, the Pentium's cache algorithm puts off writing data from SRAM to DRAM for as long as possible. Third, the cache controller wastes time in searching to see whether an item is in the cache—the Pentium reduces that time by dividing the cache into smaller caches, each of which can be searched more quickly; that technique uses a *two-way set-associative cache*.

To explain the fourth way in which the Pentium's cache is better than the 486's, I have to first make an important point about what a cache must do. You may know that a cache must guess what data and program code the CPU will need soon, and then go get that data before the CPU asks for it. But guessing what the CPU will need isn't a straightforward task, particularly when there are decisions to be made. For example, suppose the cache sees that the CPU is currently executing some instructions that mean, "Compare value A with value B. If A is greater than B, then set the value *maximum* to A; otherwise, set the value *maximum* to B." That simple statement boils down to a bunch of instructions, instructions in memory that had better be in the cache if the Pentium is going to be able to continue running without delays. But since the cache controller can't know whether the CPU will take the "A is greater than B" or "B is greater than A" fork in the road, it doesn't know which result's code to go grab and put in the cache. For years, *mainframe* cache controllers have used a technique called *branch prediction* to guess which way the CPU will go, and now the Pentium and later PC chips have cache controllers built into them with branch prediction capabilities. So that's *four* ways that the Pentium makes better use of your memory than the 486 did.

The Pentium Pro, Pentium II, Pentium III, Celeron, Xeon, and Itanium Caches

What about the Pentium Pro and its cousins, the Pentium II and III, Celeron, and both the Xeon and Itanium chips? Well, there's some good news and some bad news.

With the Pentium Pro, Intel introduced the revolutionary step of making a sort of double-sized chip, a chip that looked like two Pentium chips side by side. The second "chip," however, was a 512KB L2 memory, a built-in cache RAM. This cache was terrific in that it could talk to the CPU at half of the CPU's full internal speed (the core processor frequency), not the external bus speed. Motherboards could be designed with even more external cache, however, and some Pentium Pro systems sold with as much as 1024KB of external cache, a mix of the built-in L2 cache and some chips on the motherboard. Because any chips on the motherboard can communicate with the processor only at the external bus speed rather than the internal speed, you might call that on-motherboard cache a sort of level 3 cache. The Pentium Pro has 16KB of L1 cache, as did the original Pentium.

With the Pentium II and III, Intel created a larger rectangular package called a Single Edge Cartridge (SEC), which no longer allows external cache. You can see a Pentium III in Figure 3.4.

Figure 3.4

Pentium III in SEC
package

The result is that you can't design a motherboard for a Pentium II or III that contains any cache. The Pentium II/III has its built-in 512KB of L2 cache, but that's it. (The Pentium II/III also has more L1 cache than the Pentium Pro, 16KB of data and 16KB of instruction cache, for a total of 32KB.) And that leads to an interesting comparison of the older Pentium Pro versus the Pentium II/III. Some of the Pro motherboards had room for 1MB (one thousand kilobytes) of cache (I say this in the past tense because Pros have become scarcer than hen's teeth). Therefore, you can benchmark a Pentium Pro at 200MHz (the fastest that they were built) versus a Pentium II at 333MHz—the Pentium Pro can actually be faster, because it's got 1024KB of cache versus the Pentium II's and III's half megabyte of cache!

The Pentium II/III Xeon chip addresses that problem and offers considerably improved performance for two reasons. First, the Xeon communicates between its built-in L2 cache and its processor at full-core processor speed—a 600MHz Xeon talks to its L2 cache at a full 600MHz. Second, the Xeon comes with up to 1024KB of built-in L2 cache. As you can buy the Xeon in up to 600MHz speeds, it's the ideal platform for playing Quake . . .

But I haven't mentioned the Celeron. What kind of L2 cache does it come with? Originally it had none. But Intel's customers weren't very happy about the Celeron's missing cache, so current models of the Celeron also have cache memory (smaller than the Pentium II and PIII, but fast).

Table 3.2 summarizes the top speed and L2 cache of the major CPUs.

TABLE 3.2 Major CPUs, Their Speed, and L2 Cache

CPU	Top Speed	Clock Speed	L2 Cache Size
Celeron	550	66	128KB
Pentium II	450	66/100	256-512KB
Pentium III	1GHz	100/133	256-512KB
Athlon	1GHz	133	512KB (later version)
Via Cyrix III	466	133	256KB
Xeon	600	100	512KB, 1MB, 2MB
Itanium	1GHz	100	4MB

Itanium: Now We're Talking L3 Cache

You've already learned a little bit about the Itanium (formerly the Merced) IA-64 processor. Not only does the Itanium have the power of the Xeon-level L1 and 4MB L2 cache onboard the chip itself, it adds up to 4MB of L3 cache (with an option for an L4 cache that can be added by an original equipment manufacturer (OEM). The L3 cache, smaller than a 3-by-5-inch index card, isn't on the chip itself but is contained in the processor package. The Itanium also has its own unique form factor, Slot M, and both the 800MHz and 1000MHz editions will operate on a 100MHz motherboard.

Numeric Coprocessors

Look at an early PC or XT, and next to the 8088 is an empty socket. From 1981 to 1983, IBM wouldn't say officially for what the socket on the PC was intended. But then they announced what everyone already knew: it was for the Intel 8087, a special purpose micro-processor. The 8087 is a microprocessor that is good for only one class of tasks: floating-point numeric operations.

Since then, all succeeding Intel CPUs offered some way of incorporating a floating-point computation unit. In fact, all the current processors have a built-in *floating-point processor unit* (*FPU*).

The MMX: A Matrix Math Coprocessor

By the time the Pentium arrived, it seemed like there wasn't much to say anymore about coprocessors, because even the lowliest Pentium had the coprocessor circuitry built in.

But then a newer form of the Pentium arrived, the *MMX* (MMX, by the way, is purportedly not an acronym, because it doesn't officially stand for anything, but it basically means *multimedia extensions*). MMX technology is (since it's still around and incorporated into our PIIs and PIIIs) an enhancement to Intel CPUs that is designed to make

PCs faster and more colorful when they're handling multimedia applications (interactive video, virtual reality, and high-quality 3D) and communications applications. The enhancement is provided by MMX versions of Intel chips, which, in addition to their regular features, respond to 57 instructions that are oriented to highly parallel operations with multimedia and communications data types. Multimedia apps do lots of computation, lots of tasks in parallel, and tend to use small integer data types. The 57 new microcode instructions that constitute MMX technology were designed to help speed up the core algorithms and thus improve overall application performance. Having the MMX instructions in a Pentium chip makes it easier to build code to do multimedia operations such as simultaneous, real-time activities. An example is multiple channels of audio, near-TV-quality video or animation, and Internet communication all running in the same application. And, in fact, MMX computers that I've worked on that have video capture boards can capture much higher-quality video than comparable non-MMX computers can with the same video capture hardware.

Note

Every Pentium model since the MMX was introduced is MMX compatible—meaning that the PII, the PIII, the Xeon, and the Celeron all support the multimedia instructions packaged into the Pentium MMX.

The 57 instructions use a technique known as *Single Instruction, Multiple Data* (*SIMD*), which means that a single instruction operates on multiple pieces of data in parallel. For example, with a single MMX instruction, up to eight integer pairs can be added together in parallel. This parallel operation uses 64-bit registers. Depending on the operation, these are defined as eight 8-bit bytes, four 16-bit words, two 32-bit double words, or one 64-bit quad word.

MMX technology was designed to simplify writing things that must manipulate matrix-oriented data, applications such as:

▶ Video capture programs

- ▶ Graphical manipulation programs such as Paint Shop Pro

- ▶ Graphics-intensive games

- ▶ 2D and, to a lesser extent, 3D graphics

- ▶ Speech recognition

- ▶ Data compression

The MMX represents a specific policy goal for Intel: *let the system processor do all the computing.* Years ago, Intel sought to build terrific video capture boards around special-purpose chips designed to do one and only one thing: convert an analog video signal into a digital signal quickly. But Intel realized that they'd rather sell 100 million Pentium II chips a year than sell 50 million Pentium II chips, 5 million video capture chips, 10 million sound chips, and so on. So they started encouraging multimedia vendors to build cheaper boards that offload more and more of their work onto the main processor. The result is, of course, that people want faster and faster processors. The MMX's 57 new commands were added to the Pentium to make it easier for the processor to get those jobs done.

Does any software *require* the MMX? There are quite a few, but most of them are video games. Thus, if someone asks, "Is Windows 98 (or NT or 2000) MMX-compatible?" the answer is, "Yes." MMX CPUs have all the same operation codes (opcodes) as older CPUs, and the operating systems mentioned here have not been written to require the MMX opcodes.

What this means, of course, is that the new MMX-type processors should run all your old applications just fine. It doesn't mean, however, that you, personally, can somehow add MMX technology to your old-but-still-cranking 486 or Pentium chip. MMX instructions are new instructions directly incorporated into the processor, and this can be accomplished only when the chip is manufactured.

Which CPUs are MMX-compatible? The first MMX-capable CPU was *called* the MMX. It was a modified Pentium. But the Pentium chip didn't have enough room to be able to handle both the floating-point numeric coprocessor support as well as the matrix MMX support at the same time, so unfortunately when you're running MMX-specific software on an MMX, the floating-point support is disabled. That's too bad, because whenever you're doing matrix-specific calculations, you're likely to be also doing complex math (logs, sines, exponentials). The job still gets done, but without the floating-point coprocessor, complex math takes longer to do. Thus, the MMX gets faster on matrix operations but gets slower on floating-point. Is it a good tradeoff? Sorry, there's just no good answer to this one; it all depends upon the software you're running.

The next MMX was the Pentium II. The Pentium II is just a Pentium Pro with MMX circuits added. The good news is that the Pentium II has the power to simultaneously run both the MMX commands and the floating-point command—very cool! Clearly Intel regretted releasing a chip that made software choose between matrix and floating-point, leading some to wonder if the correct name of the Pentium II should really be the *Repent*ium chip. In any case, the Pentium II was soon joined by a lower-priced model (the Celeron) and a higher-priced model (the Xeon), both close cousins, and then by the Pentium III and soon, the Itanium—so close, in fact, that they have MMX circuitry as well.

Superscalar and Instruction Pipelines

Remember I said earlier that the Pentium and later chips try to "work smarter, not harder"? I'll explain that in a bit more detail here. As time goes on, Intel tries to speed up their CPUs. But they're greatly hampered by the need for backward compatibility. So they use another way to make the Pentium faster: basically, they put two CPUs into it.

The Pentium Pipeline Structure

As you read earlier, the circuitry that constitutes a CPU—registers, instruction decoders, and arithmetic/logic units—are all called *instruction pipelines* by CPU designers. All the Intel CPUs that I've discussed, up to and including the 486 family, had just one pipeline in each chip, which is a techie way of saying, "The 486 and predecessors could do only one thing at a time."

In contrast, there are essentially two CPUs in the Pentium chip. The first one is like a 486DX, a CPU with floating-point capabilities built right into it. The second is a 486SX, lacking a floating-point unit. (Why didn't they put two floating-point units in? It would have made the thing bigger, hotter, and more expensive.) That means that the Pentium is essentially a parallel-processing CPU, with the capability to do two things at once. Those two CPUs-within-a-CPU are called the *U and V pipelines*, and having more than one pipeline makes the Pentium a *superscalar* CPU. (Why not parallel processing or multiprocessing or dual processing, I don't know—*superscalar* is the buzzword.)

The neat part of this dual pipelining is that the Pentium uses both pipelines *automatically*. It takes a simple non-Pentium-aware program, reads it, and divides it into two pipelines. Now, that's not always possible, because some programs contain internal *dependencies*, but the Pentium does the best that it can.

For example, consider these three commands:

A = 3

B = 2

C = A + B

The first two commands, A = 3 and B = 2, are *not* dependent. You can manipulate A and manipulate B, and there's no interaction. Once they're done, then you're set to do C = A + B. As a result, A = 3 could go over the U pipeline while B = 2 goes over the V pipeline, and then C = A + B could run on the U pipeline once A = 3 was done. But now consider this sequence:

A = 1

A = A + 2

The second command can't be executed until the first command is done. Therefore, in this case, the Pentium would be forced to put the first command, A = 1, into one of the pipelines and then wait for it to finish before executing A = A + 2.

You'll see programs advertised as "designed for the Pentium" or "optimized for the Pentium." That means the instructions have been arranged so that the Pentium can keep both pipelines stuffed and busy. So-called *Pentium programs* ran fine on a 486, and even on a 386, except that they ran more slowly, because (among other things) those processors have only one pipeline.

The Pentium Pro/II/III/Celeron/Xeon Pipeline Structure

If two pipelines sound like a lot, then hold onto your hat, because the Pentium Pro/Pentium II/III/Celeron/Xeon chips contain an even more complex system with (depending on how you look at it) three or five pipelines. How does it work?

Think of the Pentium Pro family pipelines as being organized in three major pieces:

▶ Decode

▶ Execute

▶ Clean up

The decode section works as it does on earlier chips, just mainly fetching an instruction and figuring out what it needs to do—integer math, floating-point math, a memory read or write, or something else. There are three decoding pipelines, which means that the Pentium Pro can get three instructions ready at the same time. There aren't any interdependency problems with the decode phase.

The second phase executes the actual instruction. Because this takes the most time, Intel included *five* execution pipelines. Any one of them can perform very simple operations, but for more demanding (or time-consuming) tasks, there are specialists. Two of the pipelines can do only integer computations, like the V pipeline on a

Pentium. Two of the pipelines can do both integer computations and floating-point computations, like the U pipeline on a Pentium. And one of the pipelines specializes in transferring data to and from memory. As with the Pentium's two-pipeline system, there's no guarantee that all five pipelines will remain active at all times, because interdependent code may, once again, make that impossible.

Recall that the older Pentium had to examine the incoming stream of program instructions and determine the dependencies within that stream; the Pentium Pro and later chips have the same need. For nonoptimized code, the Pentium Pro family has often proven to be fast but not amazingly so. In fact, in February 1996, *BYTE* magazine reported that the Pentium Pro ran 16-bit applications (including the 16-bit parts of Windows 95) *slower* than the Pentium did, because the Pentium Pro was "tuned" to run 32-bit applications better than the Pentium. That's why if you're still running Windows 3.1 or DOS programs, *or* if you're running several of those older programs like WordPerfect 5.1 for DOS under Windows 95/98/NT, then you may not see particularly impressive behavior. You need *truly* 32-bit code (and code optimized for the Pentium Pro family) to see the performance improvements in the Pentium Pro, the Pentium II/III, the Celeron, and the Xeon (although the Celeron's lack of cache or limited cache makes it a pretty lame performer no matter what you do). And it's sadly true that there's not all that much code around that's really tuned to use 32 bits; even "new" 32-bit software such as Office 2000 and even Windows 2000 (as an operating system) still contains a lot of old 16-bit code. In my experience, the programs that are best tuned to use 32 bits are the high-end stuff—SQL database engines and file/print servers—and what some might call the low end—games. Personal productivity programs don't seem to be a priority for performance tuning; instead, the vendors seem more intent on adding thousands of features.

A final thought on superscalar architecture: it's now possible to take a second look at the Pentium OverDrive chip, the Pentium chip that fit on specially designed 486 motherboards. Was it a good idea? Well, consider what the Pentium really is: two 32-bit chips. As long as there are 64 bits feeding it, then the Pentium makes sense. But taking two 32-bit pipelines and forcing them to share a single 32-bit data path seems likely to end up creating a chip that only performs like a single 32-bit chip. (Maybe that's why Intel took so long to finally release it.)

Memory Addressable by a CPU

Megabytes are a unit of storage size—just about the amount of space needed to store a million characters. People use this term to talk about the size of primary memory—RAM, the kind of memory that goes in expansion boards, the kind of memory that Lotus can run out of if you've got a large spreadsheet—as well as secondary memory, which are disk drives. When most people say *memory*, they are talking about *primary* memory, so memory means chips or RAM. Folks usually just say *disk* memory when that's what they mean, rather than secondary memory.

Disk memory is also not *volatile*, which means that when you shut it off, it retains its data. Remove power from a memory chip (which happens whenever you turn the machine off), and it forgets whatever it contained. That's why you have to save your work to disk before shutting off the machine.

But using the same type of measurement (megabytes) for both disks and memory confuses people. I'll say, "I work with a Pentium II with 128MB of memory," and they'll think, "What good is *that*? Even I've got *six gigabytes* (6 billion bytes) on my PC." I was talking about primary memory—128MB of RAM. I didn't say anything at all about how much hard disk space I've got. *They* were thinking of hard disk space, and didn't tell me how much memory their PC has. (I hope it would be at the very least 32MB, and I wouldn't outfit a computer nowadays with less than 64MB.) End of digression.

You can't just keep adding memory to your PC indefinitely. A particular chip can *address* only a certain size of memory. For the oldest CPUs, this amount was 16,384 bytes—a 16KB memory. The original IBM PC's CPU could address 1024KB, or 1MB. Other, newer chips can address even more. The 80386, 80486, Pentium, and Pentium Pro families could address gigabytes, and newer ones still address terabytes.

Slots and Sockets

Are you feeling a bit confused about slots and sockets? If so, don't feel alone. The past few years, whenever a different approach to computer processors is taken, we end up with a different way in which the CPU is packaged for installation.

In recent modern CPU history, a *socket* was simply the place on the motherboard where the CPU plugs in—pins into holes. The Socket 7 standard created for the original Pentium-class PCs allowed for a simple insertion (or plug-in) of a CPU into the motherboard. Such CPUs feature 321 pins set in five staggered rows. A *slot* allows the CPU to slide into place, something like a tiny version of plugging an expansion card into a PCI slot.

Socket-type CPUs are cheaper to produce overall, while slot-type is an attempt to pack more speed and power into a CPU package. Put most simply, the closer you bring the cache to the processor, the better the system should perform, and the slot-type helps you accomplish that.

Although Intel moved away from the Socket 7 standard as it moved to the Pentium Pro (Socket 8, with 387 pins in five dual-pattern pin rows, and the cache built into the processor package), Socket 7 has stayed with us because alternative CPU manufacturers, particularly AMD, adopted it and used it for their line of K6 processors. Only with the Athlon has AMD broken stride, giving it a completely different Slot A insertion.

Intel, meanwhile, was shifting again. With the introduction of the Pentium II came the Single Edge Contact Cartridge (SECC), wherein the processor and cache are mounted on a *daughterboard* (secondary board) on the chip and then inserted into the motherboard. Pentium IIs and IIIs use Slot 1 technology, which has 242 pins set in two rows of 121 pins each. When Intel introduced the Itanium, change happened again, going from Slot 1 technology to Slot M.

Socket 370 was introduced during the PII reign as alternative packaging for Celerons (which in the beginning, had no L2 cache). But as Celerons were minted that included a 128KB L2 cache, the packaging turned to Slot 1, like the Pentium II itself, with an adapter available to fit a Socket 370 Celeron into a Pentium II- Slot 1-style motherboard. Table 3.3 lists CPUs and their slots or socket types.

TABLE 3.3 CPUs and Their Required Slots/Socket Types

CPU	Slot/Socket Form Factor
Pentium (classic)	Socket 7
Pentium MMX	Socket 7
AMD K6	Socket 7
AMD K6-II	Socket 7
AMD K6-III	Socket 7
Pentium Pro	Socket 8
OverDrive	Socket 8
Celeron	Socket 370
Celeron	Slot 1
Pentium II	Slot 1
Pentium III	Slot 1
Athlon	Slot A
Xeon	Slot 1
Itanium	Slot M

Details on CPU Chips

While I've talked a lot about various CPU chips in this part of the chapter, there are a few odds and ends that I haven't covered yet. I'll tie up those things here. I'll start by listing all the Intel and Intel-compatible CPUs and summarizing their characteristics—see Table 3.4. (The table is organized under abbreviated headings explained in the key that follows the table.)

TABLE 3.4 CPU Specifications and Applications

Model	ECF	ICF	WS	DP	IP	M	MC	IC	V	MMX	COMP
Intel											
8088	8	8	16	8	1	1	No	0	5	No	
8086	8	8	16	16	1	1	No	0	5	No	
80c86	8	8	16	16	1	1	No	0	5	No	
80186	16	16	16	16	1	1	No	0	5	No	
80286	20	20	16	16	1	16	No	0	5	No	
80386DX	40	40	32	32	1	4096	No	0	5	No	
80386SX	25	25	32	16	1	16	No	0	5	No	
80486SLC	25 33	25 33	32	32	1	64	No	8	5	No	
80486DX	25 33 50	25 33 50	32	32	1	4096	Yes	8	5	No	
80486SX	20 25 33	20 25 33	32	32	1	4096	No	8	5	No	
80486DX2	20 25 33	40 50 66	32	32	1	4096	Yes	8	5	No	
80486DX4	25 33	75 100	32	32	1	4096	Yes	16	5	No	
Pentium	60 66	100 133 150 166 200	32	64	2	4096	Yes	16	5 3.3	No	
MMX	66	200 233 266	32	64	2	4096	Yes	32	1.5	Yes	
Pentium Pro	60 66	166 200	32	64	3	65,536	Yes	32	1.5	No	

Continued on next page

TABLE 3.4 CPU Specifications and Applications (continued)

Model	ECF	ICF	WS	DP	IP	M	MC	IC	V	MMX	COMP
Pentium II	66 100	233 266 300 333 350 400	32	64	3	65,536	Yes	32	1.5	Yes	
Pentium III	66 100 133	500 1000	32	64			Yes	32	1.5	Yes	
Celeron	66	233 266 300	32	64	3	65,536	Yes	32	1.5	Yes	
Xeon	100	350 400	32	64	3	65,536	Yes	32	2	Yes	
Itanium/ Merced	100	500 600	64	64	3		Yes			Yes	
NEC											
V20	10	10	16	8	1	1	No	0	5		8088
V30	10	10	16	16	1	1	No	0	5		8086
Cyrix											
80486SLC	25 33	25 33	32	32	1	16	No	1	5		386SX
80486SLC	25	50	32	32	1	16	No	1	5		386SX
80486DLC	33	33	32	32	1	4096	No	1	5		386DX
80486DX	33 40 50	33 40 50	32	32	1	4096	Yes	8	5		486DX
80486DX2	25 33 40	50 66 80	32	32	1	4096	Yes	8	5		486DX2
586		100 120	32	64	1	4096	Yes	16	3.45–5		Pentium

Continued on next page

TABLE 3.4 CPU Specifications and Applications (continued)

Model	ECF	ICF	WS	DP	IP	M	MC	IC	V	MMX	COMP
6x86	75	150	32	64	2	4096	Yes	16	3.3–5		Pentium
	66	133									
	60	120									
	55	110									
	50	100									
AMD											
386SE	25	253	32	16	1	16	No	0	3–5		386SX
	33	3									
386DE	33	334	32	32	1	4096	No	0	3–5		386DX
	40	0									
486DXLV	33	33	32	32	1	4096	Yes	8	3.0–3.6		486DX
486SXLV	33	33	32	32	1	4096	No	8	3.0–3.6		486SX
486DX	33	334	32	32	1	4096	Yes	8	5		486DX
	40	0									
486SX	33	334	32	32	1	4096	No	8	5		486SX
	40	0									
486DX2	25	506	32	32	1	4096	Yes	8	5		486DX2
	33	6									
486DX2-80	40	80	32	32	1	4096	Yes	8	5		486DX2
486DXL2	25	50	32	32	1	4096	Yes	8	5		486DX2
	33	66									
486SX2-50	25	50	32	32	1	4096	Yes	8	5		486SX
Am5x86	33	133				4096	Yes	16	3.45		Pentium 75
Athlon	133	600						12			
		1000						8			

Key to Table 3.4

ECF = External clock frequency (in MHz)   ICF = Internal clock frequency (in MHz)

WS = Word size (in bits)   DP = Data path (in bits)

IP = Instruction pipelines (how many)   M = Memory (in bytes)

MC = Math coprocessor   IC = Internal cache (in KB)

V = Voltage (in volts)   MMX = MMX compatibility

Comp = Intel compatibility

Some of these chips are more powerful or less powerful. Some can actually allow you to improve the throughput of your existing PC, although most of these are in the past—CPU speeds are updated too swiftly now, so there is no real market for overdriving a CPU this way. Instead, many buy cheaper CPUs such as the Celeron and the K6-II and overclock them by manipulating clock/multiplier rates.

You'll see a bit of repetition in the following pages as I detail each processor, but that's intentional. I've thrown an awful lot of concepts at you so far; the intent in this section is to tie up all the CPU concepts before progressing on to memory, buses, and other hardware topics.

8088

The 8088 was the "Grand Old Man" of PC CPUs, although the 8086 came before it and was arguably a better design. It came in what was called a 40-pin DIP package, which means a rectangular plastic case with two rows of 20 pins. *DIP* stands for *Dual Inline Package*. Older 8088s were called 8088-1s, because they could run at only low speeds (5MHz or slower). Turbo PC/XT clones ran at 6.66, 7.16, or 8MHz. To do this, they used the 8088-2, which was rated at up to 8MHz. The 8088 was the equivalent of about 29,000 transistors.

8086

The 8086 predated the 8088 by a year and was actually more powerful than it, but the 8086 was not as well known. The 8086 was different from the 8088 in that the 8086 not only had internal 16-bit registers (a 16-bit word) but also a 16-bit data path, the doorway to the outside world. Because that required 16-bit motherboards, however, the 8086 never really caught on. The 8088 was essentially a hobbled 8086, because it had only an 8-bit data path. But that made for a cheaper motherboard, so IBM went with the 8088—and the rest is history. But a few clone makers opted for 8086-based systems because the 8086 was 100 percent compatible with the 8088 *and* faster; one example was Compaq, with a tremendously successful computer called the Deskpro.

80186 and 80188

You don't hear much about these chips, but they were souped-up versions of the 8086 and 8088. They didn't really have much in the way of new capabilities; they were just a polished version of the old chips, sort of similar to the way that the 80486 was not a big leap from the 80386, but rather a mildly improved version. The main differences were that the 186 and the 188 were manufactured in a PGA package (see the "80286" section for more on this), and had more efficient microcode. Tandy sold a computer called the Tandy 2000 that was 80186-based. It could have been a high-performance competitor to the Deskpro, but Tandy unwisely opted to make it only about 60 percent compatible with the IBM PC, forcing Tandy 2000 users to buy special versions of software. There weren't too many titles developed for the Tandy 2000, and it went nowhere.

The 80186 was the last member of what might be called the first family of PC CPUs, a family that started with the 8086.

80286

The 80286, introduced in 1981, was a major step forward for *x*86 technology. It was packaged in a square of ceramic called a *Pin Grid Array (PGA)* package. It also came in a cheaper package called a *Plastic Leadless Chip Carrier (PLCC)*. You might remember these terms from the preceding chapter. The PLCC is the more durable of the two, and is mainly found in laptops, due to its lower profile. The PGA package has an inner and an outer square of solid pins; the PLCC has curved-under legs around its perimeter. The PGA "stands" on its legs. The PLCC is surrounded by its legs. You can see chip package types in Figure 3.5.

DIP (Dual In-line Package)   PGA (Pin Grid Array)

Figure 3.5

Chip package types   Surface Mount   PLLC (Plastic Leadless Chip Carrier)

The 286 packed a lot more power into a small package than the 8088 did: the 80286 was the equivalent of about 130,000 transistors in about the same volume. Because of this, the 80286 ran hotter, and some models required extra cooling provisions such as a heat sink. *Heat sinks* are small metal caps with metal cooling fins that fit on top of a chip and enable the chip to better dissipate the heat that it generates. You see them on modern CPUs, such as Pentiums, which produce even greater amounts of heat.

The 80286 was the sole member of the second family of PC-compatible CPUs. In many ways, it was a rough draft for the 386 family, the third family of PC CPUs.

80386DX and 80386SX

The 80386, or as it was officially called by Intel, the 80386DX, was another quantum leap for the *x*86 family. Introduced in 1985, it came in a PGA package and was the equivalent of about 250,000 transistors. It incorporated a wealth of programming features, including the capability to multitask DOS programs with the help of operating systems such as Windows. The 32-bit data path sped up data access, leading to the design of buses such as the Micro Channel, EISA, VESA, and PCI buses (see the upcoming section on buses). It also differed from previous *x*86 designs in that it could address 4096MB of RAM.

The 386SX was identical to the 386DX except that it had a 16-bit data path to enable it to be more easily incorporated into AT-type hardware designs (recall that the AT's 286 had a 16-bit data path also). It was contained in a PLCC package.

The 80386 family brought a new set of instruction codes and a 32-bit programming model to PC CPUs that is essentially unchanged to this day. Look at the most modern PC programs not written specifically for a 32-bit Windows environment (Windows 95/98, Windows 2000), and many of them will run on a circa-1985 386-based system, albeit slowly.

80386SL

The SL was part of a two-chip set that was basically a combination of a 386SX and a motherboard. The two chips together constituted almost all of what's needed to build an SX computer. What made it particularly interesting was that the chip set included power management. For example, the SL system could shut down the CPU between keystrokes, saving power. The SL mainly appeared in laptops; they were in PLCC packages.

80486DX

The 80486 (officially the 80486DX) was sort of an upgraded 386. Code-named during development *P4*, it combined a tuned-up 386 with two chips that sped up a 386 system: the 385 cache controller and the 387 numeric coprocessor. The microcode was larger and faster—there were the equivalent of 1.25 *million* transistors in this chip. Depending upon what the computer was doing, a 25MHz 386 with a 385 and a 387 (cache controller and external math coprocessor) would sometimes execute only half as many instructions per second as a 25MHz 486.

Better yet, the 486 chip was actually cheaper than a 386, 385, and 387 together, so eventually 486 computers were cheaper than fully loaded 386 machines. The DX appeared in PGA packages.

80486SX

The 80486SX was more of a marketing tool than a new chip. Intel took the 486DX chips that failed the math coprocessor analysis during product testing and sold them in a new package they called a 486SX. It had a specified maximum clock speed of 20MHz and no math coprocessor. Intel then offered a math coprocessor called the 487SX that was, believe it or not, a fully functional 486DX—a CPU chip with coprocessor and all. Once the 487SX was planted in its socket, it instructed the 486SX to just go to sleep; the 487SX then handled everything, including both general computing and numeric coprocessing, just as if it were a normal 486DX system running at 20MHz.

80486DX2, DX4, and the OverDrive Chip

The 80487SX, as it turns out, was a mere harbinger of the wide variety in CPUs that was to follow. With the 486, Intel first started experimenting with product diversification, taking a basically good product (the 486DX) and repackaging it in a variety of ways.

Recall that the 80487SX was *not* a floating-point coprocessor. It was a fully functional 80486DX, but packaged a bit differently—the pins on the bottom of the chip were arranged differently from the way they were arranged on the 80486DX, so you couldn't just pop an 80486DX in the 80487SX socket. Furthermore, unlike the floating-point coprocessors of yore (the 8087, 187, 287, and 387 families), the 80487SX didn't work with the erstwhile main processor—*it took over altogether*, effectively disconnecting the 80486SX. A bit of clever marketing, eh? Buy a "cheap" 486SX and then end up buying a whole 486DX disguised as a coprocessor, with the result that Intel gets to sell more chips than if you'd bought a 486DX in the first place.

Next stop in the 486-marketing universe was the original OverDrive chip. ("Original" because the term *overdrive* has since been recycled by Intel a number of times.) The OverDrive chip was a 486DX built for a 487SX socket, as usual, *except* that they made it a clock doubler like the 486DX2.

The net effect was that the OverDrive chip did everything at least as quickly as a 25MHz 80486DX, and many operations twice as fast! So the OverDrive chip would speed up your PC by about one-third to one-half. Was it worth it? An OverDrive chip cost around $300, not a small amount, but then not a budget-buster either.

Intel then took on the market of folks who had a 486DX and wanted more speed by offering the clock doubler 486DX2. Recall that the 80486DX2, like the OverDrive chip, ran outwardly at *x*MHz, but worked internally at *2x*MHz. Thus, a so-called 66MHz 80486DX2 worked in a motherboard designed for a 33MHz chip, but ran internally at 66MHz. The value was, again, that a PC vendor needed only take one of its already existing 33MHz 80486DX models, replace the 33MHz 80486DX processor with a 66MHz 80486DX processor, and it instantly got a "66MHz 486."

The last in the Intel 486 line was the DX4, a clock tripler 486 that contained power management right on the chip, combining 386SL-like technology and clock tripling to produce a very nice processor. Its main role was in laptops, where it functioned extremely well.

486SLC and 486DLC

This one wasn't an Intel chip. It wasn't even a 486. A 486SLC was a 386SX (no numeric coprocessor, recall) with just *1KB of cache* and, of course, a *16-bit data path*. The resulting chip was somewhere between a 386SX and a 486SX in performance. The 1KB was pretty measly, so you'd have to say that the performance was closer to the 386SX than to the 486. There was also a 486DLC, a 386DX with 1KB of cache memory added, and no coprocessor. These chips were pin-compatible with the 386SX and 386DX, not the 486 line. My main gripe with them was the marketing baloney that went with them: people were told they were getting 486 technology when they bought one of these chips, but they actually got only 386 technology.

Micro technology improvement, macro sales pitches. Yup, you can always tell when a technological industry matures: the guys in the wheelhouse are marketing guys rather than engineers.

386DRU2

Another Intel competitor. It had an odd-looking name, but that was how it came to be known internally at the company. This Cyrix chip was a 386 clone, save that it was a clock doubler: you could make a 25MHz 386 into a 50MHz 386 with one of these.

That, in general, has been Cyrix's modus operandi: take what Intel does and do it better. It has not served them badly.

Pentium

In 1993, Intel introduced the processor they had code-named *P5*, known now as the Pentium processor. In some ways, it was just a souped-up 486. In other ways, it was much more, as you've seen from the earlier parts of this chapter. Here's a quick look at Pentium features besides the ones we've already examined.

Greater Raw Speed

The Pentium comes in a variety of flavors: 60, 66, 75, 90, 100, 125, 133, 150, and 166MHz, and, in its newer MMX flavor, is available up to 266MHz. Intel offers an OverDrive upgrade for chips 100MHz and under that increases the chip's speed by about half.

The 120/133MHz OverDrive processor upgrade is designed to reduce the voltage used by the 60MHz and 66MHz chips from 5 volts to the 3.3 used by the more recent chips that take advantage of Intel's Voltage Reduction Technology.

Note

Counterintuitively, you may get better performance from a 133 than a 150, because the 133 is a doubled 66MHz chip, and the 150 is a two-and-a-halved 60.

The Pentium is difficult to make because, for one thing, it's much bigger than the 486. The 486 contains 1.2 million transistors; the Pentium contains 3.1 million—over two and a half times as many.

That's an important contributing factor to the extreme heat, and it doesn't get any better with the Pentium Pro; as a laptop user, I look forward to a Hexium notebook that will serve double duty as both a fast computer and a portable hot plate for us road warrior types. (Just kidding.)

Seriously, though, I'd avoid the 60 and 66, and go straight to the 90 and 100 chips, because they're actually cooler (lower voltage, remember).

Fault Tolerance

The Pentium is designed to be used in conjunction with another Pentium on a motherboard specifically suited for fault tolerance (meaning, it would try to stand up to and operate under situations that might crash a less tolerant system). The second Pentium constantly monitors the first; if the main Pentium malfunctions, the other one jumps right in and takes up without skipping a beat. Another purpose for two CPUs on one motherboard is symmetric multiprocessing (SMP), the ability to divide the workload between multiple processors. Most dual CPU implementations are designed for SMP, and not for fault tolerance.

First MMX Implementation

Another Pentium first is the so-called multimedia support, the matrix functions in the MMX. The MMX is just a Pentium with MMX instructions included and a larger cache. The Pentium's a hot chip, in more ways than one. So hot, in fact, that you should recall that if you're still running older 16-bit apps, then you won't be all that impressed with its successors, the Pentium Pro family. So don't feel that you absolutely *must* upgrade your existing 166MHz system. In actual fact, simply adding RAM to your system may make it produce the performance you're looking for.

The Pentium Pro Family: Pentium Pro, Pentium II, Celeron, and Xeon

The Pentium Pro, Pentium II, III, Celeron, Xeon, and Itanium chips are known as the P6 line of chips. The P6s differ from their predecessors for many reasons. But are they *faster* chips? Well, yes, kind of—but, like their predecessors, the P6 family is largely limited by its heritage: it's got to be *x86* compatible.

Just looking at the P6 family shows how it's different. With the exception of the Celeron, the P6s are fairly large chips, because they contain lots of memory. The Pentium Pro chip, for example, is actually *two* chips. Inside the Pentium Pro, there is one chip (*die* is the actual word; it refers to the silicon wafer that is the actual electronics of a chip), which is the main processor. It has about 5.5 million transistors. Alongside it is a built-in 256KB external or L2 cache, about 15 million transistors' worth of static memory. You can see that in Figure 3.6.

256K L2 cache —   — Main processor die

Figure 3.6

L2 cache on the
Pentium Pro chip

The Pentium Pro incorporates three pipelines, rather than the two of the Pentium. By breaking up instruction execution into 14 steps, Intel has made it possible to do what they call *dynamic execution*. Explained earlier in the "Superscalar and Instruction Pipelines" section, dynamic execution works by using three parallel units to fetch and decode instructions; once prepared for execution, those instructions are tossed into a "pool" of waiting instructions. There's not much waiting, however, because the P6s have five execution units working side by side to try to shove instructions through at top speed. That helps because the Pentium Pro can handle groups of instructions *out of their original order*, which keeps as many of the fetch, decode, and execution units working at the highest capacity possible.

Oddly enough, the Pentium Pro has an L1 cache of only 16KB, the same as the standard Pentium, and in fact less than the Pentium MMX chips. That is offset by the large L2 cache incorporated into the chip. By putting the L2 cache on the chip, the Pentium Pro can more quickly access that memory, making it a faster "external" cache than the external caches found on Pentium and earlier chips. But 20 million transistors! That sucker is a mite toasty, so make sure there's a decent CPU fan on your Pentium Pro. Most come with a fan, as you see in Figure 3.7.

The other P6ers—Celeron, Xeon, and Pentium II—all have 32KB of L1 cache and can also suffer from heat exhaustion (the Xeon even has a sensor on-chip to detect overheating).

The later P6s' heat problems weren't as terrible as they could be, however, because Intel has again reduced the size of the transistors that make up the chip. Whereas the Pentium was built with 0.8-micron and 0.6-micron components, the Xeon is built with 0.25-micron components. That will help make the Xeon work at a decent reliability factor when running at 600MHz.

600MHz. And to think my first PC ran at 4.77MHz . . .

Speed demons that they are, depending on which operating system you're running, the P6s may not be the best choice. Recall that Intel decided to bite the bullet and sacrifice some backward compatibility with 16-bit applications in order to get better speed from 32-bit ones. Unfortunately, this means that 16-bit operating systems (including parts of Windows 95/98) don't run very well on the Pentium Pro. In fact, they may run more slowly on the Pentium Pro than the Pentium. This chip might be a better choice for those planning to run full 32-bit operating systems, such as Windows NT Workstation.

The Pentium III processors are very similar to the Pentium IIs; however, the IIIs run faster (450–550MHz), support 70 new instructions, and run on the 100MHz system bus with the original version and 133MHz on the newer Coppermines (more to come about Coppermines in just a bit).

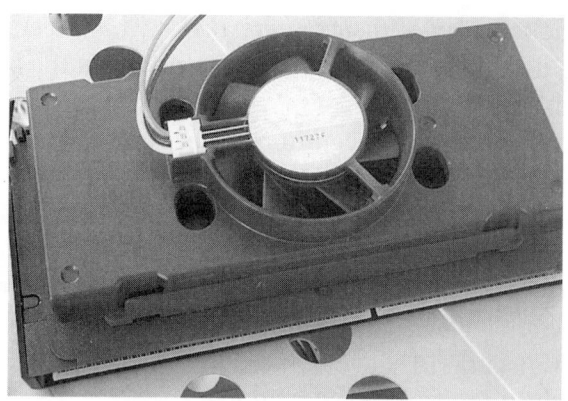

Figure 3.7

Pentium II package
with fan

Pentium II

The Pentium II (PII) made some impressive improvements to the original Pentium processor. Ranging in speeds from 233MHz to 450MHz, the PII improves not only speed, but also performance. The PII incorporates a 100MHz *front bus* interface (for the 350MHz, 400MHz, and 450MHz chips), allowing the processor to achieve greater speeds in interfacing with system resources.

The PII also has MMX technology built into the processor, thereby satisfying the new demands by users and software for faster graphics. The original PII came with 32KB of level 1 cache (16KB for data and 16KB for instructions) and 512KB of level 2 cache.

Pentium II Xeon

The PII processor was further enhanced by the creation of the Xeon family. The Xeon PII is designed for business applications and high-speed processing; up to eight processors can be combined to work together. The processor functions at 400MHz or 450MHz and can handle higher level 2 cache. The 400MHz and 450MHz are available with 512KB or 1MB of level 2 cache, but the 450MHz can handle up to a whopping 2MB.

Celeron

The Intel Celeron processor has become quite popular with home PC users. The reason for its increase in sales is due to its relatively low cost. Intel made a decision to lower processor costs (which in turn lowered PC costs) by making some changes to its existing processor families.

Recall that the new standard Pentium chips have 32KB of level 1 cache and 512KB of level 2 cache. The level 2 cache is the expensive kind, so it makes sense that if you reduce its size, you could reduce the cost of the processor, right? Well, that's what Intel did. The Celeron processor comes in speeds ranging from 300MHz to 550–650MHz (which operate at 66MHz bus speed and still have 32KB of level 1 cache). But these processors come with only 128KB of level 2 cache. Although this is a drastic cut in level 2 cache size, the reduction in price for the processor and the PCs that use it make it a very favorable choice for buyers looking to save money on a new PC.

The Celeron also had a built-in booster market. As Intel sought to make it tough for ambitious overclockers to push PIIs and PIIIs to higher than rated speeds, the Celeron became the default preference of the overclocking crowd. If overclocking techniques fail, a cheaper CPU is a lot easier to burn up than a much more expensive PIII.

Note

Check out the Celeron chip on Intel's Web site at `http://www.intel.com/celeron`.

Pentium III

Intel released its newest Pentium processor with a marketing blitz no one will soon forget. But is the new chip worth all the hype? Let's see.

First, the speeds offered by the Pentium III are getting higher. Starting out at 450MHz–550MHz, with 800MHz now available and the 1- and 1.1GHz in the pipeline, the chips also come with the MMX technology. 512KB of level 2 cache is standard. But other than the increase in speed, what's the big deal? Well, the Pentium III's strength lies in its capability to handle graphics faster and smoother than previous chips. Remember MMX? The Pentium III does MMX processing 70 instructions better! These new instructions are designed for real-time video, streaming video, and better graphics capabilities.

It's important to understand that the differences between a PII and a PIII are largely speed (the PII line stopped at 450MHz), and the 70 extra instructions already discussed. For the most part, the PIII CPU will drop right into a PII socket as a replacement on a motherboard, same as with the Xeon II/III.

The extra instructions included are useful in specific areas: streaming content delivered from the Internet (where the user doesn't have to sit and wait to receive *all* of a file before the audio and/or video begins to play) and in PC gaming. Depending on whose analysis you favor, performance with a PIII jumps about 10 to 15 percent over a PII in the areas where the extra instruction set counts.

However, the Pentium III isn't linear—there are actually two types of Pentium III. The original one was based on the same technology as the PII, but with those extra instructions. A change came about with Intel's Coppermine chip set in 1999, replacing traditional connectors with copper, and altering the process used from 0.25-micron to 0.18-micron, and offering a 133MHz system bus (original was 100 MHz), as well as a 256K L2 cache on-chip, which runs at the same speed as the processor itself. One important difference with Coppermine is that it should finally support 4X AGP, critical to helping video performance hop forward. Before this, AGP video was limited to a 1X–2X data path, which fell short of allowing AGP to truly excite the serious gaming crowd that needs speed in video. All too often, AGP was chosen not because it was wildly faster and better than PCI video cards, but because it freed up a PCI slot for another type of expansion board.

But Coppermine hasn't been a complete success in roll-out. At the time of this writing (still early in the chip set's release), there were numerous reports of problems using existing hardware in concert with the 810 and 820 chip sets, implying there are some bugs to work out. Intel's push to Rambus, a far more expensive RAM (more details to come later in this chapter), and chip shortages causing serious delays in shipping the processors have prompted many users to consider the AMD Athlon as an alternative.

Note

The Pentium Pro family of chips did well sales-wise, but it's not entirely clear that it was because of their performance; more likely, it was a matter of their big megahertz numbers. The fact that the Pentium Pro line wasn't really all that much faster than the Pentium line underscores that speeding up CPUs gets tougher the higher you go. It's not enough to provide more megahertz, more raw speed. The winner in the CPU races will be the one that uses its time most wisely, with multiple pipelines, out-of-order instruction, data bypassing, and the like.

Non-Intel Pentium Challengers: M1/M2, Nx586, K5/K6, and Athlon

For many years, chip companies competed with Intel by making clones of its chips. But the Pentium was a different story, because its difference from the 486 was not tremendous—it's a fast chip, but it's not staggeringly faster than a 486. Add that to Intel's public relations disaster back in November 1994 over the Pentium's floating-point division problems (it was noted that math computations weren't being handled correctly), and computer manufacturers soon became more open to putting a non-Intel chip in their computers.

That was the opening needed to create Cyrix's M1, NexGen's Nx586, and AMD's K5. All three of these chips are intended to be "what the Pentium should have been." They're backward compatible with 486 software, so they run Windows 95/98/NT, DOS, and the like. But they all depart from the Pentium in slightly different ways.

Cyrix's 6x86

In October 1995, Cyrix announced the shipment of its rival to the Pentium, the 6x86 (formerly the M1). Although the 6x86 is a two-pipeline superscalar chip like the Pentium, the 6x86 offers a number of other features that are also offered by the Pentium Pro (released after the 6x86). However, the Cyrix 5x86, formerly known as the M1sc, is not a rival to the Pentium, although the numbering scheme makes it sound like it is. 5x86s are pin compatible with an Intel 486, 6x86s with a Pentium.

The 6x86 features the following:

Superpipelining Instead of the Pentium's five stages, the 6x86 uses a seven-stage pipeline to avoid lags in the execution process and increase the flow of information.

Register renaming Provides temporary data storage for instant data availability without waiting for the CPU to access the on-chip cache or main system memory.

Data dependency removal Provides instruction results to both pipelines simultaneously so that neither pipeline is stalled while waiting for the results of calculations.

Multibranch prediction Boosts processor performance by predicting with high accuracy the next instructions needed.

Speculative execution Allows the pipelines to continuously execute instructions that follow a branch without stalling the pipelines.

Out-of-order completion Can process instructions out of order, making it possible to get faster-to-process instructions out of the way before spending time on the longer ones. This feature applies to the execute and write-back portions of the calculation process.

The 6x86 is a clock doubler or tripler (depending on the model). It stores calculation instructions and their results in a 16KB cache so that they can be called back into memory quickly if necessary. Cyrix also released the M2 processors, which are supposed to rival the Intel's Celeron processor line in power.

Note

The 6x86 has received mixed reviews about its Windows NT compatibility, so check Microsoft's Hardware Compatibility List before buying non-Intel systems for Windows NT use. This is less true for Windows 2000, which uses the easier Windows 98 model (mostly) for hardware, but it's always wise to check the compatibility list before you buy.

Cyrix's Joshua (Gobi and Mojave)

A disappointing last few years for Cyrix and its processors made some count Cyrix out as a serious contender to the Intel-dominated PC processor throne. While AMD CPUs began to gain in overall popularity, Cyrix began to fade until 1999, when it was announced that Via Technologies (the chip set manufacturer) had acquired them, and plans for a revamped processor line were already in production.

Originally code-named Gobi, Via is calling Cyrix's next planned release the Joshua series, and builds upon the foundation they established with the M1 and MII. However, it's supposed to have a much better speed with floating-point operations, and to support 3DNow! Technology instructions as well as MMX units (for improved multimedia capability). The on-board L2 cache, however, is limited to 256KB, or half the size of the Athlon and the Pentium II/III. The first processor in this newly-revamped line is the Via Cyrix III, with a Socket 370-type connection (like the lower-powered Intel Celeron), a front-side bus running at 133MHz, and introduced with 433 and 466 models.

Also in the Joshua series is a chip set Cyrix was calling the Mojave, a new, next-generation processor. Unfortunately, at the time of this writing, very little firm technical information was known about this processor, its potential and/or limitations.

AMD's K5/K6

The K5 is a fifth-generation processor offered by AMD. The K5 is distinct from AMD's 5x86, a souped-up version of the 486. The K5, a 64-bit version more like the Pentium, started shipping as of June 1996. The K5's most salient feature is its four instruction pipelines (twice as many as the Pentium).

The biggest difference between the K5 and the Cyrix 6x86 is that the Cyrix chip is a *CISC* (*Complex Instruction Set Chip*, an older approach to designing CPUs), whereas the K5 is a *RISC* (*Reduced Instruction Set Chip*, a newer approach). As such, the K5 must translate the complex instructions it receives to simpler ones that can be executed more quickly.

The K6 series offers some substantial gains over the K5 and proved to be AMD's most popular chip design thus far, particularly after AMD introduced 3DNow! Technology to enhance Web surfing and game playing, much as the Pentium III did (AMD's released sooner). Because the K6 can be pushed in ways the PII and the PIII can't, and due to its lower than Pentium II/III pricing, the K6-II and K6-III represent a major alternative for many users as well as PC manufacturers.

NexGen's Nx586

This chip is the oddball of the crowd. First of all, it does not support floating-point operations, making it incompatible even with some programs that run on an 80486DX. Second, it is not pin compatible with the Pentium, requiring designers to create a whole new motherboard to use it. Third, it runs at 4 volts, in comparison to the other two, which match the Pentium's 3.3-volt requirement.

It runs two instruction pipelines and can handle instructions out of order. NexGen rates chips not by their speed, but by equivalent speeds for the Pentium. The other non-Intel manufacturers do likewise. For example, the 6x86 that is rated at 100MHz actually runs at 93MHz, but Cyrix claims that it performs equally to a Pentium at that speed, and some benchmarks bear it out. The Nx586 was the first of the three to ship commercially; AMD now owns NexGen.

AMD's Athlon (K7)

The Athlon, first introduced in 1999, has sometimes been called the first PC processor AMD didn't design wholly in Intel's shadow. Like a few new processors before it, the Athlon CPU was available in some supply before the motherboards needed to support it.

Oh, there are big similarities to Intel's PII and PIII, and these are necessary, too, because you need to be able to run the same programs regardless of which PC processor is being used. Like the PII and PIII, the Athlon is mounted on a module containing separate SRAM chips making up the L2 cache, with special connectors uniting the two. Also like the PII and III, the Athlon offers a 512KB L2 cache that runs at half the speed of the processor itself.

But the differences are notable. First, the Athlon was designed around an entirely new processor core, uses a Slot A (rather than a Slot 1 of the Pentium II/III) socket, and offers a 200MHz front-side bus. The L1 cache is four times the size of what's available on a PIII, and an Athlon can decode any three *x*86 instructions at any given time. It also has the capability to dispatch up to nine internal instructions to its execution units per clock cycle, whereas a PIII can do just five. The Athlon is also credited with offering a better floating-point multiplying and adding capability for improved application and server performance, as well as enhanced gaming.

Limitations exist, however. For example, there currently is no support for using Athlon in a dual processor environment, as you might with the PII or PIII (and some brave souls have managed using the lower-rated Celeron). AMD also still suffers from a degree of industry bias, where the general rule of thumb has continued to be that if you need a solid PC processor for business use, you go with Intel. This bias is reduced today, but far from nonexistent.

As the new copper-interconnected Athlon debuts, the integrated L2 cache will run at the full speed of the processor, instead of just half-speed.

The Future: Itanium

You may know this CPU under its code name, the Merced, although it is now officially called the Itanium. It's heralded as Intel's first high-end, 64-bit central processor, the flagship of its IA-64 processor family, developed to go head-to-head with major professional server players such as IBM and Sun Microsystems' highly popular UltraSparc III, which are high-end RISC-based processors capable of performing some of the hardest tasks computers are called upon to do. In testing, this processor worked well with eight operating systems, including Windows NT 4, Linux, and various flavors of Unix.

And it's the capability to handle other than a strictly Windows-environment platform that makes Itanium a serious first entry for Intel into the powerhouse market. Intel processors have usually—intentionally or not—been designed around the Microsoft Windows platform, whether it was lower-end consumer Windows such as Windows 95/98 or higher-powered Windows NT/2000. Itanium's multiplatform support has gained the interest of major Linux distributors, for example, who formed a group called the Trillium Project to help bolster Itanium's roll-out.

Intel's theory is this: with processing demand growing at an infinite pace, we need to find ways to wed the economics (lower cost) and the workhorse-usability of personal computers with the power of server technology. Their initial market is e-business, also known as Internet commerce, a market where the current choices are either to invest heavily in the RISC-based processor environment or settle for a much less powerful server.

With all this said, you may be surprised to hear that this power-house, next-generation CPU (set to debut at 800MHz) is not a lot faster than the Pentium III. But that's OK, because in a large professional environment handling tens of thousands, if not millions, of records and files, and performing many functions, processor speed itself takes a back seat to parallel processing, whereby multiple processors work together to push through the work. Thus, an Itanium can process large databases and work with much larger amounts of memory than the 32-bit Intel chips commonly used in regular desktop systems.

At the time this book was going to print, Intel had not announced a firm date in 2000 for the release of the Itanium.

As with the Xeon, PC vendors are offering the Itanium machines in two basic configurations: workstation and server (both high-end, meaning a lot of processing power). Workstations are fitted with a dual processor (two processors) whereas servers have four processors.

PC Memory

The PC, like all computers, must have *main memory*. Main memory's job is to be the place where the PC stores the programs and data that it is working on right now. It needs to be able to access these programs and data in *nanoseconds* (billionths of seconds), rather than—as in the case of secondary memory such as hard disks—*millisandths* (thousandths of seconds).

The other name for main memory, which I've talked about before, is RAM, an acronym for the particularly unhelpful name *random-access memory*. I say it's unhelpful because *random-access* just means that it's as easy to get to the one millionth location as it is to get to the first location. By contrast, with *sequential access*, like a tape drive, you've got to fast-forward or rewind the tape to get to a particular location—the data is sequential. *Random* tells us very little because there's another kind of memory you'll meet later, named *ROM*, for *read-only memory*. That too is not sequential; the only difference between RAM and ROM is that you can both write data to RAM and read data from it, and you can only read data from ROM. Heck, even disk drives are random access. So a better name for RAM would probably be read/write memory, or RWM, but you can't pronounce RWM. You can pronounce RAM, so the term caught on.

How Memory Is Packaged: DIPs, SIMMs, and DIMMs

The most common way to find RAM today is as a series of dynamic RAM (DRAM) chips affixed to a miniature circuit board. The number of DRAM chips mounted on a side of the circuit board varies depending on type of RAM: sometimes there are eight, sometimes nine. Parity RAM adds an extra DRAM chip for error testing (for a total of nine), while non-parity RAM has eight DRAMs on a side.

If DRAM chips are mounted on only one side of a memory module, this RAM is packaged as a *Single Inline Memory Module (SIMM)*. SIMMs come in 30- and 72-pin types (with the 72-pin the "mightier" of the two, able to perform more work across less RAM). Earlier SIMMs had to be installed in pairs to work.

If, instead, DRAM chips are mounted on both sides of a memory module, this RAM is packaged as a *Dual Inline Memory Module (DIMM)*. DIMMs have 168 pins, and don't need to be installed in pairs. Most Pentium IIs and at least early Pentium IIIs typically use DIMMs.

Most motherboards have room for four banks of memory. *Bank* refers to the actual sockets for memory you see on the motherboard, where *sticks* of RAM are installed. Some of the newer machines have no memory on the motherboard at all, but instead have a large circuit board with room for megs and megs of memory.

Over the years, memory packaging has changed. Before the late '80s, you'd buy memory as a bunch of small chips (called *DIPs* because that's the type of package used), and you'd plug them into chip sockets on the computer's motherboard or an add-in daughtercard. Depending on the processor type, you'd have to add memory

in increments of 8, 9, 16, 18, 32, or 36 chips. Soon, the first generation of SIMMs appeared. Known as 30-pin SIMMs, one SIMM was the
equivalent of eight or nine DIPs, and for a time most motherboards
had sockets for 30-pin SIMMs.

Around 1992, a newer SIMM package that was the equivalent of 32
or 36 DIPs became more popular; this package is known as a 72-pin
SIMM, and most modern motherboards' memory sockets are 72-pin
SIMM sockets. Computers built around Pentium-class or Pentium
Pro–class processors require that when you upgrade memory, you
do it with pairs of 72-pin SIMMs. Since 1996, a kind of main memory
called a synchronous dynamic RAM (SDRAM) has appeared on the
market. It too is a 72-pin SIMM, but it works differently and so
requires yet another socket type. Many motherboards nowadays
have sockets for old-style 72-pin SIMMs and sockets for SDRAM
modules. You can see two kinds of SIMMs and a DIMM in Figure 3.8.

30-pin SIMM

72-pin SIMM

Figure 3.8

Single Inline Memory
Modules (SIMMs)
and a Dual Inline
Memory Module
(DIMM)

168-pin DIMM

Solving the Memory Speed Problem: DRAM, Fast Page, EDO, Burst EDO, SDRAM, and Rambus DRAM (RDRAM)

You read earlier in this chapter that it would be nice to have memory that ran as quickly as the processor, but that no one makes inexpensive, fast memory. It would seem, then, that slow memory speed would be an important pothole in the road to maximum speed, and that the smart PC buyer should be sure to spend all available money on the latest, fastest memory. PC hardware vendors have been eager to separate PC buyers from that money. In fact, fast memory *can* lead to a faster computer, but not *that* much faster.

But we have seen changes in memory bus speed over the last few years. Traditional SDRAM originally had a bus speed of 66MHz (once the PCI bus pushed up to 66MHz). Starting with the Intel BX chip set in 1998 (developed for PII and PIII processors with fuller support for newer hardware such as AGP and USB), bus speed jumped to 100MHz (PC100 RAM), which arguably provided a nice edge to overall performance as the CPUs were beginning to speed up as well. The latest Pentium IIIs have a 133MHz front-side bus and take 133MHz SDRAM DIMMs, while the Athlon K7 uses 200MHz SDRAM. The future is even faster, as you'll discover later in this chapter.

Originally, main memory was simple dynamic RAM (DRAM), a good, inexpensive memory design that you don't see anymore. Recall that there is fast memory around called SRAM—static RAM. But it's too expensive to use for all system memory, so most PCs try to strike a balance by using a lot of cheap memory for main system memory and add a little bit of the expensive SRAM to act as a memory cache. So PCs in the mid-to-late '80s tended to be a mix of a lot of DRAM and a bit of SRAM.

Memory makers wanted to build a DRAM that was faster (closer to SRAM speed), without making it too much more expensive. And that's when DRAM designers hit upon a couple of important concepts:

▶ It's impossible to make DRAM able to just grab data from any old location quickly.

▶ But once a DRAM has accessed a piece of data in *one* location, it is possible to design the DRAM so that it can quickly access data that is *nearby*.

A memory called *static column RAM* appeared in 1986 that used this information, and Compaq used it in their Compaq Deskpro 386 to squeeze good performance out of their computer. The early '90s saw another read-nearby-data-fast approach called *Fast Page Mode* memory, which was followed by *Extended Data Out*, or *EDO*, memory, which was followed by a slightly faster approach called *Burst Extended Data Out* memory.

Each memory type was faster than its predecessors, but they all shared the same basic characteristic: once a piece of data was read from a chip, nearby data could be read quickly. How near "nearby data" had to be varied from design to design, but it meant that at some point you'd exceed the "neighborhood" of the original data read. So, for example, let's assume that a "neighborhood" for a bit of data in a memory is 2048 bytes long. (Assume there's no static cache in this example.) It's the first thing in the morning, and the CPU's about to access its very first byte of the day. Because it's a DRAM access that's not near the previous access (since there *was* no previous access), that first access is pretty slow. But suppose that the next thing the CPU needs is the byte right after that first byte (which is a quite reasonable assumption). It's "nearby" to the first byte, and so its access is fast. Assuming that the CPU keeps requesting data sequentially, it'll find fast response for the next 2046. But after that, access slows again as the CPU enters another "neighborhood."

The latest kind of popular RAM solves that problem. It's called, as I mentioned earlier, *synchronous DRAM* or *SDRAM*. How it works is interesting. The CPU tells it, "Go get some data at location 10,455," and the SDRAM goes to do that. That initial access takes a bit of time, as with earlier DRAM. But what the SDRAM does next is really unique: it just starts pumping data out of the memory sequentially until the CPU tells it to stop. After the data in location 10,455, it gets 10,456, then 10,457, and so on, and *all at SRAM speeds!* Basically, the memory just goes on "autopilot" and shotguns data sequentially at the CPU. Now, *if the CPU needs a big hunk of sequential data*, then this can be quite fast, and that's why if you look at current PC advertisements, they all trumpet how much SDRAM you get, as if it really made a difference in your system's performance. But the fact is, SDRAM or any other kind of RAM really won't affect system speed tremendously. You can see two SDRAM SIMMs in Figure 3.9.

Figure 3.9

SDRAM (with Pentium III cartridge socket in background)

More RAM Is Better Than Faster RAM

To see why variations in system RAM type won't significantly affect your PC's performance, let's return to the notion of the static cache RAM. The idea with this 256KB–1024KB of memory cache is that it's obviously fast to access. So if the CPU needs the data from location x in main memory *and* the cache happens to already *have* that data, then the CPU can read the data from cache with almost no delay at all. If the data for location x isn't in the cache, that's fine—there's no hardware failure or anything like that—but access is slower, because the request for the data will have to go out to the slower main memory. But consider: if a system has, say, 256KB of cache and 32MB of main memory, then the cache has room for copies of only a small percentage of the data in the main memory. What determines which data is kept in cache and which data isn't? A memory controller circuit, either on the motherboard (in older systems) or the CPU (in modern systems). A cleverly built memory controller can get a lot of mileage out of a small amount of cache memory.

The key, then, to building a system that's both fast memory-wise and easy on the wallet is to add a small amount of expensive, fast memory as cache and then add a clever memory controller to get the most out of it. And that's what virtually every modern computer does (save for laptops, which generally don't have cache).

Note

In modern computers, well over 95 percent of the CPU's memory requests are satisfied by the static cache.

Let's do a little math to consider what that means vis-à-vis performance. Assume that about 25 percent of what the CPU does requires memory accesses. A slow memory system, then, could affect only 25 percent of the CPU's performance for good or ill. (This is a rough analysis and isn't completely accurate; it's just a back-of-the-envelope look at how memory affects performance.) But 95 percent of those memory accesses are satisfied by the nearly instantaneous static memory cache, so slow main memory could affect only 5 percent of the 25 percent of the CPU's tasks that are memory-oriented; in other words, *main memory speed affects about 1.25 percent of CPU tasks!* It may be that by the time you read this, some other new whiz-bang kind of memory has appeared to unseat SDRAM as the "fastest" memory technology, and you can be sure that its price tag will reflect its "latest and greatest" nature. But I'd suggest that rather than spending all kinds of money on faster memory, you spend that money on *more* memory. A PC with 32MB of blindingly fast memory would run Windows 98 far more slowly than a PC with 64MB of run-of-the-mill RAM.

With this said, understand that—particularly in a Windows 9*x* environment (Windows NT and 2000 handle memory more precisely)—having the proper amount of RAM for your needs can be critical. For example, if you're working with an older machine of the Pentium or Pentium MMX type with just 16MB or 32MB of RAM and hitting serious performance issues, upgrading RAM to 64MB can improve the performance more than upgrading to a faster CPU.

Rambus DRAM (RDRAM)

After what I just discussed, let's look at the future of mainstream, if Intel has its way.

As part of the move to the Coppermine (Camino) chip set, Intel wanted faster RAM not just for higher-end performance machines including servers, but standard desktops. Its choice was a new type of DRAM called Rambus (RDRAM).

On paper, RDRAM sounds almost as good as its coming reality has been controversial. RDRAM, after all, is supposed to operate at twice the clock speed and be at least 10 times faster than current SDRAM technology. It's cited as perfect for any situation requiring both high bandwidth and low latency (where you need a lot of power up front, and don't have the luxury of an often idle system). Three versions of it are intended: PC 600 (clock speed: 300MHz), PC 700 (actually 711 or 356MHz), and PC 800 (400MHz). Sounds fast, doesn't it?

Instead of SIMMs and DIMMs, Rambus comes in RIMMs, or Rambus Inline Memory Modules (see Figure 3.10). A RIMM differs from a SIMM or a DIMM in more than cost. Because these RIMMs can develop hot spots apparently related to its speed of operation, each RIMM has a heat spreader cover plate to try to diffuse the heat.

Figure 3.10

Rambus RIMMs

Beyond this, RIMMs can't be used on motherboards not designed with Rambus sockets in place. PCs currently using 66-, 100-, or

133MHz SDRAM would need to overhaul both the motherboard and the processor chip set to use Rambus.

But the controversy develops from issues such as RDRAM's very proprietary 16-bit serial bus, and limitations on how it can be used. Thornier still is the matter of cost. Not too many RAM makers jumped on the bandwagon, so supplies may be limited, production small and expensive. And talk in the press from test reports indicates the extra bang may not be worth the buck. AMD, for example, isn't embracing the Rambus route, and instead is looking at double data rate (DDR) SDRAM, which they say is fast enough and nowhere near as expensive.

At the time of this writing, with Rambus still available on only a limited basis, the price difference between a Pentium III using SDRAM and one using Rambus hovered between under $200 and over $300. It was estimated that more than 80 percent of the first Coppermine chip set–based systems shipped with SDRAM rather than Rambus.

Note

PC users have only recently begun to enjoy a time when they could seriously stock their PCs with RAM without having to take out a loan. Old-timers will remember when 16MB of RAM cost over $1000 (and there are worse stories). The RAM business has also historically been hit with a good deal of instability. A fire at a chip-related plant in Korea a few years ago, and then the earthquakes in Taiwan in 1999, drastically increased prices for several months. If you add price instability to an already costly product, you potentially reduce the number of people who can afford the technology and you make those who can afford it more inclined to consider the alternatives before they purchase a system. In today's world, you just can't do real work on an underpowered, under-RAM-supplied PC.

Stay tuned to see if Rambus revolutionizes the RAM industry, or disappears quickly as it's replaced with something that provides more performance for the price paid.

Note

You can keep up with the latest Rambus developments by visiting `http://www.rambus.com`.

Self-Healing RAM: ECC Memory

As you buy more and more memory, however, your PC becomes more fragile, because every memory byte is a circuit, and every circuit is something that can go wrong. A PC with 256KB of RAM has millions fewer failure points than does a PC with 64MB of RAM. This is not to suggest that you should buy PCs with 256KB of RAM; in fact, I'm not sure you *can* buy a machine with that little RAM. I think my microwave oven has a couple of megs these days . . .

From the original 1981 machines onward, PCs have been able to detect memory errors through a system called *parity*. Parity couldn't fix the error; it just knew that it was there. Once the parity error detection circuitry found a memory error, it made a sort of abrupt response to the problem: it just stopped the computer cold. That made people ask, "What good is parity if it just locks the system up—how is that better than just continuing to run with faulty memory?" (which is not a bad question). Parity also required a bit more memory. Early systems used either 8-bit SIMMs or 9-bit SIMMs—the difference was that the 9-bit SIMMs had parity. The same thing appears today with 72-pin SIMMs; they come in 32-bit or 36-bit varieties. The 36-bit variety includes parity.

Many systems nowadays opt not to use parity, and it's a shame, because parity has finally come into its own. Pentium II and III-based systems with parity memory cannot only detect an error, they can *correct* that error. This process is called error correction code, or ECC, memory. ECC memory's been around for mainframes and minis for years, but not for PCs save for a few expensive machines. With modern machines, however, all you need do is make sure that you buy parity memory (36-bit SIMMs rather than 32-bit SIMMs) and configure the system to use the memory for ECC—it's usually a software setting of some kind—and you get mainframe memory power for pennies. The shame is that many hardware vendors don't tell their customers about it.

Note

It's worthwhile to note that 64-bit RAM is not ECC memory; 72-bit RAM is. If you want ECC memory, 72-bit is the type to buy.

Types of Memory

So far, I've probably covered many of the terms that you come across when reading computer ads or tips on "powering up" your PC. But another bunch of terms remains—*conventional memory*, *extended memory*, and *expanded memory*. These are more software-oriented terms than hardware-oriented, but they're worth going over in case you're trying to configure software that starts asking questions about how much memory you've got.

Why so many kinds of memory? Mainly because of unfortunate planning: nobody ever thought the PC would need more than 640KB of memory. (There's a famous Bill Gates quote from the early '80s along the lines of "No one will ever need more than 640KB of memory on a personal computer.")

The familiar first 640KB of a PC's memory is called *conventional memory*. It is supplemented by *reserved areas* containing ROM, read-only memory, and bits of RAM on expansion boards; all of those RAM and ROM areas are called the *Upper Memory Area*. The 286 and later machines can address memory beyond that called extended memory. And a small-but-important number of applications can use special memory called *expanded memory*, or, as it is also known, *Lotus-Intel-Microsoft (LIM) memory*.

Note

Some memory types, such as expanded memory, are only useful in trying to support much older machines, or much older software on more recent machines. Modern computer programs really don't make use of this any longer.

Let me note here that the introduction of memory managers into DOS since DOS 5 has complicated things a bit, but I'm afraid that I'm going to have to tiptoe around the subject of memory managers. The fact of the matter is that memory management is a large topic, and I haven't got room here to do it justice.

You probably know that there are many kinds of memory these days. While you may not have heard of all of them, the three most common areas are the ones I described above. Let's take a look at these in turn:

Conventional The first 640KB of the first 1MB (1024KB) of memory, used for configuring the DOS program environment for games, etc., and loading DOS device drivers and programs that can be loaded into upper memory (640–1024KB).

Extended Windows 95/98/NT does most of its work with this type of memory.

Expanded Also called *Expanded Memory Specification (EMS)* or *LIM*, this is mainly used by some programs written in the late '80s and even used by a few modern games (the latter seems a bit odd, because it seems unnecessary).

Why so many kinds of memory? It's worth noting something before I go any further: nobody planned this. It just kind of "growed up that way."

I discussed the difference between RAM and disk memory earlier in this chapter. Just remember these three things, and you shouldn't have any problem distinguishing between them:

▶ RAM is volatile, meaning that it does not hold data when you turn a PC off, but disk drives retain the data stored on them even when the power is turned off.

▶ PCs tend to have a lot more disk space than they've got RAM space.

▶ As mentioned before, RAM is a lot faster than disk memory.

Designing a Computer's Memory: Zoning the First Megabyte

Many of the constraints that we face today have their roots in the past, a past over 20 years ago. Trust me, this isn't just a history lesson—some things IBM decided in the summer of 1980 affect how Windows 95/98/NT/2000 works today.

In the summer of 1980, IBM commenced the PC development project. The goal of the small design team was to build a "home computer" (that's what we called them in those days) that could compete with the Apple II. The PC had a good start in that it was based around a much more powerful chip than the Apple's. The chip that IBM selected was, of course, the Intel 8088, and one of the powerful features was that the 8088 could address ("talk to") up to 1024KB—1MB, or 1,048,576 bytes—of RAM. That limit shaped DOS, the need for DOS compatibility shaped Windows 3.x, and Windows 3.x compatibility constrained much of the Windows 95/98 architecture. (Think of it as The Curse of Backward Compatibility.)

Planning a new computer is kind of like planning a new community. Before breaking ground on a new planned community, a zoning board or planning board determines what use will be made of all the land space. Thus, the planners of a new community start from some unused land, perhaps fallow farmland. After acquiring the land, the next step is to plot it out into lots and then determine which lots will hold residential buildings, which ones commercial buildings, industrial buildings, local government, and so on. You could say that before any buildings are built, a planner must allocate addresses. Before any buildings get built, the planner decides that any buildings built on address *x* must be residential, and any on a given address *y* must be commercial. In the same way, planning a computer requires allocating specific contents to "addresses." Now let's take a look at how memory in IBM's first computer was designated.

IBM, too, had to worry about traffic flow (the traffic isn't cars and trucks but instructions and requests running from hardware to CPU and back), about population density (too much equipment in one place affects heat of the unit, and overheating affects a PC's performance), and resources (enough power to keep the drives, the video, and all running).

Interrupt Vectors and DOS

The bottom 1KB of memory is an area used by the CPU as a kind of table of contents of hardware support programs called *software interrupts.* The table of contents is composed of pointers to those programs called *interrupt vectors*. This area is a fixed size of 1024 bytes—400 in hexadecimal. One interrupt points to the program that controls your disk drives, another to the video board, and so on. That 1KB is reserved for the interrupt vector table no matter what operating system you're running, and no matter which CPU you're using. Above that is DOS itself. I can't say exactly how much space DOS takes up in memory, simply because first, there are many versions of DOS, and second, different CONFIG.SYS options use more or less space, and that space adds to the DOS space requirements.

Note

Do you speak hexadecimal? If you don't now, you likely will as you develop more in PC troubleshooting, because hexadecimal (also called base 16) is part of the language of math making up the computer world. Simply put, hexadecimal takes the numerals 0–9 and then takes the letters A–F and sees and uses them as if they were numerals 10–15. These letters are multiplied on a base of 16. Depending on a letter's placement in a numeric statement, it may have extra weight, and be multiplied by powers of 0, 1, 2, or 3. For more information, turn to Appendix A "Reading Hexadecimal."

Device Drivers

Directly above DOS loads a special class of programs called *device drivers*. Virtually every DOS-using computer uses at least one of these. (Under Windows, they're called Windows drivers and they are files with an extension of either 386 for Windows 3.*x* or VXD for Windows 95/98 and Windows 2000.)

Device drivers are programs that either allow DOS to support a new piece of hardware or add new capabilities to an existing piece of hardware. Device drivers are loaded in the CONFIG.SYS file with the DEVICE= statement. Some examples of device drivers include:

- A driver to support a SCSI hard disk, a Zip drive, or a CD-ROM drive

- A mouse driver, for example, MOUSE.SYS, that enables your system to recognize and control your mouse

> ▶ The memory manager drivers that many people use, HIMEM.SYS and EMM386.EXE, which make your previously useless memory above 640KB into a useful resource for your software

Sometimes the order in which you load device drivers is important in DOS. In any case, device drivers change the way that your system reacts to information from your system's hardware. When you're trying to track down a problem, it's always a good idea to boot with as few device drivers as possible, whether talking about DOS, Windows, or Windows NT.

Command Shell

Every operating system has a program that accepts inputs from users and reformulates them in a manner that the operating system can understand. In the case of DOS, the most common command shell was and is (for those of us inclined to go to the command prompt) COMMAND.COM. It loaded after the device drivers, but before TSRs.

TSR or Memory Resident Programs

Under DOS, *Terminate and Stay Resident (TSR)* programs do much the same thing as device drivers (and I say *do* because you still see many programs install TSRs), but they are loaded from AUTOEXEC.BAT, so they load after any device drivers. Here are a few examples of TSR programs:

> ▶ The program to use a 3270 or 5250 emulation board, hardware that attached your system to a mainframe.

> ▶ A small utility that came with DOS called DOSKEY that remembered the last 20-or-so commands that you typed, so if you made a mistake, you could recall a previous command, edit it, and resubmit it to the PC.

> ▶ Many virus and antivirus programs.

- Network shells and protocol stacks. (*Protocols* refer to a formal set of rules used in networking, while *protocol stacks* are a set of rules and functions that come together to help a network function as it should.)

- Many disk cache programs that speed up disk access.

- Disk compression programs, such as Stacker or DOS's Drive-Space, which were memory resident (or Windows DriveSpace that is memory resident) through either a device driver or TSR format.

DOS relied upon TSRs and device drivers, but they came with a price: they took up your precious 640KB conventional space that you needed to run DOS programs.

User Programs

Above the TSRs, you find the currently loaded program—Lotus 1-2-3 in the simple example I'm illustrating here. The remaining memory was then available for 1-2-3 worksheets. Again, the top address is 640KB minus 1, rather than 640KB, because you start counting at *zero, not one.*

The vast majority of DOS programs claimed that they could run only in the low 640KB of your PC's memory, and that's largely true. That's why the 640KB conventional memory area is so important; if your program can live only in conventional memory, and the conventional memory is full, getting more memory won't help. One of my users once said of her computer, which had only 4MB of RAM at the time, "We need to buy more memory for my PC—I'm running out of memory." She was indeed running out of memory, but with an old application that couldn't use any more memory than 640KB. As far as that application was concerned, the memory beyond 640KB didn't even exist.

Many Windows users may be feeling smug at this point, thinking that they are no longer the prisoner of that silly 640KB limitation. Unfortunately, Windows 3.1/Windows for Workgroups 3.11 are still pretty needy of conventional memory—they won't run without a certain amount of it. Windows 95/98 is less dependent on the bottom

640KB *unless* you are running old Windows 3.1 and/or DOS programs; when that happens, Windows 95/98 reverts to its old Windows 3.1 ways and gets needy of lower memory space. To be completely free of the need for conventional memory, you'd have to be running Windows NT or, mostly, Windows 2000.

Video RAM

People used to say that DOS and DOS programs had a *640KB barrier* or *640KB limitation*, but that's not actually true. DOS programs were almost all written to run on the 8088 chip (and, of course, its successors, the 286 and later). Any 8088 program could address up to 1024KB of memory—in theory. There's nothing about DOS or the 8088 (or the Pentium II, for that matter) that requires the story to end at 640KB. Nevertheless, 640KB is a very real barrier for most systems. Why?

The blame for 640KB can be laid at the feet of those 1980 PC designers.

As used in the IBM world, the video board—the circuit board that acts as an interface between the CPU and the monitor—must have some memory on it. That memory is then shared between the circuitry on the video board and the CPU. The CPU "puts data on the screen" by putting data into this video RAM. The video circuitry sees the data in the memory and interprets it as graphical or textual information.

Video memory is memory used by video boards to keep track of what's to be displayed on the screen. When a program puts a character on the screen, or draws a circle on the screen, it is making changes to this video memory. IBM set aside 128KB for video memory, but most video boards don't need or use that much memory space. The answer to the original question, however ("Where does the 640KB limit come from?") is that the video RAM must go somewhere, and the original PC designers placed it from 640KB through 768KB. Even if there were more memory for user programs above 768KB, most programs could not use that memory, and *here* you see the DOS limitation: in general, DOS programs needed *contiguous blocks of memory.*

Thus, DOS programs could start grabbing memory just above DOS itself and then keep going until they hit a pothole of some kind—and in this case, that pothole is the video memory—at which point they stop looking for memory. In general, DOS programs aren't smart enough to use fragmented memory. That's not true for Windows 3.1 or Windows 95/98/NT/2000 programs.

You'll see later that a small workaround for this problem is to load TSRs and device drivers above 768KB—a major reason to use memory managers.

You may be saying, "Why doesn't someone just build a PC with the video addresses higher up? Then there'd be more space for conventional memory." Unfortunately, that would not work. The reason is that a large number of programs are designed to directly manipulate the video hardware, and those programs are all written assuming that the video is where it's supposed to be—between 640KB and 768KB.

The current standard SVGA still uses the addresses from 640KB through 768KB, (these addresses are numbered A0000–BFFFF). This is hexadecimal (check Appendix A if that's new to you).

Used memory address space differs from total memory on board because video board manufacturers use a technique called *paging* (explained further in the upcoming section "Video Memory and Paging"). Paging enables them to put lots of memory on the video board—lots of memory means better video—without taking up a lot of the CPU's total 1024KB memory address space.

Note that the video board can be convinced to disable memory usage from B0000 to B1000, the addresses that the MDA (Monochrome Display Adapter) uses. That's so your system could run two monitors. Although it's not common, some debugging systems for programmers let you test-run your program with program output going to a VGA monitor while displaying debugging information on a monochrome MDA monitor.

Newer PCI-based video boards are quite a bit smarter about using memory, so you can put multiple PCI-based video cards into a single computer.

Video Memory Layout

The 128KB set aside for video memory isn't just laid out as one big 128KB block; rather, there are three separate and distinct video memory areas, as seen in Figure 3.11.

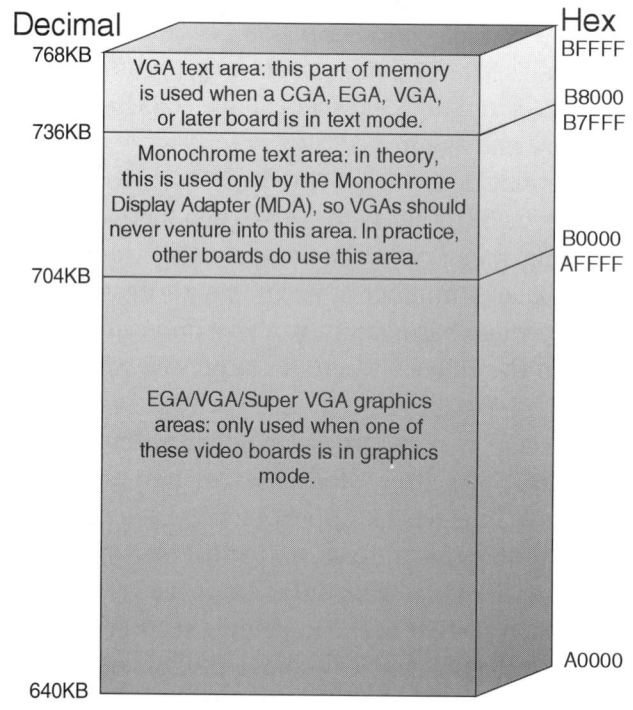

Decimal — Hex

768KB — VGA text area: this part of memory is used when a CGA, EGA, VGA, or later board is in text mode. — BFFFF / B8000

736KB — B7FFF

Monochrome text area: in theory, this is used only by the Monochrome Display Adapter (MDA), so VGAs should never venture into this area. In practice, other boards do use this area. — B0000

704KB — AFFFF

EGA/VGA/Super VGA graphics areas: only used when one of these video boards is in graphics mode.

Figure 3.11

Video memory areas   640KB — A0000

On current graphics boards, graphics activity takes place in the bottom 64KB of the video area. This is accessed only when in graphics mode. The 32KB from B0000 through B7FFF was designated for the MDA, although IBM MDAs used only memory from B0000 through B0FFF, a 4KB area. Later MDA improvements such as the Hercules Graphics Controller and clones used the entire 32KB region.

Video Memory and Paging

As you look at the VGA graphics area, a question may be forming in your mind. Anyone who's bought a video board has heard of video boards with a megabyte or two or four of memory. Where does this memory go, given that there's only 64KB of addresses set aside for VGA graphics? The answer is in the technique I mentioned earlier, called *paging*.

Recall that the video RAM is not on the motherboard, but rather on the video board. (Of course, if the VGA is integrated into the motherboard, the video RAM will be also.) Paging hardware on the VGA board enables the video board to present only 64KB of its 256KB (the amount of memory found on a normal VGA) to the CPU at a time. There are then four 64KB pages on a standard VGA and, as it turns out, they each have a job. One page governs the blue part of the screen, another the red, another the green, and the final one the intensity of an image. The actual process of generating a complete VGA graphics screen looks something like the following:

1. Issue the command to bring in (page in) the blue 64KB.

2. Draw the blue part of the screen in the blue memory page.

3. Issue the command to page in the green page.

4. Draw the green part of the image.

5. Issue the command to page in the red 64KB page.

6. Draw the red part of the screen.

7. Issue the command to page in the intensity page.

8. Designate the areas that need high intensity and low intensity.

Note

Paging is a process used commonly in the computer world to shoehorn a lot of memory into just a few addresses.

You'll see this notion of paging in many places in the computer world. Now that you've got a little insight into what's required to make *one small change* to what's visible on a VGA screen, it's easy to understand why Windows—or any graphical program—can run slowly even on a fast machine. There's just so darn much house-keeping that's got to be done every time you do so much as move the mouse! That's why a graphics accelerator (discussed in Chapter 23, "Video Adapters and Displays,") makes so much sense for today's software; in fact, most current video boards are accelerators.

The System Reserved Area

In addition to device drivers, user programs, and video, the PC needs to steal from the CPU's memory address space for the following:

▶ Small amounts of memory called *buffers* or *frames* used by some expansion boards

▶ Special memory-containing system software called ROM

ROM (Read-Only Memory)

I've talked so far about memory and RAM as if they were identical notions. As mentioned earlier, another kind of memory exists, which is not used as much as RAM, but is important nonetheless. Unlike RAM, which the CPU can both write data to and read data from, this other kind of memory cannot be altered. It can only be read, so it is called read-only memory. This is memory that someone (the computer manufacturer, usually) loads just once with a special device called a PROM blaster, EPROM programmer, or the like. So you can read information from ROM, but you can't write new information. (Well, you *can* write the information, but the ROM will ignore you. Think of ROM as a chip that can *give* advice, but can't *take* it.)

Why have a memory chip that you can store information in only *once*? Well, unlike normal RAM, the ROM has the virtue that it doesn't lose its memory when you turn the machine off—techie types would say that it is *nonvolatile*. You use ROM to store software that won't change. In essence, you can say that ROM on a circuit board contains the software that tells the system how to use a circuit board.

ROM chips are found on expansion boards such as LAN, video, or scanner interface cards, to name a few examples. ROM is also found on the system board. The ROM on the system board contains a piece of software called *BIOS*, the basic input/output system. You may recall from earlier in this chapter a reference to a set of low-level programs, called software interrupts, that directly manipulate your hardware. These programs are pointed to by the interrupt vectors at the bottom of RAM memory. Software interrupts work to help configure the working environment, while BIOS serves as something of the arbiter between the PC and DOS (or the PC and Windows). DOS relies on BIOS in that DOS doesn't communicate directly with your hardware; rather, it issues commands through BIOS. Thus, when DOS reads your floppy, it does it by calling on the BIOS routine that reads your floppy drive. That's why the BIOS is so important: the BIOS determines in large measure how compatible your PC is.

As you'd expect, IBM's BIOS is *the* standard of compatibility. Back in the early '80s, the first clone makers developed BIOS software that conformed in varying degrees to the IBM standard; so the question, "Does it run Lotus 1-2-3 and Microsoft Flight Simulator?" was the acid test of compatibility. Nowadays, I suppose it is "Does it run Windows NT/2000?" Three companies—Phoenix Software, Award Software, and American Megatrends, Incorporated (AMI)—derive large incomes from their main business of writing *very* compatible BIOS software for clone makers. This has simplified the business of cloning considerably.

I've said that ROM contains software. As you know, software changes from time to time. Occasionally a problem can be fixed by "upgrading the ROM"—getting the latest version of the ROM-based software from the manufacturer. On older systems, it means opening up the system boxes and replacing a chip. On newer systems, it's easier—all you've got to do is to run a program that rewrites the ROM. You do need to be careful about this though, because the BIOS on some systems may be designed to run some specific hardware that is present on that computer only. If you replace the BIOS on a system like that, some of the devices on the computer may not function correctly (or at all).

For this reason, you've got to know exactly what version of software is in the ROM chips in the computers that you are responsible for. In a maintenance notebook, keep track of the serial numbers or dates on the labels pasted on the backs of the ROM chips in your

PCs, or look at the PC when it boots up for an opening message from the BIOS including the software version of the BIOS. Whenever you install a board, note any ROM identifying marks. It will save you from having to pop the top to find out when you call for service.

ROM chips can usually be easily identified because they are generally larger chips (24- or 28-pin DIP chips), they are socketed (so they can be easily changed), and they often have a paper label pasted on them with a version number or some such information printed on it. ROM chips are memories, albeit inflexible ones, so they require a place in the memory addresses in the reserved area from 640KB to 1024KB.

Flash RAM

As I just said, upgrading ROM on most modern PCs is a bit different from upgrading on older PCs. Newer PCs store their BIOS on a special kind of memory chip called *Flash RAM* or, as the chips were once more commonly known, an Electrically Erasable Programmable Read-Only Memory (EEPROM, pronounced *double E PROM*).

Flash RAM is the same as a BIOS, with the one important exception: a *program* can modify the BIOS. BIOS upgrades can then be done by just running a BIOS update program.

Flash RAM modules are a great convenience on laptops, because laptops are so crowded inside that prying them apart to change a BIOS chip is an enormous hassle. With Flash RAM, however, it's child's play: just run a BIOS update program supplied by the laptop manufacturer, and the new BIOS is installed.

Ah, but there's one caveat. With added convenience potentially comes more risk. Some motherboards of today make Flash BIOS upgrading so easy, you don't even have to open up the case (a few years ago, you often had to move a jumper on the motherboard to get it to accept the "flashing"). While this innovation is a serious time-saver, viruses have appeared that are specifically written to do damage when you upgrade your BIOS (for example, the CIH virus, aka the Chernobyl virus, set to go off on the anniversary of the Chernobyl nuclear disaster or the 26th of every month, depending on the variant). The BIOS can't discern which is a good change and which is a bad one, so encountering such a virus and leaving it unchecked could damage your BIOS. When the damage is unchecked and runs its course, a motherboard replacement—or at least the BIOS chip on the motherboard—is warranted.

Buffers and Frames

A *buffer* acts as a sort of queue, or an area for storing computer messages. A *frame* refers to one complete scan of the active area of a computer display screen, containing a set number of horizontal scan lines, with a set number of pixels in each. *Frames per second (fps)* refers to the number of times the screen updates per second.

You've seen that video boards require memory to hold the current video image. They're not the only boards that use memory addresses, however; other boards also need a little memory space reserved for them. A LAN board, for example, may require some storage space. Here are a few examples:

▶ Token Ring LAN boards have 16KB of ROM that contains a sort of network-level BIOS. They also have a RAM buffer that can be adjusted to be as small as 8KB or as large as 64KB.

▶ Many Ethernet boards these days have a 32KB RAM buffer on them; that RAM buffer must have an address within the CPU's address range.

▶ Some old ARCNet cards (it's an acronym for Attached Resource Computer Network) have up to 64KB of ROM on them.

▶ Older VGA boards had 24KB of ROM on them, but super VGA boards usually have 32KB or 40KB of ROM.

▶ Many hard disk controllers have ROM, particularly hard disk controllers that offer some kind of high performance or unusual capabilities, like SCSI or enhanced IDE host adapters.

▶ Scanner interface cards, such as the one supplied with the old Hewlett-Packard ScanJet, included some ROM.

▶ An expanded, or LIM, memory board contains from 16KB to 64KB of page frame memory space to buffer transfers into and out of LIM memory.

All those memory pieces must fit somewhere in the reserved area from 640KB to 1024KB in the PC memory address space. Before you leave this section, let's add reserved areas to your memory map, as in Figure 3.12.

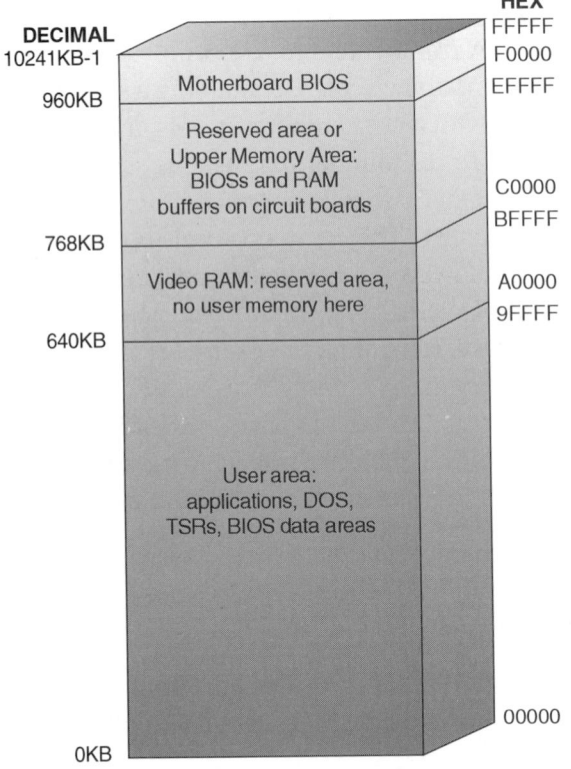

Figure 3.12

Memory map with reserved areas displayed

That's how the original PC designers laid out the first PC. The layout of that first 1024KB became a standard that no software or hardware designer dared violate, at the cost of 100 percent PC compatibility. But with more complex PCs came more memory—and a chance to get to more space.

Believe it or not, you've only gotten as far as the 8088 in this review of how software uses memory. But don't worry, the rest goes more quickly!

Extended Memory

Not content with the 8088/8086, Intel began in 1978 to develop processor chips with power rivaling that of minicomputers and mainframes. One thing micros lacked (then) that more powerful computers had was larger memory address space. So from the 80286's introduction in 1981 onward, Intel chips could address megabytes and megabytes. An 80286 could actually talk to ("address") 16MB. An 80386 or later could talk to 4GB (1GB is 1024MB) of RAM. The term for standard RAM above the 1MB level is *extended* memory.

Why did memory above 1024KB get a completely new name? Largely because the 286 and later chips had "split personalities": they could either address memory beyond 1024KB *or* run DOS programs. To use memory above 1024KB, the 286 and later chips had to shift to a new processor mode called *protected mode.* Protected mode had lots of virtues, but one big flaw: when a chip was in protected mode, it was incompatible with an older 8088 or 8086.

You see, most early CPUs used in microcomputers were more glorified calculator chips than computers—the 4004, 8008, 8080, 8085, 8086, 8088, 80188, and 80186 all fell into this category. Intel intended that the 80286 should have some powers that were mainframe-like, and in particular should be able to talk to more memory, and to *protect* that memory.

You're probably familiar with the notion that large mainframe computers can run multiple programs at the same time. Basically, the memory space of the computer gets parceled out to the applications ("Okay, text editor, you get 120KB, and database, you get 105KB, and spreadsheet, you get 150KB—no, you may *not* have more!"), and everyone's expected to stay in their places. But what about the odd program that accidentally strays from its area? If the text editor stretches a bit, it overwrites the database's area—what to do? Or, worse yet, suppose your computer were acting as a server on a LAN, and one program (a virus, or the like) tried to peek into the memory of the LAN server program itself—the *program that contains the system passwords?*

Note

The 8088, 8086, and earlier chips cannot ever address memory above 1024KB, so they can never have extended memory.

That's why memory protection is a good idea, and why mainframes have memory protection. The mainframe CPU has hardware built into it that keeps track of what application gets to use what memory. It's as if the CPU can put a "force field" around each program. As long as the program stays within its force field, it's okay. But if it tries to reach out of that area, it is stopped by the force field, and the CPU's "security system" is alerted that a protection violation was attempted. The operating system can then terminate the application (with extreme prejudice . . .). In less colorful terms, if an application tries to reach out of its space, the protection hardware senses this and stops the application, probably by ending the program and informing the user.

This memory protection is essential for any multitasking operating systems, and Linux and Windows 95/98/NT/2000 multitask. Furthermore, they work with extended memory, so you'd think that they would exploit these "force fields."

They do, but in varying ways. The oddest approach to memory protection is the one that Windows 3.x used. You see, all this placing of "force fields" must be controlled by some program, which means that there's got to be some control over who gets to set up force fields and who doesn't. That leads to the notion in the Intel world of *privilege rings*, as you see in Figure 3.13.

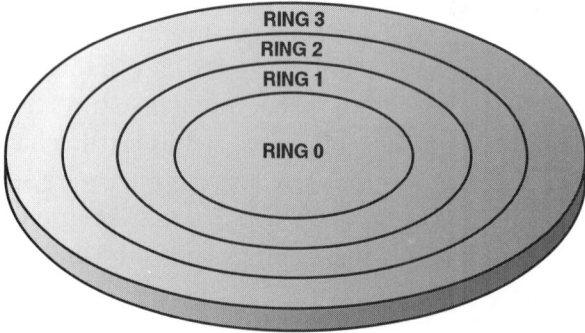

Figure 3.13

Privilege rings

Programs in ring 0 can control anything. Programs in ring 1 can control other ring 1, 2, or 3 programs. Ring 2 programs control only ring 2 or 3 programs, and ring 3 programs can affect only other ring 3 programs. Logically, then, the operating system should be ring 0, and the applications should be ring 3. That's the way that most operating systems are built.

Sadly, Windows 3.*x* didn't do that. Under that operating system, all programs were granted ring 0 privileges. *All* programs. That meant that while all programs had memory protection, all programs also had the capability to override the memory protection. No Windows 3.*x* program was safe from any other Windows 3.*x* program, leading to an unfortunately familiar error called a *general protection fault (GPF)*. Other operating systems, including Windows 95/98, are built better, but Windows 95/98 really only works protection-wise when you use programs written for Windows 95/98; older Windows applications still aren't protected.

Anyway, back to the history: until 1981, none of the Intel CPUs had this built-in memory protection, but the 286 and later chips were all built with this feature. These chips could also address memory beyond 1024KB, but *only* while in protected mode. Again, the 8088, 8086, and earlier chips could not under any circumstances address memory beyond 1024KB, so they could not ever have extended memory.

Basically, programs that run while in protected mode don't try to do *anything* with memory without first requesting memory blocks from the operating system. Then, once the OS has granted them an area in memory, the programs load their data into their spaces, and stay there.

And *that's* the problem.

The basic problem with multitasking DOS programs is that they often live up to their nickname: the "spoiled children" of PC programs. This whole notion of first asking the operating system—DOS—for permission before using memory is totally unknown in the DOS world. Programs written for DOS pretty much assume that they're the only program in the system, so they just take whatever they want without asking for it. So for the 286 to have memory protection, it would not only have to be a *different* chip, it would have to be an *incompatible* chip—incompatible with DOS and DOS programs, in particular.

Now, designing and releasing a new chip that was totally incompatible with any previous Intel offerings would be suicidal. So Intel gave the 286 and subsequent chips split personalities: when they boot up, they act just like an 8088, except faster. They can talk to 1024KB, and no more: this 8088 emulation mode is called *real mode*. You'll sometimes hear people refer to DOS programs (when speaking of Windows) as *real mode programs*. That just means they were built for the 8088. Of course, despite the fact that no one buys 8088s anymore, software is still written for the 8088 every day because of DOS's popularity. With a few instructions, it can shift over to protected mode and talk to lots of memory beyond 1024KB. But, again, once the 286 or later chip is in protected mode, it can't run programs designed for real mode—DOS and DOS programs, that is.

You may be wondering, why don't they just write an operating system that uses this protected mode? As I suggested earlier, they have—that was the whole idea of Windows 3.*x*, Windows NT, and Unix. Windows 3.*x* programs could address 16MB; some Windows programs—the ones that used Win32s—could address even more than that, although they required a 386 or 486 computer to do so.

Does that mean that DOS programs absolutely cannot use extended memory? By no means. A class of DOS programs uses software called a *DOS extender* to allow them to use extended memory. Basically, a DOS extender is a tiny operating system that unlocks the door to extended memory and provides tools that programmers can exploit to use that memory. Examples include 1-2-3 version 3.*x*, AutoCAD, and many database programs. This use of extended memory explains why, for example, 8088-based machines could run 1-2-3 version 3.

As XT-type machines were based on 8088/8086 chips, they *couldn't* have extended memory. ATs right up to the PIII and beyond *can*. When you see your computer count up to 16MB or 32MB or 64MB during the Power-On Self Test, you've got some extended memory.

Let's take a simple example—an old 286 with 1024KB of memory. There is 1024KB of RAM, all of which must be given addresses. You recall from the earlier part of this chapter that the addresses from 0 to 640KB are intended to be filled so that conventional memory space exists. Addresses 640KB through 1024KB must be left alone, because they're intended for memory from other sources, such as the video board and add-in cards. So, of the 1024KB, 640KB gets put in the 0–640KB range. That leaves 1024KB–640KB, or 384KB. Where does that memory get placed? It goes in the extended memory addresses, making it extended memory.

Figure 3.14 shows how it would look on your memory map.

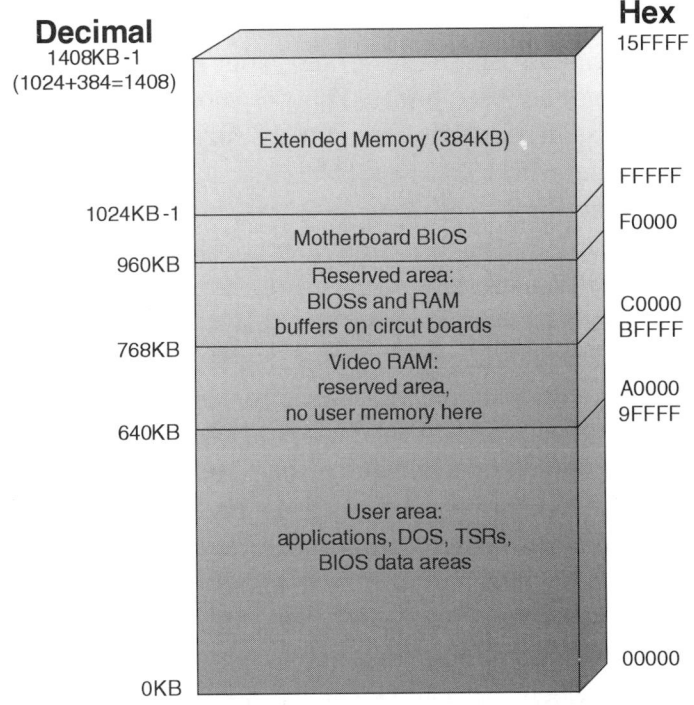

Decimal

Hex

1408KB -1
(1024+384=1408)

15FFFF

Extended Memory (384KB)

FFFFF

1024KB -1

Motherboard BIOS

F0000

960KB

Reserved area:
BIOSs and RAM
buffers on circut boards

C0000
BFFFF

768KB

Video RAM:
reserved area,
no user memory here

A0000
9FFFF

640KB

User area:
applications, DOS, TSRs,
BIOS data areas

00000

0KB

Figure 3.14

Memory map with
extended memory
included

Not to belabor the point, but this breaking up of memory causes a lot of confusion for users, so let me emphasize again why the memory gets allocated this way. The key to understanding the answer is in understanding that there's a difference between *memory* and *memory addresses.*

Remember my analogy in the beginning of this section about designing a computer versus designing a town? Well, let's suppose you're designing a town built on 1024 one-acre lots (conveniently enough). Suppose you zone the first 640 lots for residential use, the next 128 for industrial, and the remaining 256 for commercial buildings. You now have addresses, and purposes for those addresses, but nothing in those addresses. Sure, there's now a lot called 200 First Avenue, but it's only a muddy rectangle of ground: send mail there, and it just sits outside and rots.

After the town has been zoned, you start putting houses in the residential addresses—filling your PC with memory. But suppose a vendor of prefabricated houses shows up with 1024 houses? That's the situation that a computer designer faces when building a computer with 1024KB of RAM. First, she plunks down houses in the first 640 lots, filling your "conventional" addresses. But the zoning board (that is, the requirements of PC hardware compatibility) precludes her from putting any of the houses in the top 384 addresses. (Here, the computer designer plays both the roles of the planning board and the prefabricated house vendor.) The top 384 lots do not have normal system RAM (houses) in them; rather, they have special RAM. That area is filled in for a PC with some RAM physically located on the video board, and perhaps some ROM located on the motherboard or add-in boards. That, too, is worth stressing: the memory in the video area isn't taken from the system's main memory; when you buy a PC with 1024KB of memory, none of that memory is ROM or video RAM. A PC with 1024KB of RAM actually has a fair amount *more* than 1024KB of RAM, if you count the RAM on the video board and the ROM and RAM buffers on the expansion boards—and that memory is *not* counted when your system does its power-up memory count. There is simply nowhere to put the extra 384 houses, which is why XTs and PCs—8088-based computers—didn't have more than 640KB of system RAM.

Now let's move along to the 286 and later chips. They have memory limitations of 16MB or more, so now you've got to zone the addresses above 1024KB. Continuing the town planning analogy, suppose that this town has been in existence for 30 years, when a community springs up outside your original 1024 lots. You'd call that a suburb of the town; it might have a different tax rate, be governed differently, and have different levels of access to the privileges accorded town residents. For example, suburbanites might have to pay a fee to use the town parks, whereas the town residents might be able to use the parks for free. So it is with extended memory; the addresses above 1024KB are not accessible to the vast majority of DOS programs, as you've seen earlier in this discussion.

Return to the case of the vendor of prefab houses who finds herself with 1024 houses as she shows up in your new town. Again, she puts houses on the first 640 spaces and is then told that she cannot put houses on the top 384 addresses. "What will I do with these extra 384 houses?" she wails. "Take them out to the suburbs," she's told. So she puts the remaining 384 houses in the *extended* addresses, because the 384 addresses that she skipped from 640 to 1024 will be filled with buildings from another source.

So, getting back to the original question: what's happening with a 286 computer that counts up to 1024KB on power-up? First, understand that 1024KB is a count only of program memory. There is more memory in the computer—video RAM on the video board, system BIOS ROM on the motherboard, and ROM and perhaps small RAM buffers on add-in cards in the system—*that is not counted*. The 1024KB fills up the first 640KB and cannot fill up any of the addresses between 640K and 1024KB, or the PC will have program memory in the same addresses as video memory or ROM. Just as you can't put two houses on the same lot, so also two separate memories wired to the same address would both malfunction. So the extra 384KB of RAM gets addressed starting at 1024KB and going up to 1408KB.

Tip

You do not have to fill a lower memory address before filling a higher address; that's why you can have extended memory before filling the system's reserved area.

One more point that hangs some people up: I've said that the reserved area from 640KB to 1024KB contains memory, but it's not completely full. You'll usually find plenty of unused addresses between 768KB and 1024KB, a fact that created the memory manager market in the first place. Many people seem to feel that all the addresses from 0 through 1024KB must be filled by *something* before any addresses above 1024KB can be filled. But that's not true; you *could* build a computer with 128KB of conventional memory, video RAM between 640KB and 768KB, ROM between 768KB and 1024KB, and 6MB of extended memory above 1024KB. (You'd have trouble finding software that would run on it, but you could do it.)

Extended memory is simple for programmers to use, provided those programmers have a DOS extender or an operating environment that supports extended memory. The tremendous memory demands of programs today have made use of extended memory a necessity for many programs built in the '90s. But extended memory wasn't always easy to work with, which led to *expanded* memory.

EMS, LIM, Paged, Expanded Memory

In 1985, Lotus 1-2-3 version 1A was the best-selling software package in history. People used Lotus for everything. And Parkinson's Law ("work expands to fill all available resources") seemed to become an iron rule—more and more users found the 640KB limitation a chafing one. Not as chafing, however, as the 1-2-3 copy protection scheme. Copy protection was a common practice among software vendors until around 1986. 1-2-3's copy protection required that you insert a key disk into your A: drive *whenever* you wanted to run 1-2-3. No key disk, no Lotus.

So, when Lotus announced 1-2-3 version 2, people were excited. At $495 a copy, it seemed a mite pricey; but Lotus made its users an upgrade offer. "Send us $125 and your version 1A key disk, and we'll send you 2," they offered. Well, at $125, that was hard to turn down. The downside was that you had to send in the key disk, which meant that you couldn't use 1-2-3 1A *or* 2 until the upgrade arrived; but Lotus FedExed the upgrades, and people saw only a day or so of downtime. (In case you're wondering, the world was a much different place then, and people didn't rely on PCs as heavily as they do today. Nowadays, of course, an upgrade offer that took a PC out of action for a day or two would be laughed off the market.) So hundreds of thousands of users got the 2 upgrade.

This is when it became clear that there was just one little problem: 1-2-3 version 2 took up more memory space than version 1A. Which meant that any spreadsheets that packed the memory up to the 640KB rafters—and there were plenty—would not run under 2 for love or money. Worse yet, the users couldn't revert to 1A (they'd turned in their 1A key disks), leaving them stranded. "Golly," those users said. (Well, they didn't actually say, "Golly," but this book is rated "G" for general audiences.) Lotus realized that they'd better do something *fast*, so they called up Intel, the chip designers, and asked what could be done. Lotus and Intel developed a paged memory system (recall paging in the video discussion) that they called expanded memory. Using this memory system required the user to buy a new kind of memory board that Intel built called an *Above-Board*. (I'll explain the details on how it works in a bit.)

Let's finish your memory map by adding expanded memory off to the side of the standard memory column, as in Figure 3.15.

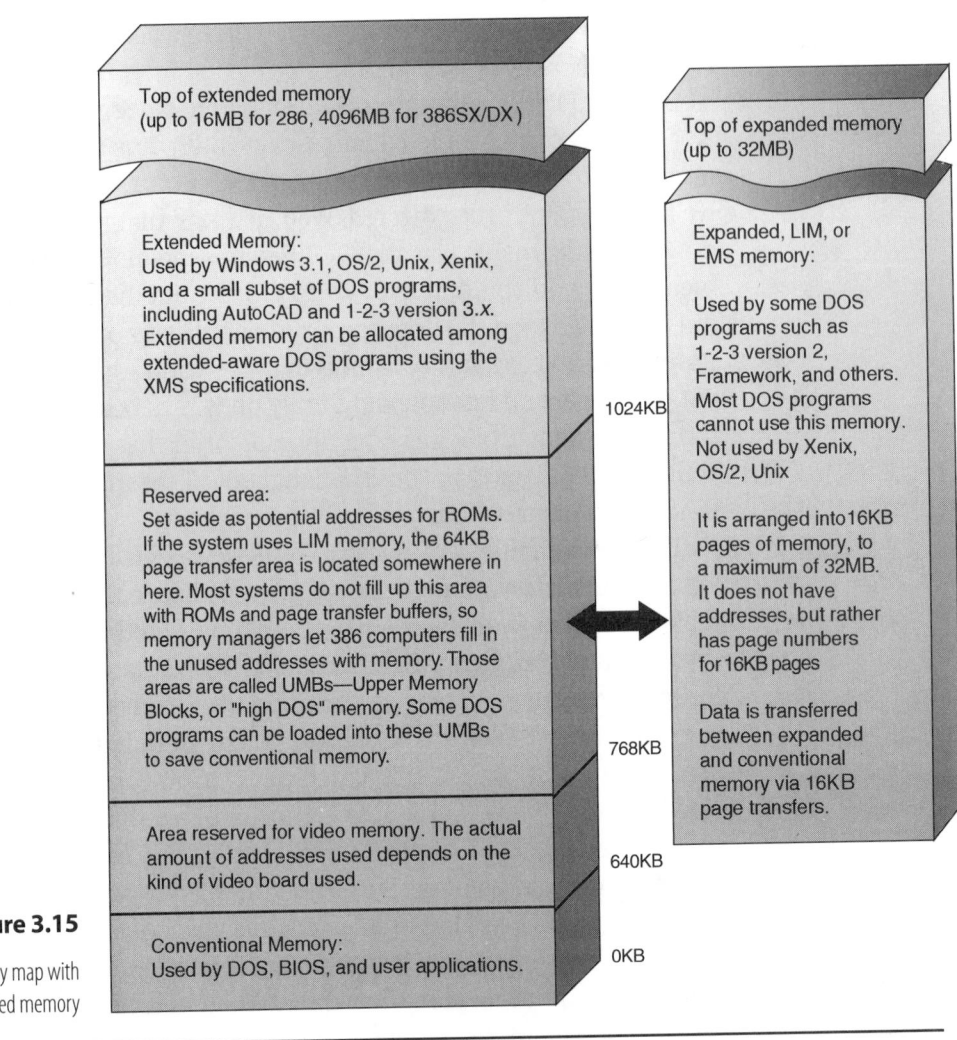

Figure 3.15

Memory map with expanded memory

On 8088 and most 80286 computers, you needed a specific memory board to support LIM: two common examples of this kind of memory board were, again, the Intel AboveBoard and the AST RAMPage cards. On 386 and later machines, you could achieve LIM compatibility with just software. That means that a 386 could make extended memory behave software-wise like expanded memory. Part of what Windows 3.1 could do and Windows 95/98/NT/2000 can do for DOS programs is to provide them with some extended memory that behaves like expanded memory. (The motherboards of some 286s could do that also, but not many.)

So now you've seen conventional, extended, and expanded memory. Let's review what you know so far:

▶ Conventional memory:

  ▶ Available to all PCs.

  ▶ Limited to 640KB.

  ▶ Virtually every program can use this memory.

  ▶ By default, DOS, device drivers, and TSRs are loaded in conventional memory.

▶ Extended memory:

  ▶ Only possible with machines based on 286 and later chips; was impossible with XTs.

  ▶ A class of DOS programs could use it.

  ▶ Used by Unix, Linux, Windows (3.*x* and 95/98/NT/2000).

▶ Expanded memory:

  ▶ Also called Lotus-Intel-Microsoft (LIM) memory or Expanded Memory Specification (EMS) memory.

  ▶ Could be used with PCs, XTs, ATs—any PC machine.

  ▶ Useful under DOS *with programs that can use it*, such as Lotus version 2.*x* and WordPerfect 5.1.

  ▶ 386 and later computers can make their extended memory act like expanded, as could a few 286-based machines.

The only problem remaining is how to tell them apart. I always remember extended versus expanded by pronouncing the latter "ex*P*anded," so I can remember that it is "*P*aged."

PC Expansion Buses

"Pentium II 128MB system with 18GB drive and AGP video for sale," reads a computer ad. The Pentium part is clearly the processor. The 128MB is the RAM part, as you've just read, and everybody (well, anybody reading *this* book) knows what a hard disk is. But what's AGP? AGP is the name of one kind of *expansion bus*. What exactly an expansion bus *is*, why you want one, and why you've got to worry about buses is the topic of this section.

What Is a Bus?

In order to be useful, the CPU must talk to memory, expansion boards, coprocessor (if the system has an external coprocessor), keyboard, and the like. It communicates with other devices on the motherboard via metal *traces* in the printed circuit, the copper lines that you'll see running around a board. That's how the SIMMs or DIMMs that probably live on your computer's motherboard communicate with the CPU, which is *also* probably on your computer's motherboard—they talk back and forth by shooting electrons along these thin metal traces.

But how can *expansion boards*, which aren't part of the motherboard, be connected to the CPU, the memory, and so on? Through the *bus*, or rather, through one of the buses—modern computers may have multiple expansion buses. And what are buses? Buses relate back to electrical engineering (as a lot of computer terminology does), and the term refers to a set of wires or tracks or conductors used to connect various parts of the PC.

Back in the early days of microcomputers, some computers didn't allow easy expansion. Take, for example, the early Macintosh computers. To expand a 128KB or 512KB Mac, you had to do some extensive engineering—which is why most people didn't mess around inside those computers. Any circuit boards that you wanted to add usually had to be mounted haphazardly inside the Mac's case; installing a hard disk required disassembling the computer, soldering connections onto the Mac motherboard, and reassembling the machine. Making modifications difficult puts the user at the mercy of the modifier, because virtually all such modifications are done at the expense of the manufacturer's warranty and service agreement, if any—and they're expensive, because they require a technician.

You don't have to do such brain surgery on a PC, thankfully. PCs have expansion slots that allow easy upgrades. (By the way, today's Macs also have expansion slots, fortunately; in fact, Macs built after 1995 have the same bus as some PCs, the PCI bus that I'll discuss soon.)

Another disadvantage of the old Macintosh approach was that the average Joe/Jane couldn't do the modifications themselves. This would be like you having to cut a hole in the wall of your house to find a main power line every time you want to use an appliance. Without standard interface connectors (that is, an outlet), you would have to find the power line, then splice the appliance into it to get power for the appliance.

This scenario, as you know, is silly, because you have standard outlet plugs. But it wasn't always unthinkable; when electricity first arrived, adding every new appliance entailed some fancy wiring work. (Kind of like adding a station to a LAN today.) Nowadays, however, you have an easy, standard way to add appliances. Any manufacturer who wants to sell you a device requiring electrical power needs only to ensure that the device takes standard U.S. current, and add a two-prong or three-prong plug. "Upgrading" your house, then (adding the new appliance) is a simple matter: just "plug and play."

Many computers adopt a similar approach. Such computer manufacturers have issued a connector standard: any vendor desiring to offer an expansion board for this computer need only follow the connector specifications, and the board will work in the computer. Even the earliest computers included such a connector, first called the *omnibus connector*, because it gave access to virtually all important circuits in the computer. *Omnibus* was quickly shortened to bus, and *bus* it has remained.

So a computer bus is an intrinsic part of a computer's hardware communication standard, an agreement about how to build boards that can work in a standard PC. For various reasons, however, there are over a half-dozen such different standards in the PC world.

The First "PC" Bus

The PC wasn't the first computer based on a chip, not by about eight years. The first commercially available microcomputer was a computer called the Altair. It consisted of a case and a row of expansion slots. It was a backplane computer, with even the CPU on an expansion card. The bus that the Altair used became a standard in the industry for years, and is still used in some machines: it was called the S-100 or Altair bus.

Although it was a standard, it wasn't ever true that every microcomputer used the S-100. The Apple II used a bus of its own, called the *Apple bus*. The original 1981 PC model used yet another bus, with 62 wires called lines. It came to be known as (you can see that this is something of a pattern, although a dull one) the *PC bus*.

The 62 lines mentioned above are offered to the outside world through a standard connector, as mentioned previously. These connectors are also called *expansion slots*, because expansion boards must plug into these slots. Some PCs have had no slots at all, so they weren't expandable; other machines have three, and most clone-type machines have eight slots. Some machines offer 10 slots. The more slots, the better: expansion slots equal flexibility and *upgradability*. (I know it's not a word, but you get the idea.) Let's take a minute, however, and look at what those 62 lines do.

Data Path

Now, remember that the original PC and XT were based on the 8088 chip. The 8088 had a data path (the "front door," recall?) of just eight bits, so the PC bus includes only eight data lines. That means this bus is *eight bits wide*, and so data transfers can occur only in eight-bit chunks. Expansion slots on a computer with this bus are called *eight-bit* slots. Eight of the 62 wires, then, transport data around the computer.

Consider the importance of data path in bus design. The eight data bits supported by the original PC bus would be pretty inadequate for a Pentium-based system; recall that the Pentium uses a 64-bit data path.

Could someone actually *build* a Pentium computer with eight-bit expansion slots? Sure. But every time that the Pentium wanted to do a full 64-bit read of data, it would have to chop that request into eight separate eight-bit reads. *Really* slow. But it could be done, and in fact there are, as you'll learn later, designs almost as bad: most P5- and P6-based systems (which incorporate a 16-bit bus to this day), and the ISA bus you'll read about in a page or two, in addition to a 32-bit bus called PCI.

Memory Size

The original PC bus included 20 wires to address memory. What's that mean to us regular user types? Well, given that each one of those address wires can carry either a 0 or a 1 signal, then each wire can carry only one of two possible values. Since there are 20 of the address lines, the total number of possibilities is $2 \times 2 \times 2 \dots 20$ times. That's 2 to the 20th power, or just over one million. However, in a sense, you already knew that, because the 8088 can address only 1MB of RAM. All those address lines are duplicated on the PC bus, accounting for another 20 of the 62 bus lines.

Memory or I/O Address?

The 20 address lines actually do double duty, because there are two kinds of addresses: the memory's addresses and *input/output addresses*. I'll discuss I/O addresses in greater detail in Chapter 6, "Installing New Circuit Boards (without Creating New Problems)." However, at this point I'll mention that the computer must be able to tell when the address lines are transmitting a memory address versus when the address lines are transmitting an I/O address; one line on the bus designates which one it is.

Additionally, there are several other lines on the bus that tell whether the data on the bus has been read from memory (or an I/O device), or whether data is to be written to memory or I/O.

Electronic Overhead

Some bus wires just transport simple electric power; there are +5 volts, –5 volts, +12 volts, and electric ground lines as part of the bus. Why are those lines there? Simple: to power a board plugged into a bus slot.

There are also a few control lines, like Reset (which, as you'd imagine, resets the processor), clock signals, and Refresh, which controls memory refresh (more on that in Chapter 8).

Interrupts and Direct Memory Access Channels

Add-in cards sometimes need to demand the attention of the CPU; they do that via hardware interrupts or IRQ (interrupt request) levels. There are six IRQ levels on the PC bus, labeled IRQ2 through IRQ7. Each gets a wire on the bus. There are also IRQ 0 and IRQ1, but they're not available on the bus.

Some of those add-in cards also need to transfer data to the system's memory quickly; they can do that via a direct memory access (DMA) channel. There are three DMA channels on the bus, labeled DMA1 through DMA3. There is also DMA channel 0, but, like IRQs 0 and 1, it's not accessible through the bus.

DMA and IRQs are both *extremely* important topics in PC upgrades, and I'm going to cover them in detail in Chapter 6.

I have given a somewhat in-depth look into the first PC bus so that you're ready to see why the many buses that followed are improvements on the original, and to help you decide which bus is right for any of the machines that you buy.

The first enhancement to the PC bus came with the IBM AT; let's take a look at that bus.

The AT (ISA) Bus

When developing the AT, IBM saw that it had to upgrade the bus. One reason was because the 80286 is a chip with a 16-bit data path.

They certainly *could* have designed the AT with an 8-bit bus, but it'd be a terrible shame to make a 286 chip transfer data eight bits at a time over the bus, rather than utilize its full 16-bit data path. So they thought that it'd be nice to have a 16-bit bus.

On the other hand, there was backward compatibility with the PC and XT to think of: it would be tough to sell a lot of ATs if they couldn't use the hardware (and software) of the existing, established PC/XT world. So IBM came up with a fairly good solution: they kept the old 62-line slot connectors and *added* another 36-wire connector, placing it in line with the older 62-line connector to provide some of these features:

▶ Eight more data lines, bringing the data bus to 16 bits in width.

▶ Four more address lines, bringing the address bus to 24 bits in width. Two to the 24th power is about 16 million, so the AT's 16-bit slots could support up to 16MB of RAM, in theory.

▶ Four more DMA channels, 4 through 7.

▶ Five more IRQ levels: IRQ 10, 11, 12, 14, and 15. I'm getting a little ahead of myself, but I know that some of you will have an immediate question. You may know—and if not, you'll learn in Chapter 6—that there are *eight* more IRQs on a machine of this type; so why do we see only five on this newer bus slot? First, IRQ9 is wired where IRQ2 previously was, saving a bus line. What about IRQ2? It's off the bus now because it's the line that makes possible the new IRQ lines. Second, IRQ13 is dedicated to the math coprocessor, so there's no point in giving it any of the bus's wires. Finally, IRQ8 is connected to the system's clock/calendar, so it also does not require a line on the bus.

These two-part connectors are called, as you'd expect, 16-bit slots. You can see these two kinds of connectors in Figure 3.16.

Figure 3.16

8-bit and 16-bit
bus slots

For a while, this 16-bit bus was called the AT bus, and you'll still hear some people use that name. Since 1988, however, most people have referred to these types of bus slots as *Industry Standard Architecture (ISA)* slots. You can tell the difference between an 8-bit and a 16-bit ISA board by looking at the edge connector on the bottom of it. Take a look at an 8-bit board, as you see in Figure 3.17.

Figure 3.17

8-bit board

Notice that it has a single edge connector on the bottom. In contrast, look at a 16-bit board, like the one in Figure 3.18.

Figure 3.18

16-bit board

Since the 16-bit slots are just a superset of the 8-bit bus, 8-bit boards work just fine in 16-bit slots, which is a good thing—no modern PCs that I know of have the simple 8-bit slots. However, almost all *do* have the 16-bit slots, making 8-to-16 compatibility good in the unlikely case that you have an old 8-bit board around that you want to use.

Years ago, you would sometimes see a motherboard with both 8-bit slots and 16-bit slots. If the 16-bit slots can use 8-bit boards, why have any 8-bit slots on an AT-type machine at all? The reason is not an electrical reason, but a physical reason. Some older 8-bit boards have a *skirt* that extends down and back on the circuit board, making it physically impossible to plug an 8-bit board with a skirt into a 16-bit connector. You can see a board with a skirt in Figure 3.19.

Figure 3.19

8-bit board with a skirt

ISA has continued on our systems for backward compatibility. Even if we use some of the latest equipment on our PCs, some of us still have ISA sound cards and even modems and network cards either installed or sitting around as a backup.

But all reigns must come to an end, and ISA's has come. ISA is being eliminated in an effort to finally move away from the antiquated slowness of the bus, and to make room for USB and FireWire, though we continue to have slower serial and parallel ports supported under the design specifications.

Since January 1, 2000, ISA slots cannot be manufactured into a motherboard on a system that will bear the "certified Windows compatible" logo, as pronounced by the Microsoft-Intel PC design specifications. Even as Linux becomes more of a player in the PC world, Windows certification is important if you want to sell PCs.

Just How Fast Is That Bus?

You learned back in the CPU section that different CPUs run at different speeds. You can't take a CPU rated to run at 25MHz and run it at 66MHz; it will fail. (You can *try*—recall that it's called overclocking—but it's not a good idea.)

Buses have clocks, as well, and those clocks drive the boards inserted into their expansion slots. That suggests a question: how is it that any board pretty much works in any kind of computer? Why does an ISA video board built for a 12MHz computer still work in a 400MHz Pentium II?

Part of the answer, you'll recall, is that the 400MHz Pentium II looks like a 100MHz chip from the motherboard's point of view; the 400MHz part is internal to the CPU chip. So the fastest bus you'd need for a 400MHz Pentium would be 100MHz. But for the rest of the story, let's return to 1985.

Early Buses Equaled Clock Rates

Prior to 1985, buses ran at the same speed as their CPUs. The PC ran at 4.77MHz, and so did the PC bus. Turbo XT clones that ran at 7.16MHz had buses that ran at 7.16MHz. When IBM released the 6MHz AT, then its bus ran at 6MHz, and so on.

But all this variation in bus speeds led to a major headache for expansion board buyers. A board designed for the 4.77MHz PC might not (and often *did* not) work in the faster machines. Part of a PC upgrader's job was to know which PC bus speeds a particular board would work in.

Compaq Tries Not to Miss the Bus

Then Compaq released its Deskpro 286/12.

In 1985, IBM was selling the AT, as you've already read. The fastest version ran at 8MHz. Compaq, as the number one IBM cloner, decided to seriously outpace IBM with their new Deskpro 286/12—the 12 stood for 12MHz.

Now, okay, 12MHz isn't such a big deal nowadays. But back then, it was like Compaq today offering a Pentium that runs at 800MHz. Nobody else even came close. But what to do about the bus? If they built a 12MHz 286 computer with a 12MHz bus, then in all probability no existing boards would work. Who'd buy a fast computer that wouldn't work with any of the add-in boards on the market?

Compaq's answer: decouple the main clock from the bus clock. They ran the CPU and much of the motherboard at 12MHz, but ran the bus at only 8MHz. Expansion boards sitting in slots would see only an 8MHz environment, so the new Deskpro could be both fast *and* compatible. And ever since, that's how everybody has built their ISA slots, at 8MHz. That's why you never have to worry about whether your computer is too slow for a particular board; from the board's point of view, every computer—including yours—runs at 8MHz. This *sounds* good, but . . .

The big drawback in having the expansion bus run at a separate clock speed than the external CPU bus is that some boards *should* run at CPU speed, such as memory boards. Imagine that you've got a 100MHz Pentium. It communicates with its motherboard at 66MHz, because it's a clock-and-a-halfer. Suppose you want to put more memory on this system, so you buy an ISA memory card. (Please *don't* do this; this is just an example.) You pop it into one of the computer's 16-bit slots, and you'll have extended your memory, but *all memory accesses will be at 8MHz, not 66MHz;* every time you access memory on that board, your system will slow down to 8MHz. Yuck. And many of us use ISA boards on a daily basis to talk to our hard disks, video monitors, and local area networks. This is a major reason why we need something other than the ISA bus as a standard, and why there are so many kinds of alternative buses available.

ISA's Not Enough: Mesozoic Local Bus

The first folks to try to set a new bus standard were, again, Compaq, a year later.

In 1986, Compaq introduced one of the first 80386-based desktop computers. Because the 80386DX is a 32-bit chip, Compaq wanted to exploit that power with a new bus slot. Remember, *they* were the guys who saddled us with the 8MHz bus slots in the first place. Standard-speed bus slots were still a good idea, but how to offer memory expansion boards that were 32-bit in data path and 16MHz (the computer's clock rate) in speed, unless by building an entirely new bus?

Compaq decided to just include a new 32-bit slot on the motherboard, a slot solely for use with a specific memory card that Compaq (and later, third-party vendors) sold. Some 386 cloners adopted this new bus format, but it never really caught on. Instead, each vendor developed its own 32-bit "standard." Intel had one it pushed for a while in the late '80s, AT&T had another, Micronics a fourth, and so on.

These buses all had several things in common:

▶ They had a 32-bit data path.

▶ They ran at the clock speed of the 386 computer—usually 16MHz, 20MHz, 25MHz, or 33MHz.

▶ They supported only one particular board, sold by the motherboard's manufacturer.

These buses came to be known as *private* buses or, later, *local* buses, because they were "local" to the processor, since there was no extra clock circuitry between them and the CPU. From 1986 to 1991, the main value of local bus boards and slots was, again, to accommodate memory for their specific computer. These were the remote ancestors of what we now call the *VESA Local Bus (VLB)* standard—what I think of as the "Mesozoic" version of VLB. I suppose that if you used one of these on a hard disk controller, you'd "Jurassic *park*" the heads on your drive. (Yeah, it was a lousy pun. But stick around; they get worse.) Discussion of VLB, by the way, is coming up in a bit; I just wanted to keep this discussion in at least moderately chronological order.

The PS/2 Bus: Micro Channel Architecture (MCA)

Not to be outdone by Compaq in the trendsetting department, IBM attempted to change the rules again in 1987 when they announced the PS/2 line. The PS/2 Models 50 to 80 (*not* the 25 or 30) got a new bus called the *Micro Channel Architecture (MCA)* bus, in order to facilitate faster data transfer within the computer, and to lower noise levels. (ISA is a *very* noisy standard, which is another reason why it hasn't gotten faster over the years.) It didn't catch on, but IBM pushed it doggedly for years before surrendering in the mid-'90s.

Introducing a new bus was a bold move (although perhaps not a very bright one), in that the MCA bus was completely incompatible with the old ISA bus. ISA expansion boards didn't (and *don't*) work in the PS/2 line. PS/2 buyers must be sure when buying a board that it's an MCA board, not an ISA board, because the ISA boards are completely useless in MCA machines.

What prompted this bold move? Well, some of the things that I've already discussed and a few others. MCA never really caught on that strongly (and I'll talk about why that's true in a minute), but some of the features that it offered have become essential for any advanced bus.

Better Speed and Data Path

As you'd expect, MCA tried to better ISA by hitting its weak points. MCA runs at 10MHz, not 8MHz. Not a great improvement, but an improvement. MCA also supported either a 16-bit data path or a

32-bit data path. It actually has a streaming mode, wherein it can transfer 64 bits at a time.

Software Board Configuration

Anyone who's installed an older ISA board (installation of boards is, again, the main topic for Chapter 6) has almost certainly struggled with small DIP switches and jumpers. These small hardware devices are used to configure older ISA boards. They're a pain in the neck, because they're often hard to change around, and you've got to remove the PC's cover to get to them in the first place.

Micro Channel boards, in contrast, are software configurable—no jumpers, and no DIP switches. You just run one central configuration program, and you can set up a computer by clicking with the mouse, rather than rooting around in the machine. This is a feature that was useful when it came out, but it's *essential* now—which is why Plug-and-Play hardware is becoming more and more ubiquitous.

Boards Can Share Interrupts

Once you start configuring boards, you'll find that the thing you're running out of most is interrupt levels. You can't put a mouse card on the same IRQ level as your local area network board, or your network connection could crash the first time that you move the mouse. That's because of how ISA was designed.

With MCA, it was *possible* to design a board that shares its interrupts with other boards. Very few Micro Channel boards *did* share interrupts, but it's possible. Why? Blame the people who write drivers. Even though several buses now support interrupt sharing, it's still almost unheard of, even in the most modern systems.

Bus Mastering Improves upon DMA

I haven't explained *direct memory access (DMA)* in detail yet, but it's basically a way for expansion boards to quickly transfer data from themselves to the system's RAM, or from the RAM to the boards.

DMA's main goal in life is speed: it makes the PC faster.

DMA can't do one thing, however. Boards can transfer data directly to RAM, or RAM to boards, but *not* boards to boards. That's handled by a kind of "super" DMA called *bus mastering*. Bus mastering was not really supported by ISA (you can have one, but only one, bus master card in an entire ISA machine), but MCA supported bus mastering.

Bus mastering is another one of those features that first appeared with MCA, but is *de rigueur* for any modern advanced bus.

MCA was neat because it was cleaner, as I said before, so it could transfer data at higher speeds than the ISA machines of a few years back. (I said "could" because it has the capability, but that capability never became important in its market.) It also included something called *Programmable Option Select (POS)*. It allowed circuit boards to be a lot smarter about how they interact with the computer. For one thing, DIP switch and configuration problems lessened considerably. More on this in Chapter 6.

EISA (Extended Industry Standard Architecture)

The MCA turned out to be pretty unimportant in the market mainly because IBM locked it up six ways to Sunday, patent-wise. Companies couldn't clone the MCA without paying a Draconian *5 percent* of their *gross* to IBM as fealty (oops, that's supposed to be *royalties*) for use of MCA. Five percent of gross is probably more than most companies are making as *profits*. For the 5 percent, you didn't even get the plans for MCA. What's supposed to happen is *first* you spent hundreds of thousands of dollars figuring out how to clone MCA— IBM offered no help—*then* you got to pay Big Blue the 5 percent.

So Compaq talked eight other compatible makers (a group called Watchzone—Wyse, AST, Tandy, Compaq, Hewlett-Packard, Zenith, Olivetti, NEC, and Epson) into forming a joint venture to respond to MCA. They created yet another new bus, one called the *Extended Industry Standard Architecture (EISA)*, which was intended to have MCA's good features, without sacrificing compatibility with the old AT (ISA) bus. Presumably, building it cost less than 5 percent of profits. It appeared in 1989 and still shows up on the motherboards of some systems that include both PCI and EISA slots. (PCI's coming up.)

EISA never got amazingly popular, but it was a kind of well-designed, solid bus that found its way into a lot of high-end servers. It was gaining some momentum around the mid-'90s, but it was overtaken by the newer, more powerful PCI standard.

What about EISA's features? Summarized, they include:

▶ 32-bit data path

▶ Enough address lines for 4GB of memory

▶ More I/O addresses, 64KB of them

▶ Software setup capability for boards, so no jumpers or DIP switches—similar to POS

▶ 8MHz clock rate (unfortunately)

▶ No more interrupts or DMA channels

▶ Supports cards that are physically large, making them cheaper to build (smaller cards cost more to design)

▶ Bus mastering

Note that EISA is *not* a local bus, because it runs at 8MHz. It runs at that poky speed because it must be, recall, hardware compatible with ISA, hence the need for slow bus slots. EISA will also run DMA at higher speeds than will ISA. The lack of local bus means, however, that EISA memory boards aren't a possibility. EISA machines either need enough SIMM space on the motherboard for sufficient memory, or the motherboard vendor must design a proprietary expansion slot for a proprietary memory card. EISA boards remain supported for use, but it's not a future standard.

Local Bus

In the XT and AT days, you expanded memory just by buying a memory expansion card, putting memory chips on it, and inserting the card into one of the PC's expansion slots. But by the time that

PCs got to 12MHz, that easy answer disappeared. As I've already said, no matter how fast your PC is—20MHz, 25MHz, 33MHz—the expansion slots still run at only 8MHz.

Now, I've been kind of beating up on slow buses, but they're not all *that* bad, in reality. Most boards in expansion slots communicate with components that are fairly slow anyway, such as floppy drives, printer ports, modems, and the like.

Only a handful of boards benefit from really high speeds. I've mentioned memory. Another board that really needs to be able to blitz data around is a video graphics board. Take a moment and calculate how many pixels (dots on the screen) you've got on a 1024 × 768 video screen. Then consider that the CPU must shove them around perhaps dozens of times per second, and you can see that having fast access to the video board is a good thing.

Hard disk interfaces benefit from high speed, and in particular SCSI hard disk interfaces. Video capture boards are another type of fast board, and local area network cards are yet another candidate for local busing.

There are two main kinds of local bus around these days: the VLB bus and the PCI bus.

VESA Local Bus

As I've already told you, the local bus grew out of a sort of nonstandard. Some manufacturers designed a special high-speed slot for the motherboard that will accommodate only a memory board. That was the first local bus.

A bit later on, vendors started including local bus slots for video cards and then selling you the video cards that fit into those slots. The problem was one of noncompatibility: the local bus video card on one machine was incompatible with the local bus video card on another machine.

Since the lack of cross-compatibility was getting in the way of video board sales, an industry group promulgated and promoted a local bus standard called VESA after the group's name—*Video*

Electronic Standards Association. It saw some moderate popularity for a bit in the early '90s but died out around 1993. It's not likely you'll run across a VESA motherboard with a Pentium or later chip on it; VESA's heyday was in the 486 days.

The VESA Local Bus (VLB) was an important step in the evolution of computers—having a 33MHz bus was cool!—but it wasn't enough. VLB is really just a 32-bit, high-speed extension of the older, dumb ISA architecture. Sometimes I describe VLB as a "big, dumb bus."

VLB actually hurt the PC world, in a way, because VLB offered improved speed but no better ways of *using* that speed: it just perpetuated the old PC approach of doing everything in a fast, brute force manner. *Brute force* here refers to the fact that the VLB did not offer most of the attractive features of the Micro Channel and EISA buses; it did not offer software setup of boards or bus mastering. VLB systems were still saddled with jumper-setting installations, and the CPU must baby-sit every single data transfer over the VLB bus. Forcing the CPU to manage each and every transfer keeps the CPU squarely in the middle of the system, making it a bottleneck to system performance.

PCI: Today's Bus

The PC world needed a better bus, because without a better bus there wasn't all that much sparkle in new CPUs. Intel was aware of this and was worried. Less sparkly new systems meant fewer new systems *sold*, and that meant fewer CPUs sold. Whatever hurts the PC world hurts Intel sales, so Intel designed an even newer, faster bus slot called PCI, short for Peripheral Component Interconnect. (Obviously, Intel believes in clinging to at least *one* PC tradition—dumb acronyms.) PCI is a good bus for several reasons, which are outlined in the following paragraphs. You can see a PCI board in Figure 3.20 and a PCI bus slot in Figure 3.21. The smaller and lighter-colored (usually white or cream or gray) slots are the PCI slots; the larger and darker (black or charcoal gray) slots next to them are ISA slots.

Figure 3.20

PCI board

Figure 3.21

PCI and ISA bus slots

Processor Independence

The PCI bus doesn't directly interface with the CPU. Rather, it communicates with the CPU via a *bridge circuit* that can act as a buffer between the specifics of a particular CPU and the bus. If you've ever looked at Device Manager in Windows 9x and Windows 2000 and wondered what the heck a PCI bridge is, this is it.

What does that mean? It means really good news for non-PC computer users. Macintosh PCs and RISC-based machines such as the DEC Alpha are now coming out with PCI slots. That means a bigger market for PCI boards and an avenue for board makers to reach the PC, Mac, and RISC markets with a single board.

Wider Data Path

PCI distinguishes itself first because it is a 64-bit bus. PCI supports a data path appropriate for the newer Pentium-based computers, which require 64 bits at each clock cycle. PCI also supports a 32-bit data path, however, so it was used in some of the last 486 systems to be manufactured.

High Speed

Like VLB, PCI originally was developed to run to 33MHz. This made the net throughput of a PCI bus as large as 132Mbps with a 32-bit board, or 264Mbps with a 64-bit board. That's one of the bonuses of PCI: it can be configured as both a 32-bit as well as a 64-bit bus, and both 32-bit and 64-bit boards can be used in either.

In 1998, with the adoption of a new specification, the PCI bus moved to 66MHz. When 64-bit PCI devices are used at 66MHz, the throughput increases to 524Mbps. For the most part, 32-bit PCI devices and 64-bit devices are interchangeable (some types of BIOS types differentiate between the two under CMOS setup). Some non-standard equipment, usually off brand, has presented some difficulties in configuration and use for the common user, but it has been, overall, one of the smoother transitions. The 66MHz PCI cards fit fine into the older PCI buses; they just won't operate at 66MHz. Meanwhile, 33MHz PCI boards go right into the newer motherboards, operating at their standard 32-bit selves.

Part of the changes in hardware over the past few years have centered around how to leave behind some of the slower buses and architecture to more adequately embrace faster technology and devices. Both Universal Serial Bus (USB) and FireWire/IEEE 1394 are part of that move.

However, as you'll learn more about in the FireWire section later in this chapter, FireWire is expensive and not easily supported. Thus, many PC manufacturers trying to keep down the price—

known in the PC industry as Total Cost of Ownership (TCO)—have been hesitant to begin putting FireWire connections on their systems. As this is written, only a handful of PC manufacturers are using FireWire (though you're seeing the connectors more and more on high-end consumer electronics equipment such as digital video cameras). Compaq includes them on servers, Sony puts them on some VAIO desktops, and Dell has one on its high-end laptop.

Instead, PC manufacturers have wanted to extend the PCI bus to give it more longevity and usefulness (and at lower cost than FireWire), in a specification referred to as *PCIx*, or PCI Extended. This seemed to draw some interest by the end of 1999, but don't look for PCIx devices with an estimated throughput of up to 1Gbps to appear in your next bargain PC system. PCIx, like FireWire, is being looked at for more serious business use, on servers and high-end workstations. It may filter down to the more modest system at a later time, but by then, we could all be using FireWire and an update to the Universal Serial Bus that makes it quite a bit faster than the USB we use today.

Backward Compatibility

Although ISA or EISA boards cannot fit in PCI slots, the common chip sets that support PCI also support ISA and EISA. That means it's easy to build a PC with PCI, ISA, and EISA slots all on the same motherboard. Typical motherboard configurations either support PCI and ISA or PCI and EISA. For some reason, the PCI/ISA motherboards support only a single processor, and in general the PCI/EISA motherboards support multiple processors. There's no engineering reason for that; it's just that the Intel chip sets for single-processor systems support PCI/ISA, and the Intel chip sets for multiprocessor systems support PCI/EISA. Nowadays, almost all motherboard makers use the Intel chip sets.

Bus Mastering

Like EISA and Micro Channel—and *unlike* VLB—PCI supports bus master adapter boards, paving the way for the "community" of processors that I referred to earlier.

Non–bus mastered data transfers require a lot of the CPU's time. For example, one author reports that a file transfer via an Ethernet network required over 40 percent CPU utilization when the Ethernet card was ISA, but only 6 percent with a similar setup and a PCI Ethernet card. Bus mastering is a good idea, and it's discussed in more detail in Chapter 6.

Software Setup

PCI supports the Plug-and-Play standard developed in 1992 by hardware vendors. There are, in general, no jumpers or DIP switches on PCI boards. There usually isn't even a board-specific configuration program. PCI setup is terrific on a Plug-and-Play system, but it can be a bit challenging on a non-Plug-and-Play system. There's an extensive discussion of that in Chapter 6.

PCI is a good architecture, and building PCI boards is relatively cheap. That's no doubt why it has become the premier PC bus.

Accelerated Graphics Processing (AGP): Local Bus Returns

The original 33MHz bus was the VLB bus. And what created the driving need for a fast bus? Video. The two things that *always* seem to drive demand for faster buses are memory and video. 33MHz was a pretty fast speed for a video board back when CPUs ran at 50MHz and 66MHz. Of course, they soon ran faster than that, so it shouldn't be any surprise that video is again screaming for more speed.

This time, however, Intel wanted to be out in front and so, before some competitor could come up with a faster bus for graphics, Intel did. They call it the *Accelerated Graphics Processing (AGP)* bus. (Note that the A stands for *accelerated*—some seem to want to rename AGP *Advanced* Graphics Processing.) It accomplishes two things:

▶ It is four to eight times faster than PCI for transferring data. CPUs on systems with AGP video boards can, then, blast video images to their video board pretty quickly.

❱ It enables a video board to supplement its own video memory with some system memory.

Think of Accelerated Graphics Processing as just the latest local bus. In addition to speed, AGP allows a CPU to put a bitmap into regular old system memory and then be able to directly use and display that bitmap for the video board. You can see an AGP bus slot in Figure 3.22. The AGP slot is the one that's darker and slightly "offset" from the other, lighter PCI slots.

Figure 3.22

Accelerated graphics processing slot

Intel clearly wants this new bus to be a very special-purpose bus. AGP motherboards have only one AGP slot, and as far as I can see, the chip sets allow only one AGP board. That's kind of a shame. In the past, new local buses *started* out as video or memory buses, but then SCSI host adapter vendors or other clever folks used the faster slots to do new and interesting things. More and more "interesting things" created a demand for faster buses, and soon large manufacturers responded with a new general-purpose bus. (That's how PCI appeared.) Because there's only one AGP slot essentially by definition, I suppose AGP won't turn out to be an intermediate step to a faster general-purpose bus.

When AGP first came out in wide market distribution in 1998, its speed (1X or 2X) was limited by other components on a PC system. The greatest issue was overall bandwidth. But changes to overall speed of a system, and the new forms of memory I've discussed, have finally allowed the production of 4X AGP cards, just beginning to appear as this book goes to press.

The new 4X AGP cards should fit fine into existing AGP ports for 1X and 2X cards, but you won't have the speed and features over 1X/2X unless you have a sufficient system—including a motherboard/BIOS updated for 4X—to handle it.

PC Card (PCMCIA): The Portable Bus

Laptop computers are an absolute must for traveling professionals and are rapidly becoming basic equipment for more casual users as well (not to mention the explosion of non-PC, Internet-connected devices such as Web phones and Personal Digital Assistants, or PDAs). I have owned *15* laptops in the past 10 years. Laptops are great because they're almost 100 percent software compatible with their bigger cousins, the desktop machines.

But until about 1995, laptops had an Achilies' heel: add-in circuit boards. I've felt for a good long time now that eventually laptops will be *all* that we'll buy, because they're portable and don't take up as much office space as do other types of computer cases. Thankfully, lower prices on laptops have allowed more people to become mobile with their computers, but laptops still generally have a fairly short life expectancy since they are much more likely to break (being dropped, jarred in transit, etc.) and laptop theft is becoming a huge issue, making people look at smaller units still, like Windows CE handhelds and PalmPilots. However, the PC Card (called PCMCIA before 1995) removes the second objection. And the new 14.5-inch LCD screens on laptops such as the IBM ThinkPads and the Digital Ultra HiNote 2000 take a serious bite out of the first.

Over the years, it's been customary to add two kinds of hardware to laptops: an internal modem and more memory. But, because laptops never had standard expansion slots, laptop owners had to buy proprietary memory from laptop vendors—often an expensive proposition. But cost wasn't the worst part of this lack of a standard bus; in fact, cost was less important than the fact that lack of a standard bus led to the lack of a *market* for add-in boards for laptops.

Japanese vendors of memory products tried to address this problem in the late '80s by founding the *Personal Computer Memory Card Industry Association*, or, in its hard-to-remember acronym form, *PCMCIA*. (The head of the group once said, "If we'd have known how important the acronym would be, we would have picked another name." Some people just remember *People Can't Memorize Computer Industry Acronyms*.) After a few years of apologetic wincing, the association renamed the bus the PC Card bus; people still say PCMCIA, however, so you'll hear both names. A PC Card/PCMCIA board is about the size of a credit card, but a mite thicker. You can see some PC Cards in Figure 3.23.

Figure 3.23

PC Cards

Type 1, Type 2, and Type 3 PC Card Slots

The standard proved extremely popular—so popular, in fact, that hardware vendors said to the PCMCIA, "Why not also support modems or hard disks?" So the memory card interface became a "PC Card Type 1 slot." A Type 1 (or *release 1* in some references) slot is 3.3mm thick, with a 68-pin connector. Again, most Type 1 cards are memory cards, either standard RAM or "flash" memory cards loaded with a piece of software (for example, 1-2-3 and WordPerfect are available on these cards).

The need for internal modems drove the Type 2 slots. While developing Type 2, an important software standard called Card Services and Socket Services was developed—more on that later. Type 2 cards can be designed to act as an object placed directly into the PC's memory address space. Why is this different from Type 1 cards? If you bought a software-on-a-card Type 1 card, like the WordPerfect example that I just gave, then the PC would have to copy the data from the Type 1 card into the PC's memory before it could run the software on the card. That took time, *and* used up some of the PC's memory. With Type 2, that's not necessary, making startup faster and increasing the amount of free memory available. Type 2 cards are 5mm thick, allowing more space for more complex circuitry. Type 1 cards will work in Type 2 slots.

Shortly after, the PCMCIA defined a Type 3 specification, one flexible enough to support removable hard disks. The main difference of Type 3 is that it's a lot thicker—Type 3 cards can be 10.5mm thick. Most laptops have room for either two Type 2 cards or a single Type 3. When purchasing Type 3 cards, be sure that what you're buying meets the standard—there are so-called "Type 3" hard disks that are 13mm thick. Xircom has also made a very cool combination modem/Ethernet card that has the connectors right on it. The connectors made it thicker, so they went to a Type 3 form factor. Yes, it takes up both slots, but it's convenient not to have to carry cables around to attach to the card.

Socket and Card Services

The PC Card standard supports the capability to remove and install a PC Card *on the fly*. All other buses require that you power down the computer before installing or removing a card, but PC Card supports *hot swapping*—the capability to swap a card while the computer is running. The computer supports this capability with two levels of software support:

Socket services The PCMCIA name for the BIOS-like software that handles the low-level hardware calls to the card. They are loaded like a device driver. Although cards can be swapped without powering down, changes in cards *do* require a reboot. (PC Card version 2.01 is the most recent version, but it is rumored that version 3 will allow changes without reboots.)

Card services A higher-layer set of routines that manage how the PC Card memory areas map into the CPU's memory area. They also provide a high-level interface supporting simple commands that are common to almost all PC Cards, commands such as ERASE, COPY, READ, and WRITE data.

In Windows 3.*x* and Windows NT, you've usually got to reboot in order to enable or disable a PC Card. In Windows 95/98, however, you can change most PC Cards at will, using them and removing them without rebooting. DOS requires a separate third-party set of programs to provide card and socket services; Windows 95/98 and Windows NT 3.51 and NT4/2000 have built-in card and socket services.

PC Card Features

Let's compare PC Cards to the other buses that I've discussed, feature for feature. Take a look at Table 3.5.

TABLE 3.5 PC Card Features

Feature	Relationship to PC Card
Memory address space	The PC Card supports a 64MB addressing capability. (This is because the bus uses 26 bits for addressing, and two to the 26th power is about 64 million.) This will be adequate for current machines, but will look sparse in a few years, as more demanding operating systems such as Windows NT/2000 become more popular.
Bus mastering	The PC Card does not support bus mastering or DMA.
Plug-and-Play setup	The PC Card not only allows—but requires—that hardware setups be done with software. Because of the physical size of a PC Card, you'll never see jumpers or DIP switches.
Number of PC Card slots possible in a single system	Most of the other buses support no more than 16 slots. The PC Card standard can, theoretically, support *4080* PC Card slots on a PC. In reality, most laptops have only two Type 2 slots. Some, like Digital's Ultra HiNote 2000 laptop, have four slots (yet another reason why I own one).
Data path	The data path for the PC Card is only 16 bits, a real shame, but one that is fixed in a later version of the PC Card called the CardBus.
Speed	Like other modern bus standards, the PC Card is limited to a 33MHz clock rate.

Years ago, it seemed to me that the smaller size of PC Cards, coupled with their low power usage, made the new bus quite attractive not only for laptops, but also for the so-called "green" PCs, desktop computers designed to use as little power as possible. I figured that for that reason, PC Cards could become an important *desktop* standard as well as a laptop standard. That didn't happen in the desktop world, *but* in the laptop world be *sure* that whatever new laptop you buy has at least two Type 2 PC Card slots. Or, even better, if it's a relatively new laptop, make sure it's got two CardBus slots.

Mini PCI (Portable PCI)

Are you asking yourself, "OK, why are we going back into PCI when we're in the middle of discussing PC Card information?" Because this is a special form of PCI device, with a much smaller form factor (actually, multiple small form factors), designed specifically for laptops and other portable devices.

Mini PCI devices are small (for example, 45-by-70-by-5.5mm for Type IB), internal expansion cards used for communications—either a modem or a network interface card. You won't see Mini PCI video cards, for instance.

This technology offers some nice advantages over the PC Card. For one, because they're smaller, they are cheaper to manufacture (PC Card technology still isn't cheap). For another, with such limited PC Card expansion in laptops, using Mini PCI frees up a PC Card slot for other needs. The Mini PCI specification also eliminates the need for dongles and proprietary I/O connectors.

Best of all, however, Mini PCI shouldn't need any special extras in order to be recognized by, or work with, your PC operating system. Your operating system should recognize the Mini PCI card as any other PCI device and work with it without a hitch. This is because Mini PCI is the functional equivalent of standard PCI, using the 32-bit PCI local bus and the same PCI BIOS/driver interface.

CardBus

First specified back in 1994, this is PC Card: The Next Generation. CardBus slots' main claim to fame is that they have a 32-bit data path rather than a 16-bit data path. They're also backward compatible: a CardBus slot can accommodate a PC Card without trouble. Other features include the following:

▶ They run at lower voltage—3.3 volts and lower, compared to 5 volts and lower for PC Cards.

▶ They can transfer data at up to 133Mbps (megabytes per second)—they're four bytes wide and run up to 33MHz.

▶ In theory, you can do bus mastering and actually have a CPU on the CardBus card, although I haven't seen that in any cards yet.

If your laptop supports CardBus, buy CardBus cards when possible. I've run 100 megabit Ethernet with both PC Card and Card-Bus boards, and the CardBus is noticeably faster. But be sure your operating system supports CardBus. That's the hard part—only some CardBus cards work under Windows NT 4. Just about all Card-Bus cards work under Windows 98 and Windows 2000.

Table 3.6 summarizes the differences between the buses.

TABLE 3.6 Bus Types

Bus Type	Maximum Speed	Number of Data Bits	Number of Address Bits	Software Setup?	Bus Master?
PC bus	10MHz (on some clones)	8	20	No	No
ISA bus	8MHz, faster on some clones	16	24	No	Only on one board
MCA	8MHz	32	32	Yes	Yes
VESA	33MHz	32	32	No	No
EISA	8MHz	32	32	Yes	Yes
PC Card	33MHz	16	26	Yes	No
PCI	33MHz	32	32	Yes	Yes
CardBus	33MHz	32	32	Yes	Yes
AGP	66MHz	32	32	Yes	Yes
Mini PCI	33MHz	32	32	Yes	No

FireWire/IEEE 1394

I think that FireWire (IEEE 1394) gets the award for Best Name of an Emerging Standard. FireWire is a new kind of serial bus not yet commercially available. It was designed to replace serial ports, parallel ports, SCSI ports, and any other port that you'd use to connect a device to your computer, with a universal six-wire connector (two power, four data) that will work for any of these.

Like the Universal Serial Bus (discussed later in this chapter), FireWire is based on a daisy-chain physical topology, meaning that devices will be able to cascade from hubs attached to the card in the computer. FireWire supports 63 devices, however, instead of the 127 that its cousin interface, USB, supports. Although it's not required that this card be PCI, the couple of early 1394 cards that I've seen on the market are PCI. When the cards are commercially available, it's probable that they will be PCI to take advantage of the local bus. This bus will need all the speed it can get, because it's intended to work with devices that will require a lot of bandwidth, such as scanners, video cameras, and the like. Although, as I said, FireWire is designed to replace all other ports, it is also designed to cope with devices that require high and variable amounts of bandwidth. The standard is designed to support speeds of 100Mbps, 200Mbps, and 400Mbps, varying the path that the signal takes in order to avoid traffic problems.

In fact, as part of the overall design efforts currently in place, it's predicted that the machine of the near future will use USB to connect slower devices, FireWire to connect faster ones, and just have a minimum amount of equipment "under the hood" such as the CPU, RAM, and video. Under this plan, drives may move outside the case in a configuration called *Device Bay*, wherein drives and other devices can be pre-installed and configured for when you need them, but can be replaced, moved, or temporarily changed without much headache.

FireWire is an important component in the integration of consumer electronics with our PC desktops, and that's also a big part of the direction in which PC hardware is heading. The home and office of the future is likely to have the PC and its functions built into or connected into a whole complex of devices, and not separate from them.

Now configuring for FireWire sounds simple, but how about *powering* those dozens of devices? Well, two of the six wires in the cable are power lines, so your add-in devices can technically use your computer's main power supply. However, providing many devices their own power supplies is probably a good idea in order to keep the strain on the system power supply to a minimum.

A lot of how FireWire works depends on drivers, and these drivers must be OHCI compliant. OHCI stands for *Open Host Controller Interface*, a standard for how FireWire and USB devices communicate with other equipment to help ensure compatibility. Adaptec, a hardware manufacturer best known for their SCSI controllers, is one of the leaders in FireWire and FireWire adapter development, but many companies (including Sony) have been working closely with Microsoft and other operating system producers to help make FireWire a PC reality over the next few years.

Before long, for example, I hope to replace my slow but wondrously portable Sony USB CD-RW with a FireWire model also being offered by Sony. The speed should be awesome! FireWire hard drives are already offered, because Macs have been ahead of PCs in that regard; USB and FireWire are old hat to the Apple crowd. FireWire should certainly simplify the process of adding or removing drives and other devices to your system, and it's meant to be fast. And there's another bonus: like USB, FireWire devices can be used regardless of whether you're using a PC or a Macintosh. That bonus becomes serious when you're maintaining an office with multiple computers, especially if you have a mix of Wintel and Apple systems. But even with all PCs, you derive a benefit from equipment you can easily trade between machines.

The standard is out, and there are few devices with an IEEE 1394 interface, as I mentioned earlier. Windows 98 already supports FireWire with major assistance from software, and Windows 2000 should offer still more support. Watch this space as more happens . . .

System Clock

The system clock, mentioned before, is the metronome for the computer system. It was implemented on the early PCs on a chip called the 8284A. The 8284A was located near the 8088 on the system board of most XTs. The early AT-class machines had an 82284 chip.

Why would you care where the clock chip on your computer is? Well, in the old days, you could install a reset switch by using the clock chip. Nowadays, however, modern PCs have the clock circuit integrated with other chips on the motherboard.

Well, you've taken a good long look at what's on the PC's motherboard; now let's look at the other parts inside your machine.

Power Supply

U.S. line current is 120 volts *alternating current (AC)*. The PC, like most digital devices, is set up to use *direct current (DC)* at 5 and 12 volts. The conversion process is done by a *power supply*. The power supply is the silver or black box to the rear and right of the inside of the PC case.

Power supplies are rated by the amount of power that they can handle: the earliest PCs used 63.5-watt power supplies, and some servers ship with 375-watt power supplies. Your power supply determines in part how many peripherals you can put into a PC. Chapter 9, "Power Supplies and Power Protection," discusses selecting, replacing, and installing a power supply. The power supply can't always cope with environmental conditions, so that chapter also discusses add-on products: surge suppressors, spike isolators, and uninterruptible power supplies. You can see a power supply in Figure 3.24.

Figure 3.24

The power supply

As I mentioned, the power supply is easy to find in the system: it's the silver or black box in the back of the chassis that has a label on it that warns you, in five languages, not to open the power supply.

Keyboard

The PC is useless without an input device, and the keyboard is one of the two input devices (the other being a mouse) used by most of us. The keyboard is subject to a number of hazards, however, so it needs maintenance—and sometimes replacement. The PC's keyboard actually contains a microprocessor of its own, called the Intel 8041, 8042, or 8048. Taking apart a keyboard isn't hard—but reassembling it *is*, and truthfully there's little point in it nowadays, because keyboards are very cheap. You can get a regular 101-key enhanced keyboard for under $20, or an ergonomic "broken" keyboard for under $75. PS/2 and "standard" keyboards are electronically identical. The only difference is the connector. Most new keyboards have either a PS/2 connector and an adapter for the larger DIN connector, or the larger DIN connector and an adapter for the PS/2.

Mouse

Nearly every computer is equipped with a *mouse,* an input device used for pointing and selecting. The *graphical user interfaces (GUIs)* on modern operating systems can work with just a keyboard, but they are cumbersome without some kind of dedicated pointing device, and the most common is a mouse.

Mice come in the mechanical and optical variety. The mechanical is the more popular type, and mice interface either via a serial port, PS/2 port (which is also serial), a "bus mouse" port, or with a cordless (usually serial) interface. USB mice and trackballs are also becoming a popular choice.

You can learn more about the keyboard and the mouse in Chapter 22, "Keyboards and Mice."

Controllers in Your Computer

Other than the motherboard, power supply, and outside peripherals, the only important things left are the expansion boards in your computer. With the exception of memory boards—and the majority of modern computers don't use memory boards because they put all of their memory on the motherboard—most of the boards in your system are *controllers* of some kind.

What's a Controller?

Every peripheral device, whether internal or external, needs something to handle communications between it and the computer. These items are called controllers, interfaces, ports, or adapters. For example, a hard disk needs a hard disk controller, the keyboard needs a keyboard controller, and the video display needs a video adapter (controller). The main reason that controllers exist is to perform these tasks:

▶ Allow for well-defined industry standards (well, *fairly* well-defined industry standards) by creating a specification that all controller boards are designed to fit and operate in

▶ Match data transfer speeds between peripherals and the CPU

▶ Convert data from the CPU's format to what the peripheral uses, as well as amplify the electronic signals between CPU and peripheral

Adaptec's 2942W PCI SCSI bus mastering host adapter is as different from IBM's original XT-type hard drive controller as a Corvette is from a Chevette, yet 99 percent of the software that was written to work with the latter works just fine (or better) with the former. The underlying hardware is a lot better, and a lot *different*, so you'd imagine there would be big compatibility problems, but the hardware has been housebroken to respond to CPU requests in the same manner (although faster) as the old Xebec-designed IBM controller. Ditto video controllers designed by ATI or Paradise: they respond to the same software as IBM's original CGA, EGA, or VGA, but are cheaper and generally work faster. Using controllers with well-defined interfaces makes building compatible hardware possible.

Remember that notion of well-defined interfaces: together, all these interfaces define what is called *PC compatible.*

You can understand the value of well-defined interfaces and modularity by looking at an automobile. Perhaps (if you're my age) you learned to drive in an old '60s or '70s car, or, if you're my Dad's age, you learned to drive in a car from the '40s or '50s. Both of us now drive cars designed and built in the '90s. The old '67 Country Squire station wagon (okay, so now you know I grew up in the suburbs) was a radically different car from the Honda that I now drive. The Hudson my dad drove in the '40s was even more radically different from his current Toyota truck. But despite our education on different cars, we're both as well prepared to drive a 2000 model as someone who's only driven '90s cars, because the *interfaces* are the same. Because I don't interact directly with the car, but rather with the dashboard gauges and controls, I don't need to know the innards of the motor. If somebody stole into my backyard tomorrow and replaced my internal combustion engine under the hood with an engine that runs on air, I wouldn't know the difference.

Back to controllers, now: most peripherals are considerably slower than the CPU in transferring data. Even the hard disk, for example, is thousands of times slower than the CPU. Most microcomputers (like the PC) have been designed to control everything in their systems, to do *all* the computing work, but that's not necessary. One of the first examples of an all-encompassing microcomputer appeared with a company named Cogent Data Systems. Years ago, they made a hard disk controller for AT-class machines with memory and a microprocessor right on it: the main CPU just makes a request of the hard disk controller, then (with the right software) goes off to do something else while waiting for the controller to do the job. Eventually, the controller informs the CPU that it's finished with the data request and that in fact the controller has already transferred the data into the CPU's memory. Truthfully, the "speed matching" benefits of controllers haven't been really exploited in the PC world yet, because intra-PC *distributed computing* doesn't really exist—again, *yet*. The power of advanced buses such as PCI was supposed to change that, but the change is coming slowly—partially because board designers tend to keep doing the same thing over and over again, and partially because Intel encourages people to put work on the CPU's shoulders. That way, consumers will demand faster and faster CPUs or multi-CPU systems.

Another controller function is simple amplification. The CPU speaks its own electrical language to other chips on the motherboard. But it's a language without too much power—a CPU wouldn't be able to "shout" loudly enough to be heard any appreciable distance on a LAN. Devices such as video monitors need signals massaged into forms that they can use. Again, controllers serve this function.

A typical system will have a controller for the keyboard, a controller for the video display, controllers for the floppy and hard disks, and interface controllers for LAN, mouse, parallel, and serial ports.

Controllers Aren't Always Separate Boards

Here's a common misconception: a controller must be on a board all its own.

Not at all. The keyboard controller is generally not a board; it's just a chip on the motherboard. The hard and floppy disk controllers *used* to reside on separate boards in XT-type machines. Then, the earliest AT-class machines put the hard disk controller and the floppy controller on the same board. Another board held the parallel port, another the serial ports, yet another the joystick, and so on.

Nowadays, motherboards incorporate all those functions and more in a single extremely integrated circuit board. These integrated motherboards can be terrific values in terms of price and performance.

For Those Who've Read Earlier Editions . . .

You may be raising your eyebrows at that last comment. What am I doing singing the praises of integrated motherboards? Didn't I once warn readers away from them? Yes, that's true: I *used* to be very much opposed to putting everything on the motherboard. So why the change?

Well, I *like* integrated motherboards now for the same reason that I disliked them before: compatibility. Nowadays there is an informal standard for these "do-it-all" motherboards; you can easily find a replacement motherboard for your Apex Clones computer from Acme Clones. My old objection stemmed from the fact that the folks who used integrated motherboards (Compaq, Dell, Gateway, and those folks) all built integrated motherboards that were not interchangeable. Hence, if a Dell motherboard went bad, you were stuck buying a replacement from Dell, at a higher price than you would have paid had the motherboard been a more generic item. New manufacturing techniques have improved the quality of these motherboards, reducing the risk of failure of one or more of the integrated components.

However, there still is a downside: many in the PC industry see this as a cost-cutting measure and not very satisfactory for those of us more inclined to upgrade our PCs and customize them rather than buy the exact same unit as those belonging to neighbors and coworkers. The percentage of motherboards including integrated components is on the rise right now, but it's being tempered by a large dissenting audience who still feel this is a poor way to go.

Let's take a quick look at the common controllers in the system.

Video Adapter

To allow the computer to communicate with a display monitor, a display adapter must be inserted in one of the PC's expansion slots. Also, you'll hear video adapter, display adapter, and video card used interchangeably. They all mean the same thing.

The basic kind of video board you find in the PC world even to this day is an enhancement of an old 1987 video standard called the *Video Graphics Array*, or *VGA*. It can display information either in a text-only form or in a graphical form.

Why is a 10-plus-year-old standard still current? Mainly because of the lack of a market leader. For years, graphical standards were created by IBM, video boards with names such as MDA, CGA, PGA, 8514, EGA, and the now-common VGA. You can see a video board in Figure 3.25.

Figure 3.25

Generic video adapter

But the lack of industry centralization has left us with no new standards; instead, there are a lot of video boards that exceed VGA's capabilities, boards generically called *super VGA* (SVGA) boards. Even though they're all lumped under the name super VGA, they're all different, making it difficult sometimes to find *drivers* (the software that controls the video board) for a particular board.

Despite their variation, video boards all have several distinct components, as you see in Figure 3.26.

RAM: Receives
and stores image
data from CPU

Image Data

ROM: Contains
VGA BIOS

Video Processor: Scans
RAM for data and
converts to digital image

Digital-to-analog converter (DAC):
Converts digital image and sends
it out the DB-15 connector to the
monitor

Figure 3.26

Video board
components

The video board contains video memory, as you learned earlier in the discussion on memory. The CPU places the video image into the video memory. A video chip on the video board then examines the data in the video memory and creates a digital image signal. That digital signal is then converted to an analog signal by a chip called the DAC, the Digital-to-Analog Converter, another chip on the video board, and the resultant signal goes out the connector on the back of the board and into your monitor.

Video boards are distinguished by their *resolution*, which is the number of dots (pixels) that they can put on the video screen, and their *color depth* (the number of colors they can display at one time). More dots means sharper pictures. They're also distinguished by how many colors they can display on those dots and by how much work the CPU must do in order to create images.

You see, on older video boards, the CPU had to do all the work of picture creation; it had to place each and every one of the pixels on the computer's screen. Nowadays, however, video boards include special circuitry called *accelerator* or *bitblitter* chips that can speed up video operations considerably. Many video boards also have hardware support for 3D rendering, allowing games to have a real-time realism that quite literally could not have happened in an under–$1 million machine 10 years ago. Other video boards include TV tuner support and/or video capture hardware.

SCSI Host Adapter

The *Small Computer System Interface (SCSI)* is a general-purpose interface that allows you to install just one circuit board in your system and use it to act as the "manager" for hard disks, tape drives, optical disks, CD-ROMs, digital cameras, scanners, and even a few kinds of printers. As you'll learn in Chapter 12, "Understanding and Installing SCSI Devices," SCSI can support up to seven devices, and more with SCSI-3.

Floppy Disk Controller and Disk Drives

The floppy disk drive is an essential peripheral, if an ancient one. The 1.44MB format has existed since the mid-'80s and has improved not a whit since then. Why? As with video, there's no market leader in the PC hardware area that can simply put a stake in the ground and say, "This *is* the new floppy standard." There are some great floppy technologies that store upward of 250MB on a floppy, including the popular Zip drives, but none has really caught on and created a critical mass. And sadly, there may *never* be an industry consensus about high-capacity floppy drives, because most modern machines can boot from CD-ROM, allowing firms to bypass floppies altogether for distribution purposes and ship CDs instead, even for operating systems (which require the distribution media to be bootable).

Since they are peripherals, floppies require an interface. This interface is called a floppy disk controller. These will, in general, not give you many problems. They *do* fail occasionally, however, so you need to know how to recognize this and address it, since virtually all PCs have the floppy drive circuitry on the motherboard. In the case of a floppy drive controller failure, you'd have to either get a new motherboard (the excuse you've been looking for to upgrade to a newer processor!) or disable the floppy controller circuit and try to find a stand-alone board that can act as a floppy controller. (More info in Chapter 18, "Understanding, Installing, and Repairing Floppy Drives.")

The much more fertile ground for failure lies in the floppy disks and floppy disk drives themselves. Floppy drives can require speed adjustment, head alignment, and head cleaning. Speed adjustment and head cleaning can be done simply and cheaply. Alignment can require some specialized equipment and is not always cost effective. Floppy drives are so cheap these days that it's usually pointless to do anything but replace them, but it never hurts to know a bit about a component's innards.

Beyond adjustment is the problem of compatibility among drive types. There are three kinds of 3½-inch floppies, something you'll need to know if you're working with old floppies. Almost all new floppies you'll come across are the 1.44MB floppies. Chapter 18 talks about floppy installation and the kinds of maintenance that you can do on a floppy drive.

CD-ROM Drives

Once a nice add-on, a CD-ROM drive is now a necessity for any home machine and a recommended peripheral for a business machine. (Why don't all business machines need CDs? Because most businesses have networks, and CD-ROM drives can be networked, reducing the need for every machine on the network to have a CD-ROM drive.)

Not only are CD-ROMs today basic equipment, but more and more, CD drives that can write and even rewrite CDs (not just any CDs, the media has to be specifically rewrite-capable) are becoming common hardware in many offices and homes. In under 10 minutes, I can burn about 650MB of data to my Sony USB Supressa CD-RW. The USB connection means it's not physically installed in my PC (it plugs into a USB port as well as into the uninterruptible power supply), so I share it easily between various PCs in my office.

CD-ROM drives are essential because virtually every software package today is distributed only on CD-ROM. Chapter 26, "An

Overview of CD-ROM," examines these issues and explains how to choose and install a CD-ROM drive.

DVD Drives

Digital versatile disc (DVD) drives are the next technology level for CD-ROMs. Whereas CD-ROMs can store up to 630MB on a 4½-inch disk, DVDs can store up to 17GB (17 *billion* bytes).

DVDs use the same kind of interfaces as CD-ROMs, either IDE (as is most common) or SCSI. They are backward compatible, which means you can read CD-ROMs in DVD drives (but not vice versa). Chapter 26 covers DVD drives as well.

Hard Disks and Hard Disk Interfaces

Most of your system's software and most of the data that you've created lives on your system's *hard disk.*

Years ago, you bought a hard disk by its size and by its interface. Normal-duty hard drives used an interface called ST-506. High-performance drives used a drive interface called the *Enhanced Small Device Interface,* or *ESDI.*

Nowadays, you still choose a hard disk by its size (see, some things never change) and by its interface; but the interface will either be the SCSI or the *Enhanced Integrated Drive Electronics (EIDE)* interface, usually called just *IDE* today. The vast majority of PCs currently use IDE, since virtually all PC motherboards have not one but *two* IDE interfaces built right on them. Each IDE interface can support two drives. As there are two IDE interfaces, then, the average PC can support four drives right out of the box. Most folks have at least one CD-ROM drive and a hard disk drive, so they've got two "openings." Good candidates to fill those openings are perhaps more hard disk drives, a DVD drive, or perhaps a tape drive or Zip drive for backups.

When a hard disk fails, your main concern shouldn't be the hard disk. Hard disks are easy to replace and install, as you'll learn in Chapters 10 through 14. Your main worry should be the *data* on your drive. Data recovery is the subject of Chapter 16, "Care and Feeding of Hard Drives."

Older disk subsystems used hard disk controllers—ST-506 and ESDI interface boards were controllers—but the newer SCSI and EIDE interfaces do not use controllers; rather, they call them *host adapters* because their job is much simpler than the job of a controller. Basically, a host adapter just rearranges the data so that it can be accepted by the bus. Much of the circuitry that once sat on the controller now lives on the disk drive itself.

Some hard disk failures—precipitous drops in speed or loss of data—can be addressed at either the controller or the drive level. Problems such as head crashes can be avoided with some simple techniques, and even the ultimate disaster—a reformatted hard disk—can be reversed in some cases. Chapter 16 provides more information.

Tape Drives and Other Backup Devices

Thinking about skipping this part and going on to parallel ports, eh? It amazes me how many people don't have tape drives on their systems. It's quite common for PCs to sport 8GB or 11GB hard disks, but no tape drive. Once you bought that 8GB drive, how did you plan to back it up, anyway—with floppies? (Let's see, now; 8192MB divided by 1.44MB per floppy equals . . . too many floppies.)

If your computer doesn't have a backup device, then ask yourself: can I really afford to lose all this data? If the answer is no, then think about getting a tape drive. Tape drives install in the same kind of slot that you'd put a floppy drive into, and they have one of three kinds of controllers. Some tape drives run off a SCSI host adapter; others connect to the floppy disk controller; and a few have their own proprietary controller. Or consider the Jaz drive from Iomega, a tool I like and use quite a bit. It's a backup system that uses removable hard disk cartridges. The benefit to this drive is that if you have a hard disk failure, you can reboot with any drive, and run your programs and read your data directly from the Jaz drive the same way you would with a hard drive. I'll discuss backups more in Chapters 10 through 14.

Parallel (Centronics) Interfaces/IEEE 1284

The most common method of attaching a printer to a computer is through a simple interface called the *Centronics* interface. The interface was named after Centronics, the company that invented it in 1976. It's more commonly known today as the *parallel port.* Another way to connect printers to PCs is through a serial port, and I'll cover them in the next section.

PCs can support up to three parallel ports. They are named LPT1, LPT2, and LPT3; the name refers to Line PrinTer one, two, or three.

Originally, parallel ports were unidirectional. They transported data only from the PC to the printer. *Control* lines led status information from the printer back to the PC, but data flowed in only one direction. For years, some parallel ports have had the option to move data backward, from the printer to the PC. That's important for two reasons:

▶ New printers can now send textual status information to the PC. Thus, it is possible with some printers for the printer to tell the PC, "I'm low on toner," or "I am a LaserJet 6."

▶ Modern PCs put things on the parallel port that aren't printers. Removable media drives and CD-ROM drives are two examples of peripheral hardware devices that can have parallel port options.

Some parallel ports not only support bidirectional data flow, they also support increased data transfer speed. These ports are called *enhanced* parallel ports, or EPP interfaces. Some parallel ports use a direct memory access (explained in Chapter 6) channel and become *Extended Capability Ports (ECPs)*, offering even more speed. The IBM PC's parallel port was originally a proprietary interface, but it's become so widely used that there is now an "official" standard describing it, IEEE 1284. You'll sometimes see parallel ports or parallel cables referred to not as parallel but as *IEEE 1284 compliant.*

Most printers require only a simple unidirectional parallel port. But if you've got a bidirectional, EPP, or ECP port, then those more advanced ports work fine with any kind of printer.

Parallel ports won't usually pose much of a problem, once you've got them installed and configured. But the printers themselves, well, that's another story.

The actual printer is the greater source of failures: printers employ a large number of moving parts. While printers are much more reliable nowadays than they were in the bad old days of daisy-wheel printers, there's always the odd paper feed or black page problems.

Worse yet, as printers get more powerful, their software gets more complex. It's a shame that so many people fail to exploit the full power of their computers simply because WordPerfect or Word 2000 isn't programmed to do the exploiting.

Modems and Communication Ports

Besides parallel ports, the other common printer interface is the serial port. Serial ports are also known as async ports, comm ports, or RS-232 ports. They are bidirectional interfaces for low- to medium-speed data transfer; most serial ports can't transfer data faster than 115,000 bits per second, but there are some serial ports that can transfer data at 345,000 bits per second.

A serial port's main job isn't usually printers, however. The two most common uses for serial ports are to attach mice or modems to your PC. Modems enable your PC to communicate remotely with other computers via phone lines and to act as a fax machine.

The DOS names for the communications ports are COM1 and COM2. It's theoretically possible to have COM3 and COM4, but they're limited in their usefulness. (More on that in Chapter 6.)

RS-232 is a source of many cable problems: either the wrong cable is configured, or environmental problems (electronic noise) cause communication errors. Figure 3.27 depicts an IBM RS-232 adapter. Data communications troubleshooting is an entire book in itself—several books, in fact—but I cover the essentials in Chapter 21, "Communications Devices."

Figure 3.27

IBM RS-232 adapter

Serial ports are the PC's general-purpose input/output devices. Hand-held machines such as the PalmPilot attach to the PC via serial ports; digital cameras do; some scanners do, modems, mice, printers . . . it seems on many systems that there are too many things to attach to a serial port and not enough serial ports. *That's* why they invented USB.

The Universal Serial Bus (USB)

It's far too easy to run out of serial ports. For instance, say you have a serial mouse and a modem. No problem, right? The mouse goes on COM1, the modem on COM2. But what happens when you add a smart uninterruptible power supply (UPS), a device that can communicate with your computer for diagnostics and software control, to the mix? At this point, you have the choice of either losing your mouse (it's possible to navigate a graphical operating system with the arrow and Tab keys, but it's no fun), losing some of the UPS's capabilities, or adding another COM port with an add-in card and hoping that one set of software will function with a nonstandard interrupt. If you don't set up COM3 to use another interrupt, then it will conflict with COM1, but not all software is prepared to deal with that.

It's a puzzle, and the problems associated with adding serial ports could keep people from using some devices that need them. But the picture has started changing, albeit slowly. It's possible that soon you won't need to worry about the number of serial or parallel ports that you have because devices are slowly being designed that use another interface called the *Universal Serial Bus (USB)*. If you've purchased a PC since 1997, you *probably* have one or two USB ports on your computer (two are required for desktops; one for laptops by today's hardware standard). If the USB standard takes hold, it could make using the plethora of new PC-related devices a little easier. But before it works, you need three things: PCs with USB ports, operating system software that supports USB, and USB-ready peripherals. You've got the first already (new PCs mainly have USB). Windows 98 supports USB, as does Windows 2000, but Windows NT *doesn't*, so you're halfway there on the second condition. USB devices for the PC were slow to emerge, but now they run the gamut from the mice and keyboards to digital cameras, printers and scanners, and drives like my Sony USB Supressa CD-RW.

I'm getting ahead of myself—what is USB, anyway?

What Is USB?

The USB, developed by Microsoft, Compaq, National Semiconductor, and 25 other USB members, is intended to take the place of the keyboard port, parallel ports, game port, and serial ports by replacing them with a single connection from which you can daisy chain *more than a hundred* USB-compatible devices. This single connection is even simpler than a nine-pin serial port, since it has only four pins. Physically, it looks either like one device (such as a keyboard) plugged into the computer, and then everything else plugged into a hub on the keyboard, or a hub plugged into the computer and then everything plugged into the hub. As in SCSI, each device can be plugged into up to seven devices and/or hubs at a time. You can see a USB connector and cable in Figure 3.28.

Figure 3.28

USB cable

Either way, it is designed to be much simpler to put together; rather than installing cards for many of these devices, you plug them into a hub and call it a day. If they're true Plug-and-Play devices (as many are planned to be) then a PnP OS should recognize them with very little help from you.

Note

Windows 98 and Windows 2000 have USB support with device drivers built into them.

USB is designed to be faster than serial ports as well. The standard describes an interface that can transmit up to 12 megabits per second, as opposed to the 100+ kilobits per second of a serial interface. The speed is meant to keep up with telephony applications, such as low-resolution video conferencing. (For higher-resolution video, you'd need IEEE 1394.)

USB recognizes four types of data transfer, divided by the type of peripheral device that uses them: bulk, interrupt, asynchronous, and control. Printers, scanners, and digital cameras, which must send a great deal of information to the PC at one time, are bulk transmitters. Keyboards and joysticks, which people use to sporadically transmit small amounts of data that must be processed immediately, use interrupt transmittal. Telecom applications, which must be delivered in a steady stream and in a certain order, use asynchronous transmissions.

The hub determines which devices are plugged into it at any given time, and from that it deduces how much bandwidth each needs, based on the kind of data transmittal the device is trying to perform.

Who Needs It?

Just about anyone should be able to benefit from the new interface, once appliances that are pin compatible with USB become more readily available. The ability to plug in a number of devices with only one port will be particularly useful to laptop owners, since laptops have limited real estate into which to plug additional devices. You don't need lots of available ports, and the hub should be easier to get to than the back of your computer. It's intended to work for just about anything that you can plug into a port in your computer: speakers, modems, keyboards, and the like.

What's Available?

As I said before, USB ports are present on most new machines (and required now for "Windows compatible" systems), even laptops (my Digital Ultra HiNote 2000 includes such a port, and Toshiba, Compaq, Dell, and IBM have notebooks with USB as well). As for devices to plug into USB ports, they've really increased over the last two years. In my office alone, USB devices include a keyboard, the external CD-RW mentioned earlier (this unit moves around between PCs to write data files to CD), a Microtek scanner, a 3Com/USR modem, a printer, a mouse, a graphics tablet, speakers, several different cameras (ranging from a simple Webcam to a very elaborate, near 35mm camera quality unit), a microphone, and a couple of Belkin USB hubs. And yes, I can hook them all up at the same time, and still use just one precious IRQ. It's something of a hardware pig heaven. But the thing I like most about USB, besides the single IRQ use and the transportability, is the fact that I can happily shelve my printer or my scanner or graphics tablet when I'm not using it. When I need the device again, I just plug it in, and it's instantly found and available for use.

If USB interests you, the next installment of USB—USB 2—should really whet your appetite. Initially planned to be about 10 times faster than the original USB implementation, USB 2 in early testing outperformed high-end SCSI *and* FireWire for throughput.

Slower devices such as mice, keyboards, and simple digital cameras won't need that kind of speed, but USB 2 might make an attractive option for those doing video editing or using high-speed drives, the same market as FireWire.

System Clock/Calendar and Configuration (CMOS) Chip

The system clock/calendar keeps the date and time even when the unit is turned off. Older XT-type systems required a separate board to support a clock/calendar, but virtually every modern computer has the feature built right into its motherboard as standard equipment.

The Clock/Calendar and CMOS Battery Issues

The clock/calendar is built on the same chip as the configuration memory circuit. *Configuration memory*, more commonly called the *CMOS*, is a small amount of memory that holds information that the computer needs in order to get started in the morning.

When you first turn your computer on, it must figure out what hardware it contains so that it can control that hardware. There's a list of the hardware in your system in the configuration memory. Most memory, however, is *volatile*, a 75-cent word meaning, "When you remove power from the memory, the memory forgets whatever was sitting in it." That's why the memory has a battery attached to it, so that the memory doesn't lose power, so it can remember while the rest of the PC slumbers.

Of course, with time, that battery will run down in power, the configuration memory will forget what kind of hardware is in your system, and the clock/calendar will no longer keep correct time. You'll have to install a new battery, of course, to fix the problem; but here's a common question about batteries and the clock.

People will tell me that their computer can no longer remember its configuration information, forcing them to reenter the configuration information into the computer every time that they turn the computer on. (They should just replace the battery but, for whatever reason, they haven't.) I explain that they've got to replace the battery, but they disagree, saying, "No, the battery's fine."

"How do you know that?" I ask.

"Because the computer keeps correct time," they respond. They're arguing that because the clock circuit still runs, the configuration memory circuit should still run. It's a good argument, but it misses the fact that running the clock requires less power *by far* than does running the configuration memory. As you may have learned from painful experience, it's possible for your car's battery to have enough power to run the interior lights and the radio, but not to crank the starter.

The vast majority of the time, the only problem from the clock will be with (1) the battery or (2) the software to use it.

The battery causes problems, of course, when it runs down and no longer keeps time. Replacement is no problem (usually $3–$10 at any decent electronics counter), save for some clock/calendar boards that *solder* the battery on the board. You kind of have to wonder if the people who designed this either (1) have parents who are first cousins or (2) want to be able to charge you $120 three years later to replace the battery. Many motherboard manufacturers nowadays have a soldered battery, but that may not be terrible news, because some of those motherboards also support a standard external battery; you just move a jumper on the motherboard to disable the soldered battery and enable the connection for the external battery. (More on CMOS and batteries in Chapter 6.)

By the way, don't confuse the clock/calendar that I've discussed here with the clock that raps out the beat that the PC dances to—the one based on the 8284 or 82284 chip. They're different circuits. The CPU clock doesn't run when the power is off to the PC, in contrast to the clock/calendar, which continues to run all the time, courtesy of its battery.

Local Area Network (LAN) Adapters

Put more than two PCs into an office, and soon you see the urge to merge: PC networks are everywhere. (Got one in your home yet? No? Don't worry; you will soon.)

Networks make it easy to share data, printers, modems, and access to the Internet. But the first step in networking your computer is to put a LAN board in every PC. They come in several flavors. The most popular kind of network is called *Ethernet*, and there are Ethernet boards for all of the PC buses. Second is *Token Ring*; Token Ring boards are usually about two to three times more expensive than Ethernet boards, and you tend to see them in large companies more than in smaller firms. Oldest in the network world of the big three is *ARCNet*, something that's pretty much dying out, but you may see one or two of them around.

There's an awful lot to say about networks, and for more information you can check out Chapter 27, "Networking Concepts and Hardware." Check around the Internet, too, because you'll see all kinds of network setups today for even the more casual of home users, including some setups that work through the wiring in your home.

Sound Boards

Years ago, Creative Laboratories introduced the Sound Blaster, a board that allowed your PC to emit squeaks, squawks, squeals, and explosions. What good was that? Well, games, mostly. But sound cards have come a long way since then. Nowadays, you can buy sound cards that can produce quality superior to that of a CD player.

Sound cards are more than just a plaything. Multimedia in PCs is becoming a business tool—it's already an education tool. For many applications, clicking the OK button will bring up an animated window of a teacher explaining how to use a program's feature, rather than just the simple text screens that we used to see in older systems.

That will be a bit friendlier, but *understanding* what the person in the animation is saying in the first place requires good sound equipment. The wrong sound card/speaker combination can make voices sound like broadcasts from bad AM radios; the right combination can provide the audio version of virtual reality.

Note

Chapter 24, "Play It Loud: Sound Cards," discusses sound cards in detail.

Other Common Boards

That's about it for the most commonly found boards. You may also see the following boards:

3270 or 5250 emulation cards Despite improvements in IBM's *Systems Network Architecture (SNA)* in the past few years, it's probably easiest to get your PC to talk to the mainframe by making it look like a dumb 3270 terminal, the familiar IBM "green screens" that you see in offices around the world. (*Dumb* in terminal parlance means it lacks stand-alone processing power.) Attachmate, DCA, and others do a nice business filling this need.

Plug one into your system, and your PC can hook up to the same old coaxial cable that's been serving IBM mainframe users for years. Just because you're attached to your company's AS/400, however, doesn't mean that you've got an emulation board. Another way to get to your firm's mainframe or mainframes is over the LAN. In that case, your LAN has a machine on it acting as a *gateway.*

Tape controllers If you want to install a tape drive for backup to your system, you'll need a controller of some kind. Many tape drives can use the floppy controller, but it's not recommended—such tapes are painfully slow, and remember that you bought the tape to quickly back up the hard disk. Some tapes are internal, some external. I'd recommend external because then you can buy a tape controller board for *all* of your machines, then buy only a few of the expensive tape drives themselves, and let the users share the occasional use of a tape drive. (That's "occasional" only when compared to the frequency of use for the hard disk. Back-ups should be near daily if you generate work of any importance at all. Yes, I know it's a pain, but can you *really* afford to lose a whole day's work? And are you sure you'd be able to re-create it if you did?) The higher-capacity tape drives all run off SCSI, but some cheaper tapes attach to the EIDE interface on your system.

Scanner interface cards Graphical and character scanners are becoming more and more popular. And with good reason—desktop publishing really shines with graphics. Today's audience demands lots of visuals. Scanners offer a way to add pictures to text in a computer-readable form. Character scanners allow easier entry of text in computer-readable form. Some scanners run off a SCSI host adapter (the preferable alternative, because there are no new boards to install once you've already got SCSI), but many scanners still use proprietary interface cards.

Finding Your Way around inside Your PC

Well, now you've learned some things about how your PC's put together. You know the names of some of the pieces in your system. But how do you figure out what's where once you take apart *your* computer? Trying to figure out what's in your computer for the first time can be tremendously disorienting. Here's my approach.

After you get the top of the computer off, find the easy stuff:

▶ Power supply

▶ Fan

▶ Floppy drives

▶ Hard disk or disks

▶ CD-ROM and tape drives, if present

After you've figured those out, only the boards are left. Figuring out the boards doesn't seem so difficult once the rest of the system has been identified.

Finding the Easy Stuff

The power supply is easy to find. It's a silver or black box with a fan on it, and it's attached to the power switch. As I've noted before, it probably has a label on it that says in five languages, "If you open me, I'll kill you."

The floppy drives should be simple to locate: just look at the slots in the front of the computer. The hard disk will be a box that whirs and has no slot in the front of it. CD-ROMs are, I hope, also simple to find; they're usually well marked. (Although there's an apocryphal story about a tech support person who was called by a user because the user had broken his "cup holder." You know, the retractable one that CDs also happen to fit into.) Tape drives are likewise usually labeled.

That leaves the tougher-to-identify components: the circuit boards. Have you started drawing your diagram yet? If not, get cracking on it. It's really simple to screw up a computer by taking it apart and not being able to put it back together.

Locating Things on the Motherboard

Your system's motherboard, once you remove it, will have a few points worth noting. I'll use a typical Pentium II motherboard for examples.

The Power Connection

Be sure to note where the power cables from the power supply go to the motherboard, as I mentioned in the last chapter. Putting them back together backward will smoke the motherboard. You see the power connection in Figure 3.29.

Figure 3.29

Motherboard power connection

Finding the CPU

The CPU on your system is often easily identifiable because many of them have a prominent Intel logo painted on them. If you're working with a much older system, look also for the distinctive names 80386, 80486, Pentium, and the like. Nowadays, finding a Pentium II/III or a Xeon is a snap; they're sitting upright in black plastic cases. You usually can't see the actual CPU, though, because it's surrounded by metal fins. Those fins are the heat sink that helps keep the chip from catching fire. (No, I'm not kidding.) You can see the processor in Figure 3.30.

Figure 3.30

Pentium II processor
on motherboard

Older CPUs are also often socketed, and most Intel-type CPUs are in PGA packages. No matter what generation of PC you own, one good method for finding the CPU is to look for the largest chip in the box; that's often it.

Remembering the Memory

Your PC's motherboard has both RAM and ROM on it.

RAM memory is usually easy to spot, because it is typically in the form of a SIMM. If you've got an older computer that uses separate chips, then the memory looks like uniform rows of small socketed chips. You see the memory in Figure 3.31.

Figure 3.31

SDRAM in Pentium III motherboard

ROM memory is usually a large chip or pair of chips in sockets, *often with a label on the top* indicating a software version number. Newer systems don't have socketed ROM, because they're flash memory and should not need physical replacing—you can just download new versions of the BIOS programs.

Slots

The only other parts that you will be sure to want to find are the expansion slots in the computer. They're obvious, in that they're relatively long, narrow electrical connectors. Refer to the bus discussion earlier in this chapter to get an idea about the differences between bus slot types. Figure 3.32 shows (from right to left) two ISA slots, four PCI slots, and an AGP slot.

Figure 3.32

Expansion slots on a
motherboard

CMOS Battery

Keep a computer long enough, and you'll have to replace the battery
or it won't be able to hold its configuration. Figure 3.33 shows that
this motherboard uses a coin-type battery.

Figure 3.33

CMOS battery on a
motherboard

Drive Interface Cables

Every motherboard I know of these days has the floppy drive controller and two EIDE host adapters integrated into its electronics. You'll have to attach and detach drive ribbon cables, so it's a good idea to locate the floppy and EIDE connectors, as you see in Figure 3.34.

Figure 3.34

Floppy and EIDE connectors on motherboard

Floppy connector   EIDE connectors

Identifying Circuit Boards

This is going to sound silly, but I use two basic approaches to identifying strange circuit boards.

The first rule is the "What is it connected to?" rule. Suppose you're trying to figure out what a board does. You notice that the back of the board is connected to a cable that goes to the video monitor. Heck, even a nonphysicist like me can figure out that the board must have something to do with video, so it's probably a video adapter.

Now, at this moment, you're saying, "Hey, wait a minute; I've disassembled the machine. Nothing's attached to it right now, so I have no idea what the board *used* to be attached to." Remember in the last chapter when I said that diagramming was essential? Here's an example of why that's true. (I hope at this stage in your PC exploration that this comment falls in the category of cautionary tale, rather than "I told you so . . . .")

The second rule of board identification is the "What kind of connectors does it have on the back?" rule. There are different kinds of connectors on the back of a PC. Take a minute to become familiar with them.

Actually, with modern PCs, the issue is often not "What does this board do?" because most new systems have pretty integrated motherboards. Most new systems have *everything* on the motherboard save for a video board and (possibly) a LAN card and/or a modem. The more important question is, "What does this *connector* on my integrated motherboard do?" Well, again, a little organization, documentation, and observation can answer those questions.

The D-Shell Connector

The *D-shell connector* is called that because if you look at it the right way, it looks like a capital *D*. You can see a D-shell connector in Figure 3.35.

Figure 3.35

A D-shell connector

D-shell connectors come in male and female varieties. They also vary by the number of pins or sockets in their connectors. You'll see DB9 (nine pins or sockets), DB15, DB25, and DB37 connectors. They're used in serial ports, parallel ports, video adapters, joystick interfaces, and some LAN interfaces.

HP or Miniature D-Shell Connector

The *miniature D or HP connector* looks a lot like a D-shell connector, but the pins are all placed next to one another. The HP connector puts 50 pins in the same space that a normal D-shell puts only 25 pins. You can see an HP connector in Figure 3.36.

Figure 3.36

An HP connector

As I said, it looks like a D-shell connector. The main application that I've seen for HP connectors is in SCSI interfaces. A 50-pin version shows up on SCSI-2 interfaces, and SCSI-3 (a later version of the SCSI standard) uses a 68-pin HP connector.

Sometimes you'll hear people call the 50-pin HP connector a SCSI-2 connector, and the 68-pin HP connector a SCSI-3 connector. Not everybody knows the HP name.

Centronics Connector

Made popular by its first big use in an interface created by a company of the same name, the *Centronics connector* looks like the drawing in Figure 3.37.

Figure 3.37

A Centronics connector

Don't confuse the Centronics connector with the Centronics interface, another name for the parallel port. The connector, which looks like an edge connector surrounded by a metal shell, is used on printers and in SCSI devices. In addition to parallel ports, Centronics connectors are used by some SCSI host adapters.

BNC Connector

A *BNC connector,* or *Bayonet Naur connector* (a bayonet is what they supposedly look like, and Naur is the guy who invented them), looks like a cylinder about 1 centimeter across with a thin tube down its center and two small bumps on its periphery. You can see several BNC connectors in Figure 3.38.

Figure 3.38

BNC connectors

In Figure 3.38, you see (clockwise, from upper left) a T connector, used to connect a single BNC connector to two other BNC connectors. Next, you see a BNC plug, and then a T connector with two plugs. At the bottom of the diagram, you see two cables with BNC plugs connected to a T connector. The T connector would then be attached to a BNC connector on the back of a circuit board.

BNCs are most commonly used in a kind of LAN called Ethernet, although they are falling out of favor (because of the RJ-45, discussed next). Ethernet attaches in several ways, known as *thick*net, *thin*net, and *10Base-T.* It is the thinnet implementation of Ethernet that uses BNC connectors. Thinnet is also known as *10Base-2.*

BNC connectors have also been used in ARCNet and 3270 (a mainframe terminal interface) connectors.

RJ-45 or RJ-13 Connector

These connectors look like the so-called *modular jacks* that you use to plug a phone into an answering machine or a wall jack. As a matter of fact, the connector that you use for a standard phone is called an *RJ-11*, or Registered Jack type 11 connector. Some networks use the slightly larger *RJ-45 connector*, which looks similar. The RJ-11 has four wires in it. The RJ-45 has eight wires in it.

RJ-45 is used in 10Base-T Ethernet connections, as well as LocalTalk connectors such as you'd see in a Macintosh network.

DIN Connector

The *DIN connector* comes from Germany; roughly translated, its name means *German national connector*. The DIN connector is a round, notched connector about an inch across, with from three to seven pins in it. DIN connectors are most commonly used in the PC world to connect keyboards to a motherboard.

Miniature DIN Connector

As the name implies, these are smaller versions of DIN connectors. You see a couple of variations on this in Figure 3.39.

Figure 3.39

Miniature DIN connectors

You'll see these used for bus mouse interfaces, InPort mouse interfaces, some keyboard interfaces, and some serial port applications.

Miniplug

A *miniplug connector* is the kind of connection that enables a set of headphones to attach to a Sony Walkman. You see these on CD-ROM players (not always, but often) or on the backs of sound cards, for microphone inputs or line input or output.

RCA Plug

RCA plugs are the kind of connectors that you might see on the back of your VCR labeled Audio In or Video In. They were used years ago for simple video output on an old kind of video board called the Color/Graphics Adapter and a later board called the Enhanced Graphics Adapter. Nowadays, you usually see them only for sound inputs or outputs on some sound cards, or for video inputs on a video capture board.

USB Connector

Universal Serial Bus systems have a *USB connector*—a kind of flat connector with a tongue in its middle, as you see in Figure 3.40.

Figure 3.40

USB connector (in center; mini-DINs on left, D-shells on right)

FireWire/IEEE 1394 Connectors

FireWire must also have its own connectors installed on the machine or provided by an adapter installed into an expansion slot on the PC itself (already available for under $150).

Boards and Connectors

Now let's put all this information together into some diagrams of common boards and connectors. Take a look at Figure 3.41.

Figure 3.41

Common boards and connectors

25-pin male: generally a serial port.

25 female: a parallel port.

EGA: 9-pin female, two RCA connectors, DIP switches.

Fifteen pins in three rows indicates VGA (Video Graphics Array) and graphics accelerators.

In Figure 3.41, you see the backs of some common interface boards. As I said earlier, note the extensive use of D-shell connectors.

Originally, video boards used a female DB9 connector to pipe out either color images, via what was called an RGB connector, or high-resolution monochrome images, via a digital monochrome video interface. That led to confusion, because it was possible to plug an RGB color monitor into a digital output; when that happened, little wisps of smoke would soon issue from atop the color monitor, and it would cease to function. Color video boards also output a kind of signal called *composite video*, which you can read more about in Chapter 25, "You Oughta Be in Pictures: Video Capture." If you see a female DB9 on a modern system, the board is most likely a Token Ring network card.

Nowadays, however, virtually all video adapters use a D-shell that is the same size as the old DB9, except that this D-shell has *three* rows of pins, not two, housing 14 or 15 pins. I say "14 or 15" because there is room for 15 pins, but some boards fill in one of the holes. You'll see those connectors on just about every video board, and *very* rarely you'll see a video board with several RCA connectors on the back; such a board is sending video out in multiple signals as is done on some high-end video equipment.

The parallel port usually employs a 25-socket female D-shell connector. I say "usually" because Tandy used a DIN connector for their parallel port for a while. And, just to confuse the issue a bit, some older SCSI host adapters use a female DB25 for attaching external SCSI devices.

Serial ports also use D-shell connectors—two kinds, in fact. Some serial ports use a male DB25. Others use a male DB9 connector. Note that oddity: most connectors you'll find on a PC are *not* male connectors, so the fact that serial ports use either 9-pin or 25-pin males is unusual. (My former girlfriend Sheila—she's mentioned in the acknowledgments—told me that she remembered that male 25s and male 9s were serial ports because most serial killers were male. A rather graphic way of remembering, for sure, but then again, Sheila is six foot one and was rated number one in the country in Tae Kwon Do, so I didn't argue with her about the little things, if you know what I mean.)

Note

Why are most connectors on a PC female? Well, designers of some kinds of interfaces have to put a connector of one gender on the PC and a connector of the opposite gender on the cable that the interface uses. Male connectors have a bunch of little pins, and pins break. Female connectors have a bunch of little sockets, and sockets don't, in general, break. Now, in the case of pin breakage, would you rather have to replace a cable ($) or an interface board ($$$)? *That's* why the female connectors go on the PC side rather than the cable side.

Let's look at some more boards, as you see in Figure 3.42.

A BNC connector helps give this away as an Ethernet LAN board. Here, the female 15-pin connector is for thicknet Ethernet cable, not games.

A 10-Base-T Ethernet card has an RJ-45 connector with a few LEDs. Some combination Ethernet boards include BNC and 15-pin connectors, too.

Two RJ-11 phone jacks: an internal modem.

Figure 3.42

Additional boards

Joysticks and standard Ethernet (thicknet) use 15-pin connectors. This may be a game card or an Ethernet LAN board.

Not all mice use a 9-pin serial connection; PS/2s use a round 6-pin mouse port.

A round port with nine holes identifies this as a bus mouse interface card.

As I mentioned earlier, Ethernet comes in three guises: thicknet, thinnet, and twisted-pair versions. Thicknet is the oldest variety of Ethernet, and it's also called 10Base-5 Ethernet. It interfaces via a DB15 female connector, and is sometimes called an *Adapter Unit Interface (AUI)* or *DEC-Intel-Xerox (DIX)* connector. Thinnet uses a BNC connector; in the board pictured in Figure 3.42, you can use either the thicknet connector or a thinnet connector. The board next to it shows the third kind of Ethernet connection, a twisted-pair, or 10Base-T, connection, with an RJ-45 connector.

Next to that board is a modem. Modems have RJ-11 jacks for interfacing to phone lines, and the RJ-11s look like RJ-45s, so it might be easy to confuse an Ethernet card with a modem card. But modems have two connectors, and Ethernet cards often have an LED or two on their backs.

Below those cards is a VGA, mentioned earlier, a joystick interface (a female DB15), and two types of miniature DIN connectors used to create a mouse interface.

Let's wrap up our look at the backs of common boards with a third group of boards, shown in Figure 3.43.

The top three boards in Figure 3.43 are varieties of SCSI interfaces, as I've mentioned earlier. Video capture boards take video inputs and convert them into digital data, and they can accept either simple composite video (like the kind that comes out the back of common VCRs), or they'll usually take the higher-quality super VHS–type connector, a miniature DIN. Below them are some backsides of some sound cards. Note that many sound cards have a joystick interface built right onto them.

Centronics 50, 50 HP, and 68 HP connectors are all used for SCSI host adapters.

Figure 3.43

Common boards

Sound cards typically have a joystick port, volume control, and audio input/output jacks.

Playback-only sound cards have headphone output jacks, line-out jacks, and volume control.

Interface cards for add-in CD-ROM drives have two audio output jacks for speakers.

Well, that was a long chapter, but now you're a certified "microbiologist." The next chapter's a bit lighter, so don't stop now: turn the page and see how to keep all this stuff working!

Avoiding Service: Preventive Maintenance

INTRODUCTION

The most effective way to cut down your repair bills is by good, preventive maintenance. There are things in the PC environment—some external, some created in ignorance by you through inattention—that can drastically shorten your PC's life.

Some of the things that affect your PC's life are common-sense things; I don't imagine that I've got to tell you not to spill soft drinks (or, for that matter, hard drinks) into the keyboard. But there are other PC gremlin sources that aren't quite so obvious; so, obvious or not, we'll get to all the environmental hazards in this chapter. There are a few factors that can endanger your PC's health:

▶ Excessive heat

▶ Dust

▶ Magnetism

▶ Stray electromagnetism (including that found in electrical storms)

▶ Power surges, incorrect line voltage, and power outages

▶ Water and corrosive agents

There's an additional factor, which is man-produced and seen more and more as PCs become more common throughout the workplace and home. This factor—believe it or not—is grease, the kind that can be found in poorly ventilated kitchens, near cooking areas, or in workshop environments like a garage. Combine grease with dust and you have a sort of sludge that can form on and within the PC, effectively gumming up the works.

Checking the Environment

Let's quickly run through the procedures and guidelines for protecting your PC that are covered in this chapter.

Be Prepared

Before you start, there are some things you may need on hand. These include:

▶ Some type of temperature gauge for checking PC internal temperatures

▶ Phillips-head screwdriver for opening up the PC case

▶ Container for placing the screws between removal and reinstallation

▶ Antistatic wrist strap for reducing the chance of stray electrostatic discharge and damaging components inside the case

1. Check power considerations:

   ▶ No heating elements (Mr. Coffee, portable heaters) in the same outlet as a PC

   ▶ No large electric motors (refrigerators, air conditioners) on the same line as the PC

   ▶ Some kind of power noise protection

2. Check temperature ranges:

   ▶ Maximum 110 degrees F (43 degrees C).

   ▶ Minimum 65 degrees F (18 degrees C). (The minimum temperature can be considerably lower, as long as the computer remains *on* all of the time.)

3. Prevent dust buildup—you can buy (from PC Power and Cooling; see Vendor Guide on CD #2 for contact information) power supplies with a filtered fan that suck air in through the *back* rather than the usual approach of pulling it in through the front.

4. Make sure there isn't a vibration source such as an impact printer on the same table as the hard disk.

5. Make sure you know or (if you're a support person) teach your users:

   ▶ That you should leave the machines on all the time.

   ▶ That cables should be kept screwed in and out of the way.

   ▶ Basic "don't do this" things in DOS, like formatting the hard disk.

6. Protect against static electricity.

Preventive Maintenance

Although this chapter discusses some preventive maintenance concerns, I mainly talk about the environmental problems that PCs face. But the fact is, preventive maintenance will save you time and headaches in the long run. These steps should take about two hours.

Be Prepared

Before you start, there are some things you may need on hand. These include:

▶ System backup software and available medium (ZIP disks, CD-RWs, or tape cartridges) for performing a full or incremental system backup of the PC to protect the data

- Diagnostics software like SCANDISK and commercial products like a disk tools suite, a virus scanner, and other system check utilities in case you have problems identifying the source of difficulty

- Nonmagnetic Phillips or Torx-head screwdriver for opening the PC case and removing expansion boards and other equipment within the case such as drives mounted in their drive bays.

- Container for placing the screws between removal and reinstallation

- Antistatic wrist strap for preventing static discharges while working inside the PC

- Commercial connector cleaner solution or a lint-free cloth or hard artist's eraser for cleaning the edge connectors

- Twist ties for binding cables together to keep them out of the way

- Slender bent piece of metal for extracting a CPU, such as described in Chapter 2, "Disassembling the PC"

- Can of compressed air for removing dust from components

---

1. Pick up the PC at its worksite. (Yes, this takes more time than having it delivered to your workplace, but you'll learn a lot just from observing its working environment.) Determine:

   - Are the connectors screwed in?

   - Have screws disappeared from the back of the machine?

   - What else is plugged into the PC's outlet? No Mr. Coffees?

   - Is the PC on a rickety table?

   - Is the PC near a window? Is it in a location that gets direct sun at some point in the day?

2. Ask if the machine is doing anything strange.

3. Ensure that the hard disk (if any) is backed up.

4. Run the machine's diagnostics. It is a good idea to run SCANDISK to see what percent of the user's drive consists of "lost clusters."

5. If it's a DOS computer, examine the `AUTOEXEC.BAT` and `CONFIG.SYS` files for any obvious problems—lack of a `BUFFERS` command, for example. If it's a Windows machine, look at the INI files for obvious tampering. If it's running Windows 95/98/NT/2000, run the computer a bit to ensure that it isn't generating a lot of error messages (stating missing devices or conflicts) or crashing in programs with specific notes about stacks or buffers, for example.

6. Disassemble the PC.

7. **Ground yourself.**

8. Clean the edge connectors with a connector cleaner and a lint-free cloth or a hard white artist's eraser.

9. Push the chips back into their sockets (this is discussed in Chapter 5, "Troubleshooting PC Problems").

10. Use canned air to remove dust from circuit boards—don't forget the circuit board under the hard disk.

11. Reassemble the PC. Ensure that all of the cables are securely in place.

12. Rerun the diagnostics.

13. Ensure that all screws are present. If they are not, add the appropriate screws.

Heat and Thermal Shock

Every electronic device carries within it the seeds of its own destruction. More than half of the power given to chips is wasted as heat—but heat destroys chips. One of an electronics designer's main concerns is to see that an electronic device can dissipate heat as quickly as it can generate it. If it cannot, heat slowly builds up until the device fails.

More and more, heat can be seen as a by-product of overclocking, methods by which people attempt to push their PC hardware for faster or otherwise more optimal performance. This is usually done through tweaking the motherboard and CPU, but it's increasingly being done with many video adapters, too.

There are several ways you can help control your PC's heat problem:

▶ Install an adequate fan in the power supply or add an auxiliary fan.

▶ Install a heat sink.

▶ Adjust your box design for better ventilation (including keeping cables from blocking proper air circulation within the PC case itself).

▶ Run the PC in a safe temperature range.

Removing Heat with a Fan

In general, laptops don't require a fan because enough heat dissipates from the main circuit board all by itself. (What you need to be careful of with laptops is that you don't block the vent(s) carrying warm air out of the unit.) However, most desktop and tower PCs will surely fail without a fan. Actually, many of today's PCs have several fans: one integrated into the power supply, one for the CPU, one for a high-performance video adapter, and sometimes more added to move heat from a hot hard drive.

When designing a fan, engineers must trade cooling power for noise. This is because the greater the capacity of the fan, the greater the noise produced— more air and more movement equal more noise. But it takes more engineering and costs more to make a very small fan that moves a fair amount of air—more than most of us would want to pay for a tiny fan. Years ago, power supplies were quite expensive, running in the $300 range for the cheapest power supply, so great care was exercised in choosing the right fan for protection. Nowadays, power supplies cost under $25, and I doubt that most PC company engineers could even tell you what kind of fan is sitting in their machines, any more than they could tell you who makes the case screws.

Now, that's a terrible shame, because the $3 fan that's sitting in most PC power supplies is a vital part. If it dies, your PC will cook itself in just a few hours.

And fans *do* die.

Fans range in quality, capacity, and purpose. As a general rule, the cheaper fans tend to wear out faster, sometimes in as little as six months to a year, while the more expensive variety made with bearings tend to endure. Such fans can often be removed, carefully cleaned of dust and debris (a pencil-sized paintbrush with a firm tip is ideal for this since you want to be careful to avoid damaging the fan), oiled, and returned to service without the need to replace the fan.

The more stuff that's in your PC, the hotter it runs. The things that make PCs hot inside include:

▶ Most chips, including memory chips, and CPUs in particular, because they have the greatest number of transistors inside them.

▶ Drive motors in older hard disks, floppies, and CD-ROMs. Some CD-ROMs run quite warm, like the Plexor 4-Plex models. Large hard disks run *extremely* hot. I've seen an old Maxtor 660MB ESDI drive run so hot that it almost burned my fingers. However, I saw the same thing on a 1.7GB Fujitsu drive. Drives in the 3½-inch half-height or third-height format run much cooler. Some circuit boards can run quite hot, depending on how well (or how poorly) they're designed.

Truthfully, heat buildup inside a PC is much less of a problem than it was in the mid-1980s. In those days, every drive was a full-height drive, and every computer had 640KB of memory built up from 90 separate 64KB chips. Add one of those early hot 8087 coprocessors, and it was common to find the inside of a PC running 30 degrees F (16 degrees C) warmer inside its box than in the outside room.

Today's PCs, however, are much more energy-efficient. A standard 180- or 230-watt power supply handles far more devices hooked to it than do hardware designs from times past. But that doesn't mean you can't exhaust the power supply's range if you install many additional drives, for example. This can require a power supply upgrade to one of 300 watts designed for more professional needs.

Before we leave the subject of fans, I should mention one debate that never goes away is whether or not it's ever wise to leave the cover off a PC for any extended period. Many of us leave the cover off short term, to make sure a new piece of equipment installed will work before we put in the screws.

However, there are a considerable number of people, including seasoned computer veterans, who believe that a PC, overall, functions better without the cover. Their theory is that much better air circulation is achieved with the bonus that you can better monitor and access the hardware.

The other side argues that today's systems were specifically optimized for overall cooling with the cover in place and that you put the PC—and operator—at some degree of risk by leaving the cover off.

Indeed, during the summer, if you have your PC cover off for any period of time, you'll notice the interior picks up almost as many dead insects as an outdoor light fixture. Operating a PC without a cover is ill-advised for anyone with small children or pets, or when your crazy cousin decides to see what happens if he moves a switch or pulls a cable. As mentioned earlier, many surfaces inside the system can be razor sharp.

For peace of mind and a cleaner PC, you probably want to keep your cover on except when you're installing or removing or checking a piece of hardware within the case.

Removing Heat with a Heat Sink

For years, electronics designers have had to struggle with hot components on circuit boards. Sometimes a fan just isn't enough, so they need more help cooling an infernal chip. They do it with a *heat sink*. A heat sink is a small piece of metal, usually aluminum, with fins on it. The heat sink is glued (using a thick substance known as heat sink compound) or clamped to the hot chip. The metal conducts heat well, and the fins increase the surface area of the heat sink. The more area on the heat sink, the more heat that can be conducted off into the air and thereby removed from the PC.

The standard Pentium II and Xeon processor packages have a heat sink and a fan integrated with the chip. The idea is that the heat sink pulls the heat off and the fan disperses it. The Celeron doesn't come with a heat sink, but that doesn't mean that it's not a good idea to think about putting one on a hot chip. You can find heat sinks in electronics supply catalogs. Adding a fan can really increase the heat sink's ability to cool its chip. I've noticed that many modern motherboards have connections to power a couple of auxiliary fans, and you can buy fans that attach to those connections from PC clone parts places (look in the back of *Computer Shopper* magazine for them).

Good and Bad Box Designs

It's frustrating how totally unaware of heat problems many computer manufacturers are. The first tower computer I purchased was from a company named ACMA, and they put together an impressive machine. There were two fans in the case—a very nice touch—as well as a CPU fan. I've got to say that they spoiled me. A later (1994) purchase, from an outfit called Systems Dynamics Group, was somewhat less enjoyable. The back of the PC chassis had room for two fans, but there was only one fan in the system. There's nothing intrinsically wrong with that, except that the cutout for the second fan—which is right next to the first fan—was left empty. The result was that the fan just sucked in air from the cutout a few inches away from it and blew it back out. Made the fan happy, I suppose, but didn't do much for the CPU.

I noticed this pointless ventilation system pretty quickly, so I took some tape and covered up the extraneous cutout. Within seconds, the air being pumped out the back of the Pentium got 10 degrees warmer. If I'd left the extra cutout uncovered, the only ventilation that my Pentium system would have gotten was the simple convection from the heated boards and drives. Even at that, however, the Pentium system—which included a 1GB drive, 80MB of RAM, a CD-ROM, video capture board, video board, SCSI host adapter, and Ethernet card—only ran 10 degrees hotter inside the box than outside the box.

Things could have been a bit worse if the case was like some I've seen, with the fan *on the bottom of the tower*! This is not too common, fortunately, but it's worth asking about so you can avoid it when purchasing a PC. This setup puts the circuit boards on the top of the tower and the fan on the bottom. I have no idea who designed this case, but it's nice to know that the banjo player kid from *Deliverance* finally has someone to look down on. The point I'm making here is to take a minute and look at the airflow in the box. Of course, even if you have a good box, you can still run into heat problems.

Dead Fans

Years ago (around 1995), I installed the Freelance graphics program on my system. Pulling the first floppy out of my A: drive, I noticed that the floppy was warm. My memory flashed back to 1982, when something similar had happened—so I knew what was going on. My system's fan had died.

Fortunately, I found the problem early and shut down the computer. I had to travel to Europe for a few weeks to teach classes and consult, but I figured, no problem—I'll just leave the computer off.

Unfortunately, while I was gone, one of my employees helpfully started up the computer—reasoning that I always leave my computers on all the time, so what the hey? So, despite the "do not turn it on" sign I'd left on it, the computer merrily melted itself down while I lectured in Amsterdam. By the time I returned, the hard disk had self-destructed, as had the Ethernet card in it.

It's actually pretty amazing what *didn't* die in the system. The CPU (a 50MHz 486DX) ran for a couple of years afterward (until it became too slow to be of value), and the Adaptec 1742 SCSI host adapter is still in service in an old server.

Heat Sensor Devices

Now, I could have avoided this problem altogether if I had had a 110 Alert from a company called PC Power and Cooling Systems. They're a name to know when you're buying power supplies. The 110 Alert is a circuit board about the size of a business card that plugs into a floppy power connector. When the PC's internal temperature gets to 110 degrees F, the alert starts making an annoying squealing noise. At 118 degrees F, it just shuts the computer down. The device is $15, and every network server should have one or one like it.

Figure 4.1

The 110 Alert thermal sensor device

While I'm on the subject of PC Power and Cooling, I should mention that this company also makes an interesting variety of power products for the PC, including power supplies with very quiet fans, power supplies with built-in battery backup, and high-quality PC cases. I use their stuff when I want to increase the odds that my PC will be running when I need it. If you have any questions about what rating of power supply to use, the company's Web site (listed, along with other contact information, in the Vendor Guide on CD #2) will give you an analysis based on information you provide about your system and your needs.

My introduction to PC Power and Cooling came with a hot 386. When I say "hot," I mean that this PC ran 25 degrees warmer inside than the temperature outside. PC Power and Cooling sells the Turbo Cool, a power supply that claimed, at the time, that it would cool your PC by 35 to 40 degrees F. Now, obviously, my 386 could not be cooled by 35 degrees, because it is only 25 degrees over-ambient—the best that a fan could do would have been to lower the temperature inside the machine to the surrounding temperature. However, buying PC Power and Cooling Systems' Turbo Cool cooled my machine from 25 degrees over-ambient to only *4* degrees over-ambient.

Additionally, several motherboard manufacturers include a thermal sensing device onboard—meaning that it's built right into the board itself and can be enabled or disabled in the BIOS.

Safe Temperature Ranges for PCs

Electronic components have an ambient (room) temperature range within which they are built to work. IBM suggests that the PC, for instance, is built to work in the range of 60 to 85 degrees F. This is because the circuit boards can run as hot as 125 degrees, but a typical machine may be as much as 40 degrees hotter *inside* than outside. And 125 minus 40 yields 85 degrees, the suggested maximum temperature.

Obviously, if you've got a good fan, the acceptable range of room temperatures expands considerably. If you have a really good fan, the inside of the machine is close to the same temperature as the outside. You don't want the inside of the PC to get any hotter than 110 degrees—hard disks can fail at that point, although, again, circuit boards can function in higher temperatures than that.

Since the temperature inside the PC is the ambient temperature plus some constant, there are two ways to cool the inside of the PC—either lower the constant with a good fan, or lower the ambient temperature. Keep the room cooler, and the PC will be cooler.

Heat also aids the corrosion process. Corrosion is a chemical process, and inside a computer, corrosion can roughly *double* in speed when the temperature of the process is raised by 10 degrees C (about 18 degrees F). Chips slowly deteriorate, the hotter the faster.

How do you measure temperature and temperature changes in your PC? Simple—get a *digital temperature probe*. Radio Shack markets one for around $30. Or you can buy one from Edmund Scientific Corp., whose address is listed in the Vendor Guide on CD #2.

The easy way to use the probe is to tape it over the exit vents by the fan's power supply. An indoor/outdoor switch lets you quickly view the PC's inside temperature and the ambient temperature.

You may ask yourself, "OK, but what's the best operating temperature range for my CPU?" Intel and other chip designers/manufacturers provide optimum operating temperatures by CPU on their Web sites, along with other specific technical information.

Duty Cycles

I said before that a device should get rid of heat as quickly as it creates it. Not every device is that good, however. Devices are said to have a *duty cycle*. This number—expressed as a percentage—is the proportion of the time that a device can work without burning up. For example, a powerful motor may have a 50 percent duty cycle. This means that it should be active only 50 percent of the time. A starter motor on a car, for example, must produce a tremendous amount of power. Powerful motors are expensive to produce, so instead, cars use a motor that can produce a lot of power for a very short time. If you crank the engine on your car for several minutes at a stretch, you will likely damage or destroy the car's starter motor. Floppy disk drive motors are a similar example: run a floppy motor continuously and you'll likely burn out the motor. *Hard* disk motors, on the other hand, run continuously and must be designed with a 100 percent duty cycle.

Duty cycle is used to describe active versus inactive time for many kinds of devices. For some components, you control some of the overall duty cycle. For example, you decide how much work your printer will do in a single day. But many devices have internal cycles to keep them working on their own on a system that's up around the clock, just as many of today's PCs operate continuously.

Thermal Shock

Because a PC is warmer inside than outside, changes in room temperature can become multiplied inside a PC.

This problem leads to a hazard called *thermal shock*. Thermal shock comes from subjecting components to rapid and large changes in temperature. It can disable your computer due to expansion/contraction damage. The most common scenario for thermal shock occurs when the PC is turned on Monday morning after a winter weekend. Many commercial buildings turn the temperature down to 55 degrees over the weekend: your office may contain some of that residual chill early Monday morning. Inside the PC, though, it may still be 55. Then you turn the machine on. Within 30 minutes some PCs can warm up to 120 degrees. This rapid, 65-degree rise in temperature brings on thermal shock.

This is an argument for leaving the PC on 24 hours a day, seven days a week. (You'll see some more reasons to do this soon.) The temperature inside the PC will be better regulated. By the way, you can't leave portable PCs on all the time, so you should be extra careful with portables to avoid thermal shock. If your laptop has been sitting in the trunk on a cold February day, be sure to give it some time to warm up before trying to use it. And give it some time in a *dry* place, or water vapor will condense on the cold disk platters. Water on the disk platters is a surefire way to reduce your drive's life.

Sunbeams

Another heat effect is caused by sunbeams. Direct sunlight isn't a good thing for electronic equipment. A warm sunbeam feels nice for a few minutes, but sit in one for an hour and you'll understand why PCs don't like them. Direct sunlight is also, of course, terrible for floppy disks. Find a shadowy area for your PC and floppies, or use drapes or good window blinds/shades to protect them from the sun.

Dealing with Dust

Dust is everywhere. It consists of tiny sand granules, fossil skeletons of minuscule creatures that lived millions of years ago, dead skin, paper particles, and tiny crustaceans called dust mites that live off the other pieces. Dust is responsible for several evils.

First, it sticks to the circuit boards inside your computer. As dust builds up, an entire board can become coated with a fine insulating sheath. That would be fine if the dust was insulating your house, but thermal insulation is definitely a bad thing for computers. As you have seen, you seek to minimize impediments to thermal radiation from your computer components. To combat this, remove dust from inside the computer and from circuit boards periodically. A good period between cleaning is a year in a house and six months in an office. A simpler approach is to use the "while I'm at it" algorithm—when you need to disassemble the machine for some other reason, clean the insides while you're at it. A tool that can assist you is a can of compressed air. (*Compressed air* isn't actually compressed air; it's some kind of compressed gas.)

Just as effective for the case and inside support assemblies is a dust-free cloth wetted with a little water and ammonia (just a few drops). Don't use the cloth on circuit boards—get a can of compressed air and blow the dust off.

This should be obvious, but when you blow dust off boards, be aware of where it is going. If you can, have the vacuum cleaner nearby, or take the board to another area. *Please* don't hold the board over the PC's chassis and blow off the dust with compressed air—all this does is *move* the dust, not *re*move it.

The second dust evil is that dust can clog spaces, such as:

▶ The air intake area to your power supply or hard disk

▶ The space between the floppy disk drive head and the disk

To combat the floppy drive problem, some manufacturers offer a floppy dust cover that you put in place when the machine is turned off. The sad part of this is that you really need the cover when the machine is on. CRT displays have an unintended, unexpected, unpleasant, and unavoidable side effect—they attract dust. Turn your screen on, and all of the dust in the area drops everything (what would dust particles drop, I wonder?) and heads straight for the display. Some of the particles get sidetracked and end up in the floppy drives.

One place that creates and collects paper dust is, of course, the printer. Printers should be vacuumed or blown out periodically, *away* from the computer (remember, dust goes somewhere when it's blown away).

By the way, another fertile source of dust is ash particles. Most of us don't burn things indoors, *unless* we are smokers. If you smoke, fine: just don't do it near the computer. An old (1985) study by the U.S. Government Occupation Safety and Hazard Administration (OSHA) estimated that smoke at a computer workstation cuts the computer's life by 40 percent. How true that holds today is unknown. But it's still not a good idea to get anything smoky, nor is it wise to leave cigarette or cigar ash near the PC where it can be drawn into the machine. Greasy air isn't good either, so avoid setting up a PC next to a much-used stove or in a garage right next to where a vehicle pulls in.

Note

Many people decide to put air cleaners/ionizers in the room where they use their PC(s). This seems to be especially true of smokers. While that's fine to do, it's best to position the air cleaner at least several feet from the PC itself. This is because smoke, dust, and other particles are apt to be drawn to the intake fan of the air cleaner. If the air cleaner is close to the PC, the PC's front vent may pick up some of the airborne debris instead.

Magnetism

Magnets—both the permanent and electromagnetic type—can cause permanent loss of data on hard or floppy disks. Most often, the magnetism found in an office environment is produced by electric motors and electromagnets. A commonly overlooked electromagnet is the one found in phones that ring using a real bell (which are not at all common these days). The clapper is forced against the bell (or buzzer, if the phone has one of those) in the phone by powering an electromagnet. If you absentmindedly put such a phone on top of a stack of floppy disks and the phone rings, you will probably have unrecoverable data errors on at least the top one. It's a good idea to get a phone with a ringer that is not a real bell to minimize the chance of erasing data inadvertently.

Don't think you have magnets around? How about:

▶ Magnets to hang notes on a file cabinet

▶ A paper clip holder with a magnet

▶ A word processing copy stand with a magnetic clip

▶ A magnetic screw extractor

Another source of magnetism is, believe it or not, a CRT. I have seen disk drives refuse to function because they were situated inches from a CRT. X-ray machines in airports similarly produce some magnetism, although there is some controversy here. Some folks say, "Don't run floppies through the X-ray—walk them through." Others say the X-ray is okay but that the metal detector zaps floppies. Some people claim to have been burned at both. Personally, I walk through an average of three to four metal detectors per week carrying 3½-inch floppy disks and have never (knock wood) had a problem. My laptops have been through X-ray machines everywhere, and I've never lost a byte on the hard disk because of it.

Airport metal detectors should be sufficiently gentle for floppies. Magnetism is measured in units called *gauss*. Metal detectors *in the U.S.* (notice the emphasis) emit far less gauss than that necessary to affect disks. I'm not sure about Europe, but I notice that the fillings in my teeth seem to set off the metal detectors in the Ottawa airport.

Another large source of magnetism is the motor in a printer—generally, it is not shielded (the motors on the drives don't produce very much magnetism, in case you're wondering).

And do you (or someone that you assist) work in a word processing pool? Many word processors (the people kind, not the machine kind) use a copy stand that consists of a flexible metal arm and a magnet. The magnet holds the copy to be typed on the metal arm. The arm can sit right in front of the operator's face so that they can easily type the copy.

The problem arises when it's time to change the copy. I once watched a word processing operator remove the magnet to change the copy and slap the magnet on the side of the computer. It really made perfect sense—the case was steel and held the magnet in a place that was easy to access. The only bad part of the whole operation was that the hard disk on that particular PC chassis was mounted on the extreme right-hand side of the case, right next to the magnet. You can start to see why I hate magnets . . .

A few years ago, I was a keynote speaker at a conference held in San Antonio, near the Alamo. As part of the "thank you" package that the conference organizers put together, we speakers got a refrigerator magnet in the shape of the Alamo. After almost placing my wallet (with my credit cards in it) on the magnet, almost laying demonstration floppies that I'd gotten at the conference on it, and almost storing the Alamo magnet in my laptop case (you know, next to the laptop's hard disk and any floppies that I had in the case), I finally gave up and threw the magnet away before I had a chance to *really* do some damage.

Oh, and by the way, *speakers* have magnets in them. Years ago, a friend purchased a home entertainment system that included a VCR, a stereo, and some monster speakers. That's when I noticed that he had stacked his videotapes on top of the speakers. I almost didn't have the heart to tell him, but I eventually advised him that his videos were history—and, sad to say, they *were*. Modern multimedia PCs all have speakers that claim to have shielded magnets, but I've got a Sony woofer/satellite speaker system that makes my monitor's image get wobbly when I put the speakers too near the monitor. No matter what the manual says, I think I'll just keep the floppies away from there.

What about preventive maintenance? My advice is to go on an antimagnet crusade. Magnets near magnetic media are disasters waiting to happen.

A sad story: a large government agency's data center bought a hand-held magnetic bulk floppy eraser. (I'm not sure why—they weren't a secret shop and thus did not have the need.) The PC expert in the shop tested it on a few junk floppies, then turned it off and didn't think about it. The next day, he remembered that he had left it on top of a plastic floppy file drawer. This meant that the eraser, even though turned off, was about an inch from the top of the floppies. He spent the next day testing each of the floppies, one by one. Most were dead. They got rid of the bulk eraser. I'm not sure what they did with the PC expert.

Stray Electromagnetism

Stray electromagnetism can cause problems for your PC and, in particular, for your network. Here, I'm just referring to any electromagnetism that you don't want. It comes in several varieties:

▶ Radiated electromagnetic interference (EMI)

▶ Power noise and interruptions

▶ Electrostatic discharge (ESD)—static electricity

Electromagnetic Interference

EMI is caused when electromagnetism is radiated or conducted somewhere that we don't want it to be. I discuss two common types—crosstalk and RFI—in the next two sections.

Crosstalk

When two wires are physically close to each other, they can transmit interference between themselves called *crosstalk*. I'm not talking about short circuits here; the insulation can be completely intact. The problem is that the interfering wire contains electronic pulses. Electronic pulses produce magnetic fields as a side effect. The wire being interfered with is touched or crossed by the magnetic fields. Magnetic fields crossing or touching a wire produce electronic pulses as a side effect. (Nature is, unfortunately, amazingly symmetrical at times like this.) The electronic pulses created in the second wire are faint copies of the pulses (the signal) from the first wire. These pulses interfere with the signal that you're trying to send on the second wire.

Crosstalk is not really a problem when applied to power lines, although I have heard of cases where the alternating current in power lines creates a hum on a communications line through crosstalk. The larger worry is when bundles of wires are stored in close quarters, and the wires are data cables.

There are five solutions to crosstalk:

- Move the wires farther apart (not always feasible).

- Use twisted-pair cable (varying the number of twists reduces crosstalk).

- Use shielded cable (the shield reduces crosstalk—don't even think of running ribbon cables for distances over six feet).

- Use fiber optic cable—it's not electromagnetic, it's *photonic* (is that a great word, or what? It means that it uses light instead of electricity to transmit data), so there's no crosstalk.

- Don't run cables over fluorescent lights. The lights are noise emitters.

I once helped troubleshoot a network that had been installed in a classroom. The contractor had run the wires through the ceiling, but the network didn't seem to work. (Ever notice how often the words "network" and "not work" end up in the same sentence? A Russian friend calls them "*nyet*works.") I pushed aside the ceiling tiles and found that the cable installer had saved himself some time and money by foregoing cable trays and instead wrapped the cables around the occasional fluorescent lamp. On a hunch, I turned off the lights and said to the people that I was working with, "Start the network up again." Sure enough, it worked.

Radio Frequency Interference

Radio frequency interference (RFI) is high-frequency (10kHz) radiation. It's a bad thing for computer communications. Sources are

▶ Nearby radio sources

▶ Cordless telephones

▶ Keyboards

▶ Power-line intercoms (intercoms that use the power line's 60Hz as the carrier wave)

▶ Motors

Worse yet, your PC can be a *source* of RFI. If this happens, the FCC police come to your place of business and take your PC away. (Well, not really. But they *will* fine you.)

RFI is bad because it can interfere with high-speed digital circuits. Your computer is composed of digital circuits. RFI can seem sinister because it seems to come and go mysteriously. Like all noise, it is an unwanted signal. How would you go about receiving a *wanted* RF signal? Simple—construct an antenna. Suppose you want to receive a signal of a given frequency? Design an antenna of a particular length. (Basically, the best length is one quarter of the wavelength. A 30-meter wavelength is best picked up by a 7.5-meter antenna. But it's not important that you know that—to learn more about it, pick up an amateur radio book.) Now, suppose there is some kind of RFI floating around. You're safe as long as you can't receive it. But suppose the computer is connected to the printer with a cable that, through bad luck, happens to be the correct length to receive that RFI? The result: printer gremlins. Fortunately, the answer is simple: shorten or lengthen the cable.

Electric motors are common RFI-producing culprits. I recently saw a workstation in Washington where the operator had put an electric fan (to cool *herself*, not the workstation) on top of the workstation. When the fan was on, it warped the top of the CRT's image slightly. Electric can openers, hair dryers, electric razors, electric pencil sharpeners, and printers are candidates. Sometimes it's hard to determine whether the device is messing up the PC simply by feeding back noise onto the power line or whether it is troubling the PC with RFI. Either way, the answer is to put the devices on separate power lines.

Your PC also *emits* RFI, which can impair the functioning of other PCs, televisions, and various sensitive pieces of equipment. By law, a desktop computer cannot be sold unless it meets Class B specifications, i.e., the FCC requires that a device that is three meters from the PC must receive no more RFI than shown in Table 4.1.

TABLE 4.1 Permissible RF Output (FCC Class B Specification)

Frequency	Maximum Field Strength (Microvolts/Meter)
30–88MHz	100
89–216MHz	150
217–1000MHz	200

RFI became an issue with personal computers when the PC came out because IBM had shielded its PC line in an effort to make life a little tougher on the clonemakers. By pushing the FCC to get tough on PCs, IBM had a bit of a jump on the market. Unfortunately, getting Class B certification isn't that hard, and just about every PC qualifies these days: clonemakers now say that their machines are "FCC Class B Certified." This has caused the reverse of IBM's original intent because the FCC certification seems a mark of legitimacy. In reality, FCC certification is not a measure of good design, quality components, or compatibility; it just means that the equipment doesn't produce excessive amounts of electromagnetic interference.

Protecting your PC from the devices around it and protecting the devices from your PC is done in the same way. If the PC doesn't leak RFI, then it's less likely to pick up any stray RFI in the area. Any holes in the case provide entry/exit points. Use the brackets that come with the machine to plug any unused expansion slots. Ensure that the case fits together snugly and correctly. If the case includes cutouts for interface connectors, find plates to cover the cutouts, or simply use metal tape.

A simple AM radio can be used to monitor RFI field strength. A portable radio is ideal because it has light headphones and a small enough enclosure to allow fairly local signal strength monitoring. A cheap model is best—you don't want sophisticated noise filtering. Tune it to an area of the dial as far as possible from a strong station. Lower frequencies seem to work best. You'll hear the various devices produce noises. I first noticed these noises when working ages ago on a clone computer that had an XT motherboard, a composite monitor, an external hard disk, and a two-drive external Bernoulli box. The quietest part of the system was the PC. The hard disk screamed and buzzed, the Bernoulli made low-frequency eggbeaterlike sounds, and the monitor produced a fairly pure and relatively loud tone.

The PC sounded different, depending on what it was doing. When I typed, I heard a machine gun–like sound. When I asked for a text search, the fairly regular search made a "dee-dee-dee" sound. It's kind of fun (okay, I guess I don't get out much), and you might pop the top on your system and do a little "radio astronomy" on it.

I've also used the radio in a number of other ways. Once, I received a new motherboard, a 486 that I was going to use to upgrade a 286 system. I installed it, and nothing happened. No beeps, no blinking cursor, nothing but the fan. So I removed the motherboard and placed it on a cardboard box (no electrical short fears with a cardboard box). Then I placed a power supply next to it, plugged in the P8/P9 connectors, and powered up. I ran the radio over the motherboard and got no response, just a constant hum. Placing the radio right over the CPU got nothing. I reasoned that what I was hearing was just the clock circuit. I felt even more certain of my guess when I noticed that the CPU had been inserted backwards into its socket. One dead motherboard, back to the manufacturer.

Power Noise

Wall sockets are a source of lots of problems. They basically fall into these three categories:

▶ Overvoltage and undervoltage

▶ No voltage at all—a power blackout

▶ Transients—spikes and surges

I'll cover these categories in depth in Chapter 9, "Power Supplies and Power Protection." Right now, however, let's look at the fourth kind of power noise, the one that *you* cause: *power-up power surges.*

In the process of discussing how to fix this, I'll have to weigh in on the Great PC Power Switch Debate.

When Lightning Strikes

In many ways, lightning fits into what you've already read about here (transient electrical charges, for example), but it's a point worth discussing separately because of the PC damage experienced each year due to it.

Anyone who lives in an area prone to serious electrical storms during warmer months knows the damage a strike can cause to a television, particularly one with an external antenna wired into it. The charge from a strike on the antenna can travel into the house, into the back of the set, and the result can be an explosion (if not a resulting fire, too).

A PC can be at least as sensitive to lightning's effects and usually costs more to replace.

With PCs, you need to worry not only about the unit itself, but anything that wires into it from a source that could be affected by an electrical storm. The most common situation is when you use a phone line connected to a modem connected to your PC, which can act much like the TV with the lead wire from the antenna coming in. When lightning strikes phone lines in your neighborhood, the shockwaves can travel along the connections and potentially travel into your home or office and into the back of the PC.

External modems, which have a separate power supply, tend to isolate the effects. Lightning may blow out the capacitors in the modem, but the damage usually stops there. Internal modems, however, are connected to the PC's motherboard itself. A charge occurring here could ruin not just the modem, but it could perhaps fry the motherboard as well. Think of what this means when you have a motherboard with the modem integrated right into the system board itself. Electricity felt on your phone line is delivered directly.

Tip

Don't underestimate the potential damage lightning can cause when you're reading about protection methods in Chapter 9. Also take lightning into consideration if your PC develops some strange problems—a malfunctioning modem, no power up, or odd boot errors—immediately following a large storm.

Leave Your Machines On 24 Hours a Day

I'd like to discuss one power-related item here: user-induced power surges. What user-induced power surges, you say? Simple: every time you turn on an electrical device, you get a power surge through it. Some of the greatest stresses that electrical devices receive are when they are turned on or turned off. When do light bulbs burn out? Think about it—they generally burn out when you first turn them on or off. One study showed that when a device is first turned on, it draws as much as four to six times its normal power for less than one second. (This phenomenon is called *inrush current*.)

The answer? Leave your PCs on 24 hours a day, seven days a week. We've done it at my company for years. Turn the monitor off, turn the screen intensity down, or use one of those annoying automatic screen savers so the monitor doesn't get an image burned into it. Turn the printer off also. Modern power management techniques (check for a Power Management icon in Windows 98/2000) let you put the hard drives and monitor to sleep on a set schedule. Leaving the machines on also regulates temperature and reduces a phenomenon called *chip creep* that I'll discuss in Chapter 5.

What? You're still not convinced? I know, it seems nonintuitive—most people react that way. But it really does make sense. First of all, consider the things that you keep on all the time:

▶ Digital clocks, which obviously run continuously, incorporate some of the same digital technology as microcomputers, and they're pretty reliable.

▶ Calculators—I've seen accountants who use calculators that are kept on all the time.

▶ Mainframes, minis, and your phone PBX never go off.

▶ TVs—part of the TV is powered up all the time so that it can "warm up" instantly, unlike older sets.

▶ Thermostats—the temperature-regulating device in your home or business is a circuit that works all the time.

Most of the things that I just named are some of the most reliable, never-think-about-them devices that you work with.

Now, consider the hard disk. All disks incorporate a motor to spin them at high speeds (depending upon the drive, they may spin at speeds ranging from 3600 to 10,000rpm). You know from real life that it's a lot harder to get something moving than it is to keep it moving. (Ever push a car?) The cost, then, of turning hard disk motors on and off is that sometimes they just won't be able to get started.

For example, back in 1984 I bought my first hard disk, an external 32MB drive. It cost $929, and while it's dead and buried now, for years I was loathe to stop using it, because nine hundred bucks is a lot of money. For a long time I kept it attached to a server and constantly running. The drive required a "jump start" when it was turned off overnight: if the thing didn't want to work, we just removed it from the system, took off the hard disk's circuit board to expose the motor, and gave the motor a spin. After a couple of spins, we reassembled it, and it would start up fine. (No, I didn't put anything important on it, but it was a great demonstration tool. And it kept data just fine.)

Here's the point: as long as we didn't turn the system off, the hard drive worked quite well, at least as well as old 32MB hard drives work. This applies to hard disks in general, and in fact to anything with a motor. Yes, the motor's life is shortened when continuously on, but even then the expected life of the motor is beyond the reasonable life of a hard disk.

Leaving your computer on all the time heads off thermal shock, which is yet another reason to leave it on. Machines should never be power cycled quickly. I've seen people fry their power supplies by turning their computers on and off several times in a 30-second period to "clear problems," and they ended up creating bigger problems.

A final word of caution, however: Leaving the machine on all the time is a good idea only if:

▸ Your machine is cooled adequately. If your machine is 100 degrees inside when the room is 70 degrees, it'll overheat when the room goes to 90 degrees on summer weekends when the building management turns off the cooling in your building. Make sure your machine has a good enough fan to handle higher temperatures.

▸ You have adequate surge protection. Actually, you should not run the machine at all unless you have adequate surge protection.

▸ You have fairly reliable power. If you lose power three times a week, there's no point in leaving the machines on all the time—the power company is turning them off and on for you. Even worse, the power that comes on just after a power outage is noise-filled. And even if you do have fairly reliable power, you may want to change your practice when there's a possibility of the kind of severe weather likely to cause temporary power problems.

Before moving on, let's take a quick peek at the other kinds of power problems—the ones we'll tackle in greater detail in Chapter 9.

Transients

A *transient* is any brief change in power that doesn't repeat itself. It can be an undervoltage or an overvoltage. Sags (momentary under-voltage) and surges (momentary overvoltage) are transients. In brief, the transient may be of a high enough frequency that it slips right past the protective capacitors in your power supply and punches holes in your chips. (No, they're not holes you can see, at least not without some very good equipment.) Transients have a cumulative effect—the first 100 may do nothing. Eventually, however, enough chickens come home to roost that your machine decides, one day, to go on vacation. (You might say that if enough chickens come home to roost, the machine "buys the farm." Permanently.) We'll talk about how to protect against these things in Chapter 9.

Overvoltage

You have an *overvoltage* condition when you get more than the rated voltage for a period of greater than 2.5 seconds. Such a voltage measurement is made as a moving average over several seconds.

Chronic overvoltage is just as bad for your system as transient overvoltage: the chips can fail as a result of it.

Undervoltage

Summer in much of the country means that air conditioners are running full blast, and the power company is working feverishly to meet the power demands that they bring. Sometimes it can't meet the full needs, however, so it announces a reduction in voltage called a *brownout*, or an *undervoltage*.

Brownouts are bad for large motors, like the ones you'd find in a compressor for refrigeration. Brownouts make your TV screen look shrunken, and they confuse power supplies. A power supply tries to provide continuous power to the PC. Power equals voltage times current. If the voltage drops and you want constant power, what do you do? Simple: draw more current. But drawing more current through a given conductor heats up the conductor. The power supply and the chips get hot and may overheat.

Surge protectors can't help you here. A power conditioner can—it uses a transformer to compensate for the sagging voltage. We'll discuss power conditioners in greater detail in Chapter 9.

Electrostatic Discharge

ESD—or, as you probably know it, *static electricity*—is annoyingly familiar to anyone who has lived through a winter indoors. The air is very dry (winter and forced hot-air ducts bring relative humidity to around 20 percent in my house, for example) and is an excellent insulator. You build up a static charge and keep it until you touch something like a metal doorknob—or much worse, your computer. On the other hand, in the summer, when relative humidity can be close to 100 percent (until 1998 I lived in a suburb of Washington, D.C., a city built over a swamp), you still build up static charges, but they leak away quickly due to the humidity of the air. Skin resistance also has a lot to do with dissipating charges. The resistance of your skin can be as little as 1,000 ohms when wet and 500,000 ohms when dry. (This fun fact is courtesy of Jearl Walker's *Flying Circus of Physics*, published by John Wiley in 1977.)

You know how static electricity is built up. Static can damage chips if it creates a charge of 200 volts or more. If a static discharge is sufficient for the average person to notice it, it is at least 2,000 volts.

Scuffing across a shag rug in February can build up 50,000 volts. This is an electron "debt" that must be paid. The next metal item you touch (metal gives up electrons easily) pays the debt with an electric shock. If it's 50,000 volts, why doesn't it electrocute you when you touch the metal? Simple, the amperage (which is the volume of electricity) is tiny. This is because even though the voltage is high, the resistance is up in the millions of ohms, and 50,000 volts divided by millions of ohms is a tiny amount of current. (As my physics professor used to tell us, "Twinkle, twinkle, little star; power equals I squared R." And people say physics is dull.) Different materials generate more or less static. Many people think that certain materials are static-prone, while others are not. As it turns out, materials have a triboelectric (the electrical discharge created when you rub two objects together) value. Two materials rubbed together will generate static in direct proportion to how far apart their triboelectric values are.

Some common materials, in order of their triboelectric values, are:

- Air
- Human skin
- Asbestos
- Rabbit fur
- Glass
- Human hair
- Nylon
- Wool
- Fur
- Lead
- Silk
- Aluminum
- Paper
- Cotton
- Steel wool
- Hard rubber
- Nickel and copper
- Brass and silver
- Gold and platinum
- Acetate and rayon
- Polyester
- Polyurethane
- Polyvinyl
- Chloride
- Silicon
- Teflon

Once an item is charged, the voltage potential between it and another object is proportional to the distance between it and the other item on the table. For instance, suppose I charge a glass rod with a cotton cloth. The glass will attract things below it on the above list, like paper, and it will attract more strongly things listed below paper.

Why does static damage PC components? The chips that largely comprise circuit boards are devices that can be damaged by high voltage, even if they're at low current. The two most common families of chips are CMOS (Complementary Metal Oxide Semiconductor) chips, (which include NMOS [Negative Metal Oxide Semiconductor], PMOS [Positive Metal Oxide Semiconductor], and an assortment of newer devices that seem to appear on an almost daily basis), and TTL (Transistor-Transistor Logic) chips. TTLs are an older family. TTLs are faster switching chips—so potentially faster chips (memories,

CPUs, and such) could be designed with TTL. Ah, but TTL has a fatal flaw: it draws a lot of power. TTL chips need much more electricity than CMOS chips, so they create more heat, and so, while fast TTL CPUs could be constructed, CPUs are tough to justify because densely packed TTLs produce so much heat that they would destroy themselves. One common family of TTL chips has ID numbers starting with 74, as in 7400, 7446, 74LS128, and the like.

CPUs and memories are generally CMOS chips. CMOS has a lower theoretical maximum speed, but it runs on a lot less power. Sadly, they are also more subject to static electricity damage. TTL chips can withstand considerably more static electricity than CMOS chips. By the way, CPUs and memories are all CMOS.

Even if static doesn't destroy a chip, it can shorten its life. Static is, then, something to be avoided if possible. Another effect occurs when the static is discharged: When the fat blue spark jumps from your finger to the computer case, a small electromagnetic pulse (EMP) is created. This isn't too good for chips. (It's the thing you've heard about that could cause a single nuclear explosion to destroy every computer in the country, except a lot smaller.) The easiest way I get rid of my static is to discharge the static buildup on something metal that is not the computer's case. A metal desk or table leg is good.

For your business, however, you may want something a trifle more automatic. The options are to

▶ Raise the humidity with a humidifier (evaporative, not ultrasonic—ultrasonic creates dust)

▶ Raise the humidity with plants or, perhaps, an aquarium

▶ Install static-free carpet

▶ Put antistatic "touch me" mats under the PCs

▶ Make your own antistatic spray (see below)

From the point of view of comfort, I recommend the first option strongly. Your employees won't feel dried-out, and the static problem disappears. Raise humidity to just 50 percent, and the problem will go away.

You can make inexpensive, homemade antistatic spray. Just get a spray pump bottle and put about an inch of fabric softener in it. Fill it the rest of the way with water, shake it well, and you've got a spray for your carpets to reduce static. Just spritz it on the rug—the rug will smell nice, and everyone will know that you've been busy. (i hear you asking, "How long does it last?" Don't worry, you'll know.)

In a similar vein, a person from a temporary services agency once told me that they tell their word processing operators to put a sheet of Bounce under the keyboard to reduce static. While this may make the area smell nice, it will have no effect on static around the computer.

Technicians who must work with semiconductors all of the time use a *ground strap*, or *antistatic wrist strap*, to minimize ESD. The idea of a ground strap is that you never create a spark—and therefore EMP—because you've always got a nice ground connection that's draining off your charges. A good ground strap is an elastic wristband with a metal plate built into it to provide good electrical connection, attached to a wire with an alligator clip. You put the clip on something grounded—the power supply case is the most common place—and put the strap around your wrist. As you're connected to a ground, you continuously drain off your charges. A resistor in the ground strap slows down the discharge process a bit (from a microsecond to a few milliseconds), so you don't end up with one of the dangerous sparks that we've discussed before. If you do a lot of board work in a dry place, ground straps are essential. Several Silicon Valley defense-contracting firms have a policy of firing employees for not wearing their ESD wrist straps when working on high-tech equipment such as satellites and military equipment.

When you must handle electronic components, take these precautions:

▶ Get an antistatic strap. They're cheap.

▶ Remember the high-tech equivalent of knocking wood—touch unpainted metal periodically. One member of my staff has suggested handling chips only while naked on a wooden floor. While this might be entertaining to some of the staff, it would not, unfortunately, prevent static charges from building up since on a very dry day even the movement of your hair can build up a charge.

▶ Reduce the chances you'll have a lot of static in the air—even though you're wearing the antistatic wrist strap, you still want to avoid raising any more stray static in the area than you have to, so if you're wearing anything acrylic on a very cold day, remove it. Also, avoid standing on an acrylic carpet without a rubberized floor pad beneath your feet, and keep long hair tied behind your back.

▶ Don't handle components in areas that have high static potential. For example, avoid carpets unless they are antistatic or in high-humidity environments. Don't wear an acrylic sweater when changing chips. Get leather-soled shoes. If your work environment allows it, you can really avoid static by removing your shoes and socks.

▶ Don't handle chips any more than is necessary. If you don't touch them, you won't hurt them.

▶ Use antistatic protective tubes and bags to transport and store chips.

▶ If possible, pick up components by their bodies. Don't touch the pins any more than necessary.

▶ Have I mentioned yet that you should have an antistatic strap and use an antistatic mat?

Use the proper precautions, and your PC won't get a big "charge" out of being touched by you.

Avoiding Water and Liquids

Water is an easy hazard to detect and avoid. You don't need any sophisticated detection devices. Shielding is unnecessary—you just keep the computer away from water.

Water and liquids are introduced into a computer system in one of several ways:

▶ Operator spills

▶ Leaks

▶ Flooding

Spills generally threaten the keyboard. One remedy—the one recommended by every article and book I've ever read on maintenance—is to forbid liquids near the computer. In most shops, this is unrealistic. Some people use clear flexible plastic covers on the keyboard, kind of like what Burger King uses on their cash registers. They've got normal cash registers, but they have a plastic skin over the keys that allows the user to spill special sauce all over the keyboard without harming it. Use the plastic covers, and they can just hose down the keyboard. (Just kidding.) With one of these keyboard "skins," you might say that you can practice safe typing.

SafeSkin is offered by Merritt Computer Products in Dallas. Their address is listed in the Vendor Guide on CD #2. They offer versions for the various odd keyboards in the PC world.

A similar disaster, flooding, sometimes occurs. Don't assume that flooded components are destroyed components. Disassemble the computer and clean the boards by cleaning the contacts and edge connectors. You can buy connector cleaner fluids; some people use a hard white artist's eraser—do not use pencil erasers! (A Texas Instruments study showed that they contain acids that do more harm than good to connectors.) Blow out crevices with compressed air. (And if you do disassemble, clean, dry, and reassemble your computer, and then find that it works, write the manufacturer a letter; they might put your face in an advertisement.)

Avoid floods by thinking ahead. Don't store any electrical devices directly on the floor; they'll be damaged when the floor is cleaned. Generally, flooding indoors is under six inches. Be aware of flooding from improper roofing; when installing PCs, don't put one in directly under the suspicious stain on the ceiling. ("Oh, that—it was fixed two years ago. No problem now.")

Corrosion

Liquids (and gases) can accelerate corrosion of PCs and PC components. Corrosive agents include:

▶ Salt sweat in skin oils

▶ Water

▶ Airborne sulfuric acid, salt spray, and carbonic acid

Your fear here is not that the PC will fall away to rust; the largest problem that corrosion causes is oxidation of circuit contacts. When a device's connector becomes oxidized, it doesn't conduct as well, and so the device does not function, or—worse—malfunctions sporadically. Salt in sweat can do this, so be careful when handling circuit boards; don't touch edge connectors unless you have to. This is why some firms advertise that they use gold-edge connectors; gold is resistant to corrosion.

You don't believe that you have detectable traces of finger oils? Try this simple experiment. Pour a glass of soda or beer into a very clean glass—preferably a plastic cup that has never been used before. There will be a noticeable "head" on the drink. (Diet soda seems particularly fizzy.) Now put your finger into the center of the head, just for a second. The head will rapidly dissolve, because the oils damage the surface tension required to support the head. It's the quickest way to eliminate a large head so you can pour a larger glass of beer. Or you could try buying a nice new 20-inch color computer monitor and see how many of your colleagues fail to understand that it is not a touch-screen device. You will end up with numerous thick, oily smudge marks on your monitor that are very visible and annoying when a dark background is displayed on it.

Carbonated liquids include carbonic acid, and coffee and tea contain tannic acids. The sugar in soda is eaten by bacteria that leave behind conductive excrement—like hiring some germs to put new traces on your circuit board. Generally, try to be very careful with drinks around computers.

Don't forget cleaning fluids. Be careful with that window cleaner that you're using to keep the display clean. If your PC is on a pedestal on the floor, and the floor is mopped each day, some of the mopping liquid gets into the PC. Cleaning fluids are very corrosive.

You can clean edge connectors with either hard white erasers (remember, don't use the pink erasers—they're acidic!) or connector cleaner products. One of the best-known vendors of these products is Texwipe. You can get a catalog of their products by writing to them at their address, listed in the Vendor Guide on CD #2.

Note

Although this chapter has discussed some preventive maintenance concerns, I've mainly talked about the environmental problems PCs face. But you should also do preventive maintenance, which means taking a machine off your desk at regular intervals, perhaps as often as every six months, and moving it to your "shop" to give it a good going-over so that you'll anticipate problems. If you missed the key preventive maintenance procedures listed at the beginning of this chapter, make sure you go back and check them out!

Troubleshooting Tips

When troubleshooting PC problems, it's important not to overlook the very environmental factors discussed in this chapter (as well as whether the system has been "pushed" or overclocked to try to bolster performance).

Ask yourself these questions when you're working on a perplexing problem, particularly one where the difficulties occur at some times of the day but not others:

▶ Is the PC in direct sunlight or positioned in such a way that strong sunlight is hitting the case or monitor for a prolonged period of time? Install a shade or blinds, close the curtains, or move the PC where it won't have sunshine heating up the PC case, which in turn heats up the internal equipment.

▶ Is the room in which the PC is located prone to severe temperature changes? For example, in the winter, is the office quite warm
during the day yet only has minimal heating during the cold
nights? Such fluctuation isn't good for any system. If possible,
move the PC into an area where the temperature remains more
even throughout the day and night. If it must stay put, then the
ambient temperature needs to be normalized before turning on
the PC.

▶ Are the problems occurring when the room temperature is very
cold or very warm but not occurring at other times? Again, moving the PC to a more climate-controlled area is a good idea.

▶ Is hardware acting flaky after a particularly bad storm or power
fluctuation? If so, the system needs to be evaluated, parts need
to be replaced (as necessary), and the system then needs to be
equipped with some type of power protection scheme like an
uninterruptible power supply or surge protector.

▶ Is the PC located in an area where large appliances cycling up or
down may cause a short flux in the power (noticeable by a brief
flicker of the lights)? The PC should be moved to a different circuit from any other equipment that may interfere with it or its
constant power supply. A power protection scheme like a surge
protector should be used.

▶ Is the area in which the PC is located prone to dampness? Dampness can cause odd behavior in a PC and can short out electronic
components. Move the PC to a dry, temperate area.

▶ Have you or the PC's user recently "pushed" the limits of the system by adjusting clock settings on the motherboard or your
video card? If so, such changes may potentially cause a heat problem inside the case, as well as account for other random errors
and device failures. Reverse the "overclocking" and then either
leave it alone, or step it up very gradually.

By now, your PC is shined to a high gloss. But what happens when
something goes wrong? For that, turn to the next chapter.

5

Troubleshooting
PC Problems

INTRODUCTION

Okay, suppose you dust out your PC fortnightly. You clean and adjust your disk drives semiannually. You have a robot that shoots anyone coming within 50 feet of your PC with food or drink. But, one day, WordPerfect refuses to print your purple prose. How do you proceed?

You might say that this is a chapter about religion. I want you to develop a process for dealing with computer repairs that you follow as dutifully as a zealot follows a religion.

Why get religious? Because people who fix PCs day in and day out—people who fix *anything* day in and day out, for that matter—have learned to do it by following some repeatable procedures step by step. The alternative method is to attack each problem in a haphazard way.

Now, I'm somebody who's tried both the religious way and the haphazard way. As such, you might say that I'm uniquely qualified to offer you some advice on how to choose which approach to take.

If you find that you're plagued with too much free time, time you've got to spend with the spouse and kids; if you just can't sleep at night and need something to fill those insomniac hours; if Saturdays and Sundays are painful tedium broken only by the occasional *Three Stooges* rerun—then, by all means, adopt the haphazard method. You'll be able to tackle all kinds of fascinating problems, most of which you created yourself while noodling around trying to fix the original problem. And, since the true haphazard fixer never takes notes, you'll get to experience the joy of problem-solving over and over, even when it's the same problem.

If, on the other hand, you want to do something with your days other than futzing around with balky PCs, then think about getting religion.

Don't get me wrong: there's nothing wrong with futzing around with a PC—you'll get some of your deepest insights and "ohhh . . . *that's* how it works" kind of knowledge through that kind of experimentation. All I'm saying is to keep the experiments and the fixing as separate as possible. And when you *must* experiment, then make sure that all your experiments are repeatable ones; taking notes should be gospel.

Troubleshooting PC Problems

Here are the key steps you should take in troubleshooting most PC problems (while remembering to stay calm and positive). Several of these steps occur before you ever power down and remove the case.

Be Prepared

Before you start, there are some things you may need on hand. These include:

- Documentation for your PC and/or its separate components (including warranty information)
- Container for placing screws between removal and reinstallation
- Appropriate screwdriver(s), such as a Phillips-head
- Antistatic wrist strap
- Connector cleaner or hard, white artist's eraser
- Boot disk and operating system installation CD (just in case)
- Diagnostic utilities

1. Check for operator errors—commands or setup that you may be doing wrong, software or hardware that you may have set up incorrectly, or instructions that you may have reversed (for example, literally reversing a cable or putting a jumper on exactly opposite from the way it needs to go).

2. Check to make certain that everything that should be plugged into either a direct power source or the PC itself is, and that the connection is secure.

3. Check the software, including program files and drivers.

4. Check for external signs of trouble, such as flickering LED power indicators or those that don't come on at all, strange sounds or lack of sound, and lack of display.

5. Run appropriate diagnostics programs.

6. Only when all else fails, disassemble the PC. Shut it down, disconnect all power, remove the case, ground yourself, and go inside to check cable and power connections, the proper seating of expansion boards and memory modules, and anything out of the ordinary.

General Troubleshooting Rules

These rules have kept me out of trouble for a long time. I know they'll be of use to you.

PC Technician's Creed

▶ "Don't Panic" and "I Will Win"

▶ Write Everything Down

▶ Do the Easy Stuff First

▶ Reboot and Try Again

▶ Simplify, Simplify, Simplify!

▶ Draw a Picture, Separate into Components, and Test

▶ Never Assume

▶ Trust No One: The Documentation Sometimes Lies

▶ Observe Like Sherlock Holmes

Although some of these suggestions are a bit tongue-in-cheek, there's a nugget of advice in every one, and they're all part of the philosophy of troubleshooting.

Remember: "Don't Panic" and "I Will Win"

You've got to have confidence in yourself as a troubleshooter. Look, this stuff isn't that hard. My technical training is as a Ph.D. economist rather than as a computer scientist or engineer, I've got 10 thumbs, and people pay *me* to fix machines. You can do it too. There's not that much to these machines. When it comes right down to it, the only thing that you really can't replace for (at most) a hundred dollars or so is your data, and you can protect that with frequent backups.

If you don't go in there *knowing* that you're going to win, you're going to get beaten—these machines can *smell* fear. A former girlfriend, a black belt in Tae Kwon Do, told me once that an important tenet of Tae Kwon Do is to "have an indomitable spirit." Sounds good to me—practice some *Tech* Kwon Do, and don't forget that indomitable spirit.

Write Everything Down

If you read Chapter 2, "Disassembling the PC" (and if you didn't, go do it), then you've already learned about the hazards of not documenting. I tend not to write things down when I'm pretty sure that the operation will be simple (it almost never is), or when it's sufficiently traumatic that I'm certain that I couldn't forget (there's always another, bigger trauma waiting). I've found that I'm more likely to write important notes down if I keep my notebook—the paper kind—handy. These notes might include, for example, special location information or notations about a problem, such as a bent pin or the actual layout being the reverse of how it appears in the manufacturer's diagram. As a bonus, writing things in your notebook means that you'll be able to find them later.

Do the Easy Stuff First

I am, by nature, a lazy person. That's why I got interested in computers: they were machines that could free me from some drudgery. The *inexperienced* and lazy troubleshooter tries to save time by not making notes, by acting before thinking, and by *swapping* components or configuration information when he ought to be *stopping* . . . stopping to consider his next move.

What I've eventually figured out is that well-planned laziness is a virtue. An *experienced* lazy person looks ahead and says, "Oh, heck, what if I *can't* fix this thing? I don't want to create any more trouble for myself than necessary." And so the lazy person keeps diagrams and writes down everything that she does so she doesn't have to tear out her hair trying to put the PC back together.

The *experienced* lazy person does the easy stuff first; if it's a video problem, and it's not software, then four things could be swapped: the motherboard, the video board, the cable, or the monitor. What gets swapped first? The easy thing: the cable.

Reboot and Try Again

Your computer is affected by fluctuations in the power supply of as brief a duration as four milliseconds. That means that if your power disappeared for only $\frac{1}{200}$ of a second, you wouldn't see the lights flicker, the microwave would still work, and the TV wouldn't skip a beat—even the digital clocks wouldn't start blinking. But several bytes of your computer's memory (not a lot of the memory, or you'd see a memory error message of some kind) get randomized. The result is that a program that has always worked pretty well all of a sudden stops dead. You'll never find out why it locked up that one time in a thousand. Maybe everybody in the building was running their photocopiers at the same time. Maybe radiation from a solar storm assaulted your memory chips (yes, that can happen, although it's unlikely; when a technician blames something on "cosmic rays," she's being facetious). It doesn't matter; the quick answer to this problem is just to start over and reboot the machine.

Now, don't get too trigger-happy with the reboot if you're in the middle of an application. It's usually a really bad idea to reboot out of Windows 95/98/2000/NT—try everything you can to get the machine to respond and let you do a graceful shutdown. If you reboot in the middle of an application, the application may leave files "open," and those files will be lost. (Such half-finished files lead to a phenomenon you may have seen called *lost clusters*. More on that when I discuss hard disks in Chapters 10 through 14.)

Simplify, Simplify, Simplify!

The average PC has about a bazillion screen savers, applications, background communications programs (such as fax receive programs), applications, and of course driver programs for sound boards, network cards, video boards, and the mouse, to name just a few. Determining the source of a problem is really hard when there are innumerable interactions between hardware and software.

That means that it's a good idea to eliminate as much as you can from a PC before trying to diagnose it. For example, boot without the network. If you're running Windows 95/98, wait for the `Starting Windows...` message and press F8. That gives you the chance to boot Windows in Safe mode. In Windows NT/2000, you can choose a configuration with a simple video driver at startup and then use the Control Panel, under Services, to stop the loading of any unnecessary drivers or programs.

I've seen this in the DOS world time and time again. Memory resident or TSR (Terminate and Stay Resident, referring to the fact that they remain in memory) programs can interfere with system functions. It may just be that the reason your drive E: will not format is because you've got your LAN software loaded. Don't ask me why—just try it. Remove all those pop-ups by rebooting without them (check your operating system for a Clean Boot option or go into your AUTOEXEC.BAT file to see what programs are set up to run there); then see whether the problem goes away. Software troubleshooting is just like hardware troubleshooting: divide and conquer. Each piece of software that you're running is a piece of the system, and you want to minimize the number of pieces that you have to deal with. TSRs are the easiest part to remove.

Draw a Picture, Separate into Components, and Test

This is a true story: A friend was once a PC troubleshooter-type for a county government in Virginia, where I live. She tells this story about another PC troubleshooter-type—let's call him Ignatz. One day, their help desk got a phone call.

"Ignatz," the caller said, "WordPerfect isn't printing with the new laser printer!"

Now, an experienced lazy person listens and says, "Gosh—how can I fix this without leaving my chair?" Many of us would probably zero in on that word, *new*. As in "*new* laser printer." The next questions might be something like, "What kind of printer did you have before the new laser printer?" "Have you ever seen WordPerfect print on this laser printer before?" (Probably not.) "Have you reinstalled WordPerfect for the laser printer?" (A confused "What?" is the probable answer.)

Ignatz, on the other hand, attacked the problem by first swapping the motherboard on the PC that was attached to the laser printer.

Yes, that's right—you read that correctly. It even kind of fixed the problem, as Iggie figured that he would reload the user's software while he was at it. Yeah, we can observe that Ignatz is, umm, shall we say, "a couple sandwiches short of a picnic" when it comes to troubleshooting. But I see people do less extreme (but just as unnecessary) things all the time. Heck, I still do a lot of dumb things myself, playing Macho Man with a Screwdriver. But I hope to get better at remembering to be lazy when troubleshooting.

Now, if old Ig had stopped to think, then he could have diagrammed the whole system. Simplified, you could say that the laser printer is attached to a cable, which attaches to a parallel port, which is connected to the motherboard, which runs the software. That kind of divides the problem into: laser printer, cable, parallel port, motherboard, and software. Each of those components can then be isolated and tested. *Testing* most hardware just means swapping it, as most of us lack the expensive equipment needed to test hardware. But software can be played with in many ways, the most fruitful of which is usually in its setup and configuration. I'd look at the software first. I always look at the software before I go after the hardware. Why? Simple: I've got a much better chance of finding the answer in software.

Never Assume

It's far too easy to assume that something is blameless. "How could the problem be the new version of ThunderWord? It's been clean for the last five versions!" Subject everything to your scrutiny, *including* the documentation. And while I'm on the subject . . .

Trust No One: The Documentation Sometimes Lies

Years ago, I bought my first Video Graphics Adapter (VGA) board. It was made by Compaq Computer Corporation, and it wasn't cheap, but I bought it from Compaq because I knew that they made a compatible, high-quality product. Since it was in the early days of the VGA, many clones were kinda wobbly compatibility-wise, so I was playing it safe.

When I went to install the board, I took the time to read the documentation. About half of the booklet that came with the board discussed installation. In particular, there were several pages about how to properly set the three jumpers that were clearly marked and even illustrated in black-and-white photos. Before even removing the board from its antistatic bag, I studied the documentation and figured out how to set the three jumpers. Donning my antistatic wrist strap, I removed the board from its bag.

But it had only one jumper on it.

I looked and looked and *looked*, but there was only one jumper on the %$#@! thing. I picked up the manual again—and a lone piece of paper fluttered from between its pages. It basically said, "Your VGA is a new and improved model. It's got only one jumper. Set it like this." Frustrating, yes, but at least Compaq provided the right documentation, albeit hidden. Jumpers are usually not the real nightmare, however; the documentation is. Almost every one of these things is badly translated from some Pacific Rim nation's language to English and, worst of all, it's usually wrong. The jumper setting for the parallel port is usually off, and I've seen incorrect documentation for the serial port jumpers as well. I've often wondered if the documentation's author didn't have a sense of humor, however: this 3-by-8-inch piece of paper is *copyrighted*.

If you're wondering, by the way, how I figured out the correct settings, then I'm afraid that there's no trick that I can share with you. When I run into one of these boards, I check my notes to see whether I've run into this particular model before. If I have, great; if not, all I can do is work by trial and error.

Today, more and more information about PC hardware (and software) is available from the manufacturers' online Web sites. If you haven't tapped this resource yet, stick with me through Chapter 30, "Using the Internet and Online Services," where you'll get a taste of some of the technical help riches out on the Net.

Observe Like Sherlock Holmes

In Arthur Conan Doyle's tales of the Great Detective, Sherlock Holmes sometimes exclaims about some new piece of evidence. He's obviously excited about it, but when Dr. Watson asks him *why* he's excited, Holmes gives nothing away. "Not yet, Watson," he demurs. "It's too early for theories."

What Holmes knew was that problem solving entails making theories, and then proving or disproving the theories with facts. But suppose Holmes had advanced an early theory aloud, perhaps in the company of the beleaguered Inspector Lestrade? Lestrade would like nothing better than to witness his harasser Holmes brought down by a faulty theory. Now, Holmes also knows that, so he's got a subconscious aversion to finding any facts that disprove this ill-uttered supposition. By keeping his mouth shut until he's got enough facts, he can offer a theory that he feels confident about.

You'll see this in your everyday troubleshooting life. Someone stands over your shoulder as you peer inside a disemboweled PC carcass. "What do you think it is?" he says.

This is a crucial moment. Learn to say automatically, "I don't know—there's not enough information yet." Otherwise, you'll find that now the game you're playing is no longer "fix the machine;"

unconsciously, you're now playing a game called "prove you're right." So hang onto the theories until you've got the facts.

When you open up a machine, you expose the machine to a certain risk that you'll do something dumb to it. PC troubleshooting differs from, say, automotive troubleshooting, in that the thing that's most commonly broken is the user. If you separate out the "user is broken" stuff (they forgot to turn it on, for example), software is the next most common problem. Honest-to-God hardware problems are actually quite uncommon compared to user and software problems. That leads me to the six specific troubleshooting steps.

Six Steps to Troubleshooting Success

The smart troubleshooter makes the troubleshooting job tractable by breaking down problems into steps. Don't panic, and remember to be methodical; otherwise, you will thrash helplessly about and get frustrated. Once you are frustrated, you are *lost*, and you start creating new problems.

Following is the method that I use. It looks a lot like methods suggested by other people, but it's not the only method. You certainly don't have to use *my* method, but find one you like and stick to it—even for the small or seemingly easy jobs. It's the "this'll take only five minutes" repairs that get me in trouble. (You know—like when someone gives you directions, saying, "You can't miss it." I *know* I'm in trouble then.) I'll assume for this discussion that you are interacting with someone else (the person with the PC problem), but you can just as easily interview yourself.

Before opening up the computer, do the following:

1. Check the nut behind the keyboard.

2. Check that everything is plugged in: power, monitor, phone lines, printer, modem, and so on.

3. Check the software.

4. Check external signs. Make notes of them.

5. Run the diagnostics disk.

Only then, if you still haven't solved the problem:

6. Disassemble the machine, clean the connectors, push the socketed chips back into their sockets, and put the machine back together.

Notice that the first five steps *aren't* hardware steps; let's take a closer look at all six.

Check for Operator Error

Operator error is responsible for 93.3 percent of PC failures. (That's a made-up statistic. But it got your attention and probably isn't far from the truth.) There are lots of things that an operator can do wrong. But one real statistic from the PC retail industry is that up to 75 percent of hardware purchases returned as defective aren't defective and worked fine on retesting.

Regardless of how inflated that statistic may or may not be, that means a lot of folks aren't installing their hardware properly. Sure, some of it can be blamed on bad instructions, but many people flat-out admit that they never look at any documentation packed with the device they're trying to install—or read it after the first three to four times a device won't install "instantly."

And since the accompanying paperwork often ends up in the trash can with the packaging from the hardware, you can end up feeling isolated and uninformed a few months later, when the device stops working. Remember the old saying about how desperate people do desperate things?

There are three main sources of problems for PCs: hardware, software, and users. Guess which one is the most likely? Users.

Software's second. Hardware is a distant third. Why are there so many people problems in the computer business? Mainly because the user interfaces still stink, even the "good" ones.

Frequently, people will ask me how to prepare a new hard disk to use in their PCs. I'll go through all the steps, and usually point them to a Web site or two that spells out the steps again for them, so they have something in print they can stare at. All too many times, however, one of these folks will come back to tell me, "It didn't work."

"What didn't work?" I'll ask.

The answer will come back, "I can't access my CD-ROM drive to install Windows" or "I followed all the instructions but the hard drive won't boot up!!!"

Invariably, I find that they didn't follow one—or more—of the steps. They either didn't FDISK or FORMAT (necessary to prep the drive) so it's not really ready for use, or they decided they didn't need to go to the trouble of installing a DOS CD-ROM driver on their boot disk, so they can't access their CD-ROM drive to install their operating system.

You see, computers are made up of hardware, and hardware for the most part is a pretty logical beast. Turn something one way, and a device becomes available for use. Turn it another way, and a device doesn't respond to you. You can't see a list of 10 steps and decide which 5 you might like to follow, because all 10 steps are likely required to get the result you want.

Still, the language of computers confuses people. You've heard the stories about users doing goofy things; well, they're true. I've seen them. I once watched a user follow the dBase III 1 installation instructions: "Insert System Disk 1 in drive A: and close the door." He inserted the disk in the drive, then got up (looking a little puzzled, I'll give him that), and closed the door to his office. If I hadn't been there to see it, I probably wouldn't have believed it. But before you giggle too loudly, consider: where was the "door?" Have you seen a door on a floppy drive lately? No, there's never been one, really—just a little latch across it or a small shutter. I mean, if you hired me to put a door on your house, and instead I installed a little plastic latch, then you'd sue me, and you'd *win*.

When teaching those same dBase classes, now and then I'd get some guy staring at the keyboard in puzzlement.

"What's wrong?" I'd ask.

"I'm looking for a key," he'd reply.

"Which one? I'll point it out," I would offer.

"The Any key," he'd say, still puzzled. I would look at the screen, where dBase was prompting, `Press any key to continue...` I had just gotten finished with my "pay attention to what the computer is doing" lecture, and so this poor soul was trying his hardest to follow my directions. (Nowadays, there is an answer for the Any key searchers. You can buy an Any key kit: it's a keytop sticker that says, "ANY KEY." You install it on ... well, any key.)

I've seen users "copy a floppy" with a photocopier. They're not dumb—they saw the "double-sided" sticker on the floppy, so they copy both sides. I once saw a bank organize their backup floppies by punching holes in them so they would fit into a small binder. True stories, all of them.

A friend at Microsoft tells the story of being called by someone who couldn't get Windows to do anything. "I've got my foot on the pedal," he said, "and it's not doing anything!" Well, mice are often found on the floor, but ...

Even worse, sometimes users will (horrors!) prevaricate slightly. "I didn't do anything. It just stopped working." Please note: I'm not one of those techie types whose motto is, "Assume that the user is lying," but sometimes it happens. More often, it's not that they lie. It's just that they don't know what's important, or they're embarrassed to tell you what they really did.

People feel defensive calling a support person (such as you). You want to collect as much information as possible. If you make them feel defensive, they'll misremember, or withhold information. Here's a trick that telemarketers are told: smile when you're on the phone with someone. It works. (As Sam Kinison said, "It creates the illusion that you care.") Being a support person can be wearing. There's a tendency to feel like "these people must get up early in the morning to think up dumb things to ask," but you can't let it get you down. Remember, these folks can't be too dumb—after all, the same company that hired them hired you, too. (Heh, heh.)

Again, think *lazy*. How can you collect enough information while on the phone to fix the problem right over the phone? The key is to not act like so many support people, the ones who don't even let you get your question out before they break in with, "Are you sure your computer is plugged in?" Stop and think about how idiotic this phrasing is. Who's going to answer "No"? It's roughly equivalent to saying "Oh! Look at that. It's not plugged in. I *am* an idiot. Sorry to bother you."

Now, don't get me wrong: you've got to ask the question—that's why it's step 2 in my six steps. But there's a right way and a wrong way. One right way is the "bureaucracy" approach: "I'm sorry that's happening to you. That must be really frustrating; I'll do whatever I can for you. But first, you know how it is here at XYZ Corp.; we've got a form for everything. Forgive me, but I've got to ask some dumb-sounding questions. Can you just double-check for me that the PC is plugged in . . ." Another good approach is to couch it in a self-depre-cating way: "My asking you if the PC is plugged in reminded me of something dumb I did the other day. The PC was plugged into the surge protector, and the surge protector was plugged into the wall. It took me 15 minutes to figure out that the surge protector was turned off! Can you believe that I did something that stupid?" If the next sound you hear is, "Ummm, can I call you back? Someone just walked into my office," then you can be pretty sure you've just engineered another fixed PC.

Best of all, however, that's a PC that your user just fixed. He's now had a success, so he'll remember that particular problem/solution combination. (Psychology tells us that people learn better with positive reinforcement than with negative reinforcement.) He'll probably end up feeling more capable, more likely to tackle the problem himself next time. "Success is a habit," said Vince Lombardi.

Another source of operator error stems from inexperienced operators. The PC isn't exactly the simplest thing in the world to master. The author of a book titled *Computer Wimp: 166 Things I Wish I Had Known Before I Bought My First Computer* observes in that book that learning to use a computer system may be the most difficult learning endeavor that a person will undertake in their post-school life. (Things like raising kids are undoubtedly tougher, but they're different kinds of learning experiences.) It doesn't take a genius to recognize that most PC hardware and software manuals aren't the easiest things to comprehend. The answer? Good education. There are tons of good books, videos, college courses, and professional seminars on PCs, one for every budget. "If you think education is expensive," they say, "try ignorance."

Make Sure Everything Is Plugged In

I know this sounds stupid, but we've all done it. A friend bought a modem and couldn't get it to work. It accepted commands all right, but could not dial out. The phone line was tested with a regular phone and worked fine. He was quite puzzled until he realized that he'd plugged the phone line into the *out* jack in the modem instead of the *in* jack. (The out jack is intended to be connected to the phone itself—not the phone line—so that the line can be shared between the modem and the phone). Another time, I ran the IBM diagnostic disk on my PC and kept getting `bad address mark` errors on my disk drives. I was all set to spend a lot of money for new drives until I realized that the disk that I was using was not formatted. (The drives were fine.)

As I just said, when you ask the user, "Is it plugged in?" be diplomatic. (Don't you hate when tech support people ask *you* that question?) But don't be afraid to ask for firm answers to the following questions:

▶ Is the PC plugged into some kind of multi-outlet strip?

▶ Is the strip on? Did the user kick off the power switch?

▶ Can the user actually see that the power strip is plugged into the wall?

▶ Are the other devices that are plugged into the power strip working? Try having the user plug a desk lamp or fan into the power strip to see whether it works.

▶ If the PC or peripheral is plugged into an outlet controlled by a wall switch, is the switch turned on?

▶ Are the peripherals plugged in? Are they plugged *into the computer*?

I know of a large communications company that kept sending technicians to try to determine why a LAN server kept dying at strange hours of the night. They'd set up the software at the user site, leave it running, and then eventually get called back to the site because after a day or two all kinds of files had been trashed. The techs would always ask, "Has this been turned off in the middle of an operation?" The users would solemnly (and annoyingly—this tech guy wasn't going to weasel out of fixing his company's buggy software *that* easily, they thought) shake their heads no. Finally, this large company sent their SuperTech—the guy who'd seen it all. He looked over the server and listened to the users' stories.

Now, this guy *knew* from the symptoms that the server was getting shut down improperly. (Remember that indomitable spirit. On the other hand, save the spirit for the machine—don't get snotty with the users.) So he looked for easy ways to turn off the machine accidentally. Noticing two light switches on the wall and only one fluorescent ceiling panel, he flipped both switches. You guessed it—the server was plugged into a switched outlet. The security staff, in making the rounds each night, would shut off the lights.

When you are checking whether peripherals are plugged in, you also need to make sure that they are in *tight*. Multiple pin connectors slowly bend under gravity unless the mounting screws are tightened. As someone stretches their legs under the desk, a loose power cord could be moved enough to disconnect it, or disconnect and reconnect it. Connectors on the floor take a lot of abuse.

I think that people don't properly secure connectors because it can't be done without one of those small straight-slot screwdrivers that are smaller than the one you've got in the kitchen tool drawer, but larger than the one you use to adjust the screws in your glasses. (Of course, we true PC repair warriors are never without our small screwdriver with the pocket clip and the logo of some company on its side, but normal humans . . .) Nowadays, you can find a remedy: many cables are sold with big plastic screws that are easily hand-turnable. (Many folks call those screws *thumbscrews,* and I guess it's as good a term as any, but I find it a bit medieval.) Whenever possible, get cables with hand-turnable screws. They'll pay for themselves in the long run.

I'm one of the worst offenders in the cable screws department. As I install and reinstall various PC components a lot, I tend to just push my serial and video cables into their sockets, not bothering with the screwdriver (I don't have the little screwdriver with the pocket clip when I don't happen to have my pocket protector around. You know, sometimes I want to work undercover, so I leave the pocket protector behind.) A few years ago, I had myself convinced that my serial port or modem was fried, because I was getting terrible error rates on my communications sessions all of a sudden. As I'd just finished giving a lecture on lightning damage to serial ports, and it was T-storm season in Washington, I figured ruefully that I'd just lost a serial port. "But," I thought, "Who knows? Maybe when lightning toasted the port, it burned up some chips—I can at least take some pictures." So I got ready to take my PC apart. Of course, one of the first things I did was to remove the cables, and that's when I noticed that the serial cable just about fell off the back of the PC when I touched it. So I returned the cables to their interfaces—making sure they were secured tightly—and, as you've already guessed, the problems went away.

Check the Software

Remember I said that more problems are software problems than hardware problems? Software problems arrive in several guises:

▶ Operator error

▶ Keyboard/screen/disk/timer conflicts with memory resident software

▶ Software that doesn't clean up after itself

▶ Software that requires hardware that isn't connected or activated

▶ Buggy applications

▶ Buggy driver programs

Software troubleshooting could be a book in itself. In fact, all the books out there on supporting Windows 95/98/2000/NT, Novell NetWare, and the like are software-troubleshooting books. But let's tackle some of the broad causes of software problems.

Virtual Device Drivers and Dynamic-Link Libraries

Modern operating systems, such as Windows 95/98/2000/NT, are built in a kind of layer-cake fashion. The application programs (such as word processing, e-mail and spreadsheet programs) sit atop the cake—they're the frosting. Your applications are supported by layers of cake and filling, layers that they need in order to work—heck, frosting all by itself is a bit much, right?

The bottom layer of the cake is the hardware. Application programs need services (such as printing, communicating with a network server, or saving files) done for them by the hardware (the printer, the network card, or the hard disk). How do applications communicate with hardware? How does your system prioritize and handle multiple requests without exploding?

Enter the operating system. If every application tries to use a piece of hardware at the same time, nothing works. What you need is a kind of traffic cop between the apps and the hardware. The OS is that cop, the piece that routes hardware requests between applications and hardware, keeping traffic jams to a minimum and "crashes" nonexistent (well, in theory, anyway). The OS acts as a "traffic cop" layer between your hardware and your applications.

Also in between your hardware and applications are two components that applications rely on to operate correctly. They are called *virtual device drivers* (VxDs) and *dynamic-link libraries* (DLLs). Both act as filling between the layers, hidden from exterior view but key to the structure of the cake. I will discuss DLLs in a minute, but first let's consider drivers.

The lowest level of system software is the set of programs called drivers that are customized to particular pieces of hardware. Drivers attach in a modular fashion to the main body of the OS (called the *kernel*). For example, in order to get Windows to recognize and use your Hewlett-Packard LaserJet model 5P, you must load a driver for that printer, adding it to the Windows system software.

Drivers can pose a bit of a problem for software stability. Most of the operating system is designed by a close-knit software development team; for example, most of the code in Windows NT was written by a few individuals working together at Microsoft. But most Windows drivers aren't written by Microsoft. Instead, the burden of writing driver programs usually falls to the hardware vendors: Diamond Multimedia writes drivers for its Viper video boards, Hewlett-Packard (HP) writes drivers for its laser printers, and so on. Programmers working at these companies don't get the same kind of support (in terms of information, resources, and time) that they'd have as IBM or Microsoft employees, and so as a result they can't always write driver programs that are well integrated into an operating system. This is not a slap at programmers at Diamond, Hewlett-Packard, or any other hardware vendor; it's just a reality that the guy on Microsoft's Windows programming team who writes the Calculator code probably plays softball on the same team as the woman who writes the Windows kernel code. And that has to mean that he'll get better answers to sticky programming questions than would someone from outside Microsoft.

Because of the way that drivers work in modern operating systems, they're usually called *virtual* device drivers. In the Windows world, the acronym for that is *VxD*. VxDs are sometimes designed to plug into a particular operating system (which means, for example, that you might not want to waste your time trying to use a Windows 95 VxD under Windows NT, unless you know that the driver will work in both of those operating systems).

The bottom line is that driver programs are often a weak link in an operating system. Windows 98 may run fine for weeks, and then you install a new version of the driver for your ATI Mach 64 video card. You try to enter Print Preview mode from your favorite word processor, and something happens, whether it's an outright lockup or some garbage on the screen. It's most likely to be that new driver.

While this isn't gospel, most operating system designers do much of their initial development on "lowest common denominator" hardware, such as VGA for video. Keep those plain-Jane drivers around and use them when possible as a kind of "known good" baseline configuration.

And a final tip about device drivers: when a new version comes along, *keep the old one around for a while!* "Latest" isn't always "greatest" when it comes to drivers. Do what a friend of mine does, and use the baby food method of testing new drivers. The first time she mentioned this to me, I was puzzled.

"The *baby food* method?" I asked her. (I'm an excellent straight man.)

"Sure," she replied. "When a baby starts eating solid food, you don't know what he's going to be allergic to. So, suppose you want to see if he's allergic to carrots. You start feeding him carrots; if a few days go by and he hasn't swollen up, then carrots are probably okay."

"I do that with device drivers. I just pop 'em into the system, try out all my applications to make sure that none of them break, and then just live with the thing for a week to see if anything new and unpleasant happens to my system. If not, I keep the driver. If I get troubles, then I document the troubles, restore the old device driver, and see if those troubles go away."

Good advice. But I'd add one thing to it. When you swap drivers on a piece of hardware, be sure to power down the system completely before restarting it. Some video drivers in particular don't work quite right unless you shut down the PC and restart after installing them

Another term you'll see turn up when troubleshooting software is *DLL*, short for *dynamic-link library*. A library is a file containing a bunch of small programs that get a particular task done. It's called a library for two reasons: first, there are usually many of those small programs in a particular library, and, second, the library file resembles a library in that it is publicly available; the programs in it are available to any application. For example, the program that tells Windows how to change the color of a part of the screen is almost certainly part of a library.

Now, the way a program finds a library is called *linking*. For most of the history of computer programming, libraries have become linked when a program called the *link editor* makes a copy of the desired library routines and incorporates those routines directly into the program. This is called *static linking*. Static linking is bad because (1) if you are running three programs that all know how to print (for example), then you're wasting RAM because you now have three copies of the print routine resident in memory; and (2) if the way that the OS wants an application to print (to continue the example) changes, then every application would have to be rebuilt.

Operating systems in use since the early '80s incorporate a different kind of linking, called *dynamic linking*. Under dynamic linking, a dynamic-link library is relinked every time the application calls for one of its library routines. Taking the example of printing, a program using static linking gets the whole library program inserted into it. A program linked dynamically to a library contains only a note that says, in essence, "When you need this routine, go out to

PRINT.DLL, load it up, and link the routine before going any further." A DLL can also be shared; once one program has PRINT.DLL in memory, any other program needing PRINT.DLL gets the one copy that's already in memory, rather than loading another one.

What's this got to do with troubleshooting? Well, sometimes an incorrectly installed program may crash, complaining of a lack of a DLL. That may be fixable by simply adding the DLL's directory to a path statement of some kind.

Or the DLL may have been accidentally erased. Or it could have been replaced.

Whenever you click File ➢ Open in Windows 95/98/2000/NT, your program calls up a DLL that contains a routine that knows how to put a File/Open dialog box on the screen. (In Windows, it's called COMMDLG.DLL.) Now and then, I've installed programs that replaced the comes-in-the-Windows-box version of COMMDLG.DLL with their own, "improved" versions.

How do you find out whether you've got a cowbird DLL in the nest? One simple way is to just compare the dates of the *other* DLLs that shipped with the OS to the suspect one. Or, as is more frequently the solution, you can simply reinstall the OS; it often saves more time than poking through DLLs looking for the "pretender."

A number of mysteries can be linked to software that doesn't recover well from disabled or nonexistent hardware. Here are some common problems:

▶ Trying to print to a nonexistent printer.

▶ Trying to print a non-PostScript formatted file to a PostScript printer.

▶ Trying to print to a printer that is offline.

▶ Trying to display graphics data on a monochrome monitor.

▶ Trying to run an old program on a computer that's too fast. Some older programs have copy protection built into them.

Unfortunately, this sometimes means that they won't run on a computer faster than 8- or 16MHz, from the days when PCs were new. These programs are still around even if the PCs they were designed for are mostly long since gone. You may have to try slowing down the system, if you've got a speed setting for your PC.

▶ Trying to run a program that needs more memory than the PC contains.

But here's my favorite hardware-induced software error. The IBM PS/2 insisted on being properly configured before it would do any work for you. If it was configured wrong—it booted up and found that it had more or less memory than it expected, or more or fewer disk drives, or the like—it printed a 162 error on the screen and waited patiently for an F1 to continue. This error typically indicates that the CMOS battery has died and that the user has lost all the PC's configuration information.

If you had an external floppy disk drive on a PS/2, it had its own power supply and power switch. If you forgot to turn on the external floppy before booting up the PS/2, you got the scary-looking 162 error. The solution was to just turn the floppy drive on and reboot. You did *not* rerun the configuration program on the Reference disk: the program would sense (assuming the floppy was still off) that there wasn't an external floppy anymore and stop looking for it. Then, when you *did* turn the external floppy on, the PS/2 wouldn't talk to it. Arggh. (By the way, there were a number of PS/2 motherboards floating around that just plain wouldn't hold a configuration for very long—that's another problem altogether.)

Faulty Software

Sometimes the problem is just plain buggy software. Even the most popular programs can misbehave when faced with a full disk, insufficient memory, or some situation that the designer didn't anticipate or didn't test.

If you experience a problem with software, try to note exactly when the behavior occurs. Perhaps it always fails when trying to save to a network drive, but not to a local hard drive. Or maybe the software always crashes when system resources on the desktop run below 50 percent. Or maybe the software will run on any PC except one with a Cyrix CPU. Any behavior like this that you can reproduce can be very helpful to a team trying to debug a program.

If you've got some experience with software and compiler/decompilers, you can sometimes check out the source code used to design the program and spot where an error might be (such as a wrong command issued).

If necessary, you can try uninstalling the suspect program to see if that sorts things out.

Check External Signs

If the computer has indicator lights, what do they indicate? Are all the lights glowing on the modem? Does the printer indicate "ready"? Is the hard disk squealing or grinding? Does the monitor image look bent? Your drives and other peripherals produce hums, whirrs, and clicks. After a while, these noises become familiar, and any variation in them signals a problem. Pay attention to these signs.

The first step in successful troubleshooting is to isolate the problem component. These signs can point the way.

It is important to document any signs here. Write down what lights are on and off, the positions of switches, etc.

Run Diagnostic Programs

Many PC-type machines come with diagnostic programs that can help pinpoint a problem—assuming, of course, that the computer is functioning well enough to run them in the first place. Other computers, such as some "no-name" clones, do not. Various public domain diagnostic programs exist. (*Public domain* means that the authors have made both their programs and the source code used to design them freely available.)

There are some very good third-party diagnostic programs, and I'm going to talk about them in a few pages.

Truthfully, diagnostic programs are not so valuable in helping to *locate* errors. They mainly make you feel confident that nothing is wrong with the PC. As I suggested earlier, they're of limited value. After all, what must be running in order to run these programs? Well, the system board must be running, the video must be running so you can see the screen, the keyboard must be active to accept commands, and the floppy must be working so the program can load. Merely loading the diagnostic program (or any other program, for that matter) tells you some things about the system. So when I talk to vendors, I question the value (in a nice way, of course) of their software.

An additional bonus of running diagnostics is that they are visually attractive; by that, I don't mean that they're beautiful—but that they look technical as heck. My friend Dave Stang says that if nothing else, running a diagnostic on a customer's machine buys you a few minutes to think about what's actually wrong. Whenever possible, diagnostic programs should be run from write-protected floppies (disks that have the tab on the back set to keep them from being written to) to eliminate viruses as culprits.

Windows Diagnostics

While not specifically for hardware, Windows 98, 98 Second Edition, and Windows 2000 include a set of System Tools (accessed via Start ➢ Programs ➢ Accessories). For example, SCANDISK enables you to perform either a surface or thorough scan of your drives and tries to fix errors it finds. The Tools menu, available when you open the System Information tool, gives you several options, including launching the Dr. Watson logging tool, which keeps track of operations performed and error messages generated; System File Checker, which seeks out missing or damaged essential files and attempts to replace them; and MSCONFIG in Windows 98/98SE, which enables you to set up a troubleshooting bootup mode and select which items you really want to load at Windows startup.

These diagnostics are not available directly within Windows 95 or Windows NT 4. Windows 95 (as well as 98/2000/NT) does include Device Manager, one of the tabs available under the System icon in Control Panel. Although it's not a diagnostic checker, vital information gets reported there that you need to check when you're having a problem. You may see an exclamation mark or red *x* on a device, indicating a device in conflict or disabled entirely. Or you may find a needed device driver not present at all when it should be. Or you may find a note on your hard drive indicating that the drive is running in MS-DOS compatibility mode (meaning Windows feels the drive isn't set to run properly in Windows, so it's running in a slower mode compatible with MS-DOS).

Third-Party Diagnostic Software

In addition to the PC hardware vendors offering diagnostic software, there is also an entire portion of the software business whose major occupation is writing and marketing diagnostic software. The types of software include the following:

Inventory These programs display and inventory what they can detect in your system. That can be useful not as inventory in and of itself; its greater value is in cataloging what the system can *see.* If you know darn well that you installed the mouse interface, but it doesn't show up on the system inventory, then you've got a problem. Before looking *too* hard for the answer, however, ask yourself first: is the driver for the mouse loaded? Diagnostic programs, like DOS and application programs, usually can't detect an unusual piece of hardware unless the driver for that program is loaded.

Burn-in When you first get a computer, it's a good idea to *burn it in.* This means to run it continuously for at least three days, running some kind of diagnostic software over and over again. Some PC manufacturers even offer a burn-in when buying a new PC.

Simple diagnostics are no good for this kind of process for two reasons. First, most simple diagnostics insist on informing you of any errors, then *requiring* you to press a key to acknowledge that you've seen the error message. Higher-quality diagnostic programs allow you to run the diagnostic in a *logging* mode, whereby any error messages are saved to a logging file, and do not require confirmation of an error. Second, good diagnostics let you run the diagnostic in a *continuous* mode, meaning it runs over and over and over until you tell it to stop. Burn-in is an important step, so don't ignore it! Of the last 10 computers I've installed, two didn't fail until after four days of continuous testing. If I'd not done a burn-in on them, I probably would have ended up with a mysterious error appearing at a no-doubt inopportune time (Mr. Murphy and his law seem to have taken up residence in my office).

Interrupt/DMA/input/output address summary As you'll learn in Chapter 6, "Installing New Circuit Boards (without Creating New Problems)," the hardest thing about installing a new circuit board is adjusting some things called the input/output port address, the DMA channel, the IRQ level, and the ROM address. (Don't sweat if you don't know what they are—they're all explained in the next chapter.) The reason that you adjust these settings is to make sure that they don't conflict with the port/DMA/IRQ/ROM of any other boards. For example, if you're putting a board in the system and that board must use either interrupt number 5 or interrupt number 7, but there's already a board in your system that uses interrupt 7, then you can't let the new board use interrupt 7. But the question arises, how do you find out what interrupts are in use on your system? Diagnostic procedures *try* to report this information. I say "try" because they unfortunately can't be trusted in this task, not due to inadequacies on the part of their programmers, but because of a simple fact: there's no way to reliably detect ports, DMAs, IRQs, or ROM addresses. How *do* you find out this information? You can look at the devices in your system by checking System in your Control Panel if you are using Windows 95/98/2000/NT.

Diagnostics A good diagnostic program should provide your hardware a workout. It will test your computer's memory thoroughly, test every possible data pattern on your hard disk, run your serial port at its maximum speed—in short, a good diagnostic program should be a sort of cybernetic boot camp for your computer.

Setup Some of these programs do things associated more with setup responsibilities than diagnostic ones. For example, most of these programs will low-level format a hard disk, an important step in setting up an older type of hard disk. Others may have a built-in system setup program that sets up the CMOS chip in a computer.

If you read these items carefully, you no doubt noticed a lot of "shoulds," as in "a good diagnostic program should . . . ." All this equivocation has a purpose, believe me: most diagnostic programs are junk. Look carefully before you spend the ton of money that you can easily spend on a diagnostic package.

It is said that one time the science fiction author Theodore Sturgeon was approached by a literary critic who said, "Ted, you write such good stuff; why do you waste your time writing science fiction?" Sturgeon asked, "What's wrong with science fiction?" The critic answered, "Ninety percent of science fiction is crap." (Well, he didn't actually say "crap," but this book is rated for general audiences.) Sturgeon is reported to have replied archly, "Ninety percent of *everything* is crap." I'm afraid that this truism, dubbed "Sturgeon's Law" by generations of science fiction fans, applies well to the diagnostics world. Let me then not waste ink beating up on this chaff; let's look at the wheat.

Norton Utilities An old classic from Symantec, with a suite of tools for reporting, diagnosing, and trying to fix various levels of PC problems (not exclusive to hardware).

CheckIt 98 A somewhat useful, inexpensive (compared to most diagnostic programs) package from Touchstone Software. It is inexpensive primarily because it leaves out some of the hardware that you need to do a system checkout. That's not meant as a negative assessment; I like CheckIt and use it quite a bit. But CheckIt does not include a few diagnostic tools, including a loopback plug for the parallel port (allowing you to test communication potential), a loopback plug for the serial port, or a digital diagnostic test disk for the floppy drive My guess as to *why* Touchstone didn't include those things is that they can be found elsewhere, and Touchstone wanted to offer an inexpensive package—adding the extra doodads can double the price. I really like two things about CheckIt: it's got a good set of motherboard checkout routines (DMA, timer, IRQ, and the rest) as well as one of the better memory testers.

First Aid A less robust system fixer and protection tool from Network Associates (formerly a Cybermedia product). It's aimed at the novice user who doesn't want to be bothered with pesky problems. I can't say First Aid has been a favorite, because some of the layers of protection built in to help newer PC users sometimes cause more difficulty when troubleshooting a tough problem. But a change of ownership for the product may mean future improvements.

Nuts & Bolts A utility from Network Associates that has long been an alternative favored by many to Symantec's ever-popular Norton Utilities. Its Discover Pro diagnostic section stands out in the Nuts & Bolts 98 edition.

PC-Technician An industrial-strength package from Windsor Technologies. I first looked at PC-Technician back in 1988, and I must truthfully say that I didn't think much of it then. But it's matured into a decent, general, inventory/setup/deep diagnostic routine. It's a bit pricier than the previous two—$195 when last I checked—but it's a complete package. There are the test disks, the loopbacks, a nice manual, and a carrying case for your tools.

(Just make sure you don't put any magnetic screwdrivers next to the disks in the case!) Windsor also sells a program that will put your PC printer through its paces, as well as a plug-in BIOS POST code. The features that I like best about PC-Technician are the memory test—again, a good one in the same league as CheckIt's—and the serial and parallel tests. All in all, PC-Technician is the best all-in-one tester, but it's pricey.

DisplayMate A utility from Sonera Technologies that checks only one thing—your display. But it does an extremely thorough job, testing aspects of your monitor that you probably didn't know were testable—*pincushioning*, for example. The accompanying manual is a tutorial on monitor problems and solutions. It won't test your memory or your printer, but it deserves a place on your diagnostics shelf.

Lost & Found More of a drive rescue utility that performs some diagnostics on a problem hard drive and then attempts to recover data from the bad drive. Made by PowerQuest (makers of the must-have partitioning program PartitionMagic). Obviously, it won't recover data from a serious crash or from true hardware damage to a drive, but I've seen it grab back most of the data from several dead drives. Look at PowerQuest's SecondChance package for periodically saving information about the current state of the PC as well.

One word of advice when running a diagnostic: although I told you to load all drivers before running the diagnostics, *don't* run your memory manager; it just confuses a memory test. As I've suggested, you can spend a *lot* of money on these programs, so it's a good idea to take advantage of the option that many computer dealers provide today whereby you can buy software and return it within a few weeks if it fails to live up to expectations or doesn't work properly with your PC setup. Better yet, check to see if there's a free 30- or 45-day trial of the program you can download and try, and then buy the full package if it works well for you.

Warning

Some vendors of diagnostic programs promote their software as *rescue* or *crash-prevention* tools, meant to help *prevent* problems with your PC or with Windows. Examples include Network Associates' (formerly Cybermedia's) First Aid and Symantec's Norton CrashGuard. However, many of these programs require you to run them all the time. These programs try to create a buffer, or a shield, between the errors you might make and the machine itself. Although this type of software can keep you from making a fatal mistake, it also may interfere as you troubleshoot PC problems—the software may not allow you to make the changes that you need to make. Over time, you may also find that the rescue program isn't working as effectively—perhaps because it's configured wrong, or perhaps because you overrode it when it suggested you do or not do something. When this happens, whole new sets of problems can crop up that may affect booting your PC, or Windows' proper operation. Thus, using this protection software may leave you needing protection from it. Use judiciously.

Look Under the Hood

Assuming that you've performed steps 1 through 5, you may actually have a circuit board problem. Many circuit board problems can be handled simply and without any fancy equipment. Step 6 just says:

▶ Take the PC apart.

▶ Clean any connectors with an artist's eraser or connector cleaner.

▶ Push all socketed chips back into their sockets.

▶ Reassemble the PC.

As you saw in Chapter 4, "Avoiding Service: Preventative Maintenance," edge connectors get dirty and make circuit boards fail. Sometimes "dead" boards will do the Lazarus trick if you clean their edge connectors.

If you examine most circuit boards, you'll see that most chips are soldered right onto the board. Soldering is a process whereby the chip is bonded to the printed circuits on the board by heating a mixture of tin and lead to the point where it is molten, then allowing the tin/lead mixture to flow over the printed circuit and chip leg, and finally solidify. Soldering is a great technique for mass-producing electronic components. The downside is that when you must fix soldered components, you must *first* de-solder the components. This isn't much fun, and most people don't have soldering skills.

Not all chips are soldered to boards, however. Some are put in *sockets*. A typical board might have 30 soldered chips and 4 socketed ones. Chips are socketed either because they've been voted "most likely to fail," or because the designer wanted to put off a decision until the last minute, or because the chip will likely have to be replaced periodically because it contains software that changes over time—remember ROM? So socketing chips makes our jobs as troubleshooters easier.

On the other hand, heating and cooling of systems make these socketed chips creep out of their sockets. That's why you should push socketed chips back into their sockets when inspecting a board for whatever reason. One particularly persnickety tech that I know takes the socketed chips out of their sockets, cleans their chip legs with connector cleaner, *then* puts the chips back in the sockets.

This should be obvious, but let me point it out anyway: don't push *soldered* chips. The best that it can do is nothing. The worst that it can do is damage a board and maybe a chip. When you push socketed chips back into a board, be sure that you are supporting the *back* of the board. If you just put a board on a table, then push down on the chips, you can end up bending and damaging the board.

I know that this kind of advice—"take it apart, clean the connectors, push the chips back in the sockets, and reassemble"—doesn't sound very dazzling. But, darn it, *it works*! Buying a board to replace a defective one is a pretty rare event for me as a troubleshooter, and I don't do much soldering. And besides, it impresses the people whose machines you're fixing—all they see you do is basically touch the boards. Eventually, you get the reputation as a person who can just "lay hands upon the board . . . and make it *whole!*" (With apologies to the evangelists in the crowd.)

Troubleshooting Tips for an Emergency

There really is a reason why I caution you to stay calm and not do anything desperate when you hit a snag. When people get scared, they do things they wouldn't even think about doing when their minds are more clear. If you lose your cool, you could end up having to fix several problems you created when trying to fix the first one.

Try to remember these considerations when troubleshooting a PC emergency:

▶ Have an emergency kit handy: a good screwdriver, a good flashlight, a boot disk or two, a floppy-based copy of a virus scanner, and diagnostic utilities.

▶ Have your operating system installation CD ready. Many problems—both hardware and software—require you to have the installation CD to reinstall or fix components. This is especially true with Windows operating systems, though not entirely unique to it.

▶ When you see the problem, stop! You need to take a moment to shift gears from working to troubleshooting.

▶ Ask yourself, "What's the last thing I did?" Understanding the steps you just took to get you into the problem can help you identify the steps necessary to get you back out of it.

▶ Do a first analysis of the "damage" before you try to change anything. The first thing you spot wrong might not be the only thing wrong, and you need all the information you can gather to make a smart choice about how to proceed.

▶ If you find yourself getting frustrated, take a break. That doesn't mean have a stiff drink (though you may feel like it), because you need your wits about you when you return to the computer.

▶ When you finally put your hands on the PC to begin correcting the problem, take it one step at a time. Try one procedure and see whether it fixes the problem. If not, undo it, and try the next. Do too many things at once, and you'll start to forget what you tried or what your results were.

▶ If you have another PC available, get on the Internet and use the resources talked about in Chapter 30 to look for help.

▶ Ask yourself why you have no backup system in place (and apologies extended if you're one of the statistical minority who regularly backs up their files . . . or even thinks about doing so until they've lost data they sorely need). Then ask yourself whether the time you're going to waste doing work over again is better than the time you thought you'd waste making a backup. If backups are taking too long, the answer isn't fewer backups, but faster, more capable backup hardware.

Installing New Circuit Boards (without Creating New Problems)

INTRODUCTION

Circuit boards and chips are fairly reliable, as long as you keep them above water and don't subject them to the ol' 110-volt torture test. So most boards that you handle won't be defective. Much more often you'll be doing upgrades to existing machines, like replacing a video board with a faster, more powerful one, adding a sound card, or adding a LAN board to a machine that isn't yet on your company's network.

Putting a new board into your system and making it work involves four steps:

1. **Installation**. Put it in the system and make sure the cables are all on right.

2. **Configuration**. Make sure the board and the rest of the system communicate.

3. **Testing**. Weed out any boards that either don't work or will soon stop working.

4. **Loading and configuring drivers**. Load the software that will help the PC use the hardware.

5. **Testing**. Try out the new device to make sure it works with the drivers.

Getting those five things done will be the focus of this chapter. This chapter begins with a QuickSteps section for those of you impatient for the basic steps of circuit board installation.

Installing a New Circuit Board

Be Prepared

Before you install a new circuit board, make sure you've got the following items on hand:

- Nonmagnetic Phillips screwdriver
- Container to hold removed screws
- Documentation for the new board
- Documentation for the motherboard on which you are installing the circuit board
- Installation disk for the new board

You'll also need to:

- Determine available resources (IRQs, memory addresses, DMA channels) that can be assigned to the device you're installing without causing any conflict.

Also, be sure before installing or removing boards that:

- You are wearing an antistatic wrist strap
- The PC is turned off and unplugged

1. Set any jumpers or switches on the new board to the resources you've already determined as available.

2. Install the board in an available motherboard slot of the correct type.

3. Boot to your operating system and install any setup software that came with the board. Even if the operating system automatically detects the device with Plug and Play, installing the setup software may add more capabilities.

4. Test the board's operation. If it doesn't work, check for resource conflicts.

5. Test all the other devices on your system to make sure installing the new board has not caused a problem with any of them.

6. Document the settings for the new board, as well as any changes you made to existing device settings.

But I Have Plug and Play, So I Don't Have to Worry about This, Right?

For several years now, PC manufacturers have attempted to make our lives easier by designing PCs around a specification called *Plug and Play* (*PnP*). If you have a PC that was built after 1996, it's almost certainly a PnP system. PnP's designers intended for PnP systems to configure themselves automatically, as you no doubt guessed from the name "Plug and Play." You just pop a new board into your system, boot up the computer, and your PC automatically loads the drivers that it needs to use the new board. In seconds, you're using your new hardware.

PnP sometimes *does* work as advertised, but only if your PC meets some fairly specific criteria—the right hardware, the right drivers, and the right operating system. If you *don't* have all those pieces in place, however, you'll find that PnP systems can actually be *harder* to configure than older systems. In fact, let's say that again, with emphasis.

Warning

PnP needs both hardware *and* software. So if you're not running a PnP-compliant operating system such as Windows 95/98/2000, your PC is not PnP, and hardware configuration can still be a real pain no matter *whose* PnP hardware you buy.

Since some folks are running PnP hardware with a non-PnP operating system (like DOS or Windows NT 4), there's a special section later in this chapter, "Making Plug and Play Work," on living with PnP's Dark Side. (In that section, you'll also learn about the "right" hardware, drivers, and operating system you need to make PnP happy.)

Installing boards in a PC of any kind isn't the toughest task in the world, but getting them to work once they're installed is made a bit difficult by a few different things. Some of the stumbling blocks can include bad board documentation (and there's no shortage of that); insufficient information about the computer that you're installing the board into (that's usually *your* fault); address, IRQ, and DMA conflicts, and PnP woes.

Those challenges are what this chapter is all about. You'll learn what all of those things are and what you need to know in order to get new circuit boards into your system and make them work. It's not difficult stuff, but it *does* need some explaining, and I promise that I'll make the whole thing as understandable as possible. As an extra bonus, the knowledge you gain in this chapter about I/O, DMA, IRQ, and the like will give you a head start in troubleshooting other problems you'll learn about later in the book.

Configuring New Circuit Boards

Most circuit boards are fully functional when you take them out of the box. But many of those circuit boards seem not to work when you install them in a PC. Why? The main reason is that the new board may *conflict* with existing boards or, more specifically, with some resource on an existing board.

Put simply, you can't have two boards that claim the same identity in a system. If you were to insert two identical sound cards into the same system, neither one would work, even if both boards were in working order before you put them into the PC.

Configuration consists of:

▶ Assigning resources to the device, avoiding any conflicts with existing devices

▶ Providing software support for the device (through the BIOS and/or device drivers)

On older boards, you specify the resources that the device should use by setting jumpers or DIP switches. Newer PnP boards almost always set resources through the BIOS or operating system.

Depending on the board, your system, and your operating system, you may need to do some (but probably not all) of the following:

- Tell a memory expansion board how much memory is on the board (older boards only)

- Tell a modem which COM port to use (COM1, COM2, COM3, or COM4, or higher)

- Tell a printer port whether it is LPT1, LPT2, or LPT3

- Select DMA channels on a board (more on this later)

- Select IRQ lines on a board (more later)

- Select I/O addresses on a board (ditto)

- Select RAM and/or ROM addresses on a board (still ditto)

- Load a driver for the board and tell the driver what I/O address you want the board to use (again, covered later in this chapter)

In many cases, the board is preconfigured at the factory to settings that will work in your PC, but not always. That's because it's usually impossible for the manufacturer to know what the proper settings should be for I/O addresses, DMA channels, IRQ lines, RAM addresses, and ROM addresses in your particular machine. Some older boards, unfortunately, are "hard-wired" to a particular configuration that you can't change. The inflexible nature of those boards may mean that you won't be able to get them to work in your PC.

Solving Real-Life Configuration Conflicts

What does a hardware conflict *look* like? Here are a few common examples of installation woes.

Scenario 1

You install an internal modem in a PC; the modem refuses to work. Worse, your mouse, which used to work, doesn't work anymore. What do you do?

Scenario 2

You install a sound card in your system and it seems to work pretty well. But now you can't print from inside Windows without crashing. What do you do?

Scenario 3

You're installing an Ethernet local area network card (LAN) in a system, and it doesn't work. So you try an identical one. It doesn't work either. As you watch the *fourth* identical board fail, you begin to suspect a pattern. What's going on?

Scenario 4

You want to install a video capture board into your brand-spanking-new 850MHz PnP Pentium III system, but then you realize that the devices in your system have already used up all the IRQs. You need another IRQ (which I'll define later, but for now just understand it's a scarce thing). You realize that you've got an internal modem in your system that you don't use, and that it takes up an IRQ. So you remove the internal modem, install the video capture board, and fire up your computer. After Windows 98 starts, it tells you that there's no way you can use the video capture board because there are not enough IRQs to accommodate the board. Clearly, Windows 98 is delusional, so how do you medicate it properly?

Each of these problems is caused by *resource conflicts.* Here are some explanations of what caused the problems.

In Scenario 1, all modern computers come with two serial ports, named COM1 and COM2. But internal modems also need a communications (comm) port—in fact, they have serial interface hardware right on them, meaning that when you install an internal modem, you're *also* installing an extra comm port.

Now, that comm port built into the internal modem is probably set up at the factory to act like COM2, but you've already *got* a COM2 on your system. That means that the comm port will conflict with the existing COM2 on your system—and if your mouse isn't working any more, then it's likely that your mouse is a serial mouse on, as you've guessed by now, COM2.

What's the answer? There are two basic approaches. First, you could disable one of the serial ports that came with your PC. The second possibility is to configure the new comm port that's incorporated into the internal modem to be a third comm port (that is, COM3). Basically, you do that by assigning a spare IRQ (trust me, I'll explain IRQs soon) to the comm port. But that can be a problem if you've run out of IRQs (an easy thing to do) or if the communications software that you're running is too dumb to be able to work with anything but good old vanilla COM1 and COM2. That happens *less* with Windows 95/98/2000/NT software than it did with DOS software, but it happens.

Now, I hear you asking, "*How* do I disable one of the comm ports on my computer or assign a 'spare' IRQ to this internal modem?" The answer is the basis of configuration: you move a jumper (see Figure 6.1), move a DIP switch (see Figure 6.2), or run a program to shut off a comm port or assign different resources to it. Whether it's a DIP switch, a jumper, or a program depends on the hardware involved. Most modern systems configure all of the I/O ports in the BIOS, so that's probably where you'll go to change the settings for your built-in COM1 and COM2.

Jumpers tend to be arranged by manufacturers in one of two ways. In the situation above, you see three sets of jumper pins. Moving from left to right, you see a jumper above the three pairs of pins, then conecting the leftmost pair, then connecting the middle pair. This might be interpreted as "jumper leftmost pins – enable BIOS," jumper middle pins – disable BIOS.

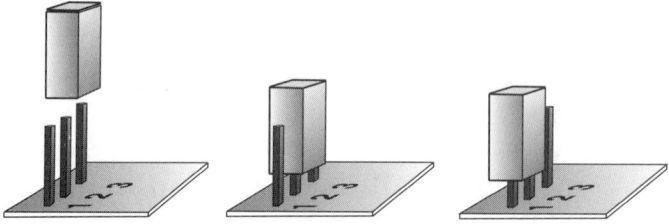

Figure 6.1

Jumpers and how they work

The alternative use of the jumpers is in triples. Here, you select an option by either jumpering pins 1 and 2, or 2 and 3. Above, you see the jumper above the pins, then jumpering pins 2 and 3, and finally jumpering pins 1 and 2. For example, jumpering pins 1 and 2 might mean "enable BIOS" and jumpering 2 and 3 might mean "disable BIOS."

Figure 6.2

Jumper and DIP switches example

Note the symptom in that first example: you installed a new internal modem and, all of a sudden, the mouse stopped working.

Note

Clue to device conflicts: if you've installed a new board and it doesn't work, don't just pull it out. Test the rest of the system with the new board in place. Does something that worked yesterday not work today? That's your clue that (1) the board is probably not broken but is conflicting with something, and (2) you now know what it's conflicting with, so it's easier to track down exactly what you've got to change to make the thing work.

In Scenario 2, the sound card needed something called an interrupt, or *IRQ* (which is an acronym for *interrupt request*). Many sound cards are set to use IRQ7, but IRQ7 is preassigned to the first parallel port, LPT1. Under an operating system like Windows 95/98/2000/NT, you can't build a conflict like this into your system because the OS notices the conflict from the beginning and attempts to correct it during installation. In contrast, DOS and Windows 3.*x* don't worry about interrupt conflicts and will simply fail. The answer? Set the sound card to another interrupt. The answer to "how do I do *that*?" is coming.

In Scenario 3, the Ethernet card has some memory on it (16K), memory that must sit somewhere in the bottom 1024K of memory addresses. When you install the Ethernet card, you tell it where to place that 16K of memory—if you don't tell it where to put the memory, it just uses a default value. If a whole boatload of these cards don't work, then it could be due to one of three things. First, all of your Ethernet cards could be faulty. (It's unlikely, but possible.) Second, it may be that the default location of the memory is the same location that some *other* memory in your system is using; for example, you might have a SCSI host adapter that uses the same memory addresses for its BIOS. In that case, you've just got to find another location for the Ethernet card's memory. Third, if you're using DOS on your system, you may be using a memory manager like EMM386.EXE, and it may have grabbed the same address range for itself. If that happens, then you've got a software conflict rather than a hardware conflict, but it all boils down to the same thing: a nonfunctional board. The answer in that case is to tell the memory manager to stay the heck away from the LAN board's territory with an exclude statement (again, the answer to "how?" is coming). Fourth, if you're running Windows 95/98/2000/NT, then the network card driver may be looking for that 16K window in the wrong place: in actual fact, the board's working fine, it's just the driver software that needs adjustment. You usually adjust drivers in a program called the Control Panel in Windows 95/98/2000/NT.

Scenario 4 illustrates why PnP is sometimes called "Shrug and Pray." (It's also a bit technical, so if you don't follow it now, don't worry, we'll return to this a bit later in the chapter.) You freed up an IRQ by removing the internal modem, which, by the way, was configured to behave as COM2. That freed up the IRQ associated with COM2, which is IRQ4. So why didn't PnP automatically assign the newly freed IRQ4 to the video capture board? Because the PnP system was designed to overlook IRQ4 when searching for IRQs; since all computers have a COM2 (which uses IRQ4 by default), it therefore assumes that IRQ4 must be occupied. How to solve this? Use the Windows Device Manager to force the computer to use IRQ4 for the video capture board. Then reboot, and the video capture board works fine. (I'll explain how to do this later in the chapter, so hang on.)

And, in case you're wondering, yes, all four of these scenarios *are* true stories. Sadly.

Resolving Device Conflicts

The simplest kind of installation problem is a conflict with the I/O ports: COM and LPT. (By the way, *LPT* is an acronym for *Line PrinTer*.)

You are not allowed to have multiple COM ports with the same designation—each port must be uniquely named. For example, you can't have more than one COM1. But you can have a COM1, COM2, COM3, and so on. You can also have an LPT1, LPT2, and LPT3, although this is far less common.

A COM or LPT conflict arises when two boards have the same COM or LPT name. If two boards both want to be COM3, then reconfigure one of them to be COM4. (You wouldn't want either to be COM1 or COM2 unless you had disabled the system's built-in COM ports in BIOS, or you would create yet another conflict.) You can reconfigure a board in one of several ways, depending on how old your machine is.

On Newer Systems: PnP

PnP systems attempt to take software setup a step further by actually eliminating the need for it—in most cases you don't even have to run a setup program. The system detects new hardware every time you boot up your computer, and appropriate drivers are automatically installed. (You may be prompted to insert the Windows CD or a disk that came with the device so that the correct driver can be retrieved.) In the case of a board that wants a COM designation, it automatically picks the next available COM number and claims it for itself. So if COM1 through COM3 are spoken for, the new board automatically becomes COM4.

Tip

By the way, if you are using a PnP board under Windows 95/98/2000 and it won't configure automatically, you may have to remove the board from the system (through Device Manager, I mean, not physically) and let Windows reinstall it for you (hopefully, correctly this time). To do this, right-click My Computer on the desktop and choose Properties from the shortcut menu. This will open a System Properties window. Click on the Device Manager tab. Then find the device that isn't working correctly, select it (by clicking once on it), and then click the Remove button at the bottom of the window. Then close the System Properties window and restart your computer. When your computer reboots, it should reinitialize the device correctly.

On Older Systems

If you've got an older machine, you will need to assign a COM port designation to each device manually, or disable the COM function altogether by doing one of the following:

▶ Alter the position of a jumper, as shown back in Figure 6.1.

▶ Alter the settings of a DIP switch.

▶ Run a program to adjust the board's "soft" switch settings. They operate just like physical switches but are modified via software rather than by physically moving them around.

But this really begs the tougher, more common question: how do you know which switch to move? I'm afraid there's no simple answer here; you've just gotta look at the documentation. People don't seem to believe this; they'll bring me a circuit board and ask me, "What does this do?" while pointing to a jumper. I just shrug my shoulders. There's no way to know without the documentation, so here's one of the best pieces of troubleshooting advice you'll ever get: become a documentation packrat—but more on documentation later.

A Word about DIP Switches

Since we're discussing configuration, here are a few points about DIP switches. There are two basic types, diagrammed in Figure 6.3: the rocker switch and the slide switch.

Figure 6.3

Types of DIP switches   Rocker switch   Slide switch

DIP switches are chip-sized things that contain between 4 and 12 small plastic switches. You'll see them even on some of the most modern PnP compatible systems. In a Perfect World, DIP switches are easy to access and labeled On or Off. Sadly, that's not always true; some say Open or Closed. If they do, just remember that Open = Off and Closed = On. Sometimes they say 1 or 0—1 = On, 0 = Off. Sometimes (grrrr . . .) they don't say anything at all. In this case, play around with them until you figure it out, and then write your findings in your notebook for future reference.

Second, if you have set the switches correctly, but the PC refuses to recognize the settings, be aware that sometimes DIP switches are defective (it's happened to me). To test this, you can remove the system board and test the switches for continuity with an ohmmeter.

Finally, remember that sometimes manufacturers mislabel DIP switches or install them upside down. It *does* happen—rarely, but it happens.

Software Switch Setup Advice

More and more boards are being designed without DIP switches. Such boards are designed to be set up through software provided with them instead or through PnP. Software setup has a good side and a bad side. The good side is that you can change settings on a board (such as making it COM1 rather than COM2) without having to open up the PC and mess with jumpers—you just run a program and you're done. The bad side is that now *you have to keep the setup program disk around forever.* What's that, you say? You're not that organized? You can barely keep track of the software long enough to get the board installed once? Okay, one solution is to get a big envelope and tape it to the side of your computer. Then put all of your setup disks in that envelope so that you'll always have them if you ever need them. Still think you might lose your diskettes? Okay, okay, maybe you don't *have* to keep the diskette around forever, but it's a real good idea since you'll need the software that it contains to reinstall the board again if your system ever fails. You may also want to make a copy of the diskettes or copy their contents to your hard disk in a folder created for that purpose.

So what do you do if you *do* lose the diskette? Your first course of action would be to check the manufacturer's Web site. Almost every board manufacturer maintains a database of the installation software for their boards online. As long as the company is around, you should be able to get the software from there. And, by the way, it might be a good idea to check that site once in a while anyway, since the companies often provide upgraded drivers there, too. Who knows, you might be able to improve your system's performance. For example, U.S. Robotics has a software upgrade for some of their 33.6K modems. All you have to do is download the new software for their 33.6K modem and it becomes a 56K modem! (See Appendix A for U.S. Robotics' contact information.)

Understanding I/O Addresses, DMA, IRQs, RAM, and ROM Addresses

I've been promising to explain those "IRQ" things in detail, and if you made it this far, you've been patiently waiting for me to keep that promise. The time has come, this is the place . . .

When I was a kid, there was a kind of standing joke about Christmas Eve. Parents would buy their kids all kinds of stuff, and the stuff would come in boxes, arranged in a way that no one could ever duplicate: once you took the pieces of the toy out of the box, you'd never be able to repack it the way it came. The really fun part, however, was the incredibly bad documentation that came with the toys. There was, for example, the story about one poor father who, when following the instructions for assembling a new bicycle, wound up building the kids a new swing set out of the parts instead. "Daddy," the son asked, the day after Christmas, "where's my new bicycle?" (I think a couple of comedians in the early '60s made a living parodying these "assembly instructions.")

The folks that made all that toy documentation needed somewhere to go as the years wore on, so they moved to circuit board documentation. They all assume that you understand five pretty important things. Those five things are

I/O addresses—Addresses the circuit board uses to communicate with the CPU.

DMA channels—Used by some devices to speed up I/O to and from the system's memory. A system has only a few DMA channels, so a system is severely limited in how many devices requiring DMA channels it can have installed at once.

IRQs—Hardware components must interrupt the CPU to force it to service them in some time-critical fashion. Each device uses an interrupt request, or IRQ, to get the CPU's attention.

ROM addresses—Many boards include some of their low-level control software in ROM (read-only memory). The ROM requires a memory address, which cannot conflict with other ROMs or any RAM in the system.

RAM buffers—Some add-in cards maintain a little (8K–64K) RAM on board to hold data temporarily. That RAM should not conflict with any other RAM or ROM in your system.

Here's the scoop on these obscure-sounding resources.

I/O Addresses

Stop and think for a minute about how the CPU talks to a piece of hardware such as a serial port, a disk controller, or a keyboard controller. You already know how the CPU talks to one kind of hardware—the memory. You know that the CPU can determine which part of what memory chip it's talking to because each location in memory has its own unique *memory address.*

Other hardware components have addresses as well and, although they're not memory addresses, the computer talks to them in more or less the same way it talks to memory. First, the computer puts the address of the device it wants to talk to on its bus, and then it either reads data from that location or writes data to that location. The address locations that the computer uses to talk to these devices are called *I/O (input/output)* addresses.

There are fewer I/O addresses than there are memory addresses—a lot fewer: any computer built with a 386 or later processor can address 4096MB of RAM or more, but only 64K of I/O addresses. That's not a serious limitation, however, since most of us won't be attaching (for example) a thousand keyboards to a single PC.

I/O addresses allow a CPU to tell its peripherals apart, as you can see in Figure 6.4.

Figure 6.4

Distinguishing peripherals with I/O addresses

The CPU communicates with the RAM using memory addresses. It communicates with other peripherals—a keyboard controller, a serial port with a mouse on it, and an Ethernet LAN card, in this simplified example—via their I/O addresses. The keyboard controller sits at address 64, the serial port at 3F8 (there's an F in the number because it's a hex number, which I'll get to in a minute), and the Ethernet card is at address 300.

What this means is that when the CPU wants to send some data to the Ethernet card, it drops it down the tube labeled 300, rather than the one labeled 3F8 or 64. (There aren't really tubes in a computer, of course; I just like the imagery of the CPU communicating with its minions via old-fashioned pneumatic tubes.)

It's Hex, but There Are No Spells

A quick word on the hex notation: you'll see that both memory addresses and I/O addresses tend to be reported in hexadecimal, an alternative way of writing numbers. There's no especially good reason for this; it's just something that techies prefer. If you've really got to understand the gory details of hex, then take a look at Appendix B, "A Short Overview on Reading Hexadecimal."

Briefly, though, hex is just another way to represent numbers. We're all comfortable with counting in the decimal system—the "normal" way of numbering: 0, 1, 2, 3, 4, 5, 6, 7, 8, 9 . . . but what comes next? Well, we're used to the next number being a 10, which is the first number—0—with a 1 stuck on the front of it. The next one is the next number, 1, except that 1 is still stuck on the front of it to produce 11, and so on.

Decimal has 10 single-character number symbols, which is why it's called "base 10." Hexadecimal is based not on 10, but on 16. Why do we use hexadecimal? Because it's a lot easier for programmers to use than binary (10011011001111011101101010101), which is the way computers actually "think." Anyway, hex starts off with the familiar zero through nine, so it's got the first 10. But after nine comes the letter A—hex uses the letter A to represent its eleventh digit. As you'd imagine, B comes next, and so on to F. You count in hex, then, like so: 0, 1, 2, 3, 4, 5, 6, 7, 8, 9, A, B, C, D, E, F . . . and then 10. See, hex has a 10 just like decimal, but it arrives later, and corresponds to the number 16 in decimal.

For example, suppose I were to tell you that the COM1 serial port uses an address range from 3F8 through 3FF. (I can hear Ford Prefect of *The Hitchhiker's Guide to the Galaxy* answer, "Why? Do you think you're likely to tell me that?") How many addresses does COM1 then take up? Well, you know that 3F8 is its first address. After 3F8 comes 3F9. Just like all the numbers you've ever known, the rightmost digit is the one that changes as the number gets bigger; nine comes after eight, so 3F9 is the next value. You just learned that 9 is followed by A, so the next address would be 3FA, then 3FB, 3FC, 3FD, 3FE, and finally 3FF. Why *finally?* Because the range is from 3F8 through 3FF, so when you get to the 3FF, you stop. Go back and count them up, and you'll see that a serial port uses eight I/O addresses.

What does a serial port do with all of those addresses? Several things. First of all, a serial port can both transmit and receive bytes at the same time. One address holds received data and one holds outgoing data. Of the other addresses, some will be used for status information, such as, "Does the modem have a connection to another modem?" Some will be wasted—because, due to a peculiarity in the PC hardware, it's easier for a circuit designer to take 8 or 16 addresses than the actual number a device requires.

Common I/O Address Uses

That's probably a bit more than you actually wanted to know. What you really need to know about addresses is, "How do you know which ones are currently taken?" Well, you can start off with Table 6.1.

TABLE 6.1 Common I/O Address Uses in PCs

Hex Address Range	User
00–0F	DMA Controller 8237 #1
20–21	Programmable interrupt controller 8259A #1 IRQs 0–7
40–43	Timer 8253
60–63	8255 peripheral controller
60–64	Keyboard controller (8742)
80–8F	DMA page registers
A0–A1	Programmable interrupt controller #2 IRQs 8–15
A0–AF	NMI mask register
C0–DF	8237 DMA controller #2
CF8–CFF	PCI bus I/O port
F0–FF	Math coprocessor (integrated into modern processors but still reserved)
170–177	Secondary hard disk controller, if present (present in most modern systems)
1F0–1F8	Primary hard disk controller
200–20F	Joystick controller
210–217	Expansion chassis
220–22F	FM synthesis interface (WAV device), Sound Blaster default

Continued on next page

TABLE 6.1 Common I/O Address Uses in PCs (continued)

Hex Address Range	User
230–233	Common CD-ROM I/O port
238–23B	Bus mouse
23C–23F	Alternate bus mouse
274–277	ISA PnP I/O Port
278–27F	LPT2
2B0–2DF	EGA (usually *not* used by modern video)
2E8–2EF	COM4 serial port
2F8–2FF	COM2 serial port
300–30F	Ethernet card (common location, not a standard)
320–32F	Hard disk controller (XT only)
330–33F	MIDI port (common location, not a standard)
370–377	Alternative floppy controller address
378–37F	LPT1 printer port
3B0–3BF	Monochrome adapter (also used on modern video)
3BC–3BF	LPT3 (uncommon)
3D0–3DF	Color/graphics adapter (also used on modern video)
3E8–3EF	COM3 serial port
3F0–3F7	Floppy disk controller
3F8–3FF	COM1 serial port
778–77F	LPT1 I/O port

Note

In PnP systems, PCI boards are assigned I/O addresses above 1000. A common I/O address for a PCI network board, for example, might be 1060–107F.

You can also see what I/O addresses are in use in Windows through Device Manager. Double-click Computer in the Device Manager (at the top of the list of devices) and choose Input/Output (I/O) to see which addresses are occupied. You can also view I/O address assignments in System Information (Start ➤ Programs ➤ Accessories ➤ System Tools ➤ System Information) in Windows 98/2000.

Many devices have only one I/O address that they can use. Using the example of COM1 again, part of the very definition of COM1 is that it uses I/O addresses 3F8–3FF. Other devices may allow you to use any of a range of addresses. For example, most sound cards default to address 220 but will allow you to reconfigure them to use some other address if 220 is not available. Reconfigure a COM1 serial port, in contrast, and it's no longer a COM1 serial port.

The key to understanding why this information is important is to know that an assigned address cannot be used by any other device; only one device is used per I/O address. To understand why this is so, I'll steal an old analogy.

I/O Address Conflicts

Think of I/O addresses as being like P.O. boxes. Say the keyboard has P.O. Box 64. When the keyboard has data for the system, it puts the data in Box 64. When the CPU wants to read the keyboard, it looks in Box 64. Box 64 is, in a very real sense, a better definition of the keyboard from the CPU's point of view than the keyboard itself is. If you plug a new device into your system and that device uses I/O address 64, then the new device won't work, and, in addition, the keyboard will cease to work as well—because you can't run two devices off the same I/O address.

Now, in reality, no one's going to design a device that uses address 64, because everyone knows that it's reserved for the keyboard. But what about a case where you have a conflict over an optional address?

For example, I once installed a Sound Blaster 16 on a PC that was already equipped with an Ethernet card and a SCSI host adapter. The Sound Blaster 16 included a circuit called a MIDI interface, and it happened to be set at I/O address 330. Unfortunately, 330 was the I/O address used by the SCSI host adapter, so I got a disk boot failure when I turned my system on. There actually was nothing wrong with the *disk*; it was the disk's host adapter board that couldn't work due to the conflict with the Sound Blaster 16. Checking the documentation, I found that the sound card's MIDI circuit offered either address 330, which it was currently using, or 300. I set the address to 300 (the Sound Blaster 16 uses a jumper to set its MIDI address), reinstalled the board, and had the situation shown in Figure 6.5.

Figure 6.5

Sharing I/O addresses between an Ethernet card and a sound card

Now the CPU's I/O address 300—that particular "post office box"—is shared by the MIDI circuit on the sound card and the Ethernet card. The system didn't complain when I booted up, because my system doesn't need either the sound card or the Ethernet card in order to boot. But when I tried to configure the sound card, it failed. You can see why in Figure 6.6.

Figure 6.6

I/O conflict between an Ethernet card and a sound card

A "play this note" message went into I/O address 300. The Ethernet card has no idea how to respond to this request, and indeed may not be prepared for any requests at all. Worse yet, the electrical signal from the CPU gets split up two ways, so it may not be strong enough to actually get to *either* board.

Why did Creative Labs, the creator of the Sound Blaster 16, build a deliberate conflict into its card? The answer is, they did not. There is no official standard for SCSI host adapter I/O addresses; Adaptec uses 330 for some of their boards, Trantor uses 350, Iomega offers a range from 320 through 350, and I'm sure other SCSI vendors have other options. Ethernet cards *tend* to sit at address 300, but that's not carved in stone. The problem is the lack of standardization. The most common conflicts occur between the types of boards that appeared after the mid-'80s, such as Ethernet cards and sound cards, because there's been no central coordinating force in the PC hardware industry since then.

How did I solve the conflict, by the way? Well, the Adaptec board offered me 330 or 300 as my only choices, as did the sound card. The Ethernet board offered 300, 310, 320, 330, or 340. I didn't want to mess with the Adaptec board, because it was the hard disk interface and if *it* became conflicted, I'd lose access to the hard disk—so I left the SCSI board at 330. That meant that the Sound Blaster 16 had to go to 300. The Ethernet board then played the peacemaker, as I set it to address 310.

More and more, I find that board manufacturers are moving from jumper settings to software settings, but in this case, the SCSI board and the sound card set their addresses with jumpers, and the Ethernet card set its I/O address with software. Which do I prefer? Well, software is, of course, nice. But suppose the sound card came preset to 330, as it did, and required that I run some software in order to get it to switch addresses? That would be a real pain. Think about it: I'd install the sound card at 330 initially, as I had no choice. That would disable my hard disk, requiring that I juggle floppies in order to run the program that would set a different address for the sound card. To add insult to injury, the setup program for the sound card works only after it's installed on the hard disk. I just might decide that getting past *that* gauntlet wouldn't be worth it and scrap the board altogether in favor of a different brand. In contrast, all I *actually* had to do was to move a jumper. So there are pros and cons to both sides.

I've already said this, but let me repeat: you probably won't have a clue which DIP switches do what without the documentation, so be sure to latch onto any switch-setting documentation you've got. Or hope that the company that made the board whose DIP switches you're trying to set still has the switch settings on its Web site.

What would I have done, by the way, if the Ethernet card was set at 300 and wouldn't accept any other addresses? How would you resolve that problem? *You may not be able to resolve all I/O address conflicts*, as not all boards even give you the chance to change I/O addresses.

Note

When working with very old computers, I occasionally run across OEM components (that is, parts that came with the computer when it was originally built) that were designed, as a cost-cutting measure, to work with only one I/O address. Some memory expansion boards were like that in 286-based PCs, as well as some modems. If you find a device like that, the best solution is probably to replace the device if possible with one that offers more flexibility.

Programmed Input/Output (PIO)

Once a hard disk controller gets some data from the hard disk, that data's got to be stored in RAM. The same thing gets done when new data comes in on a local area network card. Big blocks of sound information must be zapped out to a sound card in a smooth, reliable fashion in order for that card to produce pleasant-sounding voice or music sounds. The data originates in the system's memory, and it has got to get to the sound card.

A fundamental problem in computer design is getting data from memory (RAM) to or from a hard disk controller, LAN board, video capture card, sound card, video card—in short, to transfer data between memory and a *peripheral*. (Peripheral is easier to write than LAN card, disk interface, etc., so I'll stick to that from here on in.)

The simplest way to move data between a peripheral and memory is through *programmed input/output,* or *PIO.* With PIO, the CPU sends commands to the peripheral through an I/O address or addresses; let's see how that gets done with a simple example.

Suppose the CPU wants some data stored on one of the disk drives. Data on disks, as you'll learn in the disk section of this book (Chapters 10–17), is organized into sectors, which are blocks of data that can be anywhere from 512 bytes to as long as 32K (actually, 32,768 bytes), depending upon the size and internal data organization of your hard drive. When a PC accesses data from a disk, it can't take it in one- or two-byte chunks; the smallest amount of data that the CPU can ask for is a sector of data (which, once again, can be from hundreds to tens of thousands of bytes long). Suppose the goal for the moment is to get sector 10 from the disk and to put it into RAM. The first step is for the CPU to tell the disk interface to get the data; it does that on I/O address 1F0 on many disk interfaces, as you can see in Figure 6.7.

Figure 6.7

PIO part 1: Requesting data from the disk interface using I/O addresses

The disk interface then responds to the request, pulling all of the data in the selected sector off the disk drive. The interface then tells the CPU that it's ready, and the CPU now has the task of getting the data from the disk interface to the RAM. The CPU begins by requesting the first two bytes of data, as shown in Figure 6.8.

Figure 6.8

PIO part 2: Requesting the first part of the data from the disk controller

The CPU then stuffs that data somewhere in RAM, as you see in Figure 6.9.

Figure 6.9

PIO part 3: Putting the data into RAM

Moving those two bytes takes time, as does figuring out where to put the *next* two bytes. The CPU then requests two more bytes, puts them in RAM, figures out where the next bytes will go, and so on. Will this work? Yes, undoubtedly. Is it fast? Well, not always. Can we make this faster? Certainly, read on.

DMA (Direct Memory Access) Channels

Now, let's take a look at how PC CPUs access floppy disk drives. Suppose I want to read sector 20 from a floppy disk. Things start out very much the same as before, as you can see in Figure 6.10.

Figure 6.10

DMA part 1: Requesting data from the disk controller

The floppy disk controller is at address 1F0, so the CPU sends the initial command out over that address. Ah, but when the floppy disk controller has the data ready, it knows that having the CPU pick up two bytes and put them down and then pick up two more bytes and put them down (and so on) takes time. The idea is to get the data into the RAM, so why not cut out the middleman (as you can see in Figure 6.11)?

Figure 6.11

DMA part 2: Diversion of the CPU by the disk controller

First, there's a diversionary tactic, allowing something other than the CPU to control the bus; then, as you see in Figure 6.12, the data gets delivered to the RAM directly.

Figure 6.12

DMA part 3: Using the DMA channel to put data directly into RAM

Okay, I admit that the floppy disk controller doesn't really distract the CPU; actually, it says to the CPU, "May I have direct access to the memory?" Some of the wires on the bus are DMA request (DREQ) lines and some are DMA acknowledge (DACK) lines. A board requests direct access to the memory bus with a DREQ line, and the CPU responds with a DACK. The idea here is to allow only one peripheral at a time to control the bus. There are multiple DMA request/acknowledge lines, more commonly called DMA channels.

The original PC had a single DMA controller chip, the 8237. It allowed up to four DMA channels, and to this day eight-bit ISA slots have only four DMA channels available, numbered from zero to three, as shown in Table 6.2.

TABLE 6.2 8-Bit ISA DMA Channels

DMA	Default Function
0	Dynamic RAM refresh
1	Available
2	Floppy disk controller
3	Hard disk controller

The original PC used DMA channel 0 for "dynamic memory refresh," and as such, was not associated with a bus slot. Briefly, here's how it worked. There are two kinds of memory: dynamic and static. Dynamic sounds better than static, but it isn't. When you tell static RAM (SRAM) something, it remembers it until you turn off the power or change it. Think of memory as a container of liquid, and static RAM is a ceramic mug. You put water in it, and it stays there. Dynamic RAM (DRAM), on the other hand, is like a water cup made out of a thin sheet of paper; it leaks. Put data into a DRAM and it will forget whatever you tell it within four milliseconds (ms).

As a result, old PCs had to drop everything and do a RAM refresh every 3.86ms. This took 5 clock cycles out of every 72, or about 7 percent of the PC's time. Of course, if the CPU was doing a lot of INs, OUTs, internal calculations, or the like, then you would not notice the slow-down, as the whole idea of DMA is to work in parallel with the CPU. Wouldn't static RAM make a faster computer? Yes, in fact, it would make it much, much faster, but it's also much, much more costly. In more modern PCs, the RAM refresh is handled by a separate circuit. DRAM still needs to be refreshed in modern systems, but the CPU isn't involved, so no DMA is required, and channel 0 is free on most modern PCs.

On those old PCs, the hard disk controller used DMA channel 1, but most modern disk interfaces don't use DMA. Instead, they use PIO, for reasons I'll explain in a minute. As a result, channel 1 is available on modern PCs. The floppy disk controller has employed channel 2 since the old PC days, and it still does, so you should not assign anything else to DMA channel 2. Channel 3 is unused in general.

Any PC built after 1985 will have 16-bit ISA, MCA, EISA, PC Card, PCI, or VESA slots, all of which have *two* DMA controllers, and thus eight DMA channels to the XT's four.

Notice that this implies that you've got only *one* free DMA channel on an old XT-type machine, but seven available DMA channels on most modern PCs—just leave channel 2 for the floppy controller, and you're in good shape. However, in reality, you may not have seven free DMA channels. PCs nowadays often require two DMA channels for the sound card, and many parallel ports can be configured to be an Enhanced Capability Port (ECP), which is basically just a parallel port with, uh, enhanced capabilities—it's bidirectional and faster than the standard parallel port—but ECP needs DMA. Table 6.3 shows the DMA channels on a 16- or 32-bit ISA/PCI system. Of these, all are associated with a bus slot except channel 4, which is a cascade to channels 0–3. As with the 8-bit system, channels 0–3 have 8-bit transfer capabilities, but the added channels, 5–7, are 16-bit.

TABLE 6.3 16/32-Bit DMA Channels

DMA	Default Function	Type
0	Available	8-bit
1	Available	8-bit
2	Floppy disk controller	8-bit
3	Available	8-bit
4	Cascade to first DMA controller	N/A
5	Available	16-bit
6	Available	16-bit
7	Available	16-bit

To DMA or Not to DMA?

You're probably wondering by now what I left out of the story. I just got finished explaining that DMA allows for faster transfers of data between peripherals and memory, and modern machines basically don't use DMA. (You're supposed to go "*huh?*" at this point.)

DMA is pretty nifty, except for one thing. In order to assure backward compatibility, the AT's designers limited DMA operations to 4.77MHz—the original PC's clock speed. Lest you skim over this because it sounds like a history lesson, *ISA bus machines still do DMA at 4.77MHz.* Honest. If you've got a shiny new 850MHz Pentium III system on your desk and you do a DMA operation on it, the whole shootin' match slows down to less than *1 percent* of that 850MHz clock speed. The best the other buses (such as EISA and MCA) do when DMA-ing is 8MHz. Therefore, depending on the device, using DMA with an ISA device may actually slow things down rather than speed them up.

Fortunately, many modern ISA devices give you a choice about whether to DMA or not. Check the documentation—a device may have a jumper that turns DMA on or off, or you may be able to control DMA usage through the device's properties in Windows. You may want to try a device both ways and see which way you get better performance.

Generally speaking, ISA buses are becoming less and less common on new systems. Within a few years, you may be buying new systems with no ISA slots at all, so the question of whether to use DMA with an ISA device may be moot. PCI is the newer bus, and PCI doesn't use DMA at all.

So, in summary, if you have an expansion board that needs a DMA channel:

▶ On old PCs, the only one available is generally DMA channel 3.

▶ If you're installing a 16-bit board, try whenever possible to use the extra 16-bit-only DMAs, channels 4 through 7, so you'll leave room for the 8-bit boards in your system to use channel 3.

▶ Especially if you're out of DMAs, see if the board offers the option to disable DMA. It may be slower, or it may be faster. Try it both ways to see.

You can see common DMA uses in Table 6.4.

TABLE 6.4 Common DMA Channel Uses in the PC Family

Channel	Use
0	Dynamic RAM refresh (XT only)
1	Hard disk controller (XT only), or commonly used by sound cards in AT architecture
2	Floppy controller
3	Unused, but also used on many 16-bit sound cards (they use two DMA channels) or ECP parallel ports
4–7	Available on modern PCs

Bus Mastering

This is a slight digression, but it's important, it fits in here, and I'll keep it short.

You just learned that DMA is a neat idea that is hampered by a historical error—4.77MHz. DMA actually has another problem, although it's not one that is immediately apparent.

DMA can transfer data from a peripheral to RAM, or from RAM to a peripheral, with neither transfer requiring the CPU's intervention. But DMA can't transfer data from a peripheral to a *peripheral*. Such an operation would actually be two DMA operations—peripheral 1 to RAM, followed by RAM to peripheral 2.

Many boards built for the EISA, MCA, or PCI buses can do *bus master transfers*, allowing them to bypass not only the CPU, but RAM as well, transferring data between peripherals at the maximum speed that the bus supports. Bus mastering, then, can speed up a system in two ways. You see this diagrammed in Figure 6.13.

Figure 6.13

Bus mastering

The ISA slots in your system support bus mastering but allow only one bus master board in your ISA system. The PCI slots, in contrast (as well as EISA or MCA slots, if you're working with one of those systems), allow multiple bus masters. It's a feature worth exploiting. But bus mastering is useful for more than just peripheral-to-peripheral transfer; it's also terrific as a replacement for DMA. Designers of PCI-based boards use bus mastering to support fast peripheral-to-RAM transfers that aren't hobbled by the 4.77MHz limitation.

IRQ (Interrupt Request) Levels

In the DMA section, I described PIO. After the CPU made the request of the disk controller for the data, I said, "The disk interface then tells the CPU that it's ready. . ."—which was a trifle sneaky on my part. As far as the CPU is concerned, it initiates all conversations with peripherals; the peripherals "speak when they're spoken to." A peripheral gets the CPU's attention in one of two ways: *polling* or *interrupts.*

Polling

Let's look at how DOS controls a parallel port in order to print data. (Don't worry, we'll get to more modern methods in a minute.) The printer is massively slower than the CPU, so there's got to be some way to handshake the two. Things start off as you see in Figure 6.14.

Figure 6.14

Printing data through the parallel port

Data travels through I/O address 378, the address of LPT1, and is deposited from there into the printer. The CPU then keeps an eye on the printer, as you see in Figure 6.15.

Figure 6.15

The CPU watches the printer

The CPU sits there at the "pneumatic tube" numbered 378, just waiting for the word from the printer, much as someone expecting a letter might run out to the mailbox every 10 minutes. (I'd include the lyrics for that song that goes "Wait a minute, Mr. Postman . . ." but then we'd have to get the copyright permission, and it's too much trouble. You might just want to hum along to get into the polling frame of mind.)

The CPU essentially sits on address 378, asking, "Are you ready now? How about *now*? How about NOW?" It's a big waste of the CPU's time, but this polling method of waiting for an I/O device to finish its work is simple to design. Besides, in a single-tasking world like you see in DOS, the CPU doesn't have anything else to do anyway; it is singly focused on servicing the parallel port. Eventually, as you see in Figure 6.16, the port responds.

Figure 6.16

Response of
the parallel port
to polling

The CPU now sends another byte to the printer, and it begins all over again. As I've said, the process is wasteful but simple, and it works fine in the single-tasking DOS world.

Hardware Interrupts

But what about a multitasking world, such as most of us live in today? And even if you work in single-tasking mode, there are many peripherals on your PC, and the PC can't poll them all. That's why hardware interrupts are built into the PC.

You can see how interrupts work if we look back to the discussion of how the CPU gets data from the disk interface. Recall that the CPU stuffed a "get some data" request down I/O address 1F0. Now, it takes time for the disk to return the desired data. Why not let the CPU use that time to do other things? Take a look at Figure 6.17.

Figure 6.17

The CPU works on
other things while
waiting for the disk
controller.

The disk interface is in its "own private Idaho," as is the CPU. But most modern disk controllers (I'm equivocating because some really high-performance SCSI host adapters don't do this) have a circuit running between themselves and the CPU, a circuit called an *interrupt request* level, or *IRQ* level. The disk interface wakes up the CPU, as you can see in Figure 6.18.

Figure 6.18

Using IRQ levels to get the attention of the CPU

Once the CPU has been interrupted, it knows to start getting the information from the disk controller, as I described in the discussion of PIO a few pages back.

How Interrupts Work

PC interrupts were originally handled by an Intel 8259 prioritized interrupt controller (PIC). Nowadays, though, there's no discrete 8259 on your system; it's just built into the motherboard's chip set. The interrupt controller is *prioritized* in that the interrupt levels it controls are numbered from zero to whatever (depending upon which computer you are using). Lower numbers get higher priority. That means that if interrupt 3 and interrupt 7 both ring at the same time, it's interrupt 3 that gets handled first (*serviced,* in PC hardware lingo).

When an interrupt occurs, the interrupt controller forces the CPU to put its current work "on hold" and immediately execute a program that allows it to handle the interrupt. Such a program is called, appropriately, an *interrupt handler* or an *interrupt service routine.*

For example, in the disk drive example, when IRQ14 occurs, the CPU jumps to a small program that tells it how to grab the data from the disk controller. The computer then stuffs the data into some RAM and returns to whatever it was doing before it was interrupted.

IRQs 2–7 in XTs (A Brief History)

The original PC had only one interrupt controller (the 8259), which had only eight interrupt lines. Interestingly, the 8259 implemented only lines 2 through 7. Lines 0 and 1 weren't even on the bus because they were preassigned. What is now IRQ8 (0 on the first 8259) was attached to a timer circuit that created an interrupt about 18 times per second, and IRQ1 was attached to the 8042 keyboard controller.

Driving the keyboard interface using interrupts is a good idea because the keyboard controller is pretty dumb. It has no memory to speak of, so every time a keystroke arrives at the controller, it must hand off that keystroke to the CPU (which then puts it in the keyboard buffer) before another keystroke comes in. Essentially, once the keyboard controller gets a keystroke, it wants to say to the CPU, "Hey! Stop everything! Come service me *now* before the user presses another key!" And so it "rings the bell"—okay, not really a bell, actually it just activates its interrupt line—and the CPU stops doing whatever it's doing and executes the program that moves the keystroke to the keyboard buffer. If it didn't do this, you would have a lot of dropped keystrokes. You can see a simple block diagram of how the bus, the CPU, and the 8259 interact in Figure 6.19. (I'm showing you how the XT did it because, as you'll see, IBM had to pull a bit of a trick to expand the number of interrupts on the AT, and—surprise!—that trick is still with us today and sometimes causes mischief.)

Someone designing an expansion slot for the XT, then, could build a board to use IRQs 2 through 7; but not IRQ 0 or 1, as there simply weren't any wires running from IRQ 0 or 1 to the XT expansion bus slot connector.

Suppose a floppy disk controller wired to use IRQ6 wanted to interrupt the CPU to get serviced? Simplified a bit, here are the steps it would go through:

1. The floppy controller sends a signal through IRQ6 on the bus.

2. The 8259 receives that signal on its input number 6.

3. The 8259 then looks to see if it is currently getting an interrupt signal from its higher-priority inputs—in other words, is the timer, keyboard, or anything attached to IRQs 2 through 5 demanding the 8259's attention?

4. Assuming there are no higher priority interrupts, the 8259 then taps the CPU on the shoulder with the 8259's one "output" line, which is wired to the CPU's "incoming interrupt" line.

5. The CPU responds by putting a signal on the bus (not pictured) that says, "Okay, I'm willing to be interrupted; which interrupt number is it?"

6. The 8259 then seizes control of the *data* lines on the XT bus and uses them to transfer the value *6*, the interrupt number.

7. The CPU has a table of places where it keeps software to deal with different interrupts. There's a place there for servicing IRQ6, the floppy controller, so the CPU jumps to that location and executes that program, called the "floppy interrupt service routine."

8. Satisfied that its work is done for the moment, the 8259 resets the IRQ6 input line and is ready for the next interrupt.

Choosing IRQs

Eight IRQ lines with two preallocated for the timer and keyboard made configuring XTs a bit tricky, so PCs since the AT have all been equipped with a second 8259, bringing the total of interrupts on most PCs up to 16. *How* they added that 8259 is another story, one I'll tell you in a minute. Before I do that, however, let's take a look at which IRQs are usually free or taken; you can see the common uses for IRQs in Table 6.5.

TABLE 6.5 Common IRQ Uses in the PC Family

Interrupt Line	Device	Comments
0	Timer	Not accessible by peripherals.
1	Keyboard	Not accessible by peripherals.
2	Cascade to IRQs 8–15	Used by second 8259 to signal interrupts; not available except on XTs.
3	COM2	Can also be COM4, but only one of the two.
4	COM1	Can also be COM3, but only one of the two.
5	XT hard disk controller, LPT2	Free on most PCs. Hard disk interface used only on XTs, or alternatively for LPT2 on the unusual machine with LPT2.
6	Floppy disk controller	
7	LPT1	
8	Clock	Not accessible by peripherals.
9		Generally available but can be confused with IRQ2; see text.
10		Generally available.
11		Generally available.
12	PS/2-type mouse port	If your PC/laptop has a built-in mouse port with a small circular connector, that port probably uses IRQ12.
13	Coprocessor	Interrupt required even for modern processors with integrated numeric coprocessors.
14	Primary hard disk interface	Taken in virtually all machines as the "primary PCI EIDE interface."
15	Secondary disk interface	Taken on most post-486 systems as the "secondary PCI EIDE interface."

If you're installing a board and need an IRQ, your best bet is to first look to IRQs 9, 10, 11, or 5, in that order (it's the order of descending priority, as you'll see in a minute). If they're not available, consider disabling your parallel port, if you're not using it, to recover IRQ7, or perhaps one of your COM ports if it's idle. If you're *still* in need, and you have only one hard disk and one CD-ROM drive, then you might ensure that the hard drive and CD-ROM are both on the primary EIDE interface (you'll read more about that in Chapter 16, "Care and Feeding of Hard Drives" in the section "Recovering Data and Fixing Hard Disks") and then disable the secondary EIDE interface, freeing up IRQ15. Be aware, however, that it can be a pain to consolidate a drive and a CD-ROM on the same interface if they're not already set up that way (you might need to set jumpers on one or both devices, for example), *and* not all systems even *allow* you to disable the secondary interface.

If you're configuring an XT (in a museum, perhaps?), then your best bet for a free IRQ is either 2 or perhaps 7, but 7 is available only if you disable or remove your parallel port. And if you're configuring an eight-bit card in a modern system, the card can use only IRQs 0 through 7. Typically, eight-bit cards can use only IRQ5, because IRQ2 is not available.

Whatever you set your boards to, *write it down*! You'll need the information later.

Earlier, I suggested taping an envelope to the side of a PC and keeping important floppies there. Here are some other things to put in there. Each time I install a board (or modify an existing board), I get a new piece of paper and write down all the configuration information for the board. For example, I might note, "Intel EtherExpress 16 card installed 10 July 1999 by Mark Minasi; no EPROM on board, shared memory disabled, IRQ10 used, I/O address 310 set."

I hesitate to mention this, but you can sometimes solve device conflicts by doing surgery on the boards. Just lobotomize the chips that are performing the function that you wish to defeat. An example that I have seen a couple of times is with serial ports. A client wanted me to set up a multifunction board in a PC with clock, memory, printer, and serial ports. He already had a board installed that provided both serial ports COM1 and COM2. The jumpers on the multifunction board allowed me to set the multifunction board's serial port to either COM1 or COM2 but not to disable it altogether. What to do? A chip called the 8250 UART (Universal Asynchronous Receiver/Transmitter) is the heart of most serial ports. I found the 8250 on the multifunction board and removed it. The problem was eliminated. *Please don't try this unless you understand what you are doing.*

IRQs 2 and 9: XT Problems That Live to This Day

Take a look at Table 6.5 and you'll notice that IRQ2 is not available in post-1984 PCs, but it is available on XTs. Why did those old dinosaurs have an IRQ we don't have? Recall that I said earlier that IBM had to do some fancy designing to add more IRQs to their AT. Unfortunately, that designing built a few quirks into the AT's IRQ structure—and every PC since has been designed in the same way, even your new 850MHz Pentium III system.

Recall that the PC/XT systems had a single interrupt controller, an Intel 8259 chip. The 8259 could support up to eight interrupt channels, and the original PC/XT systems hardwired channels 0 and 1 to the system timer (a clock circuit that goes "tick" every 55 milliseconds) and the 8042 keyboard controller.

The system was wired with those interrupts because IBM wanted to make sure that the keyboard and the timer had high priorities; recall that on an 8259, when two interrupts occur at the same time, the one with the lower number gets priority.

In 1984, the first 16-bit PC-compatible system was released—the IBM AT. The proliferation of add-in devices on the market made it clear that eight interrupt levels just weren't enough. So, how to add another 8259? Just slapping the extra 8259 onto the motherboard might present some backward compatibility problems, so IBM decided to kind of slip the extra 8259 in "through the back door," as you can see in Figure 6.19.

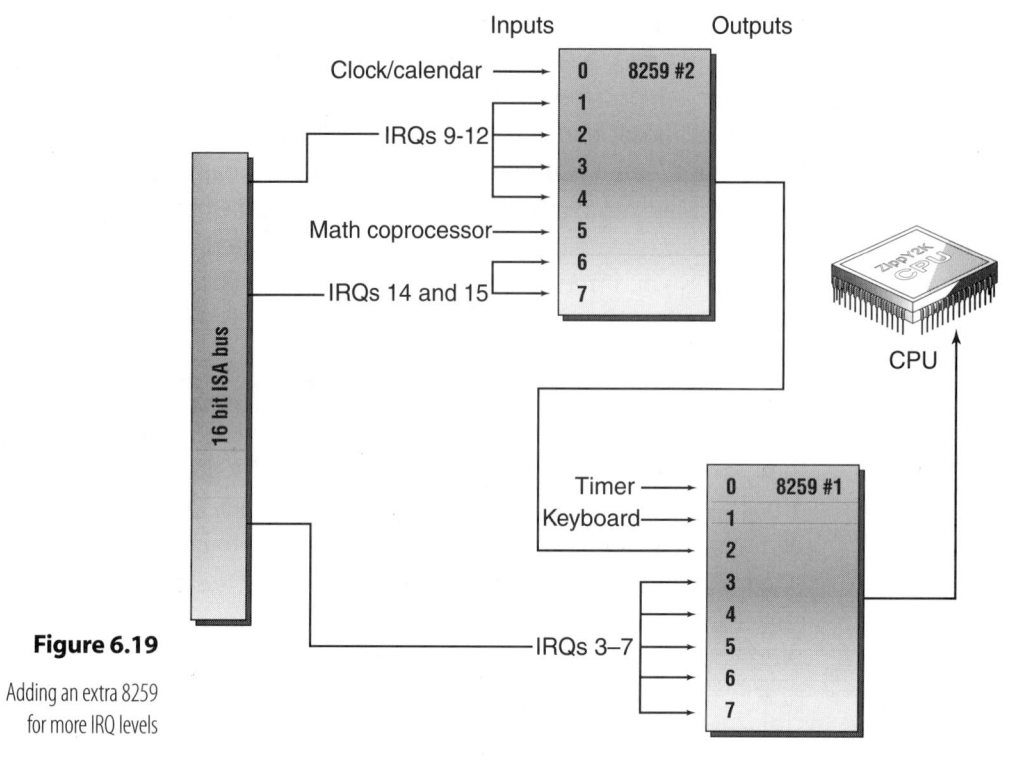

Figure 6.19

Adding an extra 8259
for more IRQ levels

First, IBM added another 8259 and used its eight inputs to create IRQs 8 through 15. Just as the old 8259 had two IRQs that never showed up on the system bus (0 and 1), so also the new 8259 had two IRQs that the system bus didn't see: IRQ8 supported the clock/calendar, and IRQ13 supported the math coprocessor chip. But how to let the CPU know when one of the second 8259's IRQs fired? By *cascading* the 8259s: the second 8259's output—its way of saying, "Hey, I've got an interrupt!"—was connected as one of the *inputs* of the first 8259, IRQ2, in fact.

Note

So, if an IRQ between 8 and 15 triggers, the second 8259 activates its output line. That shows up in the first 8259 as an IRQ2. The first 8259 tells the CPU, "I've got an interrupt for you," and the CPU of course asks, "Which IRQ?" When the 8259 replies, "IRQ2," the CPU knows that *really* means that it's now got to go to the second 8259 and say, "I hear from the first 8259 that you've got an interrupt. Which line is it?" The second 8259 replies and the CPU services the second 8259's interrupt. Incidentally, all this talk about IRQs will become unimportant in the years to come, when ISA buses are no longer part of the average new PC. The PCI bus, when unencumbered by ISA, does not require each device to have its own IRQ, so this entire system will be going away when PC makers stop putting the ISA bus in their systems. In the interim, PCI buses can do a limited amount of IRQ sharing, if the operating system supports it; see "IRQ Sharing in PCI Systems" later in this chapter.

But now notice that IRQ2 is dedicated, as were IRQs 0 and 1 before. There would be no point in leaving IRQ2 available on the ISA bus, so IBM removed the wires on the motherboard connecting the first 8259's input number 2 and the pin on the ISA bus connectors. But, they reasoned, why waste that pin—so they recycled that bus pin, giving it to the newly created IRQ9. That's fine, in general, except for one thing—if you put an old 8-bit ISA board into a 16-bit ISA slot, the 8-bit board will think that pin is IRQ2, as was the case in the 8-bit ISA days. Even the jumpers on the 8-bit board will tell you that you're using IRQ2, but you're not—you're using IRQ9. And, generally, software drivers written to go with 8-bit boards don't understand the IRQ 2/9 confusion and don't even *give* you the option to choose IRQ9. What to do? Well, avoid IRQ2 on non-XT systems if you can; if you can't, then play around with the driver and jumper settings. In some cases, lying to the board and/or driver ("Sure, you're IRQ2, trust me") will make it work. The best answer? Get those ancient 8-bit cards out of your system!

And here's one more thought about how this cascaded 8259 structure affects IRQs: priorities. In the vast majority of cases, you don't really care which IRQ you assign a board to, so long as the board has an IRQ. But sometimes you'll see two boards that won't work together—the system works with either one but not with both—even though they've got different IRQs. In that case, try swapping the IRQ levels. If that fixes it, then the problem was priorities.

But what is the order of priorities in IRQs? Well, you read earlier that back in the eight-bit XT days, IRQ 0 had the highest priority, IRQ7 the lowest. But since IRQs 8 through 15 snuck in through IRQ2, the priorities go from highest to lowest like so: 0, 1, 8, 9, 10, 11, 12, 13, 14, 15, 3, 4, 5, 6, 7.

So You Want a Third COM Port?

PCs were originally designed to support two RS-232 ports, which got the system names COM1 and COM2. But serial ports are so darn useful that many people find they need a third one—for example, on one of my PCs, I need a serial port for the mouse, another for my digital camera, one for my Palm Pilot, and a fourth for an external infrared port.

If the PC was designed to support just two COM ports, how can you have more than two? By going *outside* of the basic PC design. You can add as many COM ports as you like beyond the first two, but the system treats them like any other "unusual" device—a network card, a SCSI board, or the like. What I mean is: whether you're running DOS or Windows 95/98/2000/NT, you don't need to load any drivers to configure your operating system to support things like a standard keyboard, LPT1, COM1, COM2, a floppy drive, or a hard disk. That's because those pieces of hardware are part of the "basic PC," so to speak. But add a network card, a sound card, or something else, and you take the PC beyond the bare minimum, requiring that you load drivers for the "unusual" hardware and perhaps configure those drivers. COM3 and beyond fall into the "unusual" category of hardware.

That means you'll need to do some more configuration to make a third or higher COM port work. Each COM port needs an IRQ, so be sure you've got one free before trying to install an extra COM port. It also needs a range of I/O addresses, but there are usually enough of those around. Then you've got to get the operating system to play ball with your new port.

If you're running Windows 95/98/2000, they do a pretty good job of detecting extra COM ports automatically. But if they don't, use the Control Panel to tell Windows that you've got a COM port. Open the System applet and choose Device Manager ➤ Ports (COM and LPT), then choose the particular port and click on Properties. Click the Resources tab and uncheck Use Automatic Settings. You can then tell Windows 95/98/2000 what I/O address and IRQ your serial port is using.

Windows 3.1 also has a Control Panel, but in it, you should open the Ports dialog box and choose Advanced. There you'll find the dialog box to tell Windows 3.1 what resources the serial port uses. Windows NT 4's Control Panel works similarly.

IRQ Sharing in PCI Systems

Most modern systems today are PCI-based, and such systems can usually share a single IRQ among multiple PCI devices. For example, on my current system, IRQ11 is used for my PCI Ethernet card, my PCI sound card, and my PCI video card. PnP can set up this sharing automatically in Windows (95B/98/2000) and will report "no conflicts" even though several devices are using the same IRQ. And it's true—there are "no conflicts"—because the devices share it peacefully without any infighting for control. Such is the beauty of PCI. On a non-PnP operating system, you must check the documentation for each device to find out whether it supports IRQ sharing and go through a trial-and-error process to see which PCI devices will share with which others.

Some CMOS setup programs (which I'll talk about later in this chapter in "PC Setup Memory: The CMOS Chip") have an option that enables or disables PCI IRQ sharing (sometimes called "steering"). I usually leave this turned on unless I'm experiencing problems with the sharing, as it makes the whole IRQ situation a lot easier to deal with.

For techies only, here's a behind-the-scenes look at how IRQ sharing works. Almost all PCI devices share a single IRQ called INTA#. (There are three other PCI interrupts, INTB# through INTD#, but these are not used except by PCI devices that require multiple IRQs.) However, the PCI interrupts must be mapped by the BIOS to ISA interrupts in an ISA system. And since ISA interrupts aren't sharable, each PCI device must be mapped to a unique ISA interrupt, so you're back where you started from—out of IRQs. When you turn on PCI IRQ sharing in the BIOS, though, it passes the interrupt assignment duty to the operating system, which (if it is capable of it) can map multiple PCI devices to a single ISA IRQ. Windows 95B (OSR2, a later OEM release), Windows 98, and Windows 2000 all support PCI IRQ sharing; the original version of Windows 95 and Windows 95A do not.

ROM Addresses and RAM Buffers

In addition to I/O addresses, DMA channels, and IRQ lines, there is a fourth source of potential conflict: ROM addresses. Some adapter boards require some ROM onboard to hold some low-level code; the most common examples are SCSI host adapters, video adapters, and some network cards.

Onboard ROM makes sense on some adapters. For example, the SCSI host adapters that I use the most are from Adaptec, and most of those have ROM on them. A program stored in that ROM causes any computer equipped with the Adaptec adapter to show a message like "Press Ctrl+A to enter SCSI diagnostics" at startup. The diagnostics are a very useful set of utilities that you can access even if your hard disk isn't working (which is a good possibility, if you're installing a new SCSI adapter).

Other boards have some RAM onboard to provide memory that is *shared* between the system CPU and the adapter's circuitry. But RAM and ROM can present a configuration problem because, as before, a possibility exists that two different boards may require some software onboard, and if the two boards *both* try to locate their ROM or

RAM at the same location in the PC's memory address space, neither one will work.

Some boards let you configure the start address of the ROM/RAM (through DIP switches, jumpers, or software). However, most of the major boards that include ROM/RAM, such as the EGA, VGA, XT-type hard disk controller, and the like, should *not* have their ROM addresses changed (if it's even possible). Too many pieces of software rely on their standard addresses. The boards you'll see that typically have ROM include the following:

- Video boards, which have ROM addressed at either address C0000 (yes, more hexadecimal; memory addresses are, like I/O addresses, expressed in hex) or E0000. It's usually not a good idea to move these addresses around.

- High-performance disk interfaces, like some special EIDE host adapters or SCSI host adapters, have ROM on them, but those ROM can be safely moved if the board permits.

- Token Ring network adapters have some ROM on them; it is moveable.

- Any kind of LAN board can have ROM on it, if the PC boots from the network and not from its local hard disk. It's unusual, but some companies use this "diskless workstation" approach. Some have RAM as well.

- Some high-end sound cards may have ROM on them; the ROM contains images of prerecorded sounds, like pianos, violins, or flutes.

- All PCs have some ROM at the top 64K of the first megabyte, the memory range from F0000 through FFFFF. That ROM is called the BIOS ROM. (BIOS stands for Basic Input/Output System, as you read in Chapter 1, "Five Easy Pieces: PC Hardware in a Nutshell.")

There are two things to be concerned about when configuring memory on add-in cards. First is the obvious one: make sure that two different boards don't have memory configured to the same address.

The second thing you have to be concerned about is the effect of adapter memory on your DOS memory manager, if you're using DOS. Memory managers must know exactly which areas of memory are already filled up with adapter RAM or ROM, or the memory manager will overwrite the RAM or ROM, potentially causing lots of system problems.

Most adapter RAM and ROM ranges vary, so I can't document them for you here, but you can see the ranges that don't change in Table 6.6.

TABLE 6.6 Common ROM and RAM Buffer Addresses

Function	Address Range (Hex)	Address Length
XT hard disk controller	C8000–CBFFF	16K
EGA	C0000–C3FFF	16K
VGA	C0000–C7FFF or E0000–E7FFF	32K

Another set of heavy users of onboard RAM is PC Card boards, which brings us to our next topic.

Configuring PC Card Boards

If you've got a laptop, it's probably got at least one expansion slot designed to support a credit-card sized adapter card called a PC Card or, formerly, a PCMCIA. There are PC Card-format modems, network cards, hard disks, Global Positioning System sensors, memory cards, SCSI adapters, and sound cards, just to name a few. Under some circumstances, PC Cards offer no trouble—but in others you may have to struggle with them a bit.

PC Card Is Often PnP

In theory, PC Card boards are PnP in that they set up their own interrupts, memory, and so on. The idea is that any system using PC Cards should have some software called a *card services manager* that examines the cards in the system and sets their resources appropriately, making sure that no IRQs, I/O addresses, or memory addresses conflict. (DMA is not a problem because PC Cards can't use DMA.)

Of the popular operating systems available, Windows 95/98/2000 handle PC Cards the best because they have a built-in card services management program. Windows 3.*x* has no native PC Card support, but some PC Cards come with Windows 3.1 software that will function as a card services manager, achieving essentially the same effect.

Using a PC Card without Card Services

People running DOS on laptops without a card services manager and people running Windows NT 4 or lower on laptops will have a tougher time configuring software to use the PC Cards. Let's see how you configure a PC Card in a system that lacks a card services manager.

First, install the PC Card into the laptop; let's say for example that it's a network card. Then turn the laptop on and boot up the operating system, whether it's DOS or Windows NT. Next, load the driver for the network card. The driver's installation program will need to configure the driver, and it will ask you about the card—what IRQ is it using, what I/O address, and so on. Here's the hard part: *you have no idea what the answer is.* And the board ain't talking, at least not usually. You see, in the case where a PC Card powers up and there's no card services manager, the PC Card just picks its own resource values. That's the bad news, but it's not terrible news, as these boards are usually designed to default to some set of IRQ, I/O address, and so on.

The good news is that because the driver for the PC Card was written by the same folks who made the board, the driver usually *also* defaults to the same set of IRQ, I/O address, and the like as the board. So if you pop a PC Card into a laptop with no other PC Cards, chances are that (1) the PC Card's defaults will work just fine, and (2) when you're installing the driver, you should just take the defaults. The card will then usually work. So even if you're working with a dumb operating system (one that isn't all that bright about PC Cards), a single PC Card in a system will usually work fine. If it doesn't, just be prepared to wait on hold with the PC Card's manufacturer.

Some PC Cards Make Life Easier

Some cards work better than that, however. Given the choice, I buy 3Com's PC Card Ethernet boards when purchasing network cards for my laptop because they come with a traditional software setup program. This program lets me set the PC Card Ethernet board to whatever I/O address and IRQ that I want, and the board *stays* at that I/O and IRQ. It's way cool and I wish all PC Card manufacturers did this, as it makes setting up a Windows NT laptop leagues easier.

The 3Com cards aren't perfect, however. Recently I tried to install two 3Com 10/100 Ethernet cards in the same laptop because I wanted to use the laptop as an Internet router (it *can* be done and it actually works quite well, in case you're wondering, but it requires NT Server or a third-party router program), but the 3Com setup program was unable to address two cards in the same laptop. This surprised me, because I'd installed multiple 3Com network interface cards (NICs) in a number of desktop systems, so I called 3Com tech support. The fellow on the phone laughed and admitted that no, the setup program couldn't distinguish multiple PC Cards in a single machine, but that they didn't get too many calls for that. I had no choice but to install a 3Com card and a Xircom card in the system. The Xircom brand is a bit more of a pain to install—you can't preset IRQs and such for Windows NT installation—but with the help of Xircom tech support, I got them both working.

Handling Multiple PC Cards

But what about a system with multiple PC Cards? Again, in Windows 95/98/2000 you probably won't have a problem, as the integrated card services manager handles the conflicts if it can. But in a DOS environment without a card services manager, or in Windows NT 4 and lower, you may see a situation wherein two PC Cards clobber each other. You can easily test this: try the system with just the first card. If that works, pull out that card and insert just the second card. If *that* works, but they don't work together, then they're conflicting. What do you do about this?

Well, if one of the PC Cards is a well-designed one like the 3Com cards I mentioned a couple of paragraphs back, it's simple—just run the lame PC Card all by itself and note which IRQ, I/O, and possibly which memory it uses. Then pull that card out and insert the well-designed one, the one that lets you configure it. Set its resources to give the lame PC Card's desired resources a wide berth, and all will be well. And remember that whenever you configure a card to use particular resources, *write it down*. Put a mailing label on the PC Card and note what I/O, IRQ, and memory you set the card to.

Resolving Installation Conflicts: An Example

Ready for a real-world scenario? A few years ago, I needed to put some Ethernet cards into a half-dozen PCs. Each PC was different and had different add-on boards installed in it.

The first LAN card I installed was in a DOS-based PC with Windows 3.1. The Ethernet board I was installing used everything we've discussed—an I/O address range, a DMA channel, an IRQ channel, and some shared RAM. I left the I/O address at 300 hex, as that wouldn't conflict with the computer into which I was installing the board. The IRQ I chose was IRQ5, avoiding the more commonly used IRQ2. (I avoid IRQ2 because although it *can* be used in some systems, the fact that it cascades to IRQs 8 through 15 makes me a bit nervous; in the past, using IRQ2 had caused conflicts with Windows.) I set the DMA to channel 1 and put the shared RAM between CC000 and CFFFF, as I knew that it would not then conflict with the hard disk controller ROM between C8000 and CBFFF.

When I plugged the board in, however, it refused to function. A little fiddling around made me realize that the DOS memory manager I was using was placing its memory at the same addresses as the shared memory on my LAN board, which in turn was clobbering the LAN board. I told the memory manager to exclude the range of addresses from CC000 to CFFFF (consult your memory manager's documentation to see exactly how to do this). The board worked fine after that.

I set the second board identically in another DOS/Win3.1 PC with the same memory management software installed, and it refused to work. A quick check of my notebook reminded me that this PC had a sound card that was using IRQ5, which caused the conflict. The LAN board offered only IRQs 2 through 7, and I didn't want to use any of them—I wanted to avoid 2 if I could, and 3 through 7 were busy—so I needed an alternative approach. A quick look at the sound card showed that it could support any IRQ up to IRQ10, so I reset the sound card to IRQ10, leaving IRQ5 free for the LAN board. Problem solved.

A third PC was a Plug-and-Play system running Windows 95. I didn't worry too much about this one, because I figured that when Windows started up, PnP would kick in and reassign the sound card's resources. However, as it happened, this PC had a SCSI hard drive that also wanted to use IRQ5, so when I turned it on, the LAN board and the hard drive battled it out and neither one of them worked at all. I fixed it by removing the LAN board and rebooting, entering the SCSI drive's setup program and changing its IRQ assignment. Then I put the LAN board back in and things went smoothly.

I thought the fourth PC might be a challenge because it had all kinds of stuff installed—a sound card, a DVD drive, a CD-RW, a scanner, a printer, an internal modem—the works. A quick check in Windows 98 told me that all the IRQs were taken. So where was the LAN card supposed to go? I took a chance by installing it and booting up the system and, amazingly enough, Windows' PnP feature set it up flawlessly. Because it was a PCI system, several PCI devices were able to share a single IRQ, making room for the new device.

Still another PC was running Windows NT 4. I knew that I couldn't rely on PnP, since NT 4 doesn't support it. I started by checking out the current resource assignments in NT so I could avoid choosing resources for the new LAN board that were already in use. I did pretty well, and the LAN board installed and worked, but the user called me the next day to report that his ISDN terminal adapter was no longer working. Upon examination, I found an I/O address conflict between the two—and found that the terminal adapter had its own setup software that needed to be run to change its resource assignments. Of course, as luck would have it, the user had no idea where that software was, so I downloaded the latest version of it from the manufacturer's Web site. I ran the ISDN terminal adapter's setup program, made a change to its I/O address, and everything worked great.

I don't want to discourage you with these stories. I just want to underscore how important it is to keep documentation of what's installed in your current machines, keep the setup disks handy for every installed device, and be aware of the differences between PnP and non-PnP systems.

Where Do You Find Diagnostic Programs?

In Chapter 5, "Troubleshooting PC Problems," I mentioned the names of several generic diagnostic programs, like the Norton Utilities or Windsor's PC-Technician. You can use those to test a board like, say, a motherboard, or a memory board. They're perfectly good for that. But don't do what some folks I've seen do. I know of a group who bought a lot of PS/2s. They loaded up the Reference Diskette that came with the PS/2, told the diagnostics to run over and over, and left the machine. Hours later, they came back to see if there were any errors reported on the screen. No errors, so they shipped the machine to users. But users complained that a lot of machines had malfunctioning video. It turned out that the VGAs on Model 50s had a higher-than-average failure rate: I myself saw a classroom with 30 Model 50s develop video problems in about 20 percent of the machines. (If you have this problem, you might like to know that it seemed most prevalent when the room was above 75 to 80 degrees F. Maybe you could turn up the air conditioning.) The support staff was puzzled. How did this slip by them? Simple. Video diagnostics often require a user to look them over. If your reds are greens and blues are blacks, the monitor doesn't know. The video board doesn't know. You need an operator to audit the video tests.

Here's a cheap memory test. Build a spreadsheet that fills memory. It just consists of a single cell A1 with the value 1, then a cell A2 with the formula A1+1. Copy that cell until you run out of memory. Set Recalculation to Manual. Then write a short macro that loops continuously, recalculating, and recalculating again. If you really want to add a level of elegance, calculate the sum of this large column of numbers, and check it against the actual value. (The sum of 1, 2, 3, 4 . . . N is equal to N(N+1)/2.)

If your board includes its own diagnostic testing programs, you should use them instead of the generic testing software, since they will be more likely to test the board more thoroughly. For example, Iomega supplies an RCDDIAG program that tests the controller. Alternatively, you can test a LAN board by putting a loopback connector of some kind on it to allow it to "hear" what it broadcasts.

Note

Windows comes with a System Configuration Utility that can help in disabling conflicting drivers and startup programs. You can run it from within System Information by choosing Tools ➤ System Configuration Utility (Windows 98 and later) or running the program Msconfig.exe from the `C:\Windows\System` folder.

Making Plug and Play Work

All of this fiddling-with-jumpers and rooting-around-for-setup-programs gets old quick.

I mean, *really* quick.

In a Perfect World, you'd just insert a board into your system, turn the system on, and the system would configure itself automatically, no muss, fuss, or greasy aftertaste. It would work something like this:

1. On bootup, the BIOS would recognize the board ("This is an Adaptec 2942W SCSI host adapter").

2. The BIOS would then ask the board what IRQs, DMAs, I/O addresses, RAM addresses, and ROM addresses it needs ("It requires an interrupt, a 256-byte block of I/O addresses, and a 16K ROM range").

3. *Then* the BIOS would ask the board what range of IRQs, DMAs, I/O addresses, RAM addresses, and ROM addresses it *can* use ("It can use IRQ 5, 7, 9, 10, 11, or 14, any 256-byte block from address 60K to 64K, and any ROM address from C0000 to E0000").

4. After that, the BIOS would set the resources (IRQ, and so on) so that they don't conflict with anything already in the system.

5. Once the board—and all others—was coexisting nicely, the operating system for the PC would load.

6. Early on, the operating system would note the existence of the new board and say, "Hey, this is an Adaptec 2940W, let's load a driver for it . . . ah, here it is, in D:\WINDRIVERS . . . ask the BIOS what IRQs and such it set the board to . . . configure the driver . . . done!" And the new board works like a charm.

Sounds cool, doesn't it? I mean, after all, that's what *you've* got to do to make a sound card, a SCSI host adapter, or a LAN adapter card work. Why not let the computer do it? Well, that's the whole idea behind Plug and Play (PnP).

Way back in 1993, Microsoft, Intel, and Compaq proposed a standard called PnP. The idea behind PnP was that board manufacturers would add circuitry to their add-in boards so that the automatic setup and resource query (resource here means IRQ, DMA, I/O address, ROM address, or RAM buffer address) capabilities of EISA and Micro Channel would become available to machines with ISA buses. In actuality, no one ever made a PnP system that included EISA, VESA, or MCA to my knowledge; every PnP system I've ever seen used either a hybrid of PCI and ISA or just PCI. Although PC Cards are not part of the PnP specification, most PnP systems can configure them. Laptops using just CardBus, 32-bit bus, can be PnP.

PnP is a good idea, but it's a bit frustrating that you can't retrofit it on an existing system; it has to be built into a computer when you buy it. Today, fortunately, all new PCs are PnP-compatible, even if the boards you add into them aren't. In fact, in some cases, you can install one or two non-PnP boards, and the computer will build the rest of the system around them (as long as they don't conflict with themselves).

Booting on PnP Systems

Let's look into a bit more detail about how PnP works. PnP starts off with a PnP-compatible motherboard. This motherboard has a BIOS that understands PnP and also contains about 16K of flash memory that is a part of the BIOS. Virtually all motherboards built in the past few years are PnP-compliant; I'd hazard a guess that anything since 1995 would be PnP-compatible.

You also must have add-in cards that are PnP-compatible. These cards are configured *every time you boot*, and that configuration is done by a routine called the Configuration Manager. The Configuration Manager is usually part of the BIOS. It's possible to build a PnP system that loads its Configuration Manager off a disk, but I don't recommend it, as you end up with an only mildly PnP system. In addition to a PnP motherboard and expansion boards, you need, as I've noted a couple of times already, a PnP-compliant operating system.

In the ideal world (that is, one in which everything is PnP), the system powers up, and the Configuration Manager assumes control. It asks each board what resources it needs and what range of resources it will accept. (For example, a board might say, "I need an IRQ, and I'll take either 2, 3, 4, or 5," in the same way that the Microsoft ISA bus mouse interface does; even though there are other interrupts, its circuitry for some reason will accept an IRQ only in the range of 2 to 5.) The Configuration Manager then assigns resources to the boards, avoiding conflicts.

This means that potentially installing one new PnP card to a PnP system could cause all of the other cards to move their resources around. What does that mean for the network, SCSI, sound card drivers, and so on, that must know which resources those boards use? Well, it implies that device drivers must be a bit smarter than they are now.

For example, any DOS-based client on a Windows NT network has a file called PROTOCOL.INI on its hard disk. In that file are often references like IRQ=10, IOBASE=300, and so on. That DOS-based client doesn't work unless someone tells it what values to put in PROTOCOL.INI; in contrast, on a PnP system, the network software must take its cues from the Configuration Manager automatically, removing the need for operator intervention.

Once all boards are taken care of, the system boots in the usual way. The main difference with PnP is that the hardware shuffling of resources (I/O addresses, DMA channels, RAM windows, and the like) happens every time you boot the system, and (one hopes) quickly and invisibly.

Oh, by the way, can you force a particular board to a particular resource? Yes—that's called *locking* the resource. The Configuration Manager on your system should allow that, or your operating system may; Windows 95/98/2000 lets you do it with the Device Manager, which is in the Control Panel (Control Panel ➤ System ➤ Device

Manager). You can also get to it by right-clicking My Computer and choosing Properties, then clicking the Device Manager tab.

Configuring ATs and Beyond: Software Setup

Answering thousands of service calls that really just stemmed from incorrectly set DIP switches convinced IBM that they needed a computer that was easier to set up.

The main trouble with the XT and PC setup wasn't so much the switches as it was the fact that the PC owner would have to take the top off the computer and pull out some boards in order to get to the switches. So IBM came up with software setup on the first AT, back in 1984.

The AT wasn't totally set up with software; it had one DIP switch to set that configured its video. The rest of its motherboard configuration information was retained in a battery-backed memory. The add-in boards were left to fend for themselves configuration-wise, as the bus was ISA and ISA does not support a standard method for doing software setup on a board.

Now, this isn't just an idle history lesson: *virtually every PC since then has used the same basic approach.* Let's see how it works.

PC Setup Memory: The CMOS Chip

The nice thing about switches was that they conveyed information— if switch number three was on, you had a monochrome video board, if switch number three was off, you had a color video board, that kind of thing. This information was "nonvolatile," meaning that when you turned the PC off, switch number three stayed where it was, so that the PC could read its state the *next* time you turned the PC on.

Software setup wouldn't be as easy, the IBM engineers reasoned, unless they could either (A) put little robotic fingers in the PC's case to flip the switches when the software told them to, or (B) use some kind of memory structure to store the configuration information.

Option B sounded like the better idea (I was just kidding about option A), so they decided to stuff the configuration data into a memory chip.

The problem with using a memory chip was that memory chips are volatile (as you recall from Chapter 3, "Inside the PC: Pieces of the Picture"), and as soon as you turn off the computer, the data in the chip evaporates. So the AT engineers put a small low-power memory chip into the AT and attached a battery to that chip to keep it powered when the system was turned off.

Like most memory chips, it was built around the Complementary Metal Oxide Semiconductor, or CMOS, technology. The chip also contained a crude time and date/clock/calendar circuit. For some reason, the chip got the nickname "the CMOS chip," and that name stuck. It's a silly name on its face because *most* of the chips in modern machines are CMOS chips, but that's just what everybody calls it (and I'm surrendering and calling it that, since that's the term that others use).

The CMOS memory contains 64 bytes—not 64K, 64 *bytes*—of memory, as well as the clock/calendar. To read the data in the CMOS, your PC pushes the value's address—zero through 63—into I/O address 70 hex, and then reads it back in I/O address 71 hex. The PC writes new data by storing the requested address to I/O address 70 hex and then storing the new data to I/O address 71 hex.

The CMOS chip itself is often a Motorola 146818, 24-pin chip. It is volatile, like all semiconductor memory, and so requires a battery to maintain the integrity of its data when the system is turned off. When the battery runs down, the computer starts acting aphasic (look it up, but it means what you expect it to). Most systems use nonrechargeable lithium batteries that claim to have lives of 3 to 10 years. Others use rechargeable NiCad batteries. Some systems use a memory and battery all-in-one chip from Dallas Semiconductor. It is distinguished by the alarm clock on its face and contains a battery that Dallas Semiconductor claims is good for 10 years. When you replace it, you also replace its battery.

It's worth mentioning that, as time went on, 64 bytes just weren't enough, so EISA, Micro Channel, and PCI machines usually have a different CMOS memory configuration.

Modifying the Setup Memory: Running Setup

The most important question in software setup is "How do you do it?" It depends. Since the AT's appearance in 1984, we've seen several approaches to setup programs:

▶ Early machines had a separate setup program on a floppy disk that you'd run to modify the CMOS chip's memory or to set the time and date.

▶ Micro Channel and EISA systems usually require a setup program on floppy, as the setup program must incorporate information about new boards. Both of these architectures are nearly obsolete, however.

▶ Most 386 machines and above (including today's PCs) have a setup program in their BIOS, activated by pressing a certain key or key combination. Usually these keys must be pressed during startup, but on some older systems you can press them at any time to enter the setup utility.

▶ Pentium and higher PCI-based systems are usually a hybrid of built-in setup programs and PnP setup, wherein a system sets up at least some resources automatically with no operator intervention required.

The following sections outline some of the settings you can control from within the CMOS setup program.

Adjustable Bus Speeds

The standard ISA bus speed is, of course, 8MHz. Some clones allow you to increase the speed on that all the way up to 32MHz. It's a good idea to play with this feature, but do it carefully. I've found that most ISA cards can run just fine all the way up to 12MHz. On the other hand, if you want fast peripherals, you should invest in a machine with a VESA or PCI bus and use boards built for that interface. And ideally, your system should have an AGP bus for your video card, which further speeds up that component. Many of today's PCs have an ultra-high internal bus speed such as 66 or 100MHz; some can be adjusted, but most run at a fixed speed.

Note

Turn back to Chapter 3 if you need a refresher on AGP.

Adjustable Memory Speeds

In contrast, here's something I *wouldn't* mess around with. If you've got memory that's significantly faster than the stuff that the documentation calls for, then go ahead and play around. But be sure that you know how to restore the settings to their default state—or your system may not be able to get far enough into the boot process to even let you restart the setup program.

Keyboard Settings

I prefer a machine that does not set the Num Lock by default when powering up. (I'm old and inflexible, and the first PCs left the Num Lock off by default.) Sometimes the BIOS lets you set this.

Passwords

Be careful with these, as well. Many machines, laptops in particular, include power-on passwords as options. If you manage to forget your password, then there's usually no way to get into the machine, short of disconnecting the battery (better hope it's not soldered, like the batteries on most modern machines . . .) and waiting overnight for the power to slowly drain out of the CMOS chip. Even more annoying, once you've set a password, there's usually no way to restore the machine back to "doesn't need a password" mode.

Power Management

As onboard power management becomes chic in PC design, control of that power management often goes into the built-in setup program. You can use this to control when the computer turns itself off to save power and how often it does it.

PCI Control

Many PCI bus machines come with no control and configuration program for the boards in the PCI bus. It's an incredible oversight, but it's the case for hundreds of thousands of machines that use the PCI bus but don't support PnP.

These settings usually control a few things about the bus, but they're a sign of a poorly designed PCI machine. PCI machines should all be PnP-compatible and so should not require settings like PCI IDE interface enable/disable or the like.

Replacing the Configuration Battery

If your AT-type system insists on being set up anew every day, complete with reentering the correct date and time, you probably need a new battery. New batteries can be purchased in the $17–$30 price range. CompUSA and Radio Shack are two good places to find those batteries; so is your local PC hardware store. Alternatively, go to Radio Shack and get their Four AA Battery Holder (89 cents). Put four AA batteries in it and solder the wires from the holder to the AT battery contacts. This works, but it raises the question of where to put the battery holder (the power supply is a good place).

Note

Just like any other type of battery, the AA batteries that you use in your computer need to be replaced before they get too old, or they can leak. This problem is more common with the cheaper brands.

There are several different kinds of batteries used in PCs. Some of them look like round, flat watch batteries, held into place with metal clips; others are little barrel-shaped contraptions that look like fat resistors. In some systems, the battery is built into the CMOS chip, and the battery and chip must be replaced as a unit. Check the motherboard's documentation to find out what kind you have.

Tip

Make sure you get the right voltage of battery. Your choices will probably be 3.6v, 4.5v, or 6v. Some motherboards allow you to set a jumper to specify what voltage of battery you are using, but it's easier to just replace the battery with an identical one if possible.

When you replace some types of batteries, you may notice that the battery is connected to the motherboard with two wires, one red, and one white. If you don't pay attention when you take the old battery off, you may wonder how the new battery should be connected. In that case, remember RAP: *Red Away from the Power supply.*

Some motherboards have a lithium battery soldered onto the motherboard of the PC. When that battery runs out, you needn't solder a new one in place. Instead, these motherboards have a three-pin Berg connector that fits a standard battery. You usually have to find a jumper on the motherboard that tells the motherboard to stop trying to draw power from the soldered battery and instead pull from a battery attached to the Berg connector.

For laptop owners, there is often another type of rechargeable configuration battery, sometimes called a "standby battery." This item is actually designed to hold a charge while you replace the main battery pack; this is in order to preserve any data you have in RAM. It is recharged from your AC adapter, just like your main battery, and since it works only during the few moments when you are in the midst of a battery change, it should always have enough power. In the event that it should fail, however, you will not be able to replace it yourself. This is a "manufacturer-only" replacement item, and you should not try to work on this yourself.

Hey, Wait a Minute, My PC Doesn't Have a Battery!

Some computers do not have a CMOS battery at all. Instead they include a capacitor that gets charged up whenever the computer is plugged in. On such systems, you can leave them unplugged for up to a week without losing CMOS data. After that, they reload CMOS data from a backup on a flash ROM chip on the motherboard, which contains everything the PC needs to know about itself except the current date and time.

Other systems (especially newer, high-end ones) have a CMOS chip with a battery embedded in it. These batteries last 10 years or more, but when they die, the battery and chip must be replaced as a whole. Luckily, such chips are usually socketed, so it's easy to remove them from the motherboard. (Check the PC's manual to locate the chip.) You can order a replacement from the PC manufacturer or the motherboard manufacturer.

Parallel Port Configuration Anomalies

Here's a real PC configuration brainteaser you'll see on older systems. I have a PC with *only one* parallel port I configured as LPT2. There *is* no LPT1 in this machine. I boot it up. Once the system is running, what LPT port do I have on my system?

Answer: LPT1.

PCs have a strange feature when it comes to parallel ports. On bootup, the BIOS checks the LPTs. If there's no LPT1, it looks for an LPT2 or LPT3. If you've got an LPT2 but no LPT1, it actually converts the LPT2 to an LPT1. This is, of course, a *software* adjustment. I'll repeat: it's flat-out impossible to have an LPT2 without an LPT1. If you *do* install an LPT2 without an LPT1, the LPT2 gets made into an LPT1 on bootup time.

Nice feature. I just wish the documentation had *told* me about it. You see, it was late one night, and—oh, heck, I don't want to even talk about it. Now *you* know.

16-Bit Boards with ROM May Conflict with 8-Bit Boards with ROM

Here's an oddity you may see in older systems with a mix of 8-bit and 16-bit ISA boards.

If you have two boards in your system—one 16-bit, and one 8-bit, both with ROM on them—the 16-bit board may cause the 8-bit board to malfunction.

Why? It has to do with a characteristic of the 16-bit ISA bus. It recognizes that it must talk to some boards that are 8-bit and some that are 16-bit. It doesn't know which are which. So the extended part of the 16-bit slots have three *cheater* lines, lines that are duplicates of three lines on the 8-bit part of the slot. The way the extra lines work is this: every time a memory access is to occur, the CPU sends out a warning message on the three cheater lines, describing roughly where the upcoming memory request will be going. "Roughly" means within 128K of the desired memory address. If a board has memory that is addressed anywhere in that 128K area, it responds with an "Okay, I'm ready" signal. *But* only the 16-bit boards have the cheater lines—so if the upcoming memory access is to/from an 8-bit board, the CPU will receive no response to the warning. In that case, it just conducts 8-bit transfers.

If, on the other hand, the CPU *does* receive a response, it conducts the memory access using 16-bit transfers. To review:

1. The CPU sends out a warning message: "I'm about to do a memory access. It will be somewhere in the following 128K memory area . . ."

2. This message is audible only to 16-bit boards.

3. If a 16-bit board contains any memory—RAM or ROM—in that 128K address range, it responds, "*I've* got some memory in that range—do the memory access as 16-bit transfers." Any other 16-bit boards that happen to have memory in that range reply likewise.

4. On the other hand, 8-bit boards are deaf to the warning, so make no response, even if they did have memory in that 128K range.

5. If the CPU hears a 16-bit response, it conducts the memory access 16 bits at a time. Otherwise, it just transfers the data 8 bits at a time.

Where's the problem? What if there are *multiple* boards with memory in a given range? Well, if they're all 16-bit boards, that's no sweat. But what if, within a given 128K memory range, there were 8-bit *and* 16-bit boards? *Then* every time the CPU wanted to access the 8-bit board, it would send out a warning message that the 8-bit board, logically, would not hear or respond to—*but the 16-bit boards would!* Result: the CPU would send 16-bit data blocks to a board that could accept only 8-bit blocks—an apparent malfunction.

This sounds like a dire scenario, but it really only pops up in one area: the ROM reserve. The addresses from 768K to 896K are, you may recall, where the ROM is addressed: a 128K-sized memory area, notice. Every ROM access causes the CPU to issue a warning to the entire ROM area. If there are 8-bit boards and 16-bit boards with ROM on them, the 16-bit boards may respond to the CPU's attempts to access the ROMs on the 8-bit boards. This would result in the CPU again attempting 16-bit transfers to/from an 8-bit board. So, if adding a 16-bit board kills an existing 8-bit board, that may be a reason.

Well, some day you'll just buy a board, plug it into a system, and you *will* be able to "play" with it instantly. That day is not here yet, at least not for most of us. But for now, master the concepts in this chapter, and you'll be an expert installer.

Troubleshooting Tips

Here is a summary of some of the problems you might have when installing a circuit board, along with some possible solutions:

- If an old device stops working when you install a new one, there is probably a resource conflict. Reassign resources for one of the devices.

- Plug-and-Play devices can usually change resources through software, such as through the Windows 95/98/2000 Device Manager. Go there first to work on resource conflict issues.

- IRQ conflicts are the most common resource problem, but they're not the only kind. Check also for I/O addresses, DMA channels, ROM addresses, and RAM buffers.

- If you run out of IRQs, you may be able to enable IRQ-sharing through the BIOS in a PCI system. You can also disable one or both internal COM or LPT ports through your BIOS, freeing up their IRQs.

- On all except XT systems, you should avoid assigning IRQ2 to anything, as that's the IRQ that is used to cascade to IRQs 8 through 15.

- IRQ9 connects to IRQ2, so if you have a choice, avoid assigning IRQ9 to a device.

- If you are using PC Cards (formerly PCMCIA), Windows 95/98/2000 has a built-in card manager program to handle them. If you are using some other operating system, you should install a card manager program if possible.

- If your PC forgets the date and time each time you turn it off, it may need its configuration battery replaced. Take the old one to a computer store to get an identical replacement if possible.

▶ On some systems, the old battery is soldered into place. You may be able to set a jumper on the motherboard to use an external battery instead.

▶ Be sure to get the right voltage for your replacement battery. Some motherboards allow you to select the battery voltage with jumpers; check the PC's documentation.

Now you know how to install a circuit board. But what if you just want to repair an existing one? That's what we'll cover in the next chapter.

Repairs with Circuit Boards and Chips

INTRODUCTION

If the problem isn't software, if everything's plugged in, there are no resource conflicts, and it isn't something obvious like aburnt-out motor, a broken wire, a gummed-up printer, or an imploded display, then it's probably a defective circuit board. Step 1 is to identify the faulty part. I'll talk about diagnostic approaches in this chapter (they don't cost anything but time). Step 2 is repair. There are two levels of repair here: board level and chip level.

The more important as well as the more difficult of these operations is the first, *identification.* How do you know which board is bad? There are several approaches we'll examine here. Next, should you fix or replace the bad board? You'll see the pros and cons. Further along, as some repairs can involve chip replacements, we'll examine diagnosing and repairing memory problems—the chips you're most likely to install and replace.

Diagnosing and Solving Circuit Board Problems

This section provides the key steps for figuring out what's wrong with your circuit board. For detailed information, refer to the chapter itself.

Be Prepared

Before you start, there are some things you'll need to perform the operation. These include:

- Nonmagnetic Phillips screwdriver
- Manual that came with the board (for checking resource assignments)
- Container to hold removed screws
- (Optional) A POST (Power-On Self Test) board, which reports a code indicating at what point in the boot process a problem occurs
- (Optional) A third-party utility program for troubleshooting hardware

Also, before you open up the PC and remove/add boards, make sure that:

- You are wearing an antistatic wrist strap
- The PC is turned off and unplugged

1. Before assuming you have a bad board, check for the following:
   - Conflicts between devices (see Chapter 6, "Installing New Circuit Boards [without Creating New Problems]").
   - Software conflicts or faulty software installations
   - Hardware incompatibilities with certain programs

2. If the PC won't boot, and you have an extra identical PC, try swapping out components until you find the bad one.

or

If the PC won't boot and you only have the one machine, disconnect everything except the motherboard, power supply, and speaker. If the fan powers up and you hear beeps, turn it off and add a video card. Keep adding items until the machine fails.

Tools that may help in your diagnosis include:

- A POST (Power-On Self Test) board, which reports a code indicating at what point in the boot process a problem occurs.
- A third-party utility program for troubleshooting hardware.
- Pressing F8 while booting a Windows 95/98 PC and choosing Step by Step Configuration from the Startup menu so that you can see at what point in the boot process the PC locks up.

3. Once you've found the errant item, do one of the following:

- Replace it with a new one (usually the best bet) or attempt to fix the board (not usually cost-effective, and sometimes not even possible).
- If the bad part is integrated on the motherboard, try to disable it in BIOS and add a board that takes over that function.
- If you can isolate the problem to a single chip on a board, you may be able to replace it. Chips in sockets are much easier to replace than those soldered into place. Don't spend more time diagnosing and replacing a chip than is worthwhile given the cost of a new board, however.

How Do You Find the Bad Board?

First, let's hunker down to the tough part—figuring out which board is the problem child.

To begin with, make *sure* you've checked steps 1 to 7 discussed in Chapter 5, "Troubleshooting PC Problems." You *know* by now that a switched outlet (or one with a tripped circuit breaker) isn't the culprit. You're not ripping the machine apart to figure out why it won't boot when the last thing you did was install a new expansion board (and the machine hasn't worked since you put the board in), without first removing the new board to see if the problem goes away.

Again, just be lazy and follow the beaten path. Don't get original. Make sure you've followed the seven steps. Also, make sure you have ruled out resource conflicts as the source of the problem. Turn back to Chapter 6 if you need help with this. Remember, if the PC worked fine before you installed some new component, the problem is probably a resource conflict between something old and something new.

Assuming the machine *does* boot, you can use the machine to help diagnose its own problems. Run the diagnostics to find out if it's the keyboard or video, and so on. That'll give you an indication of what's wrong.

Suppose the problem is clearly video. What now? Again, be lazy. Before you "remove the top and begin to swap," check the easy stuff. Swap the monitor first, before the video board.

Be even lazier—is the problem specific to something like a time of day, or, more likely, a piece of software? If the video works well enough to boot the system and runs some applications but dies when you're running a particular program (games are notorious in this regard), the problem is likely software, not hardware. This may mean:

> ▶ You've installed the program incorrectly (easy to do).

or

> ❱ There's a bug in the program's code that talks to your video board.

or

> ❱ Your video card is not compatible with the program.

In this situation, if you have a second, identical computer, I'd take an exact same copy of the program and install it there. But in order to find a problem like this, it's important that the second computer be identical, right down to the version of the operating system, add-in boards, and so on. If the problem shows up on the second machine, common sense tells you that it's a software problem with the program or an installation problem or that the brand of video board that both machines have is not 100 percent compatible with the program.

If it's a hardware compatibility problem, try using a different video card. (In fact, if you have a lot of patience, you might even call the program's manufacturer and ask them which video cards work and which don't.) If it's a problem with installation, try rereading the installation instructions. Maybe you made a wrong choice when you were installing the software. (Some programs require you to turn off your virus protection before installing, for example.) If you can't duplicate the problem by reinstalling the software, check the company's Web site. Most companies have troubleshooting page(s) that list dozens or even hundreds of things that can go wrong and are easily corrected—and all of the instructions are usually right there.

If the machine doesn't boot at all, consult the next section.

Night of the Living Data: Making a Dead Machine "Undead"

Suppose the computer is completely unresponsive. You can't run the diagnostics because the machine won't talk at all. Here are two approaches to bringing your machine back from the dead, along with a few other possibilities and solutions. (Do you then run an operating system called "DOSferatu"? Better quit while I'm ahead . . .)

Identifying the Problem Board I: Two Machines

First of all, assume that there is only one problem. Ideally, you have two machines, one sick and one well. A simple strategy here is to swap boards one by one. Each time you swap a board, turn on *both machines* and note which machines are currently well. Ideally, you would like to induce the problem from the originally sick PC to the originally well PC.

By the way, did you check the old "intensity turned down on the monitor" trick? I'll turn down the intensity on my monitor for some reason, leave the machine, come back to the machine after a while (forgetting I've turned down the intensity), and panic, thinking that (at best) I've got a bad monitor.

Ghost in the Machine (Contagious Components)

Be careful here, however. Sometimes you end up with *two* sick machines. Why? I've seen components that, being damaged, damage other components. Suppose you've got a dead system, and you've stripped the system to the motherboard and power supply. You try to ascertain what's causing your problems, so you swap motherboards. Still no luck. So you try swapping power supplies. *Still* no response. What's happening?

You have a "demon" in the power supply: not only is it not working, but it also destroys motherboards. Originally it "ate" motherboard number one, and then you fed it another one. I've seen this in two situations: bad power supplies damaging motherboards and bad keyboard interfaces on motherboards damaging keyboards.

The moral is:

1. Swap the power supply before the motherboard.

2. Before swapping the keyboard, test the keyboard interface with a voltmeter to make sure the keyboard interface on the PC is not the problem, as described in Chapter 22, "Keyboards and Mice."

Identifying the Problem Board II: Just One Machine

If all you've got is one machine, here's a nice, minimalist approach. Some people call it the *min/max technique* (short for minimum/maximum).

Start with a machine that won't boot up at all and assume that there's only one thing wrong with it. Break it down to the bare essentials, then add pieces until the machine refuses to boot. *Once the machine refuses to boot, you'll know that the last item that you added is the trouble board.*

Start off by removing everything but the following:

▶ Power supply

▶ Motherboard

▶ Speaker

Turn it on. You should observe several things:

▶ The fan on the power supply should start right up. If it doesn't, either the power supply isn't getting power, or the fan's burned out. If the fan is burned out, and it *has been* burned out, then the problem's easy—you cooked your PC the last time you used it.

▶ There is *one* other reason that the fan might not start up. The power supply's pretty smart and can sense short circuits on the motherboard. If it senses such a short, it will shut down and refuse to do anything until the short's resolved.

You don't believe me? Try taking a board out while the power's on. If you do it just right, you'll create a short, and the machine will shut down. (This is not a particularly smart idea, actually, and is not recommended. You might want to just trust me on this one.)

▶ The power supply should probably also produce a "click" on the speaker (you've probably never noticed it, but it happens each time you turn most PCs on). Another aspect of the "intelligent" power supply is that once it feels that it is up to the task of getting to work, it sends a signal to the motherboard that resets the system. The result is the click. Once you hear that, you know that the power supply believes itself to be functional.

▶ Assuming that the two things listed above happened, you'll probably get one long and two shorts beep out of the speaker—the motherboard's way of saying, "I can't find the video card." You may hear a different beep combination—different BIOS configurations respond differently to the "no video" condition.

If the three things outlined here have happened, congratulations—the machine booted. (It didn't do that before, remember?) If it didn't, there are only three possible culprits: the motherboard, power supply, or speaker. It's child's play now to figure out which is the offending component: just swap the speaker, power supply, and/or motherboard. Remember what I said before about swapping the power supply first, in case it's got a demon. Remember that in the PC repair business *the cheapest and most effective piece of test equipment is a spare part.* At this point, it's a quick swap.

Assuming that the machine booted, the next step is to add the video card. Try to boot the machine. Again, if it doesn't boot, try another video card. If it boots, you'll get error messages complaining about the lack of keyboard and drives—errors 301, 601, and 1701 on an older IBM or Compaq machine, and messages in English on pretty much any current machine. Keep adding boards until the machine fails.

When you assemble (or reassemble) your computer and apply power, sometimes the system will respond with a series of beeps. (Be sure to attach the system speaker so you can hear them.) Depending upon the system, the beeps can mean a number of different things. For example, usually a single short beep or a couple of short beeps will mean "everything's okay." On the other hand, if you get a repeating pattern of not-so-short beeps, the computer is probably trying to tell you something.

Phoenix and AMI are the two primary BIOS manufacturers in the computer industry. The beep codes for the AMI BIOS are listed in Table 7.1.

TABLE 7.1 AMI BIOS Beep Codes

Beep Code	Meaning
1 beep	Refresh failure
2 beeps	Parity error
3 beeps	Base 64K memory failure
4 beeps	Timer not operational
5 beeps	Processor error
6 beeps	8042—gate A20 failure
7 beeps	Processor exception interrupt error
8 beeps	Display memory read/write failure
9 beeps	ROM checksum error
10 beeps	CMOS shutdown register read/write error
11 beeps	Cache memory bad

Table 7.2 lists the Phoenix beep codes and their meanings. The Phoenix error codes are a little different from AMI, in that the beeps occur in groups of three with pauses between the groups. So, for example, the first code would sound like this: BEEP (pause) BEEP (pause) BEEP-BEEP-BEEP (long pause) and then the pattern would repeat.

TABLE 7.2 Phoenix BIOS Beep Codes

Beep Code	Meaning
1-1-3	CMOS write/read failure
1-1-4	ROM BIOS checksum failure
1-2-1	Programmable interval timer failure
1-2-2	DMA initialization failure
1-2-3	DMA page register write/read failure
1-3-1	RAM refresh verification failure
1-3-3	First 64K RAM chip or data line failure, multibit
1-3-4	First 64K RAM odd/even logic failure
1-4-1	Address line failure first 64K RAM
1-4-2	Parity failure first 64K RAM
2-1-1	Bit 0 first 64K RAM failure
2-1-2	Bit 1 first 64K RAM failure
2-1-3	Bit 2 first 64K RAM failure
2-1-4	Bit 3 first 64K RAM failure
2-2-1	Bit 4 first 64K RAM failure
2-2-2	Bit 5 first 64K RAM failure
2-2-3	Bit 6 first 64K RAM failure
2-2-4	Bit 7 first 64K RAM failure
2-3-1	Bit 8 first 64K RAM failure
2-3-2	Bit 9 first 64K RAM failure
2-3-3	Bit 10 first 64K RAM failure
2-3-4	Bit 11 first 64K RAM failure
2-4-1	Bit 12 first 64K RAM failure
2-4-2	Bit 13 first 64K RAM failure
2-4-3	Bit 14 first 64K RAM failure
2-4-4	Bit 15 first 64K RAM failure
3-1-1	Slave DMA register failure
3-1-2	Master DMA register failure
3-1-3	Master interrupt mask register failure
3-1-4	Slave interrupt mask register failure

continued on next page

TABLE 7.2 Phoenix BIOS Beep Codes (continued)

Beep Code	Meaning
3-2-4	Keyboard controller test failure
3-3-4	Screen initialization failure
3-4-1	Screen retrace test failure
3-4-2	Search for video ROM in progress
4-2-1	Timer tick interrupt test in progress or failure
4-2-2	Shutdown test in progress or failure
4-2-3	Gate A20 failure
4-2-4	Unexpected interrupt in protected mode
4-3-1	RAM test in progress or address failure > FFFFh
4-3-3	Interval timer channel 2 test or failure
4-3-4	Time-of-day clock test or failure
4-4-1	Serial port test or failure
4-4-2	Parallel port test or failure
4-4-3	Math coprocessor test or failure

Note that this isn't gospel—your machine, depending on the manufacturer, may do something different from these expected outcomes. *Try it* sometime on your functioning PC. Note the outcomes. Do it *before* your computer breaks down, so you'll have a reference.

Note

Again, I must stress this strongly: do this on a healthy PC so you can see what *your* healthy machine looks like at various stages of reassembly. If you don't know what healthy looks like, you can't recognize disease.

Now, you may get down to the last board, the machine may be booting fine, and you insert that last board, thinking, "Aha! Gotcha. Now to prove it . . ." But then the machine boots fine. (Grrrr . . .) Why? One of the following may be true:

> It just wanted some attention.

> It fails when boards are hot, and the disassembly and reassembly cooled it to the point that it works.

> You didn't do the greatest job the first time you took it apart, cleaned it, and put it back together.

What Makes Boards Fail?

If you're reading this, you may already have a dead board. I've suggested that you just replace it, but in case you're interested, here's what generally zaps boards.

Most component problems boil down to either environmental trouble, damage due to mishandling, or faulty manufacturing. The most common ailments (and their antidotes) are the following:

> Socketed chips can creep out of their sockets due to expansion and contraction. (Push them back in.)

> Bad solder joints can disconnect or cause short circuits. (Replace, or you can try resoldering if you feel up to it.)

> Weak components can fail under heat. (Replace them, if possible.) By the way, one easy way to find a component that is failing under heat is to put a handful of cotton swabs in the freezer for an hour (keep them dry). Then put the tip of a swab on the suspected component(s). If they come back to life, you've found your culprit.

> PC board traces can be scratched. This is something you can usually see if you look carefully (or use a magnifying glass).

> Dirt and dust can build up heat. (See Chapter 4, "Avoiding Service: Preventive Maintenance.")

> Edge connectors or chip pins can corrode. (Clean off corrosion with a pencil eraser.)

▶ Electromagnetic interference from other devices can cause impairment. (Keep unshielded devices such as speakers well away from PC components.)

Other Problems and Solutions

The remaining chapters in this book cover peripherals in depth, but here are some ideas for solving some kinds of problems, along with pointers to other chapters for more information.

Hard Disk Problems

If you seem to have a hard disk problem, look at the extensive discussions of drive recovery in the hard disk chapters (Chapters 10 through 14).

Keyboard Problems

Keyboard problems are covered in detail in Chapter 22, but here are a few possibilities:

▶ The system board may be at fault. Test the keyboard test points (see Chapter 22 for more information).

▶ Is the keyboard plugged in securely? On some machines you need to push firmly to seat the keyboard plug in the socket.

▶ Is it a PS/2 keyboard plugged into the PS/2 mouse port?

▶ Are you leaning on the spacebar (or any other key) accidentally, or is anything resting on a key?

▶ Are any keys stuck?

Many Beeps when Booting, No Video

If you boot your PC and get one long beep and two short beeps and then the drive A: light goes on but there's no display, the problem is most likely the display board. Assuming you have a floppy diskette in drive A:, type **dir a:** and press Enter on the keyboard. If the drive A: light comes on, the system is responding—you just can't see it. Swap the video board. Take a look at Chapter 23, "Video Adapters and Displays."

Drive A: Light Stays On

You try to access drive A: and the floppy light comes on and stays on. You probably put the floppy cable on backwards. Check Chapter 17, "Understanding, Installing, and Repairing Floppy Drives." Ditto if the floppy light comes on immediately when you start the PC and stays on.

There's another possible reason—are you loading a program from a floppy? The problem could be insufficient memory to run your application. Try your backup disk also.

Parity Check Error (Memory Error)

See the section "Test Memory" in Chapter 8, "Semiconductor Memory." Note that not all memory errors are caused by bad memory; see also the section "Causes of False Memory Errors" in that same chapter.

Fix or Replace Boards?

Assuming (as we'll discuss presently) that you can find the bad board, do you just replace it, or do you try to fix it? Sure, it's macho to get out the soldering iron and fix an errant board. But, in general, you won't find it cost-effective to repair a circuit board. This is basically because (1) the inexpensive boards are far cheaper to replace than to repair, and (2) the more expensive boards require even more expensive equipment to repair.

Inexpensive boards, such as one of those ubiquitous video or sound boards, can be had for a reasonable price. Chips on these boards are primarily soldered, not socketed, and so can only be fixed by someone trained to solder chips without destroying them.

Add the hourly cost of this person to the cost of replacement chips, and the amount soon adds up to an amount in excess of the cost of a new $15 board. In addition, more and more boards are four-layer boards, which are tough to solder correctly. Four-layer means the board has not only printed circuit traces on the top and bottom, but two layers in the middle! Even if it is a simple two-layer board, don't forget that time is wasted inserting the board and powering up the computer after each chip replacement.

Maintenance Considerations for Integrated Motherboards

These days, most motherboards are of the all-in-one variety. The disk controllers, parallel and serial ports, mouse, and keyboard controllers all exist on proprietary chips that are mounted directly on the motherboard. Some of them even have built-in video and sound support. Arggh! Worst-case scenario for troubleshooting! If one of the onboard controllers fails, you may have to replace the whole motherboard!

But it's not *all* bad news. Now there are fewer boards to worry about and fewer DIP switches to fuss with. Also, reducing the chip count should produce a more reliable machine overall, and indeed it often does. But it can limit PC troubleshooting to an all-or-nothing matter because there's just one board in the system, and, as I've already said, it's just not reasonable to fix those kinds of surface mount components.

Tip

What can you do if one of the onboard subsystems fails? In many instances, the BIOS on newer boards gives you the option of disabling one or more of the onboard circuits. So if, for example, your system board's IDE controller wanders off to the happy hunting grounds, you may be able to turn off the onboard circuitry and simply install a new IDE controller card in one of the available slots on your motherboard. Then all you have to do is move the data cable(s) (the flat, ribbon cables) to the new IDE card, and you're back in business.

Understanding the PC Boot Process

Part of bringing a dead machine back to life is understanding how PCs get started in the first place. In this section, you'll learn in great detail what steps a PC goes through to boot, from the time you flip the power switch to the time that the operating system loads. Basically, three things affect whether or not a PC will boot:

1. The hardware must work.

2. The processor must start up and run a program in the BIOS called the Power-On Self Test (POST). (I mentioned BIOS in Chapter 6, and I'll cover it more thoroughly shortly.)

3. The BIOS must load the operating system from the active partition of the boot drive.

Let's start with a quick overview, and then we'll look at each step of the booting process in greater detail.

First, the system needs power from the wall (at least until solar-powered PCs appear) or a battery (in the case of a laptop), and the power supply had better be able to use it; a faulty power supply means a useless PC.

Second, at least a few pieces of the motherboard itself must work. In particular, the CPU, the system's cache RAM, the clock circuit, and the bottom 64K or so of system RAM must be functional, or you won't get anything on the screen at all.

Then, assuming that the basic hardware can function, you'll recall that each PC has a set of software built into a ROM, called the *basic input/output system*, or *BIOS.* That BIOS is a collection of important programs—programs that control the video board, the disk controller, the keyboard, and the system clock, to name a few—but perhaps the most important of those programs is the one that starts up the PC. That program determines what hardware is in the system, does a basic checkout of that hardware, and senses the presence of BIOSlike programs associated with expansion boards in the PC. If those programs exist on the expansion boards, the BIOS will yield control to them so that *they* can do the initialization.

Once the BIOS startup and checks work out all right, the BIOS then attempts to load the system software from the floppy or hard disk. Once the operating system gets loaded from disk into the computer's RAM, the BIOS passes control to the operating system, and the computer is ready to use.

That's the overview; now let's look at the details.

Step One: PC Power

The computer first requires power. I'll handle that in greater detail in Chapter 9, "Power Supplies and Power Protection," so I won't elaborate on the point here. But remember: the power supply in the PC can be the culprit, rather than the power coming from the wall.

Step Two: Check the Hardware

Once your system is getting power, there's got to be some functioning computing hardware to use that power. The familiarity of computers and CPUs sometimes makes us forget exactly how many microscopic components have to work together in order for the PC to get up and running . . . but the PC doesn't forget. What I mean by that is that the BIOS software's first job is to look at what hardware is in your system and to check that it works.

The ROM and Bootstrapping

Why do we need BIOS? It has to do with how CPUs work. When a CPU powers up, it doesn't know how to communicate with anything—the keyboard, display, disk drives, you name it. Before it can communicate with, say, a hard disk, a CPU needs a program in memory that tells it *how* to communicate with a hard disk. Virtually all PC programs must be read from disk before the PC can run them. This kind of leads to a chicken-and-egg problem: the CPU needs a disk-reading program before it can read anything from disk, but it loads its programs from disk. From where, then, does the CPU read that first disk-reading program at the start of the day? It might seem like a good idea to just leave that program in memory in the first place, and that's the idea with ROM (read-only memory). Normal RAM chips lose their contents when you shut down power on a PC; ROM does not forget.

One of ROM's most important jobs is to store low-level programs that control disks, keyboards, and the like. These programs are used not only at startup, but also throughout the day. The other part of the BIOS is the part that's used only when you first power up the computer, as seen in Figure 7.1.

Figure 7.1

Step 1 of the boot process

All Intel chips have one feature in common: when they power up, they immediately start executing instructions located at an address 16 bytes below the 1024K level or, more specifically, at address FFFF:0000. That's why the main system BIOS chip gets a location up in the range of 960K through 1024K—so it can fill the need of the PC's CPU to have instructions to execute when it powers up. Take a look at Figure 7.2, which illustrates this concept.

Figure 7.2

Location of BIOS in
memory

The BIOS's initial main job is to *inventory* and *initialize*: to figure out what's in your PC and then get it ready to do some work, testing it in the process. Now, this gets a little involved, so let's look at how BIOS does this in parts.

There are five steps to the BIOS initialization process:

1. Test some low memory.

2. Scan for other BIOS.

3. Yield to other BIOS.

4. Inventory the system.

5. Test the system.

Test Low Memory

In order for the BIOS to function, it needs some RAM to work with. So for most BIOS, one of the first things done is to test the bottom part of the system's RAM. Now, if that test crashes, then most BIOS can't recover. That leads to the following observation . . .

One major reason for a dead PC is that the lowest bank of RAM has failed. Therefore, one troubleshooting step is to replace the first bank of RAM.

Note

Replacing the first bank of RAM may not be possible on older machines because some motherboards have their first bank of memory *soldered* in place. (Thankfully, this is very rarely the case anymore except in a few proprietary systems.)

Scan for Other BIOS

The BIOS in your PC can't support every possible piece of hardware—such as LAN boards, unusual video boards, you name it—so the important functions of inventory and initialization have to go somewhere else. That is why many add-on boards have some ROM on them, as you may have noticed when installing boards. What you may not know is that those ROM chips contain some initialization code for those boards. For example, a hard disk controller ROM might do a quick read of the hard disk—kind of an "are you there?" test. A video board ROM might test the memory on the video board. A LAN board ROM might broadcast its network address over the LAN, testing that it has a unique network address.

Note

Add-on ROM chips are supposed to be easy for the main BIOS to find and should contain three signature bytes. The first bytes are hex 55, then comes AA, and then a number indicating how long the BIOS will be. That number is the length of the BIOS divided by 512. If you want to see this for yourself, try this little exercise, which shows you the BIOS signature on a video card. (This may not work in Windows NT/2000 systems.)

1. From the DOS command line, type **debug** and press Enter.

   You will see the prompt for DEBUG (-).

2. Your VGA ROM is either at hexadecimal address C000:0 or E000:0. To see it, type **d C000:0 L 3** and press Enter. If that doesn't yield a 55 AA *xx* code, try typing **d E000:0 L 3**.

The main system BIOS allows the add-on boards to do *their* inventory and initialization first. Now, before that can happen, the main system BIOS must *find* those other BIOS. It does that by examining memory in the ROM area—the addresses between 768K and 960K. Once it finds BIOS, it can go to the next step.

Yield to Other BIOS

Once it has found a BIOS on the add-on board, the main system BIOS passes control to that BIOS so that it can do whatever inventory and initialization the add-on BIOS requires.

The main system BIOS allows every add-on card's BIOS to initialize itself before doing its own inventory and initialization. Notice what that means: the software contained in the ROM on an add-on board gets to run *before* the system BIOS, and it also runs before your operating system gets loaded—we haven't gotten near to loading the operating system yet. For an example, consider a VGA board. As you saw in the exercise above, it's got a BIOS chip on it, one that contains a setup routine. That setup routine usually announces that the board is up and ready by putting a copyright notice on the screen. That copyright notice is probably the first thing you see when you turn on your PC.

When your PC is booting, the VGA message appears *before* the memory test occurs and before the PC checks for the drives. Again, the point here is that this VGA ROM assumed total control of the system fairly early in the boot process, as will each ROM that's on an add-on board in turn. If anything goes wrong with a program in one of those ROM chips—and such things *do* happen—then a PC that functions properly before adding in the board will refuse to boot after that board has been installed. I'll come back to that notion in a minute, but let's finish up with the last two steps of this BIOS initialization.

Inventory and Test the System

Once all of the add-on ROM chips have gotten their time and, *assuming that their programs ran properly and returned control to the main system BIOS*, the main system BIOS will inventory the items that it will control, items that vary from system to system. At a minimum, one of the items that the system BIOS must inventory and initialize is the system memory.

What does "inventory and initialize" mean here? You've seen at least one example of it a million times—the memory test. Ever notice the quick flash of the drive lights on the floppy and hard disk drives? That's the inventorying of the storage devices.

Hard Disk Time-Outs

Now let's put this information to use. Ever seen a computer do the memory test, then seem to lock up and not boot? The problem may be the disk drive. The simple are you there? test that the main system BIOS does every time you turn on the computer involves a quick disk read. But if the disk drive doesn't respond immediately, the BIOS doesn't give up—it waits, hoping that the drive will respond. The amount of time that it will wait is called the time-out period. I've seen more than one system BIOS with a time-out period of four minutes. That means that if the system has a bad hard drive, it could wait *four minutes* before reporting failure! The trouble is, most people aren't patient enough to wait four minutes—they just see the fact that their computer isn't doing anything. The logical verdict is that the computer is dead, and it's time for a new PC. So be *patient* when your computer doesn't respond on boot-up; give it a few minutes, literally, to report a disk drive time-out.

If the hard disk does time out and report an error, the first thing to check is the cabling connections. Is the ribbon cable firmly plugged into the drive and into the motherboard's EIDE connector? Is it plugged in with the red stripe on the cable to pin 1?

Note

You'll learn more about EIDE drive troubleshooting in Chapter 11, "Installing an IDE Hard Drive."

Inventory Lockups

Another manifestation of BIOS initialization problems that makes your PC look dead, is, as I've mentioned, the "inventory and initialize" function of add-on BIOS. I once installed an ESDI hard disk system in a computer and powered up the computer to test the system, which consisted of a matching controller board and drive. I turned the system on and it did almost nothing: the fan whirred, but that's it—nothing on the screen. This, of course, panicked me, as the system that I tried the board in was a $5000 high-powered workstation that I was trying to make even faster: the client wouldn't be very happy if I smoked her computer. So I tried removing the new ESDI controller board, and the system booted up just fine. Restored the board, and the system wouldn't boot. The problem was that the high-speed ESDI board's initialization routine just wasn't written well and happened to crash on that particular system. Replacement ROM solved the problem.

You'll recall from Chapter 5 that the POST gathers a large amount of testing information about its PC that it never tells the PC's owner—*unless* the PC's owner has one of the POST boards that I mentioned in Chapter 5. If you're tracing a boot failure, don't overlook the POST board step.

CMOS Setup Information Read

I've known people who thought that they had a bad drive because of a CMOS error, but what they *really* had was incorrect information in their CMOS. The CMOS has a battery that maintains startup information. If the battery dies, the system might not boot up, or it might boot up with default (and possibly incorrect) information about the hard disk or other components. When the CMOS battery fails, the computer goes back to the factory default BIOS settings. So, for example, if the default is "one floppy drive" and you actually have two, your second floppy drive will not function unless you go into the BIOS setup program and remind it about that other floppy drive. Your next step, of course, would be to get and install a replacement battery, as I described in Chapter 6.

Load MBR

First, the BIOS looks for a drive that's ready. The BIOS is usually set up to begin by first looking at A:, your primary floppy drive. If there is nothing in A:, the BIOS then looks at C:, your primary hard drive. This default setup allows you to use a bootable floppy disk to boot from drive A: if you want to run hard drive utility programs, install new operating systems, or run any program that needs to run before your installed operating system boots up. While this may not actually be the greatest idea in this virus-plagued age, sometimes you just have to boot from your floppy. (We'll look at virus issues in more depth in Chapter 15, "Viruses.") Of course, to boot from C:, just leave the floppy drive empty. Once the BIOS has detected a drive that's ready, it loads the first sector of data from that drive, the sector whose coordinates are cylinder 0, head 0, sector 1.

Some BIOS setup programs enable you to set a boot drive order, so you could, for example, set the system to check drive C: first and to check A: only if C does not contain the needed startup files. That makes the PC boot slightly faster, because it doesn't have to check A: every time. However, if for some reason the startup files on the hard disk have a problem and you need to boot from a floppy, you will need to go into the BIOS setup program and change the boot order so that the PC will look in A: before it hits C: and becomes stymied.

Things work slightly differently for floppies and hard disks, but the hard disk procedure is actually just the floppy procedure with a few steps added, so let's focus on hard disks. That first sector on a hard disk is called the Master Boot Record (MBR). It's just 512 bytes, so it should load easily into memory, although if it doesn't, the system won't boot and it probably will not show any error messages— it'll just lock up. Additionally, if the MBR is blank, the system will also lock up because it depends on that MBR to contain a meaningful program. If that happens, consult the troubleshooting procedure in Chapter 16, "Care and Feeding of Hard Drives," in the section "Recovering Data and Fixing Hard Disks."

Find a Bootable Partition

Once the MBR is in memory, the BIOS passes control of the PC over to it. The MBR contains a very small program that is the next link in the chain of events that leads to a successful boot. As you may know, PC hard disks can be *partitioned*, allowing you to make one physical hard disk seem like several hard disks, or perhaps to put multiple operating systems on a single hard disk. The MBR program just finds a bootable partition, loads the first sector of that partition into memory, and then passes control to the newly loaded sector. The MBR finds the bootable partition using a small table contained in the MBR itself called the *partition table*. That program is created and maintained by the DOS FDISK program, so you've probably modified a few partition tables in your time if you've set up hard disks. Anyway, if the MBR can't find a bootable partition, it'll issue a message that says `Missing Operating System`. Assuming that it can find a bootable partition, it'll load the first sector from that partition into memory and pass control to that sector.

By the way, you may know that the majority of computer viruses are called *boot sector viruses*. If your system is infected with one of these, this is the point where the virus becomes active. That's why cold booting from a floppy bypasses a virus if one exists on the MBR. (Of course, the floppy should be write-protected to prevent the virus from infecting it too.)

The DBR Loads and Executes

The first sector of the bootable partition goes by different names for different operating systems, but in the DOS world it's called the DBR, or *DOS boot record*. The DBR is another very brief program whose sole job in life is to find the two so-called "hidden" programs, called `IO.SYS` and `MSDOS.SYS` for those of you who use MS-DOS. Windows 95/98 also boots from `IO.SYS` and `MSDOS.SYS`, just like their DOS ancestors, but Windows NT and 2000 do not. You may have heard people say that Windows 95/98 runs on top of DOS or is DOS-based, but NT is not; this is what they mean.

Before loading the two hidden files, of course, the DBR must check to see that they're on your disk in the first place. If it can't find them, or encounters problems while loading the two files, it issues the possibly familiar message `Non-system disk or disk error: insert boot disk and press any key when ready.`

Assuming that all is well, the DBR yields the stage to the two hidden files.

The Hidden Files Execute

Once the DBR loads the hidden files, the DBR passes control to the first hidden file (IO.SYS) and disappears. The first hidden file then *double-checks* that it has been loaded properly and checks the second hidden file. Once up and running, the first hidden file loads CONFIG.SYS. (The process is slightly different in Windows NT and Windows 2000 systems, but they have their own hidden files that execute on the way to starting up.)

CONFIG.SYS Loads and Executes

Assuming that you have a CONFIG.SYS file, the system executes the commands in CONFIG.SYS at this time. It first executes the BUFFERS, FILES, STACKS, DOS, FCBS, and LASTDRIVE commands, and then loads any device drivers. In a Windows 9x/NT/2000 system, you will not always have a CONFIG.SYS; those operating systems typically take their settings from WIN.INI, SYSTEM.INI, and/or the Windows Registry. (The same goes for AUTOEXEC.BAT.)

Error information on drivers is fairly sparse, but if CONFIG.SYS can't load a driver, it will say something like Bad or missing XXXX.DRV. If you're using Windows 95/98/NT, you can slow down the process by pressing F8 on bootup and then choosing Step-by-step Confirmation from the Startup menu that appears. This forces the system to display one line at a time on the CONFIG.SYS, requiring a keystroke from you to continue to the next line. Some badly written drivers will simply crash the system without any error messages.

COMMAND.COM and AUTOEXEC.BAT Load

The next step is to load something called the *user shell*; typically, it's the COMMAND.COM program. If CONFIG.SYS contains a

SHELL statement, the hidden files will use that to locate a command shell, but, in the absence of a SHELL statement, the hidden files will next load COMMAND.COM from the root directory. Saying that COMMAND.COM is the "shell" of DOS means that it is the program that accepts user commands and loads programs at the user's request.

Your PC can run into trouble here if COMMAND.COM is missing or if it's not of a version that matches the hidden files.

Finally, COMMAND.COM loads and executes AUTOEXEC.BAT, executing any commands stored in there, and starts the graphical user interface of the operating system (Windows 9*x*/NT/2000).

There are two common places where these last few steps can go wrong. First, CONFIG.SYS contains statements that can load device drivers, complete programs in their own right. Any bugs in a device driver can stop the system dead, so part of your troubleshooting approach might include temporarily renaming CONFIG.SYS to nullify its effects. If there's a SHELL statement in CONFIG.SYS, double-check that it makes sense: does it point to a bona fide copy of COMMAND.COM, and are all of the COMMAND.COM options correct?

Note

If you have MS-DOS version 5 through 6.2, or you have upgraded to your current version of Windows from one of those DOS versions, onscreen help is available for DOS commands such as COMMAND.COM. To access it, type **HELP** and then the command name at a DOS prompt, like this: **HELP COMMAND.COM**. If you try this and get a Bad command or file name message, the DOS help file is not available on your PC.

Second, if there's a SHELL statement, check to see if there is a corresponding SET COMSPEC statement in the AUTOEXEC.BAT file, as you see here:

CONFIG.SYS:
```
SHELL=C:\DOS\COMMAND.COM /E:512 /P
```

AUTOEXEC.BAT:
```
SET COMSPEC=C:\DOS\COMMAND.COM
```

Note in this example that the SHELL statement shows that the COMMAND.COM file is in the DOS subdirectory, and the SET COMSPEC statement agrees with it. If the two don't agree, you may see an error message like `Cannot reload COMMAND.COM, system halted`. That leaves AUTOEXEC.BAT as a source of troubles, and it's not without its share: load a buggy TSR program in AUTOEXEC.BAT, and the system will freeze at boot.

So, to review, you've seen how the PC starts up. A basic core of hardware must have power before anything can start. Then BIOS performs inventory and initialization. BIOS kicks off the DOS load process and, once DOS loads, your PC is ready to go to work. Now you understand the underlying mechanics so you can recognize where the boot process is failing. That, in combination with some of the other techniques in this chapter, should help you get a dead PC up and running.

Finding and Replacing Bad Chips

Okay, you *insist* on trying to fix some boards? Sometimes you *can* be a real hero and actually fix a circuit board. Most maintenance shops do very little board repair, instead returning boards to the manufacturer or, more often, just disposing of them. Board repair can be time consuming and therefore expensive, so it's not a great idea when most boards cost somewhere in the range of $100–$200 or even less. You'll spend a minimum of an hour and a maximum of forever fixing a board.

This is not to say that it should never be attempted. In fact, since the most expensive parts on your motherboard are usually socketed, the easiest chips you can troubleshoot are

- Memory chip

- Replacement microprocessor

- Coprocessor

- ROM (read-only memory)

If you're going to handle chips, please first take a look at the section on chip handling, "Chip Sockets and Chip Insertion/Removal" later in this chapter. In general, bad chips are found in one of the following ways:

▶ Manufacturer notification

▶ Software identification of chip malfunction

▶ Temperature testing

▶ Digital probe and pulse testing

▶ Use of specialized (and expensive) signature analyzers

▶ Exhaustive chip replacement

Chip "Recall"

The most common method of finding bad chips is the first: manufacturer notification. That is, the manufacturer will send you a replacement chip and a notice that says something like, "Some boards built in 1996 malfunction due to a faulty 65X88 chip. Enclosed find a replacement 65X88. . . ." Kind of like a car recall.

Software Chip Testing

Software identification is possible when the chip is not so vital to the system that the system can't run without it. Many memory problems can be identified with software, as can some problems with some major chips, like the 8284 clock chip and the 8237 DMA controller. ROM often contains a checksum (an error check) that can be used to verify that the contents of the ROM haven't been damaged. You usually get the program that checks the checksum with the board that has the ROM in question. For example, most PC system diagnostics know where the checksum for the BIOS ROM is, and they check that as part of their routine.

Temperature Chip Testing

Some faulty chips can be traced through their temperature or lack thereof. A properly functioning chip should be slightly warm to the touch—warmer, at least, than after a night of deactivation. A completely cool chip, particularly a large one (large chips tend to run warmer) is probably dead. Similarly, a very hot chip—finger-burning variety—is probably dead or dying.

A worse situation occurs when the device works *sometimes*, then fails after a while (generally just before you were going to save your work). Heat can make a marginal component stop working, and the marginal component may not seem unduly warm. In this situation, how do you locate the bad component? By controlled application of heat and cold.

First, start up the device—PC, modem, whatever—with the cover off. Then blow warm air (I *did not say hot*—100 degrees will do nicely; I mean, we're talking a burn *in* process here, not burn *up*) onto the circuit board: use a hair dryer. The intermittent chip will fail eventually. Now get a can of component coolant and direct the cold blast directly onto the suspect chip. If there is no particular suspect chip, start with the big ones. Now try to restart the device. If it starts, there's a good chance that the cooled chip is the bad one. If it doesn't restart, try another chip. As always, keep notes.

Finally, there is the brute force method. Get a digital probe and pulser and test each chip, one by one. Surefire, but slow.

Identifying Chips

As long as we're trying to replace chips, let's see how to find the silly things in the first place, and let's look at what those numbers atop the chip mean. A chip can be described by its function, its identification number, and its manufacturer.

Chip Function

Physical size is some indication of a chip's complexity, but it is not tremendously important. Memory chips are fairly small, but they are complex.

Identification Number and Manufacturer

When a manufacturer designs a new chip, it gives it an identification number. For example, an 8088 is a particular microprocessor chip, and a 7400 is a quad two-input NAND chip. Generally, chip designs are patented, so another manufacturer must be licensed before it can offer a chip that it did not design. For example, back in the XT days, Intel designed the 8088, but Advanced Micro Devices (AMD) probably made more of them than Intel ever did. I do not know who developed the first 256K x 1 dynamic RAM chip, but virtually everyone in the chip business makes them now.

Prefixes and suffixes may be added to a chip's ID number. The suffixes refer to the package that it is in (usually DIP—Dual Inline Package, which is indicated by the suffix AN), or the temperature range (S is military specification, N is normal). Thus, 7400AN refers to a 7400 chip in a DIP package. A two-letter prefix refers to the manufacturer. Some manufacturer codes are HD for Hitachi, WD for Western Digital, DM for National Semiconductor, and R for Rockwell. Another code may be present, like B9544. This means (ignore the B) that the chip was made in the 44th week of 1995. Some vendors, like Intel, do not put a date code on their chips. Instead, they put a serial number on the chip (for example, a motherboard in front of me has a chip with serial number L5450275).

Other suffixes refer to performance, as with the old 8088-1 and 8088-2 microprocessors. The -2 ran up to 8MHz, and the -1 ran reliably only up to 5MHz. In the case of memory chips, there are more specific speed codes, as you'll learn in Chapter 8.

Soldering and Desoldering

If you're going to change chips, a few words about soldering.

It isn't hard, but it *does* take some practice. *If you have never soldered before, the place to learn is not on your PC!* Get some practice elsewhere, or just decide not to bother with soldering tasks. We PC fix-it people seek to minimize the amount of soldering required by choosing components that use sockets instead of solder whenever possible. More on sockets later.

The trick with soldering is to heat up *both* components to the desired temperature, then apply the solder. You want just enough heat to melt the solder, but not so much as to destroy whatever it is that you're soldering.

Soldering irons come in various powers or wattages. For PC work, you want a low-power iron, like a pencil iron fewer than 50 watts. Here are a few tips to remember when soldering.

- Use a 60/40 solder with rosin core (*not* acid core), ⅟₃₂-inch width.

- Do not apply the tip for more than 10 seconds—this should be more than sufficient.

- For desoldering, *do not* use solder suckers or vacuum bulbs unless they have grounded tips. They can build up static charges. Use wire braid instead.

- Remove the board first. Don't try to solder things on or off boards that are installed in the PC.

- When replacing chips or transistors, socket them first (see next section).

- Buy a solder jig (sometimes called a "third hand") so that you have enough hands to hold the board, the soldering iron, the chip, and the desoldering tool. Many electronics stores sell different varieties of this product; Edmund Scientific (see Appendix A) sells a reasonably priced one called the Extra Hands Work Station.

Note

By the way, a techie student once claimed that I was dead wrong about solder jigs, as true techies scoff at them. To the true techies, I apologize. I've used the things, and I like 'em.

- If you are replacing a diode, transistor, or capacitor, draw a picture of how the original is installed. Memory (the human kind) gets faulty when faced with the normal frustration of soldering. It doesn't matter which way you insert a resistor.

▶ When desoldering a chip from a circuit board, don't desolder each pin in order. This builds up too much heat in one area. Jump around. Use a heat sink. Alternatively, use a solder tip designed for DIPs.

▶ As mentioned before, many system boards are now four-layer boards. They are *very* tough to work on competently with the usual inexpensive soldering equipment.

Chip Sockets and Chip Insertion/Removal

Most chips are soldered directly onto the printed circuit board, but they need not be. Chip *sockets* (as in light bulb "sockets") are available as an alternative. As long as you're removing and replacing a chip, think about installing a socket for the replacement.

The advantages of socketed chips are that they are easy to remove and replace, and it's a lot harder to damage a chip while inserting it in a socket than it is while soldering it in place. On the other hand, a soldered chip saves money—no socket must be bought. Also, it can't creep out of the socket.

As mentioned before, a socketed chip's problem may simply be that it has crept far enough out of the socket to impair electrical connection. Recall that an early step in troubleshooting is to push all socketed chips gently back into their sockets.

Whether installing a socketed or directly mounted chip, you must be sure to install it with the correct side up. Chip pins are numbered with the furthest pin on the left side labeled 1, then counting down on the left side and finally up the right side (counterclockwise). You can see this in Figure 7.3.

Figure 7.3:

Chip numbering

A chip can fit into a socket in one of two ways. The top of the chip generally has a notch to orient you when installing. To make things even easier, most circuit boards are designed so that all of the chips face the same way. This is *essential*: insert a chip with the notch facing the wrong way and you may destroy the chip. Figure 7.4 shows the correct orientation of the chip notches; consult the documentation for the chip if you cannot determine the correct alignment.

Notch or equivalent

Figure 7.4

Chip notches

Troubleshooting Tips

If you've tried everything else and finally determine that the problem you're having is indeed the circuit board, keep the following in mind:

▶ Beeps (more than one) when starting a PC usually indicate a problem with one of the primary components, such as the keyboard, video, or motherboard. Refer back to Tables 7.1 and 7.2 to find out what a particular string of beeps means.

▶ The power supply is more likely to be the problem than the motherboard in a no-power situation; further, a bad power supply can ruin a good motherboard, so do not swap a good motherboard into a system with a possibly bad power supply.

▶ Problems that occur only with one program usually signal an incompatibility between that program and your hardware. This problem can sometimes be overcome by a software patch from the manufacturer of either the hardware or the program.

▶ A heat source (like a hairdryer) and a cooling source (like spray coolant or a frozen cotton swab) can help you check for heat-related problems. If applying heat makes the component fail and cooling it makes it work, overheating is the culprit.

▶ Soldering and desoldering is not usually a cost-effective repair on a board, and it is difficult for beginners to do it correctly. If you do decide to solder or desolder, use a pencil iron under 50 watts and 60/40 solder with rosin (not acid) core, $\frac{1}{32}$-inch width.

Now let's move on to that essential part of everyone's PC: the memory.

8

Semiconductor Memory

INTRODUCTION

I said in the last chapter that you generally won't handle trouble-shooting down to the chip level. There are, as I noted, exceptions. Memory is one of them. So let's talk about the chips that you *will* replace. No discussion of circuit board and chip problems would be complete without some talk of memory chips. Memory (or RAM) chips are the chips that you are most likely to have to mess with. Generally, you'll handle *dynamic RAM* (*DRAM*), but some older computers use *static RAM* (*SRAM*).

DIMMs are, by far, the most common type of RAM sold these days. Prices for RAM can range from $65 for 32MB to over $2000 for a 512MB module. For some perspective, consider the 4GB (yes, *giga*byte) RAM kit available for the Silicon Graphics (SGI) Onyx Reality. It's bargain priced from BuyComp.Com at $19,321, a savings of over $7100!!! Get yours today!

This chapter acquaints you with memory characteristics and tells you how to handle and install memory chips. You'll also learn about the kinds of problems that can lead to false memory errors and the tests used to detect memory problems.

Installing RAM

Installing RAM is, in theory, easy, but is often an exercise in frustration. Why? Depending on who you bought your machine from (or who made it, as that's likely whom you purchased it from as well) and what market it was targeted for, there can be all kinds of nifty snafus, shortcuts, skimpings, and other annoyances. I have a Packard Bell that I purchased for $700 to use as a test server. You have to remove the motherboard power coupling to install or remove RAM if you want to put anything the size of a 3.5-inch hard disk in the lower drive bay, which I did. Then, even though the motherboard's IDE subsystem supports four devices, the cable had only one terminal on it, so I had to replace it in order to get another drive installed.

I've come across many systems like this, with wires pulled taut because the manufacturer probably didn't want to spend the extra $.0015 on an additional inch or two per cable, using unmarked IDE cables to save even more, and drive bays accessible only from the front (how do you get the cables attached?). One of my favorites is arbitrary power supply terminal length. There are usually a few extra terminals that snake from the power supply cable trunk that can be attached to drives and other internal devices. After you've cut off all the restricting zip ties, you find that they are also forever intertwined in a way that disallows most of the terminals to reach beyond 5 or 6 inches from the power supply. Everything is, of course, 6.5 to 10 inches away.

Ah. Fresh cynicism is great. A good bet here is that if you have an opportunity to get a great deal on RAM (128MB SDRAM DIMMs were going for about $110 in June 2000) and installation for free, do it. If nothing works, you can blame them. Let's press on, shall we?

Be Prepared

Before you start, there are some things you may need on hand. These include:

- Phillips-head screwdriver to remove the case screws.

- Small cup or other receptacle to place the screws in.

- Antistatic wrist strap or antistatic pad with a strap to prevent zapping (highly technical term) of the RAM, possibly causing failure.

- Your motherboard's manual for settings, location, and jumper references.

- A smattering of replacement jumpers. These can be found at just about any electronics supply shop at $1–$2 for 20. Get the medium-sized ones. If you do a lot of board crawling, it's good to have these around.

To install the RAM, follow these steps:

1. Shut down the system and remove the power cable.

2. Place the case on a flat, stable surface. Remove the screws from the rear of the case.

3. Slide off the cover. This is different for each maker, but new machines are starting to make it easier. Place tower systems right side down. Desktop systems should be oriented so that the ports on the rear of the case face left.

4. Locate the three DIMM or four RIMM slots. They are approximately 4 inches (10cm) long, are very close to each other, are near the CPU, and have large white or gray tabs at each end. There should be a diagram in your motherboard material.

5. Move the tabs away from the slot. They swing on sturdy hinges near the bottom of the slot.

6. Identify the pegs inside of the slot. There will be two. Match those with the notches on the RAM and orient accordingly.

7. Lower the module into the slot. Apply only slight pressure to each end. This should kick up the tabs on each end.

8. Feel the module's positioning with your fingers along the top edge. If it slides or otherwise feels loose, reseat it.

9. When you feel confident that the notches match the pegs, the tabs are in the upright position from your slight pressure, and you feel comfortable that the module is ready, push firmly on one end of the top edge near a tab.

10. If all things go well, which is likely, you should feel and hear a taut snap as the module enters the pin array and the tab locks over the end.

11. Repeat with the other side.

12. Start the machine.

Tip

If you have a Dell, Hewlett-Packard, Packard-Bell, Micron, Gateway, Toshiba, Sony, Acer, IBM, or other top-tier machine, you will invariably view a company-specific splash screen when starting. To defeat this, tap the Del key a few times. If this does nothing and the system enters Windows boot, reset the machine and try again with the F1 key. One of these will open the ROM BIOS settings applet. Check your BIOS material for the procedures needed to turn off the vendor-specific splash screen and to turn on verbose RAM checking. Turning on RAM checking will allow you to see the RAM POST when the BIOS checks for faults.

13. If the RAM is not recognized or the system does not start correctly, shut down, unplug, and reseat (stop, drop, and roll!!). If repeated attempts to do this result in failure every time, return the RAM for a replacement.

VISUAL UPGRADE

Removing and Installing SDRAM Modules

1 Pull the plastic clips at both ends of the slot away from the SDRAM module.

2 Gently pull the SDRAM module from the slot on the motherboard.

3 A motherboard with all of the SDRAM memory modules removed.

4 Carefully insert new SDRAM memory modules into the slot.

5 Press the SDRAM memory module into the slot until the plastic clips lock. (If it doesn't snap into place, press the lever inward.)

6 An SDRAM memory module properly seated in its motherboard slot.

Introducing Memory Sizes, Speeds, and Shapes

You'll see memory referred to as *DIPs, SIPPs, SIMMs, DIMMs,* and so on. What do all these terms mean?

Chips are distinguished by their

▶ Package type, which can be

   ▶ *Dual Inline Packages* (*DIPs*) look a lot like all the other standard chips in your computer. They are little, black, plastic bricks with two rows of metal legs, one on each of their long sides, hence the name *dual inline. Single Inline Pin Packages* (*SIPPs*) are small circuit boards that contain several memory chips on them and have a single row of pins across the bottom.

   ▶ *Single Inline Memory Modules* (*SIMMs*) and *Double Inline Memory Modules* (*DIMMs*) are also small circuit boards containing several memory chips. They each have an edge connector across the bottom.

   ▶ *PC Cards* (also known as PCMCIA cards) and *CompactFlash* are small, thin modules that plug into a special socket found mostly on notebook computers, digital cameras, and personal digital assistants (PDAs).

   ▶ Various proprietary, vendor-specific chip packages.

▶ Access speed (how quickly the chip fetches data), which is measured in nanoseconds. Common access times are 40-, 50-, 60-, 70-, and 80ns for normal memories, and as low as 8ns for expensive, high-speed memories. Lower numbers are faster.

▶ Memory capacity; modern DIMM capacity ranges from 32MB to 1024MB for memory modules.

Memory Package Types

Let's take a quick look at the kinds of packages in which you'll find memory supplied.

DIPs are just simple memory chips. SIMMs come in a 30-pin format and a 72-pin format. The 30-pin format is the equivalent of about nine DIP chips. The 72-pin format is the equivalent of about 36 DIP chips. The SIMM itself may have three, eight, nine, or more chips on it—the actual number of chips on a SIMM is only loosely related to its memory capacity or type.

SIPPs look just like SIMMs except that they don't have an edge connector on the bottom; instead, they've got pins on the bottom. SIPPs enjoyed a brief popularity in the late '80s, but you won't find them around much anymore.

Modern computers use 168-pin DIMMs or, on occasion, some kind or proprietary memory type. Figure 8.1 shows some DIMMs.

Figure 8.1

DIMMS

30-pin SIMM

72-pin SIMM

Laptops in particular have made heavy use of proprietary memory modules, and there's rarely any rhyme or reason to the design. Some of these memory cards look like—but *aren't*—PC Cards. Others are just chip packages. Typically, though, they are designed to meet the limitations of the interior of the machine. The Small Outline

DRAM (SO-DRAM) DIMM was designed to meet this challenge and to proffer a standard RAM format for portable systems. (More on that a little later.)

DIMMs have replaced SIMMs primarily because they are simply more efficient and they can pack twice as much memory into the same space. They do so by mounting DRAM chips on both sides of the inline memory module and by using two sets of contacts, one on each side of the module board (SIMMs use only one set). And before you ask: No, you can't upgrade your computer simply by installing DIMM modules into your SIMM slots, because the actual package— the module board—has a different interface. Both the electronics and the connectors are different.

Note

The primary reason that DIMMs have a superior physical design over SIMMs is that they contain twice the contacts of SIMMs, a set on each side. This allows one DIMM to act as two SIMMs and eliminates the need to mount duplicate banks of RAM. In reality, modern systems with three physical banks for SDRAM DIMMs actually see six banks of RAM. One DIMM is already a pair. So simple, it's brilliant!

Will you need to keep boosting memory? Silly question. Speed and capacity largely drive the computer market. More is always better, and memory sizes thought to be really spiffy last year are called "brain dead" this year. Just stay tuned. Memory chips are a hot technology area and, other than CPUs, have the most influence on what you can do with your box.

Motherboard Chip Sets and DIMM Slots

When Intel designs a CPU, it also designs a series of support chips that manage the operations of the systems around that CPU. One of the primary systems is RAM operations and management. I have a 333MHz Pentium II with 128MB of 66MHz RAM. This arrangement sits on a BIOStar MicroTech M6TLC PII motherboard, which runs the Intel 440LX chip set.

Warning

The LX chip set has a known limitation wherein it is unable to cache beyond the first 64MB of RAM, even if there's more. Not nice! If you need caching access to more RAM—that is, for Computer Aided Drafting and Machining (CAD/CAM), 3D design/animation, graphic arts—then I suggest something along the lines of a Pentium III 500 or better with a 440BX chip set. That's just me, though.

Systems today operate with a combination of Intel's 440BX chip set, capable of using 100MHz SDRAM (PC-100), and the new 8*xx* series (810e, 820, etc. . . .) that can use 100 and 133MHz SDRAM DIMMs. (I'll explain *SDRAM* later.) So, you can see that the motherboard chip set defines the type of CPU, how fast it can run, what features it offers, and, most importantly, what types of RAM it can take.

This is expressed in two ways: (1) by the chip set and the types of RAM it can recognize, and (2) by the number of slots on the motherboard. Most motherboards come with three DIMM slots, and the chip sets limit most of these systems to a maximum of 384MB of RAM (128MB DIMM × 3). Some motherboards exceed this limitation, such as the ASUS P3V4X Apollo Pro133A (`http://www.asus.com`). This motherboard can accept up to four 512MB SDRAM DIMMs, for a total of 2GB of RAM.

Memory Banks on 64-Bit Computers

Every Pentium or Pentium Pro-based motherboard I've seen either uses a proprietary memory module, or takes 72-pin SIMMs. You'll need two 72-pin SIMMs to make a bank on these computers. Many of these motherboards have four SIMM sockets, making two banks. However, more modern Pentium II/III/Celeron and AMD Athlon machines commonly use three banks of DIMM slots.

This is because, as mentioned before, DIMMs are the logical representation of two SIMMs; one DIMM slot is the equivalent of two SIMM slots. Interleaving is eliminated, and since interleaving operations can be handled at the chip level and not handed off through a much slower bus, speeds increase multifold.

RDRAM comes in sets of two, but can operate independently, not requiring an operational partner. RDRAM systems typically ship with four RIMM slots.

Dynamic RAM

As computers are built faster and faster, all the components must get faster and faster to make plopping a 700MHz Pentium III onto a motherboard worth it. Design a system around a 700MHz chip, and you need a lot of very fast components—including RAM.

Note

Static RAM (SRAM) is the simplest kind of memory to understand, because when you put data into it, the data stays there. Now, your response might be, "Big deal—isn't that the whole idea of memory? What good is memory that *doesn't* hold onto the data that you give it?" Well, to build that kind of memory, you've got to build about six transistors into each bit storage location. That kind of memory—SRAM—can be quite fast, but also quite expensive. If you used SRAM for your PC memory, then there'd be no trouble with getting memories that kept up with your CPUs; but, on the other hand, you wouldn't be able to *afford* those computers, because SRAM is about 10 times more expensive than the DRAM that people are used to buying. SRAM is also physically larger than DRAM and generally runs much hotter. Of course, all these negative aspects drove the market to adopt DRAM and see SRAM move into a supporting role (it's typically used for Video RAM, L1 and L2 cache RAM, or other similar RAM needs). Fortunately, things have speeded up quite a bit over the past few years.

Dynamic RAM (DRAM) was the economical answer to the earlier SRAM. Each DRAM bit is built of a single transistor and a capacitor, in contrast to SRAM's six transistors.

DRAM has two problems from the point of view of a PC designer. First, the *dynamic* in its name means that it forgets the data that you give it almost as fast as you can give it the data. That means that

DRAM-based systems require refresh circuitry to get around this electronic amnesia.

Second, the way that DRAMs are built to be cheaper is that they are organized not simply into a set of addresses; rather, each bit in a DRAM has a row address and a column address. The slow part of accessing any part of a DRAM is in getting to its row. Once you're in a row, subsequent intra-row accesses can be quite fast. In fact, that's the area with the most advances recently, in DRAMs that can access data quite quickly. This brings me to Table 8.1, which outlines the types of DRAM.

TABLE 8.1 The March of Time with DRAM

Type	First Used	Clock Rate	Bus Width*	Peak Bandwidth	Voltage
FPM (60, 70ns)	1990	25MHz	64-bit	200MBps	5v
EDO (50, 60, 70ns)	1994	40MHz	64-bit	320MBps	5v
SDRAM (66MHz)	1996	66MHz	64-bit	528MBps	3.3v
SDRAM (100MHz)	1998	100MHz	64-bit	800MBps	3.3v
SDRAM (133MHz)	1999	133MHz	64-bit	1.1GBps	3.3v
RDRAM (Direct Rambus)	1999	400MHz (× 2)	16-bit	1.6GBps	2.5v
DDR SDRAM (100MHz)	2000	100MHz (× 2)	64-bit	1.6GBps	3.3v
DDR SDRAM (133MHz)	2000	133MHz (× 2)	64-bit	2.1GBps	3.3v
SLDRAM	____	400MHz (× 2)	16-bit	1.6GBps	2.5v

* Indicates the maximum module data width, not its external bus width. 64-bit external pathways began with the 75MHz Pentium.

Data courtesy of CMP TechWeb and Kingston Technology © 2000

As you can see in this table, it took four years to get from quite slow Fast Page Mode (FPM) RAM to Extended Data Out (EDO) RAM, which produced only a marginal increase in performance. At that time, adding 16MB of RAM to a 16MB system yielded an approximate 30 percent boost in overall performance. Going beyond that resulted in little more than an additional 5 percent, if even that.

That diminished return ad infinitum changed with synchronous dynamic RAM (SDRAM) and its 66MHz bus. This also, as mentioned before, marked the point when RAM speed became tied to the CPU speed. This is important because timing is crucial to efficient data transfer in systems that are defined by time, such as our computers. 1998 ushered in 100MHz SDRAM, or PC-100. 1999 showed us 133MHz SDRAM, and RDRAM from a company named Rambus.

Note

RDRAM is interesting, in that instead of increasing the pipe that the data passes through, it makes it *smaller*. Quite a bit smaller, in fact. Most RAM operates at an internal 64 bits with a variable external data path (which these days is almost always 64 bits as well). RDRAM uses a 16-bit data path. Now, this yields only a 500MBps-faster performance over 133MHz SDRAM, but its internal operations move at an intense 400MHz. RDRAM I/O can be doubled to two paths, which increases the logical speed to 800MHz, though real life doesn't operate like that.

Ovonic Unified Memory

Even more interesting is a new memory type that may be emerging, and quickly, if technical hurdles and cost restrictions can be overcome. It's called Ovonic Unified Memory (OUM) and it's based, believe it or not, on the same phase-change technology as CD-RW (rewritable) disks.

To quickly explain, the addressable surface of the CD-RW media is such that applying a laser to it changes the addressed location of a thin-film material to crystalline or amorphous, on or off, 1 or 0. Now,

CD-RW drives have gotten as fast as 8x, but they're limited by the laser, which can move only so fast or it begins to write gibberish. (By the way, CDs can be read a lot faster because of several factors, not the least of which is the laser's capability to scan several regions at one time through various technologies and ever-increasing stability at very high rotation speeds.)

Ovonyx (`http://www.ovonyx.com`), the company that's developing OUM, states that it is as fast as DRAM because an OUM array uses transistors instead of lasers to apply charges that spark the metamorphosis. There are a few interesting factors to reflect on that OUM brings to light. First, think of the CD-RW. It's basically a CD that has a special layer that can be structurally altered by a laser but retains the ability to be read by legacy CD-ROM drives (under most circumstances. For a more detailed explanation of CD technology look to Chapter 26, "An Overview of CD-ROM"). So, as proven, the OUM technology applies a charge to the surface of the rewriteable material and changes its state as dictated by the incoming data in a very similar fashion to CD-RW and DVD-RAM. CD media costs about $1 a piece to produce. Think about it. Need more?

Second, a CD-RW disk can hold up to 640MB of data on its aggregate surface area. With the ability of chip makers such as Intel and IBM to pack millions of transistors, several layers of these combination thin-film/transistors arrays could be packaged into the space traditionally taken by SDRAM DIMMs, provide dramatically greater storage space, and consume less energy. Less energy? That's right, read on . . .

Last, all of this is what is called *nonvolatile*. Currently, all RAM is *volatile* in that when the power is taken away, everything there gets wiped. See now? Nonvolatile RAM, much like Flash RAM used in digital cameras, retains whatever you put on it without needing a charge to retain it. You see, SDRAM arrays must be constantly refreshed (read: electrified) or their states are lost and the array is reset. OUM doesn't have that problem. Like a CD-RW, once it's written, it becomes a feature of the medium, not a magnetic signature.

Unfortunately, although Intel has invested in Ovonyx and the OUM technology, don't expect to see it this year or maybe even next year. Engineering on this scale can take some time, and it's crucial to make sure there are *no* kinks or fumbles. You have to admit, though, it's very, *very* cool. I can clearly imagine spending only a few hundred bucks for four or five *gigabytes* of RAM and never having to reboot my machine. Ever. Very cool indeed.

The dark gray section that encompasses the last three items in Table 8.1 is what appears to be our RAM future: RDRAM, double data rate SDRAM (DDR SDRAM), and synchronous link DRAM (SLDRAM). These are not far off at all, really. Of course, seeing this, you may wonder what's wrong with all of us, that we aren't all using RDRAM. Heck, it's so darned fast already! The answer is simple; cost. Rambus, like most other companies, likes to make money. The design is theirs, and Intel has invested heavily in it. They also like to charge for the privilege of use. This privilege often results in systems costing $2500 or more, easily placing RDRAM well out of reach of the average consumer who expects their machines to cost little more than $1200.

Note

RDRAM comes in a package format called Rambus Inline Memory Module (RIMM). RIMMs come in 64-, 128-, and 256MB modules, ECC and non-ECC, and at speeds of 600-, 700-, and 800MHz. That's *fast*.

FPM and EDO DRAM

FPM and EDO DRAM types are not used anymore. You may have one or the other in your PC that you are upgrading with the help of this book, but in the end, they will go the way of the woolly mammoth (unless you have another old machine that could use more RAM, but then that's another set of problems).

There is one instance where EDO DRAM can still be used, but it's mostly a crutch for backward compatibility. The motherboard I mentioned earlier, the BIOStar MicroTech M6TLC PII, is capable of handling up to 384MB of SDRAM (128MB DIMMs), but can take up to 768MB of EDO DRAM (256MB DIMMs). As, however, with all pre-SDRAM DRAM types, EDO DRAM suffers from less efficient transfer speeds and reduced capabilities. If you need that much RAM, then you don't need a motherboard like this one and you certainly don't want EDO DRAM!

SDRAM

Synchronous Dynamic Random Access Memory (*SDRAM*) is a variant of DRAM that includes an on-chip burst counter. This burst counter can be used to increment column addresses and increase the speed of memory access.

Note

SDRAM typically comes in either SIMM or DIMM formats, though DIMM is the dominantly common format today.

Although faster is generally considered better and speed is pursued for its own sake, the reason behind the SDRAM is that CPUs are getting faster. With their increasing speed, they require ever faster memory in order to function within earshot of their potential. With SDRAM, the CPU and RAM are locked together by the same clock. Thus, the speed of the RAM and the CPU are linked, or synchronized.

Note

Another solution to the problem of speeding up RAM is *cached RAM,* which boosts the overall speed of the memory by adding a static RAM area on the dynamic RAM chip itself. This small amount of fast SRAM acts as a cache to the DRAM.

Normally, memory chips answer data requests. Cache memory can anticipate the CPU's needs. When the CPU asks for data, the memory already has it waiting and ready to go. Some cache memory implementations also include a pipeline. The pipelined architecture has a design in which one stage can fetch an address while other stages present the data for output. The cache memory concept has the advantage of being a simple, elegant replacement for older chips; it just plugs into the system and goes.

SDRAM modules come in 72-, 144-, and 168-pin packages and can range from 4MB to 512MB in capacity. There are generally two types of SDRAM DIMMs; *unbuffered* and *registered*. The 72-pin SO-DRAM was designed to meet the specific needs of portables and their space limitations. The problem was that upgrades required two modules, eliminating the savings in space. Thus was born the 144-pin SO-DRAM variant of the full-sized DIMM. 168-pin packages are solely for use in systems that do not have space limitations.

Note

Unbuffered memory is simple memory that relies on a controller to function predictably. This is the most common type of RAM and one of the reasons why RAM is inexpensive. *Registered* memory has a register array onboard, generally allowing for more orderly operations. It's also more costly to make, and that cost gets passed on to you, the buyer. Fortunately, it's really only important that you know which type your system requires. A general rule of thumb is when in doubt, it'll probably take unbuffered. Don't worry. Nothing will break.

To Error Correct or Not to Error Correct

You will probably note that some types of RAM are labeled ECC, which is short for error-correction code. If you have seen this, you likely wondered why it was more expensive than non-ECC RAM. Well, the answer is simple. ECC RAM does more than conventional RAM. Of course, if you need ECC RAM, you can probably afford to buy it, since it's mostly used to help prevent costly and damaging errors, faults, and mistakes. Now, if you're already buying ECC or if you already have it, then you don't need to read this section and can move on.

Good to see you stick it out. Now, how does ECC work? Good question. The answer is that ECC uses special algorithms to watch, evaluate, and fix various problems that appear in the data stream, either incoming or outgoing. This means greater stability for data-intensive applications such as CAD/CAM and audio and video editing, though I doubt you'll need it at home.

DDR SDRAM

As noted earlier, *DDR* is short for double data rate, and it maximizes output by using both the leading and following edge of the clock tick to perform operations. This means that DDR can locate and pass an address in one tick as opposed to two. DDR has great potential for making speedy systems, as long as the system it is installed in takes advantage of the new speed. The architecture of the overall system can be lacking if the front-side bus (FSB) is not fast or wide enough to handle the additional traffic. Current FSBs are not up to the task of utilizing DDR technology, but they'll get there.

DDR SDRAM is not yet common, but there are some vendors and chip makers that are supporting and making it—IBM, for one, although their initial focus is on servers, with their first DDR SDRAM stick being a whopping 256MB module. Samsung is in the throes of engineering 128MB and 256MB versions, with the 128MB version in testing as of this writing. Micron, the guys behind Crucial Technologies (RAM makers), are also on the bandwagon. Others joining in are AMD, Mitsubishi, NEC, Toshiba, Hyundai (not the car guys), Fujitsu, and a few others. In general, the industry seems to be rallying around DDR and ignoring Rambus DRAM, an investment of Intel's.

VIA's (`http://www.viatech.com`) MVP3 motherboard supports DDR SDRAM modules, and most video card makers have opted to use DDR SDRAM in their latest 3D accelerators, a market segment always out to ride the bleeding edge. Though I was unable to find any per-unit pricing information at this early stage of the game, all indications say that DDR won't cost significantly more than current SDRAM offerings. Additionally, those prices should drop swiftly if support grows with industry acceptance and implementation.

Note

Those 3D video cards I mentioned earlier? They seem to be averaging around $250 to $350 per unit.

SLDRAM

Synchronous link DRAM is what is called a protocol-based technology. Unlike other RAM, a *protocol-based technology* works on the premise of a facilitating object being involved in the transfer of data to and from one place and another. In this case, the data being transferred is stored in RAM. Think of the CPU as a client and the SLDRAM bus as a server. When the client requests data from the server, it's sent. Requests occur in both directions. This makes for a more intelligent data manipulation interactivity. It's potential is very strong.

To make it as fast as possible, SLDRAM uses a mulitiplexed bus to move data in and out, bypassing the limitations of traditional pins. SLDRAM can currently handle I/O speeds of up to 1.6GBps with a very fast theoretical cap of 3GBps.

Blast from the Past: Memory Interleaving

Some systems attempted to minimize the loss of speed incurred by charging capacitors by arranging the RAM into *interleaved banks*. The idea was this: memory is organized into banks, or logical groups. With interleaving, memory subsystems always have an even number of banks. Memory addresses are then *interleaved* so that when one address (in the first bank) is being accessed, the following address (which is in the second bank) is being charged up. That way, when it's time to access the second bank, it needn't be charged, because the following address is ready to go. While reading that address in the second bank, its following address (back in the first bank) is being charged up, and so on.

Notice that this works only if the CPU's memory accesses tend to be in consecutive memory addresses. That's a pretty good assumption, but if the program running in the system jumps all around the RAM for data, then interleaving is defeated, and memory accesses slow down.

Interleaving was a good idea for its time, but it was effective only for the first access in a row, and it required an even number of memory banks. It was rather awkward.

If you're upgrading an older system, keep track of whether it requires memory to be interleaved, or you might be confused as to why that old 80486 doesn't work, especially since you just put in fresh RAM.

Matching System Memory to Cache Memory

All the information mentioned earlier in this chapter on SDRAM and cache RAM points to one large problem in the personal computer industry: There is an increasing disparity in clock speeds between processors and DRAM. Combine this with an increasing degree of processor super-scalability, and you get a situation in which effective cache management becomes a critical factor in obtaining optimal application performance. System main memory access now can take anywhere from tens to hundreds of CPU clock cycles. Hence, the difference between finding information in the on-chip cache instead of in main memory can completely dominate the effective speed of an application, or even an entire system. There are a variety of techniques that make more effective use of the processor caches. These techniques can be divided into two types: those focusing on programs and those focusing on processors.

Better Programs

An important aspect in effective data cache management is how, and how well, an algorithm accesses the data that is in the cache. Since accessing memory whose addresses are adjacent or close together speeds up cache performance, structuring program code with the memory system in mind is often the best way to increase speed. Programmers can use a couple of design strategies to improve performance, such as making greater use of large element arrays instead of arranging data in multiple, individual structures. Additionally, code can be written to make use of processor-specific features. For example, most CPU instruction sets provide the user the ability to manage the data cache via software.

Better Processors

Although writing better programs is a good place to look for better matches between system memory and cache memory, what about something for those of us up in the cheap seats—those of us who aren't involved in program creation? The best thing (perhaps the only thing) to do is look for systems that have already addressed this problem and look to the chip vendors to provide increasingly faster iron.

Some Pentium system designs use two or more processors with dedicated caches for each processor. The advantage of such a multi-processor design is that each processor communicates freely with its own cache and thus provides highly efficient bus utilization. More efficient bus utilization equals more rapid cache access (equals a faster computer). Simple. The problem, of course, it that this kind of multiple processor design tends to be expensive and complex. Each dedicated cache requires an additional cache controller and

SRAMs, and each cache also requires its own data-path, memory-bus, and interrupt-control circuitry. Big money. Big headaches.

A bit different is a design that uses two processors that share a single secondary cache. This design is simpler and less expensive. You need only one cache controller and some SRAM. It's not as fast as dedicated caches but according to Intel, it typically improves system performance by 50 percent to 80 percent with a secondary processor installed.

Causes of False Memory Errors

Memory often gets blamed for problems arising from other sources. In most cases, memory that has been working for a few weeks will work forever. While memory hardware failures were common up to the late '80s, the quality of memory chips has improved considerably since 1988. Reliability has increased substantially over the last 12-plus years as well. Rare is the case when RAM goes bad. That said, potential problems still exist, especially in older systems that are still in use, a growing practice in today's ever-more-common multi-PC home. These older systems still need to use the older RAM and, if these systems have had RAM augmented and not replaced, these older problems can still occur.

Power Drops and Surges

Memory is often falsely accused for a simple reason: the memory is so demanding in its need for constant, clean power. If the power drops out or surges for just a few millionths of a second, the memory loses its contents, causing a memory error. This wasn't an error caused by the memory—it was a power error that just *showed up* in the memory. Think of it as the canary in the coal mine of your PC.

Along the same lines, a static electric surge looks just like a power surge. Scuff across a shag rug on a dry day, touch your computer, and you're likely to cause a memory error—but please *don't* try this out, because you may cause permanent memory damage. A failing power supply may, in the same way, cause apparent memory failures. So will noisy power being fed to a perfectly good power supply.

The telltale signs in this case are the addresses reported by the memory errors. If you've truly got a memory error, you'll see the same address reported as bad over and over. But memory errors that always report different locations—locations that test fine when tested a few minutes later—likely point to power problems.

Is there *enough* power? Insufficient power can cause parity errors. This one can be a real pain, since it waits for some large disk access to trigger the parity error—for example, when you try to save your data to disk.

You see this one with underpowered clones: your application works fine until you want to save the file, then you get a parity check. The problem is that you're running the power supply to the poor thing's limits and then want to fire up the hard disk. Not enough power, the memory gets shortchanged, and, BANG! A memory error happens.

And, while it's unusual, improperly shielded sources of RF noise can alter memory, causing parity errors. I remember a 64KB chip made back in the early '80s that was built in a chip package that was accidentally built out of a ceramic material that was a very low-level emitter of alpha particle radiation. Once in while, an alpha particle would zip through the chip, causing a nonrepeatable error. I'm glad I don't have to troubleshoot *those* chips any more.

Mismatched Chip Speeds and Manufacturers

If you need a chip that has an access speed of, say, 80ns, but you can get only a faster chip—say, one that runs at 60ns—can you use the faster 60ns chip to replace the slower 80ns chip? Yes, *but* you must replace the entire bank of chips when you do that. Putting a single 60ns chip into a bank of 80ns chips will often cause the 80s to appear to have errors.

Whenever possible, avoid mixing *manufacturers* in the same row. I flatly cannot explain this, but I have seen cases where it caused problems. For instance, I have two rows of chips—one entirely Mitsubishi, another entirely Toshiba—that work fine. Then I mix the rows. Errors occur. Restore the rows, and the problem disappears.

Memory Tests

Modern RAM is pretty reliable, but you may come across a RAM failure of an odd sort on some SIMMs: *soft failures*. These are failures that show up only with very specific tests.

Note

DIMMs of SDRAM varieties rarely have faults. When they do, the faults can often be traced back to a fabrication error.

Walking Bit Test

Years ago, a manuscript of an early edition of this book suddenly started growing typos. And odd typos they were, too: now and then, a letter would show up wrong for no reason. I first thought that the printer was failing, but checking in the file on the disk, I found that the typos were *there*, too. I thought this extremely odd, because I'd proofread the text—as had many others—and these obvious typos didn't appear. I began to be certain that the problem was machine-induced.

I suspected my mass storage device, a Bernoulli cartridge system, and so I started saving the document on my hard disk instead. Still, the errors were cropping up. That's when I also noticed that some files were being corrupted when I copied them.

It was starting to look like the problem was in the system's memory. Whenever a piece of data passed through the system's memory, it would sometimes—very rarely, actually—become corrupt. Finally, I ran a *walking bit* test.

You see, standard memory tests just go to a particular location and test the heck out of it, stuffing different combinations of 1s and 0s into a particular byte, and then reading them back. Tests of that kind were coming up zero for errors. But what about interactive problems? It turned out that there were two memory locations, at roughly 560KB and 600KB, that were in cahoots with one another, so to speak. Test either location, and there was no problem. But put a 1 into the 560KB location and, lo!, a 1 popped up in the 600KB location.

This kind of error is called a *walking bit* error, and it's a problem on the memory address circuitry rather than the memory itself. It really doesn't matter where the error originates, however, because the answer is the same: replace the problematic memory units. More on how in a little bit. It takes software to test this properly, and there are two programs that test a very wide range of things, including this.

Mountain/Valley and Checkerboard Tests

Here's another example of memory problems that will never be detected by single-byte testing. Consider a set of bit memory cells, as you see in Figure 8.2.

Figure 8.2

Set of bit memory cells

But suppose one kind of bit can "leak over" into another kind of bit, as you see in Figure 8.3.

Figure 8.3

Set of bit memory cells with a "leak over" into another bit

The effect is that the 0 bits leak over into the 1s, eventually turning them into 0s. Filling each bit with a 0 and then surrounding it by 1s, and vice versa, is called the *mountain/valley* test. The *checkerboard* test lays out a pattern of 1s and 0s like the light and dark squares of a checkerboard.

All three of these tests are incorporated into the two memory tester programs (CheckIt and PC-Technician) that I recommended in Chapter 5, "Troubleshooting PC Problems." I strongly recommend running one of these programs overnight when you first install some new memory.

Tips on Installing Memory Chips

A lot of manuals include some really scary instructions for installing memory chips. I've probably installed a terabyte or so myself (64MB chips have made it easier to get to the 1GB level), so here's what works for me.

First, as always, be aware of static electricity. Your acrylic sweater and the soles of your shoes are powerful producers of it. If I'm worried about the static level of an area, and I'm not prepared with an antistatic strap, *I take my shoes and socks off.* I know it sounds a little bizarre, but I kill very few chips in my bare feet—probably less than a half dozen in all the time I've been installing memory.

Second, the memory chips go into slots on the motherboard. As before, don't insert a module into a board while the power is on. Push the white or gray knobs on the ends of the slot out from the center so you have room to slide in the module. Orient the module so that the notches in the pin array match the pegs in the slot on the board. Then push the chip into the socket firmly with your thumb.

Tip

Some people who have been around it long enough call any RAM package mounted on a printed circuit board a *stick* of RAM. Heck, I do. I will, for the sake of clarity, not refer to them here as sticks, but as modules.

Note

Remember that *patience* is the keyword here: look at what you're doing and take your time if you're new to the process.

How do I upgrade my old 486? How do I remove SIMMs? Between removing and installing, removing SIMMs can be the harder task, depending on how chintzy the motherboard manufacturer was. Figure 8.4 shows you how to remove SIMMs.

Figure 8.4

Removing SIMMs

First, *gently* pull aside the plastic tabs that hold the SIMM in place. Be careful, as the tabs are easily broken.

Once the tabs have been pushed outward, rotate the SIMM forward. It then comes right out of its socket.

There is an unfortunately frequent occurrence in the classes that I teach on PC repair that concerns SIMM removal. In every class, I tell students, "Don't remove SIMMs until I show you how to do it." Now and then, I'll get some prize idiot who decides that he'd rather figure it out himself. So he grabs the SIMM and yanks it out—and sure enough, he *did* figure out how to remove a SIMM! Unfortunately, however, that SIMM socket will never again hold a SIMM, because he has broken off the little plastic tabs that hold SIMMs in place. Even *more* unfortunately, that means that memory can't be installed on the motherboard, which means that someone—he—is going to have to buy a new motherboard. So, unless you plan to exercise the old MasterCard when you attack SIMMs, follow this procedure.

The key to removing SIMMs (and DIMMs) is to push the little tabs outward *gently*. They hold the SIMM in place. If you push too hard, you can break them off. Some SIMM sockets are better designed, and use metal spring tabs to hold the SIMMs in place—it's harder to break these off—but an unfortunate number of sockets use plastic tabs. Push the tabs outward either with the blade of a small screwdriver, or with your fingernails. Err on the side of caution. You'll feel the SIMM move a bit, and that will be your signal that you can try to pull it a bit forward. Once you've got one tab and one side free, work on the other side.

Reinserting SIMMs (and DIMMs) is similar. You place the SIMM angled forward in the SIMM socket, then push it back into place. As the SIMM contacts the tabs, relieve the pressure on the tabs by helping them outward. The SIMM will snap into place—start over if it doesn't—and all will be well. Memory is one of the most sensitive parts of your PC, both electronically and mechanically. Now that you know more about memory chips, your machine will run that much better.

Troubleshooting Tips

Before you start, this is where I get tough again. Now, I've already talked in detail about what can go wrong if you don't take the proper steps to protect yourself and your hardware before jamming your hands inside the case. I've also discussed the necessity of having any static discharge eliminated with an antistatic pad or wristband, so have your solution ready. Last, don't forget to disconnect the power cable completely. I cannot stress the importance of these precautions enough, unless, of course, you have money to burn on replacement parts.

Tip

For more details on safety precautions, look over Chapter 4, "Avoiding Service: Preventive Maintenance" again.

There can be only a few problems with RAM itself. Either it's bad or it's been statically "zapped." A few other problems can occur with installation. Here are some Q-and-A-type problems and solutions:

Q: I added a 64MB module to match my already installed one, but I still get only 64MB of RAM.

A: The module is not seated correctly. First, never put the case back on and screw it tight until *after* you have verified that all systems and subsystems are working properly. Second, using your fingertip, gently wiggle the top of the module. If it moves, remove and reseat it.

Q: I installed new RAM a few *weeks* ago and everything worked fine until today, when I went from 64MB to 32MB. I reseated the DIMM several times but to no avail. What now?

A: Replace the DIMM with a new one. You can do this either through the retailer or the manufacturer. If this does not fix the problem, then it's likely a problem with your motherboard or another chip-level component. This is when you need to take the box in for service.

Q: I installed new RAM a few *months* ago and everything worked fine until today, when I went from 64MB to 32MB. I reseated the DIMM several times but to no avail. What now?

A: If something is going to go wrong with RAM (or any other chip component for that matter), it will happen in the first several weeks. Most manufacturers warrant their products for 3 to 12 months, others for the lifetime of the product. Make sure you keep all your warranty information in the same, easily remembered place and *register your stuff*! Once they officially know you bought it, it's hard for them to deny you service.

Power Supplies and Power Protection

9

Personal computers (at least, desktop PCs) don't come with batteries included. You plug them into the wall socket and they work. But the PC itself does not directly use wall current because it is 120-volt alternating current in North America, 220–240 in Europe and the U.K.

By the way, a word to European readers. Everything I say here applies to you *except* for references to the mains. As I just mentioned, your mains are not 120 volts, but more like 200+, and the power frequency is 50 cycles per second, not 60. *Do not* try any of the tests here that refer to the actual alternating current, unless you already know about working with the mains safely.

The PC doesn't need AC; it needs DC, usually 3.3 or 5 volts for its chips, 12 volts for the motors on older drives—newer drive motors run off 5 volts. But the wall sockets provide AC—so how does the PC convert the juice? With the power supply. The power supply actually doesn't *supply* power—it *converts* it from AC to DC.

There are two kinds of power supplies: linear power supplies and switching power supplies. The PC's power supply is, in every PC *I've* ever seen, a switching power supply. Both linear and switching power supplies have their positive and negative aspects.

Linear power supplies are based on transformers. That makes them hot, heavy, and impervious to changes in current levels, while rendering them vulnerable to voltage swings. Linear power supplies are an older design than switching power supplies, and you still find them on monitors and some external drive cases. Even small linear power supplies generate a relatively large amount of heat, which is why you should never cover the holes atop a monitor; you can fry a monitor quickly that way.

Switching power supplies are digital in nature. They step down voltage by essentially "switching" it on and off, hence their name. Think of how they work in this way: suppose you had a 1000-watt bulb in a light, but you only wanted the lighting value of a 100-watt bulb. You could get 100 watts' worth out of the 1000-watt bulb by switching it on and off but leaving it off 90 percent of the time. I know it sounds goofy, but if you could switch the light on and off quickly enough, then *you'd never see it flicker.* (In fact, that's how fluorescent lights work. They're actually very bright, but they flash off and on 60 times per second, too quickly for most eyes to register—and they're off over 90 percent of the time.)

Switching power supplies are less sensitive to fluctuations in input voltage, although that is still a problem. These power supplies generate heat but a lot less of it than linear power supplies.

Why do we care about power supplies? Mainly because power supply troubles can be mysterious and annoying. Just as bad are similar-looking troubles with the supplied power itself. This chapter looks at both.

Replacing a Power Supply

Here are the essential steps for replacing a power supply. The rest of this chapter provides more detailed coverage about power supply hardware.

Be Prepared

Before you start, make sure you have the following handy:

❯ Nonmagnetic Phillips screwdriver

❯ Container to hold removed screws

Also, before you start working with the motherboard, make sure that:

❯ You are wearing an antistatic wrist strap

1. Turn everything off and unplug the power supply from the wall outlet.

2. Unplug the power supply connectors from the motherboard and the drives.

3. Remove the four screws holding the power supply in the case and lift the power supply out.

   or

   If an AT, remove the screws holding the power switch to the case.

4. Insert the new power supply and secure it with the screws you removed in step 3.

   or

If an AT, attach the power switch to the case with the screws removed in step 3.

5. Connect the power supply to the motherboard:

   ▶ In an AT system, make sure P8 and P9 plug into the motherboard with the black wires toward the center.

   ▶ In an ATX system, the plug fits only one direction.

6. Plug the power cord into the power supply. On an ATX system, flip the power switch on the power supply (if present).

7. Press the power button on the front of the PC. If you hear the fan(s) spinning up, the power supply is working. Turn the power off again.

8. Connect the power supply connectors to the drives on your system. The floppy drive gets the little connector (the Berg); all other drives get the large ones (the Molex).

9. Turn the PC back on and confirm that all devices are working.

VISUAL UPGRADE

Replacing a Power Supply

1 Position the new power supply unit at the rear of the case.

2 Fasten the power supply to the chassis with four screws.

Screw #1

Screw #2

Screw #3

Screw #4

3 Connect the power supply's largest connector(s) to the motherboard. The connector(s) is keyed so that you cannot connect it incorrectly.

4 Connect the other Molex and Berg connectors to the fan, hard and floppy drives, CD-ROM drive, etc.

5 Plug the computer's power cord into the new power supply unit.

Components of the Power Supply

The power supply is the black or silver box in the back of the PC with the large yellow label telling you in five languages not to open the box up and warning you that it is dangerous to do so. Despite the fact that I can only understand a few of the multilingual messages, I'm inclined to take them at their word.

The reason is mainly due to a thing called a *1000-microfarad capacitor,* which is inside the power supply. The capacitor is utilized to smooth out some power glitches. Big capacitors look like miniature soda cans, sized anywhere from about a couple of centimeters (about an inch) long to perhaps four times that size. Capacitors are kind of like holding tanks for electricity. If you've got some power that needs to go from point A to point B, but it tends to fluctuate a bit in the process, then an electronics designer can smooth it out a bit by putting a capacitor between A and B. The downside of a capacitor is that it's a part of a circuit that retains electricity even after you turn the circuit off. I once got a zap from a monster capacitor in a television that had been sitting unplugged in my family's attic for a few years, and I'm told that I'm lucky that I didn't do anything worse to myself.

The upshot of what I'm telling you is that the capacitors inside power supplies tend to argue against your trying to fix them. Power supplies can cost as little as $25 for an entire new unit, so just replace them if they're faulty. I recommend replacing and not repairing floppies just because it's a pain to repair them, but I recommend not repairing power supplies because they can hurt you.

Power Supply Connections

The motherboard needs power, and connectors from the power supply provide it. There are two kinds of power supplies available today, which correspond to the two kinds of motherboards: AT and

ATX. (Some motherboards and some power supplies are dual-purpose and can support either.) On an AT, two separate connectors, called P8 and P9, plug side-by-side into the motherboard. On an ATX, a single, 20-pin connector plugs into the motherboard to supply it with power. We'll look at them more closely in a minute.

AC power comes into the power supply from a wall outlet. On some systems (mostly the ATX ones), there is a power switch directly on the power supply that turns this power influx on/off. Other systems don't have a switch on the power supply; whenever it's plugged in, it's automatically on.

However, just because the power supply is receiving juice from the wall doesn't necessarily mean that it is using that power to run the PC. The PC's on/off switch is separate, and it's usually on the front of the PC. That switch has a wire running from it to the motherboard; when you press the switch, the motherboard says to the power supply, "Hey, I want to turn on now, send me some of that power!" or "Okay, I'm ready to shut down, stop sending me power now." The point is, the power supply is the master of the power coming into the system—it receives it, converts it to DC, and doles it out as needed/requested to the components plugged into it.

As I mentioned, the connectors that plug the power supply into the motherboard are different depending on whether you've got an AT or ATX system. First, let's look at the AT model. P8 and P9 are identically sized and shaped; the only difference is the colors of wires and the order in which they appear. You have to get them plugged in right or you will irreparably smoke your motherboard. Just keep this in mind: *black together*. Both connectors have a black wire; when the connectors are plugged in properly, the black wire on P8 will be next to the black wire on P9. Figure 9.1 shows P8 and P9 connectors.

Figure 9.1

Power supply
connectors to the
motherboard for an
AT system

P9
Connector

P8
Connector

The ATX design fixes that potential for confusion. On an ATX power supply, there is a single connector that goes to the motherboard, shown in Figure 9.2. There's no way to get it plugged in wrong, because it fits in only one direction. Just one of the ATX's many design improvements!

Figure 9.2

Motherboard
connector for an ATX
power supply

When you buy a computer, the case, the motherboard, and the power supply work as a team: they're all AT, or they're all ATX. (Some motherboards can go either way, so they have both AT and ATX connector sockets. Figure 9.3 shows an example of such a beast.) So if you ever buy a replacement for any of those components (a replacement power supply, for example), you need to make sure you get the right kind so it will work with your other pieces. You also need to make sure that you get a power supply with enough wattage (235 is decent for AT, or 250 for ATX) to run all the devices you want to have in the system.

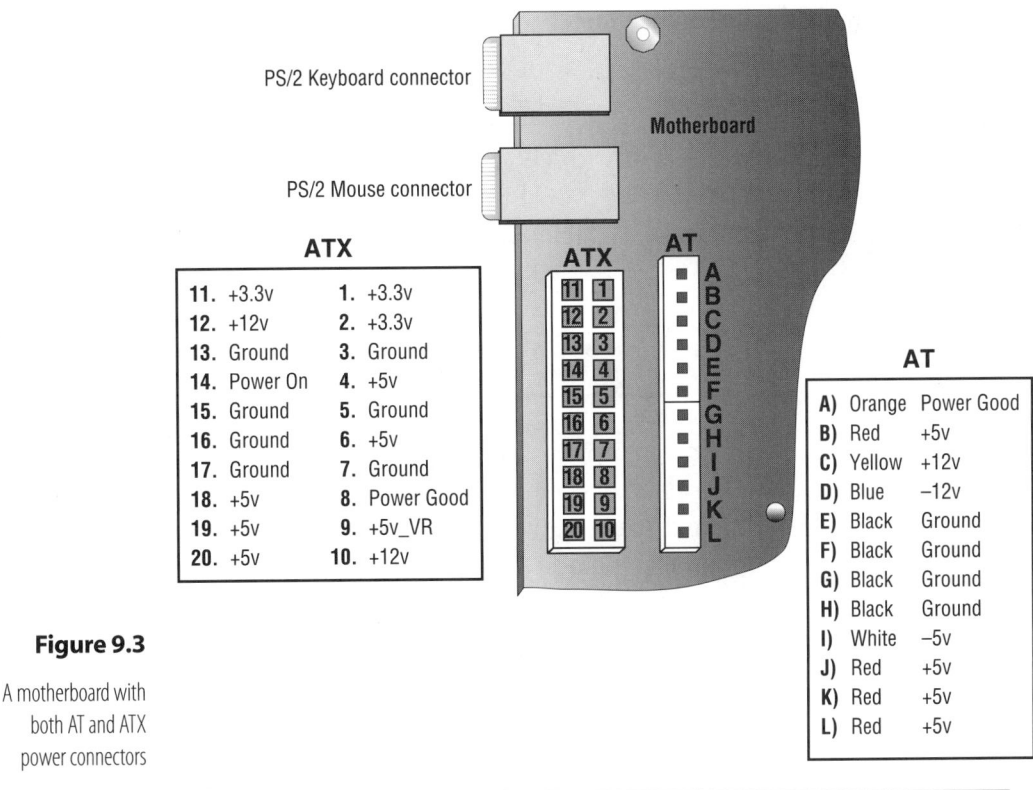

PS/2 Keyboard connector

Motherboard

PS/2 Mouse connector

ATX

11.	+3.3v	1.	+3.3v
12.	+12v	2.	+3.3v
13.	Ground	3.	Ground
14.	Power On	4.	+5v
15.	Ground	5.	Ground
16.	Ground	6.	+5v
17.	Ground	7.	Ground
18.	+5v	8.	Power Good
19.	+5v	9.	+5v_VR
20.	+5v	10.	+12v

ATX **AT**

AT

A)	Orange	Power Good
B)	Red	+5v
C)	Yellow	+12v
D)	Blue	−12v
E)	Black	Ground
F)	Black	Ground
G)	Black	Ground
H)	Black	Ground
I)	White	−5v
J)	Red	+5v
K)	Red	+5v
L)	Red	+5v

Figure 9.3

A motherboard with both AT and ATX power connectors

A bad power supply (either one that doesn't work at all or one that works erratically) can cause all kinds of problems in a system. If in doubt, test the power supply with a multimeter. The power supply lines can be tested against a ground (any of the black wires). If you are actually testing a power supply, all of the black wires should be tested.

You can then perform a resistance test of the motherboard. The tests are conducted on the power supply pins. Table 9.1 contains the *minimum* resistance for each connection. If the measured values are less than this, the motherboard is definitely faulty.

TABLE 9.1 System Board Resistances

Common Lead (Black Probe)	VOM (Voltage-Ohmmeter) Lead	Minimum Resistance (Ohms)
8	10	0.8
8	11	0.8
8	12	0.8
5	3	6
6	4	48
7	9	17

All power supplies, regardless of type, sport several identical Molex connectors for attaching to drives (hard disks, floppy disks, and tape drives). Figure 9.4 shows one of these. Most modern power supplies also include the smaller Berg connectors used to power 3½-inch floppy drives, shown in Figure 9.5. If your power supply doesn't have any Berg connectors, but you need one (or more), you can buy adapters at Radio Shack or a computer store that will convert a Molex to a Berg.

Figure 9.4

A Molex connector; your power supply has several of these.

Figure 9.5

A Berg connector supplies power to 3½-inch floppy drives.

You don't need to use all of the drive power connectors. Just because you've got four drive power connectors doesn't mean that you must have four drives. (I get asked that now and then.) Just make sure that the unused power connectors are tucked out of the way. I once saw a system freeze solid because one of the ground wires (the two black wires in the middle) on an unused drive power connector made contact with a test point on a motherboard.

Power Supply Maintenance

Good news here: there isn't any maintenance required. The fan and the power switch are the only moving parts. If you suddenly notice that the PC is very quiet but still operating, your fan may have died. If that happens, save everything and *shut down immediately!* The computer's own heat can quickly damage or destroy itself if the fan isn't present to dissipate it.

This is a real concern. Twice in my PC experience, I've taken a floppy disk out of the PC's drive and realized that it felt too hot. In both cases, it meant that the power supply's fan had died. In the first case, it was an original PC packed to the gills with heat-producing devices, and even though I turned off the PC as soon as I realized the problem, I was too late. Over the next six months, things failed, one by one, inside the system. The next time, the main casualty was a $1000 hard disk.

Don't block the vents that the PC uses for cooling. And take compressed air and blow the dust out of the fan now and then. (Remove the power supply from the PC case first so the dust doesn't immediately settle on the inside of computer.)

Saving Power

More and more of us are buying electronic things—from "smart houses" to microwave ovens to fax machines to . . . well, to *PCs.* All that electrical demand is not, sadly, matched by the corresponding electrical supply; we're not building power plants fast enough. That, in conjunction with a general concern for the earth, has lead to a rating offered by the American Environmental Protection Agency called Energy Star. More generally, there is a lot of interest in power saving or "green" PCs.

The thesis of the green computer movement is that we need to design, build, and use computers that require less electrical power. Green PC research is good for consumers first because, obviously, less electricity used means lower power bills and a planet that's easier to live on. But it's got another side effect: we're building better *laptops*, PCs that run on their batteries for longer. Green PCs save energy in a few ways.

Turn Things Off When You Don't Need Them

One of the main sources of power savings for green PCs is just to turn off interfaces when they're not being used. Laptops spend a fair amount of power keeping parallel and serial ports active when they're not in use. Green machines shut down circuits that aren't doing anything. Unfortunately, that includes hard disks, but I'll have more to say on that in a minute.

Run Chips Slower

The power output of a circuit is related to its frequency. Run a CPU and its memory at a lower clock rate, and you use less power. Many green machines will slow down a CPU when the system is idle . . . or when the system *thinks* it is idle. One oddity of green PCs is that they sometimes go to sleep when you don't want them to, so when troubleshooting systems, turn off the power saving features first, either in the BIOS setup or in the operating system (Windows' Power Management icon in the Control Panel will provide the controls).

Build Lower Voltage Systems

Power is related to voltage as well, so lower voltage means less power. Older PCs used 12 volts for the fans and drive motors and used chips that ran at 5 volts. Newer systems have chips that run anywhere from 2.2 to 3.3 volts for the processor and 5 volts for the smaller logic chips, fans, and motors.

Green Cautions

Having said all that, I've got a few complaints about green PCs. First of all, I think the green PC technologists have missed the boat by focusing on hard disk and CPU power savings. The fact of the matter is that on your average desktop PC, the color monitor consumes two-thirds of the power. A desktop PC often consumes 150 watts, 100 of which are used by the monitor.

In contrast, consider the laptop that I'm writing these words on. It's got a color display, 64MB of RAM, a 400MHz processor, and 6.5GB of mass storage. All that power comes at a cost of no more than 15 watts for the whole thing, display and all. The answer seems easy: just move us away from energy-hungry CRTs and offer desktop LCD panels. Such monitors have already been introduced for desktop PCs, but they are still rather pricey. (This will change in the next few years, and we'll all be able to afford them.)

Further, it's a really bad idea to save a smidgen of power by turning the hard disk on and off when it's not used. You end up cycling the power on the hard disk dozens of times a day and saving a small amount of power, *but* you reduce the length of life of your hard disk. And if you're concerned about power use, consider how much power Seagate uses to forge the disk platters, build the semiconductors, solder them to the boards, make the shipping cartons, and send the drive to you . . . doesn't seem like much of a win, does it? Green PCs are a good idea. But don't play with the power settings for the hard disk.

Upgrading the Power Supply

Years ago, desktop PCs lacked the power to drive all of their peripherals. It was common to find a PC start failing because it couldn't provide enough power to, well, *drive* its drives.

This experience led me to a preference for external peripherals, a preference that I retain to this day, even though today's PCs usually have power supplies with plenty of oomph. Whenever I'm buying a CD-ROM, large hard disk, or backup device, I buy it in an external case whenever possible. That means that every peripheral has its own fan and, as a bonus, its own power switch. Sometimes it's convenient to have the ability to disable a drive without popping the PC's top. It also means that the peripheral doesn't heat up the inside of the PC, *and* it doesn't strain the PC's power supply.

Even if you don't have my "powernoia," however, you'll probably never have to worry about getting a larger power supply on your machine. *But,* if you're building a server with 512MB of RAM and a full height 50GB hard disk, as well as a couple of CD-ROMs, a SCSI host adapter, and two LAN cards, you might think about one of the 300-plus-watt power supplies.

Better, however, is this advice: don't just get a *big* power supply. Get a *good* power supply, one of the ones made by the PC Power and Cooling people. I referred to them in Chapter 4, "Avoiding Service: Preventive Maintenance," and their contact information is listed in the Vendor Guide on CD #2.

When buying a power supply, don't confuse "watts capacity" with "watts used." Will a 300-watt power supply use more power than a 150-watt power supply if it's put in a PC that draws only 100 watts? No. However, a 300-watt bulb uses more power than a 150-watt bulb because there, "watts" means watts used. The description "300-watt power supply" means a power supply that can convert *up to 300 watts.* Notice the *up to*—putting a 300-watt power supply on a system that only requires 50 watts will cause the power supply to convert only 50 watts. A lot of folks misunderstand that—even an IBM engineer in 1983 warned me that putting an XT's 130-watt power supply on an IBM PC would "burn up the motherboard." He was wrong, but I didn't know any better at the time.

But pushing a power supply too far isn't a good idea. How do you know how much power your machine is using? One simple way is to use a device like the Power Meter from PARA Systems. The Power Meter looks like a power strip with a gauge on it. You just plug it into the wall and then plug your system unit into the Power Meter. It has a wiring tester, so it tells you if your outlets are wired correctly. (See the section "Protecting the PC from the AC," coming up.) Then turn the system unit on and look at the needle on the gauge. It measures amperes of current flowing. You'll get a value between 0.5 and 3. Just multiply that ampere value by 58 and you'll get the number of watts that your system unit uses. If it is close to its rated power supply, it's time to get a bigger power supply.

Why 58? You may know that Power (Watts) = Volts × Amps, and that you ordinarily get 120 volts from the wall outlet. Why not multiply amps by 120? Simple—this isn't direct current, where amps and volts are always in phase. Instead, we're dealing here with AC, alternating current. In AC, current and voltage follow a sine wave–like path, a path that can fall out of step. That means multiplying amps by 120 would overstate the total actual power requirements. To calculate the correct wattage, you need to take a kind of "average" of the power used. This is called the *RMS power*.

When buying upgrade power supplies, consider the fan. I've seen far too many tower cases that put the drives and other hot things above the fan. And for heaven's sake, don't buy those dumb plug-in boards that have a fan on them. Your PC is built to circulate air in a particular direction. Those fans may actually work *against* the system's fan!

Also avoid the newer power supplies with fans that shut down "when they're not needed." They've got a thermocouple in them—a circuit that measures heat. If the heat in the system drops below some level, the fan shuts off. This is a terrible idea. PCs can suffer from "hot spots," areas that are considerably hotter than the average PC temperature. Just because the air going through the fan is, say, 100 degrees F, it doesn't mean that there isn't a 130-degree section over the processor. (And speaking of processor fans, if you've got one, check it occasionally. They're made incredibly cheaply, and tend to die after nine months or so, leaving you with a useless fan that actually *increases* the heat on the processor.)

Speaking of replacement power supplies, remember the discussion of the power supply lines in Chapter 6, "Installing New Circuit Boards (without Creating New Problems)"? You may have noticed the first line on P8, called Power Good. This is a digital signal enabled by the power supply once it views itself as warmed up and ready. A flaky Power Good leads the computer to issue a long beep or short beeps or generally unusual noises. Some inexpensive replacement power supplies cause computers to emit a loud or long beep, then settle down to good service. I have experienced this myself, and I can only account for the beeps if the power supply doesn't wait quite long enough to first enable Power Good. A little initial up and down activity on the line induces the clock to issue a RESET command to the PC.

Determining If You Need a New Power Supply

You turn the computer on and nothing happens at all. It is plugged in, so it's not that—what next?

The Power Supply Troubleshooting Trail

First, check the wall outlet. The outlet should be providing between 104 and 130 volts AC current. Just set the voltage-ohmmeter (VOM) to read AC voltage and put one lead in each hole of the outlet.

Second, check the power cord. It should be firmly plugged into the power supply.

Third, is power getting to the power supply? The fan gets it first, so if it isn't turning on, the power supply isn't getting power. When some power supplies are first turned on the speaker emits a low click.

Fourth, check to make sure the power supply is connected to the motherboard using the right connectors, whether P8 and P9 (AT) or the single-piece 20-pin ATX connector.

If all those things check out correctly, try swapping in a different power supply. The following section outlines how to remove and replace one.

Replacing a Power Supply

If you suspect the power supply, replace it. It's simple.

1. Open the PC case.

2. On the back of the PC, you will see four screws bolting the power supply to the chassis. Remove these.

3. Disconnect the power cables from the motherboard and drives. Draw a picture and make notes of what connects to what. Note wire colors: the black wires on the P8 and P9 connectors (if it's an AT system) are always next to each other.

4. If it's an AT, detach the screws that hold the power switch in the front of the computer. These screws may be difficult to reach without removing drives in some cases.

5. Install the new power supply by reversing the procedure.

6. To be extra careful, strip the PC down to the minimum circuit boards. Then power up and run whatever diagnostics you use.

Protecting the PC from the AC

You can control a lot of things in your environment, but you have little control over one aspect of the PC environment: the power delivered by the electric company. For various reasons, it may not come out clean and regular like it's supposed to. Worse yet, you can't always blame the power company—sometimes it's your fault or your building management's fault.

Do You Have Power Problems?

Power or wiring problems can show up as:

▶ The computer mysteriously "freezing up"

▶ Random memory errors

▶ Lost data on the hard disk

▶ Damaged chips on a circuit board

▶ Data transmission noise and peripheral errors

Years ago, I was at a hotel doing a presentation that involved a demonstration PC. The PC did the strangest things:

▶ Once, it stopped the memory test at 128KB and froze.

▶ Another time, it gave a memory error message around 400KB.

▶ The hard disk wouldn't boot about 30 percent of the time, despite a fresh format.

▶ It stopped talking to the keyboard a few times, requiring the "Big Red Switch" (the power switch).

What was the problem? The old "hotel power problem." When the coffee machine was on, the PC did strange things. Additionally, the PC shared an outlet with two 600-watt overheads in continuous use and a slide projector. I moved it to another outlet, and the problem disappeared.

Having said that, what can you do about power problems? The four steps to power protection are:

▶ Check that your outlets are wired correctly.

▶ Find out what else is on the power line.

▶ Provide a common ground for all devices.

▶ Protect against noise—surges, spikes, and under- and overvoltages.

Following are the facts to "empower" you to solve your line problems.

Check Outlet Wiring

AC outlets have three wires: a large prong, a small prong, and a center cylinder. The cylinder is the safety ground, the prongs are the "hot" or *phase* line (the official term is "phase," but anyone who's ever accidentally touched it calls it "hot") and the *return*, also called common, or neutral. The wires in the wall are supposed to be wired so that green is ground, white is return, and whatever's left (usually black) is phase.

It's not unheard of for the hot and the return to be reversed. This actually isn't a problem as long as *everything* is wired backwards. But if you plug, say, the PC into a correctly wired outlet and a printer into a wrongly wired outlet, and if one of the devices connects the ground and the common—again, not an unusual occurrence—*and* there is a break in the neutral, then you'll get 120 volts across the cable from the printer to the PC. Lots of destruction will follow. Worse yet, miswired outlets can hurt you: if you touch both the PC and the printer at the same time, you are the electrical path.

You can buy circuit-wiring testers from most hardware stores. I got mine at Sears for $6 some years ago—they're probably a bit more now, but well worth it.

Check What Else Is on the Line

Ensure that there isn't any equipment on the same line as the PC that draws a lot of power. That includes the following:

▶ Large motors, like the ones you find in air conditioners, refrigerators, or machine tools

▶ Heating coils, such as in small space heaters or coffee makers—"personal coffee makers" are included here

▶ Copiers and their cousins, laser printers

Anything that draws a lot of current can draw down the amount of voltage being delivered to a PC on the same breaker or fuse. Worse yet, heating coil devices like coffee makers inadvertently create something called a *tank circuit* that can inject high-frequency spikes into the power line, noise that can slip through your power supply and go straight to the chips on the circuit boards.

One simple solution is to just get a dedicated power circuit to the computer. Another is to get an isolation transformer such as are found in a power conditioner. An RF (radio frequency) shield between the primary and secondary coils of the transformer removes the high-frequency noise.

Some laser printers draw 15 amps all by themselves. That implies that, like it or not, you've got to put a 20-amp breaker in for *each* laser printer/PC combination. PCs *without* lasers don't draw much power and don't require a separate breaker.

Ensure Common Ground among Devices

Electrical ground is intended, among other things, to provide an electrical reference point, a benchmark value, like sea level. A computer communicates ones or zeros to a modem, for instance, by varying voltage relative to ground: greater than +3 volts means 0, less than –3 volts means 1. Close to 0 volts means "nothing is being transmitted."

The problem arises when the two communicating devices don't agree on the value of ground. If, in the above example, the modem's ground is a 7-volts potential below the computer's ground, the modem and the computer each think that the other is sending data when actually neither is.

Generally, it's not that bad. But if the computer's ground is 3 volts different from the modem, the occasional bit will be lost or garbled.

The answer? Simple—just ensure that all devices plugged into your PC share the same ground. A simple six-outlet power strip will do this. There is one flaw in this approach, however: what about local area networks (LANs)? Basically, a LAN is one big ground problem. Some people have suggested grounding the shield of the network cables every hundred feet or so. The only true solution is to use fiber optic LANs, but they're still a wee bit expensive.

Note

Ensuring that all equipment has a *common* ground has nothing to do with having a *proper* ground. A proper ground is mainly for safety, not data protection. (If someone insists that you must have a good ground for proper data transfer, ask him how airplanes and spaceships manage it, hmmm?) We'll look at proper grounding soon.

Protect Against Power Noise

We've already discussed undervoltage, overvoltage, spikes, and surges in Chapter 4.

◗ *Undervoltage* is undesirable because the power supply reacts to too *little* voltage by drawing too *much* current. This heats up and may destroy components.

◗ *Overvoltage* can damage a chip because too much voltage destroys the circuits inside the chip.

When some outside force causes your power line to deliver more voltage than it is supposed to, this is called an overvoltage condition. Such conditions are, in general, dangerous to the computer.

The physics of it is this: the heart of the computer resides in its chips. A chip is a specially designed crystal. Crystals are highly structured molecules: many of them would be happier in a less structured environment. Applying electronic and heat energy to the crystals allows this breakdown in organization to occur. One spike might not do it, but it leaves damage that is cumulative. Even small spike damage is cumulative. Damage is proportional to energy. Energy is voltage, multiplied by current, multiplied by time.

Brief overvoltages of under a millisecond in length are called *spikes*. Longer ones—milliseconds to seconds—are called *surges*. *Spikes* may be of high enough frequency to introduce RFI (radio frequency interference)-like problems.

You (or your boss) may be skeptical about the actual seriousness of power problems. This may all be, you suspect, a tempest in a teapot. If you don't think that you have power problems, spend $130 on a simple device that can monitor the quality of your power. Called the AC Monitor, it's from Tasco Ltd. in Colorado. They're listed in the Vendor Guide on CD #2.

This device will continuously monitor the voltage that you are receiving at the outlet, and it will indicate power drops, surges, or spikes (no frequency variation, sadly) with a light and an audible warning.

The big three conditions that you wish to avoid are

◗ Surges and spikes

◗ Low voltage

◗ No voltage (power outages)

Solutions to Power Problems

Solutions to power problems fall into three categories:

▶ Isolation

▶ Shielding

▶ Proper grounding

Isolation means isolating the noise (surges, spikes, and so on) from the computer—draining it off harmlessly. This is done with filters, transformers, gas discharge tubes, and *metal oxide varistors (MOVs)*. An MOV is an important part of a surge protector. When a surge comes in, an MOV shunts it off to ground. Unfortunately, the MOV is a kamikaze component—it "throws itself onto the grenade." Each MOV is only good for one big surge or a bunch of little surges. (No, there's no easy way to test to see whether an MOV is still working or not, at least not without a $2000 tester.) Power conditioners and surge protectors provide isolation in varying quality.

Shields minimize high-frequency noise. Shielding is evident in the filter capacitors in surge protectors, RF shields between the primary and secondary coils in a power conditioner, the metal case of the computer, and in the shield in shielded cable.

Some people view grounding as a magic answer to noise problems. Just run a wire from the device in question to a metal stake pounded into the ground (called a *ground stake*), and all of your ground problems go away! (Kind of like an electronic Roto-Rooter: "... and away go troubles down the drain.")

Nahhh.

First, having a proper ground *is* important. It makes electronic equipment safer (because it keeps you out of the circuit), but, as we've seen, a *common* ground is important to minimize communication errors between devices. So the main reason for a proper earth ground is safety.

The idea behind a ground stake (ya know, years ago, I thought ground stake was just hamburger ...) is to provide a nice electrical path to earth ground. It *doesn't* eliminate noise, however: two ground stakes a few yards apart will pass current and noise between themselves. Ground stakes are less effective when there's a drought. I once heard of a ground stake that provided a better connection to ground than others on a particular site because it was, er, "watered" by local fauna. (No, I'm not sure I believe it, but ground *is* magic, and magical stories accompany it.)

A final thought on grounding: some companies are extra careful to ground their computer rooms, thinking that this will somehow protect their data. They're not so careful about the other areas in the building, however, so you've got a computer room with a cleaner ground than the rest of the building. Step back for a moment and ask what effect differential grounding would have on lightning protection. If lightning were to strike the building, it takes the easiest path to ground. If the easiest path to ground is through your computers, so be it. Basically, if you ground your computer room well and *don't* ground the rest of the building well, it's like putting a big "EAT AT JOE'S" sign on the computer room, as far as lightning is concerned.

Devices to Remedy Electrical Problems

Okay, now we've seen the problems and the approaches to solutions. Now let's look at what's available on the market to solve the problems.

If you're looking here for a recommendation, please understand that I haven't got good news. Electric power in the twenty-first century in most of the Western world is getting worse and worse due to aging equipment and lack of new capacity being pitted against ever-growing energy demands.

The PC really needs cleaner power than the stuff that you feed your refrigerator, Mr. Coffee, or desk lamp. The only absolutely reliable way to get clean power is to rectify the power, put it in a battery, and then use the DC power in the battery to reconstruct the AC power. A device that does this is a *UPS (uninterruptible power supply)*. A good one will cost you about a hundred bucks, but in the long run will save many hundreds on new computer components and lost data. On the other hand, there are some fairly effective alternatives like surge suppressors, *SPSs* (*standby power supplies*), and power conditioners. Me? I'm building a faraday cage for my office (just as soon as I get some time and money . . .).

Surge Suppressors and Spike Isolators

Many of us have purchased surge suppressors, or as they are also known, surge protectors or spike isolators.

The idea with suppression devices is that once they see a large surge coming, they redirect it out to the electric ground—kind of like opening the floodgates. The most common redirection device is an MOV, which we talked about a couple of sections earlier. It is an impassable barrier between the supply voltage and protective ground *until* the voltage reaches a certain level. *Gas discharge tubes* and *pellet arrestors* are slower but beefier devices. *Coaxial arrestors* fit somewhere in the middle.

The best suppressors use several lines of defense: MOVs, coax arrestors, and gas discharge tubes, for example.

Of course, an overzealous surge suppressor can redirect *too much* power for too long and create a worse surge of its own.

Another important question is *what* voltage level triggers the surge suppressor? They're not waiting for 120.00001 volts to get going: some will pass 1000 volts before calling in the Marines. By then, your PC is toast.

PC Magazine started doing tests of surge suppression devices years ago and published the results in the magazine. They created spikes and measured how much of the spike was allowed through. Some suppressors emitted smoke and flames when subjected to a real surge. Others died quietly, not informing the owner that they no longer protect the PC (they still pass electricity, so there's no way to know.) You can see a surge protector in Figure 9.6.

Figure 9.6

Surge suppressor

The Bad News about Surge Suppressors

You see, I can't, in good conscience, recommend them to you (with a few exceptions).

As I've said, the best suppressors use several lines of defense, and the heart of those are MOVs. As we've said before, MOVs are one-time-only devices. One surge and they're history. Worse yet, they can't be tested.

Yes, some surge protectors come with a little light that goes out when the surge protector doesn't protect any more. But those little lights can't be trusted, either. The light is in series with a fuse, and the fuse is in series with the return from the MOV—it's called a *bleeder fuse.* Given a large enough surge, the fuse will blow (along with the MOV, you recall) and the light will go out. In that case, the case of a single large surge, the light *is* effective. But an MOV can also be destroyed by a number of smaller surges. In that case, the fuse would be unaffected, and the light would stay on.

Summarizing, there's no way to know whether or not your surge protector is still protecting. If you've got a light on your surge protector and it goes out, you definitely have a dead surge protector. But if the light's on, that's no guarantee of surge protector effectiveness.

Meanwhile, another company has built a renewable surge protector. The company's name is Zero-Surge, and their product is (likewise) called the Zero-Surge Protector. It's a good product, but be prepared to pay a bit for it, as you would for any quality device: models range from $150 to $200. Zero-Surge's contact information is in the Vendor Guide on CD #2.

Power Conditioners

Between a surge protector and a backup power supply is another device, also in-between in price, called a *power conditioner*. A power conditioner does all the things that a surge protector does—filters and isolates line noise—and more. Rather than relying on MOVs and such, the power conditioner uses the inductance of its transformer to filter out line noise. An isolation transformer is a far superior device for removing noise to a capacitor or an MOV. Additionally, most power conditioners will boost up undervoltage so that your machine can continue to work through brownouts.

Recall that the surge protector's MOVs fail with no sign, so there's no good way to know whether your surge protector is doing any good. Power conditioners don't have that problem—when a transformer fails, you know it—the power conditioner just plain doesn't provide any power.

Which power conditioner is right for you? I have used the Tripplite LC1800. I've seen it in mail-order ads for as little as $179. One firm that sells them cheaply is Altex Electronics, which is also listed in the Vendor Guide on CD #2.

The LC1800 even shows you your incoming voltage via some LEDs on its front panel. *Do not* plug your laser printer into the LC1800, as it is only rated for 6 amps. (Remember that lasers draw up to 15 amps.)

Backup Power Supplies

In addition to protection from short power irregularities, you may need backup power. I have lived in a number of places in the north-eastern U.S. where summer lightning storms will kill the power for just a second—enough to erase your memory and make the digital clocks blink. Total loss of power can be remedied only with battery-based systems. Such systems are in the range of $150 to $1200 and up. Figure 9.7 shows how UPSs and SPSs work.

When power is normal, an SPS passes current through to the PC
– spikes and all – while siphoning off a bit of the power in order to keep the battery charged.

When the power is interrupted, the SPS supplies power to the PC from the battery for as long as the battery lasts. The SPS must also sense the power-down condition and get the battery on-line quickly enough that the PC can continue to work uninterrupted.

A UPS, on the other hand, sends power from the socket right into the battery, keeping it constantly charged. The computer draws the power from the battery instead of the line.

Figure 9.7

How UPSs and SPSs work

When power is interrupted, the UPS continues to supply power to the computer from the battery. Benefits: constant surge protection and zero switching time.

There are two types, a *standby power supply* (SPS) and an *uninterruptible power supply* (UPS). SPSs charge the batteries while watching the current level. If the power drops, they activate themselves and supply power until their batteries run down. A fast power switch must occur here, and it's important to find out what the switching time is—4ms or under is fine, and 14ms, in my experience, is not fast enough.

A UPS constantly runs power from the line current to a battery, then from the battery to the PC. This is superior to an SPS because there is no switching time involved. Also, this means that any surges affect the battery charging mechanism, not the computer. A UPS is, then, a surge suppressor also.

A UPS or SPS must convert DC current from a battery to AC for the PC. AC is supposed to look like a sine wave. Cheaper UPS and SPS models produce square waves (see Figure 9.8). Square waves are bad because they include high-frequency harmonics, which can appear as EMI (electromagnetic interference) or RFI to the computer. Also, some peripherals (printers in particular) can't handle square-wave AC. So, when examining UPS, ask whether they use square wave or sine wave. Some produce a pseudo-sine wave. It has the stair step look of a square wave, but it doesn't have as many harmonic problems.

Figure 9.8

UPS AC waveforms

Sine wave

Square wave

Ordinarily, the purpose of a UPS is to allow you enough time to save whatever you're doing and shut down gracefully. If you are in an area where the power may disappear for hours, and may do it regularly, then you should look for the ability to attach external batteries to the UPS so that you can run the PC for longer periods.

Remember that a sine wave UPS is the only way to really eliminate most power problems. The reason *everyone* doesn't have one is cost.

A decent compromise can be found in a fast (4ms) square-wave SPS. I know I said that square waves are bad for your peripherals, but consider how often the SPS will actually be doing anything. Not very often—remember that it supplies power only when the line voltage drops out, which is not a common occurrence. The brief minute or two each month of square wave power that your peripherals end up getting won't kill them. And you'll save a pile over a UPS.

On the other hand, remember that a UPS is *always* online, and so must produce sine wave output. But UPSs do have the benefit that they provide surge protection by breaking down and reassembling the power, and SPSs *do not* provide this protection. You must still worry about surge protection when you buy an SPS, but that's not true if you buy a UPS. So make the choice that your budget allows.

Something to look for in backup power supplies—both UPSs and SPSs—is a serial port.

A serial port? Yes, a serial port. Most operating systems can monitor a signal from a serial port-equipped UPS/SPS. When power fails, the operating system is informed by the backup power supply of that occurrence, and the operating system does a graceful shutdown in the battery time remaining. This function is also called a *heartbeat.* Table 9.2 summarizes what we've covered about power problems and solutions.

TABLE 9.2 Power Problems and Solutions

Protection Method	Remedies Surges	Remedies Low Voltage	Remedies Outage
Power conditioner	yes	yes	no
SPS	no	no	yes
UPS	yes	yes	yes

Before buying an SPS or a UPS, however, be aware of just one more thing—many people are selling SPSs under the name of "offline UPS." Real UPSs are nowadays being called "online UPS."

So What Should I Buy?

Sounds like you can spend a pile of money on power protection and, sadly, that's true: a real, honest-to-goodness UPS will set you back four figures. (As I mentioned, cheaper ones are SPSs that marketers call "offline UPS." Kind of like calling a car "wingless ground-based airplane" or calling those salespeople "honesty-challenged.") The best compromise that I've come up with is a neat little combination of a power conditioner and an SPS with, of course, a serial port attached. Called the Smart-UPS 450, it's made by American Power Conversion (APC) and I've found them for about $300. It's a complete power solution, and they've worked wonderfully for me for the past four years, through storms and power company screwups. You can find contact information for APC in the Vendor Guide on CD #2.

The Granddaddy of Power Problems: Lightning

When Thor's hammer falls near your site, you won't need any special equipment to note its passing. Curled-up, blackened circuit boards are pretty easy to spot.

I travel around North America and Europe teaching troubleshooting classes. You know what *everyone* tells me? No matter where we are, the natives tell me that they're in the "lightning capital of the world." (I know, hearing something *shocking* like that makes you want to *bolt*.) Take a look at Figure 9.9 to find out where you rate.

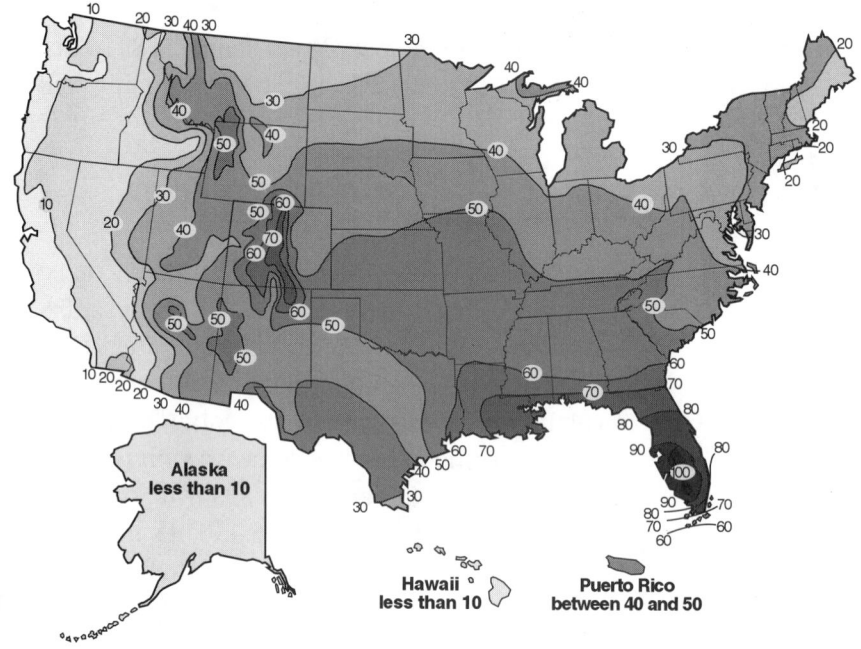

Figure 9.9

Mean annual number
of days with
thunderstorms

Looks like central Florida can lay claim to the "Thunderstorm Central" title. Here's what we know about thunderstorms:

▶ Lightning affects your system even if it doesn't strike your building.

▶ It is *good* to leave a machine plugged in—the lightning has an easy path to ground.

▶ As mentioned earlier, taking special care to ground the part of the building that the big computers are in just makes those computers more vulnerable. A better-grounded path is the one that lightning will take.

▶ Lightning arrestors can reduce the likelihood of lightning damage.

▶ Newer high-tech lightning rods are being used in some sites. They look like umbrellas built of barbed wire standing about 30 feet tall.

▶ A cheap lightning protection: overhand knots in the power cord.

Believe it or not, some researchers found this last one out. It makes the lightning surge work against itself and burn out the power cord, *not* the PC. And it works—Washington had the biggest thunderstorm it had in years in the summer of 1989, and the stuff with knots in the cords rode it out without a hitch. The TV didn't have knots in the cord, so I did have to buy a new TV.

The following year, a bolt hit my *telephone line*. It literally toasted the line from the telephone pole to my house; crispy brown little bits flaked off at the touch. But once inside, the bolt hit my five knots, and nothing inside was fried. Why did I tie the knots? I got tired of losing a modem every summer to lightning. There are also surge suppressors for telephone lines—APC makes a good one, and they're not expensive, about $30, I think.

Power's not the sexiest part of PC hardware, but it sure can be the most troublesome. Get a Smart-UPS and a decent power supply, buy external peripherals, and you'll be electrified with the results.

Troubleshooting Tips

If you are not getting any power to the PC (no fans, no nothing), do the following:

▶ Check whether power is coming from the wall outlet to the power supply.

▶ If you are using a power strip, confirm that it is on. (Most power strips have a rocker on/off switch.)

▶ Check for loose connections from the power plug to the power supply or from the power supply to the motherboard.

▶ In an AT system, confirm that the black wires of P8 and P9 are together, not at opposite ends of the power connector on the motherboard.

- In an ATX system, make sure that the power switch on the power supply itself is on before you press the power button on the front of the PC.

- If the power supply has a voltage switch (110/220), make sure that it is set for the currency in the location in which you are working (110 is standard in the U.S.).

If you are having other problems with the PC that you suspect might be power-related, do the following:

- Check that your outlets are wired correctly.

- Make sure no other high-wattage devices are sharing the power line.

- Make sure that your outlets are grounded and that all your devices share the same ground (plugging them all into the same power strip will accomplish this).

- Install equipment that can protect against surges and spikes, low voltage, and/or power outages. This might include a surge suppressor, an SPS, or a UPS.

In the next chapter, we'll take a general look at the hard drive before moving on to specific types of drives.

10

Hard Disk Drive Overview and Terminology

INTRODUCTION

Hard disks are where most of a PC user's data lives. Since the data on your system is the most valuable part of the system, it stands to reason that the hard disk is, in some ways, the computer's most important part.

That's why this book has so many chapters on hard disks. In this one, we'll look at disk-ese and get a bird's-eye view of disk technology.

Disk Types and the Future

Before we begin, it's important to note that there are two basic types of disks: magnetic disks and optical disks. Examples of magnetic disks include floppy disks, hard disks, and hard disks with removable cartridges that can you can mount either internally or externally.

Examples of optical disks include CDs, WORMs (write once, read many), DVDs, and erasable optical disks. Briefly, the disk controller writes data to an optical disk by burning microscopic holes on the surface of the disk with a laser. The disk controller reads the data by shining a second laser on the disk surface and reading any changes in the reflection pattern that the holes cause. Refer to Chapter 26, "An Overview of CD-ROM," for information about optical disks.

No single technology can provide the storage solutions to all segments of rapidly expanding markets. Advancing disk technology employed by some disk drives allows the storage of ever-increasing amounts of data on a disk and improves data transfer rates.

Special niche markets might consider using the holographic storage techniques that are currently being developed. Holographic storage technique stores data in two- or three-dimensional boundaries inside special containers. While not commonly used, it could be particularly useful in multimedia applications and for storing the many variants of image files.

Wet disk technology is another technology now being used by some manufacturers. Wet disk replaces the air cushion over the hard disk with liquid and allows the heads to get closer to the disk surface to read dense data.

As the number of individuals and businesses using computers (and the Internet) increases, so does the demand for larger storage capacity and higher disk access speeds. Disk technology will continue to improve and come up with innovative methods to meet these needs. Indeed, it is quite conceivable that a few years from now completely new and very different storage techniques may be available.

Hard Drives and Interfaces

All peripheral devices need some way of communicating with the computer. A hard disk subsystem consists of the hard drive itself, a disk interface, and the cable or cables connecting them. Disk interfaces are either host adapters or controllers, depending on the type of disk technology. Older drive technologies use controllers, newer ones use host adapters.

A controller is a device that controls the transfer of data (in both directions) between the computer and the peripheral device. Controllers can be built into a single chip or chip set or they can be on expansion boards.

Host adapters are physical devices that contain the necessary circuitry to support a device. Host adapters can be built into the main circuitry of a computer or they can be separate add-on boards.

Disk terms are relevant either to a hard drive or to a drive interface. For drives, Table 10.1 summarizes these terms.

TABLE 10.1 Hard Disk Terms

Drive Characteristic	What It Means, Why It's Relevant
Number of cylinders	Part of capacity determination. Hard drives store data on a stack of aluminum or glass platters. Each surface of each platter (top and bottom) consists of magnetically divided circular tracks. A cylinder is a stack of corresponding tracks. For example, track 20 on each of the platters (tops and bottoms) would make up one of the cylinders of the hard drive.
Number of heads	Part of capacity determination. There are two heads for each platter of the hard drive (one on the top and one on the bottom). The heads read and write the data on the platters.
Number of sectors	Part of capacity determination. Each track on every platter consists of divisions or sections (the sectors). In general, each sector contains the same number of bytes of data.

Continued on next page

TABLE 10.1 Hard Disk Terms (continued)

Drive Characteristic	What It Means, Why It's Relevant
Zone Bit Recording (ZBR)	Describes whether the number of sectors per track is constant. If the number of sectors per track remains the same on all tracks, the tracks divide the platters more or less like slices of pie. This makes the center tracks denser than the outer tracks. In order to make the data readable in the inner tracks, the data in the outer tracks is spread out; this compromises capacity. Therefore, most drives today vary the number of sectors per track to optimize the total disk area.
Head positioning mechanism	A drive design element, a tradeoff of speed versus cost. Older hard drives use a *stepper motor* to move the heads back and forth so they can access each of the tracks (cylinders). Today most hard drives move the heads using a voice coil. Refer to the Voice Coil and Stepper Head-Positioning Mechanisms" section for more information.
Access time	Drive design characteristic. This is the amount of time it takes for the heads to locate a specific piece of data in the hard drive. The components of access time include controller overhead time, latency, and seek time. Usually manufacturers specify the "average access time," because the actual seek time varies depending on the location of the heads and the next bit of data.
Data transfer rate	The data transfer rate (also called media rate) is the speed at which the system copies data from the hard drive to the computer or from the computer to the hard drive and consists of a two-step process. The first is the Internal Data Transfer Rate (the *sustained rate*) and involves actually reading or writing to the disk. The second is the External Data Transfer Rate (the *burst rate*) and involves the transfer speed over the interface between the hard disk and the rest of the PC.
Drive interface type	Configuration issues determine what kind of interface your computer will need to communicate with the hard drive. Most today employ Enhanced Integrated Drive Electronics (EIDE). The other popular interface in use today is Small Computer System Interface (SCSI).
Direct memory access (DMA)	Direct memory access is a popular hard drive interface data transfer method. DMA is a mechanism for transferring data between the hard drive and host memory that virtually eliminates the CPU from the transfer process. The use of DMA requires an operating system device driver and a basic input/output system (BIOS) that supports the DMA specifications. (For more information refer to the "PIO and DMA Protocol Transfer Mechanisms" section in this chapter.)

Continued on next page

TABLE 10.1 Hard Disk Terms (continued)

Drive Characteristic	What It Means, Why It's Relevant
Programmed input/output (PIO)	PIO is the most popular hard drive interface data transfer method. It has five modes, each of which defines a different maximum transfer rate and uses the CPU in the data transfer process. PIO transfers data to and from the disk controller through the I/O ports. The CPU manages throughput at the I/O ports. (For more information refer to the "PIO and DMA Protocol Transfer Mechanisms" section in this chapter.)
Write precompensation cylinder	On older hard drives, the heads required higher current output to write to the inner cylinders because the data was so close together that the heads switched on and off more quickly there. Therefore, the platter needed more oomph to write the data reliably onto the inner tracks. The write precompensation cylinder specification told the computer when to boost the current to the write heads. Most current hard drives don't need the boost because they keep sector lengths constant.

Drive interfaces have characteristics as well. Table 10.2 summarizes some of them.

TABLE 10.2 Drive Interface Characteristics

Interface Characteristic	Relevant to Host Adapter, Controller, or Both	What It Means, Why It's Relevant
Logical block addressing (LBA)	Host adapter	A method that allows computers to access all of the data on hard drives larger than 528MB.
On-board cache memory	Both	Some controllers have some memory on them for keeping copies of data that the computer frequently requests.
Sector translation	Both	Alternate method of getting the computer to support larger drives.

Continued on next page

TABLE 10.2 Drive Interface Characteristics (continued)

Interface Characteristic	Relevant to Host Adapter, Controller, or Both	What It Means, Why It's Relevant
Interface to system bus	Both	Which PC bus is this interface built for? Possible types are ISA, EISA, MCA, PC Card, VESA, PCI, USB, and even parallel ports (see Table 10.3). Alternate method of getting the computer to support larger drives.
Max error burst/ ECC length	Both	How many bad bits can this controller recover from?

We'll tackle everything in Table 10.2 in this chapter. Once you've gone through this, you should be ready to learn how to install, protect, and repair hard disk subsystems.

System buses provide pathways to move data and control signals between the various components within the computer. Current PCs can include several types of buses, including an expansion bus, a data bus, and a local bus.

Expansion bus Also an external bus or input/output bus. Provides a path for adapter cards and external devices to the internal system bus.

Data bus Provides for the transfer of data between system components and provides direct access to memory on the system board.

Local bus Also an internal bus. Connects the microprocessor with the system controllers. Transfer rates over a local bus are close to the processor speed of the unit.

Table 10.3 briefly describes some of the system bus/interface types from Table 10.2.

TABLE 10.3 PC System Bus/Interface Types

Bus Type	Acronym Definition	Description
EISA	Extended Industry Standard Architecture	An open standard PC bus architecture in systems with Intel Pentium, 80386, and 80486 that can transfer data at 32 bits per second. A few high-performance PCs use EISA. Most high-performance PCs use the PCI bus because it is more flexible (see the description of the PCI bus in this table).
ISA	Industry Standard Architecture	A standard PC bus architecture in IBM PC/XT and PC/AT systems that allows 16 bits at a time to flow between the computer, its expansion cards, and associated devices. ISA is usually used for slower peripherals. In the early '90s, the higher performance PCI bus started replacing ISA, and today ISA is almost obsolete as Intel and Microsoft continue to move the industry away from its use.
MCA	Micro Channel Architecture	An interface between one or more computers, their expansion cards, and other devices. A proprietary nonstandard system from IBM for its PS/2 computers.
PCI	Peripheral Component Interconnect	Originally a local bus interconnection, PCI is no longer a local bus architecture. Currently you can implement PCI (PCI 2 and up) as a 64-bit bus or 32-bit bus that synchronizes with the clock speed of the microprocessor. PCI uses all active paths to transmit both address and data signals and, in addition, supports burst data.
USB	Universal Serial Bus	A Plug-and-Play interface between a computer and an add-on device. If a computer has a USB, you can add a new device without adding an adapter or turning the computer off. USB supports a data speed of 12Mbps. Today, most new computers and peripheral devices have USB.
VESA (VL Bus or VLB)	Video Electronics Standards Association	The VESA local bus, sometimes referred to as VL Bus or VLB, was the first popular local bus. VESA is a technology that provides fast data flow

Continued on next page

TABLE 10.3 PC System Bus/Interface Types (continued)

Bus Type	Acronym Definition	Description
		between the expansion cards and the microprocessor. It is a 32-bit bus that is a direct extension of the 486-processor/memory bus. VESA is usually associated with systems with advanced video cards and is sometimes associated with disk controllers because it provides them a more or less direct connection to the processor. With the advent of the Pentium processor and the PCI bus, VLB has become obsolete for new systems. All Pentiums and higher use PCI.

Disk Geometry: Heads, Tracks, Cylinders, and Sectors

If I wanted to tell you how to get to my house, I might say something like, "Travel west from Washington, D.C. for five miles on I-6 to Dreller Avenue, then turn left on Dreller and take it south for another mile until you reach Garner Drive. Take a right onto Garner and I'm two blocks up on the right." In order to understand what I'm talking about, you'd have to understand *west, south, block, left,* and *right*. In the same way, you can't even think about doing disk work without understanding terms like *cylinder, head, sector,* and *track*— words that are basic to disk discussions.

Disk geometry refers to the electronic organization of any type of disk drive, the actual physical number of heads, cylinders, tracks, and sectors. The physical geometry of a disk stores data on disks in bytes and organizes the bytes into 512-byte groups called *sectors*. Sectors are the minimum unit of data that you can read from or write to a disk. A specific number of sectors group together into *tracks* and tracks on hard drives are grouped together into *cylinders*.

A disk has at least two surfaces. The system addresses the sectors on a hard drive using a matrix of cylinders, heads, and sectors. You can see a cutaway view of a hard disk in Figure 10.1.

Platters

Actuator arm
and disk heads

Figure 10.1

Cutaway view of a
hard disk

Before going into detail about hard disks, however, it's easiest to explain hard disk structure with a simpler storage medium—a 1.44MB floppy diskette:

▶ A floppy diskette is typically made of Mylar. Jackets covering the Mylar disk can be flexible or semirigid. The read/write heads access the Mylar surface through the drive gate.

▶ A floppy diskette has two *sides* (surfaces), which require two *heads* to read them.

▶ Each side contains data.

▶ Each side has 80 concentric *tracks*. There is a related notion called *cylinders* (we'll discuss them in a moment), so we say a 1.44MB floppy has 80 cylinders.

▶ Each track has nine divisions or *sectors* (like nine pieces of a pie).

▶ Each sector stores 0.5K (512 bytes) of information.

In contrast to the Mylar of a floppy diskette, a hard disk drive contains rigid metal or glass disks, called *platters*, stacked up on a spindle inside an air-filtered enclosure. For example, the original XT 10MB drive had two platters. Other drives may have fewer, some others many more. Again, a floppy diskette is like one "platter," but it's not rigid.

The platters have a coating of a special material on both sides that allows the computer to store information in magnetic patterns. Each platter is capable of holding billions of bits of data per square inch. A special motor on the spindle drives the platters at high speeds.

A hard disk also has electromagnetic read/write heads and a logic board or controller. The sealed enclosure prevents foreign contaminants such as dust particles, fingerprints, or smoke particles from affecting the various components and operation of the disk drive. Foreign contaminants can cause a head crash, which can occur when the head makes contact with the disk surface itself or by the head touching particles on the disk surface.

Disk Heads

Like a floppy diskette, the hard disk has an electromagnetic read/write *disk head* for each side of each platter. For example, some drives have four heads: two heads for each platter (one on top and one on the bottom) × two platters. The read/write heads mount on an actuator arm that moves the heads over the surface of the platter on a very thin cushion of air to the proper track. Feedback from the servo system accurately positions the read/write heads. A rotary voice coil at one end powers each actuator arm. The actuator arms lock together and move from track to track as a single unit.

The disk controller (usually a microprocessor) controls the servo system and translates digital data into magnetic pulses that the read/write heads store on the platters. The read/write heads transfer the magnetic pulses back to the controller, which then converts them back into digital data for the CPU.

Remember, the disk drive is sealed and contains the mechanical components of the drive. You don't have to worry about aligning or cleaning these heads, and besides, you couldn't do those things even if you wanted to because they're inaccessible.

Manufacturers today are including magnetoresistive (MR) heads with separate read and write elements in disk drives. These heads make it possible to place more data under a single head. Having separate heads allows the construction of wider write and narrower read heads to suit differing operating needs.

Disk Tracks

Each side of each platter (each *surface*) contains concentric tracks, like a floppy and similar to the annual rings of a tree. A *disk track* is a path that contains the reproducible information on the magnetic media. Track counting starts at zero at the outer edge and increases as it moves inward.

A floppy like the 1.44MB example I use in Figure 10.2 typically has 80 tracks, but some of the oldest hard disks start at 305 tracks and go up from there; I've seen hard drives with over 16,000 tracks (cylinders). Today, 3½-inch is the most common hard drive size in use today. This means that the platters inside the drive are 3½ inches in diameter. Most laptop computers use 2½-inch drives. New technologies make it possible to store nearly as much data on one of these drives as on a 3½-inch drive.

Track 0

Track 1

Track 79

Figure 10.2

A 1.44MB floppy diskette

Disk Cylinders

A platter has two sides with concentric tracks. A pair of tracks on the opposite sides of a platter makes a *cylinder*. If there are two or more platters, all pairs of tracks that line up with each other form a cylinder. If there are three platters, each cylinder has six tracks (three pairs). In other words, taken together, the tracks become a virtual cylinder. You can see the relationship between tracks and cylinders in Figure 10.3.

The number of tracks per surface is identical to the number of cylinders; therefore, most manufacturers do not report the number of tracks, they report the number of cylinders. Although the two terms mean different things, people use cylinder and track synonymously.

It's easier to store data on the same track on each platter – it can all be accessed without moving the read/write head back and forth.

All of the same tracks on each platter are collectively known as a cylinder.

Track on one platter

Platters

Figure 10.3

The relationship between tracks and cylinders on a disk

Hard drives usually have more than one platter; so most hard disks have four or more read/write heads. The heads lock together and attach to an *actuator arm*. That means that when the actuator positions head 0 (as in most of the rest of the computer business, here we count 0 to 3, not 1 to 4) over track 142 on surface 0, it also positions head 3 over track 142 on surface 3. Each head is always physically at the same track number or cylinder number. It is impossible to independently position the disk heads. Here's how it works.

To read a particular sector, the disk hardware goes through three steps. First, it must move the read/write head over the desired track. Second, it must wait for the disk to rotate so that the desired sector is under the head, and, finally, it must read.

In general, moving the head takes the most time. This means that the disk hardware can most quickly read a file whose sectors are all on the same track and *whose tracks lie above one another*—one head move can read a pile of data. Thus, if a large file starts out on, say, head 0, track 142, it's a good idea to make sure that the next track that file uses is head 1, track 142, and then head 2, track 142, and so on. There's no need for a head movement, but the disk can suck up a lot of data.

Disk Sectors

Each platter surface is figuratively cut into wedges like a pie. These wedges are called *sectors*. A sector is the smallest accessible unit on a disk. When you format a disk, the disk controller establishes the sector size. Floppies typically divide tracks up into 8 to 18 sectors apiece. See Figure 10.4.

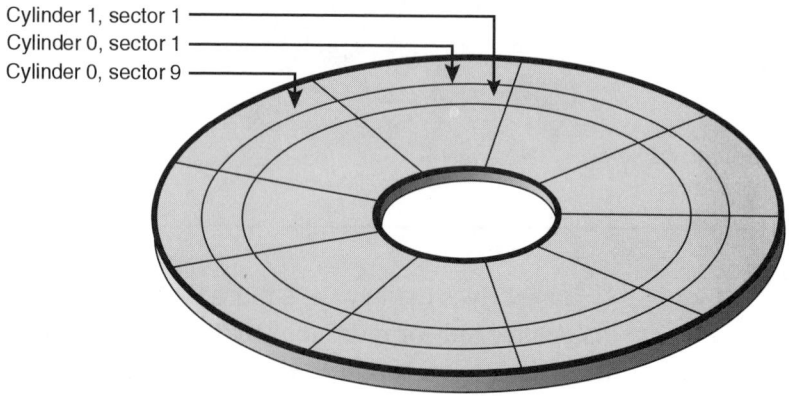

Cylinder 1, sector 1
Cylinder 0, sector 1
Cylinder 0, sector 9

Figure 10.4

Tracks and sectors
on a floppy

Both hard and floppy disk devices typically store 512 bytes on a sector—0.5K of data, as 1K = 1024. (See Figure 10.5.) In addition to containing data, each sector also contains a few more bytes dedicated to error detection and correction and internal drive control.

Figure 10.5

Each sector typically contains 512 bytes of data

1 sector = 512

Summarizing, then, a 1.44MB floppy consists of:

- ▶ Two sides or surfaces (or heads)
- ▶ 80 tracks or cylinders per side
- ▶ 18 sectors per track
- ▶ 0.5K bytes per sector

So:

- ▶ $2 \times 80 \times 18 \times 0.5K = 1.44MB$

Now compare the specs on a 10MB XT hard disk, the simplest hard disk I've ever seen.

▶ Four surfaces

▶ 305 tracks on each surface

▶ 17 sectors to a track

▶ 0.5K bytes on each sector

So:

▶ $4 \times 305 \times 17 \times 0.5K = 10{,}370K$ bytes

As you examine other disks, you will find that the 512 bytes per sector is constant. The number of tracks, the number of platters, and the number of sectors vary. Most manufacturers do not report the number of platters but instead the number of heads, which equals the number of surfaces. For example, consider a more modern disk:

▶ 16,383 cylinders

▶ 16 heads for storing data

▶ 63 sectors per track

▶ 512 bytes (0.5K) of data on each sector

Total all that up, and you get roughly an 8.4GB drive. (One costs about $100. Let me tell you about the 32MB drive that I bought for a thousand bucks in 1983 . . .)

Zone Bit Recording

Before leaving the subject of sectors, it's worth mentioning that the diagrams that you've seen in this book so far have all shown drives as having a constant number of sectors per track. That's not always the case.

The outer track on a disk is typically double or more the circumference of the innermost track. With an equal number of sectors on each track, data on the outer track is quite loose, while data on the innermost track is quite dense.

Placing differing numbers of sectors per track on a disk surface is called *Zone Bit Recording,* or *ZBR.* You will also hear the terms multiple zone recording or even just zone recording in place of ZBR. Consumer demand for greater and greater capacity on smaller and smaller drives, in combination with cheaper and faster electronics, has led to a growth in the use of ZBR.

Here's how it works. Based on their location on a disk, the ZBR program groups the tracks into zones. All tracks within a specific zone are given a constant number of sectors. Movement through the disk from the innermost zone to the outer zone passes you through multiple zones, each with a higher number of sectors than the one before.

Most software that you run on a computer won't know that your disk has ZBR. Because most computer software assumes that there are a constant number of sectors per track, ZBR drives keep that software happy by pretending that their drives contain a constant number of sectors per track. One kind of disk that you'll run into that is *always* ZBR is a CD. Rather than concentric tracks, CDs have one long continuous spiral similar to the grooves of a phonograph. CDs solve the varying numbers of sectors problem by actually varying the speed of the drive motor, depending on which part of the disk is being read; more on CDs and CD-ROM drives in Chapter 26.

Physical and Logical Geometry

As mentioned previously, *physical geometry* refers to the electronic organization of any type of disk drive—the actual physical number of heads, cylinders, tracks, and sectors. In the '80s, the physical geometry of a disk was relatively simple and BIOS setup contained the number of heads, tracks, and sectors. The PC could easily access the drive.

There have been changes in disk geometry, but there have been very few changes in the original setup parameters in the system BIOS. The BIOS mostly limits the number of sectors to 63 per track.

This means that you need to fool the system to make sure that the old BIOS standards and the new disk drive are compatible.

Because the system BIOS handles only one number for the number of sectors per track, any drive that uses ZBR needs to hide the physical geometry of the disk from the system. The disk subsystem accomplishes this using *logical geometry*. The manufacturer establishes the logical geometry of a disk that is a set of bogus values for the cylinders, heads, and sectors on the disk. The disk controller gives these bogus values to the BIOS. The hard disk controller provides automatic translation between the logical and physical geometry. The physical geometry is totally hidden. Table 10.4 is a sample of the difference between a drive's physical and logical geometry (it contains the specifications of one of my hard drives).

TABLE 10.4 Sample of a Hard Drive's Physical and Logical Geometry

Parameters	Logical Geometry	Physical Geometry
Cylinders	7480	6810
Heads	16	6
Sectors per track	63	122–232
Total sectors	7,539,840	7,539,840

Sector Translation and Logical Block Addressing

Until around 1994, the BIOS on most PCs had a limit of 528MB for hard drives. Newer BIOS versions correct this limitation and theoretically work with hard drives in excess of 8.4GB, although some BIOS are unable to handle hard drives over 2GB or 8.4GB. Early on, the biggest problem with the BIOS-driven constraints for disks wasn't that it was hard to support drives with 500 heads, because there weren't any of those around. The biggest problem was that there were a *lot* of drives with more than 1024 cylinders. There are a number of translation schemes that address these problems, two of which include sector translation and logical block addressing (LBA).

Note

Why are some hard drives limited to 2GB while others have a whopping 8GB? Refer to the section "BIOS and Operating System Capacity Barriers" for more information about disk capacity. Refer to your hardware and software specifications for details about your particular system.

Sector Translation

When you install a hard disk in a computer, as you'll learn in the next few chapters, you've got to tell the computer how many cylinders, heads, and sectors that new drive has. Strictly speaking, you're putting that information into your system's CMOS (Complementary Metal-Oxide Semiconductor) chip.

Some BIOS won't let you enter a value for cylinders above 1024. (Some newer systems allow you to enter larger numbers.) Now suppose you have a drive that has 1600 cylinders and four heads. If you try to tell most systems that the number of cylinders is 1600, they'll just laugh. To compensate, some drive systems *fib* to the PC, saying that it's not 1600 cylinders and four heads, but rather 800 cylinders and *eight* heads. This cylinder/head/sector (CHS) translation divides the number of cylinders by an integer (in this case 2) and multiplies the number of heads by the same integer when passing CHS values from the drive to the operating system. Do the math, and you'll see that the capacity is the same either way, but now the BIOS is happy. The BIOS then issues commands to an 800-cylinder, eight-head disk, and the drive subsystem translates those imaginary coordinates into a 1600-cylinder, four-head set of "true" coordinates. The name for this translation is *sector translation* or *cylinder/head/sector (CHS) translation.*

Some SCSI and IDE systems take sector translation to new heights by internally keeping track of only the total numbers of sectors on the entire drive. Ordinarily, system software would say to a disk interface, "Get me the sector on cylinder 100, head 3, sector 20." This is a "three-dimensional" sector address. But for these SCSI and

IDE systems, the system software would just say, "Get me the 143,292th sector on the disk." The numbering scheme for all sectors is sequential, one after the other, with no concern for their head or cylinder location. Such a sector-addressing scheme is a *linear addressing scheme.*

So why is this a problem? Usually, it's not. But if you're running a low-level disk fixer, the program may have to reformat particular tracks on the disk. When it requests the controller to low-level format, say, cylinder 10, head 5, the controller understands the request to mean, "Format the *real* cylinder 10 on the 1600-cylinder drive—not the *logical* 800-cylinder." In the process, the low-level format ends up destroying data that the disk fixer did not originally intend to destroy and could in fact render the hard disk useless. SpinRite is a disk utility that detects sector translation and thus avoids these problems, but not all disk utilities do.

Note

Disks smaller than 528MB use the CHS translation mode. The BIOS directly uses the logical geometry that the disk presents to it. Disks over 528MB use either Extended CHS (ECHS) mode or logical block addressing (LBA). ECHS takes the logical geometry of the hard disk and translates it into an equivalent geometry that makes the BIOS happy. LBA does the translation in a different manner from CHS, as described in the next section.

Logical Block Addressing

Sector translation gets a bit strange for larger drives where the disk drive uses logical block addressing. Instead of referring to a cylinder, head, and sector number, LBA assigns each sector a unique sector number starting at zero and going up to the total number of sectors on the disk less one (that is, if there are 18 actual sectors on the cylinder, LBA would number them 0–17). The translation is similar to ECHS translation but instead of translating to the drive's logical geometry, translation occurs directly to a logical block number (a sector number).

If you look at the BIOS listings for some of the newer drives, you'll find that some have specs that don't seem to make sense. For example, some claim to have *64 heads*! How huge is *that* drive? Well, physically, it's about the size of a pack of playing cards. How do they fit all of those heads—let's see 64 heads would be 32 platters—into a drive about an inch high? The answer, as you probably suspect, is that they *don't*. The drive claims to be 64 heads, 63 sectors, and 611 cylinders. That's a total of 1,231,776K, 1203MB, or 1.17GB. (Remember that a megabyte isn't 1,000,000 bytes, it's 1,048,576 bytes. Similarly, a gigabyte isn't 1,000,000,000 bytes; it's 1,073,741,824 bytes. Don't be surprised, however, if manufacturers conveniently redefine the definitions to 1,000,000 and 1,000,000,000.) Let's say I have a drive with 2448 cylinders, 16 heads, and 63 sectors, which is about the same size as the drive described above.

Careful readers will be scratching their heads at this point and saying, "Hey, wait, 64 heads were definitely impossible for a drive that is one inch high, but *so are 16 heads.* What's the story?" It's true; the drive does not have 16 heads. But that's what I had to tell the computer when I set it up.

You see, this drive, like many modern high-capacity drives, uses ZBR encoding. That means that there are a variable number of sectors per track. The problem is that your PC's BIOS insists on knowing the number of cylinders, heads, and sectors per track on your drive and will refuse to use any drive until you provide that information. But my technical specifications for my drive say that it's got 3854 cylinders and six data surfaces, and there's no information on sectors per track. There's no way a modern BIOS can just say, "It has 3854 cylinders, six data surfaces, and a variable number of sectors."

In response, the design of my drive's on-board electronics makes the PC happy and appears to provide a nice, consistent number of sectors per track. No problem, really—it's a kind of sector translation. The real problem is that the drive geometry that the drive exposes to the CMOS is 2448 cylinders, 16 heads, and 63 sectors. Sixteen heads and 63 sectors are no problem; 2448 cylinders are a problem.

My host adapter and my drive work together to solve the problem by using LBA. In the case of this drive, LBA rearranges the apparent geometry of the disk, which ends up producing an apparent drive with fewer cylinders and more heads than the system sees.

Usually, the disk interface supplies the LBA feature. Occasionally, however, I've seen jumpers on a drive that you must move in order for LBA to work with that drive. LBA's main job is to bypass DOS's quirkiness with drives over 504MB.

Comparing Translation Modes

To reiterate, there are three translation modes: Standard CHS, Extended CHS, and LBA.

▶ Standard CHS uses

  ▶ Physical geometry between the physical drive platters and the disk interface

  ▶ Logical geometry between the disk interface and the BIOS

  ▶ Logical geometry between the BIOS and operating system and applications

▶ Extended CHS uses

  ▶ Physical geometry between the physical drive platters and the disk interface

  ▶ Logical geometry between the disk interface and the BIOS

  ▶ Translated geometry between the BIOS and operating system and applications

▶ LBA uses

  ▶ Physical geometry between the physical drive platters and the disk interface

  ▶ Logical block addressing between the disk interface and the BIOS

  ▶ Translated geometry between the BIOS and operating system and applications

Voice Coil and Stepper Head-Positioning Mechanisms

Most of today's hard drives use voice coils in the actuator motor to move the heads back and forth. Earlier hard drives used a stepper motor mechanism to move the heads; many of today's floppy drives still use this mechanism.

Voice Coil Mechanisms

Named after the voice coil circuit in telephone electronics, the hard disk voice coil is a *closed control system*: it is self-correcting. The head moves, but it looks to the data on the disk to figure out exactly where to stop. A hard disk voice coil has a cylindrical rod at its middle. Energizing the coil moves the rod in or out of the coil, depending on how much energy the coil uses. The rod connects to the heads, so energizing the coil moves the heads in or out. The controller senses the position of the head by reading the magnetic servo pattern that the manufacturer prerecords on the drive. The magnetic servo pattern is in addition to any data on the disk. You can see a voice coil in Figure 10.6.

Figure 10.6

A voice coil

Coil—

Pivot point—

Head actuator arm

The actuator and control electronics determine how far to move the heads by reading the servo patterns and making the necessary adjustments for proper positioning of the heads. There are two types of servo systems: embedded servo and dedicated servo.

Some drives intersperse the head positioning information, allowing all surfaces to be used for data—this is an *embedded servo* positioning mechanism. The manufacturer lays servo information down on the disk by either restricting the servo signals to a wedge or sector of the tracks, or distributing the signals and embedding them into every sector.

Other drives dedicate an entire surface to this information— which is why you'll see some drives report an odd number of sides, such as the old Seagate 4096 that claims to have nine surfaces, but actually has ten. Such an approach is a *dedicated servo* positioning mechanism. A dedicated servo system is faster and has more accurate tracking than an embedded system, but it has the disadvantage of losing a whole disk surface to servo data and the requirement of a separate servo head.

When you turn the machine off, a spring holds the heads against the center of the disk. This means that whenever you shut down the computer, the drive parks itself! Note that if the system goes bad, all you can do is either buy a new drive or send it back to the manufacturer.

Stepper Motor Mechanism

Generally, the stepper motor system is found now only in floppy disks where the track density is relatively low. The stepper is an *open* system: it is not self-correcting. A stepper system assumes that cylinder 40 will always be 40 clicks away from cylinder 0. As time goes on, its position drifts further and further from the actual data.

The stepper motor rotates in small, consistent increments and moves the drive read/write heads in individual steps. Specifically, the shaft of a stepper motor has magnets permanently attached to it. Energizing one or more of the coils that are around the body of the motor creates a magnetic field that interacts with the permanent magnets on the shaft of the motor. Turning these coils on and off in sequence causes the motor to rotate forward or reverse.

Disk Performance Characteristics

One of the jobs of a hard disk is to read and write data as fast as possible. Some disk/controller combinations are faster than others are. Many performance factors are interrelated. Drive speed is measured by looking at two disk performance characteristics: how long it takes to find a particular piece of data (*access time*) and, once found, how quickly it can be read off the disk (*data transfer rate*).

The access time is a combination of the seek time and latency and involves finding the correct location or position on the drive. The average seek time is the average time that the heads require to move from one track to any other track. Data transfer rate involves the speed at which the drive reads and writes (transfers) data.

Note

A drive's average access time is the interval between the time a request for data is made by the system and the time the data becomes available from the drive. While the average access time metric is sometimes used to assess hard disks, it is more frequently used to assess CD-ROM drives.

Seeks and Latency

How quickly you can find and read a sector involves access time. Reading a particular sector involves two steps. First, move the head to the correct track. Then, once the head is over that track, wait for the sector to spin under the head, then read the sector. You see this in Figure 10.7.

Reading a particular sector involves two steps:

Figure 10.7

Reading a sector on a disk

First, move the head to the desired track. That is called seek.

Then, once the head is over that track, wait for the sector to spin under the head. The wait is called the latency period.

Now, moving the head takes a lot longer than waiting for the sector to come around. So low seek times (the time to move the head) are critical to good disk performance.

The formula to remember is shown in Table 10.5.

Table 10.5 Access Time Formula

Access Time	=	Seek Time	+	Rotational Latency Period
Time to find a sector	=	Time to move to the sector's cylinder	+	Time to wait for the sector to rotate around and appear under the head(s)

The two components are called *seek time* and *latency period or rotational latency period*. Seek time is the time required for the head to position itself over a track. The latency period is how long it takes the desired sector to move under the head.

Typical Seek Times

Of the seek time and the latency period, the seek time is usually the longer wait. Seek time is normally expressed in milliseconds (ms). It varies according to how many tracks the heads must traverse. A seek from one track to the next track is usually quick—5 to 16ms, but most seeks aren't so convenient. Remember, the lower the seek time, the better. Note that in current PCs, a millisecond is a long period, considering that the measure for modern PC memory is in nanoseconds. This means the system may have to wait for the hard disk.

A common measure of an average seek is the time the system requires to travel one-third of the way across the disk. Most benchmark programs use this measurement. You might wonder, "Why not halfway across the disk, rather than one-third?" The reason is that most accesses are short seeks—just a few tracks.

Years ago, companies sold hard disks with seek times of almost 100ms; by the mid-1980s, seek times were down to the high 30s. However, IBM still considered it acceptable to deliver a system with a seek time of 84ms on its PS/2 Model 50. Nowadays, the range of acceptable seek times is considerably narrower.

The worst seek time you should accept from a new product is about 10ms. The best you'll find will probably be no better than about 4.7ms. In general, the low speed depends on what you're willing to spend.

For example, my 1997 desktop system has a 3.82GB EIDE hard drive with a seek time of 11ms—not too bad for those days but a bit high for today's guidelines.

Seek times are built into a drive. There's no way for you to improve on a drive's seek time, short of getting a new drive.

Rotational Latency Period

Once a head positions itself over a track, the job's not done: now the head has to wait for the correct sector to rotate under the head. How *much* time is a matter of luck: if you're lucky, the sector is already there; if you're really unlucky, you just missed it and will have to wait an entire revolution. As I mentioned before, this waiting time, whether large or small, is the *rotational latency period*. A common number cited is *average latency period*. This makes the simple assumption that, on average, the disk must make a half-revolution to get to your sector. Manufacturers calculate the latency period from the spindle speed. Latency, like seek time, is normally expressed in milliseconds.

Depending on the model, disk drives rotate between 3600 and 12,000rpm (revolutions per minute). The usual spindle speed for a new disk varies between 5400 and 7000rpm. For a disk rotating at 3600rpm, one-half revolution then takes 1/7200 of a minute = 60/7200 second = 8.33ms. This contributes to the amount of time that the system must wait for service (the rotational latency). The higher the spindle's speed (rpm), the lower the average latency. Reducing the latency improves system performance. Table 10.6 lists some standard spindle speeds and the corresponding average and worst-case rotational latency period (in milliseconds). Calculate the average latency based on a half rotation of the disk; calculate the worst-case latency on a full rotation of the disk.

TABLE 10.6 Rotational Latency and Spindle Speeds

Spindle Speed (rpm)	Average Rotational Latency (in ms)	Worst-Case Rotational Latency (in ms)
3600	8.3	16.7
4500	6.7	13.3
5200	5.8	11.5
5400	5.6	11.1
6300	4.8	9.5
7200	4.2	8.3
10,000	3.0	6.0
12000	2.5	5.0

Table 10.6 shows that the higher the speed of the spindle, the lower the latency. As new technologies reduce drive costs, manufacturers are increasing the spindle speeds of the newer and more

expensive drives. Reducing latency is particularly beneficial for users who frequently access random sectors on the disk.

Note

Manufacturers are also using cylinder and head skewing to reduce latency and include any necessary skewing in today's high-speed disk and disk controllers. It is not possible for users to adjust the cylinder and head skewing.

Data Transfer Rates, Interleave Factors, and Skewing

Once a disk has found the data, how fast can it transfer it to the PC? This is called *data transfer rate*. Specifically, the transfer rate is a measure of the amount of data that the system can access over a period of time (typically one second). It involves the external data transfer rate that is the speed of the communication between the system memory and the internal buffer or cache built into the drive. It also involves the internal data transfer rate that is the speed that the hard disk can physically write or read data to or from the surface of the platter and transfer it to the internal drive cache or read buffer. A number of factors can influence the data transfer rate including interleaving factors and cylinder and head skew.

The Internal Data Transfer Rate

In a disk, the transfer rate is a measure of the communication between the CPU and the controller and the controller and the disk drive. The internal transfer rate under discussion here is the rate that data is written to and read from the disk. Transfer rates vary depending on the density of the data on the disk, how fast the disk is spinning, and the location of the data.

There are two types of density when discussing hard drives: areal density and track density. *Areal density* refers to how much data (bits) the disk can store in a square inch. Areal density impacts the seek time and data transfer rates. *Track density* is a part of the calculation of areal density and is a measure of the density of the tracks on each platter.

To calculate the density of the disk, multiply the bytes per sector by the number of sectors on the disk. Determine the number of revolutions of the spindle per second by dividing the spindle rpm value by 60. The following gives you the transfer rate in megabits per second:

Data Transfer Rate = (Spindle Speed / 60 × Sectors-Per-Track × 512 × 8) / 1,000,000

Remember that there are only 512 bytes in a sector. This means that whenever an application requests, say, sector 1 of track 100 of side 2, it'll probably next need sector 2 of that track and side. In fact, most times when you need *one* sector from a track, you'll end up needing them all. So what's the best arrangement of sectors to allow them to be read at maximum speed? Read on to find out.

Interleave Factor

The interleave factor refers to the way sectors are organized on the disk. A 1:1 interleave factor means the sectors are arranged sequentially around each track. A 2:1 interleave factor means that consecutively numbered sectors are separated by an intervening sector around each track.

The speeds of a modern controller mean it can handle a 1:1 interleave factor without any problem. It is not possible—nor necessary—to adjust the interleaving factor on modern disks.

Interleaving is not a factor on modern IDE, EIDE, or SCSI disk drives. All of the new Pentium-based PCs use IDE, EIDE, or SCSI, so if you have a newer PC, the following interleave factor discussion is irrelevant; it's included for historical information only.

On older PCs, the process of low-level formatting a hard or floppy disk laid down milestones (sector IDs) that separated sectors from each other.

The numbering of sectors on a disk is logical so the system can address the sectors to read or write data. Logical sector 1 does not have to be the same sector as physical sector 1, nor does it have to be physically adjacent to logical sector 2. The number of physical sectors that occur between logical sector numbers is the interleave factor.

Interleaving was necessary because older controllers were not fast enough to finish reading or writing data for sector 1 until part of sector 2 was already spinning under the read/write heads. On 1.44MB floppies, the 18 sectors are laid out like numbers on the face of a clock, as shown in Figure 10.8.

Figure 10.8

1.44MB floppy interleave order

```
            17  18  1
        16              2
     15                    3
    14                       4
    13                       5
    12                       6
       11                 7
         10   9    8
```

That's because the floppy disk spins slowly enough so the controller can read all of the sectors on a 1.44MB floppy in one pass. 1.44MB floppies have nine sectors on a track, and the disk rotates only five times per second. The most burden a floppy could put on its controller would be to throw it 0.5K sector × 18 sectors/rotation × 5 rotations/second or 45K per second. Heck, the serial port on most PCs can run at almost that rate—consecutive sectors on a floppy are no big deal.

Early IDE and SCSI hard disks didn't work that way. The problem was that hard disks rotate many times faster than floppies. In addition, hard disks packed more sectors on a track. To see the problem, suppose you had a hard disk with a 1:1 interleave, meaning the sectors were in numerical order, as shown in Figure 10.9.

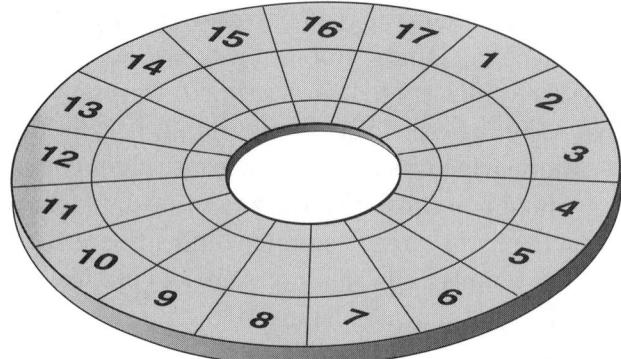

Figure 10.9

A 1:1 interleaved
hard disk

As the hard disk rotated, the minimum this disk would throw at the controller per second would be 0.5K/sector × 17 sectors/rotation × 60 rotations/second = 510K/second! Most hard disk controllers (and some computers) couldn't handle a half-megabyte per second. The computer had to both read the data and check the data for validity before transferring it to the computer's memory.

So let's look in detail at what happened when the computer reads two sectors in succession on a 1:1 interleaved disk.

1. The operating system and BIOS requests that the hard disk controller read a sector.

2. The controller instructed the disk head to move to the track and read the sector, as shown in Figure 10.10.

3. The head reads the data and transmits it to the controller.

Step 1: An instruction to read sector 1 on a given track is executed. The head has been positioned over the right track, and now the data is read as the disk turns under the head.

Figure 10.10

How interleaving
affects disk speed
(part 1)

4. Because hard disks are fragile devices, the controller always includes extra data when it writes information to the disk. This information, when read back, enables the controller to detect whether or not errors arose in the data. The information is called the ECC (error-correction code) and allows the computer to both detect and correct errors in the data read from the disk. It involves a mathematical function and takes a little while to compute: see Figure 10.11. (The microprocessors on hard disk controllers aren't the fastest things in the world. I mean, you don't find too many Pentiums on disk controllers.) Meanwhile, the disk continues to spin, as in Figure 10.12.

Suppose these numbers have been stored on a hard disk.	317 491 802

Now imagine that some of the data has been obscured. Without the extra information, we have no hope of recovery.	317 ■1 802

Figure 10.11

How disk error
correction works

An ECC (error-correction code) adds redundant information to the data on disk so that in the event of damage some data can be recovered. A simple example of redundant data is a sum.

317
491
802
————
1610

With the sum, however, the controller can work backward and deduce the value of the lost data.

317
■1
802
————
1610

Must be 491

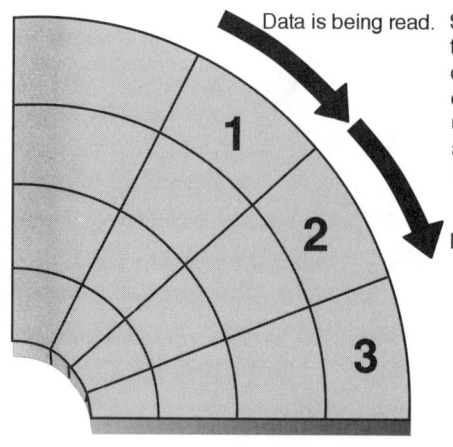

Data is being read. Step 2: The data has been passed from the disk head to the controller. The controller checks that the data was not corrupted while on disk. It does that check using a mathematical computation called an Error Correcting Code (ECC) test. Meanwhile, the disk keeps turning.

Data is being checked.

Figure 10.12

How interleaving affects disk speed (part 2)

5. Once the controller checks the data, it passes it to the BIOS and the operating system, both of which are also paranoid about hard disk data loss. The BIOS and the operating system have their own small amount of overhead—proportionately less than the controller's, but relevant nonetheless. Meanwhile, the disk continues to spin: see Figure 10.13.

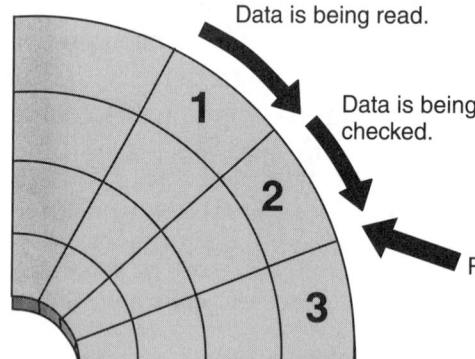

Data is being read.

Data is being checked.

Step 3: After the controller pronounces the data okay, the operating system and BIOS must be consulted again. Finally they're ready to request sector 2–but sector 2 has just passed by! We are in the perfect location, however, for sector 3. Why not, then, put sector 2 where sector 3 is now?

Request issued for sector 2.

Figure 10.13

How interleaving affects disk speed (part 3)

6. Now that everyone is happy with the data, the operating system wants the next sector. But the disk continues spinning while the controller, operating system, and BIOS take a long time with the last sector's data. If sector 2 comes right after

sector 1, the controller always misses the subsequent sector. That implies that the controller has to wait a whole rotation to get the next sector.

Thus, with a disk with the sectors laid out clock-fashion, in numerical order, the controller always ended up reading only one sector per rotation. As the disk rotated at least 60 times per second, the controller read 60 or more sectors/second. Each sector held at least 0.5K, so the data transfer rate from this disk was 30K/second, a rather poor transfer rate. (A 1.44MB floppy could outperform this disk because it transfers data at 45K/second!)

But suppose the sectors were staggered to give the controller time to get ready for the next sector. IBM did that on the XT, as shown in Figure 10.14.

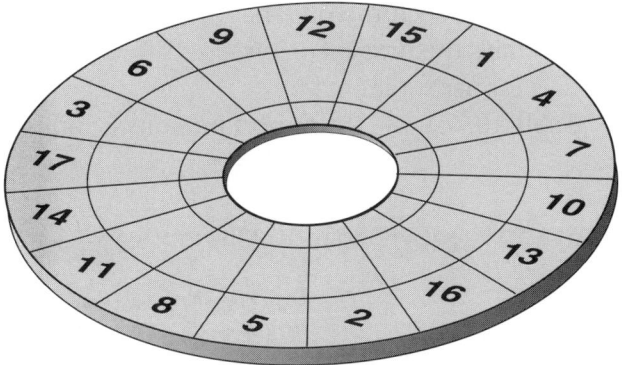

Figure 10.14

Hard disk with a 1:6 disk interleave

This is a 1:6 interleave. Start at 1, then count clockwise six sectors. You're now at 2. Count six more. You're now at 3. And so on. This gave the XT time to do computations and still catch the next sector. Inspection will show that the XT could read three sectors on the first rotation, or about 180 sectors/second. That means that you could get three times the throughput from an XT by using a disk with a layout of 1:6.

As controllers got faster, they were able to compute error-correction codes faster. IBM interleaved the AT disk more tightly, as shown in Figure 10.15.

Figure 10.15

Hard disk with a 1:3 disk interleave

This is a 1:3 interleave factor. Here the computer could read six sectors on a single rotation. Remember why interleave had to be a 1:3 disk—the sectors would be too close, and the controller would always miss the next sector. The net effect would be like getting only one sector per rotation.

Table 10.7 shows the importance of the interleave factor.

TABLE 10.7 The Importance of the Interleave Factor

Drive Type	Max Data Transfer (K/Second)	Sectors Read/Rotations
Hard Disk (17 Sectors/Track)		
1:6	85	2.8
1:5	102	3.4
1:4	128	4.3
1:3	170	5.7
1:2	255	8.5
1:1	510	17.0

You can see that reformatting from IBM's default 1:6 interleave to a 1:5 interleave improved disk throughput by 20 percent. Changing interleave on an IBM AT from 1:3 to 1:2 increased disk throughput by 50 percent. The right interleave factor means that the controller, the computer, and the disk are right in step, pulling data off the disk as quickly as is possible. The kind of controller you have determines the optimal interleave factor.

Remember, the interleave factor is set when you low-level format a hard disk. Some software writers used to offer interleave fixer programs. These measured the disk's optimal interleave, then allowed the disk's interleave factor to be reset without backing up, reformatting, and reloading. Their approach was really a simple one: just read a track, store it in memory, reformat the track to the proper interleave factor, and rewrite the original information.

Cylinder and Head Skew

Modern controllers eliminate the need for interleaving on modern disks. But other conditions can cause a less than optimal data transfer rate. For example, switching between tracks causes a time delay, as does switching from one head to another. Today's disk drive manufacturers design cylinder and head skewing to reduce latency when the read/write request causes a switch between consecutive heads or cylinders.

Note

The design of modern disks makes it no longer possible for the user to adjust either cylinder or head skewing.

Suppose the first sector of each track is physically in the same position on the platter. If we are reading the entire contents of two consecutive tracks, the controller reads all the sectors of the first track in order and then gets ready to switch to the first sector of the second track. At this point, the first sector of the second track is on top of the previous first sector, and the controller has yet to physically move the heads to the second track. This takes some time.

As the heads move to the second track, the first few sectors go by and the controller needs to wait an entire revolution of the platter before it can continue reading the data. To avoid this problem, the manufacturer might program the drive controller to offset the first or start sector of adjacent tracks from each other. For example, they could establish the first sector of track two to be adjacent to the third sector of track one. This is *cylinder skew*, and movement is horizontal.

A similar time delay problem occurs when switching from one head to another within a cylinder. Each track in the cylinder is accessible by one of the drive heads. Switching between heads is a purely electronic process and takes time, although there is no physical movement. Here too, the manufacturer might program the drive controller to offset the first sector of tracks within the cylinder from each other. This is *head skew*, and movement is vertical.

Error-Correction Code (ECC)

No electronic data transmission or storage system is perfect. Each system makes errors at a certain rate. Modern disks have built-in error detection and correction mechanisms. While this isn't really a disk performance feature, I mentioned this in passing a few pages back, and I want to give you more of the information on how disks can self-correct errors.

Disk systems are great as storage media, but they're volatile. From the first second after you lay a piece of data on a disk, it starts "evaporating." The magnetic domains on the disk that define the data slowly randomize until the data is unrecognizable. The disk itself and the media may be fine, but the image of the data can fade after x years. Put another image on, and it'll last for another x years. (If you're taking videotapes of your baby in the hopes that you can use them to embarrass her in front of her dates in 15 years or so, physics may thwart you because the videotape is magnetic.)

Disk subsystems are aware of this, and so include some method of detecting and correcting minor data loss. The disk subsystem can detect but not correct *major* data loss. The controller includes *extra* data when it writes information to the disk. When the controller reads back this information (the *error-correction code*, or ECC) it lets the controller detect whether or not errors have arisen in the data. We saw an example of ECC back in Figure 10.11. The basic idea is that the controller stores redundant information *with* the disk data at the time that the data is originally written to disk. Then, when the data is later read from disk, the disk controller checks the redundant information to verify data integrity.

The ECC calculations are more complex than a simple checksum. The ECC that most manufacturers implement in hard disks (and CD-ROMs) uses the Reed-Solomon algorithm. The calculations take time, so there's a tradeoff; more complex ECCs can recover more damaged data, but they take more computation time. The number of bits associated with a sector for ECC is a design decision and determines the robustness of the error detection and correction. Quite a number of modern disks use over 200 bits of code for each sector.

Some controllers let you choose to use an *x*-bit ECC. In this example, *x* refers to the number of consecutive bad bits that the ECC can correct. The original AT hard disk controller, for instance, could correct up to 5 bad consecutive bits. That meant that it had a "maximum correctable error burst length" of 5 bits. Newer controllers, including drives in newer AT-type clones and many Pentium machines can usually correct up to 11 bits (11 is better, if you can get it). Note that, a newer controller may have to stay at 5 bits if you use it in an actual IBM AT—the IBM AT BIOS can support only 5-bit ECC. Some of the newest drives installed in the latest Pentium-based machines are using special high-speed controller hardware to do *70-bit* error correction! They can correct 70 bad bits in a row—quite amazing.

Getting Good Data Transfer Rates on Modern Systems

I said earlier that interleave adjustment is of value only on older systems. So how can you crank the maximum data rates out of your hard disk? Most of it boils down nowadays to choosing good hardware and, to a lesser extent, to tuning device drivers.

Modern SCSI-3 and EIDE host adapters can deliver megabytes and megabytes per second if they're set up right. Here are the big things to look for:

▶ The drive must have a good data transfer rate. Most drives nowadays have a small amount of cache memory on them. A small amount of cache can be useful to have but note that that same cache can fool test programs into thinking that the drives are faster than they actually are. Read the "External Transfer Rate Dependencies" and "Caches in Drive Subsystems" sections for more information.

▶ You also need a fast disk interface. On IDE drives, a host adapter with the Enhanced IDE (EIDE) interface is a good choice because it can transfer data more quickly.

▶ Avoid using an ISA board. If one is present, swap it out and use a PCI or VESA board instead. The fastest disk interface in the world will run slowly if it's an ISA board. Fast disk interfaces must be built on top of fast buses.

▶ Avoid buying disk interface boards with tons of cache memory on them. Read the "Caches in Drive Subsystems" section to see why.

Once you've got the hardware in place, you may have to tune a device driver on your PC. My EIDE system, for example, will run just fine without any special drivers, but the performance that it turns in isn't stunning. Add the drivers that came with the disk interface card, however, and the data transfer numbers I get improve.

External Transfer Rate Dependencies

The external transfer rate depends on the type of drive interface in your PC and the modes that it supports. Support for modes existing in the drive interface need to be present in both the drive and the system BIOS. Higher external data transfer rates are possible if your EIDE interface supports the industry-standard PIO mode 4 and DMA mode 2 protocols. PIO stands for *programmed input/output*. DMA, as you recall, stands for direct memory access. Both of these protocols consist of a set of rules for operating the physical interface.

The system or host adapter BIOS needs to support these protocol modes. If this support is not present, the drive defaults to whatever slower transfer rate the BIOS and the disk drive support. The PIO and DMA transfer modes also require that the interface is running over a high-speed system bus such as PCI or VESA. You can read more about these transfer modes in the section "PIO and DMA Transfer Mechanisms."

Caches in Drive Subsystems

Disk drives are slow, I mean, really slow. Your computer uses RAM memory that responds to requests in tens of nanoseconds, but the disk drive responds to requests in tens of milliseconds—that's six orders of magnitude difference in speed! Most operating systems set aside a small area of memory as a disk cache.

A disk cache seeks to use the speed of memory to bolster the effective speed of the disk. The cache is held in memory chips and is usually one to a few megabytes. The operating system can access data previously placed in the disk cache on an as needed basis. Using this disk cache can cut down on the number of physical seeks and transfers from the hard drive itself. Smart caching algorithms generally mean that there is no need to change the size of the disk cache.

The disk's adapter or controller board contains a cache that separates the internal read/write operations from transfers over the bus and holds recently accessed data. Most drives nowadays have at least 64K of cache RAM right on them.

The amount of RAM on a disk drive is usually small, between 32K and 1024K. This cache buffer acts as a holding area for one or more tracks or even a complete cylinder's worth of information in case you need it. The point of buffering an entire track is simple: it would be just about impossible to manage one-to-one interleaving otherwise, and besides, the built-in sector translation that virtually every drive does nowadays requires some buffer space to juggle sectors around. This cache buffer can be effective in speeding up both throughput and access times.

As an example, let's say there are two drives in a system, a high-performance EIDE drive, and a lower-performance IDE drive. The EIDE drive turns in a buffered read value of 4688K/second, and the IDE transfers data at nearly the same rate, 4448K/second. Sounds like the two drives are equal—but they're not. It's just more likely that they both have 64K of similar-speed RAM chips on them.

You can see the difference between the two drives when you compare the next transfer value, the sequential read value. There, the EIDE drive transfers data at 3664K/second, but the IDE falls way behind to 1280K/second.

A word of caution: if you increase the size of these caches, you could run out of memory to effectively run programs and manage data. This could force your PC to rely on virtual memory to run the programs.

Computers running modern operating systems have efficient caching algorithms built into them, so they have the benefits of caching. On-board caches on disk interface boards just add another layer of data shuffling and, in my experience, real-world tasks don't get done any faster with them. Think of it this way: buying 4MB of cache RAM for your disk interface card costs the same as buying 4MB more for your system, but that interface card RAM does only one thing. Buying 4MB for the system is general-purpose—you can use it for anything that computers need RAM for.

Another reason to avoid on-board caches on interface boards is write caching. Interfaces with memory on them will delay actually writing data to the disk in order to make the disk subsystem seem faster. It's not a bad idea *except* that sometimes your system resets itself without warning the disk interface. As the system didn't warn the disk interface, it didn't write the data to the disk, and you have the equivalent of turning off the computer in the middle of a disk write.

This is *not* mere paranoia; every "version 1.0" of an operating system that I've ever installed on a controller with delayed writes caused major problems. That's why my bottom line recommendation on cached disk interfaces is: Don't use them.

BIOS and Operating System Capacity Barriers

The BIOS and interfaces in older and modern PCs can impose limits on the size of the hard drive. Additionally, PC operating systems have some inherent characteristics that can limit disk size.

BIOS and Interface Limitations

The interface from the PC system to the hard disk controls the operation of the disk drive through the addresses and commands that it sends to the hard disk. On the system side of the interface, the BIOS provides software routines that let different applications access the hard disk. File manager routines provide the mapping from file names to locations on the disk and then send read/write commands through interrupt 13 (INT 13) Application Programming Interface (API) to the BIOS. The INT 13 is operating system independent and is the primary interface to the BIOS. BIOS routines convert INT 13 requests into IDE/ATA interface requests for the disk drive to perform read/write functions. Note that manufacturers update the BIOS routines and INT 13 functions from time to time. The size of IDE hard drive that the computer will recognize is dependent on a combination of requirements of the BIOS and the IDE/ATA interface.

Note

ATA (AT Attachment) is the real name of what is widely known as IDE.

The INT 13 Interface Addressing

The use of INT 13 requires specific hard drive parameters and exact head, cylinder, and sector addressing. Conventional INT 13 functions use 24 bits to represent the disk geometry, as shown in Table 10.8.

TABLE 10.8 INT 13 API 24-Bit Allocation of the Hard Disk

Number of Bits Allocated	For the . . .	For a total of . . .
10 bits	Cylinder number	1024 cylinders (2^{10}) that the system can address
8 bits	Head number	256 heads (2^{8}) that the system can address
6 bits	Sector number	63 sectors ($2^{6}-1$) that the system can address

Therefore, for conventional CHS addressing, using the values $1024 \times 256 \times 63$, it is possible to address up to 16,515,072 sectors. And at 512 bytes per sector, you get a theoretical disk capacity of 8.4GB. LBA addressing views the available address bits as a single number. Larger disks require a BIOS and operating system that support INT 13 extensions or an operating system that bypasses the BIOS and INT 13. INT 13 uses 24-bit addressing.

INT 13 Extensions

By the early '90s, the disk-drive industry had increased the capacity and functionality of disk drives to such an extent that the BIOS INT13 interface specifications no longer provided adequate support. During the following years a number of extension were made to the specifications. These extensions permit

▌ The attachment of more than two drives to the system

▌ Accessing drives in excess of 528MB

▌ The use of BIOS translation algorithms (CHS and LBA)

▌ Commands to assign the order that the system is to access drives

INT 13 extensions now make it possible to use faster versions of the PIO and DMA transfer modes. When the 8.4GB capacity barrier was encountered, BIOS developers included new extended INT 13 functions that use 32 bits to represent addresses.

If a disk drive has a capacity greater than 8.4GB, using INT 13 extensions requires changes to the BIOS and the operating system. Note that Windows 95/98 and most other newer operating systems already support these extensions. Windows NT and Linux do not. Windows 2000 setup does not determine if BIOS INT 13 extensions are enabled or available for use before allowing the creation of a system partition with more than 1024 cylinders or typically larger than 8.4GB.

The ATA Interface Addressing

IDE/ATA interface recognizes a drive and figures out its capacity by looking at the logical geometry of the drive: the number of cylinders, heads, and sectors per track that it contains. Before 1994, drives and the BIOS only supported CHS addressing. Today's drives support both CHS addressing and LBA addressing.

Today's IDE/ATA interface uses 28 bits to represent the disk address as shown in Table 10.9. The BIOS records the information in defined registers; it records the starting address of the data on the disk, the length of the data transfer, and the read or write command (read or write).

TABLE 10.9 IDE/ATA Interface Disk Addressing

Number of Bits Allocated	For the . . .	For a Total of . . .
16 bits	Cylinder address in the cylinder register.	65,536 cylinders (2^{16}) that the system can address
4 bits	Head address in the head register.	16 heads (2^4) that the system can address
8 bits	Sector address in the sector register. The first sector is number 1 as there is no sector 0.	255 sectors (2^8-1) that the system can address

Therefore, for CHS addressing for the IDE/ATA interface using the values $65,536 \times 16 \times 255$, it is possible to address up to 267,386,880 sectors. And at 512 bytes per sector, you get a theoretical disk capacity of 137.4GB. IDE/ATA uses 28-bit addressing.

Capacity Barriers

As we have seen, the IDE/ATA and INT13 BIOS standards use a different number of bits for the disk geometry. It is necessary to observe the limitations of both standards, which means the system can use only the smaller of each geometry number as shown in Table 10.10.

TABLE 10.10 Combined IDE/ATE and INT 13 Allocation of Bits

Standard	Bits for Cylinder Number	Bits for Head Number	Bits for Sector Number	Total Bits for Geometry
INT 13	10	8	6	24
IDE/ATA	16	4	8	28
Smallest	10	4	6	20

The 528MB Barrier IDE/ATA (EIDE/ATA) disks have a limit of 16 logical heads. To compensate, these disks always have a large number of cylinders, but because of the INT 13 limitation they can only see 1024 of the cylinders and 63 sectors. When the system has a nontranslating BIOS, the capacity will be $1024 \times 16 \times 63 \times 512$, or 528MB. This is the well-known 528MB barrier.

To overcome this limit, BIOS designers implement one of two translating algorithms for converting the INT 13 API address to the ATA address. The first is BitShift translation that changes the cylinder and head values so that the total number of sectors remains the same. This is the most common translation method. The second algorithm is the LBA assist translation. A system can use this translation only if the drive supports LBA addressing.

The 2.1GB Barrier Although relatively rare, some BIOS can have a problem translating the disk geometry if the number of cylinders exceeds 4096. A BIOS with this problem could report the disk as 2.1GB although it could be larger. There is also a 2GB capacity barrier that is an operating system issue and has to do with the file allocation table (FAT).

The 4.2GB Barrier There are some operating systems that store the number of heads as an eight-bit value. This can cause a problem if the BIOS reports 256 heads and BitShift translation is in use. If this is the case, the maximum capacity is 4.2GB. Note that the LBA assist translation never reports more than 255 heads so the problem does not exist where the drive and BIOS support LBA.

The 8.4GB Barrier The BIOS limitation of 8.4GB ($1024 \times 256 \times 63 \times 512$/per sector) causes this barrier. New extended INT 13 functions have recently been added to overcome this barrier. The new extension passes a 64-bit LBA address in a device address packet. Extended INT 13 passes the packet through host memory rather than through host registers. If the drive supports LBA, the BIOS passes the lower 28 bits of this address directly to the ATA registers. If LBA support is not present, the BIOS converts the LBA address to a CHS and passes that address to the ATA registers.

The 32GB Barrier Information about this barrier is still scarce. In some systems, the motherboard BIOS cannot address drives greater than 32GB. This is an LBA addressing limit in the particular BIOS code on the motherboard. Most BIOS manufacturers have now made corrections in their core BIOS. Contact your motherboard manufacturer for information and for a BIOS update if necessary.

Microsoft and others have found that the protected-mode (graphical) version of SCANDISK can misreport cluster sizes on IDE hard drives whose capacity exceeds 32GB and the BIOS uses the BitShift translation algorithm to report the disk's geometry. If the BIOS uses the LBA assist translation algorithm, there is no problem. A fix for this problem for Windows 98 is under development. For the current status, go to Microsoft's Web site and the Microsoft Knowledge Base article "SCANDISK Errors on IDE Hard Disks Larger Than 32GB." Windows 95 does not support storage media larger than 32GB.

Circumventing Drive Size Limitations

You can circumvent this artificial limitation either by bypassing the BIOS or fooling the BIOS during CMOS setup. The bypass method is for operating systems such as NetWare and UNIX and is referred to as *auto-configure*. It uses the Disk Parameter Table (DPT) instead of the BIOS to pass information about drive capacity from the IDE drive to the operating system.

The "fool the BIOS" method is called *auto-translate*. DOS and Windows machines can use auto-translate. When you choose this method during CMOS setup, you tell the BIOS to create an Enhanced Disk Parameter Table (EDPT) during the Power-On Self-Test. The initialization process fills this table with the appropriate values for all the drive characteristics, along with a checksum value to ensure the accuracy of the parameters. This type of table allows the system to support drives with more than 1024 cylinders or more than 528MB.

The EDPT contains a set of drive parameters that come from two sources. The first set of drive parameters comes from the Identify Drive command. The second set of drive parameters is from the BIOS and includes a number of extended INT 13 functions (see below). The EDPT provides information about the translation mode(s) that the drive and BIOS use. The information that the EDPT presents to the operating system is a translation of information taken from the drive. The information is not dependent on how the CHS and IDE bit fields match up.

BIOS Translation Support

The BIOS supports two types of translations based on information that the Identify Drive command returns.

▶ One provides a straightforward translation of BIOS CHS information to IDE/ATA CHS information. This is referred to as IDE CHS.

▶ The other translates the CHS information that passes to the BIOS into a 28-bit logical block address (LBA). The BIOS receives this LBA information and sends it to the drive's task-file register where it then sets bit 6 of the drive's select drive head register to indicate that the information in the task registers is LBA rather than CHS. From then on, the drive uses the LBA value to fetch the appropriate physical block from the disk.

The result of either of these translations is that the Enhanced Drive Parameter Table can now let the enhanced IDE interface access drives as large as 8.4GB. You need no software or operating system change to support high-capacity drives. The IDE CHS and the IDE LBA translations are mostly transparent to the operating system. Western Digital calls its IDE LBA-enabling driver FASTDISK.

Fortunately, virtually all newer systems have upgraded EIDE hard drive software, making it possible to use drives as large as 20GB with no modifications at all.

Operating System Limitations

In the PC world, the operating system limits the partition size, which restricts installation of the operating system to the first 8.4GB of the disk. For example, the Windows NT bootstrap process has inherent hardware and software limitations beyond which Windows NT cannot operate. These limitations prevent Windows NT 4 from using a partition larger than 8.4GB as a system partition. Logical partitions in Windows NT can be much larger. Additionally, Windows NT limits the first partition, or boot partition, to a maximum of 4GB; because of this, a drive larger than 8.4GB must have at least two partitions.

Windows 98 and Windows 2000 were written after the development of the BIOS INT 13 extensions and can boot from larger partitions. Windows NT 4 was developed before the INT 13 extensions and is unable to use its features.

In the Windows world, operating systems that use the 16-bit versions of the file allocation table (FAT) have an inherent limitation in the operating system that restricts a partition to 2.1GB. With 32-bit FAT and new technologies, the next limitation with the Advanced Technology Attachment (ATA) interface is expected to occur at 137GB, when the 28 bits of addressing on the ATA bus run out.

No version of Windows 95 supports hard disks that are larger than 32GB. If you want to use media larger than 32GB on a Windows 95 machine, Microsoft recommends that you upgrade to Microsoft Windows 98, NT, or 2000. If you are using Windows NT, it must be Windows NT 4, and you must be running Service Pack 4 or higher.

PIO and DMA Protocol Transfer Mechanisms

The most popular hard disk interfaces that modern PCs use are ATA-2 (EIDE) drives running with PIO (programmed input/output) mode 4 or multiword DMA (direct memory access) mode 2. Both PIO and DMA protocols consist of a set of rules for operating the IDE and EIDE interfaces. The PIO data transfer method depends on the processor to handle data transfers. DMA is a transfer mode for moving data between the hard drive and host memory that virtually eliminates the CPU from the transfer process.

The IDE/EIDE interface usually employs PIO since, back when IDE first came on the scene, PIO was faster than DMA. DMA was slower because it was tied to bus speed, and the ISA bus of the time was quite slow indeed. When interrogated with an Identify Drive command, a hard disk returns information about the PIO and DMA modes it is capable of using.

PIO Modes

PIO modes are a range of protocols for a drive and IDE controller to exchange data at different rates that the manufacturer implements in a chip set. PIO transfer modes use the CPU in the data transfer process. Because of CPU involvement process, PIO is ideal for lower-performance applications and single tasking. PIO modes do not require any special drivers.

There are five different PIO modes (mode 0 through mode 4) and each one defines a different maximum transfer rate. Different IDE/ATA standards support some or all of the PIO transfer modes. PIO transfers data to and from the disk controller through the I/O ports to memory. The CPU manages throughput at the I/O ports.

For optimal performance, a controller should support the drive's highest PIO mode (usually PIO mode 4). The transfer rate of PIO modes is the external data transfer rate for the drive and represents the speed of the interface. It does not represent the speed of the drive itself. Note that modes 3 and 4 both require the use of a PCI or VESA local bus and specific BIOS support.

The VL Bus uses both PIO and block PIO (BPIO). Block PIO deals in larger chunks of data but otherwise works the same way as standard PIO. For example, where PIO transfers a single block of 256 words (512 bytes), BPIO transfers *n* blocks of 256 words. If you want to use BPIO, you need special drivers from Western Digital.

Note

VL Bus is an enhanced version of the VESA (Video Electronics Standard Association) bus.

DMA Modes

Many IDE/EIDE drives support DMA transfer modes as an alternative to PIO. The DMA data transfer method lets the drive take care of data transfer after the processor takes care of initial setup. DMA allows the drive to move information directly to or from RAM, which is a boon for multitasking PCs. Early versions of DMA use a controller built into the chip set to effect the transfer. Modern DMA uses the device itself to effect the transfer.

Faster DMA and EIDE came along hand in hand with the introduction of faster buses. The EIDE interface supports these faster buses with Type B DMA (transfer rate of 4Mbps) and Type F DMA (for PCI local bus, transfer rates up to 8.33Mbps). Both Type B and Type F DMA require device drivers or BIOS changes that support the DMA specifications. Single-mode DMA is relatively slow and is now rarely used. Multi Word DMA 1 and Multi Word DMA 2, however, are very fast and can use a transfer rate of 480ns or more. The Peripheral Component Interconnect (PCI) interface also supports a new type of DMA transfer called scatter/gather. Scatter/gather is useful in computers that use virtual memory management. In such a system, the computer can scatter a block of memory (four 4KB blocks) across the hard disk in many different physical locations. Normally, the interface would use four separate requests and DMA instructions to fetch that block of memory. With scatter/gather, a single I/O request "gathers" up the four 4KB blocks into a single 16KB block and delivers it. Since you're using one request instead of four, you get faster response.

Modern ATA Standards

ATA, or AT Attachment, defines the standard drive interface as attached to an AT-style machine. ATA is a disk drive implementation that integrates the controller onto the drive itself. Simplistically, ATA defines the physical, electrical, transport, and command protocols for the internal attachment of storage devices and the communication between a PC and the hard drive.

ATA Specifications

The original ATA specification, commonly known as IDE, was an ANSI standard for connecting drives to the ISA bus. The interface was little more than a simple buffer. Today's AT Attachment interface (ATA-2), also an ANSI standard, is also known as Fast ATA-2 or Enhanced IDE (EIDE). ATA-2 pushes the data transfer rate up to 6.67Mbps, or 10Mbps for a cache-hit burst. It connects directly to the local bus that, in turn, has higher bandwidths than previously and consequently a higher throughput rate. The ATA-2 interface supports:

▶ PIO modes 3 and 4 and DMA modes 1 and 2

▶ Block transfer commands

▶ Logical block addressing

▶ ATAPI support for non-hard-disk IDE/ATA devices

ATA is for hard disks only. The advent of tape and CD drives for PCs stimulated the development of the ATA Packet Interface (ATAPI) standard for non-hard-disk devices that plug into an ordinary ATA (IDE/EIDE) port. ATAPI requires BIOS and driver support. The ATAPI protocol allows these devices to share the ATA bus with traditional ATA disk drives.

ATA-3, also known as EIDE, adds some improvements to ATA-2. ATA/ATAPI-4 along with ATA/ATAPI-5 are both under development and are trying to merge ATA-3 and ATAPI into a single standard.

▶ ATA/ATAPI-4 (also known as Ultra-ATA or Ultra-DMA/33) incorporates support for a theoretical burst data transfer rate of 33Mbps.

▶ ATA/ATAPI-5 incorporates support for a theoretical burst data transfer rate of 66Mbps. This version also provides support for the Universal Serial Bus (USB) devices through a UDMA ground bus 80-wire cable requirement and cyclic redundancy checking (CRC).

EIDE and Fast ATA-2

ATA and ATA-2 are the interface standards. Fast ATA, Fast ATA-2, and EIDE are marketing terms invented by disk drive manufacturers. All use fast transfer PIO modes 3 and 4 and multiword DMA modes 1 and 2. Enhanced IDE (EIDE) is a Western Digital trademark. Both Seagate and Quantum use the term Fast ATA. Note that vendors tend to use these terms loosely, which can create some confusion. Additionally, some manufacturers label hardware as EIDE even when they implement only a part of the EIDE features set. The difference between the two schemes is mainly in the scope of EIDE. Table 10.11 shows some of the differences.

TABLE 10.11 Differences between EIDE and Fast ATA-2

Feature	EIDE Drives Support	Fast ATA-2 Drives Support
Fast transfer modes (see above)	Yes	Yes
LBA mode	Yes	Yes
Four devices on the interface	Yes	Maybe
ATAPI support	Yes	Maybe
Block mode	No	Yes
Western Digital's Enhanced BIOS	Yes	No

We've discussed the theory behind the hard disk drives, now let's move on to actually installing them. In the next chapter, you'll learn all there is to know about installing an EIDE drive.

Installing an IDE Hard Drive

INTRODUCTION

For as long as I can remember, hard disk prices have been in free fall. And that's good news for everybody—well, mostly. It's not entirely good news because just when I think I'm pretty happy with my computer, the drive prices go down, and I start eyeing a newer, larger, faster, cheaper (arggh!) hard disk. So, eventually, I give in, and I buy that new hard disk.

And then I've got to install it. Sound familiar? Then you've come to the right chapter. Here you'll learn how to put in an IDE hard disk. You'll learn how to jumper, cable, and install the drive, and how to set up a dual-drive system. You'll also learn how to configure the CMOS—where hard disk information is stored.

Installing an IDE Hard Drive

If you're in a hurry, you are in the right place. Collected here, for your convenience, are the basics steps that you will perform to install an IDE device.

Be Prepared

Before you start, there are some things that you may need on hand. These include:

- Hard disk drive or other IDE device.

- Manual for the device and other configuration information.

- Adapter kit, if needed. Some systems come in small desktop cases and others in roomy tower cases. Regardless of which, check inside to see what drive bays you have free. All drives today are designed to fit either 5¼-inch or 3½-inch bays. Most hard drives are 3½-inch and most CD-ROM, CD-R/RW, and DVD drives are 5¼-inch. If you have only a 5¼-inch bay free for that new 20GB hard disk, you'll need an adapter kit.

- Flashlight, if not required, at least recommended.

- Phillips-head screwdriver with a medium tip.

- Small plastic cup for placing screws in. Personally, I lay out screws in a pattern so I can return them to the place I removed them. I work left-to-right, top-to-bottom. That way I can just repeat the process and get the right screw in the right hole.

- Antistatic wristband—although not exactly necessary for installing drives and other similar devices, it's a good idea to have one handy. It's best not to harbor any stray static electricity if you happen to touch a component that you're not working on, which is altogether possible.

▶ Toe or fingernail clippers—also not required, but handy. These are great for cutting those hampering zip ties (those plastic little strips that bunch wires together). Just be careful not to snip a wire or two. Of course, the cutting area of nail clippers is not very big, so there's little chance of this occurring if you pay attention.

Pardon me if this whole thing sounds like I'm a chef going through the throes of baking pastries for a big party, but there are ingredients (that are listed above) and clear-cut directions for mixing it all together (that are listed below) into a tasty digital treat.

1. Gather the ingredients and open the case.

2. Jumper the drive as appropriate. If you intend for the drive to become an adjunct to the existing main drive, then set it to Slave as per the drive's manual. Almost all hard disk and CD-based drives ship in Master mode by default.

3. Insert the drive into its intended bay. This may be easy, or it may be nigh impossible. I've dealt with both many, many times. The newer budget systems are the worst as they were not designed to be upgraded. I've had to remove RAM, motherboard power taps, twisted cable, and other drives just to place a drive in a bay, sometimes all at once!

4. Locate an IDE cable terminal extending from the motherboard. The existing drive will likely be at the end of the cable with another terminal several inches behind that. Also locate a power tap. These small, white blocks have four small holes and can be installed in only one way. Cable the drive.

5. *Now* you can put the screws in. Allow the drive to be mobile while cabling or be content with the space there is between the back of a mounted drive and the power supply. The new Hewlett-Packard budget PCs give you just enough room to cram your fingers in there, without the drive mounted.

6. Leave the case open, check all your cable terminal points, and attach the monitor, keyboard, and mouse. The other cool stuff can come later. Power it up. You should see the drive being identified if you mounted and configured it correctly, although there are circumstances out of your control that could cause that to not happen (there's more detail further in the chapter).

7. Configure the system's CMOS so that it knows that there's a drive there.

Of course, there's more to it than that. And that's why there's an entire chapter on the process and its details. First, though, you can work through these steps visually. This should help quite a bit.

VISUAL UPGRADE

Installing an IDE Hard Drive

1 Mount the new drive in the computer chassis (or removable drive bay). Be sure to use two screws on each side!

2 If the computer has a removable drive bay, mount it into the computer's chassis and lock it into place.

3 Check the drive's documentation (either in the manual or on the drive itself) for the drive's Master/Slave settings.

4 Set the jumper at the rear of the drive to signify either Master or Slave status.

5 Connect the drive data cable to the EIDE connector on the motherboard (if you are installing the first or third EIDE in the computer).

6 Connect the free end of the EIDE data cable into the connector at the rear of the hard drive.

7 Connect the power supply's Molex plug into the power connector at the rear of the hard drive.

Molex plug

Warnings and Apologia

Before you go on, however, let me warn you: hard disk installation has a lot of details to it. That's not because it's hard—it is not—but because of the radically different types of hard disk subsystems that have grown up and become popular over the years.

Even though we generically call them *hard drive subsystems*, there are really two distinct kinds of disk installs that you might have to do, in roughly descending order of likelihood:

▶ IDE

▶ SCSI

These drive types aren't as different as night and day, but significant enough differences exist that the actual installing of SCSI drives is covered in the next chapter. Chapter 13, "Partitioning and Formatting EIDE and SCSI Drives," covers how to *format and partition* both types of drives once you've handled the hardware installation.

The IDE Mish-Mash

Okay, I admit it's a veritable nightmare. Given the alphabetical resources of every single IDE protocol, you could write completely new IDE protocol! There are a number of versions of IDE that have poked their heads up over the years. If you'd like to make soup, here are the ingredients: IDE, EIDE, ATA, ATA2, ATA3, ATA4, ATAPI, PIO Mode-0, PIO Mode-1, PIO Mode-2, PIO Mode-3, and PIO Mode-4.

Steps in Hard Drive Installation

Putting in an IDE hard disk requires following the steps outlined in the QuickSteps section at the start of this chapter, plus two more: partitioning the drive so that it will act as one large drive or several smaller ones, and formatting the drive to make it ready for your operating system. Again, for any given drive type, a step may vary or may be left out altogether, but the general sequence is the same.

As time has gone on, this process has sometimes gotten easier, and sometimes harder. Here's how to approach all but the last two steps. As I said earlier, these are covered in Chapter 13.

Assemble Compatible Hardware

The hardest part about this step is just buying the right stuff. In the preceding chapter, you got some insights into the main decision points entailed in choosing the right disk subsystem. Remember to stress compatibility, size, and speed in making your decisions.

Since you have chosen IDE over SCSI (because you're reading this chapter), then your system will be based on IDE. Don't bother with cache memory on the host adapter; buy memory for your computer instead. When you're buying a drive, buy as much space as you can afford; believe me, you'll fill it up quicker than you can imagine.

Note

Remember, since it's IDE, chances are the drive will plug directly into the motherboard. Very few motherboards are made today that do not have primary and secondary IDE channels built into them.

When you buy an IDE drive and interface, it's not a bad idea to check with the interface's manufacturer to ensure that it's compatible with the drive, and to check with the drive's manufacturer that the interface is okay. Despite the disk "standards," particular drive/interface combinations often have quirks. In the IDE world, problems often arise when trying to interface two different drives.

Master/Slave Jumpers

You've read that most drive systems can support more than one physical hard disk. But if you put two identical hard disks into a system, how do the disk interface card and the operating system know which is which? Which is (for example) C:, and which is D:?

When you install a *second* IDE drive, you have *two controllers in the same system*, which is, as you'd imagine, a prescription for trouble. (If you've forgotten why, look back to Chapter 6, "Installing New Circuit Boards (without Creating New Problems)," for a reminder about circuit board conflicts.) Modern IDE drives are equipped for this problem and have a provision to essentially shut off their onboard controllers. Installing two IDE drives in the same system, therefore, boils down to getting one of the controllers on one of the IDE drives to control *both* drives, and getting the other drive to essentially shut off its controller. In IDE terms, you say that one controller is the *Master* and one is the *Slave,* or that you must *slave* one controller to the other in order to make them work together.

Note

Few systems leave the factory with motherboards that do not have IDE drive subsystems already installed and tested. The vast majority of these systems also have the capability to support up to four IDE drives, two Masters and two Slaves—one of each on the primary and secondary buses. My personal workstation (amongst my vast LAN system) has two 8GB hard disks, a 24x CD-ROM drive, and a 4x-4x-12x CD-R/RW drive, for a total of four drives. I do *not* have any controller cards in this system.

This isn't a permanent selection, so you may choose to retain your old drive as Master, adding the new drive as Slave, then use a transfer utility to move your working OS to the new drive. Or you may opt to make your old Master a new Slave and install a fresh copy of your favorite OS to the new drive, a freshly minted Master.

Some IDE drive vendors phrase Master and Slave configurations differently. You may see the following options:

◗ Only drive on an IDE channel

◗ Master in an IDE channel with two attached drives.

◗ Slave in an IDE channel with two attached drives.

Jumper, Cable, and Install the Drive

I'm going to combine some of my steps for discussion purposes, but they still happen in the order I originally described: first look at the drives and set their jumpers correctly, then install them in the machine.

Cabling methods vary among the different drive interface types; I'll start out with the ones you're more likely to see, and then move to the older, less likely ones.

IDE Configuration

A typical IDE hard disk has connections like the ones you see in Figure 11.1.

Figure 11.1

Typical IDE hard disk connections

40-pin connector   Jumper block   Power connector

Like all drives, the hard disk needs a power connection. It uses the same old Molex connector that CD-ROMs, tapes, and other hard disks use. There is only one cable for data and control information, a 40-wire cable. The jumper block on the back of the drive enables you to set whether this drive is a Master or Slave; usually, if there's only one drive, then there's a third setting—but check the drive's documentation to be sure. In Figure 11.2, you see example jumper settings that could come from pretty much any IDE drive.

Jumpers are little plastic blocks that have a bit of copper inside. They are formed so they can slide firmly over two posts. To close a pair of posts, you slide a jumper block over the two. They must be immediately adjacent to each other, and the hardware engineers design the post blocks to operate in this fashion. Common are two rows of three or four posts with the left-most posts in each row representing Master or Slave status. The drive makers also often place a jumper on a single post with the same effect as not having a jumper so you, the user, will have one if and when you want to install the drive as a Slave. The default, of course, is for the drive to be configured for Master status.

Figure 11.2

Configuring drive jumpers

Configuring drive jumpers for a Western Digital AT-IDE 540MB hard disk drive

You don't put any jumpers on this drive at all if it's the only drive in the system, but put a jumper on the extreme left-hand position if it's the Master, or jumper the middle if it's the Slave. (Of course, you'll note that the text and Figure 11.2 do not match. That was done deliberately to point out that no two drives are the same. All right, they are if they're the same model, but that's it!) When installing a multiple-IDE system, try to use the newer and faster of the two drives as the Master, and the slower one as Slave. The reason I say "try" is because not every drive will slave to every other drive. If one way doesn't work, try it the other way. The only other jumper you might have to set on an EIDE drive would be an LBA jumper to enable or disable logical block addressing. Most drives don't require this, but I ran across it on an IBM machine once.

Once you've got the jumpers in place, then cable the hard drive to the host adapter. You'll see two kinds of cables, as shown in Figure 11.3.

Figure 11.3

Types of hard drive cables

Hard drive cable   Cable for two hard drives

A multiple-drive configuration would look like Figure 11.4.

Figure 11.4

Multiple IDE hard drives and a host adapter attached via a cable

Note that it doesn't matter which connector the Master or Slave goes on. If you've put everything on right—no upside-down pin header connectors or forgotten Molex power connectors—then you're ready to proceed to CMOS configuration.

Configure the System's CMOS

I could have called this section "Introducing the Hard Disk to the Computer's Hard Disk BIOS." Your computer has low-level software, a set of built-in machine language programs whose purpose it is to control your hard disk hardware. That software must be in ROM on your system.

Why Must the Disk Startup Software Be in ROM?

Because if you want to boot from a storage device (such as a hard disk), then the software to control that storage device must be already *built in* once you turn the computer on. Otherwise, the computer won't know how to access the storage device and load whatever operating system is on that device. It's kind of a chicken-and-egg problem: you need software to be able to read the hard disk, but you bought a hard disk in the first place so that you could put all your software there. This software "vicious circle" is broken, of course, with ROM, because it enables a PC designer to ensure that a small amount of software is automatically present in the computer's memory just as soon as the computer powers up. All that startup software is collectively called your computer's BIOS (basic input output system), as you've read earlier in this book.

The BIOS doesn't contain software to control every possible peripheral, simply because it doesn't *have* to. There's no need for the BIOS to support a scanner or sound card; you don't need them to boot. Most LAN boards have no need of BIOS, unless you have a diskless workstation and therefore need to boot from the LAN card itself.

Unfortunately, there's more to making a disk work than some generic software. The BIOS software must know some of those intimate details of hard disks that you examined in the last chapter: cylinders, heads, write precompensation, and the like. Which leads to another chicken-and-egg problem: where to store the details of a hard disk?

Well, one obvious answer would be to put the information into some kind of ROM. But that's not a very good answer, because ROMs were a pain to make in the early '80s. It would be ludicrous to tell a PC buyer that she'd have to go find somebody with a ROM burner to make her a configuration chip every time she bought a new hard disk. Nowadays, flash memory is cheap enough that someone could easily design a little flash memory into a system to keep track of disk characteristics, but nobody had ever heard of flash memory in 1982.

Personally, I think the best answer would have been to store the disk's hardware configuration information on the disk itself, on the first sector. There wouldn't be a chicken-and-egg problem because every hard disk has a first sector with the coordinates cylinder 0, head 0, sector 1. But that didn't occur to the first PC hard disk system designers, and, by now, you've probably figured out where the hard disk configuration information goes: into the system's CMOS. Most computers will store hard disk configuration information in the CMOS. *Most* computers? Sure. SCSIs don't need CMOS, and what about XTs?

The Evolution of CMOS Drive Tables

The first time I set up an AT-type system, I ran the SETUP program that came with the AT. Things started out pretty well, because it asked me easy stuff—"What day is it?" "How much memory does this computer have?" (Piece of cake—just count up the chips.) "What kind of floppy drives does this have?" (Still easy.) Then it asked what kind of hard drive I had.

"Heck, no problem," I thought, and typed in Seagate ST-225. (For the youngsters in the reading audience, that's a 21MB ST-506 drive that was just the cat's pajamas in 1983. I told you, I've been at this for a long time.)

After I typed ST-225, I *swear* snickering came out of the tiny little disk of metal and paper that thought it was a speaker. You see, the AT wants a *drive type number,* a number from 1 to 47.

In order to fully understand what a drive type number is, you should know a little history. The XT world usually saw controllers that could support only a very small group of disks. In an effort to combat this, the original AT had a table in its ROM describing 14 common drives of the time. Remember, a big difference between the XT BIOS and the AT BIOS is that the XT BIOS didn't come with hard disk support; ATs, in contrast, were all built assuming that they'd have hard disks, and so their BIOS contains support for hard disks. The idea was that when you bought a hard disk for your AT, then the hard disk would look a lot like one of these 14 drives. If it didn't, then you couldn't use the drive.

Now, supporting 14 common drives sounded like a good idea; after all, 14 supported drives was better than 4 to 8 supported by older XT controller boards. Of course, it seemed like a good idea only for a while, because drive types proliferated, and the next model of the AT had a BIOS that included descriptions of 25 common hard disks.

Do you suppose 25 drive types was enough? Nah, of course not, so the following generation of AT BIOS software included 47 drive types.

And then it stopped.

IBM's 1986 decision to use 47 built-in drive types has been adopted by most manufacturers to this day. And it had led to some troubles over the years. Today all computers come with a fixed drive table, an extra drive type called the *user-defined drive type,* and an Autodetect function. If the drive you're installing doesn't fit anything on the drive table, then you just select the user-defined type and specify the number of cylinders, heads, sectors, and write precompensation on the drive.

I suggest you select the Autodetect function. It's the easiest. All drives have identifying codes that enable them to be recognized by name. Current BIOS technology (and this has been so for the last several years) can detect the size of the drive installed and extrapolate the dimensions.

Pretty much all drives of all types are detected in this fashion today. CD-ROM, CD-R, CD-RW, DVD, LS120, Zip, and other such drives are all recognized by Phoenix and AMIBios CMOS BIOS chips. It's really much easier. The amazing variety of drive geometries today makes autodetection of user-definable drive types a necessity, and most computers designed in the mid to late '90s include these options.

Blast from the Past:
IBM PC-AT Drive Recognition Options

Just how far have we come since the halcyon days of the i386 and ROM BIOS that could not recognize a hard drive? Things have changed drastically since then, and thankfully, for the better (mostly).

Back in the old days, it used to be the case that if you tried to match your drive to your AT-type machine's drive table, and there was nothing on the drive table even remotely like your drive, you still couldn't match write precompensation even if you were willing to settle for a monstrous loss of cylinders. Or, if you were installing an RLL controller that formatted 26 sectors per track: nothing in your drive tables matched, as most of the drive tables out there were strictly MFM 17-sector entries.

In this case, you had three options:

▶ Get a new BIOS, one that included your drive type, or a user-definable drive type, or get a BIOS custom-burned with your drive type. Again, that chip went on your *motherboard*, not the disk controller board.

▶ Buy an add-on ROM in addition to the BIOS ROM.

▶ Use a device driver such as SpeedStor or Disk Manager.

If you couldn't get a system BIOS ROM for your AT-type machine that allowed user-defined types (not everybody offered them), you might have discovered that a newer system BIOS was all you needed. A lot of old IBM ATs out there had only 14 drive types in their ROM: an upgrade to the more-common 47 types would do the trick (assuming that you needed this particular computer). Or you could have tried a custom ROM from the BIOS with any drive you liked. A custom ROM was about three times the cost of an off-the-shelf unmodified ROM. Most older 286- and 386-based AT-type machines had room for an extra pair of ROMs. Some vendors sold add-on ROM solely to enlarge the AT drive table.

Finally, there were software answers, such as products called SpeedStor or Disk Manager. The way they solved the BIOS compatibility problem was to format most of your drive as something other than a hard disk, then require that you load a device driver to read the drive.

The idea behind these device drivers was that they required only a small DOS-compatible partition on the front of the drive, a partition just large enough to boot from. The rest of the drive was invisible to the system's BIOS, but that was okay: the device driver handled that.

The strength of the device driver approach was that the device driver presented the remainder of the drive to DOS as a generic storage device. DOS was actually unaware that the device driver's space was a hard disk; all DOS knew was that there were lots of sectors that were available for storage. There was no limit on the number of sectors or tracks as far as the device driver was concerned.

The weakness of the device driver was that once you'd installed the driver, the system had to use the driver to access your hard disk. That posed problems for alternate operating systems or even for games that stretched the limits of the PC a bit.

The least desirable option was to use a device driver to communicate with your hard disk. One reason was that it was *another* piece of software that needed to function properly for your programs to use the hard disk and thus complicated your troubleshooting hassles. Another was that a ROM was usable for any operating system, so you'd have no trouble moving to Novell, Windows NT, or Unix at some point.

12

Understanding and Installing SCSI Devices

INTRODUCTION

Small Computer System Interface, or SCSI, is somewhat of the dark horse of system hardware. It's popular, but has always remained just behind IDE in commonality due primarily to its higher cost and the difficulty that most people have understanding SCSI. Apple was enlightened for many years, having used two SCSI buses (one internal, the other external) in the vast majority of their systems. Recently, they too have turned to the lower cost of IDE despite the somewhat weaker performance and reliability. Prices, however, are stabilizing and soon (within the next year or two) "ever the twain shall meet," as it were. In this chapter, you'll learn about what SCSI does, how it works, how to physically install SCSI devices, and how to set up software to support SCSI devices. Once you know that, you will be better equipped to attack problems with SCSI.

Installing a SCSI Card

If you're in a hurry, you are in the right place. Collected here, for your convenience, are the basics steps that you will perform to install a SCSI device.

Be Prepared

Before you start, there are some things that you may need on hand. These include:

▶ Hard disk drive or other SCSI device.

▶ Device's manual and other configuration information.

▶ Adapter kit, if needed. Some systems come in small desktop cases and others in roomy tower cases. Regardless of which, check inside to see what drive bays you have free. All drives today are designed to fit either 5¼-inch or 3½-inch bays. Most hard drives are 3½-inch and most CD-ROM, CD-R/RW, and DVD drives are 5¼-inch. If you have only a 5¼-inch bay free for that new 20GB hard disk, you'll need an adapter kit.

▶ Flashlight, if not required at least recommended.

▶ Phillips-head screwdriver with a medium tip.

▶ Small plastic cup for placing screws in. Personally, I lay out screws in a pattern so I can return them to the place I removed them. I work left to right, top to bottom. That way I can just repeat the process and get the right screw in the right hole.

▶ Antistatic wristband—though not exactly necessary for installing drives and other similar devices, it's a good idea to have one handy. It's best not to harbor any stray static electricity if you happen to touch a component that you're not working on, which is altogether possible.

▶ Internal or external terminator, if your device doesn't have one built in.

▶ Toenail or fingernail clippers—again, not required, but handy. These are great for cutting those hampering zip ties (those little plastic strips that bunch wires together). Just be careful not to snip a wire or two. Of course, the cutting area of nail clippers is not very big, so there's little chance of this occurring if you pay attention.

If you went through the IDE chapter before this one, you'll note that I'm using pretty much the same recipe. Why? Because the installation of SCSI drives is similar to IDE drives. The differences are in setup and in the need to also install a card for SCSI (most of the time), whereas IDE support is built into most motherboards. There are, however, motherboards that have a SCSI bus or two built right in. Now, lets get to cookin' up some SCSI stew!

1. Gather the ingredients and open the case.

2. Jumper the drive as appropriate. If you intend for the drive to become an adjunct to the existing main drive, then set it to a higher SCSI ID number than the boot drive as per the drive's manual. Almost all hard disk and CD-based drives ship set to ID 0 or 1 by default.

3. Insert the drive into its intended bay. This may be easy, or it may be nigh impossible. I've dealt with both many, many times. The newer budget systems are the worst, as they were not designed to be upgraded. I've had to remove RAM, motherboard power taps, twisted cable, and other drives just to place a drive in a bay, sometimes all at once!

4. Now, either install the SCSI host adapter or, if you're installing a SCSI drive to a system with SCSI support built into the motherboard, move to the next step.

5. Locate a SCSI cable terminal extending from the motherboard. The existing drive will likely be at the end of the cable with more terminals several inches behind that. Also locate a power tap. These small, white blocks have four small holes and can be installed in only one way. Cable the drive.

6. Now you can put the screws in. Allow the drive to be mobile while cabling or be content with the space that exists between the back of a mounted drive and the power supply.

7. Terminate the SCSI chain.

8. Leave the case open, check all your cable terminal points, and attach the monitor, keyboard, and mouse. The other cool stuff can come later. Power it up. You should see the drive being identified if you mounted and configured it correctly, although there are circumstances out of your control that could cause that to not happen (there's more detail further in the chapter).

Of course, there's more to it than that. And that's why there's an entire chapter on the process and its details. First, though, you can work through these steps visually. This should help quite a bit.

VISUAL UPGRADE

Installing a SCSI Card

1 SCSI cards have connectors for both internal and external devices.

Internal connector

External connector

2 Connect an internal device to the connector at the top of the card.

3 There are several types of external connectors for SCSI cards; be sure to match the correct cable to your card and device.

4 Insert the SCSI card into a PCI slot.

5 Insert the connector from an external device into the connector at the rear of the card.

Target ID number

SCSI

Termination switch

6 Set the target ID number for the external device (in this example, a JAZ drive). Be sure the last device on a SCSI chain is terminated (in this example, the JAZ drive has a switch on the back that sets the termination).

SCSI Overview

Prior to the mid-'80s, every type of storage device had its own kind of controller. If you wanted to add a scanner, a hard disk, a tape backup device, and a CD-ROM to your computer, then you'd have to install one board into the system that would act as the interface for the scanner, another for the hard disk, one for the tape, and one for the CD-ROM. That meant not only four controllers, it also meant having to *configure* four separate boards.

The computer industry responded to this issue with the following idea: build PC peripherals that have controllers built right in, so those peripheral/controller combinations are configured correctly, right out of the factory. The only interface problem that would remain would be interfacing the controller/peripheral pair to the bus of the target system—the PC, in this case, but it would be just as easy to interface (in theory) to a Macintosh or a Unix workstation. A new interface arose called the *Small Computer System Interface*, or *SCSI*.

SCSI Benefits

The benefit of putting a controller on each device in the SCSI world is that you know that the controller and drive are a matched set. In particular:

▶ The cables between the controller and the drive, which are a troublesome source of noise, can be extremely short, leading to much lower noise levels. In general, the longer the cable, the more opportunity to introduce interference. To paraphrase a well-known car advertisement series, Shorter Is Better.

▶ The controller and the drive (or the peripheral) can be more closely matched. When both the controller and drive come from the same maker, everything there becomes a known quantity and all external influences can be more easily dealt with (I'll get to those a bit later). That also means that built-in diagnostics can be included on the SCSI device.

SCSI peripherals can be focused to do a particular task, but they lack the capability to talk to any real-world bus. SCSI devices don't know what a Macintosh, a PC, or a Sun computer is. That's where the SCSI board that you install in your system comes in. The SCSI "controller," then, is not a controller at all; it's just a kind of universal translator that enables any SCSI device to communicate with a particular computer's bus. The SCSI *host adapter* (its true name) is, then, the glue that cements your SCSI devices and your computer.

The trick to SCSI is that it makes disk drives, all of which come in different shapes and sizes, into generic storage devices. That was the goal of the original SCSI. As time has gone on, SCSI has been expanded to include all kinds of storage devices, as well as printers and scanners.

Note

As time has passed, traditional interfaces such as parallel have grown faster, and new ones such as USB are already fast enough for peripherals (for example, scanners and printers). Therefore, SCSI has become primarily the domain of those who want or need fast disk access.

Some Basic SCSI Concepts

Understanding SCSI requires knowing a whole new bunch of terms. I'll describe some of them in a minute, as I take you step by step through planning and configuring a SCSI installation. But here's a quick introduction to some SCSI concepts.

SCSI-1, SCSI-2, and SCSI-3

The original SCSI specification appeared in 1980 as a hard disk interface. It lacked agreed-upon standards, leading to a plethora of different—and incompatible—SCSI implementations. SCSI-2 made some big steps toward standardizing SCSI, improved data transfer rate, and supported new types of devices. SCSI-3, or Ultra SCSI, increases the number of devices that a SCSI subsystem can support, their data transfer rate, and cable lengths, as well as providing for simpler cable schemes. More on this below.

Single-Ended versus Differential SCSI

Some SCSI implementations use an electronic signaling system that is called *single-ended* in the SCSI world and is known as *unbalanced* in much of the data communications interface world. Single-ended SCSI systems will not work if the total length of their cables exceeds 6 meters. Differential SCSI uses a balanced approach that requires twice as many wires in a cable but can support up to 25 meters on a cable.

Note

You may wonder why distance is important if all these devices are just sitting inside your PC case. Well, SCSI is a popular tool for network administrators as SCSI's format practically begs to be configured as a RAID (Redundant Array of Inexpensive Discs). A great number of these in a corporate server room or series of server rooms can start to create a wide gap. Consider the length needed to run a cable over a door frame as opposed to just across the carpet and you'll get an idea of how long cables can get.

SCSI IDs

Because SCSI is a bus, multiple devices share it. One device is distinguished from another on the bus by its SCSI ID, a number from 0 to 7 on SCSI-1 or SCSI-2 systems, 0 to 15 on a single-channel SCSI-3 system, or 0 to 31 on a dual-channel SCSI-3 system.

Active and Passive SCSI Terminators

The electronics of SCSI require that both ends of the chain of SCSI devices contain a circuit that *terminates* the system. Older systems used a simple circuit called a *passive terminator.* Most systems nowadays require an *active terminator.* The problem is that many SCSI devices with built-in termination offer only passive termination, and that means that you've either got to buy an active termination device or put up with flaky SCSI performance.

SCSI Underview

Sure, we've sort of glanced at SCSI, so now let's get our hands dirty. At this point, the different generations make little difference, as much modern software can't make full use of the modern SCSI generations. But some can, and that makes it worthwhile knowing about and purchasing more advanced SCSI. Here's a rundown on the SCSI generations.

SCSI-1: The Beginning of a Good Idea

In 1981, Shugart Associates—the company that eventually became Seagate—developed a parallel block-oriented transfer protocol called the Shugart Associates System Interface, or SASI.

SASI became the Small Computer System Interface, or SCSI, in 1984, when the ANSI's X3T9 committee formalized the specification.

SCSI-1 Interface

SCSI is an eight-bit parallel interface between a SCSI host adapter and a SCSI device. (*Eight-bit* here has nothing to do—or very little to do—with your bus interface.) The standard runs at 5MHz, meaning a throughput of eight bits, 5 million times a second, for a maximum data transfer rate of 5Mbps. It incorporated a command set that could be only partially implemented by a vendor, but the vendor could still claim that its device was SCSI compatible.

SCSI-1 Device Types

SCSI-1 defined several generic device types:

- Random access devices (hard disk)
- Sequential access devices (tapes)

❱ Printers

❱ Processors (host adapters)

❱ WORM optical drives

❱ Read-only random access devices

These types changed in SCSI-2, as you'll see later.

Asynchronous and Synchronous SCSI

SCSI-1 defined a SCSI notion that has remained with us, a set of rules for transferring data across the SCSI bus. You'll see references to it in some SCSI software, so let's take a minute and define asynchronous versus synchronous SCSI interfaces.

The most basic kind of data transfer over a SCSI bus goes something like this: the initiator requests a byte, the target responds by sending the byte over the SCSI bus, and the initiator says, "Got it," signaling to the target that the transfer went okay.

That "got it" message is called a *handshake* or an *acknowledgment.* Each handshake takes time, however, and introduces a fair amount of overhead; in fact, one of the main failures of SCSI-1 was the amount of time spent on overhead.

This method of handshaking every byte is called *asynchronous SCSI.* There's a faster method, whereby the initiator acknowledges big blocks of bytes, rather than every single byte. That's called *synchronous SCSI.* It's essential for high-speed disk access. Double-check that both your host adapter and your drives support synchronous access.

You can have asynchronous and synchronous devices on the same SCSI bus, but nobody talks synchronous if the host adapter can't.

SCSI-1 left so much undefined that it was nearly inevitable that the actual SCSI-1 implementations on the market would be incompatible.

SCSI-2 Improves on a Good Thing

SCSI-2 was being developed even prior to formalization of the SCSI-1 standard by ANSI in 1986. The point at which SCSI-1 was finalized and SCSI-2 began was rather arbitrary and had more to do with simply deciding to get the standard published on a particular date than a quantum jump in specifications. The specification simply reflects where the state of progress was at the date of publishing. SCSI-2 enhancements include new command sets, wider data paths (16 and 32 bits), and command queuing.

Scripting and Disconnects

SCSI-2 incorporates scripting, whereby a series of transfers can be "batched" across the bus. For example, a hard disk could be backed up to an optical drive—with no processor intervention.

SCSI-2 also allows disconnects, whereby the host adapter sends a command to a slow device such as a tape drive—a rewind command, for example—and then disconnects the drive from the SCSI bus, so that the whole bus doesn't have to remain idle while the tape rewinds.

Kinds of Devices

SCSI-2 defines a slightly different set of generic device types than did SCSI-1:

- Random access devices (hard disk)

- Sequential access devices (tapes)

- Printers

- Processors (host adapters)

- WORM optical drives

- CD-ROMs and CD-R/RW (which replaced the former)

- Scanners

▶ Magneto-optical drives

▶ Jukeboxes (the data storage type, not the music type)

▶ Communications devices

The first five are the same, the sixth changed, and the last four are new types.

Fast and Wide SCSI

As originally defined, SCSI is an eight-bit parallel interface between a SCSI device and a SCSI controller. Several variations have been defined in SCSI-2.

Fast SCSI doubles the data transfer rate over the existing data path. If SCSI-1 eight-bit transfers are 5Mbps, then Fast SCSI eight-bit transfers are 10Mbps. Fast SCSI works on either single-ended or differential SCSI, but if you set up Fast SCSI on single-ended cables, your total cable length can be only 3 meters.

Wide SCSI uses an extra cable to increase the data path to 16 or 32 bits. Using nondifferential cables and interface, Wide SCSI can increase data transfer rate to 20Mbps.

Fast-Wide SCSI uses a greater data transfer rate over a wider cable to support a data transfer rate of up to 40Mbps, but 20Mbps is more common.

SCSI-3, or Ultra SCSI

During the '90s, processor and data-transfer performance increased by factors in the hundreds. Now the disk subsystem has become a real bottleneck. Ultimately, Fibre Channel, with its incredibly high speeds, will resolve this problem. However, the solution will take time, will not be backward compatible, and will likely prove too expensive for many situations. In the meantime, Ultra SCSI serves as an interim solution. It's twice as fast as SCSI-2, multichanneled, and can use all that SCSI-1 and SCSI-2 hardware you have accumulated over the years.

For Ultra SCSI, ANSI separated the single SCSI standard into a collection of standards that are extensions of the SCSI-2 interface standard.

More Devices

SCSI-3 will support up to 16 devices, rather than the current eight.

Device Types

The command set has been expanded. There are now device types for Digital Audio Tapes (DAT) and for file server–type devices as well.

Expanded Number of I/O Channels (MultiChannel)

Give an Ultra SCSI drive an additional I/O channel, and you have MultiChannel SCSI, as it expands the number of I/O channels available to the system. For example, instead of a single channel supporting seven devices, the Adaptec 3940 has two channels, each with its own independent RISC processor. The 8-bit AHA 3940 Ultra SCSI version can support up to 15 devices and move data at up to 40Mbps. The 16-bit AHA 3940 Wide Ultra SCSI version doubles this to 31 devices, and it can move data at up to an incredible 80Mbps.

Performance is greatly enhanced by this strategy (as well as by doubling the internal clock speed), since faster devices can have their own channel. Slower devices can use another channel, so they are no longer a bottleneck impeding the speedier peripherals.

Another advantage of having multiple channels is the ability to use only one of your valuable PCI slots for hardware mirroring.

Shorter Cables

As data transfer speeds are increased with Ultra SCSI, transmission noise and signal quality become problematic over the entire length of the cable connecting the host and the device(s). To address this problem, the cable specification for Ultra SCSI was shortened to 1.5

meters. Bus extenders can be added to increase the total cable length to 7.5 meters.

Mandatory Active Termination

SCSI-3, as I've already mentioned, also forces the termination circuits to get a bit more complex. Instead of simple passive resistors, SCSI-3 termination must include voltage regulation circuits that keep the bus voltage between 4 and 5.25 volts. That means a less noisy bus, but it also spells trouble for a SCSI-3 configuration with an old SCSI-1 or SCSI-2 that doesn't support active termination. Again, many SCSI-1 or SCSI-2 devices do support SCSI, but there's no guarantee. And, like SCSI-2, SCSI-3 requires SCSI parity.

Bridging into Serial and Fiber SCSI

SCSI-3 introduces a lot more wires with a 68-wire connector. That's because of the parallel nature of SCSI, in combination with the new 32-bit data bus. But there's another approach, as well—serial SCSI.

Serial SCSI is a six-wire version of SCSI. It's easier to cable and used for greater distances; serial SCSI can run for over a kilometer of cable! Additionally, SCSI-3 is defined for optical fiber, paving the way for even faster systems. I'll talk more about Fibre Channel in a bit, but I mention it here because some aspects of this technology are included in the SCSI-3 standard.

Comparing SCSI-1, SCSI-2, SCSI-3

Table 12.1 compares SCSI-1, SCSI-2, and SCSI-3. Table 12.2 shows SCSI types and specifications.

TABLE 12.1 SCSI-1, SCSI-2, and SCSI-3 Compared

Standard	Bit Width	Cable Name	Pin Count	Max Transfer Rate MBps	Max SCSI Devices	Description
SCSI-1	8	A	50	5	8	Asynchronous
SCSI-2	8	A	50	10	8	Fast
SCSI-2	16	A+B	50+68	20	8	Fast-Wide**
SCSI-2	32	A+B	50+68	40	8	Fast-Wide**
SCSI-3	16	A	50	10	8	Fast
SCSI-3	16	P	68	20	16	Fast-Wide*
SCSI-3	32	P+Q	68+68	40	32	Fast-Wide**

* with one cable   ** with two cables

TABLE 12.2 SCSI Types and Specifications (New, Combined)

SCSI Type	Max Device	MBps	Bus Width	Pins	Cable Name	Max Length	Note
SCSI-1	7	5	8	25	A	19.7	Asynchronous
SCSI-2	7	5	8	50	A	19.7	
Fast SCSI-2	7	10	8	50	A	9.8	
Wide SCSI-2**	15	10-20	16	50+68	A+B	9.8	32-bit with 2 cables
Fast-Wide SCSI-2**	15	10-20	16	50+68	A+B	9.8	32-bit with 2 cables
8-bit Ultra SCSI-3	7	20	8	50	A	9.8 (to 4 devices) 4.9 (for 5 or more)	
16-bit Ultra SCSI-3*	15	20-40	16	68	P	9.8 (to 4 devices) 4.9 (for 5or more)	
8-bit Ultra2 SCSI-3**	7	40	8	68+68	P+Q	39.4	16-bit with 2 cables
16-bit Ultra2 SCSI-3**	15	40-80	16	68+68	P+Q	39.4	32-bit with 2 cables

* using one cable   ** using two cables

Fibre Channel

Hewlett-Packard, IBM, and Sun Microsystems began the Fibre Channel Systems Initiative (FCSI) in 1993. The goal of this initiative was to create an industry standard for I/O interconnection that would increase I/O performance and allow for more configuration flexibility. This technology is so complex that an entire book could be devoted to it. Therefore, I will give only an overview here.

Fibre Channel Storage Area Networks

Imagine for a minute that your current SCSI cable connects to your computer in the same way your network cable does. The other end of the cable connects to a hub, which in turn connects to a 100MBps "network" of hard drives (or other peripherals). If you are using copper cables, these other devices may be located up to 30 meters away. If you use fiber optic, these devices may be in various buildings or even up to 10 kilometers apart. All your data I/O now travels through this cable rather than through the regular network. This configuration roughly defines a storage system implementation of Fibre Channel.

Terminology

The concept of the interconnecting Fibre Channel network is called the *fabric*. Each point of connection, whether it be a hard drive or a server, is called an *N-port*, or *Node port*. When Fibre Channel is used to network storage devices, the term *SAN* is used, meaning *Storage Area Network*. Fibre Channel implementations that use a dual-loop configuration roughly analogous to Token Ring are called *Fibre Channel Arbitrated Loop*, or *FC-AL*.

Note

Token Ring, an IBM innovation, is a token-passing, ring-shaped local area network. Unfortunately it was more expensive than Ethernet and sort of worked itself out of the industry due to its higher costs. Those costs, however, were quite warranted as Token Ring (especially the FDDI implementation, which is like two Token Rings for the same workgroup) offered greater reliability and fewer dropped packets. Though Ethernet/802.3, at 100Mbps speeds, came out quite some time ago, it was only in 1999 that 100Mbps Token Ring was accepted as a standard.

Fibre Channel and Clusters

Clusters are groupings of servers that are accessed by a common group of clients. The main benefit of clustering is *fail-over* capabilities. If a client is running an application from a server that fails catastrophically, another server in the cluster will dynamically take over, with no disruption to the client. Some applications can also scale by using clustering technology.

Fibre Channel complements clustering technology in several ways. Since it offers the ability to add more devices than other SCSI technologies, Fibre Channel offers the capability of creating larger clusters. Further, unlike older SCSI technologies, Fibre Channel can be configured not to give priority to any node, improving cluster performance.

Defining a SCSI Configuration

Making SCSI work requires understanding the following items and issues. This is just an overview; you'll examine each of these issues later in this chapter in detail.

SCSI Host Adapters

Issues:

▶ The host adapter must be compatible with the system's bus.

▶ The host adapter must be able to support the same level of SCSI (SCSI-1, SCSI-2, or SCSI-3) as the peripherals.

▶ When you're buying a SCSI host adapter, you're buying the ambassador between all those expensive, fast peripherals you bought and your CPU and memory. Now, more than ever, bus mastering and 32-bit interface SCSI host adapters are preferable.

▶ The host adapter must be assigned a SCSI ID between 0 and 7, or 0 and 15 on a single-channel SCSI-3 host adapter (most common for PCs).

▶ The host needs a SCSI driver that follows the same SCSI standard as the SCSI drivers on the peripherals. There have been three standards here: Advanced SCSI Programming Interface (ASPI), Common Access Method (CAM), and Layered Device Driver Architecture (LADDR). ASPI has become the primary standard. These are *not* related to SCSI-1, SCSI-2, and SCSI-3; this is a different dimension in SCSI compatibility.

SCSI-Compatible Peripherals

Issues:

▶ Each SCSI peripheral needs a SCSI driver that is compatible with the SCSI standard on the host's SCSI driver.

▶ All SCSI devices follow SCSI-1, SCSI-2, or SCSI-3 cable standards; it may be important to know which level the device follows when installing it.

▶ Each peripheral must be assigned a unique SCSI ID from 0 to 7, or 0 to 15 for single-channel SCSI-3.

▶ Devices can be mounted internally or externally.

▶ Some devices have optional built-in termination (see the next item); others may have termination that's *not* optional (this is *very* bad, but more common than you'd hope), and still others do not include termination of any kind.

▶ Terminated devices should support active termination, but some will support only passive termination.

> Devices should be able to be daisy chained, so they should have two SCSI connectors if they are external.

SCSI Cabling

Issues:

> There are several kinds of SCSI cables and even variations between SCSI-1, SCSI-2, and SCSI-3. (See Table 12.1.)

> You can't run cables more than a few feet, or the SCSI signal degrades and the peripheral doesn't work.

SCSI Termination

Issues:

> Each SCSI system needs two terminators, one on each extreme end of the chain of devices.

> There are two kinds of terminators: passive and active. You're supposed to be able to use either type for SCSI-1 or SCSI-2, but active is usually a better idea. SCSI-3 requires active termination.

> Some devices have built-in terminators; others require separate termination devices.

> The host adapter probably supports termination of some kind. This should be considered when terminating the system.

SCSI Drivers

Issues:

> The SCSI system needs a driver for each SCSI device, as well as a driver for the host adapter.

▶ SCSI hard disks may not require drivers; instead, they may have an on-board BIOS that serves that function.

SCSI Installation

Actually putting SCSI adapters and peripherals into your system is pretty much the same whether you're using devices that are SCSI-1 or SCSI-2. So let's look at physical installation first.

SCSI Physical Installation

Basically, putting a SCSI device into the PC requires the steps outlined earlier in the QuickSteps section. Software installation follows the physical end of a SCSI setup, but for the moment let's continue focusing on the physical part.

Choosing a SCSI Host Adapter

Many computers—more and more—have SCSI support right on their motherboards; others come with SCSI adapters in a slot as standard equipment. If this is true for you, then skip to the next section. But otherwise, just a few thoughts about choosing host adapters:

▶ There are host adapters for 8-bit ISA, 16-bit ISA, 16-bit MicroChannel, 32-bit MicroChannel, 32-bit EISA, VL-Bus, and PCI. The wider your interface, the better your maximum data transfer rate.

▶ Many SCSI host adapters use bus mastering to improve their performance. *Bus mastering* is very similar to direct memory access (DMA) in that it allows the host adapter to transfer data straight into memory without having to involve the CPU. But DMA allows only high-speed transfer from peripheral to memory or memory to peripheral—not peripheral to peripheral. Bus mastering makes peripheral-to-peripheral transfers possible without CPU intervention, often leading to higher-speed data access. Anyone who's heard of bus mastering has probably heard that the PCI and EISA buses support it. While it's not generally known, bus mastering is possible with ISA bus machines. Adaptec makes an AHA1542 controller that's almost jumper-free and that will do bus mastering on an ISA bus machine, providing some admirable data transfer rates.

Tip

By the way, there's another benefit to bus mastering: it means that your host adapter doesn't need to use one of your precious DMA channels.

- Some SCSI devices come with *optional cache RAM*. While it sounds like it'll make your system really scream, what it mainly does is make the benchmarks look good. A system that provides no hurdles between the bits on the platter and the CPU's RAM will provide pretty good data transfer rates that are real data transfer rates, not bogus ones. Bus mastering should reduce or remove the need for cache RAM on the controller.

- Look for an adapter that supports SCSI-2 or SCSI-3 if you have the budget, and potentially one that supports Fast SCSI, Wide SCSI, and Fast-Wide SCSI.

- If you need to support more than seven devices, or if you have a slow device that is monopolizing the bus and preventing faster devices from giving you the performance you need, consider a multichannel SCSI host adapter. That way, you can put the faster devices on one channel and the devices that are slowing things down on a separate channel.

- Make sure that your adapter has drivers that support the ASPI standard. (See "SCSI Software Installation" for more information.)

Tip

Choosing the wrong host adapter isn't the end of the world, but it can mean more installation and troubleshooting headaches.

And if you're in a tight spot and need to interface a SCSI device with a computer that doesn't have slots, look into the MiniSCSI Plus from Adaptec. It costs about $79 and will convert your parallel port into a SCSI-2 adapter. The software provided with it is ASPI compatible, as well.

The MiniSCSI does suffer from one serious problem. It will not work unless the item at the end of the SCSI chain includes an active terminator. Most SCSI-1 devices don't provide termination power, but many SCSI-2 devices do. As a result, the MiniSCSI will work with only a subset of the SCSI devices. Try it before you buy it. (More information about termination later in this chapter.)

Installing the SCSI Host Adapter

Putting a SCSI host adapter into the PC is pretty much the same as installing any board. SCSI adapters are a bit more of a pain than the average board to install because they typically require DMA channels, IRQ levels, I/O addresses, and a ROM address.

It's usually possible to connect SCSI devices to a host adapter both internally and externally. In Figure 12.1, you see that there is a 50-pin header connector on the SCSI host adapter for internal connections, and a Centronics 50-pin female connector for attaching external devices.

Figure 12.1

SCSI connectors

More recent SCSI adapters will use a miniature 50-socket D-shell connector. A note of interest here—some SCSI adapters with three interfaces (an internal Wide 68-pin connector, a 50-pin connector, and an external connector) will allow connection to only two of the three interfaces at the same time. Thus, if you have internal wide and narrow devices, the external connector cannot be used. You should consult your documentation for the particular adapter.

Assigning a SCSI ID to the Peripheral

Now consider the SCSI peripheral that you're going to install.

SCSI is a parallel interface. SCSI-1 (and most SCSI-2 implementations) defined eight wires to communicate data, an 8-bit data bus. Now, the SCSI designers needed a simple way for a number of devices on a SCSI bus to say, "I want to talk!" and they all needed a way to say that all at the same time—so they couldn't share a wire to signal that they wanted to use the bus. Every device needed a separate wire.

What, then, was the easiest way to let multiple devices signal that they wanted to use the bus? To let the data lines do double duty. Each data line is also a SCSI ID line, and, as the original SCSI design called for eight data lines, there are eight SCSI devices that can go on a SCSI bus.

A basic SCSI configuration assigns this identification number, called a SCSI ID, to each device on the SCSI system. The values for this ID range from 0 to 7, and the host adapter typically is set to 7. Other, more advanced, configurations can handle IDs from 0–15 and even 0–31. You typically can change the host ID from 7, or, in the case of the more advanced configurations the last ID in the chain, but don't—you'll expose yourself unnecessarily to software incompatibilities.

You typically set a SCSI ID with a DIP switch, a jumper, a thumb-wheel, or the like. There are just a few rules for setting SCSI IDs:

▶ Each device on the SCSI chain must have its own ID.

▶ The lower the SCSI ID, the higher the priority of the device. If two devices both want the bus at the same time, the one with the lower number wins. Hard drives need ID 0 or ID 1 because they should have highest priority.

▶ Do not use ID 0 or ID 1 for anything but hard disks. If you plan to boot from a SCSI hard disk, make it ID 0.

▶ Check your system documentation to see if it expects a device at a particular ID. For example, my advice to put a hard disk on ID 0 or 1 is really DOS- and Windows-based advice. Other operating systems (SCO Unix, for example) may not care about which ID you use for a boot drive. At the same time, SCO must see any CD-ROMs at ID 5.

▶ Regardless of what I recommend, or what your documentation says, the only way to solve some SCSI problems is to just try out different ID combinations until something works. I've never fixed anything by fiddling around with the adapter's ID, but I've fixed things by messing with other IDs.

▶ IBM PS/2 machines with SCSI drives use ID 6 for bootable hard disks.

Does this sound a bit haphazard? Well, it is, to an extent: SCSI is still something of an evolving standard.

Something new to help us out is SCAM (SCSI Configure AutoMagically). With this newer functionality, devices and the host adapter configure SCSI IDs automatically. The hitch is that both the host adapter and devices need to support SCAM in order for this to work.

Targets, Initiators, LUNs, and LSUNs

So far I've been talking about SCSI IDs. But say that while installing my Adaptec SCSI hardware—Adaptec is the SCSI market leader and a manufacturer whose products I can recommend—I see a message upon bootup that says

```
Host Adapter #0 - SCSI ID 6 - LUN 0: NEC CD-ROM
DRIVE: 841 1.0
```

And a later message says

```
Host Adapter #0, Target SCSI ID=6: NEC CD-ROM
DRIVE:8411.0
```

First of all, `Target SCSI ID` is the same thing as `SCSI ID`. *Target* simply indicates that this device, a CD-ROM, is a target rather than an initiator.

In the SCSI world, any communication is initiated by one device and acknowledged by another device. The device that starts the conversation is called an *initiator*. The device that responds is called a *target*. In general, the host adapter acts as initiator and the SCSI peripherals act as targets. It is possible, however, for the two to reverse roles in some communications, but the *Target SCSI ID* message references the fact that the CD-ROM is usually a target.

The *logical unit number (LUN)* refers to the capability of a SCSI device to have subdevices. For example, consider the (now obsolete) Iomega 44 + 44 Bernoulli backup device. It is a metal case containing two 44MB cartridge drives, and it is SCSI compatible. If I connect an Iomega 44 + 44 cartridge device to one of my SCSI systems, I'll see a new SCSI ID, which refers to the 44 + 44 system. But the two drives will be distinguished not by different SCSI IDs, but instead by different logical unit numbers under the same SCSI ID.

This is actually fairly unusual in the SCSI world and as a result will probably give your system heartburn—that is, your drivers may not be able to address the second 44MB drive. But now you'll know what *LUN* refers to. Again, the vast majority of devices include only one LUN.

In theory, each SCSI device can have up to eight LUNs. If one of the SCSI IDs is taken by the host adapter, that leaves seven for peripherals. If each peripheral had eight LUNs, there could be 56 SCSI logical units on a single host adapter.

To make things even worse, each LUN can have a sub-subdevice called an *LSUN*, or *logical sub-unit number*, which can range from 0 to 255. Let's see, 56 logical units, each with 256 logical subunits. . . that's 14,336 devices on a single host adapter! Not bad, eh? Well, actually, this wouldn't work for several reasons. First, a standard PC SCSI host adapter wouldn't get too far having to keep track of 14,000 devices. Second, there's a maximum cable length of 6 meters and a minimum cable length of 10 centimeters. Third, I don't know of any PC SCSI software that supports LSUNs.

Notice also the NEC CD–ROM. . . information. That's actual descriptive information in English that the CD-ROM gives to the host adapter about what it—the peripheral—is.

Enabling/Disabling SCSI Parity

The SCSI bus can detect and use parity signals to detect errors in transmission over the SCSI cabling. Errors can and do occur, particularly as the cable gets longer from end to end.

Tip

To use SCSI parity, all devices must support it. If only one device does not support SCSI parity, then you must disable it for all devices on the chain.

Some operating systems, such as Windows NT, will not work at all with a SCSI CD-ROM unless it supports SCSI parity. That implies that you should plan to support SCSI parity from the very beginning and buy only devices that support SCSI parity (and SCSI-2 and -3, by the way).

SCSI Daisy Chaining

Many of you will end up putting only one or two SCSI devices on a PC, but SCSI can easily support seven peripherals off a single SCSI host adapter (15 for SCSI-3), or it could theoretically support hundreds of devices with a lot of rocket science. (The "hundreds of devices" concept works if you put eight SCSI adapters in a system, and each is connected in turn to eight SCSI adapters—that's possible; remember LUNs? The second-level SCSI adapters can be externally connected to other SCSI adapters, leaving the possibility of lots of devices. As I said a page back, it's impossible to find PC software that supports such a thing, so forget it.)

Multiple devices are attached to a single SCSI host adapter via daisy chaining. There are several kinds of cables in the SCSI world.

Types of SCSI Cables: SCSI, SCSI-1, SCSI-2, and SCSI-3 (Wide or Ultra Wide)

External SCSI devices tend to have two 50-pin female Centronics connectors, as you see in Figure 12.2, which shows the back of a SCSI device.

Figure 12.2

Connectors for external SCSI devices

A 50-pin male connector, such as you'd see on a SCSI cable, looks like Figure 12.3.

Figure 12.3

50-pin male connector for SCSI

Some external SCSI cables have a Centronics connector of this type on both ends of the cable. Such a cable is called a SCSI peripheral cable, or SCSI cable, and is pictured in Figure 12.4. Use it either to connect between SCSI-1 host adapters and SCSI devices or when daisy chaining from SCSI device to SCSI device.

Figure 12.4

SCSI peripheral cable

Other older SCSI cables have a male DB-25 connector on one side and a Centronics 50 conductor connector on the other side. Those are called Macintosh SCSI, or SCSI-1, cables and are pictured in Figure 12.5.

Figure 12.5

SCSI-1 cable

Newer SCSI adapters often do not employ a Centronics connector for external devices, but rather use a miniature 50-socket D-shell connector; some people call it an *HP-50 connector*. You can see the male version of that connector—the version that you'd see on a cable—in Figure 12.6.

Figure 12.6

SCSI connector—
50-socket D-shell
(HP-50 connector)

The cable incorporates two buttons on either side that you must squeeze together in order to connect or disconnect the cable to or from the adapter. You will see this connector instead of the Centronics on some peripherals (more and more, as time goes on) and more commonly on the backs of SCSI adapters. Since 1993, Adaptec has put them on the backs of their 1742 adapters in lieu of the more common Centronics 50. Such a cable—Centronics 50-conductor connection on one side, mini DB-50-pin connector on the other—is popularly called a SCSI-2 cable. Take a look at Figure 12.7.

Figure 12.7

SCSI-2 cable

Through Thick and Thin: Not All Cables Are Equal

While I'm discussing cables, let me relate a short war story that taught me an important lesson about cables.

I installed a CD-ROM onto a server so that I could install Windows NT on my LAN. The CD-ROM was an external drive that used the 50-conductor Centronics connector, so I walked over to my cable pile and pulled out a standard SCSI cable with 50-conductor Centronics connectors on both ends. I plugged the CD-ROM into the SCSI adapter's interface port on the back of my PC, and the problems started. My existing tape drive and hard disk drive—both internal SCSI—started acting up.

After an hour or two of playing around with the system, I found that if I downgraded the SCSI system from SCSI-2 to SCSI-1 (I did this by reconfiguring my SCSI host adapter, an Adaptec AHA1542C), the problems went away. I had vague forebodings about losing SCSI-2 compatibility—SCSI parity doesn't work under SCSI-1, recall—but everything seemed to work, so I figured that I'd live with it.

Then came time to install NT. The README file said, "The SCSI and CD-ROM support built into Windows NT require that CD-ROMs provide SCSI parity to function properly." Great, I thought, and started fussing with the SCSI devices to get the CD-ROM to support SCSI parity. I mean, there was a jumper specifically included on the CD-ROM to control whether SCSI parity would be used, so why wouldn't it support SCSI parity?

Just on the off chance that I had a bad cable, I went back over to the cable pile to see what else I had. I found another dual 50 Centronics cable identical to the cable that I was using, and another dual 50 Centronics cable that was about twice as thick as the first two. I tried swapping the original thin cable for the other thin cable—no difference. But when I used the thicker cable, everything started working! I got full SCSI-2 support, as well as SCSI parity functionality.

A few calls around to cable places brought the information that, yes, there were two kinds of dual 50 Centronics cables. The thin ones work fine for SCSI-1 but not for SCSI-2. The thick ones are good for both.

Internal SCSI Cabling

External devices, as you've read, tend to have two SCSI connections on them so that they can support the SCSI daisy chain. Internal devices, in contrast, use only a single 50-pin header connector. Internal SCSI cables are just ribbon cables with 50-pin IDC connectors, as you see in Figure 12.8.

Figure 12.8

Internal SCSI cable

Because the connectors are sitting in the middle of the cable, one connector does the job for daisy chaining.

Terminating the SCSI Chain

Before popping the top back on your PC, there's one more thing that needs doing: you must terminate the SCSI chain.

Note

SCSI-1 termination was a simple resistor. SCSI-2 termination requires a small amount of power applied by the SCSI device (600 milliamps at 4–5.25 volts). Some devices do provide termination resistance, but not termination power, making them potential troublemakers in a SCSI-2 setting.

Whenever I discuss termination in class, people start referring to killer cyborgs from the future, but *termination* just means providing a voltage and resistance on either end of a cable, so that the entire bus has a particular set of electrical characteristics. Without this resistance, the SCSI cables cannot transport data around without significant error rates. (It will work sometimes, despite what some people claim, but it won't work reliably.)

Note

Actually, on short SCSI chains, your peripherals *might* work, but there's no reason not to terminate properly. Problems occur in unterminated chains when packets "reflect" off of an inactive terminal point.

Active and Passive Terminators

SCSI-1 specified two kinds of termination, active and passive. Active was pretty much ignored until SCSI-2 became popular. Passive terminators are just a resistor network; if you're interested in how they work electronically, you can see that in Figure 12.9.

If you don't speak schematic, don't sweat it: the jaggy-looking things are resistors, *passive termination* refers to a source of electricity, and the triangle standing on its head represents electrical ground, the place that the power from Termpower is seeking to go. The main thing to notice is that the only thing going on here is resistors; there are no chips, and no amplification is going on. Passive termination is basically an adaptation of the simple terminators found in ancient floppy disk or ST-506 systems. Back in the SCSI-1 days, the designers figured that the major use for SCSI would be to hook up a couple of hard disks to a host adapter, all with no more than eight inches to a foot of cable.

Figure 12.9

Passive SCSI termination

Passive termination

If, on the other hand, you intended to run longer cables and put a lot of stuff on them, then you need some kind of booster for termination power; that's active termination. It's represented schematically in Figure 12.10.

Figure 12.10

Active SCSI termination

The LT 1086 chip's job is to provide amplification power when necessary. Active termination is, then, a bit more expensive than passive, but there is no more than a few cents' difference.

So, in a modern setup, do you need active or passive? As in the old SCSI-1 configuration, if all you're going to do is to hang a single drive on a host adapter, then it probably doesn't matter. But if you want to use longer cables, external devices (they usually need longer cables), and more than one or two devices, then active termination is a good idea. The problem, as you'll see in the next section, is that termination is built into the SCSI devices themselves, and some vendors get cheap and simply add passive termination.

You can mix passives and actives on a SCSI chain, putting a passive on one end and an active on another.

Internal and External Terminators

You've seen that some SCSI devices are installed internally in the PC (and connect to the host adapter with a ribbon cable), and that other devices are installed externally (and connect to the host adapter with a SCSI cable of some kind). There are also internal and external terminators, as well as SCSI devices that have terminators built right in. As I have mentioned, some vendors build active termination into their devices, some build passive termination in, and some don't build in termination of any kind, forcing you to buy a separate termination device of one kind or another. Most SCSI devices with termination let you disable that termination, but some are boneheadedly designed without any provision for disabling termination, forcing you to put those devices on one of the extreme ends of the SCSI chain.

If you've got to disable a terminator, you'll find that devices let you do that in one of these ways:

▶ An internal, *Single Inline Pin Package (SIPP)* terminator on the host adapter and/or a hard disk.

▶ Some host adapters, such as the modern Adaptec adapters, let you enable or disable termination via software.

▶ Many devices adjust termination with a DIP switch or a jumper.

If you must buy an external terminator, then you'll need to choose the right one for whatever SCSI connector type you have. In Figure 12.11, you can see a Centronics terminator.

Figure 12.11

Centronics terminator

They clip onto one of the Centronics connectors on the back of the last external device on your SCSI daisy chain. I've also seen external SCSI terminators for the mini DB-50/HP-50 connectors and the old Macintosh-style DB-25s.

SIPP-type terminators often show up on the host adapter itself, as it needs termination and SIPPs don't take up too much space. You can see a SIPP in Figure 12.12.

Figure 12.12

A SIPP-type terminator

If you have a host adapter that uses SIPPs for its termination, then there are typically three of these SIPPs on a host adapter. You'll also find SIPPs on many internal SCSI hard disks. You just remove them (gently, as you may need to reinstall them one day) by working them out with needle-nosed pliers. Once you've done that, put them in an envelope, seal it, label it "SCSI Terminators," and put it somewhere.

If you look at the back of the external SCSI device, you may notice a switch labeled "termination." It can be flipped on or off, so if this SCSI device is the last on the chain, then all I need do is to flip it on; otherwise, I flip it off.

Sample SCSI Setup: One Internal Drive

When I say, "Put terminators on the end of the chain," it's worthwhile taking a minute and making sure that you know what I mean. With that in mind, let's look at a few sample SCSI applications. Take a look at Figure 12.13.

In this setup, you've got just a SCSI hard disk. There must be terminators on each side, but there are only two sides, so it's simple to figure out where the terminators go. Both terminators are probably SIPP-type terminators. The host is ID 7, the hard disk is ID 0; this means that you're intending to boot from the hard disk.

Hard disk ID 0
(Terminated)

Host adapter ID 7
(Terminated)

Figure 12.13

SCSI setup: one
internal drive

Sample SCSI Setup: Two Internal Devices

Now let's make it a bit more complex (see Figure 12.14).

CD-ROM ID 6
(Terminated)

Hard disk ID 0
(Not terminated)

Host adapter ID 7
(Terminated)

Figure 12.14

SCSI setup: two
internal devices

Now I've added an internal CD-ROM. It needs to have a different ID, so ID 6 is good. Remember, I want to avoid ID 1 for anything other than a hard disk and I want to have a higher number and therefore lower priority. The CD ROM isn't a high-priority device, anyway, so assigning it a higher SCSI ID versus a lower SCSI ID won't be that noticeable to a user. The hard disk terminators must be removed, as the hard disk is in the middle of the chain, and the CD-ROM is terminated.

Sample SCSI Setup: One External Device

Now let's do the same things, but with external devices, as shown in Figure 12.15.

Figure 12.15

SCSI setup: one
external device

Now there's just one external device, a cartridge storage device that I won't try to boot from. I've set the Bernoulli box to ID 6 and terminated it, as it is the extreme end of the chain.

Sample SCSI Setup: Two External Devices

Continuing, I'll now add a second external device, as in Figure 12.16.

Figure 12.16

SCSI setup: two
external devices

This time, I'll make the CD-ROM ID 5, as ID 6 is taken. The Bernoulli box shouldn't be terminated, as it is now in the middle of the chain, and the CD-ROM is terminated.

Sample SCSI Setup: Internal and External Devices

For the grand finale, let's put two external devices and two internal devices on this system (see Figure 12.17).

CD-ROM ID 4 (Terminated)

Hard disk ID 0 (Not terminated)
Host adapter ID 7 (Not terminated)

Scanner ID 3 (Terminated)

Bernoulli box ID 6 (Not terminated)

Figure 12.17

SCSI setup: two external and two internal devices

The important point to notice about this scenario is that the termination has been removed from the host adapter, as it is now (for the first time) in the middle of the chain. The external devices are attached to the external connector on the back of the SCSI host adapter (the Centronics or miniature D connector), and the internal devices are hooked to the internal 50-pin header connector. Every device has a unique SCSI ID, and there's termination on the ends of the chain. Additionally, I've assigned them SCSI IDs in roughly the order that their speeds warrant—the Bernoulli box is faster than the CD-ROM and scanner, and so you assign it a lower priority than the peripherals, resulting in equal access speeds.

Special Termination Issues for SCSI-3

There are some special termination issues that apply to SCSI-3. On the external connector of a SCSI-3 host adapter, you can daisy chain both 8-bit SCSI (SCSI-2) and 16-bit (SCSI-3) devices. This can present some unique termination problems.

For example, suppose I attach to the external connector a SCSI-2 CD-ROM with a standard Centronics type SCSI-2 connector. To do this, I get an adapter that converts the 68-pin SCSI-3 connector on the host adapter to the 50 pins the SCSI-2 device uses. What is the result?

Think about it this way: a SCSI-2 device has 8 data bits or pins plus ground wires and other assorted signals. A SCSI-3 device uses two sets of 8 data bits, or 16 data bits total. You can call one of these two sets *a high order set* of 8 data bits and the other a *low order set*. When I connect a converter to the SCSI host adapter, I pass only the low order data bits to the SCSI-2 devices that are attached. Remember that the last device is terminated. What does it terminate in this scenario? Only the low order data bits! For that reason, it is critical that the adapter connected to the external port of the host adapter not only converts the 68 pins to 50, but that it terminates the high order data bits and associated ground signals.

SCSI Software Installation

Much of the SCSI installation process is like a normal hard disk's installation process: low-level format, partition, and high-level format. Doing those things isn't much different from doing them on non-SCSI hard disks, except that you may have to use a special program for the formatting and/or partitioning; check your SCSI software documentation for an example.

The tough part about SCSI software installation, however, is the drivers. There seem to be a million of them, and none of them appear to be on speaking terms with one another—and what do they do, anyway?

Until a few years ago, SCSI drivers were proprietary. You were crazy to buy a SCSI hard disk and host adapter unless you got them from the same vendor, a vendor that supplied drivers for the two of them. But since 1991, several *universal driver* standards have appeared. Figure 12.18 shows how they work.

Figure 12.18

Universal SCSI driver standards

Rather than trying to create a hard disk driver, a CD-ROM driver, a scanner driver, and a tape driver that are all compatible with the operating system, a universal driver system defines an intermediate standard and supports that with a driver specific to the host adapter. The SCSI device drivers then need only be written to work with the intermediate standard defined by the host adapter's driver. The primary and exceedingly dominant standard is ASPI. Its two competitors, CAM and LADDR, are all but gone. Additionally, no discussion of drivers can fail to include the INT 13 BIOS interface found on many SCSI host adapters.

The idea here is that you buy a host adapter from anyone and get a driver for that adapter that supports the ASPI standard. Since the driver on your host adapter board speaks ASPI, and your device's driver speaks ASPI, everything will work out fine. And if you decide to replace your current SCSI host adapter board with one that's faster or better in some way, then all you need is a new driver for that board—you don't even need to change the device driver for the tape drive. (It should be stressed that this is the idea; of course,

ASPI compatibility is not a black-and-white thing in the real world. You should experience little incompatibility until you get into the really interesting SCSI drive farms, super-big device chains, or RAID arrays.)

With Bootable Hard Disks, You Don't Need SCSI Software

I'm going to discuss this in detail in a few pages, but if you are in the process of installing a SCSI hard disk on device 0 or 1, and in a hurry, then I wanted to note here that you needn't worry about SCSI software; you don't need it. Hard disks on device numbers 0 and/or 1 have built-in BIOS support and don't need separate SCSI drivers. Hard disks above device 1 or removable hard disks do require separate drivers.

Installing SCSI Software

If your SCSI device didn't come with a driver, you can use the generic driver provided by Adaptec called EZ-SCSI. Here's a section from a CONFIG.SYS file built with EZ-SCSI:

```
DEVICE=C:\ADAPTEC\ASPI4DOS.SYS /D
DEVICE=C:\ADAPTEC\ASPIDISK.SYS /D
DEVICE=C:\ADAPTEC\ASPICD.SYS /D:MSCD001
```

Taken in order, these three device drivers (1) load the base ASPI support for the host adapter, (2) provide an ASPI-to-hard-disk interface for a removable SCSI hard disk (a Bernoulli box), and (3) provide an ASPI-to-CD-ROM interface for a SCSI CD-ROM. If the first driver didn't load, then the second and third drivers could not load.

EZ-SCSI comes with drivers for CD-ROMs, removable cartridge hard disks (such as Bernoulli boxes), and fixed hard disks. EZ-SCSI does not include drivers for scanners, WORM (optical Write Once, Read Many times) drives, WARM (optical Write And Read Many times) drives, scanners, or tape drives. If you get a device that supports ASPI later, then you can easily add it to a configuration that started out from EZ-SCSI. EZ-SCSI also comes with formatting and partitioning utilities for storage devices, a tape backup program, a scanning utility, and a benchmarking program.

Warning

EZ-SCSI is *not* free, and it's doubtful that Adaptec will ever make it so. Neither does Adaptec, nor any other SCSI hardware vendor for that matter, make it easy to add SCSI to your system unless you buy something from them. Quite a distasteful attitude, I think. Why would you want SCSI if you don't have SCSI peripherals? IDE/ATAPI CD-R and CD-RW drives require an ASPI layer to be installed in order to be accessed and written to as such a device and the makers of these devices are often asked to pay very large ASPI software licensing fees. Unfortunately, it's not always possible.

The ASPI Standards

ASPI was invented by Adaptec, and the first time I read anything about ASPI, the A stood for Adaptec. But ASPI has been adopted by other hardware manufacturers, and, as you've read, it is the home of two very fine suites of SCSI drivers. I'd personally recommend that you stay within the ASPI standard, as it's easiest to find drivers that are ASPI compatible.

Let me underscore that there is no such thing as an "ASPI-compatible SCSI hard disk." The compatibility question relates to the drivers, not the hardware.

SCSI without Drivers: On-Board BIOS Support

After all this talk of mixing and matching drivers, you may be getting a bit queasy. But if all you're going to install is a hard disk or two, then you may never have to trouble with drivers.

Why SCSI Adapters Have BIOS

Using SCSI hard disks, if you think about it, can lead to a sort of chicken-and-egg problem. The SCSI device isn't accessible until the SCSI device drivers are loaded, and device drivers are generally loaded from the hard disk. But how can you load SCSI drivers from a SCSI hard disk? I suppose one answer would be to boot from a floppy and then not reboot, but it's a somewhat cumbersome answer.

The answer to the problem of, "How does my PC boot from a SCSI hard disk?" is that most SCSI adapters have an on-board BIOS that contains enough software to run the hard disk, even if there are no SCSI drivers loaded. That's a real lifesaver, enabling us to use SCSI hard disks without having to worry about drivers. However, they must be configured as SCSI IDs 0 and 1.

When to Disable a BIOS

Many SCSI installations that I do are not intended to support a hard disk. For example, installing a CD-ROM in an already running system means that I've already got a functional IDE drive in the system, so there's no point in replacing it with a SCSI drive.

In that case, I don't need the BIOS, so I disable it. You do that either with setup software or with some kind of physical setting, like a jumper or DIP switch. That's a real benefit, as it creates more space in my Upper Memory Area for larger Upper Memory Blocks. So disable your BIOS if you are not booting from a SCSI hard disk.

Troubleshooting SCSI

First, it's important to note that Windows 95, 98, 98SE, NT3.51, NT4, and 2000 all sleep, eat, and breathe SCSI. In fact, they all need translation drivers to understand IDE/ATAPI, the type of drive shipped in a huge percentage of new systems for years!!!

Next, you'll be disappointed to find out that Windows 2000 does not have an ASPI layer built in, as NT did in previous versions.

Finally, the names *SCSI-1 cable* and *SCSI-2 cable* are misleading. What I've called SCSI-1 and SCSI-2 cables are not universal terms. Whenever you buy a SCSI cable, be extremely careful to specify the kinds of connectors you want on either side. Be triple careful about the mini DB-50 or HP-50 connector; everyone seems to have a different name for it, so make sure you're getting what you want.

Note

Note that there is a difference between the terminology used and the physical characteristics of the cable. Although Wide SCSI has more pins (68 versus 50), the cable is not wider than a SCSI-2 cable. In fact, the SCSI-2 cable is the physically wider of the two. *Wide* refers to the data path—a 68-pin cable has 16 bits of data, whereas a SCSI-2 has only 8 bits or pins devoted to the data path.

Installation Troubleshooting

Now that I've drilled into your head the idea that you should have only terminators on either side of the chain, let me offer an exception.

Note

The sum total of your SCSI cables should not exceed 18 feet. In general, the shorter your cables, the better.

Sometimes a SCSI setup doesn't work. You check and recheck the SCSI IDs, but there are no duplicated IDs. You've terminated properly, but things still don't work. What do you do?

Remember that the sum total of cable lengths must not exceed 6 meters. Lower-quality cables mean that distance shrinks.

Things to try:

▶ Most SCSI host adapters display a sign-on message listing the recognized devices on the SCSI bus. Use that information as your first diagnostic. If the device is seen on the bus, but you can't get it to do tricks, then the problem is probably a driver problem rather than a hardware installation problem.

▶ If you encounter *phantom disks*—disks that you can see but cannot read or write—then you've probably put two devices on the same SCSI ID.

▶ Sometimes the ID-setting device is defective. I've seen a tape drive that, when set for ID 4, would show up as ID 6.

▶ Sometimes cables are defective, or combinations of cables don't get along.

To check whether it falls under the last item on this list, try this:

1. Install only the host adapter and its driver. Boot the system and make sure that the host adapter is working—no DMA/IRQ/IO address conflicts. It may even come with a host adapter diagnostic; run it.

2. Turn off the PC, add the first SCSI device, and power it up before you reboot the PC. SCSI devices often must be active before the host adapter can recognize them. (Also be sure that everything is terminated correctly.)

3. Once you've got that device in place, power down the PC and the existing SCSI device (if it's external), and add the next SCSI device. Test it as you just tested the first SCSI device.

I find it most convenient to install the internal devices first, then the external devices. I usually remove the SIPP terminators from the host adapter, and just place an external SCSI terminator on the connector on the back of my host adapter if it's a Centronics-type connector. Otherwise, I get a SCSI cable, attach it to the back of the host adapter, and then terminate that.

Warning

Remember to power down all the SCSI devices before adding or subtracting from the daisy chain.

13

Partitioning and Formatting IDE and SCSI Drives

INTRODUCTION

Now that you've installed your hard drive, it's time to make use of it. In order to use your hard drive, you'll have to perform two tasks: partitioning and formatting. (With a SCSI hard disk, you may need to perform an additional task first, low-level formatting, but I'll get to that in a minute.)

Partitioning a drive means that you tell the computer how the space on the physical hard drive should be apportioned to various drive letters (*logical drives*). You might choose to make your entire hard drive one big C: drive, or to chunk up the physical drive into C:, D:, and E:, or more. Partitioning also chooses a file storage system, such as FAT16, FAT32, or NTFS.

Formatting your hard drive structures the drive's space into well-organized compartments that can be used to store data. Each logical drive you create with partitioning must be formatted separately.

Take special care when using the information in this chapter on existing drives. Partitioning and formatting are "destructive" activities—they erase whatever data was stored on the disk. Once a drive has been partitioned and formatted, you will seldom need to redo it. You'll more likely find yourself partitioning and formatting a brand new drive you're adding to your system, or reformatting after some catastrophe (such as a virus) has trashed everything on the disk, leaving nothing left to lose.

Partitioning and Formatting a Hard Disk

Whenever you install a new hard drive in your system, you'll need to follow several steps to prepare it to accept files.

Be Prepared

Before you start, there are some things you'll need to perform the operation. These include:

- A bootable floppy, used to start the PC (unless you are configuring a second disk for the PC, and the primary hard disk is still bootable).

- Access to the MS-DOS programs FDISK and FORMAT. On a Windows PC, they're in the `C:\Windows\Command` folder. If you created a startup disk using Windows 9x, those programs will be there; otherwise, you can copy them from a working PC to your bootable floppy.

1. If you're configuring the PC's primary hard disk, boot your computer from a bootable floppy disk.

   or

   If configuring a new, secondary disk, you can start the PC from your hard disk normally.

2. Run FDISK and partition the new hard disk.

3. Exit FDISK and reboot your computer.

4. Format each new partition that you created in step 2.

5. Reboot your computer (not necessary in all cases but usually a good thing to do).

If you need to install your operating system, during your last reboot make sure you boot from the Setup disk required for installing your OS. If you are partitioning and formatting a secondary drive, you won't need to reinstall your OS. You may, however, need to reinstall certain programs if any new drive letter assignments change the location of previously installed applications.

Low-Level Formatting

Low-level formatting divides the disk's tracks into a specific number of sectors, creating the intersector and intertrack gaps and recording the sector header and trailer information. It also fills each sector with a dummy value or a pattern of test values.

Low-level formatting is typically done at the factory, so you should not have to worry about it, especially on IDE drives. There are utilities that will let you low-level format an IDE drive, but I don't recommend doing it because you'll mess up the optimal head and cylinder skew factors for the drive that were set at the factory, as well as the map of physically defective sectors on the drive.

In the past, SCSI drives sometimes would come from the factory without low-level formatting, but this has changed in recent years. Should you need to low-level format a SCSI drive, you'll find a utility to do so built into the SCSI adapter's BIOS. As you boot your PC, you'll see a message onscreen about the SCSI adapter, telling you to press some certain key to enter its setup. Do so and then hunt around for the low-level hard disk formatting utility. But again, and I stress this strongly: don't low-level format a drive if you don't have to. Try partitioning it first (see the following section), and if that goes okay, just forget you ever heard about low-level formatting.

In the unlikely event that you should need to low-level format an IDE drive, check the manufacturer's Web site for a utility. Each IDE manufacturer has its own methodology for low-level formatting, and you can't get good results by using the utility for one brand with another brand's drive. Here are the Web sites to look for:

Seagate `ftp://ftp.seagate.com/techsuppt/ seagate_utils/sgatfmt4.zip`

IBM `http://www.storage.ibm.com/techsup/ hddtech/welcome.htm`

Quantum `http://support.quantum.com/menus/ soft_menu.htm`

Western Digital `http://www.wdc.com/service/ftp/wddiag/wd_diag.exe`

Maxtor `http://www.Maxtor.com/library/ide.html`

Partitioning

Partitioning a drive tells it how to allocate the available physical space among various drive letters. You must partition a drive in order to use it. Even if you're going to give the drive all to a single drive letter, you've still got to create a partition.

How It All Began

In 1983, IBM ushered in the era of hard disks in PCs with their XT. Nobody was surprised that IBM would introduce a computer with a hard disk, but we *were* surprised by the large size of the hard disk—*10MB*! Back then, that was huge.

Why did IBM put the large drive on the XT? Because they wanted to sell us *two* operating systems—DOS and *Xenix*. For those who don't know, Xenix was a Unix variant that Microsoft was pushing for a while, back before they started selling OS/2, and *way* before Windows.

The problem with having both DOS and Xenix on the system was that they didn't get along. Xenix didn't like DOS's file format, and vice versa. So the only way to get them to peacefully coexist was to draw a line down the center of the drive, saying in effect, "This is *yours*, DOS, and that's *yours*, Xenix."

So Microsoft and IBM came up with a way to essentially make a 10MB drive into two 5MB drives. (Or a 6 and a 4, or a 2 and an 8, or whatever; you can chop up a drive just about any way you like.) That "chopping up" became known as partitioning.

The program used most often to partition a drive is FDISK, a venerable old program that has been around since the early versions of DOS, and that still comes today with the latest releases of Windows. You can use other, third-party programs, such as PartitionMagic, but the freebie FDISK works just fine.

Most people prefer to allocate all the physical space to a single hard disk letter (C:). However, different situations may call for different configurations. For example, suppose you had a single 18GB drive. You could create two partitions, C: and D:, and install Windows 98 on one of them and Windows 2000, or Linux, or some other operating system on the other. Then each time you started the PC, you could choose which drive to work from (and which operating system to load). This is called *dual-booting,* and it's possible only with multiple partitions.

Partitioning Options

Through the years, partitioning a physical hard disk into multiple logical drives has fallen in and out of fashion. Back when hard disks were small and MS-DOS was king, most people just partitioned their 20MB drives as one big drive and thanked their lucky stars that they had such a large drive. Then, in the mid-'80s, people started buying drives bigger than 32MB, which caused problems because DOS 3.3 couldn't support partitions larger than that size. As a result, people with drives larger than 32MB had to partition their drives into multiple 32MB logical drives. Real power users in those days had 120MB drives that they had to divide into a 32MB C:, 32MB D:, 32MB E:, and 24MB F:. It was a pain, but it was the only option. Then DOS 5 came out, with support for larger partitions, and everybody started having single-partition drives again. Then hard disks got bigger. Windows 95 and MS-DOS 6 supported hard disks up to 2.1GB in size, which seemed like plenty—but then hard disks got bigger again, and people found themselves carving up their 6GB drives. And so it's gone, over and over throughout the years, with hard disk capacity and operating system capability leap-frogging one another.

The latest versions of Windows (95b/98 and above, and NT/2000) provide *large disk support*, which allows you to have a single drive letter with up to 2TB (that's terabyte, which is the next step above a gigabyte), so there's virtually no operating system limitation anymore. Given that, people partition their drives into multiple logical drives for two main reasons: to support multiple operating systems, or as a matter of personal organizational preference. With Windows 95/98 as your operating system, there is also a related issue that fewer people consider: partition efficiency, as I'll explain in the next section.

Efficient Partitions: Clusters and Disks

What do I mean by *partition efficiency*? Well, first of all, I'm talking about systems using FAT16 or FAT32 file systems (essentially, MS-DOS and Windows 95/98 systems). Windows NT/2000 and OS/2 systems have their own native file systems and don't have the efficiency problem that I'm about to describe. For example, Windows NT/2000, by default, uses the NT File System, or NTFS, although it can run on FAT16 or FAT32 if needed (not as efficiently, however).

The file system used in MS-DOS and Windows 95/98 is called the *file allocation table (FAT)* system. (You'll learn more about FAT in Chapter 14, "How Hard Drives Organize Data.") One of the cornerstones of FAT organization is that a FAT-based system allocates space to files in units called *clusters*. A cluster is an area on a hard disk ranging from 2KB to 64KB. (Floppies can have smaller clusters.) The important part about clusters is this: when a program writes a file to disk, it gets the disk space allocated to it by the operating system. When a FAT-based operating system allocates space, it does so cluster by cluster. Each cluster is allocated to one, and only one, file.

There are two variants of FAT: FAT16 and FAT32. *FAT16* is the older of the two. It's a 16-bit file system and has been used since the MS-DOS days. *FAT32* is a newer, more efficient 32-bit version that originated with Windows 95b and continues in Windows 98.

The *size* of a cluster on a logical drive is determined by the size of the logical drive and the file system (FAT16 or FAT32), as you can see in Tables 13.1 and 13.2. Notice that the cluster sizes are smaller on a FAT32 system, making it a more efficient file storage method with less wasted space on the drive.

TABLE 13.1 Relationship between Logical Drive Size and Cluster Size: FAT16

Size of Logical Drive (in MB)	Cluster Size (in KB)
0–15	8
16–127	2
128–255	4
256–511	8
512–1023	16
1024–2047	32
2048–4095	64

TABLE 13.2 Relationship between Logical Drive Size and Cluster Size: FAT32

Size of Logical Drive (in GB)	Cluster Size (in KB)
< 8	4
8–16	8
16–32	16

To understand this whole thing about storage efficiency, and how the FAT system and your disk size play into it, let's look at an example. Suppose you save a 400-byte file on an 80MB logical drive. (I know that's a really tiny drive, but bear with me, just for the sake of discussion.) Clusters on an 80MB drive are 2KB in size, or 2048 bytes, and so those 400 bytes are placed in this 2048-byte cluster, wasting 1648 bytes in the cluster. That's wasteful, but consider the greater amount of wasted space if you stored that 400-byte file on a 3GB logical drive, where clusters are 64KB—65,536 bytes long. The cluster would have 400 useful bytes, and 65,136 bytes thrown away. Because cluster sizes are controlled by logical drive sizes, keeping logical drive sizes down keeps cluster sizes down, which leads to more efficient disk space usage.

Looking at Table 13.1, you see that with the FAT16 file system, the range of logical drive sizes that offer the smallest cluster is the range from 16MB through 127MB. If you had a drive that was

1024MB, then, you could divide it into eight logical drives C:, D:, E:, F:, G:, H:, I:, and J:, each 127MB in size, and you'd even have a bit left on the end for a small logical drive K:.

Is that the right way to divide up a disk? Well, yes and no. If you make one big logical drive of it, then you'd end up with clusters 32KB in size, and that's bad because of all the wasted space. On the other hand, one logical drive is easier to manage, search, and back up. Windows-based programs are so large these days, you might not be able to fit even a single program on one of those 127MB logical disks. So it's a matter of temperament and taste.

Warning

DOS, early versions of Windows 95, and Windows NT 4 cannot recognize FAT32 partitions, so they will not be able to boot from a drive that has been converted from FAT16 to FAT32. Carefully consider your needs before proceeding.

One attractive solution to the whole tiny-drive-versus-wasted-space dilemma is to use FAT32 instead of FAT16. FAT32 makes it much easier to use a single partition on your drive because of its enhanced capacities and smaller cluster size, as seen in Table 13.2. With FAT32, that 1024MB drive could be partitioned into a single logical drive and still have a cluster size of only 4KB. Most drives sold today are much bigger than 1024MB—they're more in the neighborhood of 10GB to 36GB. But when you have a drive that monstrously large, a few wasted clusters are probably not your biggest worry anyway.

Note

All new computers sold today that come with Windows 98 are set up to use FAT32. If you have installed Windows 98 as an upgrade over Windows 95, you can run the FAT32 converter included with Windows 98 to convert the drive from FAT16 to FAT32 without losing any data. (This is an exception to the general rule that you can't mess with the partitions without wiping out the disk content.) You can also buy third-party products such as PartitionMagic that can do the same conversion, plus some other nice things like change the allocation of the space between partitions.

Warning

One little caveat here: you can't convert a drive from FAT16 to FAT32 if you've run a disk compression program on it, such as DriveSpace or Stacker. The two technologies are incompatible with one another. If you have a compressed drive, the best thing to do is copy all your important files off it, then repartition it as a FAT32 drive and reformat it.

FAT16 and FAT32 are by far the most popular file systems in use today, but not the only ones. NTFS is a powerful file system that provides many awesome features for NT/2000 users and system administrators. When you install Windows NT/2000 on an empty drive, you're prompted to choose whether you want to use FAT or NTFS. NTFS will make Windows NT/2000 run most efficiently, but if you later want to remove Windows NT/2000 and install Windows 95/98 on that drive, you'll have to repartition and reformat the drive in order to do so.

How to Partition a Drive

I've talked about the *why*, now let's look at the *how* of partitioning.

Let's suppose you have a 4GB hard disk that you want to divide into three logical drives of 1.5GB, 1.5GB, and 1GB. You use FDISK to partition the drive into two partitions initially, a *primary DOS partition*, and an *extended DOS partition*. (Partitions that use the FAT16 or FAT32 file system are called DOS partitions, regardless of whether you will later load MS-DOS or Windows 95/98 on the drive.) The primary DOS partition can have only one logical drive: C, so you allocate 1.5GB for the primary DOS partition. But you can create as many logical drives as you want out of the space on the extended DOS partition (in this example, two), so you allocate the remaining space (2.5GB) for the extended partition and then create a logical drive D: with 1.5GB and a logical drive E: with 1GB out of it.

If you're working with an additional hard disk (not the system's main one), you can find FDISK in the C:\Windows\Command folder on your main hard disk.

If you're setting up the primary hard disk on a PC, you'll need to boot from a startup disk that contains FDISK. If you create an emergency startup disk using Windows 95/98, FDISK will automatically be included on it.

To partition a drive, follow these steps:

1. At a command prompt, type **FDISK** and press Enter.

2. If your copy of FDISK came from Windows 95b or higher, you'll see a warning like the one in Figure 13.1 asking whether you want to enable large disk support. Choose Y and press Enter.

Figure 13.1

Enable large disk support if prompted.

```
Your computer has a disk larger than 512 MB. This version of Windows
includes improved support for large disks, resulting in more efficient
use of disk space on large drives, and allowing disks over 2 GB to be
formatted as a single drive.

IMPORTANT: If you enable large disk support and create any new drives on this
disk, you will not be able to access the new drive(s) using other operating
systems, including some versions of Windows 95 and Windows NT, as well as
earlier versions of Windows and MS-DOS. In addition, disk utilities that
were not designed explicitly for the FAT32 file system will not be able
to work with this disk. If you need to access this disk with other operating
systems or older disk utilities, do not enable large drive support.

Do you wish to enable large disk support (Y/N)...........? [Y]
```

The main FDISK Options menu appears. Figure 13.2 shows the one from the version of FDISK that comes with Windows 98. Other versions are similar.

Figure 13.2

The FDISK Options menu.

```
                    Microsoft Windows 98
                   Fixed Disk Setup Program
           (C)Copyright Microsoft Corp. 1983 - 1998

                       FDISK Options

Current fixed disk drive: 1

Choose one of the following:

1. Create DOS partition or Logical DOS Drive
2. Set active partition
3. Delete partition or Logical DOS Drive
4. Display partition information


Enter choice: [1]




Press Esc to exit FDISK
```

3. First, check for existing partitions by choosing option 4, Display Partition Information. Existing partition information appears, if any. Figure 13.3 shows a single, primary DOS partition, for example.

Note

If the disk already has a partition, you might not need to partition the drive again—you can simply press Esc until you exit the program and then format the drive(s) with the existing partitions.

```
                        Display Partition Information

Current fixed disk drive: 1

Partition    Status    Type    Volume Label    Mbytes    System    Usage
  C: 1          A      PRI DOS                   4120     FAT32     100%



Total disk space is  4120 Mbytes (1 Mbyte = 1048576 bytes)




Press Esc to continue
```

Figure 13.3

This drive has a primary DOS partition and no extended partitions.

4. If you found existing partitions and you want to delete them and repartition, press Esc to go back to the FDISK Options menu and then do the following:

   a. Choose option 3, Delete Partition or Logical DOS Drive.

   b. If you have logical DOS drives on an extended partition, delete them first (option 3, see Figure 13.4). You can't delete an extended partition until you have first removed its logical drives.

   c. After you have deleted all the logical drives from the extended partition, delete the extended partition itself (option 2, Figure 13.4). You can't delete the primary partition until you have first deleted the extended one.

d. After you have deleted the extended partition, delete the primary partition (option 1, Figure 13.4).

e. After deleting all partitions, press Esc to return to the FDISK Options menu.

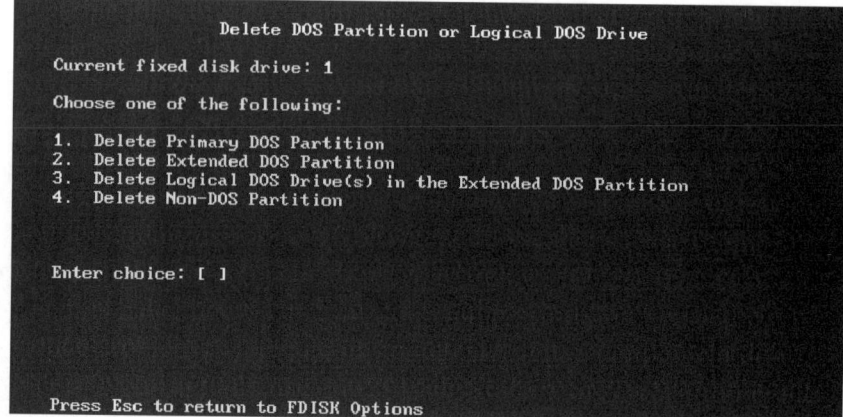

Figure 13.4

Delete logical drives and partitions here.

5. Now create the primary DOS partition by doing the following:

a. Choose option 1, Create DOS Partition or Logical DOS Drive.

b. Choose option 1, Create Primary DOS Partition.

c. When asked whether you want to use the maximum available size for the Primary DOS partition, choose Yes or No. If you want to follow along with the example I'm working through here, where you create three logical drives, you would choose No.

d. If you answered No, enter the amount of space, either in megabytes or in percentage, that you want to allocate to the primary DOS partition (that is, the C: drive). For example, to create a 1.5GB partition, type **1500**. See Figure 13.5.

e. Press Esc to return to the FDISK Options menu.

```
                        Create Primary DOS Partition
Current fixed disk drive: 1




Total disk space is  4120 Mbytes (1 Mbyte = 1048576 bytes)
Maximum space available for partition is  4120 Mbytes (100% )

Enter partition size in Mbytes or percent of disk space (%) to
create a Primary DOS Partition.....................................: [ 1500]


Press Esc to return to FDISK Options
```

Figure 13.5

Allocate space for the
primary DOS
partition.

6. If you chose not to allocate all the space to the primary partition, it is not set automatically as the active partition. It must be active in order to be bootable. To make your primary partition active, do the following:

a. From the FDISK Options menu, choose option 2, Set Active Partition.

b. Type **1** to select partition 1 as the active one and press Enter.

c. Press Esc to return to the FDISK Options menu.

7. Next, set up your extended partition using the remaining space, by doing the following:

a. From the FDISK Options menu, choose 1, Create DOS Partition or Logical DOS Drive.

b. Choose option 2, Create Extended DOS Partition.

c. Leave the default setting for the extended partition size, which is all of the remaining space, and press Enter.

d. Press Esc to verify the drive integrity. You're then prompted to define the logical drives.

e. Enter the amount of space to allocate to the next logical drive (D:). Leave the default to use the entire extended partition for it, or enter a specific size in megabytes or percentage. For our example, to make D: a 1.5GB partition, you would type **1500**.

f. Enter the amount of space for the next logical drive (E:). For our example, leave the default to use all remaining space on the drive.

g. When you are finished assigning all the remaining space on the extended partition, press Esc to return to the FDISK Options menu.

8. You're done partitioning! Press Esc to exit FDISK and then reboot your PC.

Warning

Do not attempt to format or use the drives until you have rebooted. That's because drive letter assignments change when you partition, and the drive letters you booted with will no longer be correct.

How DOS Names Partitions

Your operating system assigns drive letters to the various logical drives on your system, but how does it decide which logical drive gets what name? The answer may surprise you.

If you have one physical drive with three logical drives defined on it, as in the example in the preceding section, the naming is simple. The logical drive in the primary DOS partition is named C:, and the two in the extended partition are named D: and E:. But suppose you have *two* physical drives that are each divided into three logical drives? How are *they* named?

Answer: it depends on whether there's a primary DOS partition on the second drive. It is acceptable for the second physical drive to contain only an extended partition, unlike the first physical drive, which *must* have a primary DOS partition before it can have an extended partition. It is also acceptable if the second physical drive has both a primary and an extended DOS partition.

▶ *If the second drive has both a primary and extended partition*, then the primary partition on the first drive is C:, the primary partition on the second drive is D: (surprise!), the two (in our example) logical drives in the extended partition on the first drive are named E: and F:, and the two logical drives in the extended partition on the second drive are named G: and H:.

▶ *If the second drive has only an extended partition*, then the primary partition on the first physical drive is C:, again, and this time the logical drives in the extended partition on that first physical drive are named D: and E:. The three logical drives in the extended partition on the second drive are named F:, G:, and H:.

Partitioning Large Drives with Device Drivers

If you have an old computer that you want to add a new, very large hard disk to, you may run into a little snag. Very old systems, which were built before gigantic hard disks were even dreamed of, can't recognize and take advantage of *logical block addressing (LBA)*. LBA is a method used to translate the cylinder, head, and sector specifications of a large drive (over 528MB) so they're usable by the system. In this case, we're talking about the physical hard disk, not a logical drive. Without LBA, a PC can't use a hard disk larger than 528MB (roughly half a gigabyte).

The solution is to use a driver that functions as a BIOS extender. It loads when the PC starts, and helps the PC recognize and work with the drive to its full potential.

Here's how it works: When you use a driver-type installer for a disk, it reworks your partitions so that you have a small primary DOS partition and a large non-DOS one. It then boots your PC from the small, recognizable partition and uses a driver in CONFIG.SYS to trick the operating system into thinking that the large, non-DOS partition is actually the primary, bootable drive.

Most hard disks sold today come with a SETUP disk that installs the needed drivers to configure the drive on an older PC. It's important to use the disk that came with the drive, because the program is often tailored to work specifically with that drive manufacturer's hardware. You can usually download the program for free from the manufacturer's Web site if you get a second-hand disk that no longer has a SETUP disk with it.

For the most part, this driver-based drive setup works fine. Here are a few caveats, however:

▶ Driver-based drive setup is not compatible with every old PC. Older PCs are worse than today's in terms of standardization, and some older PCs are not 100 percent compatible. I have run into systems that it wouldn't work with, notably some older Compaqs. You won't know until you try.

▶ Non-DOS operating systems, as I've mentioned before, cannot access these alien partitions set up by the driver-based drive setup. You would be unable to run OS/2 or Unix on a system employing it.

▶ It's one more source of bugs. I'm not saying any one brand of program in particular is buggy. But the more software, the more bugs and potential software conflicts.

▶ The driver requires a line in your CONFIG.SYS file in order to load. If CONFIG.SYS gets deleted, the drive won't be recognizable.

With slightly newer systems, (circa 1995 or so), you may run into another problem: the BIOS does not support drives larger than 2GB or 8.4GB (depending on the system age), even with LBA. Such limitations can't always be overcome with the free utilities that come with the hard disk. It depends on the utility and its capabilities. On such a system, the BIOS may acknowledge the drive's existence but claim that it is a smaller size than it is, or it may not acknowledge the drive at all.

If you run into this situation, you have two choices. You can let the drive function as the size that the BIOS thinks it is, regardless of its larger actual size (if the BIOS sees the drive at all), or you can buy a third-party disk management program. There are several good programs on the market that overcome the BIOS drive size limitation. You may want to investigate Disk Manager DiskGo! (by OnTrack), Drive Up (by FWB Software), and EZ Drive (by MicroHouse). These programs work by telling the BIOS that the drive is a smaller size, and then using a driver loaded at startup to amend that data so that the full size of the drive can be recognized by the operating system when it loads.

Warning

The only caveat you need to be aware of is when booting from a floppy. Usually drives that are installed this way need to self-boot to load the drivers they need to access all the space. Booting from a floppy can prevent this. So check the instructions on the driver. To boot from a floppy, you may need to press a key at boot time. This loads the driver and then returns you to a prompt that lets you run a floppy afterward.

Backing Up Partition Information

Having gone through all that work to create the DOS partition, you may wonder, *what happens if the partition information is destroyed?* This is a real problem: in this situation, the PC will refuse to even recognize that a disk exists. The data's not erased, but it might as well be. The way you solve this problem is with prevention: back up the partition information. There are several ways to do this, and I'll show you a number of them in Chapter 16, "Care and Feeding of Hard Drives."

Formatting

Finally, you run the FORMAT program. Formatting a disk does not actually overwrite the data on the disk; rather, it wipes clean the record of what's stored on the disk, marking the data area of the disk as available for data storage.

What does that mean, exactly? Well, I'll get into all the details in Chapter 14, but for now, just understand that there are more areas on a disk besides the data area, where data is stored that you copy to the disk. One of these areas is the FAT, which keeps track of which files are stored in which locations. When you format a disk, the FAT is re-created, along with a few other special system features of the disk, but the data area is left untouched. That means that your data is still there on the disk, even after reformatting. Utility programs such as Norton Utilities can sometimes be used to *unformat* a disk to retrieve some of that information.

The process for formatting a hard disk depends on the operating system. In MS-DOS, you use the FORMAT *drive letter*: command at the command prompt. You can do the same thing when booting from a startup disk created with Windows 9*x*.

When you install Windows (95/98/NT/2000), if the hard disk on which you are installing has not been formatted, the installation program will format it for you—no muss, no fuss.

To format a hard disk from *within* Windows (95/98/NT/2000), you can right-click the drive icon and choose Format from the shortcut menu. Of course, you can't do this to your boot hard disk (that is, the one that contains the files that are running Windows); you can do it only with a secondary hard disk you are adding.

A Note about Bad Areas

You may have heard it said that reformatting a hard disk will get rid of bad areas on the disk. This isn't true—not exactly, anyway.

When you format a disk, it runs a cursory check of the disk for bad areas and excludes those bad areas from the formatting. However, not all bad areas are immediately obvious.

Bad areas have either *hard* errors or *soft* errors. Hard errors are problems in the disk surface itself, wherein it cannot record data at all. They are caused by manufacturing defects or later abuse. Soft errors, in contrast, occur when some data has faded on the disk to the point where it cannot be read. Disk repair programs, such as ScanDisk and Norton Utilities, fix such errors by retrieving any data they can from the area and then cordoning off the area as "bad" so it won't be used again (kind of like a hazardous waste dump for your system).

When you reformat a drive, it retains its memory of the hard errors, but not the soft ones. Some of the areas previously marked as bad therefore appear to be good again, but any data that you copy to them may be in peril.

Therefore, after reformatting a hard disk that contained many errors, you should run a disk utility such as ScanDisk in its Thorough mode to thoroughly check each physical sector of the disk for errors. ScanDisk comes free with Windows 95/98/2000/NT.

Third-Party Partitioning and Formatting Tools

You may be surprised that you don't have to use the tools shipped with DOS and Windows to partition and format your drives. There are several very good third-party tools available, for a moderate cost, of course.

The leading third-party partitioning tool is PartitionMagic. Not only can you partition and format your hard disks, but you can also install multiple operating systems on your computer, each independent of the others, and choose which one to boot each time you start your PC. PartitionMagic also enables you to reallocate the disk space between logical drives on the same physical hard disk without losing any of the data on the drives. You can also switch between FAT16 and FAT32.

System Commander, by V Communications, is another top-notch tool with similar capabilities. You may also want to check out Disk Manager DiskGo! (by OnTrack), Drive Up (FWB Software), and EZ Drive (MicroHouse), all of which I mentioned earlier for partitioning help, but which offer a full range of partitioning and formatting utilities.

Troubleshooting Tips

Patience is said to be a virtue, and with hard disks that truism is, well, true. Basically, if you make a mistake while using FDISK or formatting a drive and catch it before you install an operating system and several hundred megabytes of software, you can pretty easily recover. If you don't find out until days later, well . . . here are some tips.

▶ If your computer won't boot from your hard drive, run FDISK again and check to see that the partition you have your OS installed on is set as the active partition.

▶ If FDISK reports a disk size that isn't true, your BIOS may be incorrectly identifying your hard drive. Run your BIOS setup program and confirm that the size is correct, and try running FDISK again.

▶ An older BIOS may not recognize newer hard disks, especially those over 2GB or 8.4GB (depending on the system age). If this is the case, you should update your BIOS if possible. You may have to use special software provided by your hard disk manufacturer to fool your BIOS into recognizing the disk.

▶ No access to FORMAT? Perhaps, not a problem. If you are planning to install Windows on the new hard disk, you may not need to bother with formatting the drive. Simply boot from your Windows CD (if your system allows you to boot from a CD—check the Boot Sequence settings in your BIOS) and let the SETUP program format the disk for you.

▶ Formatting a disk does not automatically make it bootable. If you've started the PC with a startup floppy made with Windows 95/98, use the /S switch with the FORMAT command (FORMAT C: /S) to copy the system files needed to boot along with the formatting operation.

14

How Hard Drives
Organize Data

I n the last four chapters, I've talked about the details of how your disk hardware works. But disk repair requires understanding disk software more than disk hardware. In this chapter, I'll show you how DOS (and Windows of all varieties in one form or another, for that matter) stores data on your disk.

You may be telling yourself, well, even I know about FAT32. What's all this with DOS? That's a good question with a good answer. Understanding the low-level DOS file structure, FAT, is the easiest and fastest way to understand all other file systems. DOS is easy to learn and quick to understand. Get the basics in DOS and you'll move forward swiftly.

This chapter also covers NTFS, the file system native to Windows NT and Windows 2000. We'll take a look at its main features and benefits.

The Basics

In simple disk-based systems, all you need to know about files is their location. In one early disk-based computer that I worked with, you'd keep track of files by noting their cylinder/head/sector location. It didn't have much of a user interface—you specified the address of a file, then the computer read it and executed it. You'd generally start up the system by loading the word processor (not a great one, as you'd expect, but better than a typewriter). This was a bit cumbersome because, you see, if I lost the address of my word processor, that meant I essentially lost the word processing program forever. I couldn't say "execute the program WP," which would have been preferable, but rather "execute cylinder 0, head 0, and sector 1."

After the word processor loaded, however, things looked much nicer. You could pick out a text file by name, load it, and work with it—you didn't have to know its address. That was possible because the word processor took a certain number of sectors for itself, sectors that it used to store documents. I didn't have to know the document's address because the word processor kept its own little directory to the sectors that it had taken over for documents. You'd ask for a file, say LETTER1.DOC. The word processor would look up LETTER1.DOC in its directory, see that LETTER1.DOC started in some cylinder/head/sector, and note how many sectors it was. Then the word processor would load up those sectors, and away you went.

That was a nice, simple system, but it had a few major drawbacks. The biggest problem was that only the word processor knew that the files existed. The BASIC interpreter or the simple database manager that came with the system was totally ignorant of the files because it was totally ignorant of the directory that the word processor kept for its own personal uses. The system also lacked most of the pieces of basic file maintenance. Space wasn't recovered well when files were erased, data recovery tools didn't exist, and if the disks hadn't been small floppies, the system probably would never have worked. Using such a system to manage a hard disk would be silly.

That's a major reason why we have DOS and Windows (despite the Microsoft claims, up until FAT32 was introduced in 1995, DOS and Windows pretty much stored data in the same way). DOS provided a central space and file management unit. An area that Lotus 1-2-3 sees as a file named `FINANCE.WK1` is the exact same area that WordPerfect sees as a file named `FINANCE.WK1`. That way, any program can find any file, and no program will inadvertently write over another program's files (unless something goes very wrong).

Note

FAT32 doesn't change things drastically; it just allows for the space of larger drives to be used in a more efficient manner. It also allows for better long file-name support, something DOS still doesn't do without help. I'll talk more about FAT32 later in this chapter.

In this chapter, you'll learn that DOS manages files with a tree-structured directory and a construct called the file allocation table (FAT). You'll learn that space is managed with groups of sectors called clusters, a topic that I've discussed briefly already, but that I'll go into in more detail shortly.

How DOS Organizes Disk Areas: Overview

You're now familiar with some terms: you know of tracks, cylinders, and such. Each OS organizes data in its own way. DOS sees data in the following way:

▶ Disks are divided into *absolute*, or *physical*, sectors.

▶ Absolute sectors map to *DOS* sectors.

▶ The DOS sectors are grouped into clusters.

▶ A file's *directory entry* includes the first cluster number in the file. That is the initial pointer into the FAT, which keeps track of where files are located.

▶ The FAT contains information that DOS uses to locate the remaining clusters. There's a FAT entry for each cluster.

A FAT entry can be:

- ◗ A number, which acts as a pointer to another cluster
- ◗ A zero, indicating an unused cluster
- ◗ A bad sector marking
- ◗ An end of file (EOF) indicator

Absolute Sectors and DOS Sectors

Identifying an area on a disk by its cylinder/head/sector refers to what DOS folks call its *absolute sector:* cylinder *x*, head *y*, sector *z*. This is illustrated in Figure 14.1. I have referred to this form of addressing as *three-dimensional* elsewhere in this book.

1. Finding the sector at head 5, cylinder 40, sector 1 is a three-step process.

3. Then, cylinder 40 narrows it to track 40 on surface 5.

Figure 14.1

Three-dimensional addressing: identifying an area on a disk by its cylinder/head/sector

2. First, head 5 defines which surface the sector is on.

4. And finally, sector 1 shows the sector.

DOS doesn't directly use absolute sector locations. Instead, it refers to sectors with a single number called a *relative sector number* or *DOS sector number*. The number system is called relative rather than absolute because it numbers the sectors in order from front to back of a disk. There's no "cylinder 100, head 2, sector 1," instead there's "sector 15,421."

When using relative sector numbering, DOS orders sectors by starting at cylinder 0, head 1, sector 1: this is *DOS sector 0*. (Note that cylinder 0, head *0*, sector 1 does not have a DOS sector number designation: it is "out of bounds," as far as DOS is concerned.) The remaining sectors on the track are DOS sectors 2 through 16, assuming that a track has 17 sectors. DOS then moves to the next head, head 2. The 17 sectors on cylinder 0, head 2, are the next 17 DOS sectors, numbers 17 through 33. DOS keeps moving up the heads until the cylinder is exhausted, and then moves to head 0 of cylinder 1. It continues in this fashion, moving farther and farther inward toward the center of the disk.

You can relate the absolute address of a sector to its relative sector if you know the following information:

DH Head that the DOS Boot Record (DBR) is located on (more to come on the DBR later in this chapter)

DC Cylinder that the DBR is located on

DS Sector that the DBR is located on

NS Number of sectors per track on this disk

NH Number of heads on this disk

Assuming that you have a C, H, and S (cylinder, head, and sector) address for a sector, you find its relative sector (let's call it RS) like so:

$$RS = NH \times NS \times [(C - DC) + NS] \times [(H - DH) + (S - DS)]$$

For example, suppose you've got a logical drive D: with its DBR on cylinder 100, head 1, and sector 1. The disk has 4 heads and 17 sectors per track. What is the relative sector number of the sector at the absolute address of cylinder 140, head 3, and sector 4?

DH = 1

DC = 100

DS = 1

NS = 17

NH = 4

Relative sector = $4 \times 17 \times [(140 - 100) + 17] \times [(3 - 1) + (4 - 1)] = 2757$

The relative sector number is 2757.

How about computing the absolute location of a sector from its relative sector? Before you can do that, let me define some notation: DIV and MOD. *DIV* means do a division, but throw away the remainder. For example, 7 DIV 3 equals 2, not 2.33. *MOD* means do the division but *keep* the remainder—throw away the quotient. So 7 MOD 3 equals 1, because when you divide 7 by 3 you get 2 with a remainder of 1.

Given the same definitions of RS, DC, DH, DS, NS, and NH, you find the absolute cylinder, head, and sector by using the following formulas. Remember, this time you already know RS, NS, NH, DH, DC, and DS, and you're looking for C (cylinder), H (head), and S (sector).

S = (RS MOD NS) + DS

Temp = RS DIV NS

Temp is a temporary variable you use and then throw away. It makes writing the formulas easier.

H = (Temp MOD NH) + DH

C = (Temp DIV NH) + DC

Let's try it out on the example you've already done. You've got relative sector 2757 on a disk with 4 heads and 17 sectors per track. The sector's logical drive has a DBR on cylinder 100, head 1, and sector 1.

Collect what you know so far:

$DC = 100$

$DH = 1$

$DS = 1$

$NH = 4$

$NS = 17$

$RS = 2757$

And then start calculating:

$S = (2757 \text{ MOD } 17) + 1 = 3 + 1 = 4$

$Temp = 2757 \text{ DIV } 17 = 162$

$H = (162 \text{ MOD } 4) + 1 = 2 + 1 = 3$

$C = (162 \text{ DIV } 4) + 100 = 140$

So relative sector 2757 turns out to be at cylinder 140, head 3, sector 4.

This sector-numbering notation is also known as a *linear sector address*. Why use DOS (relative) sector numbers in the first place? One reason is that they are hardware independent. All DOS assumes about the drive is that it consists of a bunch of sectors, and each sector contains 512 bytes. Another possible reason is that every four or eight sectors are grouped into a cluster, and it's easier to divide up a one-dimensional number like a DOS sector than it would be to have to constantly figure out that cluster 200 is on cylinder 40, head 2, sectors 15–17 and cylinder 40, head 3, sector 1. (I just made those numbers up, so don't try to figure out where I got them from.)

Clusters

Next, as I mentioned previously, DOS sectors are grouped into clusters.

A *cluster* is the minimum space allocated by DOS when DOS gives space to a file. For example, if you create a file that is 1 byte long, you don't take up just a byte on the disk, but instead the minimum allocation—a cluster. Cluster size varies with the disk type and size, as you can see from Table 14.1. Floppy disks use clusters that are just one sector long, but a 10GB hard disk uses clusters that are many sectors long—4096 bytes (4KB). That means that a 1-byte file on a single-sided floppy would take up 512 bytes on the disk, as would a 500-byte file. On the other hand, a 1-byte file would take up thousands of bytes on a 10GB disk drive. Note that Table 14.1 includes cluster sizes for NTFS, a non-DOS-based filing system which I discuss later in this chapter.

TABLE 14.1 Cluster Sizes

Disk Type	Cluster Size (Bytes)	Sectors per Cluster
Single-sided floppy	512	1
Double-sided floppy	1024	2
3½" 720KB floppy	1024	2
3½" 1.44MB floppy	512	1
5¼" 1.2MB floppy	1024	2
0MB–15MB logical drive	4096	8
16MB–127MB logical drive	2048	4
128MB–255MB logical drive	4096	8
256MB–512MB logical drive	8192	16
512MB–1024MB logical drive	16,384	32
1024MB–2048MB logical drive	32,768	64
2048MB–4095MB logical drive	65,536	128
4096MB–8GB	4096 (FAT32 only)	* 64
9GB–16GB	8192 (FAT32 only)	* 64
17GB–32GB	16,384 (FAT32 only)	* 64
32GB and above	32,768 (FAT32 only)	* 64

Continued on next page

TABLE 14.1 Cluster Sizes (continued)

Disk Type	Cluster Size (Bytes)	Sectors per Cluster
2048MB–4095MB	4096 (NTFS only)	8
4096MB–8GB	8192 (NTFS only)	16
9GB–16GB	16,384 (NTFS only)	32
17GB–32GB	32,768 (NTFS only)	64
32GB and above	65,536 (NTFS only)	128

* Note: FAT32 allows for cluster counts between 65,526 and 268,435,456 clusters

Think of the following analogy. Two airline shuttles operate out of Ronald Reagan National Airport, in Washington, D.C., where I live. They both promise a seat, with no reservation required, on a jet flying from Washington, D.C. to New York every hour. Say you're the person running those shuttles and that the jets used can accommodate 100 people. How many jets must you run this hour? If you've got 1 to 100 people, run one jet. Just one person—the 101st person—forces you to go to a second jet. There are no half jets.

Depending on what kind of storage medium DOS uses, different-sized "jets" are used. First the floppies appeared, then the 10MB disk drives, then the 1.2MB floppies, and now the 16⁺MB drives. DOS versions 4.*x* and later support drives up to 512MB in size—they use a 16-bit FAT (65,536 entries) and clusters of size 8192. Today, all new systems can support drives that contain many gigabytes of data.

You've seen that cylinders and heads are counted starting at 0, and that sectors start at 1, so it won't be *too* strange when I tell you that clusters start at number *2*. By the way, clusters start only in the data area, after the FAT and directory.

Note that the largest logical drives available are the 4GB drives. That's because DOS is built upon a processor architecture that can handle data objects up to only 64KB, and the 4GB drive requires 64KB-sized sectors. A bigger drive would require bigger sectors, and DOS can't handle sectors that big.

DOS Boot Record

The starting point in the DOS partition is the first sector, called, you will recall, DOS sector 0. That sector always contains an important piece of program code called the *DOS Boot Record* (*DBR*). That's the code that's used to boot up the system, in combination with the partition record and the so-called "hidden" files. I'll explain in greater detail what the DBR does a bit later, but for now understand that it resides in the first DOS sector.

As DOS has evolved into its various versions, the DBR has also taken another important role. A table in the beginning of the DBR contains a bunch of disk ID information. Early versions of DOS pretty much ignored the table, but later versions need it. One byte on the table is pretty deadly—if set to a particular value, it keeps the system from booting from either the hard disk *or* the floppy. You'll see more about that in Chapter 16, "Care and Feeding of Hard Drives."

The FAT and the Directory

As I said earlier, the directory and the FAT work as a team in locating files. The directory tells you the names of your files, and the FAT tells you each file's location. Take a look at Figure 14.2.

The FAT immediately follows the DBR on the disk—it always begins on sector 1. The operating system then stores two copies of the FAT—the primary FAT and one for backup—right next to each other. The FAT's size will vary according to how large the partition is.

The FAT is then immediately followed by the root directory. Directory entries are 32 bytes long, and the root contains space for 512 entries on a hard disk, or fewer entries for floppies, depending on the floppy type. The exact number of root entries is stored in the DBR. The data then follows the root on the disk.

Table 14.2 compares FAT/FAT32 and NTFS, Windows NT's file system that I'll discuss later in this chapter.

Each file has a directory entry telling DOS the file's name, size, last date altered, and the like.

Figure 14.2

The file allocation table (FAT) and the directory work together to locate files.

The entry then includes a pointer to the FAT, which tells DOS exactly which sectors the file resides within.

TABLE 14.2 FAT/FAT32 and NTFS

FAT and FAT32	NTFS
Cluster size determined by disk volume size	Cluster size determined by disk volume size and is adjustable
Files are placed in first free location on disk	No special areas on disk requiring file placement
Supports only READ-ONLY, SYSTEM, ARCHIVE, and HIDDEN attributes	Supports FAT/FAT32 attributes and additional Time Stamp and compression
Eight characters for a filename, and three characters for a file extension (255 for filename in FAT32)	Supports long filenames and FAT 8.3 filenames
Only one file allocation table (increased chance of corruption/lost data)	Multiple copies of Master File Table kept on disk

A file's name and extension are self-explanatory. Of course, while DOS and Windows 3.1 are limited to eight characters plus a three-character extension, Windows 95/98/2000/NT can have filenames that are as long as 255 characters. You may not know about the attributes, however. The one-attribute byte is viewed by DOS as eight attribute *bits*, six of which are used:

ARCHIVE Is set (= 1) if the file has not been backed up, reset (= 0) otherwise.

HIDDEN If set, the file is invisible to most DOS functions.

READ-ONLY If set, tells DOS not to allow changes or erasure of the file.

SYSTEM Says, "Don't move this file."

LABEL Indicates that this directory entry is not a file entry at all, but the disk label. That's why disk labels can be up to 11 characters—the label name uses the space taken up by a filename and a file extension.

DIRECTORY Means that this directory entry does not point to a normal file, but rather to a subdirectory. Subdirectory information is stored in a file-like construct, hence the directory entry.

By the way, the read-only and archive bits can be manipulated by DOS's ATTRIB command. Set a file to read-only with ATTRIB + R *filename*, and you won't accidentally erase it (−R removes the read-only status).

The starting cluster number tells DOS where a file begins; the FAT tells where the rest of the file is. The starting cluster number is vital, then, as it is your link into the FAT. Finally, the last four bytes contain the file size in bytes.

Each cluster on the disk has a corresponding FAT entry. Given an entry for cluster x, the entry must be one of the following:

0 Indicates that the cluster is unallocated.

EOF (actually any value from hex FFF8 to FFFF) Indicates that it is the last cluster in a file.

BAD (actually hex FFF7) Indicates that the cluster contains a bad sector or sectors and should not be used.

Nonzero cluster number Is a pointer to the *next* cluster in the file that x is a part of.

Figure 14.3 shows an excerpt from a FAT with entries relevant to the ORDERS.DAT directory being added to that directory.

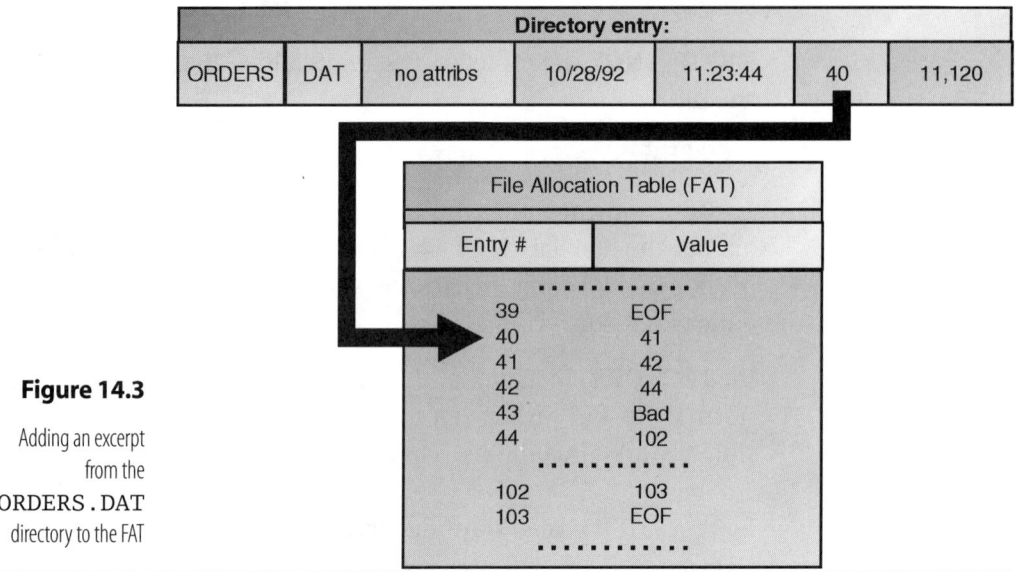

Figure 14.3

Adding an excerpt from the ORDERS.DAT directory to the FAT

Reading this FAT excerpt, you can see that cluster 39 is the end of some file—you don't know which file. You start looking for ORDERS.DAT in cluster 40 because the directory entry *told* you to: entry 40 contains 41, meaning that 41 follows 40 as the next cluster in ORDERS.DAT. Entry 41 contains 42, meaning that 42 is the next cluster in ORDERS.DAT. Entry 42 contains 44, telling you to skip 43, which was skipped because it is a cluster with unusable areas in it—a bad cluster. Entry 44 tells you to skip to cluster 102 for the next cluster, and 102 points you to 103, which is the end of the file.

Note that each cluster's FAT entry in a file links to the next cluster's FAT entry in that file. This is called a *one-way linked list*, one way because you can follow it in only one direction. (If this is unclear, look only at entry 103, the EOF for ORDERS.DAT. Looking only at that entry, what would tell you that 102 was the previous entry? Nothing. On the other hand, the FAT *will* tell you to go from 102 to 103.)

Subdirectories

Now let's add subdirectories to the preceding example.

The subdirectory structure in DOS is implemented with very little change over what I've said so far. Subdirectories look like files, as far as DOS is concerned, except (1) they have a size equal to zero, and (2) their DIRECTORY attribute bit is set. The subdirectory itself resides in a cluster or clusters, and is arranged identically to the root directory, *except* for the first two entries. You know the "." and ".." files that you see whenever you type DIR in a subdirectory? They actually have file entries. The "." and ".." are stolen from old Unix terminology. The ".." entry refers to the subdirectory itself, and the "." refers to the parent of the subdirectory. Those entries, like other subdirectory entries, do not have sizes. The entry for "." (the self-referencing one), reports the *starting cluster* equal to the cluster that the subdirectory *itself* exists in. The entry for ".." reports the starting cluster of the parent directory. If the parent is the root, the cluster value is set to 0. I know that sounds complicated, so here are some examples.

Suppose you have a subdirectory called C:\JUNK, and the subdirectory was created on December 31, 1998. Let's further suppose that the subdirectory itself is in cluster 5000. This does *not* mean that the files in the subdirectory are in cluster 5000—it means that the actual information about the names and such of the files in \JUNK can be found in cluster 5000. The root entry for \JUNK in the root directory would look like this:

Name	Ext	Size	Date	Time	Cluster	Attribs
JUNK		0	12/31/98	8:03 p	5000	directory

Suppose further that \JUNK contains only one file, A.TXT, created on January 1, 1999, that it starts in cluster 6000, and is 100 bytes long. If you looked in the contents of cluster 5000 to see the actual subdirectory structure of \JUNK, you'd see the following.

Name	Ext	Size	Date	Time	Cluster	Attribs
.		0	12/31/98	8:03 p	5000	directory
..		0	12/31/98	8:03 p	0	directory
A	TXT	100	01/01/99	7:00 p	6000	no attribs

Silly though they seem, those two entries must be the first two entries in a subdirectory, or CHKDSK says that the subdirectory is invalid. (CHKDSK's "cure" is worse than the complaint, so when CHKDSK offers to convert the subdirectory to a file, tell it to take a walk. More on this later in Chapter 16.)

A.TXT was a simple example, as it takes up only one cluster. (Why? Because it's 100 bytes long.) If the file were longer than one cluster, DOS would simply follow the same procedure as with ORDERS.DAT—look in the FAT for entry 6000, read what's in there, and follow the FAT chain to the end of the file.

Let's summarize how a file in a subdirectory is read by DOS. Say you're reading the file ORDERS.DAT from the subdirectory you've just examined, C:\JUNK. DOS performs the following steps:

1. DOS looks in the root directory for an entry with the name JUNK that has its DIRECTORY attribute set. It notes the starting cluster of JUNK—suppose it is 5000, as in our example.

2. DOS goes to the FAT and looks up entry 5000 to see if the subdirectory information extends over several clusters. Most subdirectories can fit easily in one cluster, so DOS probably sees EOF in entry 5000. (Why do most subdirectories fit in one cluster? Most hard disk clusters are 2048 bytes, and each directory entry is 32 bytes long. That's enough space for 2048/32, or 64, directory entries. Most subdirectories don't have more than 64 files in them.)

3. DOS reads cluster 5000 and assumes that the data is formatted as in the root directory. It looks for a directory entry called ORDERS.DAT and notes the starting cluster. Suppose the starting cluster is 40.

4. DOS returns to the FAT and examines entry 40. Suppose 40 contains 41; that means that the file is not only in cluster 40, but also in 41.

5. Next, DOS continues examining the FAT, looking in entry 41. Suppose 41 contains 42; the file continues in cluster 42.

6. Assume that the remainder of the file search goes as in the earlier ORDERS . DAT example. Then DOS is done.

Notice that finding ORDERS . DAT in a subdirectory was the same as finding it in the root, except for the first two steps.

Logical Drive Structure

Ever since PC-DOS 3.3 (MS-DOS 3.2), it's been possible to create multiple logical drives out of a single physical drive. This section explains how they are organized.

In the case of a simple disk system, the PC looks first to the partition table to find where a partition exists; the partition entry then points to the first sector of the partition, which, by the way, contains the code to boot from that partition. You've already seen how that works with the primary DOS partition. Suppose there were a 16,384-cylinder, 16-head drive that contained a primary DOS partition in the first 8192 cylinders and a Xenix partition in the last 8192 cylinders. That's one 4.2GB logical drive for DOS and one 4.2GB logical drive for Xenix. (Note that the drive has 63 sectors per track.) The disk structure would then look like Figure 14.4.

Cylinder 0, head 0, sector 1: MBR

Figure 14.4

Disk structure of a 16-head drive with a 4.2GB primary DOS partition and a 4.2GB Xenix partition

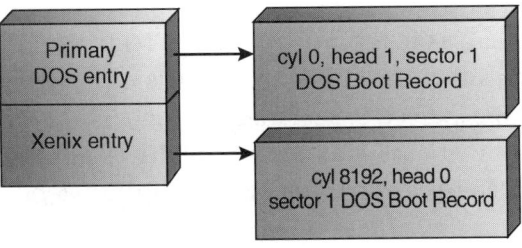

It would seem that a similar arrangement occurs with a logical drive (let's call it drive D: in this case) in an extended DOS partition: the partition points to the DBR of drive D:, and everything is normal.

But it doesn't work that way. It *can't* work that way, as there can be *multiple* logical drives in the extended partition. You would have a way to find the first logical drive, but how to find the others? There's a one-to-one relationship between partition table entries and DBRs for primary partitions, but not for extended partitions.

DOS makes one extended partition look like multiple drives by creating a set of fake Master Boot Records for the extended partition, one for each logical drive in the extended partition. The real MBR's partition table points to the extended partition. The first sector of the extended partition is not the DBR for a logical drive, but an extended partition table (EPT)—the first bogus MBR. Examining that EPT, you see a record pointing to the next track, where the DBR for drive D: (the first logical drive in the extended partition) resides. Let's use the 16,384-cylinder drive again, but this time make the second 8192 cylinders an extended DOS partition with a single logical drive. Take a look at Figure 14.5.

Figure 14.5

Disk structure of a 16-head drive with a 4.2GB primary DOS partition and a 4.2GB extended DOS partition

Cylinder 0, head 0, sector 1: MBR

| Primary DOS entry | → | cyl 0, head 1, sector 1 DOS Boot Record for C: |

| Extended DOS partition entry | → | cyl 512, head 0, sector 1 Extended Partition Table: Primary DOS partition | → | cyl 512, head 1, sector 1 DOS Boot Record for drive D: |

Note that, as in the case of the real MBR, the EPT wastes the rest of the track that the EPT is on. There is nothing in the sectors in cylinder 8192, head 0, sectors 2 through 63.

What if there are multiple logical drives in the extended DOS partition? Then there is a chain of EPTs. If the extended partition in our example were divided into two logical drives named D: and E:, the first EPT would contain two entries—the primary DOS entry for D: and an extended DOS entry pointing to the start of drive E. Examination of the sector pointed to would show *another* EPT, this time with only one entry—a primary DOS partition for drive E: To illustrate this, assume that cylinders 8192 through 12,000 are used by logical drive D:, and 12,001 through the end by logical drive E:. Take a look at Figure 14.6.

Cylinder 0, head 0, sector 1: MBR

Figure 14.6

MBR-to-DBR relationship with three logical drives

So the only way that DOS can find logical drives other than C: is to wend its way through the chain of EPTs on the disk. That's why FDISK shows a slight pause when moving from the Create Extended Partition function to the Create Logical Drives part—it's searching the chain. Once FDISK is done, the hard drive is partitioned, After that, all you have to do is format the partitions, and it's ready to store data.

FAT32

FAT32 was somewhat of a fix for the limitation in FAT16 and Microsoft's way of catching up to the quickly growing hard disk market. FAT32 provides a number of enhancements over any previous FAT, but is still lacking in areas of security and advanced data management, so it can't take over for NTFS. Here's a quick look at what's been enhanced:

▶ It can see up to 2TB (terabytes!).

▶ Clusters are as small as 4KB for drives up to 8GB.

▶ It is not limited to storing the root directory at the top of the drive.

▶ Root directory limitations have been removed because it is now a cluster chain, which can be located anywhere on the drive.

▶ FATs are more recoverable and flexible.

▶ It can be dynamically resized.

FAT32, however, is *not* security oriented, the way NTFS is. Any modifications can be made by any user to a FAT32 directory structure. The big gain comes to you, where you can save as much as 20 percent of your original drive space that previously went to oversized clusters. The optimal drive size for FAT32 is really 8GB as it is the maximum size drive that can be structured in 4KB clusters.

One of the biggest problems older users face, though, is not thinking drive compression. Most users of older systems used drive compression of one sort or another to optimize that tiny space as much as possible. FAT32 can't deal with drive compression, nor will it allow itself to be compressed by such antiquated techniques as Microsoft DriveSpace.

NTFS

NTFS, or NT File System, was developed specifically for Windows NT/2000 as an advanced file system for Windows NT/2000 networks. Because Windows NT/2000 are not DOS-based operating systems, NTFS is not a DOS-based file system—you can only employ it if you're running NT or Windows 2000. The main characteristics of NTFS are:

- System security; advanced file permission settings

- Supports Windows 2000 file encryption, disk quotas, volume mounting, and data compression

- Logging of activities in case the system goes down

- Inaccessibility if the computer is booted from a DOS floppy

- Maximum volume of 1024GB

- Filenames up to 256 characters long

- Extensive customization features which allow you to optimize disk performance

NTFS is based on a tree structure—all objects, files, and directories are treated as files, or records. The *Master File Table*, or MFT, is a key component. The very first record, or file, of the MFT is named $Mft. It is essentially an index of all the files that reside in an NTFS volume. All filenames and their time stamps are included in the $Mft file. If a file is too large to fit all of its attributes in the $Mft file, the rest of the file is allocated to other parts of the volume. This approach provides more direct means of access to files than FAT, and therefore, faster access to directories and files.

The MFT also includes a mirror file, which provides a backup index of the entire volume in case the MFT is corrupted. Another way that NTFS differentiates NTFS from FAT is that it keeps track of all changes to the disk structure. Should your system go down, NTFS is able to recover the disk back to the last valid disk structure. Note that this tracking feature cannot recover user data that wasn't already written to the disk at the time a failure occurs, but the volume's structure will remain intact.

In a nutshell, this is how NTFS gets a file from disk to memory system: NTFS is file-based, as I explained above. When it is asked for a file reference, it looks it up in the MFT and passes the parameters of the associated Logical Cluster Number (LCN) back to the controller so the file system driver can place the referenced LCNs in what's called a *run*, which is really just a chain of contiguous LCNs (nothing gets moved, just a bunch of run flags get turned on). A full complement of runs makes a file, and the name of that file is the name under which the *runlist* is stored. When the file is called, the runlist is triggered, and all associated LCNs are read into memory.

NTFS 5 made its debut as part Windows 2000, and with it came these features:

Disk quotas Administrators can define the amount of space that a user is allocated. Additionally, they can define whether it is merely tracked or actually enforced by the server.

Encryption NTFS can now encrypt and decrypt data in real time as it is read and written to disk.

Reparse points Applications are now able to capture data from open processes and perform operations on them before returning them to the system object that requested the initial operation. One of the key uses of this is for data redirection, allowing one object (that is, directory or file) to look like another. Hmmm, very Unix-like, that.

Sparse files This is a rather interesting new capability. NTFS can allocate space to a file, but allow that file to remain very small. Okay, that's vague. VMWare, a virtual machine emulator for Windows NT and Linux, actually does this. If you tell VMWare that you want a 2GB drive container (a file that acts like a drive) to install Windows 98SE in your Windows NT 4 Workstation installation and use up only 800MB of that space, that's all it will use. If you look at the drive container file on your hard drive, it will say it's only 800MB.

Windows 2000 does this a little differently. First, when an object asks for space, the system checks to see whether there's room. The "No" is obvious, so I'll do the "Yes." The system then *soft* allocates that space to the object. The object can load anything into that space it wants, even if it's only a fraction of what it asked to be allocated. The system then keeps track of how much is being used of that soft allocation and will use the unused space as needed. Once the object starts asking for its requested space, the system makes sure it's available. This is a very useful feature.

USN journaling USN journaling offers a more finely-tuned way of tracking every minute operation transacted on the system. (USN stands for *update sequence number*, the format that defines and localizes file system changes.) As it stands with NT 4, there are a finite number of operations and activities that NT can monitor before it's swamped. Journaling is a way for the system to account for itself; each operation must log its activity as opposed to the system watching everything getting done and recording it. Journaling is much less CPU intensive than *not* journaling; event traps are resource hogs.

Tip

If you're running a Windows NT or Windows 2000 network, the only time you really shouldn't use NTFS is when you need to support other operating systems on the same computer as Windows 2000.

Preventive Tip: Backing Up Your Master Boot Record

I strongly suggest that you back up your Master Boot Record very, very often. I have found Ranish Partition Manger (RPM) to be the most useful utility in both protecting systems from boot record viruses and the silly ineptitudes I practice on occasion that seem to result in the destruction of a Master Boot Record. The last version I've been using is 2.38 Beta 1.9, and you can find it at this site:

```
http://www.users.intercom.com/~ranish/part
```

It's stable, fast, relatively easy to use once you get the hang of it, and is very, very small. A 96KB download, to be exact. Save yourself gobs of trouble and add backing up your MBRs as a regular measure.

Tip

Since partitions and logical drives don't get changed very often on systems that are intended for consistent use, make sure to date the MBR copy on the floppy. It's also best to maintain an RPM disk for each machine instead of trying to remember which oddly named file was which machine's MBR copy.

An Overview of Viruses

INTRODUCTION

Writing most of this book is a lot of fun. Fixing things is like putting together a puzzle—it's challenging and provides rewards in the end (a completed puzzle or a recovered hard disk). In either case, your only opponent is bad electrical power, buggy software, or (if you're supporting others) inattentive users.

Viruses are a whole different story. With viruses, you actually have a human opponent and sometimes a competent one.

People often ask at this point, "Why do people write viruses?" I wish I didn't have to answer this question. The answer is, viruses are written by computer criminals. Some people just plain get their jollies making other people's lives difficult, and they think it's clever to write viruses. The fact is, they're just childish. Virus authors exploit not cleverness but rather trust. Most viruses attack PCs via portals that exist because of *trust* in the computer community, not stupidity on the part of users. It's rather like this: suppose you lived in a community where everyone knew everyone else, so folks didn't lock their doors. How clever need one be in order to be a thief? Not very—the thief *knows* that it's easy to get into any house. Would you applaud or be impressed with the skill of such a thief? Of course not. That's what today's virus authors are—mere children screaming for attention.

There *are* people who get their kicks that way, however, and that's why antivirus software can be a nice support tool. It does the job that you and I have neither the time nor the knowledge for—monitoring the PC for common viruses and suspicious virus-like behavior. Good antivirus software should be able to prevent, detect, and remove viruses without destroying valuable data. It must also be easy to update, since new viruses are created every day, and software that can detect and clean every virus except the one you've currently got is less than useless. Good software, combined with educated users and regular backups, can make virus attacks less likely—and less serious.

This chapter provides an overview of viruses, including the most common terminology, most common ways a virus enters your system, and tips on how to prevent and detect a virus.

Types of Viruses

Virus is the generic term that people are using these days to describe any of a group of programs designed to replicate itself and spread (much like life, if you think about it). Some are pranks and do no damage, whereas others are intentionally destructive computer programs. This section outlines various types of viruses, how they enter your computer, and the type of damage they do once they've infected your machine. You'll explore the following:

▶ File infectors and boot sector viruses

▶ Macro viruses

▶ Worms

▶ Web applet viruses

Note

Viruses cannot harm your hardware—they affect only the data stored on your computer.

In the past, classifying viruses was much simpler than it is today. The two most common types of viruses a few years ago were file infectors and boot sector viruses. But just as life continues to get more complicated as technology evolves, so do viruses. These days, a virus can be classified as, for example, a file infector macro virus, or a polymorphic stealth Web applet virus. Virus creators are constantly reinventing the wheel in order to develop the killer, undetectable virus. I'll cover how to protect your system from viruses later on, but for now let's take a look at the types of viruses and their techniques.

File Infectors and Boot Sector Viruses

File infectors begin their dirty work whenever the executable file to which they are attached is run. They may proceed directly to certain areas of the disk where specific files sit (such as the partition tables or COMMAND . COM) or hide in memory for just the right moment. (File infectors are also called *program infectors,* or *parasitic viruses.*)

Another strain of file infector is made up of two split programs. One is the top program that will not register as a virus when a virus scanner runs, and the other contains an algorithm that, once the first program is resident, changes part of the first program's code to make it a virus. It's sort of like a terrorist who gets through the security checkpoints at the airport, apparently unarmed, and then converts his umbrella into a shotgun once he's on the plane.

The following list summarizes the three-letter extensions of the types of files susceptible to viruses:

▶ EXE

▶ COM

▶ BIN

▶ DLL

▶ SYS

▶ DRV

▶ OVL

▶ VXD

Boot sector viruses are not as common as they used to be. They infect your system when it reads an infected drive or floppy disk. These types of viruses generally prefer hard drives, but a minority, including the Stoned virus, infect floppies. They are loaded into memory when the PC is booted from a drive that contains an infected disk. You're probably wondering, "What if the disk is not really bootable (in other words, it has no COMMAND . COM file) and the screen displays the message `Non-system disk error`? That doesn't stop anything, unfortunately. Once the computer attempts to boot from the infected disk, it's too late—the PC has to read the boot sector of the floppy to know it isn't bootable. During the read, the virus wakes up and springs into action.

Macro Viruses: Melissa Isn't the Girl Next Door

Macro viruses are one of the most widespread viruses around. You can infect your system simply by opening a document with a macro virus attached. As their name implies, macro viruses reside as macros in a document.

How do macro viruses work? Macro viruses are written in the macro language of an application. Applications that currently permit the use of macros, such as word processing programs and spreadsheet programs, are at risk not only of infection, but also of infecting others. Macro viruses spread when infected documents are transferred. Most of the macro viruses around right now are designed to infect Microsoft Word (versions 6.x and later) and Microsoft Excel.

Many macro viruses do nothing or almost nothing: they spread, but that's about all. Some people believe that these relatively unobtrusive examples of macro viruses are not the product of hackers at all, but are mutations that first appeared as the result of random bit scrambling in somebody's download and wound up propagating, unseen and unnoticed, as time passed. On the other hand, there are destructive macro viruses that overwrite data, modify the contents of documents, and even send documents via e-mail.

Melissa, Concept, DMV, and Nuclear are names of some macro viruses. Melissa, which infects Microsoft Word 97 and Word 2000 documents, was so widespread that it brought computer viruses to the evening news. Once an infected document is opened, the virus locates the user's Microsoft Outlook Address Book, and if it finds one, e-mails a copy of the infected document to up to 50 people. Microsoft included security against macro viruses in Word 2000, but Melissa is intelligent enough to disable those security dialog boxes, so users would not be aware that the document they are trying to open is infected.

Note

Melissa is not only a macro virus, but she's a *worm*, too. To understand more about worms, see the section titled "Worms."

Concept and DMV work pretty much the same way: they force you to save documents as templates and replicate themselves to your other documents. The main difference between the two is that DMV uses the AutoClose macro to install itself in the Normal template, while Concept uses AutoOpen. Nuclear can be destructive, however. On April 5, it deletes COMMAND.COM, and zeroes out MSDOS.SYS and IO.SYS, so that not only will your system not boot because it has no command shell, it won't tell you what the problem is because the SYS files are missing.

That's the bad news. The good news is that Microsoft got on the ball and created the Word Macro Virus Protection Tool (available from www.microsoft.com) to alert you of the presence of macros in your documents (not macro viruses, just macros) and allow you to open documents without activating the macros. Once they're open, you can look at the list of attached macros. If you see anything called Insert Payload or Payload, you've got the Nuclear virus. AAAZAO and AAAZFS indicate the presence of the Concept virus. Other tools can clean the viruses from your system.

A Day in the Life of a Macro Virus

Here's a relatively benign example of how a macro virus works: ShareFun is a Microsoft Word macro virus that attempts to spread over e-mail attachments. Every time somebody opens an infected file in Word, the chance of the virus becoming activated and spreading is one in four. You might open the document once, twice, or even three times and you might luck out, but open it a fourth time and the virus will activate. This means that if Microsoft Mail is running at the same time, the virus will try to send e-mail messages to three people randomly selected from the local MSMail alias list. (It's harmless if you're not running MSMail.) The subject of the messages is always the same: "You have GOT to see this!" The message is empty of text, but it contains a link to a file attachment called DOC1.DOC, which is infected by the virus. If the recipient double-clicks on the attachment, he or she will get infected by the virus and could spread the infection further with their own MSMail. As of this writing, the virus does nothing destructive; it merely propagates, and only when the circumstances are there for it. (Incidentally, this virus is not technically an "e-mail virus," because the recipients do not literally get infected from your e-mail; rather, they get infected by trying to open the attachment.)

ShareFun also has code to protect itself: if you try to analyze the virus in Word for Windows by looking at the "macro" by using either Tools ➢ Macro or File ➢ Templates, the virus will execute and infect your Word NORMAL.DOT template.

Worms Wiggle Their Way through E-mail

The major trait of a worm virus is to propagate via e-mail. A worm program is sent as an e-mail attachment. Once you open the attachment, the worm locates your e-mail address book and sends out the infected attachment. You can imagine how quickly this type of virus can spread, considering how many of us rely on e-mail as a means to send documents, whether personal or work related.

As you learned previously in this chapter, our friend Melissa was a worm—she propagated by locating Microsoft Outlook Address Books and sending herself, infected Word document that she was, to your friends and colleagues. But alas, poor Melissa, she's lost her place as the most popular worm. The most famous worm to date is the Love Bug virus. In simplest terms, thousands of people received e-mails with the subject line "ILOVEYOU." Thousands of people threw caution to the wind when they read the subject line and opened the attachment. Oooops. The ILOVEYOU worm went right to work, wiggling its way into users' Outlook Express Address Books and propagating itself. (At least it wasn't propagation without love.) Not only did the Love Bug propagate via e-mail, but it scanned users' PCs for passwords, which were sent back to the originator of the virus. It also copied itself over numerous file types including MP3, JS, and JPG.

Warning

A good way to avoid worms is to never open any file attachments from unknown sources and to listen to, or read, the national news. Viruses and their creators have been getting a lot of attention in the press lately. Press reports alerted computer users about the Love Bug and so limited the damage it caused.

Web Applet Viruses

Danger, Will Robinson—browsing the Web may be hazardous. The newest type of virus can exist in three popular Web scripting languages: ActiveX, JavaScript, and Java. While these languages allow for much of the gee-whiz features of the Web, such as 3D animation, it's possible for these languages to transfer virus programs to your system. The transfer is triggered by you simply opening a Web page that contains infected ActiveX controls or Java/JavaScript code. Once the virus makes its way into your system, it may corrupt files or directories, or do other types of damage—what happens depends on the actual virus.

To date there hasn't been an outbreak of a Web applet virus. However, as more and more consumers log on to the Internet, it's a safe bet that you'll be hearing more about this type of virus in the future.

Note

For information on how to protect yourself from Web applet viruses, see the "Tips for Protecting Your PC against Viruses" section.

Virus Naming Conventions

How are viruses named? First, you'll see a prefix, such as W97M. This is normally the platform where the virus operates. W97M is a Word 97 Macro virus. Next, you'll see the virus family name, such as Melissa. Sometimes you'll see a suffix, such as .a. This indicates the variant of the virus. In certain situations, a virus will have an alias that is more commonly known than the official name. W32/Ska, also known as Happy99, is one such virus.

Here's a list of some common virus prefixes:

WM Word Macro viruses native to Word 6 and Word 95.

W97M Word Macro viruses native to (and applicable only to) Word 97.

XM Excel Macro viruses native to Excel 5 and Excel 95.

X97M Excel Macro viruses native to Excel 97.

XF Excel Formula viruses.

AM Access Macro viruses native to Access 95.

A97M Access Macro viruses native to Access 97.

W95 Windows 95 viruses. These may affect Windows 98 too.

Win Windows 3.*x* viruses.

W32 32-bit Windows viruses.

WNT 32-bit Windows viruses that can infect Windows NT.

Trojan/Troj Trojan horses.

VBS Viruses written in Visual Basic Script.

AOL America Online Trojans.

Java Viruses written in Java.

Techniques of Attack

Virus creators get their kicks from tricking us—the more complex the virus, the longer it takes investigators to figure out how it works and how it spreads. A virus may use one or several sneaky modes of operation covered in this section.

Polymorphic Viruses

A *polymorphic* virus changes, or mutates, so that it cannot be detected by antivirus software. For example, back in 1998, a polymorphic macro virus, named Excel8_Extras, appeared. It created an infected spreadsheet in the Excel startup directory, then added a *randomly-generated* macro and module name to infected documents. Because the virus was able to randomly generate new names, it took longer for investigators to pinpoint the virus.

Multipartite Viruses

Just to make things maximally confusing, some viruses have a boot sector portion *and* a program infector portion; these are called *multipartite* viruses. For example, researchers discovered that the Hare virus was a polymorphic, multipartite virus that infected COM and EXE files as well as Master Boot Records (MBRs) on hard drives and boot sectors of floppy disks. Upon execution, the virus infects the MBR and goes resident, infecting any COM or EXE file that is executed.

Stealth Viruses

Some viruses are said to be stealth viruses. A *stealth* virus attempts to hide itself by keeping a copy of the parts of the disk that it infected, *before* it infected it. Then, when it detects that a virus scanner is looking for it, it shows the scanner the uninfected copy of the file, as if to say, "Nobody here but us chickens." Now, note that the stealth feature of a virus works only if the virus is active in memory, which will not be the case if you've first booted from a clean, write-protected DOS floppy. Always do that before running an important virus scan.

Warning

Many program infectors (and all boot sector viruses) become Terminate and Stay Resident (TSR) programs—which is a good reason to install a TSR scanner that can constantly monitor your system for viruses. TSRs take system memory, which tips you off that you may have a virus. If your system memory doesn't add up to 640K, then you might have a virus.

Trojan Horses

A *Trojan horse* program acts like the Trojan horse of Greek mythology. A malevolent program is hidden inside another, apparently useful, program. While the "useful" program is running, the malevolent part does something nasty, like erase your FAT and directory.

The only good thing about Trojans is that they're self-limiting: once an evil Trojan erases your hard disk, it has erased itself, also. Today, instead of running on private e-mail systems like BBSs as they did in the past, Trojans (which now typically have a replication component) are finding their way to the Internet and the World Wide Web.

Pure Trojans seem to have gone out of style. Trojans instead show up in the virus world as the initial source of infection for some viruses. A virus that injects itself into COM or EXE files is also a Trojan, as it is waiting for you to run that formerly useful program: once you run an infected copy of dBase, you are waking the virus up.

Time Bombs and Logic Bombs

Then there is the bomb. There are *time bombs* and *logic bombs*. The *bomb* is a piece of code embedded in a program or the operating system itself that waits for a particular event to occur. When that event occurs, the logic bomb "goes off," doing some kind of damage.

Logic bombs have been around nearly since the beginning of computing. An early one showed up in a mainframe payroll program. The program's creator had inserted a clause in the payroll program that said, "If you find I'm not on the payroll, erase all payroll files."

Bombs show up as the more destructive part of viruses. They include instructions such as, "If it's Friday the 13th, erase the hard disk," or "If the worm has succeeded in making 10 copies of itself, erase the hard disk."

An Example of a Virus at Work

By now you know that a virus can use a combination of approaches in attacking your data. A virus might work in the following way:

1. Assume that you double-clicked on one of those animated holiday cards sent to you in an e-mail as an EXE file—an executable program. The virus is then introduced to your system via the infected EXE file (an example is a Trojan horse). Either this Trojan is hidden in an application program that has been doctored by the virus creator, or it is the Trojan portion of a virus that is injected into a program file or the boot record by the worm portion.

2. Once the program with the Trojan is activated by a certain event, such as your running a particular application, the virus is awakened. It installs itself in the operating system as a logic bomb, waiting for an opportunity to (1) activate the worm and/or (2) activate the destructive portion of itself.

3. The logic bomb activates the worm portion whenever an acceptable host presents itself. Some viruses replicate only onto floppies from the hard disk. Other viruses infect any program file that gets activated, whether on the floppy disk or the hard disk. Every time the worm copies itself onto another disk or program, it activates a built-in counter that keeps track of how many copies it has made.

4. Eventually, the destructive part of the virus may be activated, either by an event, such as running a program, a date occurring

(such as Friday the 13th), or by a certain number of replications. When the destructive portion activates, the virus may do something as innocuous as flashing a message on the screen or as damaging as erasing the hard disk.

Virus Hoaxes

As if viruses, and the very real threat they pose to computer users everywhere, aren't enough to cause you concern, there is a cottage industry springing up that is intended to cause panic and anxiety: hoaxes. Hoaxes are just that. They are fake virus warnings initially transmitted by a malicious person who relies on the likelihood that people will send them to everyone they know thinking they are doing a good deed. Sadly, no threat is averted, no virus is exposed, and no one is helped. What actually happens is a great deal of wasted time, confusion, and higher blood pressure.

To avoid falling into this trap, if you get a virus warning from anyone, you should first check with an authoritative antivirus Web site and do some research to see whether the message you are reading is about a real virus or a hoax. (See the "Resources: Stay Informed" section for a list of helpful Web sites.) If it's a hoax, please pass that on to the person who sent you the message and inform them of this tragic misuse of the Internet.

Tips for Protecting Your PC against Viruses

The most effective way to avoid catching viruses is to shut off your computer . . . permanently. Don't like that idea? How about just removing your floppy disk drives, disconnecting from your network, and never connecting to the Internet?

Effective as those means are, they're not much good in the real world. Never opening e-mails so as not to catch viruses is sort of like cutting off your hand so as not to get a hangnail. Sure, it prevents what you were trying to prevent, but it doesn't give you much good use of your hand—or your computer. In the real world, what can you do about viruses?

▶ **Purchase virus protection software, install it on your system, and use it.** See the "Antivirus Software" section for a list of the best virus protection/detection software.

▶ **Be sure to update your virus protection software.** Some software will automatically link to the vendor's site and download detection code for the newest viruses. Or, you can check their site from time to time to make sure your software is up to date. However you do it, do it.

▶ **Don't open e-mail attachments from people you don't know.** This is critically important because many newer viruses spread by sending infected files over the Internet as e-mail attachments. Sometimes, this includes people you do know, who may be unwittingly passing on an infected file to you. It's important to note that simply opening an e-mail with an infected attachment will not introduce the virus into your system.

▶ **Don't download files from the Internet unless you have virus protection software that scans them for viruses.** Also, think twice about the site you're considering downloading from. Is it a company with its reputation at stake, or an unknown individual?

▶ **Consider disabling your browser's ability to handle pages that contain JavaScript, Java code, or ActiveX controls.** This doesn't necessarily mean that you won't be able to view the page—just the parts that contain ActiveX controls or Java/JavaScript. You can always reset your browser to handle those components if you need to.

▶ **If you don't want to disable your browser for ActiveX, Java, and JavaScript, consider the source before entering a site.** If you know nothing about the site, think twice before entering. There are a lot of people out there who have Web sites, a lot of time on their hands, and nothing to lose.

‣ **Keep up with the news.** Major outbreaks are reported on national, even local (depending on where you live) news, in newspapers and on the Web in sites such as www.cnet.com.

‣ **Back up your data frequently.** I've already said this: viruses are scary, but not backing up regularly is scarier. Any of a large number of random external events—flood, fire, power surges, vibration—could destroy data on your hard disk, and it could happen at any time. Backing up regularly is more important than keeping up to date on the latest virus buster programs.

‣ **If you're managing a network, centralize your applications.** Install all programs used in the department on one computer (preferably one not used as a workstation) and then back up all the application software from that computer. Protect this computer from virus infection with your life. If you get a virus, you can use either the files from the computer or backup floppies to restore applications to the newly cleaned computer.

‣ **Don't use pirated software, especially games.** First of all, it's not nice to use commercial software that you didn't pay for. Most software companies are fairly small operations, no more than 10 to 15 people. These are not large, faceless corporations that "deserve" (in the eyes of some people) being taken down a peg or two. Most software operations are Mom-and-Pop operations that just barely get by. Using copies of software you didn't buy is just plain theft. People who use illegal copies are thieves, plain and simple—and cowardly thieves, to boot. There's good, cheap software in all areas, so "just say no" when someone offers you a copy of a program. More relevant to the present discussion, many virus attacks that I've heard of seem to have come from pirated software—another good reason not to use copies.

‣ **Don't trust bundled CD-ROM software.** Although you might think all software distributed on CD-ROM is virus-free and safe to use, there have been cases where companies inadvertently distributed a virus on their CD. Word Macro viruses are a particular problem, so be sure to scan those files before opening them.

▶ **Avoid Web sites that cater to self-proclaimed "hackers."** These tend to mainly have pirated games anyway, and the software generally isn't screened. The same idiots that think it's okay to crack the copy protection on a game and give it away free also think it's okay to insert a virus in the cracked game. In some odd Robin Hood manner, they view it as "just punishment" for anyone *else* who uses illegally copied software.

▶ **Be wary of shareware programs without documentation.**

▶ **Stick to big shareware download sites such as Tucows or PC Magazine, and Web sites that register their users.** Most reputable Web sites these days ask that you register when you get on. Then they don't let you upload files until they've checked that you are who you say you are. That way, if you upload a virus, they can come after you. This makes people less likely to upload viruses.

▶ **Write-protect any floppy that you put in your drive, if possible.** This is particularly important when installing a new piece of software: you don't want your master copy of a program to become infected. Some programs require that the disk not be protected while installing—I certainly hope that vendors move away from this practice. Also, get in the habit of leaving the floppy drive empty. Boot sector viruses can't get at your hard disk if you don't boot from an infected floppy. You can read and write data on a floppy with an infected boot record for years and never be infected. But boot from the floppy—even if it's not a bootable floppy—and you've got the virus. If you're not careful, you'll find that now and then you try to reboot the machine with a floppy in drive A:. Keep the drive empty and it won't happen.

Antivirus Software

There are quite a few antivirus software packages on the market that will search your PC for viruses and alert you if incoming files are infected. The following products are well worth consideration.

- Command AntiVirus for Windows 95/98 (Command Software Systems Inc.; `http://www.commandcom.com`)

- F-Secure Anti-Virus (F-Secure Corp.; `http://www.datafellows.com`)

- McAfee Internet Guard Dog (McAfee Corp.; `www.mcafee.com`)

- McAfee VirusScan for Windows 95/98 (McAfee Corp.; `www.mcafee.com`)

- Norton AntiVirus 2000 (Symantec Corp.; `www.symantec.com`)

- PC-cillin (Trend Micro Inc.; `www.antivirus.com`)

Resources: Stay Informed

First of all, understand that we're on shaky ground here. There are really no totally reliable sources of data on virus prevalence. As I said earlier, the people doing most of the yelling about what a big danger viruses pose to life on Earth are generally the people who stand to gain the most from the panic—vendors of antivirus products. Personally, I am concerned about viruses, but I have not panicked and I do not advise panic on your part.

The following URLs provide current lists of the top viruses, as well as virus descriptions and recent news about viruses, including hoaxes:

- Network Associates: `http://vil.nai.com/villib/alpha.asp`

- Symantec: `http://www.symantec.com/avcenter/`

- Trend Micro: `http://www.antivirus.com/pc-cillin/vinfo/`

- The WildList Organization International: `http://www.wildlist.org/WildList/`

▶ F-Secure: `http://www.f-secure.com/virus-info/`

▶ ICSA: `http://www.icsa.net/html/communities/antivirus/index.shtml`

▶ Virus Bulletin: `http://www.virusbtn.com/`

Viral Symptoms

How can you tell if your PC is infected with a virus? Here are some of the most common symptoms:

▶ Files or programs become corrupted or aren't working properly. For example, a Word document that was fine an hour ago now includes text or formatting that you did not insert.

▶ New programs or files appear mysteriously in a directory.

▶ Odd warning messages, error messages, or random dialog boxes appear onscreen.

▶ A drive name has been renamed.

▶ Programs or files suddenly disappear from directories.

▶ Memory problems occur, for example, not enough memory when you should have no problem running the applications and files that you're running.

Troubleshooting Tips

The following procedures have been helpful to me in coping with a virus attack. I recommend that you make a form for yourself from this list, arranging the list in two columns so that you've got one side free for checking things off and for your notes.

1. Calm down.

2. Grab a pen and pad so you can write out the diagnostic steps you take. It might be hard to believe that you could forget important details, but under the stress caused by a virus attack, anyone could be subject to bouts of amnesia. To keep from forgetting anything, make two lists. The first list should record what you've done in the recent past that may have allowed entry, such as opening an executable file from a friend of a friend. The second list should detail the steps you take to detect, isolate, and hopefully destroy the virus. To remember what you've done as the hunt continues, you will want to reread your notes for the next few days—or months. Writing down what you are about to do also forces you to think about the next step. That mental pause may prevent you from taking an unnecessary step or making a dangerous error.

3. If you haven't already powered down the computer, record all information being displayed onscreen inside the virus dialog box: the type of virus reported, in which files it is contained, the exact DOS or Windows message.

4. Note your most recent actions and computer symptoms (leaving the screen on for this step may help your memory).

5. In the rare case that your PC was infected by a floppy disk, note the names of all floppy disks lying around, and whether you received any disks from anyone recently (if so, did you insert them in the floppy drive?) or gave any disks to anyone else recently. Remove all floppies from drives and remember to discard all the floppy disks that were around the infected PC.

6. If you must save your onscreen data, save it to an empty floppy and mark the disk *immediately* as "Potentially Infected."

7. If at all possible, access the Internet on another system and look up the most recent virus list. Compare the reported symptoms with those manifested by the computer.

8. If there's a match, determine whether your antivirus software needs updating in order to detect the virus infecting your PC.

9. Power down (just rebooting may not oust the virus). Then reboot from the hard drive and run your antivirus software. Download the latest virus detectors from your antivirus software vendor's site.

10. Write down all files reported as infected. If no backups or hard copies exist for infected files, consider making copies to another floppy. If you make backups, mark those floppies as "Potentially Infected."

11. Re-scan the hard drive with your antivirus program.

Don't let fear of viruses destroy your use and enjoyment of your PC. The analogies between safe sex and safe computing, although now trite, are very accurate. Have a good time, but use protection. At the very minimum, use antivirus software and back up data regularly. Don't put original program floppies in your PC's drives unless they have write-protect tabs on them.

On a final note: if you know someone who's a virus author, report them to the authorities. Viruses are computer terrorism, and terrorists should be caught and punished.

16

Care and Feeding
of Hard Drives

I discussed some of these things earlier, but here's a summary of what you can do to make your disk hardware live longer. Some of this has been covered earlier; for the others, I'll expand upon them in a few pages.

As you read in Chapter 4, "Avoiding Service: Preventive Maintenance," leave your computers on all the time: it's easier on their drives not to have to start up every day.

Also, get good power protection. You read in Chapter 9, "Power Supplies and Power Protection" about buying power conditioners, UPSs, and SPSs to protect your hardware—and the hard disk is no exception. Surges go through the *whole* system. Including the drive heads. And if the drive heads happen to be near the FAT or partition record . . .

A few more tips:

▶ Use the proper mounting hardware for your drive, and mount it according to manufacturer's guidelines.

▶ Don't smoke around drives. Smoke raises the particulate level in the air around you. Dust is, in general, not good for the hard disk.

▶ Attend to squeaky drives. Not only are they annoying, they may be trying to tell you something.

Let's take a closer look at the last few items.

Protecting Your Hard Drive

There's not much to be done in the way of regular maintenance on the sealed Winchester drive: you can't clean the heads, and you can't align them. If the drive itself is fried, then about all you can do with it is cut it open and leave it on your bookshelf as a conversation piece.

What kills hard disks?

▶ Dust and smoke

▶ Rapid temperature change

▶ Vibration

▶ Excessive heat

It's important to avoid these killers and, in addition, to have a data protection plan.

Dust and Smoke

Even though there's an air filter on the drive, the filters aren't perfect, and dust can slip into a drive. When a dust or smoke particle sits on the disk, the head whips around and crashes right into it. Then it drags it around the platter, leaving scratches in its wake. On a 3½-inch platter rotating at 5400rpm, a particle on the outermost track would travel at 56 miles per hour. The outermost track is, by the way, the most important track, as it contains the directory information for the rest of the disk. The space between the head and the platter is infinitesimal compared to the size of dust, dirt, or hair, as you see in Figure 16.1.

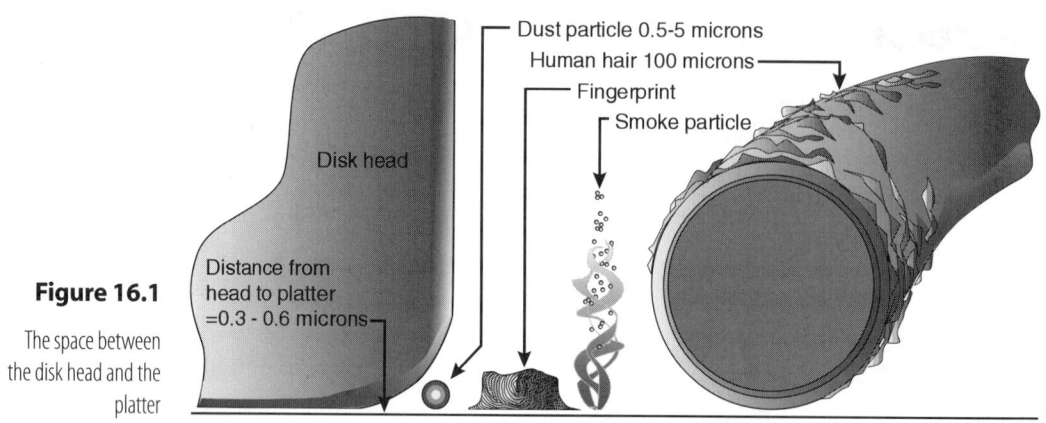

Figure 16.1

The space between the disk head and the platter

Ziplock Bags Keep Your Cool

Quick temperature changes aren't good for drives, either. A drive, while cold, may not respond properly. There is, of course, an easy fix for this—just let it warm up. But there's a related problem that's much worse. People leave a laptop with a hard disk in their car overnight on a cold night, then bring it into the office, and the hard disk dies. Even when heated up, the drive refuses to function. It's quite mysterious.

What kills a drive isn't so much temperature change (although a lot of temperature changes can kill a drive or make it appear dead), but condensation. A drive sitting in cold, dry air that makes a quick transition to the warm, moist air inside a heated building in winter leads to condensation of water droplets on the platters.

The same thing happens with hard drives that are being transported. Suppose it's Friday, and you know that on Monday you must drive to another of your company's offices to install a hard disk. So you test the hard disk, see that it is okay, and put the disk in the trunk of your car. The weekend goes by too quickly, as always, and the hard disk spends it in the trunk of your car. Then, arriving at the PC's site on Monday, you install the hard disk—but it does not work.

Now you know why it happened, but what can you do to keep it from happening again? Before you take the drive into the building on Monday, put it in a Ziplock bag and seal the bag. That will allow you to bring the drive into the building with its own bubble of dry air. Then let it warm up for about 30 to 45 minutes in the bag. Once the platters are no longer cold, it's safe to take the drive out of the bag, and no condensation will occur.

Vibration

The other evil, vibration, is a problem because of the way in which the head travels above the disk platter. Recall that the head travels above the disk on a cushion of air. The distance between the platter and the head (called the *head gap*) is very small. Any bouncing around while the drive is running can cause the head to literally crash into the platter below. This plows a small furrow in the platter and grinds down the head.

Don't put your PC on the same table as any equipment that vibrates, such as some inkjet printers or subwoofers. All that shaking is no good for it. It's easier to lock the corral today than it is to explain to the boss tomorrow why all the horses are gone.

Excessive Heat

Most disk cases nowadays leave enough space for you to mount two 3½-inch disk drives, meaning you've got enough room to put that second IDE drive into your system without having to get rid of the existing IDE drive. That's nice, except for the fact that there ends up being no space between the two drives. While 3½-inch drives don't generate as much heat as did older drives, they still run warm, and stacking them one on top of the other isn't a good idea. Think about just drilling new holes or finding a disk chassis that leaves some air space between the drives, or you may be able to mount the second drive in an extra floppy bay if you have one.

Data Protection

The essence of data protection is simple: back up data areas (they can be lost in a number of ways), periodically rewrite all information back onto your disks (as magnetism fades), and keep half an eye peeled for computer viruses. The different areas on your disk should be backed up at different intervals with different tools. A complete backup program consists of the following steps.

▶ Backing up:

  ▶ The drive type (if you are using an older system or hard drive)

  ▶ The MBR, including the FAT and directory (daily)

  ▶ System files

  ▶ The user data (regularly)

▶ Making an "emergency" boot floppy for each system.

▶ Taking whatever measures you can to minimize the probability of an accidental format.

Note

Although it may sound strange to accidentally format your hard drive, it's possible. Take my word for it, it's been done. Of course, you'll most likely avoid such catastrophes by simply working in a GUI like Windows or KDE for Linux, but these are still no guarantees.

▶ Testing and refreshing the disk media at least annually. This means you should, each year:

  ▶ Back up, format, and rewrite your whole drive to refresh the sector IDs and data.

  ▶ Test the disk media with a specialized media tester of some kind.

It also can't hurt if you:

▶ Periodically defragment the data to ease any data recovery problems.

▶ Utilize the verification features of the operating system and some applications.

▶ Understand the threat posed by computer viruses and know how to protect yourself from them. By the way, the best way to avoid computer viruses is to never download anything from the Web unless you are certain that the source computer is virus-free. Also, never, ever copy programs from friends' disks. Not only is this illegal (unless the program is shareware or freeware or specifically states that it may otherwise be copied for distribution), it's also one of the most common ways to contract a virus.

It looks like a lot, but it's not really: Let's take a look at each item.

Backing Up Your Hard Disk Drive Type

Note

Today, virtually all computers and hard drives auto-configure when they are installed. As such, you never need to set the drive type in CMOS and you can skip this section. If, on the other hand, you are using an older system, it's very important that you save the hard drive configuration data contained in your CMOS.

The most important part of the CMOS information is your hard disk's disk type. Not that the other information in your CMOS memory isn't important, but it's that incorrect or missing hard drive data that will crash your system. The other information (like the time and date) will be nothing more than an inconvenience. To look at your CMOS data, run your computer's BIOS setup program and you'll see (among other things) the drive type displayed.

Looking at the list of information in the BIOS, you'll find a number of drive specifications (either two or four drives will be listed). Chances are that only one of the drives will have actual data. The others will generally say "not installed" or some other similar note.

Your drive will either be a prebuilt drive type, like drive type 15, or it will be a user-definable drive type. The user-definable drive type is usually numbered 47, although not all computers use 47; in many older Compaq computers it is a number in the low 60s.

If your drive is of a user-definable type, be sure to make a note of not only its drive number, but also the number of heads, cylinders, sectors, and write precompensation. Some computers require that you note the ECC length, so take that down if the Setup program shows it.

Better yet, stick a paper label on the drive with the drive number on it (or, if you're so inclined, a permanent marker works well, too). If you ever move the drive to another computer, however, you may not be able to use the same drive type number in the new one. Each computer's BIOS is different, and what is drive type 35 for one computer may be drive type 42 for another. But if you write down the specifications for the drive (heads, sectors, and so on), you'll always be able to enter the data into your new system and get the drive to work.

Backing Up and Restoring Your MBR with DEBUG

You may recall that the Master Boot Record (MBR) resides on cylinder 0, head 0, sector 1. Without your MBR, your computer will never boot. Unfortunately, because the head spends a lot of time there— the root directory and FAT are in that area, among other things— cylinder 0 is more prone to problems than most cylinders.

I have seen strange things kill cylinder 0, and when cylinder 0 is dead, the whole disk might just as well be dead. Lose the MBR, and the operating system has no idea how to communicate with the disk. So back it up.

As a matter of fact, it's a good idea to back up not only the MBR (which is the first sector of the first track), but the entire first track at cylinder 0, head 0. Various programs squirrel important information onto these otherwise-unused sectors: for example, a dual boot system relies on sectors 2 and 3 of the track, and Disk Manager stores information about a drive's geometry on sector 8.

The EXE Files: Using DEBUG

Although DOS 5 included an MBR backup program, it was removed from DOS 6 and subsequent versions of DOS and all versions of Windows, so chances are you won't have one. You can back up the MBR with the Norton Utilities, if you have a copy. You can also back up your MBR if all you have is DEBUG (and that's available on even the most current systems). But be careful: DEBUG is a very powerful utility and can damage a file. If it is not used correctly, you will no longer be able to use the file. If you do use DEBUG, it's a good idea to use it on a copy, not an original file. That way, if you make a mistake, you still have an undamaged original. Use a *bootable* floppy that contains DEBUG.EXE (MS-DOS users) or DEBUG.COM (PC-DOS users). If you're using Windows, put a copy of DEBUG onto a Startup floppy before you begin. You can make a Startup floppy from the Control Panel. Type the program lines into DEBUG as shown below in bold type. (The case doesn't matter, but I'm showing the words in caps for clarity's sake.) I've placed underscores where blanks should go. Line 1 starts DEBUG and creates a new file called MBR.DAT.

1. **DEBUG_MBR.DAT**. You will see a `File Not Found` message—because the file didn't exist before. Don't worry about the message.

2. **A**. This tells DEBUG that you want to assemble something.

3. **MOV_DX,9000**. This command tells DEBUG to move the value of segment 9000 to register DX. Since you can't write

anything to a register, you have to move this information to an extra segment.

4. **MOV_ES,DX**. This command moves any information in register DX to the extra segment (called ES).

5. **XOR_BX,BX**. BX is the offset; XOR is a programming trick to set it to zero.

6. **MOV_CX,0001**. This command stores the value of track 0 and sector 1 in register CX.

7. **MOV_DX,0080**. Here, you're storing the information at head 0 of drive 80 (your A: drive is drive 00, your B: drive is drive 01, your C: drive is drive 80, and your D: drive is drive 81—these are all physical drives, not logical drives) into register DX.

8. **MOV_ AX,0201**. This command tells DEBUG to read 1 sector.

9. **INT_13**. This is the BIOS disk call.

10. **INT_20**. This tells the BIOS, "I'm done!" and signals that it won't get any more commands and can leave memory.

11. Press Enter to stop entering commands.

12. **G** runs the program. When it's done, you should see a message that says `Program terminated normally`.

13. **R_CX**. This command asks DEBUG to show you the value of register CX and lets you edit it.

14. **200**. This is the size of the file that DEBUG will write.

15. **W_9000:00**.

16. Type **Q** to exit DEBUG.

Congratulations! You have just created a file called MBR.DAT. Here's a sample screen of this operation.

```
A:\>debug mbr.dat
-l 9000:0
-a
25A4:0100 mov dx,9000
25A4:0103 mov es,dx
25A4:0105 xor bx,bx
25A4:0107 mov cx,0001
25A4:010A mov dx,0080
25A4:010D mov ax,0301
25A4:0110 int 13
25A4:0112 int 20
25A4:0114
-g

Program terminated normally
-q

A:\>
```

The process of restoring your MBR is similar to that of saving it. To restore your MBR, first start from a bootable floppy that contains both DEBUG (.EXE or .COM) and the correct MBR.DAT—do *not* try restoring an MBR.DAT from one machine onto another machine unless the two machines are identical! Once you're set, change to the A: drive and type the following (again, underscores should be typed as blanks):

1. **DEBUG_MBR.DAT**. This time, if you get a File not found message, *stop and exit* DEBUG (type **Q**) *immediately!* If you continue at this point, you could blast your MBR. (Seeing that message means that you didn't save it properly.)

2. Type **L_9000:0** to direct DEBUG to load the information to 9000:0, where you'll tell the program to look for it.

3. Assuming that all went well, now type **A** to let DEBUG know you want to assemble a file.

4. **MOV_DX,9000**.

5. **MOV_ES,DX**.

6. `XOR_BX,BX`.

7. `MOV_CX,0001`.

8. `MOV_DX,0080`.

9. `MOV_AX,0301`. This command tells DEBUG that you want to *write* 1 sector.

10. `INT_13`.

11. `INT_20`.

12. Press Enter to stop entering commands.

13. **G** runs the program. When it's done, you should see a message that says `Program terminated normally`.

14. Press **Q** to exit DEBUG. Your screen will look like the previous graphic.

Backing Up System Files

It's no secret that operating systems are getting more and more complex these days. Your operating system's default system files, for example, include a bunch of configuration files that tell your operating system how to work and how your applications should work with it. Lose those files, and it's all over.

16-Bit Applications

To 16-bit applications, such as Windows 3.*x* and all applications created for it, the important files have the extension INI. Each application that you run has its own "innie" file that defines the environment in which it operates. For example, my copy of Ami Pro has an initialization file called `AMIPRO.INI`, which defines the default document template used, the default location to which files are saved, and so forth.

The Windows operating system itself has several initialization files:

SYSTEM.INI Contains the hardware information for Windows.

WIN.INI Contains the Windows user environment.

CONTROL.INI Describes the color schemes and printers used with Windows.

PROGMAN.INI Defines the contents of all Windows program groups and how the Program Manager works.

WINFILE.INI Defines how objects appear in the File Manager.

This isn't the place for a complete discussion of the INI files, but if you'd like to know more, the Windows Resource Kit has a very good description of all the INI files and what they do.

Note

INI files are generally kept in the Windows directory. You can view (and edit) an INI file in a text editor such as Windows Notepad. It's not a good idea to open it in a word processor lest you save it as a word processor file.

What does all this mean in terms of rebuilding your system if necessary? When backing up, even if you normally only back up data rather than system files, it's a very good idea to back up all INI files as well. This way, if you must reinstall the operating system, you'll be able to restore your system exactly the way it was when you backed it up—application files and all. To restore INI files, just copy them back to the Windows directory, replacing any existing files. (Of course, be very sure that the backed-up files are the ones that you want to use.) The only restrictions are that this will work best if you're restoring the system information to the same computer you took it from. Other computers may not work with the memory configuration or fonts that you set up on the original system.

Registry-Oriented Operating Systems (Windows 95/98/2000/NT)

Windows 95/98/2000/NT organizes its configuration information differently. Rather than having a bunch of INI files, almost all information relating to the operating systems and most 32-bit applications stored therein are stored in a central database known as the Registry. The exact files of which the Registry is composed depends on the operating system: for Windows 95, it's two files, USER.DAT and SYSTEM.DAT; for Windows NT, it's five *hive* files, each of which describes a part of how the operating system works. But whichever operating system you're talking about, all the files are combined to make one Registry. The only exceptions to this are any 16-bit Windows apps on your system. They don't know how to look in the Registry for configuration information, so they maintain INI files and copy their contents to the Registry.

Note

There actually are a number of true 32-bit applications that still use INI files. The simple fact is that it's easier, faster, and more reliable to store information about an application's configuration in a local file, that is, an INI file that resides in the same directory as the application. Most commercial applications add entries to the Registry, but the majority of shareware and freeware titles use INI files.

The good news about the Registry is that it's centralized: only one Registry to back up, not five or more individual text files. Most of the time, you make changes to the Registry in the same way that you usually make changes to INI files: by changing the settings in the Control Panel.

Your method of backing up the Registry depends on the operating system you're using. If you're using NT and have a tape drive, you can back up the Registry at the same time that you back up your other data. When you restore the data, you can choose to restore the Registry at the same time, so long as you restore it to the same drive that it came from. If you're using Windows 95 or later, you can export the Registry as a text file from the Registry Editor, and then import it as needed. Backing up the Registry on a regular basis is a *very* good idea, as the Registry is required to boot the operating system.

Rebuilding the Operating System

Whichever operating system you're using, the process of rebuilding the system with its backed-up configuration is about the same:

1. Reinstall the operating system.

2. Install any patches (e.g., Service Packs) that were installed when you backed up.

3. If necessary, restore or reinstall any applications that were not backed up.

4. Restore the data and the configuration files.

This should put your system back to the way that it was when you last backed up.

Backing Up User Data

If you're concerned about data integrity, I shouldn't have to tell you to back up regularly, but . . .

Quick, now. How many of you have backed up your hard disk in the last seven days? Hmmm . . . not too many. How about in the last month? Last year? *Ever?*

There are two kinds of hard disk users: the ones who have had a disk failure and lost data that wasn't backed up, and the ones who are *going* to. (Actually, I first heard this as, "There are two kinds of dead pilots: the ones who have landed and forgot to lower their landing gear, and . . .")

You seek to stay in the latter category as long as possible.

I can't stress this strongly enough: at the first sign of unusual behavior, back up the entire disk.

Backup Options

When hard drives were smaller, it was semireasonable to back up an entire drive's data to floppies. These days, however, floppies just don't cut it for mass storage. Of my workstations, the one with the *small* disk has 1GB of storage space; one of the really monstrous systems has 17GB. For just a couple hundred dollars today, you can buy a drive with 20GB or more (it's true! Check out the Quantum Fireball CX line). There's no way that I'm backing up one of those drives to 1.44MB floppies—it would take more than four *thousand* floppies!

Over the years, backup options have improved dramatically. In the past, you had three choices when it came to data protection: tape drives (controlled either by their own tape controller or from the floppy controller), removable drives such as Bernoulli Boxes, or floppies. These days your options include:

▶ Tape drives

▶ Removable media drives such as Zip and Jaz drives

▶ Optical (MO, or magneto-optical) drives

▶ Writable\rewritable CDs

▶ A second hard drive (hard disks are cheap now: why not?)

We'll discuss these options in more detail now.

Tape Drives

The traditional means of backing up a large hard disk is the tape drive. These devices are simple, they're a known quantity, and they're cheap. Although some tape drives still run off the floppy controller (which is bad, as it's slow), you can also buy SCSI or IDE models that can plug into your system's host adapter. When looking for a tape drive, keep the following in mind:

▶ An external tape drive may cost a little more, but you'll be able to use it to back up more than one system.

⟩ Preformatted tapes save a great deal of time, since tapes can take up to an hour to format.

⟩ The same tape software that works with Windows 9x may not work with other operating systems, such as Windows NT. Similarly, the data on those tapes may not be readable to NT-compatible tape software.

Tape drives come in a wide range of capacities and formats: models range in size from 250MB to 8GB and higher digital audio tape (DAT) format.

Removable Media Drives

Removable media drives are exactly what they sound like: they're magnetic storage units that allow you to remove the media and put in a new set, giving you virtually unlimited storage capacity. They're not the fastest storage units out there, but they're cheaper than most and work pretty well. They have other advantages as well. Because they can connect to your computer via the parallel port, you can use them to back up just about any system, even laptops. Plugging a removable drive into the parallel port doesn't mean that you can't use your printer, either: it goes between the parallel port and the printer.

Tip

Removable drives are a handy way of transferring data from a laptop back to your office workstation, if your laptop doesn't have a LAN connection to the other PC.

Iomega made the first popular removable drives for the PC in the form of the Bernoulli Box. Although I've still got my Bernoulli Box and like it, I find its cartridges to be a touch expensive, and it's bigger and heavier than a Zip drive without offering much more in the way of storage capacity (150MB as opposed to 100MB). The cartridges are physically bigger, too. Iomega now has some new offerings for backup: Zip and Jaz drives.

For small systems, or for those users who only want to back up part of a drive, there's the Zip drive. These units, which plug into your parallel or SCSI port, hold 250MB or older 100MB cartridges. Zip drives are about as cheap as you'll find in the realm of largish-scale backups: the new 250MB drives are about $200 and the cartridges are about $15. (I've seen them offered in 10-packs for $100.) Even if 100MB doesn't back up most modern drives, backing up to five cartridges isn't too bad. The unit weighs about a pound, so you can even take it on the road. The cartridges are about the size of a 3½-inch floppy disk, except thicker.

For larger systems, Iomega makes Jaz drives. These removable drives have cartridges that can hold 1 or 2GB—not too shabby. They're pricier than Zip drives, but they're fast (in fact, faster than most hard drives. A Jaz drive backs up 1GB of data in about five minutes.) and can back up most hard drives with only one cartridge.

CD-RW Drives

Note

Magneto-optical (MO) drives aren't necessarily gone, but they're not proliferating either. The MO looks a lot like a pygmy CD and is a little thicker. They often come in mountable cartridges to prevent direct handling, and they are slow. Quite a bit slower, in fact, than a basic 2X CD-R drive. Today, with 8X CD-R/RW drives available for as little as $300, the MO is not really a sensible option.

For those with larger storage needs, consider CD rewritable (CD-RW) drives. They range in capacity from standard CDs (650MB) to DVD-RAM drives that can store up to 5.2GB. And, unlike the older (and slower) magneto-optical drives, CD writers are quite inexpensive, starting at as low as around $200 for the 650MB. The DVD drives are more expensive (around $700) but are well worth the expense if you are managing enough data to merit their use.

Another Hard Drive

Hard disk space has gotten so cheap that it's feasible to just get a second hard disk and keep a copy of your data on both disks. Depending on which operating system you're using, you'll need to do this by periodically XCOPYing your data to the second hard disk, or, if you're running Windows NT, you can use its Disk Administrator to set up the two disks as a mirror set.

Note

A *mirror set* is a group of two physical drives that are set up so that when data is written to one, it is written to the second as well.

Of course, an extra hard drive isn't as portable as some of the other options that we've talked about here. Another disadvantage is that, unless it's an external drive, you can't switch it to another computer easily and, if it's part of a mirror set, you'll only be able to use it on a computer that has the compatible software installed. But for a high-speed and simple backup solution, it's very workable.

What Software Do You Need?

The answer to this question really depends on what you're installing and what operating system you're using. For example, if you're using Windows 95/98 and decide to get a CD-ROM drive, the setup process is limited to telling Windows about the new hardware (you do this with the Add New Hardware utility in the Control Panel) and rebooting the machine.

Other hardware varies in its software requirements, for example:

Tape drives You'll need to install the tape controller software. This may either come with the drive or be part of the operating system.

Removable drives They'll have installation utilities. The Zip drive, for example, works with Windows 95/98.

A second hard disk You'll need to set it up as you would any other hard disk.

CD-R drives and optical drives Like CD-ROM drives, they'll have setup software. Some operating systems will be able to detect compatible types, but you'll need to see what CD-R types are supported first.

Once the software is installed, you'll be able to back up files. When using devices such as CD-Rs, removable drives, or optical drives, you could use the DOS XCOPY command to copy files and directories from your hard disk. However, it's easier to take advantage of the graphical interface of today's operating systems. Just drag the icon from the drive you want to back up onto the icon for your backup drive.

Backup Strategies

Having the tools to back up is only part of the solution. For complete data protection, you've got to make sure that you use them. I know it's a pain, but you've got to back up your data on a daily basis if you generate anything of importance at all. Even losing one day's work can be bad, so how would you recreate a week's worth?

First, centralize your data as much as possible. If you're responsible for backing up more than one networked computer, consider storing all data on a file server for backup. It's much easier to back up one computer than ten.

Second, create a schedule and stick to it. I've found that a rotating backup schedule that combines full and differential backups works quite well. On Monday, for example, you might do a full backup of the system. Then, on each day of the rest of the week, you can do a differential or incremental backup so that you only copy the files that have changed.

Note

A *differential* backup copies those files that have changed since the last backup of any kind; an *incremental* backup copies only those files that have changed since the last full backup.

Name each backup tape, disk, or cartridge with its date, the machine it belongs to, and the type of backup it is. For example, a full backup of my workstation might be labeled "08/05/00 Full backup of INTEVA."

Finally, don't rely on your memory. Make yourself a backup schedule and put it on the wall or someplace very visible. Posting your backup schedule in a prominent place has two advantages. First, you know at a glance when you last backed up (initial each backup after you've completed it). Second, it reminds you to back up until it gets to be a regular habit.

Carbon Copier

Ghost from Symantec and DriveImage from PowerQuest (see the Vendor Guide on CD #2 for contact information) are utilities that can make a complete copy of a drive and "paste" it to another drive (although it doesn't *just* paste—it can also format and resize the partitions). Think of it as software that acts as a Xerox machine for hardware.

The principle is simple; they copy every bit from the source drive, cluster for cluster, to a file that the program understands, typically with some sort of compression. When you're ready to create a duplicate drive, merely plug in the drive and tell the utility to copy the selected image to it.

Both DriveImage Pro and Ghost support multicasting for distributed network installations that cut down on excessive traffic. DriveImage comes with a very cool little tool called MagicMover. Let's put it this way: have you ever removed an application from one machine only to have to install it on another *and* reconfigure everything by hand? MagicMover allows you to migrate installed applications wholesale. It can track down every instance of a drive path that the application might require and reset it to the new drive's path structure.

But wait, that's not all! If you have media large enough (multi-gigabyte tape or DAT backup device) you can make an image of your drive and save it for restoring later. Test a lot of machines? When one bites the dust, slap a new disk image onto it. It beats having to reconfigure everything from scratch.

Pick one. They're both great buys.

Preparing Boot Floppies

Once you've got the important places backed up, make sure that you can get your computer up and running without the help of your hard drive. This means that you must make sure you've got a boot floppy for each of your systems, and it should be a bootable floppy with whatever device drivers you regularly use to boot your system. This is for emergencies when your PC won't boot from the hard disk.

If you're running Windows 9x, you were given an opportunity to create a boot disk when you first installed the operating system. If you *didn't* create a boot disk, all you need to do is to open the Control Panel, click Add/Remove Programs, choose the Startup Disk tab, and select the Create Disk option.

Windows 2000 doesn't allow you to cancel the creation of a bootable floppy, so make sure to be prepared with a single floppy when you install Windows 2000.

No matter which operating system you're using, you should be sure that you've got a boot floppy or some kind of recovery disk handy.

There are a few caveats, though. For one, the boot floppy it makes has no clue about CD drives. So a recovery by reinstalling Windows from CD is out. Early versions of Windows, particularly Windows 95, did not come with a CD driver, even though it shipped on a CD. You were either expected to already have a CD driver installed in Windows 3.*x* or to create one from scratch. It was a pain.

Well, Microsoft heard and obeyed. With Windows 98, they shipped a floppy disk that had generic drivers for most standard IDE and SCSI CD-ROM drives. It is *this* floppy that you must prize above all. It is the single most important tool you have in the recovery of any non-NTFS system, since it can boot pretty much any system that has CD-ROM support.

Now you have access to just about any utility that will run from a CD-R that you can cram into it. Do you have several utilities spread throughout CDs and floppies? This floppy will make most, if not all, of them available without having to reboot over and over again.

But what about NT and 2000? Windows 2000 is a complicated beast, but NT is almost as easy as Windows 9x. Just back up the Registry (those are the SYSTEM.DAT and USER.DAT files that are located in your C:\Windows directory) Unlike Windows NT, however, simply backing up the Registry in Windows 2000 isn't enough. There are a few more variables involved that Microsoft calls the System State. These items make up the System State for a domain controller:

▶ Active Directory

▶ Boot files

▶ COM+ class registration database

▶ Registry

▶ The SYSVOL

Just run a complete backup to tape or DAT and it will include *all* of the files necessary to back up your system. You should almost never back up just a handful of the important files—always back up everything you can.

If you don't have the space, however, back up the files that you cannot afford to lose. In a worst case scenario, you'll have to reinstall the system and all of your applications, but that's not nearly as inconvenient as losing all your work and having to do it all over again.

Performing Media Tests Annually

No disk medium is perfect. Greater use of voice coil head positioning and sputtered media has greatly improved disks, but there's always the chance that a part of a platter isn't coated perfectly. Worse yet, there's the chance that all that bad treatment most PCs get has led to a disk scratch or two.

That's why there are so many "disk tester" programs around. A popular example is the Disk Doctor program that's been a part of the Norton Utilities for years. Basically, all these kinds of programs do is try to read your data, sector by sector. If there's a sector that they have trouble reading, they attempt to move the data elsewhere, then mark its cluster as bad in the FAT. Of course, once an area is marked bad, the operating system sidesteps it.

There are two problems with this approach. First—through no fault of their own—these programs miss most of the disk problems until they're just about disasters, and second, the way they mark bad areas (the FAT) is too transient. Take a look at Figure 16.2.

Figure 16.2

How the operating system handles disk errors

You see, with disks, there are a lot of problems that the operating system doesn't tell us about. If the operating system detects a read error, it performs several retries without informing the user. If the retries succeed, the user never knows there is a problem. Even *before* the operating system retries occur, however, the BIOS can retry. When the BIOS sees errors, it will respond by executing retries of its own or, if the retries don't work, employing the error correction hardware. (You may recall that hard disk controllers use an ECC—error-correction code—that allows them to not only detect faulty data on the hard disk, but also to correct it—or a short burst of bad data anyway.) If BIOS retries have been sufficient, the operating system discovers nothing of the problem. However, if the BIOS had to use ECC to reconstruct data, it informs the operating system when it hands the data over. But believe it or not, the operating system actually has a small section of code whose job is to filter out these messages so that it can ignore the BIOS error messages.

"Ignore?" Yes. Upon bootup, the system sets up pointers to various important areas in the BIOS. These pointers are called "software interrupts"—different from hardware interrupts, they're basically "canned" utility programs easily available to any program running on the system. One of them, INT 13, points to disk routines. As provided by the BIOS manufacturer, read and write attempts with INT 13 will return messages that inform INT 13's caller of required error correction. Upon bootup, however, the operating system actually substitutes some of its *own* INT 13 code that ignores the fact that the sector had to be error corrected! That means that an application program can't even recover the error correction information if it *wants* to. This is dumb, as it would have been nice for Norton and the gang to be able to bypass the operating system and utilize INT 13 directly, employing the fact that there had to be an error correction to warn users of disk areas that are causing problems. This also means the operating system ignores the early warnings of data and reports nothing until disaster strikes. It also means that it'll be tough for *any* tester program to do meaningful media tests, as both the BIOS and the operating system seem to discard the early warning signs.

Pattern Testing Methods

In order to generate the problems that prompt retries and ECC corrections, a program's got to *do* something—read or write the disk. So disk tester programs write and read data to/from the disk. You wouldn't think it would matter exactly *what* a test program writes, just that it writes—it seems that a test program has only to write out "Mary had a little lamb" or the like zillions of times all over the disk, then read it back, and the disk's tested. Believe it or not, however, there's a science to the choosing of test patterns.

Recall that data is encoded on the disk using either MFM (modified frequency modulation) or some kind of RLL (run-length limited). Both encoding schemes seek to merge the clock and data signals into a stream of pulses on the disk. It turns out that not all patterns are equally simple to encode and decode: some are less reliable. A read/write test writes out these problem patterns that are encoding method–specific.

Think of it this way. Suppose you wanted to test the degree of color definition of a TV picture tube. You might do this by displaying letters against a background on the tube, then measuring from how far away the letters are still readable. Would you display white letters on a black background? No, hopefully not—that would be cheating. It would be much better to use, say, blue on purple, or red on brown. Pattern testing is the disk equivalent.

Problems with Newer Controllers

As I'm writing this, changes are occurring in the disk world that may require another rewrite of the disk fixers.

You've already seen that it's common for a controller to automatically retry its current operation, and in fact to retry it from 8 to 30 times. Only if the retries haven't worked does the controller use the ECC information. So having to resort to an ECC correction is a fairly infrequent event, and it's one that should cause some worries.

However, that's changing as disks get smaller, physical size-wise, but larger, data capacity-wise. The original IBM specification for hard disks required that the drives read no more than one bad bit in 10^{12} (an American trillion or a European billion). The smaller, denser disks, however, can see one bad bit in only 10^7, or one in ten million. To combat that, the disks are using a *76-bit* ECC! (You may recall that the old XT-type WD1002 controller gives you a choice between 5 and 11 bits. That's probably fine, for the older, more reliable drives.)

File Defragmenters

After running for a while, the files on your hard drive can become *fragmented* or *noncontiguous.* This means that a given file may be stored partly in clusters 30–40 (one contiguous group) and partly in clusters 101–122 (another contiguous group). A file is said to be noncontiguous if (logically) it has more than one contiguous block of disk space. Noncontiguous files are bad for two reasons, as demonstrated in Figure 16.3.

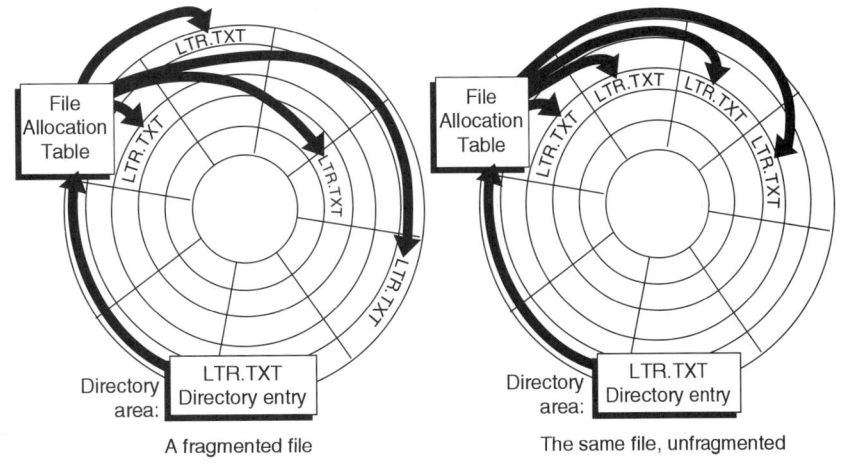

Figure 16.3

A fragmented and an unfragmented file

A fragmented file

The same file, unfragmented

First, noncontiguous files take longer to read. The fact that the disk head must go chasing all over the disk to read them slows down disk access. Putting the whole file together makes read operations quicker: move the head once, and all of the data can be read.

Second, you have a higher probability of recovering a deleted file if it is not fragmented. Keeping disks defragmented just pushes the odds a little further in your favor. Think of it this way: suppose you've got to find and piece together a file on a disk whose FAT has been zapped. Would you rather have to find a file in clusters 100, 120, and 1521, or a file in clusters 100 to 102? If the files are always defragmented, data recovery is easier.

Note

Most systems utilities, such as Norton Utilities for Windows, cache up to the last 1500 deleted files for improved recovery odds. It is *not* a good idea, though, to go about deleting things willy-nilly.

How do files become fragmented? When the operating system needs a cluster, it basically grabs the first one available. When the disk is new, only a few clusters have been taken, and the rest of the disk is one large free area. New files are all contiguous. But as files are deleted, they create "holes" in the disk space. As the operating system looks for more clusters, it takes the first sector available. This can easily lead to a new file being spread out over several separate areas.

You can easily defragment files using the defrag utility that is included in all versions of Windows. It's located at Start ➤ Programs ➤ Accessories ➤ System Tools ➤ Disk Defragmenter (see Figure 16.4). Just fire it up and run an analysis on the disk first to find out if it even needs it. If it does, it's suggested that you do run the defragmenter. For FAT12, FAT16, and FAT32 file systems, I suggest that you close all running applications and anything else superfluous. For NTFS 4 and NTFS 5, it's all right to leave things running since it's designed to handle network server operations, but it's preferred to have as little running as possible.

Figure 16.4

The Disk
Defragmenter utility
in Windows 2000
Server

Note

Windows NT 4 does not come with a defragmenting tool, but ExecSoft is nice
enough to offer Diskeeper Lite, a manually operated version of their award-
winning Diskeeper. It's free of charge to anybody who needs it. If you want
automation, you can pay for the big version and enjoy fast, convenient, nonde-
structive active defragmentation all the time. It even works over a network. See
the Vendor Guide on CD #2 for contact information.

One last thing to keep in mind is that only fragmented files will
be defragmented while the disk they are on is the boot drive. Booting from a floppy or other device is essential if you want to defragment an entire drive, top to bottom.

Recovering Data and Fixing Hard Disks

The linchpin of the Windows 9*x* space allocation system (not to mention DOS) is the file allocation table (FAT). The FAT and the directory structures allow Windows (and DOS) to keep track of the data stored on the device and where and how that data is stored. FAT troubles are what cause all of those cryptic CHKDSK woes. (And when I say CHKDSK, I'm also talking about SCANDISK, as it does basically the same thing except with a prettier interface.) You see, CHKDSK *doesn't* check the disk, it checks the FAT. A lot of folks think that they're doing something good for their disk when they run CHKDSK. "I run CHKDSK now and then to look for bad areas on the disk," they say. That's totally wrong. CHKDSK just checks and reports on the state of the FAT. It doesn't do a new media check.

CHKDSK in Action, Such as It Is

All CHKDSK does when it reports numbers of bad sectors is to scan the FAT, counting up all the clusters marked as bad. Then it multiplies the number of bad clusters by the number of bytes per cluster and arrives at the number of bad bytes on the disk. Any new bad areas are *not* discovered by CHKDSK, but rather by one of the disk test programs that I discussed in Chapter 5, "Troubleshooting PC Problems." CHKDSK does only a few things:

▶ It counts up the available clusters, used clusters, and bad clusters.

▶ It searches the directory structure to ensure that it makes sense: all subdirectories must have the proper format (for example, the "." and ".." files must be in place). It examines the entire subdirectory tree.

▶ It examines all files' directory entries and FAT chains. The directory entry, you will recall, records the file size in bytes. The FAT chain tells how many clusters a file uses. Those two numbers must agree: there have to be enough clusters allocated in the FAT to accommodate the number of bytes referenced in the directory.

▶ It checks that all FAT chains make sense.

Understand before we go any further that CHKDSK errors do not point to hardware errors. They either indicate bad software or dumb operators.

The simplest kind of problem (simplest to repair, that is) is one where the directory or the FAT has been damaged or modified in some way that you don't want. For example, if you delete a file, it isn't really deleted—at least not at first, so it's easy to undelete it. Another directory/FAT problem is a formatted disk; believe it or not, you can often *un*format a hard disk! Yet another is something you've probably seen before, a *lost cluster*. You can repair all of these problems by manipulating the FAT and/or directory structure and leaving the data alone.

Somewhat harder to solve are the problems that come from actual disk damage in one part of the disk; these are the `Sector not found` errors. You usually fix them by telling the disk to avoid the affected area, then reloading backups on that area. Yes, I said backups; there's just no guarantee that you'll be able to recover data on an area that's been "cratered."

At the end of this chapter, we'll look in detail at how to resurrect dead drives. But first, the easy problems . . .

What Happens When a File Is Deleted

Sometimes carelessness and haste carry a painful price: accidental deletion of files. There are lots of ways to do this, and I need not dwell on them. Let's see how to recover from the problem.

Hold on a moment. Recover from *deletion*? Undeleting? Isn't that kind of like unpainting a house or unwatering a lawn?

Nope. First of all, understand that the operating system is lazy and doesn't really rub out much of *anything* when it deletes files.

Deletion is not done by blanking out clusters but instead by changing the first letter of the name of the file still stored in the directory. The operating system doesn't go to the trouble of erasing the clusters, so they just sit there, available for use the next time a new file is created (or an old file is expanded). *As long as you undelete before a new file is created, the file can be saved.* Figure 16.5 shows the FAT and directory entries of an example file, HAMLET.TXT, when it doesn't have any problems. HAMLET.TXT starts in cluster 100 and runs (contiguously) through cluster 104. Its file size implies that the file will be five clusters long, and indeed it turns out to be five clusters long.

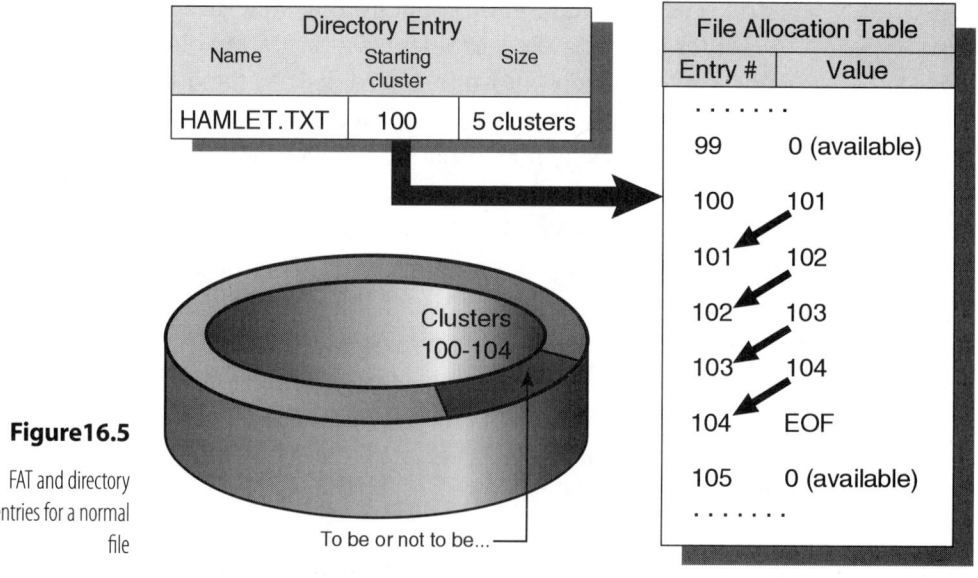

Figure16.5

FAT and directory entries for a normal file

Figure 16.6 shows what HAMLET.TXT would look like if it was deleted. The first character is changed, and the FAT entries are changed to zero, making them available.

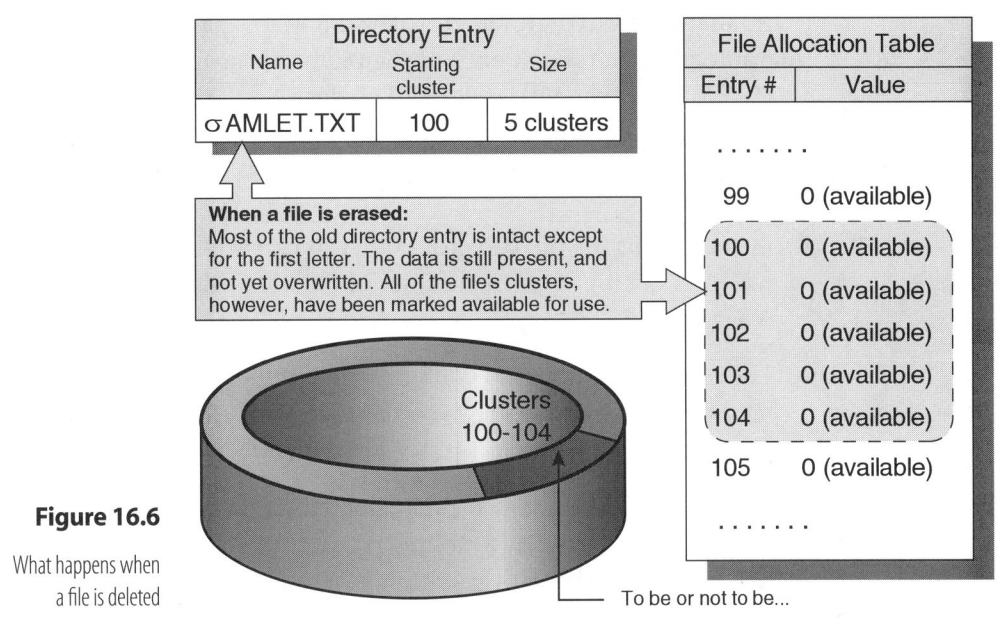

Directory Entry		
Name	Starting cluster	Size
σ AMLET.TXT	100	5 clusters

When a file is erased:
Most of the old directory entry is intact except for the first letter. The data is still present, and not yet overwritten. All of the file's clusters, however, have been marked available for use.

File Allocation Table	
Entry #	Value
. . . .	
99	0 (available)
100	0 (available)
101	0 (available)
102	0 (available)
103	0 (available)
104	0 (available)
105	0 (available)
. . . .	

Clusters
100-104

To be or not to be...

Figure 16.6

What happens when a file is deleted

Basic Unerasing

For some reason, Windows 9x/NT/2000 does not have any undelete facilities except for the Recycle Bin, which only allows you to undelete files if you deleted them by putting them in the Recycle Bin. If you deleted a file from a DOS command prompt, there aren't any undelete possibilities. The process could be done by hand with a lot of patience and DEBUG, but fortunately, for both Windows and DOS, there are products to do this for you. The best known product is, of course, Norton Utilities. The original included UnDelete, and since version 3.1, it has included Quick UnDelete (QU).

Note

The Recycle Bin is really just another directory on your hard drive. When you trash files in Windows, you are moving those files from one folder to another.

No matter how you undelete, please understand that it's not a guaranteed matter. Look back at the picture of what happens to HAMLET.TXT when it's deleted. The data's still there, and so is most of the directory entry, but the FAT chain has been zeroed out. What, then, does an undelete program know? Well, it knows that:

▶ By looking at the old directory entry, it can see how large the file was and so compute the number of clusters that must be reassembled.

▶ The directory entry also contains the number of the starting cluster. So you know, in the case of HAMLET.TXT, that it (1) occupied five clusters and, (2) started in cluster 100.

▶ Looking at the FAT, you see that cluster 100 is available, so you can attempt undeletion. If QU found 100 occupied, that would mean that the file had been overwritten. Not only is 100 free, but the next four clusters are free, too. Assuming that the file was contiguous before it was deleted (as most files are), QU would just reassemble HAMLET.TXT out of clusters 100 through 104. On the other hand, if HAMLET.TXT had actually been in clusters 100, 200, 250, and 301, the unerasing program would have reassembled the file completely incorrectly based on its assumptions.

It should be obvious that there's some guesswork here. Can you reduce the guesswork? Well, you've seen now that undeletion is mainly a matter of manipulating the FAT. An even easier and more reliable approach to reassembling the FAT chain would be to back up the FAT every day so that if a file were deleted, the old FAT image would be around and available to assist the unerasing program.

To summarize: when you've got a deleted file that you want to undelete, don't create any new files, and undelete with a commercial program like Norton Utilities.

Here's a true story to underscore how important this is. I've got a friend who's a PC support person. He worked in a department with a woman that he *really* wanted to get to know better—I mean, he wanted her to suffer a data loss in a *big* way. One day, Fate offered him his chance. She called up, explaining that she'd accidentally deleted a couple of files on her hard disk. He assured her that he could help her and raced over to her workstation with a copy of Norton Utilities. To make the program more convenient to work with, he (you guessed it) copied it to the hard disk. Arggh. The poor boy lost the data—*and* the date.

Unerasing Partially Overwritten Files

Someone calls you up. "I accidentally deleted a file," he says. "No problem," you reply, eager to don the cape and cowl and go save the day as Dataman, the finder of lost data.

"I'll be right over," you say. "Just be sure not to create any files until I get there." You arrive, and find him typing away at the keyboard. Dataman (that's you, remember) is aghast.

"I told you not to create any new files! What are you doing?" you cry.

"Oh, I lost a *WordPerfect* file. *This* is an *Excel* file I've just now created. That won't affect a deleted WordPerfect file, will it?"

"Users . . ." you mutter. No point in explaining now that there's only one FAT for the system and that it's not subdirectory-specific.

The previous is a true story, and it happened to me. Here's what I did.

1. First, as the new file was created in a different subdirectory, the original WP file's directory entry was not overwritten. I pulled it up with Norton and saw that the file was five clusters long and started in cluster 300. Thank goodness it was a file that contained text; partial text files are usually recoverable—partial spreadsheets often are not.

2. A look in the FAT showed that cluster 300 was, indeed, taken by the new Excel file. But clusters 301 through 304 were open.

3. I decided to create a directory entry with Norton and then string the FAT entries together by hand. Before I could do that, however, I needed to know which clusters used to contain the WP file. There are two approaches to getting this information: one is to just assume that clusters 301 through 304 are the

ones you're looking for. The other is to search the disk. I decided to search the disk.

4. Norton has a Text Search program. You give it some text to search for and tell it whether to search all of the disk or the deleted part of the disk. (Deleted here really means available areas. It will search just within a file, a range of sectors or clusters, or the whole disk, if you like.) In this case, I asked if there was a hard copy of the document around. There was, so I searched for random phrases that I typed in from the hard copy.

5. Once the match is found, Norton shows you exactly what it found and where it found it (cluster 20, sector 77). I kept notes on all the clusters that matched text from the hard copy and found that the text had probably been in clusters 300 (I knew that from the directory entry), 301, 302, 310, and 311—it had been fragmented!

6. Then I hand-assembled a file out of the remaining clusters.

Do be careful about using this search technique. There were also old versions of the document on the disk, and I kept finding them when trying to locate the remains of the deleted document.

So unerasing a partially overwritten file boils down to (1) finding out which clusters remain from the file and (2) building a directory and FAT chain by hand with Norton or the equivalent.

How Programs Save Files

The way that most programs save files actually increases the chances that you can recover a lost file. Suppose I'm in my favorite word processor, Ami Pro, working on a document called BOOK . SAM. When I tell Ami to save the file, it goes through these steps:

1. It saves the file in its current state to a file called SAMSAVE0 . TMP.

2. It waits for the entire file to be written out safely.

3. It deletes the previous BOOK.SAM and renames
SAMSAVE0.TMP to BOOK.SAM.

The effect is that not only do I have the current BOOK.SAM on
disk, I've also got a whole bunch of "free" space that actually contains
the previous version of the file. What about the next time I save the
file—will Windows overwrite the old BOOK.SAM? Probably not. In
order to minimize fragmentation, the operating system starts looking for free space after the cluster where it appeared previously. For
example, suppose all of the disk's free space is contiguous. When I
start up the PC in the morning, my BOOK.SAM might start at cluster
1000. Let's say that the free space starts at cluster 1500. Suppose
also that BOOK.SAM is 50 clusters long. That means that the first
time I save the file, the operating system will look for the first free
cluster, which will turn out to be 1500. It will then save the file starting in clusters 1500–1549 and will mark clusters 1000–1049 as
available. The next time I save the file, the operating system won't
put the "new" file at cluster 1000; instead, it will look for a free cluster by remembering the last free cluster that it saw, which would be
cluster 1550, and start from there. The net effect is that the space
from 1000–1049 is left alone, at least until you run out of space on
the disk or until you reboot.

I've used this to my advantage. Once, I accidentally managed to
destroy both this whole book *and* my backups. (Don't ask.) As I very
rarely reboot, I had all of my work for the past week or so sitting in
the "available" part of the disk. A little search and stitch work, and it
was all as good as new.

Recovering Accidentally Formatted Hard Disks

Formatting is kind of like erasing, only more so. Unformatting can
be like undeleting, only a *lot* more so.

Accidental formats are a painful problem, as they zap the whole
disk in one fell swoop. Remember that the DOS FORMAT command
does not actually delete sector data but only deletes the boot record,

the FAT, and the root directory, creating a set of blank FATs and a root directory in their place.

One of the primary reasons disks are not completely formatted is because of the immense amount of time that would be involved in *actually* erasing the data. In reality nothing is ever "deleted" per se. To "erase" implies removal. Nothing is ever removed from a disk, just redefined. So, to make all data on the disk vanish you must convert the bits. Everything gets turned into 1s, and *that* makes the data unrecoverable and unreadable.

So the sectors are all there, but how to sew them back together? (A 17GB hard disk has more than 16 million sectors.) There are two approaches, which I call Class I and Class II unformatters. Class I can recover an entire disk but requires some preparation *before* the format occurs. Class II, on the other hand, can't recover the entire disk but will work even if you haven't prepared the disk prior to the format.

Class I Unformatters

The Class I approach is to keep a copy of the FAT, the directory, and the boot record in a specific physical location. As long as you keep it up to date, the disk can be easily restored. See the section "Backing Up and Restoring Your MBR with DEBUG" for how to do this.

Class II Unformatters

The alternative approach to unformatting, which I call the Class II approach, can only recover information in subdirectories, and even then there are no guarantees. Recall that subdirectory information is maintained in files, and those files are recognizable by their format: the ".." and "." directory entries. Unformatting programs first locate these files, then use the information in them to reassemble data files.

The subdirectory files contain a link to the first FAT entry. Since the FAT is a blank FAT, its only use is to tell you what the first sector was. It also tells you how many clusters the file used to take up. Unformatters just take a number of contiguous clusters and tack them together as the file. This means that fragmented files cannot be saved in their entirety, and garbage sectors may be tacked on the end of data files. But it's better than nothing, and your chances of success can be improved by running a defragmenting program now and then (see the "File Defragmenters" section). The defragmenting program should be run *before* formatting the disk. Defragmenting a freshly formatted disk accomplishes nothing. It also means that any files kept in the root directory cannot be restored.

Fixing Lost Clusters

Ah, yes. Lost clusters. These are the words in the CHKDSK error message that it seems everyone has seen in the past. People confuse lost clusters with bad clusters, so the lost cluster message strikes fear in users' hearts. It needn't, however: it generally just means some sloppy internal housekeeping on some program's part.

When CHKDSK reports lost clusters, it basically means loss of the pointer from the directory to the FAT. Recall that the *pointer* is just the "starting cluster" entry in a file's directory entry.

Lost clusters occur when the FAT entries for a file are written, but the starting cluster value for the file hasn't been put in the directory. Why would the FAT reflect a file's status while the directory would not? Generally, this happens because you can't report how large a file is until you've seen it and it's been stored on disk. Disk storage involves allocation of clusters, so as the clusters are allocated and filled, the FAT gets updated, little by little. The directory entry for a file, however, is the last part of the file to go on the disk, mainly because the directory contains the file's size, and the operating system can't know that until it's finished writing the file out.

As the directory entry with the starting cluster value is often the last thing written when the file is created, this means that a program that "died" in the middle of manipulating the FAT could easily have created some FAT chains without yet having written the directory entry. But why would a program "die"?

▶ The computer may have been shut off by a user in the middle of a file operation, perhaps because the user thought that turning the computer off would abort some mistake that was made.

- Buggy software. It either tries to bypass DOS and handle the FAT and directory stuff itself (incorrectly), or it just freezes up in the middle of the file write operation.

- Along the lines of buggy software, there are a fair number of programs that create "temporary" files for their own use. The programs are supposed to delete these files upon exit, but some don't do a very good job of erasing the files. Lost clusters result.

As I've explained, lost clusters are a chain of FAT entries—allocated clusters—with no directory entry. A lost cluster is, then, a "file with no name." (Sounds kinda like there's a country-western song in there: "Ah wrote a letter to my babe / but the disk went lame / an' now those purty words / are in a file with no name . . ." Okay, so I'm not Kenny Rogers.) You can see a chain of lost clusters in Figure 16.7.

Figure 16.7

A chain of lost clusters

What do you do about lost clusters? First, remember that this is either a temporary file that's trash anyway or it's a file whose write operation was never finished properly. In either case, there's probably nothing of value there. The main reason that you want to clean up lost clusters is to make CHKDSK happy and to get the space back on your hard disk that those lost clusters are wasting.

If you run CHKDSK on a disk with a lost cluster, you'll see a message like this:

```
Errors found, F parameter not specified.
Corrections will not be written to disk.
1 lost clusters found in 1 chain. Convert lost
chains to files (Y/N)
```

Nobody ever knows what those first two lines mean, and they seem innocuous anyway. What gets people's attention, however, is the "lost clusters" part. First, CHKDSK is saying, "You have lost clusters." Most people are kind of panicky at this point, thinking, "Gee, I didn't even know I *had* clusters—much less that I could lose them." "Lost" gets confused with "bad" in most users' minds. They're not quite sure what's going on, but it seems that CHKDSK is offering to fix the problem with the "Convert lost chains to files?" question. So they say "Y" in response.

Those first two lines in the CHKDSK message *are*, in fact, important. CHKDSK, when run without the /F (Fix) option, does not actually do anything to the disk. What it's really saying is, "Even if I *say* I'm going to fix something, ignore me. I'm lying." If you tell CHKDSK to convert the lost chains to files, you'll get a response looking something like

```
XXXXXX bytes total disk space
XXXXXX bytes in XX directories...
2048 bytes would be in
1 recovered files...
```

You've got to read the fine print: 2048 bytes *would be* in 1 recovered files. It didn't actually *do* anything. Run it again, and you'll get the exact same response. Since it's not doing anything, it can easily *keep* doing nothing forever. I know this all seems pretty obvious when I explain it, but you'd be surprised how many users wonder why there are lost clusters every single time that they run CHKDSK. The answer is simple: they always run CHKDSK, not CHKDSK/F, and so the few lost clusters that they have never get fixed.

How *would* you fix a chain of lost clusters? Just as CHKDSK says, it will convert the chain to a file. Lost clusters are just a file with no name, so CHKDSK creates a directory entry for the lost chain. The entry includes a bogus file name, FILE0000.CHK. If there's already a FILE0000.CHK, CHKDSK uses FILE0001.CHK, and so on. Those files are put in the root directory, by the way. For those people using DOS 6.2x and Windows 95 or later, SCANDISK will do the same thing, and you don't have to bother with the /F parameter.

Here's a *very important point:* if, for some reason, you have loads and loads of lost clusters, you may see a File creation error message when CHKDSK is trying to convert the chains to files. That's because CHKDSK puts all the files in the root directory and the root, you may recall, only has room for up to 512 directory entries. So if you had 600 chains of lost clusters, CHKDSK would be able to create directory entries for the first 500-odd (depending on how many files you already have in the root), but would fail thereafter. The answer here is to handle the first 500-odd FILEXXXX.CHK files, then delete them, freeing up both their space and their directory entries. Then run CHKDSK again to handle their remaining lost clusters. Take a look at Figure 16.8.

Figure 16.8

Fixing a chain of lost clusters

Once CHKDSK has put a filename on a chain, what can you do with this file? As I explained before, such files are usually temporary files and contain no valuable information. Data loss problems usually do not result in lost clusters.

On the other hand, it can't hurt to use a text editor or Norton to examine the file. There just may be some data that you thought you had lost.

Invalid Subdirectory Errors

As you've seen, a subdirectory's information is contained in a file. The subdirectory must have the "." and ".." files as its first entries. If they aren't there, CHKDSK assumes that the directory has been corrupted and issues a message like this one:

```
C:\PCNET Invalid sub-directory entry.
Convert directory to file (Y/N)?
```

CHKDSK is offering to take the actual subdirectory information and convert it to a file (not a particularly tough thing to do). The fact is, the operating system could work with the subdirectory without any trouble, even *if* the first two entries are corrupted.

CHKDSK, on the other hand, moves you from the frying pan into the fire. It is offering to *eliminate* the subdirectory as a directory. There are files in that subdirectory. Think about it: if we take away the directory, what do we have? FAT chains without directory entries because their subdirectory has been zapped. And what are they exactly? You got it—files with no name: lost clusters. Allowing CHKDSK to convert the subdirectory to a file instantly converts all the files in that subdirectory (and any subdirectories *under* that subdirectory) to lost clusters. Sheesh! Nice job, CHKDSK. SCANDISK does the same dumb thing.

As I said, you can probably get to all the files even *if* the subdirectory is screwy. Try copying them elsewhere. Failing that, first print out the directory listing of the subdirectory.

Now CHKDSK sees a whole lot of FAT chains without directory entries because their directory is gone. It then converts these to

FILEnnnn.CHK files. Your problem is to match up the CHK files with the former subdirectory contents. Your hints are the order and size of the files. The sizes may not match exactly, as CHKDSK just reports entire cluster size. The directory, which had more specific file size information, is gone, so the best that CHKDSK can do is to add up the number of bytes in the clusters and report that as the file size.

Here's an example. Imagine that you have the following files in an invalid subdirectory:

▶ ORDERS.TXT—2010 bytes

▶ NAMES.DBF—3000 bytes

Say that this is a hard disk, with 2048-byte sectors. After CHKDSK mauls the subdirectory, you find you have two new CHK files:

▶ FILE0000.CHK—2048 bytes

▶ FILE0001.CHK—4096 bytes

Notice that the file sizes have been rounded up to the nearest 2048 multiple. To finish the recovery job, first rename the files. Second, use Norton Utilities to revise the directory file size. *This is important,* as Lotus will refuse to read a file that has been completely recovered but has the wrong directory file size.

Or, try to fix the subdirectory yourself. You know what the subdirectory is supposed to look like—recall the ".." and "." files. Load the damaged subdirectory file with Norton Utilities and see if the damage is only minor. Perhaps you can do a little surgery and fix the problem without resorting to CHKDSK's extreme methods.

Allocation Error Message

Occasionally, you will see CHKDSK complain about an *allocation error.* That means that the directory and the FAT do not agree about how large a file is. CHKDSK's response is to assume that the FAT has better information than the directory and to just set the directory's size entry equal to the number of clusters times cluster size—the total number of bytes that CHKDSK can find for the file in the FAT. Take a look at Figure 16.9.

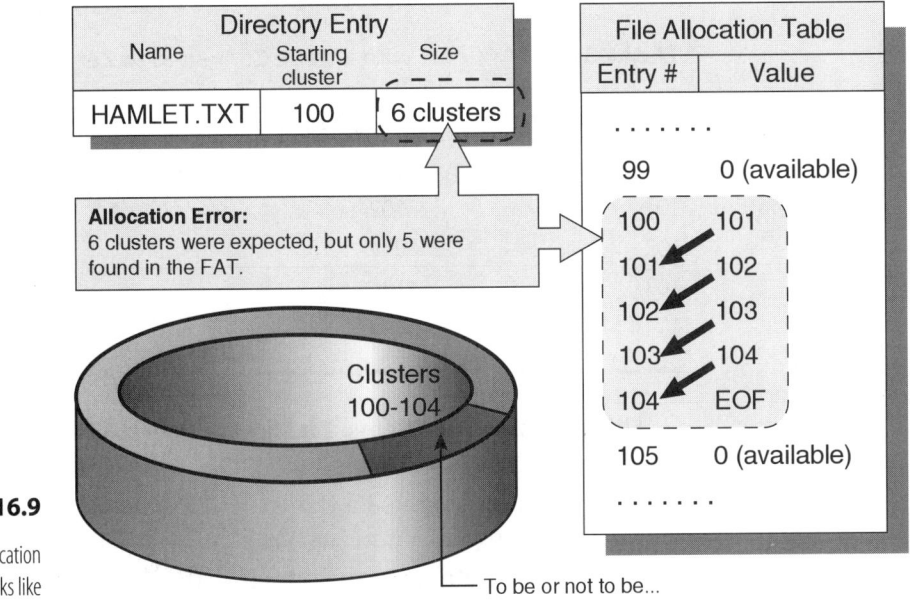

Figure 16.9

What an allocation error looks like

File Has Invalid Cluster Message

If a FAT chain leads to either a zero (an "available" cluster), or a "bad" marker, there's something wrong. CHKDSK responds by truncating the file at that point. For example, if a file were in clusters 100 through 104, a normal FAT chain would look like Table 16.1.

TABLE 16.1 Theoretical Normal FAT Chain

Entry Number	Entry Value
100	101
101	102
102	103
103	104
104	EOF

However, if, through a software error, the value in entry 102 were converted to zero, the chain would look like Table 16.2.

TABLE 16.2 FAT Chain with a Value Converted to Zero

Entry Number	Entry Value
100	101
101	102
102	0
103	104
104	EOF

This poses two problems. The first is that 101 points to 102, indicating that cluster 102 is "taken." There's a conflict, however, because with a zero in its FAT entry, 102 claims to be available. Further, 103 and 104 have now been cast adrift: there's a chain from 103 to 104, but nothing in the directory points to it. So CHKDSK would report both an allocation error (because 102 contains 0) and a chain of lost clusters.

When CHKDSK reports an allocation error, ask yourself: "When did I last modify this file?" That's when the problem was created. If you can nail down what program or, more likely, what *combination* of programs caused the bad FAT chain to be written, you can keep it from happening again.

Cross-Linked Clusters

Another CHKDSK complaint is *cross-linked clusters.* It refers to multiple pointers into the same cluster. It means that more than one file thinks it owns a disk area: cluster 14 (for example) is reported to be owned by more than one file. Figures 16.10 and 16.11 show a normal pair of files and a pair of cross-linked files, respectively.

Figure 16.10

A pair of normal files

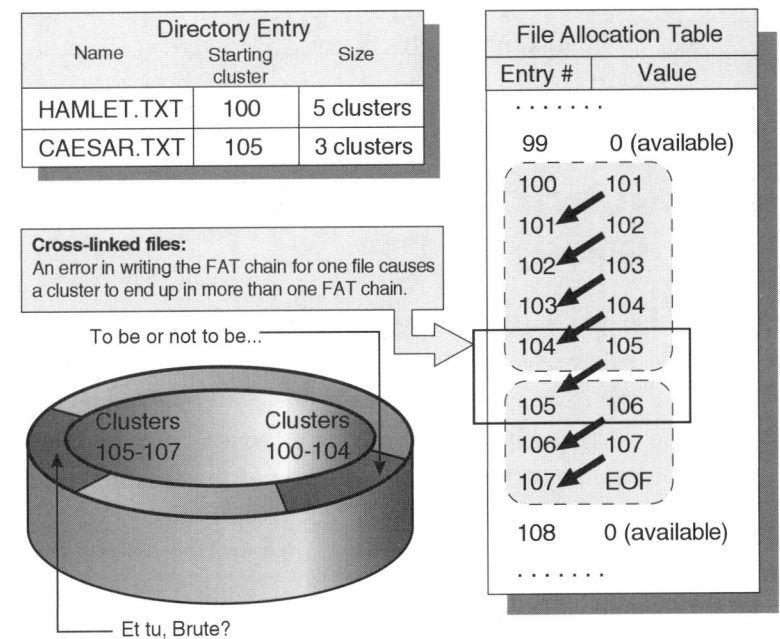

Figure 16.11

A pair of cross-linked files

Files generally become cross-linked because there is more than one program running on the PC at the same time in some kind of multitasking mode, a mode of operation very common and familiar to Windows users today. There are different ways to handle multitasking, but in an old approach you ran two programs simultaneously by modifying DOS so that you could run two DOS environments simultaneously and then run programs under these copies of DOS. Then program 1 asks DOS copy 1 to write out a file, and program 2 asks DOS copy 2 to also write out a file. As both copies of DOS are running simultaneously, each grabs for the same cluster. Result: cross-linked files. This will not necessarily happen with multitasking systems like Windows, Unix, and the Macintosh OS, but it does occasionally.

CHKDSK won't fix this for you; it'll just complain about it. The fix is to first copy all affected files to other files, then delete the original affected files. In the example in Figure 16.11 there are two files, HAMLET.TXT and CAESAR.TXT, that are cross-linked. Copy them to HAMLET.BAK and CAESAR.BAK, respectively. Then delete HAMLET.TXT and CAESAR.TXT. The copied files will have as much data as can be recovered. In all probability, some data has been lost. Again, this is not a hardware error, but rather is caused by software.

Understanding and Repairing Media Errors

Some problems aren't solved as easily as patching the FAT. Sometimes part of the drive just stops working. It could be that a part of the rusty coating on the drive that stores your data flaked off. Or perhaps the drive arm started to wobble a bit and can't get to a particular part of the disk. Whatever the reason, you may find yourself with a dead—or dying—part of a disk.

There are two very different problems facing a user of a hard disk with a media problem. First and foremost is data recovery. There *is* such a thing as "too late" when it comes to disk media errors, so, as I've said before, I strongly counsel adopting a religious attitude to backups. Second is the question, "Can I continue to use this drive?" The answer is, "Maybe," and, with some tricks you'll learn in this chapter, you can turn that into "Probably."

Data Recovery: A Case Study and Some Tips

Late one night, I was working on the first edition of this book, concentrating on a fairly large chapter. I saved my document to my laptop's floppy disk drive (this was before laptops had hard disks) and tried to make a backup of my file (let's call it TEXT). The drive ran for a bit and then I heard a bone-chilling sound: the grinding noise of a misreading drive! Sure enough, seconds later I saw this:

```
Data error reading drive B:
Abort, Retry, Ignore?
```

What to do? I'd followed all the rules of good data integrity—I tried to back up as soon as I exited the application, but the dumb word processor hadn't verified the data when it wrote it out.

The first thing to try, of course, was *Retry*. It actually *does* work in some circumstances. Remember that your data doesn't actually disappear altogether, it just fades, albeit sometimes a *lot*. Before you get your hopes up, however, remember that Retry is almost always a wasted effort on hard disks, inasmuch as there may have been 90 retries even before you saw an error message. With floppies, it's a different story.

No luck. What now? Remember to go for the easy stuff first. I took the diskette out and resat it in the drive. (It works sometimes.) Still no luck. I tried another drive. Still no luck.

Now the chill began to grow down my back. But I knew what to do about that.

Get up and take a walk.

I'm serious. If you were in the position that I was in at that moment, you'd be panicked. Panic is a sure cause of problems.

Next, write-protect the diskette. Why? Simple. Most people do exactly the wrong thing at this point—they call in the big guns like

Norton Disk Doctor. NDD is a nice program, but it's a surgeon. Surgeons get paid to *cut*. There's a time and place for surgeons, don't misunderstand me. But before you go to the surgeon, you get X-rays or MRIs, as a good doctor uses the most noninvasive techniques possible to figure out what the problem is before cutting.

And, for God's sake, *don't* run Norton SpeedDisk or Defrag! I have heard of no less than *five* cases in the last six months where someone wanted to recover data from a disk, so the "expert" first ran SpeedDisk. Arggh. In case it's not clear why this is an incredibly stupid idea, go back and read the "File Defragmenters" section. (Do I sound harsh? If so, it's because few things annoy me more than "experts" who don't have the courage to say the magic three words "I don't know," and instead just blunder along in the hopes that they can solve the problem. That may work with some problems, but, believe me, it sure doesn't work with data.) The job of these defragmenters is to move data that's in files so that each file is all in one place. That's data *in files*. In files means files that are good, readable, without problems. Delete data, and those areas that the data was once in are now available to be overwritten, and believe me, SpeedDisk will overwrite the data. Never, never, *never* run a disk defragmenter on a disk that you're trying to recover data from!

Warning

One of SpeedDisk's features is the ability to erase all blank space. See how that could be a problem?

Now, try to make a copy to work from. There are two approaches to copying a file, each with its own pros and cons.

▶ COPY the file elsewhere. When it gets to the bad part, and asks `Abort, Retry, Ignore`?, tell it Ignore. Ignore says to take the data, warts and all. Better to have a file with a creepy cluster or two than to have no file at all.

▶ DISKCOPY the disk. DISKCOPY "Xeroxes" a disk—it copies the disk sector by sector. The problem is that when it hits a bad sector, it skips the whole track. It doesn't try to copy it at all, and in fact if there were data on the target disk before, DISKCOPY doesn't even bother to delete the track. But the resulting disk has the same structure as the problem disk.

Sometimes the DISKCOPY command can get a few bytes that the COPY can't, and vice versa. Remember, these are the noninvasive techniques, so you can play to your heart's content without making things worse. Try the following techniques on the copies first. If that's no good, only *then* do you actually work on the *original* damaged disk.

Again, I wanted to affect the disk as little as possible, so I first "disconnected" cluster 612 from the file. It was simple: I just used Norton Utilities' NU program and changed the FAT. The FAT previously said to go from cluster 611 to 612 and from 612 to 613. I changed it so that it went straight from 611 to 613, and I marked 612 as "bad," intending to look at it more closely later. Then I copied TEXT without a hitch. Terrific—most of the file was back, 1024 bytes to go.

Next, I went into NU and tried to read cluster 612. Now, as it turns out, clusters on a lot of floppy disks are just pairs of sectors— a sector on the bottom head and a sector on the top head of the floppy. No reason, therefore, to assume that the *whole* cluster was bad; it was quite unlikely that both sides would be damaged. So I asked NU to read the cluster, and sure enough, it got over half of it: one side (512 bytes) was totally undamaged, and some of the sector on the bad side was readable. Result: I got back about 800 bytes of the missing 1024 bytes, wrote them to another cluster, and again repointed the FAT to use the newly written cluster. Only 200 bytes remained of lost data, and 200 bytes is about a sentence or two, so it was a piece of cake to reconstruct. You'd nvr evn knw thr ws a prblem. (Just kidding.)

To summarize, when you get the dreaded Abort, Retry, Ignore? message:

1. First choose Retry. If that does it, copy the data and throw away the problem disk.

2. Try another drive.

3. Stand up and walk around. Calm down.

4. Write-protect the problem disk before going further.

5. Try to DISKCOPY or COPY the file before going further. Do the surgery on the copy if possible. Remember that DISKCOPY throws out entire tracks and COPY only loses a bad cluster.

   Do not run invasive utilities like Norton Disk Doctor or SpeedDisk. If you *do* run Disk Doctor, don't let it make any of the "fixes" that it offers to do unless you've exhausted all other possibilities. *Under no circumstances* should you run Norton SpeedDisk on a disk with files that you're trying to recover.

6. Run SCANDISK or the like to determine where the bad clusters are. Then run DiskEdit and try to read these clusters. DiskEdit will read the good data as well as the bad. Copy the cluster to somewhere else and rearrange the FAT to use that cluster. Don't forget to modify *both* FATs.

It bears repeating: as soon as your hard disk starts showing spontaneous new bad sectors, back up the whole disk *immediately* and get ready to replace it—it's on its way out.

Assuming you've recovered your data, do you throw the drive away? Sometimes, sometimes not. If you choose to keep it and try to bring it back to life, read the next section.

Resurrecting Dead Hard Disk Drives

Unerasing and Sector not found errors are really just the opening act for the big one—doing the Lazarus trick on your hard disk. Before you go further, you might review the section "Understanding the PC Boot Process" in Chapter 7, "Repairs with Circuit Boards and Chips."

Remember Your Priorities

Fixing a dead hard disk is really three different kinds of tasks. In order of importance:

1. You want to get your data off the hard disk.

2. You must make the disk hardware respond to the system.

3. You may want to make the disk bootable again and perhaps keep it in service.

Keep those priorities in mind. Many times, folks focus on the third and least important goal. Data recovery is the foremost goal, although you can't recover any data until the disk talks to the system in at least a minimal fashion.

The boot procedure is integral to the drive initialization process, the method whereby the system identifies the hard disk or disks in the PC. As I already mentioned, look back to the boot description in Chapter 7 for more information on that. I'll build on that information immediately by presenting a flowchart of the drive recovery process and follow that with a section on each phase of the recovery process.

This discussion assumes that we're talking about a drive that worked yesterday in the very same machine with the very same controller. You didn't drop it from the back of a truck, and you didn't add any new boards between then and now. If you're having installation problems, look back at Chapter 11, "Installing an IDE Hard Drive," or Chapter 12, "Understanding and Installing SCSI Devices," to find information on drive installation.

Tracing a Disk Failure

Understanding the boot process might lead you to try to first verify the hardware, then the partition, and so on—and that's how I'll do it, basically. But verifying the hardware involves popping the top, and I'd like to avoid that if possible. So I've arranged the troubleshooting steps into a master hard disk troubleshooting flowchart designed for minimum effort. You can see it in Figure 16.12. It's an overview, and I'll expand on each box, but it's still useful as a roadmap of the drive resurrection trail.

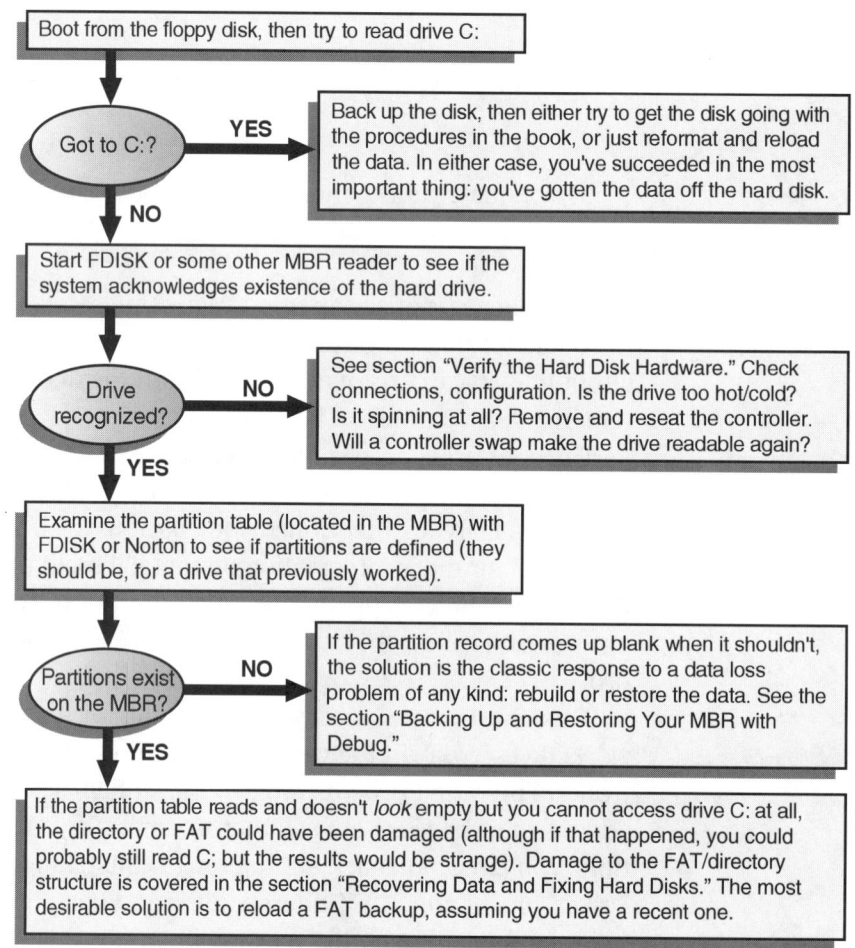

Figure 16.12

A simple flowchart example

There's a lot of detail in the following sections, so it's easy to get lost. If you do, come back to this flowchart to orient yourself.

Recovery Step 1: Boot from a Floppy

Get your "toolkit" floppy ("panic" floppy, some people call it) that I suggested creating before. Boot from a floppy with whatever device drivers your system uses and then try to read C: (or D: or whatever). If the drive is accessible, just copy all the data off the drive. Then you can figure out why it's misbehaving with less stress. You also don't need to go any further in this chapter: just reinstall the drive.

Recovery Step 2: Try to Read the MBR

The first and most important piece of data on the hard disk is the Master Boot Record (MBR) and the table that it carries within it, the partition table. Trying to read the MBR is a quick test of (1) the hardware's ability to recognize and read the drive and, (2) the integrity of the MBR data itself.

There are a number of programs that will read an MBR on a disk. The DOS FDISK program is one such program, although a fairly limited one. The Norton Utilities' DiskEdit program will also read an MBR, as you saw in Chapter 15, "An Overview of Viruses."

Whichever program you use, fire it up and try to read the MBR. If there's something seriously wrong with the MBR, you'll get a message along the lines of "you've asked me to read data off a disk, but the disk is not present," or the like. If you don't get that message, and it reads the MBR without complaint, skip the next subsection and go to "Recovery Step 3: Is the Partition Table Blank?"

Blast from the Past: Verify the Hard Disk Hardware

Many of the shortcomings that this guide represents are hurdles that have been long cleared. Of course, I still have a Toshiba T2200SX laptop (386SX20) and a 486DX33 desktop box in service that use hardware old enough to be this section's grandmother. All right, maybe not grandmother, but aunt at the very least. For tips on verifying modern drives see the text after this sidebar.

If a cable's loose, the controller's got a couple of cooked chips, or the drive motor doesn't want to start spinning, you've got a hardware problem. The BIOS generally detects that something is wrong during the initial POST (Power-On Self Test). You may see a message like one of the following. These messages are some of the first to appear when the system powers up, so watch carefully!

▶ `0 hard disk(s) found` message on boot

▶ `1701, 1780, 1781, 1790, 1791,` followed by `press F1 to continue,` and finally BASIC pops up on your screen

▶ `Drive failure, Hard disk failure`

▶ `Invalid configuration—press F1 to continue`

▶ `Run SETUP—configuration lost`

If you see one of these messages, don't panic. You can fix most hardware problems without a soldering iron and a schematic—a screwdriver and some patience will do the job in the majority of cases.

Try to resolve apparent hardware disk failures with the following steps:

1. Check that the PC has not lost its SETUP information.

2. Check that the drive has warmed to operating temperature: not too hot, not too cold. Simply touching it should tell you if it's room temperature or not.

3. Ensure that the cables are completely in place, or try swapping the cables. Also, make sure that cable terminals that do *not* have guide notches are matching pin 1 to pin 1.

4. Verify that the drive platters are spinning. It's not a good idea to open the case to take a peek, but you can still judge whether or not it's spinning. If it gets hot really quickly and there's no "rushing air" sound, it's likely had a catastrophic spindle crash and is not spinning. If you do hear the rushing air sound but it is interrupted by a "shingsh" sound, then you've either got a

head crash or a minor spindle crash. If none of these symptoms are detectable, it's either very good at hiding its own ailments or you need to look elsewhere for the problem.

5. If it is a band-stepper, watch the stepper motor to see if the head moves on power-up.

6. Reseat the chips.

7. Swap the controller. Older (and I mean *older* drives) had separate controllers. Modern drives, however, have controllers on them. Look underneath the drive and you will see a circuit board held in place by four to six screws. You'll need a #9 or #10 Torx wrench that you can get at your local hardware store for a couple of bucks. Take off the screws and remove the card, and you'll see that it's connected to the drive itself by pressure tabs. Swap in another controller from a drive of the same model (also match the revision) and plug it in.

Check That the Drive Hasn't Lost CMOS

A drive won't work if it isn't recognized, as when an AT, PS/2, or 386 or later has lost its SETUP info or the information is wrong.

Did you see a message like "`Invalid configuration information—press F1 to continue`"? If the battery's run down on your 286/386/486 or later computer, it may have forgotten that it has a hard disk or, worse, it may *misremember* what kind of hard disk it has. Run the SETUP program for your computer to check to see that the computer remembers correctly what kind of hard disk it has.

But what if you've lost the drive parameters? Well, you should look it up in your documentation. You *did* keep track of your documentation, didn't you?

A 1790 or 1791 error almost always points to invalid configuration. AT-type systems first seek to cylinder 0, then out to the highest cylinder. If the seek to 0 fails, that's a 1780 or 1781, depending on whether it's the first or second hard drive. A 1780/1781 could be caused by a lot of things, so don't assume that the problem is configuration. If the seek to the highest cylinder fails, however, that's a 1790/1791—almost certainly a configuration problem. Why?

Suppose a misconfiguration tells the system that the disk has 700 cylinders, when it actually has 500. The attempt to seek out to 700—200 cylinders further than the disk can handle—will fail, and 1790/1791 will result.

Is the Drive Too Hot or Cold?

The drive won't work normally if it is too cold, or, less likely, too hot.

Is it Monday morning? Did you just bring the drive in from the outside, if the computer is a laptop? Make sure the drive is warmed up to room temperature before you try to use it (this goes double if you're about to format it). Alternatively, could it be too hot? If a temperature probe indicates that your computer's insides exceed 110 degrees F (43 degrees C), your drive may be overheated.

One quick way to overheat the inside of a PC is if the PC's fan isn't working. Is air flowing through the chassis?

Check the Drive Cables

Perhaps the drive's cables have come loose or have been reconnected incorrectly, or they may just be bad. Do you have another set of cables? Give them a try. Have you been inside the computer recently? I know, I know—you didn't touch the hard drive. But removing the case could accidentally move cables around. Just reach down behind the drive and make sure the cables are snugly in place. I taught a "hands-on" class recently where we used 10 identical machines. One of the machines kept experiencing hard disk failures. In each case, all that was needed to fix the drive was to just reach around behind the drive and reseat the 34-wire edge connector, which kept slipping off.

Verifying Modern Drives

Drives these days are quite bulletproof. As such there are only a few things you need to do to check a drive. First, there's a pre-problem checklist.

▶ Have you moved the drive to another bus?

- Have you changed any jumper settings?

- Was the drive, case, or anything containing the drive dropped or was it otherwise traumatized?

- Have you modified the BIOS settings?

- Did you change any drive letter or path assignments (Windows NT/2000 only)?

Then there's the post-problem checklist:

- Are the cables seated properly?

- Is the drive abnormally warm to the touch?

Note

Keep in mind that drives already run warm. A drive that is uncomfortable to the touch should cause concern.

- Is the drive recognized by the BIOS? That is, does the drive's name and model number appear in the POST information?

Tip

Most big systems vendors (i.e., Compaq, Dell, Hewlett-Packard, etc.) ship their systems with a custom BIOS that displays their logo instead of the normal text-based startup. This is extraordinarily annoying to the seasoned user. If you've got one of these systems, check your BIOS for a setting marked "Show POST Testing" or "Test RAM" that is disabled. Enabling the option should make the obnoxious advertisement disappear and the text visible.

- Does it make noise above and beyond the normal?

- Does the drive click or make a scraping noise?

- Does the drive work but heat up quickly and become unreliable?

All of these factors may indicate a physical problem that could preclude any further steps at all. It's likely that you'll need a recovery service or, if you're extremely lucky, special disk recovery software that uses simplified drivers to minimize drive activity.

BIOS Autodetection

Since all BIOS are capable of autodetection routines today, vendors rarely, if ever, set specific drive values, instead relying on the BIOS to take care of that chore. As the BIOS recognizes and registers each drive, it prints the drive's vendor-specific information to the screen. For a typical system that has a CD-R/RW and an 8.4GB HDD, the BIOS POST might appear like this:

```
130,600KB RAM OK

ATA BUS0
Master - Maxtor 8.4GB 90845D4
Slave - None

ATA BUS1
Master - Ricoh CD-R/RW MP7040A
Slave - None
```

If you've paid attention to this over a long period of time, you'll notice immediately when something goes differently. Maybe the drive doesn't appear. Maybe it takes longer to be recognized. These two things are the biggest pointers to potential problems with a drive.

Recovery Step 3: Is the Partition Table Blank?

If the previous steps worked, stop: you needn't continue. On the other hand, if they didn't, we'll now examine the partition table (PT).

The previous step read the MBR mainly to see if the hardware was functioning in even a minimal way. Now we'll examine the PT to see if the partition definitions are still intact. (In the next step, we'll see if they make sense.) If the PT is blank, *you will not see any error messages at boot time.* DOS just ignores a nonpartitioned drive. If there isn't a bootable floppy in drive A:, the system will request that a bootable floppy be inserted in drive A:.

Returning to the flowchart in Figure 16.12, we're now at "Examine the partition table. . . ." You've got the MBR. Is the partition table blank—does FDISK report that there are no partitions?

The partition table should not be blank on a drive that was previously working, so something has deleted it. If it *isn't* blank, go to the next step. Perhaps the first thing you should do if you've got a blank partition table is to just reboot. You fix a blank partition table/MBR as you would any data loss problem. Try to restore the data from a backup (or rebuild, if you didn't make a backup). If the drive won't take the data, reformat cylinder 0, head 0 to restore the sector IDs on that track. And if the format won't work, there's physical damage on 0/0, and you need to get a new hard drive.

The Final Step: Send Your Drive to the Mayo Clinic

Still can't get it to talk to you? Hey, look—even Dr. Kildare lost a few. If you *really* need that data, there is a last hope. It ain't cheap—from $500 to $20,000—but you can send it to a service. They disassemble the disk and remove the data, then send it to you on a CD or pretty much any media you require. These services can charge $200 to diagnose the problem, then you negotiate over the recovery cost. The negotiation will be colored by the time period you want it recovered in and how difficult the recovery is. Expensive, yes, but cheaper than going out of business.

> **Note**
>
> Note that I said, ". . . how difficult the recovery *is.*" When you do send your drive to a service to be recovered, they take it and prepare the drive for recovery, making a list of recoverable files in the process. This means that they're already in a position to recover your data the instant you say go. Of course, you can opt to say no, and they'll return the drive to you, toss it out, or send it to the manufacturer. It's up to you. You only pay the $200 evaluation fee for testing, setup, and a list of files. If the list doesn't contain any files that you want to recover, at least you've only spent 200 smackeroos.

You'll find a list of data recovery services in the Vendor Guide on CD #2. They may have specialties, so shop around a bit before sending your poor infirm hard disk to these wizards.

But I hope after getting through this chapter you needn't even contemplate bringing in outside help. This finishes the section of the book on hard disks; next, we'll take up backup tools.

Troubleshooting Recap

We obviously covered a lot of very technical information in this chapter. In case it's made your brain tired (it has mine, and I'm exposed to it every day!), here's a recap:

Remember your priorities You want your data back, you want your disk to work, and you'd like to use the drive again, if possible, in that order.

Step 1 Boot from a floppy. Try not to go too far without an emergency boot floppy. Give it time, and the "crash" will creep up on you when you least expect it.

Step 2 Try to read the MBR. This can rescue you from a lot of trouble. Remember to have a backup.

Step 3 Check to see if the partition table is blank. If you saved all of your partition table data, you can rebuild it.

The Final Step Send your drive to the Mayo Clinic. Wrap it up and send it off. These guys can often rescue data from seemingly unrecoverable drives.

17

Understanding, Installing, and Repairing Floppy Drives

INTRODUCTION

Now that we've covered hard drives, let's take a look at floppy drives. Floppy drives are the venerable old grandfather of data storage; the original IBM PC stored data and programs using a 360KB 5¼-inch diskette. The technology has improved since then, but at its heart floppy technology is the same as it was 13 years ago. Today's 1.44MB 3½-inch floppy disks may soon be superseded by new, more efficient storage technologies, but for the next several years, floppy disks will continue to play a part in most of the computer systems that you service. In this chapter, you'll learn something about their maintenance and repair.

Replacing a Floppy Drive

Be Prepared

Before you start, there are some things you'll need to perform the operation. These include:

- Nonmagnetic Phillips screwdriver
- Container to hold the removed screws
- The new floppy drive

And as usual, before working on a PC, ensure that:

- The PC is turned off and unplugged.
- You are wearing an antistatic wrist strap. Floppy drives themselves are not especially sensitive to static electricity, but installing one involves connecting it to the I/O controller (usually the motherboard) with a ribbon cable, and the motherboard can be easily harmed by ESD (electrostatic discharge).

Warning

Before replacing a floppy drive, make sure the problem is not with an individual disk. Try the drive with several disks.

1. To replace a floppy drive, first turn the PC's power off and remove the cover.

2. Disconnect the ribbon cable and the power connector from the drive. Notice which direction the red stripe on the ribbon cable points (toward the center or the outside of the drive).

3. Unscrew the screws holding the floppy drive in place (unless it is held in place by clips and drive rails; in that case, release the clips). Pull the drive out of the PC.

4. Install the replacement drive using screws or clips, as the case requires.

5. Connect the power cable (the small Berg one).

6. Connect the ribbon cable with the red stripe going to pin 1. The drive may have a little 1 next to one end of the connector to tip you off; if not, connect it the same way that it was connected on the old drive (see step 3).

7. Turn on the PC and test the new drive by trying to read a disk from it.

VISUAL UPGRADE

Replacing a Floppy Drive

1 Mount the floppy into the computer's chassis or drive bay.

2 If you are installing the first floppy drive, connect the floppy data cable to the connector at the edge of the motherboard.

Berg connector

3 The power connector on the back of a floppy drive requires a Berg connector from the power supply unit.

4 Connect the Berg connector from the power supply to the rear of the floppy unit.

5 One of the other connectors on the floppy data cable will connect to the gold connector pins at the rear of the floppy drive.

6 If you are installing floppy drive A:, use the connector with the twisted wires in the cable. If you are installing a second floppy drive, use one of the other data connectors on the cable.

7 Connect the floppy data cable to the connector pins at the rear of the floppy drive unit.

In the Days before Floppies

I didn't buy my first four microcomputers (a Netronics Elf, a TRS80 Model I, an OSI Challenger 1P, and an IBM PC) with floppy disk drives. Floppies cost too much money at that time so most of us micro users in those days used cassettes. *Cassettes?* Yup, cassettes. There was a standard interface called the "Tarbell interface" that let micros read and write data to standard $40 cassette machines at a rate of 600bps. They were a pain and not very reliable, but there wasn't much else available.

Note

Cassettes were so popular, in fact, that the IBM PC was shipped with a cassette port and the first PC I bought didn't have a floppy drive or floppy controller. I couldn't afford them anyway at first, but eventually I could. When the system booted up without an attached drive, it defaulted to a version of the BASIC language stored in ROM. This was, again, no great innovation—most microcomputers shipped with BASIC in ROM in the late '70s and early '80s. To this day, if you have a PS/2 that can't boot from the floppy or the hard disk, BASIC appears on the screen. You're seeing the same old cassette BASIC that's been part of the IBM PC system ROM since 1981.

The Post-Floppy Era

For the last 13 years or so, virtually all PCs made have included floppy drives. Floppies are a marvel of construction. The number of moving parts that they possess makes it surprising that they are in the least bit reliable, but in fact they are fairly solid these days, with some exceptions. If you asked a PC repairperson in the early '80s, "What's the least reliable part of the PC?" you'd be told that it was probably a toss-up between the floppy drive and the daisy-wheel printer. But nobody uses daisies anymore, and their laser-based replacements are quite trouble-free. There's good news in the floppy department also, as floppies are less troublesome than they once were. This is partly because they are manufactured better and partly because they're used less: hard disks are the medium of choice for many home users and most corporate users. The floppy's role nowadays is mainly as a program distribution medium and an archival device. As most hard disks can't travel, most computers still rely on floppies to get information from the outside world. (By the way, ask that repairperson what's the most troublesome part of *today's* PCs, and the answer will be the hard drive.)

Floppies used to be de rigueur in a system because they were the only removable disk type available. If you needed to "sneaker-net" a file from one PC to another, a floppy was your only option. (LANs and the Internet have introduced two alternatives to file transferring since then.) Over the last couple of years, a revolution has been afoot to omit regular floppy drives from the newest systems because better and more reliable removable storage devices have become available, including LS-120 (super-floppies), Zip drives, writable and rewritable CD-ROMs, and others. The phenomenally popular I-Mac computers have led the way by making the floppy disk an external option rather than an integral part of the package. So you will gradually begin to see fewer and fewer floppy drives over the coming years, until eventually they go the way of the computer cassette tape drive. In that sense, we really are living in the "post-floppy" era!

Floppies Nowadays

Floppy disks are cheap enough these days that they're basically disposable—if a disk comes up with an error, just throw it away. Floppy drives are fairly cheap these days too, such that it's cheaper to replace a floppy drive (about $20) than it is to spend an hour of a technician's labor troubleshooting the broken one.

Because of the popularity of CD-ROM as a program distribution medium, floppies are also not as heavily used as they once were. Once, it was possible to ship commercial software on floppies. That's still happening, but having to load 30 floppies to install one's word processor is becoming a bit silly. A single CD-ROM is not only more convenient for the consumer, but also much cheaper to manufacture than the floppy disks required to hold the same amount of data.

Although the floppy drive is an "aging" technology, you will still frequently encounter them in the systems you work with for many years to come, so you'll need to know something about how they work. In the rest of this chapter, I'll explain the mechanisms behind a floppy drive and its disks and tell you a little about troubleshooting and repairing floppy drives should you decide that it's worth your while to do so.

The Floppy Subsystem

The floppy disk subsystem is, like the rest of the PC, modular. That's useful because you will see that you can use this modularity to "divide and conquer" in order to solve problems. The subsystem consists of four parts: the floppy disks themselves, the drive, the disk controller, and the cable connecting the drive to the controller.

Part 1: The Floppy Disk

A floppy, when extracted from its case, looks like a thin 45rpm record, only quite a bit smaller. It's a Mylar disk with iron oxide affixed to it. (Who would have imagined that we'd rely every day on a data storage medium made out of the same plastic that weather balloons are made of with rust glued onto it? Maybe that's why I can't read my backups on rainy days.) We worry so much about dust getting on our hard disk surfaces that we seal up the disk drive. Should we have the same concern about floppies? Is there some way to "clean" a disk? Those of us over, say, age 30 may recall getting out the Discwasher and cleaning an LP prior to playing it. For some people, a ritual like this was comforting. For those people, I must sadly report that no such ritual occurs with floppies.

Floppies are stored inside their own Discwasher: a semi-rigid case lined with fleecy material. As the disk rotates inside the case, any dust is picked up by the material. The case has a hole cut in it so that the disk can be read/written without having to remove it from the case. In general, there is no need to clean a floppy disk. You can see some floppy disks in Figure 17.1.

Figure 17.1

Floppy disks

A reasonable life expectancy for a floppy disk is said by disk manufacturers to be about three to four years. There are, of course, better and worse disks. There are different coatings on higher density disks, generally incorporating less iron oxide (a cheap ingredient) and more cobalt or barium (expensive ingredients). Table 17.1 lists the specs for the three types of 3½-inch floppy disks out there—double-density (DD), high-density (HD), and extra high density (ED), as well as the older 5¼-inch DD and HD models. Of these, you will probably encounter only 3½-inch high-density; the other standards are all but obsolete.

TABLE 17.1 Floppy Disk Specifications

	5¼" DD	5¼" HD	3½" DD	3½" HD	3½" ED
Tracks per inch	48	96	135	135	135
Bits per inch	5876	9646	8717	17,434	45,868
Primary coating	Iron oxide	Cobalt	Cobalt	Cobalt	Barium
Thickness (micro-inches)	100	50	70	40	100
Recording polarity	Horizontal	Horizontal	Horizontal	Horizontal	Vertical

Tip

You should not archive data on a floppy disk that you expect to need after several years because floppies tend to develop surface errors over time that make certain sectors (it's a crapshoot which ones) on the disk unreadable. Try to store important archives on CD-R, or at least Zip disks.

Part 2: The Floppy Drive

3½-inch, 1.44MB floppy drives have been the standard for many years now; you'd be hard-pressed to find one of the old 1.2MB 5¼-inch drives anymore except on the very oldest PCs. (And even if you did find such a drive, finding a floppy disk for it that has not gone bad would be an even greater challenge! Remember, the average life of a floppy is only a few years.) The very first 3½-inch floppy drives were 720KB in capacity, rather than 1.44MB, but again, such drives will appear only on systems 10 years and older.

A 3½-inch drive connects to the drive controller (normally built right into the motherboard) with a ribbon cable, the same as a hard drive or CD-ROM drive (except the ribbon cable the floppy drive uses is slightly narrower). It also requires power. Recall from Chapter 9, "Power Supplies and Power Protection," that a floppy disk uses the smaller, Berg connector from the power supply and not the normally chunky connector.

Tip

Most power supplies come with only one Berg connector, so if you have two floppy drives you will need a power cable adapter. Your computer's motherboard or power supply/case may come with such an adapter; if not, you can pick up an inexpensive one at a computer store.

Part 3: The Disk Controller

Whenever a computer wants to interface with an outside device, it needs a controller to act as a "go-between" to allow the outside device—a floppy, in this case—to talk with the CPU. XT-type machines generally had a separate controller board. AT-type machines usually put the floppy and hard disk controller function on the same board. Most motherboards today put the floppy and hard disk controllers right on the motherboard. A single floppy controller can handle up to two floppy drives.

Part 4: The Cable

The last piece in the floppy subsystem is the cable that connects the controller to the drive. Cables sound insignificant, but this one isn't: I've fixed a pile of floppy problems by swapping cables. The drive is connected to the controller by a 34-wire ribbon cable. Most of the cables have three edge connectors: one for the drive controller, one for drive A:, and one for drive B: (although very few computers nowadays have a second floppy drive). As the cable is 34 wires wide, you'd think that the interface between the floppy and the controller is a parallel interface—eight bits wide—but it's not. Floppy-to-controller interface is serial, transferring one bit at a time.

It's important that you plug your floppy drive into the right connector on the cable. The connector from the drive controller to B: (the middle connector on the cable) is a "straight-through" cable—i.e., pin 1 on the drive controller side is connected to pin 1 on the floppy side, pin 2 is connected to pin 2, etc. The connector to A:, at the other end from the controller, has a twist in it, however. It is this twist that identifies A: as different from B:; you can see this in Figure 17.2. The ribbon cable has three connectors: one on one end and two on the other end. The lone end goes on the controller. The one in the middle goes on drive B:. The one on the other end goes on drive A:. If you're likely to forget (as I am), get a magic marker and write "controller," "B:," and "A:" on the appropriate connectors before disassembling the whole thing.

Figure 17.2

Floppy cable with twist for the A: drive

B: drive connector

A: drive connector (after cable twist)

Floppy controller

It never hurts to have a couple of extra ribbon cables around. The cables are inexpensive and available from many mail-order houses or computer discounters, so it's easy to keep an extra one around.

Simple Preventive Maintenance for Floppies

Failure on the floppy can be a scary, potentially disastrous thing if you have stored some critical data on a floppy disk. (That's not a very good idea, by the way. Never put your only copy of something important on a floppy.) What can you do to lower the probability of a floppy disaster?

Anyone who has a VCR and rents videotapes on a regular basis probably knows about the need to clean the VCR's heads. Something like that can be done for the floppy as well, although you'll probably never need to. And a few diagnostic tests can point out upcoming floppy problems.

To Clean Heads or Not to Clean Heads?

Like your VCR, floppies have an electromagnetic read/write head that does most of the drive's work. In the process of accessing the disk, the head may rub some of the coating off the disk and onto itself. It seems reasonable, then, to assume that head cleaning kits are good things.

When you can't see something, you get superstitious about it. We can't see the junk on floppy heads (or the data on magnetic disks, for that matter), so we play it safe and purchase a floppy head cleaner to ward off floppy evil spirits. Once procured, however, the first question is: *how often should I clean the floppy heads?*

The instructions on the head cleaner say to do it every week. That doesn't seem to be a good piece of advice, as shoving a floppy head cleaner in a drive could misalign a disk head. The floppy cleaner is a relatively thick piece of cotton shaped like a floppy. Worse yet, some floppy cleaners are *abrasive*—they wear away some of the floppy head with every use. (One has to look askance at this procedure. Scraping away some of the head to find a clean part seems somewhat like using sulfuric acid to clean one's teeth.)

Personally, I clean my heads only when the drive fails. I have some computers on which I've *never* cleaned the heads, and they work fine. My recommendation: clean the heads only when you start experiencing read/write errors. (Of course, for only slightly more money than a good-quality head-cleaning system, you could have a whole new floppy drive, so weigh your options.)

As I hinted before, *be careful* when choosing a floppy head cleaner! Don't buy an abrasive cleaner—make sure it uses a cotton floppy and some cleaning fluid.

By the way, there's an issue related to cleaning the heads called *demagnetizing* them; it's done with some audio recording heads. People sometimes ask me if floppy heads need to be demagnetized—they don't.

Defending Disks

Did you ever notice the "do not" cartoons on the back of a floppy disk jacket? Do not expose the disk to heat, cold, magnets, or dust, they warn. They lead you to believe that floppies are very fragile items. A little practical experience with disks teaches you that it isn't really true. Yes, disks must be taken care of, but you needn't get crazy about it. Don't put them on the radiator or leave them on a shelf that gets three hours of direct sunlight every day. Don't store them under the roof leak or use them as coasters. Given the choice, store them upright, stacked left to right rather than on top of each other. And keep them away from magnets.

When it comes to temperature extremes, you've got to be concerned about something called *thermal shock.* If your portable computer has been sitting in the back of the car in freezing temperatures overnight, bring it in and let it warm up before using it. Just a little heat expansion/contraction can temporarily realign your drives or make the motors respond a little differently. In addition, condensation from rapidly warming items can build up on the electronics, and the moisture can cause electrical shorts. Extreme temperatures can damage the disks: vendors claim that disks should never be stored below 50 degrees nor above 125 degrees. Cold isn't as much of a problem as heat. I've ordered software through the mail and had it sit outside in January in my mailbox for a week and have had no problem reading the disks.

Dust, smoke, and dirt can cause damage to the head and/or to a disk. Everybody knows smoking is not good for you, but you may not know just how bad it is for your drives. If you're in a dusty environment, think about getting a power supply with a filtered fan. Running the air through a filter before pushing it through the system removes the vast majority of the dust particles.

As you read in Chapter 4, "Avoiding Service: Preventive Maintenance," magnets—both the permanent and electromagnetic type— can cause permanent loss of data on hard or floppy disks. Something I have yet to understand is the little plastic paper clip holder with the circular magnet near the opening. Why is the magnet there? Are people afraid the paper clips will get out if not magnetically restrained? (As one of the members of Monty Python might say, "Are you suggesting paper clips are *migratory?*") One day, you'll put a floppy on top of the paper clip holder. It'll be sad. Or you'll use one of the paper clips—now magnetized by their proximity to the magnet—to clip a document to a floppy. Arggh.

Warning ....

Watch out for less-obvious magnetic sources, too. Unshielded stereo speakers, for example, have powerful magnetic pulls. And some older telephones have magnets in them, too.

Removing, Configuring, and Installing Floppy Drives

You generally won't repair drives, you'll replace them. That means it's most important to be able to rip 'em out and slap 'em in.

Removing Floppy Drives

Floppy drives are removed in three steps:

1. Remove screws from mounting brackets.

2. Remove power connection.

3. Remove data connection.

I covered the physical extraction part pretty thoroughly in Chapter 2, "Disassembling the PC," so I won't repeat it here.

Installing Floppy Drives

Installing a floppy is just the reverse of removing one, except that the drive must be configured. To configure a new floppy, you must:

▶ Connect it to the twisted connector if it's drive A: or the non-twisted connector if it's drive B:. You can't have a drive B: in a system without a drive A: so your primary floppy should always be A:, at the opposite end of the cable from the controller.

▶ Attach a power connector. Again, you want the smaller power connector, the Berg, for the floppy drive.

Note

Most PCs use a standard size floppy drive, but some proprietary systems (the Compaq Presario is particularly notorious in this regard) use a nonstandard floppy drive with offset positioning that requires you to buy a replacement directly from the original manufacturer (and typically at two to three times the cost of a generic replacement!). So if you are replacing a floppy drive in someone else's PC, it pays to examine the old drive before buying a replacement for it.

The Future of Floppies

No discussion of floppies would be complete without a little look at where floppies are going, and going *soon*. Several companies are vying to set the next standard in floppies. Toshiba, among other companies, has put forth a 2.88MB floppy disk standard, but it has received a less-than-enthusiastic welcome in the market, and you will seldom see such drives or disks for sale. (Most BIOS programs support them, however, so if you happen to have one, you're not stuck.) A more promising contender is the SuperDisk (aka LS-120), which can write to a 1.44MB floppy disk and can also read and write special "super floppies" that hold up to 120MB. Most computers made in the last several years include BIOS support for these. Zip drives, which hold up to 250MB per disk, have also cropped up as floppy drive alternatives in some systems.

However, the floppy drive as a whole may soon be a thing of the past. The newest PC standards do not even call for a floppy drive. Increasingly, rewritable CD-ROM drives are taking over the functions that used to be relegated to floppy disks, including backup and data transfer. And, as I discussed at the beginning of this chapter, new software almost universally comes on CD-ROM these days, rather than on floppy.

Will the floppy drive go the way of the dinosaur? Probably. But for many more years, you will probably continue to upgrade and repair systems with floppy drives.

Troubleshooting Tips

The mechanical nature of floppy drives makes them prone to a host of ills. In the following sections I'll catalog a few of them.

A Disk Cannot Be Read

Pop a disk in the drive, try to read it, and the message says `Data error reading drive A:`, or `Sector not found reading drive A:`, or perhaps the dread `General failure reading drive A:`. Such a message is even better than your morning coffee to get the ol' blood pumping, particularly if the disk contains your only copy of the football pool.

What to do:

1. Press R for Retry. Sometimes it'll work. Ignore the painful grinding sounds. After three or four unsuccessful retries in a row, you may safely conclude that it's not going to work. But if the disk seems to read a little bit of data before repeating the error, keep trying—you may be able to kludge the disk into reading the file—perhaps just this once—before it goes kaput completely.

2. Remove and replace the floppy. I've seen 3½-inch drives that are unreadable until you take them out and put them back in. The hub centering is fairly critical.

3. Take the floppy out and try it in another drive. The read/write head on one machine may be aligned just slightly differently than on another, and that little difference might make one drive read a disk that another cannot.

   If one drive can read a disk that another cannot, either the disk drive's head could be misaligned, or the floppy disk could have been formatted by a different disk drive and *that* drive's head was misaligned. Try to find the drive that created the disk. (If it's the one you've been fooling with, obviously this advice isn't too useful.)

4. If you *still* haven't solved the problem, you're basically in the same boat as someone who's suffered a media failure on his or her hard disk. See Chapter 16, "Care and Feeding of Hard Drives," for information on hard disk data recovery.

The Drive Refuses to Function

When the drive won't read or write properly, there are a bunch of possible causes. I am assuming here that this is a drive that worked fine yesterday and to which you haven't done anything that would obviously cause drive problems.

1. Did you see a floppy drive controller failure error on the screen when the system booted up? Such a Power-On Self Test (POST) error message means that drive A: did not respond. The system no longer realizes you have a floppy drive. This means that your CMOS battery has failed (in which case it would recognize only floppy drive A:, not B:), the floppy controller has failed (in which case both floppies would be dead), the floppy drive itself has failed, or the cable is bad.

2. If there wasn't a POST error, try other disks in the drive. If only one disk gives the drive fits, the problem more likely lies in the disk.

3. Clean the disk heads. It's easy and takes only a minute. (But see my earlier caveats about drive-cleaning in the section "To Clean Heads or Not to Clean Heads.")

4. Try to format a disk. If you can format a disk all right but that disk is unreadable by other drives, your drive head is probably misaligned. If it's misaligned, toss it. New floppy drives are about $15 to $20 today and realigning a floppy drive is not a project, it's a career.

5. Finally, swap the relevant components: the controller, cable, and drive. Swap only one component at a time, and when swapping a component doesn't solve the problem, replace the component.

6. Again, don't overlook the lowly cable. Cables can get nicked when installing boards, replacing drives, or just removing the cover. How bad that is depends on which line gets nicked. One cable on an old laptop that I once owned kept the change line from working, so that when I put in a different floppy, the file listing still showed the previous disk I was looking at. It takes only a two-minute swap with another cable to find out for sure. For more information about change lines, see the section "Drive Shows Phantom Directories" later in this chapter.

Intermittent Disk Errors Cannot Be Solved by Changing the Drive

Or the controller, for that matter. Suppose you get periodic data loss and have changed the drive and controller—what next? The power supply. Malfunctioning power supplies often show up as gremlins in the system. Try swapping the power supply.

Disk Rotation Speed

Small variations in disk speed (plus or minus 1 percent) are okay, but greater differences can make the floppy nonfunctional or dangerous.

Dangerous? Yes. Many years ago, when copy protection schemes were in vogue for programs distributed on floppy disk, I was asked to install a copy of a program I was using. It was a perfectly legal copy. When I went to install it, it informed me that it was an illegal copy and refused to load. I tried installing it on other machines. It didn't work. The software publisher first told me that I was lying or mistaken, and finally (after threats of violence), sent me another master disk.

What had happened was this: the floppy drive on the computer was slightly out of correct speed. Not so different as to render it unusable for normal uses, but enough to upset the finicky copy protection system on the program disk. Worse, the copy protection system being used on the disk permanently altered disks that it saw as illegal copies so that they would always seem bad. That was why the disk wouldn't run on other computers.

Drive Shows Phantom Directories

The symptom here is that you do something, give a DIR command, for example, on a floppy. Then you remove the disk and put a different disk in the drive. Do a DIR, and you see the *directory of the previous floppy, not the one in the drive now!*

If you see this on a computer, this is a RED ALERT! Don't use the thing until you get the problem fixed. Reason: say you put a floppy in the drive and do a DIR on it. Then you put a different floppy in the drive and write some data to the floppy. *The PC writes data to the new floppy using the old floppy's directory!* That means the newly written file is probably okay, but everything else on the floppy is trashed. (Let me tell you about how I lost four pages out of a chapter in a book I wrote many years back.) Where does this problem come from? It's something called the *change line signal.* I mentioned this earlier in the chapter, when we were talking about cables.

Time for a little history. Back in the old days, when floppies were the major storage medium for micros, software designers wanted to squeeze the most performance from those floppy drives, mainly because they were pretty low-performance. (I know, you were expecting one of those boring "old-timer" stories about how I used to have to write my own BIOS hacks and make cables using my teeth to bare the wires and so on. Not just now, but buy me a couple of Flowers' Bitters sometime, and I'll tell you about how I used a matchbook cover to repair a hard disk and saved the free world in the process.) One way to do that was to avoid, wherever possible, rereading information on a floppy. What information gets read the most? The directory and FAT.

Way back before DOS even existed, there was an operating system called CP/M—Control Program for Microcomputers. To get better speed, some CP/M applications read the directory only when a disk was first inserted in a drive. That meant that if you were going to swap a floppy while in WordStar, you had to tell WordStar about the switch, or it would trash your floppy. It was a real pain.

The original IBM PC guys remembered the CP/M experience and (I'm guessing) decided that they'd sacrifice a little speed for reliability. So the IBM PC and XT (but not all XT clones) BIOS always read the disk directory and FAT prior to doing anything dangerous—they didn't assume that the floppy stayed in the same place. And all was well with the world.

But some makers of compatibles, looking to outdo IBM performance-wise, sold computers with slightly different floppies: these floppy drives had something called *change line support*. No big revolution: in fact, it had been around since the CP/M days. One of the signals from the drive to the controller was a "change line" signal—it signaled that the floppy door had been opened since DOS had last looked at the drive. (Back then, floppy drives had little door flaps you opened and closed.) If the change line was activated, DOS would reread the floppy; if not, it wouldn't bother. That meant that writes did not need to be preceded by directory reads, as in the IBM XT case.

The IBM AT design team, looking to show the competition who was boss, added the change line feature to the AT. That means there is a minor difference between XT floppy drives and AT floppy drives: the XT drives don't really use line 34 on the floppy edge connector, but the AT drives use 34 as the "change line" line. To complicate matters, this question of whether or not change line support is really needed is determined by what BIOS your computer has. Some XT clones need it, some don't. Some AT clones need it, others don't. The IBM AT needs it, as does every other computer made since then—including the computers you work on today.

If you have a computer that needs change line support and you install a floppy drive that lacks it, the computer will display the phantom directory (and possibly trash a floppy someday). These days, however, it is virtually impossible to buy a floppy drive without change line support, so you don't need to worry about it. We're talking ancient history lesson here, with the XTs and ATs and such.

Now you know what change line support is and that some computers need it (including almost all the PCs that are still alive today). Suppose you find yourself with a change line problem—phantom directories. What do you do?

First, check the floppy cable. Try substituting a different floppy cable, and see if that doesn't clear up the problem. You can also try the following:

Fool the controller into thinking that there have been lots of change line signals. If you're a techie with cable-building capability, construct a cable that disconnects line 34 on the drive side and cross-connect lines 34 and 20 on the controller side. As line 20 is activated with each head step, the controller will believe that it is seeing many change line signals.

Ctrl+C between disk accesses. This one works only if you're working at a DOS prompt (which few of us are anymore). Remember to do a Ctrl+C keystroke, and you've changed the floppy. It forces DOS to reread the disk directories. Not great, but a good emergency measure.

Floppy Troubleshooting Recap

There are several things to try before you give up on a floppy drive:

▶ Always try other disks in the drive before assuming that the drive itself is bad.

▶ If the floppy drive light comes on and stays on all the time, you have installed the ribbon cable backwards.

▶ If the floppy drive light does not come on at all, check the power connector.

❿ If you see a floppy drive controller error at startup, check in the BIOS to ensure that it recognizes your floppy drive. If the CMOS battery fails, it may forget about all drives except the first floppy drive (A:).

❿ If you switch disks but the PC still shows the previous contents of the drive, check for a damaged ribbon cable.

❿ Intermittent disk access errors often indicate a bad power supply in the system.

❿ Data errors reading the disk can mean a bad disk. You might also try cleaning the disk heads using a disk cleaning kit.

❿ Try to format a disk. If it works, but that disk is then unreadable by other drives, the drive head is probably misaligned. Throw the drive away and get a new one.

❿ If replacing the drive does not help, try replacing the cable. If that doesn't work, the problem is probably the disk controller. If it's built into the motherboard, you may need to disable it in the BIOS and install a separate I/O controller card to use instead.

Now, let's move on to the subject of printers. In the next chapter, we'll talk about troubleshooting printers in general. Then we'll get specific about particular printers.

18

Troubleshooting Printers

INTRODUCTION

Printers, like any other mechanical devices, can be real maintenance headaches. Whenever you've got moving parts, you have the potential for wearing out, breaking down, or otherwise conking out.

However, it may surprise you to learn that most printer problems that people have are *software*-related. That is, the operating system or a particular program isn't sending the right information to the printer to get the desired printout. (You know the old saying—garbage in, garbage out!) For example, when a printer spits out endless sheets of paper with mysterious junk characters on them, it's a good bet that the printer driver is not speaking the printer's language.

I'll spend the next couple of chapters talking about printers. This chapter eases into the topic by discussing the general preventive maintenance you can perform on a printer, the various interfaces that printers use to connect to a PC, and some general printer troubleshooting. Then, in upcoming chapters, I'll go into laser printers and inkjet printers in greater detail.

Connecting and Testing a Parallel Printer

Here are the basic steps for connecting a printer. For in-depth coverage on printers and how to troubleshoot printer problems, refer to the rest of this chapter.

Be Prepared

Before you start, there are some things you'll need to perform the operation. These include

▶ Printer's manual

▶ Computer's manual

▶ (Optional) Extra parallel cable to swap with, in case there is any doubt whether the current one is working

Before you connect a printer to a PC, make sure that:

▶ The computer is turned off

▶ The printer is turned off

1. Set up the printer and turn it on. Run its self-test to confirm that it's working properly.

2. Turn the printer off and connect the printer to the computer with a parallel cable. If you want to use ECP or EPP, make sure you have a parallel cable capable of that.

3. Turn on the PC. If needed, enter the PC's BIOS setup program and make sure the parallel port type is set correctly (ECP, EPP, Bidirectional, etc.).

4. If you're using Windows, run the setup software that came with the printer to install its printer driver.

   or

   If you're using a DOS-based program, configure the program to use the printer.

5. Print a self-test using the printer's Windows driver or utility program.

   or

   In a DOS program, create a simple document or drawing and print it as a test.

Printer Maintenance

Keeping your printer in top condition means giving it a little maintenance attention now and then. Printer maintenance varies depending on the type of printer, so let's look at the maintenance on some of the most common printer types.

Dot Matrix Printers

If you're still using a dot matrix printer, you are either seriously strapped for cash or you need to print multipart forms. I'll assume the latter. Since dot matrix printers strike the page with the print head (printers that use this type of technology are known as *impact* printers), they can print through multiple layers of carbon (or carbonless) copies, and some businesses need that capability.

Note

The only kind of impact printer you'll find for sale these days is a dot matrix printer. Daisy wheel printers, which used to rule the marketplace 10 to 15 years ago, are all but extinct. (Okay, you might find a daisy wheel printer at an estate sale, or in a mysterious forgotten crate in a government warehouse.) And even dot matrix printers are over the hill.

To clean a dot matrix printer, use a dry, soft cloth to clean both the paper path and the ribbon path. Most manufacturers suggest cleaning every six months, as the ribbon path can build up a film of inky glop that causes the ribbon to jam. To do this, go to a drug store and buy a dispenser box of 100 clear latex gloves. Use them when working on the printer (but don't use them when you're working on chips and boards—that latex can build up some mean static) so that you don't have to wash your hands for hours to remove the ink.

Tip

When working on a printer, it's easy to get ink on yourself and your clothes. Here's a tip that will help you clean up. A friend once told me that hairspray will remove ink from fabric. So another friend and I experimented with her hair mousse stuff—you know, the spray that you use to make your hair defy gravity? It did nothing. Then we tried some Aqua Net, a hairspray that hasn't changed since Jackie Kennedy used it in the White House. The result? We found that cheap hairspray works a lot better than the expensive stuff. Spray it on the fabric and rinse with cold water. A little soap will pick up the rest.

You can also vacuum out the paper chaff periodically from the inside of the printer. The continuous-feed paper used in impact printers is somewhat more prone to leaving dust behind than normal single sheet paper is. You may find it unwieldy to use the same vacuum on the printer as you use on the living room carpet. Purchasing a tech vacuum of some sort may be best because it is smaller and easier to use in tight areas, and it won't suck key tops right off your keyboards.

On an impact printer, the print head moves back and forth across the page, which means there is probably a drive belt. Determine if there is a belt tightening mechanism for the printer and find the correct tension values. Keep a replacement belt on hand. (Believe me, they're no picnic to find in a hurry).

Warning

Some dot matrix printers have ribbon cables that are used to carry the data to the print head. They often look like drive belts, but they are definitely not. Tighten these and they'll usually break. If they do, you can say goodbye to your printer.

Most impact printers never need to be lubricated. In fact, oil can do considerable damage if applied to the wrong places. If you thoroughly disassemble the printer, you will probably have to lubricate various points as you reassemble it. If you intend to do this, I strongly recommend that you get a maintenance manual from the manufacturer.

Here's a tip that will extend the life of both the ribbon and the print head: put some WD40 lubricant on a used ink ribbon. Let it soak overnight. It'll produce good output the next day, and you won't damage the print head—WD40 is a good lubricant for print heads. Let me stress, however, that this only applies to ink ribbons. If you have any other type of printer, this will not work. So don't go soaking that laser toner cartridge in anything, okay?

The expensive part of a dot matrix printer that dies is the print head. Luckily, almost all dot matrix printers these days have a thermistor (basically, a temperature sensor) that detects when the print head is getting too hot, and it shuts the printer down until it cools off. To avoid excess heat build-up around a dot matrix printer, avoid stacking things around it—leave a clear path for airflow on all sides.

Replacing the print head is not economical on many printers because of the high price that manufacturers charge for replacements. For example, the print head replacement for a good-quality wide-carriage dot matrix printer might cost $100 or more. Fact is, in almost every case, it makes no sense to replace a dot matrix print head unless you have one of the very expensive, high-speed dot matrix printers. You can buy a brand new printer for about the cost of a replacement dot matrix print head.

Inkjet Printers

Inkjet printers have come a long way since their introduction back in the '70s. At one time, they clogged pretty regularly because the ink would dry in the tiny holes in the heads. Today, the jets are designed to resist drying, and the heads are generally protected by a rubber boot that keeps the holes from drying out. Also, on some models, the heads are built into the ink tanks so that when you replace an empty tank, you're also getting new jets. This keeps the print on these printers looking like new.

If you let an inkjet printer sit too long without using it, the ink in the jets (and/or in the ink cartridges) dries out, and one or more colors won't print. This can result in some odd-looking printouts with amusing (but definitely not lifelike!) colored stripes. If this happens, run the printer's built-in head-cleaning utility. You can do this by pressing certain buttons on the printer itself, or in most cases through the printer's driver in Windows 95/98/2000. (Right-click the printer in the Printers window [Start → Settings → Printers, or choose Printers from the Control Panel] and choose Properties, then look for the cleaning command, usually on the Utilities tab.) After cleaning the heads, run a nozzle test, which you can also do through the printer's buttons or its Properties box in Windows. The nozzle test prints some basic geometrical pattern of lines on the page in each of its colors, so you can see which color, if any, is failing to print. Sometimes several cycles of cleaning followed by testing are required to clear out the dried-up ink residue.

You may see advertisements for refilled ink cartridges, or even kits that promise to let you refill the cartridges yourself, but this is seldom a good idea. True, it can save you money, but on many models, as I mentioned, the heads are built into the ink cartridges, so that you get new heads when you get new ink. This is by design. If you continue to print with the old heads tankful after tankful, the print quality will definitely suffer, and you may harm your printer.

Note

On some inkjet printers, moving the ink cartridges into view so you can replace them can be a real exercise in coordination. On certain Epson models, for example, you have to hold down two little tiny buttons simultaneously for several seconds, then press another button. Check the printer's manual to find out what the procedure is for your specific model—that's usually the only way to find out (other than visiting the manufacturer's Web site and searching for the info).

Thermal-Transfer Printers

When you were a kid, did you ever make pictures by coloring with crayons onto a piece of heavy paper and then using an iron to transfer the colored wax to another piece of paper? (If not, just nod politely and keep reading—we'll get past the "when you were a kid" stories in a minute.) Thermal-transfer printing works something like that. Very hot pins are pressed onto a wax- or wax/resin-coated ribbon, and the wax or resin melts and is transferred to the paper beneath it. The difference is that the paper has to go through the process four times, once for each color (normally cyan, yellow, magenta, and black). This kind of printer produces excellent quality color images—better than an inkjet, and arguably better than color lasers—but are rather expensive in terms of consumables. You won't find them for sale in the typical office supply store—they're a specialty item. (Refills for them are also generally not available at your regular retail outlets.) Some of these also require special thermal paper, which of course is a lot more expensive than normal paper.

The issues involved with thermal-transfer printers are much like those with other printers: keep them cool and keep them plugged in. If you're having problems with print quality, such as smearing, you might try using another manufacturer's paper or ribbons.

Laser Printers

Laser printers are important enough that I'll devote the next chapter to them. As a result, I'll limit my discussion of them here.

The laser printer is very similar to a copy machine. Having said that, it's amazing that they are as reliable as they are.

You may be surprised to learn that many different brands of laser printer operate using the same basic innards. The most common laser engine is made by Canon. Many of the HP LaserJets, Apple LaserWriters, and Canons (obviously), as well as the older QMS Kiss and others, are built around the Canon engine. These need very little maintenance except for a new cartridge every few thousand copies or so. The cartridges cost in the neighborhood of $70 to $120, and, according to HP, contain all that is needed for routine maintenance. So, every time that you change your cartridge, you'll perform routine maintenance like cleaning the corona wires and paper pickup pawls.

It's okay to buy recycled toner cartridges, but make sure your refill company completely rebuilds the insides, including replacing the photoelectric drum. Avoid the "drill and fill" vendors, as they don't replace the insides, and using that kind of refill will lead to a lower-quality print image and may damage the laser printer. If you don't refill them, many of the cartridge manufacturers provide a way to mail in the used ones for recycling (and sometimes a rebate).

Laser printers require proper ventilation and a fair amount of power. Other than that, don't pour any Cokes in them and they last a long time. Never ship a laser with a toner cartridge in place. It can open up and cover the inside of the laser with toner. And don't take the toner cartridge out and wave it around, or toner might spill out and make a mess. You will also want to wipe out any stray toner in the printer's insides every time you change the toner cartridge.

Tip

To get the last little bit of life out of a toner cartridge, you can take it out and shake it gently from side to side. But don't turn it on end, and don't shake it up and down, or toner might spill out.

On some models, a new toner cartridge comes with a long, thin felt strip mounted on a piece of plastic. You drop this into some slot or other on the printer, replacing the old and cruddy strip that was there before. Not all laser printers have this, though.

Printer Interfaces

The parallel port is far and away the most common type of interface between printer and computer, so it's important that you understand its basics. But it's also important that you're aware of the other ways that a PC can communicate data to a printer.

Parallel Ports

The vast majority of printers connect to a PC via the parallel port, a female 25-pin connector that's typically built right into the PC. In an ATX design, it's a built-in part of the motherboard that sticks out of the back of the PC; in an AT design, it's a connector attached to the motherboard with a ribbon cable. As with other peripheral trouble-shooting, you should start your diagnosis by checking this connection at all junctures. Is the parallel port functioning? Is the printer cable connected firmly at both ends? If it's an AT system, is the little ribbon cable inside the PC from the connector to the motherboard snugly plugged in?

The History of Parallel

The parallel port was originally devised as a high-speed, low-cost alternative to a serial port for printer interfaces.

Until 1976, serial ports were the established way of hooking up a printer to a computer. The problem was that serial port hardware was expensive. Adding a serial port to a computer could raise the computer's price by anywhere from $250 to $1000. That got in the way of selling printers, and so a printer company, Centronics, decided to do something about it—they created the Centronics parallel interface, which is essentially the parallel interface that PCs still use today.

There were some drawbacks to parallel interface, however (and there still are today). While RS-232 (another term for serial cables) allows cables of more than 50 feet in length, the Centronics interface is reliable for only 15 feet—actually, less for modern ports. RS-232 is bidirectional and quite flexible as to the kind of things it can support. Originally, the Centronics parallel interface was designed to be unidirectional and was aimed only at printers. RS-232 is serial, employing only two wires for data; Centronics is an eight-bit parallel interface, with eight wires for data. The circuitry required to implement a parallel port, however, is much simpler than that required to implement a serial port because data in your computer is also parallel. The computer simply transmits the data as it is, so the cost of making a parallel port is much lower. The result was a Centronics interface that was easy to cobble together for just a few dollars and offered terrific throughput, as much as 500,000 bits per second (bps) compared to RS-232's 20,000bps.

Today's Parallel Ports

Since then, the parallel port has continued to evolve. First, some laptops offered bidirectional parallel ports. Then those bidirectional parallel ports were further modified to become *enhanced parallel ports (EPP)* and *extended capabilities ports (ECP)*. ECP is more commonly used for printers, while EPP is more common for other parallel devices such as scanners. These newer port types let you print with the speed of the wind, between 500,000 and 1,000,000bps. They also let printers form a lasting relationship with computers based on communication—the printer not only listens to the computer but also communicates its own problems, like being out of paper or having a paper jam. Using an ECP port, you don't need to go to the printer to discover that it didn't do its job—a message will pop up on your monitor telling you so.

To use an ECP port, you need four things: an ECP or EPP/ECP port, an ECP-capable printer, an IEEE 1284–compliant parallel cable, and Windows 95/98/2000 which, at the time of this writing, is the only operating system out there with ECP capability. Once you have installed these features, you will begin to print with unparalleled speed (excuse the pun). If your parallel port's controller is built-in to the motherboard (as almost all are these days), you can set its mode in the BIOS setup program. Normally, the BIOS lets you choose a parallel port mode, such as Output Only (the old, unidirectional mode), Bidirectional (a simple bidirectional mode), ECP, or EPP.

The expanded capabilities of the parallel port have led to the parallel port's use in more areas than just printers. The parallel port now sees use as a file transfer interface (for removable media drives or external CD-ROMs), as a connection to a local area network adapter, or as a connection to an input device such as a scanner. Trouble is, you have only one parallel port on most systems, so how can you have more than one parallel device at once? Well, you can continually switch cables, or you can attempt to share the port among the devices. Some nonprinter parallel devices, such as scanners, have a built-in pass-through that lets you connect the parallel devices in a sort of daisy chain, like SCSI. This works on some systems better than others. Generally speaking, inkjet printers have a harder time sharing a parallel port than do other printer types, and different BIOS settings for the parallel port can sometimes make the difference between sharing success and failure.

Windows 95/98/2000/NT has support for up to three parallel ports, LPT1 through LPT3. Parallel port addresses are hex 3BC, 378, and 278. The PC has a peculiar process for relating I/O addresses to LPT addresses. First, it looks for address 3BC. If there is a port at that address, it assigns it LPT1. If not, it looks for 378 and, if it exists, assigns *that* to LPT1. If that's not available, it finally tries for 278. Once LPT1 is assigned, it looks (in the same order) for LPT2 and LPT3. This means that if you put a first parallel port into a machine and the port has address 278, you'll end up with an LPT1, even though 278 is intended for LPT3. But install a second port at 378, and the next time you boot up, the 278 port will become LPT*2*. Most systems have only the one port, LPT1, but you can easily add expansion boards with extra ports (both parallel and serial).

Serial Ports

The original printers connected to computers via serial (RS-232) ports. It's still possible to connect printers serially today, provided the printer has a serial interface (not all do). But I don't recommend it. Serial port printing can be very slow, and with today's graphics-heavy print jobs, that can mean frustration and waiting around.

Some printers have both a parallel and a serial interface so, in theory, you could hook up two different PCs to the same printer, each through a different interface. However, because of the speed issue with serial, I recommend instead that you share the printer through some other means—perhaps using a switch box or on a network.

Infrared Ports

For members of the "virtual office" who have no desk but only a laptop to carry around and plug in as needed, there's a way to eliminate at least one of the cables you need to plug in: printers with infrared ports are available. Rather than requiring a parallel cable to connect the printer to your computer, a ray of infrared light shines between a transceiver on the computer and one on the printer.

Note

There's no reason why desktop computers can't use infrared printers as well, but most desktop machines are not equipped with infrared capabilities. In contrast, most laptops made in the last few years do have this capability.

Data travels between the computer and printer via an infrared connection. Light and electric impulses all pulse at a certain rate per second; this rate is called the *frequency*—the more pulses, the higher the frequency. Signals with higher frequencies can transmit data more quickly (each pulse can carry a bit of data). However, they have a shorter range and are more prone to interference than lower-frequency signals because anything that interferes with the signal will affect more data than it would if there were fewer pulses per second. Infrared light has a high frequency. Thus, the computer sends a beam of infrared light to the receiver on the printer. The devices have a pretty good range, but it is usually limited to line of sight. (You can't print from an office around the corner.)

If you're having trouble with a wireless printer, check the following:

▶ Are the infrared ports on the printer and computer both clean and unblocked?

▶ Does it help to move the printer/computer to one side?

▶ Did someone stand between your printer and computer during the print job?

Other than that, troubleshooting an infrared printer is much like troubleshooting any other printer. The tricky thing about wireless printers is making the connections.

Network Printing

Most businesses today don't want to be tied down to providing a printer to every single PC—or, conversely, limiting each PC to printing on only one printer. Thus was born the network printer.

There are two ways to use your LAN to print. One is to connect the printer to a PC and then share that printer on the LAN. Although the printer "belongs" to the person using that PC, anyone on the network can send printer jobs to it. The other way to share a printer is to hook it directly into the network. This requires a network-capable printer. Some printers come network-ready; others can be made ready by installing an upgrade card in them. (It varies among manufacturers, but HP offers a JetDirect card for some models that make them network-capable.)

There are, however, a few caveats to using these marvels of technology. First, like any network device, you must be using the same protocols on your server that you use on the printer's network interface, since the printer driver is actually installed on a server, then shared. Standard protocols supported are TCP/IP, IPX/SPX, EtherTalk, and DLC. Unlike other protocols, DLC is used only for printing and mainframe access in the Windows environment, so you may not have it installed. You must also be sure that the protocols are configured correctly—if you are using TCP/IP, for example, you must have an IP address and a subnet mask for the printer. It is also a very good idea to be sure that your network cable is securely plugged into the card and hub.

Common Problems

It's hard to discuss printer problems and troubleshooting them without delving too deeply into the specifics of the thousands of models out there. I haven't got the space to do that (or, truthfully, the time to get to know all of those printers), but there are some generic pieces of advice that I can pass along. And I'll tell you more about lasers and inkjets in upcoming chapters.

Isolate the Problem

As always, try to isolate the problem. Something in the computer or its software? The printer interface? The cable? The printer? Is the printer plugged in, cabled, and *online*?

The steps I use are as follows:

1. Check if it is online, is plugged in, has paper, and is turned on.

2. Turn the printer off and then on again. Reboot the computer, and try it again.

3. If it is a network printer, check the network configuration (such as the IP address and subnet mask on TCP/IP).

4. Use the printer self-test to see if the test page prints correctly. The printer's manual usually tells how to do this.

5. Check that the software is configured for the printer and that the correct drivers are loaded for it in Windows (if used).

6. Swap the printer cable to make sure your cable isn't faulty.

7. If it is a network printer, try printing from another computer.

8. Swap the printer with a different one of the same model, if possible.

Some other things to check right off the bat:

▶ Do a DIR from the command prompt, then try a screen print using the Print Screen key.

▶ If you are dealing with a network printer, check the queue at the server to be certain there are no stuck jobs. If there are, then purge the queue.

▶ Check the printer manufacturer's Web site to see if an updated driver is available for your version of Windows or for the particular DOS-based program you want to print from.

Cable Lengths

The role of cable lengths in noise and interference has been discussed before in this text. But another problem is overly long cables. Serial cables aren't supposed to be longer than 50 feet, and older parallel cables should not exceed 6 feet. Newer IEEE 1284 (ECP and EPP)–compliant cable can actually go to 15 feet. If you're using long cables and getting mysterious errors, the cables may be the culprits.

There are parallel port extenders—check the Black Box catalog (you can find their contact information in Appendix A) to find them. This will let you run your parallel cable up to a kilometer.

Something I've noticed in recent years is that modern parallel port chips don't put out all that much power. I used to be able to share a printer between two computers with an A/B switch, but now it's often the case that it won't work unless the A/B switch has amplification power. The moral seems to be to keep those parallel port cables as short as possible. It is also not recommended to use an A/B switch with laser printers unless you have a powered switch.

Printer Emulation Problems

A more and more common problem is emulation mode. Many printers nowadays will emulate a Hewlett-Packard LaserJet of some kind. Unfortunately, some vendors' idea of "Hewlett-Packard–compatible" is a blend of fact and fantasy. Anyway, if you've got your Acme Laser Printer set up for HP emulation, don't tell your software you've got an Acme—tell it you've got an HP. This sounds simple, but you'd be surprised at the number of people that get tripped up on that one.

Another emulation option is international capability—that is, the ability to specify what country the output is being prepared for distribution in. Many printers speak foreign languages. If you set up your printer for British, you may get the pounds sterling sign rather than a dollar sign. Oh, and by the way, most printers nowadays don't have DIP switches; they support some kind of software setup. Many of the newer printers not only support multiple emulation modes, but they know enough to automatically switch modes based on the driver being used to print. Check the printer's documentation to see how yours handles it.

Port Problems

As you know, printers can have a serial or parallel interface. On the PC, the only visible difference between the two is that the parallel port has a female connector and the serial port has a male connector.

Electronically, they are radically different, however. The parallel interface uses different voltages and handshakes from the serial interface. Most printers today come with only parallel, or, less commonly, with both parallel and serial. As I mentioned before, given the choice, use parallel. It's a cleaner and faster interface.

As laser printers get faster and, more particularly, support higher resolution, more high-speed interfaces will appear. For example,

Apple uses an AppleTalk 230,000bps interface to an Apple Laser-Writer. Some printers interface with SCSI, and some use proprietary CPU-to-printer interfaces.

Some printer cables fasten with clips; others fasten with screws. You should tighten the screws if your cable uses them; don't just plug it in and hope nobody comes along to bump it. I saw a situation where an Okidata printer printed consistently incorrect characters. I tried to understand the problem by comparing the ASCII codes of the desired characters to the codes actually printed. I found in each case that bit 6 was *always 1*. It turned out that the wire for line 6 was not fully seated. Securing the connector did the job.

I found a similar problem with a broken wire in a cable. Here's an example. Suppose I try to print "Hello" but get "Iekko." Compare the codes of the desired and actual characters in Table 18.1.

TABLE 18.1 An Example Printer Cable Problem

Desired Character	Code	Actual Character	Code
H	01001000	I	01001001
E	01100101	E	01100101
L	01101100	K	01101101
L	01101100	K	01101101
O	01101111	O	01101111

The "E" and "O" aren't affected, but "H" and "L" are. Notice that in all cases the low bit is "1."

The serial port, being the versatile interface that it is, allows you to set several communication settings for it:

▶ Speed (1200, 2400, 4800, 9600, 14400, or 19200)

▶ Parity (Even, Odd, or None)

▶ Number of data bits (7 or 8)

▶ Number of stop bits (usually 1 or 2)

You can set these settings in the Properties box for the port (from the Device Manager) in Windows. However, you are more likely to find a serial printer used in a very old system that doesn't have Windows 9x. In that case, you can do it at the command prompt, like so:

```
MODE COM1: speed,parity,data bits,stop
bits,p
MODE LPT1:=COM1:
```

In the first case, an example would be:

```
MODE COM1:9600,N,8,1,P
MODE LPT1:=COM1:
```

Meaning: "9600 bits per second, no parity, 8 data bits, 1 stop bit." The "P" means that it's a printer.

If you are using one of those new-fangled ECP parallel ports for your printing needs, you may run into problems like garbled text or graphics. This is because some printers on the market haven't quite reached IEEE nirvana yet and therefore don't work so well with ECP. There are two things to do in this instance: in Windows, change the printer spooling properties from EMF to RAW; if that doesn't work, change the port back to Bidirectional or Output Only mode in your BIOS setup program.

If you're having other port problems, did you install something recently? Could something be conflicting with the printer port?

The Weather

Everyone talks about it, but . . .

A printer repairman told me about a day that he'd had the previous October. He said that all over town a particular model of printer was failing left and right. He couldn't figure it out. We thought about it. Around the middle of October, we turn on the heat in Washington. That dries out the air and, in turn, the items in the work area. Chips don't mind being dried, but what about capacitors? Could a paper-type capacitor be malfunctioning because it was drying beyond a certain point?

A repair memo came around from the manufacturer a couple of months later. Sure enough, a particular capacitor didn't like it too dry. The answer: either put a humidifier near the printer, or change the capacitor to a similar, less dry-sensitive replacement. Moral: be suspicious when the seasons change.

Troubleshooting Tips

Like a bad cable TV connection on the night of the big pay-per-view fight, printers are notorious for going on the fritz when you've got two minutes to print and fax vitally important documents. Here are some additional troubleshooting tips to help you avoid resorting to the ultimate show of frustration: whacking your printer upside its paper-tray as if it were a vending machine gone bad.

Printer Won't Print at All

If the printer won't print at all:

▶ Check that the printer is getting power, is online (check the Online button), and is connected to the PC.

▶ Turn the printer off, and then on again. The same for the computer.

▶ Look on the printer for any error codes or flashing lights that could give a clue as to the problem.

▶ See that the printer has ink, toner, or ribbon, and that it's installed correctly.

- ❱ Turn off the computer and run the printer's self-test to see if it can print as a separate entity from the computer.

- ❱ Check to make sure the correct driver is installed on the PC.

- ❱ Check the printer queue, and purge any print jobs that appear to be hung up.

- ❱ Turn the printer off, let it sit for 10 minutes, and try again. Overheating can shut down a printer temporarily.

- ❱ Try a different printer cable.

- ❱ Try hooking up the printer to a different computer.

Printout Has Quality Problems

If the printout isn't all it should be:

- ❱ Ensure that the correct printer driver has been installed.

- ❱ Check the printer to make sure it is using the right print emulation mode if it has more than one available.

- ❱ On a dot matrix printer, ensure that the belt is adjusted properly.

- ❱ Replace the ink, ribbon, or toner cartridge if needed, along with any other replacement parts, such as the felt pad in some laser models.

- ❱ Clean the printer according to the instructions in its manual.

- ❱ On an inkjet, clean the nozzles using the printer's built-in utility for that purpose.

Now, just as I promised, we will delve more deeply into the workings of specific types of printers. Next up: inkjet printers.

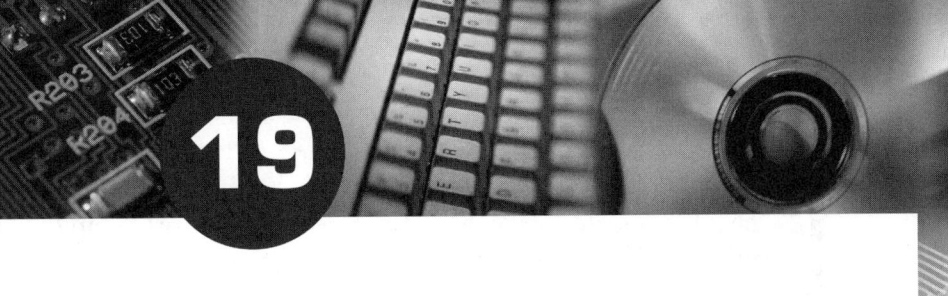

19

Troubleshooting Inkjet Printers

INTRODUCTION

The inkjet printer began as a "poor man's laser," producing near laser quality black-and-white output at a fraction of the cost of a real laser printer. As the technology continued to develop, affordable color inkjet printers became available (while color laser printers were still way beyond the reach of ordinary people), and inkjet printers exploded in popularity because they provided an affordable way for the average home or small-business user to get color printouts.

Today, inkjet printers still cost less than laser printers. Inkjet output is not quite as crisp as output from a laser printer; you can tell the difference if you look closely. Inkjet output can also sometimes smear if you touch it immediately after it exits the printer. However, the difference is minor, and inkjet output looks professional enough for almost any home or business use. The drawbacks? Inkjet printing speed has traditionally been slower than that of laser printers (2–4 pages per minute, as opposed to 6–10), and their per-page cost (of the ink versus laser toner) is higher.

As with laser printers, most problems associated with inkjet printers can be attributed to either human error or ignorance. You see, inkjet printers aren't like television sets. You can't just plug them in, turn them on, and expect them to work flawlessly for their entire life without a little Tender Loving Care.

Getting the most out of your inkjet printer means getting it to work right and then maintaining it in good working order. Once you learn the ropes of regular preventive maintenance and some emergency troubleshooting, you'll be able to get quality printouts every time you hit Print.

Parts of an Inkjet Printer

Inkjet printers are fairly simple machines in concept. They all have several common pieces:

▶ An outer case to hold the inner parts

▶ A paper-feed mechanism

▶ Printer cartridges, which hold the ink and can be black or a combination of black and color

▶ Inkjets that control the distribution of ink on the page. These are often built into the ink cartridges, so you don't see them or work with them separately.

▶ A carrier that holds the printer cartridges and moves them back and forth over the paper

▶ A paper-exit tray

Some printers are multifunction devices that also include scanning, faxing, or copying capabilities. Such units will have additional parts; check the manual to learn more about them. Most of these devices are not inkjets, however, but rather simple laser or optical black-and-white printers.

The Case

Inkjet printer cases come in all shapes, sizes, and even a few colors. Ultimately, the type of case depends on the model of printer you have. Each manufacturer has designed their case to fit a variety of design and mechanical factors, so they aren't compatible with each other.

Most printer cases have some sort of lid or hatch that lifts up to give you access to the ink cartridges. You will not need to remove the entire outer case for routine operation. Should you need to perform more drastic operations on the printer, however, you can (on most models) remove a few screws and lift off the entire outer plastic shell.

You won't find any sort of manual for removing the printer's outer casing, as the manufacturer doesn't want you to do it. Instead, they want you to send your printer to an authorized repair center if there are problems that necessitate removing the case. However, I once took my Lexmark 5700 Color Jetprinter apart to clean the inner workings (it was all gunked up with ink) and was able to disassemble it and put it back together with no problems. The key is to work slowly and examine carefully how each piece fits with the others.

Did I mention that the case probably won't be just one piece? That's true. The Lexmark I took apart had something like eight pieces to its outer case. Two pieces make up the supporting base, three or four parts fit together to form the outer front of the printer, and a few more hold the paper-feed and paper-exit trays.

Whatever you do, don't force anything. Carefully note where all the screws are and remove them one at a time, putting the screws in a safe place so you don't lose them. If the screws are different sizes, write this on a piece of paper. When you try to put the case back together, this information is invaluable. After you take off one piece of the case, set it aside and move on to the next. As you remove the pieces of the case, look closely to see how they all fit together. Sometimes it seems like a jigsaw puzzle, so write some notes if you need to, so you remember the details.

When you disassemble your printer, you can clean each piece of the outer case with an alcohol-based cleaning solution and a soft cloth or paper towel. This is a good idea if ink has sprayed on any inner surfaces or you happen to get inky fingerprints on any of the pieces (as I did).

The Paper-Feed Mechanism

The paper-feed mechanism usually holds approximately 100 sheets of paper or more (it really depends on your printer), and feeds the paper into the printer. On some printers, there is a separate, removable tray that holds the paper; on other printers you simply stack the paper up against the feed mechanism. Most inkjet printers allow you to use different sizes of paper, including standard letter, envelope, and greeting card–sized paper. An adjustable feed guide helps you position various types of paper correctly for feeding.

Some printers have the capability of feeding paper in from either the front or the back. Typically, the front is for normal paper, while the back is an optional-use feed for some special media type such as envelopes. Other printers have a manual feed feature, which you can use to manually insert a single page at a time of some non-standard paper size that the printer doesn't normally support.

Over time, the gears on the paper-feed mechanism can become worn and start failing to pull paper into the printer smoothly and evenly. On some printers, the gears start making an annoying squeaking sound too, and oiling them doesn't help much. In such cases, it's usually worth it (to me, anyway) to take the printer to an authorized service center and have the feed mechanism refurbished. It's not that you can't do it yourself, but the authorized service centers have better access to the needed parts.

Printer Cartridges

The printer cartridges hold the ink that your printer uses. Make sure you use printer cartridges that are compatible with your make and model of printer, as they come in different shapes and sizes. Most look like little boxes, and some have carefully designed nozzles and electronic contacts built in. Other, simpler styles of printer cartridges are simply ink reservoirs that feed into the printer cartridge carrier, which has the more complicated parts.

Almost all color inkjet printers today have both color and black ink cartridges that you can replace separately. (On older, cheaper models, cyan, yellow, and magenta had to be combined to make black, and it resulted in a somewhat muddy gray.)

Some color printers have the three primary colors in one cartridge, whereas other models allow you to purchase and install each of the three colors separately (magenta, yellow, and cyan). The primary disadvantage to the "three colors in one box" type is that you may not use the three colors at the same rate. If you run out of cyan, for example, you have no choice but to replace the entire cartridge to restore your color printing capability, or live with your inability to print blues.

Printer cartridges are manufactured with a protective piece of plastic and transparent tape that covers the nozzles and contacts. Make sure to remove this prior to installing.

At the end of this chapter, I'll tell you more about cartridges, including how they can be refilled (and why you may *not* want to do so).

The Printer Cartridge Carrier

The printer cartridge carrier holds the printer cartridges and moves back and forth over the paper while ink is being sprayed onto the paper. To install printer cartridges, you may have to move a lever or press a button on the printer to put the carrier in a position to accept the cartridges, and then snap them into place. On some printers, the cartridge carriers come out of the printer completely, and then go back in with the new cartridge.

The Exit Tray

The exit tray holds the paper after it comes out of the printer. Many models of inkjet printers have sliding pieces to the exit tray, enabling you to retract the tray in order to save space when you're not using it. When you print, extend the tray to its full length to catch the paper.

Some printers have a lever you can flip to make the output come out at the opposite end of the printer from normal. For example, if the output normally comes out the front, you could make it come out the back. Why would you want to do this? Primarily to get a straight path through the printer. If you are printing on some stiff medium, such as cardboard, you can avoid the otherwise-inevitable curling by allowing the paper to exit the printer in a straight line from the spot where it entered, rather than curling around a roller on its way out.

How an Inkjet Printer Works

At the most basic level, inkjet printers work by blowing jets of ink onto paper. The older generation of impact dot matrix printers use a mechanical print head that physically impacts a ribbon, thereby transferring ink to the paper. In contrast, inkjet printer "heads" don't physically touch the paper at all. Instead, these printers force ink through nozzles and spray the ink right onto the paper. Depending on the printer and its technology, there can be between 21 and 128 nozzles for each of the four colors (cyan, yellow, magenta, and black). By mixing the colors, the printer can produce almost any color.

There are two types of inkjet printers: thermal and piezo. These are two different technologies used to force the ink from the cartridge and through the nozzles.

Thermal inkjets use the older of the two technologies. They heat the ink in the cartridge (to about 400 degrees Fahrenheit), causing vapor bubbles in the cartridge that rise to the top and force the ink out through the nozzle. The vacuum caused by the expelled ink draws more ink down into the nozzles, making a constant stream.

Piezo printing uses an electric charge instead of heat. It charges piezoelectric crystals in the nozzles, which change their shape as a result of the electric current, forcing the ink out through the nozzles.

Piezo is the preferred technology these days. Heat is never good for hardware, and piezo printing eliminates the need for it; therefore, the printers can use better (less heat-durable) inks that are less prone to smearing. The nozzles also last longer because they aren't punished by high temperatures day in and day out.

Common Problems and Possible Solutions

Just about all printer problems can be easily fixed if you know where to look. Although I attempt in this section to give you a good general sense of what problems might occur and how to prevent them, you should read the manuals that came with your printer carefully.

The list of things that can go wrong with printing is fairly large, but you can organize them into general categories to help you troubleshoot. The point is to try to remove problems that might not be affecting you and to point you in the right general direction. Try thinking along these lines to categorize your printer problem:

▶ Your printer seems to be working, but nothing is printing.

▶ There are color problems.

▶ The printer appears dead.

▶ Printing seems very slow, but is working.

▶ The quality of your printouts is poor.

▶ The output is garbled or formatted incorrectly.

▶ The paper is jammed or not feeding correctly.

I'll cover each of these symptoms in turn.

Printer Works but Nothing Prints

This problem may be as simple as running out of ink. Most printers come with software status controls built into their Windows driver. Right-click the printer's icon in Windows, choose Properties (it works basically the same in all Windows versions), and look for a status monitor in the Printer Properties dialog box that indicates the ink level. Replace any cartridges that indicate they are out of ink. Figure 19.1 shows the ink levels for an Epson printer.

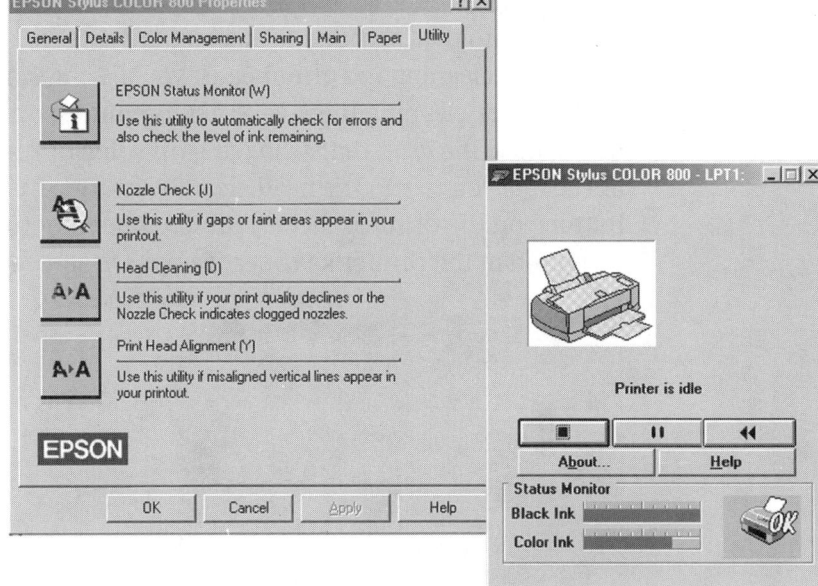

Figure 19.1

This status monitor for the Epson Stylus Color 800 shows the color and black ink levels.

If that doesn't work, try running the nozzle check and/or print head cleaning routine that is a part of your printer control program. Your nozzles might be clogged up. This is sometimes a problem if you haven't printed in a long time. A nozzle check prints a test pattern using all the jets, so you can see whether any are malfunctioning. Head cleaning self-cleans each jet. You will want to run these two utilities, first one and then the other, to check the current nozzle functioning and to improve it. Head cleaning uses up a small amount of ink, however, so if you do it a lot, you'll end up wasting ink.

True story: One time I was working with a printer that hadn't been used in over a year. Nearly all the nozzles were clogged, so I had to run the head cleaning routine 20 times in a row. The quality kept getting better and better, and I was feeling encouraged, but then the blue nozzles just quit. Kaput. Nothing. I panicked. Had I ruined the printer by repeated cleaning? Nope, I had just depleted all the blue ink. So I installed a new cartridge, and it worked perfectly. Incidentally, on many printer models, installing a new ink cartridge also takes care of any clogged nozzles, because the inkjets are built into the cartridge. (This isn't the case for all models.)

If, after cleaning the print heads, you see intermittent output on the page, try cleaning them several more times; this can sometimes break loose the crud that's clogging up some of the jets. Most printers enable you to run the head cleaning routine by pressing certain buttons on the printer (check your documentation) or by choosing an option in the printer's Properties box (as shown in Figure 19.2).

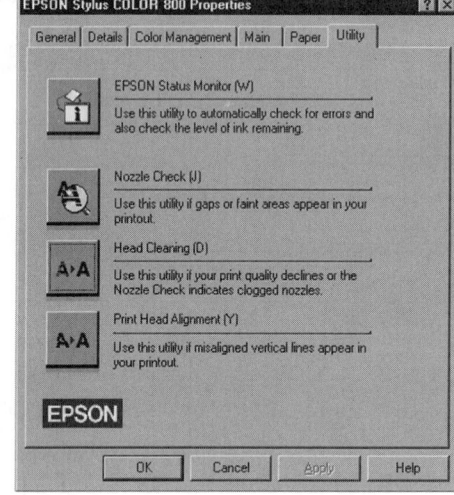

Figure 19.2

Most printers have utilities such as nozzle checking and head cleaning built into the driver.

If that fails, take your print cartridges out and check whether any obstructions might be blocking the ink. If you've recently replaced your printer cartridges, check them to make sure you removed all the protective coverings from the print nozzles and contacts.

Warning

The documentation for some printer models claims that if you remove an ink cartridge after initially inserting it, it becomes useless and you can't reinsert it. I have reinserted a cartridge in one such printer successfully, despite the instructions, but if you have a printer that claims this, try all other troubleshooting first before you resort to removing the cartridge for examination and reinsertion.

Color Is Wrong

If the colors on your printout don't match what you see onscreen, the most likely problem is that one of the color jets is clogged. Check the printout—do all greens look yellow, and is the blue missing? That means you're out of cyan. See the instructions in the preceding section for replacing an ink cartridge and/or cleaning the print heads.

If the color problem is more subtle (all colors appear, but they look too dark, too blue, or whatever), the problem might be with your monitor's color calibration. If your video card ships with a utility that allows you to calibrate your monitor's color, you should run it. There might also be a utility built into your printer driver or video card driver; try displaying the device's Properties to look for one.

Printer Doesn't Print at All

Ah, the dead printer. Fear not, the problem is usually simple.

First, check that the printer is plugged in and the power is on. Then, check your printer cable connections. Try removing the printer cable and reseating it at both ends.

If these aren't causing the problem, make sure that the printer appears in your operating system and that it is online and currently selected as the default printer. In Windows, check the Printers list (Start ➢ Settings ➢ Printers); a checkmark next to the printer's icon indicates that it's the default. Right-click it and choose Set as Default if needed. Sometimes strange things happen and this gets messed up. I've seen cases of printers disappearing or suddenly going offline.

If your default printer is a network printer, make sure your network connection is up and running. If the printer appears "faded" or "grayed out" in the Printers window, it's because the printer is not available for some reason (usually due to a failure in the network connection to it).

Next, open the print queue for your printer (by double-clicking its icon in the Printers list) to see whether printing is currently paused. (The title bar will read `Paused` if it is.) Choose Printer ➢ Pause Printing to unpause it. You might have paused printing and forgotten to reset it.

If the printer's status is User Intervention, that means the printer is waiting on something. If it's a network printer, there could be a warning or error message on the host computer's screen, waiting to be answered. Or the printer could be out of paper or have a paper jam.

Printing Is Slow or Intermittent

Slow or intermittent printing could be caused by a couple of things. First, double-check your cable connection to the printer. If your printer is capable of bidirectional communications, make sure your printer cable is also. (Most printer cables bought today are bidirectional, but an old one you found in someone's junk drawer may not be. You can't tell by looking at them, but it will say on the packaging of a new one you buy.) Bidirectional communications enable the printer to communicate with the operating system (and vice versa), so that your printer control program can communicate with the printer and return error messages and ink levels. Bidirectional printing must also be enabled for the port that the printer is using (probably LPT1) in your PC's BIOS.

Slow printing could also be caused by your printer driver settings. In most cases, you can choose to print in draft, normal, or high-resolution mode. The higher the quality, the more time the printing will take. If you're printing at 1200dpi (dots per inch), your printout may take a very long time. If you want it to print faster and don't need the higher quality, lower your print quality settings through the printer's print settings. You can set these by displaying the printer's properties (right-click it and choose Properties), or, within some applications, with a PRINT SETUP command.

Finally, slow printing can be the result of using the wrong driver for your printer. If you let Windows autodetect your printer instead of running the setup software that came with the printer, you may not be using the best possible driver. Dig through the documentation that came with the printer and find its SETUP CD, and run that to install the specific driver for your printer.

Quality Is Poor

If the printer prints, but the output isn't as good as you think it should be, you've got some investigative work to do to find out why.

First, check to see what quality mode the printer is set to operate in. As I mentioned earlier, the higher the quality, the slower the printing. Sometimes people set their printers to draft quality (the fastest, lowest-quality setting) and forget that they've done so. Check the printer's Properties box to view and change the quality setting. Figure 19.3 shows an example.

Figure 19.3

Most printers enable you to choose from several quality settings.

While you're there looking at the quality setting, see also whether there is a Media Type or Paper Type setting. With inkjet printers, plain old copy paper doesn't produce as good an image as special inkjet paper with a shinier surface and less porous "holes." The less porous the paper, the higher the dpi setting you can use for the printout. Using a very high dpi (such as 1400) with plain paper can actually result in a printout that looks *worse* than a printout at a lower resolution (720, perhaps) because the paper can't handle the dots being that close together because of its porousness. For best results, buy paper made specially for inkjet printers, because it enables you to print at higher dpi.

Next, clean your print heads through the printer control program, as described in the previous "Printer Works but Nothing Prints" section. A clogged nozzle can result in stripes on the page (*banding*), or "bald" patches where there is no printing.

Your print heads may also be out of alignment. Run the print head alignment routine from your printer (probably built into the printer driver, as with the other utilities you've seen so far in this chapter). This aligns the print heads and nozzles so that the black and color ink cartridges print at the same location on the page. This one does its stuff the first time, so you should not have to do it multiple times for best results (as with head cleaning).

Check your ink levels. Low ink results in banding or streaking. If you're low on color ink, your printout will appear washed out or oddly miscolored. You may be out of one of the three primary colors used in color printing.

If your printer allows it, remove your print cartridges and inspect them manually for defects or blockages. You may need to clean them with a clean rag. Reinstall them and make sure they are properly seated in the carrier. Remember that not all printers allow you to reinsert the same cartridge after removing it (at least not according to the documentation; you might still be able to do so.)

If you have problems at the edge of the page, such as output being cut off at the edges, you may be trying to print material outside of the effective print area of your printer. Many printers will not let you print across the full width of a standard sheet of paper.

Output Is Garbled or Formatted Incorrectly

If you print a nicely formatted word processing document, but it comes out with the wrong fonts, skewed margins, or junk characters, the problem is probably a corrupt printer driver.

To repair a driver problem, delete the printer from the Printers list and reinstall it using the disk that came with the printer. If you don't have such a disk, download the needed setup software from the manufacturer's Web site. Windows comes with drivers for many popular printers, and you can use the Windows-provided driver in a pinch, if one from the manufacturer is not available. (The Windows version may not have as many features, so I try to always use the manufacturer-supplied drivers whenever possible.)

The driver is not always to blame, however. One time I had a very frustrating service call, in which the printer was printing the output scrunched up on the left side of each page. The printout would appear perfectly in Print Preview onscreen, but without fail, each page came out distorted. I tried reinstalling the driver. I tried resetting the printer. I tried printing from DOS. Nothing worked. Finally I checked inside the printer and noticed that the ink cartridges were not completely seated in their holders. I gave them a firm push into place, and violà! Problem solved. Weird but true.

Paper Is Stuck or Not Moving

If paper jams in your printer, stop what you are doing and carefully but firmly pull the paper out of the printer. Try not to rip the paper as you pull it out, because you don't want to have small pieces of paper caught inside the printer. When you've removed the jammed piece of paper, throw it away and resend your job to the printer.

If paper fails to feed at all, check that the paper is seated correctly in the paper tray. If any obstructions are blocking the paper, carefully remove them. If a piece of paper is bent, it may not feed correctly. You'll have to throw it away.

You should also check to ensure that you haven't overloaded the paper feed tray. Too many sheets in the tray can easily cause jams or feed problems. Sometimes using very thick or very thin paper can cause feed problems too. Try to use a standard paper weight (20 lb or so) whenever possible.

Most printers also have paper guides that snuggle up against your paper and keep it straight as it feeds into the printer. These guides can be set for different sizes of paper. Make sure the guide is properly set and isn't loose.

Finally, make sure your printer is on a flat, stable surface. If it is tilted at an angle or on a shaky table, that might cause feed problems.

Common Error Messages

Although each printer will have error messages that are unique to its particular make and model, here are a few error messages you might encounter.

Ink Low

This signifies that your printer cartridge is running out of ink. You should replace the printer cartridge soon. Some printer manufacturers recommend that you don't change an ink cartridge until the printer reports that the ink is completely out. You can make that call yourself, but it's nice to have the advance `Ink Low` warning so you can make sure you have a new cartridge available.

Warning

Ink cartridges tend to dry out on the shelf. Don't stockpile ink cartridges; after six months or so they lose their freshness.

Out of Memory

Laser printers are page printers—they print entire pages at a time, so they must have a lot of memory in them to store a whole page. In contrast, inkjet printers are line printers—they print line-by-line, so they don't typically need a great deal of memory. You seldom hear of memory upgrades available for inkjet printers because it's simply not an issue.

Therefore, if you get an `Out of Memory` error message onscreen as you print to an inkjet printer, it most likely refers to a lack of memory on your PC, rather than on your printer. Usually it does not really mean that you should add memory to your PC; rather, it means that memory-hogging programs you have run on your PC have allocated all the available memory, and there isn't enough left for the printer driver to spool its output to the printer. In such a case, it's best to restart your PC and resubmit your print job after doing so.

Out of Paper

You are either completely out of paper, or if your printer has multiple paper sources, you may have designated an empty tray. You'll have to load more paper in your printer or switch to another paper tray to continue.

Paper Jam

Paper has jammed somewhere in your printer, preventing it from continuing. Carefully but firmly pull the paper out of the printer, hopefully in one piece. Depending on where the paper jam occurs, you may have to pull it out of the top (or paper-feed area) or the bottom (the paper-exit tray). If you can't reach the paper easily, you might have to open the access panel to reach inside your printer.

Print Head Failure

If your printer cartridges are not working correctly, you might receive a `Print Head Failure` error message. Dirty, fouled, or clogged printer cartridges can cause this problem. Clean your printer head through your printer control program, and if necessary, remove the ink cartridges and clean them with a clean cloth.

Preventive Maintenance

If you own a car, you're probably used to preventive maintenance. You change your oil every 3,000 miles or every three months, check the air in the tires, check other fluid levels, and routinely put gas in it so it will run. Printers also require some regular maintenance, although it is far less troublesome than what you need to do for a car.

Clean the Print Heads

Although you don't want to overdo it, you should clean your print heads periodically by running the head cleaning utility (as discussed earlier in the chapter). This should remove any built up "gunk" or ink on the print heads and help ensure consistently high-quality printouts.

Align the Print Heads

Every time you install new printer cartridges, you should also align your print heads. This keeps the color and black ink cartridges aligned so there are no gaps between black and color portions of your printout. Your printer may do this automatically, but it doesn't hurt to do it manually by using the head alignment utility in your printer driver (again, covered earlier in the chapter).

Realigning print heads might also be necessary after moving your printer or bumping into it accidentally.

Complete Overhaul

It may be necessary to take your printer apart and clean the inner parts. You shouldn't take this step unless you are comfortable with it, but if you print a lot and find that your printouts aren't very good and you've run through the standard steps to fix quality problems, your printer may just be dirty inside.

Carefully remove the outer case and disassemble your printer, cleaning each part as you go along with an alcohol-based cleaner. This will remove any ink that has dried on the parts. You may have to soak some pieces to get the ink off them. A small glass jar works well for the smaller pieces. Just soak them for 15 to 30 minutes and wipe them off with a cloth or towel. When everything is clean, reassemble your printer and print out a test page (after you've realigned the print heads).

Refilling Ink Cartridges

Due to the cost of today's inkjet printer cartridges (usually over $30 for black and upwards of $40 to $50 for color), the cottage industry of refillable inkjet cartridges has emerged. It should be said that most manufacturers do not recommend this, but what they don't know won't hurt them. In fact, some manufacturers make their printer cartridges very hard to get into by yourself, thus making it hard for you to refill them without special tools or equipment.

You should be able to purchase kits made specifically for your brand of printer and model of printer cartridges if your printer is popular enough. This method gives you some assurance that your new cartridge will contain ink with the same characteristics as the retail printer cartridge. If not, you may be stuck with buying the officially designated replacement cartridges.

Refilling ink cartridges involves removing the lid of the existing printer cartridge and simply refilling it. Due to the wide variety of existing printer cartridges, you should carefully follow the instructions provided with the kit you buy.

You should not refill a cartridge more than once. That's because, on most printers, the print jets are built into the cartridges. When you replace the ink cartridge, you also give yourself a brand-new set of jets. If you continually refill and reuse the same cartridge, you're never getting new jets, and your print quality can start to suffer. You'll get clogged jets more and more often, resulting in more head-cleaning, which in turn wastes ink, and before you know it, you're caught in a vicious circle. Yes, it's okay to be a little thrifty and refill occasionally, but don't be so cheap that you cheat yourself out of decent quality printouts.

Troubleshooting Tips

Here's a summary of the troubleshooting procedures covered in the chapter:

▶ For print quality problems, check the utilities built into the printer's driver. (Right-click the printer and choose Properties to display the available tools and settings.)

▶ Use the nozzle checking utility to see whether any jets are clogged; then use the head cleaning utility to clean them. This uses ink, so balance the need for cleaning with your need not to waste ink.

▶ If the color is seriously off, one of the ink colors is probably out, or its nozzles are clogged. If the color problem is more uniform, check the color calibration for the video card and/or the printer. One or both may have a color correction utility.

▶ If the printer doesn't print at all, check all your connections, and make sure the printer is installed correctly in your operating system.

▶ Make sure the printer isn't offline, paused, or requiring user intervention (such as adding more paper).

▶ If the printer is accessed through a network, make sure your network connection is up and running.

▶ If the printer prints slowly, try decreasing the quality setting for a draft print. You can usually do this through the printer's Properties box. Slow printing may also be the result of using the wrong driver.

▶ Poor print quality can mean you are running out of one or more colors of ink, that the print heads are misaligned or clogged, or that you're using a draft quality setting.

▶ Garbled output indicates a problem with the printer driver. Remove the printer from Windows (or other operating system) and reinstall.

Troubleshooting
Laser Printers

INTRODUCTION

L aser printers are actually pretty reliable. Most of the printer problems you'll see are not printer problems at all, but rather problems with the humans trying to use them. As I told you in Chapter 5, "Troubleshooting PC Problems," you should first check the part of the equation that walks and talks.

Once the human component has been checked and cleared, exercise a methodical approach to testing the rest of the system. Break the problem down into its possibilities/probabilities, testing and eliminating them, one by one. Start with the easy stuff first. It's always possible that the only thing the printer needs is more paper.

Parts of a Laser Printer

Let's start out our discussion of laser printers by looking at its parts.

Interface Controller

Much of a laser printer is actually a computer—that is, it's comprised of the same basic stuff as your desktop computer: circuit boards, memory chips, ports, and so on. As in your computer, the laser printer has a large printed circuit board that receives, modifies, and outputs data. Different manufacturers call it by different names, but in this book I'll go with the generic name *interface controller*.

The interface controller is the printer's motherboard, and it handles some pretty important tasks. Here's some of what it does:

▶ Communicates with the PC that wants to print using an input interface (parallel, serial, network, or infrared)

▶ Manipulates incoming data for translation to the print engine

▶ Monitors the Control Panel (usually a button panel on its front) for user input

▶ Provides information on printer status at the display and through various LEDs

▶ Stores configuration and font information

Of these, the input interface is the one you will deal with most directly, so let's look at it more closely.

Input Interface

Depending on the printer, the input interface may provide only for parallel connection, or it may offer other options too, such as serial, network, or some other special I/O such as infrared.

Parallel Ports

As you learned in Chapter 18, "Troubleshooting Printers," parallel connectivity uses eight wires to transfer the data, with each bit traveling in parallel down a separate wire. A full byte (eight bits) of data at a time will travel the cable.

The Achilles' heel of the parallel port is the fact that it is quite limited in terms of distance. Most manufacturers want the parallel interface cable to be limited to about 15 feet for laser printer applications. The parallel interface is by far the most common printer interface type, and nearly all printers support it.

Serial Ports

Serial, as the name implies, is used to send data in a bit-by-bit fashion, using one wire to send and another to receive. This is a rugged and flexible interface when compared to the parallel port. It can be configured to change several parameters including speed and can be found on everything from mice to modems.

If a decent, shielded, twisted-pair cable is used in a quiet environment (one without lots of radio frequency or electromagnetic interference), it is possible to send and receive data through a serial port at distances of several hundred feet. However, its transmission speed is limited by its very nature—since it sends each bit one at a time, or serially, it can't rival a parallel port that sends eight bits at once. Therefore it's a less common interface, and some printers don't include it at all.

Network Interface

In Chapter 18, I explained the two ways a printer can hook into a network—through a networked PC or with its own network connection. You can connect to Token Ring or Ethernet, 10 or 100Mbps, coax, or twisted pair, depending on the network interface that your printer comes with or that you install in it.

Optional I/O

Some printers support additional I/O possibilities, such as infrared or Macintosh connection. For example, on HP laser printers, there's an optional I/O, or "video" port, located at the back of the printer next to the standard serial and parallel ports. This is the receptor of many upgrades and emulation enhancements. One of the better known among them is the LaserWriter upgrade board that allows the printer to communicate with Macintosh computers.

This is also used as the interface for many other after-market enhancements such as printer sharing devices.

CPU

Just as your computer's motherboard holds its CPU, the printer's interface controller also holds the main brain of the printer, its CPU. No matter which port receives the data, the CPU controls its processing. Most laser printers today use a RISC processor (which, by the way, stands for Reduced Instruction Set Computer), as opposed to your PC, which uses a CISC (the C stands for *complex*). However, the basic processing concept is the same.

Printer RAM

It's important to remember that a laser printer is a page printer—it composes an entire page in memory first, and then transfers it to paper. So there must be enough RAM in the printer to hold an entire page, or it can't print. How much is "enough"? It depends on the page being printed. More and larger graphics, and more fonts, means more memory required.

When laser printers first appeared on the market, they came with a measly amount of memory (often only 512KB) that wasn't enough to compose a full-page graphic. People using those printers would get an error message when printing complex pages and, naturally, they complained about it bitterly to the manufacturers.

The manufacturers responded by offering to sell memory upgrades. But these upgrades were typically a proprietary type of memory, which cost quite a bit more than normal computer memory (which, at that time, was no bargain either!). Sometimes it was actually cheaper to buy a whole new printer with more memory than it was to pay for one of these RAM upgrades!

Manufacturers have learned their lesson somewhat in recent years and have made printers that accept regular DRAM SIMMs (that is, the same type of RAM that computers use). That, combined with the dropping cost of memory in general, has made it a lot more economical to have a printer with a decent amount of memory (say, 4MB for an average home office).

Print Language

The printer communicates with the PC's software in a special language. When you install a printer driver, the driver knows what language that printer requires, and "speaks" it.

The most common language for laser printers is Printer Control Language, or PCL, developed by Hewlett-Packard in the early 1980s. The following table lists the various iterations of PCL and what printers they were originally used in.

PCL Version	Year Released	HP Printers
PCL 3	1984	LaserJet, LaserJet Plus
PCL 4	1985	LaserJet Series II, 3100 (all models), 3150 (all models)
PCL 4e	1989	LaserJet IIP, IIP Plus
PCL 5	1990	LaserJet III, IIID, IIIP, IIIsi, HP-GL/2, 4V, 4MV
PCL 5e	1992	LaserJet 4, 4M, 4L, 4ML, 4P, 4MP, 4 Plus, 4M Plus, 5P, 5MP, 5L, 5L-FS, 5Si, 5Si NX, 5Si MX, 5Si Mopier, 5Lxtra, 6L, 6Lxi, 6Lse, 6Lxi, 6MP, 1100 (all models)

PCL 5c	1994	Color LaserJet 4500, Color LaserJet 8500, Color LaserJet 5, 5M
PCL 6	1996	LaserJet 5, 5se, 5M, 5N, LaserJet 6, 6P, 6Pse, 6Pxi, 6MP, 2100 (all models), 4000 (all models), 4050 (all models), 5000 (all models), 8000 (all models), 8100 (all models)

You don't have to worry about which version of PCL a printer uses, in most cases. The driver will automatically handle the communication. If, however, you don't have the correct driver available for some reason, you can sometimes use a driver that speaks the same PCL version as the printer you have and get away with it. You can use Table 20.1, later in this chapter, as a guide for picking a substitute driver if needed.

The other major language that laser printers use is PostScript, which was developed by Adobe in 1985. PostScript offered many features that PCL lacked in the beginning, such as scalable typefaces, so it quickly became the standard in desktop publishing and graphics. It failed to catch on with the average mainstream user, however, because printers that used it were more expensive.

Nowadays, almost every laser printer supports PCL, and many support both PCL and PostScript. (You choose which language you want to use by selecting one driver or another in your software.)

Printing Mechanisms

The parts I've talked about so far are all computer components but, obviously, a printer must have some mechanical parts too. The paper needs to be taken in, printed on, and spit back out again. Different laser printers handle the paper input/output in different ways, but the process of actually creating the printed image on the page is fairly standard among laser printers. You'll learn about this printing process in the following section.

How a Laser Printer Prints

Laser printing is a multistep process. Understanding the process is more than just a techie exercise; it's essential to understanding what can go wrong and how to fix it.

I'll explain this in detail shortly, but the overview on how a laser prints is roughly like this: the printing drum is cleaned, an image is "painted" onto it with electrostatic charges, print toner moves to the charged areas, the toner is transferred to a piece of paper, and, finally, the toner is fixed onto the paper permanently with a heated metal roller. You can see this in Figure 20.1.

3. Laser beam selectively hits part of the EP drum, making that part conductive. The conductive part loses voltage, dropping to -100V.

Mirror

2. Main corona puts –6KV charge on drum surface.

4. Developer roller squeezes toner (represented by the #4 area) into a uniform layer on the EP drum. The parts that are charged to -6KV, however, repel the toner. Toner only remains where the laser has touched, as it is the most positively charged part of the drum.

1. Eraser lamp clears residual charge from drum.

Rotating EP drum

Paper movement direction

Figure 20.1

How a laser printer works

6. The image now only sits on the paper as fine, dustlike toner. The toner must be fixed to the page. The fuser roller actually melts the toner into the page with heat at a temperature of 180 degrees C.

5. The paper is pulled under the drum, which now contains the desired image written in toner. A second corona, the transfer corona, emits a positive charge, drawing the toner from the drum to the paper.

Figure 20.2 shows a laser printer with paper ready to start running through the printing process.

Figure 20.2

Laser printer beginning the printing process

Paper

> The paper feeds from the left. The rollers and the print cartridge are on the right.

Data Input

When an application has data ready to be printed, it establishes communication with an output port in the PC. The PC then determines that there is indeed an output device attached to that port and satisfies itself that the device is waiting for data.

The laser printer responds in a favorable manner to the overtures of the computer by signaling on the strobe line (pin 1) on the parallel interface or DTR (line 20) on serial. This indicates that the printer is inactive but receptive.

When the application begins to deliver the data, it is received by the printer buffer—that is, its RAM. The printer's RAM holds the data until it can be processed by the printer's CPU and printed using the printer's print hardware.

Once the data is ready for printing, the hardware goes through a preparatory process before the laser actually begins to define the image.

A significant percentage of the printing process involves the electrophotographic cartridge. There are several things that need to happen within the cartridge each time that the interface controller receives data. The first of those things is drum preparation.

Drum Preparation

The heart of the print process is the photosensitive drum, an aluminum cylinder coated with a photosensitive material. The drum's job is to pick up laser printer *toner*—a fine black dust that is the "ink" of the laser printing process—and deposit it on the paper. Figure 20.3 points out the photosensitive drum.

Figure 20.3

Photosensitive drum
in a laser printer

Photosensitive drum——

Cleaning the Drum

Since the same photosensitive drum is used to print every image (it actually rotates almost three times during the printing of each letter-sized page), it must be prepared for the newer image by completely purging the previous one. If the drum weren't completely purged, then subsequent pages would have ghostly images from previous pages. You know how hard it is to completely clean a blackboard when you erase it, and parts of what was on the blackboard previously kind of hang around? That's what we're trying to avoid in laser printing.

The cleaning process is accomplished in two parts. Physically, excess toner is constantly wiped from the drum by means of a rubber cleaning blade.

The drum is then cleaned electrostatically by five erase lamps found in the hinged top cover on the early printers and by another drum—a charged drum—in the later printer models. On the printers with lamps, the lamps can shine onto the photosensitive drum via one of the two narrow hinged covers on the top of the cartridge, which open automatically when the cover is closed. These lamps neutralize residual charges by illuminating the photosensitive component of the drum.

The photosensitive component can be permanently damaged by exposure to light; therefore, the illumination from the lamps is red filtered. Pop the top on certain laser printers, and you'll see red plastic; those are the filters for the lamps.

Conditioning

After the original preparation, the drum requires conditioning for the next image. This process involves the application of a uniformly negative charge to the surface of the drum by the primary corona assembly (the one in the cartridge) in the early printers or a charged drum in the later ones. The high-voltage power supply provides a –600v charge to the corona wire or charged drum, thus creating an electrical corona, kind of like some major-league static electricity. That –600v charge is applied by a very important thin wire called the *primary corona* located in the disposable laser cartridge. The corona must actually emit a *–6000*v charge in order to get the –600v applied to the drum.

Air is a natural insulator (it's true—in double-paned thermal windows, the air between the panes is as good an insulator as the glass panes are), and that could get in the way of transferring the charge from the corona wire to the drum. But when a corona wire produces a charge, it causes the air in the area of the wire to be ionized with the net effect so that it no longer provides insulation between the drum and the corona. The –600v charge is therefore transferred to the entire surface of the drum.

The voltage buildup on the surface of the drum is uniform because it is filtered by a grid that is attached to a varistor in the high-voltage power supply. Take a look at Figure 20.4.

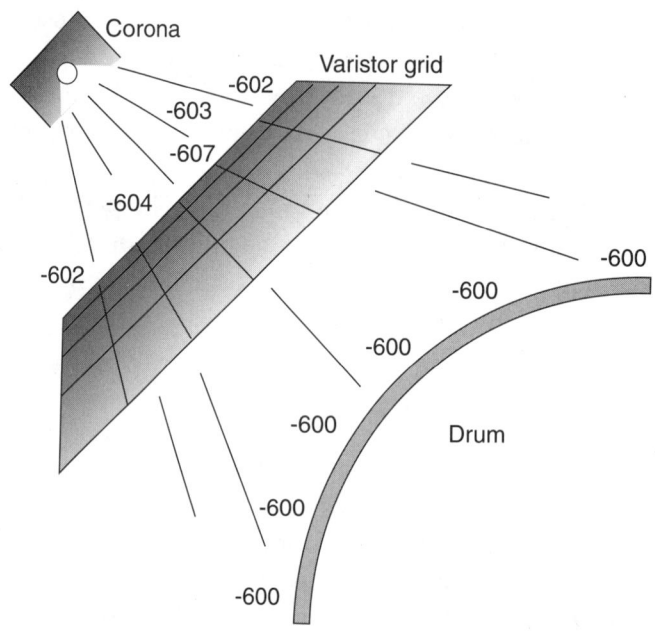

Figure 20.4

Corona, varistor grid,
and drum

A varistor is so named because it is a *variable resistor.* It will not conduct electricity until a specific voltage level is achieved. This, of course, is the characteristic that allows it to be useful in this particular application.

Writing the Image on the Drum

Now that it's conditioned, the drum is ready for the image.

First, the photosensitive drum is scanned by the laser unit. This is done in a fashion similar to that of a CRT, with a repeated horizontal sweeping motion of the beam. (As a matter of fact, the interface cable on PostScript and optional I/O printer interfaces is referred to in some HP technical documents as a *video cable.*)

Once a character definition has been determined by the interface controller, the laser light is provided by turning a laser diode on and off at the appropriate times in the current beam position, which in turn is determined by its reflection from the rotation of a polygonal mirror.

On the LaserJet III and earlier, the on/off status of the laser diode could be changed 300 times for each inch of the beam's progress across the drum, hence the 300-dpi (dots per inch) resolution of those printers. This creates a map of the appropriate portion of the character on the drum by causing a discharge of the voltage potential in the affected areas, thus creating an invisible electrostatic image with the laser. More modern laser printers have even higher resolutions, up to 1200 dpi or more.

The laser access to the drum is through the second hinged door on the cartridge, as you see in Figure 20.5.

Figure 20.5

Laser access to the printer drum

The beam continues its sweep in perfect synchronization with the rotation of the drum so that each incremental horizontal sweep of the beam is offset by $\frac{1}{300}$ of an inch from the previous one. The process continues until the entire drum has thus been mapped.

The affected points of the drum are neutralized to about –100v.

The fact that the drum rotates $\frac{1}{300}$ of an inch with each horizontal sweep of the laser and that the laser diode is able to change states 300 times per inch results in the 300×300 dpi resolution of the printer.

How Color Laser Printers Differ

While color laser printers are expensive, they are gaining a following due to the glorious graphics and text they produce. The professional-looking output produced by these printers makes them a boon to people who do their own advertising or graphics printing.

Color laser printers work in much the same way as their cheaper black-and-white cousins. The technical details of the print process vary somewhat depending on the manufacturer. Some color lasers print each color on the page individually, making several passes (one for black and one for each of the toner colors), much like the color separation printing that's done by commercial presses. Because the printer has only one drum, the whole printing process repeats several times for each page, layering the toner.

A color printing method that is gaining more popularity is the "Direct-to-Drum" method used by many of the Hewlett-Packard color lasers. In this print method, the charging corona places the negative charge on the drum, and the laser then gently sweeps over the drum and creates an image for the yellow toner (the first of four primary printing colors) to attach to. After the yellow toner has made itself at home, the drum is again charged by the corona, and the laser works its art on the drum and creates an image for the next printing color, magenta. This same process happens again for the final two colors, cyan and black. After all four colors have been applied to the drum, the image is transferred onto the waiting paper. This method allows a single dot on the page to have a blended color, rather than the dithered colors of images produced on inkjet printers and cheaper color laser printers.

Note

An inexpensive alternative to color laser printing uses LED (light-emitting diode) technology rather than lasers. Okidata's OKICOLOR 8 printers use this technology. These printers print quickly because they make only one pass, as with an inkjet, but the quality is arguably not quite as good as with a real color laser.

The problems people have with color laser printers are virtually identical to the problems with black-and-white models. One exception is color registration—that is, a failure of the colors to align properly on a laser printer that prints by making multiple passes over the paper.

(Because fewer and fewer color lasers work that way these days, this problem is confined to only a few brands and models.) This problem is often a symptom of the paper not being fed through the printer precisely, so your difficulty is probably with the feed rollers rather than the printing process itself. Check your printer's documentation or the manufacturer's Web site to see what can be done.

The Paper Feed

When the drum has been conditioned, the paper sensor/feed roller assembly draws the paper into the printer. You can see this in Figure 20.6.

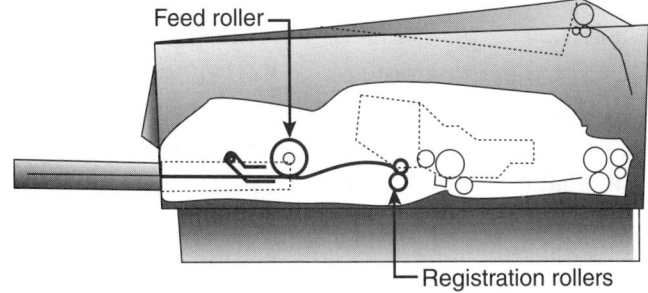

Figure 20.6

Paper sensor/feed roller assembly

Notice that the paper is bowed slightly upward. You might have also noticed at some time that the printer draws the paper from the tray an inch or so and hesitates before continuing. Both occurrences are related to a procedure that ensures that the top edge of the paper is perfectly aligned with the top of the image on the drum.

The paper is presented to the registration rollers, which impede its travel until a carefully timed release causes every part of the process to be synchronized.

Image Development

After the image is mapped on the photosensitive drum, there is then the simple application of a basic law of nature and of magnetic properties: opposites attract.

The developer component of the cartridge contains a rotating metallic cylinder with a permanent magnet running its length, a toner reservoir, and a toner height control mechanism. The height control is to regulate the amount of toner that may travel with the cylinder.

The metallic cylinder is situated adjacent to the photosensitive drum. Its sole purpose is to collect toner from the reservoir and present it to the drum in a usable form. This device is called the developing cylinder.

The developing cylinder rotates with a portion of its surface in contact with the toner in the toner reservoir of the cartridge. Its magnetic personality (not to mention the fact that its surface is given a highly negative –600v charge by the high-voltage power supply) causes an irresistible attraction to the tiny neutrally charged particles of toner, which then cling to the cylinder.

The toner that adheres to the cylinder adopts its charge by the time it travels to the image area of the photosensitive drum.

The toner is made of plastic resin particles (the part that melts) bonded to iron oxide (the part that is attracted by the electrical charges).

While the toner-laden developing cylinder rotates toward the image-ready photosensitive drum, a scraping blade removes the excess toner, thus delivering a uniform supply of it to the image process.

The electrical properties of the magnetized developing cylinder are further enhanced by a DC bias and an AC potential.

You can adjust the DC bias via the print density control knob on the printer. Its purpose is to regulate the density of the toner that ends up on the printed page. Counter-intuitively, selecting a *higher* number on the green wheel results in *less* toner being offered to the photosensitive drum and therefore results in a lighter image being put on the page. As the developing cylinder presents the now highly negatively charged toner to the laser-affected areas of the photosensitive drum, they are attracted to the invisible electrostatic image because it, although still negative in charge, is much less negative than the toner itself.

The remainder of the drum, not having been struck by the laser, remains at a –600v charge and effectively repels the similarly charged toner.

The AC component on the developer roller affects the DC potential, thus causing the toner, in a reciprocal process, to escape the negatively charged roller at the moment of highest potential, only to be reattracted to it when the AC component swings high. This happens 60 times per second, effectively presenting a fog of toner to the laser-affected areas.

Those particles of toner that find their way to the electrostatically defined image are not drawn back to the developing cylinder. Take a look at Figure 20.7 for an overview of the process.

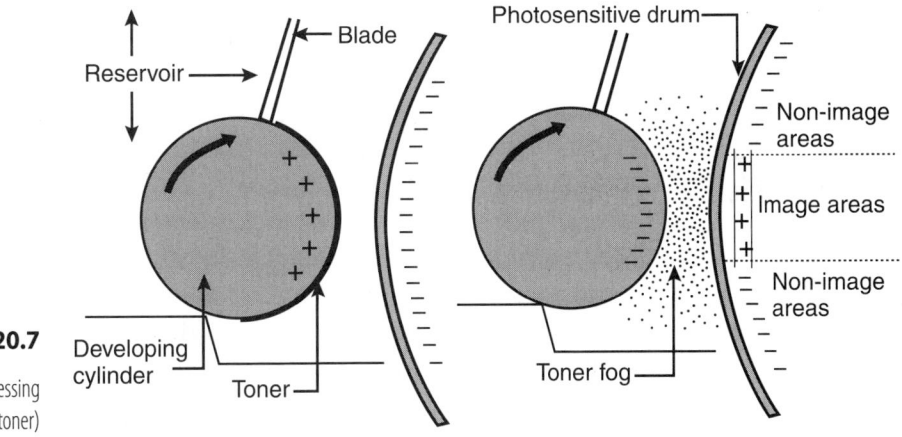

Figure 20.7

Image processing (toner)

Image Transfer

The desired image now exists on the drum in the form of fine toner particles. Toner is about 50 percent iron oxide, 50 percent plastic. (You can actually get toner out of fabric by rubbing a powerful magnet across the surface.) Next, the laser printer transfers the toner to paper by giving the paper a strong (+600v) *positive* charge. That charge is applied by the *transfer corona*, another very important thin wire permanently mounted in the printer. The toner then jumps from the drum to the paper. Once the toner is on the paper, the paper runs past the *static charge eliminator*, which reduces the paper's charge. The image is now transferred to the paper. Take a look at Figure 20.8.

Photosensitive drum

Figure 20.8

Transfer corona

Transfer corona

Fusing the Image to the Paper

Once the drum has yielded the image, separation of the paper from it (the drum) is not a foregone conclusion. However, as the paper advances, its natural stiffness facilitates the separation due to the fact that the drum circumference is relatively small. Thinner papers might adhere to the drum, however, so separation is also assisted by the static eliminator, a row of teeth with a highly negative charge that aids in the neutralization of the potential between the positively charged paper and the negatively charged drum.

The paper proceeds to the fusing station with its toner image in the precarious condition of being held to the paper by only gravity and a weak electrostatic charge.

The fusing station assembly is composed of a fuser roller, cleaning pad, thermistor, thermo-protector, and pressure roller.

The fuser roller is a Teflon-coated cylinder that has a high-intensity quartz lamp inside it to provide the heat for the fusing process. If the heat builds beyond acceptable levels, there is a detection/protection mechanism called a *thermistor*, located near the fuser roller, which will shut the printer down.

Just how hot are we talking about here? Well, the temperatures of the LaserJet III's fuser were 165 degrees C (330 degrees F) when on but inactive and 180 degrees C (355 degrees F) while printing. The temperatures are higher in the LaserJet 4 and later models. Given these temperatures, caution is advised in the insertion of any gummed, plastic-coated, inked, or raised image media (not to mention your fingers). I have heard multiple reports of people inserting nonrated Mylar or acetate to make overhead projection display sheets. Put simply, if you try to print on something that melts below 180 degrees C, you'll probably have to buy a new fuser roller. They make special transparency film just for laser printers, so make sure you buy that kind if you need some.

The cleaning pad is positioned so as to remain in constant contact with the fuser roller. It collects any contaminants that seek to become part of the process and provides the already slippery fuser with a silicone film. This ensures that the paper with its now fused image will continue on as planned and not have a tendency to stick around (pardon the pun).

As I mentioned in Chapter 18, a critical part of the cartridge change is the replacement of this pad. It wears out, just like your printer runs out of toner, and needs to be replaced to maintain your printer's longevity and print quality. Without the silicone film, the hot fuser will be much more likely to receive permanent contamination. The replacement toner cartridge should come with a replacement cleaning pad; if it doesn't, check your printer manual to find out what to do.

The pressure roller is a rubber roller that is situated against the fuser roller in such a way that the paper is pressed between them as it passes through. The fuser roller is one of those strong personality types that leaves a lasting impression, so every few minutes the printer will rotate this assembly to keep the rubber roller from receiving a permanent indentation in the area where the rollers are being social. That's the odd noise that your laser printer sometimes makes for no obvious reason.

If you are unfortunate enough to get a paper jam prior to this point in the process, it will become immediately obvious that the image on the paper has not yet been fused. As you remove the affected sheet, liberal amounts of toner will remain on anything it gets in contact with.

As the paper proceeds along its path, it's very important that it not wobble off to the left or right, but instead cleave to the path of the straight and narrow. That is accomplished by the feed guide assembly.

As it passes between the fusing roller and the pressure roller, a combination of heat and pressure ensures that the deposited toner will not become random particles of plastic and iron at the slightest disturbance (see Figure 20.9).

Figure 20.9

Fusing roller and pressure roller

After the image is safely fused in place on the paper, the copy is ready for delivery utilizing the fuser roller and the exit delivery rollers. The exit area paper guides direct the paper to the facedown delivery tray at the top of the machine or the faceup delivery tray at the rear of the machine. Some printers have only one exit tray, usually the facedown one on top. Others allow you to choose by flipping a switch or lowering a tray.

When you're printing with heavy stock or fragile items, you can spare them the final turn by using the delivery tray at the back if your printer has one; just open the door and the paper comes out the back.

I've noticed that my envelopes don't wrinkle quite as badly if I let them exit at the back. This is because the exit delivery area at the top of the printer has the most acute angle that the paper encounters in the entire process. Unfortunately, the LaserJet 4 doesn't offer an option in paper delivery. It can be made to deliver out the back (check the printer's manual to find out how), but it can be tricky, particularly with older models. Take a look at Figure 20.10.

Exit delivery rollers

Fuser delivery rollers

Figure 20.10

Rear exit for paper on printers

During this whole process, the printer uses sensors located throughout it, which report to the CPU as soon as they see the paper. The printer knows how long it should take to get from one sensor to the next; if a sensor doesn't report "seeing" the paper within a particular window of time, then the printer's CPU assumes that the paper's jammed, and it stops the printing process and reports a jam.

Printer Disassembly Dependencies

Now that you've got some feeling for how laser printers operate, we'll move along to handling some common repairs. If you find yourself disassembling a laser printer, use the chart in Figure 20.11 to determine what you must disassemble before getting to a particular piece.

Figure 20.11

Laser printer
disassembly
dependencies

Common Symptoms and Solutions

Now that you know how a laser printer works, you can see what can go wrong. There are lots of *potential* problems with lasers, but I'll confine this to the most common problems only; then we'll take a look at the more rigorous testing you can do.

Vertical White Streaks on the Page

Since the paper is transported top-to-bottom through the laser printer, the paper also passes the coronas top-to-bottom. If a part of the corona were covered with toner, it couldn't transmit all of its charge, leaving either the drum (if it's the main corona) or the paper (if it's the transfer corona) with insufficient charge. That would lead to a vertical stripe with little or no charge, thereby leaving no toner—a white stripe. The answer: clean the coronas.

The main corona is, recall, in the toner cartridge, so if you are being barraged with support calls at the time and you need a quick fix, you can just change the cartridge. But some printers come with a little brush or other cleaning tool with which you can clean your corona. On an HP LaserJet, for example, open the printer and you won't be able to miss the green plastic brush. Note that one side of it is gray and has a suedelike feel. That's for cleaning the main corona. Now remove the cartridge. Note the slot atop the cartridge. You'll see that the suede end of the brush fits nicely into the slot. Just run it across the slot once and the corona's clean. Some cartridges don't allow you to clean the corona (notably the LaserJet 4 model and several non-HP models). Take a look at your manual for details.

The transfer corona is a permanent fixture in the laser, so it *must* be cleaned on *all* laser printers. Its exact position, again, varies depending on the make and model. On an HP LaserJet II, IID, III, or IIID, for example, open up the printer and, fairly close to the front of the printer, there's a metal trench that runs the width of the printer. It's protected with a webbing of monofilament threads. The monofilament keeps the paper from accidentally feeding into the trough and getting crunched up and snapping the delicate corona.

Shine a flashlight into the trench, and you'll see a hair-thin wire: that's the transfer corona. With the printer off, dip a Q-tip into some rubbing alcohol and carefully clean it end to end. (And, as my friend Brock Meeks says, "Once you clean the Corona, it's Miller Time.") Some printers don't let you get at the transfer corona (notably the HP LaserJet IIP and IIIP, among others), so check your printer manual if in doubt. And be careful with the wire! Don't break it, or your printer won't work and you're in for an expensive repair.

Smearing on the Page

Well, what keeps the toner from smearing? The fusing roller. It is covered with a Teflonlike coating to keep stuff from sticking to it, but it can become scratched or junk can just get baked onto it. In either case, the heat doesn't get transferred to the page. Try cleaning the roller with a soft cloth and some alcohol, but *let the thing cool down before you mess with it!*

Another cause of smears is trying to print double-sided on lasers that are designed to print single-sided. It seems tempting to create double-sided documents by running paper through the laser twice, but it's not a good idea. For one thing, there are rubber rollers that grip the paper so as to pull it through the printer. Ordinarily, they grip the underside of the paper and cause no trouble. But if you're printing on two sides, they end up gripping the underside of the paper—and the underside of the paper has printing on it. The rubber rollers smear the already printed side. This is less of an issue with newer laser printers than with some of the older models.

Horizontal Streaks on the Page

If you see a regular horizontal line on your output, it's more than likely caused by an irregularity in one of the many rollers that the paper must pass by on its journey from the paper cartridge to the output bin. The key to identifying *which* roller is in measuring the distance between the lines. If the horizontal lines are always spaced the same distance apart, then *that distance is the circumference of the bad roller.* Use the numbers shown in Figure 20.12 as a handy-dandy key: just measure the distance between the regular horizontal lines with a ruler and then read off the name of the bad roller. Whether or not you want to try to *replace* the problem child is up to you: getting to some of those rollers is a bit hairy. In my experience, however, the most common distance is 3.75 inches—the circumference of the photosensitive drum.

Figure 20.12

Diagram of printer problems

Cloudy, Faded Output

This sounds like an ad for a laundry detergent; it's what you see when the whites aren't white and the blacks aren't black. The probable cause is either low toner or a dirty or damaged corona wire.

Recall that image creation and transfer requires two corona wires. The coronas attract toner, which can eventually get caked all over the wire and render it less useful. So you need to clean coronas now and then. Refer back to "Vertical White Streaks on the Page" earlier in the chapter for instructions on how to clean them.

Black Line Down the Side of the Page

I don't know why this happens, but you'll see it when the toner is low or the toner cartridge is faulty. Replace the cartridge.

Memory Overflow Error

If you get an out of memory error, or memory overflow, or 20 MEM message (on the LaserJets), it means that you asked the printer to do something that it doesn't have enough memory to do. One common reason for this is that you bought a printer without enough memory for the jobs you do. (Remember, I said earlier that many laser printers come with only 512KB by default, which is not enough for a full-page graphic.)

The answer is generally to get more memory. But another possibility is that you've filled the printer's memory with *fonts*. They take up space in memory, too. I find that I can keep the printer from running out of memory under Windows 95/98/2000 by making these modifications to the printer's Properties in Windows:

▶ Print TrueType as graphics.

▶ Use raster graphics rather than HP-GL graphics.

Those are both settings you can control in Windows 95/98/2000 by right-clicking on a printer in your Printers folder and choosing Properties.

55 Error on Startup

Sometimes you'll get a 55 error when you turn a LaserJet printer on. It's pretty scary, particularly when you get out the shop manual and look it up.

There are two circuit boards—oops, PCAs—in lasers that are relevant to this problem. The DC controller board handles charging and discharging the coronas, and the interface board controls the parallel and serial interfaces. If you smoke your interface with a switchbox, just replace the interface PCA. (In case you've never heard, HP says you can damage your LaserJet Interface PCA with a parallel port switchbox. If they catch you at it, they void your warranty.)

Anyway, when powering up, the two boards do a communications test to ensure that they're talking all right. If there's noise in their communication, the 55 error pops up. The HP shop manual says that you must replace the cards if you see this error, but don't sweat it too much: this error can just crop up due to the normal inrush surge that you get when you turn the machine on. I had a LaserJet Series II printer that was giving me 55 errors about every other day on power up. I thought I'd have to do some surgery on the printer, but then I happened to move it to another outlet. Bingo! The error never returned. It seems that power noise of any kind on power up shows up as a 55 error.

Fonts Do Not Appear on Page

Once you become a desktop publishing maven, you dazzle others with your documents—documents replete with fonts galore. But one day you find that a *really* font-intensive page will not print. What's going on?

You've come up against a printer shortcoming, I'm afraid. Older HP lasers (the II and III) can print only 16 different fonts per page. Remember, the printer defines *font* as a combination of typeface, size, stroke weight, etc., so Courier regular 10-point is one font, Courier 10-point bold is another, Courier 12-point bold still another, and so on.

Actually, 16 fonts should not be a great hindrance. The strangest page in this book has no more than 10 fonts on it.

While we're on the subject, the LaserJet II can hold only 32 soft fonts in memory at any one time (that is, fonts other than the ones resident in the printer itself). That can be a real problem for a printer on a LAN, as it may have to serve *multiple* desktop publishing mavens. Can't you just hear it now? "I want four sizes of Helvetica, with italics and bold, and . . ." "But I *must* have Times Roman!" "*Times Roman*? You use *that* old woofer? You want to knock out my Palatino for Times Roman? Your name Gutenberg or something?" And the PostScript guys are just smiling in the corner . . . Luckily, almost all of the more modern laser printers can handle a lot more fonts, both per page and in memory generally, so you should seldom run into any walls.

Printer Picks Up Multiple Sheets

Believe it or not, this usually isn't the printer's fault. It's usually the paper. You need dry paper in order to get proper feed. Is the paper sitting in the tray for weeks at a time? Not good. When paper is removed from its ream wrapper, it's supposed to be dry. So how do you keep paper dry afterward? If it gets used in a day or two, there's no problem. But if it sits in the tray for longer, it could pick up some humidity. Here are two thoughts. First, keep the paper in a large Tupperware lasagna carrier. It'll keep it dry as long as you burp it when you put the paper in the Tupperware. Another approach—if the paper is already damp—is to dry it out with a microwave oven. And make sure you've got the correct side of the paper up when you put it in the printer. (Look at the package for the arrow.)

Paper Jams

Trying to print double-sided can cause this. The first time you run the paper through the printer, the paper gets a slight curl imparted to it. Turn it upside down and run it through the printer again and that slight curl can sometimes translate to a paper jam. Another cause of paper jams is printing on the wrong side of the paper. There are, believe it or not, two different sides to a sheet of paper, called the *wax* and the *wire*. Paper will have a "print this side up" indication on the wrapper: pay attention to it. Paper can acquire a curl in humid environments, but the wrapper keeps the paper dry, so don't take paper out of the ream until you're ready to use it. Using cheap paper can also lead to paper jams. Also, old laser printers may have rollers that get out of round, leading to jams.

Basic Testing

If you've got a serious laser problem, you may still be able to avoid taking the thing apart to fix it. Here are some tests to try before doing the heavy-duty screwdriver work.

Printer Power

Relative to your other office devices, laser printers are power hogs. Over seven amps of constant current draw put this device in the same league as an entire well-equipped *kitchen*. Since the printer uses this much energy, it's critical that everything related to the electrical system be in top condition.

We've discussed outlet wiring before, back in Chapter 9, "Power Supplies and Protection." With lasers, however, it's doubly important because of all the power that they suck up. Ideally, you (as the technician) will have an electrical wiring diagram for each building you support, even if it's just your home. Then, when someone starts to plug a Mr. Coffee into an outlet on the same circuit as one of the workstations, you can offer appropriate and eloquent opposing arguments (all mainly consisting of "don't plug other things next to the laser unless you want to buy its replacement"), complete with documentation if necessary. You need to remember that it's a good idea to keep lasers on circuits of their own.

Resetting the Printer

Like the PC, the laser printer can become confused—it is a very complex piece of equipment performing very complex operations. Things go wrong. On occasion, you may find it necessary to reset the printer.

As with the PC, there are different levels of reset for a laser printer. The most severe reset of all for a PC is the power-down, or cold reboot. Cold reboots aren't usually the best way to handle PC problems because you might be using an application that must be shut down a certain way in order to start up again without problems. (Windows 95/98/2000 is like that.) Printers don't have the same problem. As a matter of fact, the power-down reset for the printer only clears the print buffer; it doesn't clear any downloaded fonts or other system data. This can be a useful feature but, although it can temporarily get you past a difficulty, it won't always solve everything, and you'll still have to address the cause of the initial problem.

> **Tip**
>
> If you reset the printer while your computer is still spooling data to it, when the printer comes back online the data may continue flowing to it. And since the first part of the job is now gone, you're likely to get garbage characters instead of your print job. Cancel the job from your print queue first, and then reset the printer.

You can also reset a laser printer using the buttons on its front panel. (Check the documentation to find out how.) If you do this, however, you'll lose any fonts or macros that you've downloaded to the printer.

On some color lasers, if the printer does not calibrate itself correctly at startup, the printer may work but the colors will appear too dark. If you see this, turning the printer off and then back on again gives it another try at the color calibration routine.

The Cable and Ports

Next, take a look at the cable and the I/O ports.

Secure Connection

If your printer and computer don't seem to be communicating, check the printer's power cable and the data cable to make sure that they're both snugly seated. Pay special attention to the connections at both ends of the data cable: if the little screws on the cable hood aren't screwed in all the way and securing the cable, it's very easy to dislodge the cable, even by doing something as minor as stretching your legs under your desk and knocking the data cable aside.

Cable Length

So long as it can reach from your computer to the printer, it's not possible for a data cable to be too short. It can easily be too long, however. HP recommends that a parallel cable be no longer than 15 feet. As with many manufacturer standards, I have found that to be quite conservative. I've seen printers work fine with parallel data cables well beyond twice that length.

A serial cable can be much longer than a parallel cable because the signal voltages are higher. Although slower, serial communication is more rugged and flexible than parallel.

What We Have Here Is a Failure to Communicate

If the printer is printing but isn't printing what you sent it, try swapping the data cable for another one. Cables can have flaws that show up only after you've handled the cable a little. If a data pin in a parallel cable breaks, the results could be something like the "Iekko/Hello" example from Chapter 18. If the cable is fine, check to make sure you are using the right driver for the printer.

Parallel Cable Type

In Chapter 18, you learned about the various modes for a parallel port—ECP, EPP, and so on. Not all parallel printer cables support these modes, so select one carefully. The original parallel printer cables were not bidirectional, so they did not include the needed circuitry to manage port modes in which information flows not only to the printer, but also from it.

Generally speaking, any new parallel printer cable that you buy today will work with an ECP or EPP port. Beware, however, of old cables fished out of someone's stash of extras.

You don't have to worry about this for serial cables, by the way, because they are by their very nature bidirectional. However, serial ports do not support ECP or EPP printing modes.

Environmental Considerations

You may not see these concerns on Greenpeace bumper stickers, but it's important that you consider them when setting up and using your printer.

Heat

A laser printer can pump out some serious heat. This is one reason that it is important that it be placed in a well-ventilated area. Because of this, systems furniture, or any furniture that attempts to fit every part of your workstation into a neat little cubbyhole, can be bad news. It's sometimes built without regard for the fact that the equipment needs to breathe properly. While arranging a workstation, see to it that all your devices have air circulating around them so that heat can dissipate. If you use your printer when it's in an unventilated area, its heat-sensitive components are likely to cook and fail prematurely.

Light

Always guard the toner cartridge from direct contact with strong light, as white light will shorten the useful life of the photosensitive drum. (The light that is used to bathe the drum for print preparation is red filtered, as in a darkroom.) Don't slide the toner cartridge's door open to see the photosensitive drum, unless, of course, you're planning to recycle the cartridge right away.

Ammonia

Ammonia can be detrimental to the laser printer's ability to neutralize ozone (discussed below) and can also permanently damage the toner cartridge. The chief sources of ammonia in an office setting are the chemicals used for cleaning and those required in the blueprinting process. If you work in an office where blueprinting is done, keep a watchful eye on the fume hood fan and general ventilation in the area of the machine itself.

Ozone

In recent years, we've heard a lot about ozone and the ozone layer. Ozone is a pale blue gas naturally produced whenever a lightning bolt occurs. It's in the upper atmosphere as a by-product of the reaction of oxygen to solar ultraviolet rays. Ozone production doesn't require anything so dramatic as a lightning bolt, however. It's also a natural by-product of the ionization that takes place during the laser printing process.

Ozone is great stuff in the outer areas of the earth's atmosphere but is not good for humans and can be anything from a minor irritant to downright dangerous in significant concentrations. If it is present in concentrations greater than one part in 20,000, it is irritating to the mucous membranes and is poisonous. You can't generally see it, but its odor is most often described as pungent. Most people can detect the presence of ozone at a concentration as low as one part of ozone per 10 million parts of air.

Not only can ozone be harmful to humans, but, as a super-effective oxidizer, it can also cause deterioration of components in the machine itself. Therefore, ozone buildup is one more reason to make sure that your printer is properly ventilated. You're more likely to have problems with ozone if:

- There are several active laser printers and/or copiers in a small, confined area.

- The relative humidity is very low.

- There is improper or nonexistent ventilation.

- The ozone filter is in need of replacement.

- Any combination of the above conditions exist.

You should replace the ozone filter in the laser printer after about every 50,000 prints, if your printer has one that's replaceable (check the manual). If office ventilation leaves something to be desired, or if you've got a lot of laser printers in a small, enclosed area, I recommend that you replace the filters more frequently. Mind you, all of this only applies to printers that actually use a corona in the printing process; the LaserJet 4si, for example, would be exempt from this process.

Paper and Media Issues

Just think of this as an up-to-date version of "garbage in, garbage out."

Paper Type

Every kind of laser printer has its own paper type and quality requirements. If you follow those requirements, you'll be less likely to run into paper jams and distortion problems. In general, the better the quality of the printer, the better the quality of paper it will require. At the very least, higher quality paper may give you higher quality printouts. High humidity can also affect the performance of paper in a laser printer (not to mention the fact that it can cause the printer to seal your envelopes).

The Paper Feed

You'll need to inspect the feed assemblies periodically. Over time, the feed rollers become glazed and thus less efficient at picking up one sheet of paper at a time from the paper tray. Replacing the rollers is not a major production, but many people that I have talked to find immediate (but temporary—isn't that always the way?) gratification by abrading the feed rollers somehow. You might try rubbing pencil erasers or *very fine* sandpaper over the rollers.

The separation pad (it's just beneath the feed rollers) plays a major role in letting the feed roller pick up only one sheet at a time. Over time, however, it wears thin. It's a good idea to replace the feed rollers and the separation pad about every 100,000 prints. You can buy them in a kit of other like items for those heavy-duty printer maintenance sessions.

Contaminants

Laser printers are powerful, yet delicate, machines. Foreign objects in the printer can really affect its performance for the worse. Therefore, you must be very careful about what you feed your laser printer: no foreign objects, only the paper recommended by the manufacturer, and no labels or other printables not intended for laser printers.

One of the nastiest things I ever heard of anyone feeding the laser printer was a piece of paper that had a staple in place. This is almost certain to do damage to the fuser assembly. If the Teflon of the roller has scratches in it, your prints will have vertical white lines on them. There's nothing to be done about this; you have to replace the fuser assembly.

Another common contaminant is any printable not intended for a laser printer. If labels aren't specifically manufactured to be used in a laser printer, don't use them—this is one thing you really can't fudge on even if you've got extra plain labels. Also, letterhead that has raised ink may not fare well when run through the printer.

On a final note, there may be partial sheets of paper buried in the rest of the ream. They won't gum up your printer, but they could cause it to jam. Also, don't use textured paper since the toner does not stick to it.

Never Jam Today

There are several paper jam sensors in most laser printers. Some of them are timing sensors, which make it highly unlikely that a jam could occur anywhere in the process without the printer alerting you. One major cause of jams is improper media; stock that is thicker or thinner than the printer is prepared to handle can cause a fair amount of difficulty.

If a jam occurs before the paper reaches the fusing assembly, there are two things that you'll need to note:

▶ Any toner that has not gone through the fusing assembly will end up all over everything when the jam is fixed. The stuff is hard to get out of clothing or carpeting, so be careful when handling paper with loose toner on its surface.

▶ Carefully remove any paper jam in the area of the transfer corona, so as not to damage the wire or its attendant monofilament.

Paper Curl and Wrinkling

The major cause of curling is the effect that the fusion heat has on the paper composition—the amount of curl is generally directly proportional to the ash content of the paper. If you follow the manufacturer's recommendation for paper type, you're less likely to have problems with curling than otherwise.

Wrinkling will usually be the result of stiff paper negotiating the tight turn at the top of the printer near the facedown tray. It is most evident with heavy stock or envelopes. If the printer is equipped for it, you can avoid the problem by allowing heavy paper to feed from the faceup tray or output faceup to the rear of the printer instead of facedown at the top.

Advanced Testing

What you've already read are the easiest to fix and most common problems. Sometimes, however, the problem requires more work than a change in paper or a tap of the Reset button.

Voltage Tests

If, when you turn it on, the printer doesn't respond normally, the printer's power system is probably malfunctioning. To find out for sure, you'll need a voltage meter. A basic multimeter is a must for the printer technician, but a good digital unit is quite a bit more accurate; you should be able to obtain one for about $30. Using a digital multimeter makes it possible to check for high and low AC and DC voltages, resistances, and continuity.

Location of DC Voltage Test Points

The DC power supply provides three different DC voltages to the system's components. All three can be checked at an interface labeled J210; it is a 20-pin female interface with pin 1 located at the lower-left corner and the odd numbers along the bottom row, left to right.

Using the multimeter, check the indicated pins (every other pin along the bottom, left to right, starting at 1) for the following voltages (frame ground is the reference):

▶ pin 1 = +5v

▶ pin 5 = –5v

▶ pin 9 = +24v

▶ If *none* of the voltages are present, check the fuse on the DC power supply.

▶ The AC power.

If *one or more* of the voltages is missing, you'll need to do at least one of the following:

▶ Remove all optional devices, including memory.

▶ Replace the DC power supply assembly.

▶ Replace the DC controller PCA.

Testing the Host's Interface

When it comes to testing the host's I/O ports, a breakout box is a handy thing to have around. A breakout box is a diagnostic tool that will indicate with LEDs what the activity on the tested port happens to be. You can also use a breakout box to design a cable if you happen to be working with something that is nonstandard.

Charting Printing Problems

You can sometimes tell which printer component is causing problems from where the problem appears on the page. Figure 20.12, shown earlier in this chapter, can help you track down errant components.

Diagnostic Software

If you're having output problems and want to see exactly what is going from the computer to the printer, you can capture printer output in a file by means of a utility program. Your printer may have come with its own diagnostic software, or you may be able to download a testing utility from the printer manufacturer's Web site.

Testing the Engine

There are many things that could be wrong if you send a print job to the printer and nothing happens; one of the worst is a problem with the laser engine. To determine whether the laser engine is functioning properly, you need to bypass the interface controller where data is received and force the printer to do a direct print from the engine itself.

On newer Hewlett-Packard printers, like the LaserJet 4 or higher, the engine can be tested by using the Self-Test menu on the printer (not the Print Test Page command from Windows).

But if you still have one of those older models hanging around, then on the side of the printer that is opposite the memory upgrade socket there is a hole (it's exposed on the LaserJet II but has a plastic cover on the LaserJet III). Push a ballpoint pen or the like into the hole. This will force a print direct from the laser engine circuitry. Try it now, while the printer's working, so you can compare it to tests you run when the printer is malfunctioning. Your good control test indicates:

▶ The laser engine and engine circuitry are functioning correctly.

▶ Laser alignment is correct (shown by side margins).

▶ Feed timing is correct (shown by top and bottom margins).

▶ There is sufficient toner.

▶ None of the major components is significantly damaged or contaminated in any way (there are no smudges or repeating anomalies).

Setting a Baseline

It's hard to get any information from a test print if you don't know what a good print looks like. Now, while the printer still works, you should print a test page using the Self-Test menu on the printer itself. Some older models may not have menus to work with; in that case, you should consult your manual to find the exact instructions since they vary from printer to printer. Keep this test print somewhere, and you can compare it with your test prints later to see how the new print compares with the baseline test print. A test print shows various gray scales, text, horizontals, and verticals. The tightest horizontals and verticals will appear to the average viewer as single heavy lines but, if you look at them closely, you'll see multiple lines in those areas.

Understanding Error Messages and Fixing Printer Problems

One sure way to know that you've got a problem is for your laser printer to *tell* you that you've got one. In Table 20.1, I explain what each printer error message is on most HP LaserJets, what causes it, and what you should do to try to fix the problem that it describes. When the situation or the response required is not obvious (and sometimes even when it is), I have indicated the path to a (hopefully) happy ending. If your printer's manual has a similar table, consult it instead, as its codes will be specific to your printer.

TABLE 20.1 Printer Error Messages

Message	Meaning	Solution (Where Applicable)
00 READY	The printer is ready.	
02 WARMING UP		Wait a few moments for the printer to signal "ready."
04 SELF TEST	Continuous self-test printing.	

TABLE 20.1 Printer Error Messages (continued)

Message	Meaning	Solution (Where Applicable)
05 SELF TEST	Self-test in progress (on some printers, this will result in a print).	
06 PRINTING TEST	Self-test printing.	
06 FONT PRINTOUT	Printing sample characters from all installed fonts. Or printing PS configuration pages.	
07 RESET	Returns all printer settings to the default and clears buffered pages, temporary soft fonts, and macros.	
08 COLD RESET	Returns both the Configuration and Print menu selections to the factory settings.	
09 MENU RESET	Returns all Print menu items to factory settings, clearing buffered pages, temporary fonts, and all macros.	
10 RESET TO SAVE (HP LaserJet only)		Press and hold Reset to confirm the acceptance of Print menu selections (you'll lose any temporary fonts, macros, or buffered data), or press Continue or On Line (no changes to selections will be made).
11 PAPER OUT (HP LaserJet only)		Add paper to the input tray.
12 PRINTER OPEN		Close the top cover assembly.
13 PAPER JAM	Sample jam codes (vary among printers):13.1—internal jam, 13.2—input jam,13.3—duplex jam, 13.4—output jam	Open the printer, clear the jam, and press Continue or On Line to reprint the page.
14 NO EP CART		Install the toner cartridge.
15 ENGINE TEST	Engine test with printout preceded by pressing the Test Print button.	

TABLE 20.1 Printer Error Messages (continued)

Message	Meaning	Solution (Where Applicable)
16 TONER LOW		Replace cartridge (rotating the existing cartridge briskly can result in more prints even if the message remains).
17 MEMORY CONFIG (HP LaserJet III only)	Indicates memory configuration in progress (happens when Page Protection is set to On).	
18 SKIP SELF TEST (HP LaserJet III only)	Skips the ROM and RAM tests on startup and is activated by holding down the minus key. Don't do this routinely.	
18 MIO NOT READY (LaserJet 4M or 4Plus)	The Modular I/O (network card) is not ready.	Power down the printer and make certain the card is seated properly in the socket. A new card may be needed if this persists.
20 ERROR	Indicates that memory capacity has been exceeded by the volume of data received.	
21 ERROR	Indicates that the memory received is too complex for the printer to process.	
21 PRINT OVERRUN		Enable page protection or reduce the complexity of the job (more printer memory may be required).
22 ERROR	Communication handshake was unsuccessful.	Rate of transmission or configuration may need changing.
22 I/O CONFIG ERR	Wrong handshake protocol (XON/XOFF, DC1/DC3, and DTR handshake protocols are supported).	
40 ERROR	An error occurred during data transmission (an error occurs if you power down the computer while the printer is online or an attempted transfer uses unmatched rates).	Turn the printer off and cancel the print job in Windows. Wait a few seconds and turn it back on again. Then resubmit the print job.
41 ERROR	A temporary page-creating error occurred.	Press the Continue key to repeat the page.

TABLE 20.1 Printer Error Messages (continued)

Message	Meaning	Solution (Where Applicable)
42 ERROR	Communications problem has occurred between the Interface/Formatter PCA and an optional interface device.	Reseat the optional I/O device and press Continue to resume printing.
43 ERROR	A communications problem has occurred between the Interface/Formatter PCA and an optional interface device.	Power off the printer and check your optional devices. Power on and try again. If the problem persists, contact the manufacturer for troubleshooting help.
49 REMOVE PAGE	Paper was in the manual feed guides when the printer was turned on.	
50 SERVICE		Power off the printer for at least 10 minutes. If the problem persists, you may have to repair or replace the fuser assembly.
51 ERROR	Indicates loss of laser beam for more than two seconds.	
52 ERROR	Scanner motor unable to maintain appropriate speed.	
53-x ERRORUNIT	Error detected on optional memory card.	Verify that the correct revision level (B or greater) is installed.
54 ERROR	Problem with the duplex unit shift plate.	
55 ERROR	Communications problem between the DC Controller PCA and the Interface/Formatter PCA.	Do a test print to verify functional DC controller. If the problem persists: check DC voltages at J210, replace the Interface/Formatter PCA, and replace the DC Controller PCA.
61 SERVICE	A checksum error in the Interface/Formatter PCA's ROM was detected during self-test.	
62 SERVICE	Checksum error occurred in the Interface/Formatter PCA's internal font ROM.	
63 SERVICE	Error was detected in either the Interface/Formatter PCA's dynamic RAM or in optional memory.	Remove any optional memory and retest.

TABLE 20.1 Printer Error Messages (continued)

Message	Meaning	Solution (Where Applicable)
64 SERVICE	Indicates a laser scan buffer error.	Turn the computer off and back on.
65 SERVICE	An error occurred on the dynamic RAM controller.	Turn the computer off and back on. If that doesn't work, replace the Interface/Formatter PCA.
67 SERVICE	A miscellaneous hardware or address error has taken place on the Interface/Formatter PCA.	Reseat all cables, font cartridges, and optional devices. If that doesn't work, replace the Interface/Formatter PCA.
68 ERROR	A recoverable error has occurred in NVRAM (nonvolatile RAM).	Press Continue to clear, then verify the Control Panel menu settings; one or more items will have reverted to their factory defaults.
68 SERVICE	NVRAM failure has occurred.	Replace the Interface/Formatter PCA. You can temporarily operate the printer without VRAM, but all Control Panel volumes revert to their factory defaults and the 00 READY message becomes 68 READY/SERVICE.
69 SERVICE	Time-out error has occurred between the Interface/Formatter PCA and an optional I/O device.	Remove the optional device and retest. If the message persists, replace the Interface/Formatter PCA.
70 or 71 ERROR	Improper cartridge application.	Turn the printer off and back on. If the error persists, verify with the cartridge vendor that the cartridge was designed for that printer.
72 SERVICE	Font cartridge removal error. May also result from a malfunctioning font cartridge or poor connection.	Turn the printer off, wait a few seconds, and turn it back on again.
79 SERVICE	Miscellaneous problem.	Turn printer off and back on. If the problem persists, remove the memory modules and any installed font, macro, and personality cartridges one at a time. If the problem still occurs, and the printer has an optional I/O device installed, try a different interface (parallel or serial) if possible. If the problem continues, replace the

TABLE 20.1 Printer Error Messages (continued)

Message	Meaning	Solution (Where Applicable)
		Formatter PCA. If the problem is intermittent, temporarily remove any non-HP hardware/firmware and test the printer. If it keeps failing, replace the Formatter PCA.
CONFIG LANGUAGE	This message is the result of holding down the Enter key while powering on the printer.	Following the self-test, select a display language with the +, –, and Enter keys.
EC LOAD (envelope size)	You've requested an envelope size not currently installed in the printer, or the tray is out of envelopes.	Load the correct envelope in the envelope tray. Insert a loaded tray and select the loaded envelope size from the Control Panel or press Continue to override. Envelope size may be COM10, MONARC, C5, or DL.
PC LOAD (paper size)	You've requested a paper size not currently installed.	Same as above, only for paper. Paper size may be EXEC, LETTER, or LEGAL.
PE FEED or MF FEED	You've made a request to manually feed paper or envelopes of the indicated size.	
PE TRAY = (envelope size)	The printer wants to know the size of the paper or envelopes you're using.	Use the + and – keys to select a size and then press Enter. Press On Line or Continue to proceed.
FC (LEFT/RIGHT/BOTH)	You removed font cartridge(s) while the printer was offline and contained buffered data.	Reinsert cartridge(s) and press the Continue or On Line key.
NO FONT	The printer could not read the font cartridge(s).	Reinsert the cartridge(s) and try again.
FE CARTRIDGE	You removed a cartridge while the printer was online.	Turn the printer off, reinsert the cartridge, and turn the printer back on.
USER MAINTENANCE (LaserJet 4si only)	Has printed 200,000 pages.	
MENUS LOCKED	Administrator has a security lock on the Control Panel.	See your network administrator.

Other Things to Consider

If you're still looking for the source of a problem, one of these remedies may help.

The Toner Cartridge

If you install and maintain the toner cartridge properly, you shouldn't have problems with it. In these days of greenery, many people wonder whether they should use recharged cartridges. You're a lot safer using retreads than you used to be: the folks recycling them are either doing a better job or are using better components (or both); the recent efforts are far superior to many of the early ones. Still, keep an eye out for unscrupulous recyclers. A properly redone cartridge includes a new photosensitive drum. Beware of what are called "drill and fill operations," which drill a hole in the cartridge and refill it with toner but don't replace any of the parts inside.

Color laser printers require four separate toner cartridges, and the method for replacing them depends on the printer make and model. The printer should let you know when one of the cartridges needs replacing, but if you start seeing a particular color dropping out, check its toner level and replace as needed. Some color laser printers offer a color-by-color self-test, much like inkjet printers do, so you can gauge the quality of each individual cartridge's output.

Even first-time cartridges can cause print anomalies. If the cartridge is running out of toner, you might see vertical white streaks on your prints. Rocking the cartridge gently around its long axis usually lets you get about a hundred more prints out of the cartridge (depending on the amount of white space and toner density adjustment).

When new, toner cartridges sometimes make noises. Don't worry too much about them—incidental printing noises are quite common and are not usually a matter of concern. Just watch for any print anomalies that might be related to the sounds you hear.

Image Problems

There are several components that could cause image problems.

Mirror

In many laser printers, there's a mirror in the lid assembly. If it gets dirty, your prints may have fuzzy edges. Tobacco smoke is the most common culprit, so use a good glass cleaner and lens-cleaning material to get it back in shape, and chase smokers away from the printing area.

Vertical Lines

We talked earlier about what scratches on the feed rollers do to your print jobs: they will almost always leave vertical lines on the print. Scratches don't just appear—they're generally the result of someone running things through the printer that don't belong there (staples or labels or transparencies not meant for laser printing). Since even running paper through the laser printer twice generally isn't a good idea, there's no reason why staples should be anywhere near the printer paper in the first place.

Distorted Images

If your printed images look stretched, the printer's feed components are probably slipping, or its gears are not functioning properly. The gears may not be gripping on the shaft, as they should be. To restore the printer's feed capability, get new feed rollers, separator pads, and assorted bushings in a kit, and replace the worn-out components.

Squeaking or Groaning Sounds

Laser printers can make some pretty bizarre sounds. Some of these sounds indicate developing problems, and should, therefore, receive appropriate attention, but a perfectly healthy and properly functioning printer can also make noises that sound as though the printer is malfunctioning. The most noticeable noises are generally part of the paper feed process.

A noise that I have been asked about more than any other is the one that comes every few minutes from an idle (but powered on) laser printer. This noise sounds like the printer's electric motor beginning, as though it's about to print, and then stopping abruptly. There's a good reason for that description: that's exactly what the sound is. Since the fuser assembly remains hot even when idle, the printer needs to rotate it every so often. Otherwise, the hot metallic fuser roller would burn a permanent depression into the rubber pressure roller with which it is in constant contact.

Maintenance Issues

Here are a few things you should check to keep your laser printer in good working order.

Errant Toner

When, in the course of printer events, you are called upon to clean up toner, the method will depend on the amount and location. You can clean up minute amounts on the inside of the printer along the paper's path with a slightly dampened cloth or a swab dipped in alcohol. If there are larger amounts of toner, more drastic measures are called for.

Warning

Never, ever, ship a printer with a toner cartridge still inside.

If a cartridge is dropped or jostled improperly during shipment, it is possible that there will be larger quantities of toner to deal with.

Warning

Don't get out the Electrolux! Toner is a plastic resin bonded to iron particles, a deadly combination to hot electric motors (like those in vacuum cleaners). If you try to vacuum up the runaway toner, it will blow straight through a normal vacuum cleaner bag and into the motor, where the plastic will melt and the iron will play havoc with the armature and brushes. The particles that don't stop in the motor will fly through the air and cover the vicinity (and you) with tiny black particles that are very difficult to wash out of clothing.

If you get toner on your clothing or skin, remember its properties; use only cold water and plenty of soap. You're likely to get toner on you if you have to clear a paper jam that happened before the paper got to the fusing assembly, so be careful. If you have a large toner spill in the printer, take it outside and use a compressed air canister to clean out the printer.

Cleaning

Like getting exercise and balancing your checkbook, printer cleaning rarely gets done as often as the manuals recommend. Each of the printer's components needs to be cleaned regularly, however.

The Clean Command

Many printers, including most of the HP LaserJets, have a self-cleaning routine that you can run. One of the kindest things you can do for your printer is to run the self-cleaning routine every time you change the toner cartridge. If your printer doesn't have a clean utility, you might be able to download one from the manufacturer's Web site.

The clean command will usually print a large black box on a piece of copier grade paper. This sheet of paper is then placed facedown and sent through the process again. This is the only time you should refeed a piece of paper without the luxury of a duplex unit! Sending this sheet through again will reheat the toner that was placed on the paper the first time, causing it to become slightly adhesive. Any miscreant toner particles or small pieces of paper stuck to the innards of the printer will now be pulled out. The way to tell if the clean command has performed up to par is to check the black box that was printed on the first pass—if it is covered with shiny black specs, then you know it worked. You may need to do this more than once just to be sure you get all of the little varmints attached to your rollers.

Corona Wires

There are two corona wires in most printers. (Check your manual to find the exact locations.) You should clean both of them regularly or whenever there is a problem with the printer that might be caused by excess toner on the wire. Clean the primary corona in the toner cartridge once at the midpoint of the life of the cartridge—you've got no excuse to avoid doing so, as HP and many other printer manufacturers thoughtfully provide a plastic brush for the job. Insert the suede end of the brush into the slot in the cartridge and slide it from one end to the other.

The transfer corona is in the bottom of the printer beneath the paper path. On most printers, several monofilament lines protect it from damage in the event of a paper jam. Clean it with a cotton-tipped swab (which may come with your replacement cartridge), gently stroking it in each direction and on each side between the monofilament segments. I recommend that you do this in good light, so you can see how much pressure you are putting on the corona, as, if you break it, the entire corona assembly must be replaced.

Usually the products of your labor will be pretty innocuous: perhaps some toner or a little dust. The winner in the most-disgusting-corona-problem category, however, is the time one technician reportedly found several well-done roaches in the transfer corona channel. The only reason the users discovered the cockroaches was because the insects' bodies were making the pages turn black.

Some printers, such as the LaserJet 4, don't use a corona that you must clean; they use charging rollers. That's why it's important to check your printer's manual to find out exactly what parts you are expected to clean and how to access them.

Registration and Feed Guide Assemblies

Here, maintenance is pretty easy: you need only occasionally wipe with a damp cloth to clean up that errant toner (unless, of course, some foreign object happens to stop in this area). You'll need to clear paper fragments away periodically, as it's here that paper fragments or partial pages will usually stop.

Fusing Assembly

I really can't overemphasize the importance of keeping the fuser roller free of contaminants. Because of the high temperatures at which it operates, this critical part of the printing process will have a tendency to hang on to a little bit of everything that touches it: paper curls up and stays with it, letterhead ink melts on it, etc. To keep this from happening, the roller itself is coated with Teflon and the brush that rides on top of it (on HPs, it's underneath the fuzzy green lid) is permeated with silicone.

I've seen people leave the cotton tip on the silicone pad that cleans the fuser. This is not a good idea, as this causes the pad to fit its slot too tightly instead of floating easily on the roller.

Separation Pawls

Push back the lid behind the fuser assembly, and you'll see a set of four clawlike things called *pawls*. The pawls facilitate the separation of the paper from the fuser. Over time, however, they get a gradual buildup of contaminants that could eventually begin to scrape the Teflon from the fuser roller. If they scrape off the Teflon, the effect is the same as that of a staple fed to the printer: broad vertical lines will begin to appear on the print.

You can't repair scratches on the fuser roller; you'll need to replace the entire fuser assembly. To avoid making a habit of this, regularly use an alcohol-dipped swab to clean each of the pawls thoroughly.

Improving Print Quality

There are some amazing differences between the printers that are available today and the ones we started with many years ago. Many of the best models today print at 1200×1200 dpi and use ultra-fine toner to produce some impressive printing. No matter which printer you use, however, there are things that you can do to improve the quality of its output.

Paper Quality and Feed Continuity

The type of paper and the quality of the toner can differ along a surprisingly wide range. A close inspection will reveal the difference. And, as you read earlier in this chapter, the wrong type of paper can cause paper jams.

Keep the paper-feed mechanisms in top condition to avoid paper slippage and, with it, image problems. The key items are the feed rollers and the separation pad, located just inside the printer and near the paper tray receptor.

Image Formation

The image formation components are the laser engine, beam mirror, toner, developer roller, primary and transfer coronas, and photosensitive drum. With all these items involved, you might worry that the imaging components of the printer will be a troubleshooting nightmare. It's not that bad, though: if you keep the cartridge changed and the coronas cleaned, that's usually all you'll need to do to keep the print sharp.

A few last tips: as I've mentioned before, it's best to use a fresh ream of paper, not one that's been sitting in your laser printer's cartridge for the last two weeks soaking up moisture and developing a curl. Distribute the toner in the cartridge. Take the cartridge out of the printer and rotate it 15 times. Then shake it side to side 15 times. You can also help the laser's toner transfer process by "clearing its throat" and printing three to five *totally black pages*. You can do that with a little LaserJet program. Here's the command sequence; keep it handy:

```
esc&10Eesc&10Lesc*p0x0Yesc*c2400a3300B
esc*c0PescE
```

That'll print a black page. The "esc" stands for the ASCII escape code, ASCII 27.

Laser Printer Rumors and Truth

I'd like to end this chapter with these rumors. I know they sound goofy, but I hear people ask this stuff in class, so here are the top laser rumors, and, where I can supply it, the Truth.

Toner Is Made of Powdered Chicken Bones

When I heard this one, I thought I'd make a million bucks organizing a chicken bone recycling center. No go, though. (I *did* mention it to some execs at a well-known fried chicken chain, however, so if you end up seeing separate trash cans for the bones, you know whose fault it is.)

Elvis Is in the Printer

Rumor has it that, on HP LaserJets, if you press a certain set of keys on the laser panel, a full-page graphic of Elvis prints out, with the caption "The King Lives." So goes the tale.

HP swears it ain't so, and I believe them. Here's why: there isn't enough ROM on the laser circuit boards to store a bitmap of Elvis, even *before* he gained weight. I swear I heard this from someone in class, and others had heard of the rumor also. My guess is that HP brought it on themselves with the Secret Service Test Mode. (Why not tell everybody about it, anyway?)

Cartridges Are Designed to Self-Destruct

The rumor: there are pieces of glass in the toner of Canon-type cartridges that slowly chew up the print drum so it is completely unusable by about 8,000 copies. This supposedly is done to discourage rechargers.

I just don't know. HP denies it, but Canon's patent application for the toner includes "silica particles"—conceivably another name for pieces of glass. That's for the next book, I suppose.

The official HP spec sheet on toner says that toner is composed of the items listed in Table 20.2.

TABLE 20.2 LaserJet Toner Ingredients

Component	Percentage by Weight
Styrene acrylate copolymer	55–65
Iron oxide	30–40
Salicylic acid chromium chelate	1–3

Now, salicylic acid is *aspirin*. Maybe *that's* why it's no headache at all to set up a laser printer . . .

Troubleshooting Recap

Here's a quick review of the troubleshooting tips covered in this chapters:

▶ Vertical white streaks on the page can indicate a dirty transfer corona. Clean it with a cotton swab.

▶ Vertical black streaks indicate scratches on the feed rollers, perhaps caused by running staples or other hard foreign objects through the printer by mistake.

▶ Smeared ink could mean a scratched or dirty fusing roller. Clean it with a soft cloth and some alcohol (after it has cooled down). Ink sometimes also smears when you run double-sided pages on printers not designed for it.

▶ A distorted or stretched image probably means the printer's feed components are slipping or the gears are not functioning correctly. To restore the printer's feed capability, get new feed rollers, separator pads, and assorted bushings in a kit, and replace the worn-out components.

▶ Horizontal lines are usually caused by an irregularity in one of the many rollers that the paper passes through. To identify which roller, measure the distance between the lines. Figure 20.12 shows a chart to help.

▶ Cloudy or faded output usually means it's time to change the toner cartridge, or you've got a dirty or damaged corona wire.

▶ A black line down the side of the page can indicate the toner is low or the toner cartridge is faulty.

▶ Error codes that appear on the printer's LED panel can be looked up in the printer's manual or on the manufacturer's Web site. Table 20.1 lists the codes for Hewlett-Packard LaserJets.

▶ A printer that picks up multiple sheets is usually fine—it's the paper that's your problem. Make sure it is dry and well fanned. Dry it in a microwave if needed.

▶ Paper jams can result from trying to print double-sided or from curled or cheap paper.

▶ Many printer problems can result from using the wrong printer driver in Windows or other software you're using. Make sure you have the correct driver. Most printers come with a driver disk.

▶ If a printer that usually works fine gets an error or starts printing out garbage pages, try turning it off and then back on again after a few seconds.

▶ If you want the printer and computer to communicate using an ECP or EPP parallel port, make sure you have the parallel port defined in the computer's BIOS as ECP or EPP, and make sure you have an ECP- or EPP-capable cable.

▶ Avoid stacking anything that blocks the airflow around a laser printer. And avoid placing it in a low-ventilation cubbyhole in a computer desk.

▶ Keep toner cartridges away from strong light, as it's bad for the photosensitive drum.

▶ If your output is wrinkling, check the paper quality. You may be able to set the printer to eject the printed pages from the back, faceup, reducing the amount of turns the paper has to make to get to the exit, and perhaps reducing the wrinkling.

In the next chapter, we'll look at communications devices and how you can make your computer talk to other computers.

Communications Devices

21

INTRODUCTION

When computers first appeared on the scene many years ago, each was an island. But it didn't take us long to figure out how to connect to each other's machines, and soon the first computer bulletin board was born. Modems were the essential devices for getting digital data over phone lines, and low-priced modems made computer bulletin boards the craze of the mid-'80s. Today, we are starting to see the real emergence of broadband. (I'll cover *broadband*, the term used these days to collectively refer to high-speed Internet access through cable, DSL, or other forms of access, later in this chapter.)

Even into the year 2000 we're still using modems, but now they're not just for bulletin boards. Many people use modems on their systems so that they can fax things back and forth right from the PC. Others use their modems to hook up to the biggest bulletin board of them all—the Internet.

In this chapter, I'll look at asynchronous communications: how they work, what goes wrong, and how to make things connect right. After that, I'll show you broadband options and technologies, what can go wrong, and how to troubleshoot it and get it working right. Trust me, it's nothing like working with modems.

A PC troubleshooter dealing with serial communications must understand:

▶ What RS-232 is

▶ How RS-232 is supposed to be used

▶ How RS-232 is actually used

▶ How to test RS-232 components

To deal with broadband issues you need to understand:

▶ TCP/IP

▶ Ethernet cabling

▶ Network interface cards

▶ How to protect yourself

The Global Network

The last several years have seen an immense leap in technologies surrounding the Internet that make it even more exciting. Certainly, as PCs have grown faster and relatively easier to use, the Internet has also become more usable. This is partly because of the analog modem. Speeds have improved over the past few years, especially since the 33.6 modem replaced the 28.8. The primary evidence in this was the V.90 protocol wars of the late '90s. Two distinct technologies developed by two industry groups, X2 and k56flex, allowed the traditional analog modem to attain speeds of up 53Kbps.

Note

Despite claims, V.90 cannot yet connect at a true 56Kbps. At best you may connect at a consistent 50.6Kbps or slightly better. Why? Ask your local telephone company. Existing current (electrical, that is) limitations prevent telephone companies from extending beyond 53Kbps in total analog bandwidth per connection.

Of course, after a spat, X2 disappeared and was replaced by V.90 with backward compatibility to k56flex, the apparent winner in the previously mentioned V.90 war. Today, the vast majority of systems, portable and otherwise, ship with a V.90 modem. So, this is where I begin; the modem. Let's take a closer look at this thing.

How Analog Modems Work

Let's start off with a look at each of the pieces of the serial picture, as serial is the way data gets into and out of your PC when talking about modems. Of course, analog signals from analog modems are not the only way of getting data to your PC. There's also the matter of Ethernet, broadband's favorite medium. But we'll talk about that later.

The Asynchronous Port

On the computer end, the computer must be able to speak the language of asynchronous communications. A device to allow this to happen is called an asynchronous port, asynchronous adapter, communications port, or RS-232 or 232C port. (RS-232 and RS-232C are the same thing. In fact, the "official" name nowadays is TIA/EIA-232D.)

Note

By the way, something that is *asynchronous* is generally the essence of all that is serial. Serial is one after the other, just like those old movie serials like *Rocketman* and *Superman*. It's the opposite of *synchronous*, also known as parallel (which you can think of as that parallel universe in the old *Star Trek* episode where there was an insane, evil Kirk that got switched with the cool Kirk), which means occurring at the same time.

The connector type used is generally the standard 25-pin DB25 type connector, such as you would find on the back of most modems and that you can see in Figure 21.1. Ever since the advent of the AT, some adapters have used a 9-pin connector. You won't miss the other 16 pins—asynchronous communication doesn't use them anyway. The signals are the same. You *may* have a cabling problem, however. We'll discuss cables later.

Figure 21.1

Standard 25-pin
DB25 type connector

Most folks don't buy an asynchronous adapter on a board by itself. Instead, it usually appears as a connector (or two, for COM1 and COM2) right on the motherboard.

The UART

This is going to sound like techie stuff, but it's important. You see, serial ports are not all created equal—even some of the newer serial ports.

Serial ports are based on a chip called a *Universal Asynchronous Receiver/Transmitter (UART)*. The original was a National Semiconductor 8250 designed back in the late '70s. It worked great on the slow XTs and PCs. Unfortunately, computer manufacturers kept on using them all the way through to the 486 compatible computers, and thereby hangs a tale.

One of the big performance criteria with a UART is how quickly it resets after an interrupt. Interrupts occur whenever data arrives in the serial port, so you can imagine that they're pretty common occurrences. The 8250 reset in 1000ns, which was no problem when it was used by the older PCs. The PCs would access the 8250 in *2000*ns, so the fact that the 8250 was taking forever to reset was no big deal from the PC CPU's point of view—it was a lot slower.

Problems began appearing as soon as turbo XTs appeared. At 10MHz, an XT could access the 8250 in just about the same amount of time that it took the 8250 to reset, leading to a potential "not ready" problem for the UART. To correct this problem, a new chip, the 16450, was built by National Semiconductor, with a reset time five times faster than the 8250—200ns. That basically solved the bottleneck problem between CPU and UART.

Multitasking and higher transfer speeds, however, posed another problem. The CPU can only be in one place at a time, and if you're running five programs, the UART might find itself full of data with no CPU to transfer the data to. By the time the CPU would say to the UART, "Whatcha got for me?" the UART may have been forced to discard some data. The 16450 UART can hold only one byte. If that space is full, and the CPU hasn't come around to get the byte, any incoming bytes get discarded due to "buffer overflow." (The one byte in the 16450 is the "buffer.")

Enter the 16550. It's got a 16-byte buffer. That may not sound like much, but have you done a file transfer under Windows and then opened up a new program? The resulting disk access to load the new program means that the CPU ignores the UART for hundreds of nanoseconds, and you usually drop a block or two of data. That's not the end of the world, as most communications software uses an error-checking scheme that detects the dropped block and resends it, but it still makes your system a bit slower and less reliable. And dropping a block at a critical time may mean losing your communications connection. The 16-byte buffer in the 16550 is the answer.

Note

As discussed in Chapter 3, "Inside the PC: Pieces of the Picture," the Universal Serial Bus (USB) is the challenger to the "of course the modem goes in the serial port" mindset. This new port type provides a single four-pin connection for a number of devices (among them, compatible modems) to be daisy-chained from the computer, like a SCSI chain.

What Happened to the External Modem?

Nothing, per se. Well, I guess you could say that the Internet happened to the external modem. The more the Internet grows and shapes the way we live in very profound ways, the more the technology around us becomes Internet-enabled. And what's the most well known Internet appliance? Why, the personal computer, of course. With everyone wanting Internet access with their new systems and new PC sales even being driven by the Internet, a modem must be included or the vendor will not fare well against competition. It's expensive to add $50–$150 in plastic, cabling, and extra power supply into a new system that's going to retail for less than $800 (okay, $799) when they can slot a $15 internal "Winmodem" into the box instead.

And, pray tell, what is a Winmodem? There is an ancient mythological creature called a Doppelganger. Its ability was to take the form of another and take advantage of said imitation. Sadly, in the process, the copied individual or animal died. The Winmodem performs similar magic in that it mimics a real modem by acting like one, but in reality it is co-opting your CPU's precious clock cycles to do its bidding. The Winmodem is actually unable to do anything even vaguely modemlike on its own.

Of course, you can still buy "real" external modems and even internal versions of those expensive ones, but you typically don't have to, unless you plan on using an operating system other than Windows. The Winmodem, due to its "special capabilities," has limited support outside of Windows (hence the name). It is, however, unlikely that you will receive a "real" modem bundled with a system, even a system that costs over $2000.

The Cable

Communications cables are the bane of a PC expert's existence. The problem is that no manufacturer follows the RS-232 standard exactly. Many manufacturers use a different connector, or they rearrange the order of the pins. Neither is a fatal problem—just a pain in the neck.

Cables can have broken wires and loose pins, or they can be wired incorrectly. The section "Common Cables: A Configuration Cookbook" includes wiring diagrams for common PC cables.

Note

There are now two (different) common internal serial cables being used by motherboards, and they are incompatible. In general, motherboards will include the internal (ribbon) serial cables, so all you need to remember is to keep the cables that came with the motherboard together with that motherboard.

The Modem

The most common use for a serial port is as an interface to a modem. Modems allow computers to communicate via regular phone lines. They've been around for decades. In the PC world, Hayes Microcomputer Products introduced the Smartmodem (now called the Smartmodem 300) in the early '80s, starting a whole new generation of communications devices. Now 56Kbps modems are pretty much the norm.

Modems are designed to follow certain modem standards so that they can communicate with other modems. The one that you're likely to hear of is the V.90 standard. Why are some modems called "smart" modems? Because they're programmable. What does "programmable" mean? Well, back in the old days, you had to flip switches to do things like:

▶ Turn echo on/off

▶ Adjust speed, parity, data bits, or stop bits

▶ Turn a monitor speaker on/off

Additionally, you had to dial your calls by hand. You can send programmable modem commands via software in the computer. Thus, you can write a program to set some communications parameters, dial a number until it answers, log on to the computer at that number, download a file, and log off, all without the operator having to be present. This is the way that companies like Prodigy and America Online have automated e-mail and Internet communications.

Also, it's important to understand that a 56Kbps modem usually doesn't actually deliver 56Kbps. High-speed modems adjust their speeds according to the perceived quality of the phone line. On a bad day, you might only get 10,000bps.

The Communications Software

If you have a programmable smart modem, as most of us do these days, be sure that your communications software understands the modem's language. Most smart modems claim to use the same language as the market leader, Hayes, but if you're using a clone modem of some kind, it can't hurt to check with the software vendor. Most software will work fine on the more popular clones, like the U.S. Robotics, Intel, or Practical Peripherals modems.

Modem Maintenance

For the most part, modems are solid-state and so have no moving parts. Modems can tend to run hot, as many are designed around one or two fairly dense chips, so don't pile books atop an external modem—make sure the area around it is ventilated. I know the ads all show a phone perched on top of a modem, but I'm not sure it's such a good idea. I know for a fact that it's *not* a good idea to stack up modems. I've had a fair amount of heat-related modem trouble. Be sure that you know where the modem's warranty information is. (Most modems have two-year warranties, so don't throw that information out.)

The usual stuff applies: as they are large connectors with tiny pins, screw in the cables. Don't make the cables longer than they need to be: it increases the noise level in the cable, and if a loop of cable dangles down behind a table it may get caught in something or be idly kicked. I know of an analyst who routinely braced his feet against the cable—just a nervous habit. The cable was even more nervous.

In Chapter 9, "Power Supplies and Power Protection," I mentioned power problems. *The same surge problems can appear on phone lines.* If the line from the phone company switching station to your computer is above ground at any point, think seriously about getting a phone line isolator (sometimes called a modem isolator). These are commonly featured on the standard electrical strips that you buy at your local national hardware or discount franchise. This isolator sits between the modem and the phone. Another measure of prevention is an RS-232 isolator, which sits between the modem and the PC. I'd rather smoke a modem by itself than a modem and the rest of my system.

Now, there used to be companies that offered optical isolators for RS-232, which solved *all* communications power surge problems, but they seem to have disappeared. I don't quite understand it, but it's certainly become difficult to find optical RS-232 isolators.

You may be wondering why I beat up on surge protectors in Chapter 9 but am suggesting them now. Mainly, cost. Surges really don't occur that often over the phone line, save in the event of lightning strikes. When that unlikely lightning strike occurs, you want something that'll take the brunt of the impulse and hopefully burn out in the process, cutting off the connection between your expensive equipment and the lightning. (I suppose you could also try knots in the phone cord.)

Understanding RS-232

You know, for a "standard," RS-232 sure provides a lot of headaches. Buy a device from Vendor A with an RS-232 port on it and a device from Vendor B with an RS-232 port on it, and try to hook them up. When it doesn't work (a common outcome), you start calling people.

Vendor A: "Trouble with our unit? Gosh, we don't really ever get bad reports on . . . Wait! What are you trying to connect to? *Vendor B?* That's your trouble. That guy hasn't designed an interface that follows specs since the day he got into business."

So you, reasonably, are annoyed by the temerity of Vendor B, and call him. He is jolly.

Vendor B: "Vendor A? Is that old rapscallion (not the actual word used) still lying about me? His problem is that he builds 'em to the standard, all right—the *1964* standard. He's building RS-232-A ports. We follow the 1984 conventions, and . . ." (soothing noises follow).

If you could get these two guys in the same room, you know what they'd say?

"Your problem is the cable—it's the wrong one." You wait, expectant, for the solution. But they demur.

"Oh, no—we don't sell cables," they chorus, and then leave.

You'll probably face about two big RS-232 compatibility problems per year, and you'll be a happier person if you can take a swing at fixing them. Look, if a simple country economist like myself can do it, so can you.

So here's the world's shortest course on what RS-232 is and how it works.

Why Is There RS-232?

Problems like the above aside, RS-232 exists so that different vendors can offer equipment that can communicate with each other's equipment. I can buy a modem built before the PC was even designed, and it'll work with the PC just fine because they use RS-232 to communicate. RS-232 is an example of a *physical interface*—an agreement among vendors about how to make equipment communicate.

For a simpler and more familiar example of a physical interface, think of the plug in your wall socket. It supplies 120 volts, 60 cycles per second, also called hertz (Hz) alternating current. If you plug in something that uses, say, 220 volts, 50 cycles per second, you'll get very unpleasant results, up to and including burning your house down. So when did you last check to be sure that something used 120-volt, 60Hz current? Probably never: you just figure that if you buy something with a regular power plug on it, it'll use the juice okay. And you're right. There's a standards agency—Underwriters Laboratories (UL)—that concerns itself with power and safety, so you won't see a UL sticker on something that you could plug into a wall socket and damage yourself with.

So the plug itself seems important. Can I, for instance, use my U.S. microwave in London? Nope—they have different power. The first problem I'll run up against is, again, the plug—my plug won't fit into any wall sockets. Can I just snip off the plug, install a British-type power plug, and use the wall current? No again: it's 220 volts, 50Hz.

Why use different plugs, then? Simple: the plug is a *reminder* about where the equipment can and can't be used. The plug tells us something else, too: what devices *supply* power, and what devices *use* power. Female connectors indicate a device (like an extension cord) that supplies power. Male connectors indicate a device that uses power. This way, you don't plug a toaster into a microwave oven and think that something will come of the marriage.

Behind the plug lies a lot of information about the interface standard. Know what plug you've got, and you don't have to worry about things like how many volts or hertz the power is. Well, RS-232 does something similar.

Just as there are two members of the power interface—the user and the supplier—so too are there two kinds of RS-232 interfaces. RS-232 was basically designed to allow computing devices called *data terminal equipment (DTE)* to talk to communications devices called *data circuit-terminating equipment (DCE)*. So there's a DTE-type RS-232 interface and a DCE-type RS-232 interface. RS-232 is designed to allow DTEs to talk only to DCEs. RS-232 uses DB25 and DB9 connectors. Male connectors go on the DTEs; female connectors go on the DCEs.

DTE-type interfaces are most commonly found on PCs and printers. Devices with DCE-type interfaces include modems, mice, and scanners.

How RS-232 Works

The original specification for RS-232 is a digital interface with 25 separate wires, each with its own task. RS-232 is defined for both synchronous and asynchronous communication, so there are a lot of lines in the 25 that you'll never use in asynchronous communications. In fact, for the most basic RS-232 applications, you only need three wires: transmit, receive, and ground. As mentioned before, lines are either "on" (with a voltage level of +3 volts or more), "off" (below –3), or "neither" (in between). *Flow control* is an important part of RS-232's purpose. Flow control allows a receiving device to say to a sending device, "STOP! My buffers (a small amount of memory in the receiving device) are overflowing—hang on a second and I'll get right back to you."

There are 10 important asynchronous lines in RS-232, as shown in Table 21.1. It's important to understand that each line is controlled by either one side or another. Line 2, for example, is viewed as input by one side and output by the other side. If both viewed line 2 as input, then both would be transmitting information that was never received, so each line (except grounds, which are just electrical reference points) is controlled by one side or another. Note, by the way, that there is also a 9-pin version of the RS-232 connector. When I refer to pin numbers, I'm referring to the 25-pin numbers, not the 9-pin.

TABLE 21.1 RS-232 Leads

Description	Pin # (25 Pin)	Pin # (9-Pin)	From	Abbreviation
Power On Indicator Leads				
Data Set Ready	6	6	DCE	DSR
Data Terminal Ready	20	4	DTE	DTR
Leads That Announce That an Outside Event Has Taken Place				
Data Carrier Detect	8	1	DCE	CD
Ring indicator	22	9	DCE	RI
Ready to Send/Receive Handshake Leads				
Request To Send	4	7	DTE	RTS
Clear To Send	5	8	DCE	CTS
Data Leads				
Transmit Data	2	3	DTE	TD
Receive Data	3	2	DCE	RD
Ground leads				
Signal ground	7	5		SG
Protective ground	1			FG

Here's the sequence of events for a normal RS-232 session.

1. Both devices are powered up and indicate "power up" status. The DTE powers up line 20 (DTR, Data Terminal Ready). The DCE powers up line 6 (DSR, Data Set Ready). A well-designed RS-232 interface won't communicate further until these two lines are activated. The DTE waits to see a signal on line 6, the DCE on line 20. Lines 6 and 20 are supposed to be "equipment check" signals that only indicate device power status, but they're sometimes used as flow control lines.

2. The modem connects with another modem. This is where the communication in "data communication" comes in. In a modem/terminal situation, the situation envisioned by the RS-232 designers (see "A Note on Reality" for what often really happens), a distant modem is dialed up. The modems exchange carriers (the high-pitched whine that you hear when modems connect), and the modem (DCE, recall) tells the terminal (DTE, recall) about it over line 8, DCD (Data Carrier Detect). If you've got an external modem with red lights, by the way, you see the preceding in the lights: line 6 is attached to the light labeled MR, Modem Ready; line 20 is attached to the light labeled Terminal Ready; and line 8 is attached to the light labeled CD (Carrier Detect).

3. The terminal (DTE) asks the modem (DCE) if it's ready. The terminal activates line 4, RTS (Request To Send). The modem, if ready, responds with line 5, CTS (Clear To Send). Now the handshake process is complete. Lines 4 and 5 are flow control lines.

4. Data is exchanged. The terminal (DTE) passes information for the modem (DCE) to transmit along line 2. The modem passes information back to the terminal along line 3.

And that's all there is to RS-232.

A Note on Reality

The above description is nice and complete so far as the standard goes, but most RS-232 interfaces aren't complete. Most PC software, for example, only looks at one handshake, such as 8 (Data Carrier Detect), 6 (Data Set Ready), or 5 (Clear To Send), and ignores the rest. Some software doesn't look at *any* control lines, so DTR, DSR, DCD, RTS, and CTS become irrelevant. That makes cabling easier, but it ignores the question of flow control.

Flow Control

Flow control is implemented in *either* hardware or software. Software control uses signals, such as the following, which are sent as data to the receiving computer:

▶ XON/XOFF

▶ ENQ/ACK

Hardware control sends control pulses along special wires (control lines) in the cable, and it's done with one or more of the control lines, usually one of the following:

▶ DSR

▶ CTS

▶ DCD

The software approach is to send "STOP!" characters back and forth when one side's buffers are overflowing. The hardware approach simply deactivates a line when the receiver needs a rest. Again, here's where your cable design is vitally important: if you neglect to include the particular handshake wire in your cable, there's no way for the computer to know that the printer is overflowing its buffer.

Another handshaking problem shows up when one side is using one method and the other side a different one, as when the PC is looking at CTS and the printer is using XON/XOFF.

You can test your handshake easily. Say you're hooking up a serial printer. Have the computer send a bunch of information to the printer to be printed and then do something like pull the paper tray out or take the printer offline. Once that's done, see if the computer figures it out—does it stop sending information to the printer? Then put the paper tray back in or put the printer back online and see if it picks up where it left off. Keep switching protocols until one of them works for you (or refer to your product manual!).

Common Cables: A Configuration Cookbook

Well, now that you've had the complete RS-232 overview, here are a few basic cable diagrams, including:

◗ Serial DB25 connector to a modem (Figure 21.2)

◗ Serial DB9 connector to a modem (Figure 21.3)

◗ Serial DB25 connector to another PC, or a printer (Figure 21.4)

◗ Serial DB9 connector to another AT or a printer (Figure 21.5)

◗ Serial DB9 to serial DB9 (computer to computer) or computer to printer (Figure 21.6)

Figure 21.2

25-pin DTE to 25-pin DCE cable

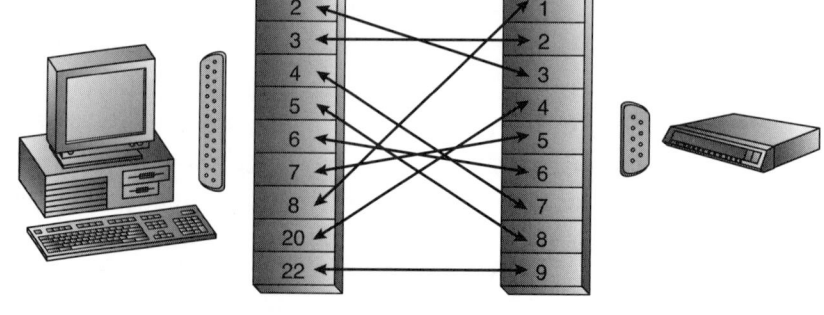

Figure 21.3

25-pin DTE to 9-pin DCE cable

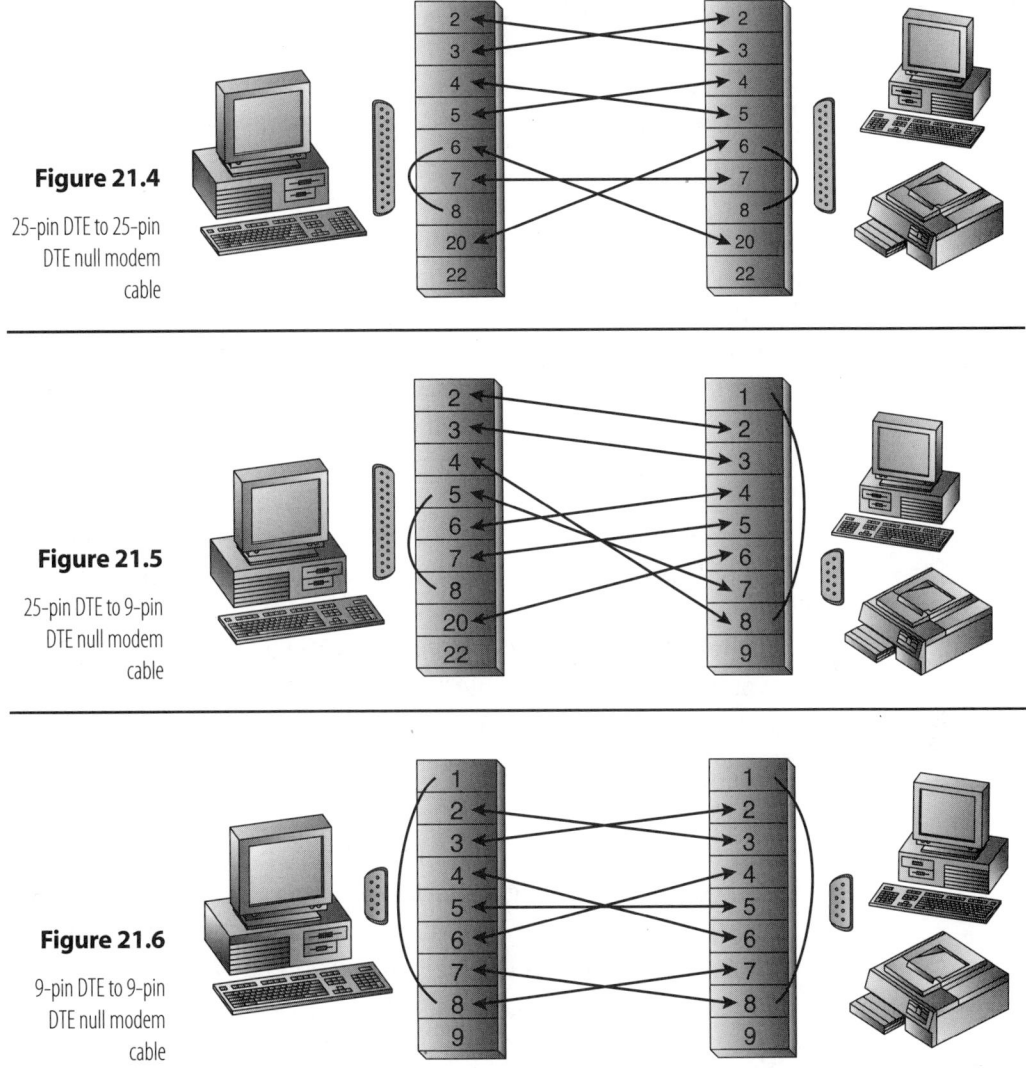

Figure 21.4

25-pin DTE to 25-pin DTE null modem cable

Figure 21.5

25-pin DTE to 9-pin DTE null modem cable

Figure 21.6

9-pin DTE to 9-pin DTE null modem cable

Welcome to Broadband

Ah, broadband at last. We're not there entirely, but this last year has seen the rollout of many forms of broadband access over most of the country, predominantly DSL. For those of you who don't know what broadband is, you may be sorry you asked, depending on where you live, of course. Broadband is very high-speed Internet access via digital connections or other means that are faster than the aforementioned analog modems.

As I've mentioned, analog modems are limited to what they do in the performance arena, but cable, satellite, and DSL are not nearly as limited. Why? Easy. Let's look at each type of broadband access real quickly:

Cable modems This format has been available longer than any other broadband access. There have been cable modems in one form or another for the last four years or so. More, if you count the test markets. Cable modems work just as you'd think they would, through your cable TV line. That's a big pipe since it has to handle all those channels.

Satellite Though pretty much unknown in metropolitan areas, satellite is often the only option for decent access in the hither and yon. Really, this is just a format variant of cable access that's done with dishes. Plug a special card into your system, plug in and tune the dish, and go. Not too hard, but there are speed and access limitations. In fact, they make you pay big if you exceed your contracted usage per month.

DSL Possibly the most anticipated Internet technology ever. If you're willing to shell out the funds, DSL can give you access to the Internet on par with T1, a long-established, very fast digital connection typically used by business interests. T1 happens to cost about $1500 a month, which makes it prohibitive in cost and maintenance fees for the average Internet user. In comparison, a DSL connection at around 384Kbps downstream will run you about $40–$65 a month—and that usually includes ISP service.

All About Digital Modems

To make a long story short, the combination of upper modem limits and too many graphics on the Internet is beginning to make a faster modem connection look very attractive. Since modems are almost at the end of their rope, that faster connection is going to be digital—probably the *Integrated Services Digital Network (ISDN)*.

What Is ISDN?

If you already know what ISDN is, you can skip this part. For the uninitiated, however, it's a high-speed digital telephone line with two data channels that can each transmit 64,000bps, or they can be combined for a single-channel throughput of 128,000bps. Not too shabby. If you keep the channels separate, you can run two conversations via the same telephone connection. For example, you can talk on the telephone while using the modem.

Depending on two circumstances, you may be able to use ISDN to dial into the Internet or your favorite online service provider. The first circumstance is whether or not you can get an ISDN connection to your home or office. Depending on where you live, getting the connection can be mildly aggravating or just plain impossible. Washington, D.C., for example, is one of the only "mildly aggravating" areas, as ISDN has been offered here for several years now. Getting my ISDN connection up to connect my company's two offices three years ago was only slightly less painful than having a root canal (the telephone installation guys were so new at it that they had to take the shrink-wrap off the ISDN installation kit before they used it), but the process has become somewhat easier of late.

The cost of an ISDN connection varies significantly throughout the United States—so significantly, in fact, that it's impossible to quote usual charges with any amount of accuracy. Most often, the charges are based on a flat monthly fee plus a per-minute connection time charge. If you're connecting two places within the same calling zone or are able to wrangle a deal with your ISDN provider, you *may* only have to pay a flat monthly fee. If you can get such a deal, I highly recommend it, as it will probably save you money if you're the kind of person who goes online enough to need a high-speed connection.

Besides being able to afford the connection, you'll need an ISDN connection at your service provider. Just as you can't make a 56Kbps connection unless the modems on both ends of the connection support speeds that high, you can't dial up using ISDN unless there are ISDN devices on both ends of the connection. (Really, it's a bit more complicated even than that, as an analog modem wouldn't know what to do with a digital signal if you did call it, but the end result is still the same: unless your provider offers an ISDN connection to the Internet, you can't have one.) These can be a little tricky to come by even if you live in an area that offers ISDN, so you may have to shop around a bit for a provider.

Of course, all this matters little considering that ISDN costs significantly more than DSL or cable, not to mention that DSL and cable are also significantly faster.

ISDN-Capable Modems

Assuming that you've got an ISDN line and an Internet provider with an ISDN line, you'll need an ISDN modem (typically called a "terminal adapter"); this will let your analog modem use a digital line. (In the early days of ISDN, you would have needed another device called an NT1 to plug the ISDN device into, but many new models are including the NT1 in the device itself.)

Note

If you intend to use additional devices on an ISDN line, you'll either need digital versions of the device or a converter. Converters are about $150. Considering that your analog phone is probably worth about that much, save some money by making sure the ISDN line is dedicated.

If you've already got a modem and telephone and don't feel like getting new ones, you can use a device such as Motorola's Bitsurfer to connect. This little box has two analog ports that you can plug devices into.

If you plan to upgrade, you can replace your old modem with an ISDN model. These aren't cheap, but their cost is proportional to the increase in speed that you see. Some ISDN modems have more features than others do. For example, 3Com's IQ ISDN modem has user-controlled band allocation so that you can combine the two data channels to get 128Kbps. If the telephone rings while you're connected, however, the channels will separate so that you can answer the telephone while keeping the original connection; they'll recombine once you hang up.

To recap, here's what you'll need to use ISDN:

▶ An ISDN telephone line

▶ Someone with an ISDN telephone line and associated equipment to call

▶ An ISDN modem and/or telephone, or a converter that you can plug analog equipment into

Once you've got all that, you can surf with speed, scoffing at the masses that you whiz by.

Digital Subscriber Line (DSL)

The slow, "upstream" portion of the line between us and the local ISP is the major hang-up with broadband because of the limitations of the connection between the phone company's Central Office (CO) and the home. Now, along comes digital subscriber line (or *loop*, to some) (DSL), which is meant to address just this issue. Upstream data flow (from the computer user to the ISP) is a fraction of the data flow at the bottom of the data stream. The upstream data flow is typically measured in kilobits per second (Kbps) while the downstream data flow (from the ISP to the computer user) is measured in megabits per second (Mbps). Table 21.2 shows DSL speeds and distances.

TABLE 21.2 A Look at DSL as It Stands Today

DSL Type	Upstream Speeds	Downstream Speeds	Max. Dist. from CO
ADSL	64–800Kbps	.5–8Mbps	12–18,000 ft.
ADSL Lite	64–384Kbps	1–1.5Mbps	22–25,000 ft.
VDSL	1.6Mbps	13Mbps	1,000–4,500 ft.
	3.2Mbps	26Mbps	1,000–4,500 ft.
	6.4Mbps	52Mbps	1,000–4,500 ft.
HDSL	768Kbps, 1.544 and 2.048Mbps	768Kbps, 1.544 and 2.048Mbps	12,000 ft.
SDSL	384 and 768Kbps	384 and 768Kbps	5–10,000 ft.
V.90 modem	33.6bps	53bps	N/A

The most common DSL being rolled out is ADSL (asymmetric digital subscriber line), which means that the streams are not the same. Typically, upstream speed is slower than the downstream. ADSL specifies that there is a circuit connecting two ADSL modems on each end of a twisted-pair telephone line, creating three channels. One of these channels is a plain old telephone service channel (POTS), the second is a medium-speed bidirectional channel, and the third is a high-speed downstream data channel.

DSL is far faster, more versatile, less costly, and more reliable than ISDN. Its proponents point out that it is supposed to be capable of providing simultaneous telephone and data transmission service over the same single pair of copper wires. Furthermore, analog devices like fax machines can be used on the POTS channel, whereas ISDN requires digital devices in most cases.

If you live in a large metropolitan area, it's likely you already have access to DSL. You need to contact a local provider or even your telephone company and inquire about its availability. Chances are that if it's not available, it will be soon.

How DSL Works

DSL is very cool, and it doesn't work much differently than ISDN or even cable modem technology.

All forms of DSL are based on the ability to split existing phone lines (POTS, or plain old telephone service) into two or three frequency bands. This is called a frequency spectrum. If there are two frequency bands, as there are in HDSL and VDSL, one band is used to provide upstream data flow and the other is used to provide downstream data flow. If there are three bands, the third "channel" is used for standard voice. POTS takes up only a small portion of the total capacity of the available bandwidth, so adding this is trivial.

Physically, there has to be a connection between the provider and you. It's relatively easy enough for your local telephone company to pipe a T1, T3, or faster connection into your CO, but they also need to add what's called a DSLAM, or DSL access multiplexer (just another fancy name for splitter). The Internet connection goes into the DSLAM, and the POTS lines pass through it. If there's no terminal adapter, your DSL modem on the other end of the DSLAM does nothing and simply acts as a fancy wire holder for the POTS lines.

On the other hand, if you *do* have a DSL modem, an ATM (Asynchronous Transfer Mode, a very high-speed protocol link) is established.

It's in the so-called Last Mile that most of the problems with DSL can occur. The Last Mile, which is owned by the big telcos (such as Bell Atlantic, Southwest Bell, Bell Canada, and Pacific Bell) is essentially just simple POTS line, also known as twisted-pair, and this is why there is a distance limitation. Copper wire can only retain so much cohesion for so long. After a certain point, the signal begins to degrade and it is no longer useable.

The ISP comes in to provide you access to the overall Internet. Typically, you are given a static IP, but some providers offer only DHCP (allocating whatever IP number happens to be available, but since you're connected all the time it doesn't really matter), and some now use PPPoE (PPP over Ethernet).

Installing and Configuring DSL

Having DSL installed is a process, to be sure. It took two months for mine to get installed and that's in the D.C. area! Now, for the most part, the process is the same everywhere and involves no real technical know-how at all. First, call a provider like Flashcom or Concentric Networks and order service appropriate to your price range and needs. Simple 300+Kbps service can be had for about $50 a month with a free modem and installation.

Whomever you order from will typically make arrangements with an independently owned company or a telco. An independently owned company (also called a "partner"), such as Covad or GTE, has to make arrangements with whichever telco owns your phone line.

Once that's done, a representative of your local telco comes to your office or domicile to test the line to see if the "loop" is good. This means they are checking the POTS (plain old telephone system, or good ol' copper wire) lines to see if they can handle the connection and will pass clean data.

Note

As mentioned above, DSL is limited to the distance from the Central Office and that CO's installed DSLAM (DSL access multiplexer). If that distance is exceeded, you cannot have DSL. If it were installed despite the long distance, it would be unreliable or not work at all.

If a partner is involved, they are notified by the telco that the line was tested and informed what condition it is in. If it is acceptable, the process moves onward and the partner representative comes over to make the installation. The telco marks the line tested for DSL, which is typically an existing phone line. The installer finds it and prepares it, installs an RJ-45 jack at the wall plate you specify, and plugs it in to test it.

If the telco handles it all the way, they'll probably be the ones to install the line into your office or domicile—exactly the way the partner would but with one less entity to deal with.

The installer will bring a modem with them (unless you made arrangements to provide your own). They'll also need to plug into your Network Interface Card. What? You don't have one? Okay, important note here. In order for DSL, cable modem, or satellite access to work, it needs an Ethernet connection. This means that you need to install an Ethernet card. You can find them at your local PC store for around $30–$40. Don't go cheap here. Spend the few extra bucks and get the PCI card. NetGear makes particularly compatible and reliable cards.

Anyway, once the installer has the modem connected and everything appears to be working correctly, it's time to configure. There are a few things you'll need:

 A static IP number

If your provider does not provide a static IP number, get another provider. Period.

 A gateway IP number

 At least two DNS IP numbers

 Your POP3 and SMTP server IP numbers

Now, write all these down and put the list in a safe place. Repeat this three times. Even fast minds like ours can get all in a twist and only remember one clever and crafty hiding place at a time, so it's best to hedge one's bets. Now we can get to the configuration (this procedure assumes you're working with Windows 9x):

1. Go to Start ➤ Settings ➤ Control Panel and open Network.

2. Enter the appropriate information on the tabs. Do not activate WINS.

3. Click OK.

4. Restart the machine.

5. Enjoy your speedy connection.

Securing Windows in a DSL System

There is one big negative about DSL with a static IP: crackers. These mean and nasty people are called "crackers" because they crack into your system. (You've probably heard them called "hackers," but *hacker* actually means someone who enjoys working with computers "very close to the metal." Hackers are not mean and malicious; crackers are.) Crackers like to gain access to systems that are not their own and destroy data, take things, or just leave evidence of their illicit presence.

To do this, they need what are called exploits, or shortcomings in the system that allow them to get around established security measures. Windows is very, *very* bad in this respect (bad, *bad* OS . . . BAD!) in that it practically broadcasts its presence. So, how do we prevent this from happening? Easy. Follow this very complicated list of instructions:

1. Turn off file sharing.

Obviously, this is a simplistic answer to a potentially complex problem, but if you only have one computer connected to the DSL, there is absolutely no need whatsoever to share your files with the world. Of course, there are more factors in real life and hence, more options. To turn file sharing off, go to Start ➢ Settings ➢ Control Panel and open the Network item. Click on the File/Print Sharing button in the lower half of the dialog and uncheck both items. You're done.

If you are sharing an Internet connection with a housemate via home networking of some sort (i.e., peer-to-peer Ethernet, LAN, wireless, phone line–based, etc.), file sharing may be required. There are software packages that are specifically designed to allow the sharing of a single modem connection (or DSL, of course) that also have built-in protection from caustic elements. Vicomsoft is a superb example of a company that provides a number of solutions at various price points for both Windows and Mac.

Note

You can find contact information for Vicomsoft in the Vendor Guide on CD #2. If you have only two or three home-based users to consider, examine SurfDoubler and SurfDoubler+ ($75 for two users, $100 for three). These products are also great if you have children around as they incorporate CyberNOT filtering service. For more complex jobs, consider the overwhelmingly cool Internet Gateway, also from Vicomsoft (it's woefully undernamed—it should be something like Internet Dazzler). A five-user package runs at about $250, but an unlimited user package is only about $730. For a small office, that's quite the bargain.

Internet Gateway uses NAT, or Network Address Translation, to make one IP address available to as many computers as are behind the server. The security benefit to this is that if the server is secure from attack, so are all the machines that it serves because they all appear to be one machine: the server. NAT works because the server records which internal machine sends a request, tracks the data from server to server, and delivers the data to the requesting client when it comes back. Only the server knows the real address of the machine that requested the data, and it just makes the translation for it.

Of course, the best protection is to turn off the computer or otherwise disconnect from the Internet (i.e., turn off the modem) when you're not using it. That way you might notice peculiar and unfamiliar activity if it goes on for a long time. One good indicator of "peculiar" would be lots of activity when you're doing nothing and no Internet-related software is active.

Troubleshooting Tips

Communications troubleshooting can provide you with hours of mind-exercising delight, *if* you're the kind of person who likes puzzles. Let's see how to deconstruct the problem and isolate the bad component. There are a few possibilities to look at when you're troubleshooting communications:

▶ The software

▶ The hardware

▶ The phone line

▶ The port

▶ The modem

▶ The cable

Common Communications Software Problems

If you are connecting to another PC by modem, you'll need to set up some parameters that you don't need to worry about when you are connecting to the Internet. You must ensure that both parties in the communication have agreed on the *communications parameters*:

▶ Parity (can be even, odd, or none)

▶ Number of data bits (can be 7 or 8)

▶ Number of stop bits (generally 1, could be 2 or even 1.5)

▶ Local echo on/off

All direct communications packages, such as Windows Hyper-Terminal, have the ability to set these values. Don't worry about what the parameters mean—just be sure that they match. Common symptoms that may be software problems include the following:

- Cannot connect

- Cannot see input

- Input is double

Cannot Connect

Check the parameters. If you cannot connect, or if you connect and see garbage ("{" characters in particular), you've probably got a speed or data bits mismatch.

Cannot See Input

You type, but you can't see what you're typing. Try a simple command, such as whatever command you would use to get a file directory from the distant system. If the command gets a proper response from the other side, even though you can't see what you typed, you must set your local echo to On. "Local echo" tells your PC whether or not to display the characters that you type.

Sometimes you want to disable local echo, as the remote site will echo characters, meaning that you press a key, the key goes out to the remote site, the remote site echoes, and *then* you see the character that you typed. Whether or not you need local echo is determined by whether or not the other site provides echoes.

Input Is Double

You type a character and two characters appear on the screen. Output from the other computer is normal. Answer: set your local echo to Off.

Sometimes, there is no local echo command. In that case, the command has been misnamed (it's a common mistake) to "duplex." (Duplex is something completely different—an engineering concern in data communications.) If you've got the duplex command, then:

- ◗ Half duplex = local echo on

- ◗ Full duplex = local echo off

Again, it's incorrect terminology, but who cares as long as you can get the problem solved?

Is Your Software Set Up to Talk to Your Modem?

You instruct most modems to dial a number by sending the command ATD, followed by the phone number. Some modems *don't* do it this way, however. (IBM sold an internal modem for their luggable PCs for a while that used a strange command set.)

Simple Hardware Problems

Along with software problems, basic hardware incompatibilities can also keep your communications from working successfully.

You're set up to dial the distant computer, but the modem doesn't respond. There are lots of possibilities:

- ◗ Is the modem plugged into the phone jack? If you share the modem's phone line with a phone, you may have forgotten to plug the modem back in after using the phone.

- ◗ Is the modem plugged into the computer? Did the serial cable fall out? (It won't if you screw the connectors in.)

- ◗ Is the phone line working? Plug in a phone. Is there a dial tone?

- ◗ Is it your phone system? If you have an in-house phone system, like a ROLM or Northern Telecom system, you may have to issue extra commands to dial out of your PBX (private branch exchange) system. Check with your telecommunications manager.

Warning

BE WARNED! Plugging an analog modem into a digital system *will cause damage to the modem*. If you plan on traveling, avail yourself of Hello Direct's LineStein digital adapter, which converts pesky digital jacks to analog in seconds. A mere $120 gets you the unit and another $40 gets you a battery pack (it normally plugs into the wall, but . . .). A few replacement laptop modems definitely cost more than that! The gizmo can "learn" the particulars of practically any digital PBX system. Just plug it in to the wall and line and press the Learn button. A green light means a good line.

Phone Line Noise and Quality Problems

Sometimes it isn't hardware or software; it's the phone line itself. There are a few simple things you should try first. Can you try the call on another line? Is it a multiextension phone—could someone be picking up the phone as your modem tries to dial?

There are a few other areas that you should also check:

▶ The quality of the communications provider

▶ The in-house wiring

▶ Whether call-waiting is interrupting modem sessions

The call-waiting is easy enough to check. Just make sure that you have a "*70" (don't include the quotes, of course)—or whatever your phone company's call-waiting turn-off arrangement is—in front of the ISPs dial-up access number. As for the first two items, experience and lots of dirty clothing are the only ways to solve them.

Check the In-House Cable Plant

You may find that line noise is being created by the wiring in your building. It could be that old wires don't transmit as well as they once did or that someone ran the wires near the high-voltage lines in the elevator shaft—any number of a million things could go wrong with the in-house cable plant. Inspect your cable plant periodically. I had phone noise trouble in my building, so I restrung my phone lines and the problem went away. (I actually found that my termination block was made out of four wood screws driven into a rafter in the basement!)

Check the Ground

Did you check that the modem and the PC share a common ground? You may recall from Chapter 9 that plugging the PC and a peripheral into different outlets can lead to slight differences in the value of "electrical ground," which in turn can lead to noisy communications.

Check the Voltage

The phone line has four lines, one each colored red, green, yellow, and black. Only the red and green lines are used. Each pair should offer 48 volts of DC power with all devices on-hook. Each off-hook device will draw about 3 to 9 volts (although some go as high as 12). Get seven phones off-hook on one line, and it will not have enough juice to power any of them, although the one closest to the main junction box might work. If your phone varies greatly from this, call your repair office.

Warning

The voltage on a normal phone line is enough to be felt. If you happen to measure the line while the phone is ringing, the voltage shoots up to almost 100 volts. Only do this test if you know what you're doing, please. We'd miss you.

Or, you could try checking out the phone line with a phone line tester. IBM makes one called the Modem Saver for about $29; it's not the greatest thing in the whole world, but it does the job. You just plug it into the modular phone jack and little lights tell you whether or not the line is working. You can find the information for this product in the Vendor Guide on CD #2.

The Other Side

Half of the possibility for problems comes from the folks that you're trying to communicate with. Double-check their parameters with them. Try calling out to another computer, if possible. Have they recently installed a new revision of *their* communication software or a new, "completely compatible" modem?

Going Further

There are devices called *analog channel test units* that will actually test the phone line between you and the other party. They are, however, quite expensive. You can also get an oscilloscope, which can help you measure the frequencies being produced by your modem to see if they are within specification. Again, you may not want to go this far, as the required investment in test equipment is not trivial.

Port Problems

Since the RS-232 port is a bidirectional device (it talks as well as listens), you can use a *loopback* to allow it to test itself. Serial ports *do* become ill. I don't know why—on my system, I presume it's something to do with the plugging and unplugging that I do (I do a large amount of communications consulting, so I try a lot of equipment out on my system). For instance, years ago I bought two Toshiba 1100+ laptop computers and they both had something wrong with the serial port: Receive Data in the first one, Ring Indicate in the second. Probably 20 percent of the expansion boards that I've worked with had a serial problem. So it's worthwhile knowing how to diagnose such a problem.

To test the port, you need to see what is happening on the various control lines. I recommend that you get a breakout box to assist you in testing the communications port.

A breakout box allows you to prototype a serial cable without soldering or pin crimping (the two most common methods of cable assembly). That's convenient because you can figure out what the correct cable configuration should be even if you don't know how to solder or crimp. Then you can give that cable configuration to someone in your company or a technical service house to make up the cable for you. You see, getting the cable made (soldered) isn't too hard, once you've settled on a cable design. But making sure that it's designed correctly *is* difficult, so you want to do it yourself; a breakout box makes that possible.

Regular 25-wire RS-232 type cables come in one side and go out the other. All 25 lines are represented on each side with large round metal posts. The breakout box comes with about a dozen wires that terminate in small plugs that mate with the posts. The way the box works is that you design a cable, run wires from post to post to make the connections necessary for the cable, and plug in the breakout box (it serves as the cable) to the two devices that you want to interface. The cable design either works or it doesn't.

As an example, say I'm trying to design a cable to allow my laptop to transfer data to my PC. The cables on either end are too short to connect the two devices, so I need to first run a couple of extension cables. I run a regular straight-through cable from the PC to one side of the breakout box and another regular straight-through cable from the laptop to the other side of the breakout box.

Now I'm ready to start prototyping. I figure I'll start my cable design with a cable that just connects 2 on the PC side to 3 on the laptop side, 3 on the PC side to 2 on the laptop side, and 7 on the PC side to 7 on the laptop side. (See the section, "Common Cables: A Configuration Cookbook," for basic cable diagrams.) To set this up, I just run one of the wires from 2 on the PC side to 3 on the laptop side, and from 3 on the PC side to 2 on the laptop side. I actually don't have to run a wire from 7 to 7, as there are DIP switches for each of the 25 lines, and any time I want a "straight-through" connection all I need do is to close the DIP switch for that particular line. (Make sure the others are all set to "open," or you'll have lots of "wires" in your cable that you didn't intend to have.)

Some breakout boxes have red and possibly green lights to indicate activity levels for various inputs and outputs in the RS-232 connection. Red lights indicate the presence of voltage in excess of +3 volts (interpreted as 0), and green lights indicate the presence of voltage below –3 volts (interpreted as 1). The signal used to indicate "active" on the control leads is 0.

Modem Problems

Some modems have loopback capabilities built right in. In that case, you can do simple loopback tests, as described in the section "Port Problems." If not, the best first procedure is just a modem swap. They're small and don't require much work to swap.

Do the front lights tell you anything? Put a breakout box inline between the modem and the computer. You should see the correspondence as shown in Table 21.3.

TABLE 21.3 Modem Front Panel Light/RS-232 Line Correspondence

Modem Light	Red Light on Breakout Box
TR	20
MR	6
RD	3
SD	2
CD	8

When a specific modem light is on, the corresponding breakout box light should be on.

Are the connections correct? Many modems have two phone jacks—one to connect to the wall and one to pass through to the phone. Connect the "phone" one to the wall and you'll dial up okay, but disconnect as soon as the other side answers!

Note

Obviously, there are some things described here that do not apply to an internal modem—the lights, for instance. Although some internal modems do have lights on their back panel, it's uncommon since most people don't orient the rear of their CPU case to point at them (although some do, and I've been known to keep a test unit uncased and backward for months on end). For an internal modem that is *not* a so-called Winmodem, make sure it's properly seated in its port and that the cable is working and properly seated in the *correct* jack. Also, double-check your driver installation. For Winmodems, do the same, but also make sure you're running Windows. Seriously, don't feel bad about reinstalling the drivers. That usually resets anything that was incorrectly modified.

Cable Troubleshooting

To check out the serial cables, detach the breakout box from the computer, then connect the cable that you usually use to the computer. Connect the breakout box to the free end of the cable, and rerun the cable tests. If one fails, you have a broken wire.

Remember that with cables, speed trades off for distance. If you have a 100-foot RS-232 cable, you won't be able to run it at 38,400bps. But the exact same equipment and a two-foot cable might be able to do it at that speed. The only difference is in the length of the cable.

On the other hand, if you're reading this because the cable has never worked, refer to the sections "Understanding RS-232" and "Common Cables: A Configuration Cookbook."

Now that you know how to talk to other computers, let's go back to the one on your desk. In the next chapter, we'll discuss keyboards and mice.

Keyboards
and Mice

INTRODUCTION

The design of the PC keyboard has apparently kept IBM fairly busy since the original PC's inception. Every time a new PC is released, a new keyboard follows. They're all the same to troubleshoot, however.

The near-universal acceptance of graphical user interfaces (GUIs) means that everybody needs some kind of pointing device. We've tried electronic stylus devices, light pens (I wanted to call this chapter "Of Mice and Pens," but I couldn't really justify it), and even a Headmouse that tracks the way that you are facing. Still, the consensus pointing device seems to be the mouse. Mice can be more of a pain than keyboards, however, so I'll tell you how to handle them, too, in this chapter.

Installing a Keyboard, Mouse, or Trackball

Installing a new keyboard, mouse, or trackball is among the easiest installations you'll encounter.

Be Prepared

Before you start, there are some things you may need on hand. These include:

▶ Your new keyboard, mouse, or trackball

▶ Documentation that came with the product, to ensure proper installation

▶ Software or drivers ready to install, if required

To install a keyboard, mouse, or trackball, follow these steps:

1. Turn off your computer.

Note

USB devices are designed to be *hot-swappable* and should not require you to turn off your computer or reboot.

2. Unplug the old device (keyboard, mouse, or trackball).

3. Plug your new device into the appropriate port (keyboard, mouse, or USB) on the back of your computer.

4. Turn your computer on.

5. Install any special software or drivers for non-Plug-and-Play devices. Plug-and-Play devices should be detected by Windows, which will prompt you to install the correct drivers.

Keyboard Types and Components

With all of its moving parts, the keyboard has many potential sources of problems. Understanding those sources requires understanding the types of keyboards and their parts; here's a look at them.

Keyboard Types

There are a number of IBM-type keyboards, but you're most likely to come across one of these three:

Original PC or XT keyboard (generally called the XT keyboard) This has 83 keys and the benefit of a nice "clicky" feel to it. When you press a key, it offers some tactile feedback. Pretty much all the IBM keyboards do that, but over the years many clone keyboards have adopted a mushy feel. The numeric keypad and the cursor control keys are integrated into one 5-by-3-inch area on the right side of the keyboard.

Original AT keyboard (generally called the AT keyboard) Improvements over the XT keyboard include a larger Enter key and the addition of a SysReq (or SysRq) key intended for use with OS/2. It also has 10 function keys along the top of the keyboard (labeled F1–F10). It's still my favorite keyboard layout, but it's been largely superseded in the marketplace by the 101-key keyboard.

The 101-key PS/2 keyboard (generally called the enhanced keyboard) This appeared in 1987 and has the big benefit of being compatible with every other keyboard interface. The extra keys were added by separating the cursor and numeric functions from the numeric keypad, as well as adding two more function keys, F11 and F12 (see Figure 22.1).

Figure 22.1

PS/2 keyboard

The main difference between the XT and AT keyboards is that the XT keyboard puts the keyboard microprocessor in the keyboard, and the AT keyboard assumes that the keyboard microprocessor is on the system board. They are generally incompatible: you can't use an XT keyboard on an AT, or vice versa. Clone keyboards generally get around this by putting an XT/AT switch on the keyboard. The enhanced keyboard, on the other hand, will work on any machine without modification.

The "broken" keyboard designs (also called ergonomic keyboards), such as the Microsoft Natural Keyboard, look like a 101-key keyboard to the PC hardware. Figure 22.2 shows what they look like to the user. Since they're compatible with the existing hardware, they're easy to install, and although they take a little getting used to, they're easier on the wrists than standard keyboards. People who do a lot of typing might prefer these.

Figure 22.2

Microsoft Natural
Keyboard

Note

Many newer keyboards have additional keys that can speed up your productivity. There are Windows keys that open the Windows Start menu, menu keys that operate like a right mouse click, and keys that help you connect to and browse the Internet. There are even multimedia keys that you can use to operate your CD-ROM and multimedia applications. Some keys, through the help of drivers and special software, can be configured to perform your favorite tasks or to work with programs of your choosing; these are called *HotKeys*.

Switch or Contact Design

The hardest part of designing a keyboard is in creating the right *action*—the right *touch*. Anyone who learned to type on a keyboard expects the keys to move about a third of an inch when pressed, and some keyboards do that correctly—I find those kinds of keyboards preferable. Newer keyboards, on laptops in particular, don't move as much ("don't have as much travel," is the actual lingo), less than half that amount. Let's see . . . this book is about 2 million keystrokes . . . one sixth of a wasted inch per keystroke . . . comes out to almost 5 miles of extra finger work I'm doing with this old-fashioned keyboard! (And to think they say writing isn't strenuous.)

You'll find two basic kinds of keyboards:

▶ Switch-based

▶ Capacitive

The switch-based keyboard uses, as you'd imagine, microswitches (very small switches that turn on and off when a key is pressed) for each key on the keyboard. The switches can become dirty. They can be cleaned sometimes, but often it's easier to just replace them. They're sufficiently cheap that when a problem of any magnitude occurs, perhaps you should just throw away the keyboard and buy a new one—I've seen them for as little as $6. Clones tend to use this switch-type approach.

The IBM and AT&T keyboards are capacitive: in the bottom of the keyboard is one large capacitive surface. Each keyboard key pushes a spring, which in turn pushes a paddle. The paddle makes an impression on the capacitive module. The capacitive module sends out signals, which are interpreted by the 8048 microprocessor in the keyboard. It then sends the key's ID, called a *scan code*, to the PC. The PC then figures out what the key means.

Note

The capacitive design sounds more complicated (it is) and is more expensive than its switch-based counterpart, but it consists of one large module rather than a lot of prone-to-fail switches, which means it is less likely to fail. Unfortunately, it limits you a bit as to what you can do to repair the keyboard. Repairing a switch-based keyboard will be less expensive if the problem lies with a switch or key, as opposed to trying to repair a malfunctioning capacitive module. Truthfully, the most you can do to fix sticking keys on most keyboards is to clean them or just get a new keyboard.

System Board/Keyboard Interface

The interface between the keyboard cable and the system unit is the keyboard interface. This is a DIN (or mini-DIN if it's a PS/2) plug that has five (or six, for mini-DIN) pins. Figure 22.3 shows the connector *on the system unit side*. You can get adapters for DIN to mini-DIN, or mini-DIN to DIN, for a few dollars.

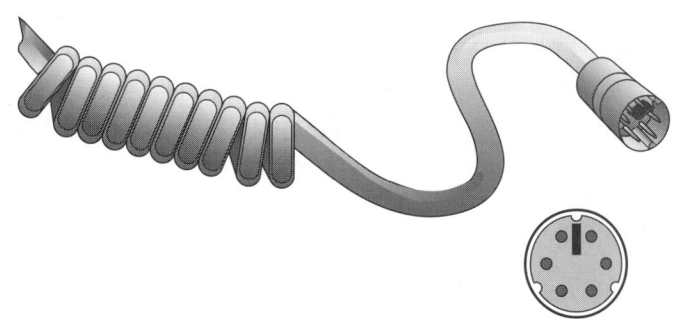

Figure 22.3

An old-style DIN keyboard connector with five pins (top) and a new-style PS/2 mini-DIN keyboard connector with six pins (bottom)

The USB interface is becoming more popular for keyboards, and some models may, in fact, require you to use a USB port unless you have a USB-to-PS/2 adapter to make your USB keyboard compatible with the PS/2 keyboard port. The Microsoft Natural Keyboard and several Microsoft mice are examples of devices that are USB by design, although some versions may include a USB-to-PS/2 adapter with the product. There are several benefits of USB devices, which mostly derive from USB being a newer, faster technology. A USB connection is faster than the other, older I/O ports on your computer such as COM and parallel ports. In addition, a USB device doesn't require special device drivers for it to operate. (A driver is required, but USB drivers cover a wide range of devices, so, for example, a USB pointing device driver covers mice, touchpads, and writing boards.)

You simply plug the device in and it works (ideally, that is). USB devices also require no conflict resolution for competing resources such as COM ports, which require IRQs and other precious system resources to operate.

About the only drawback to using a USB device is backward compatibility. Windows 95 and NT 4, for example, are not USB "aware" and therefore incompatible with USB devices.

Keyboard Connector

The keyboard cable runs from a DIN connector, which attaches the system unit to a flat-jaw type connector inside the keyboard housing. The cable has five wires, and can be checked for continuity quickly with an ohmmeter: disconnect the cable inside the keyboard and test each line. (See the "What To Do When a Keyboard Fails You" section in this chapter for details.) On the other hand, once you're inside the keyboard, then you're kind of making a choice: do you really want to spend four hours playing around inside a keyboard, four hours that may be totally fruitless, or do you just spend a few bucks on a new keyboard?

Keyboard Maintenance

The major aspect of maintenance for keyboards is *abstinence*. Abstinence, that is, from spilling things into the keyboard. The SafeSkin was discussed in Chapter 4, "Avoiding Service: Preventative Maintenance;" this is one protection approach. Another is just to be careful.

Periodically disconnect the keyboard and remove it from the general area of the PC. Pull the keytops off of it (I hope this needn't be said, but I'll say it anyway: be sure you have a similar keyboard nearby so that you can put the key tops back in the right order, unless—heh, heh—this is a keyboard for someone you don't like). Then hold it upside down and blow it clean with compressed air. The keytops aren't that tough to remove—I use one of those "chip puller" tools that come with PC toolkits (recall that they're dangerous to use to actually pull *chips* with), and find it to be *just* the tool for the job. If the keyboard is particularly messy, you can use a spray cleaner. In extremis, you can soak a sticky keyboard in water overnight—but make sure it's completely dry before you try using it.

What To Do When a Keyboard Fails You

Since most keyboards are so inexpensive (with the exception of some ergonomic and wireless keyboards), you may want to view the keyboard as disposable. There are some simple things you can do before throwing out a keyboard, however.

Make Sure It Is Plugged In

On the back of computers that use PS/2-type connectors are two identical ports, the mouse port and the keyboard port. Make sure you've plugged the keyboard into the correct port. You will get an error when turning on the computer if the mouse and/or keyboard are connected to the wrong port.

Make Sure BIOS and Windows See It

When your computer boots up, you should see a message if there is a keyboard failure. Pay close attention, and if you see it, try checking the connection first before you move on to more drastic measures.

If the BIOS doesn't display any errors onscreen (such as `Keyboard not present` or `Keyboard failure`) when you boot up, make sure Windows recognizes your keyboard by checking the Device Manager. You can access the Device Manager in Windows 95/98 by opening the Control Panel and double-clicking the System icon. Select the Device Manager tab from the System Properties dialog box. Your keyboard should be listed in the Keyboard category. If it is listed, make sure it is the proper make and model.

Fix Bent Pins

Check your PS/2-type connector that plugs into the motherboard for any bent or missing pins. This often happens if someone (usually children, although adults can do this too if they aren't paying attention) tries to force the connection in the wrong orientation. What happens is that the pins that aren't lined up with the correct holes on the motherboard connector get bent back as you force the connection. There's simply no place for them to go but sideways. If your pins are bent, carefully straighten them with a pair of slim, needle-nosed pliers. Be careful not to break off the pins as you straighten them.

Connect It to Another Computer

If you're fortunate enough to have more than one computer in your home (most businesses have several), you can try swapping keyboards with a machine that you know isn't suffering keyboard problems. If the keyboard that you suspect is having trouble doesn't work on the "good" computer, you know that keyboard is bad. If the new keyboard doesn't work on the machine you're testing, you may have a faulty keyboard connection on the motherboard. Unfortunately, there's not much you can do about this yourself. If your computer or motherboard is under warranty, or you have a maintenance agreement, you might be able to send your computer to the manufacturer and let them replace the keyboard connection. If you're doing the work yourself, you may have to replace the motherboard.

Check the Keys

If only one key is malfunctioning, check the spring under the key to see whether it springs up and down like a key should. Remove the key by grabbing it with your fingers and pulling up. For the tough keys, fashion a hook from a paper clip or, again, use a chip puller. You will see a spring under the key. Replace the keytop and see whether the problem goes away. If not, try pulling the spring out *just a little*. Then replace the keytop.

Some keyboards use rubber cups instead of springs. Either way, the cup or spring is designed to keep the keys from being "on" all the time.

Test Pin Voltages

Voltage between all pins and pin 4 should be in the range of 2–5.5 volts DC. If any of these voltages are wrong, the problem probably lies in the PC—the system board in particular. If they're okay, the problem is probably in the keyboard. Note that the pins are not numbered consecutively for either a DIN or a mini-DIN.

If you hold a DIN so that the pins are at the top and count from left to right, the pins are numbered 1, 4, 2 , 5, and 3; the number 2 pin is at the top center point. Holding a mini-DIN with the single groove in the connector at the top, and starting from the bottom left and moving clockwise, the pins are numbered 1, 3, 5, 6, 4, and 2; the groove is between pins 5 and 6. Check the keyboard cable next.

Check the Cable Continuity

Next, test continuity of the cable. Turn the keyboard upside down so that the cable is coming out of the back of the keyboard, to the right. Remove the two screws. The bottom plate will swing back and up for removal.

You will now see that the cable splits to a single wire, which is grounded to the bottom plate and a cable with a flat-jaw connector. Push apart the jaws of the connector to release. You can then use an ohmmeter to test each of the five wires for continuity. An ohmmeter is a device that electricians (and computer technicians) use to test electrical circuits for power and detect short-circuits.

Completely Disassemble It

Not recommended for the fainthearted. You've got a good chance of making things even worse, so don't do it unless there's no other hope.

Warning

This step will take about four hours once you've taken the keyboard apart, put it back together wrong, figured out what you did wrong, taken it apart again, accidentally spilled all the pieces on the floor, etc., and then finally managed to reassemble the thing.

Remove the main assembly from the keyboard case. With a vise, or C-clamps, set up a support for the keyboard assembly on the sides. If you don't connect the clamps to the sides, you're in for a surprise when you remove the back metal plate. (Remember those springs on each paddle?)

Alternatively, you can make your life easier by removing all the keytops. But, again, don't do it unless you've got another keyboard around that you can use as a guide to replacing the keytops.

Note

One way to remember which keys go where is to put the keyboard (keys facing down) on a photocopier and make a picture of the keys.

A printed circuit board with capacitive pads on it is held against a metal plate by 10 metal tabs—five above, five below—and a hex screw. You must use pliers to unbend the tabs enough to remove the plate. Position the assembly so that the plate is on top (not the printed circuit board), then remove the metal plate.

The plate has been holding dozens of plastic paddles against the printed circuit card, one for each key. These are small, flat, easily-broken pieces of plastic shaped like the outline of a castle turret, or the rook piece in chess. What you are looking for is a broken paddle. Replace any broken paddles and then put the metal plate back on.

The other reason to attempt this is if you've poured hot coffee into the keyboard. Very carefully remove all the paddles and clean them, as well as the bracket that they sit in. Then use alcohol to clean the capacitive PC board. Then reassemble and pray. I *have* seen this work, but only once.

Putting the metal plate back on is a bit difficult. Position it correctly, then use clamps to hold one side together while you bend the tabs on the other side into place. Again, it is easy to damage paddles at this point. Where do you get replacement paddles? No one that I know of sells them. Get them from the first keyboard that dies: it's good for 101 replacement paddles.

Replace the Keyboard

If you've gotten this far and have had no luck, don't despair. Many keyboard problems can't be fixed, and the things aren't that expensive anyway.

Keytronics, Datadesk, and Northgate make good replacement keyboards. Datadesk's are a bit cheaper, and they have one that is programmable. This means that you can move that annoying Esc key somewhere else, set up your keyboard as a Dvorak keyboard, and the like.

Note

The Dvorak keyboard has all the keys in different places than the traditional keyboard layout, which is derived from the typewriter and created in the 1870s. The Dvorak is supposed to make typing easier and faster.

Keytronics offers a keyboard with an in-line bar code reader. Other software enables you to print bar codes with a dot matrix or laser printer. One firm I know of uses bar codes at the top of their document-tracking forms so that secretaries don't have to key (and sometimes miskey) a 12-digit document-tracking ID every time they have to update the document-tracking database.

Several companies are now offering "broken" keyboards designed to lower hand and tendon stress, as I said earlier. I've used the Microsoft Natural Keyboard, and if you're looking for advice, I'd suggest that you find someone with one of these and borrow it for a while before you buy it. It definitely feels easier on most of my hand, but my left index finger has to do enough reaching that sometimes it feels like it's going to separate from the rest of my hand.

Mouse Types and Components

Mice are in some ways simpler devices than keyboards; after all, most have only two or three buttons and maybe a wheel as compared to the average keyboard's 101 keys. (Some new mice do have up to six buttons.) But all mice have some moving parts that can go seriously wrong.

Mouse Types

Basically, mice work in this way: you move them, they figure out somehow how much you've moved them, and then they transmit that information to the computer. The "how they figure out how much you moved them" and the "transmit the data to the computer" parts are how mice vary.

Buttons and Wheels

All mice have at least two buttons: left and right. You can't go wrong choosing a two-button mouse, but a number of more modern mice have extra buttons and wheels to make scrolling, zooming, and selecting much easier. Microsoft's IntelliMouse Explorer (see Figure 22.4) has five programmable buttons that can be used with standard programs and Internet-related applications; it also has a wheel (located between the left and right mouse buttons) that zooms in and out or scrolls.

Figure 22.4

Microsoft
IntelliMouse Explorer

Mouse Positioning Methods

Most mice are mechanical, meaning that they use some mechanical method for detecting motion. On most mice, the primary mechanical part is a ball on the bottom of the mouse. Take the mouse apart (remove the retaining ring, turn the mouse over, and the ball falls out, generally rolling under something), and you'll see three little wheels that turn when the ball moves against them.

Two of those wheels are monitored electronically; when they turn, they transmit how much they turned to the computer. The two wheels are perpendicular to one another, so one tracks X-axis motion and one tracks Y-axis motion. The third wheel just balances the first two.

Another, less common, mechanical mouse manufactured by Rockwell uses two wheels that are on the outside of the mouse, They are positioned horizontally and are tilted slightly to detect the X and Y movement. These mice are totally sealed and never need cleaning. Unfortunately, they are somewhat difficult to find.

The third kind of positioning mechanism is in the optical mouse. This has no moving parts. The mouse has optical sensors on the bottom of it. As you move the mouse across a special mouse pad with a grid, its sensors see the grid lines running across the pad and report them to the PC.

Newer optical mice, most notably from Microsoft, require no special grid or mouse pad of any kind. I recently purchased one for my laptop and simply love it. I can use the laptop downstairs while sitting on my living room couch and use the couch as a mouse pad, or travel in the car and use my leg.

The Microsoft optical mice operate by using a red LED to take 1500 snapshots per second of the surface below it. By comparing the images dynamically, they can determine speed, direction, and distance.

Note

The new Microsoft optical mice are a boon to gamers. In addition to having precise positioning, they are all USB mice. Normal mice operate at 40MHz (the frequency their position is updated by Windows) due to the interface, but USB mice operate at 120MHz. With frame rates of some games shooting well over 40MHz, having a mouse that can keep up with your game is a must.

Trackballs

Trackballs are pointing devices that have the ball (normally located underneath and inside of a mouse) on the top of the unit. Instead of moving a mouse around, you move the trackball with your finger. It's just like the trackballs on old arcade machines such as Atari's Missile Command.

Many people prefer trackballs to standard mice because you have fine control over the position of the cursor and don't have to move anything around on your desktop. Trackballs are ideal for certain professions, such as architects and graphic artists, who need a high degree of pointing precision as they work. Trackballs are also an attractive alternative for young children and people with certain disabilities because they often find them easier to use than mice. Some laptops even use this technology as their primary pointing device.

Mouse Interfaces

Most mice connect to a PC via a serial port. Some use a USB connection or proprietary interface.

There have been several proprietary mouse interfaces over the years, but the most common are the Microsoft bus mouse interface and the IBM PS/2-type interface, which is very like yet another Microsoft interface, the InPort interface. All three interfaces use a mini-DIN connector as a plug.

The Microsoft bus mouse interface is a bit brain damaged in that it works only with interrupts 2, 3, 4, or 5. The PS/2-type interface is typically integrated into a motherboard—I see it on a lot of laptops—and it's usually hard-wired to IRQ12.

Mouse Cleaning

On a mechanical mouse, the little wheels get gunk stuck to them or hair wrapped around them, so you must clean them. Just remove the mouse ball and examine the wheels. I've used rubbing alcohol, a toothpick, and a cotton swab to get the gunk off the wheels. You may also need to clean the ball with a bit of alcohol. Clean the mouse about twice a year— or more if your desk is covered with dirt or dust, as dirt and dust are just gunk in its fetal stages.

On an optical mouse, clean the sensors; you can often just polish them with a soft cloth. Keep the mouse pad clean as well so that the grid lines are clearly visible to the sensors.

For optical mice that do not require special mouse pads, simply clean the exterior of the mouse with a soft cloth.

What To Do When Your Mouse Fails You

You can troubleshoot a mouse by following these steps:

1. First, make sure your mouse is plugged in securely.

2. Next, check the driver. Is the mouse driver set up correctly? Is it there in the first place?

3. Clean the mouse and shake any debris off of the mouse pad.

4. Check the interface at the end of your mouse cable and at the motherboard, whether it is USB, PS/2, or the serial port. See if there are any obvious problems such as bent pins (for PS/2 and serial port mice only) that can be straightened.

5. Ensure that Windows recognizes the mouse and it is listed in the Device Manager as properly installed.

If all this fails, and your computer is not the culprit, you'll need to replace your mouse. Simple mice are very inexpensive, but if you've got a real fancy mouse you might have to pay upward of $50 to $75.

Wireless Input Devices

This chapter discussed the issues involved with using cabled mice and keyboards. However, interest in wireless input devices has been picking up. What is there to know about these devices?

They work like this: you get a receiver with the device (mouse or keyboard) that plugs into your computer, usually through the keyboard port. This cabled receiver then sits on top of your monitor or anywhere else handy that's within 45 degrees of the line of sight with the transmitter on your keyboard.

Most of these devices use infrared frequencies to transmit data, meaning that they've got high bandwidth (not really an issue with something that transmits as little data as a keyboard or mouse does) and are pretty much immune to outside interference. Use a cordless telephone or other infrared devices (such as a TV remote control) in the same room, and it will have no effect at all.

Radio-controlled wireless keyboards are another matter. One such device operates at the 49MHz frequency, about where older cordless telephones operate (most new cordless phones operate in the 900MHz range). This means that if you use both devices at once, then they'll interfere with each other. On the other hand, if you can get around the interference problem, radio waves are looser and thus much more flexible than infrared waves. If you've ever used a CB radio, you'll know that you don't have to be within the line of sight to transmit data via radio. The radio-controlled keyboards have a range of about 30 feet under optimal conditions, as opposed to 15 feet for most infrared devices. (Some manufactures claim a larger distance, but as you probably know from operating a TV remote-control device, it's easier to point accurately from a short distance than from 20 feet away.)

Generally speaking, wireless devices are more expensive than wired devices, and input devices are no exception. Although one manufacturer's advertising extols wireless keyboards as a wonderful way to reduce cabling needs, the lack of one or two cables doesn't make up the price difference. You can find the cheapest keyboards for under $20, and the expensive wireless models are running in the $70 range.

If you're just interested in typing at a desk, I'd stick with the standard cabled keyboards. They're cheaper, you don't have to point them or keep the transmitter and receivers dust-free (a thick layer of dust causes a keyboard to stop working), and they're simple to use.

Troubleshooting Recap

Here's a summary of troubleshooting tips for your keyboard:

▶ Make sure that the keyboard is plugged in and the connection is secure.

◗ Ensure that there are no BIOS warnings at bootup and that Windows recognizes the keyboard.

◗ Check the cable connector for any bent or missing pins.

◗ Swap the keyboard you suspect is malfunctioning with one that you are sure works to see if the problem lies with the computer and not the keyboard.

◗ Check the keys for proper functionality. They should all spring back to their original state when you press and release them.

◗ Test pin voltages on the keyboard cable.

◗ Check for cable continuity within the keyboard housing.

◗ Disassemble the keyboard and check all internal parts.

◗ Replace the keyboard if none of the above works and your computer is not at fault.

And here are a few things to try when your mouse isn't working correctly:

◗ Ensure that the mouse is plugged in securely.

◗ Check the mouse driver in Windows to make sure it's correctly installed.

◗ Clean your mouse to remove built-up "gunk."

◗ Check for bent pins on the cable.

◗ Replace your mouse if nothing else works.

23

Video Adapters and Displays

INTRODUCTION

The display on a computer is the primary output device. Because of that, your personal comfort when using a PC is wrapped up in the display, and video taste tends to be a personal kind of thing. What's behind the screen? How can you choose the best equipment for you? And how much can you fix when it fails?

This chapter will help you select and install a video card. We'll also take a look at the parts of a video board, as well as their image resolution, color depth, vertical frequency, and 3D capability.

Shopping for a Video Card

1. Decide what your needs are—business, entertainment, gaming, or general purpose.

2. Budget yourself. Today's prices range from under $50 for a low-end VGA card to around $300 for a high-end consumer 3D card.

3. Pick your favorite 3D API (application programming interface), if necessary for gaming. Many games support multiple APIs (DirectX, OpenGL, and Glide) but some will specialize in one over the others. Check to see what the requirements are of the games you have or want to buy, and look for a card that supports those APIs.

4. Choose a manufacturer such as Creative Labs, Diamond Multimedia, or Matrox. (Contact information on these manufacturers can be found in the Vendor's Guide on CD #2.) Check out online or magazine reviews of different cards to see how they match up.

5. Decide on an AGP (Advanced Graphics Port) or PCI bus card. This is dependent on your motherboard. Many older PCs do not have AGP. If you have an AGP slot, choose that type of card for better performance.

6. It's usually best to get the most memory you can afford, although general purpose and business computing video memory needs are less demanding.

Installing a New Video Card

Be Prepared

Before you start, there are some things you may need on hand. These include:

> ▶ A container for screws

> ▶ The manual for your computer

1. Begin with a clear tabletop so you have room to work.

2. Make sure your computer and peripherals are turned off, and ground yourself by touching something metallic.

3. Unplug all the connecting cables, including the power.

4. Remove the screws that hold the outer case of the computer, put them in your container, and carefully remove the case.

5. If you are replacing an old video card, find the old card inside your computer and remove the screw that attaches it to the computer chassis.

Note

If you have a system with on-board video circuitry (you can tell if you do because the monitor will plug into the case of your computer rather than to an expansion card), you must disable the on-board video system before an add-on card will work. This usually involves moving a jumper on your mother-board. Your computer's manual should have a jumper diagram that will tell you how to do this.

6. Gently but firmly, ease the old video card out of the slot on the motherboard and remove the card from your computer.

7. Insert the new card into an open, compatible slot (AGP, PCI, or ISA) on your motherboard.

   ▶ If the slot is the same as the card you just took out, you can insert the new card into the slot you just vacated on your motherboard.

   or

   ▶ If your new card requires a different slot, you may need to remove a metal plate that covers an expansion card opening at the back of your computer. Unscrew the plate, remove it, and cover the opening that's left by the card you removed.

8. Mount the card securely by screwing the video card's rear plate into the computer's chassis.

9. Put the cover back on your computer and screw it on.

10. Reattach all the external cables.

11. Turn your computer and peripherals back on.

12. If your system and video card are Plug-and-Play compatible, when Windows boots up it should install the proper drivers for your card. You should have the disks or CD-ROM that came with the card handy at this stage. If Windows fails to detect your new video card, you should install the drivers manually. Either way, read through the manual that came with the video card for instructions on how to ensure the drivers are installed correctly.

VISUAL UPGRADE

Installing a New Video Card

1 Never handle a circuit board by its edge connector; oils from your fingers can cause connectivity problems.

Internal connector   Expandable memory

Processor

2 Most video cards have expandable memory, a processor, and an internal connector.

3 The internal connector on a video card is called a feature connector; most commonly it is used to connect a television tuner or other video device to the computer's video card.

Feature connector

4 A video card's 15-pin D-shell connector is the standard plug for all computer video monitors.

5 Align the video card with the slot and press it down until it clicks into place.

6 Mount the card securely by screwing the video card's rear plate into the computer's chassis.

How a Video Board Works

The parts of the board that you must understand in order to see how video works and how it can be tuned up include:

◗ The system CPU

◗ The system bus and its interface to the video board

◗ The video memory on the video board

◗ The video imaging chip on the video board

◗ The Digital-to-Analog Converter on the video board

Consider this: how does the CPU get an image onto the computer's display? I'll start from the CPU and end up at the monitor in this explanation.

A basic video board looks like the one shown in Figure 23.1.

RAM: Receives and stores image data from CPU

ROM: Contains VGA BIOS

Image Data

Video processor: Scans RAM for data and converts to digital image

Digital-to-analog converter (DAC): Converts digital image and sends it out the DB-15 connector to the monitor

Figure 23.1

An AGP video board

The CPU and Video Images

The primary objective of a video board is to take information from the CPU and display it on a monitor. When a program wants to display data, it does so by telling the CPU to store data in the video board. Exactly *how* a CPU does that varies, as there are two basic kinds of video boards: dumb frame buffers and coprocessor/ accelerator boards. I'll take up those two types in a bit, but for now just understand that the CPU controls the video board.

What that implies, for anyone trying to speed up a video subsystem, is that a faster CPU will make for faster video, all other things being equal.

The System Bus

Recall from Chapter 6, "Installing New Circuit Boards (without Creating New Problems)," that in a system with an ISA bus, any board in a PC runs at a mere 8MHz. Spend all the money you like for a fast Pentium III, but anything in an ISA (or EISA, for that matter) slot runs at 8MHz. Whenever Windows manipulates the video board, your "screamer" whispers at 8MHz.

The CPU is connected to the video board through the system's bus. The speed of that bus can be a constraint on how fast the video system can update. What's the fastest rate at which data might be zapped into a video board? Well, the video system need not update the picture on the screen more often than 72 times per second, as you can't perceive images faster than that. High quality video boards have 32MB of RAM on them, so the maximum amount of data that a video board might have to work with would be 72×32, or 2304MB per second. The PCI bus runs at 33MHz and is 32 bits wide, so the maximum video data throughput for PCI video cards is 133MB per second. What does all that mean? Simply this: the faster your bus interface, the better for your video board. That suggests that when you buy a video board, you should buy a video board that uses an AGP bus, provided you have a motherboard that is AGP-compatible. AGP runs at 66MHz and is 64 bits wide, providing a maximum video data throughput of 528MB per second!

Aside from its increased speed, the most distinguishing characteristics of an AGP bus are that it is a dedicated video bus and that an AGP video card can use system memory as an extension of its own local frame buffer memory. AGP 4X, the latest innovation in video bus subsystems, is able to move data between the video card and your CPU at double the rate of today's standard AGP 2X speeds, to around 1GB per second.

In fact, the peripheral that probably benefits the most from a fast bus is the video board. How important is a local bus? Well, a video card in a standard ISA bus slot can only transfer data 16 bits at a time, at 8MHz. That's only 16MB per second. A video card sitting in an AGP slot can potentially transfer video data 33 times faster!

The Video Memory

The video image is then stored in the video memory. As with all memory, faster is better and more is better. (Why is more better? I'll discuss video resolution and color depth later, but the answer is, briefly: the more dots you want to put on your screen and the more colors that you want to be able to use for them, the more memory your video board needs.) But video memory has some special needs in that it is usually addressed in blocks, and it is addressed simultaneously by several chips—in particular, the CPU and the video imaging chip.

Dual Ported Memory: VRAM

Let's look at that second characteristic first. Ordinarily, a RAM chip is addressed by the CPU and no other chip, unless there's a DMA operation going on—and when that happens, the CPU doesn't access the memory.

In contrast, memory on a video chip has no choice but to talk to two chips at the same time; the CPU shovels image data into the video memory, and the imaging chip pulls it out. On video boards with normal RAM, this presents a performance problem, as normal RAM can only address one chip at a time. Video boards with normal RAM just make the CPU and the imaging chip take turns, slowing things down.

Some video boards use a special kind of memory originally called Dual Ported RAM, but which most people call VRAM, for Video RAM. There's nothing intrinsically video-ish about this RAM; it's just that its most logical application is in video boards.

Dual-Ported, Block-Addressable Memory: WRAM

But another thing about memory is its blocky nature. Modern graphical user interfaces tend to address memory in large blocks, rather than on a byte-by-byte basis. For example, to draw a colored background, the CPU must say to a whole large block of memory, "store value X," where X is the value that sets the desired background color. A CPU does that by arduously working on several locations one at a time.

Window RAM (WRAM) makes that task easier by allowing blocks, or "windows," of memory to be addressed in just a few commands. WRAM is a bit more expensive, but it's a good buy in video boards.

Newer Video Memory: MDRAM, SGRAM, and DDR

Multibank DRAM (MDRAM) is aimed at the cost-conscious user who still wants good performance. MDRAM allows you to add memory in 32KB chunks, which lets you calculate exactly how much you need and install just that much. You therefore aren't wasting money on excess video memory that you may not need. MDRAM is much faster than VRAM and WRAM.

Synchronous Graphics RAM (SGRAM) operates at higher speeds than other video memory. It is capable of operating at speeds between 66MHz and 80MHz.

Double Data Rate RAM (DDR SDRAM) doesn't increase the memory clock speed, but it does move twice as much memory per clock cycle, thereby doubling the rate at which video data is moved.

Video Aperture

Some high-performance video accelerators (I'll discuss accelerators in a few pages) get their speed by mapping their video memory right into the computer's memory address space. This video is called the *video aperture*, and you've got to understand it to solve some configuration problems.

Let's see how a video board uses memory. In graphics mode, an EGA, VGA, or newer video board only uses the addresses between 640KB and 704KB for video memory. But think for a moment, and you'll see that this doesn't seem to make sense. From 640KB to 704KB is just 64KB, and even a simple VGA board has 256KB of RAM on it. Super VGAs can have 1 to 16 or more *megabytes* of RAM on them. How does all that RAM fit into a 64KB address space?

Simple: a little bit at a time.

The VGA uses its 256KB of RAM within a 64KB constraint by taking the 256KB and chopping it up into *four* 64KB-sized areas. Most of the video memory is invisible to the CPU at any instant in time. To update the VGA, a VGA-aware program first asks the VGA to make the first 64KB area visible to the CPU. The 64KB is defined to describe the red part of the image. Once the red 64KB is made visible to the CPU—*paged in* is the correct term—then the VGA-aware program can modify the red part of the VGA image. The red 64KB—the *red page*—is then paged out, and the next 64KB—the green page—is paged in and modified. The same is done for the third page (the blue page) and the fourth page (the intensity page).

Stop and consider what had to happen just to update a single VGA screen: move in the red page, modify it, and move it out; then move in the green page, modify it, and move it out; then move in the blue page, modify it, and move it out; and, finally, move in the intensity page, modify it, and move it out. That's a lot of work. The reason so much work must be done is because of the severe memory address constraints of DOS-based programs, which in general must live in the bottom 1024KB of PC memory.

Now think about what happens with a super VGA board with 2MB of RAM. If the super VGA board is built like most super VGA boards, the 64KB-page approach is still used. But 2MB is, however, *32 different 64KB pages*. That means that a super VGA video driver for a 2MB video board must page in and out 32 different pages in order to update the video screen just once. *Now* it should be obvious why high-resolution super VGA screens can be so terribly slow.

Some super VGA boards take a totally different approach. They reason that they are not being used by DOS-based programs but by

Windows programs. Windows can easily rise above the 1024KB address range, so some super VGA boards place the whole 2MB of RAM right into the PC's address space, just like the RAM that the system uses to run programs. The value of this approach is that now the video RAM can be updated in a straightforward, *fast* way, without having to wait around for 64KB-sized blocks to be paged around. The range of addresses used for this 2MB block of memory is called the *video aperture*.

Mapping video memory right into extended memory is a good thing, in general, as it significantly speeds up video operations. But there's one catch. As you've learned in several places in this book, you can't have two things located at the same address. If the video RAM is directly mapped into the PC's extended memory address space, then you've got to be careful that it doesn't end up in the same address as some of the PC's installed extended memory. For example, if your PC has 8MB of memory, be sure to put the video aperture above 8MB so that it will not conflict with your system memory.

Video aperture is usually an *option*; you can usually choose to just use the standard 64KB-at-address-640KB-page approach. While disabling video aperture and using the small page approach will slow you down, it might be the only way to get a system to work. IBM's accelerator board, the Extended Graphics Array (XGA), will optionally allow you to set its 2MB of video RAM to a video aperture—*but* that aperture must be somewhere in the bottom 16MB of memory addresses. That's a shame, as many Windows "power users" will have at least 32MB of system RAM. The video aperture must appear in the bottom 16MB of addresses, but those addresses are already filled with RAM, so the XGA user would have to disable video aperture. That's not a problem for *every* high performance board user, however. For example, the ATI mach32 system can use any address in the first four *gigabytes*—and I somehow suspect that before any of us puts 4GB on a computer, there will be some quite significant changes in video.

The bottom line is that you should do the following:

▶ Look for video aperture as an option for high performance video systems.

▶ Make sure that the video aperture can appear *anywhere* in the address range of 0GB–4GB.

▶ When experiencing video troubles, check to see if the manufacturer has already enabled the video aperture and perhaps accidentally addressed it on top of some system RAM. (I've seen that happen with an XGA system sold with 16MB of RAM and the XGA RAM addressed at the 8MB level. The system kept crashing Windows until the video aperture was disabled.)

The Video Imaging Chip

Once the image is in the video RAM, that image must be converted into a digital video image format. That's done by the "display chip," "video chip," or "imaging chip," depending on who's talking about it. Over the years, there have been many different imaging chips. Nowadays, however, the main question to answer when looking at video chips is this: is it a dumb frame buffer or an accelerator/coprocessor of some kind?

Frame Buffer Chips

Most video chips in the PC world before 1992 were frame buffers. *Frame buffer* means that the board is populated with memory chips, as you've just learned, and the memory chips hold an image that closely resembles what shows up on the screen. Each dot (*pixel*) on the screen has a corresponding location on the video memory. Set it to one numeric value, and one color appears on the pixel. Another value, and another color appears in its place.

The problem with frame buffers is that every one of those pixels must be arranged by the CPU. That can be a lot of work for one CPU—which is where accelerators and coprocessors come in.

Smarter Video Chips

Newer video chips take some of the burden off the main processor and put it on themselves. These kinds of chips are coprocessors called *video accelerators*.

Back in Chapter 3, "Inside the PC: Pieces of the Picture," you learned about numeric coprocessors, special-purpose CPUs that are particularly good at a small group of jobs.

Video coprocessors are just another kind of special-purpose CPU. As you'd expect, they're designed to shove pixels around quickly. Your math coprocessor is just a single chip, but video coprocessors are generally entire circuit boards. Coprocessors can be very fast, but unfortunately they're also expensive. It's not unusual to have to spend over $1000 on a coprocessor.

Accelerators typically include VGA circuitry on-board; coprocessors typically complement a VGA, requiring that you have both a VGA board and a coprocessor in your system. Coprocessors require that you link them to a normal video board via a "feature connector," a pin header or edge connector that you'll commonly see on video boards.

Related to a coprocessor is a less expensive alternative called an *accelerator.* The difference is that a coprocessor is a full-fledged microprocessor that's programmable to do just about any task that the main CPU can do. An accelerator, on the other hand, is not a general-purpose CPU, but rather a special-purpose chip that knows how to do a few particular graphical tasks quickly. Most accelerators are good at something called *bit blitting.* As you probably know, a term commonly used by GUI users for pictures is *bitmaps.* Windows wallpapers are bitmaps, screen captures are bitmaps, and any picture created with Paintbrush is a bitmap. Much of what slows Windows down is placing bitmaps on the screen, either transferring them from memory to screen, or moving them from one part of the screen to another part of the screen. Moving a bitmap is technically referred to as a *bitmap block transfer,* which is abbreviated *bitblt.* A number of inexpensive Windows accelerators are just VGA boards with a bitblitter chip on-board. The large number of bitblt operations that Windows does makes this combination of VGA and hardware bitblt support very cost-effective. Accelerators may also know how to build simple geometric shapes like lines or circles.

The fact that accelerators are a one-board approach in contrast to the video-board-and-coprocessor approach may make an accelerator a better buy. It's certainly a cheaper option, but be aware that an accelerator board's dual nature means that it has both generic VGA circuitry and accelerator circuitry, and the two circuits are unrelated. It's quite common to see incredibly fast accelerator chips paired with painfully slow VGA circuits, and the result is that running Windows is quite fast (the accelerator is at work) but that games run very poorly, as the slower VGA circuit is now active. When looking at benchmark results for an accelerator, look for times for both the VGA circuit and the accelerator.

Digital-to-Analog Converter (DAC)

The video board's work is almost done; the digital image has been produced by the imaging chip. Only one more thing to do—convert the image from digital to analog. That's done with a special chip called the Digital-to-Analog Converter, or DAC.

About all there is to say about the DAC is that it comes in varying abilities to produce color. The 15-bit DAC produces 32,768 colors; the 16-bit DAC produces 65,536 colors; and the 18-bit DAC produces 262,144 colors. The 24-bit and 30-bit DACs produce 16 million and 1 billion colors, respectively.

You usually can't upgrade DACs; whatever your vendor built in is what you're stuck with.

Video Board Characteristics

Now that you know the parts of a video board, how do you choose between video boards? RAM type, bus attachment, and video chip are all important, but so are image resolution, color depth, vertical frequency, and 3D capability. You'll learn about those in this section.

Note

If your needs are more specialized than for general computing or playing games, look for a video board that has a TV-out or digital flat-panel connection, video capture, or TV-tuner capabilities. Others support dual-monitor connections and may come with DVD software.

Resolution and Colors

Resolution on a video display is the number of horizontal and vertical dots that make up the picture. For example, the most basic resolution today is 640×480, which means that the image is 640 dots wide by 480 dots high. Most VGA boards nowadays are super VGA boards, even the cheap clones. You can pick up a no-name VGA board for about \$15–\$30, and in addition to standard VGA, it will probably support 800×600 mode. The more expensive VGA boards (\$200–\$300) will support at least 1024×768 and usually 1280×1024 or higher. More resolution means more dots on the screen, which means that the video board needs more memory.

A video board's memory requirements are determined by two things: its resolution and the number of colors that it can display. For instance, the basic VGA can display a resolution of 320×200 with 256 colors, but when in the higher 640×480 resolution, it can only display 16 colors. That has nothing to do with the constraints of the monitor, or even of the VGA board, *except* for the amount of memory on the board. A normal VGA comes with 256KB right on the board. Table 23.1 shows a summary of resolutions available for common video boards throughout PC history.

TABLE 23.1 Video Board Resolutions

Board Type	Resolutions Supported	Colors Supported
Color Graphics Array (CGA)	320×200 640×200	4 2
Enhanced Graphics Array (EGA)	CGA resolutions 640×350	16
Video Graphics Array (VGA)	CGA and EGA 320×200 640×480	256 16
Super VGA	CGA, EGA, VGA $640 \times 480, 800 \times 600, 832 \times 624,$ $1024 \times 768, 1152 \times 870, 1280 \times 1024,$ $1360 \times 1024, 1600 \times 1200$	256, 32K, 64K, or 16 million+ (ranges from 4-bit to 32-bit color)

Resolutions like 1024 × 768 with 256 colors obviously require more memory—that's why you see ads for VGA cards with an option for 256KB, 512KB, or 1024KB on the board. If all you're doing is regular old VGA, you need only 256KB—there's no point in spending the extra money for 512KB or 1024KB. Table 23.2 shows the amount of memory that a video board needs for some sample resolution/color combinations.

Note

Note that cards can come with as much as 64MB of video RAM built-in, such as #9's 64MB digital video card especially built for SGI's 1600 × 1024 LCD monitor. Most PCI and AGP cards ship with 8–16MB of video RAM.

TABLE 23.2 Memory Required at Various Color Depths

VGA & Apple 13"—640 x 480

Resolution and Color Depth	Minimum Memory Required
AT 16 colors (4-bit color)	256KB
AT 256 colors (8-bit color)	512KB
AT 32K colors (15-bit color)	1MB
AT 65K colors (Thousands) 16-bit color	1MB
AT 16.7M colors (24-bit color) true color	1MB

Super VGA (SVGA)—800 x 600

Resolution and Color Depth	Minimum Memory Required
AT 16 colors (4-bit color)	256KB
AT 256 colors (8-bit color)	512KB
AT 32K colors (15-bit color)	1MB
AT 65K colors (Thousands) 16-bit color	1MB
AT 16.7M colors (24-bit color) true color	1MB

TABLE 23.2 Memory Required at Various Color Depths (continued)

Nonstandard SVGA—832 x 624

Resolution and Color Depth	Minimum Memory Required
AT 16 colors (4-bit color)	512KB
AT 256 colors (8-bit color)	1MB
AT 32K colors (15-bit color)	1MB
AT 65K colors (Thousands) 16-bit color	1.5MB
AT 16.7M colors (24-bit color) true color	2MB

Extended SVGA (XGA)—1024 x 768

Resolution and Color Depth	Minimum Memory Required
AT 16 colors (4-bit color)	512KB
AT 256 colors (8-bit color)	1MB
AT 32K colors (15-bit color)	1.5MB
AT 65K colors (Thousands) 16-bit color	2MB
AT 16.7M colors (24-bit color) true color	2.5MB

Nonstandard XGA—1152 x 870

Resolution and Color Depth	Minimum Memory Required
AT 16 colors (4-bit color)	512KB
AT 256 colors (8-bit color)	1.5MB
AT 32K colors (15-bit color)	2MB
AT 65K colors (Thousands) 16-bit color	2.5MB
AT 16.7M colors (24-bit color) true color	3.5MB

1280 x 1024

Resolution and Color Depth	Minimum Memory Required
AT 16 colors (4-bit color)	1MB
AT 256 colors (8-bit color)	1.5MB
AT 32K colors (15-bit color)	2.5MB
AT 65K colors (Thousands) 16-bit color	3MB
AT 16.7M colors (24-bit color) true color	4MB

Continued on next page

TABLE 23.2 Memory Required at Various Color Depths (continued)

1360 x 1024

Resolution and Color Depth	Minimum Memory Required
AT 16 colors (4-bit color)	1MB
AT 256 colors (8- bit color)	1.5MB
AT 32KB colors (15- bit color)	3MB
AT 65KB colors (Thousands) 16- bit color	3MB
AT 16.7M colors (24-bit color) true color	4.5MB

1600 x 1200

Resolution and Color Depth	Minimum Memory Required
AT 16 color s (4-bit color)	1MB
AT 256 colors (8-bit color)	2MB
AT 32KB colors (15-bit color)	4MB
AT 65KB colors (Thousands) 16-bit color	4MB
AT 16.7M colors (24-bit color) true color	6MB

Vertical Scan Frequencies: Interlacing and 72Hz

Your video monitor displays information by projecting a narrow beam of electrons onto a phosphor-covered glass panel—your monitor screen. Wherever the beam hits, the phosphor becomes excited ("excited" here is a relative term) and the phosphor lights up for brief period of time (see, excitement *is* relative here), then fades out. Because it fades very quickly—in hundredths of seconds—the electron beam must retrace its path constantly to keep the image on the screen. How often must it travel across the screen? Well, the electron beam in the back of a video monitor must repaint or "refresh" the screen at least 60 times per second, or your eye will probably perceive flicker. (Why "probably"? Hang on for a sentence or two.) And that brings me to a story about the IBM 8514 video system.

Interlacing and the 8514

The 8514 was an early IBM high-resolution (1024 × 768) video system; as a matter of fact, the 8514 video system is important because it was the first mass-market PC-based video system to support a resolution of 1024 × 768. But, in order to save money on the monitor, IBM cut a corner on the system. Now, in order to get high-resolution images, you need a high-quality (read: expensive) monitor. One way to get higher resolution out of a cheaper screen is to refresh it less often. The 8514 does not refresh 60 times per second, but rather at 43 times per second.

This isn't the first time we've seen this less-than-60-refreshes-per-second approach to high resolution; it's called *interlacing*. What was significant was that *IBM* did it, so the practice of interlacing became acceptable.

But, you see interlacing is *not* acceptable, at least not from a quality standpoint. The result of interlacing is a flickering screen and eye-strain headaches. That's why you've got to be careful when buying a system with 1024 × 768 resolution. Check that it's *non*interlaced.

By the way, if you do have an interlaced monitor, there may be a few things that you can do to reduce the effects of flicker. Several factors affect flicker—that's why I said "probably" a few sentences back. First, you see flicker better with your peripheral vision, because the center of your vision is built around low-resolution color receptors called cones on your retina. Surrounding the cones are high-resolution monochromatic receptors called rods.

Peripheral vision images fall on the rods. Sailors know this because when searching for a ship on the horizon, they don't look right at the horizon—they look below it, so the horizon falls on the high-resolution rods. In any case, the closer you are to your monitor, the more of its image falls on the cones, which are less flicker-prone. You can demonstrate this with any monitor. Stand so that your monitor is about 60 to 80 degrees to your left: if the direction you're facing is 12 o'clock, the monitor should be at about 10 o'clock. Hold a piece of paper in front of you and read the text on it. You'll notice that you're seeing the monitor out of the corner of your eye, and that it's flashing. This also suggests that you should buy a small monitor, as a large image will end up falling more on your rods; but 1024×768 on a 12-inch screen is, well, suboptimal. Glare screens will also reduce flicker. Another antiflicker tactic is to keep your room bright. When the ambient light is bright, your pupils contract, which has the side effect of reducing the amount of light that gets to the peripheral rods. You'll also find that certain color combinations exaggerate the flicker—black and white is one problem combination—so play around with the Windows colors to make the screen more readable.

The Benefits of Fast Vertical Refresh Rates

Since I've brought up the subject of video with low refresh rates, it's worthwhile looking at the opposite end of the spectrum—video systems that refresh at more than 60 screens per second. The more common use of larger monitors means that more people notice flicker on normal 60Hz VGA. Furthermore, people nowadays use their computers all day, so anyone who has even the slightest sensitivity to flicker will get some eyestrain. As a result, vendors nowadays are offering VGA and super VGA boards that put out much higher vertical refresh rates. Indeed, 72, 80, and 120Hz cards have flooded the market. Investing in the highest refresh rate you can afford is well worth it, in my opinion. My eyes rest much more easily on an 80Hz screen than a 60Hz screen.

There are, of course, a few caveats. First, you need a *monitor* that can handle the vertical refresh rate you want; a basic cheap $200 VGA monitor can't handle an 80Hz signal. Before you buy a video board, find out what kind of monitor you currently have and ask the video board's vendor if your current monitor can use all of the video board's features. If not, either don't buy the board, or plan to buy a new monitor with your new board. (Don't you just love it when some computer expert tells you to go spend some money? Kidding aside, believe me, better video is worth it.)

The second caution is actually kind of funny or sad, depending on how you look at it. Every single computer I've set up in the past four years had a video system that came out of the box configured for a lower refresh rate than it could actually handle. Now, reconfiguring the video for a faster refresh rate usually isn't any harder than just running a short program that comes with the video board, so it's not like I unlocked some hidden feature of the video board. It's just plain inexplicable why a computer company would sell a superior video product as part of its PC but wouldn't take the two minutes to utilize those features.

So, if you've got a recently purchased computer, take a close look at the video documentation that came with it. I've been able to bring more than a few surprised smiles to the faces of owners of PCs by running the video setup programs that were sitting right on their hard disks.

3D Video Boards

Three-dimensional graphics are all the rage today, especially in the gaming world. Although these video boards are also very important to a segment of the computer-aided design and graphics industry, it is through gaming that they have enjoyed their vast popularity.

Quite simply, 3D-capable video adapters are able to make you believe you are seeing action in three dimensions. They do this through the illusion of adding depth to a scene, creating powerful lighting effects, mapping textures to polygons, and other special effects.

While they share a common overall objective, there are different types of 3D video boards that implement 3D in substantially different manners. Each video board manufacturer relies on special chip sets, which are in turn created by other manufacturers. It is the video chip set that has the greatest effect on the 3D capabilities of the card. Two prominent chip set manufacturers today are nVidia, which produces the TNT, TNT2, and GeForce chip sets, and 3Dfx, which produces the Voodoo line of chip sets.

In addition to the chip set, the 3D API (application programming interface) is also important. The top three APIs are DirectX, OpenGL, and Glide. DirectX is a 3D graphics API that was created by Microsoft for computers running Windows. A latecomer to the 3D party, DirectX now vies with OpenGL as the standard 3D API for Windows-based 3D applications. OpenGL, originally created by Silicon Graphics, is a 3D API supported by an independent industry consortium that is compatible with other operating systems besides Windows. Glide is a proprietary API used by 3Dfx's Voodoo line of chip sets.

Video Monitor Characteristics

Now that you've got a board, what monitor goes with it? Monitors aren't as complex as video boards, but there are a few terms to work with.

Perhaps the most important thing to understand about the monitor/board partnership is that the video board calls the tune, and the monitor dances—if it can. Virtually all modern computers (except for some older laptops) have video circuitry that can produce 1024 × 768 signals, but some computers don't have monitors of a quality to actually *display* that signal. Having 120Hz is nice, but both the video board and the monitor must support it.

Monitor Mumbo Jumbo: Horizontal Scan Frequency

As I explained earlier, a monitor works by directing a beam of electrons against the inside of its screen. Phosphors on the inside of the screen become "excited" and glow. Making phosphors glow or not glow defines images on the screen. From a computer's point of view, a video display is just an array of pixels. *Resolution* is the number of dots that can be put on the screen. The electron beam sweeps across the tube, painting lines of dots. CGA used 200 lines top to bottom, EGA used 350, and VGA uses 480. As it uses higher resolutions, super VGA uses even more lines.

Consider the number of horizontal lines that a monitor must draw per second. In a basic VGA, each screen has 480 lines, and there are 60 screens per second. So 480 times 60 is 28,800 lines per second. That is called the *horizontal scan frequency*, as it is the number of times that the beam sweeps horizontally per second. It too is measured in hertz (Hz) or kilohertz (kHz)—thousands of hertz. Actually, a VGA has a somewhat higher horizontal scan rate than 28,800Hz (28.8kHz), as the monitor has extra lines that you can't see (they're called *overscan*). How *many* extra lines a monitor has varies from video mode to video mode. A CGA has a horizontal scan frequency of 15,750Hz, or 15.8kHz. EGA uses 21.8kHz, and VGA uses 31.5kHz. So the horizontal scan frequency your monitor needs to serve your board is determined in part by two important factors: the number of horizontal lines on the screen and the screen's refresh rate.

Dot Pitch

Some monitor ads tout "0.28mm dot pitch." What are they talking about?

We've seen that more resolution means more dots (pixels) on the screen. The distance between the centers of the dots on the monitor is the monitor's *dot pitch*, and it's measured in millimeters (mm). The smaller the dots, the closer together they can be and the higher the resolution that a monitor can show in a crisp and readable manner. A larger monitor can have a larger dot pitch without sacrificing resolution, simply because the monitor's screen is larger.

In reality, you'll see four dot pitches for VGA monitors: 0.34, 0.31, 0.28, and 0.26 mm. Avoid 0.34 on 12-inch VGA monitors, but you may find it quite acceptable on 14-inch monitors—go take a look at one before you buy it. You'll find 0.34 on a 14-inch or 0.31 on a 12-inch monitor is fine for VGA only, but buy 0.28 if you plan to use a super VGA with 800×600 resolution, and buy 0.26 for a super VGA using 1024×768 resolution.

Monitor Size

Monitors range in size from small 14-inch models to professional-caliber behemoths that have a display of 21 inches or more. The factors you should weigh in choosing the right monitor for you are price, space, and use.

It almost goes without saying that the larger the monitor, the more money it will cost. Generally speaking, you can expect to pay between $200 and $1000 for a monitor, with the smaller monitors available at the low end of this spectrum. Seventeen-inch monitors fall in the middle, while19- and 21-inch monitors can go off this scale.

In addition to price, space can be an important consideration. The larger monitors take up more desktop space—sometimes much more. Of course, the width of a 21-inch monitor will be larger than a 15-inch model, but the depth is of much more concern because of the size of the cathode ray tubes (CRT) used in larger monitors.

Finally, how you plan to use your computer is an important factor in determining the right monitor to buy. If the primary role of your computer is general computing, you can get by with a 15- or 17-inch monitor, but if you spend much time with graphics, a larger monitor will help greatly.

Another important point to remember when you choose a monitor is that the size of the screen you can actually use will be smaller than what is advertised. A 17-inch monitor, for example, may only have a viewable dimension of approximately 16 inches. This is caused in part by the fact that monitor sizes are based on the measurement of the CRT diagonally from one corner to the opposite, and also because computer monitors underscan. Underscanning creates an image that is smaller than the overall size of the CRT and leaves a black frame around your picture.

Flat-Panel Displays

Recently, flat-panel LCD displays have emerged in larger numbers and are becoming quite popular for desktop computers. Their main benefit is their space-saving nature. Based on the technologies that power laptop displays rather than the traditional CRTs used in everyday monitors, flat-panel LCD displays take up significantly less desktop space. Flat-panel displays are costly, however. You can expect to spend over $800 for even the smallest models.

Multifrequency Monitors

The last monitor feature is *multisyncing,* the ability to handle multiple resolutions automatically. Recall that the horizontal frequency that you need to display an image is determined by the refresh rate (the vertical frequency) and the horizontal resolution. Until 1986, monitors were fixed-frequency in both the horizontal and vertical directions. When you bought a CGA monitor, it could only do one set of frequencies: 15.75kHz horizontal, 60Hz vertical. The EGA monitor had to be able to do double duty, as it could be attached to either CGA or EGA boards, and so had two sets of frequencies: 15.75kHz/ 60Hz for CGA boards and 21.8kHz/60Hz for EGA boards. The VGA knows of three sets of frequencies: one for CGA modes, one for EGA modes, and 31.5kHz/60Hz for its native standard VGA mode. So a "vanilla VGA" monitor is a fixed-frequency monitor that only supports CGA, EGA, and VGA—no super VGA modes.

In 1986, NEC changed that with its Multisync monitor. The Multisync could detect and synchronize with any horizontal frequency from 15kHz to 31.5kHz and with any vertical frequency from 50Hz to 70Hz. That meant that a single monitor could work on any kind of video board that was out at the time. More important, when IBM introduced the VGA in April 1987, the Multisync was ready—it could handle VGA's 31.5kHz horizontal frequency with no problem.

Now most video vendors offer their own Multisynclike monitors: they're generically called variable frequency monitors (VFMs). NEC doesn't sell the original Multisync any more, but they have Multisync models from the 3FGX (31.5–38kHz horizontal, 50–80Hz vertical) to the 6FGX (30–66kHz horizontal, 50–90Hz vertical). The competition is not asleep, however.

At the moment, my pick for the best reasonably priced monitor is the ViewSonic E771. This is a terrific monitor for several reasons:

▶ It syncs up to a wide range of frequencies, including 1280 × 1024, and can do 1024 × 768 at 87Hz.

▶ It is crisp and clear.

▶ It automatically sizes itself. I don't have to play around with the size controls every time I change resolution or frequency.

▶ It's a 17-inch monitor, the smallest size I'd recommend for use day in and day out.

This is the monitor I'd pick for a new machine, without question. (Contact information for ViewSonic can be found in the Vendor's Guide on CD #2.)

Resizing Screens with Multisyncing Monitors

You'll notice on some of the cheap Multisync monitors that the screen size jumps around when you change resolution. Change from 640 × 480 at 60Hz to 640 × 480 at 72Hz, and the screen gets smaller.

That's due to the higher frequency of the beam writing the image on the screen. On those simple monitors, you must move size and position knobs in order to get the image just right.

This is normal, unfortunately. To combat it, you should buy "autosizing" monitors.

Reference: Older Display Types

This section provides you with some background on pre-1987 displays. You may need this information if you ever find yourself working on an old system.

Before 1987, video standards basically came from IBM. Big Blue controlled the market, and whatever IBM did, everyone else would follow. After 1987, however, the disastrous performance of the PS/2 in the market left the marketplace without a leader. The top-of-the-line video in 1987 was the VGA, which is the baseline standard today. But what preceded it?

There are several basic kinds of older monitors:

▶ Composite monochrome

▶ Composite color

▶ RGB

▶ EGA monitors

▶ Direct-drive TTL monochrome

Table 23.3 offers one way to understand these monitors.

TABLE 23.3 PC Monitor Types		
	Analog	**Digital**
Monochrome	Composite monochrome	Monochrome TTL
Color	Color composite	RGB: CGA (640 × 200), EGA (640 × 350), VGA (640 × 480)

Composite monitors are a step better than a television set. They offer greater resolution than a TV, but that's about it. They offer low expense and good quality.

RGB (Red, Green, Blue) monitors offer better resolution for color text than do color composite monitors. The IBM Color Display and the Princeton Graphics HX12 are RGB monitors. RGBs are more expensive, offer somewhat better quality than composite color, and attach to a display adapter with a nine-pin D-shell connector. You see very few composite monitors in the PC world these days.

More expensive than regular RGB, EGA (Enhanced Graphics Adapter) monitors are RGB monitors with higher resolution. Characters are sharper and the display steadier. In addition, these monitors can display 43 lines of text on a screen rather than the usual 25. This isn't as great as it sounds: most programs won't support the 43-line mode. Notable exceptions are dBASE and the IBM Personal Editor, but more and more are joining the crowd: OS/2 even directly supports 43-line displays with the MODE command. An example of an EGA monitor is the IBM Enhanced Color Display. As I've already mentioned, EGA has been supplanted by VGA, an even higher resolution display standard (it can display 50 lines of text where EGA can only do 43).

Direct-drive TTL monitors are monochromatic (generally amber and black or green and black) and offer high-resolution, steady images. An example of this is the IBM Monochrome Display. They are connected with a nine-pin D-shell connector like the RGB, but don't plug one of these in where RGB is expected or vice versa. You honestly will get smoke.

Fairly expensive, but most versatile, are the multiscan monitors. These can serve as an RGB or an EGA monitor—they sense at what rate data is coming in and adjust their scan rates accordingly. Most modern monitors are multiscan monitors.

The second part of a display subsystem is the controller board. There are quite a few in use currently, and they all have their characteristics. Table 23.4 summarizes them.

TABLE 23.4 Common PC Adapter Types

Adapter	Maximum Resolution/ Colors	Char. Box Size	Monitors Supported	Graphics Supported?
Color/Graphics Adapter (CGA)	640 × 200/2	8 × 8	RGB	Yes
			Composite	No
Monochrome Display Adapter (MDA)	720 × 350/3	9 × 14	Mono TTL	No
Enhanced Graphics Adapter (EGA)	640 × 350/64	8 × 14	RGB	Yes
			EGA	No
			Mono TTL	No
Hercules Graphics Controller (HGC)	720 × 350/3	9 × 14	Mono TTL	Yes
Multi Color Graphics Array (MCGA)	640 × 480/2	8 × 16	Analog RGB	Yes
Video Graphics Array (VGA)	640 × 480/ 262, 144	9 × 16	Analog RGB	Yes
Super VGA	Up to 1024 × 768/256	9 × 16	Analog RGB	Yes
8514/A	1024 × 768/ 262, 144	9 × 16	Analog RGB	Yes
XGA	1024 × 768/ 262, 144	9 × 16	Analog RGB	Yes

Several display adapters were used throughout the late '80s:

▶ The IBM Monochrome Display Adapter (MDA)

▶ The Hercules Monochrome Graphics Adapter

▶ The IBM Color/Graphics Adapter (CGA)

▶ The IBM Enhanced Graphics Adapter (EGA)

▶ The IBM Professional Graphics Adapter

The PGA It never really caught on, but it was the first real attempt in the PC world to add intelligence to a video board. That led eventually to the graphic accelerator boards that are becoming standard equipment on many modern PCs.

The IBM Video Graphics Array Sporting PGA-quality graphics and a much more reasonable price (the PGA ran around $3000), the VGA made its appearance in 1987 with the PS/2s. This board is, as I've said, the baseline for video today.

The IBM 8514/A Very High Resolution Graphics Adapter
A video coprocessor in the tradition of the PGA. More successful than PGA, but still not a big smash hit. It was replaced by the XGA.

The IBM XGA (extended graphics array) Built to do Windows and OS/2 quickly. Never really caught on, but if you buy a modern PS/2, you'll have it built right into your motherboard.

Refer to Table 23.4 for details about these boards.

Video is an important part of your PC, but its lack of moving parts means that the best medicine for video problems is to understand how it works and how to attack its problems. The wide variety of so-called Super VGA boards has led to a plethora of drivers and video setup programs. Make sure you've got the most up-to-date drivers and a monitor that matches your board, and all will be well.

Troubleshooting Tips

Once you have a system in place, how do you attack video problems? Here are a few suggestions.

Some of the dumbest monitor problems are the easiest to resolve:

▶ Is it turned on?

▶ Is the brightness or contrast turned down?

▶ Is everything plugged in? Is it plugged in to the right place?

▶ Did you hear one long and two short beeps indicating a bad video card?

▶ If the display is dead, do you hear the power supply fan? There are nonvideo reasons for a display "malfunction," such as when the power supply has killed the computer.

▶ If the computer is okay but the display is bad, you will see the drive light come on. Use a sound-emitting program to see if the computer is functioning.

The quickest test is a monitor swap. If that does nothing, swap the display cards. *Don't* try to service the monitor. As I've said before, you can hurt yourself doing that.

If the display is rolling and you can't see enough to check the video modes, restart the computer in Windows Safe mode (press the F8 key when you reboot and you'll be given a menu with Safe Mode as one of the options). This will start Windows in standard 640×480 in 16 colors, so you can use almost any card and monitor to test your system.

Speaking of drivers, sometimes you'll see a case where you reboot your operating system, only to lose synchronization—the screen turns into moving bands. That probably means that you told your video board to exceed the capabilities of the monitor. Drop back a bit in resolution and you'll be okay.

Now that we've talked about what you can see, let's talk about what you can hear on your computer. The next chapter is all about sound.

Play It Loud: Sound Cards

INTRODUCTION

In the early days of PCs, the only way that a PC could make noise was with its built-in speaker. Even the best PC speaker is tinny, however, and the best we could hope for were squeaks, squawks, and the occasional boom (though even that was more like a crackle). One ambitious 1984 program called PC Parrot attempted to make the PC speak, but it was limited by the sound equipment possibilities.

That's not true any more, and it hasn't been for many years. Sound equipment on the PC is so good that I didn't type much of this chapter, I spoke it, using a voice recognition product that allowed me to talk—it typed what I said. Although that's a sophisticated use for a PC sound card, even the least sophisticated cards can handle it. And the best part is that sound's no longer expensive—basic sound cards can be had for under $30. (IBM and Lernout & Hauspie (commonly known as L&H) are just two of the companies competing in the voice recognition software market. Both offer packages for anywhere from $30 to $50 for the average user, and they include headphones with a microphone.)

In this chapter, you'll learn how sound cards work, what features to look for when choosing one, and what you're likely to run into when you install a sound card. As my voice dictation system shows, sound isn't just for games.

By the way, you may notice that there are no QuickSteps in this chapter. That's because installing a sound card is very simple and best explained through the following visual guide. The tools you will need to have on hand are listed in the "Be Prepared" sidebar. You will not need anything special for the sound card itself.

Be Prepared

Before you start, there are some things you'll need to have on hand. These include:

- The card's manual and other configuration information. The Web is a great place to look up sound card installation data and cabling schematics.

- Phillips-head screwdriver with a medium tip.

- Container for placing screws in. (I like to lay out the screws in the same pattern I removed them, working left-to-right, top-to-bottom. That way I can just repeat the process and get the right screw in the right hole.)

You might also like to have on hand:

- An antistatic wristband

- Flashlight

- Nail clippers. These are great for cutting those hampering zip ties (those plastic little strips that bunch wires together). Just be careful not to snip a wire—but the nice thing about nail clippers is that the cutting area is not very big, so there's little chance of this occurring if you pay attention.

VISUAL UPGRADE

Installing a Sound Card

1 Sound cards have several internal and external connectors.

Internal

External

2 The rear of most sound cards has a joystick port in addition to miniplug jacks for speakers, line in, and a microphone.

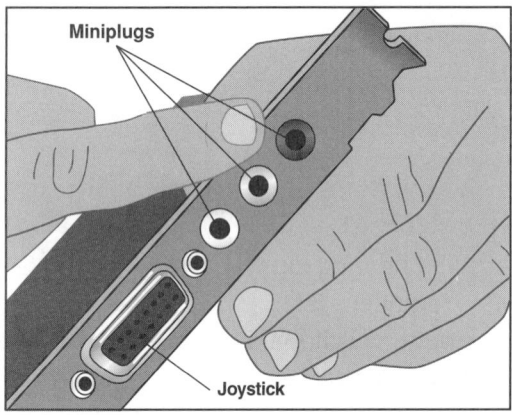

Miniplugs

Joystick

3 Insert the sound card into a free slot (ISA or PCI, depending on the type of card).

4 Screw the back plate of the card into the computer's chassis.

5 Connect one end of your CD-ROM's audio cable into the internal CD IN connector on the sound card.

6 Connect the other end of the audio cable to the Audio connector at the rear of the CD-ROM drive.

Audio Connector

Sound Synthesis

The goal of sound cards is to record and play back sound. How they do it varies considerably, however. There are three main methods of sound reproduction:

◗ Sampling

◗ FM synthesis

◗ Wavetable synthesis

We'll look at these three methods later in this section. But first, let's discuss what sound *is*.

Sound Characteristics

Sound consists of a set of waves of varying pressure created in the air by our vocal cords, musical instruments, or natural forces. A picture of a sound is called a *sonogram,* and you can see one in Figure 24.1. It's a sonogram of the word "hello" being spoken (by me, in this case).

Figure 24.1

A sonogram of the word "hello"

Understanding a bit about sounds requires understanding a bit about signals. The dimensions of this signal are called *amplitude* and *frequency*. Amplitude and frequency probably conjure up visions of trigonometry and physics, but—I promise!—there's nothing tough about this.

Sine Waves

In order to discuss signals in a bit more detail, I've got to talk about another potentially scary topic—sine waves. Take a look at Figure 24.2.

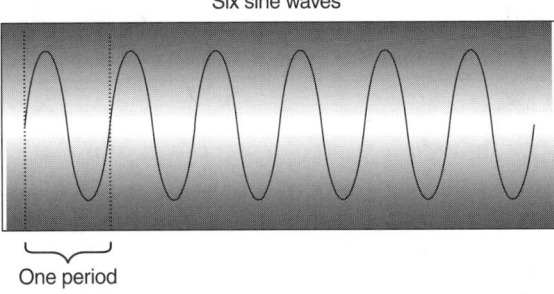

Six sine waves

Figure 24.2

Sine waves

One period

A wave starts anywhere, makes one upturn and one downturn (unless you start later in the signal, in which case it makes one downturn, *then* one upturn), and then ends up at the same height at which it started. That's one wave. But what does this have to do with data communications?

The imagery of waves works to describes signals because of the up-and-down (*periodic* is the more exact term) nature of waves. Turns out the sine wave is the building block of *all* waves.

What do I mean by "building block?" A mathematician by the name of Fourier proved that *any* wave phenomenon could be built by adding together the right series of waves. *Finding* the right series of waves to build any one signal is not a simple task—it's called a "Fourier decomposition"—but it *can* be done with the right tools (read: computing power). We won't do Fourier decompositions in *this* book; I just want you to understand why sine waves are so important to any study of signals. To see an example of sine waves adding up to a signal, look at Figure 24.3, which shows a number of sine waves superimposed on one another.

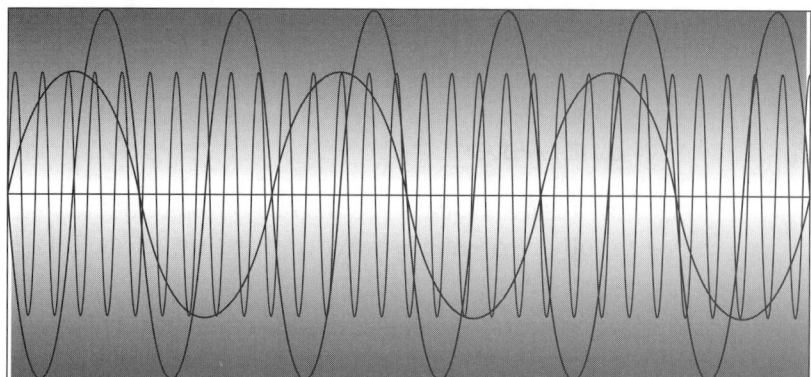

Figure 24.3

Several sine waves superimposed upon one another

Notice that some jump up and down more quickly, some reach higher or lower, and some stretch a bit further left and right, but they're all sine waves. In Figure 24.4 we can add them all together.

Figure 24.4

Sum of the sine waves in Figure 24.3

The sum is no longer anything *like* a sine wave. Any signal, no matter how bizarre, can be broken down into sine waves, which is why they're so important to a good understanding of signaling limitations. With that in mind, let's look at two aspects of a sine wave—amplitude and frequency.

Amplitude

This should be a familiar concept, as we talk about amplitude all the time—we just call it *loudness* or *volume.*

In human voice communications, volume carries meaning, such as urgency, or it may be used so that a voice will carry far. From a sine wave's perspective, amplitude means *height.* Take a look at Figure 24.5.

Smaller amplitude   Greater amplitude

Figure 24.5

Amplitudes of a
sine wave

In signals, amplitude also relates to *power* used for transmission. When transmitting data, communications engineers must overcome the fact that transmitting data over a distance reduces a signal's amplitude, weakening it or *attenuating* it. You can partially restore a signal by *amplifying* it; all an amplifier does is try to boost the amplitude of the signal.

Communications systems use power, or amplitude, to describe two things:

▶ The raw transmission power of the communications medium

▶ Perhaps more important, the *clarity* of the communications medium—a ratio of the power of the *noise* to the power of the *signal*, known as the *signal-to-noise ratio*

Frequency

The other sine wave characteristic is its *frequency*. Frequency describes how often a wave goes up and down in a given time. You can see this in Figure 24.6.

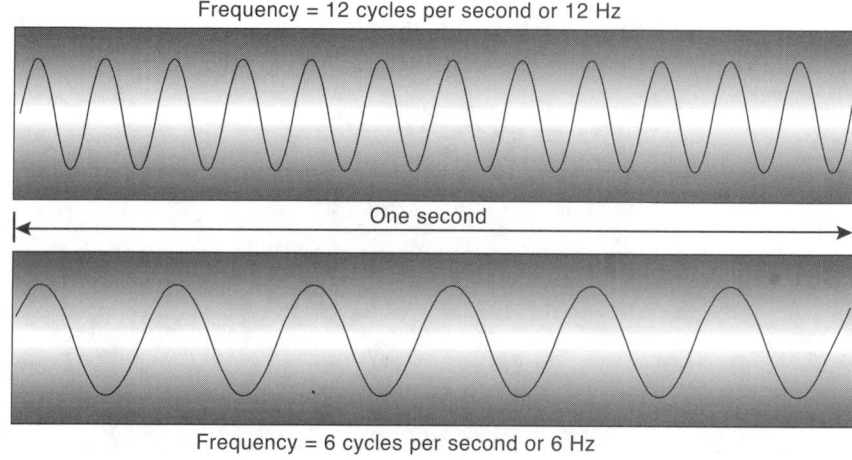

Figure 24.6

Comparative frequency of two sine waves

In this figure, you see two waves diagrammed over the course of one second. The top wave goes up and down 12 times in that second, the bottom one only 6 times. That means that the top wave has a higher frequency.

Frequency is measured in *cycles per second*, which is abbreviated CPS, or, more commonly, the term *hertz* is used. It's a unit that means, as you'd guess, "cycles per second," and is named after Gustav Hertz, a German physicist whose work on the nature of electrons won him a Nobel Prize. Hertz is usually abbreviated Hz. Look back at Figure 24.5, and you'll see that the two waves in that picture had the same frequency. Conversely, the two waves in Figure 24.6 have the same *amplitude* but different frequencies.

We talk about frequencies when talking about sound; if you say that someone has a "high-pitched voice," you mean that person has a voice that produces a range of frequencies whose average is somewhat high, as human voices go.

Signals to Bits: Sampling

In order for your sound card to use a sound, the sound has to be converted from its analog self into a more bit-friendly format. The main method of converting analog sounds into digital is called *sampling*. (Before I learned how this was done, I called it "digitizing" the audio. I've since learned that expert types always say "sampling," so file "sampling" in your list of good-stuff-to-know-at-cocktail-parties, and *never* say "digitizing.") It's done with a method called *PCM*, or *Pulse Coded Modulation*.

Suppose we are trying to convert the simple analog signal shown in Figure 24.7 into digital.

Figure 24.7

A simple analog signal

Under PCM, the signal is sampled many times per second, and the height of the wave is recorded. (Actually, what is recorded is the *logarithm* of the height—remember that sound volume is perceived logarithmically.) You can see an example of sampling in Figure 24.8.

Figure 24.8

Sampling a signal

The lines represent the height of the signal at various times. It's impossible to measure the height of the signal at all times, so we can only measure a limited number of samples—hence the "sampling" name.

That doesn't seem like a lot of information about the signal, and it isn't. To get a better picture of how to reconstruct the original audio signal, we'd do better to get more samples in the same time period, as you see in Figure 24.9.

Figure 24.9

Reconstructing the original audio signal by getting more samples

This underscores an important point, which is emphasized in Figure 24.10: more samples mean a higher-quality signal once reproduced. In Figure 24.10, you can see an original signal for a second's duration. Below that is the result of sampling it 20 times in that second, and the result of sampling it 40 times per second.

There are more values in the more frequently sampled signal, and so the reconstructed signal will be of higher quality.

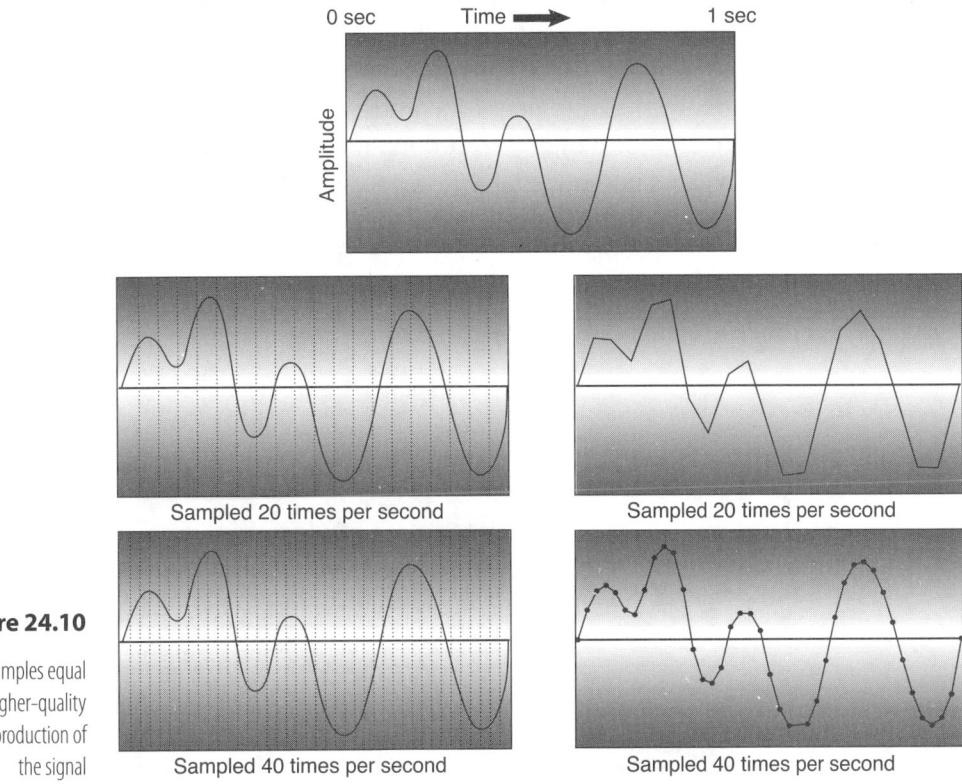

Figure 24.10

More samples equal
a higher-quality
reproduction of
the signal

How many samples do we need per second? For the answer to that, we turn to Nyquist's Theorem. It says that to completely capture a signal, you've got to have N samples, where

$$N = 2 \times \text{signal bandwidth}$$

The bandwidth of our ears is considered to be well within a 22,050Hz range. Twice that would be 44,100 samples per second, which is the sampling rate of a music CD. Higher sampling means more data must be stored per second.

But that's not all there is to sampling with PCM. Suppose the recorded values can range from –127 to +128, and they can be only integers. Since the total possible number of values is only 256, each signal value is encoded with eight bits here.

Why not use 16 bits per sample? Using 16 bits would allow for many more nuances of sound—65,536 values for 16 bits compared to 256 for 8 bits—but it doubles the amount of data needed to store a given audio signal. Of course, with the size of today's hard disks, there's little stopping you from using 16-bit encoding, at least as far as space goes. You can see the difference in bit sample sizes in Figure 24.11.

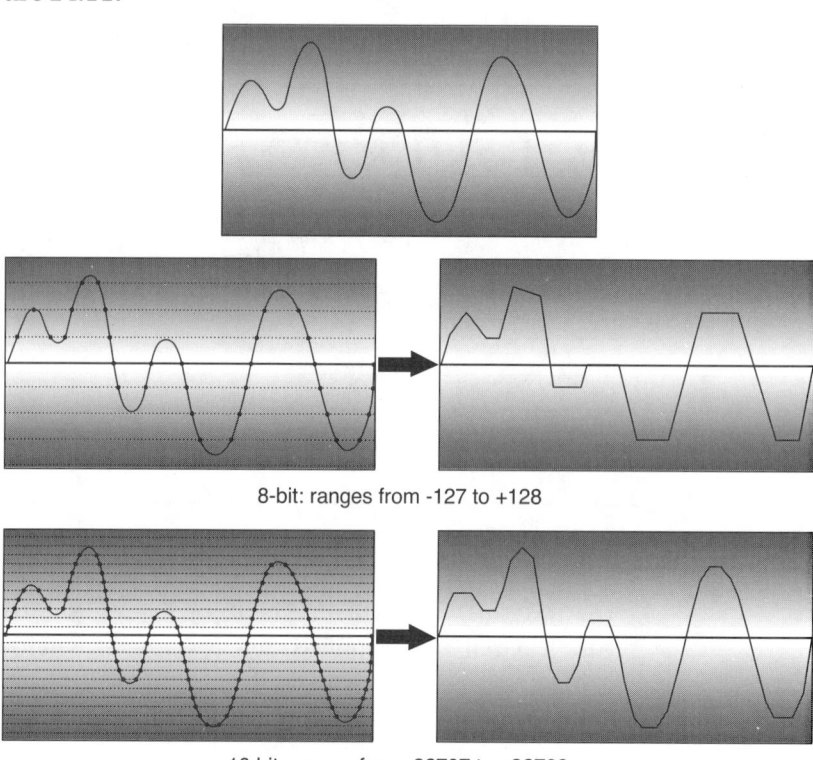

8-bit: ranges from -127 to +128

16-bit: ranges from -32707 to +32708

Figure 24.11

The difference in bit sample sizes

Music CDs sample 16 bits per sample, 44,100 samples per second.

The cheapest sound cards can only sample at 8 bits per sample; more expensive ones can sample up to 32 bits per second. For most voice and music uses, 16 bits is fine, which yields about as much quality as the human ear can directly perceive.

Note

There is a new use for this information today, and it's called MP3. You may have heard of it. I will cover MP3 technology, in detail, shortly.

FM Synthesis

Sampling works well for recording sounds. But to assemble entirely new sounds, PC software authors need ways to tell a sound card, "Play an 'A' as it would sound on a harpsichord." One method for that is with FM (frequency modulation) synthesis. It's usually implemented as a *MIDI (Music Instrument Digital Interface)* circuit.

I'm simplifying here, but the idea behind FM synthesis is that musical sounds follow a four-part cycle, as you see in Figure 24.12.

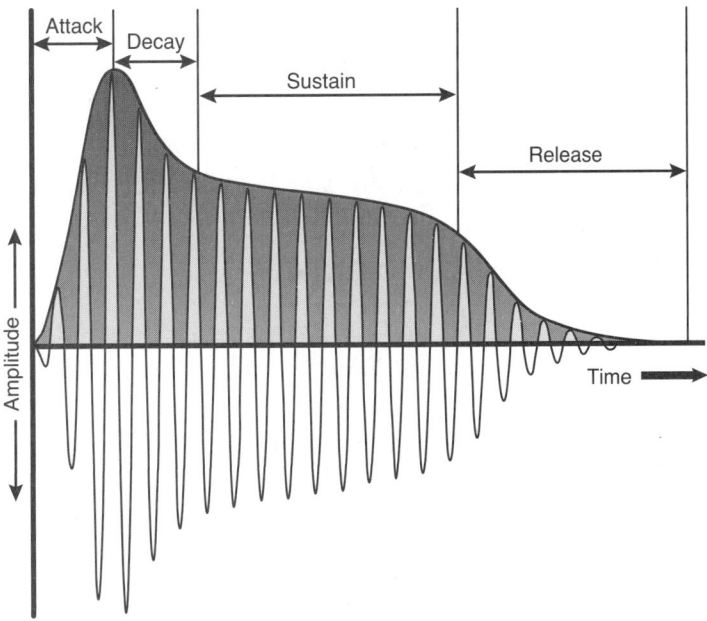

Figure 24.12

The four-part cycle of musical sounds

The notion in FM synthesis is to describe an instrument's waveform in terms of the size of the attack, decay, sustain, and release (ADSR) parts of the cycle. These four elements are generally the basis for sound in terms of waveforms. Attack is the speed at which a sound begins. Decay describes how the sound begins to release. Sustain describes the actual length of the sound. And finally, release describes when the note is "turned off."

Wavetable Synthesis

FM is an easy model to encode, and it allows for some very compact music files in orders of magnitude smaller than sampled files. But the simplistic nature of the ADSR model limits musical fidelity.

Some sound cards get around that by storing entire instrument waveforms in a ROM on the board. That's called wavetable synthesis. If you want the best quality musical synthesis, it's the way to go. (Of course, alternatively you could just buy CDs and play them on your stereo, but that wouldn't be as fun.)

Sound Card Characteristics

The variations of sound cards include how they create sounds, how fine a resolution they use for it, and what "extras" they carry onboard, such as a pass-through audio circuit or a CD-ROM interface.

8-, 16-, 32-, or 64-Bit Sound?

Thus far in this book, a "16-bit card" has meant one that has a poorly aging 16-bit ISA slot connector on it. The card can pass 16 bits worth of data at one time to the bus, but the only impact it has on sound is being a potential bottleneck when large amounts of data need to be passed at one time. When it comes to sound cards, 16-bit means something else entirely: it refers to sample types.

> A sample is a recording of a sound, such as a musical instrument, for the purposes of playback. In this context, it is for the express use of attempting to reproduce an instrument's sound in a digital format. To more accurately reproduce an instrument's sound requires many samples that represent its entire scale of sonic capabilities. A typical collection of samples to cover a wide range of musical instruments is around 4 to 8MB in size, *after* compression. An accurate representation of a piano requires 16 to 24MB of space!

Eight-bit samples are good for very simple game sounds or music. However, you really need a board with the ability to play back and record 16-bit sounds to do good multimedia. The Sound Blaster 16 from Creative Labs was a good example of a good 16-bit card. Today there are 32- and 64-bit cards such as the AWE32 and AWE64, but they are commonly shipped as OEM (Original Equipment Manufacturer, or no-name parts that are built by companies that also build a model for consumer availability) as well as retail versions. Creative Labs, the most ubiquitous sound card maker and the developer of technologies by which most other cards are defined, has recently released the Sound Blaster Live! 64-bit sound card. Compared to older cards, even others from Creative Labs, the Live! card is intense. Capable of up to 1024 discreet voice polyphony and hosting 32MB of samples, it is one of the most powerful consumer-grade sound cards available. The Platinum version sound card is available for a mere $150 compared to the professional boards of two years ago that ranged from $300 to $2000 with similar capabilities.

> Keep in mind that the recent spate of sub-$500 systems has produced a new class of personal computer: the Minimalist. Gone are the days when everything was on a card so that if you wanted something new you could simply add it. Most budget systems ship with video and audio subsystems built into the motherboard. Couple this with only two or three PCI slots and a single ISA slot (or none), and there's not much to work with there. Almost invariably, one of the PCI slots is taken by the modem, which leaves only one or two slots available for upgrades. See Chapter 3, "Inside the PC: Pieces of the Picture," and the section "PC Expansion Buses" for a detailed discussion of this.

IRQ or DMA Sound Recording?

When you try to capture sound in combination with video you'll find that the lame multitasking structure of Windows 3.*x* and 95 (and even NT4), if you still use them, can make total audio/video capture difficult. Windows 9*x* and the upcoming Windows Millennium Edition (as well as Windows 2000) make strong improvements in these areas and make it a lot easier to get that total multimedia experience due to a more efficient multitasking environment and improved conflict management.

The point is that most simple sound cards are driven by interrupts, which chew up CPU time when the CPU needs to be able to just hunker down and pay attention to the video capture board. There are, however, some audio cards that aren't built to be interrupt-driven, but are rather DMA-driven; Turtle Beach's cards are one good example. As they don't lean on the interrupts, you'll get smoother audio/video interleaving on your recordings.

Note

On a similar note, some older sound cards can only handle MIDI and can only play back MIDI files; others can only play back sampled files, usually called WAV (pronounced "wave") files because that's the name that Windows gives them. Most game music is MIDI, and most multimedia sound is WAV, so it would seem that having both capabilities in your card would be right and good, correct? Correct! No cards or chip sets shipping today in the consumer channel are limited to one or the other.

Pass-through and/or CD-ROM Interfaces?

Many sound cards have a small Berg connector on them designed for a cable like the one in Figure 24.13.

Figure 24.13

Berg connector on
a cable

This is an audio pass-through cable. It lets you play music CDs from a CD-ROM in your PC through the speakers on your sound card. This used to be a problem because getting this audio cable required complying with each manufacturer's proprietary requirements. Things have settled down a bit these days, and there is no longer a need for a veritable wig of cables just to make sure you have the correct one. CD-ROM drives coupled with standardized cabling for digital audio/video make it easier to install such devices.

So in a pinch, you can always install a poor man's (or woman's) pass-through cable: run a cable from the headphone output on the front of the CD-ROM to the Line In input on the back of the sound card.

Some sound cards have CD-ROM interfaces for proprietary CD-ROMs. I recommend that you avoid these, as they're a compatibility headache. Even the sound cards with SCSI interfaces implement slow SCSI interfaces. If you have a SCSI CD-ROM, my advice is to just get a good SCSI host adapter and hang the CD-ROM off that. On the other hand, with IDE/ATAPI drives as fast as 52X with bus speeds of anywhere from 4 to 33MBps (Ultra ATA), more expensive SCSI devices are often a waste of money for the casual user.

Note

SCSI is in no way a waste of time or money for the video or media specialist who needs SCSI's special capabilities, speed, and reliability. There's no match for SCSI when it comes time to edit video live or for any number of the hundreds of other uses for SCSI drives and devices.

Speaker Systems

All this sound stuff is of no value unless you've got some speakers so that you can hear it. You *can* run some sound cards through the internal PC speaker, but *don't*: it's monaural and of pretty low quality.

The speakers you'll get will be likely stereo speakers. They can either be externally powered or run off the sound card's output; in general, a simple pair of speakers should not require power. More specialized woofer/speaker sets will pretty much always include an amplifier, so plan for a power outlet near the PC for the speakers if you can.

Double-check that the speakers are shielded (most are) so that the magnetism they create is minimal. They'll be sitting near your PC, so it's quite likely that you'll end up putting floppies near them; an unshielded speaker can damage data on a hard or floppy disk if the disk is close enough to the speaker.

If you're a real computer music or game aficionado, it would behoove you to pick up a speaker/woofer combination. In fact, most major vendors (Compaq, Dell, Quantex, Micron, Hewlett-Packard, etc.) ship their systems with high-quality speakers. Quantex, in particular, ships their systems with Altec Lansing–powered speaker systems. You can add a subwoofer to the lower-end systems; the more expensive systems already come with one. Hewlett-Packard ships with Polk Audio speakers, a very well respected manufacturer of world-renowned home and professional speaker systems.

Tip

If you did not get a nice set of speakers with your last system, there is hope. You can buy some! Don't despair, they're quite reasonable. You can purchase a quality set of speakers complete with subwoofer for as low as $35 or pop for a complete surround sound setup for only . . . hold onto your seat . . . $150! That's four satellite speakers, a subwoofer, and a center channel speaker! Just make sure your sound card supports all of the features you want in a speaker system, or you'll incur another charge.

Installation Tips

Truthfully, there isn't much to say about installing sound cards that is special, except for two things.

First, if you plan on using normal, unshielded speakers, be careful where you put them. Depending on the size and type of magnets used by your speakers, they can have a profound effect on your viewing and storage pleasure. The magnets in unshielded speakers can literally bend the electrons away from their intended destination as they're fired at the glass, resulting in distortion. I briefly mounted my Sony satellite-and-woofer system atop my monitor, and the picture looked like it was melting around the edges. As for storage media, I only have one thing to say: Magnets erase data.

Second, when you install that sound card on an older machine, document everything. The Sound Blaster 16, a popular sound card, requires *three* I/O addresses, *two* DMA channels, and an IRQ ("in a pear tree . . .") to top it all off. Newer motherboards, BIOS chips, and architectures, as well as Windows 98/2000 and a number of other operating systems, do quite well in allocating and managing the resources necessary to support all these features. Windows in particular is able to automatically sense and install the proper drivers for all Sound Blaster series products (with the exception of Live!, a more recent product).

Nevertheless, things can go wrong, so make sure you take notes!

Tip

If you are clueless about what's in your machine before you install such a board, then it's high time that you do an inventory. Whip out a pen and some paper and write down what you have.

The Reason for All of This: Multimedia

Multimedia. Yes, multimedia. It's all about having your PC do everything you want. Fast 3D games, poundingly loud and clear digital music, and speech recognition for love letters. Whether you've noticed it or not, sound, specifically music, is a major component for most life on this planet. One of the biggest players in this growing space is MP3 technology.

MP3 Audio Files

This audio format is actually called MPEG Layer-3, and it deals specifically with compressing high-quality sound while retaining as much of the original quality as possible. It does this by removing those ranges of sounds that we cannot hear, which is produced in audio. There is always a measure of "waste" sound that is included in all recordings. Call it an imperfect world. Now, as more compression is applied, the complex algorithms used to determine what sounds a human is able to hear based on psychoacoustic models trim more and more inside of the human hearable range. So, the greater the compression, the lower the quality.

Needless to say, MP3 audio files have made quite an impact on the music industry. First, they're not secure so they can be "ripped" from a CD and traded (and they are, with great vigor I might add). Second, they can get quite small and still sound great. I'll do the numbers in a minute, but as an overview, you can get DAT-quality sound (that's right near CD-quality or White Book Audio with slightly more dramatic losses in the higher spectrums) compressed down to a megabyte per minute.

There are two factors that make up the quality of MP3 files. These are kHz and Kbps (kilohertz and kilobits per second, respectively). The kHz is in direct relation to the bit depth of the sample. A 16-bit recording is on par with a 44.1kHz recording, also known as White Book or CD-quality audio. Making it 22kHz reduces its reproduction quality by only one-third. Kbps are the other piece to this two-part puzzle. Where kHz can be correlated to the sharpness of a picture, Kbps can be correlated to how smooth the sound plays back; Kbps are often referred to as frames.

To use a familiar analogy, in cartoons the more "frames" there are, the smoother the apparent motion. Simply put, 60 pictures showing the stages of a person moving their arm over a period of five seconds will result in a more natural movement than will 15 frames. Sound works the same way and is represented in Kbps. 144Kbps at 44kHz makes for an MPEG Layer-3 file that sounds as good as digital CD audio but only takes up a fraction of the space. Considering this, Layer-3 can compress a CD-quality audio file to fit about a minute's worth of sound into roughly a megabyte of space. Your typical three- to five-minute song would end up being anywhere from 3 to 6MB in size.

Warning

MP3s are often used to facilitate the illicit exchanging of copyrighted music. Persons of uncouth character copy their CDs to MP3 files and distribute them over the Internet to people who do not own the CD, thereby removing any potential revenues earned by the artist. It is estimated that billions of dollars in revenue are lost on a yearly basis due to piracy using MP3 and other technologies.

MP3: How to Get It and the Gear You Need

Gadget fans, get ready (I'm one, so I understand). MP3 has been examined by the hardware industry and consumers alike and deemed very, very cool. Why? Here are the facts real quicklike:

▶ Near digital-quality sound.

▶ Very small files.

▶ As many options for storing the files as there are storage options.

▶ Can be extremely miserly on batteries.

▶ Everyone is getting on the MP3 train. Portable, home, and car MP3 audio components are either shipping or about to.

And then there are some nonhardware or software issues that make MP3 (well, any compressed digital audio format for that matter) a very attractive format, indeed:

▶ It drastically reduces the requirements for publishing music to a worldwide audience. Artists who had to wait for a record label executive to stumble along and fortuitously catch their act to "discover" them can record their music and publish it on sites like mp3.com and be heard by people everywhere.

▶ There are no additional costs (unless you don't have a computer, of course). Boatloads of freeware, shareware, and commercial software are available for doing pretty much anything you might want to with MP3s, and with the state of today's sound cards, even a bargain PC can serve as a low-end studio.

▶ CD collections can be a thing of the past. Think about it. You can move from your music shelf to the CD player, endlessly swapping CD for CD, or you can reach over, click a few times, and listen to as many albums as you have storage room for. That big HDD is looking mighty nice.

MP3, to the consternation of the record industry, is not secure. This means that it cannot be protected from theft and piracy. Real's RealJukebox can encode your personal music, recorded from CD, into a proprietary RMX format that makes it secure, but the security can be turned off and it's not really an MP3. There are also efforts to make MP3s secure so that the music industry as a whole will accept it for more than a pirate's trading ground or a home for unsigned bands. Even if this happens, though, MP3s still hold immense promise for in-home media storage.

Note

You may hear the term *codec* come up now and again. It's a fake word made up of two real words, *compression* and *decompression*. It's sometimes incorrectly used to describe either compression or decompression, so a codec can be a way of encoding media, decoding media, or (correctly) both.

Note

The only really secure codec is Liquid Audio's format. These tracks can also be recorded in CD-quality but have the added ability to "time out" (meaning you can't listen to them anymore) after a specified period, specified either in days from first use or on a certain date. The renowned art rock band Yes recently advance-released their single "Lightning Strikes" from their new album of the same name over the Internet in Liquid Audio. It timed out the day the album was released to the public. As you can see, this offers artists security and also acts as a great way to publicize a new recording and boost sales.

MP3 Hardware

There are already a number of products available for the MP3 buff. Most of them are portable players, similar to a Walkman, but with RAM instead of tape or CD. The trend was started by Diamond Multimedia with its popular RIO. With 64MB of RAM and a $150 price tag, it was a welcome novelty to most. Now that the novelty has worn off and people take MP3 seriously, there are similar products available from Sony, Creative Labs, and many others.

Here's a quick list of companies that make MP3 hardware:

Best Data The guys that probably made your external modem in the early '90s have jumped into the MP3 market. The Cabo is about $240 with 64MB of RAM built in.

Creative Labs The sound card pros typically stay on the leading edge of most new technologies having anything to do with sound. They also innovate a lot. Prime example is the 6GB Nomad Jukebox that's shaped like a portable CD player.

Diamond Multimedia The company that started it all, they make the aforementioned RIO. 'Nuff said.

Sony Those innovative electronics guys are at it again with various ways of getting MP3s to play in way out places. The MC-P10 Music Clip is a Sharpie-shaped MP3 player that has 64MB of RAM packed into its slim fuselage.

Other manufacturers include:

▶ Audiovox

▶ D-Link

▶ I-JAM

▶ RCA

▶ Sensory Science

See the Vendor Guide on CD #2 for contact information on these companies.

Some companies are releasing units that can be used in cars (remove the faceplate and stick in the cradle to upload files for the next day or for that road trip you've been planning on taking), outside (imagine a boom box that can play regular CDs and CD-Rs with MP3s on it), and in the home (a 50GB HDD makes a nice media storage component).

A good place to look up the latest MP3 player reviews is at `www.cnet.com`. Once there, click on Consumer Electronics and then MP3 Players. This site includes solid reviews and honest (sometimes scathingly so) criticism. It's worth a look just for its lowest price finder.

MP3 Software

There are a number of different solutions for playing and managing MP3 files on your personal computer. Here they are, listed by platform:

Windows
WinAMP Possibly the most well known MP3 player there is—so much so that AOL bought the company. They also pioneered streaming MP3 with their ShoutCast technology.

RealJukebox With the recent release of their 2.0 version, Real Networks has joined the ranks of the "skinners" and the "visualizers." No, these are not punk groups, they're ways of customizing the look of your player.

Sonique One of the early commercial skins-based players with visualization capabilities. It works well but is more visually oriented, with its main highlight being animated menus and other controls. Sonique relies on Windows Media Player for its audio capabilities.

Windows Media Player Microsoft likes to have its foot in as many doors as it can. MP3 media is now no exception. Not surprisingly, it's taking on QuickTime and Real's two products by offering a staggering array of tools and features. Unlike most Microsoft software vying for leadership in an existing market, this is actually pretty easy to use.

Unix/Linux

MP3blaster A console player that has an integrated playlist. Nice, fast, stable, and an app that only a Unix devotee could love.

XMMS Possibly the most well known MP3 player in the Linux world, it's an exact clone of WinAMP. You'll need an X-Window server to use it.

KMP3 A very capable MP3 player for the popular KDE desktop manager.

MPG123 The granddaddy of them all (well, it's not *that* old) only plays from the console and doesn't have an interface, but there are many interfaces for X-Window and other Window managers.

See the Vendor Guide on CD #2 for contact information on these companies.

In addition to its other features, Real has jukebox software that can organize your MP3s and digitize your CD collection. The Windows Media Player also has extensive playlist and file management functions.

QuickTime 4 and the Internet

MP3 is hot, but QuickTime is older, wiser, and more capable. Quick-Time, an Apple technology, ironically, is pretty much the standard for digital media on computers of both the Windows and Macintosh varieties. The problem, until recently, was that the versions for QuickTime on the Mac and Windows did not share parity. Soon after version 3, however, Apple released their first feature-for-feature version for both Windows and Macintosh. This act alone created millions of new users because it allowed any QuickTime-compatible file to be viewed on either platform without modification. All of a sudden, Windows users were no longer left out in the cold.

This brings us to the Internet and its impact on QuickTime. Let's just say that QuickTime is not the only kid on the block anymore. Enter players Real and Microsoft. Real offers RealPlayer 8 and RealJukebox 2 for Windows and RealPlayer 8 the Macintosh. Microsoft offers the Windows Media Player (WMP) for Windows and MacOS. Both deal almost exclusively in streaming media from the Internet. Real has been doing this since 1994 and has the distinction and advantage of being what's called "first in space," a term used to describe the first to release a technology into a particular market. Windows has the ubiquity afforded by its operating system that lets it easily distribute and integrate their software into the market.

Note

Streaming is a technology that tries to get something very large from one place to another in a very short period of time. How do you get a 35MB file to someone using a 33.6 or 56K modem? A process like this would normally take *five to seven hours*. Most people are unwilling to wait that long. The smart people over at Real came up with a way to compress the media and allow the user to view the media as soon as enough of it was downloaded, usually only a small percentage of the total file.

What QuickTime has that the others do not is threefold: name, ability, and innovation. The name comes from years at the top and an unwillingness on Apple's part to walk away from this franchise. The ability comes from being able to handle over 200 different types of digital media with aplomb, something very few can claim. QuickTime can also act as a 3D media viewer, a virtual reality machine, a personal video editor, a television, a radio, and a complete multimedia center all rolled into one. It lacks for little, although it could use a nice way to organize and play media files stored locally. Finally, QuickTime's innovation lies in Apple's ability to find something fresh and new and strike it while the proverbial iron is hot.

Interestingly enough, in this case, Apple was sneaking in the back door. This, of course, is where the tale winds back to Real and Microsoft. Both of these QuickTime competitors stream media to their clients. Both can, to a degree, display the formats of the competitor (WMP has a distinct disadvantage when it comes to Quick-Time formats despite Apple's Technology Sharing agreement with Microsoft). It is, however, QuickTime that plays all formats. And now, it too streams. Apple shipped a hastily developed package with the MacOS X Server package that allowed it to become a streaming Quick-Time media server. Since that day, several large players in the Internet media content field have jumped on the QuickTime streaming media bandwagon, including HBO, MTV, and National Public Radio.

Troubleshooting Tips

There's nothing like troubleshooting a sound card, especially when you just installed it.

The first tip—one that you should regard as a very close friend—is to *limit yourself to doing only one thing at a time.* This way, if you get in a jam, it's much easier to backtrack and figure out what caused the problem.

One of the most common problems occurs when setting up a Creative Labs brand Ensonique ES1371 or 1370 sound card (also called the Audio PCI64) for use in Windows MS-DOS mode. This is almost invariably a conflict with, oddly enough, LPT Interrupt Sharing, which is meant to resolve these kinds of problems. It's easy enough to disable. Go to My Computer ➤ Properties ➤ Device Manager ➤ Sound, Video, Game Controllers and get the properties for your PCI 64 card. Go to the Settings tab and uncheck the Allow LPT Interrupt Sharing check box. If that doesn't fix the problem and there are no other conflicts, it's likely that your card and game are simply incompatible.

A supposedly common problem with Turtle Beach's popular Monterey and Tahiti cards is that the microphone does not work. This is actually not the case because they do, just not in a way people expect. These cards require a line-level input, a state that is commonly mistaken for being nonpowered. Simple microphones don't output any significant amount of current, so, unless you have a microphone capable of producing line-level output (–10dBV to +4dBV) or a microphone preamplifier, you'll need another path to getting microphone input. You can buy a relatively inexpensive inline preamp made specifically for microphones, or you can get a mixer.

If you need input now and cannot wait, try to locate that old auto tape deck you stashed in the attic when you got your car CD player (it's probably next to the turntable). Most mid- to high-end tape decks have a line-level out so, with a gender changing cable (RCA to minijack) that you can get at Radio Shack for $10, you can connect it straight to the sound card. Remove the tape deck's door cover or leave it open, set it on Pause, place your finger on the little metal plunger in the top-left of the tape bay, and set it to record. Once it's running, you have a nice little mixer for your microphone and a line-level input going to your card.

Cards are much more delicate than sound equipment and can fry easily. Make sure you place the correct current line to the correct jack, or you might end up with a card that doesn't do anything.

Now you know how to get the most of your computer's sound—how about an accompanying picture with that? In the next chapter, we'll cover everything you need to know about video capture.

25

You Oughta Be in Pictures: Video Capture

INTRODUCTION

Once, we transferred most of our technical knowledge through books. All you needed to receive information from a book was sufficient light to read, functional eyes, literacy skills, and the desire to learn. Computers could display the written word, but truthfully in a lower-quality manner than could books; it is considerably easier to read text from a book than from a video screen. Nevertheless, computers have been until recently little more than electronic books.

The pervasiveness of television and videotape has made nonwritten communications popular and, actually, *more* than popular—it's something of a requirement in some sectors. In response to this, moving video is being integrated more and more into PC software.

In addition to the uses of video on the computer, the speed and power of personal computers has improved to the point that the home user can capture, edit, and return to tape finished video productions that rival those done by professionals. With the advent of low-cost consumer digital camcorders in the digital video (DV) and Digital-8 formats and the FireWire digital connection on new computers, the quality can in fact equal professional results.

E-mail can be affected by video: for less than $100 you can get a simple video camera that looks like a golf ball. You clip the camera to your monitor, hook the camera to your video capture board, FireWire, or USB port, and you record your message in full motion video and sound. Then you package the video clip into an e-mail message, and your recipient can hear your voice and see you. With a product such as Microsoft's NetMeeting, you can hold interactive video conversations.

Just a few years ago, the state of the art in computer-assisted presentations was pretty color graphs. Now it's pretty color graphs with inserts of moving, talking figures. Video editing and production was the domain of the professional and the serious hobbyist. Producing your own feature movie was not even a fantasy. Now all these can be done with simple consumer video equipment, off-the-shelf consumer computers, and inexpensive video-editing software. One of the most famous examples of the desktop movie revolution was the creation of the movie *The Blair Witch Project*, shot on consumer analog and digital video camcorders and edited on desktop computer equipment. It grossed untold millions of dollars and launched a desktop video revolution.

How do you accomplish all these moving-video feats? With video capture hardware and software. In this chapter, you'll learn what kinds of hardware and software you'll need, how to install them, and how to make them work.

Installing a Video Capture Board and a PC Cam

Installing a capture board is relatively simple in current PCI bus computers. Installing a PC cam on computers with USB ports is also easy. For both procedures, the main thing to remember is to follow instructions and take your time.

Video Capture Board

Be Prepared

Before you start, there are some things you may need on hand. These include:

- Plenty of light so that you can see into the computer case when opened
- Screwdriver or other tools required to open your computer case and install the capture board
- Small container to hold removed screws
- Windows installation CD for any drivers required upon software installation
- Antistatic wristband

1. Open your computer case.
2. Select the appropriate slot in which to plug the capture board.
3. Remove any chassis plugs that will interfere with the external connections to the board.
4. Plug in the board and replace the screws to hold it in place.

5. Follow the board manufacturer's instructions for installing software drivers and other software utilities.

6. Follow the board manufacturer's instructions for testing and implementing the board itself.

PC Cam

Be Prepared

Before you start, there are some things you may need on hand. These include:

▶ PC cam documentation. Read the installation instructions thoroughly before you begin installation.

---

1. Plug the PC cam's USB cable into a USB port on your computer.

2. Plug the PC cam's power cable into the device and attach it to a power source.

3. Follow the PC cam manufacturer's instructions for installing software drivers and other software utilities.

4. Follow the PC cam manufacturer's instructions for testing and implementing the board itself.

Video Capture Overview

There's a lot to learn about doing video capture. Summarized, it looks like Figure 25.1.

Figure 25.1

Creating video
capture clips

There's a lot to that; don't worry, I'll explain it all in this chapter. Briefly, however, creating video capture clips requires three main steps:

1. Connecting and configuring the video capture hardware and software.

2. Capturing the image with video capture hardware.

3. Running the resulting video file through an offline compressor for long-term storage.

The last step is useful because video compression software today will enable you to make your files much smaller, thereby taking up less storage space, and still maintain pretty good sound and image quality.

Video Capture System Components

Let's go shopping for video capture stuff. I'm not going to tell you which brands of things to buy—at the speed that this business moves, any brand-name specifics would probably be obsolete by the time you read this. Instead, I'll highlight the kinds of equipment you'll need.

A video capture system includes four pieces:

▶ The video camera

▶ The cable connecting the camera to the video capture board

▶ The video capture board or digital video connections

▶ The rest of the PC doing the capture

These pieces are illustrated in Figure 25.2.

Figure 25.2

The pieces of a video capture system

To do video capture you need a camera, cable, video capture board, and your PC.

All four components rely on each other, making the whole process like a chain, no stronger than its weakest link. Get a lousy camera, and you get lousy images. Great cables and the world's best video capture system will ensure only that you get really full-fidelity reproductions of the camera's lousy images. A million-dollar camera's super-high-quality images are useless if your capture board can't capture anything bigger than 160×120 pixel images. You're wasting your time unless you've got a good camera, good cables, a good capture board, and a powerful PC to back it all up. It doesn't matter if the camcorder you select is analog (VHS, 8mm, Hi8, S-VHS) or digital (miniDV or Digital-8); the camera part of the system is governed by the same rules. These rules are outlined in the next section.

The Camera

Video cameras come with a lot of options these days, with names such as Electronic Image Stabilization, autofocus, autoshutter, and tons more. Don't get distracted by the doodads; camera image quality boils down to three facts:

▶ You've got to have good lighting and composition on your subject.

▶ You need good optics—that is, the lens or lenses—on the camera.

▶ The camera must receive the image with a high-quality imaging chip, an internal component in the camera.

▶ The composition and lighting I leave up to you; but let's take a look at the optics and electronics end of image generation.

Lens

The light from your image goes first through the camera's lens. Some lenses are plastic; some are glass. Although glass is better, I wouldn't worry much about a camera's lenses if you're doing video capture. Why? The low resolution of video capture (as compared to film) means that even the worst camera optics will deliver resolution beyond video capture's capabilities.

While plastic lenses can produce a credible video capture image, they are *much* easier to scratch than are glass lenses, so be sure to keep the lens cap on your camera when you're not using it, and clean the lens with a soft cloth and a lens cleaner. If you need to use special lenses for your video capture, then you might look into the higher-end camcorders that allow you to use standard camera lenses.

CCD Chip

The lens focuses the image onto the part of the video camera that records it. While most video images are stored and transmitted in analog formats (videotape is analog, and so are the two most common video interfaces), the image is originally recorded digitally, believe it or not. Modern cameras capture video images with a chip that's similar to a memory chip, a chip called a *charge coupled device*, or *CCD*. A simplified version of how it works is something like this: a CCD is a memory chip that doesn't have a cover on it, just an array of memory cells. The camera electronics fill up all the memory areas, and then the lens applies the light to the exposed memory cells. Light affects how much data remains in the memory cells, so the camera circuitry figures out how much light is on various parts of the image by reading data in the various parts of the memory array.

CCDs vary in size, which is measured by the total number of pixels that they detect. The total number of pixels on a camera's CCD ranges from about 250,000 to 570,000.

While that sounds like lots of pixels, it's really not. In order to store color information, the light from the lens is passed through a *stripe mask,* a colored filter that filters out all but red from some pixels, blue from some, and green from others. As a result, some of the pixels then become red sensitive, green sensitive, or blue sensitive. Each complete *color pixel,* then, is composed of three of the chip's original pixels, so divide the original pixel count by three to get the total number of colored pixels that the camera truly has. Then, as the CCD is a square array of elements, take the square root of the resulting number to determine the CCD's horizontal and vertical resolution. You can see the composition of color pixels in Figure 25.3.

Blue-sensitive pixel
Green-sensitive pixel
Red-sensitive pixel

CCD chip

Figure 25.3

Three pixels make up a single color pixel.

For example, one common CCD has 270,000 elements. That becomes 270,000/3 = 90,000 color pixels. The square root of 90,000 is 300, so a 270,000-pixel CCD yields a color image with a resolution of 300×300.

Basic VHS cameras usually have CCDs with 250,000 to 280,000 pixels, for resolutions of 300 to 306 pixels horizontally and vertically. If you're going to buy a VHS camera, then it really doesn't matter which one you buy, as the CCD on one will be about the same as any other.

Better cameras, in contrast, are equipped with an essential interface, the super VHS, also known as the S-VHS, or Y/C, interface. (I'll explain the details of the Y/C interface a little later.) When I surveyed the consumer camcorder market, I found that about one-fifth of the camcorders are equipped with a Y/C interface. Those Y/C-equipped cameras have CCDs with pixel totals of 380K (356×356), 410K (370×370), 470K (396×396), and 570K (436×436), with the 470K chip most common.

My recommendation is that you purchase the cheapest Y/C-equipped camcorder that you can find; there's not all that much difference between the most common resolution, 396×396, and the highest I found, 436×436. If, on the other hand, you want much better quality and can afford to spend more money, you can get cameras with *three* CCDs: one for red, one for green, one for blue; *each* CCD has a resolution of about 640×640. I don't recommend that because, as you'll see, about the maximum resolution you'll see out of a video capture system is 420×483.

No two chips and no two lenses are the same. Every year sees improvement in the CCD market. To find the best camera for your money, your best bet is to go to a showroom that sells lots of cameras. Connect different cameras viewing the same image to the same monitor, one at a time, to get the best idea of which camera produces the best image.

Don't presume that the most expensive camera is the best. Remember that it's not a camera—it's a *camcorder*. An exception to this comment is the three-CCD camcorder. The presence of three CCD devices significantly improves the resolution and color quality of the camera. A camcorder is a camera *and* a VCR, so you're paying for both. In a VHS camcorder, S-VHS camcorder, and Hi8, DV camcorder, the terms *VHS*, *S-VHS*, and *Hi8* and *DV* do *not* describe the camera; they describe the videocassette recorder that is part of the camcorder. You should get the best-quality camcorder you can afford, but be assured that reasonable quality digital video can be produced by the least expensive contemporary camcorder.

PC Cams

Another inexpensive alternative to using a camcorder for video capture is the PC cam (short for PC camera). These devices are small, but fully functional, video cameras that plug into the USB or parallel port or into proprietary interface boards. They are designed to be used for capture as well as to serve as live video sources for Web-based conferencing, e-mail video attachments, and other links to the Internet. These cameras range from $50 to $250 and all seem to deliver a similar quality. The results will not be adequate for serious video production but are fine for occasional use, as a video source for a Web cam, or for video conferencing as designed. PC cams usually don't have microphones and if they do they are poor quality. If you are capturing audio with video, you will need to provide an external microphone attached to the audio circuits of your computer.

Popular PC cams are the Intel PC Camera, Logitech QuickCam Express, IBM PC Camera and 3Com HomeConnect PC Digital Camera. All are available in USB and parallel versions. The USB versions are much simpler to install and seem to have fewer conflicts with other hardware and software installed on the computer. Installation is simple.

Web Cams

Web cams are video sources that are linked to a Web page and that provide continuous streaming video via the Internet. Web cams are used for fun, promotion, and security. Web cams generally use a PC cam device for the video source and utilize streaming video software such as RealVideo to establish the Web page component. Instructions for creating and maintaining a Web cam can be obtained from www.realaudio.com and other sources on the Internet.

VCR

What are the differences between digital versus analog VCRs? The most significant difference between a digital and an analog camcorder, at least for the consumer, is that the digital camcorder captures the analog video from the camera, digitizes it, compresses it, and stores it as a digital computer file on the tape, whereas an analog camcorder records only the analog video on tape. In the case of the digital camcorder, the video file can be transferred directly to the computer's hard drive without any further capturing and compression process. In the analog system, the analog video collected by the camera and stored on tape still needs to be captured, digitized, compressed, and stored on the computer's hard drive.

In digital camcorders, much of the concern I discuss later about loss of quality in generational copying is not an issue, and you are encouraged to store the video on digital tape for later transfer to the computer.

If you *must* capture to analog tape, use S-VHS or an 8mm format in preference to VHS. That's because of all the recording formats in the video world, VHS is the absolute worst: it retains a low-resolution image. In fact, in ascending order of desirability, VHS is the worst; super VHS is better, and Hi8 is better yet. In the consumer video world (and professional as well), the digital formats (miniDV and Digital-8) are the best of all, besting even Hi8 and rivaling professional systems.

What does "better" mean? Talk to TV people, and you'll find that they speak a different language than you and I speak when it comes to resolution. First of all, video formats—whether broadcast, S-VHS, VHS, Hi8, laser, or whatever, all share the same vertical resolution—483 visible pixels. The TV paints 483 horizontal lines as its electron beam travels from the top of the screen to the bottom of the screen. Actually, it paints *525* lines, but some of them get lost in TV overhead, making 483 the best number you can get for vertical resolution.

The difference in video products is, believe it or not, *horizontal* resolution. No one *ever* quotes vertical resolution because everything shows 483 lines top to bottom, at least in theory. But everyone quotes *horizontal* resolution. Horizontal resolution is defined something like this: if I were to point a camera at a piece of paper with a bunch of parallel vertical lines on it, how many of those lines could I fit on a screen before they blurred into each other?

The lowest answer to that question is VHS, which will show only about 200 lines. Therefore, VHS resolution in computer terms is about 200 pixels wide by 483 pixels deep. S-VHS is about 420×483. Broadcast video is about 360×483 in resolution. The composite interface can support about 240×483, and the Y/C (S-VHS) interface, like the tape format, is near 420×483 in resolution. The differences in resolution are illustrated in Figure 25.4.

Figure 25.4

Comparing video resolution

| VHS: 200 pixels wide by 483 pixels deep | S-VHS: about 420 pixels wide by 483 pixels deep | All video formats: 483-pixel vertical resolution |

Note

I'm virtually certain that I'm going to get letters on this, so I'd ask that the video experts in the audience please note: no one in the video industry publishes vertical by horizontal pixel equivalents, at least not ones that can be tested and agreed upon as standard. I spoke to four people who were all undoubtedly experts on video, and got different resolutions—sometimes *very* different resolutions—from each. Please don't write to tell me that I'm all wrong unless you've got a repeatable, definitive reference for your resolutions.

Digital video conforms to the same limitations, at this time, that the analog systems do. This is because the digital video information must be translated back to analog video that conforms to a North American standard in order to be broadcast or viewed on the currently dominant analog television systems. (You'll learn more about this standard, called the National Television System Committee, or NTSC, standard, later in this chapter.) This will change in the next few years as digital video and High-Definition TV, or HDTV, become the legal standards for broadcast and come to dominate the consumer marketplace for televisions. But I am getting ahead of reality. Currently television is dominantly analog, and there are millions of analog camcorders that need to interface with computers.

The Camera/PC or VCR/PC Video Interface

Once you've got the information in the camera, you've got to get it to the capture equipment. Cameras and VCRs tend to have one or more of three kinds of outputs.

▶ Some cameras and all VCRs have a radio frequency (RF) output, the kind that goes directly into a television's antenna connection. Your video capture equipment probably won't support this interface, and because the image quality is very low, you wouldn't want it in any case.

▶ Most cameras and VCRs have an interface known as an NTSC, a composite, or simply a video interface. It's one of two common interfaces on a video capture board. It is the minimum quality interface that you'd use to connect a video source (a camera or a VCR) to a video capture board.

▶ As I mentioned earlier, better-quality consumer camcorders and VCRs have an output labeled S-VHS, known as a super VHS, or Y/C, interface. It is the preferable interface between a video source and a capture board.

If you are using DV or Digital-8 and are connecting to your computer by FireWire or other devices in the digital domain, most of this information is irrelevant because when you transfer digital video into your computer via a FireWire or another digital connection, you are not capturing the video but are transferring a file from the tape to the hard drive and back. This eliminates image quality loss and many of the other problems discussed below. When you are transferring digital video from the computer into analog formats, then the interface rules above apply with a vengeance.

To understand these interfaces in detail, you've got to understand a bit about how video information gets shuttled around in the video and TV world. Explaining them will require that I take RF, composite, and Y/C a bit out of order.

Component versus Composite Interfaces

Color signals all boil down to three simple, or *primary*, colors: red, green, and blue. You can describe any color as a combination of those three colors, as you can see in Figure 25.5.

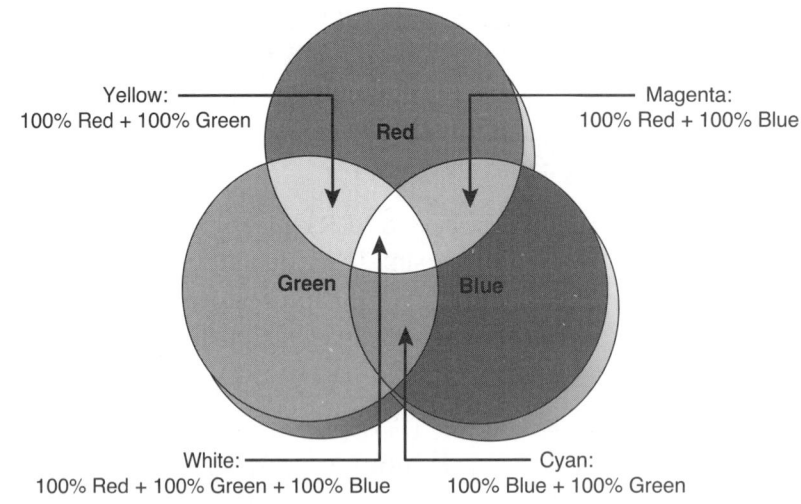

Figure 25.5

Primary colors
combine to form
other colors.

Basically, color video cameras record pictures by breaking a picture down into a grid of dots called *picture elements*, or *pixels*. The camera senses the degree of red intensity, green intensity, and blue intensity of each pixel, transmitting that information to the recording equipment (the VCR, tape deck, or whatever). Figure 25.6 illustrates how this works.

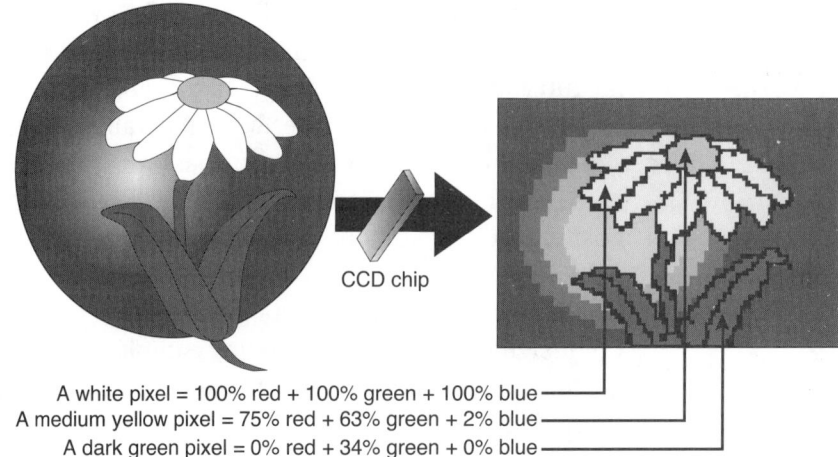

Figure 25.6

The camera records
pictures as an array of
pixels containing red,
green, and blue color
information.

Professional-quality video cameras connect to videocassette recorders of similar professional quality via an interface with *five* cables—one each for the red, green, and blue signals, and two more cables for synchronizing the signal. (Ever adjusted the Vertical Hold or Horizontal Hold knobs on a TV? That's what those cables transmit: vertical synchronization and horizontal synchronization information.) An interface of that type, a video interface that uses separate cables for each primary color, is called a *component* interface. Not all video interface types are component interfaces, however; alternative approaches blend the red, green, and blue signals together into a single-cable *composite* interface. Video interfaces are, then, either component or composite in nature. The two are contrasted in Figure 25.7.

Component interface:

Red signal

Green signal

Blue signal

Horizontal synchronization data

Vertical synchronization data

Composite interface:

Combined red, green, and blue signals

Horizontal synchronization data

Vertical synchronization data

Figure 25.7

Component versus composite video interfaces

Component interfaces are preferable, because keeping the color signals separate allows higher-quality signal transmission. Composite video, on the other hand, is cheaper to build hardware-wise, and so most camcorders and VCRs in North America support only a composite-type interface called NTSC. As I mentioned earlier, NTSC stands for National Television System Committee. It's the North

American standard video interface format for broadcast color TV and was developed in 1953 (an earlier black-and-white version of the NTSC standard was established in 1941). Y/C is an example of a kind of component interface. You see a variation of the Red Green Blue (RGB) component interface on the back of some high-quality computer monitors; not only do they have the common 15-pin VGA D-shell connector, they may also have five BNC connectors for the professional RGB component interface that I described in the preceding paragraph.

From Black-and-White to Color

Before getting any further into this, let me warn you: understanding video interfaces is a bit difficult because the video industry "just growed that way." If the video business were starting out now, every piece of video equipment would probably use the simple, intuitive five-cable RGB interface. Like the muddle of extended, expanded, and conventional memory, no one planned this—it just turned out this way.

As you know, video didn't start out with *color* transmission; the first TVs were black-and-white, or monochrome. Actually, neither term is really correct; it's better to describe colorless video images as *grayscale*. In grayscale, video images are represented as pixels, as in color video, except each pixel can assume only a shade of gray. But what is "gray"? Technically, gray is any color created by mixing equal amounts of red, green, and blue light. No red, green, or blue yields black; full intensity red, green, and blue yields bright white. Varying intensities in between create lighter or darker grays. Although we're used to a world of color, we can easily interpret grayscale images; we do it whenever we see a black-and-white TV show or movie, or most pictures in newspapers. The combinations of red, green, and blue that produce some various shades of gray are illustrated in Figure 25.8.

White: ← 100% red, 100% green, 100% blue

75% gray: ← 75% red, 75% green, 75% blue

50% gray: ← 50% red, 50% green, 50% blue

25% gray: ← 25% red, 25% green, 25% blue

Black: ← 0% red, 0% green, 0% blue

Figure 25.8

Combinations of red, green, and blue produce various shades of gray.

The original video equipment and TV broadcast equipment was designed in the grayscale-only days for grayscale-only signals. Basically, black-and-white TV signals consist of a series of information about the intensity of each pixel on the TV screen, information that tells the TV how much to light up each part of the screen, producing black-and-white images. A whole industry grew up in the '50s around grayscale TV: TV networks and studios invested millions of dollars in equipment that they obviously wouldn't want to see become obsolete. Millions of households invested hundreds of millions of dollars in TV sets that they wouldn't want to see become obsolete.

Which is why the advent of color TV in the 1960s posed a problem.

You see, everybody *wanted* color TV. Colorful pictures are more interesting than grayscale pictures to look at. But nobody wanted a new color system that would make the existing black-and-white TVs obsolete. NBC couldn't just say, "As of 1 January 1953, we're going to stop broadcasting old-style black-and-white signals and start broadcasting the new color signals. Now, the color signals won't work with your old TVs, so it's just too bad for all of you who've faithfully watched our network all this time—you'll have to go out and buy a new, expensive, color TV."

So the broadcast companies devised a method for transmitting color signals whereby the old grayscale signal still got transmitted, but with a separate color portion added. Old black-and-white TVs wouldn't look for the color information, and so they would still work fine, displaying grayscale images. But color TVs would know to look for that extra color information and display it. As the color information got pasted on the back of the existing grayscale signal, there wasn't much room for the color information. As a result, NTSC color video isn't of a very high quality. That's why the television industry recently began broadcasting the new HDTV. Remember that the color signal starts off as three pieces of information: its red value, its green value, and its blue value. Each of those values is measured in *lumens*, a measure akin in some ways to voltage; it actually measures the number of photons striking some small area. Black-and-white TV equipment converts the red, green, and blue values to a single gray scale value called the *luminance* of the pixel, or the Y value. (Y isn't an abbreviation of any word, it comes from a 1930s color model that described colors in terms of a set of X, Y, and Z axes, rather than red/green/blue.) The formula used to create the grayscale pixel (depicted graphically in Figure 25.9) looks like the following:

Luminance of the grayscale pixel (Y of a video signal) =

$0.59 \times$ (luminance of green, or G) +

$0.11 \times$ (luminance of blue, or B) +

$0.30 \times$ (luminance of red, or R)

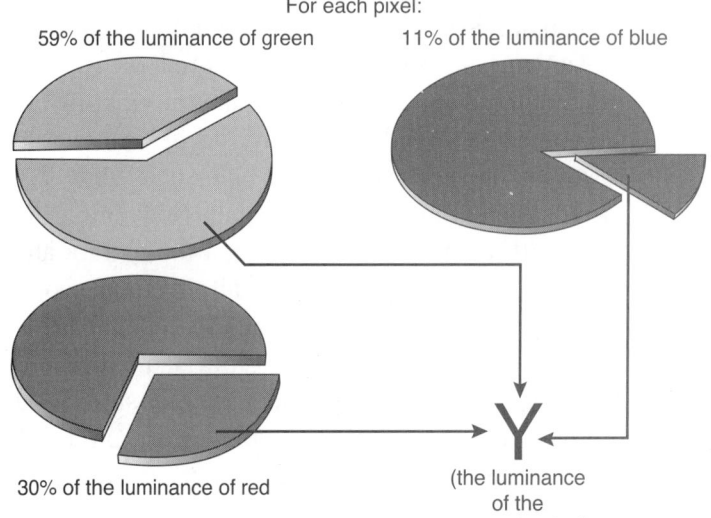

Figure 25.9

Formula used to create the grayscale pixel

For each pixel:

59% of the luminance of green

11% of the luminance of blue

30% of the luminance of red

Y

(the luminance of the grayscale pixel)

You see that Y can be derived arithmetically from R, G, and B. Notice that green has the highest coefficient, 0.59—nearly 60 percent of the colors that you see depend on green! Of course, no one knows exactly *why* we see green so well, but one theory works something like this: most animals *lack* color vision, and see only in gray scale. Millions of years ago, however, our many-times-removed ancestors lived in trees as pre-primate, lemur-like creatures. Living in the green, leafy canopy of a jungle means having to detect predators who attempt to mimic the colors of the jungle, like the green of a tree-living python or the shadow-like stripes of a tiger. There are two ways to detect predators: by their movement and by color sense. Most animals detect other animals by motion. Our ancestors added a remarkable ability to see extremely fine differences in color, like the few-wavelengths difference in color between a green snake and the leaves that it hid in. Since a lot of their world was the green of leaves, green played a disproportionate role in their color sense, as it does today to *our* color sense. Notice also that you're most insensitive to blue; that's one reason why many people find blue to be a calming color. Looking at blues doesn't excite the optic nerve as much, which means that the ancient parts of our brains that are still looking out for predators can rest for a while.

Despite the fact that luminance contains red, green, and blue, it's not possible to deduce the original amount of red, green, and blue from a given luminance, any more than it's possible for me to ask you, "If I made $50,000 this year, some from consulting and some from writing, then how much did I make from consulting, and how much did I make from writing?" I haven't given you enough information to deduce the answer to my question. If you just transmit the luminance information, you haven't sent enough information to allow a color TV to reconstruct the R, G, and B.

But suppose I rephrase the question this way:

"I made $50,000 dollars last year from consulting and writing. I made half of my income from consulting and half from writing. How much money did I make from consulting, and how much from writing?" You see, I asked you to derive two values—consulting income and writing income. But when I gave you only one piece of information—the sum of both incomes—I didn't give you enough information to compute the separate income amounts. When I added the second piece of information, however—the ratio of the two incomes—you had enough information to solve the problem. So, to solve for two values, you need two pieces of information.

In the same way, the color TV engineers knew that black-and-white TV was already using Y, so they wanted color TVs to *continue* to use Y (so that they'd be backward compatible with black-and-white signals). Y is derived from R, G, and B, but Y is only one piece of information. They'd need to add two more pieces of information onto the TV signal in order for a color TV to be able to reassemble the R, G, and B information.

Here's where it gets ugly: they decided to create two more signals composed of R, G, and B, but, unlike luminance, these two new signals, named I and Q, really don't correspond to anything in our experience. (Remember that Y corresponds to the grayscale part of the picture, the part you'd see if you turned down the color adjustment knob on your color TV set). For the curious, the formulas for I and Q are illustrated in Figure 25.10.

Figure 25.10

Computing values for I and Q

$$I = [0.74 \times (R - Y)] - [0.27 \times (B - Y)]$$

$$Q = [0.48 \times (R - Y)] + [0.41 \times (B - Y)]$$

The I and Q signals are blended so that they can be easily broken apart with a technique called *Quadrature Amplitude Modulation*, or *QAM*. The entire process of QAM is a bit complex, but you'll get the idea of how it works if you think of it this way: with QAM, you start with a baseline signal called a *carrier wave*. Like all waves, it has an *amplitude*, a *frequency*, and a *phase*. QAM modifies the carrier wave's amplitude to match the I signal, and changes the carrier's phase to store the Q value. Phase and amplitude are different characteristics of a wave, like the height and weight of a person, so they can be modified somewhat independently of each other. The combined I/Q signal is called *chrominance*, which is usually abbreviated C.

So, to sum up where you've gotten so far: R, G, and B don't get transmitted as R, G, and B, because luminance, or Y transmission, has been central to television broadcasting since TV was invented. Color television tiptoes around the limits of Y-based black-and-white transmission by creating separate I and Q signals, then combining them with the Y signal in such a way that they're separable by the receiving TV. The combined Y, I, and Q signal is the composite video signal that I've discussed in this section and that is illustrated in Figure 25.11.

Figure 25.11

The composite video signal

Composite interface:

Combined red, green, and blue signals:

Y, I, and Q

Horizontal synchronization data
Vertical synchronization data

Those composite signals are then converted into broadcast TV waves, where they are received by TVs, both color and black-and-white. Black-and-white TVs don't know to look for I and Q, so they see only Y, and are happy. Color TVs separate out (decode) Y, I, and Q, convert them to R, G, and B, and then display color on their screens.

As you've seen, the composite signal is also known as an NTSC signal. It blends Y, I, and Q. Separating them back out isn't a perfect process, which is one reason why a composite interface isn't the best available interface. The other kind of interface that you find on some video equipment is the S-VHS, or Y/C, interface, as I said before. Now you're in a better position to understand why it's called that: there are separate wires in the cable for the luminance (Y) signal and the chrominance (C) signal. Note that I'm going to call this interface the Y/C rather than the S-VHS because there are both an interface and a video tape format called S-VHS; there's only a Y/C interface, reducing any confusion.

The RF inputs and outputs that you see are for the broadcast TV signal, which is the messiest of all the interfaces: not only is it composite, but it also has been modulated onto a radio frequency carrier, adding even more noise. No video capture board that I know of accepts RF signals, although the PC-TV boards that allow you to view television in a window on your PC screen have RF inputs.

Before leaving this topic, there's another format to discuss. You've learned about RGB and YIQ, but there's one more format used in video capture—YUV. The Y in YUV is the same as in YIQ, but U and V are just two different ways to represent chrominance. Video capture boards may store the capture data as Y, U, and V data rather than R, G, and B data.

The Camera/PC Audio Interface

If you want to capture audio with your videos, you'll discover that most video capture boards do not capture sound. Instead, you'll have to have a PC sound card of some kind. To capture video *and* audio, you'll probably have to limit the quality of your audio recordings to 8-bit, 11kHz monaural formats. When transferring digital video, the audio tracks are already contained in the file and need not be captured separately and reintegrated into the computer file as it does in analog capture.

The Cables

Just one piece of advice: get good ones. The skinny S-VHS cables that come with the VCR or camcorder can't provide the noise resistance that a third-party cable such as a Monster cable can (they're the company that makes what are probably the best audio and video cables; you can find their stuff in higher-end electronics stores).

There are composite cables and Y/C cables. They look like the ones in Figure 25.12.

Composite video cable   S-VHS video cable

Figure 25.12

Video cables

Even if you don't buy the really high-quality cables, buy *some* third-party cable. The cables that ship with video boards are usually of minimum quality, and a place like Radio Shack can sell you a better cable.

The shorter the cable, the less signal loss, so keep your cables as short as possible.

FireWire (IEEE 1394) digital video transfer cables have a different connector type than do analog cables. They consist of four- and six-pin male connectors on the cables. They are also susceptible to quality (that is, the quality of the signal is tied to the quality of the cables), and so the best cables you can afford are best. Also limit the length of the FireWire cable to as short as you can get away with for your installation.

When selecting a FireWire cable for your systems, you need to note that two types of connectors are used on camcorders, digital VCRs, and computers. Some connectors have four pins and some have six pins. The result is the same, but in order to connect the cable to the device, you must have the proper number of pins on the connector. The cables come in four-pin-to-four-pin, four-pin-to-six-pin and six-pin-to-six-pin. Check your devices before purchasing cables!

The Capture Board

The thing that makes your PC able to accept and record moving video is the video capture board. There are two fundamental types of capture boards: analog and digital. Both are described below.

Before buying either type of board, first make sure that the capture board can capture *moving* video. There are a few video capture boards out there in the $100 price range that sound like a good deal, but they capture only stills.

Do stills sound like all that you need? Then these boards are *still* (no pun intended) not a good deal. Unless your image is totally still, then your capture gets a visual side-effect that makes it look like you're viewing the image through venetian blinds.

Digital Interface Boards and Connections

The primary digital video interface that is used on consumer digital video and computer equipment is the IEEE 1394 standard digital interface connection. Apple has a version that conforms to the IEEE 1394 standards called FireWire. There is no practical difference between IEEE 1394 and FireWire, and because of Apple's marketing program, FireWire has become the default name for the interface. Sony also has a marketing version of IEEE 1394 called iLink, and it is also compatible with other 1394 and FireWire products. IEEE 1394 is used not only for video transfer, but also as a high-speed connection for multimedia of all sorts, hard drive connections, and any other data transfer required. It was intended to make it easy to connect a wide variety of digital devices without the need for a proprietary board plugged into the bus.

In the case of digital video, FireWire makes the connection and transfer easy to accomplish. IEEE 1394/FireWire connectors are now common as standard equipment in low-cost computers, both desktop and laptop. In this case, no additional hardware is required to transfer digital video from a digital camcorder to your computer. If your computer does not have one, it can be added as a PCI board or as a PC Card (PCMCIA card) on a laptop. It can cost as little as $100 with driver and video transfer software utilities. More elaborate video transfer systems using FireWire are available and may be integrated into boards that also perform analog video capture. These systems allow you to use both digital and analog video sources in editing programs on the computer.

Examples of both dedicated FireWire add-on boards and integrated boards are the DV-200 FireWire card and the DC-500 integrated digital and analog capture/transfer card, both from Pinnacle Systems (www.`pinnaclesys.com`).

Analog Capture Systems

Analog video boards differ in a few ways:

▶ Some video boards support *overlay,* a feature whereby you can see video displayed in real time in a window on your computer.

▶ Most video boards support some kind of on-board real-time compression hardware. The exact method for doing that compression varies, leading to more- or less-effective compression options.

▶ Some video boards can't save moving video and are capable of grabbing only still pictures.

▶ Most video boards have both a composite and a Y/C connector, but be sure that whatever board you buy has a Y/C connector.

As always, a faster board requires a faster bus interface. Of the factors that I just mentioned, let's get the important ones out of the way.

Analog capture systems include boards that plug into a computer's bus, devices that plug into parallel, USB, and PCMCIA connectors. The boards have the fastest transfer rates and will allow the highest-quality capture with the least problems. There are, however, several very good systems that are external. The best example is the Dazzle Digital Video Creator device manufactured by Dazzle Multimedia (www.`dazzle.com`) and that comes in both a parallel port and USB version. This system (I recommend the USB for its reliability and ease of use) captures MPEG2 compressed video that can be edited and transferred back to tape, used on CD-ROM or hard drive, or delivered on the Internet at a very good quality. In general, analog capture boards confront many issues not present in digital video transfer. These are considered in the subsequent sections.

Real-Time Compression Features

You've already seen why compression is so important to video work. Those 320×240 windows are pretty small, but even at 15 frames per second (fps) they produce about 3.5Mbps of data in a completely raw format. Shove that much data down most hard disks' throats, and you'll end up with a lot of lost data. While you *can* capture data to RAM, which is faster than disk by a good bit, most of us can't afford a few gigabytes of RAM with which to capture. How, then, to get high-volume video data onto a relatively low-speed drive? By pre-crunching the data down to size. Video capture boards do that with on-board compression hardware.

Virtually all video capture boards do some kind of real-time compression as they capture the video data. Most offer the option of a compression technique called YUV9, which is pretty standard, and another technique, which can compress data better, but which is specific to that particular capture board.

The downside of the board-specific real-time compressor is that while it greatly improves your ability to capture long video sequences, it significantly reduces the video image quality. As I'll explain in an upcoming section, you usually *don't* want to capture data compressed by the video board, as the compression technique causes this degradation of image quality. If you can live with some image degradation, however, then the proprietary real-time compression support on most video capture boards will be useful; again, this will be clearer when I explain captures to memory versus captures to disk.

Overlay or Preview?

Analog video capture boards show you either the actual video signal as it arrives to the capture board, or the image that they're processing. In the first case—an *overlay* is the term—you see a window within your Windows screen (I'll assume that you're using Windows, although there are a few tools around for other operating systems) and full-motion video. In the second case, you see the image that's been processed by the video card, or the *preview* of the captured image. Previews will always be inferior in quality to overlays, as previews are limited by the color depth of your video board—if your video board shows only 256 colors, then you'll see a 256-color rendering of the 16-million-color image. As I've said before, today's computers and capture boards can't keep up with the 30fps speed of broadcast video signals. In a preview window, the colors will look "muddier" because Windows attempts to take the millions of colors in the incoming image and convert them into combinations of its 256 colors, a process called *dithering*. For example, if you had a video screen that could show *only* red, green, or blue in one intensity—each color was just "on" or "off," instead of capable of varying intensities—then you could fool your eye into seeing yellow by displaying a lot of green pixels interspersed with an equal number of red pixels. That would be a dithered yellow.

It sounds like an overlay board is more desirable than a preview board, but I'd tend to disagree. Overlay boards show you a nice, colorful, smooth picture, but that's usually not the picture that you end up with, so it's not very helpful. Further, overlay boards are more difficult to install.

When I described overlays, you may have wondered just how an overlay board can display 16-million-color video on a Windows desktop with a video driver that supports only 256 colors; sounds too good to be true, eh? Overlay boards accomplish this by modifying the way your video board works. Most every VGA board has an edge or pin-header connector on it called the *feature connector*. An overlay board requires that you run a cable from the feature connector on the VGA to a similar connector on the overlay board, and that you then disconnect the monitor from the video port on the back of the VGA and connect it to a similar-looking connector on the video capture board. This means that now the video capture board can "process" the signals from the VGA board before they get to the monitor. It is the hardware on the video capture board that allows full-motion video and 16 million colors. Essentially, it makes a window on your screen into a TV set. In fact, there are some boards available that are not video capture boards at all, but simply overlay boards. Equipped with an antenna input and tuner circuit, they allow you to watch TV in a window on your Windows desktop.

An odd side effect of the overlay is that the TV part of the window is not under the control of Windows (or whatever operating system is being used); it's just a kind of "hole" that the hardware fills. That means that if you try to capture an overlay window with the Alt+Print Screen or Print Screen key, then you won't get the image. As the operating system doesn't control that portion of the screen, it cannot capture that part of the screen.

The CPU, Bus, and Disk Systems

I hope I've made clear by now that the whole name of the game in analog video capture is data transfer. There's lots of data to shovel around, and no room for your hardware to stop and "catch its breath," so to speak. That argues for a fast, wide bus.

Add audio capture, and you've got an extra problem: now two boards with real-time demands are running simultaneously, throwing interrupts at the CPU, and, again, there's no time for either board to "catch its breath." That argues for bus mastering, so that both boards can transfer data to memory or disk without having to wait for the CPU. It would seem, then, that the optimal bus for video capture would be PCI, offering speed, width, and bus mastering.

In digital video transfer, the connection (FireWire/IEEE 1394 usually) the speed of transfer, and system requirements become a non-issue. These only become problems when you are transferring back to analog directly from the computer.

The best hard drives to use for capturing analog video are Fast-Wide SCSI hard drives that are audiovisual (AV) rated and can capture that highest-quality video at the lowest compression. In fact, a Fast-Wide SCSI system can capture, in a fast and properly configured computer, uncompressed full-screen video. In digital transfer, the drive speed is not generally a consideration—although if you are playing back to analog video, the drive speed does matter.

Installing a Video Capture Board

Installing a video capture board is just like installing any other board. Most video capture boards come with a software setup routine, and you must pick an I/O address, a hardware interrupt, and sometimes a memory overlay window. Virtually all the current boards and recent computer systems—certainly those that are up to the task of video capture and edit work—are PCI systems with automated installation processes. The section below points out some of the issues involved in manually configured systems.

Before you try to install the board, make sure that you've got a video source around that you can use to test the board. Every video capture board I've ever installed came with a self-test program; run it. The self-test will test for basic interrupt, memory, and I/O address conflicts. Then it will try to display the image coming in from the video source (the camera or the VCR). Now, if you pass the IRQ, I/O address, and memory test, then you still may not see an image. Here are some things to try if that happens:

- Check that the cable isn't loose or incorrectly connected. S-VHS cables in particular seem to need to be firmly pushed into their sockets.

- If the video source is a camera and the screen is black, don't forget that most video cameras will shut themselves off after a while if they're not recording. Perhaps it's better to just run a tape in a VCR as a video source so that you don't have to worry about whether there's a test signal.

▶ Most video capture boards have both composite and S-VHS inputs. They automatically figure out which input is active, but sometimes they guess wrong. The video capture software that comes with your board will usually allow you to force the board to use either the composite or the S-VHS input.

▶ Even if you pass the I/O address, IRQ, and memory tests, double-check that you don't have a conflict on one of those. You can do this by using the hardware installation diagnostic in Windows.

Once the board is up and running, it's time to try out the video capture software.

Running the Video Capture Software

The point of all your hard work so far was to grab a video. Now let's try it.

Start from a Known Video Source

The best bet for your first time around is to use a fairly good-quality video to practice with. I'd recommend that you hook up a VCR to your video capture board and just continuously run a commercial videotape. It's only VHS quality, granted, but it's going to be correctly color balanced, show decent brightness and contrast, and will serve as a good reference point.

You should be able to see the actual video image on a video monitor in addition to your PC's monitor. Set up the VCR and a TV near the table. Most VCRs have both an antenna output and an NTSC composite video output—it's usually just labeled Video Out, or the like. Connect the TV to the Antenna Out connector, leaving the Video Out connector available for you to connect to the video capture board.

Note that you should record off a VCR only while you're getting comfortable with video capture. Remember that you should do your captures straight off the camera into the capture board; saving to tape, then capturing from tape, adds a generation of the "photocopy" effect. Of course this is not a problem in digital VCR or camcorder video transfers, as the video is already digitized in the camcorder and is only being transferred to the computer's hard drive. In this case, the use of tape makes the process much easier since you can get it right with the camcorder before transferring it to the computer.

In the next sections, you will look at the capture and transfer process for both digital and analog video.

Digital Video Capture and Transfer

Digital video transfer is simple. Using the transfer and editing utilities supplied with your computer, FireWire transfer card, or video device, the process is a version of file transfer similar to copying data files from one hard drive to another. Most video transfer software can even control the operation of your digital VCR for starting, stopping, and fast-forward and reverse. With the cables properly connected and the equipment turned on, you need to use the controls to find the clip that is to be transferred, select a folder on the hard drive to store it, and begin the transferring process. Be sure to read the video transfer software and video device manuals for details of their specific features and processes.

Analog Video Capture

Now I will cover the basics of the more complex analog capture and compression process.

Use the Right Video Mode on Your PC

Before going any further, find a video mode that works well for your capture. You want a low-resolution driver, as high-resolution drivers must keep track of more pixels and so slow down the system. As video is very colorful, however, you want a 16-million-color driver if possible. The best video mode is probably a 640 × 480 mode with 16 million colors. Whatever your options are, just pick 640 × 480 resolution and then choose the most colors that your board will support.

Adjust Contrast, Brightness, and Color

Now that you've got the TV showing you what the video *thinks* that it should look like, run the video capture software on your computer and take a look at the picture in the overlay/preview window. You're likely to see that the colors on the pictures are different from those on the TV. Use the video capture software's VIDEO SOURCE OPTIONS command or the like (every program has a different name for it) to adjust brightness, contrast, and colors.

Some systems provide separate slider controls for red, green, and blue. Others offer sliders with labels such as Saturation, Tint, or Hue.

Saturation refers to the purity of the color. Shine a red light on a white wall, and you'll see a red area on the wall. Shine a red light *and* a white light on the wall, and the resulting wall color changes; we'd say that it is "washed out." Adding white light *desaturates* a color. Pure colors are saturated; impure colors are desaturated.

Tint and *hue* are intended to mimic dials and knobs with similar names and functions on a TV set. They're compromises, and (in my opinion) not very good ones. As there are three things to adjust—red, green, and blue intensity—it's obviously impossible to provide all possible red/green/blue combinations on a single dial. Instead, then, these dials enable you to bias the colors between extreme red, extreme green, and anywhere in between. The bad news, then, about these controls is that they don't let you play with the blue setting. But, then, recall that blue is the least important of the three primary video colors.

Choose Frame Size and Frame Rate

Next, you'll actually capture some moving images. You must choose frame size and frame rate. You'll usually have frame size options up to 320×240 for moving captures, and 640×480 for still captures. You can set any frame rate.

A 320×240 frame of 24-bit color will require 230,400 bytes to store. Using 15 frames per second would provide a raw data rate of $230,400 \times 15$, or 3,456,000 bytes per second, as I've said before. The relationship between frame size and data rate is illustrated in Figure 25.13.

1 frame (320 x 240 pixels, 24-bit color) = 230,400 bytes

Figure 25.13

Relationship between frame size and data rate

15 frames/second = 3,456,000 bytes/second

That's a lot of data to shovel around. In contrast, 15 frames of size 160×120 at 24-bit color require only 864,000 bytes per second transfer. Assuming you had a high-performance hard disk that could, say, capture data at about 1.7MBps (not an impossible rate for a wide SCSI drive), then you'd be able to capture about 30 frames per second straight to disk.

The whole idea of 160×120 captures certainly sounds like it'll make your captures easy, and it will, because small frames don't require as much horsepower to record as do large frames. But you can't *see* small frames. My recommendation is that you do whatever is necessary to capture at 320×240 resolution, and at least at 15 frames per second.

Capture to Disk

If you capture to disk, you'll have to reduce the flow of video capture data so that you don't overwhelm the maximum speed of the disk interface. You can do that in these ways:

▶ The capture process can't be slowed down by any extra DOS housekeeping. That means that it's much faster to allocate disk space on a defragmented disk drive, so defrag your disk before doing video capture.

▶ As I explained in the previous section, keep the frame rate low; 320×240 data at only 5fps produces a raw data rate of about 1.2MBps, which a fast hard disk can keep up with. Again, that's not the frame rate that I *recommend*, but if you must capture to disk, then it's one option.

▶ Again, use a smaller frame size; going from 320×240 to 160×120 cuts the data flow by a factor of four.

▶ Keep the audio sampling rate low, at eight bits per sample and 11,000 samples per second.

▶ Capture data with a compressing codec (see the next section for more information about codecs), so that there's less data to have to store to disk. The downside of this is that the compression technique will lose some of the video capture data; again, see "Which Compression Format/Codec to Use with Capture?" later in this chapter for more information. Compression is a tradeoff, so different applications will have greater or lesser compression requirements.

▶ The CPU's speed is important as well. A 600MHz Pentium can capture more data per second than can a 200MHz.

Disk capture imposes limits that you'd rather avoid, but unless you've got lots of RAM, it may be your only option.

Capture to RAM

In contrast, if you capture to RAM, you won't have to worry about dropping frames until you run out of RAM. You can address that by buying more RAM. Many computers today can accept as much as 256MB of RAM or even more. In the final analysis, it is the best way to get captures done.

256MB can capture about two minutes of video data without data loss. Your system will, of course, be different from mine, and the numbers may be way off compared to your experience. Find out early on how much you can capture by just doing captures of different time lengths: try capturing five seconds. When the capture program is done, it will announce how many frames it dropped. Now, hopefully, a five-second capture will show no dropped frames; if it does, then you're probably capturing 640 × 480 moving video, or have very little RAM. Keep upping the length of time of the memory capture until you start dropping frames; you'll then know how long your captures can go.

Which Compression Format/Codec to Use with Capture?

You're almost ready to capture some video. You've got just one more decision to make: which codec to use.

Codec? That's another acronym, one that stands for coder/decoder. Its job is to compress the video data as it's captured, and decompress it as it's being viewed or edited. The program that supports the compression and decompression—the codec—is kind of like a driver. (Just to make things more confusing, some very simple codecs don't compress at all; they're called codecs for simplicity's sake.) Some codecs are specific to particular boards; some are generic.

Lossy and Lossless Compression

There are lossy and lossless compression methods. *Lossless* compression techniques enable you to compress data and then decompress it without losing any information. For example, expressing a price of forty-nine dollars and ninety-nine cents as $49.99 takes up less space, and yet you don't lose any information in translating from the one format to the other. *Lossy* compression techniques don't exactly decompress back to the original data. Storing forty-nine dollars and ninety-nine cents as $50 yields a terrific amount of compression, and is probably fine for many uses, but it's not exactly right when decompressed into fifty dollars.

Most computer data cannot be subjected to lossy techniques; you certainly wouldn't want a spreadsheet to store your financial data *almost* accurately. But image data withstands compression without corrupting its message terribly.

For example, on my hard disk I have an image of a forest. It is about 740KB in size. Stored in the Windows BMP format, there's no compression, and so it ends up as a file that's 740KB in size. The simplest kind of compression is *run-length* compression, where you analyze the image for repeated bytes, and store the pattern only once. For example, if you've got a horizontal line of 500 blue pixels, you wouldn't store them as "blue, blue, blue . . . ;" instead, a run-length approach would store the information "repeat 'blue pixel' 500 times." Stored in a run-length format, the file drops to a size of only 249KB. A run-length format is lossless, recall. A common *lossy* compression technique is called JPEG (after the group that invented it, the Joint Photographic Experts Group) compression. Stored as a JPEG file, the 740KB file becomes 95KB in size. Put the two images side by side, and you don't really see the differences.

There are many techniques besides run-length encoding and JPEG. One technique is *Variable Content Encoding (VCE)*, where the codec scans the image for repeated patterns of bytes. For example, if the pattern "r, r, b, b, r, r, b, b, r, g, g, g, g, g, r" appeared several times in the image, then the codec would build a *dictionary* of that and other common patterns. It would give each pattern a short identifier, which it would then use in the stored file. I'm vastly oversimplifying here, but it would be kind of like if the codec stored an image of a flagpole, calling it `image01`, and then encoded an image of the United Nations building. Instead of having to represent all the flagpoles in front of the UN building, the codec could skip all the pixels devoted to representing flagpoles, storing just the one image of a flagpole and putting the instruction `insert image01 here` wherever a flagpole went. This is related to another lossless method called *Huffman encoding*. If you've ever used a file compression program such as PKZIP or LHARC, then you've used Huffman encoding.

Yet another lossless technique is *delta encoding*. In delta encoding, video files are stored as groups composed of complete, or key, frames, followed by a series of *skeleton frames* that record only the differences from the previous frame. At 15fps, most of the screen does not change from one frame to another. If the video is of a person sitting and talking to the camera—what is known as a *talking head*, the phrase from which David Byrne took the name of his musical group—then the background remains unchanged, perhaps throughout the entire video. That background can be three-quarters of the entire image, meaning that the delta frames need not store information about those three-quarters of the screen. The delta idea applies not only from frame to frame, but also within a frame. A codec could, for example, encode a horizontal line of the image, and then note that the next horizontal line of the image was almost identical; it wouldn't store the whole line, then, but just the changes— the *deltas*, in math and engineering terminology—for that line.

The idea of key frames matched with delta frames is common to many codecs, both lossy and lossless.

Codecs can do a lot of compression without loss, but the big gains are in lossy methods. Most lossy techniques rely on people's higher sensitivity to the grayscale image (the Y) than to the color (the C or the U and V, depending on the image encoding you're talking about).

The Intel Smart Video Recorder, for example, claims to record 24-bit data, but it doesn't; it uses a method whereby it captures and analyzes a 4×4 pixel area. Consider that 16 24-bit pixels are 48 bytes. The Intel capture board views each 3-byte pixel as having a byte that describes the Y (luminance) part of the pixel, and U and V bytes that describe the color, the chrominance. The raw Intel capture codec doesn't touch the Y byte, but scrutinizes the U and V bytes, compressing them to 1 bit! How? Well, a 4×4 pixel area is pretty small. As a result, you're not likely to see large color changes from pixel to pixel. For that reason, Intel can do a kind of compression called *color sub-sampling*. It takes only the U and V bytes for the entire 4 × 4 "pixel group," and averages them. The average of the 16 U bytes is 1 byte, and the average of the 16 V bytes is 1 byte. There is now 1 U byte and 1 V byte, or 16 bits, to spread out over the 4 × 4 area. The 16 pixels in the group each take 1 bit, and so each pixel has its untouched 8 bits of Y information, and 1 bit of the communal U/V information. This process is illustrated in Figure 25.14.

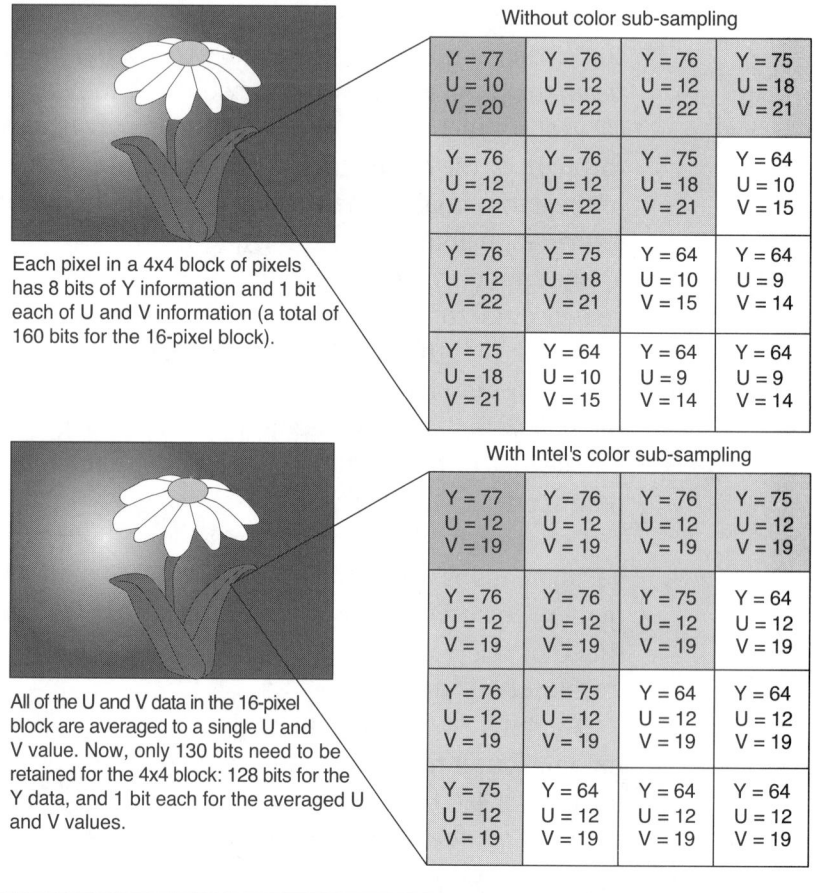

Without color sub-sampling

Y = 77 U = 10 V = 20	Y = 76 U = 12 V = 22	Y = 76 U = 12 V = 22	Y = 75 U = 18 V = 21
Y = 76 U = 12 V = 22	Y = 76 U = 12 V = 22	Y = 75 U = 18 V = 21	Y = 64 U = 10 V = 15
Y = 76 U = 12 V = 22	Y = 75 U = 18 V = 21	Y = 64 U = 10 V = 15	Y = 64 U = 9 V = 14
Y = 75 U = 18 V = 21	Y = 64 U = 10 V = 15	Y = 64 U = 9 V = 14	Y = 64 U = 9 V = 14

Each pixel in a 4x4 block of pixels has 8 bits of Y information and 1 bit each of U and V information (a total of 160 bits for the 16-pixel block).

With Intel's color sub-sampling

Y = 77 U = 12 V = 19	Y = 76 U = 12 V = 19	Y = 76 U = 12 V = 19	Y = 75 U = 12 V = 19
Y = 76 U = 12 V = 19	Y = 76 U = 12 V = 19	Y = 75 U = 12 V = 19	Y = 64 U = 12 V = 19
Y = 76 U = 12 V = 19	Y = 75 U = 12 V = 19	Y = 64 U = 12 V = 19	Y = 64 U = 12 V = 19
Y = 75 U = 12 V = 19	Y = 64 U = 12 V = 19	Y = 64 U = 12 V = 19	Y = 64 U = 12 V = 19

All of the U and V data in the 16-pixel block are averaged to a single U and V value. Now, only 130 bits need to be retained for the 4x4 block: 128 bits for the Y data, and 1 bit each for the averaged U and V values.

Figure 25.14

Color sub-sampling

Other boards do similar things. For example, the Video Spigot has a YUV 4:2:2 option that also employs a 4×4 group, but that puts a bit more emphasis on the color information (2 bits for U, 2 bits for V) and a little less on the grayscale image (four bits for Y).

The Intel Indeo codec takes things a step further by doing the 4×4 averaging not only on the U and V information, but on the Y information as well. If Indeo requires even greater compression, then it can average information over 4×8 or 8×8 pixel groups. The Indeo codec also drops one bit of the eight bits of Y information, so that what was YUV9 information becomes essentially YUV8 information.

Vector quantization is yet another lossy technique related to the delta encoding lossless technique. Under the delta encoding technique, you store delta frames that vary from a key frame, and deltas within a frame. But if you examined the patterns of deltas, you'd see that *they* had some common patterns, as well. For example, imagine a picture of a sunset. A codec encodes each line of video image as pixels. But if you examined each horizontal line of the image, you'd see a gradient pattern from midnight blue to blue to reds to the orange of the sunset. That's a smooth gradient; even as the sky gets darker, the relative change in darkness as you go from the top to the bottom of the sky is pretty constant. That gradient can be expressed as a table of deltas, and the Intel Indeo codec contains a number of these prebuilt tables. The Indeo codec then tries to find one of these prestored delta tables that resembles whatever image it is working on, and essentially shoehorns the image into that delta table.

That's been a very quick look at compression. Here's what I want you to understand from all this: good compression involves a lot of analysis and a lot of CPU time. Video capture boards just don't have the horsepower to do a really good job of compression in real time; heck, nothing short of a massively parallel computer could do a really good job of compression in real time. Now, most video boards come with a video editor program that will subject your video to *offline* compression, which can take an hour to compress one minute of video. I'll talk about offline compression in a minute, but understand at this point that offline compressors can do a fairly good job of compacting your video data while doing the minimum damage to it; real-time compressors can't. It sounds like I'm saying that you shouldn't do any kind of compression when capturing, but that's probably not a realistic bit of advice.

Data transfer limitations on modern PCs mean that you'll probably have to accept *some* kind of real-time compression, but my advice is to play around a bit with the codecs that your system supports to find the one that does the least damage to the image as it compresses. As you'd expect, the codecs that reduce the data transfer rate the most also do the most violence to the original image. Start out with a no-compression codec, if that's an option. Record some reference data—something on a videotape, so you can ensure that you're getting identical recording conditions—and see how much data you can record with each codec before you start dropping frames. Then go with the lowest compression codec that you can stand to work with, and get to work. (I say "that you can stand to work with" because slower codecs mean shorter captures, which mean more time spent editing and splicing.)

Consumer digital video utilizes an industry standard DV compression mode based on the JPEG format. It is lossy but at a level that is minimal and cannot be detected without laboratory test equipment. It is above the minimum broadcast digital video standards. Recompression can be done, once the basic DV file is on the computer's hard drive. This would usually be necessary for Internet playback, CD-ROM playback, and transfer to analog video tape.

Using Offline Compression

Once you've got your video captured or your digital video transferred, you'll find that it's kind of huge. You may want to trim off some needless intro and exit frames. That's where a video editor is useful: it lets you take a subset of a capture file and then save it by using some kind of offline compression. The choices you must make at this stage are:

▶ The type of codec to use to compress the data

▶ Whether to set key frames

▶ Either the target data transfer rate of the output file or an index of quality

▶ Whether to pad the data for CD-ROM storage

▶ How to process video into a streaming format

Offline compression uses a codec, just as capture does; it may even have the same name as the capture codec. But offline compression can compress at much greater ratios than capture compression. There's a price to pay, of course—two prices, in fact. First of all, really dramatic compression rates require lossy compression techniques, with all of their tradeoffs. Second, compression takes time and ties up your computer. It only takes time once for each video, as you've got to capture each video only once, but it still takes time.

Let me revisit the reasons why you want to capture data in as pure a state as possible. The offline compression that you're going to do is lossy by nature. But if the data was first recorded with a lossy codec, and you compress it further with an offline codec, then you end up with data that's been "smeared" twice. That's why you should either capture without compression or with a codec that's as noninvasive of your data as possible.

Choosing a Codec: Don't Recompress Until You're Done!

After editing a captured video, you'll resave it to disk. At that time, the video editing software will use a codec to encode the video data, just as the capture software did. Choosing a codec is easy. The big question is: are you done working on this AVI (audio/video) file? If you are, then use the codec that will give you the most compression. If not, then resave without any new compression. You'll compress even if you're not worried about the space that the file takes because of the data transfer rate required to play back the video clip. Playing back a raw Intel YUV9 video clip at full speed requires the computer doing the playback to read the file off its hard disk at about 1.3MBps, so it's a good idea to compress the data so it can be played on slower systems if you want to.

Suppose you're building a video out of five smaller clips. Each time you splice one of the smaller clips into the master clip, you save the intermediate result. If you use a codec with lossy compression to save these intermediate videos, then you'll end up reapplying lossy compression to your video several times, resulting in an awful-looking video. *This is very important.* For example, suppose you'd captured several small clips using a 24-bit RGB codec. This codec stores the entire image to disk or RAM, meaning that you won't be able to save very long clips before frames start dropping, so you'll be doing lots of editing. Suppose you've got pieces A, B, and C that you want to splice into video D, and suppose that your video editor lets you splice together only two files at a time. First, splice A and B, producing video IV1, for intermediate video 1. Also save it by using the 24-bit RGB codec. Then splice IV1 to C, saving it to D. As D is the final product, it's fine to go ahead and use a lossy compression codec. The process is illustrated in Figure 25.15.

Figure 25.15

Reserve the lossy compression for the last save.

Setting Key Frames

Tell your video software that you want to set the compression type and options, and you'll probably see a dialog box something like the one shown in Figure 25.16.

Figure 25.16

Setting the
compression type
and options

You can see the Compressor list box that lets you choose a codec. The compression software next lets you establish how often to set key frames, and whether you want to control the number of key frames. Tell the software that you do not want to control the number of key frames and concentrate instead on the data rate. Key frame adjustment is just fine-tuning. When you've got your video just the way you like it, try saving it with slightly different frame rates, and you can sometimes adjust the picture quality and data transfer rate. In general, however, you can unselect the box and forget it.

Setting Data Rate and Compression Quality

The example dialog box also shows a slider bar for Compression Quality and a check box for Data Rate. Actually, these options are the same thing. If you try to control one of them, you negate any control over the other.

Codecs have to make tradeoffs in order to compress data. Remember that less data means less data transferred per second. Putting the same image into less data means, logically, getting a lower-quality image; ergo, lower data rate equals lower compression quality.

The fact that the Compression Quality slider takes values between 0 and 100, and you can punch in any value that you like for the data transfer rate (from 10KBps to 16,000KBps) makes it seem that codecs must have infinite options in crunching your data. In truth, that's not the case. The Intel Indeo codec basically chooses whether to do its pixel averaging on the basis of a 4×4, 4×8, or 8×8 pixel group. That means that if you take the same video and save it with dozens of varying data rates, *you'll end up getting only two or three variations of the same file.*

This is important. If you tell a codec, "Make this a 405KBps file," then all the codec will do is examine the file and say to itself, "Well, I could *really* compress this, and get it down to 100KBps, or do a kind of average job, and get it to 267KBps, or do a really basic job, and that'd probably work out around 624KBps. I guess I'd better do the 267KBps job, as that's less than or equal to what I've been asked to do."

Padding for CD-ROM

One option that you see in video editors is Pad output for CD-ROM, or something like that. This means to make sure that each frame's size is an even multiple of 2KB. CD-ROM drives read data from a disc in sectors of 2KB. For that reason, you'd like each video frame to come off right on a sector boundary. CD-ROM padding makes sure of that, writing enough zeroes at the end of each frame to ensure that it ends on a sector boundary, and so the next frame *starts* on a sector boundary. It's done to make the video play more smoothly.

Using RealVideo Files for Internet Streaming

You will need to recompress your video to a streaming format for delivery as streaming video over the Internet. The most common formats used are RealVideo, Quicktime, and Microsoft's AVI. RealVideo has the largest user base. It is possible to capture directly to RealVideo by using the RealVideo Producer software, and it is also possible to stream directly from your camera to the Internet without capturing the files. The most common process, however, is to capture and edit the files destined for Internet streaming and then to recompress the files into RealVideo files. The RealVideo Producer software is available in a basic version free to download from `http://www.realvideo.com` and can be upgraded for a fee to more sophisticated and full-featured versions.

Getting around Bugs in the Video Capture Software

This really isn't your job as a hardware fix-it kind of guy or gal, but you'll find that after you've done all the setting up, you'll have to deal with the worst part of analog video capture: software bugs.

Every programmer must grapple with memory when designing a program. Programs store all their data in memory areas called *heaps*, *arrays*, or *variables*, all of which must be properly allocated and provided for by the programmer. For example, if the programmer of a financial analysis program knows that he's going to allow the program to track just 10 people's portfolios, then he's got to allocate enough space to store 10 portfolios. If the user tries to input an 11th, then the program should contain built-in safeguards that would intercept that attempt and reject the request. If the program *didn't* reject the request to create an 11th portfolio area, then it would end up creating that 11th portfolio area on top of some other program's memory space, "clobbering" the program.

In the Windows world, the word for clobbering memory space is a *general protection fault*, or GP fault. GP faults happen when a program tries to utilize memory that it doesn't have the right to use, an area that may be in use by some other program. Similarly, a program may try to utilize memory that just plain doesn't exist, as in the case of a program trying to allocate the space from 32MB to 64MB on a 64MB system. Basically, GP faults happen because of sloppy programming.

Note

I bring this up because if you're running analog video capture software, you're going to run up against a lot of GP faults. Look at the kind of data rates that video can generate, and you can understand how the memory needs of video capture programs could easily exceed the amount of available memory. The GP fault may be caused by the video editing program, or it may be caused by the codec software, but no matter what's at fault, it still crashes your system.

How do you avoid GP faults in your video capture system? First, have as much memory as possible on your computer. If the program never exceeds physical memory, then it's less likely to result in a GP fault. Second, allocate a big paging file, as that gives your video program a little "elbow room." Third, believe it or not, some Windows programs are sensitive about the amount of conventional memory available on your computer; they can't run unless you've got a certain amount of conventional RAM available. Finally, I've found that one way to reduce the number of GP faults created by the Microsoft Video 1 and Indeo codecs is by previewing a few frames. Most video editing programs have an option to allow you to select which compression codec to use, and in the resulting dialog box there's usually a Details button. Click it, and the dialog box unfolds, showing a Preview box and a slider bar that lets you control which frame you will see. Just let it build a few frames, and then the GP fault is less likely to occur. I have no idea why this works, but I've often found that it does.

Video capture can enable you to build some state-of-the-art presentations and programs as well as enable you to edit and produce video productions that range from montages of the kids to business marketing videos and even "desktop" movies. Now that you know how to do it, go try it!

Troubleshooting Tips

Q: How do I obtain the best-quality video?

A: Use the best camcorder you can obtain. Cameras with three CCD chips are best, and digital is best.

Q: I am having trouble with my cable connections. What can I do?

A: Use the shortest and highest-quality cables for connectors. Cables wear out from use. Use fresh cables. Gold plated connectors eliminate problems caused by corrosion.

Q: Can I produce high-quality video with an external device?

A: For analog capture, external capture devices are inexpensive, easy to install, and produce good-quality video. Plug-in boards, however, produce the highest-quality captures.

Q: I am dropping frames when capturing to my hard drive. What is the problem?

A: Your hard drive is not fast enough. If possible, use a Fast, Wide, Ultra SCSI hard drive rated for AV for highest-quality analog capture.

Q: I can't afford a SCSI drive. Can I use a USB external drive?

A: The USB port is not fast enough for video capture to hard drives, though for general file storage it is OK. Good results can be obtained with FireWire external hard drives, if a high-speed drive is selected. SCSI AV drives are still best.

Q: How much difference does capturing directly from the camera rather than from tape make?

A: Not a great deal. Capturing video directly from the camera eliminates generational quality loss but lacks the convenience of multiple "takes" and portability afforded by capturing from tape. Choose the method most comfortable to you.

Q: Which format is best, MPEG, Quicktime, or AVI/Microsoft?

A: They are all good file formats and all afford good-quality video. Select the appropriate format based on your target audience and its likely preference.

Q: I am having trouble with quality when recompressing my video from 640 × 480 to smaller RealVideo formats. What is the problem?

A: When recompressing to streaming formats for use on the Internet, capture analog video at the same aspect ratio, if possible, that your finished streaming file is anticipated to be. This will result in the best quality.

Q: My streaming video jumps, drops frames, and leaves out chunks of video content. What is happening?

A: When shooting video primarily for use on the Internet, avoid pans, zooms, and scene and background changes. These effects increase the file size and result in dropped frames and poor-quality streaming video.

26

An Overview
of CD-ROM

INTRODUCTION

CD-ROM drives are no longer the luxury item they once were—having one is a necessity. Almost all software sold today comes on CD-ROM, so you'll need one to install any new programs you buy. CD-ROM drives also play audio CDs through your PC's speakers, and let you play large, graphics-intensive games without making room on your hard disk for the entire program.

As CD technology continues to evolve, new kinds of drives are being made available, including high-capacity DVD drives, and CD recordable and rewritable drives (CD-R and CD-RW). In this chapter, I'll untangle the specifications of each drive type and tell you how to install, maintain, and troubleshoot all kinds of CD-ROM drives.

Installing CD-ROM and DVD Drives

No matter what kind of CD-ROM you are installing (including DVD), the physical installation of the drive is basically the same. DVD requires a little bit of extra cabling if you are also installing an MPEG-decoder card (required to watch DVD movies onscreen), but other than that, they're very similar.

Be Prepared

Before you start, there are some things you may need on hand. These include:

▶ Phillips-head screwdriver for mounting the drive in the case

▶ Small dish to hold the screws as you work

▶ Any instructions that came with the drive

▶ (Optional) Antistatic wrist strap, to protect electronics from static electricity

1. If the drive requires a separate adapter card, install it in the PC. Most CD-ROM drives run off the motherboard's existing IDE interface, so this may not be necessary.

2. If you're installing DVD and you have an MPEG decoder card to install, install it in the PC. These are usually PCI cards. If it's an IDE drive you're installing, set Master or Slave settings. If SCSI, set the SCSI ID number and/or termination as needed.

3. Install the drive into an open bay.

4. Attach the power cable to the drive.

5. Connect the interface cable to the drive interface (on the motherboard or adapter card) and to the drive.

6. (Optional) Attach the sound cable from the CD-ROM drive to the sound card if you want to be able to play audio CDs.

7. If installing an MPEG decoder card as part of a DVD installation, attach a loopback cable from your computer's video board to the DVD decoder Video In port, then connect your monitor cable to the DVD decoder Video Out connector.

VISUAL UPGRADE

Installing a DVD Drive

1 Install an internal DVD drive into an open 5-¼" drive bay in your computer.

2 Most DVD drives use a hardware decoder board that must be installed in an open PCI slot.

Master/Slave settings

Power connector

Data connector

3 The rear of the DVD drive has several areas: the Master/Slave settings at the left; the data connector in the center; and the power connector at the right.

4 After setting the Master/Slave jumper, connect the IDE data cable to the drive. Then connect the power connector to the drive.

Jumper

5 The DVD decoder card has two video connectors: one for input and one for output.

Decoder Video In

System Video Out

Decoder Video Out

6 Attach a loopback cable from the computer video board's Video Out connector to the DVD decoder's Video In connector. Then connect your monitor's video cable to the DVD decoder board's Video Out connector.

Types of CD-ROMs

Several types of CD-ROM drives are available:

▶ "Normal" CD-ROM drives, which read regular data and audio CDs

▶ CD recordable (CD-R) drives

▶ CD rewritable (CD-RW) drives

▶ DVD drives

Note

In discussions in this chapter, I'll use the term *CD-ROM* or *CD-ROM drive* to refer to a drive and *CD* to refer to a disc.

When choosing a CD-ROM, think about what it's for. Do you need to be able to read DVD discs? If so, DVD is your choice. Do you need to create your own CDs? Then go with CD-R or CD-RW. If you need neither of those capabilities, go with a regular old CD-ROM, and save yourself some money.

Tip

When I bought my last PC, I shelled out the extra $150 to get a DVD drive instead of a regular CD-ROM. I thought it would be useful, but to be honest, except for the one time I played a movie on it just to see what that's like, I have not used the DVD capabilities. Since then, better and faster DVD drives have come out. If I had waited until I really needed one, I could have had a better DVD drive, not to mention spent less on it. Don't let the PC industry hype you into thinking that you need a DVD drive if you don't think you'll use one.

Regular CD-ROM Drives

You'll see a CD-ROM drive in virtually every computer sold today. These ubiquitous devices read data CDs, just like you read the contents of any other disk on a PC. They also play audio CDs, provided you have a CD player program installed on your PC. For details about their mechanics, see "How CDs Store Data" later in this chapter.

CD-R and CD-RW Drives

CD-R and CD-RW are two technologies for recording your own CDs. *CD-R*, the older technology, writes only once to a blank, writable CD. After you write to the CD, it can't be written to again (except in the case of a multisession disc, which I'll get into later.) It's great for data archiving or creating music CDs.

However, CD-R has its drawbacks. If the recording process falters, you've just wasted a blank CD (and they cost about $1 apiece these days). CD-R is also not great for backing up data that changes frequently, because you have to use a new CD every time something changes to make sure you have a current backup. That's where CD-RW comes in.

A *CD-RW* drive can write to a blank, rewritable CD multiple times, just like with a hard or floppy disk. You can erase files stored on a CD-RW disc and make changes to them, so CD-RW is an ideal format for backing up constantly changing data, such as data files from an accounting program that you use every day. You can write to a typical CD-RW disc over 1000 times before it "wears out." Although CD-RW blanks are more expensive, they last longer because you don't have to throw one away when the data on it becomes outdated.

Most CD-RW drives sold today are dual-purpose drives that can do CD-R as well as CD-RW, depending on the type of blank you insert in them. I'll explain the specifics of both technologies later in the chapter.

DVD Drives

Like CD, *digital versatile disc (DVD)* is known mostly by its initials. Basically, the DVD format squeezes more data onto a single disc than is possible with a regular CD. CD-ROMs can fit about 630MB onto a disc, whereas DVD can fit as much as 17GB. DVDs are mostly used to distribute movies, but, increasingly, game manufacturers are releasing games and business applications on a single DVD that would otherwise have required multiple CDs.

A DVD drive can also function as a regular CD-ROM drive, so you don't need to have both in your PC; a DVD drive can replace your existing CD-ROM.

There are two types of DVDs: DVD-video and DVD-ROM. *DVD-video* is what you buy at your local video store. These discs are optimized for the storage and playback of digital movies through a player connected to your television. These discs are analogous to audio CDs that you play in your stereo. DVD-ROM is the computer counterpart and, as such, is more similar to a CD-ROM that you use at your computer every day. Your DVD drive in your computer will play both types of discs, but playing DVD-video discs requires a special adapter card called an MPEG decoder. Some DVD drives you can buy come with the needed decoder card; others make you buy it separately. These decoder cards used to be very expensive but they have recently come down in price, so that you can buy a decent one for about $100 if you didn't get one with your DVD drive.

As of this writing, a few companies are starting to develop DVD-RAM drives, which will let you create your own DVD discs. However, such devices are not available to the mainstream user yet, and even when they do become available, they'll be expensive.

Cross-Platform Format Compatibility

All the specialty types of CD-ROMs (DVD, CD-R, and CD-RW) can function as regular CD-ROM drives, in addition to their special functionality. Therefore, in theory, anyway, you could replace your existing CD-ROM drive with one of these specialty drives. A lot of people do replace their CD-ROM with DVD, in fact.

However, think twice before you replace your only CD-ROM with a CD-R or CD-RW. Think about it—what's one of the main things you'll want to do with a writable CD drive? *Copy CDs.* And you won't be able to do that unless you have an additional drive in your system that can read CDs.

In past years, compatibility between drive types has been a little shaky. The early CD-R drives produced discs that normal CD-ROM drives couldn't always read, nor could audio CD players in stereo systems. Things have gotten a lot better lately, however, so you should not have any problem playing a CD-R disc almost anywhere.

CD-RW discs, however, are a different story. Their lower reflective capability makes them difficult to read in some older CD-ROM drives. However, drives of 24x speed or above can usually read CD-RWs. Look for *multiread* capability when shopping for a CD-ROM to determine whether it can read a CD-RW disc.

How a Drive Reads a CD

After you insert a CD into the drive, the electronics within sense the disc, and a controller tells the spindle motor to begin spinning. A laser device (which uses a low-intensity gallium-arsenide laser mounted on a swing arm) is invoked, and focus-control circuits adjust the optical beam to the size of the pits on the disc (more on pits in a minute). The laser beam runs over the surface of the CD, reflecting light back to a photodetector that measures the reflected light and encodes it into a digital signal. This signal then transfers to the drive electronics, which give the signal to the computer.

The key part here is what's on the surface of the CD, because that affects how the light gets back to the photodetector. The recorded CD has *pits* in it (or dots that looks like pits to a laser—the pits are tiny indentations burned into the disc to represent data). To the CD player, however, the important part is not the pits, but the spaces between them, called the *land.* When the laser reads data, it senses the transitions between the lands and the pits. As you know, computers use the binary system (1s and 0s) to record data. A transition on a track is interpreted as a 1, and no transition is interpreted as a 0. The binary patterns are bounced back to the photodetector, which sends the data to a component that can interpret binary data back to its original format of sound, text, or graphics.

Now that you know how the CD reader works, let's take a look at how each of the various types of CDs stores that data for it to read.

How CDs Store Data

In order to understand how CDs store data, you have to understand several things about them: how the data is organized on the disc, what the disc is made of, and how discs are read and written. Those specifics are different for each of the CD types, so let's delve into each of them separately.

Physical Composition of Regular CDs

Compact discs are optical storage media that are read with laser light. The surface of the disc is arranged as a single spiral that begins at the inside of the disc and travels outward toward the edge of the disc. The commercially produced ones are made of injection-molded plastic formed from a stamper disc, are coated with an aluminum film to make them reflective, and are then lacquered to protect the surface. (CD-R and CD-RW are different, as I'll explain later.)

Compact discs aren't big (physically, only 4.72 inches in diameter) but from 527MB to 742MB will fit on a disc, depending on the number of sectors on the disc and the format used on it. Standard discs use the same size spiral as an audio CD (60 minutes) with 270,000 sectors and up to 99 tracks. The typical disc used in a computer-based CD-ROM drive stores 630MB using 333,000 sectors.

Compact discs are physically organized a little differently than hard disks. Whereas hard disks lay individual tracks in concentric circles, compact discs define a track by the length of a specific file; one file equals one track. The tracks on compact discs are laid sequentially on a continuous spiral. This spiral is a staggering 3 miles long and can contain more than 2 billion pits.

Commercially produced CDs are made up of a polycarbonate (plastic) wafer, about 1.2mm thick. This wafer is coated with metallic film, which is then covered, for protection, by a plastic polycarbonate coating. CDs are single-sided; the player reads data from only one side.

Regular CDs store data by arrangements of pits on the CD (about 0.12 microns deep and 0.6 microns wide). The pits produce areas of less reflectivity, so when a laser hits the disc, the light does not bounce back as strongly. Just like with 1s and 0s in binary computer code, this "pit/no pit" system stores binary data on the CD, as I said earlier.

Physical Composition of DVD Discs

A DVD disc is much like a regular CD, except everything is smaller and closer together. There are two kinds of DVD discs as of this writing: a single-layer kind that stores up to 4.7GB of data (or 135 minutes of video) , and a dual-layer kind that stores up to 9.4GB in one layer or 17GB in two layers.

DVD discs can store more information than regular CDs because they have a smaller pit length, less space between pits, a slightly larger data area (less wasted space around the outside and inside), and a few other minor design improvements. The primary difference is that the pits are much smaller and much closer together.

These new two-layer DVD discs are a wonder of technology. The second data layer is written to a separate substrate below the first layer, which is semireflective to allow the laser to penetrate the top layer to read the substrate below. This enables the disc to hold more than twice the data on the same surface area. Is that cool, or *what*?

And the technology is improving every day, so that in the future there might be many layers on a single DVD disc.

Physical Composition of CD-R Discs

Recall from the preceding discussion that regular CD-ROMs are composed of metallic film on a plastic disc, and the disc is pitted to store the data by reflecting or not reflecting light from the pit/no pit areas.

Commercially available *recordable* CDs, on the other hand, are coated with metal in a process similar to electroplating and are overlaid with photosensitive organic dye. When the laser burns data into the CD-R media, it heats the metal and the dye together, causing the area to diffuse light in the same way that a pit would on a mass-produced CD, such that CD-ROM drives are fooled into thinking that a pit exists. There is no pit, though—just a spot of less reflectivity.

Physical Composition of CD-RW Discs

As you learned in the preceding section, the dye on a CD-R disc changes as a result of mixing with the underlying metal, into a non-reflective state. That change is permanent, which is why you can't make changes to a CD-R disc's content.

In contrast, CD-RW discs also contain material that changes reflectivity when exposed to a laser, but not permanently. The CD-RW disc contains a silver-indium-antimony-tellurium alloy that is naturally reflective. When the CD-RW drive writes, the laser uses a high-power setting (called Pwrite) to heat the alloy to about 500 to 700 degrees Celsius, causing it to liquefy. After being liquefied, a spot loses its reflectivity when it hardens again, making an artificial pit. By reheating the area to a lower temperature (about 200 degrees Celsius, a setting called Perase), the laser makes the material revert back to its reflective state again. In this way, it is possible to write to CD-RW discs many hundreds of times.

Before you can use a CD-RW disc, you have to format it, much like you format a hard disk, but with a special utility that comes with the

CD-RW software. Early CD-RW drives took a long time to format (more than 30 minutes in some cases), but more modern drives can format a CD-RW disc in about 30 seconds. Formatting lays down a grooved spiral on the disc, ensuring accurate alignment of the burned-in data.

Standards: An Issue of Compatibility

If you've spent any time in the computing world at all, the concept of standards is not new to you. Parallel ports meet a standard, so that you can buy a parallel cable off the shelf and plug it into your printer. Data on your disks must follow the FAT format, so that your operating system and programs can read it. Internal hard drives follow standards that enable them to fit into drive bays, and so on.

Standards, both physical and logical, apply to CD technology as well, so that the discs can be read and the user can find the data on them. In this section, I'll discuss some of the particulars of those standards and where they came from.

The Genesis of Standards

To make sure that all compact discs of a particular kind will work with a corresponding drive, data must be stored and indexed on all discs the same way.

The CD of today fared better than its forefather, the *laser videodisc*, which was a large disc (about the size of a record album) that played movies on a TV. Philips and Sony were early, prominent developers of both videodisc and CD-ROM. They learned from their experiences with videodiscs that incompatibility can frustrate the user and subsequently restrict growth in the marketplace. Licking their wounds and vowing not to make the same mistake twice, they put their corporate heads together and developed a set of standards for CD-ROM discs. Since that time, technology has progressed, necessitating the creation of new standards and extensions to existing standards. Before I jump ahead, let's briefly review and define the original standards.

A color system was used to designate CD-ROM primary standards: red, yellow, orange, green, and white. To simplify matters, think of these standards in the following manner:

Red Book Digital audio

Yellow Book Data storage

White Book Video CD (movies)

Orange Book Writable CDs, including CD-R and CD-RW

Green Book Combination of Red Book and Yellow Book (for interactive presentations and kiosks)

Of these, Red and Yellow are by far the most important for PC users to know about. They're described in the following sections, along with High Sierra, ISO 9660, and CD-ROM/XA, which are all extensions of Yellow.

Red Book

The *Red Book* was the original specification defining how digital audio information is stored and indexed. It was developed for music CDs, which were the first CDs commercially available, and almost all music CDs conform to this standard today.

Yellow Book

The *Yellow Book*, also named *ISO 10149* (ISO stands for the International Organization for Standardization), extends the Red Book audio specifications and deals specifically with the more interactive requirements of CD-ROM: random-access capability and multimedia. The specifications concentrate on storage and indexing of data and error correction.

This standard supports several file formats for the different computer platforms that use CD-ROMs. These include Native Macintosh hard disk format, Digital Equipment Corporation's (DEC's) VMS, Apple's Hierarchical File System (HFS), and ISO 9660. I'll tell you more about ISO 9660 in the following section.

High Sierra and ISO 9660

In 1985, CD-ROM companies formed an alliance to produce a standard CD-ROM file structure independent of the operating system. The result is commonly known as the *High Sierra* standard. After some modifications, the standard was formally accepted by the ISO and was named *ISO 9660*. It sets forth a standard file system with a hierarchical directory structure of eight levels. This *Compact Disc File System (CDFS)* is similar to the FAT architecture familiar to DOS users. This ISO 9660 format is the standard format for all data CDs produced today.

Note

Theoretically, if a drive is an ISO 9660–compatible drive, it can, for example, read the information whether it is a Windows-based system or a Macintosh. However, this alone does not ensure compatibility because applications may contain instructions that use the resources of a given computing platform and that are not available on another platform. Thus, reading data and executing the program code is not the same; you can't execute programs written for Windows on a non-Windows machine such as a Macintosh, even if the Mac can detect the CD. Before you buy a CD, check its packaging to see what operating system it supports.

CD-ROM/XA

The CD-ROM/XA standard is another extension to the Yellow Book. The *XA* stands for extended architecture, and this standard does exactly that. By defining the way in which different data types may be interleaved (that is, woven together) on a CD, the XA standard really makes multimedia CD-ROMs possible. It also allows for multisession recording.

A common application requiring the interleaving of sound and motion can be demonstrated through a multimedia presentation. Suppose you're giving a presentation with pictures of a person speaking and have sound to follow along. In order for the movement of the speaker's lips to match the spoken words, the sound and the pictures must be synchronized. To accommodate this, tracks on a CD-ROM/XA disc can contain interleaved video/picture, audio, and computer data.

Briefly, here's how it works. A normal CD-ROM track contains only Mode 1 data-type sectors. With CD-ROM/XA, a track contains only Mode 2 sectors. There are two form types within a Mode 2 sector. Form 1 contains user data (2048 bytes) and error-detection code (EDC) and error-correction code (ECC) data. Form 2 contains raw data (2324 bytes) such as audio or voice.

In order for a CD-ROM to be fully XA-compatible, it must have the following capabilities:

▶ Read data from two differently defined data streams. These streams are Mode 2, Form 1, which is static information, and Mode 2, Form 2, which is time-dependent information.

▶ Allow data from each stream to be buffered and delivered to the CPU and video subsystem as required.

▶ Translate the adaptive differential pulse code modulation (ADPCM). *ADPCM* is a standard for audio compression, usually a 4:1 ratio. In other words, the CD-ROM must be able to send the audio signal to the speakers properly decoded and decompressed.

Be careful of manufacturer claims that their drives are XA compliant. XA-compatible drives are still evolving, and unless they are able to read Mode 2, Form 2, they are not compatible. In addition, ADPCM translation is not always embedded in drives listed as XA-compatible. To get full compatibility, you may need to purchase a new interface board.

The increased visibility of multimedia CD-ROMs has increased customer interest in XA compatibility, but to date most manufacturers have concentrated on interpreting images, not standardization.

Although this is not really an issue now, expect it to become one as more titles with full XA functionality become available.

Multisession Capability

Recall from our earlier discussion of CD-R that you can write to a CD-R only once. Multisession capability provides a way out of that limitation, but at a price.

Say you have a 640MB capacity disc, and you write your daily backup of your data files to it. That takes up 100MB. The next day, you want to back up your data files again. You can create a second session on the same disc, and write the next day's backup to the new session. The only gotcha is that once you create the second session, the first session is gone forever. You can't access multiple sessions, only the last one written to the disc.

A multisession CD-R drive has the capability to write multiple sessions. A multisession CD-ROM has the capability to *read* a disc that contains multiple sessions. (That is, it can read the last session written to the disc. No drives can read the older sessions.)

If you want to use Photo-CDs (the kind you get when you develop your film at the local drugstore, that have your pictures in digital format), you will want to ensure that your CD-ROM has multisession capability, because of the way pictures are stored on the disc. Multisession capability is good to have even if you are not interested in Photo-CDs. In the corporate world, CD-R data discs are being used and recorded in multiple sessions for archiving purposes. In addition, the newer, portable CD-ROMs (such as Sony's MMCD portable) support XA format. If you intend to use a given CD on a portable and stationary drive, both should be XA compatible.

Choosing the Right CD-ROM

CD-ROM drives aren't all the same. They vary in terms of their hardware interface, speed, drivers used, access to additional hardware, and where they attach to the computer. So that you can select the right one for your needs, I'll go through the details of those characteristics now.

Physical Characteristics

Physically, most CD-ROM drives look pretty much alike. The front panel typically has a power on indicator, CD busy signal, an Eject button, a manual eject hole, an audio jack, and a volume controller of some kind.

Disc Loading

Not all computer-based CD players load discs the same way, as you may know from using the audio devices. Although they are becoming less and less common, some players require that you place the CD in a *caddy* (a protective storage case that minimizes exposure to contaminants) for loading, and then insert the caddy into the drive. If your drive uses caddies, get a separate caddy for each CD, rather than sharing a caddy between discs. This avoids the hassle of finding a caddy when you need it, and will keep the disc protected. Other drives have a tray in the drive that the disc goes directly into. Once you put the disc into the tray, it slides back into place in the drive, and the CD starts spinning.

Although some caddy-style drives will play when the drive is on its side, so that the disc is positioned vertically rather than horizontally, many CD-ROM drives must be in a horizontal position to run. Do not attempt to run a CD player when it's on its side unless the drive is specifically listed as being able to support this position.

Internal or External

Many CD-ROM models are available in both internal and external flavors. If you've got an empty drive bay and don't mind opening up your system to install the drive, internal drives are often the best choice. They tend to be less expensive than external drives, and more models are available. Additionally, some interfaces (such as

IDE, for example) aren't available at all in external models, so if you've got an IDE controller that you want to use with the drive, internal is your only choice.

External drives are good for those with a SCSI interface who don't like cracking the case, don't have an extra drive bay, or are running into a bit of a power crunch from too many devices making demands on the power supply (external drives have their own power supply). They do tend to be more expensive than comparable internal drives, but (assuming that you have a SCSI host adapter installed in your computer), they're much easier and faster to install. Plug an external drive into the SCSI chain and plug in its power cable, make sure it's terminated properly, reboot … and there's your drive.

Performance Characteristics

All CD-ROM drives look pretty much alike (within the limits of being internal or external drives), but looks are not the measure of performance. You can buy drives with various spinning speeds, access/seek times, data transfer rates, buffering techniques, and so forth. All these features directly affect drive performance.

Some factors external to the drive can also affect its performance, such as CPU speed, physical interface, and the video system. However, unless you're planning to replace the entire system, there's not much that you can do about system effects on CD-ROM performance, except to be aware of them. A slow processor or inadequate video system will keep the fastest CD-ROM drive from maximizing its potential. The fastest drive will not perform well on a slow 486—best to save your dollars for your Pentium system.

Data Transfer Rate

If you're buying a CD-ROM drive, you've got several choices: the slowest drives available today are 32x and the fastest ones are more than 50x. Speeds are relative to the original (1x) CD-ROMs that were introduced back in 1981. The *x* factor measures the drive's capability to transfer data to the PC. Faster is better, to a point, but as the speeds get higher, the difference becomes less apparent. You'll notice a big difference between a 2x drive and an 8x one, but very little between a 32x and a 50x, because other factors intervene, such as the limitations of the other system components.

Data transfer rate, measured in kilobytes per second, is the measure of the quantity of data supplied to your computer at the onset of the first read operation. I talked about the specifics of data transfer rate in Chapter 10, "Hard Disk Drive Overview and Terminology," and it works pretty much the same way on CD-ROM drives. Table 26.1 shows typical transfer rates.

TABLE 26.1 CD-ROM Speeds and Data Transfer Rates

Drive Speed	Transfer Rate (KBps)
1x	150
2x	300
3x	450
4x	600
5x	900
8x	1200
10x	1500
12x	1800
16x	2400
18x	2700
24x	3600
32x	4800
36x	5400
40x	6000
48x	7200
52x	7600
100x	15,000

Access Time

Access time is the amount of delay between the drive receiving the command to read and the actual beginning of the reading. It's measured in milliseconds (ms). The measurement is just an average; the actual speed depends on where the data is located on the disc and how quickly the read mechanism can get to it. The closer to the center the data is, the quicker it can be accessed.

Don't expect an access time from your CD-ROM that even approaches the access time you see from your hard disk. I've got one hard disk with an access time of 9ms, but a common CD-ROM access time is more than 100ms. Generally speaking, most hard disks are 10 times faster than most CD-ROM drives.

Table 26.2 lists some typical access times for various drive speeds. Lower numbers are better. Notice that unlike data transfer rate, the access time does not get better at a constant rate as the drive's *x* rating goes up.

TABLE 26.2 Typical CD-ROM Drive Access Times

Drive Speed	Access Time (in ms)
1x	400
2x	300
3x	200
4x	150
6x	150
8x	100
10x	100
12x	100
16x	90
18x	90
24x	90
32x	85
40x	75
48x	75
>48x	75

Caching

Disk caching temporarily stores recently accessed or frequently accessed data to the hard disk, to take advantage of its higher access rates. Most CD-ROM drives have a small amount of memory in them for this purpose. Typically, the directory of the CD-ROM is cached. Caching the directory enables the computer to more quickly navigate subdirectories and makes the CD-ROM drive appear to be faster. However, the actual reading of the data is still slower.

Buffers

A cache uses some form of logic to figure out what to store: depending on how it's set up, it will temporarily store the most recently accessed or the most frequently accessed data on the hard disk. Buffering is similar to cache, except that there's no logic to how data goes into it. Data is stored in the buffer until the CD-ROM drive is ready to send the data to the CPU for processing. Buffer sizes can vary from 32KB to 1MB. Although bigger is always better, you should look for a buffer of at least 256KB.

The efficiency of the use of the drive buffer is in part based on the firmware in the drive. Two approaches for buffering are used, one to increase throughput to the CPU, and one to reduce seek time. Circular buffer read-ahead enables the drive to continue reading with one interrupt to the CPU. As a result, the buffer is kept full, and throughput is increased. In the other approach, the root directory of the drive is copied into buffer memory, which helps to reduce random-access time.

Interface Type

You can connect CD-ROM drives to the rest of your computer via an IDE, SCSI, EIDE, USB, or parallel port. Although you should be familiar with these first interfaces from earlier chapters, I'll briefly review them here.

Before I begin, however, I'd like to point out a couple of things about CD-ROM drive interfaces. First, they work in pretty much the same way as hard disk interfaces or floppy interfaces, so if you've got a handle on those, you're set. Second, most interfaces will do a credible job (with the exception of the parallel port, which is extremely slow). You can run into problems while installing CD-ROM drives with any of the interfaces, as illustrated in the upcoming "Troubleshooting Tips" section. Most conflicts will revolve around resource conflicts and outdated drivers.

SCSI drives have the best overall performance. However, the cost is higher, especially if you don't already own a SCSI controller. IDE drives cost less, and since most computers today have an integrated IDE interface, they are simple to install. Proprietary interface drives are usually easy to install and comparatively cheap, but they won't work with all operating systems. Today, the push is toward EIDE, an interface that is similar to IDE but quite a bit faster.

IDE

Integrated Device Electronics (IDE) came into being around 1985. IDE uses the AT-Attachment specification (ATA). The ATA specification took form in 1984 due to the collaborative efforts of Western Digital and Compaq Computer Corporation, which developed the idea of building an AT-compatible controller directly into the drive electronics. More than any prior specification, IDE places drive- and host-interface electronics directly into the drive. As a whole, this significantly reduced the price of the hard disk subsystem. It also enabled vendors to make improvements to the capacities and performance of drives with less risk of incompatibility.

Historically, IDE drives worked well with the host adapters from other vendors. Problems still arose when users mixed drives from different manufacturers in a Master/Slave configuration. The ATA specification standardized the communications between the Master and Slave drives. Most current drives now follow this standard.

The motherboards of most ISA bus PCs include an IDE interface, but the drive houses the controller logic. The 16-bit parallel interface can support two drives (either two hard drives, or one hard drive and one CD-ROM). When attaching both a hard drive and a CD-ROM to the controller, the CD-ROM should be configured as the Slave device. (On an IDE interface, one drive must be designated as Master and the other as Slave. This prevents the two drives from trying to "talk" over one another.)

Since IDE interfaces are already on most PC motherboards, many CD-ROM drives use IDE. IDE drives are a good, cost-effective solution for text and graphics applications. They don't work as well for CDs using multimedia, as IDE does not support multitasking. For multitasking, you need to move up to SCSI.

SCSI

If you're using a Mac or Unix system, you probably don't have any choice about using SCSI, because the OS requires it. You can either take this time for a soda break or keep reading to learn more about the interface. For Windows users, however, SCSI is not a foregone conclusion unless one of the following applies to you:

▶ You already have SCSI-compatible peripherals attached to your system.

▶ You plan to install multiple peripherals.

▶ You are looking toward the high-speed CD-ROMs (which normally have a SCSI interface).

SCSI is a good choice for those who need high performance and system flexibility. One SCSI host adapter card can provide a system interface for up to seven devices (one or more of which can be the CD-ROM), and SCSI devices have a high data transfer rate.

EIDE

Enhanced IDE (EIDE) is a technology that can support one or two devices on a single cable. Since most computers have two EIDE connectors, you can connect up to four EIDE devices in your computer at once. Most current CD-ROM drives use a subset of EIDE called AT Attachment Packet Interface (ATAPI). The same connector is used for IDE, EIDE, or ATAPI. Therefore, an IDE/ATAPI CD-ROM drive can be installed on a spare IDE connector.

USB

Some external CD-R and CD-RW drives are connected to your computer through your USB port. This type of connection is fast and far easier to set up than the others. You simply plug your CD-R or CD-RW drive into your USB port, and that's about it. You don't have to worry about resource conflicts, and since USB is *hot-swappable*, you don't even have to turn off your computer to connect your drive.

Multimedia Kits

Back in the days when CD-ROM drives were first becoming popular, lots of people bought them as upgrades for their non-CD-equipped PCs. The problem was that at that time, standardization was a problem. Unlike today, when most CD-ROMs have an IDE or SCSI interface, back then there were way too many interface choices. Some CD-ROMs ran off proprietary SCSI-like interface cards; others used true SCSI; still others ran off a sound card. Beginning upgraders were often not sure of what they were getting and how it would fit with their existing systems.

Enter the *multimedia kit*. These package deals consisted of a CD-ROM drive, a sound card (usually one that doubled as the CD-ROM interface board), speakers, and a bundle of CD-ROM-based games and applications. The advantage: everything was guaranteed to work well together. The disadvantage: the CD-ROM often ran off the sound card, so if the sound card went bad, the CD-ROM sometimes wouldn't work either, and you had to scrap the whole kit (except the speakers, of course). These kits also tended to have cheap, tinny-sounding speakers compared to the sold-separately models.

These kits are less popular today, now that IDE is the standard CD-ROM interface, and any sound card will work with any CD-ROM drive to produce multimedia, but you may still find these kits for sale. Nowadays, they're often DVD equipped too.

Installation

Installing a CD-ROM drive is fairly easy these days. The BIOS in most systems recognizes an IDE CD-ROM immediately upon startup, and most operating systems (including Windows 98/2000 automatically detect your CD-ROM without any prompting. Just hook up the drive to your IDE or SCSI interface, run the cables, and turn on the PC.

If you are installing a CD-ROM in a non-Windows environment or in an older PC, you may need to do some driver and/or BIOS setup after the physical installation to allow your system to see the new drive. But I'm getting ahead of myself here—first things first, the physical installation.

Physical Installation

Before you start the installation, think about where you're going to put it and set any jumpers on the drive accordingly. If it's an IDE drive, you'll need to connect it to one of your system's two IDE interfaces. If it'll be the only drive on that interface, it'll be the Master. If it's joining an existing device on that interface (on the same cable), it'll be the Slave. Set the jumpers on the drive accordingly. If it's a SCSI drive, make sure you set its ID number if there's a jumper on the drive for that, and make sure you have the termination for the chain set correctly. (This is just like the stuff you did for hard disks earlier in the book, so I won't belabor it here.)

You'll also need to free up a drive bay in your system if it's an internal model you're installing. Pop the plate off the front and slide the drive into the bay.

Next, connect the power plug and the interface cable (the ribbon cable), taking care to match up the stripe on the ribbon cable with pin 1 on the connector (usually indicated by a little *1* etched into the metal around it).

Finally, secure the drive in the bay with screws (usually provided with a drive), and fire up the PC to see if the new drive works.

BIOS Configuration

You may not need to tell your BIOS that you have a new drive—it may come up with that information on its own. As your system boots, you'll probably see a list of detected hardware; if your new CD-ROM appears on that list, the BIOS has figured it out.

Even if you don't see anything indicating that the BIOS has detected the drive, go ahead and let your operating system load. If the new drive appears there, you're fine—*no worries, mon.*

On some systems, you must enter the BIOS setup and set the drive type for the IDE interface to CD-ROM (or Auto, if there's no CD-ROM setting).

Drivers

Most CD-ROM drives come with a driver disk containing a SETUP program. If you plan to use the drive in MS-DOS or some other non–Plug-and-Play operating system, you will need to run the SETUP program on this disk before you can use your drive.

On Windows PCs, you should not need to load any drivers in CONFIG.SYS and AUTOEXEC.BAT to drive the CD-ROM. It should appear, ready for use, in My Computer. If it doesn't, you might try loading the device drivers and see whether that makes any difference.

To operate a CD-ROM drive in MS-DOS, the following drivers need to be loaded:

▶ If it's a SCSI CD-ROM, there needs to be a line in CONFIG.SYS that loads the driver for the SCSI adapter. This driver comes from the SCSI card's manufacturer. It might look like this: `DEVICE\C:\SCSI\SCSIDRV.SYS`.

▶ In `CONFIG.SYS`, there needs to be a line that installs the driver for your specific model of CD-ROM. This driver comes from the CD-ROM drive's manufacturer. It might look something like this: `DEVICE=C:\MYCD\NECCD.SYS /D:mscd001`.

▶ In `AUTOEXEC.BAT`, the Microsoft CD extensions need to be loaded (`MSCDEX.EXE`). That like would be something like this: `C:\DOS\MSCDEX.EXE /D:mscd001`.

If you need a driver for a specific SCSI card or CD-ROM drive, check the manufacturer's Web site. There are also generic drivers that might work. You see them at work on a startup disk created with Windows 9*x*, for example; they enable you to start your system and use your CD-ROM drive when you are not in Windows. In a pinch you can copy those drivers to your hard disk and use them for running in MS-DOS mode.

Recording Compact Discs

The basic process of creating your own CDs is fairly straightforward. Of course, you need the CD-R or CD-RW drive. You also need special CD recording software. Your drive should come with its own software, but there are other applications available that you can buy. Shop around and read a few reviews of other CD recording software if you are unhappy with what came with your drive.

Essentially, you create a CD by selecting the files and directories you want to write on the CD within the CD recording software and telling it to record. That's about it. You'll need to take special care that you choose the right standard so that your filenames appear correctly. Some standards support long filenames, whereas others do not. In addition, you can create hybrid CDs that can be read by both IBM-compatible and Macintosh computers.

One of the most frustrating parts about making a CD-R disc is encountering an error called a *buffer underrun*. This occurs when the drive you are reading from can't keep up with the CD writer's "need for speed," and makes it wait. The problem is—it can't wait. It has to keep moving, and writing, at a more-or-less continuous rate. If it's ready to write but the data hasn't arrived yet, a buffer underrun occurs, and you've just wasted a blank CD.

Buffer underruns can happen because of any of the following:

▶ Some other application is hogging the processor's attention, so the processor can't tell the source drive to send the data to the CD-R fast enough. Try not to use any other programs, or even move the mouse around, while a CD is being created.

▶ The source drive can't operate as quickly as it needs to because of its own limitation. In that case, try transferring the files for the CD to your hard disk first, and then making the CD from there instead of going CD-to-CD.

▶ You don't have a large enough data buffer set up. A data buffer holds information read from the data source, so that even if there's a pause in the data-reading, the writer can keep writing without a wait. You typically set this up in the drive properties.

▶ You don't have DMA enabled for the source drive. DMA modes transfer data and with less CPU intervention. Try displaying the drive properties and turning on DMA transfer if possible.

▶ You are trying to record at too high a speed. Many CD-R drives advertise that they can record at up to 8x speed, but if you find you get buffer underrun errors at that speed, try 6x or even 4x and your errors may go away.

In general, SCSI CD-R drives are less susceptible to buffer underruns than IDE models. (But then they also cost more, too.)

Maintenance

The majority of maintenance entails caring for your CDs properly. By caring for your discs, you are doing preventative maintenance on the CD-ROM drive, reducing the opportunity for contaminants to enter the drive.

Dos and Don'ts of Compact Discs

Here are a few pointers to keep your CD-ROM drive up and running:

▶ If a disc needs to be cleaned, use a soft, clean, *dry* cloth and wipe in a radial motion from the inner hub to the outer hub. Do not use a circular motion.

▶ Do not use cleaning agents, as many solvents used in them can damage a disc.

▶ Do not use a wet cloth.

▶ Avoid cleaning the label side of the disc.

▶ Use a caddy to transport discs.

▶ Avoid exposure to extreme heat or cold.

▶ Avoid excess humidity.

▶ Avoid direct sunlight and high-intensity UV light.

▶ Don't put your CDs in a microwave. It'll make them unusable, and send up some spectacular sparks.

Troubleshooting Tips

First, let's take a look at problems common to CD-ROM drives. Then I'll move on to DVD drives.

Common Reasons for Difficult CD-ROM Installations

Installations of CD-ROM drives can be fraught with challenges for a variety of reasons, but the most common problems stem from balancing the needs of the drive against the needs of other peripherals within the system. The following list identifies some common reasons for difficult installations:

▶ BIOS needs to be told to look for IDE CD-ROM drive

▶ Problems with software drivers (applicable mainly if not using Windows):

  ▶ MSCDEX not loaded in AUTOEXEC.BAT

  ▶ Wrong version of MSCDEX

  ▶ CD-ROM driver not loaded in CONFIG.SYS

  ▶ Wrong CD-ROM driver being used

▶ Missing cables or forgotten cables:

  ▶ Missing audio cable

  ▶ Inverting the ribbon cable so it is connected upside down (pin-1 rule)

▶ Improper SCSI termination or SCSI ID.

▶ I/O, DMA, and IRQ conflicts.

▶ CD-ROM and host adapter incompatibilities. Check with the adapter's manufacturer for a list of supported drives.

If you've checked all the items in the preceding list and the drive still doesn't work, it's possible that either the drive or the controller is dead. (Obviously, it's the drive if something else is plugged into the controller and the other device works.) Check the following:

> ❱ Is the controller board seated properly? Reseat it, and if that doesn't work, try swapping it with an identical working board.

> ❱ Does the drive unit even work? If you've got one, try connecting an identical working drive in its place.

Slow Initialization of the Drive

This error message can be symptomatic of having the buffer parameter in the MSCDEX.EXE statement set too high. Set the buffers to four or five for each CD-ROM drive attached to your system. Modify the /M: parameter in the command line. If using SMARTDRV, try setting this parameter to 0. This is not an issue in Windows, because MSCDEX is not required. However, if you have Windows 9x and you are still using MSCDEX.EXE in your AUTOEXEC.BAT, you can save some startup time by disabling it there.)

DVD Troubleshooting

Are there black borders at the top and bottom of the screen when a movie is playing? If so, this is normal if you're playing a movie in *widescreen* format. This is the same aspect ratio that you see in movie theaters. Because the widescreen presentation is wider than the aspect ratio of computer monitors (and most televisions), the black bands appear at the top and bottom of your screen.

If you have CDs that won't work in your DVD drive, first check to make sure the disc is clean. A dirty disc can be temperamental to read. If that fails, your DVD player might not be able to read the CD. Some CDs won't work in early DVD drives because the DVD laser isn't reflected off of the dye used in creating the CD. In other cases, such as with Photo-CDs, you may be completely out of luck. Some DVD drives don't read Photo-CDs (the newer ones do, however). It's best to try a DVD drive before you invest a significant amount of time and money in a certain technology. If it works, stick with it.

If you have a DVD drive that has an external DVD decoder board, check to make sure you have the connecting video cables attached to the right ports. You should run a cable from your video card to the Video In port on the decoder card, then attach your monitor cable to the Video Out port on the DVD decoder card.

The sound quality of DVD movies on a computer system can be problematic. Most DVD movies have stereo surround sound and other hi-fi gimmicks, which may not be supported by your computer's sound system. If this is the case, you may experience unusual audio echos and other oddities.

For DVD drives with software decoders, make sure you have the correct drivers installed. Visit the Web site of the drive's manufacturer to see whether updated device drivers and DVD player software are available. Manufacturers (good ones, anyway) continually refine their drivers and software to fix bugs and problems in previous releases.

27

Networking Concepts and Hardware

INTRODUCTION

Okay, you're convinced—your office is never going to enter the 21st century until you get those PCs connected. Linking your computers means being able to share files, applications, peripherals (such as printers), and internet connections among other benefits.

You've already got the computers. But what else do you need to make them start talking to one another? First, you'll need to understand some basic networking concepts. That's where this chapter comes in. Then, once you've got the basics, I'll tell you about all the components needed to set up your network—from network cards to cabling—and how to make them work.

If you've already set up a network, don't just skip over this chapter. I'll tell you what you need to extend your network or to link it to another one.

Installing a New Network Card

If you have already installed any other type of card, installing a network card is straightforward.

Be Prepared

Before you start, there are some things you'll need to perform the operation. These include:

- Antistatic wrist strap.

- Container to hold screws.

- Floppy disk or CD with software drivers that shipped with your card.

- Inventory of used IRQs, I/O address spaces, and (rarely) DMA channels so that you can be sure to assign your new card available resources and thereby avoid system conflicts. You can obtain this inventory by accessing Control Panel ➤ System ➤ Device Manager and double-clicking Computer at the top of the list.

If you're removing another card to insert the new one, follow these steps:

1. Power down your PC, open the computer case, and identify the card you want to remove.

2. Make sure that the card is disconnected from any outside cables.

3. Unscrew the small screw attaching the card to the PC case and lay it aside.

4. Pull gently on the card, using both hands to wiggle it back and forth slightly to disengage it from the connectors.

5. Once you've got the card out, wrap it back up in its original sheath, if you kept it and plan to use the card again. Don't

touch the gold connectors on the card; the oils in your skin can corrode the gold and degrade connectivity.

To install a new networking card, follow these steps:

1. Power down the PC, open the computer case, and find a slot in the PC that's free and fits your specific network card. Try to choose a slot that's not next to another card to maintain a good airflow.

2. Install your new card by first unwrapping the card, being careful not to touch the gold connectors, and setting it aside.

3. Unscrew the plate that covers the slot's opening to the rear of the computer and set the plate and screw aside. (You may need the plate later, and you'll need the screw in just a minute.)

4. Align the card with the slot in the PC and push gently but firmly to seat the card in its slot. You may need to push fairly hard, which can be somewhat intimidating if you're not used to inserting cards. If you've got the right slot and push straight in, then the card should snap into place.

5. Using the screw that you set aside in step 3, screw the card in to hold it in place. This extra step will keep the card from sagging or working loose.

6. Close the case and, if the cables are already in place, connect them to the card.

7. Install the network card's drivers. The process for installing drivers depends on your operating system. Follow the instructions that come with the network card. (Check the manufacturer's Web site to make sure you have the most recent drivers for your card).

8. Configure your card's interrupt, I/O address space, and (if applicable) DMA channels. (If your card is a PCI card, you won't have to worry about this step because it is Plug and Play.)

Basic Networking Concepts and Components

In this section, I'll cover the basic elements of a local area network, including network cards, cables, and connectors.

What Is a LAN?

Strictly speaking, a *local area network (LAN)* is a group of computers connected within an enclosed area, such as a building. LANs can vary greatly in size. They can consist of two Windows 98 workstations in the same room or several hundred workstations spread out over several floors in an office building. The key to the definition of a LAN is that all the computers on the network are grouped together in some fashion and connected somehow, and are in the same building. On most LANs, the medium of connection is some sort of cable. However, as I will discuss later in this chapter, some LANs use wireless communications to link their computers.

Note

If the network extends beyond the borders of a single building, it's no longer a LAN but some type of *wide-area network (WAN)*. There are a couple of kinds of WANs. If the network is big enough, it's just a WAN, but the smaller ones may be named somewhat differently. For example, a WAN that extends through a major urban area may be referred to as a *metropolitan area network (MAN)*. A WAN that connects the buildings of a university might be identified as a *campus area network (CAN)*. Generally speaking, LANs are contained within the confines of a single building, and WANs are not.

That's the textbook definition, but in the real world LANs are generally defined more by their function than by their physical characteristics. In this more usual sense, a LAN is a means of linking computers to allow them common access to individual hardware. That is, subject to security restrictions, all computers on the LAN can access each other's shared hardware (printers, scanners, CD-ROM drives, hard disks, modems, and so on) as though that hardware were available locally. Because the members of a LAN can share hardware, they can share the data on that hardware, too.

Therefore, not only can all computers on the LAN access certain parts of each other's hardware (subject to security restrictions, which I'll discuss later), but they can also use that hardware as though it were available locally. This implies that the users of these computers can share data.

Although the first office computers—mainframes and terminals—were networked, the first personal computers (PCs) in an office setting were typically stand-alone devices. The oldest form of the LAN is commonly referred to as *SneakerNet*, an official-sounding name for an unofficial way of doing business. In this arrangement, one PC user would copy data from his computer to a floppy disk, then walk that floppy over to another computer, either to print out the data at the printer attached to that computer or to give a copy of the data to someone else. If you don't have all that much data to transfer, it's not a terrible solution (and for some situations, it still works just fine) but it's got several serious drawbacks:

- The risk of losing data to lost or accidentally formatted floppy disks is high.

- It's difficult to keep all versions of a document current if more than one person needs to work on it.

- Floppy disks hold up to only 1.44MB of data, and modern files may be quite a bit larger than that.

- What if both users don't have the same applications on their machines? The second user may not be able to open the shared file.

- Security is a problem—how do you keep those floppy disks from walking out the door?

- It's quite time-consuming for users to have to copy files, walk them to another PC, and then wait for the file's recipient to copy or print the data in question.

For anything other than very simple purposes, SneakerNet is not the way to go. In modern offices, you need a solution that permits:

▶ Easy sharing and transferring of data, and protection of that data

▶ Sharing of applications

▶ Easy interaction with other users on the network

▶ Sharing of peripheral devices

Let's take a look at these needs in some more detail.

File Management

Sharing, transferring, and securing information between computers on a network is generally known as *file management.* One of the primary purposes of a LAN is to provide a common storage area so that a number of people can access the same files. The PC that shares the files or directories is called the *file server.*

File sharing can help ensure that only one version of a file is going around, and that anyone who uses that file is always working with the most recent version of the information. If you don't want to share a file with the network but you need someone else to do some work on it, you can transfer it to that person—just move it from your hard disk to theirs, or else send it as an e-mail message.

The act of sharing a file with the network does not automatically give everyone on the network access to it. In modern network operating systems, you can restrict access to shared files or directories based either on a password system or on a user account. This capability may be fine-tuned to permit a variety of types of file access—at a minimum, read-only or full access. Therefore, you can keep others from seeing your work or just stop them from making changes to your work when they're not supposed to.

What about protecting that data from loss? The most valuable asset your company has is its data. This data is far more valuable than the putty-colored boxes called computers on your desk, which are already obsolete from the moment you bought them and inherently replaceable. If your data is lost or corrupted, that signifies a disaster of monstrous proportions. The good news is that networking can make backing up all that data much simpler than it is with stand-alone computers. You can either store all the data on a single server and back up that server regularly, or provide a central backup system on the network to which each PC user must copy all important files from his or her computer's hard drive. If managed properly, LANs can provide a degree of data security unheard of in stand-alone computing environments.

Sharing Applications

One of the great advantages of a LAN is that it can make the process of distributing applications to the users in your office much easier. Many applications—not all, but most—will permit you to install them on a central computer called an *application server* and let people access these applications from the network.

Note

A *server* is a network-capable computer dedicated to servicing requests for resources from other computers on a network. A *client* is a computer on a network (or the person using that computer) that subscribes to the services provided by a server.

Installing applications in this manner has a couple of advantages. First, as the bulk of network-installed applications will reside on the server rather than the client, this means that less disk space is needed on clients than if the application were installed on every PC. This is no small consideration in a world where a popular office suite requires almost 2GB of space to install fully. As common as large disks are nowadays, you won't necessarily have those large hard disks installed in every computer in your network. Second, installing and upgrading applications is much easier if you can install the program files on a single point instead of on all computers in the network. Although this doesn't work for all applications or in all situations, when application sharing is feasible, it can save a lot of time and energy.

How does this work? When a client PC connects to the copy of an application installed on an application server, a copy of the application is loaded into the client's memory. As the client interacts with the program, it interacts with the copy stored in its own memory, not the one on the server, so more than one client can access the same application simultaneously.

Note

One word of caution, however: installing applications on an application server for use by the rest of the network does not mean that you have to buy only one license for that application. Typically, you must buy one license for each user of the application, whether concurrent or total. (The requirements differ depending on the application.) If you don't have proper licensing for all your applications, you are guilty of software piracy, which is a federal crime. You don't think that anyone will know or care? This is not necessarily the case. The sole purpose of the watchdog organization called the Software Publisher's Association (SPA) is to care about piracy issues, and it will prosecute violations against its member organizations.

Enhancing Office Interaction

As offices get larger, it can be hard to keep people apprised of important events and to get them together. Networks can help encourage office cohesion by use of e-mail and group scheduling software.

Group scheduling was once probably one of your office manager's favorite ways of accumulating gray hair. It can be made much easier with the use of a network and some specialized scheduling software. Without these tools, organizing departmental meetings can be a nightmare as the organizer tries to sort through everyone's schedules to find a compatible time to meet. Group scheduling software can make this task much more approachable. The idea is this: everyone enters their schedules into a calendar program. Only they or selected people can see their own schedules, but the times are stored in a central database. When you want to call a meeting, you enter the names of the people you want to be present, then pick a time. If all the people listed are free at that time, the scheduling software will notify you. If not, it will notify you that there's a conflict and with whom, and (depending on the package) may be able to suggest the first time when all the people listed will be free. Once a time has been set, you can use the scheduling program to e-mail everyone invited to the meeting, telling them of the date and time.

Speaking of e-mail, it's useful for a lot more than just scheduling office meetings. E-mail is probably the most ubiquitous networking application today. A lot of e-mail–related network traffic may entail tired jokes, but it's also invaluable as a method of asking for quick answers to quick problems, or scheduling private meetings between people. E-mail is good for communication too simple to require scheduling software between people who are sufficiently busy that they can't just drop everything for each other's convenience. Not only is it faster than dropping by someone's office to ask a question or talk, it's more private. Everyone notices if the boss stops by your cubicle, but if she sends you an e-mail asking you to stop by for your performance evaluation, then no one knows about it except you and her. Essentially, think of office e-mail for any communications that require relative privacy, mass dissemination, or brevity.

Another advantage of e-mail over telephone calls or in-person meetings is that most e-mail systems permit you to attach binary files to e-mail messages. For example, you can send someone a file to review with your comments separate from the document itself. The recipient of the message can just open the file and read or edit the data. Sending binary files in this way is like sharing the file with the network, but it has four main advantages for some applications:

▶ You can explain anything confusing about the data in the e-mail message or emphasize the importance of the information.

▶ You can ensure that the recipient is getting the intended file and you don't have to worry that they will open the wrong one by mistake.

▶ You don't have to worry about setting the proper permissions on the file or muck around with passwords because only the recipient of the e-mail message will get a copy of the file you send.

▶ You can send files to people with whom you don't share a LAN connection, such as those to whom you only have e-mail access via the Internet.

In short, the introduction of LANs is one of the best things to ever happen to office communication and information-sharing.

Sharing Peripheral Devices

A *peripheral*, or *peripheral device*, is simply any piece of hardware that attaches to the motherboard of your computer, whether directly or indirectly. Not all peripheral devices are external to the computer case, and not all can be shared. However, for those that can be shared with the rest of the network, peripheral sharing can be a good way to make these devices available to everyone and make it easier for people to use them. For example, rather than having people line up at the PC with the printer attached, they can send print jobs to it as though it were attached to their machine and pick up those jobs at their leisure.

Sharing peripheral devices can save network users both time and money. It's true that even without a network, you don't have to buy printers or CD-ROM drives for every computer on the network. One or two devices distributed throughout the office can work just as well if demand isn't high or people don't mind standing in line to use them. However, if people must waste time waiting for a device to be free, then the money saved by not having a printer at every desk may be spent in lost productivity.

Like shared folders, shared peripheral devices aren't necessarily available to everyone on the network or at the same level of control. Thus, you can share that color printer that uses the really expensive cartridges with the network but protect it so that only the graphics people can access it, not every Tom, Dick, and Harry with a rough draft to print out.

These are the basics of what you can do with a LAN. Now let's take a look at the pieces of the backbone that make all of this possible: cards, cables, and connectors.

Understanding Network Components

To create a simple network, you'll need hardware to connect your computers: network cards, some sort of cabling, and connectors to affix the cables to the cards inserted in each PC. I'll explain each of those items in this section.

Door to the Outside World: Network Cards

The *network interface card (NIC)*, known also by such aliases as the *network board* or *adapter*, is the add-in card that you'll plug into the motherboard of your computer to provide an interface to the network. A network card really isn't fundamentally different from any other daughtercard: it plugs into a slot on the motherboard, requires certain resources in order to operate, and has a jack on the side that sticks out the back of the computer into which you can plug the tool into the card controls. If this were a sound card, you'd plug in speakers to produce sound. Since it's a network card, you plug in a network cable to produce connectivity.

You can divide NICs into categories in a few ways. First, there's the type of network they support. As I mentioned in Chapter 3, "Inside the PC: Pieces of the Picture," there are two main LAN types: Ethernet and Token Ring. These two types represent two fundamentally different methods of communicating. Unfortunately, you can't make Ethernet cards and Token Ring cards talk to each other without the help of internetworking devices. And although Token Ring is still being used in smaller networks, it is going out of style due to higher implementation costs and lower speeds than Ethernet is capable of. Therefore, I will discuss only Ethernet here.

Second, there's the type of cable that the cards support. The jack on the back of the card must be of a type into which you can plug the cable you want to use. The good news is that many modern cards support more than one type of cable. For example, Ethernet cards often support the type of Ethernet that requires coaxial cable as well as the kind that requires unshielded twisted-pair (UTP) in a single card. You could use this type of card to start out your Ethernet network with coaxial cable. Then, you could switch to UTP (which uses an RJ-45 connector) as the network gets larger without having to install new network cards. Figure 27.1 shows the back of a network card that includes ports for both types of interfaces, as well as an attachment unit interface (AUI) port.

Figure 27.1

A dual-jack network card for both UTP and coax

Coax port   AUI port   RJ-45 port

Third, there's the card's bus type, which governs how fast the NIC can talk to the motherboard. Most modern cards for desktop machines will be available with the Peripheral Component Interconnect (PCI) bus type. As noted in Chapter 3, Industry Standard Architecture (ISA) bus types still exist but are quickly becoming obsolete. So it's a good idea to always use PCI network cards—even if their ISA counterparts are much cheaper.

Note

Laptop users must use network cards with the PC Card interface. PC Cards were formerly called the Personal Computer Memory Card International Association (PCMCIA) cards.

The main difference between the ISA and PCI buses is one of speed. PCI, which is faster than ISA, communicates with the motherboard at a rate of 32MBps and a clock rate of 33MHz. ISA communicates with the motherboard at 16MBps and 8MHz, which is how fast PCs operated when the ISA standard was originally developed. For reasons of backward compatibility, this hasn't changed.

Note

External data transfer rates are typically described in terms of bits per second (bps), whereas internal data transfer rates are typically described in terms of bytes per second (Bps). Remember, one byte equals eight bits, and one ASCII character can be expressed in one byte.

Fourth, there's external data transfer rate, typically measured in megabits per second (Mbps). The data transfer rate that the network card you choose can support isn't the only factor that determines network speed, but it's one of them. Ethernet runs at either 10Mbps, 100Mbps, or 1Gbps. Although you can plug a PC with a 10Mbps card into a 100Mbps network, for example, the speed of the PC's connection to the LAN will be determined by the speed of the card connecting it to the LAN.

Note

The faster version of Ethernet, Gigabit Ethernet, supports transmission speeds of up to 1 billion bits per second (Gbps). The NICs designed for these high speeds are very expensive and designed for the high-end server market, rather than for client PCs or ordinary servers.

The Silver Link, the Silken Tie: Network Cabling

Sir Walter Scott may not have been talking about network cables when he wrote of these bonds, but the description fits: network cables are indeed the sometimes almost invisible but essential pieces for tying together a network. The types of information that will be sent between computers (text, complex graphics, video, or audio), the distance between computers, and the environment in which those cables must operate are all determining factors for the type of cable you will need to use. As each type of cable is used for a particular kind of network, the kind of network you want to create will determine which cable type you choose.

Note

Copper wire, used within twisted-pair and coaxial cable, may be either stranded or solid. *Stranded wire* is made of smaller wires combined, while *solid* is a single wire. Stranded cables are more flexible than solid and thus better for short runs requiring stress to the cable that might break a solid wire, but they are also more vulnerable to signal loss.

What are the options? There are several, divided between copper wire and fiber optic. Each of them is designed to solve, in a different way, one of the most nagging problems facing any kind of transmission: interference, *radio frequency noise*, or *RF noise* (terms you may remember from Chapter 4, "Avoiding Service: Preventive Maintenance"). The problem is that copper wire was originally chosen as a medium for network transmissions because it conducts signals terrifically well, but that same capability makes it susceptible to interference from other sources of electrical signals, thus endangering the integrity of the original transmission. To get around this, the various cable types use one method or another of protecting the wire from outside interference or even making it immune to such interference.

The less susceptible cabling is to interference, the faster it is, because transmission speed along analog channels (such as copper wire) is a function of frequency. Before your eyes glaze over, understand that this is important. Copper cables are sometimes described in terms of the frequencies they can support, so if you don't understand what this means, then you're not going to understand those descriptions.

Frequency describes the rate at which electrical impulses travel through a certain area. As you learned in Chapter 24, "Play It Loud: Sound Cards," frequency is expressed in hertz, or cycles per second, the cycles being how fast the pulses can be created. They can be illustrated as sine waves (see Figure 27.2). In other words, a signal that runs at 8MHz can run 8 million cycles in one second. The higher the frequency, the faster the data is traveling because more 1s and 0s are being packed into a single second.

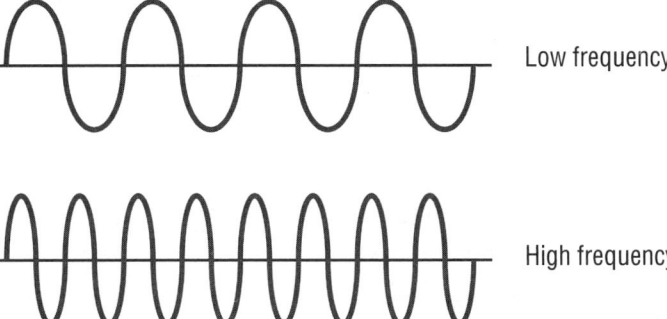

Figure 27.2

The more bumps of a sine wave in a given time period, the higher the frequency

Low frequency

High frequency

Higher frequencies are more susceptible to interference than are lower frequencies because more data is compressed into a given instant. If you're unsure as to why this is so, take a look again at Figure 27.2. Suppose that something interfered with both the low-frequency signal and the high-frequency signal for a half second (a long time, but this is to make the point, not to show precise measurements). During that half-second, the data transmitted along those channels would be corrupted and lost. In the case of the higher-frequency signal, you've lost a larger proportion of the data because more data was crammed into that half second. The lower-frequency signal lost much less data.

The maximum frequency supported by a given cable does not imply that the data transfer rate of that cable always uses that frequency, but indicates only what the physical medium of the cable is theoretically capable of supporting, if undamaged and installed correctly. For example, Category 5 UTP (discussed in the following section) operates at a maximum frequency of 100MHz; but to support speeds of 100Mbps, a frequency of only 62.5MHz is required. That's just how fast the cable could transmit data under ideal conditions if the data were pushed through it that quickly. I'll discuss frequency and its relationship to signal strength and carrying power further under "Wireless Networking," later in this chapter.

Another variable in physical cable types is their reach. When reading the descriptions of the cable types, you'll notice that they vary in the length of the cable that they can use. That's due in part to a phenomenon called *attenuation*. Again, as you learned in terms of sound waves, attenuation is the degree to which a signal weakens over distance. The more vulnerable the cable is to interference, the more it will be affected by attenuation. The good news is that devices, such as repeaters, can rebroadcast the signal on long cables so they can run for longer distances.

Interference versus Attenuation

Although interference and attenuation have similar effects on data transmission (they're not good for it), they're not the same thing.

Interference is a stray electronic signal that distorts the signal being transmitted, possibly corrupting the data being carried by adding extra humps in the sine wave or otherwise interfering with the signal. *Attenuation* is the increasing weakness of a signal as it travels. Just as a sound loses power from the time it leaves its source, but may still be audible at any given distance from its source, all signals experience attenuation. The problem arises when the signal is so severely attenuated because it has traveled farther than it was meant to that the fading signal can distort the data.

Both interference and attenuation work a lot like sound. Interference is the problem that you run into when a lot of people are all talking at once and it's difficult to sort out who said what, or even to distinguish the sound of one voice as it gets overrun by the sound of another. Attenuation is the problem you run into when someone's too far away for you to hear their voice properly and you may misunderstand them. Interference problems are resolved by shielding out other "conversations;" attenuation problems are resolved by boosting the signal.

Twisted-Pair Cable

If you wrap one good conductor around another one, they form a field that protects the conducting wires from RF noise. That's the approach taken by twisted-pair cable. There are two types of twisted-pair cable: unshielded twisted-pair (UTP) and shielded twisted-pair (STP).

There are two differences between the types of twisted-pair cable. First, UTP has four pairs of wires, and STP has two. Second, and the key to the difference in their names, STP has an extra conducting layer surrounding the twisted wires to give the cable an extra level of protection from interference. This does not necessarily imply that STP is always better protected from RF noise than UTP, but only that the two cable types take different approaches.

The theory with UTP is that the two wires wrapped around each other individually conduct noise, but cancel out each other's noise. The theory with STP is that the conductors are best protected with a layer of conducting wires rather than the two conductors being wrapped around each other. This extra layer of protection can make the STP cable hard to work with because it stiffens the cable and the shielding only works as long as it's both properly grounded and not torn. Figure 27.3 shows the difference between UTP (top) and STP (bottom).

Foil shielding

Figure 27.3

Sections of UTP and STP

Note

UTP is used in Ethernet networks (10Base-T and 100Base-T) and occasionally in Token Ring networks. STP cable is commonly used in Token Ring networks, which are not covered in this chapter.

The Electronics Industry Association (EIA), Telecommunications Industry Association (TIA), and National Electrical Manufacturers Association (NEMA) established a five-grade standard for UTP. They then commissioned Underwriters Laboratories to certify and grade cable sold in the United States according to these standards. The higher the grade number, the more twists per foot and the more often the pattern of these twists must vary to throw off RFI. Thus, although no cable is entirely uninfluenced by interference, the higher the grade, the more immune that category of UTP is to RFI and EMI and the faster it can accurately transmit data. Technically speaking, Category 3 cable, rated for transmissions of up to 10Mbps and with at least three twists per foot, is LAN-capable, and may be found in existing LANs. However, any new LANs using UTP will most likely use Category 5 cable, which is rated for transmissions of up to 100Mbps and capable of extending up to about 90 meters.

Beyond Category 5

Note that Category 5 cable is the highest *certified* standard of twisted-pair cable. As of this writing, there are also a couple of not-yet-certified standards: enhanced Category 5 and Category 6.

Enhanced Category 5 cable is like Category 5 (high-speed UTP) except, well, it's enhanced. It's got more variance in its twist patterns and uses a higher grade of wire than does ordinary Category 5 cable and can typically support frequencies of up to 200MHz. It's not certain how the standard will define enhanced Category 5 cable— whether this will be the frequency rate required or if it will have to be as fast as 300MHz.

Category 6 cable is a kettle of fish of a different color because it requires a foil wrapping around the twisted-pair cable and is thus STP, rather than UTP. It's unclear as yet just how high its frequencies will be when and if a standard is defined. On the low end, one possibility is 350MHz, but on the high end, rates of 600MHz are bandied about. There are a lot of hang-ups attached to a Category 6 standard, such as what type of connector to use, the fact that it's STP instead of UTP, and the speed at which it's supposed to run. So Category 6 products are not likely to be widely available in the United States until some of these issues are sorted out.

Category 5 cable is able to keep up with the needs of Fast Ethernet, which supports data transfer rates of up to 100Mbps. Why are faster cables needed? Mostly because of the specter of Asynchronous Transfer Mode (ATM) and Gigabit Ethernet networks, which require frequencies in the hundreds of megahertz (350MHz for ATM) to keep up with them. These high-speed networks make Fast Ethernet look like your father's Oldsmobile. At a top frequency of 100MHz, Category 5 cable can't keep up with those needs, so the options are either to improve UTP performance or switch to fiber optic cable.

IBM also maintains standards for a variety of types of twisted-pair cables (and two types of fiber), organizing them by function rather than in order of immunity to RFI. The twisted-pair types are as follows:

Type 1 Is solid-wire STP used for data transmission. It has two pairs of wires in each cable.

Type 2 Combines four unshielded solid wires and two shielded solid wires in the same sheath. The UTP is intended for voice transmission, and the STP is for data.

Type 3 Contains four pairs of solid-wire UTP to be used for voice or data.

Type 6 Contains two pairs of stranded-wire cable. It's essentially like Type 1 except that it uses stranded wire instead of solid.

Type 8 Is a special type of STP designed to be flatter than ordinary cable so it can be run under carpets.

Type 9 Consists of two pairs of STP covered with plenum rather than polyvinylchloride (PVC) and is meant to be used between floors in a building. PVC emits toxic smoke when it burns, so plenum is required to meet some fire codes.

Twisted-pair networks typically connect each individual NIC to a centrally located switching area, either a hub or a *punchdown block* connected to a hub, which is a place to plug in lots of cables. I'll talk about hubs in the "Additional Networking Hardware" section.

Coaxial Cable

Coaxial cable, often referred to as either BNC cable or thinnet, is made of a single copper wire encased in insulation and then covered with a layer of aluminum or copper braid that protects the conducting wire from RF noise. As you can see in Figure 27.4, coaxial cable has four parts:

▶ The central wire, called the *inner conductor*

▶ A layer of insulation, called the *dielectric,* which surrounds the inner conductor

▶ A layer of foil or metal braid, called the *shield*, which covers the dielectric

▶ The final layer of insulation (the part you can see), called the *jacket*

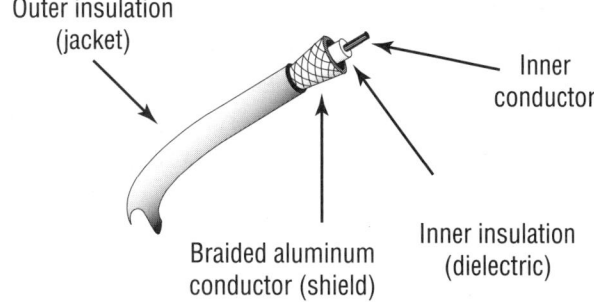

Figure 27.4

Coaxial cable

With a top data transfer rate of 10Mbps, coaxial cable is slow by modern standards, but it's got a couple of advantages over UTP for some installations. First, it can extend for longer runs. The top length for UTP cable runs is 100 meters, but coaxial cable can extend for more than 800 meters. However, after 185 meters you'll have to boost the signal with a device called a *repeater*, which I'll describe later in the chapter.

The second advantage is that you can use coaxial cables to connect PCs to each other directly (rather than to a central hub) in a daisy-chain effect. This can be handy for those who have only a couple of computers in the same room to connect and don't want to go to the expense of a hub.

Note

There's actually a second kind of coaxial cable known as *thicknet*, which is used in older networks but not often installed new today. This cable can stretch for longer distances than can thinnet cable, but it's much harder to work with. One contractor I know who used to have to work with thicknet refers to it as "frozen yellow garden hose" because of its stiffness. Thicknet doesn't actually connect to the PCs themselves, but forms a backbone to the network that the PCs connect to with short patch cables.

Fiber Optic Cable

One way of getting around the problem of how to protect your data medium from EMI is to whack that Gordian knot in two. Make that cable utterly immune to EMI by not using electronic signals for transmission at all. That solution is called *fiber optic cable.*

Fiber optic cable is indifferent to RF noise because of the difference in its conductive medium; rather than using electronic pulses to send data, it uses light. The light is conducted through a hair-like glass or plastic fiber that is covered with a thin insulating layer called *cladding.* The cladding is then surrounded with a plastic jacket to protect the delicate fiber. You can see a drawing of fiber optic cable in Figure 27.5.

Figure 27.5

Fiber optic cable

Sheath   Insulation   Cladding   Fiber core

As you'd expect, the fibers are the crucial element of data transmission. At each end of the fiber is a device called a *codec,* or coder/decoder. The codec is responsible for encoding the data into light pulses and then decoding them back into the electronic impulses that a computer can understand. To transmit data, a light-emitting diode (LED) or a laser at one end of the fiber sends signals along the cable. When those signals reach the other end, they're decoded into their original form.

It might sound as though traffic through a fiber optic cable is limited to a single path of data, but this isn't true for a couple of reasons. First, fiber optic cable may have more than one fiber in it, meaning that multiple data pathways exist. The more fibers a cable has, the more data can pass through it at once, just as a four-lane highway can carry more traffic than a single-lane road.

Second, there are two types of fiber optic cable:

Single-mode fiber Sends transmissions along a single path, like a flashlight. This beam of light is intense, so single-mode fiber can carry more data for longer distances and is thus suitable either for applications that are traffic intensive or need to travel for long distances.

Multimode fiber Allows multiple modes to pass through the cable at once. There are two kinds of multimode fiber: step index and graded index. In *step index fiber optic cable,* the light beams bounce around inside the cable in a zigzag pattern. *Graded index cable* has a more rounded pattern to the light movement, like a sine wave (see Figure 27.6).

A *mode* is a ray of light entering a fiber at a particular angle.

Figure 27.6

Step index system: Light bounces along an angular path inside the cable.

Multimode cable sends more than one beam of light down the fiber at a time.

Graded index system: Light follows a more rounded path.

Both kinds of multimode fiber optic cable are prone to *modal dispersion*—spreading of the received light impulse—due to the number of light beams traveling through the cable. When the signal spreads, it moves more slowly, so single-mode cable transmits faster than multimode cable. To understand this behavior, try imagining what would happen if you threw a ball down a pipe. If you threw just one ball and it went through without hitting the walls of the pipe, it would move faster and more accurately than if it bounced off the walls of the pipe. Just as bouncing off the walls of the pipe slows down the ball's travel speed, bouncing off the walls of the cable slows down the light signal.

Note

Single-mode cable is more expensive than multimode and can extend further without requiring the signal to be boosted. Multimode cable is more often used within buildings; single-mode is reserved for inter-building use.

Fiber has had notable success as a LAN backbone, combined with UTP taps to each workstation, for those with high-traffic networks and deep pockets. Fiber's not often run to the desktop at this point for a couple of reasons. First, it costs more per foot than does UTP and requires some specialized knowledge to install it, driving that cost up as well. Second, with the advent of Fast Ethernet (which as I mentioned earlier supports speeds of up to 100Mbps over copper wire), UTP is much faster than it used to be, not quite reaching fiber's speed when used in a Fiber Distributed Data Interface (FDDI) network, but rivaling it. However, as higher speeds are required for some applications and the costs of fiber drop, you can probably expect to see fiber run to the desktop more often.

If fiber's too expensive to run to the desktop and no longer always hugely faster than UTP, then why use it at all? First, it *is* really fast and eminently suited to demanding sorts of traffic such as video. Second, since it transmits light, not electricity, fiber optic cables are completely resistant to EMI and RFI, so signals are sometimes able to travel several miles without any degradation. Some kinds of fiber can transmit up to three miles in LAN environments and across the country via a high-powered laser device in WAN environments. Fiber optic cable is also useful in hazardous environments because it can't spark (as electric transfer cables potentially could). Furthermore, it doesn't contain any metal, so it resists corrosion. Finally, fiber optic cabling is harder to tap into than is copper-based cable, so it's more secure and therefore popular for top-secret communications.

A relatively new kind of high-end fiber network called *Fibre Channel* seeks to blur the distinction between individual devices and the network even more than the LAN does already. Fibre channel can operate at even higher speeds than does FDDI.

Wireless Networking

Wireless networking is less esoteric than it may sound. Essentially, it's any method of connecting two devices without having a cable running between them. It's best suited for the following situations:

▶ When wiring isn't possible or is prohibitively expensive because of logistical problems

▶ When clients (such as laptop users) join and leave the network frequently, or don't have access to a desk with a network connection

▶ When network clients need to move around a lot

Unless there's a specific reason to make a network or part of it wireless, it's not a good idea. Wireless networks are slower than their wired counterparts and more prone to interference. That said, at times they're invaluable—for example, doing inventory is much easier with a wireless laptop that you can carry around than with a wired terminal that you must keep running to in order to enter numbers.

Wireless networks operate on the same principle as do wired networks; signal strength and speed are a function of frequency, or how often information can be passed during a given interval. The frequencies used depend on the signal, but generally speaking, wireless types can be divided into two classes: radio signals and infrared signals. *Radio signals* have a wider range and (like radio) are relatively immune to most barriers, but in exchange have a low transmission speed. *Infrared signals* have a very high frequency and high speed, but are easily disrupted.

Getting Connected: Cable-NIC Connectors

Getting NICs and cables is a large part of the business of putting together a LAN, but you still need something to make those NICs talk to those cables, and that's where connectors come in.

Coaxial Cable Connectors

Three types of connectors are associated with coaxial cable:

▶ T connectors

▶ BNC connectors

▶ Terminators

You saw illustrations of these connectors in Chapter 3. I'll repeat some of those illustrations here as I describe how these connectors fit into a LAN.

T connectors (see Figure 27.7) plug into network cards, where they stick out the back of the PC and provide an interface for plugging in the BNC connector.

Figure 27.7

A T connector creates the interface into which you plug the BNC connector.

A BNC connector (see Figure 27.8) plugs into the T connector attached to the NIC. This links the card and the cable, with the cable forming the crossbars of the "T" (see Figure 27.9), and may also be used to link sections of coaxial cable.

Figure 27.8

The BNC connector may link coaxial cables to each other or to T connectors.

Figure 27.9

The BNC connector
attaches the
T connector to the
coaxial cable.

BNC connector

T connector

Network interface card

The terminators are the final piece of the coaxial puzzle; they are used to define the ends of the cable. If you don't have terminators at each end of a coaxial segment, then the signal will "echo" from the end of the cable and *shadow packets* will result. Shadow packets slow down network speed by increasing traffic and may corrupt data if confused with real packets. Terminating the segments ensures that packets will be destroyed when the signal reaches the end of the segment.

Note

Terminators are made for either 50-ohm or 75-ohm cable. The standard is usually a 50-ohm terminator. Pay attention when you're buying terminators because they won't work if you mix them up. Most coax network cable systems require 50-ohm terminators.

Twisted-Pair Connectors

Most UTP cable uses RJ-45 connectors, which, as you learned in Chapter 3, look like chunkier versions of the connectors used to plug your telephone into the wall (see Figure 27.10). The RJ-45 connectors are attached to both ends of the cable; one end plugs into your computer card and the other plugs into a hub or a punchdown block in the wiring closet. Essentially, it looks like a somewhat bulkier version of a telephone cord.

Figure 27.10

Each end of UTP network cable has an RJ-45 connector on it.

Okay, I lied—not all UTP cables connect a hub and a network card. You can use crossover cables in some implementations to daisy chain computers together. *Crossover cables* are wired to perform the function of a hub.

STP cable doesn't use the same connectors as UTP cable. You'll use a D-shell connector (see Figure 27.11) with STP to connect the cable to the NIC. You'll need an IBM Data Connector (Figure 27.12) to connect it to a multistation access unit (MAU) or hub.

Figure 27.11

A D-shell connector connects the cable to the machine's network card.

Figure 27.12

An IBM Data Connector connects the cable to the MAU.

Warning

You may notice that the D-shell connector used to connect to a Token Ring card is the same one that is used to connect to a video card. Be careful not to plug the network cable into your monitor.

Fiber Optic Connectors

Unlike copper-wire cables, in which the transmission medium is the biggest source of signal loss, fiber optic is most susceptible to signal dispersion at its connectors. Fiber optic cable uses two kinds of connectors: screw-mounted adapters (SMA) and spring-loaded twist (ST). The ST connector uses a spring-loaded twist to clamp to the cable, whereas the SMA screws onto the end. ST connectors (see Figure 27.13) are more common than SMAs.

Figure 27.13

An ST connector and a connector cover

Summary of Cable and Connector Types

Having trouble assimilating all these cables and connectors? Table 27.1 lists the cable types discussed, their speeds, their maximum lengths, and the means they use to minimize electrical interference.

TABLE 27.1: Cable and Connector Types

Cable Type	Top Speed	Maximum Length Supported	Anti-Interference Measures Used	Connector Used
Coaxial	10Mbps	2500 feet	Copper braid around transmitting wires	BNC
Unshielded twisted-pair (UTP)	100Mbps	300 feet	Twisted-pairs	RJ-45
Shielded twisted-pair (STP)	100Mbps	300 feet	Twisted-pairs combined with metal shielding	D-shell
Fiber optic	155Mbps or greater	10Km	Transmission without electrical signals	ST or SMA

Networking Protocols and Application Programming Interfaces

For data to get from point A to point B on the LAN, you need not only hardware, but also networking software to package that data for transmittal. That networking software consists of three main parts:

▶ A redirector to send requests to the network instead of the local hard disk

▶ Network card drivers to provide communications between the operating system and the network card

▶ Networking protocols to send the data on its merry way and pick it up at the end of its journey

So, for example, if Fred tries to save a Microsoft Word file from his computer to a shared drive on the network file server, the following happens:

1. Fred clicks Save and chooses to save the document to his drive G:, which is in fact a network connection to drive D: shared from the file server.

2. The redirector examines the request to save, notes that drive G: is not locally available, and redirects the request to a part of the operating system called the *network file system driver.*

3. The file system driver passes the request to the network card driver.

4. The network card driver passes the request—and the data—to the network card.

5. The network card packages the data for transmission across the network and sends it.

6. The file server's network card notes that a package has arrived for it, and receives it.

At this point, the process is reversed: the server's network card driver passes the request to the file system driver in the operating system, and writes the file to the local drive.

If you're building a network, chances are excellent that sooner or later the network you create will be connected to another one in some manner or other. After all, that's how the Internet itself got started; local networks were given the means to connect to each other in a larger whole. Most networks grow in stages, rather than emerging full-blown in their final form, so they often include a hodgepodge not only of hardware but of network operating systems and communications needs as well. This, in turn, means that the network needs more than one type of redirector, must use more than one type of network protocol, and that not all the cards use the same driver. In short, sometimes even with careful planning it can be a bit of a mess as networks grow and merge. In this section, I'll discuss the various parts of the networking process so you can better understand what you're dealing with when it comes to managing networking software in all its varied parts.

First, I'll discuss the role of the redirector in arranging communications between applications and the operating system to reach network-accessible data. Second, I'll look at the role of the network card driver. Finally, I'll examine the three transport protocols used most often in PC-based networks.

The Role of Redirectors

From the perspective of the PC initiating a network request, the first actor in the networking process is the redirector. Its role is to fool an application on the local machine into thinking that it is getting data from a local drive, rather than from a network drive. The point is that it shouldn't matter where the file being requested is stored; it should be accessible in the same way, no matter what.

For example, what happens if you are running Word and open a file stored on a network drive? From Word's point of view, there *is* no network. It knows only that there are one or more disk drives available with names consisting of a letter and a colon, as in A:, B:, C:, and so on. Like other application software, Word was not built to accommodate storage devices that aren't on the local machine. Thus, there must be a layer of software (placed just below Word) whose job it is to present a common drive-letter interface to Word when supplying data stored on the network. Word thinks that it is addressing local drives, but its requests for information from network drives must be *redirected* to network requests. So, if you tell Word to get the data from directory DOCS on the server named BIG-DOG, the redirector software initiates the request.

Note

Redirectors are often referred to as *clients* (as in, the Windows 98 Client for NetWare Networks) because they're a required part of a client machine.

Therefore, before you can join a network, you must install a redirector that's compatible with the network type. Not all network operating systems use the same redirectors, so you must install the one that corresponds to the operating system on the network to which you're connecting. For example, Microsoft networks use Server Message Blocks (SMBs) to pass data back and forth, so they need a redirector that can phrase things in terms of SMBs. Novell networks use NetWare Control Protocols (NCPs) for the same job. So, to make requests of a NetWare server, you must use a redirector that can phrase requests in terms of NCPs. Note that having a transport protocol such as TCP/IP in common is not enough—you must have a redirector that works with the operating system to which you're connecting. The good news is that redirector support can overlap if the Presentation layer protocol is the same for more than one operating system. Thus, if you're using Windows 98, you can use the SMB-supporting Client for Microsoft Networks to connect to any operating system that supports SMBs.

Redirectors and APIs

Most user applications are unaware of the network or networks that they use. But some, such as e-mail or groupware programs, must be cognizant of the network and exist only *because* of the network. They need to be able to "plug in" and communicate with other programs running on other machines in the network.

Programmers build network-aware programs to be tailored to sets of commands that a network offers to applications programs. Those sets of commands are called APIs, or *Application Programming Interfaces*. Think of an API as being somewhat like the dashboard of a car. Your car's dashboard is the interface that you see, and you must learn to use it in order to operate the car. You actually have no idea while you're driving about what's under your car's hood—you just push down on the accelerator and the car goes faster.

Thus, you don't have to know precisely how a car works to drive it. Not only that, but once you know how to drive one car, you can drive just about any car because the controls—the API—are the same.

(I discovered while driving a friend's Volkswagen one night that Volkswagens do not use the same API for "reverse" that other manual shift cars do, but this analogy generally works.)

A dashboard consists of just a few primitive commands: brake the car, accelerate the car, shift the car's transmission, and so on. There is no command for "back the car out of the driveway," and yet you can still back a car out of a driveway by just assembling a number of the primitive commands into the actual action of backing a car out of a driveway. You have, in a sense, built a program with your car's dashboard controls arranged in a certain order.

Your computer's API functions in pretty much the same way. Your network services, like the redirector, can sit on top of different transport protocols. Without an API, the programmers of your network software would have to develop one redirector program to connect Microsoft NT to IPX/SPX and a different redirector program to connect Microsoft NT to TCP/IP. It is the same redirector; it is just talking to different transport protocols. The way to avoid this is to provide a common "dashboard" for all the network services. Thus, the redirector service is not written to a protocol, but rather is written to an API (in our example, NetBIOS). NetBIOS can sit on top of IPX/SPX, NetBEUI, and TCP/IP. This means that the transport protocol can change, but you do not have to rewrite your network service because it is written to the API (NetBIOS).

Sockets are a well-known type of API. They are temporary communication channels set up for passing information between a client program and a server program. These programs can be running either on the same machine or across the network. There are three network APIs that you'll probably come across in the networking world:

▶ Novell Sockets

▶ NetBIOS

▶ TCP/IP Sockets

The API will take your network request and perform the task through the proper transport protocol.

File System Drivers

The redirector is the piece on the end of the connection that's making the request. Its counterpart on the end of the connection that's complying with that request is the *file system driver.*

File system drivers aren't used just for networking, but are part of any request for access to storage media. In Windows NT, for example, the network file system driver is one of the supported file systems: FAT, NTFS, CDFS, and the network.

Note

I introduced FAT and NTFS in Chapter 14, "How Hard Drives Organize Your Data." CDFS is the Compact Disc File System, used by PC-based CD-ROM devices.

In general, the role of *any* file system driver is to organize data on the storage media with which it's used. To take a commonly used disk drive file system that you're already familiar with, FAT numbers each cluster and notes which files are stored in which cluster. You will recall from Chapter 14 that if a file's data requires more than one cluster to hold it all, then each cluster will also include a pointer to the next cluster on the disk that's used to store that data; the final cluster has an end of file marker so the FAT file system knows when to stop looking. How does the file system know where the clusters are? When you format a disk, you're cataloging the space on it with the file system you use

When you ask to retrieve a file, the FAT file system is in charge of finding the data you want and making sure that all of it is retrieved (as chances are excellent that not all data will be in the same cluster). Similarly, when you attempt to save a file to disk, the FAT file system finds the first free space on the disk and stores the data associated with that file in those clusters, marking the clusters to point to the next one used as required.

Note

Depending on where disk space is available, those clusters may not be contiguous. The file system doesn't look for the first group of unused clusters that's large enough to store the file; it looks for the first unused cluster, period. If all the file's data won't fit into that space, then the file system will store the remaining data in the next free cluster, wherever that cluster happens to be on the disk.

The network file system is just one more interface for reading disk space. The only difference is that it's used for network access instead of local access as are the other file systems. Thus, on the server end, when the server receives a request for disk access from some network client, the request goes to the network file system, which does what must be done—retrieve data, store a file, or whatever. The important aspect to this is that the network file system makes the local format of the server's hard disk immaterial to the client. Even if the file system with which the disk is formatted is not supported by the client, it doesn't matter because the local file system isn't the one used to satisfy network requests. So long as the client can talk to the server, the server will interpret the file system for the client.

The Role of Network Card Drivers

Now you know how a request gets from the application to the operating system, or is satisfied on the operating system side. How does that request get to the network? That's the role of a piece of software called a *network card driver.*

As you know, any device driver is a piece of software that lets an operating system and a piece of hardware talk to each other. Network drivers are responsible for managing any extra-computer communications, including those required to access the Internet. You'll have one network driver installed for each model of card used. Thus, for example, if you have a PC with a cable modem connection to the Internet and a network connection, you'll need two drivers installed. If you have more than one network card installed (perhaps if your PC is acting as a router) and they're of different kinds, you'll have one driver installed for each. However, if you have two network cards of the same type installed, you'll only have to install the one driver. Basically, these drivers install Data-Link network support for the PC, allowing it to access an Ethernet network, for example.

Network Binding Interfaces

Modern drivers use a tool to bind the network cards to the transport protocols. (I'll explain transport protocols more fully in the next section.) In general terms, this tool is called the *network binding interface.* It serves as the interface between a NIC driver and a collection of protocols called a transport stack.

Note

If you're familiar with the concept of binding a protocol to a network card, then the network binding interface is where the binding takes place. It's essentially a means of "marrying" a NIC driver and a network transport protocol.

What's going on here is fairly straightforward. The network binding interface clumps each installed driver with each installed transport protocol. The name of the clump depends on the network type—for example, NetWare networks call them *modules.* Communication between modules is handled by a program called LSL under NetWare and PROTMAN.SYS under Microsoft networks. Any configuration information required for the binding interface is contained in a text file, such as PROTOCOL.INI for Microsoft networks, or NET.CFG for NetWare networks. However, if the default values for the drivers are used, there won't be much information in these configuration files.

The Ties That Bind

I've said that one of the handy things about network binding interfaces is that they permit you to use more than one transport protocol with each network card driver. By default, all network transport protocols are bound with all installed network card drivers. When you attempt to send data across the network, and more than one transport protocol is installed, which protocol gets used? The answer depends on the order in which the transport protocols were bound. You can edit the binding order to place the protocol that will be used most often first, so as to reduce the number of retries required to find the protocol needed to access a particular server.

If you want to cut off communication to a server that's using a particular protocol, you don't have to uninstall it—just remove it from the list of protocols bound to the network card.

There are two competitors for the title of world standard network binding interface: Novell's Open Datalink Interface (ODI) and Microsoft's Network Driver Interface Specification (NDIS). These two binding interfaces have a lot in common in terms of what they do and how they do it. The main difference between them is that ODI-compliant drivers operate in real mode. As you know, this means that they must use memory in the first 640KB of the memory installed in your machine, and that they can't cooperate with other drivers that may be installed in the system. NDIS-compliant drivers, in contrast, run in protected mode so they can multitask with other drivers and don't use scarce conventional memory.

Why use ODI-compliant drivers if they can't run in protected mode? Mostly because your redirector sometimes requires them. Not all redirectors will work with the NDIS-compliant drivers. If you're not sure, check the documentation for your operating system to find out the requirements of your particular redirector. Generally speaking, both NDIS and ODI work with all transport protocols; any limitation is on the driver side.

Network Transport Protocols

Sneakily, throughout this part of the chapter I've been referring to transport protocols without ever really explaining what they are. First, what *is* a protocol? One of the best ways to understand a protocol is to know that it is simply a standard or set of rules.

You are confronted with protocols in various aspects of your daily life. For example, if your phone in your house rings, you pick it up and say, "Hello?" Why do you say "hello" first? Why doesn't the caller identify himself first? The answer is that it's a tradition. It is the custom in the United States that the person answering the phone should respond first. In other words, this is the American *protocol* for answering the phone. If you were in mainland China, you'd pick up the telephone and wait for the other person to say, "Wei," to signal that they were there. When you meet someone, do you hug, kiss, or shake hands? Once again, the answer is determined by protocol.

How does this apply to networks? Network transport protocols determine how data is transmitted across the network, and how that data is packaged and addressed. For two computers on the same network to communicate, they must be using the same network transport protocols because the protocols used determine how the data is packaged and delivered.

The good news is that modern operating systems can simultaneously support more than one protocol, so you can use one for each type of connectivity you need. The bad news is that not all operating systems support all transport protocols; in fact, they tend to specialize, and even some like-named protocols are not usable across all platforms. However, today there's enough overlap that some degree of communication and interoperability is possible across all major operating systems.

Tip

Loading more than one network transport protocol uses up RAM, so even though it's possible to load more than one transport protocol with modern operating systems, it's a good idea to install support only for the ones you need.

Please be aware that the following sections are *introductions* to the three main protocols used in PC networking, and are not complete. TCP/IP, for one, is an enormously complex protocol with sufficient configuration options to write a book about them, or a lot of books. What's here is simply intended to help you understand the basics of how each of these protocols work and what's involved in it.

The NetBEUI Protocol

Back when IBM first started marketing their PC network, they needed a basic network protocol. They had no intention of building large networks, just small workgroups of a few dozen computers or less.

Out of that need grew the Network Basic Input/Output System, or NetBIOS. NetBIOS is just 18 commands that can create, maintain, and use connections between PCs on a network. IBM soon extended NetBIOS with the NetBIOS Extended User Interface, or NetBEUI, which is basically a refined set of NetBIOS commands. Over time, however, the names NetBEUI and NetBIOS have taken on a different meaning. NetBEUI is the transport protocol, whereas NetBIOS is the set of programming commands that the system can use to manipulate the network; it is actually an API.

NetBEUI is one of the fastest protocols that you can use, in terms of its speed when slapping data into packets for transmittal and unwrapping said data on the receiving end. It's also beautifully simple to set up: you install it and bind it to a network driver, and it works. No configuration is required, and the address of the computer is an easy-to-remember name that you assign.

Computer names on a network using NetBEUI are actually NetBIOS names. They can be up to 16 characters long and are not case-sensitive.

However, there is one problem with NetBEUI, and this problem really limits its usefulness: you can't route it. In other words, if your needs are larger than those of a single segment, you can't use it to transport data beyond your local segment. (A *segment* is a piece of a network that can operate on its own or that has been subdivided simply for better management purposes. For example, within a network comprising several floors of a building, a segment might be on one floor.)

It's also only supported by Microsoft operating systems and OS/2, so if you planned to communicate with the Unix file server or NetWare print server, well, you're out of luck.

Today, NetBEUI's usefulness is somewhat limited. TCP/IP is faster than it used to be, so NetBEUI doesn't have the performance advantage it did at one time. As Internet access becomes ever more ubiquitous, you need TCP/IP anyway, as it is the protocol required to use that network. Even though some NetBIOS applications require support that NetBEUI can give, you can now use NetBIOS over IP to get the same effect.

In short, NetBEUI's not useless, but its usefulness is limited to small, single-site networks that don't need Internet connectivity, and not a lot of those are around.

The IPX/SPX Protocol

IPX/SPX, Novell's proprietary transport protocol, is actually two protocols—IPX and SPX. IPX, or Internet Package Exchange, is a network-layer connectionless protocol. It's responsible for finding the best path for packets to take to reach their destination, or for picking them up when they arrive. Packet addressing and routing are handled by the IPX protocol. So, logical network addresses (as opposed to the hardware ones that are burned into the network card at production) are assigned at the IPX level. An IPX address consists of a 4-byte (32-bit) network number and a 6-byte (48-bit) node number.

What do these numbers mean? The *network number,* also called the *external network address,* identifies the physical segment to which the computer is attached. If two or more servers are on the same network segment, then they'll all use the same external address.

Note

External network addresses are assigned only to NetWare servers. Client machines on a NetWare network inherit their external network addresses from the server they log in to.

The *node number,* or *internal network address,* is usually the hardware address of the network card inside the PC. This is handy, as it means that no translation has to take place from software-assigned names to hardware-assigned names. When installing a Novell NetWare server, you are asked to accept or change the internal IPX number. It then becomes that server's ID number. If you type **slist** from a workstation, you'll see this ID for each server listed.

Figure 27.14 shows the format of a complete NetWare IPX address.

Figure 27.14

A NetWare logical address

Note

For those occasions when NetBIOS support is required, you can enable support for NetBIOS over IPX/SPX.

Note that *routing* is handled by the IPX protocol. In other words, IPX/SPX is a routable protocol, unlike NetBEUI, and can therefore be used to connect network segments separated by a router. To find the most efficient paths, every 60 seconds, IPX issues a broadcast with the Routing Information Protocol (RIP) or the NetWare Link Services Protocol (NLSP) and sends it to an expected location along all available paths. A sort of echo returns from this broadcast, and IPX determines the shortest path to the known location by how long it takes for the packet to get back. The only trouble with this method is that it makes IPX/SPX a rather "noisy" protocol prone to generating a lot of network traffic as it attempts to keep up to date with current routes.

As IPX includes no support for error handling, for some purposes it's supplemented by the services of SPX, the Sequenced Package Exchange. This protocol is connection oriented, which means that it makes sure that a solid connection has been established before it attempts to send data across the network. Because it's reliant on a valid connection, the SPX protocol is responsible for handling lost packets and other errors. Its main function lies with client/server computing, which is dependent on error-free communications.

Even though IPX and SPX are proprietary to Novell, their usefulness is not limited to Novell networks because of IPX/SPX-compatible protocols that aren't the original protocol but can communicate with it. These compatible protocols have been instrumental for permitting Microsoft networks to communicate with Novell ones, as the two network types have no other transport protocols in common. NetWare IP and Microsoft's TCP/IP are not mutually intelligible.

The TCP/IP Protocol

The Department of Defense developed the Transmission Control Protocol/Internet Protocol (TCP/IP) in conjunction with ARPANET (Advanced Research Projects Agency Network) to handle the problem of connecting networks with dissimilar hardware, for example, Sun systems talking to mainframes and mainframes talking to PCs. Each of the two halves of the name TCP/IP describes a different task.

Note

Strictly speaking, TCP/IP has more than two parts—it's actually a suite of protocols. However, the best known are IP and TCP, so I'll concentrate on them here.

Working at the network level, the *Internet Protocol (IP)* provides a standard set of rules and specifications for the different networks to follow if they want IP to route their packets from one network to another. IP is designed for communications between both LANs and individual machines. The *Transmission Control Protocol (TCP)*, on the other hand, takes network information and translates it into a form that your network can understand. In this way, it supports process-to-process communication between two machines or clients. You could think of IP as the part of the protocol that sets the rules of communication and TCP as the part that does the interpreting.

You can tell how good TCP/IP is at its job by its current task. It's the transport protocol for the Internet, the system that connects thousands of individual computers and networks over the world. Although originally designed for use by universities and the military, TCP/IP is becoming more popular for business applications. It can be used to connect LANs, Unix hosts, DEC VAX minicomputers, and many other kinds of computers.

What happens when a Mac in a remote office wants to send data to a PC in headquarters? First, TCP establishes a connection that provides full duplex error-checking (error-checking of data in both directions) between the two platforms. Second, IP lays down the rules of communication and connects the ports of the PC and the Mac. At this point, TCP has prepared the data, so IP takes it, breaks it into smaller pieces if the original was too big, and puts a new header (a "forwarding address") on the packet to make sure it gets where it's going. The TCP packet is also labeled with the kind of data it's carrying and how long it is. Next, IP converts the packet into a standard encoded format and passes it to the PC at headquarters. Finally, the PC's TCP translates the encoded packet back into "PC-ese," that is, its own networking protocol. You can see the process in Figure 27.15.

Figure 27.15

Sending data from a Mac to a PC through a TCP/IP network

●=Data

TCP/IP has become the default protocol for many of the world's networks. It's the only universal communicator that permits computers of all types—PCs, Macintoshes, and Unix workstations—to communicate, and it's required for communication on the Internet. It is a little slower than NetBEUI, but its wide support more than makes up for any performance hit. It's better to be a little slow and able to talk to the whole world than really fast and able to talk to only small groups.

Configuration Requirements for TCP/IP

One catch to TCP/IP is that it can be difficult for novices to set up, as there are so many addresses and servers to assign. As I've discussed already in this chapter, NetBEUI and IPX/SPX are pretty simple to set up addresses for. In the case of NetBEUI, you assign a computer name, and in the case of IPX/SPX you assign a network identifier and let the system assign its own node identifier based on the hardware address of the PC's network card. However, TCP/IP can require a whole slew of addresses, including:

▶ A local IP address

▶ The IP address of the Domain Name Service (DNS) server, which translates an easy-to-remember name, such as `computer.company.com`, into an IP address, such as `192.168.0.100`.

▶ On NT networks using NetBIOS names to identify computers, the IP address of the Windows Internet Naming Service (WINS) server, which translates NetBIOS names into IP addresses

▶ The default gateway (that is, the portal to the next network segment), which is even required for Internet access

▶ The number (called the *subnet mask*) that identifies the network segment to which your computer is attached

▶ If dynamic IP addressing is enabled, the IP address of the server assigning IP addresses

If you've spent any time on the Internet at all, you're probably familiar with the concept of IP addresses. Simply put, they're a 32-bit (four-byte) number that identifies a computer on the network. This is the software address of the PC, as opposed to the hardware address burned into the network card. In its binary form, an IP address might look something like this:

```
11000000 01101010 01111110 11000001
```

It's not wildly easy to read by anyone but a programmer or a computer, so for the convenience of humans, IP addresses are normally written in what's called *dotted quad* format, converting each byte of the 32 bits into a number using the base-10 system, as shown below:

192.106.126.193

Each network card attached to a TCP/IP network has a unique IP address that identifies it on the network—not just the physical segment to which it's attached, but the entire network.

Where does this IP address come from? How do you know what numbers to include in it? The answer depends on the scope of your network. If you're creating IP addresses for a local TCP/IP network that will never have any contact with the Internet whatsoever, then you can more or less make them up if you want to, just so long as no two network cards have the same IP address. However, if you want to connect to the Internet, you'll need to get unique IP addresses, and that's where an organization called the InterNIC comes in.

The InterNIC, simply put, is an organization in charge of assigning Internet addresses to companies and organizations that request them. In broad terms, it assigns groups of IP addresses to organizations based on their sizes, by assigning specific numbers for the first byte (or first two, or first three) and then letting the organization use any numbers they like for the other addresses. So, for example, if you requested a set of Internet addresses from the InterNIC, they might give you the set 192.106.*X*.*X*. This would mean that all your IP addresses would have to start with the 192.106. prefix, but that you could assign numbers (up to 255) as you chose for the final two quads of the address. The parts assigned by the InterNIC are called the *network* portion of the address, and the parts assigned internally are called the *host* portion.

Note

If your eyes aren't boggling at the idea of having to assign an IP address for each computer in your organization, they should be. Not only must you assign the numbers, but you must also create a file that maps computer names to the IP addresses. The file with the name mappings must be kept up to date on every computer on the network. To reduce the complexity of this problem, you can run a Dynamic Host Configuration Protocol (DHCP) server to assign IP addresses from a pool, and then use a WINS or DNS server to resolve name-address mappings. WINS servers take care of NetBIOS names, and DNS servers take care of domain names.

A key part of Internet addressing lies in identifying not just a specific computer, but identifying the *subnet,* or part of a network, to which it belongs. That's done not with an external network number, as with IPX/SPX addresses, but with the subnet mask. The subnet mask is a number that can be overlaid onto the IP address. If the network portions of the IP address match the subnet mask, then the IP address is on the same subnet. If the network portions don't match, then the two IP addresses are on different subnets.

It's easy for two computers on the same subnet to communicate with each other; TCP/IP broadcasts the data, and the computer with the destination address that matches the one in the IP packet picks up the data. If a computer on one subnet wishes to communicate with a computer on another subnet, then the request must go to the router that connects the two subnets. The router looks at the network address of the destination address, decides whether that address is on the local subnet, and if it isn't, forwards the packet to the next subnet. Then that router examines the destination IP address, decides whether the address is on *that* subnet, and either broadcasts the message for pickup or forwards the packet again to the next subnet. This procedure continues until the correct subnet is found.

When a packet arrives at its destination, a protocol called the *Address Resolution Protocol (ARP)* resolves the IP address to the network card's hardware address. ARP is also responsible for translating the addresses for outgoing data.

Multiple Transport Stacks

Two things should be obvious by now. First of all, there is no single best network protocol. Second, you may conceivably want to run all three of the protocols (NetBEUI, IPX/SPX, and TCP/IP), each for a different reason, and the good news is that you can. One of the values of the current networking model is that it supports multiple transport protocols. This is shown in Figure 27.16.

Figure 27.16

A network using
multiple transport
protocols.

In this example, you see that the client machine has four transport protocols loaded and the server has one protocol loaded. This
could happen if the client machine connected to more than one
server. The IPX stack might talk to a Novell server, the TCP/IP stack
might talk to an Internet server, and even NetBEUI might be used for
local access with Microsoft machines. Each transport protocol binds
to the drivers and redirector installed on each machine. As discussed earlier in the "Network Binding Interfaces" section, you can
change the binding order for the various protocols so that IPX/SPX
(or a compatible protocol) may be used first when connecting to a
NetWare server, or TCP/IP for connecting to the Internet.

Installing Cables

Most of what I'm going to talk about here concerns how to prepare
for a contractor's help and what you need to know about your

physical installation before the cabling process begins. This is not a complete tutorial in cable installation. First, I don't have room. Second, it's difficult to tailor such instructions when you can't see the environment in which the cable will be installed. Third, complex cabling is often a specialist's job. Therefore, I'll talk about the basics, so far as you need to know them for simple cabling jobs or for overseeing someone else doing a more complex one. After reading this, you'll be better prepared to instruct the cable installer in what you need done. Outsourcing this kind of work isn't cheap, and the meter's always ticking, so it's best to be prepared.

Plan Ahead

This is one of those really obvious but easily overlooked hints: don't just think about what your needs are now, think about what they'll be five or ten years down the line. Cabling a building is not so much fun that you're going to want to do it twice, so plan ahead.

First, know your situation. Get the blueprints for the building you're in and study them. Where is the ductwork? Where's the electrical wiring and how is it shielded? Are there any surprises waiting to happen? What are the fire codes for your area? What do they say about where you can use PVC-coated cable and where you must use plenum?

Get the fastest cable you can afford. Even if you don't need it now, the chances are excellent that sooner or later you'll use it, when your company starts implementing databases or video to the desktop or some such thing. Buy that 100Mbps Category 5 now, or even fiber if you can justify it, and you'll save yourself money later in not having to pay for two cabling installations.

Give Yourself Some Slack

Don't plan out your cabling needs to the last foot, but anticipate quite a bit of extra cable. First, you'll need this because you can't just plug PCs into the network on top of each other.

Tip

Conveniently, some coaxial cable comes with marking every 10 feet, so you can tell how far apart to make the connections.

In addition, the extra room will give you flexibility. If you have just enough cable for your needs, then sooner or later Joe User is going to want to move his PC five feet to the left, and that's going to completely throw off your entire network if your plan has no flexibility built into it. When running the cable along the ceiling or floor, leave a few loops (6 to 8 feet for backbone cable) at each corner, or each doorway, or anywhere that there's a permanent physical feature in the building so you can find it again. Secure the loops with electrical tape to keep them neat and out of the way. When you need a little more length in your cable, you'll have it. Otherwise, you'll have two options: splicing the cable yourself, or paying someone else to do it. Contractors typically charge not only for the length of the cable they run, but also for the number of terminations they must do. Splicing the cable means paying for two useless terminations that don't do anything but give you more length that you could have had from the beginning with a little planning. Similarly, when running taps from a backbone or hub, give yourself a spare 10 to 15 feet so that you can move the PC at a later time if you need to do so.

Warning

If you haven't planned for flexibility and need to extend your cable, splice it rather than attempting to stretch it. Stretching can damage cable—especially stranded cable—and damaged cable is far more prone to interference.

Giving yourself elbow room applies to conduit, too. In big installations with high security needs, you'll often have a central backbone run in a large duct, with smaller conduits branching off from it. This is an expensive configuration, and larger conduits will make it more expensive yet. Regardless, you should seriously consider getting conduit a little larger than you need now. For example, if the ½-inch variety will let you run two taps from the backbone, get the ¾-inch variety so that you can run three or four taps if you need to do so. Once again, even if it's more expensive up front, giving yourself room to grow will save you money down the road, when you don't have to buy new conduit, pay to have it installed, and scrap the stuff you already paid for.

Neatness Counts

Keep in mind that you're going to have to deal with this cable at some point after it's installed, so make it as easy to get at as possible. When it comes to ceiling installations, you may be tempted to just throw the cables across the floor because it's less work. It's true, this is less work initially, but when you have to work up in that ceiling later, you're not going to like it if you have to trip over cable snaking across the floor. To avoid this, tie the cables to something such as the supports of the drop ceiling; clamps are made for the purpose, or you can use the plastic snap ties. You may also want to consider attaching the cables to air conditioning or heating ductwork.

As a last resort, leave all the cables on the "floor" of the ceiling, but bundle and tie them so that they're out of the way. That way, if you have to move them, you have to move only one lump, not six individual cables all tangled up together.

Note

Not all drop ceilings can support cable, so you may have to tie the cables to the supports or ductwork to make this work at all.

Running cables under the floor requires similar planning. Again, lay the cables neatly so that they're easy to get to. If you've got the money, consider getting ductwork to run the cables in so that they stay in one place. Also, put the cables somewhere that you can get to them *after* the furniture has been put into the room. It might look neater to have the cables running along the wall, but the chances are excellent that cubicles or an extremely heavy table will be along the wall. The middle of the room, where there's less likely to be furniture, is a better bet.

If you're running cable *on* the floor, then the rules are a little different. In that case, you'll do well to keep the cables against the wall and out of harm's way. That way, people will be less likely to trip over them (injuring themselves and/or the network in the process). Also, janitorial staff are less likely to damage them with enthusiastic cleaning. Tape down cables as best you can to avoid the chances of them being tripped on or wandering away.

Finally, label *everything*. At troubleshooting time, you're going to want to know which cables go where without doing this routine: "Okay, Karen, when I say 'Go,' shake the cable so I can tell which one it is." That exchange is typically followed by this routine: "Okay, it wasn't that cable. When I say so, shake the one next to it."

To avoid this, you can use different colors of electrical tape wrapped around the ends of the cables, or little adhesive numbers, or (if you've got deep pockets) color-coded cables themselves. These make it easier to tell which cable you've got at the end and also make it possible to tell which cable you're holding when you're crouched in the ceiling. I don't recommend hand-printed labels, as they can be hard to read. Unless you've got a really complicated cabling system that requires extensive description, symbols are probably the way to go. You can identify them at a glance and don't have to decipher someone else's handwriting or turn the cable over to read the whole thing. A little more than 10 percent of the male population can't tell red from green, so consider using symbols or avoiding green and red cables.

Tip

Keep a legend of cable codes around so people can tell what they're looking at even if you're out of the office.

Play Well with Others

Finally, think about what's going to be running in the same place as your network cable. Got lots of interference-producing devices around? Consider cable with extra shielding, such as coaxial or STP, or, better yet, RFI-immune fiber.

Fluorescent lights emit a lot of EMI, so don't run cables over the top of them.

Are electrical cables already in place? Don't run your network cables parallel to them, particularly if you're looking at big bundles, such as those leading up to a fuse box. If new electrical cables are going in after the network has installed, avoid introducing new interference problems by asking for armored cable (run in a metal sheath) rather than the ones enclosed in the plastic sheath. Once again, it will cost more up front, but these extra precautions may save you money later.

Things to Know Ahead of Time

I've talked about some of the specifics you need to be aware of before the cabling process begins. Here are some questions for your contractor. Figuring out these details early in the process can save you time, money, and lots of headaches.

Do you have wiring conduits? Many buildings provide you with built-in places in the walls and ceilings where you can run your cable. Often, these wiring conduits are themselves plenum-rated. This means that you *may* be able to use a cheaper PVC cable.

How are you testing your cables? You will want to know the precise method that is being used to test the cables after they are installed. Common sense reigns supreme on this issue. (Keep in mind that common sense really isn't that common.) Make sure that you get a written description of the testing method and follow the testing logic from start to finish to ensure that it makes sense for installation.

How are you documenting your cables? Make sure that the cables are being documented and labeled according to your company's set standard. If your company has not set one, then it should do so. You want to be sure that the labeling system makes sense to you, so I recommend that your company set the labeling standard, not the contractor.

What is the repair policy for the cable installation? You will want at least a 24-hour on-site response from your contractor. Many contractors say they have a 24-hour response to cable problems, when what they mean is, "We will call you back within 24 hours, and it may take us up to a week to actually get there." You don't want that; you want the contractor at your site in 24 hours or less. Cable problems are mission-critical problems.

Can you get at least three local references from the contractor? You will want three local references from your contractor so that you can personally see the quality of their work and documentation of it. Most companies will not mind taking you on a tour of their cable systems if they are happy with the work the contractor has done. Don't forget to reciprocate when prospective clients call you to come see your expertly designed and installed cable system.

Are you following building and fire code requirements? To ensure the safety of all your employees, follow all local building and fire codes. You want to select a contractor who can demonstrate by experience and references that they are well versed in the local regulations. When in doubt, call the city or county offices and ask questions.

Do you need to notify anyone else in your building or locale of your plans? You may need to check with other tenants in your building to make sure that the cable installation will not conflict with their workflow. This is usually more of a courtesy than a requirement. Often, if you notify building management, they will notify all the other tenants in your building.

How long is the guarantee on the cable installation valid? Verify the length of time the contractor will guarantee their labor and the cables. A one-year service contract is advisable. Reasonable costs for an annual service contract should not exceed 12 percent of the overall cable installation cost.

Wireless Networking

Preparing for a wireless network—or, more likely, a wireless portion of a wired network—isn't significantly different from preparing for a wired one. You still have to think about environmental factors and how the data is going to get from point A to point B.

As I said earlier, two kinds of wireless networking are used in LANs. Most common are the radio-frequency (RF) wireless networks, which can be used to connect PCs and servers over a fairly wide area, but have low transmission speeds (around 1Mbps). More specialized applications, such as wireless printers and keyboards, use infrared (IR) technology to create a high-speed, short-range link.

Interference is the biggest problem you're likely to encounter with wireless networks. Infrared communications have an extremely high frequency, so in order to use them, the sender and receiver must be close and in the line of sight. If you can't stretch a piece of string between the sending device and the receiving one, they can't communicate. Therefore, if you've got an IR printer, it's a good idea to place it somewhere that IR notebook users can access it without people walking between the two devices.

RF devices are less prone to interference because their lower frequencies mean that the signal can more or less go around obstacles instead of being blocked by them. For this reason, although IR devices are confined to the room in which they operate, RF wireless devices can roam up to about 300 to 500 feet away from their source if indoors, or 800 to 1000 feet away if outdoors. Thick walls or metal barriers will interfere with the signal, but otherwise they're pretty flexible.

Installing and Configuring Network Cards

The cables are in. Now, you're ready to attach them to something. If you're not familiar with cable installation and configuration, read on. You'll learn how to get the card in the box in the first place and how to make it work with the other cards in the box once it's in there.

Installing Network Cards

If you have any experience at all in installing cards in a PC, the mechanics of installing a network card are pretty straightforward. Power down the PC, don your antistatic strap, open the computer case, and find a slot in the PC that's free and fits the kind of card you have.

Tip

If you can, choose a slot that's not next to another card in order to keep the air-flow inside the PC's box as open as possible.

If you're removing another card to insert the new one, follow these steps:

1. Make sure that the card is disconnected from any outside cables.

2. Unscrew the small screw attaching the card to the PC case and lay it aside.

3. Pull gently on the card, using both hands to wiggle it back and forth slightly to disengage it from the connectors. This may take a little tugging, but if the card doesn't come fairly easily, stop and make sure that the card is indeed fully disconnected from the PC.

4. When you've got the card out, set it aside. Wrap it back up in its original sheath, if you kept it and plan to use the card again. Don't touch the gold connectors on the card; the oils in your skin can corrode the gold and thus reduce the card's connectivity.

Installing a card is much the same process, in reverse:

1. Unwrap the card, being careful not to touch the gold connectors, and set it aside.

2. Power down the PC and open it up.

3. Find an open slot on the motherboard that matches the bus required by the card. An ISA card needs an ISA slot; a PCI card needs a PCI slot.

Note

PCI is the card type you're most likely to be dealing with. MCA and EISA cards are very rare, and I'd be surprised if you found a network card that required that you use either bus type. It's possible to find EISA network cards, but they're fairly uncommon.

4. Unscrew the plate that covered the open slot's opening to the rear of the computer and set the plate and screw aside. You may need the plate later, and you'll need the screw in just a minute.

5. Align the network card with the slot in the PC, and push gently but firmly to seat the card in its slot. You may need to push fairly hard for this to work, which can be somewhat intimidating if you're not used to inserting cards. If you've got the right slot and push straight in, then the card should snap into place.

6. Using the screw that you set aside in step 4, screw the card into the little hole in the case to hold it in place. If the card is

in all the way, this extra step won't affect the card's position-ing all that much, but will keep it from sagging or working loose.

7. Replace the case and, if the cables are already in place, con-nect them to the card.

Installing Network Card Drivers

The process for installing the drivers for the card depends on your operating system. Like other add-in cards, network cards come with a floppy disk containing drivers. To install these drivers, follow the instructions that come with the network card. The setup process is usually initiated with really complex operations, such as running INSTALL from the A: drive. This type of installation program will have an interface like the one shown in Figure 27.17.

Tip

The operating system may include drivers for the card, but if the operating sys-tem is more than a year old, the drivers that come with the card itself are likely to be newer.

Figure 27.17

Installing network cards from a floppy disk

More recent versions of operating systems may include drivers for the cards that you can load by using an interface within the operating system. For example, Windows 95/98 includes the Add New Hardware Wizard, which you can use to detect the card and automatically load the required driver. That said, you may end up using the disk anyway, as the drivers on the floppy disk may be more recent, or may be better optimized for the card than are the drivers included with the operating system. Consider the 3Com EtherLink III NIC used for the previous example (see Figure 27.17). When installing the card for use with NT, you're not supposed to use the drivers that come with the operating system. Instead, you should manually select the card to be installed and install the drivers from the floppy. Not sure what you should do? Read the documentation for the card included in the package or (often) on the manufacturer's Web site.

Speaking of Web sites, if you've got Internet access, you may not want to use the drivers provided on the floppy disk or in the operating system because they're both extremely likely to be outdated. Instead, turn to the Web site for the network card's manufacturer and find the section for software downloads. Select the type and model of card you're using. There will often be a page from which you can connect to download sites for that particular model of card.

Any responsible company will prominently display the date that the drivers were released. Compare the dates listed on the site with the dates of the drivers on the floppy disk in order to determine whether there are more recent versions of the drivers for your particular card. This tip about downloading drivers from the Internet applies not only to network cards but also to any device you're installing. Not all device drivers are frequently updated, but it's always worth looking.

Configuring Card Resources

In a lot of ways, installing the card physically is the easy part: you plug it in and you're ready to go. Configuring it is another matter entirely. In the "Networking Protocols and Application Programming Interfaces" section, I talked about the logical addresses that the cards use. I also discussed how those addresses must be unique on the network, but that's not the hard part. The hard part lies in making sure that the network card has access to the CPU and a place to store its data while it's waiting for the CPU to process that data. In other words, it needs its own interrupt, I/O address space, and (rarely) DMA channels. You should recall these terms from Chapter 6, "Installing New Circuit Boards (without Creating New Problems)," where they were covered in detail. In the next few pages I will review what they mean in terms of configuring your network card.

Tip

On modern cards, interrupts, I/O buffers, and DMA settings are software configured, either with a SETUP program or by automatic detection in the operating system. On older cards, some of these settings may be set with hardware jumpers or switches on the card itself. So, before installing a card in the machine, note whether the card is software configurable or hardware configurable.

Tip

If you're using only PCI cards and have installed an operating system that supports Plug and Play, you don't have to worry about any of the configuration issues mentioned in the remainder of this section. PCI cards support Plug and Play, in which the cards are self configuring. The cards still use the same resources described here—you just don't have to hand-configure them.

Getting the CPU's Attention: Interrupt Requests

The network card is in charge of sending and receiving information across the network. However, it can't *do* anything with that information. All number crunching, moving to main memory, or data manipulation must be handled by the CPU.

This is fine, but every other device in the PC or attached to it—the keyboard, hard disk, video card, sound card, and what have you—is also contending for access to the CPU. As you know from Chapter 6, the CPU uses *interrupts* to manage this communication.

When the network card has packets waiting to be processed, they're stored in the NIC's memory. When a packet arrives in the "waiting room," or memory, on the NIC, the NIC goes over to the CPU, taps it on the shoulder, and says, "Excuse me, CPU, but there is some information sitting in the memory of the NIC. When you get a chance, will you please interrupt what you are doing and process this information or move it over to main memory?" When the NIC does this, it is making an *interrupt request.*

Once the CPU receives this request, it goes ahead and continues working. However, when it gets a free moment, the CPU will then go over to the NIC and start processing the information or move the information from the NIC to main memory.

Generally speaking, each device on your network that needs an interrupt must have a different IRQ line assigned to it. If you assign the same IRQ to both the network card and the LPT2 port, sometimes one won't work, sometimes the other, and sometimes neither will work.

How do you find out which interrupts your network card can use and which of those are free? The first question can be answered by reading your network card's documentation. Somewhere, it should list supported interrupts. Most network cards support two or three interrupts, one of which is likely to be IRQ 5.

Tip

If no supported interrupts are available for your network card but some interrupts are available, look to see whether a device in your system could switch to the one that's free. For example, suppose that your network card supports only IRQs 5 and 10, but IRQ 7 is the only one available. If your sound card is using 5 but will support 7, switch the sound card's interrupt to 7.

You can answer the second question in a couple of ways. One method is to meticulously document each interrupt, I/O buffer area, and used DMA channel and write them on a sheet of paper that's kept in an envelope taped to the computer case. There are a couple of advantages to this method. First, you can always get a good idea of your system's configuration, even when the computer is turned off. Second, it's easy to see the configuration at a glance—something not always true when dealing with software diagnostics. The only catch to this method is that you *must* keep it updated, or you're lost.

Well, not entirely lost. Although software diagnostics have historically not been all that great at correctly identifying which devices were using which resources (including IRQs), with Windows 95 the situation got a lot better. The Device Manager tab in the System applet available in the Windows 95/98 Control Panel can tell you what resources some devices are using. (In Windows NT/2000, this information is available through Control Panel as well.) As shown in Figure 27.18, select the device for which you want information, then click the Properties button. You'll move to the Properties sheet for the device. Turn to the Resources tab, as shown in Figure 27.19, and you'll be able to see the system resources that a particular network card is using. (Note that the Resources tab is not available for every device in the Device Manager window.)

Figure 27.18

The Windows 95 Device Manager

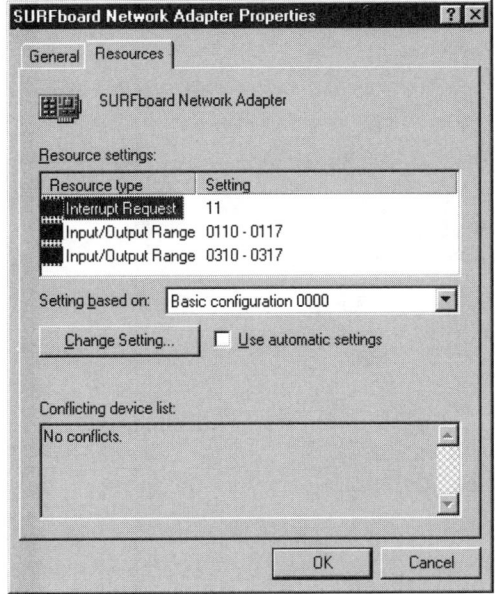

Figure 27.19

The properties of a network card

You can use the Device Manager not only to determine current system configuration but also to change it. To change the interrupt a device is using, click the Change Setting button on the Resources tab and enter a new IRQ number in the space provided. If you choose an interrupt not supported by that device, Windows 95/98 will tell you and offer you another option. If you choose an interrupt that *is* supported but is already in use by another device, the Device Manager will alert you to the problem, as shown in Figure 27.20. If you insist on making the devices conflict, the Device Manager will show the problem device in the list with an exclamation point next to it (see Figure 27.21).

Figure 27.20

The Device Manager will warn you if you assign an interrupt already in use by another device.

Figure 27.21

Devices currently not working will have an exclamation point next to their entries in the list of installed devices.

An exclamation point next to a device in the list of installed devices doesn't necessarily indicate a resource conflict, but could herald some other problem with the device that keeps it from working.

Warning

Another option for Microsoft Windows users is Microsoft Diagnostics (MSD), the DOS-based system information tool. You can use it to get configuration information about your system, but unless you run it from DOS (not from a DOS window in Windows), then it's likely to be inaccurate. For example, note that the network adapter shown in the previous example is using IRQ 5. When I run MSD on the same computer, it reports that IRQ 5 is free and open for use; that is a troubleshooting nightmare waiting to happen.

Where Does This Data Go? Choosing a Base I/O Address

Now you know how the network card gets the CPU's attention when it has information to pass along. Where is this information stored? For that matter, when the CPU passes instructions to the peripheral device, where are those instructions stored?

The answer to both questions lies in the I/O addresses. Remember, they're like a mailbox that the CPU can use to pick up data waiting for it and to drop off instructions for the device to which that I/O area belongs. Each device must have its own I/O area so that the CPU will drop off the appropriate instructions to each device; it's going to cause no end of confusion if the CPU asks the network card to play a sound. Therefore, you'll either need to tell the device which I/O addresses to use or let the system configure itself to avoid conflicts. The *base* I/O address is the one defining the bottom of the range.

Note

Normally, you'll configure the base I/O address, and the rest is taken care of for you. However, some cards require you to define a range, letting you pick from one of the ranges supported by that card.

Converting Hexadecimal Addresses

As you learned in Chapter 6, I/O addresses and memory addresses are written in hexadecimal, a base-16 numbering system like the familiar base-10 numbering system. You can do conversions if you want to, but for most of us, the simplest way to convert hexadecimal to decimal is to break out the Windows calculator and run it in Scientific mode. Make sure that the calculator is set to display in the number system you're starting out in (say, hexadecimal), type in the number, and then change the display to the numbering system to which you're converting. This doesn't impress people the same way that converting in your head does, but you don't have to *tell* anyone you used the Windows calculator.

Getting Information to the CPU: Direct Memory Access

Once the CPU knows that there is a packet of information sitting on the NIC, how does the information actually get from the NIC to main memory?

By using *direct memory access (DMA)*. You already know that when a packet arrives at your workstation, it goes to the memory of the network card. At that point, the network card issues an interrupt to the CPU to ask it to do something with this data that it's just received. The next step is for the CPU to tell DMA chips on the motherboard, "Please move this information for me and let me know when you're finished." The real power of direct memory access is that the DMA chips can move information back and forth while the CPU is busy with other tasks.

When the DMA chip is finished moving the information, it lets the CPU know that it is done.

As with IRQ lines, every device on your network that needs to use DMA must use a unique DMA channel to avoid traffic jams and system crashes. There are really no software utilities that document this information well. The best way to keep track of your DMA channels is to document the settings of your cards as you install them. As most cards—especially newer ones—don't use DMA channels, this isn't too hard to do.

DMA isn't just for motherboards. A special type of network card known as a *bus-mastered network interface* card (actually, as you should recall from Chapter 6, this could be any kind of card) has a DMA chip on the card itself.

With its own DMA chip, a bus-mastered network card can communicate with main system RAM without additional processing intervention by the CPU.

Additional Networking Hardware

It's not enough to create a single LAN. These days, the chances are excellent that your LAN will either start out connected to another network or it will be connected at some point. That's when you've got to move on from simple networks and start dealing with internetworking and intranetworking devices.

Intranetworking *and* internetworking devices? Yup. The basic difference between the two is that *intra*networking devices extend your LAN, and *inter*networking devices connect two different LANs or networks of any size or breadth. This isn't a perfect division, by any means. Why? Because it's sometimes hard to tell where one network ends and another begins. Some devices include both extending and linking capabilities, but the internet/intranet division is a start for organizing networking hardware.

Models of Network Functionality

You can fit some aspects of networking hardware into a simple model, so long as you don't strain the model overmuch.

Physical layer devices, such as repeaters, operate like an extension of network cable, allowing the network to transmit its signal farther than would otherwise be possible.

A *Data-Link layer device* has some functions specific to a particular kind of network, such as Ethernet or Token Ring. The degree of complexity of these functions varies with the device. For example, hubs are mostly concerned with connecting the members of a network indiscriminately; switches may forward information to only the particular segment where a frame's destination address may be found; and bridges may actually permit two disparate network types to be connected. However, the basic idea remains the same; they're concerned with hardware only. A Data-Link layer device doesn't know or care what networking protocol is in place on the network, what network operating system is in place, or what applications are running on the network.

The Data-Link layer is not itself monolithic, but it is divided into two sublayers: the Media Access Control (MAC) and the Logical Link Control (LLC). The MAC layer is concerned with hardware addresses and connectionless data transfer, whereas the LLC layer actually makes connections before passing along data. Most Data-Link devices are more concerned with MAC functions than with the LLC functions, but bridges may use some capabilities defined at the LLC level.

Network layer devices, such as routers, are concerned with networking protocols, such as IPX/SPX or TCP/IP, not with network type.

Repeaters Extend the Network's Reach

Repeaters are devices that regenerate an electronic or photonic signal so as to increase the distance that that signal can travel—basically, to boost it at some point after its original transmission. All repeaters do is strengthen the signal by repackaging and rebroadcasting; they do not connect disparate networks, filter packets, or route data to other subnets.

The sole purpose of a repeater is to reduce the effects of attenuation. As you may recall, that's the tech-ese for "signals get weaker as they travel." As signals get weaker, they're more easily corrupted by other signals. This shouldn't be news to anyone who's ever used a radio while on the road. Say you're driving along, listening to Bela Fleck. As your drive approaches the end of the broadcast area, Bela doesn't immediately disappear, but has a disturbing habit of suddenly breaking off and sounding like the Bee Gees, because the radio station in the new broadcast area is having a "Best of Disco" show. Bela fades out, and the Bee Gees fade in. What happens with radio also happens to networks; no matter what type of signal it is, how well it's shielded, or how immune to interference, sooner or later it will fade to the point at which it's no longer intelligible at its destination.

You can take two approaches when it comes to solving the problem of attenuation. First, you can boost the signal with increased voltage, which is what your radio station is doing when they start boasting about getting a new transmitter. The new transmitter will have no effect on the signal's quality for the original broadcast area. However, it will improve it on the outer edges of the broadcast area and extend it to new areas. Sooner or later, the signal will still fade, but with the stronger original signal, it will travel farther before doing so.

The second approach, and the one taken by networks and inherent in repeater design, is to repeat the signal, so as to start it out fresh again.

What Can Repeaters Do for You?

In repeating the signal, repeaters can have a couple of beneficial effects. First, in Ethernet networks they can help you avoid collisions, or allow you to have a bigger network and spare you from worrying as much about collisions. Second, they can allow you to isolate parts of your network.

Note

All segments of a network connected with repeaters must be using the same Data-Link and Network protocols. That is, you cannot use a repeater to connect a Token Ring network to an Ethernet one, or to connect an Ethernet network running IPX/SPX to one running TCPI/IP. Both networks must be of the same type (Ethernet) and both running the same transport protocol.

Avoiding Collisions

Like other baseband networks, Ethernet networks have only a single "path" on which data can travel at a time. Collisions occur on Ethernet networks when two or more PCs' network cards begin transmitting data on the network at the same time. Therefore, before a PC on an Ethernet network begins transmitting, it listens to the network to make sure that all's quiet on the western front before it begins. However, a PC can hear only so far, and if a node too far away to hear—but on the same segment—is already transmitting, then they'll collide. Admittedly, collisions are inherent in the Ethernet design and to be expected on a properly functioning network, but they can slow down the network by requiring retries. You don't want to have collisions more often than is strictly necessary. Repeaters can help you avoid excessive collisions by boosting the signal so that all PCs on the network can "hear" each other.

Isolating Segments

Ethernet segments are vulnerable to downtime caused by breaks in the cable connection. If you've got some parts of the network that are more prone than others to network downtime, then a repeater could isolate those segments, letting them go down in flames without affecting the rest of the network. For example, say that you're running a PC training firm and want your instructors to get lots of hands-on experience. Therefore, you set aside part of the network to let them mess with it and with testbed servers. After all, the last person you want within reach of the mail server is someone playing, "What happens if I do *this*?" However, if that segment is connected to the rest of the network, then removed cables, forgotten terminations, and other network problems could have a bad effect on network functionality elsewhere. That is where the repeater can help you; even if the cable segments are shorter than the 185m maximum, you can still use a repeater to keep the dead bits of the network from affecting the living ones.

How Do Repeaters Work?

So now you know that the function of a repeater is to regenerate a signal so that it can travel further. Strictly speaking, this isn't quite true; rather than just boosting the signal, repeaters repackage a signal and rebroadcast it. Essentially, what happens is this: when data packets arrive at the repeater, the device takes them apart and repackages them in the same form in which they started out. The repeater isn't actually affecting the data, or touching the addressing information. However, it is revitalizing the signal from scratch, not just resending the original signal. That said, there's no error control built into this process. If a packet is corrupted when it gets to the repeater, it will be corrupted when it leaves the repeater.

On Ethernet networks, every device is a repeater.

Repeaters versus Extenders

You'll have gathered that repeaters don't just repeat, but actually repackage. There *is* a device that just repeats; it's called a LAN *extender*, and this device fulfills the function that you'd expect from something called a repeater. Extenders function similarly to repeaters in that they permit you to have longer networks without increasing the chances of collisions, but they don't add to your repeater count. What's repeater count? You can have up to only four repeaters in a single network, and the number you have is called your *repeater count.*

There's no reason to *not* use a repeater in place of an extender, except that you can use only so many repeaters in a network and you're not limited in the number of extenders that you can use.

The sidebar contrasting repeaters and extenders refers to repeater count. Again, you can have up to only four repeaters in a single network, or else Bad Things (such as network failures or delays) can happen. There are two reasons for this.

First, overuse of repeaters can actually increase the number of collisions on the network. Every time a package is disassembled and reassembled, there's a tiny delay. This delay isn't long enough to matter when a package is being reassembled only once, but the more repeaters on the network, the more tiny delays you'll have. Eventually, the delays will accumulate until, at some point, a sending node is waiting too long to receive any acknowledgment of its transmission and resends its data. The trouble is that when the sending node does this, its original packet is still in transit. If the sending node resends the data while the original transmission is still limping on toward its final destination, then the two packets will collide. Once again, collisions are to be expected in an Ethernet network, but you don't have to go looking for them.

The second potential problem with too many repeaters is data corruption. Each time a repeater breaks down and reassembles a packet, there's the chance that it's putting the data back together incorrectly, perhaps substituting a 0 for a 1 at some point along the line. (If that doesn't sound like a big deal, then consider this: 11001100 binary is 204 decimal, but 11101100 is 236 decimal. Someone just got an informal raise.) It's like the old game of Gossip that perhaps you played in grade school. Person A whispers something in the ear of person B, and person B whispers what they heard in the ear of person C, and so forth around the circle. Finally, person O says what he or she heard, and it turns out to be an extremely garbled version of what person A said in the first place. Funny then (at least fourth-graders get a big kick out of it), but not good when what's getting garbled is not tongue twisters but your network's data.

The four-repeater rule is not carved in stone; your network will not work perfectly with four repeaters, then crash in flames as soon as you add the fifth. However, it will become more unreliable as you increase repeater count, and four hops is the recommended upper limit.

Hubs Connect the Dots

Hub is a catch-all term for a device that connects networked devices to each other. The term is used most often to apply to devices used in Ethernet networks. Token Ring networks use multistation access units (MAUs), which, like the network itself, function differently from the Ethernet hubs. However, both hubs and MAUs serve the same basic function of joining the PCs on the LAN.

The Types of Hub Models

Most hubs come in one of three forms:

▶ Stand-alone

▶ Stacked

▶ Modular

Stand-alone hubs are what they sound like—powered or (more rarely) unpowered devices that may or may not include the capability to connect to other hubs with a short run of cable, perhaps fiber or twisted-pair, in which case they're stacked. Stand-alone hubs, both in stand-alone and in stacked form, are shown in Figure 27.22.

Figure 27.22

Stand-alone hubs may be used alone or linked to other hubs.

Unmanaged stand-alone hubs are generally pretty inexpensive (I picked up one LinkSys hub with five PC ports for $59), but hubs get more expensive as more ports are added. If you don't need management capabilities, buying two stand-alone hubs and linking them may be cheaper than buying one big one.

Modular hubs are built with a backplane that hub cards can plug into, as shown in Figure 27.23.

Figure 27.23

Modular hubs look like add-in cards plugging into a motherboard.

Add-in card for additional ports

If built to be "intelligent" (I'll discuss this in the following section), the hubs in a modular or stacked design may be managed by one hub that's the Master, while the rest are Slave hubs. Why choose a modular or stacked hub? Mostly, it will depend on how your network will grow. You can add modules to a hub chassis, or you can get stackable hubs to distribute them throughout your building, wherever they happen to be needed.

Some Hubs Are More Equal Than Others

Hubs come in a variety of forms, ranging from extremely simple designs that act as a cable interface to those that offer some advanced management techniques. You can theoretically divide hubs into three categories:

▶ Passive

▶ Active

▶ Intelligent/managed (two terms for the same thing)

Passive hubs are unpowered devices, such as patch panels, that provide an interface for cables to transfer data back and forth. They're appropriate for some applications, such as wiring a house for a network, but you're more likely to find an active and/or managed hub in most LANs.

Note

All completely passive devices are unpowered, as a powered hub regenerates the signal and is therefore active.

An *active hub*—that is, any powered hub—has repeating qualities, repackaging and regenerating the signal as described in the earlier section on repeaters. Otherwise, active hubs serve the same functions as passive hubs, blindly making sure that data put on the network is broadcast to each connected segment so that whomever the data is for can pick it up. One advantage that most powered hubs have is *status lights.* If a PC's connection to the network is working, then the light for the port it's plugged into comes on. If the PC isn't connected to the network, then the light is out. Another status light on one hub I have shows a scary-looking red light whenever collisions take place, but recall that some collisions are a normal and expected part of Ethernet operations.

Intelligent, or managed, hubs have a module that allows them to do a bit more than just shove data along the network; they can be used to help you troubleshoot or keep tabs on your network. If you see a hub sold with a managed device interface (MDI), it's an intelligent hub.

Management protocols, such as the Simple Network Management Protocol (SNMP), have two parts. A monitor runs on a management server, and an agent runs on the devices to be managed. The monitor and the agent can communicate. In the case of SNMP, the most common generic management protocol, the monitor queries the agent and collects information from it, perhaps including the following:

▶ Hub and/or port-level status and activity information

▶ Performance statistics on a per-port basis

▶ Network mapping of all SNMP-capable hardware on the network

▶ Event logging of network errors and activity

You can also use management software to do things to managed devices, such as:

▶ Change network security by denying unauthorized people access to the hub

▶ Set tolerances for activity, error levels, and performance so that if those tolerances are exceeded you know about it

Note

This is a sample of the kinds of information that may be available with managed hubs, not a complete list or one that will apply to all managed hubs. The precise information that the management software delivers depends on the agent installed and may vary with the model.

Managed hubs aren't always necessary. If your network has only a single hub and this hub is easy to get at, you can probably check it out in person as easily as you can call up diagnostic software. The more PCs that are on the network, and the harder the hub is to get at, the more complicated troubleshooting gets. What's simple with one hub becomes a nightmare when you've got 10 hubs with 16 PC ports each. In that case, some kind of management software can help you keep your sanity when it comes time for troubleshooting.

Tip

When choosing managed hubs, look for management modules that can be upgraded with flash ROM. That way, when improvements become available, you can upgrade the module rather than replace it.

Hub Architecture

At its most basic level, a hub is a device that offers an electrical connection for cables that can't be hooked into each other directly. *Ports,* or the little holes you stick the cables in to connect them (see Figure 27.24), are relevant to the definition of any hub.

Figure 27.24

Inserting STP cables into a hub

Ports are important; the ports in a hub determine

▶ The cable type that the hub supports

▶ The number of PCs that may be connected with a single hub

▶ Whether the hub is expandable and may be remotely managed when the network is down

Like network cards, hub ports are designed to accommodate only particular kinds of cable connectors. For example, thin coaxial cable and UTP require different ports, and STP requires ports different from those used by fiber. Like other network devices, hubs can be used only with the type of cable with which they're compatible. Also like other devices, they're logically compatible once the cables fit. That is, if you buy a hub that supports connections to RJ-45 connectors like those used with UTP, then you should be able to use that hub for your 10Base-T network whether the hub came from Ye Olde Hub Shoppe or 3Com—the physical interface remains the same. To make a live network connection, you provide power to the hub and plug in the cables.

Note

Some hubs have ports for various sorts of cables. This allows them to connect to more than one type of network so that you can physically connect, say, an AS400 to your PC-based 10Base-T LAN. Or, you can connect hubs with backbone cables made of thick coaxial cable or fiber optic cable.

Those ports won't do you any good unless there's some mechanism to connect them internally so that packets from one cable may be passed to the rest of the network. To let ports—and thus the nodes plugged into those ports—communicate, there's an internal bus system inside the hub providing each port with a receiving connection and a sending connection. The way that data is sent to each port depends on the type of network involved. For example, Ethernet networks broadcast data to all parts of the network, leaving it to the nodes to sort out whether a packet is intended for them or should be ignored. Thus, data coming into a hub from a PC on a 10Base-T Ethernet network is broadcast to all segments plugged into the hub, as illustrated in Figure 27.25.

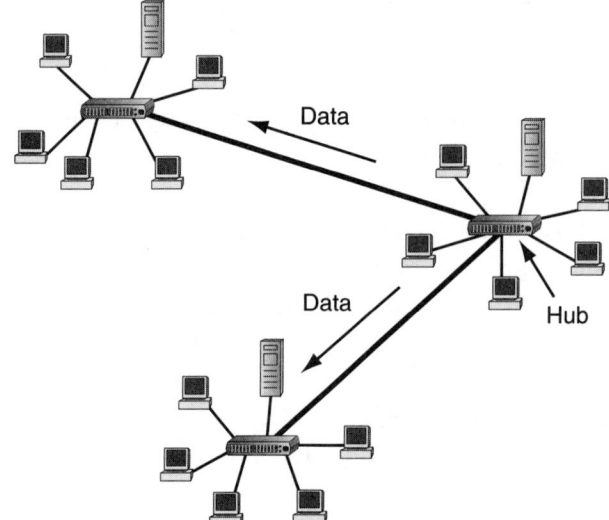

Figure 27.25

Data sent on a 10Base-T network is broadcast to each PC plugged into a hub via the ports.

Some intelligent hubs note the physical address of the network card associated with a particular port. These hubs may either be preprogrammed with a static list of address-hub mappings or they may create mappings through discovery. Static address mappings can be used to keep unauthorized people off the network. As shown in Figure 27.26, if a hub is given a static list of port-address mappings, and a PC with a physical address not found in that list attempts to connect to the network, a smart hub can isolate that port. Once isolated, the unauthorized PC can't actually connect to any of the other PCs plugged into the hub.

Figure 27.26

Intelligent hubs can use static lists of authorized physical addresses to keep unauthorized PCs off the network.

The internal bus of the hub operates at the same speed as the network, or, more precisely, the speed of the network is determined in part by the speed of the hub. Therefore, if you want to run a 100Mbps network, you'll need a hub with an internal bus that supports that speed.

Not all the ports in a hub are for plugging in computers. One, the AUI port, may be present to let you connect the hub to another hub or to another device such as a bridge or router, as shown in Figure 27.27.

Figure 27.27

Use the extra port to link hubs to each other or to internetworking devices.

Models with AUI ports typically list the number of ports like this: 5 + 1, meaning that the hub has five ports for PCs to plug into and one AUI. The type of cable that plugs into the AUI port depends on the hub; some models may use fiber or thick coaxial, while others may use RJ-45 and look like one of the PC ports. More expensive hubs may have fiber AUI connections. However, even the cheap $59 hub that my network supports can connect to other hubs at 100Mbps because its AUI supports Category 5 cable.

Tip

The more ports a hub has, the more expensive it's likely to be, and the expense may be greater than the cost of another hub with the same number of ports. Check costs—it may be cheaper to attach two hubs with their AUIs rather than to buy a single hub with the number of ports that you need.

In addition to their AUI ports, some hubs will have a serial port interface. This interface enables you to connect the hub to a PC or modem and thus get remote management capability that isn't affected by network crashes not related to the hub itself. Such management is referred to as *out of band* management, as it takes place independent of ordinary network transmissions.

Switching Hubs

You'll notice that some smart hubs don't just blindly shove data onto all the segments of the network that are plugged into them. Instead, they notice the MAC addresses of the network cards associated with each port and can discriminate based on those addresses. Switches carry this capability somewhat further to identify the destination's MAC address and forward the packet only to the segment on which that address is located.

The distinction between an ordinary hub and a switching hub is the difference between the office switchboard operator getting an incoming call and paging the intended recipient to pick up the call, and calling a specific office and patching through the call directly. Figure 27.28 illustrates this concept.

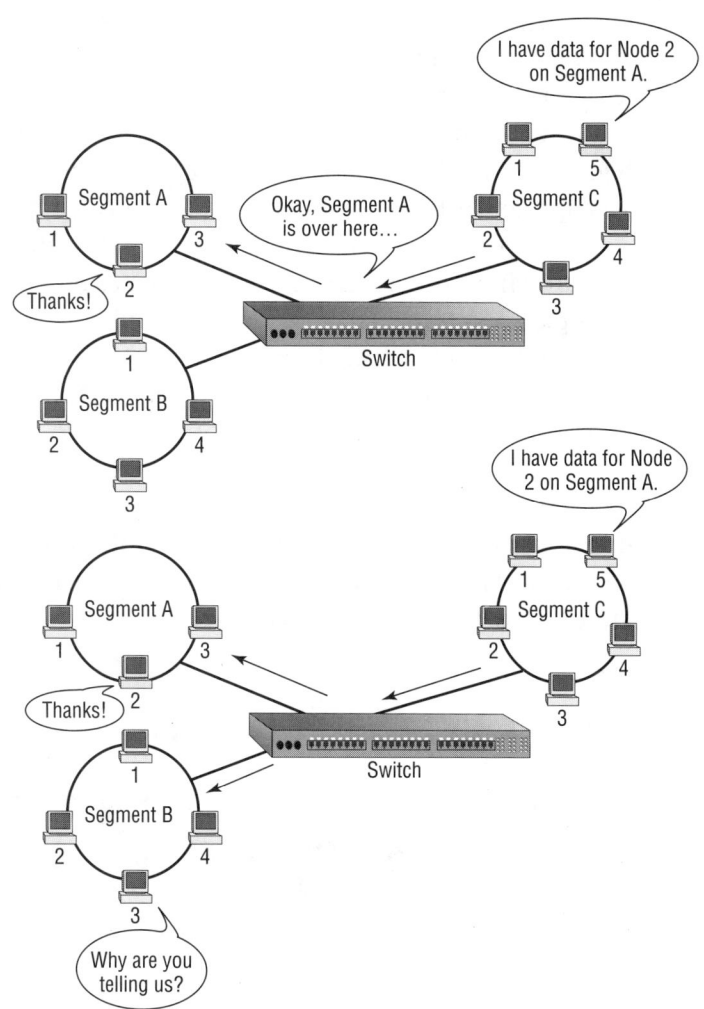

Figure 27.28

Switching the signal (top) versus broadcasting the signal (bottom)

Why bother with switching the signal instead of broadcasting it? One major reason is traffic control. If every time there's a telephone call into the office, the switchboard operator makes everyone listen to the page and then decide whether to pick up, that's more of an interruption to the office than it is to directly notify the call's target. Similarly, when a hub broadcasts all frames to all segments attached to it, then every PC on the network has to stop and "listen" and can't talk lest they cause a collision. If the signal is switched only to the part of the network where it needs to go, then the rest of the network isn't bothered. It can transmit data on the other segments without interfering with the first transmission.

Switching also makes it possible to reserve more bandwidth for high-traffic applications. With ordinary hubs or repeaters on a 10Mbps network, all ports share the same 10Mbps pipe. With switching, each port can have its own 10Mbps pipe, unencumbered by traffic from other ports. Switching makes it possible to connect multiple LANs to get all the advantages of being linked without the disadvantages of sharing bandwidth.

The role of a switch is a bit more complex than simply that of a hub with a little more on the ball than average. As illustrated in Figure 27.29, you typically don't plug individual PCs into a switch, but plug hubs into the switch's ports so that each segment of the network has its own port. Depending on where you put the switches in the LAN, you can use the switch to isolate portions of the network at the workgroup, departmental, or backbone level.

Figure 27.29

Use switches to isolate parts of the network, not to isolate individual PCs.

Note

Although switches are often used to connect LAN segments, you can connect an individual PC to one if you want to devote a large amount of bandwidth to a single power user or server.

Switching Methods

Most switches use one of two methods to accomplish their mission: cut-through or store-and-forward. In *cut-through switching,* the switch reads only the MAC address in the frame to be switched. (*Framing* is the act of packaging data into segments called packets, or *frames.*) The switch starts forwarding the frame to the appropriate port on which that MAC address is to be found as soon as the switch knows where to send it—usually after only 20 to 30 bytes of information have entered the switch. (Recall that an Ethernet frame has about 1500 bytes of information in it, so this pause to inspect 30 bytes of the frame represents very little latency.) Thus, cut-through switching operates essentially at line speed.

Store-and-forward, a function also found in bridges, receives the entire frame and then inspects it to determine its destination MAC address and checks the frame for errors. Only frames that are in good shape get forwarded.

Figure 27.30 illustrates the difference between the two methods.

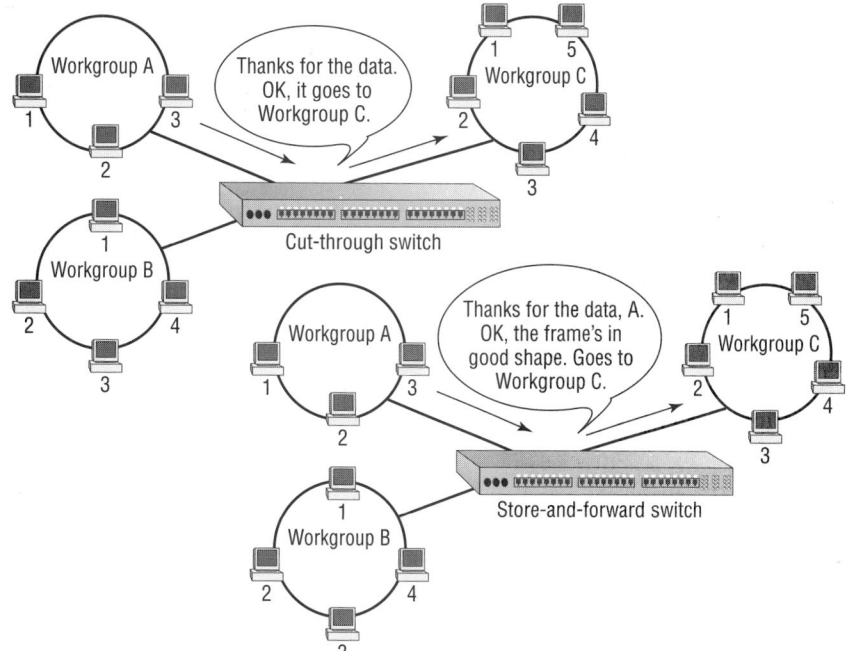

Figure 27.30

The switching method you choose depends on whether it's more important for your network to be error free or very fast.

Which method is better? Cut-through switching is generally faster, as the frames can be shoved onto the appropriate segment as quickly as they arrive at the switch. However, this method carries the hazard of forwarding damaged frames and thus increasing network traffic with useless bits. Store-and-forward switching is slightly slower, as each frame must be inspected for errors before it's forwarded, but is less likely to propagate errors on the network. It's not slow, exactly, but there's a degree of latency found with store-and-forward switching not found with cut-through switching, and the larger the frame, the greater the delay. This is an issue that affects bridged networks as well.

Therefore, cut-through switches are best for networks that need high throughput more than they need to reduce the chance of error propagation; smaller, simpler networks can benefit from them. Store-and-forward switches may be necessary for more complex networks that can't take the chance of wasting time on garbage frames.

Note

Some switches support both methods. Ordinarily, they use cut-through switching and monitor error rates without storing the frames. If error rates exceed a predetermined tolerance, the switches change to store-and-forward switching.

28

A Buyer's Guide to PCs

INTRODUCTION

If you're the kind of person who fixes your own or someone else's PC (and if you weren't, why would you be reading this book?), you're likely to be the kind of person who's often looking to the next PC, the latest-and-greatest machine. Perhaps your palms itch when you see that someone else owns a dual processor Pentium III system when all you can afford is a Pentium II. You eye 26GB hard drives the way some teenaged boys (and many grown men) eye Corvettes.

Or maybe you're not that way. Maybe your computer is just a tool for you, a platform upon which to get some work done. But you've found that your current platform just isn't fast enough to support today's software and you need to know how to either upgrade your existing machines or buy new ones that won't offer as much trouble when it's time to upgrade again in a year or two.

Note that if you check out the system requirements of Windows 98/2000, they'll appear ridiculously low. Windows 98 can supposedly run on a 486DX/66 machine with 24MB RAM, and Windows 2000's minimum system requirements are a 133MHz Pentium-class CPU with 64MB RAM. Don't fool yourself into thinking that these machines will even remotely be satisfactory unless you plan to use your computer as a doorstop.

It's a good time to upgrade; with prices these days, everybody can own some of the fastest PCs on the planet. Buyers with tons of money don't currently have much advantage over the rest of us. (Unless, of course, you've *got* to have an 850MHz Pentium III-based system with the digital, active matrix, flat panel screen, and 26GB drive.)

But *which* one to buy? Well, I'm not going to tell you *that*: there are zillions of honest vendors out there who deserve your money. I'd just like to give you some advice on how to make sure that your vendor is one of the good ones.

I tell my clients that when they're going to buy a PC, they should consider four things: compatibility, upgradability (I know, it's not a word), serviceability, and price/performance.

Because I'm concerned about those things, I recommend that home users and small businesses avoid many of the big names in the PC business and buy a *generic* computer rather than a *proprietary* computer. For larger corporations that have such things as technical support, on-site service, warranties, and other programs in their technical budget, however, dealing with large, name-brand computer companies is more cost-effective and desirable than buying generic computers.

Note that an odd fact about the computer industry is that while the technology is always changing, you can expect to spend roughly the same amount of money on a new system today as you would five years ago. Of course, the new system will be much more powerful in an objective sense than the one five years ago, but the new PC will occupy the same relative position in the marketplace. In other words, a mid-range PC five years ago cost somewhere between $1500 and $2000. And, guess what? That's what they cost today!

Parts of a Generic PC

Now, I've discussed this before, but before I go any further, let me remind you what I mean when I say "generic" and "proprietary." *Generic* refers to machines designed like the IBM AT, even if the machine is built around a Pentium III. Generic machines are PCs consisting of a few separate industry standard parts. Those parts include:

Standard case If you buy a computer with an unusually shaped case, such as the "slimline" PCs or the micro towers, you may find that all of the boards inside the computer are unusually shaped as well. That means that you probably won't be able to easily locate affordable replacement parts should you need them. It also means that you can't put an industry-standard ("generic") power supply in your system. That's undesirable because there are some very nice power supply alternatives these days, such as super-quiet fans or power supplies with built-in battery backup. The choice of whether you get a desktop case or tower model is completely up to you. Desktop cases tend to save space on your desktop (you can put your monitor on them), but towers are nice and roomy inside. You can also place tower cases on the floor if you want to.

ATX case This is a newer case style, which actually rotates the processor and expansion slots 90 degrees inside the case, giving you room to add more cards. A side-mounted fan on the power supply does a better job of cooling the system than the standard version. But the most visible difference is the double-height aperture in the back where the keyboard, mouse, and ports are located; these ports are all piled on top of one another. A standard motherboard will not fit in an ATX case, and vice versa. Some cases have additional buttons (usually located right on the front of the case) for "Turbo mode," a reset button, and a power switch. The Turbo button, now obsolete, does the opposite of what it says. It actually slows your computer down. The reset button allows you to "warm boot" your computer. In other words, press the reset button to reboot your computer without turning the power off. The power switch/button, obviously, turns your computer on or off. Power switches that are located on the front of the case are the most convenient. It is sometimes a pain (especially if you have a tower case under your desktop) to reach around and grope for the power switch just to turn your computer on.

Motherboard The largest circuit board in the case, the motherboard holds the CPU, memory, and expansion slots. On that motherboard there should be *eight* expansion slots, rather than the three that you find on some computers these days, so that you can add expansion boards to your PC now and in the future. Three slots just aren't enough. Today's motherboards should have mostly (or all) PCI slots and one AGP slot. You can't tell how many or what kind of expansion slots there are from looking at the back of the computer. You'll have to ask a salesperson or read the marketing material closely. Motherboards built at around a 100MHz bus speed will feature the most advanced Pentium III processors and have a distinct performance advantage over older, 66Mhz bus systems. 133MHz bus systems are also available, if you're willing to shell out big bucks for them. New motherboards may also support the AGP 4X standard, which is an improvement over the widely deployed AGP 2 standard, resulting in faster video performance if you have an AGP video card that supports AGP 4. Finally, look for a system that has USB ports.

I/O This used to be a separate entity, but now it is built into most motherboards. It's good to get a motherboard with two EIDE controllers that support Ultra ATA/66 transfer rates. EIDE controllers allow your hard drives to talk to the CPU, and two of them let you have up to four hard drives or CD-ROMs. Since there are two EIDE channels, if you put more than one device on a channel they will be in a Master/Slave configuration. The parallel port resides here as well; get one that is ECP/EPP so that you can connect to a nice, fast printer. There should be two PS/2 ports for your mouse and keyboard so that you don't need to waste a perfectly good serial port. Speaking of which, serial ports and floppy drive connectors are considered I/O as well; not much to concern yourself with here, just be sure you have the standard setup of one floppy controller and two communication (COM) ports.

Video adapter board This is the component that allows the PC to display images on the monitor. Look for a video board that can display screen resolutions of 1024×768, support true color, and is a 3D board if you play games. AGP video boards are faster, so look for that as well.

That's just a generic overview. I'll zoom in on particular features you should be looking for in a few pages.

Problems with Proprietary PCs

How is one of these generic PCs different from a proprietary PC? Well, you find all of the same functions in a proprietary PC, but you find all of them on a single circuit board, a kind of "workaholic" motherboard. The big problem with proprietary computers is that you can't upgrade them easily, nor can you fix them for a reasonable price. Proprietary computer motherboards are typically shaped differently from each other and from generic motherboards, making it impossible for you to replace an old or damaged proprietary motherboard with anything but another motherboard of the exact same make and model. As motherboards of that particular make and model are available only from that particular vendor (by definition, since the motherboard is proprietary), it may be expensive or impossible to get a replacement. Likewise, it's almost certainly impossible to get an upgrade.

For more specific problems with proprietary designs, let's return to my four criteria.

Compatibility is at stake because if the vendor did anything wrong (for example, if the company chose a mildly incompatible video chip, as AT&T did for some of their systems), you must either throw away the computer or hope that the designer was farsighted enough to allow you to disable the built-in video function so you can go out and spend more money on a separate video board.

Upgradability is a concern because not all boards are built alike. Take, for example, the Compaq Deskpro systems. Although they work very well, they are difficult to upgrade (the motherboards especially, because they are not a standard shape). You must buy a new motherboard from Compaq, as opposed to running to your local vendor and picking up a newer, faster one when it comes out.

Serviceability is a problem for reasons touched on above. A generic design like a Gateway 2000 is a safe buy in many ways, not the least of which is that even if Gateway goes bankrupt tomorrow, the entire machine is composed of generic parts that can be bought at *thousands* of clone houses around the country. And this isn't brain surgery; you've seen in this book that you can break down and rebuild a PC in about 30 minutes and leave it better than when you started.

And what about *price/performance*? First of all, notice that I put this last. That's because compared to what computers used to cost, *any* PC is a bargain, even if you pay list price for one made by IBM. In regard to the proprietary computers, in theory, a single-board design can be faster and cheaper for many reasons. You don't see that in actual fact because single-board designs tend to be embraced by the big-name companies that need to pay for four-page color spreads in *Byte* and *PC Magazine*.

You don't need to buy a big name to get big performance, reliability, or flexibility. Look in your local paper's business section for the names of companies near you that sell generic PCs. It couldn't hurt if the company offers service through a national service company like Wang or TRW. Then choose that fire-breathing 850 MHz Pentium III you've been eyeing, put it to work and smile, knowing that you've bought the security of easy upgrades and independence from having to buy from a single vendor.

Choosing a Market Niche

What PC are you going to buy? As with any consumer product, there are differences between "name-brand" computers and those that are "generic."

Name-brand computers are built by well-known companies such as IBM, Compaq, Dell, Gateway, and Micron and can be found in most computer retail outlets. You can also buy them direct from the manufacturer by using a toll-free number, the Internet, or mail order. Some of these companies shoot for top-notch quality, service, and other value-added options, so you may not get much of a bargain price-wise. You will, however, get a name-brand computer that is supported by a company that is visible in the marketplace and has a significant service and support operation.

Generic computers, on the other hand, are a mixed bag. You'll probably get a lower price than you will with a comparable name brand computer, but you won't have access to a bunch of extras such as an extensive software bundle that comes with the computer or 24/7 customer support.

Many generic computers do use high-quality components, so the overall quality of the computer and its compatibility with other components is comparable to name-brand computers—but you need to do some research to make sure this is the case. At the lowest end of the generic spectrum are computers you should stay away from. They are built from the cheapest components and are more unreliable than the other computers I've mentioned here.

Choosing PC Parts

When choosing a PC, I look at what it's made of in order to decide if it's the kind of machine that I'm looking for. Let's look at the important parts of a PC and summarize what you should consider when buying a PC. All of these items are discussed elsewhere in the book; this is just a summary. Consult the index to find out where to read more about any given topic.

CPU

If you're buying today, you should buy a Pentium III or an equivalent processor from another manufacturer. Midrange Pentium III chips are coming down in price and are quite fast. Most games written today are, in fact, written to take advantage of the Pentium CPU.

The fact of the matter today is that CPUs are leveling out in speed. To explain: a 386 was twice as fast as a 286 at the same speed, thus a 386/20 was twice as fast as a 286/20. Same difference between the 386 and 486, and the Pentium and 486 again. Yet what about the difference between the Pentium II and the Pentium? Between the Pentium II and Pentium Xeon, or how about the Celeron? They are a little faster in clock speed only; the real difference is in the way these processors handle their work—Xeon, for example, gives access to more memory than a Pentium II, but it is not twice as fast.

What's *not* getting faster are the peripherals. CPUs today are hundreds of times faster than XT-level CPUs; modern peripherals, however, are only dozens of times faster than XT-era peripherals. Take the money you're saving by not buying the latest and greatest CPU and spend that on a faster bus and faster peripherals. (There are exceptions; some processes are very CPU-intensive and will benefit from a faster processor.)

Be certain to get enough cache memory. There are two types of cache memory, L1 (or level 1) and L2 (level 2). Cache memory is used by the processor to access frequently used pieces of data and can speed up your system. L1 cache is resident on the CPU and doesn't require a bus to transport data between the cache and the processor. L1 cache is usually 32K. L2 cache also resides on the CPU but requires a bus to transport data, slowing it down by comparison to L1 cache. L2 cache sizes range from 128K on the Intel Celeron to 512K on Intel's Pentium II and III chips.

"Upgradable" PCs

What about modular "upgradable" PCs? The idea *sounds* good, but the upgrades are proprietary and can be quite expensive. Generic PCs are the original upgradable PCs.

System Bus Speed

66MHz is now becoming obsolete and 100MHz is the new standard. 133MHz bus speeds are now available. Faster is always better, but faster is also more expensive. System bus speeds are used with the speed of your CPU and a clock multiplier to determine the ultimate speed of your system. Bus speed also affects the type of RAM you can install later on. RAM chips are compatible only with the system bus speed they are originally designed for.

Expansion Card Bus

You need a fast bus to drive fast peripherals. You want a *smart* bus so that your system works with Plug and Play and so that you can set up new boards easily. There's really only one smart and fast bus: PCI.

Most new boards are coming out with more PCI slots (which is good; you should look for this in a board), a few EISA slots for backward compatibility, and an AGP slot, which is currently reserved for high-speed video. Which brings me to my next bus requirement: Plug and Play. Make absolutely sure that your new machine will support Plug and Play (through its PCI and AGP slots) as implemented by Windows 98; I say "as implemented by Windows 98" because a good number of vendors have a kind of loose interpretation of what Plug and Play means. The simplest hard-and-fast test is to ask, "Does it work with Windows 98?"

Not every board you plug into your system needs to be a PCI board, although that is preferable. You should be pretty sure, however, that the following adapters are PCI:

▶ SCSI host adapter

▶ Any LAN cards

▶ Any video capture or sound capture hardware

RAM

Remember this simple mathematical equation to help you buy the right amount of RAM: More = Better. Today's operating systems like RAM (especially Windows NT). Get a system with at least 64MB of RAM. And, if you can afford it, I suggest getting 128MB of RAM. You can never have too much RAM!

ROM BIOS

This is an important part of compatibility. Make sure your system has one of the big three—Phoenix, Award, or AMI. That way, it's easy to get upgrades. Nice BIOS features include:

▶ User-definable drive types

▶ Bus speeds that can be set in the setup

▶ Processor cache enable/disable

▶ Plug-and-Play capable

▶ Flash upgradable

Motherboard/System Board

Motherboards come in a variety of flavors, depending on the number and type of ports you need and the form factor of the case. They also have different bus speeds. The system bus speed determines the speed at which the CPU and the motherboard communicate. 100MHz is the current standard, although 133MHz is coming on strong. You'll also need to ensure the motherboard has USB ports if you plan on expanding your system in the future with USB devices, and it should also have an AGP slot for an advanced video card. If the USB ports and AGP slot are built in, and the PC has their associated devices already installed when you purchase it, you're won't have to worry about it.

Disk Drives

You're probably going to end up buying EIDE-type drives, mainly because they're so amazingly cheap, fast, and reliable. Just back the silly things up *regularly*, because there is a limited array of repair options open to you. Look for a minimum size of 12GB for your primary hard drive.

Floppy Disks

I've seen too many problems with Mitsubishi drives to recommend them; TEACs seem the most trouble-free. I recommend getting an Iomega Zip or Jaz drive also, if you need a lot of data storage space.

CD-ROM and DVD Drives

At a minimum, you should have a CD-ROM drive in any computer you buy. If you don't (come to think of it, I don't know if they even sell systems without them nowadays), you won't be able to install any software. Virtually all software these days is distributed on CD-ROM, except for some unique system utilities that require you to boot from a floppy drive. Since DVD is becoming more widespread, I suggest you go for a CD-ROM/DVD drive. That way, when software and games are more prevalently distributed on DVDs, you'll be able to buy them without worrying about being able to use them. As an added bonus, you'll be able to play DVD movies on your PC. Not a great productivity-enhancer, but they are fun! The one trade-off you'll make if you get a DVD drive is a bit of speed. CD-ROM drives max out at 48X or more, while DVD drives tend to be a bit slower. Most of the time, you'll never know the difference.

Video Board

Get a 3D AGP video accelerator board to support modern graphical operating systems, applications, and games. (See Chapter 23, "Video Adapters and Displays," for more about video.)

Video Monitor

Buy a 17-inch monitor. You'll save on eyestrain, regardless of the resolution you choose. If you consistently work in high resolutions such as 1024×768, this size monitor is a must.

Sound Card

You should look for a system that has a sound card. Although all systems have an internal speaker independent of a sound card, few programs take advantage of it.

Speakers

Most PCs ship with some sort of speaker system to complement the sound card. The common little cubes are perfectly functional, but you might consider going with a speaker set that has a subwoofer. The sound will be much richer, and music or games will really blow you away.

Mice

Any of the Microsoft mice seem the best of all the ones I've worked with. The newest mice don't have balls—they use infrared pulses to determine how far, fast, and in what direction you move the mouse. They come in USB and don't even require a mouse pad.

Printers

Although laser printers used to be the standard for high-quality output, today's inkjet printers are excellent. In fact, some, like the Lexmark 5700 series printers, actually support up to 1200 ×1200 dpi. Additionally, these printers can produce photo-quality color. And inkjet printers are usually only a couple hundred dollars, while color laser printers can cost from $300 to many thousands of dollars.

Serial Ports

Look for serial ports based on the 16550 UART chip. It's built for multitasking.

Parallel Ports

Make sure that your parallel ports are enhanced parallel ports or ECP/EPP interfaces. They're faster and bidirectional. Bidirectional parallel ports are essential for modern printers, which send status information back to the PC over those ports.

Universal Serial Buses (USBs)

How many things do you currently have attached to your computer? A modem, monitor, sound card, more? Eventually, on a standard system, you'll run out of room for more additions. USB is designed to solve this problem—you can have up to 127 devices attached to a USB port. Not only that, you can simply plug in the device and forget it—no messy configurations or even reboots. When you get a system, look into one with USB ports on the motherboard, since so many people are coming out with compatible add-ons.

Many systems come with two USB ports on the motherboard, which works great if that's all you need. But if you need more ports and can't daisy chain devices together (many USB devices for PCs do not have USB ports on them so you can't connect them together), you should consider buying a USB hub. These connect to a USB port on your computer and offer more open ports for you to use.

Modems/Network Adapters

Many systems come with an internal modem so you can connect to the Internet. Don't take anything less than a 56K modem that supports the V.90 standard. If you're working on a network, you'll need to get a network adapter card. These come in a wide variety of flavors, and the type you get depends on what type of network you have. The most common type is the Ethernet network, which operates at speeds of either 10Mbps or 100Mpbs. You can also get dual modem/network adapter cards, which will allow you to connect to the Internet over a phone line and be connected to your network at the same time.

From Whom Should You Buy?

When I ask this question, I don't mean whether you should buy from Dell, IBM, or Jeff and Akbar's House of Clones; instead, I mean, "Should you buy directly from the manufacturer, via mail order, or at a store?"

Well, if you're a really large company, then it probably makes sense to go straight to Compaq or whomever and negotiate a specific deal. But if you're a hobbyist or a SOHO (small office/home office) shop, then you'll have to examine your strategies.

You can probably buy cheapest from mail order. *But* if you do that, then returning defective merchandise involves shipping things around, getting RMA (Return Merchandise Authorization) numbers, etc. That can be a hassle.

Going to a big computer retailer is just a fast way to waste money, so I don't intend to shove you into the arms of Computerland or the like. There are many small businesses whose main line of work is to sell computer parts, software, supplies, and systems at a reasonable price. These local vendors often offer prices that aren't much more expensive than mail order. (Besides, the nice thing about local stores is that I like my vendors within choking distance. . .) And patronizing your local PC store means that when you need that disk drive on Saturday, you need only run down the street to get it, rather than waiting a week for it to ship.

That's not to say that mail order doesn't make sense. Mail order firms are more likely to have the latest and greatest software and hardware. Their prices will, again, sometimes be lower than the local store's. They may even know more about the product than a local vendor might. But take it from a veteran, there are a few things to be sure of:

▶ First, use a credit card. It's your first line of defense when mail order companies get nasty. If you didn't get what you wanted, just box it up, ship it back, and cancel the charge. Years ago, Dell used to charge a 15 percent "restocking fee." (They may still, but I refuse to do business with them, so I wouldn't know.) They sent me a hard disk that had clearly been dropped. When it worked, it registered seek times in the hundreds of milliseconds, despite what their ad promised. They tried to convince me that the drive was just what I wanted, but I knew better and sent it back. They tried to charge me a restocking fee, so I just complained to Citibank, and Dell backed off.

▶ Second, find out whom you're talking to. If the person responds, "Operator 22" (I suppose his friends call him "22"), ask to speak with a supervisor. You're about to give this guy your name, address, phone, and credit card number, and he won't even tell you who he is? Write the name down. Also get a confirmation number or order number.

▶ Third, buy the product only if it's in stock. Back-ordered things can take months to arrive, and by the time they do, you'll be charged the older (and higher) price. Get the salesperson to check that it can ship today. If not, don't place the order.

▶ Ship it overnight or second-day. By default, mail order companies use UPS ground, which can take anywhere from one week to a millennium to arrive. Second-day is usually only a few dollars more, and that way you can get a guaranteed delivery date out of the salesperson.

▶ Once you have the product, keep the carton that it came in for 30 days. That way, if a problem arises, it's easy to ship it back. And if you do have to ship something back, then by all means insure it.

▶ Another way of buying computers is over the Internet. Many computer manufacturers will sell directly from their Web sites. Some of those that do are Compaq, Dell, and Gateway. What's nice about these sites is that you can custom-design your own system right online, choosing your CPU, memory, video display, and so on. Once ordered (usually with a credit card) the company builds your system to order and ships it to you within days.

Just follow those rules and you should have good luck getting things through the mail.

System Comparisons

Ultimately, the type of system you buy should do the tasks you need it to do. If you are just going to connect to the Internet, you'll need a much less powerful system (which also means less expensive) than someone who wants to play the most advanced games on the market. Before going out and buying your new PC, see if you fit one of these categories:

Family You'll use your computer for everyday tasks such as financial planning, writing letters, doing homework, and connecting to the Internet.

Gamer You want to play all the great games out there.

SOHO Your home computer is used for business, and you might even have a home network installed.

Big business You're concerned about networking and compatibility.

Note

You can purchase "Internet systems" (sometimes called "NetPCs") for between $100 and $500. These are optimized for Internet use only and therefore don't have the full range of features found in most desktop systems.

Table 28.1 lists what types of components are typical of these systems and gives you a general price range you can expect. Of course, you can play with the components and go up or down the technology scale. Getting more advanced components will raise the price of the system—some dramatically. Another area to watch for is other peripherals that I haven't listed. These might be a CD-RW drive, printers, scanners, external storage drives, tape backup drives, etc.

TABLE 28.1 Computer Features versus Needs

User Category	System Features	Cost
Family	Intel Celeron 466MHz processor 64MB RAM 6GB hard drive 40X CD-ROM generic sound card generic speakers 15" monitor 8MB AGP SVGA video card 56K V.90 modem standard mouse standard keyboard Microsoft Windows 98SE	$800–$1500
Gamer	Intel Pentium III 850MHz processor 256MB RAM 25GB hard drive 12X DVD/CD-ROM 3D sound card speakers with subwoofer 19" monitor 32MB AGP 3D video card 56K V.90 modem Microsoft IntelliMouse with IntelliEye standard keyboard Microsoft Windows 98SE	$2500–$3500
SOHO	Intel Pentium III 600MHz processor 128MB RAM 25GB hard drive 40X CD-ROM	$1000–$2000

Continued on next page

TABLE 28.1 Computer Features versus Needs (continued)

User Category	System Features	Cost
	generic sound card	
	generic speakers	
	17" monitor	
	8–16MB AGP SVGA video card	
	56K V.90 modem	
	standard mouse	
	ergonomic keyboard	
	Microsoft Windows 98SE or Windows 2000 Professional	
Big Business	Intel Celeron 466MHz processor	$1000–$2500
	64MB RAM	
	6GB hard drive	
	40X CD-ROM	
	generic sound card	
	headphones	
	15–17" monitor	
	8–16MB AGP SVGA video card	
	56K V.90 modem or network card	
	standard mouse	
	ergonomic keyboard	
	Microsoft Windows 98SE, NT 4 SP2, or 2000	

Shopping Tips

The two essential laws of buying a new PC are to never sign anything and never hand over any money until you're absolutely sure you are getting the system you want and need. Knowledge, as they say, is power. Make sure you read all the literature concerning your prospective PC and understand everything. It's also very helpful to perform a cost-tradeoff analysis. Sit down and decide what you absolutely need and calculate the price of the system, then start upgrading components and recalculate the price. Stop when you reach the top limit of your budget and decide whether you'll be happy. If not, can you reduce anything to make room for that component you really, really want?

You can also purchase with an eye toward future upgrades. For example, you may want a 25GB hard drive but can't afford it right now. Hard drives are relatively easy to upgrade, especially if you plan on adding a second one in the future. Maybe you can compromise on a 16GB hard drive now and get another 16GB hard drive within a year. Your total storage space would reach 32GB—more than the 25GB you would have originally purchased.

Other components, such as the CPU, are more expensive to upgrade later. I recommend getting the fastest CPU and the most amount of memory you can afford the first time around.

When you take your new PC home (or it arrives via mail order), the first thing you should do is carefully unpack it and read through the documentation that comes with it. Then, find a place to set it up and put it together. Make sure to connect everything to the correct ports. Turn it on and give it a test drive. In fact, test all the components so you know they are all working. Print something, connect to the Internet or your network, play a game that makes use of your 3D video card, etc. If something doesn't work, recheck all your connections and reread any manuals. If you can't resolve the problem, call the service/support division of the company you bought the PC from and start getting their help. The bottom line is, if something doesn't work and it's not your fault, you need to get it fixed or replaced by the manufacturer/reseller immediately.

Tip

Leave your new system on for two to three days straight, even if you usually turn it off each time you're done using it. This helps the components to get "settled." This little endurance test will weed out components that have flaws and are going to fail anyway. Better to get it over with sooner rather than later.

Once you're sure everything works and you're happy with your new system, start installing other applications that you own and have fun with your new PC!

29

Notebook/Laptop Computers

INTRODUCTION

In some respects, upgrading and maintaining your laptop or notebook computer is much simpler than taking care of a desktop machine. On one hand, the jobs you can take care of on your own usually are plainly indicated in your owner's manual and often require nothing more than unplugging an old module and plugging in a new one. On the other hand, you must leave some things in the hands of experts with specialized equipment. Again, your task is simple: put your laptop in a box, ship it off, and pay the nice people who are taking care of you.

In between these two clear extremes are upgrades and fixes that require taking the laptop apart and doing the kind of minor surgery that, with a little instruction, you can usually handle on your own. In this chapter, I'll identify which types of upgrades and fixes fall into each of the above-mentioned categories, and give you instructions for accomplishing them. Here are some examples of all three classes of upgrade:

▶ Say you want to add a modem. For most laptops, the process is simple: you locate the PC Card slot on your laptop, open the cover, and slide in your new credit-card-sized modem. Okay, you'll need to install the drivers too, but with PC Cards it's almost automatic.

▶ Say you've decided to install a larger hard disk or more memory. These are two tasks you *can* handle yourself, but both entail opening a system that was not really designed to be taken apart easily. If you're adventurous, handy with small tools, and want to save some money, you can do the job. If you have a lot invested in your laptop and don't feel that experimenting is such a good idea, companies that specialize in laptop upgrades will do the job quickly and for relatively little money, and will usually guarantee their work.

▶ Say you want to upgrade your Pentium laptop to a Pentium III processor. This you cannot do on your own. Reason: Laptop

CPUs are generally surface mounted rather than socket mounted. You cannot remove a surface-mounted laptop CPU on your own. It takes special tools and expert skills.

I'll be spending time in this chapter on the first and second categories in the preceding list. Let me also reiterate that such items as hard drives and memory modules, while designed to be easily replaced, do involve opening your system. Whenever you do your own upgrading, be mindful of several important factors:

Warning

You should read and reread the terms and conditions of any service agreements and/or warranties that came with your laptop. In some cases, opening up your laptop and tinkering with its innards can void such agreements.

▶ Depending on which brand of laptop you have, opening the system could mean removing the screen and/or the keyboard before you can get to the object of your replacement tasks. Getting from point A to point B in a laptop usually requires a detour or two, so don't get frustrated. Plan your moves carefully, but expect to be sidetracked.

▶ Refer to your owner's manual early and often. If you've lost it, write to the manufacturer and get a new one.

▶ In all cases, be even more aware than usual of cleanliness and antistatic precautions. Real estate inside a laptop is cramped; loose bits of dust, crumbs, and cat fur really need to be kept out. Not only can they cause components to not fit right, they can cause electrical shorts and can trap and hold excess heat. You can get away with a little dust in a big desktop box; there's usually enough room to let the system fan work and enough space to dissipate the heat. Laptops don't give you that luxury.

▶ Always assume that cables and connectors have no slack. Again, space is so tight inside a laptop that everything has been measured down to the last millimeter. Never tug, bend, or twist anything.

▶ Never handle new parts anywhere but along the edges, if at all possible (and, if there's a choice, along the plastic edges instead of the metal edges). Latex hospital gloves are really handy, as well as cheap; consider wearing one glove for basic moves such as picking up objects and taking them out of a bag, and keep your other hand free for performing the moves that require more dexterity.

▶ Go out and buy the correct tools if you don't already have them. A set of jeweler's screwdrivers with rotating barrel bodies will save you more grief than you can even guess at, and for $5 or $10 a set you don't have to break the bank to add them to your toolbox.

Modern laptops have been purposely designed to keep those of us who love to tinker firmly in the back seat. The parts you can mess with are clearly marked. The parts that are off-limits should be scrupulously avoided. In a lot of respects, these are delicate, precision instruments, and the best way to really screw one up is to start hacking around with the assumption that you can make something fit by pushing just a *little* bit harder.

Upgrading and Maintaining Your Laptop

These QuickSteps summarize how to upgrade your laptop's memory, install a new hard drive, and replace your battery.

Upgrading Your Memory

Be Prepared

Before you start, there are some things you may need on hand. These include:

▶ Memory purchased from laptop manufacturer or reputable third-party vendor

▶ Small Phillips-head screwdriver, for removing the cover over the memory panel on the laptop

▶ Documentation for the laptop, to tell you where and how to insert the memory

▶ (Optional) Latex gloves, to keep the inside of your laptop and all components clean

▶ (Optional) Antistatic wrist strap, to guard against static electricity damage

1. Turn off the PC and unplug the power cord.

2. Consult the laptop documentation to find out where the memory goes.

3. Open the computer to gain access to the memory. On many laptops, there is a panel on the bottom that you remove by unscrewing a few small screws. On some others, you must remove the keyboard and place the memory underneath.

4. Remove the old memory, if needed. Consult the documentation; the procedure varies from system to system.

5. Insert the new memory. Again, see the documentation.

6. Put everything back together, replacing any components or panels you removed to get access to the memory.

7. Turn on the PC. It should detect the new memory automatically.

Upgrading Your Hard Disk

Be Prepared

Before you start, there are some things you may need on hand. These include:

▶ Hard disk designed to work with your laptop. (Consult the manufacturer to find out what you need.)

▶ Bootable floppy disk, to restart the PC after installing the new hard disk.

▶ Documentation for the laptop, to tell you where and how to insert the hard disk.

▶ Small Phillips- and flat-head screwdrivers, to remove screws on access plates (if necessary) and mounting hardware (if necessary).

▶ Hex or Torx screwdriver on some computers, to remove screws on access plates (if necessary) and mounting hardware (if necessary).

▶ Needle-nosed pliers, in case you drop something into the system and need to fish it out.

- Pencil and paper, to write or sketch the current physical layout of cables and connectors.

- Software to partition and format the new drive, if you have bought what is known as a *bare* drive, which has not been partitioned and formatted by the manufacturer.

- (Optional) Latex gloves, to keep the inside of your laptop and all components clean.

- (Optional) Antistatic wrist strap to guard against static electricity damage.

---

1. Back up your important data on your hard disk.

2. Open your laptop's case. Refer to the laptop documentation to find out what you need to remove for access to the hard disk.

3. Remove the existing hard drive. The exact method varies; the documentation should tell you how.

4. Install the new hard drive.

5. Boot from your floppy startup disk and partition/format the new drive.

6. Install your operating system.

Replacing Batteries

Be Prepared

You don't usually need any special tools to install a battery, because on a laptop batteries are designed for quick swapping in and out. But before you start, there are some things you'll need to perform the operation. These include:

▶ New battery, specifically chosen to work with your laptop. (There are many kinds out there, only a short list of which will work with any one particular laptop.)

▶ The documentation for the laptop, to tell you where the battery is located and how to access it.

1. Turn off the computer.

2. Disconnect it from the AC adapter and remove any cables to printers, modems, networks, etc.

3. Find out where your battery is located by checking the laptop documentation, and remove any access panel or flip open any hatch needed to access it.

4. Pull the old battery out.

5. Insert the new battery quickly. Some laptops can't hold their BIOS setup configuration for more than a few minutes without a battery.

6. Close up the laptop.

7. If this is a brand new battery, keep the machine off and connect the AC adapter. Fully charge the battery before you turn on the computer.

Memory Upgrades

Upgrading the computer's memory is probably the most common improvement that people make, as well as one of the easiest to accomplish. Most laptops come with specific instructions on how to do it and provide the specifications for exactly what kind of memory to buy.

Most laptops use proprietary memory modules, rather than standard SIMMs or DIMMs. That means you must buy very carefully, and only after consulting your laptop documentation and/or its manufacturer. You might be able to order a memory module from a company that specializes in various brands of memory, but as a fallback plan you can order it from the laptop's manufacturer.

Many laptops use a modular system for memory. A certain amount of memory is built into the system, and you can't remove it. (On modern laptops it's usually some basic amount like 32MB.) Then there is an expansion socket into which you can plug one additional memory module, of whatever size you want. So, for example, suppose your current PC has 64MB of memory—32MB built in and a 32MB expansion module. You will need to remove the 32MB expansion and replace it with a higher-denomination expansion module to increase your overall memory.

Preparing for the Upgrade

As long as you follow some basic, preliminary precautions, there is little you should worry about when it comes time to upgrade the memory on your laptop.

Back Up Your Important Data

Making sure that you back up your important data from your hard disk before you do any work on your computer is always a good idea. The chances that you'll do some damage are slight, but you have to lose everything only one time to understand the value of backups.

Prepare Your Workspace

Before you start, clear off your workspace. The kitchen table will do just fine (wipe it down first). Have a flat surface to work on with plenty of room to lay things out. You don't want your screwdriver rolling onto the floor just when you need it. I like to work on a clean, white towel (not a terry-cloth towel, though—you don't want to introduce lint). The color provides contrast, and the softness reduces ricochets and adds a little traction for fast-moving, small items such as screws. Lay out your tools (a small flat-blade screwdriver, small- and large-head Phillips screwdrivers, and maybe small needle-nosed pliers just in case). Some systems require little hex-head screwdrivers, but most do not. The tools will vary; just make sure you've got your toolkit close at hand. You may want an antistatic strap that you can wrap around your wrist or ankle to keep static from building up while you work, but for a short job like this you probably won't need one.

Disconnect Everything

When installing any kind of internal components in your laptop, including memory modules, always double check that the computer is turned off and disconnected from the AC adapter. Remove the battery pack from the computer. Remove all cables to components such as printers and external modems, and so on, and any PC Cards.

Ground Yourself

Make sure that you are well grounded and always touch something metal before you touch the delicate stuff inside the laptop. That way, if you've collected any static, you'll discharge it onto the metal object instead of into your computer. Those little blue sparks that come off your fingers can have hundreds or even thousands of volts, and that's definitely not good for electronic components that run on 2.2–5 volts. Filing cabinets, light fixtures, coworkers, and door frames are good things to touch to see if you're sparking.

Also, please make sure that none of your tools are the magnetized kind that come in so handy in other situations around the home. They're good for fishing lost screws out of the sink, but you don't want them anywhere near your computer.

Keep It Clean

So, touching some things is good to get rid of static. On the other hand, there are other things you never want to touch at all. For example, do not touch the metal conductors on the memory modules. Even minute amounts of dust, grit, skin oils, and sticky crud left over from lunch can be a real problem. Also, try not to touch cables, wires, and other components you're not working on. Maybe it's picky, but the fewer things you mess with, the fewer things you'll have to check later if the system doesn't work the way it's supposed to. Remember the latex gloves I mentioned earlier? This is a good time to take them out and put them on.

Make a Map

With some laptops, you may need to unplug something else (such as a hard drive or a battery) before you can get to the memory module adapter, or slot. If you do, sit back for a minute, grab a pencil and paper, and make a sketch of what plugs into what before you start pulling things apart. Don't worry about making it pretty or exactly to scale; just make sure everything in the sketch is accurately identified and labeled. This is especially important for any wires you need to move out of the way. You can't rely on your remembrance of things past to make sure they all go back exactly the way they need to go back. With bigger machines, such as desktop computers or car engines, you can get away with tagging wires with masking tape. You won't have that kind of room inside a laptop and you really don't want gummy tape glue inside your system.

Get Motivated!

At this point, you may be asking yourself whether you really want to do this kind of upgrade on your own. You may think that all these precautions signal something difficult or dangerous. That is really not the case. All I'm trying to do is point out that you need to take your time and proceed in a careful, well-planned manner.

Look at it this way—installing memory in your laptop will take you 10 to 15 minutes. These things are made to be upgraded, after all. Now, if you pay someone at the local computer store to do the upgrade for you, it will take them the same 10 or 15 minutes to do the job. It will also cost you about $85. That's the going hourly rate for most PC repair jobs, and you'll pay for a full hour regardless of how little time the upgrade really takes.

At the very least, you should try doing the installation yourself and, if you get to a place where you really don't want to go any further, then take it down to the shop. But first give it a shot yourself. You'll be surprised at how easily most of these systems come together and you can use the $85 you save to treat yourself to dinner and a movie.

Doing the Installation

Increasing the memory on your laptop is probably the easiest upgrade option available. The following sections detail the steps involved.

Access the Memory Module

The first thing you have to do is open up the computer so you can get at the memory modules. Most laptops have access hatches that you open from the bottom, so close the screen, turn the laptop over, and work from the bottom of the laptop system unit. Sometimes you have to unscrew a cover plate to open the memory hatch; with other laptops, you push small locking tabs and lift the cover plate away from the body of the machine. In either case, the correct hatch should be marked with something that indicates which is the correct one. It might say *memory*, it might have a stylized drawing of a memory module, it might have something arcane, like the term *exp*, but it will usually have something to indicate that this is where the memory lives. If there are other hatches, they too will be marked. You're smart—you'll figure it out.

Some laptops require you to remove or simply lift up the keyboard in order to access the memory area. For these systems, open up the screen, unlatch the keyboard (by sliding the unlocking latches on the side or at the back), and work on the system from the top.

The top-access systems usually still have the memory modules down at the bottom of the system, so you may also have to move the disk drive or hard drive to get at the memory. If you have to move a drive, it will usually come equipped with a plastic tab that you use as a handle. Always use the tabs or handles they give you. Do not put a screwdriver under the drive and try to lever it out. Look before you pull. There may be little plastic or metal devices that the manufacturer used to hold the drive in place. There may be small screws that hold it down. Refer to your owner's manual to see whether you need to remove any of these things or whether the whole unit should slide out as a single piece.

Even on systems you access from the bottom, you may still have to move something else out of the way before you can reach the memory area. Some laptops, for example, require that you remove the hard drive by sliding it out of its socket and removing it from the machine.

Look Around

Once you have exposed the memory area, you'll want to stop for a minute and study what's in front of you. Does your system have slots that accept SIMM or DIMM memory modules, or is it the kind that uses prepackaged proprietary memory modules?

If you have the latter, you'll simply insert the new, two-plug memory module into the sockets that are provided. These machines are usually limited to accepting only one upgrade module, so if something is already in the upgrade sockets, you'll have to remove it before you can add the new module.

Even if you have the kind of laptop that accepts ordinary SIMMs or DIMMs, you need to see what kind of room you have. Such systems as Toshiba's or IBM's have slots that accept SIMM or DIMM modules, and they can accept more than one module before the system is fully loaded.

Do you have empty slots, or are all of them filled? If you have empty slots, you can go ahead with the addition of your new memory. If your slots are all filled, you'll have to empty one or more of them so you have a place to put your new memory.

Out with the Old

If you have to remove memory, look for something that indicates which slot has the highest number (for example, there might be a small 0 or 1 printed on the board next to the slot). You will usually want to replace existing memory starting with the highest numbered slot. (This is where your owner's manual or the company's tech support people can be most helpful, by giving exact instructions if you can't find a clear indicator just by looking at the slots.)

To remove any memory modules you have to get rid of, look for the locking latches on both edges of the socket. Unhook the latches from the module by pressing them away from the module. These latches can sometimes be fairly tight, but don't get carried away and apply too much force; you don't want to snap them off. Just a gentle push outward should be enough. Once the latches are released from the edges of the module, you can tilt the module upward and slide it out. Do not touch the gold or tin connectors.

Set aside any modules you've removed and save them for possible future use. You never know when they might come in handy. You may be able to sell your old memory. My local computer store has a bulletin board for people to advertise old parts that they want to sell or buy, including used chips. Failing that, try giving them to a school. Taxpayer revolt being what it is, the school's probably pretty desperate for any charity you care to offer, and you can probably take a tax break by deducting the value (or a percentage of it) when April rolls around. (Ask your tax preparer, just to be sure.)

In with the New

If you have empty slots and don't have to take anything out before you add the new memory, or if you've freed some room by following the instructions above, pick up your new module by the edges and slide it into the socket. It will go in at an angle and then pivot down until it locks into place. Make sure it's fully seated in the slot before you pivot it down.

Most memory modules are keyed by having little notches cut into the side so that they will fit into the slot only one way. If you have any doubts (for example, if the module seems really hard to fit into the connector), take it out and try it the other way. (This is also why you took a few minutes to make a sketch of what things looked like before you started.) Never try to cram something into a place where it doesn't seem to want to go. It might be misaligned, something might be blocking the way, or it might be upside down. These things slide in easily. If yours doesn't, it's the wrong way around. Turn it and try again: dust it off, line it up and make sure it goes in straight; just don't force it.

Put Everything Back

Once you have the new memory correctly installed, by whichever method your laptop requires, replace whatever you took out, or off, in exactly the same way you removed it. Replace the drives, battery packs, and access covers in reverse order from the way they came off. Reconnect any cables you disconnected and turn the machine on. It will go through its normal boot cycle, only this time you should see a bigger number on your screen when it does the memory check. If all goes well, you're done. For example, if you installed a 64MB module in a computer that already had 32MB of memory, the boot sequence should confirm that all went well by showing that you now have 96MB of memory.

If you get an error message or if the amount of memory the computer recognizes does not match the amount you should now have, don't worry about it. Sometimes the BIOS gives you that, and you enter the BIOS program, and then exit it, and everything is fine from then on.

If you continue to get BIOS error messages regarding the memory at startup, however, you'll have to turn off the machine and go through the installation process again. If you have to reopen the computer and do it all again, it'll probably be because the new memory module isn't fully inserted into the slot. Make sure that it's straight and fully seated, so the locking tabs snap into the notches on the module. And if that doesn't fix it, send the memory back, because it's defective.

Hard Disk Upgrades

The capacity of your laptop's hard disk drive can be increased by installing compression programs, such as Microsoft's DriveSpace, that will effectively double the amount of space you can use. But that won't work if you're using one of the newer versions of Windows that uses FAT32. And at some point, you may decide that you've compressed everything as far as you can and you still need more room. You have these options:

▶ You can attach a removable media drive, such as a Zip drive, via your laptop's parallel port.

▶ You can slip a PC Card hard drive into your laptop.

▶ Some laptops will let you replace the floppy disk drive or CD-ROM drive with a second hard disk.

▶ You can remove your current hard drive and completely replace it with a new, higher-capacity model.

The last of these options is the one most people choose. The others have certain drawbacks. External removable media drives force you to carry extra gear and, although they're good for special occasions such as hauling around huge graphics files, they tend to be cumbersome and somewhat slow. PC Card hard drives are handy and work quite well, but using one means giving up, at least temporarily, access to PC Card modems and other devices that use the same slot or slots. Replacing your floppy drive or CD-ROM with a second hard drive is a tempting solution, and some people are happy to trade their floppy for something bigger. However, others rely on their floppies to load new files and programs, or need to keep their CD-ROMs for the large reference works they have in their CD libraries. Additionally, not all laptops have controllers capable of supporting a second hard drive. If you have one that will, such as an IBM ThinkPad, I'll go into that upgrade option shortly. For now, though, let's take a look at what you need to do to replace your current hard drive with a new one.

Finding the Right Hard Disk

The only real trick in replacing your hard drive is getting a new one that will work with your laptop—and that isn't really much of a trick. Almost all laptop computers use 2½-inch hard drives. If your laptop was made before 1996, it probably has a *full-height* hard drive, about 18 millimeters high. If your laptop was made after 1996, it probably has a *slim-line* hard drive, about 11 millimeters high.

A slim hard drive will usually work in an older (pre-1996) laptop, but a full-height drive won't fit in a laptop made for the 11mm drives. If you find a really good deal on a full-height drive but aren't sure whether it will fit into your newer laptop, the best way to check is to remove your current drive (see "Taking Out the Old Hard Drive" later in this chapter) and take a ruler to its height. Just measure the height of the drive, not its supporting brackets. If it's 18mm, you can use a new drive that is either 11mm or 18mm. If it's 11mm, you need to specify the same (a slim-line model) for your new drive, too.

Verifying the BIOS

Another factor you have to watch out for is what kind of BIOS you have. Some older BIOS chips will not let you have a hard drive larger than 540MB (or, on slightly newer systems, 4GB or 8.4GB is the limit). If you have this kind of BIOS, you will need a software BIOS *extender* (software that enables the BIOS to recognize larger hard drives) for your notebook/laptop, or you will need to send your laptop to an upgrade company that will update your firmware BIOS. I talked about this in great detail in Chapter 13, "Partitioning and Formatting IDE and SCSI Drives."

The good news is that most mail-order sources will either include the BIOS upgrade software as part of the price, or will upgrade your firmware BIOS if you send them the computer. The bad news is that if you have to send your laptop away to be upgraded, you're going to be without it for a few days. Generally speaking, however, most laptops will do just fine with a software BIOS extender, and you won't have to send your machine out into the cold cruel world on its own.

Obtaining Mounting Hardware

Finally, some laptop hard drives are manufactured in such a way that their supporting brackets are built right into the drive itself. If you have this kind of hard drive, you will need to get new mounting hardware along with your hard drive, and you may have to hunt to find it. A lot of retailers don't carry a large variety of brackets. Your best bet in such a case is to call your laptop's manufacturer, or the hard drive vendor, and find out where you can get the hardware you need to attach the new drive to the laptop. Seems like such a minor item, but details like these can give you the biggest headaches.

Note

Need some pointers on how to locate a source for laptop hard drives? Again, the best way to find one quickly is to use one of the search engines on the Internet. Just run a search for **laptop + hard drive**.

Backing Up Your Data

Things can go wrong—remember Murphy's Law? It's always better to be safe than sorry when messing around with your hard-earned data. Do not remove your old hard drive until it is entirely backed up, either on the new hard drive or by some other means.

To back up your data, you have a number of options, as presented in the following paragraphs.

Network Backup

If you have access to a network, the easiest way to back up your hard disk is to copy everything from your laptop to the server and keep it there until you are done installing your new hard drive. You will need to make sure you have all your configuration software on a floppy disk, however, or your machine won't be able to access the network to let you download all your files when you are ready for them.

External Drive

If you have an external tape drive or a Zip drive, you can use MS Backup or some other backup program (Norton Backup is good) to move all your files to the external drive and then restore them to the new hard drive after you finish installing it.

Second Laptop or Desktop Computer

You can use a commercial program such as LapLink to copy all your files to another machine and then restore them to the new hard drive after you finish installing it.

Second Hard Drive

If you have a laptop that will accommodate two hard drives (by removing the floppy disk drive or CD-ROM, for example), you can install the new hard drive, XCOPY everything from the old drive to the new drive, remove both drives, install the new drive in place of the old drive, and finally, reinstall the floppy drive or CD-ROM. This is a lot of work, but sometimes you have to get creative if you want to get anything done.

Alternatively, you can use the Seagate FileCopy program. FileCopy will make an exact, bootable duplicate of the original hard drive on another hard drive that has as large or larger capacity.

Programs such as Norton Ghost and Drive Copy make complete copies of your hard disk content, onto whatever media you choose (another hard disk, a writable CD-ROM, etc.). That way, you can back up everything just as it is and then "transplant" it onto the new drive later. Such a program can save you hours in reinstalling Windows and all your Windows programs and recopying all your files.

Preparing for the Hard Drive Upgrade

You've got the hard drive and mounting hardware. You've backed up all your files. You have a bootable floppy disk at hand and another floppy with all your network access software. If you've backed up your old hard drive to a server and removed all boisterous children and kittens to another room, you're all set to begin. Before you start, however, make sure you have all the necessary tools handy. Refer back to the QuickSteps at the beginning of this chapter for a list of what you might need.

Hard Disk Upgrades   **1189**

Installing the New Hard Drive

You're all ready to go. You have your hard drive. You have your laptop. You have a flat, clean surface on which to work. Your tools are all laid out where you can reach them. You have grounded yourself. Let's get started.

Opening the Laptop

In order to get to the hard drive of some laptops, you need to completely open them up. With others, you may just have to lift off the keyboard by unsnapping it. And some have drives that simply slide out (my favorite).

First, make sure you know the location of the hard drive.

You may be lucky and have a drive caddie that slides out from the computer, no screws required. Another easy replacement job is for machines in which the keyboard or other piece unsnaps or lifts up to reveal the hard drive. Only slightly more involved are laptops in which a top or bottom piece is unscrewed and removed to get to the hard drive. More difficult are the laptops that have a top or bottom piece that is unscrewed and removed, and then require that one or more components be removed to get to the hard drive. The hardest type is the kind of laptop in which a top or bottom piece is unscrewed and removed, and most components, including the system board, are removed to get to the hard drive.

If you have a computer that comes with a hard drive caddie, you can ignore most of this information because you just slide out the old drive and slide in the new one.

Work slowly and carefully. Don't try to pry apart your computer once the screws are removed. Many of the notebook computers have extremely thin plastic snaps that align the top and bottom and help to hold them together. In addition, some types of notebooks also require you to remove a keyboard mask, while others may have this keyboard mask built into the top cover piece. Slowly pull away the plastic cover while carefully looking for connecting cables. If you find any, you will need to disengage them before you can completely open the system.

Finally, many laptops have quite a bit of mounting hardware, which has to be removed before you can gain access to the drive.

Taking Out the Old Hard Drive

Once you can see the hard drive, find the proper screwdriver among the tools you have thoughtfully laid out within reach and unscrew the mounting bracket. Remove the mounting bracket along with the drive.

Make sure to carefully detach the drive interface from the interface connector, and remember which way the drive was positioned. Consider drawing a sketch to help you remember the proper position.

Remove the hard drive from its mounting bracket. It will probably just slide out, but you may have to push it a little. Make sure you're not pushing at an angle and be careful not to push too hard. If you don't detect any movement while applying moderate force, check it for small screws or plastic tabs that may be holding it in place.

Putting In the New Hard Drive

First, install the new hard drive in the mounting bracket. Next, carefully place the new hard drive (in its mounting bracket) into the same spot where the old one was positioned. Pull out the sketch you made when removing the old drive and make sure you're putting the new one in the same way the old one came out. Also, be extra careful that the drive interface pins are properly aligned with the cable or connector to which they attach. These parts are really small and often quite delicate, and it's easy to wind up with the top row of pins in the bottom row of the connector.

That's really all there is to it. Carefully align and replace any covers, keyboard masks, plastic snaps, and so on, in the same order you removed them, but don't try to permanently close up the system just yet. Make sure any screws you do install go in all the way, but don't over-torque them. Make sure you don't have any pieces left over. If you drop a screw and it rolls down into the system, get it out before you do anything else. These are small machines. It didn't go very far. Pick the system up and roll it from side to side (like one of those kid's toys with little ball bearings that you try to roll into the clown's nose). The little screw will eventually rattle into a place where you can see it and grab it with your nonmagnetized needle-nosed pliers. Dental picks and hemostats are also handy for this kind of work, although they're usually not things most people have in their toolboxes and are too expensive unless you do this kind of thing a lot.

Finally, while you have everything open, you could spray it with a can of compressed air to get out any dust. Don't try to wipe away the dust with a cloth or a paper towel, though, as you'll likely scratch something or leave lint or paper fibers behind. Also, don't blow on the inside of your laptop. Your breath may be minty fresh, but it's also very humid.

Testing the New Hard Disk

Now, before you put the system completely back together, put the battery pack back in and turn the laptop on. If the system runs through its memory test, you can breathe a sigh of relief. If the system won't run the memory test, the most likely culprit is the hard drive interface or one of the other connections. Check all the connections. If you don't find anything obvious, try replacing the old drive and try again. If this works, something is wrong with the new hard drive.

If the memory test succeeds, you'll probably get an error message such as HDD Configuration Error. Don't worry. You want it to say this. Your CMOS is looking for the hard drive you took out and just doesn't recognize the new one yet. Get into your CMOS setup routine (with the SETUP disk, or by pressing one or more keys while the system is booting) and set the hard drive to the correct type as indicated by the information that came with the new unit.

You may have to identify it by number and you may need to fill in several parameters, such as number of heads, number of cylinders, number of sectors, etc. All this information should be in with the packing slip and the bubble wrap in the new drive's shipping box. On the other hand, you may not need to do anything except reboot.

Now that there is nothing on your hard drive, you'll need to boot your computer from your bootable floppy disk (a floppy that has COMMAND.COM on it). After you've formatted the drive, you should be able to boot right from the new hard drive.

If you've transferred your CONFIG.SYS and AUTOEXEC.BAT files from your old hard drive, your system may not boot from the new hard drive because something in these files is not configured correctly for your new drive. Refer to to Chapter 11, "Installing an IDE Hard Drive," and Chapter 13. Dealing with a laptop hard disk is the same as with any other computer.

Closing Up

Once everything seems to be working, you can close up your computer. Put the keyboard back in place. Screw down any access hatches you had to remove. Connect your laptop to the network, Zip drive, external tape drive, or whatever you used to hold all your backup files, and then partition and format the drive, as described in Chapter 13. Reinstall the operating system and copy your data onto your new drive.

Installing a Second Hard Drive

With some laptops, such as the IBM ThinkPad 760, you can replace the floppy drive or CD-ROM drive with a second hard disk. Often, however, you will need to buy a second hard disk holder since you can't just let the new hard drive rattle around in there. Other laptops, such as the Dell Inspiron 7500 series, have additional bays for sliding in an additional hard drive (or extra battery).

When you put your secondary hard drive into its caddie, make sure that any slots, connectors, or projections on the hard drive match the corresponding slots, connectors, and projections on the caddie. Then press it firmly into the caddie until you hear it click into place. If it doesn't seem to be going in after you've applied a moderate amount of force, don't keep pushing. It's probably not lined up right. Take it out and reinsert it. You may have to wiggle it a little to make sure everything is lined up correctly.

Next, remove the disk drive or CD-ROM drive. On laptops that have removable keyboards, this requires the following steps:

1. Make sure that no disks or CDs are in the drive you're taking out.

2. Turn off the power.

3. Disconnect the AC adapter.

4. Unplug any cables that attach to printers and modems.

5. Unlatch the keyboard and swing it up out of the way.

6. Remove the battery.

7. Use the attached handles, tabs, or straps to remove the CD-ROM drive or disk drive.

If you're replacing a disk drive with a hard drive, you will have a hole in the front of the laptop where you used to insert disks. You can cover this with a shaped piece of plastic called a *bezel*. Remember the baggie with all that unidentifiable stuff from when you brought your laptop home and unpacked it? Your bezel's in there. If you saved the box, go rummage around in the closet until you find it. If you threw the box away, you can usually get a bezel at your local computer store. Generally, they are shipped with new hard drives, but you might make a note to ask just to be sure. Some bezels are made to be installed from the inside of the computer while the drive bay is empty. Others are designed to be pushed into place from the outside. Either way, make sure you cover the hole in the front or side of your laptop. Holes like that are invitations to all sorts of problems.

If you're replacing a CD-ROM drive with a hard drive, you can usually just slide the new hard drive into the space vacated by the old, unwanted CD-ROM. If that space was previously unoccupied, you may have to remove a bezel so the front of the hard drive can be seen from the outside (so you can see the drive's activity light) and then finish up with the following steps:

1. Firmly press the new hard drive holder until it clicks into the connector.

2. Replace the battery.

3. Reattach the keyboard and reconnect the AC adapter and whatever cables you just took off.

Installing PC Card Drive Cards

PC Card hard drives, sometimes also called hard cards or credit-card hard drives, offer an extremely simple way to add storage capacity to your laptop. They generally come in the size known as a Type 3 PC Card, which means that they take up two card slots in your laptop and can store upward of 1GB. You can get Type 1 and Type 2 PC Card hard drive cards, which take up only one slot, but they tend to be quite small in terms of capacity.

Figure 29.1

PCMCIA card (Xircom network adapter/modem combo FR)

Installing a PC Card hard drive requires nothing more than making sure you have installed the device driver software that comes on a disk with the card and that you have the card pointed the right way. Make sure the notched edge on the card goes in first. Press the card firmly into the connector. Usually, there will be an Eject button either inside the PC Card opening or on the side of the computer next to the card slot. You'll know when the card is fully installed because the Eject button will pop out. On some laptops, the IBM ThinkPad for example, you then pull the Eject button out a little bit and fold it toward the front of the laptop.

Other Kinds of Upgrades

Now I've covered upgrading memory and hard drives, but what if you want to upgrade your laptop in different ways? Say you want to increase its utility in the office instead of just using it at home or on the road. The following sections go into some of the other things you can do to put more life in your laptop.

Laptop LAN Adapters

You can connect your laptop to the company network by connecting a LAN adapter to the parallel or SCSI port of your laptop or inserting a LAN adapter card into your PC Card slot. Some have telephone jack–type connectors (RJ-45) for 10Base-T connections, and some have coax cable connections (BNC). You'll need to find out which kind you need, as well as making sure that your laptop is configured with the correct software for networking. Prices can range from about $75 to several hundred dollars, depending on the type of network you have and which vendor you choose. Also, prices change rapidly, as with everything else involving computers, so be sure to get the most recent price quotes from whomever you choose.

There are dozens of resources on the Net that make information about LAN adapters easy to find. Computer Shopper has a wonderful set of utilities that enable a person to select, compare, and choose which system they want peripherals for. CNET has similar information, as does ZDNet and dozens of other sites, both retail and editorial.

PC Card LAN Adapter Cards

A different type of LAN adapter is the PC Card type. Instead of plugging a cable with an attached adapter into a port on your laptop, you insert the PC Card LAN adapter card into the PC Card slot in the side of your laptop and connect to the network by means of attaching the network cable to it. There are many kinds, from many manufacturers. Lots of current information about them is available online.

Wireless LAN Cards

If you're the type of person who thinks it's more than a little pointless to have a walkabout computer that's shackled to a desk by its LAN connection, you can upgrade to a wireless LAN card. These are more expensive than the ones discussed in the preceding sections, but they do give you more mobility.

As mentioned earlier, your best source for current and accurate information about wireless LAN cards is the Internet, since technology and pricing changes so rapidly.

Working with Laptop Batteries

When you're on the road, without access to AC power, your laptop battery is your lifeline. Without it, your laptop is just another seven-pound paperweight. This section looks at charging, replacing, and extending the life of the battery's charge.

Battery Care

Most laptops come with specific instructions on how to deal with their batteries. They are not all the same. In general, however, you will have a recharger and/or AC adapter you can use when your battery power runs low. The AC adapter will recharge the battery at the same time that it provides power to keep your laptop running. Some batteries will fully recharge no matter when you plug in the AC adapter. Others will not. The IBM ThinkPad, for example, carries this warning: "Repeatedly charging a battery pack that has not been completely discharged shortens the battery operating time. To preserve battery operating time, discharge the battery pack completely, then recharge it."

Always be especially careful that the adapter you use with your laptop is the one that came with the computer or is a replacement specifically recommended by the manufacturer. The plug from your cordless electric drill's adapter may very well fit your computer, but there is little chance that the voltage and amperage requirements will match as well, and you'll be really sorry if you use it to recharge your laptop.

Warning

A battery is not just something that can hurt your computer. It is something that can hurt you. Batteries can and do explode if you handle them carelessly.

Keep these tips in mind when handling your laptop battery:

- Keep the battery away from fire.

- Keep the battery away from water.

- Never try to take it apart.

- Don't drop it, throw it, or bang it on the table.

- Always use only the battery designed especially for your particular make and model.

Something else to pack into your carrying case is a small, one- or two-socket surge protector. If you're going to be using your laptop from hotel rooms, conference centers, airport lounges, and other such places, you'll need one. You can't be any more confident of the quality of the electricity out there than you can back in the office—and you've got a surge protector on the floor under your desk, right?

Finally, it's a good idea to have more than one battery for your laptop. This is not just to let you keep working when you're out of reach of electricity. Many batteries need to be completely depleted before being recharged, so an extra battery lets you completely drain a battery, swap it out, and plug it into a recharger while you use the laptop with the backup battery. Completely draining a battery before recharging it often adds significantly to its useful life.

Charging a Battery

Keep your battery healthy by following the manufacturer's guidelines for first use and for when and how to recharge it. For example, the battery pack in many computers will be low or "dead" when you first buy it. You have to plug in the AC adapter and let it take a charge before you can use it. Furthermore, many batteries will require that you charge them, drain them completely, and charge them again (sometimes repeatedly) before they will accept and hold their maximum charge.

New batteries and those that have not been used in a long time will not take a full charge the first time you connect them to the AC adapter. With some types of batteries, such as the lithium-ion battery pack that IBM uses in the ThinkPad, you will have to fully discharge and then recharge the battery up to a half-dozen times before the battery is operating at peak performance.

Batteries do not like to be recharged until they are completely empty. You might think you're helping the battery to a longer life by keeping the laptop connected to the AC adapter all the time, but just the opposite is true. They wear out a lot quicker. Always run them down before you plug them in again.

With some laptops, you are advised not to run them while their batteries are charging. The competing demands of accepting a new charge while simultaneously losing charge as part of normal operation cause internal problems that shorten the battery's life.

Some batteries need to be completely discharged and then recharged from time to time. It cleans them out, so to speak, the same way you sometimes drain and refill the radiator in your car. Some power management utilities that come with the laptop, or that you can buy at your local computer store, have discharging functions as part of the program. For example, the discharging program for the IBM ThinkPad works like this: (1) Connect the AC adapter to the computer. (2) Click the Discharge button on the Fuel-Gauge program. (3) The battery automatically drains. (4) When it hits bottom, it starts to charge up again automatically.

Replacing a Battery

Regardless of how well you care for your battery, there will come a time when you have to take it out and put in a new one. Since this is one of the things most people will have to do fairly routinely, most laptops make it pretty easy.

1. Turn off the computer.

2. Disconnect it from the AC adapter and remove any cables to printers, modems, networks, etc.

3. Find out where your battery is located. On some laptops, you will access it through a hatch on the bottom of the computer. Generally, the hatch will simply slide out, but in some cases you will need to take out some screws or release a locking mechanism. On other laptops, you reach the battery from the top by first lifting off the keyboard. Check your owner's manual if you're not sure how the keyboard comes off.

4. The battery is usually right on top. Once you get the hatch or access panel off, the battery is the first thing you see. Make sure, however, that you don't need to remove something else before you go to work on the battery. If your laptop has a

CD-ROM, for example, you may have to remove it before you can pull the power pack.

5. Some batteries have plastic tabs or handles that you use to pull them away from their sockets before lifting them out. Others are unplugged simply by sliding them out of the connectors by hand. If yours has tabs or handles, use them.

6. Don't pull out the battery and then go home for the evening. Put the new one in right away. Some laptops depend on their batteries to hold their CMOS configurations for more than a few minutes or seconds.

7. Close up the laptop in the reverse order you opened it.

8. If this is a brand new battery, keep the machine off and connect the AC adapter. Fully charge the battery before you turn on the computer. Also, you may have to completely discharge and then recharge the battery a few times before the battery will operate at maximum capacity.

Buying a New Battery

Sometimes the information printed on the side of the battery can be confusing or obscure. The Internet has a plethora of information about batteries for just about every laptop and notebook available.

Note

Several good online sources are available on the Internet for finding more information about batteries for your laptop. Just run a search on **laptops + battery**.

If you still can't find a battery for your machine, the technical support people who work for the online supply houses will generally be able to locate the information (and the battery) you need. For some of the more obscure or older makes, you may have to send your old battery to the supplier and have it rebuilt. Doing so can sometimes take a week or more.

Conserving Battery Power

Many laptops now have power-management functions, either built into the BIOS, operating from within Windows, or available by using special drivers. These functions monitor whether the system is on and whether anybody is using it. After prescribed periods of no input from the keyboard or mouse, the laptop "goes to sleep." It doesn't turn itself off but slumbers until you wake it up. The advantage is that power-consuming features of the unit, such as the screen display, are no longer drawing down the charge in the battery. Preserving the life of the battery is obviously preferable to replacing it, so there are several things you can do to make sure you get the most use out of yours.

Most laptops today have power management features in the BIOS. When you enable power management, you allow the laptop to help you save battery power by shutting itself off in various degrees when you leave it running without AC power. My laptop, for example, has three degrees of power management to choose from in the BIOS: Max Performance, Balanced Power Saving, and Max Power Saving. They control when and if the hard disk will stop spinning, the display will turn off, and so on.

Some laptops come from the factory with a small, non-DOS partition on the hard disk that they can use to Suspend to Disk. This copies the contents of memory to the small partition when you issue a command to do so, or when the battery power gets critically low, so you can stop using power completely without having to shut down your PC.

Windows 9x provides power management functionality too. Use the Power applet in the Control Panel to control how long Windows waits before turning off the display and/or hard disk action to save power. See Figure 29.2.

Figure 29.2

Windows 98's power management controls, accessible through the Control Panel. Windows NT and 2000 have similar controls.

Laptop Maintenance Issues

Although keeping your laptop in good condition requires many of the same considerations as a desktop machine (for instance, keep it clean and dry, and feed it high-quality electricity), its portability adds a few factors to the equation and makes some of the ordinary issues especially important.

One of the most important things you can do to keep your laptop in good shape is to make sure you have a good carrying case. Sounds trivial, maybe, but it's not. Your laptop is a traveling companion and, as with any situation where you leave a secure, controlled environment, it will be subject to the same bumps and knocks as you.

Modern carrying cases are especially designed to save you and your notebook lots of grief, and it's well worth the investment to get one you can count on. I don't necessarily mean you have to spend hundreds of dollars for one of those aluminum suitcases, either. A good padded shoulder bag will give you all the protection you'll usually need, will make it easier for you to get through doors, into cars, and onto airplanes, and will keep you from having to reinvest in new laptops.

So, don't carry your laptop outside without a case. It may look power-chic in a TV commercial, but it's probably the worst thing you can do. People drop things, even important things, and no ordinary laptop will survive a tumble onto concrete.

When you're looking at carrying cases, check to make sure that it's made of a nonporous material. Even if you like the look of a canvas-type bag, make sure there's some kind of inner liner that will keep it from transferring moisture to the inside. Raindrops on the outside are OK. When they soak through and fizzle your laptop, they're not OK.

Check the hardware between the bag and the carrying strap. If the connection is a simple spring latch, never pick up the bag with the computer inside without first making sure the "tongue and groove" pieces are straight before pulling on the strap. Sideways pressure on many of the latches that I've had experience with will cause most of them to release. You will get to find out how much a new case (or perhaps a new computer) costs when the case opens and the computer lands on one of its corners or slams into something hard (such as airport steps).

You also want to make sure that the case you get has separate compartments for things you carry with you. Pens, pencils, mice, and modems rattling around and bumping into your machine can cause damage.

Make sure the outer walls of the case are well padded. The padding doesn't have to be extremely thick, but you want something between the case walls and your computer to distribute the shock of accidental bumps.

Finally, don't put anything in your case that doesn't belong there. I know people who have packed socks, toothbrushes, and candy bars into their carrying cases and treated them as overnight bags for emergency business trips. These people also tend to buy more new laptops than my other acquaintances. Putting anything in the bag that is damp, pointy, or crumbly is always a bad idea.

The weakest link on your laptop is the hinge that flips the screen up and down. It's not that the hinges are designed badly, it's just that they get the most exercise and, unlike people, exercise makes them weaker instead of stronger. Unfortunately, the only thing you can do to keep a hinge from croaking before its time is just don't fool with it too much:

▶ Never pick up the laptop by the open screen.

▶ Don't slam it shut because you're in a hurry.

▶ Don't yank it open and bend it too far.

▶ Don't open and close it repeatedly as a way to ease nervous tension.

Generally, you should not oil the hinges. They really weren't made for that kind of maintenance, and oil is a tremendous attractor of dust, grit, and pollen, all of which will only gum things up even worse.

The other areas you have to watch are the openings in your laptop's case. The floppy drive has a latch, flap, or door that closes when there's no disk in the drive. If this gets stuck in the "open" position, you'll collect lots of dust and your floppy drive, at least, could be ruined. On a lot of laptops, the floppy drive flap is pretty flimsy and can be quite easily pushed aside (which makes another good reason to have a laptop carrying case that gives you separate compartments for business cards, paper clips, and pencils). You don't want a stick of chewing gum wedging into your floppy drive after you've packed up your laptop for a business trip.

The other area that exposes the inside of your laptop to the outside world is the bay with your PC Card slot openings. Your computer probably came with plastic covers to seal up any slots that are not in use. Or it may have hinged flaps that come down when the slot is empty. Make sure these slots are closed or sealed. The connectors inside the slots are especially tiny, and even minute amounts of foreign material can cause big problems.

When it comes to the monitor screen, there are really only a couple of precautions you have to keep in mind. First, when you clean it, use a soft, lint-free cloth. Dry is best; very slightly damp is okay if you have really sticky garbage caked onto the screen; wet is never recommended. Try not to use paper towels since the cheap kind can scratch. Second, don't twist the monitor, which means don't grab it when you want to swivel the computer around to show somebody what's being displayed. You can damage the screen as well as the hinges that hold it to the computer. If your computer uses one of the film technologies for display (such as a thin-film transistor, or TFT, display), then pushing, hitting, or twisting the screen can warp the film. Screens are not repairable items. If yours gets broken, you have to replace it.

PC-to-Laptop Syncing

Most people who have a laptop also have a desktop PC. Keeping files updated between them can be a real challenge.

If both PCs are on a network together, you can transfer files between PCs using the network connection. If not, you can connect them directly with a null modem cable (basically a straight pass-through serial cable) and then use special software to manage the connection. Windows comes with a Direct Cable Connection utility that does the job just fine.

Windows (versions 9x and higher) also comes with a synchronization feature called My Briefcase that's specifically designed for keeping files matched up between your desktop and your laptop PCs. For example, suppose you are working on a report at work, and you want to take the latest draft home with you over the weekend. You copy the report from your desktop computer to the Briefcase on your laptop (using either a disk or your LAN). Then, you work on the report at home, and when you return to the office, you synchronize your Briefcase, copying the latest version back to the desktop to overwrite the older version.

You can use My Briefcase either with a floppy disk or on a network. To do it on a floppy, first copy the files on your main PC into the My Briefcase icon on your desktop in Windows. Then drag the My Briefcase folder onto the floppy drive icon to move it there. On a network, start at the remote PC (the laptop) and access the files on the main PC through Network Neighborhood (or My Network Places, depending on the Windows version you have). Drag them to the My Briefcase icon on the remote PC to copy them there.

Then, to sync the files from a floppy, copy the My Briefcase folder back to the desktop from the floppy disk. Then open the My Briefcase window and click the Update All button. Or, on a network, make sure both PCs are connected to the network and open the My Briefcase folder on the remote PC. Then click Update All to update the copies on the main PC.

Syncing Data with Palm Devices

Many people these days use Palm devices, made by 3Com. Popular models include the Palm III (see Figure 29.3), the Palm V, and the Palm VII. All use the same operating system.

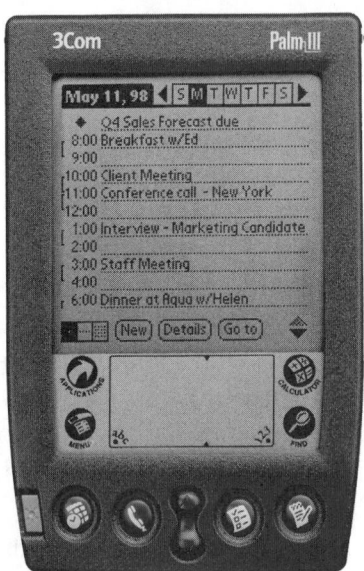

Figure 29.3

Palm IIIc

The primary purpose of a Palm device is to store addresses, appointments, and task lists in a portable, easy-to-update format.

You can use a Palm device as a stand-alone tool, but it's most effective when combined with a computer. You can enter and update your data on the computer, and then transfer it to the Palm device by syncing. *Syncing* updates the information on both sources—the Palm device and the computer—by comparing the dates of various additions, edits, and deletions and placing the most current information in both places.

Palm devices come with their own custom software, called Palm Desktop. You can use it to store and edit your information if you like, or you can use any of a variety of other programs instead if you prefer. The Palm devices work with Microsoft Outlook, Lotus Notes, and several other popular programs through special drivers called conduits. Most Palm models come with conduits for popular applications that you can install when you run the setup software for the device on your PC.

To sync a Palm device, simply place it in its cradle (which is attached to the PC via a serial or USB port) and press the button on the cradle. (There's only one button; you can't miss it.) You can also initiate a sync from the PC, by clicking the Synchronize button in the program you have set the device up to sync with. In Outlook, for example, installing the conduit places a Synchronize icon on Outlook's toolbar, and you can click that icon to begin the sync.

Troubleshooting Tips

Troubleshooting laptops and handheld computers involves some similar techniques to those you would use for a desktop computer, but there are some important differences. The similarities (at least for laptops) lie mainly with the operating system and software you use. Windows 98 running on a laptop is the same operating system that you have on your desktop. The main difference is that all your components are connected together internally, and you have an internal power supply (that is, your battery). You don't really have to check cable connections or mess with add-in cards like you do for a desktop model. Instead, the trouble might have to do with configuration and battery issues.

If your computer won't turn on and is unplugged, your battery may be dead. Try plugging in the laptop's A/C adapter so you know you have power and try it again. Most of the time, that's the problem. If your laptop still won't turn on, it may already be on but be in a power-saving sleep mode. Try pressing a key on the keyboard to wake it up, or move your mouse/cursor/touchpad around a bit. In some cases, you may have to press and hold the power button down for a few seconds to get it to wake up.

As with desktop computers, make sure all your drivers are updated. On my Dell Inspiron 7500, I regularly check for updates at the Dell Web site for my major components:

▶ Integrated video system

▶ DVD-ROM drive

▶ Touchpad drivers

▶ Modem/network adapter PC Card

▶ Sound card

Laptops are the computer of choice for more and more people every day because of their unique combination of features and convenience. Now that you know how to keep yours in good repair and to care for it properly, you're ready to join the ranks of the computing road warriors.

30

Using the Internet and Online Services

INTRODUCTION

Do you know the single most important reason why you need to get online if you own a computer? Because going online gives you the tools you need to master the PC— from the hardware to the operating system to the software— and tips on the future technology that you need to prepare for now to handle tomorrow.

I just spent one hour on the Net (I'm not joking—the time spent was 62 minutes, 11 seconds) and quite literally solved a week's worth of PC hardware concerns. In that hour, I grabbed two brand new drivers for equipment I use, researched the pros and cons of a motherboard I'm planning to buy, read a couple of articles on Rambus memory, arranged to beta test some new diagnostic software, looked up technical notes on terminating some network cable, exchanged Net messages with a friend at 3Com who pointed me to a solid ISDN modem for my new office, and performed a bandwidth test to see if my current modem is operating at maximum speed for my phone line. That's a lot of necessary ground to cover in an hour, all made possible because of the phenomenal amount of material available on the World Wide Web today.

And today, you can't think of this kind of Internet access as a luxury; it's essential.

By the time you buy a new printer or motherboard and get it home, the drivers or the motherboard BIOS may already be months out of date. Sure, you can call a tech support line and request the drivers be sent to you on CD, but then you'll sit waiting for a week or two or more for them to arrive. That's pretty unrealistic in a world in which the PC has become an essential part of our daily lives, and not some little appliance that sits in the corner and that you dust more than you use.

Getting Online Help

Gathered from the information presented in this chapter, here are a set of steps for getting online help for problems you may experience with your PC.

Be Prepared

Before you start, there are some things you may need on hand. These include:

▶ Paper and a pen/pencil, for taking notes and for keeping information you need to provide handy (or maybe you already have these things stored in a database or text file on another PC

▶ Basic information about your PC (type of CPU and motherboard, video card chip set used, exact version of your operating system), so that you can provide these necessary details when posting or calling to get assistance

▶ Prepared short synopsis of the problem (for example, what you may have installed, removed, or modified just before the problem cropped up; exact symptoms you're seeing; what you've already tried and what behavior changes, if any, you saw as a result) so that you can report it when posting or calling for technical assistance

▶ Product registration information and/or the model and serial number of the malfunctioning device, to provide to the manufacturer if you're reporting the device (and especially, if you need to return it for a working one)

▶ The problem PC or device nearby when you research, post a message online, or call for support, so that you can double-check settings and walk through a set of steps—it makes it a lot harder when you don't have the system right there

1. Dial into the Internet as you normally would.

2. Select one of the resources mentioned in this chapter—for example, one of the Web search engines, or Web-based computing support such as CNET or The Microsoft Network, or others.

3. Identify a helpful site from those you visit.

4. After checking out any online instructions for posting, prepare your post by giving necessary information about the problem you're having, including exact error messages. Then provide background information about your PC, such as which operating system and version you have, recent changes you've made to the configuration, and your type of PC.

5. Post your note per the instructions provided.

6. Note where you posted your message, so you can easily find your way back.

7. Start checking back anywhere between 2 to 48 hours later to see what responses you may have (and respond appropriately).

8. Analyze the information you've received and proceed with your troubleshooting.

Problems with Traditional Methods

Getting the information you need through traditional means can be difficult or impossible. You've got problems to solve, new drivers to track down and acquire, newer and fancier hardware to install, and new software versions to learn about. Many good trade magazines are available, and some are free to computer professionals, but the problem is that they give you too much to look at. It's easy for me to accumulate a dozen magazines and journals in a week while I'm out of town. How can I read all of that and pull out the information that I need in time to get through the next lot when they show up the following week?

Some problems can't be solved by magazines, either. A lot of knowledgeable people read them and write for them, but the problem is the time lag. If I'm installing a new board, and it's not working no matter what I do, I want to know how to make it work *now*, not weeks or months from now. Writing a letter to an advice columnist at my favorite computer magazine, waiting for the letter to be published, and then waiting for a reply isn't going to help me. Calling the board manufacturer's tech-support line might work, but then it's on my nickel (ever notice how few tech-support lines are 800 numbers?), and I might not get the right answer anyway.

Then there's the problem of acquiring updated drivers, software patches, hardware documentation that the maker assumed that I wouldn't need, and just plain new product information. Working with computers often involves a fair amount of isolation and not a lot of free time, and it's hard to keep up with all that stuff. I need a way to throw questions into the ether for anyone and everyone to answer, to acquire drivers without waiting for the manufacturer to get around to sending me a disk, and to learn about new products.

Here are some examples of the frustrating situations you can run into when trying to get information you need *now*. At the very least, these are some reasons why *I* learned to use online services for tech support and getting software.

Journey into Faxback Hell

In concept, faxback services are a nice way of answering common customer questions. Why hire staff to run a telephone line when 75 percent of the people who call have the same question? It's much simpler to prepare documents that answer the most frequently asked questions, and then make those documents available via fax to those who request them.

The catch is that you usually have to know exactly what you want before these services work, and be able to provide a document number for it. No document number, no fax. Even if you get one of the rare faxback services in which real people handle telephone questions, that real human probably doesn't know which document you need. Usually, the only way to get a document number is to order the catalog from the faxback service, at which point you have a list of titles with document numbers next to them. In other words, you still can't be sure that you're ordering the document that you need.

Facing the Muzak: Technical Support Lines

I don't want to pick on those who man tech-support lines. That's got to be one of the most thankless jobs around. Callers are stressed out from worrying about their problem, probably snappish from being kept on hold, and prone to ask what sound like stupid questions because the tech-support rep has answered that same one six times already that day. (See where faxback services come from?)

But tech-support lines aren't usually any fun for the caller, either. Many people have a hard time explaining a particular chain of events to someone they can't see. Others wait on hold for 20 minutes to hear a tech-support guy tell them, "Gee, I've never heard of that problem before. Can you hold on a minute (or 2, or 10) while I get my supervisor?" Unlike sales lines, the lines to tech support are often not toll-free, which means that if you're at work, you may have to explain to the business manager all those long-distance charges on your code, or if you're at home, you have to swallow the long-distance bill yourself.

Far too many tech-support lines are 9-to-5 propositions, which means that weekend warrior types can be stuck until Monday if they have a problem. And then there's that period of being on hold. I'm never sure whether it's more annoying to hear violin renditions of "Purple Haze" or a comforting male voice repeatedly assuring me that my patience is appreciated. (How do they know that I'm being patient? Maybe I'm grinding my teeth smooth while waiting to get back to something productive.) Then there are the tech-support lines (such as Microsoft's Windows NT support line) that won't even talk to you until you've given them $250.

The *idea* of tech-support lines is wonderful—that a company will provide a team of experts to answer your questions on demand. The reality is often less wonderful, for both the caller and the tech-support person.

Making Friends and Influencing People

Often, one of the best ways to answer a question is to find someone who's got more experience than you do. Unfortunately, this is sometimes easier said than done. You may not have anyone around to ask (often the case for home PC-ers), or you may be the person with the most experience. Sometimes, your circle of personal resources just doesn't have experience where you need it. Or they may profess a great deal more expertise than they actually have, and some of the poorest PC tech is done over the water cooler. If you've been a NetWare person all your life, and all the people you know are NetWare people, then you could be stuck when setting up that Windows NT Server machine and something obscure goes wrong. At this point, you need more friends and work associates.

Then, too, friends don't always give you written instructions when answering your questions. Either you try to remember what they told you or you write it down yourself, but there's always the possibility of misinterpreting or outright forgetting what they told you. I leave it to your imagination to envision how ugly *that* can get.

Read All about It

As I noted at the beginning of this section, there's just too much for one person to keep up with—hundreds of pages show up on my doorstep every week. Then there's the problem of money. Not all these magazines come cheap, especially if you can't demonstrate that you work in the industry (not difficult to do, but a consideration) and therefore warrant a professional courtesy rate. And for some magazines, such as *PC Week*, you pay full price no matter who you are. Even if the subscriptions are tax deductible for you, it adds up.

What's Out There?

So what help can you get from cyberspace? Let's take a look at a few things you can expect to find.

New Product Information

Unsurprisingly, there's lots of new product information on the Web, as people try to make the idea of the marketplace on your desk a reality. Sometimes, getting cold hard facts about how something actually works can be difficult, but at least you can learn that a product exists.

Reviews

Product reviews—both professional and real-user anecdotes—are available everywhere on the Internet, often ahead of print journals. The lack of print delay means the reviewers are working with later versions or drivers, especially when reviewing a product in testing. When new hardware, a new driver, or a patch debuts, you don't have to be a guinea pig by being the first to buy and try it. Instead, you can take a few days to read about the response the item is getting from users posting to newsgroups and Web-based message boards before you invest your money and/or time.

White Papers and Background Information

White papers are wholly different from short question-and-answer help and quick troubleshooting pieces: they're sort of the mini-thesis or novella of the tech world. They take a specific topic (the effect of older analog phone lines and wiring on dial-up connection speed with modems, or configuring for optimal security under Windows NT/2000, for example) and explore it in some detail. Sometimes, such papers include an industry-wide perspective, and, sometimes, they provide in-depth comparisons of different chip sets or features.

Typically authored by an expert in the field (a senior project manager, a senior product developer, etc., at a company responsible for the product or issue being discussed), they can provide quite a bit of background that several short technical articles or product information churned out by a company's marketing department don't provide.

Frequently Asked Questions (FAQs)

Because certain topics come up as questions again and again ("How do I update a driver?" or "How do I get this device to work under Windows 98?"), one Internet information resource stable is Frequently Asked Questions (FAQ) pages, listing the most common questions about a product along with their answers.

Product Documentation

This is not *always* available in cyberspace, but sometimes it is there when you need it. Some hardware is sold without its documentation (as if you didn't need the documentation to set up the hardware?), and going online is the easiest way to get it, if it's available. Many times, too, documentation updates covering ground originally missed or documented incorrectly will appear online only.

Device Drivers and Utilities

Lots of these. Device drivers are crucial to getting your old hardware to work with your new software. For instance, when Windows NT came out, the HP scanners wouldn't work with the old drivers, so I eagerly awaited the arrival of new NT drivers for the scanner. As this is being written, I'm seeing some of the same patterns with the Windows 2000 debut, as people scramble around online to download the latest 2000 drivers and patches. Shareware and freeware PC utilities are also commonly available.

Advice

Today on the Internet, more and more technical sites are cropping up that either give you step-by-step how-tos for hardware installation and troubleshooting (PC Guide at `http://www.pcguide.com`, and Service911 at `http://www.service911.com`), or provide some assistance for free while letting you "rent" an expert for a fee (Expertcity at `http://www.expertcity.com`, and MyHelpdesk at `http://www.myhelpdesk.com`), or work by a bonus system whereby you answer questions on one topic for someone and then earn points toward getting your questions answered by someone else (Experts Exchange at `http://www.experts-exchange.com`).

One big advantage is that you can often learn from people who use a product much like you do. The downside tends to be that there are a lot more so-called experts out there than may be able to fix a PC. One tip is to look around such sites for people who seem to be well-respected and able to explain things clearly. A good tech tends to have a big following, so with a little reading, it often becomes clear who you should listen to and who to ignore.

Warning

Advice that you'll get from other users of online services is not any more universally accurate than advice that you get from other people. Check your sources before doing anything drastic based on anyone's posting!

The Advantages of Gathering Information Online

Earlier, I discussed some disadvantages of obtaining information by traditional means. Information culled from cyberspace has some advantages over information gathered via traditional means. Let's take a look at a few of those.

It's Often Cheaper

Cost comes in two main categories: money that you spend, and money that you lose—or, as we old-country economists would have it, explicit and implicit costs. Let's assume that you have a telephone and a modem, and that you live in an area that has local access to the Internet (in case you're not sure what this means, I'll be discussing that later in this chapter). If you call tech support with your problem, the process goes like this:

1. Call the tech-support line (almost certainly long distance), probably between 8 A.M. and 5 P.M., when telephone rates are highest.

2. Wait on hold.

3. Talk to the tech-support person.

4. Possibly wait on hold again while the tech person looks up the problem or consults with someone.

5. If all goes well, get the answer.

Every bit of that process occurs while the meter is ticking.

If you post the question, on the other hand, the process looks more like this:

1. Create a forum/newsgroup message.

2. Connect to your online service.

3. Post the message in the appropriate forum or newsgroup.

4. Close the connection.

5. Periodically dial in to see whether you have waiting messages. (Some forums even will e-mail you alerts that an answer or comment has been posted to your question.) Download the messages.

6. Close the connection.

7. Read your messages.

Now, the process differs a little bit when you're talking about posting to a Web site for help. You can't usually compose a message offline or grab your messages to read offline. What you can do, however, is compose your message in something like Windows Notepad and paste it into the browser message window. If you post a question to more than one message area, or more than one Web site, doing so means you won't have to retype all those nitty-gritty details again (and you're less apt to forget to include something important).

None of this costs you anything above the monthly service charge for your online connection (usually about $20). And at no time do you have to sit on hold, listening to elevator music or some inane greeting.

It's Convenient

One of the biggest hassles of tech-support lines is the time spent on hold. If you have something else that you could be doing, it's annoying to have to wait, tied to the telephone, for someone to answer your call. If instead you post your question to a newsgroup or forum, then you can do something else while waiting for an answer. Check back in a couple of hours, and you may already have an answer. If you need an answer *now*, posting a question to a newsgroup may not be good enough—you may get the answer you need in 10 minutes, tomorrow, next week, or never. But if it's something that you want to know but don't have to know right this second, newsgroups and forums are great.

Another aspect to the convenience of online services and the Internet is that they run on a 24-hour clock. I've found that one of the best times to post a question to a newsgroup is after the normal workday. This may have something to do with geography—I live on the East Coast, so 5 P.M. comes earlier to me than it does to most of the country. But it's also due to the fact that a lot of techies check into their newsgroups (or Web-based message boards) when they get home from work, or late at night. If I post a question at 5 P.M. EST, then by morning I often have a collection of answers.

For example, I once posted a message about a problem that I was having installing Windows NT Server on a new machine. All the hardware conformed to NT's compatibility requirements, but on reboot the dratted installation would just tell me that it couldn't find NTLDR, one of the required components for starting the system. NTLDR was on my hard disk—I could see it when booting from a DOS floppy—but darned if the installation program saw it. I gave up late that night (trying to fix things when you're tired can be a great mistake), posted a message that outlined the problem and described the error messages that I saw, and resolved to check in the following day. When I returned, I discovered that three people had posted responses to my original posting, and one of those responses did the trick. I updated the system BIOS, and the installation worked just fine.

The convenience isn't limited to question-and-answer sessions, either. Want to see what applications are out for Windows 98, but it's 3 A.M.? How about looking up the technical specs on Advanced Micro Device's latest CPU? You can use a search engine (more on those in a bit) to search the Web for sites containing information about the subject. Once you've found some Web help sites, you can review them to see which one you want, then copy it to your computer. If you've got an unlimited-access account, then you can even read at your leisure on the Web without filling up your hard disk with information you won't need past that minute. You can also download drivers and evaluation software at your convenience, not at the convenience of someone else.

Posting online also gives you the option of cutting and pasting significant portions of your configuration files—for example, the contents of your CONFIG.SYS if you're having a problem with conventional memory in DOS. You can also supply screenshots of errors or strange-looking screens to further document your problem.

Initial Results May Be Better

One of the nasty truths about today's very inexpensive (relative to the past) hardware, coupled with the burgeoning population of first-time PC users, is that a lot of tech companies have had to scale back some of their support services, or at least not beef them up as much as might be needed to handle a high volume of user phone calls.

As one cost-saving measure, many manufacturers *outsource* their first-tier product support, meaning they hire an outside support firm to handle initial calls from users. Then, follow-up, if any, is provided by more experienced technicians supplied by the manufacturer.

This means that during your first call for support, it's possible you won't reach someone actually employed by the manufacturer. In some cases, you may not even reach someone who has ever used the product for which you need help. Heck, the person you talk to may be more of an operator than a technician. Many agencies use script books or computer databases to look up your question and offer an answer based on the closest match they can find. Throw them a question not in the script, and you may be in for a long wait or several calls.

Follow-up Is Often Better

One of the best aspects of the interactive parts of newsgroups and forums is that those who answer your questions are generally doing it not because they're getting paid for it, but because they're trying to help you. I've found that that translates to good follow-up. Until you post a message saying that all is well with your problem, you can almost certainly count on people trying to help you through the process, if you're polite and respond to messages posted to you.

For example, on one occasion I was helping a friend figure out how best to get PowerPoint 95 (a PC application) to people in a largely Unix-oriented office. We were deciding whether it would be better to provide the users with individual machines that could run the application, set up a PowerPoint workstation or two for those times when they needed it, use some kind of PC emulation on the Sparc 5s and 20s that the users already had, or what. (For those of you raising your eyebrows at the thought of buying users a second computer just to run an application, this office was an intelligence shop that had some money to spend on the project.) I posted a message outlining the situation on a couple of relevant forums, one for the PowerPoint side of the problem and one for the organizational side of the problem. The answers that I received about the organizational aspects of the problem sparked some new questions, which I asked, and then some other people got into the question and raised some more issues. By the time things wound down a couple of days later, I had what I needed and far more background besides.

Internet Choices

In the old days (pre-1995 or so, when most people first discovered the Internet), you rarely if ever heard the term *Internet Service Provider* (ISP). To go online, you either used your modem to dial into local (sometimes free, sometime subscription) bulletin board services often run by hobbyist computer operators, or you signed up with one of the major "soup-to-nuts" online services (in those days, CompuServe, America Online, Genie, Delphi, or Prodigy). The Internet was largely restricted to the government, the military, and educational institutions.

If solid computer technical support was what you wanted, and you needed access to patches and new drivers and some of the best PC technical minds, you really had just one choice: CompuServe, the so-called "granddaddy" of online services and one of the oldest.

Times change. CompuServe, as I'll discuss shortly, lost its technical luster several years ago, and users aren't looking so much for access to one closed online network (like America Online and most of them used to be), but easy access to everything they can find on the Internet.

With rare exceptions, the better technical content now tends to reside globally on the Internet (mostly through Web sites) rather than locked behind a subscription wall requiring you to be a member of CompuServe or AOL or MSN to access help areas or forums. Although there is still content (special chats, fancy communication features, and editorial articles) you can get only by being a member of an online service, the most popular sites are on the Internet itself, accessible by any provider. Thus, there aren't usually clear choices on what Internet provider or service to sign up with, particularly if your focus is on getting information on and support for your PC.

Because the Internet became the big draw instead of the proprietary content that the big services developed, most of these services have evolved today to provide a portal to the Internet. A *portal*, simply put, is an entrance way, or lobby, that highlights various things that can be found on the service or the Internet. Portal providers (such as AltaVista, Excite, Lycos, MSN, and Yahoo!) highlight categories of topics (computing or hardware/software, real estate, or health) along with sites they think their users will want to visit, and package it along with ads from companies. Most portals are free to the user to visit; they get their money from the advertising they carry.

You can access information on the Internet by using either a local or a national ISP. Local ISPs usually provide only access to the Internet, in varying degrees of reliability and speed. National ISPs—such as EarthLink, Juno, and PSI/FlashNet—often provide special help areas for members on their Web sites but don't typically have exclusive, serious PC help content.

Before choosing a provider, you should know which parts of the Internet you wish to access and then make sure the provider you choose provides full access to those areas.

Parts of the Internet

For purposes of research today, the Internet has three important parts: the World Wide Web, FTP sites, and Usenet newsgroups.

(*Gopher holes*, or sites that held information on a variety of topics, have been more or less superseded by the Web as sources of new information, although they still maintain a small following.)

The World Wide Web

Originally a method devised by a Swiss think tank to make its papers on physics available to other scientists, the Web has become one of the most hyped aspects of the Internet over the last five years. The graphical side of the Internet, it offers papers that you can read online, files that you can download, and links that you can follow to related sites. Search engines make it possible to easily find information on a particular topic.

Right now, the Web is at a crossroads of sorts. On the public side, it's becoming a favorite marketing ploy, much to the disgust of many people who've been involved with the Internet for a long time and like its ideals of shared information for the public good. (Ever notice all the television advertisements nowadays that close with invitations to visit the product's Web site?) In many circles, electronic commerce exhibits the same kind of bad taste as handing out business cards at a private barbecue. On the other hand, thousands of Web sites are run by people who create Web pages for the sake of information-sharing, not to sell anything. (Then there are the *vanity pages* created by people who assume that the rest of the planet wants to know what they're doing that week, but those aren't really relevant here.) I'm hoping that the marketing side of the Web doesn't drown out the information side, as it's a good place to do preliminary research. Many serious tech types, however, find you have to wade through a lot of shopping and "fluff" sites to locate the real meat of research material. So they find a few good focused sites and/or newsgroups, and concentrate there.

One change occurring is that Web-based message boards for users to post questions and get answers are becoming more and more common, often in addition to newsgroups or as a replacement for newsgroups (Internet-based public messaging divided into specific categories of interest—more about that in a moment).

Web-based messaging is still in its infancy and has some draw-backs. For example, it tends to be a bit clunky and not as well fea-tured as a Network News Transfer Protocol (NNTP) newsreader at its best. (An *NNTP newsreader* permits the reading of Internet-standard newsgroup messages; both Internet Explorer and Netscape Naviga-tor built a mail/newsreader into their total package.) Also, Web-based messaging until recently has mostly attracted those who didn't have access to newsgroups, or felt it was too difficult to con-figure information to use the newsgroups. Thus, the questions tended to be very basic and the answers tended to suit the less-experienced clientele.

However, Web-based messaging makes sense from a company's perspective, because it gives them a way for users to ask questions or post comments, and support staff to respond, all within a Web site. It's easier to monitor traffic to a Web site alone than it is to monitor traffic on a system that "mixes its media," so to speak, by having a Web page for some information, and newsgroups for others.

Web-based messaging is also convenient and far more accessible than newsgroups because you're much more likely to have a Web browser available to you at most computers, whereas you won't always have access to NNTP newsgroups or private e-mail. It's likely to become the standard just because we're beginning to change the way we connect to the Net, by using devices other than the PC (such as Web phones, Personal Digital Assistants, or PDAs, and very soon, refrigerators—of which the first generation built with Internet access allows the refrigerator to dial in your grocery order). When a Web browser and Net connectivity can be built into almost anything, it makes sense for people to communicate through the Web itself and not have to find a way to accommodate separate programs such as mail and newsreaders.

Some manufacturers' Web sites even find a way to accommodate both those who prefer to use newsgroups and those who want to post through the Web. Intel, for instance, has a much-respected NNTP-to-Web gateway that allows users to read and to post ques-tions and replies by using whichever standard they prefer.

FTP Sites

Before the Web became so popular, the easiest way for a hardware or software manufacturer to get new drivers, utilities, or patches to its customers was to set up a server that customers could dial into and download the files by using *file transfer protocol*, or FTP. Servers set up this way are called *FTP sites*. Even though Web pages are often used to present files for download, the sources for some of those files are still FTP sites that are available to the Web page via a link created by the page's author.

Usenet Newsgroups

Newsgroups are discussion groups that are part of a service called Usenet. They cover all kinds of topics, from bicycle maintenance to cat stories to problems associated with configuring hard drives to . . . you name it. If you haven't found a group that covers exactly the topic that you want to discuss, either you should look a little harder or one will probably pop up soon enough.

What Is Usenet?

Usenet, also called NewsNet and NNTP, is similar in many ways to e-mail, with one major difference: you don't need a Usenet address. Usenet is a collection of topic-related messages that are stored on special NNTP servers. You access the messages using an NNTP-compliant client, such as Outlook Express. Usenet groups have names similar to Web site domain names but they are often longer and hence, more descriptive. An example of a Usenet group address is `comp.os.ms-windows.apps.compatibility .win95`, a group dedicated to discussing application compatibility issues with Windows 95. Other Usenet addresses can get quite silly, such as the obvious dislike for a beloved purple dinosaur shared by the list members of `alt.barney.dinosaur.die.die.die`.

Beware, however, as Usenet is also used by unscrupulous individuals to pass illicit and illegal information and/or material with mature content, including child pornography. Groups that carry this type of information often have descriptive names with *sex* in the title. If you are careful, you'll never see such material, but be aware that it is out there (the Internet is anonymous, especially Usenet). Also remember that many people *cross-post* (distribute the same message to a number of other groups) and send such material to groups that do not dwell on those things.

Of course, newsgroups can be a powerful tool if used properly, and a number of ISPs and other organizations offer smut-free NNTP access. You need merely make the choice.

Most newsgroups are unmoderated, meaning that no one's watching the message content to ensure that subject discussions stay on track, or that people are polite (or even not downright obscene) to each other, or that people don't post totally irrelevant messages in the wrong forums (called *spamming*, and considered to be impolite). Although there's a lot of garbage in newsgroups (on the order of offers of nude celebrity pictures), newsgroups have been around for a long time and are good places to find people with lots of technical experience. Technical newsgroups, after all, are frequented by those interested enough in talking shop to do it online.

Note

Because thousands of newsgroups exist, a server that holds traffic for all of them may be able to keep only a few days' worth of traffic at a time. To keep current with a newsgroup, you may want to check in fairly regularly.

Normally, your access to newsgroups works like this: your ISP maintains a news server that stores as many of the postings in all or selected newsgroups as possible. (Note that this means that you may not have access to all newsgroups—if it's not on your news server, you can't reach it.) Rather than connecting directly to Usenet, then, you dial into the news server and read the messages posted there. Any messages that you post to a newsgroup will be uploaded from the news server to Usenet itself.

CompuServe

As I said earlier, CompuServe used to be *the* online service to join if you were into computers or wanted access to the people shaping the computer industry. A decade ago, it was pretty easy to join a whole host of computer forums available only on CompuServe and rub elbows with top decision-makers and senior support brass at companies such as Microsoft, Novell, Lotus, and Digital Equipment Corporation (DEC). You paid for the privilege, too: for a very long time, you paid a monthly subscription in addition to up to $24 per hour connection fees.

Some of those top names are a bit faded now, and CompuServe's supremacy in online technical material faded even faster, even before the Internet became the place to go.

Today, CompuServe is owned by America Online (AOL), and its technical content is far more limited than it used to be. Most of the old guard contingent of experienced professionals who could answer almost any computer question have disappeared. You can still join and participate in computer forums there and download files, but it's usually easier to locate the same material—or better—on manufacturer Web sites or from popular technical sites such as AnandTech (http://www.anandtech.com), WinDrivers (http://www.windrivers.com), and Tom's Hardware (www.tomshardware.com).

Thus, computing support has largely shifted from CompuServe to specific manufacturer Web sites (such as Intel's); heavily promoted Web-based user forums (for example, those on CNET and ZDNet); smaller, newer contenders (such as MyHelpdesk); and a base of about 30 professionally managed technical forums comprising Computing Central on The Microsoft Network.

All-in-One Online Services

What about all-in-one online services such as The Microsoft Network (MSN), America Online, and EarthLink? The options that they offer are similar to those available from a local ISP or CompuServe, the main difference being that these online services come to you—you don't have to go out of your way even a little bit to get access to cyberspace. The Microsoft Network comes with Windows 95/98, America Online will mail you their startup software, and startup software for EarthLink is available at the www.earthlink.com Web page.

These online services are designed to offer you universal (or, at least countrywide) access to both the Internet (chat groups, Usenet newsgroups, and the Web) and to special forums that they operate. They have some advantages: no negotiating with a provider, easy acquisition of software, and you can set it up either as you install the operating system or from the Add/Remove Programs utility in the Control Panel.

So Which Should I Choose?

Unlike just a few years ago, people today often make their choice of Internet provider (or provider and online service, as is the case with AOL and MSN) based on these factors:

▶ Ease of signup and use

▶ Reliability of service (people generally don't like their Net service to be unavailable, or to have to wade through a lot of busy signals before they can connect)

▶ Connection speed and support (good dial-up connection rates or support for using cable and digital subscriber line, or DSL, high-speed access)

▶ Price (typically from $9 to $25 per month, depending on whether you want additional mailboxes or a fixed Internet protocol (IP) address

 ◗ Ability to access from other locations (important for those who need to travel for business or tend to take off on weekend trips)

 ◗ (Increasingly), the ability to access from other than a proper PC (using wireless Web phones, PDAs such as a Palm, etc.)

Less-experienced people—or those with less of a desire to learn all the details—often sign up for one of the national services such as AOL or MSN, whereas more-experienced folks tend to choose a large, well-supported Internet service provider (EarthLink, Juno, etc.).

There's also a new breed of Internet service available: the "free" ISPs, such as freei (`http://www.freei.net`) and NetZero (`http://www.netzero.com`). They're free in that you don't pay a monthly service fee to connect to them, but you usually get extra advertising built into their browser windows (which helps pay for your free access).

The Tools You Need

What do you need to explore cyberspace? Not much: a PC (since you're reading this book, I'll assume that you've got that much), a modem, an account with an ISP, and some communications software.

Modems

Modems were discussed in detail in Chapter 21, "Communications Devices," but they're worth a little attention here. Most systems nowadays come with a modem already installed. If you're just gearing up for exploring cyberspace, you may be wondering just how fast a modem you should get. Really, it depends on what services are available in your area.

If you live remotely, outside of a large population area, you may be stuck with older, analog phone lines that usually won't utilize the full speed possible of a standard 56K, V90 modem. In urban, high-population or technically-dense areas (lots of tech companies), you may be able to use cable modems (with service provided often by the same firm providing your cable TV) or one of the DSL variants I'll talk about more in a moment, which can get you speed of between 20 and 100 times what a standard dial-up modem connecting at 28.8Kbps can achieve. If you have more than one PC in your office or home, you can network them together to share an Internet connection, so you don't have to pay for two or more accounts (unless you choose to do so).

Many modems today support 56K connections, theoretically. Unfortunately, almost none can really run at that speed. You'll be lucky if you get more than 33K using a dial-up modem, though some areas get 40K or better.

If you can't get a 56K connection, should you look for a lower-speed modem or go with the best available? I'd do the latter. First, it's often hard to find modems that aren't the latest and greatest unless you're looking in a place that sells used hardware. Second, modems aren't expensive equipment. Third, many online connections are increasing in speed, as providers realize that they've got to give their customers a faster path to cyberspace. If you can't get a high-speed connection now, you may be able to do so in the near future—particularly if you're talking about Internet access, in which case several companies in the area may be competing for your online dollars.

You may have seen or heard of Winmodems and wondered why they are so much cheaper than other modems. Winmodems are designed to work only with Windows, so if you try to use a non-Microsoft operating system with a Winmodem, you'll find that there are no drivers for it and the modem won't work. Although Winmodems can be considerably cheaper than other modems, their limitations and unreliability make them a poor choice.

What about internal versus external modems? Although they're a touch more expensive, I like external modems. First, their position outside of the PC means that you can watch the status lights, so if a problem occurs you may be able to tell the point at which the problem occurred. External modems are also much easier to swap out if you're using the swap method for troubleshooting. Second, using an external modem saves that slot in your PC for something else, such as another board, or just for air circulation. The only real downside to using external modems is that they usually use up a serial port.

Besides, modems that beep and flash make you feel that they're *doing* something. Most techies I know get warm, fuzzy feelings from status lights of any kind.

Increasingly, modems are of the cable or digital subscriber line (DSL) variety, meaning much better speed because your computer is no longer talking through those old, noisy telephone lines. Unfortunately, though, major speed avenues are still only available to those who live in large population centers (DSL lines, for example, require the customer to be within 1500–3000 feet of the station in order to receive), or randomly across various cable television systems. The cost is typically between $30 and $200 per month for a connection rate from several times to 100 times faster than a traditional analog connection of 28.8K, and you usually still need to subscribe to a separate ISP for your actual Internet account to be used with your fast connection.

On-ramps to the Information Highway

The Internet isn't one entity but a group of components, and Web sites (locations on the World Wide Web) are the most visible. But there are other components of the Internet as well, including Internet Relay Chat (IRC) for real-time online chatting, FTP for uploading/downloading files, gopher searches (largely replaced by big Web search engineers), and more.

So, how you connect depends a bit on what part of the Internet you want to reach, and what your goals are once you reach there.

Connecting to the Internet

To connect to the Internet, whether you want to reach the Web, FTP sites, or newsgroups, you'll need to be running several communications programs, including a Web browser, an FTP client, and a mail/newsreader client like those included with Internet Explorer and Netscape Navigator. In the early days of the Internet, you would have to install and set up all of them yourself. These days, however, most connection software automatically installs and sets up all of them for you. In this section, you'll take a look at what each of the communications programs is and what it does.

TCP/IP is the transport protocol used by the Internet. It's actually two protocols working in tandem: the *Internet Protocol* (IP) shuffles data between source and destination, and the *Transmission Control Protocol* (TCP) makes sure that the data gets to its destination in one piece and in the proper order.

The *Serial Line Interface Protocol* (SLIP) and the *Point-to-Point Protocol* (PPP) are two ways of doing the same thing: making the Internet think that your system has its own IP address, so that it can receive images directly instead of having to view them on the connection server at the ISP. If you can get it, go with PPP—it's faster than SLIP and has some features (such as data compression and error correction) that SLIP does not have. It's also easier to use, as it doesn't require you to create a login script to negotiate your connection to the Internet.

Tip

If PPP isn't available, see if you can get *CSLIP*, a compressed version of SLIP. It doesn't have all the features of PPP, but it's a little faster than regular SLIP.

How much will the connection cost you? It depends on where you are in the country and what kind of connection you get. Many ISPs offer two classes of Internet connection: one in which you pay a flat monthly rate for a certain number of connection hours, and then a per-hour charge for any hours beyond that; and one in which you pay a somewhat higher rate for an unlimited access account. At $25 per month, the unlimited Internet dial-up access account I was able to get seemed a bargain. When browsing the Web or reading newsgroups online, it's easy to stay up longer than you actually meant to.

For those offline readers that don't disconnect you when they're done downloading messages, it's nice to know that you haven't blown your entire free connection time allotment because you forgot that the line was still open.

Tip

When choosing an ISP, be careful to choose one that has a local access number. Otherwise, you'll run up long-distance charges while connected.

What about Connecting with ISDN?

Integrated Services Digital Network (ISDN) connections to the Internet are beginning to be available in most areas of the United States. Getting an ISDN connection can speed up your connection more than fourfold (a potential 128Kbps versus 28.8Kbps), significantly reducing your connection time when downloading large files or browsing graphics-intensive Web sites. Rather than waiting for images to slowly develop on your screen, they appear instantly. I use it and like it very much.

ISDN is faster than dialing in with a regular modem, but it's also much more expensive, both in terms of startup costs and monthly charges. ISDN rates vary across the country (I've heard of prices that range from about $20/month to $*800*/month). It's impossible to say how much it will cost you, but think about this: to connect to the Internet requires a modem, a telephone line that you've already got, and an account with an ISP. Connecting via ISDN can require some or all of the following:

▶ ISDN line (outside) installation fee

▶ Measured service connection charge (that is, measured by hours, by bandwidth used—how much you upload/download, etc.)

▶ Site-specific fee for additional inside wiring

◗ Terminal adapter/NT1 equipment

◗ Ethernet network interface card with 10Base-T connector for your computer, if it does not already have one

None of these items come cheap: one ISP offering ISDN in central Virginia estimates that your start-up costs will run from under $100 to $1000 depending on the kind of setup required.

Communications Software

Once you've got the connection, you'll need some communications software to go with it to get to the resources out there. The software you need depends on the type of connection you choose to go with. For example, if you've got AOL or MSN and you're using the latest version of their software, you'll have a newsreader and a Web browser in addition to a forum reader. On the other hand, if you've got an Internet connection through an ISP, you may have to get your own newsreader and browser.

Note

When you sign up for Internet access with an ISP, they'll usually include an e-mail package in the deal.

Some of this software can overlap. For example, if you like, you can also use your AOL or MSN interface or Web browser to FTP and browse newsgroups. None of this software is expensive, some is free on the Web, and some comes with the connection you get.

Tip

Tucows (www.tucows.com) is the ultimate resource for Internet software for all platforms. Each item is rated and accompanied by a short description of what it does. WinFiles.com (www.winfiles.com), now owned by CNET, comes in a very close second.

Quick Guide to America Online Forums and Getting Mail

Since AOL is the best known of the online services also offering Internet access, let's go for a fast little tour around functions you may use in trying to get technical support on AOL.

AOL puts most of their main interest areas, for example, mail and support areas such as Computing, on their main two introductory screens to make it pretty easy to navigate the process. These two intro screens are the main sign-on screen (where your mail, if you have any, is announced to you) and the Channels screen. On most versions of AOL software, these open automatically when you sign on to the service. If you don't see the Channels screen pop up, just click on AOL Channels from the sign-on screen.

From the Channels screen, you click the Computing icon to be directed to computing forums (PC and Mac) that are offered on the service. Also, AOL is built around the use of keywords to help you swiftly move from one place to another. Click the keyword icon on the AOL screen or press Ctrl+K to bring up a dialog box, type in **Computing**, and then hit Enter.

AOL isn't a techie haven, and it shows as you begin to familiarize yourself with the AOL Computing channel. While AOL used to operate its own technical forums divided between operating systems, applications, and hardware, today's AOL Computing channel is mostly tied to links to CNET reviews. Beyond that, AOL maintains just a small area for simple questions, almost none of them relating to hardware.

Browsing the Web

If you're a Windows user, it's getting hard *not* to have a Web browser these days. Windows 98 comes with a built-in version of Microsoft Internet Explorer. There are many other browsers (such as Netscape Navigator) that you can download from the Web, for Windows 95/98/NT/2000.

Tip

You can buy Netscape or other browsers as part of an Internet starter kit.

The aforementioned Tucows Web site provides free downloads of most available browsers.

Reading Newsgroups

You've got a lot of options when it comes to reading newsgroups, including these:

▶ AOL

▶ CompuServe

▶ Web browsers

▶ Third-party newsreaders

America Online (AOL)

To get to the newsgroups on AOL, all you need to do is select the keyword *newsgroups.* When you first sign on, it will walk you through the steps needed to enable junk-mail filtering. You can change the settings any time you like afterward. AOL also has its own proprietary message boards, which are not accessible through the Internet; you must be a member and logged in using AOL software to participate.

Web Browsers

Most Web browsers today have a mail/NNTP newsreader built in, as I've already mentioned. This is better than using a gateway interface to the newsgroups, as you find through AOL, but still leaves some things to be desired. One problem with this is that for some, configuring the newsgroup reader can be a little tough (in that it requires lots of little details) and there's a lot of variation between types of newsreaders.

To find a newsgroup on a particular subject, then, you must either scroll through the thousands of groups out there, or, as illustrated in Figure 30.1, use the Find function to search for text that may help you find a group. Once you're *in* a newsgroup, however, the interface is fairly straightforward, and it's easy to move between messages and back to the main list. When performing a page text search in a Web browser to find a particular newsgroup, be as specific as possible. For example, the Find tool in Internet Explorer will locate every instance of the text string you specify on that page, whether it's a whole word or not.

Figure 30.1

When using Internet Explorer's Outlook Express to read newsgroups, you can search for text strings to find newsgroups covering a specific topic.

Internet Explorer, the most popular Web browser, offers a newsgroup reader through its Outlook Express mail/newsgroup component.

Third-Party Newsreaders

If you've got access to the Web, however, you've also got access to dozens of freeware and shareware newsreaders. The Tucows Web site contains links to many of these, including descriptions, licensing information, and file sizes.

If you don't have an unlimited access Internet account, you may want to consider using an offline newsreader, such as Free Agent, TIFNY, or X News, which are available from the Tucows Web site.

So many newsreaders are available for downloading from the Web that you can experiment with them to see which one you like best. Using one of the search engines discussed later in this chapter, try searching for *newsreader*. With so many options, it's worth spending a little time finding the one that will make researching easiest for you.

Finding and Getting What You Want

First of all, what do you want? Help solving a problem? Utilities? Background information? What you want drives where you go to look for it.

Getting Advice

Due to their interactive nature, forums and newsgroups are the best places to get problem-solving advice. (Web site message boards come up third, but are improving, as stated earlier.) Sometimes, you can get lucky and someone's asked the question before you did, but most of the time it's easiest if you go ahead and ask anyway.

Tip

If the forum or newsgroup in which you plan to post a question has a list of Frequently Asked Questions, read the FAQs before posting to make sure that your solution isn't in it.

Reading and Posting in Newsgroups

Earlier in this chapter, I discussed some of the places in which you can find newsreaders and some of the decent features you can look for. When you're first using a newsreader, one of the features that you'll *definitely* want is a good sort mechanism that makes it easy for you to find newsgroups to post to or read.

Why? I just updated the list of newsgroups that one of my newsreaders knows about. Guess how many newsgroups it knows about? 500? 2000? 5000? I lost track at 28,000.

Browsing more than 28,000 newsgroups takes more time and energy than I have, so there's got to be a way to organize them. There is, in the form of the newsgroups' prefix. Many (not all) newsgroups are sorted by domain:

alt. Stands for *alternative*—the discussions here are probably a little weird, as just about anything goes in these groups.

comp. These newsgroups are, broadly speaking, computer-based. They may be computer-related humor or Sound Blaster installation hints. The exact nature of the discussion depends on which group you're talking about, but the discussions should in some way touch on computers (even if it's about how evil they are).

misc. Hard to fit into any particular category, these groups might cover topics such as good techie books, militia activity, and home schooling.

news. These newsgroups generally cover network and newsgroup-related technical issues.

rec. These groups are recreation-oriented, covering just about any topic that you could think of for recreation.

soc. These groups deal with social and cultural issues.

talk. These groups are for those who like debate. Whatever you feel like arguing about, it's probably covered here.

There's a lot of crossover. You can probably start a flame war on a `comp.` newsgroup that would do credit to an `alt.` newsgroup by posting an "NT is better than Linux!" message if you're so inclined, but that's more or less how the usual domain breakdown shakes out. Not all newsgroups fall into one of these domains, however. Thus, it's useful to have a newsgroup reader that sorts groups not only by domain, but by topic. For example, as shown in Figure 30.2, the Offline Usenet Interface (OUI) from Dvorak provides a place for you to enter keywords by which to sort newsgroups.

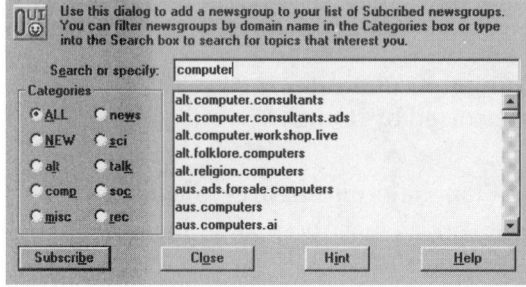

Figure 30.2

Some readers let you sort newsgroups based on keywords.

As you can see, a search for *computer* gets newsgroups not in the `comp` or `news` domains. Note, however, that this list does *not* include some newsgroups that I know (from personal experience) are computer-related, because those newsgroups don't have the word *computer* in their names. In other words, don't assume that if the keywords you supply to find information about your Super-Sender modem don't net anything, then no one is talking about your SuperSender modem. You just need to start surfing the groups themselves to see what people are talking about, or you can search by using one of the Web search engines such as AltaVista (`www .altavista.com`), Lycos (`http://www.lycos.com`), Tech-Web Search (`http://www.techweb.com`), Northern Light (`http://www.northernlight.com`), or Google (`www .google.com`). Many search engines today will pick up Web-based messaging as well as (sometimes) newsgroup messaging and include them as searchable topics.

When you need help with a problem and you don't know where to start looking, think about keywords associated with your difficulty. In your newsreader, you can see the way that newsgroups are named. Based on that naming scheme, identify the parts of your problem that might be in the name of a newsgroup. For instance, if you want to ask advice about choosing a SCSI controller to work with your system running Windows NT Workstation, that gives you several good potential keywords: *SCSI*, *NT*, and *configure*. In this case, I'd probably start with SCSI, since that's really what the problem is about. You can see one result of this search in Figure 30.3.

Figure 30.3

Results of a search for *SCSI* in newsgroup names

From this, you can choose a newsgroup that looks likely (perhaps `comp.periphs.scsi`), go to it, and read a little of the message traffic already posted to see whether it looks like people are talking about subjects related to your problem.

If no SCSI newsgroups seem to fit the bill, you can try *NT* instead. There's a trick to this one, though: newsreaders aren't case-sensitive, and most don't let you distinguish between searching for whole words only and searching for part of a word. Therefore, if you search for *nt* only, you'll get the NT hits, but you'll also get any other newsgroups with names that have *nt* in any form. (Obviously, this point doesn't apply to just NT, but to any combination of letters that have significance on their own but can also be part of a word.) So this time, if you search for *.nt*, you'll get results like the ones in shown in Figure 30.4.

Figure 30.4

Results of a search for *.nt* in newsgroup names

This search still found some newsgroups not focused on Windows NT, but it's better than the results that you would have gotten by searching for *nt* by itself. Scrolling down the list, you notice that there's a newsgroup called `comp.os.ms-windows.nt.setup.hardware`. That looks more promising, so you go to it, read some of the messages already posted, and post your question if it doesn't look like it has already been asked recently. Then, you can check back into the newsgroup at intervals to see whether anyone has replied to your posting.

Warning

There isn't much that you can do about this, but be advised that if you post to a newsgroup, you're likely to get on the mailing list for get-rich-quick schemes—even ones having nothing to do with what you posted about.

Netiquette

This chapter is about research, not manners, but manners can play a significant role in determining whether your research results pay off. Remember, no one *has* to answer your questions.

- DON'T WRITE IN ALL CAPITAL LETTERS. THIS IS CONSIDERED SHOUTING AND IS RUDE.

- The more traffic a newsgroup or forum experiences (that is, the more new messages are posted each time you visit), the more likely it is that someone will see your posting and reply to it.

- Be specific in message headers. "Help!" is too vague to grab my attention; "Need to restore hard disk configuration information" is more effective.

- Explain your situation briefly, but completely, at the beginning of the message. If it's a troubleshooting question, describe what you've done so far and any relevant parts of your configuration. People are more likely to reply to your posts if they know the background.

- Don't make posts longer than they need to be. First, reading onscreen is harder than reading hard copy, and paging through messages is wearisome. Second, people are paying to download and read your messages—don't give them junk.

- Don't post a question in more than one section in an online forum. If it's in the wrong section, the forum sysop will move it to the correct one. (Posting a question in more than one forum at a time is sometimes appropriate, however, if you're trying to get different points of view.) Posting the same question to more than one newsgroup is sometimes acceptable if the groups are not too similar in topic and the question fits into more than one category, but keep it to a minimum.

- Be polite. The people who are replying to your posts are doing *you* a favor. For heaven's sake, don't be rude to them, even if you disagree with their conclusions. Everyone can see your posts, not just their intended recipient.

- If you encounter anyone breaking these rules, don't lecture them about it. If the forum or newsgroup is moderated, the moderator will do so. If it isn't, I assure you that someone else will take care of it and you won't have to look like a scold.

Getting Patches, Drivers, or Utilities

Web sites, MSN forums, FTP sites, and newsgroups devoted to binary files may have drivers, utilities, or patches available for downloading.

Note

Newsgroups actually aren't a terrific source of utilities. Many of the groups devoted to binary files have names such as `alt.binaries.pictures.hamster`, and the ones devoted to computer-related binary files don't get much traffic.

As always, when downloading files, keep these things in mind:

▶ Shareware is not freeware. If you use a shareware product, then you're implicitly agreeing to pay the shareware's author for the software once the evaluation period has expired.

▶ Downloading large files can take a long time, and if there's an error on the line during the download, you may have to repeat it. If the telephone line that you're using for your modem has call-waiting, disable it before connecting.

Tip

To disable call-waiting before connecting to the Internet, preface the telephone number to dial with *70. For example, if the number to your local node was 555-1234, you'd configure your system to dial *70,555-1234.

▶ It's rare that a virus is uploaded to a moderated forum, but it can happen. Before running any program on your system, it's a good idea to virus-check it first. (PC viruses, recall, can exist only in executable files or Office documents containing macros, so other binary files and message threads don't need to be checked for viruses.)

▶ Copyright laws apply to electronic documents. You can't, for example, download a white paper that someone's written, remove their name, and substitute your own.

Web Sites

Unless you know the exact URL for the Web site that has the file you want to download, it's usually easiest to use one of the many Web search engines to search for the *type* of file that you want (see "Using Web Search Engines" later in this chapter). If you want benchmark tools, search for *benchmark*; for newsreaders, search for *newsreader*, and so forth. For drivers, try searching for the vendor's name plus the word *driver*. The parts of the Web are so interlinked that many utilities and drivers are available from more than one site.

Once you find a site with files for downloading, click the link to the file and choose to save it to your machine.

Sometimes the official product Web site isn't the best place to look for documentation. For instance, on one occasion I was looking for the documentation for an Adaptec SCSI host adapter, the AHA-2490. Intrepidly, I searched first for *AHA-2490 documentation* with AltaVista. When that engine produced no useful-looking sites, I tried the same search with Excite (if I don't find anything that looks close in the first 10, I tend to assume that I need to change either the query parameters or the search engine). Bingo! Six Adaptec sites topped the list! (Of course, number seven is a site for ordering skin-care products, but I resisted temptation and didn't check it out to see how in the world the name of a SCSI host adapter netted me an online beauty salon.) So, after entering Adaptec's personal space and moving to the Support section, I used the site's internal search engine. I searched for the word *documentation* to see where I should be looking for the files I needed. Unfortunately, this is what I saw when I got the results:

```
Q. Is technical documentation available for
   Adaptec hardware and software products? How
   do I get it?
```

A. You can call Adaptec's Literature Hotline at (800)-934-2766, and request Technical Reference manuals or User's Guides for our hardware. Software manuals are available with the purchase of Adaptec software.

Hmmm. This wasn't exactly the answer that I wanted—I wanted this documentation *now*, not after it was mailed to me. (Internet access really encourages instant gratification.) As it happened, using a slightly different search, I found the documentation at the Memory Lane Computers site, but the point is that Adaptec's site didn't contain the documentation with jumper settings that I required—a third-party site did.

A good rule of thumb when researching via the Internet is to go to the manufacturer's Web site first, learn everything you can, and then expand your search to related sites (tech sites with reviews of a product, or sites where users may be asking questions and getting help with that product) and newsgroups.

FTP Sites

FTP sites are servers that hold collections of files available for downloading. Although Web sites are now the most common places to find files for downloading, some FTP sites are still good resources for information, software, and drivers.

Unless you've got an account on the FTP server that you're trying to reach—if you're not sure, you probably don't—you'll have to log in anonymously, providing your e-mail address for a password. (Providing your e-mail isn't always necessary, but it is polite because that lets the FTP administrator know who's been there.) Not all sites support anonymous login, but most of the ones that you're likely to need do.

How can you get to FTP sites? One way is through your Web browser.

In the address space where URLs are displayed in your Web browser, type the address of the FTP site you want, starting with *FTP* instead of *HTTP*. For example, the address might look like this:

`ftp://ftp.megatrends.com`. (For the curious, you can pull down utilities and Windows NT information from this site.)

Tip

If you don't know the address you want, you can check out an FTP Web search site (such as the one operated by Lycos at `http://ftpsearch.lycos.com/`).

When you use a Web browser to FTP, you are automatically connected to FTP sites with anonymous login—no extra steps required. If a site does not support anonymous login, then you'll know it: you'll be prompted for a password that you won't have and have to cancel out in disgrace.

By the way, it's easy to find drivers on the Web. A number of driver sites maintain complete listings of all available and updated drivers. Two that come to mind are DriverGuide (`www.driverguide.com`) and the CNET site I mentioned earlier, WinFiles (`www.winfiles.com`). DriverGuide offers a free membership in the "users helping users" system of driver collection. WinFiles maintains a large database of driver information from practically all the vendors that exist. Plus, almost all vendors that have a Web site have a Support link on their home page and a relatively easy way to locate driver downloads.

Cautions about Online Troubleshooting

Throughout this chapter I've been talking about how online services and the Internet can be a marvelous help to you when you're trying to research something related to your computer or to get help with a problem. They can help, but now it's time for some cautions to go along with the cheerleading. (Most of this stuff will probably seem really obvious, but bear with me.)

Don't Believe Everything You Hear

There's a lot of misinformation in the PC world. It's not actual lying, but it's stuff that's misheard, or corrected later but the person telling you missed the correction, or misunderstood because the listener didn't have enough background to remember the information correctly. The trouble is that a lot of this misinformation gets repeated until it has a life of its own. Some is harmless, such as an assertion that I saw repeated that Microsoft was responsible for changing the PCMCIA card's name to the PC Card (they weren't), but some is not. If someone suggests a drastic measure in response to a problem that you've posted a question about, I suggest that you hang on for a little while and see whether you get any other responses. Surely you've met people in person who claim to know more than their experience covers; they exist in cyberspace, too— and they're harder to strangle when you follow their suggestion and something goes desperately wrong.

When in Doubt, Check for Viruses

First, a dose of reality: viruses aren't a problem for most sites. FTP sites, for example, rarely allow anonymous logins to upload files to their sites. No company wants the public relations nightmare of being responsible for a virus infection.

That said, you might just be careful of sites that are not representative of a particular company and cater to those who might enjoy a little rule-breaking before breakfast. If you come across a site that offers to let you download games and (possibly) pirated software, or quite openly caters to hackers, it's a good idea to check the files that you download before running them. Once again, only executable files can contain PC viruses, so you needn't worry about document files (with the exception of Office documents that have macros in them) or messages.

Note

Macro viruses represent the first cross-platform virus and the only PC virus that can be contained in a document. This class of virus is discussed in more detail in Chapter 15, "An Overview of Viruses."

Don't Give Out Personal Information

When posting in public areas such as newsgroups or forums, don't give out any personal information that you don't want the world to know about, such as your home address, your telephone number, credit card or checking account information, or the like. This information isn't impossible for someone who's got a little time on their hands and nothing better to do to figure out, but that doesn't mean that you have to make it easy for them.

Places to Go, People to See

In the course of this chapter, I've identified some of the ways that you can find what you're looking for in the far reaches of cyberspace. However, in the course of my travels, I've found some useful places (or keywords to places) that I'll include here, to perhaps save you a little time.

Note, however, that in all these online services, groups and sites come and go (especially when you're talking about Web sites). Also, the character of existing groups or Web sites may change. This information is not guaranteed.

Note

I've probably left out dozens of useful sources of information, but this is meant to be a starting point, not a definitive guide to researching online. If you know of a newsgroup, forum, or Web site that I haven't mentioned here but you think could be helpful to those repairing or upgrading their PCs, please *don't* e-mail me with the information. I'll find it.

Finding Helpful Web Sites

Use the Web search engines I've already suggested to start, and then begin asking friends, colleagues, and other Web users which sites they recommend for help.

Some of these sites will have reviews and information only, while others may have that plus areas where you can post questions, get answers, and maybe even help out someone else. An unspoken rule of the technical Internet is that in exchange for getting help from those more knowledgeable than you, you in turn help someone else less experienced than you are.

Finding Helpful Usenet Newsgroups

As I've discussed, there are tens of thousands of newsgroups out there. Not all of them will be available from your news server (some subscribe to only a limited number, and there's not much that you can do about that), but there's enough that you should be able to get help with almost anything.

The best troubleshooting groups seem to have the word *hardware* in them. This keyword nets you a plethora of useful newsgroups:

▶ If you're building a computer from scratch, you might be interested in checking out `alt.comp.hardware`. The discussions that I've seen there tend to focus on what components will work together and pricing, with some postings advertising components for sale.

▶ An even better how-to site in terms of traffic (more traffic means more people to see your posts) is `alt.comp.hardware.homebuilt`. (An apparent offshoot of this one, `alt.comp.hardware.homedesigned`, gets less traffic, some of which is cross-posted from `alt.comp.hardware.homebuilt`.)

Note

`alt.comp.hardware.homebuilt` is a good source of advice for those building or repairing homemade machines, but not those upgrading store-built machines. If you've got questions about IRQ settings on a sound card you're installing, better to stick with `alt.comp.hardware` or `comp.hardware`.

▶ Finally, `comp.hardware` is an active newsgroup and covers many repair and installation issues.

Why *hardware* and not more-specific words? Traffic levels, mostly. More-specific groups devoted to particular hardware questions (such as I/O transfer) seem to have too little traffic to do any good. I recommend checking out the newsgroups discussed above, as the IBM and Microsoft sites generally don't look as good as the generic sites in terms of response rates and relevant material.

Oddly enough, some seemingly computer-related keywords really don't net you much help in the hardware department:

Setup The groups with this word in their name seem to be software-related, particularly operating systems. (Then again, if you've got the PC trouble taken care of and you're ready to move on to software, these newsgroups might be able to help you after all.)

Boot Typing this word gets you music and video bootleg groups. Not much good there.

Computer This nets computer-oriented newsgroups, but so many newsgroups—technical or not—have the word *computer* in their name that the results of a search are a bit overwhelming. Searching for *comp.* has a similar problem—even though the `comp.` domain is computer-oriented, the hundreds of newsgroups that have *comp.* in their name are not necessarily so. Try being more specific about what aspect of the computer you want to talk about.

CPU   This nets hardly any results (and of three CPU groups on my news server, one is in Chinese, and one is a newsgroup currently holding nothing but a get-rich-quick scheme—you can tell how little traffic the group sees because no one has bothered to tell off the poster yet, and it's a week old.)

Using Web Search Engines

Keeping up with the Web sites out there (and listing every Web site that might be potentially interesting to you) is an impossible task. The most important thing that you need to know about researching on the Web is which search engine will make researching easiest. These aren't all the search engines available, but these are some of the ones that I've used most or like best.

Note

Before deciding that a particular topic isn't referenced on the Web, try a few search engines. For example, a search for *cyrix* under Yahoo! netted 12 hits; the same search under WebCrawler netted 434. One of the reasons for this is that not all search engines work the same way. Some, for example, list hits by the number of times that your query criteria appear in a document; others by how early the hit appears in a document.

Northern Light

Although it's one of the newer search engines in the Internet neighborhood, Northern Light (`www.northernlight.com`) works pretty well, and helps categorize the search results you may get by querying (searching) on something like *Iomega Zip drives* or *alternative backup drives*.

TechWeb

Although TechWeb (`www.techweb.com`) is an Information Technology (IT) Web site and not strictly a search engine per se, use their Advanced Search option to investigate various computing topics. Also check out their links at the bottom of the page.

Ask Jeeves

Ask Jeeves (`www.askjeeves.com`) is a search engine dressed up as a proper butler where you perform searches phrased as regular questions, such as "Where can I buy a DVD-ROM drive?" or "What kind of ISDN modems are available?" Here, you still have to sort through the chafe to get to the fiber, but Jeeves will attempt to interpret what you want several different ways, so you can usually get in the neighborhood of where you're trying to go.

Yahoo!

I find Yahoo! (`http://search.yahoo.com`) to be less useful for technical topics than social ones. Its indices are limited and it puts too much extra text in the search results for my taste. If you're not quite sure what you're looking for and just want to browse, Yahoo's browse function is pretty good. Skip the word search function altogether, and choose Browse to move to the Computers section.

Lycos

One of the original search engines, Lycos (`www.lycos.com`) is still a default standard for many. I just performed a few searches on Lycos for newer types of PC drives coming on the market, and noticed the search brought up a nicely balanced mixture of independent technical articles and reviews, manufacturer sites, references to them posted on various Web message boards, and vendors selling these faster drives.

Google

Like Northern Light, Google is a relative newcomer to the Web search engine competition, but it provides an interesting alternative. For instance, I just searched using Lycos and Google on the words *Firewire drives* and got different hits on each.

This underscores another point: don't necessarily get yourself locked into using one search engine. Sometimes, the best results can be had by regularly hitting at least three to do the same search and comparing results. Different search engines may use different criteria, giving you much different results even when you search on the same phrase.

WebCrawler

I like WebCrawler (`http://www.webcrawler.com`) quite a bit. First, it shows you more hits per page by default than most other search engines do: the usual number is about 10, but WebCrawler shows 25. This is possible because, by default, the search engine shows only the titles of pages that meet your criteria, not a summary. (Because many search engines use quotes from the page text as summaries, they usually aren't very helpful, so I don't find this to be a drawback.) Like most other engines, WebCrawler also lists the total number of hits that your search produced.

Excite

When researching, I tend to use Excite (`http://www.excite.com`) fairly frequently, mostly because it turns up the more technical topics rather than marketing-oriented ones. Excite also comes with a fair text-searchable newsreader—you can search for messages with certain words in the text, but the reader does not do thread handling, so you can't read messages before or after the one that came up in the search. However, even this limited capability can help you identify newsgroups that you'd like to visit. Excite can also search Internet classifieds—nice if you're interested in picking up used hardware.

For me, the main faults of this search engine are twofold. First, it doesn't report the total number of hits generated from a search (a valuable feature of many search engines that helps you determine whether you should refine your search a little). And although it provides useful information about the size of a page, this information is hard to pick out of the entries because of the font used and the way that the entries are structured. On the plus side, however, the search logic tends to come up with useful hits.

AltaVista

AltaVista (`http://altavista.com`), now owned by Compaq, is another useful search engine. First, it's one of the most complete search engines available. Second, it tells you not only about how many hits your query found, but also (if you queried using more than one word) how many hits each of the words found. Best yet, you can use the advanced search techniques to use a limited set of Boolean operands (AND, OR, NOT, and NEAR) to refine your search. AltaVista also does Usenet searches as well as Web site searches.

That's a flying look at some of the search engines available on the Net. If none of these do the trick, try Infoseek (`www.infoseek.com`) or HotBot (`http://hotbot.lycos.com`). Or, to access a number of search engines all at once, check out Microsoft's search page at `http://lg.home.microsoft.com/search/ie5/searchsetup.asp`.

Picking a Search Engine

In general, these are the features that I find desirable in a search engine:

▶ A report of the total number of hits generated from a search—while a few hits are easier to read through, a lot of hits may yield a lot more information for you; a Web search engine that traditionally gets only a few hits on a major topic may not be a very robust search engine.

▶ A large number of hits displayed simultaneously (I find it faster to scroll down a page than to move to another page to see the next 10 hits).

▶ As little extraneous text surrounding the hits as possible, so that the links are easy to see, or the capability to customize the query results to show more or less surrounding information.

It's often quicker to go to nonofficial Web sites that link to the official ones, rather than going to the opening page of an official site and wandering through a maze of linked documents. For example, if you need HP scanner drivers, go first to a third-party site that contains links to a bunch of different manufacturers' scanner download sites. When you activate the HP link there, you'll move immediately to the part of the HP site where drivers are stored.

Finding Useful FTP Sites

FTP sites are sufficiently numerous that it's easier to suggest ways to find the one you want than to provide a list of all sites that hold files pertaining to a particular topic.

FTP with the World Wide Web

It's easy to find FTP sites from the Web: just look for one of the many index pages with links to them. Following are two that I've found to be helpful—both incorporate a search engine, so you're not dependent on the (limited or nonexistent) search capabilities of your Web browser.

The best way to get access to public FTP servers is by downloading a copy of CuteFTP from Tucows. The free version is advertiser supported, but it includes a complete list of public and corporate FTP servers. Use one of the search engines mentioned earlier to look for a current (many are quite old and outdated) list of anonymous FTP servers, since these can change pretty rapidly. The freeware FTP/2 from Kaufman Software does not have a list of servers, but it also has neither the overhead nor the advertisements that CuteFTP does.

Finding Microsoft Network Forums

For the purposes of researching how to upgrade and maintain your PC (check the title), the Hardware forum on MSN/Microsoft Computing Central is probably your best bet. It's got an active membership, and a variety of question topics and skill levels are represented. (I haven't seen anyone laughed at for asking a newbie question yet.) In fact, one very basic question about what RAM was got some people out of the woodwork admitting that they didn't know either; thanks for asking. The traffic there is not as heavy as some hardware-related Usenet newsgroups, but it's not bad.

In all, MSN Computing Central (`http://computing central.msn.com`) maintains about 30 computing forums, running through a range of operating systems (not just Microsoft-based: Unix, Linux, and OS/2 too), telephony and PC communications, games, and Safe Computing (virus and network security).

If you're looking for more product-specific information, you might want to check out one of the vendor forums. The easiest way to find a forum that discusses the topic in which you're interested is to use the Find tool (discussed earlier in this chapter) to search for instances in MSN of a particular keyword.

Troubleshooting Tips

Getting assistance from a remote source always presents some degree of difficulty, just because the person who is helping you can't see your system. This puts the responsibility squarely on your shoulders to present your problem as clearly as possible, erring on the side of offering too much rather than too little information.

In a recent informal survey of several managers who run online technical support forums for MSN Computing Central, almost all reported the same thing: users often don't give enough information when first presenting their problem to get useful help.

These are real examples taken from just one morning's online help requests:

"Help. I'm getting an error message. What do I do?" is all one user writes, not mentioning *which* error message, let alone where it was observed, or what might have happened as a result.

"Why doesn't the drive I just added work?" writes another, failing to provide even basic details about what kind of drive, how it was prepared and configured, or what operating system is being used.

"My PC beeps. What do I do to stop it????? Also, why does it crash when I use my favorite program??? Huh???? That's really dumb!!!!!!!!!!!!!!!! And why couldn't I install Windows 2000???" types another person. All PCs beep unless they're dead, but because no information is provided, we don't know if it's beeping unusually. We don't know what program is causing the user's PC to crash, or whether the user is getting any error messages before the crash that might give an indication of what's wrong. As for why Windows 2000 wouldn't install, we're left wondering here, too, because there's no information on what happened trying to install it. Finally, this exemplifies a common myth about online tech support: that more punctuation—like exclamation marks to highlight frustration—will take the place of providing details about the PC and its problem. Sadly, it doesn't.

If you find someone able and willing to help you, the last thing you want to do is force the person into a position of having to pull teeth to extract information from you—it's a waste of their time and yours—and you probably want to solve this sooner rather than later. So present basic details about your system and the problem at hand when you post the first time, and if you reply, reference the previous messages. You don't have to write a book, but you need to offer basic facts. Important details to include are:

- Type of machine, such as Pentium II, and a quick overview of what you have installed (that is, 64MB RAM, 4GB hard drive with 2GB free).

- Operating system used—check your version and report it.

- If receiving an error message, provide the *exact* wording and whether it can be reproduced when it occurs.

- The last thing(s) you were doing before the problem was noticed or reported, including any hardware, software, or upgrades installed or removed.

- Exact steps you've taken already to try to resolve it (important in case something you tried was in error, and a second problem could mask the solution of the original problem).

- Any other relevant information, such as noting an LED power indicator not on when it should be, or failing to boot, or the PC beeping a specific number of times on bootup.

That's about all there is to researching online. At this point, you should have a good idea of how you can get connected to the outside world, the tools available to you, and how to find what you need. I'll see you out there.

Whether you're connecting to AOL, the Internet, or The Microsoft Network, the rules are much the same:

▶ The answer is probably out there somewhere. Don't give up too easily.

▶ Most people like nothing more than to give advice, so never be afraid to ask.

31

This Old Computer

INTRODUCTION

I've been working with computers in one way or another now for decades. As a result, I've seen computers evolve from giant, room-filling monsters such as the Univac that predicted the presidential election results in the early days of television, all the way to computers so small that they fit easily in the palm of a hand. And in all that time, one thing I've learned has been universally true: every new computer is faster, smaller, and cheaper, and has greater capacity than the last.

What does this mean to you? Well, for starters:

▶ Any computer you buy today will already be becoming obsolete while you're taking it home.

▶ The options you buy for your computer today will be cheaper tomorrow.

▶ No matter what your computer can do today, you'll want it to do something new tomorrow.

What can you do? The answer is actually pretty simple: *never buy anything for your computer that you won't be using now.* Why? Because (as I just mentioned) the thing you want today will be faster, cheaper, and generally better tomorrow. So if you won't need it until tomorrow, wait until tomorrow to buy it.

A common mistake newcomers to computers make is assuming that they are buying an appliance, like a refrigerator, that will be good for 10 years. Computers just aren't like that. While it's true that the computer you buy today will be capable of performing the same *tasks* in 10 years (assuming nothing breaks), *your needs will be different.* If you buy your computer and never upgrade its components, your computer will become obsolete in three to four years. If you're adventurous, however, you (or your favorite service rep) can selectively upgrade your components over time and extend the life of your computer, and its capability to make your life easier.

The March of Technology

Back in the "good old days," personal computers were not a business at all. They were a hobby. They were the hobby of people who loved technology. They dabbled in electronics. Actually, a lot of them did much more than dabble. Most were also engineers. Engineers who designed and built radios, TVs, and just about any kind of electronic test equipment that you might be able to think of.

These people were engineers because they loved the technology. So back in the mid-'70s, when Intel produced the 4004 chip, the first microprocessor (they originally called it a microcomputer), it opened the door to a new world for us. Interestingly, Intel really didn't know what they'd done at first. They developed the 4004 processor to solve a problem for one of their customers. Figure 31.1 shows the 4004 processor.

Figure 31.1

Intel's 4004 microprocessor chip

The problem Intel needed to solve was that their client, Busicom, was competing with several companies that were producing new versions of their circuits very quickly. Busicom needed a new way to bring their new designs to market faster. Intel found a way.

At that time, whenever a company developed a new circuit design, it took them months to lay out new circuit boards and manufacture them. It was a process that had been refined and refined, but they had hit a wall. They couldn't get any faster.

Intel proposed something revolutionary. To understand what they did, you need to know that electronics firms were beginning to use components called Programmable Array Logic (PAL) integrated circuits. These devices contained small arrays of logic circuits that could be customized to perform specific tasks by burning certain circuit paths in the chip. The PAL enabled companies to bring new products to market faster because they could include a number of these customizable parts in the design and make changes to the circuit without redesigning the board.

Trouble was, the PALs had limitations. First, they were small and contained only a few logic gates. And second, they could be customized only once. After that, they were as unchangeable as any other chip; so if you wanted to make another change, you had to get new PALs. (Today's PALs are a *lot* more powerful than the ones we had back in the old days.)

Note

Computers compute with the help of logic, and *logic gates* using Boolean algebra are the components on the chip that make this possible. The logic gates are hardwired into the chip while Boolean algebra dictates the form of the gate and how we use it. Electrical signals (the things that make up bits) go into the logic gates and are compared using logical operations such as AND, OR, and NOT. For example, an AND gate compares at least two values and results in TRUE (or 1 using binary notation) if they are both identical. If not, the result is FALSE (or 0).

Intel's idea was to use a programmable device that could perform many tasks based upon programming. And that device could be reprogrammed at any time, even when it was running another program. They had developed a part that was designed to replace a lot of logic chips. In fact, though, what they had invented was the first single-chip computer. (Well, not quite, since it required some support chips, but it was amazing nonetheless.)

The 4004 was programmed in products to couple the processor with a ROM chip. The program was stored in the ROM, and the computer did whatever task was programmed into the ROM. Later, EPROM (Erasable/Programmable Read Only Memory) chips were developed. To erase one of the EPROMS, you exposed the logic wafer inside the chip to ultraviolet (UV) light passing through an open window on the top of the chip.

Intel's programmable chip (the 4004) was a great idea, but in the end Busicom backed out, and Intel was left with a part that was developed but had no customers.

What could Intel do?

They sold it to hobbyists, engineers, and anyone with the "bug." Remember the people I was talking about before? The ones who loved technology? They became the first real customers for Intel's 4004 chip. But it wasn't long before they wanted more. You see, Intel never intended to make computers—just a chip that enabled circuits to be made faster and easier. Now they were being asked to take their relatively simple, 4-bit processor and turn it into something that hobbyists could use to make a real computer . . . a *personal* computer.

So Intel made the 8008—the first 8-bit microprocessor—and the rest is history.

Hobbyists who were passionate about technology were initially Intel's primary customers for this new class of product. Intel sold parts faster than they could make them, because they had customers who were obsessed. Their own engineers joined in the frenzy, which resulted in newer, faster, more capable parts streaming out of the new technology. Computers doubled and tripled in speed and power in a heartbeat. Initially, it was passion for technology that drove the market. But in the end, it was money that drove the market.

More and more people in the computer business were becoming multimillionaires, and soon the drive was on to make better, faster, and cheaper parts because it meant making more money. That's why the computer industry moves so quickly. It's designed to make the makers rich.

But it also makes the end users confused. In the early days of computing, most people had no interest in computers. In fact, most people were only barely aware of them. But with the introduction of a single computer program—VisiCalc, the first "killer app"—people found themselves compelled to buy computers. A company, noticing that its competitors had computers, felt compelled to buy them so as to compete more effectively. And once again, the rest is history.

The whole point of this history lesson is to show how (and why) computers got here as they are, and to explain why technology has advanced so quickly. This is a business in which the only way you can stand still is to "run as fast as you can." So grab your hat, your checkbook, and your old computer—we're going to start running.

Worth Their Weight in Chips

Okay, so now you have a decision to make. Is your computer an old computer?

C'mon, didn't you read the previous section? If you have a computer, you have an old computer. The question is, *how* old is your computer? There's a saying I used to hear when I was a kid: "worth its weight in gold." It meant that something was very valuable. Nowadays, gold is worth about $300 an ounce. That's about the weight of a silver dollar. Today, we have a new measure of value: silicon. Well, not exactly silicon, but the circuits that we implant onto the surface of silicon. Figure 31.2 shows a microprocessor on the tip of a finger, weighing maybe $1/50$ of an ounce. Depending upon the actual part, one of these can be worth more than $1000! And sometimes much, much more.

Computers are made of these silicon chips with circuits built into the very structure of the chip (hence, integrated circuits). How much they're worth depends on a lot of factors, but nothing has more influence on the value of a microprocessor than its age. For example, when 80286s were first introduced, they were worth hundreds of dollars. Today they are worth only a few cents.

Figure 31.2

A microprocessor on
the tip of a finger

What to Keep and What to Toss

The fact that a computer is old doesn't necessarily mean that you
should throw it away lock, stock, and barrel. Let's take a look at
which components you can salvage, and which ones you should consider replacing.

New Life for a 486?

Let's take a look at an old 486DX/66 system. It includes a 486 motherboard; 8MB RAM; a 1.2MB, 3½-inch floppy drive; a 124MB hard
drive; a 14,400bps modem; a 15-inch VGA monitor; an early inkjet
printer; a 4X CD-ROM drive; and ISA sound and video cards.

Why did I start with a 486? Because anything older wouldn't be
worth upgrading, and there are almost no parts that you can use to
upgrade them. And everything newer can be upgraded. Of course,
the newer they are, the easier they are to upgrade.

So what can you do to make this system more current? Here's the
list, but be aware that upgrading all these components will cost

about the same as putting together a totally new system, will be more trouble, and will not work as well.

"All right," I hear you asking, "if it's a bad idea to upgrade a 486, why should I even read this information?"

Because you don't need to replace all the components. The best advice I can give you for a computer as old as a 486 is to keep using it, as it is, for as long as it does what you need and as long as the parts keep working. This, by the way, is good advice for any computer that you have. If you need a faster computer, save your data and get a new system. In Chapter 32, "Building the Ultimate Computer," I'll talk about the benefits of buying a new computer versus building one yourself.

If you decide to keep using your old computer but parts such as your CD-ROM drive or monitor start to fail, you can replace some of the parts one or two at a time to keep it alive. So if your old 486 is still adequate for your needs, but something is broken, here's what you can replace:

Video card If your old VGA card bites the dust, you can replace it with a new card, but most of the new ones are PCI and AGP, ports not available on a 486 motherboard. You'll need to search for an old ISA video board to replace your bad one.

Floppy drive Standard 3½-inch floppy drives haven't changed much over the last several years, so you should be able to replace a defective one with a minimum of fuss.

Hard drive If you need to replace your hard drive, make sure to get one that is compatible with your BIOS, or upgrade your BIOS at the same time. Older machines don't recognize drives larger than 512MB, and an old BIOS may not even recognize your new drive. You should also make sure to purchase the same type of hard drive that you are replacing. Replace a SCSI drive with another SCSI, or IDE with an IDE.

Power supply This component fails more often than any other in older systems. This is primarily because the power supplies that came with the systems were often designed to meet the needs of the basic system but had very little to spare. So when users added boards or drives, they exceeded the capacity of the supply. If the power supply on one of the older systems dies, you may need to get a new case as well, since many of the new power supplies won't fit in older cases—they're too small.

Motherboard This is it. The big upgrade. When you're done with this one, your faithful old 486 will have a new brain. It can even become a Pentium III. But since you'll probably want to replace a lot more than the motherboard if you do this upgrade, (putting old, slow parts with a new, fast motherboard is a bad idea) you should probably read the next chapter before proceeding. There you'll learn how to build your ultimate computer from scratch.

Save Your Data!

When people think of a computer, they generally think of the actual physical equipment—the CPU, monitor, keyboard, and so on. But the fact is, the most important part of your computer is the information that it contains. You can always replace the CPU, the keyboard, or the mouse. But once data is lost, the only way to get it back is to reconstruct it. The process of reconstruction can be, by far, more expensive than the entire computer. It's the information in the computer that makes it *your* computer. It has your bookkeeping, your addresses, your letters, your taxes, and your games—everything that you do with your computer that *makes* it your computer lives in the data.

So when you upgrade your system, make sure that your data follows you. Here's how you do it.

Backing Up to Removable Media

There are a few kinds of removable computer media. There are cartridge hard drives such as the Zip and Jaz drives (shown in Figure 31.3), tape drives such as HP's Colorado drives, and CD writers (and read/write CDs). All of these have their upsides and their downsides. The real benefit to removable media is that you can easily transport your data from one place to another. The only real down-side to removable media is that it loads more slowly than it does from your primary hard drive.

Figure 31.3

Removable media drives

To move your data to a removable drive such as a Jaz or Zip drive, install the drivers for the unit you have and reboot with the drive connected and powered up. In Windows, it will appear as another drive in your My Computer window. Once installed, every removable drive behaves essentially like another hard drive.

You can also use Windows' Backup Wizard to save your data to a backup drive. To access Backup from Windows 95/98, choose Programs from the Start menu. Then choose Accessories ➢ System Tools ➢ Backup. Make sure that you have your backup drive plugged in and ready to go before you begin. Once there, the Backup Wizard will guide you through the process.

Backing Up to Tape

Backing up to a tape drive is similar to backing up to removable media, but since it's a serial device, not random access, it has some subtle differences. You can't just drag and drop files with most tape backup systems. You have to use a backup program to manage the process. Most tape drives come with some kind of backup software. If you don't like the features of the backup program that came with your drive, there are plenty of alternative programs out there to select from.

Backing Up Directly to Another Hard Drive

If you're going to be upgrading to a new hard drive, the fastest and probably best approach is to copy files directly from your old drive to your new one (see Figure 31.4). Most new drives include software to facilitate this. For example, Seagate drives have a program called FileCopy. This program creates an exact duplicate of your old drive's data on your new drive, where it can be run as if it were the original.

Figure 31.4

Hooking up both your new and old hard drives to the same system is probably the best way to transfer files from the old drive to the new drive.

When you install a new drive without removing the old one first, you need to run a program that tells your computer which drive is the old one and which is the new one. Then you set up the drive parameters (it's mostly automatic), partition and format the new drive, and go into Windows. From there, run FileCopy or a similar program, and the computer automatically transfers the files.

Once you're done, you can either remove your old drive or leave it in as a secondary drive. Either way, you switch the new drive to primary (since the newer one is usually both larger and faster), and off you go. If you remove the old drive, you can hold onto it as it is and you'll have an image backup of your system for emergencies. Remember though, that magnetic data is not everlasting—it needs to be renewed every few years if you want it to maintain its integrity. To do this with your old hard drive, just plug it in as your secondary drive and run SCANDISK. Then put it away for another five years or so.

Whatever you do, don't wait 10 years like I did with one system drive. The drive read once, and then the data became unreadable (yes, reading does remove a tiny bit of the signal strength). Under normal operating circumstances, you'll never run into this problem because you read and write data regularly. Your data, therefore, is always relatively current. But on a drive that's been sitting around for years, you can't read it to check what's there before you copy the data, since you may get only one read out of the drive.

You can transfer the entire content of the old drive to a new one, even if the new drive is not the same capacity, by using a program such as DriveCopy or Norton Ghost. These programs make a sector-by-sector copy of the complete contents, so the new drive looks identical to the old PC. This can be a great time-saver, because you don't have to reinstall Windows and all your programs on the new drive. After copying the old drive onto the new, you can then remove the old drive from the system and discard it, or reformat it and reuse it elsewhere.

Choosing an Upgrade Path

There are many reasons why you might want to upgrade your computer system. Many people upgrade because they learn about a tool or program and decide that they must have it, for one of these reasons:

▶ Their friend has it.

▶ They saw it in an ad.

▶ A salesman said it was cool.

These, by the way, are all the wrong reasons to upgrade. If you find yourself considering an upgrade because you want another "thing" on your computer, you're asking for trouble. The more "things" you have attached to your system, the slower it will perform and the more likely it is to crash. Every time you add another device driver or use up another IRQ or address line, there's a chance that all the other stuff on your system will stop working. (By the way, this is also true of any software you install.)

Most people add software and peripherals to their computers much as they would add a new CD to their music collection. Trouble is, unlike a music CD, programs alter the way your system works. Before you add another program (or anything else) to your system, make sure you really want it and will have a good use for it.

The right way to choose a peripheral or a new program is to find that you need your computer to be able to do something that it can't, then do some research to be sure that the new item will actually provide your computer with that new capability. For example, let's say that you have a true color ISA SVGA card in a machine without PCI or AGP slots. If you go out and buy the latest 3D 4X AGP video card and try to install it in your system, you're in for a nasty shock. It won't be possible. You'll have to take it back to the store and reinstall your older, less capable card.

Getting the picture?

In the preceding scenario, you went to a lot of trouble just to wind up in the same place you began. You logged wasted time and maybe lost money as well. If you had done a little research up front, you could have saved yourself all that time and effort.

If you really need an upgrade, then it's worth it. But if you don't *really* need it, look out—you may be asking for a lot of trouble for nothing. So be careful not to upgrade your computer just because you see or hear of something that sounds interesting. The best decision-making process to use for upgrading your computer is as follows:

1. Decide whether you need new functionality.

2. Research products/tools/techniques to determine which one(s) best meets your needs, and be sure they will integrate easily with your existing system to provide the functionality you seek.

3. Acquire new products/tools/techniques and install necessary components.

Ready to start upgrading? Okay then, let's go.

Upgrading a Computer

Before you begin any type of upgrade to your system—even installing a new software program—be sure that you've backed up all necessary data on your hard drive. If you haven't, stop reading and do it now. Skipping this step would be a terrible mistake.

Planning Your Upgrade

Computer owners usually have one of two basic types of computer systems—a home PC or a business PC (or a combination of the two). While these two categories often involve basically the same hardware, the computers tend to do different kinds of things. One is optimized to do home applications, and the other is optimized for business applications. When planning an upgrade, the decisions you make should be based on the type of system you have.

First, make a checklist of what you need the computer to do. Should it be faster? I know the answer to this is always "yes." But you need to ask yourself how much you're willing to pay for increased speed. Do you need new capabilities? Components that can provide these would include modems, networks, printers, scanners, and video cameras . . . you get the idea.

The following list includes most traditional computer hardware and peripherals; use it as a guide to create your own checklist for planning your upgrade. You may choose to add other unusual or esoteric components to your own list.

▶ Motherboard

▶ Microprocessor

▶ Memory

▶ Hard drive

▶ Floppy drive

▶ Removable media drive

▶ Tape drive

- Modem

- Home networking components

- Scanners

- Printers

- Cameras

- TV tuners (enabling you to receive television signals through your computer just like in a television)

The sections that follow discuss some of the individual components that you might consider upgrading.

Motherboards

Although your microprocessor is really the heart of your computer, virtually everything plugs into the motherboard. And today's motherboards have most of the I/O circuits on them as well. Current motherboards have the following:

- EIDE controllers for your:

  - Hard drive(s)

  - CD-ROM drive(s)

  - Internal removable media drive(s)

- Floppy controller

- Serial ports

- Parallel port

- USB port(s)

- PS/2 keyboard port

- PS/2 mouse port

- Video chip set (on some boards)

- Sound chip set (on some boards)

- PCI expansion slots

- ISA expansion slots

- AGP video slot (on some boards)

- Cache memory

- Memory slots

- Microprocessor socket and support circuits:

  - ZIF socket (on some boards)

  - Variable voltage circuitry

  - Variable processor bus speed

Although some of these items are pretty obvious, some are not so obvious. Let's take a look at what each of these does.

Before going out to buy a brand new motherboard, make sure it will fit your existing case. There are several different form factors for motherboards, which are all designed to fit the various cases that exist. These are broadly classified as AT or ATX.

EIDE Controllers

Most motherboards have two of these, labeled Primary and Secondary. Figure 31.5 shows a typical pair of EIDE connectors. By the way, as you may recall from earlier in the book, EIDE adapters will talk to both IDE and EIDE drives. In fact, some older boards actually have one EIDE (the Primary) and one IDE (the Secondary) instead of two EIDEs.

When you connect the data cables to the EIDE/IDE connectors, make sure that you align pin 1 of the cable with pin 1 of the connector.

EIDE
Connectors

Figure 31.5

Typical EIDE/IDE
connectors on a
motherboard

The other end of the data cable goes into the connectors on the appropriate drive. They are also labeled, usually on the bottom of the drive.

When you connect your drives, connect your boot hard drive to the Primary connector. Also, be sure to set it to Master. There's a jumper that determines whether a drive is the Master or the Slave drive. Every drive has a host adapter built into it that has the capability to control two drives. This allows two drives to share a single data cable. So when you set one of the drives to Slave, it turns its host adapter off. Setting it to Master sets it up to control two drives. On some drives, you need to remove all jumpers for a single drive. Others can control one or two drives if they are set to Master.

Microprocessor

Choosing an upgrade microprocessor can be a tough decision. At any given moment, a variety of processors are available from several manufacturers. The top three manufacturers are Intel, AMD, and Cyrix. Intel, of course, is the market leader. They invented the microprocessor and they lead the pack. That is, they set the standards. Everyone else has to follow the leader. AMD traditionally makes compatible processors that are almost always a little (or sometimes a lot) faster in one way or another than comparable Intel processors. Cyrix is usually the fastest of the pack for a given part, but they often sacrifice total compatibility for speed.

Another fact to be aware of is that the newest, fastest processors are almost always much more expensive than those that are just a bit slower. For example, recent pricing for a 500MHz Intel Pentium (which was the fastest processor at the time this book was being written) was about $800. The AMD K6-III-450, which is rated at 90 percent as fast as the 500MHz Intel Pentium, was about $250—less than a third of the price.

Floppy Controller

The floppy controller on the motherboard can control up to two floppy drives. The floppy drives also use a single cable, but instead of setting jumpers on the drives to select which is drive A: and which is drive B:, the cable itself is modified. The A: drive must be plugged into the connector that has a twist in the middle (see Figure 31.6).

Figure 31.6

The floppy cable that has a twist in it is for drive A:.

B: drive connector

Floppy controller

A: drive connector (after cable twist)

Serial and Parallel Ports

The serial and parallel port cables should be plugged into the motherboard in the same way as the EIDE/IDE connectors are plugged in (be sure to align pin 1). The trick to installing these connectors is that most are supplied on a metal bar that attaches to a slot in the back of the computer that could hold an expansion card. To avoid losing a potential expansion slot, take the connectors off the metal bar and mount them in the mounting holes in the back of the case, as shown in Figure 31.7.

Figure 31.7

Installing the serial and parallel port connectors in the back of the computer

USB Ports

Two varieties of USB ports are available. For motherboards that have the USB circuitry onboard, you'll get a pair of connectors, mounted on a metal bar, just like the serial and parallel ports described earlier.

In this case, however, leave the connectors on the metal bar—there's no place to attach the USB ports individually on a standard case.

For motherboards that don't have USB circuitry onboard, you can get a USB adapter card that will plug right into a PCI slot (see Figure 31.8).

USB connectors

USB cables

motherboard

Figure 31.8

Installing USB ports

(cutaway side view of case)

Keyboards, Mice, PS/2, and DIN

Now this is a confusing bunch of connectors. Depending on your motherboard, either you will have a single, large DIN connector or you'll have two mini-DIN (PS/2) connectors. The older style keyboards use the larger DIN connectors, and new ones use the smaller PS/2-style connectors. The main problem you may run into is that the PS/2 keyboard and mouse connectors look almost exactly the same, so look for the labels before you plug anything into them. And *never, never* force them!

Video and Sound

Years ago, personal computers were text-based and had no sound. Then one day Mr. Sim came to America. He brought with him the first Sound Blaster card and he, not Steve Jobs, changed computers forever. In essence, he created multimedia. Today almost every application uses some kind of sound and graphics. Even Microsoft uses multimedia. People understand sound and graphics, and if your system isn't capable of multimedia, you should probably consider upgrading your capability with new sound and video cards. Lots of motherboards today actually have sound and video right on the board. If they do, then all you need to do to set them up is plug them in. Windows 95/98/NT/2000 will identify these ports automatically and prompt you for the included driver disk(s).

PCI, ISA, and AGP

These are the expansion slots that you'll find on your motherboard. Most new boards are PCI boards. They are the new standard for expansion slots because they are much faster than the older-style ISA slots. On the other hand, even new motherboards include at least a few ISA slots so that you can still use some of the older ISA expansion boards. The AGP slot on newer motherboards is a high-speed expansion slot that you can use for the new, fast video cards. Figure 31.9 shows the ISA sockets, PCI sockets, and an AGP connector on a motherboard.

Figure 31.9

PCI, ISA, and AGP connectors

Most new motherboards have several kinds of memory and memory slots, such as the DIMMs, SIMMs, and cache memory shown in Figure 31.10. Most boards have at least 256KB of fast cache memory. In most cases, you can increase that to as much as 1MB, and sometimes even 2MB.

DIMM
Sockets
(memory)

Cache
Memory

Figure 31.10

DIMM sockets and
cache memory on the
motherboard

Note

If you have the option of using DIMMs or SIMMs, choose DIMMs if you can. They
are available in faster speeds, and some motherboards that will run at only
66MHz using SIMMs will run at 100MHz with DIMMs.

The Microprocessor Slot and Control Circuitry

The microprocessor socket is very special. It's called a zero insertion force (ZIF) socket, and it's shown in Figure 31.11. It enables you to insert or remove your expensive microprocessor in the socket without putting any stress on its leads. If you look at it closely, you'll see that there's a lever on the side of the socket. When the lever is in the up position, the holes in the plastic top align with the electrical connections below them, so the socket will slide in easily. Once the chip is in place, move the lever to the down (locked) position, and the top of the socket slides over and presses the leads of the processor tightly against the electrical contacts inside the socket.

Figure 31.11

A ZIF socket with the microprocessor out and the lever up

Near the ZIF socket, you'll find a few groups of jumpers. By putting the jumpers in the right places, you can set both the voltage and the frequency for the processor. Details are printed in the motherboard manual and often on the motherboard itself.

Making Final Decisions

Okay, so now you're familiar with your motherboard, you know what goes where, and you know how to plug things in. Time to make the final decisions. What new capabilities do you want to add to your system? In this section, you'll take a look at the choices you have and what each does for you.

Communication Options

No matter what kind of computer you have today, you're almost certainly going to want to have communications capabilities. These include Internet access, e-mail, perhaps a home network, and possibly even video conferencing. All of these things are forms of communication.

For the most part, computer communications consist of sending and receiving digital information between computers. In addition to a requirement that both computers be compatible, there are two other limiting factors when it comes to digital information. First, can the computers handle both the type and the speed of the data being sent? Second, can the medium used to connect the computers support the data speed? The *medium*, as you probably know, is the vehicle that carries the data, such as phone lines, cable, or satellite.

Modems

The most basic kind of computer communication today is modem to modem. Modem, by the way, is a word that was created from the term *mod*ulator/*dem*odulator, which describes what a modem does. During modem communication, the signal is initially digital. The modem receives data from your computer and converts that data into a series of tones (which, by the way, are what you hear as screeches and beeps when the modem is connecting—sometimes referred to as *white noise*). Once the modem connects, the speaker is usually programmed to shut off. It makes that lovely sound only so you know it's trying to connect.

Choosing a modem is pretty easy if all you want to do is connect to your ISP. There are basically two kinds of modems: internal and external. Internal modems plug into a card slot in your motherboard and external modems connect to a serial port on the outside of your computer. That is, unless you have a USB modem (not common yet). Actually, if I were choosing an external modem, I'd get the USB kind since they won't use up any of my precious COM ports. But frankly, I almost always choose internal modems because they are more convenient. No extra wires to fall over, no extra power connectors to deal with.

Home Networks

Home networks are becoming more and more common these days. Quite a few homes today have more than one computer. A home network enables you to share data as well as resources. For example, with a home network, everyone can print using the same printer. And if you do have more than one printer, any computer connected to the network can print to any printer that is also connected to the network. So if you have a laser printer in your home office, for example, then your son could write a report on his computer and print it on your laser printer (if you'll let him). Similarly, if you want to print some color photos, you could load glossy paper into junior's color inkjet printer and print your photos on that printer.

There are a couple of kinds of home networks. One connects your computers via standard Ethernet cables. Another, which is gaining more acceptance these days, is the phone line network. With the advent of USB technology, home networks that run through USB connections are now possible, although they are typically slower than a conventional 10Mbps Ethernet network.

Note

To learn more about USB connections, go back to Chapter 3, "Inside the PC: Pieces of the Picture." And for more information on home networks, check out Chapter 27, "Networking Concepts and Hardware."

Ethernet networks connect computers via special cables and sometimes hubs. There are two popular Ethernet cabling systems, *twisted-pair* and *coaxial*. Twisted-pair cabling looks like phone wires with a gland problem. The wires are thicker, and the connectors are the same basic shape as telephone cable connectors, only larger. Coaxial cabling is similar to the cable used for cable TV, and uses bayonet-type screw-on connectors.) For most home installations, twisted-pair or phone line networks are the best choice. They are far easier to install, and generally are quite a bit less expensive than coaxial.

Phone Line Networks

Phone line networks use your existing telephone wiring. The assumption is that you already have telephone wiring to the same places that your computers will be located. Each computer in your network will need a phone line adapter card. The cards transmit and receive data over the same lines as your phone without interfering with phone service, because they operate at a different frequency than the phones.

As an example, consider Diamond's Home*Free* Phone Line Network. The package comes with two network adapters (one for each of two computers), phone cords, and all the software you need to set it up. (Actually, you may need to use your Windows 95/98 setup CD to load some of the network protocols, so keep it handy.)

To set up the network, all you need to do is plug the cards into the system, use the cables to connect the cards to a nearby telephone jack, and run the setup software. Once the network's installed, you can share files, resources (such as printers and modems), and even drives (including removable media drives). One very useful feature of Diamond's phone line modem is its capability to let up to three users log onto the Internet from a single account.

Playing Games

Did you know that game playing is the second most popular reason that people buy computers? (The top reason is Internet access.) What do you need to have in order to really get the most out of game play on your computer?

You need a high-performance computer. In fact, video games are really "pushing the envelope" of multimedia. So if you're planning to play games, get a fast 3D video card with at least 16MB of video RAM. You should also get a great sound card, such as Creative Labs' Live card, speakers, the best monitor you can afford, and whatever game controllers you will need to make your game playing more realistic.

The Next Step

Well, that's about it. If you have an older system and you want to convert it to a new system, go through your checklist and replace the parts you want to upgrade. But choose carefully. Remember, never buy more computer than you expect to need right now. Buying parts that you think you may need in the future is usually a waste of money, since those parts will probably be faster, smaller, and less expensive then. And by the way, when it comes to computers, the future can be as soon as tomorrow . . . or even later on today.

And one final note: If, after reading this chapter, there's more you want to do to your system, read on. As I said earlier, in the next chapter you'll look at building the ultimate computer. Of course that, too, is a moving target. So all I can really do is give you the basics, since by the time you get this book there's almost certainly going to be yet another generation of components.

32

Building the Ultimate Computer

INTRODUCTION

Well folks, this is it. In this chapter you're going to build the ultimate computer. Sounds like a tall order? All right, I'll admit that building any system from scratch is a big project. But by now, you've already done the toughest part: figuring out what to put into your ultimate system. (You have decided, haven't you?)

On the outside chance that you're still not sure, stick around, 'cause in this chapter you're putting one together from beginning to end. So grab your parts, clear a big table, and let's get started.

Building the Ultimate Computer

Because there are so many components involved, this series of QuickSteps is only an overview of the steps necessary to build a computer. Refer to the appropriate section in this chapter for the details of each step; refer to the appropriate chapter for more information on the individual devices and hardware being installed.

Be Prepared

Before you start, there are some things you'll need on hand. These include:

- All of the hardware that is going to become your new computer.

- The documentation that comes with the components. I can't emphasize this strongly enough. Although the procedures I lay out are correct in the general sense, the manuals that come with your hardware are going to give you a lot more specific information that you should abide by.

- Lots of room to work with.

- A clean tabletop.

- Containers for screws and other small objects you don't want to lose.

- Patience.

- More patience.

- Software, including an operating system such as Windows 98SE.

- Device drivers required by individual components such as a modem or video card.

1. Gather all your parts.

2. Open the case and remove the power supply and drive chassis.

3. Set up your motherboard.

  ◗ Install the CPU.

  ◗ Install main memory.

4. Install the video card and test it.

5. Install the hard drive(s) and floppy drive.

6. Configure the BIOS.

7. Install your CD-ROM or DVD drive.

8. Install the operating system.

9. Install the sound card.

10. Install your other expansion boards, such as an internal modem and DVD decoder board.

11. Put it all together:

  ◗ Install the motherboard.

  ◗ Install the power supply.

  ◗ Attach the add-on boards.

  ◗ Install the drives.

  ◗ Conduct another system check.

  ◗ Install the rest of the boards.

  ◗ Install the parallel and serial port connectors.

  ◗ Connect the front panel lights and speaker.

Step 1: Assemble All the Parts

The first thing to do is look over all the parts you have, just to make sure that you've got everything you need. I'll briefly recap what you should look for when you go out to buy the items discussed in this section, but almost everything listed here has already been covered in more detail earlier on in the book. So if you want more information, check the index or table of contents for pointers.

Computer Case

There's more to this important item than meets the eye. The case provides a framework for your whole system. It's the main part of the computer that you'll see, and it includes the power supply that will run your computer. So choose one that looks nice (if that is important to you), has lots of room to work in, and is sturdy and solidly built. Figure 32.1 shows an excellent case. The power supply is up out of the way of the rest of the system, and the metal frame that holds the drives is removable, which is very important.

Figure 32.1

Computer case with removable drive frame

Notice that the power supply is at the top of the case. Always make sure that the power supply is near the top if you are getting a tower case. This is important because heat rises, and the fan in the power supply pulls air out of the top of the case; cooler air is pulled in through the bottom. A power supply near the middle or bottom of the case would draw heat across the CPU, drives, or whatever is between the fan and the top of the case.

Depending on your personal taste and needs, there are several different types and sizes of cases you can purchase. Above all, make sure you match the case with the motherboard you plan to purchase with regard to these common case styles:

Desktop This type of case lies flat on its widest side, and people typically set their monitor on top of it.

Slim-line Like a desktop model but squashed so it's not as tall.

Mini-tower This case stands up (think monolith) and is fairly short with perhaps two large and two small externally accessible bays.

Mid-sized tower Like a mini-tower but slightly taller with a few more bays.

Tower (or full tower) A big tower case with lots of expansion bays, suitable for power users or network servers.

Plan ahead and get a case with enough bays to hold all the equipment you plan to install, such as hard drives, floppy drives, and a CD/DVD-ROM drive. Table 32.1 shows the common types of computer cases and how many internal and external bays they have.

Note

Table 32.1 has two columns, Internal Bays and External Bays, which warrant further explanation. Internal bays hold devices that don't require external access to operate, such as a hard drive. Once you install a device in an internal bay and put the computer case back together, you can't get at that device without removing the cover. Internal bays are primarily used for additional hard drives. An external bay is designed to hold a device that requires external access to operate, such as a floppy or CD-ROM drive. Both of these examples require access to "the outside world" because you must be able to insert and extract floppy and CD-ROM disks to use the drives. For example, if you plan on installing two hard drives, a floppy drive, a CD/DVD-ROM, and an internal Zip drive, you will need at least two internal and three external bays.

TABLE 32.1 Common Computer Case Types and Sizes

Case	Size	Internal Bays (Hard Drives, Etc.)	External Bays (Floppy Drive, CD-ROM)
Full tower	large	6+	3–5+
Mid-sized tower	medium	5	2–4
Mini-tower	small	4	2–3
Desktop	small	4	1–2
Slim-line	smallest	3	1–2

Finally, you must consider what motherboard form factor you will be using and buy a case that it will fit into. Cases are classified into two broad form factor categories: AT and ATX. An AT motherboard will fit only into an AT case, and an ATX motherboard will fit only into an ATX case. In general, smaller cases tend to be AT and larger cases tend to be ATX, but you can usually find both form factors available in the case type you want.

Motherboard

The motherboard forms the basis of your PC, so it's important that you choose one with the features you need to put everything else in place. Here are some factors to consider when choosing a motherboard:

Processors accepted This is your primary decision factor. Choose the processor model and speed that you want to build your system around first and shop only for motherboards that accept that processor.

AT versus ATX form factor Make sure the motherboard matches up with the case in this regard. ATX is the newer type and has a number of advantages over AT, including better cooling, better power management, and on-board parallel and serial port connectors (so you don't have to run ribbon cables from the motherboard to the connectors inside the case).

Type of memory used If you want to reuse memory from an old system, make sure the motherboard will support it. Many new motherboards support only a certain speed of memory, such as 100 MHz or 133 MHz; your old SIMMs and DIMMs may not work in such a motherboard.

Number of ISA and PCI slots Newer motherboards are phasing out ISA slots, offering perhaps only one, or even none. That's fine, unless you have old ISA devices such as a modem, network card, or sound card that you were planning to reuse in this system. In that case, shop for a motherboard with enough ISA slots for everything you're moving over.

USB support This is almost a no-brainer these days—all motherboards have it. But some motherboards offer only one USB port, while others offer two. Two is better, obviously.

Built-in video Some motherboards come with a built-in video card. It's not usually an outstanding video card, but it's adequate for a business system (probably not for a serious gamer, however). You can usually disable it in the BIOS if you don't want it. However, such motherboards seldom have an AGP slot into which you can put a replacement video card (see below), so you would be stuck using a PCI video card.

AGP slot AGP is the latest and greatest (and fastest) system bus type, used only for video cards. Make sure the motherboard has an AGP video slot unless you plan to use built-in video.

Built-in sound   Some motherboards have a built-in sound card, often an Ensoniq model (a division of Creative Labs, the Sound Blaster people). It's good enough for casual use, but those with serious sound demands, such as gamers or musicians, may find it inadequate. Like the built-in video, it can usually be disabled in the BIOS if you don't want it.

Video Card

Video cards are one of the hidden bottlenecks in computers. You can have the fastest system (you're building one), but if you use a slow video card, it'll still perform like it's on vacation in the Bahamas.

For your ultimate system, you'll use an AGP video card with lots of built-in video RAM. Recall that AGP is a type of system bus corresponding to a slot on the motherboard. You may see both PCI and AGP video cards for sale when you shop. If your motherboard will accept an AGP model, that's what you want; if not, PCI will do. AGP performs somewhat better because it has a faster path to the processor than PCI.

When you go to buy a video card, the two basic things you should look for initially are speed, memory, and 3D capability.

Speed on video cards is measured in lots of different ways. One is a measurement of "millions of polygons per second." Polygons are the shapes used to create 3D graphics. The more polygons per second, the faster the card can produce images.

Another speed measurement that is often listed is something called the "frame rate." A frame in computer graphics terms is the same as a single frame on movie film. To get smooth, realistic, full-motion video, you should have a frame rate of at least 30 frames per second, which is comparable to the number of frames per second you see in a movie at the theater. As the frame rate goes down, the image gets jumpy. For a business system that isn't going to be playing a lot of graphic-intensive games, a rate of 15 frames per second would be minimally acceptable.

Video cards have their own built-in memory that's used for video processing. The higher the resolution and greater the color depth, the more video memory is required for that operating mode. For example, a video card with 2MB would be able to display 16.7 million colors at 800 × 600 resolution, but only 256 colors at 1024 × 768 resolution. The amount of memory a card has does not have anything to do with its speed of performance.

In case you're interested, here's how the maximum resolution/color depth is calculated. If you have a 16-color display, you need four bits to control each dot because 16 combinations are possible with a four-digit binary number (2 to the 4th power, or 16). If you multiply the number of dots in the resolution by the number of bits required for each dot, you have the amount of memory required to display that resolution. For example, 640 × 480 with 16 colors would be 640 × 480 × 4, or 1,228,800 bits. There are eight bits in a byte, so that would be 153,600 bytes (approximately 154KB). Therefore, if your video card had 1MB, you could have any of the following combinations: 640 × 480 in 24-bit color, 800 × 600 in 16-bit color, 1024 × 768 in 8-bit color (256 colors) or 1280 × 1024 in 4-bit color (16 colors). Most video cards today come with a minimum of 4MB, which should be plenty unless you have a huge monitor that you want to operate in very high resolutions with 24-bit color depth. (If that's the case, get out your calculator and use the formula I just described to decide what you need.)

You also need to think about inputs and outputs. The basic function of a video card is to accept data from a computer and to output images to a video display. But many video cards today do a lot more. Some accept video input from video cameras and output to television sets, and others will output to the new digital flat-panel displays. If you think you might be interested in any of those capabilities, make sure you shop with them in mind.

Sound Cards

People love for their PCs to make noise—to play music, to make game sounds, to talk back to them. And whom can we thank for it? Creative Labs and their amazing Sound Blaster cards. Okay, there are other sound cards out today. But the Sound Blaster was the first and, for a long time, it's been the best. They made the rules for sound cards, much as Hayes made the rules for smart modems. So today, even though Hayes is long gone, their modem's AT instruction set is still the standard (along with a lot of new extensions). And, as far I can see, Creative Labs will be with us for a long time to come, and the Sound Blaster's standard will continue to be the template for all other sound cards.

When you go out to buy a sound card, the first thing to look for is Sound Blaster compatibility (unless, of course, you're getting a genuine Sound Blaster of some sort). If you get a card that isn't Sound Blaster–compatible, there's a chance it won't work with some of the programs you may want to run.

The next thing to look for is the card's specifications. There are three factors to be concerned about with a sound card: its number of bits, its wavetable capability, and its input and output jacks.

Number of bits Almost all sound cards today are 16-bit cards. A 16-bit card can process 16 bits of data at once. Don't accept an 8-bit card.

Wavetable capability There are two kinds of sound cards: FM synthesis and wavetable synthesis. The latter is preferable. Wavetable cards have prerecorded, built-in sounds, such as the sounds of various instruments playing different notes. (FM synthesis cards simulate those notes instead, which doesn't sound as good.) Wavetable cards commonly have 32, 64, or 128 voices that they can play at once.

Note

If you hear of a sound card that has 16 in its name, it is probably referring to its bits and it probably does not contain wavetable synthesis (check the box to be sure). If, on the other hand, there is 64 or 128 in the name, the numbers probably refer to the number of wavetable voices.

Input and output   The important question is this: does the card have the jacks you want? Jacks come in many varieties, and not everyone needs every kind. You will, at the minimum, want a speaker output, a microphone port, and line in/line out. You may also want to look for MIDI input, which enables you to plug in a keyboard or other digital instrument, and an auxiliary input.

Most sound cards also have a built-in joystick port like the one shown in Figure 32.2. Joysticks are primarily for games, but they can also be used for some accessibility programs that let people with disabilities use a PC. Joysticks don't really have anything to do with sounds but have traditionally appeared on sound cards because people who like sounds usually like games too.

Figure 32.2

Joystick port on the sound card

Modems

Want to connect to the Internet? To get on, you need a device that will connect your computer to it. For most of us, this is going to be some kind of modem.

The traditional type of modem is a modulator/demodulator that translates digital signals from the PC to analog format for transmission over a phone line. That's the kind that most people have, and that's what I think of when I hear the term "modem." There are other kinds of modems available today, such as cable modems and ISDN modems, but these are not really modems in the strict sense of the word. Like a modem, they do connect you to the Internet or other online service, but they do so differently. Rather than converting between analog and digital signals, they simply pass along the digital information as-is across a network or digital phone line.

If you're getting a standard modem, the things you should look for are the speed (almost all are 56K), data translation capability (these days you should get V.90), and any extra features you may want to have, such as voice and fax. Most modems today do faxing, but not all have voice capabilities. This allows you to hook up a speaker and microphone so that the computer will operate as a speakerphone or answering machine. You may also want to get a modem that can handle a video camera so you can have two-way videophone communications.

The final decision you need to make regarding your modem is whether or not to get an internal or external one. External modems have LEDs on them (see Figure 32.3) that let you see what the modem is doing from one moment to another. They also don't use any of the system power or system slots. On the other hand, most of us don't need to know exactly what the modem is doing and rarely use up every slot in our systems. Also, an external modem uses up either a serial port (there are only two of them) or a USB port, which will cost you more money.

Figure 32.3

External modem showing indicator lights

For these reasons, and because I don't like to have so many extra things hung on the outside of the computer, I usually recommend internal modems. For this system, that's what you'll use.

By the way, don't think you can save a few dollars by using a generic modem. Why? When using a modem, the driver is very important, and brand-name modems tend to have better-written drivers than the off-brand ones. In my opinion, 3Com and U.S. Robotics are some of the best available.

For my dream PC, I wouldn't go with a standard modem at all— I'd spring for a cable or DSL connection. But if that's not available (it depends on your location), my choice would be a 3Com V.90 56K modem.

Hard Drive

The hard drive holds the most valuable thing in your computer— your data. Choose your new drive carefully. The drive should be fast, reliable, and large enough to handle more than double the data you'll need to store.

"Double?" you say? Yep, double. Fact is, once a drive gets half full, it starts to slow down. So (for example) if you think you'll need 10GB, get a 20GB or larger drive.

Note

When you get a hard drive, buy it as a complete kit. That way, you'll get all of the extra bits and pieces you need to install it easily. For example, mounting rails are not always needed, but they're great to have on hand if you discover you need them for the slot you're trying to mount the drive into in your case.

Hard disks have two critical performance measurements:

Average access time The time it takes for the drive head to reach and read the average bit of data, measured in milliseconds. Lower is better. A decent speed is 10 to 12ms.

Data transfer rate How quickly data moves from the hard disk to memory. Higher is better. Look for a rate of 11 to 16Mbps at the minimum.

Floppy Drive

For this new computer, you're getting a SuperDrive. This is a floppy that can read and write to the 3½-inch 1.44MB floppies but can also read and write to the new 120MB floppies. This means that with one drive you've got compatibility and high capacity. After all, the reason you use floppy drives is because you want to be able to exchange data with computers that aren't connected to your computer. 1.44MB floppies are the standard. Virtually every computer today has one. But you also know that 1.44MB isn't very much space today. So the SuperDrive provides a reasonable upgrade that's built-in and includes all of the hardware you'll need to install the drive, as well as some software and usually at least one of the 120MB disks. If you happen to purchase one that doesn't include a disk, be sure to purchase a disk separately when you get the drive so you can test your installation.

Zip Drive

Okay, I hear you. You're asking, "Since I've already got a SuperDrive (120MB drive), why should I also get a Zip drive?" Well, one reason is that you might need to exchange files with someone who has a Zip drive. They're very popular, and the chance that someone will need you to have one of these is greater than the chance of someone needing you to have a SuperDrive.

Although the Zip drive is more of a marketing achievement than an engineering achievement, it is, nevertheless, useful for transferring large files. Depending on the model, Zip disks hold either 100 or 250MB of data, which is more than enough capacity to transfer even the largest graphic files, PowerPoint presentations, or other files for business or pleasure.

When you buy your Zip drive, I recommend getting at least one 10-pack of disks. First of all, most dealers will give you a deal if you buy them when you're getting the drive. And second, you'll want them later. I usually get the ones that come in a variety of colors. This makes it easy for me to see which disk I want quickly.

I guess if your budget will only allow you to get one or the other, I'd suggest getting a standard floppy (which you can now get for about $10 if you look around) and get the Zip drive. I like the Super-Drive better, although it's not the standard at this time. But, hey, you can put one into this system because it's the dream machine . . . the ultimate computer! So grab your drives, and let's move on.

CD-ROM/DVD Drive

Now this is something that always gets me excited. Don't ask me why. I guess that I'm still a kid when it comes to movies, but the technology of DVD movies is just plain incredible.

DVD drives can hold more than two hours of high-quality, full motion picture video as well as CD-quality, 3D stereo sound! And I can watch it on my computer (my own personal movie theater) or connect it to a big-screen TV and hi-fi stereo system and share it with my friends.

Like SuperDrives, DVD drives are backward compatible to audio CDs and CD-ROMs. So if you get a DVD drive, you can use any of the standard format CDs or DVDs. The kinds of things to look for when you go out to buy a DVD drive are speed and features.

Now, when I say "features," I'm not kidding. DVD drives can be purchased as a drive only or they can be purchased as a kit. You should buy the kit, as it contains some items that you'll definitely be glad to have. Notice the small circuit board? This is something that you really, really want. It provides you with hardware decoding. You see, when the DVD image is put onto the disc, the information is compressed so that the manufacturer can fit more stuff on it. This stuff includes alternate languages (yes, Kermit the Frog speaks Cantonese on some DVDs) and different screen proportions, such as standard and wide-screen (also called letterbox). They also usually include the promos and trailers and sometimes include extra goodies like a director's cut of the movie or the director commenting on what they were doing or other behind-the-scenes information.

Anyway, the data on the DVD disc has to be decoded. There are two kinds of decoders available: software and hardware. The software decoders are slower than the hardware decoders are, so they produce an image that's not as sharp as it can be. The hardware decoder produces an image that is razor sharp. Remember that this is the ultimate computer, so you're getting the kit with the hardware decoder.

Networking

You may think that just because you have a home system or a small office system, you don't need networking. Well, you may want to think again.

The only people who don't really need a local area network are people with just one computer. Everyone else will benefit from it. This is true even if the other computer is your kid's computer. A second system can really save you if you ever crash. One of the best things you can do with your network is back up the data from one computer onto another. Or better yet, back it up onto a removable media drive that's connected to another computer. Then, if one of the systems goes down (I should say *when* it goes down, since eventually they all do), you can go over to the other computer, download the files you need from the removable media drive, and continue working while the sick one is being revived. And, by the way, make sure to install the drivers for the removable media drive on both machines so that it can be run from either computer.

Now, getting back to networking. There are a lot of options available for networking (as you may recall from Chapter 27, "Networking Concepts and Hardware"). The fastest of these today is Ethernet. So, as you probably guessed (ultimate computer, you know the routine) . . . you're getting Ethernet.

To set up a small Ethernet network, you will need the following, most of which can be purchased together in some sort of network starter kit at your local PC store.

A network interface card (NIC) for each PC There are two speeds available: 10Base-T and 100Base-T. 100Base-T is better and faster, so go with that if you can afford it.

Hub You'll need a hub to connect the various PCs and networked devices together. Make sure you get one with room for expansion. For example, if you currently have three PCs, get a five-device hub.

Cables You'll need a network cable to run between each NIC and the hub. Check the plugs on the NIC and the hub, but you'll probably want RJ-45 plugs on the cable.

Extra Interfaces

The idea of extra interfaces might surprise you. Don't worry, you'll use them later—for now, just get them. One is USB, pictured in Figure 32.4, which you may already have built into your motherboard. It's getting to be another standard interface like serial and parallel, and most of the new motherboards have them. If yours doesn't, get it and add it. A lot of new devices are being offered with USB connections, and they make adding other devices to the system very simple. No IRQs or other complications to consider. Just plug it in and the system recognizes it.

The other connection I'm recommending is FireWire, also known as IEEE 1394. This new interface is quite fast and, for now, it's the only way to get (for example) full motion, digital video from a DV camera. If you aren't concerned about getting the video as a digital signal, you can use a standard NTSC or S-video interface, but neither is as sharp as digital.

USB Card

USB Cable Connectors

Figure 32.4

USB card and cables

Step 2: Start with the Case

Now that you have everything you need and you're ready to roll, you need to find a large, open space that's big enough for you to open the case and work on any side of it easily.

Get a couple of cups, an egg carton, or some other convenient containers to hold all of the loose screws that you'll be taking out of the computer case. Typically, there are at least two sizes of screws used in computers. If you have more than one container, you can keep them separated by size.

You're using a tower case for the ultimate computer. Find the cover screws and take them all out (see Figure 32.5). Leave the screws for the power supply in place for now.

The power supply screws will generally be only in the back panel of the case, while the case screws will go through the cover and the back panel and will be nearer the outer perimeter of the back.

Figure 32.5

Removing the cover screws from a tower case

Once the cover is off (put it somewhere you won't trip over it), you can see inside the cabinet.

You can mount the motherboard directly into the case and do all your diagnostic testing from there, but it can sometimes be difficult to work with a motherboard when it's down inside there. That's why I like to test the motherboard before I mount it in the case. To do so, you may need to remove the power supply from the case, because the power supply is required for testing (you've gotta have some power to fire it up and see if it works). You can try leaving the power supply in the case and see whether the cables will reach to where you've got the motherboard sitting, but it's probably easiest just to undo the couple of screws holding the power supply in the case and pop it on out. On an AT case, the power switch is screwed to the front of the case; you can remove it or leave it in place if the cables will reach.

Tip

During the initial configuration and diagnostics (before putting the motherboard into the case), some people like to set it on a book or box that is about 2 inches high and roughly 9 × 11 inches. You can even use the box that the motherboard came in for this purpose. This will help later when you're installing circuit cards in the motherboard because it allows you to press a card down firmly without bending the little metal lip that may hang down from a circuit card past the bottom of the case when the cover is off.

Step 3: Set Up the Motherboard

Now remove your motherboard from its protective plastic bag and open up the motherboard manual that came with it. This is an extremely important document. When you're done here, put it in a safe place. It contains information that you must have to be able to use the motherboard.

Installing the CPU

Take a look at your CPU. It will be a square chip with pins on the bottom (AMD K6-III), as in Figure 32.6, a black cartridge (Athons and Pentium IIIs), or a rectangular circuit board with a square chip mounted on it (Celerons).

Figure 32.6

The AMD K6-III-450 processor

Open up the motherboard manual to the page that shows a diagram of the motherboard layout. It should be labeled with all of the locations of the various control jumpers, interface connectors, and components. Find the jumpers that control the CPU and system voltage. Figure 32.7 shows a motherboard with a Super7 processor slot (for the K6-111 in Figure 32.6); your motherboard may look different.

Figure 32.7

The motherboard layout showing all of the major components, connectors, and jumper locations

Setting the Voltages

Now take a look at the page that shows the jumper positions for different voltages on the motherboard. The *core voltage* is the voltage that the CPU uses for its internal operation. The *I/O voltage* is the voltage it uses to communicate with the rest of the system. Depending upon your motherboard, you will need to set either one or the other of these voltages.

To set the voltages, you'll need to put some jumpers in the right places on the motherboard. You should find a table in your motherboard manual that looks a lot like the one in Figure 32.8. Placing or removing these jumpers sets the correct voltages for the CPU and system I/O. Set them incorrectly, and you can say goodbye to your expensive CPU—so set the jumpers carefully.

Figure 32.8

The motherboard's voltage settings table

Setting the Clock Speed

Before you go any further, on the outside chance that your CPU isn't imprinted with information about on what frequency to set it up, the motherboard manual usually contains a table that covers that information for most current processors. Table 32.2 is an example of such a table. (This is just an example; you should use information relevant to your CPU.)

TABLE 32.2 Operating Frequencies and Multipliers for CPUs

CPU Type	Frequency (MHz)	System Bus Clock (MHz)	Multiplier
Intel			
Pentium 166 MMX	166	66	2.5
Pentium 200 MMX	200	66	3
Pentium 233 MMX	233	66	3.5
Celeron 400	400	66	6
Celeron 433	433	66	6.5
Celeron 466	466	66	7
Celeron 500	500	66	7.5
Celeron 533	533	66	8
Pentium II 233 MMX	233	66	3.5
Pentium II 266 MMX	266	66	4
Pentium II 300 MMX	300	66	4.5
Pentium II 333 MMX	333	66	5
Pentium II 350 MMX	350	100	3.5
Pentium II 400 MMX	400	100	4
Pentium II 450 MMX	450	100	4.5
Pentium III 450 MMX	450	100	4.5
Pentium III 500 MMX	500	100	5
Pentium III 550 MMX	550	100	5.5
Pentium III 600 MMX	600	100	6
Pentium III 533B MMX	533	133	4
Pentium III 600B MMX	600	133	4.5
Pentium III 550E MMX	550	100	5.5
Pentium III 500E MMX	550	100	5
Pentium III 600E MMX	600	100	6
Pentium III 650 MMX	650	100	6.5
Pentium III 700 MMX	700	100	7

Continued on next page

TABLE 32.2 Operating Frequencies and Multipliers for CPUs (continued)

CPU Type	Frequency (MHz)	System Bus Clock (MHz)	Multiplier
Pentium III 750 MMX	750	100	7.5
Pentium III 800 MMX	800	100	8
Pentium III 533EB MMX	533	133	4
Pentium III 600EB MMX	600	133	4.5
Pentium III 667 MMX	667	133	5
Pentium III 733 MMX	733	133	5.5
Pentium III 800EB MMX	800	133	6
AMD			
K6-166	166	66	2.5
K6-200	200	66	3.5
K6-233	233	66	3.5
K6-266	266	66	4
K6-300	300	66	4.5
K6-II-300	300	66	4.5
K6-III-300	300	100	3
K6-II-333	333	95	3.5
K6-II-350	350	100	3.5
K6-II-366	366	66	5.5
K6-II-400	400	100	4
K6-III-400	400	100	4
K6-III-450	450	100	4.5
Athlon 600	600	200	3
Athlon 650	650	200	3.25
Athlon 700	700	200	3.50
Athlon 750	450	200	3.75
Athlon 800	800	200	4
Athlon 850	850	200	4.25
Athlon 900	900	200	4.5
Athlon 950	950	200	4.75
Athlon 1000	1000	200	5

Setting the clock speed is very similar to setting the voltages. Let's say that the CPU runs at 900MHz. If the motherboard manufacturer tried to make the all of the components operate at 900MHz using today's technology, you'd have a system either too expensive to buy or one that would work only if it were all on a single chip. Bottom line: the rest of the system has to run slower. How much slower? Well, bus speeds in today's systems range from 66MHz to 200MHz. On a 900MHz Athlon system, for example, the bus speed is 200MHz (as you saw in Table 32.2).

The Multiplier

Some motherboards autodetect the processor speed, but others must be told by setting a multiplier jumper on the motherboard. Check Table 32.2 to find your processor and then set the appropriate multiplier, if needed, on your motherboard. Figure 32.9 shows some sample jumper settings you might find in a motherboard manual to help. The multiplier for a 900MHz processor running on a board with a 200MHz bus, for example, would be 4.5.

Figure 32.9

A sample CPU clock multiplier settings table; check your motherboard manual for yours.

Plugging in the CPU

All your CPU settings should be complete now, so get ready to install the CPU. There are two main types of CPU connectors in use today, and you should have already chosen the correct motherboard for the type of CPU you have.

Pin Grid Array (PGA) A square, ZIF (zero insertion force) grid of holes with a little handle that lifts up to open and goes down to close. The processor has little pin "feet" that fit down into the holes. There are various sizes of these:

▶ Socket7 is what the original Pentiums used.

▶ A variation called Super7 is the current standard and is used by many AMD and Cyrix processors.

▶ There is also a Socket PGA-370 version that some of the newer Celeron processors use.

Slots These slots look somewhat like the slots in the motherboard that circuit cards fit into, but they're designed to accept only a processor. The processor is in a rectangular cartridge that fits snugly into the slot. Sometimes there are plastic support brackets at either end of the slot to ensure that the processor doesn't fall over. You typically mount a cooling fan to the outside of the plastic cartridge.

▶ Slot 1 holds Pentium II processors, which come in a cartridge. Inside the cartridge are the processor and the L2 cache, both mounted on a common circuit board. It can also accept the older type of Celeron and Pentium III processor, which was mounted on a bar circuit board (no plastic cartridge around it), with a fan strapped directly to the processor chip.

▶ Slot 2 holds higher-end Pentium II and Pentium III cartridges and also Xeon processors. It's the same design but a larger slot and a larger cartridge.

To install a PGA type processor, lift the lever on the CPU's ZIF socket. Then carefully align the pins on the CPU with the holes in the socket as shown in Figure 32.10.

Be sure to align the diagonal pin array
on the CPU with the diagonal hole array
in the socket.

Figure 32.10

Aligning the CPU pins
with the holes in the
ZIF socket

Processor
(bottom view)

ZIF Socket

Warning

Be sure to align the holes correctly. One corner of the CPU has a pin missing and one corner of the socket has a hole missing. If you don't align the CPU properly, it won't go in correctly, and you may damage one or more of the delicate pins, making the CPU unusable.

The CPU should fit into the socket with absolutely no resistance. If it's tight, check the locking lever to make sure it's not partly locked. It should be up and back as shown in Figure 32.11.

Figure 32.11

Opening the locking lever fully

Once the CPU is fully seated in its socket, lower the lever and lock it into place. It should click into position behind a molded clip in the socket's side.

Next, squeeze a bit of heat sink compound from its tube into the center of the metal top of the CPU and put the heat sink/fan on top of the CPU as shown in Figure 32.12. Finally, clip the heat sink/fan on both sides, and you're done installing the CPU.

Heat Sink Fan

Motherboard

ZIF Socket with Processor Inserted

Figure 32.12

Installing the heat sink/fan on the CPU

To install a slot-type processor (Slot 1 or Slot 2), first install the plastic mounting brackets that came with the motherboard. This can be frustrating because the directions are often vague as to where and how the brackets should be positioned. But persevere—this is often the hardest part of a Slot 1 or Slot 2 installation, and once it's over with, you're home free.

Align the cartridge over the slot, making sure it's facing the right way. Note the positioning of the trench in the slot and match it up with the edge of the circuit card sticking out of the bottom of the cartridge. Then firmly press the cartridge into the slot so that the mounting brackets hold it in place.

Installing Memory

The next thing you need to do is plug the memory into the motherboard. Today there are two kinds of memory available, SIMMs and DIMMs. To get maximum system speed, use DIMMs since there are DIMMs that can run at the 100MHz bus speed. The fastest SIMMs can run at 100 MHz and higher bus speeds.

Following the rule that you should never buy more computer than you know you'll need immediately, install 128MB of RAM in this system. Although there are 256MB and 512MB SDRAM/RDRAM DIMMs available, nothing this computer is doing will require that much memory. So, ultimate system or not, 128MB is all it'll get. If the need arises, you can always put another 128MB SDRAM/RDRAM DIMM in the other DIMM slot.

Note

The most important thing about installing memory is making sure you buy the right kind. DIMMs are the standard for new PCs today, and there are two kinds. The older kind, SDRAM, is standard in most PCs. A newer kind, RDRAM, is more expensive and more efficient and speedy, but not all motherboards accept it.

To install the DIMM, first take a look at the DIMM and then take a look at the DIMM socket.

Although it's not initially obvious, there are small notches in the edge connector of the DIMM that align with mating plugs in the DIMM socket. Turn the DIMM so it lines up correctly and press it straight down into the socket until the latching levers on either side start to lock into position. Once the DIMM is fully seated, pull the latches up the rest of the way to lock in the DIMMs.

Step 4: Install the Video Card and Test the System

At this point, I feel I should tell you about a good friend of mine. This friend—we'll call him Jim—loved to build computers. Trouble is, most of the time they didn't work . . . well, not at first, anyway. I don't know if it was the parts he bought, a negative attitude, or what, but if he ever assembled a computer right into the case without testing the parts first, it never . . . I mean *never* worked.

I can't tell you why. He'd take the same parts, lay them out on the test bench, and plug them together first, and they'd work just fine. But skip the test, and the system would be doomed. Oh, he'd get it running eventually, but in the end, he always wound up taking it apart and putting it together again piece by piece on the test bench first.

So let me give you some advice: put the whole thing together first outside of the case. Once you're sure everything is working, *then* assemble it into the case. This, by the way, is good advice even if you don't have the same little black cloud following you around that my friend had.

Plug In the Video Card

The next step in building your computer is to plug in the video card. Although the philosophy at this point is to plug the system in and test it with as close to nothing plugged into it as possible, without a video card you'll have a real hard time telling what's going on in the computer. This system has an AGP video card, so find the AGP slot.

(If your motherboard has built-in video, you won't have an AGP slot, of course, but neither will you need to plug in a video card.) Press the video card firmly into the slot.

Next, connect the monitor to the video card. Before you test the system, you'll need to make sure the monitor is plugged in and powered on, of course, but that'll come a bit later.

Providing Power to the Motherboard

First, you'll need to plug the power supply into the motherboard. Look at the wires coming out of the power supply and locate the long one (ATX) or two short, different-looking ones (AT). That's what plugs into the motherboard; refer to Chapter 9, "Power Supplies and Power Protection," if you need more assistance.

Next, find the little pair of wires that run from the case's power button and hook them up to the corresponding pins on the motherboard. The motherboard manual's layout diagram will tell you which ones to use.

Tip

You may also wish to connect the wires for the speaker (mounted in the case) to the appropriate pins on the motherboard so that you can hear any warning beeps that the motherboard may emit during the startup process. They can help you in troubleshooting problems.

On many ATX systems, there are actually two power switches: one on the power supply itself and one on the case. The one on the power supply is the "hard shutoff" that turns power off or on to the whole shebang; the button on the front of the PC controls whether the motherboard *thinks* it's on or off. When you turn on the power switch on the power supply, you may hear the PC's fan kick on for a second and then back off again. That means that the motherboard is receiving power but has not gotten the signal from the power button to turn on.

Some power supplies have a power switch permanently connected to them with a long, thick wire. That switch mounts in the front of the case and functions as the sole power switch for the system. If you've got such a switch dangling on a wire from your power supply, be careful with it. The wires are not always well insulated on these. You might want to wrap it with black electrician's tape before you go further.

Finally, plug the power supply's power cable into the wall and flip the power switch on the power supply. If there is a separate power button on the case, push that too, and the system should begin to start up. You'll hear the power supply fan, and you should see some messages on the monitor indicating that something is happening.

The First System Test

Take a look at the monitor. Did the name of the video card come up? Did it count up as much memory as you installed? (Note that 64MB comes up to about 65 million, and 128MB reaches about 131 million.) If the system got that far, it's doing well. Turn everything off and move on to the next step. If it didn't make it, you need to recheck all of the steps you've taken so far.

The most frustrating problems to troubleshoot can be those where you don't see anything onscreen at all. Here are some tips.

▶ No power supply fan noise:

   ▶ Are both power switches on? Some systems have two, as noted earlier.

   ▶ Is the processor installed correctly?

   ▶ Is the memory installed correctly?

   ▶ Are you sure the power supply is not defective?

▶ Fan goes on but nothing appears onscreen:

   ▶ Is the video card installed correctly?

> Is the memory installed correctly?

> Is the monitor on and connected to the video card?

In my PC-building career, I have spent more time troubleshooting at this point in the process than any other. Fortunately, there are a finite number of things that could be causing the problem. Sometimes swapping out the motherboard, processor, memory, video card, and power supply, one by one, and replacing them with known good ones is the only way to pinpoint the problem.

After you get something onscreen, you might choose to go ahead and mount the motherboard in the case. (Skip to "Putting It All Together" later in this chapter for details). Everything you add from that point on can be added directly into the case, although less intrepid persons may decide to continue adding components outside the case and putting it all into the case only after the entire system has proved itself.

Step 5: Install the Drives

Now that you're sure the motherboard, memory, and video card are all working, the next thing you need to do is (as you may have guessed from the rather large lettering above) install the drives. Well, okay, not all the drives, just the floppy drive, hard drive (you're only using one in this system), and the CD-ROM or DVD.

All these drives need to go in next because it takes one or more of them to install the operating system.

Installing the Floppy Drive(s)

Figure 32.13 shows a floppy drive and its data cable. See the dark stripe along one edge of the data cable? This marks the wire that goes to pin 1 on the connectors. Another thing you should look for is a twist in the cable. The twist is positioned just before the connector for drive A:. The floppy drive controller is wired to detect this twist and assigns the drive nearest the twist to drive A:. Except for the cabling, there's no difference between an A: drive and a B: drive unless one is a (shudder) 5¼-inch drive.

Figure 32.13

Floppy drive and cable (notice the twist near one of the connectors)

If you look at the back of a floppy drive, you'll see that there are two connectors back there. One is the data connector and the other is the power connector. Although many drives print where pin 1 is on the circuit board, some don't. When that happens, just plug the data cable in so that the dark stripe (usually red) is nearest the power connector.

Installing the Hard Drive(s)

Like floppies, two hard drives can also share a single flat ribbon data cable. These, however, are not twisted to define the drives. Instead, they are set up as Master and Slave. Figure 32.14 shows the back of a typical IDE/EIDE hard drive. There are three connector areas. The largest area is for the data cable, the area with large pins is the power connector, and the center area is the control block where you place the jumpers for the Master and Slave settings.

Data Cable   Control Block   Power
Jumpers   Cable

Figure 32.14

Location of the
connectors on a
hard drive

There are usually two IDE/EIDE connectors on the motherboard. One is called Primary and the other is called Secondary. To specify a hard drive as drive C: (also called the boot drive), plug its data cable into the Primary connector and set its control block jumper to Master.

Now plug in the data cable and the power cable. Be sure to position pin 1 of the data cable nearest to the power connector and to align the angled corners of the power plug with the angled corners of the power connector.

Setting Up the BIOS

As you may recall, there are a number of different ways to get the computer to go to the BIOS setup screen. Since this one has an AMI BIOS, it's very easy. Shortly after the computer begins to boot up, it displays a message on the screen like the one shown in Figure 32.15.

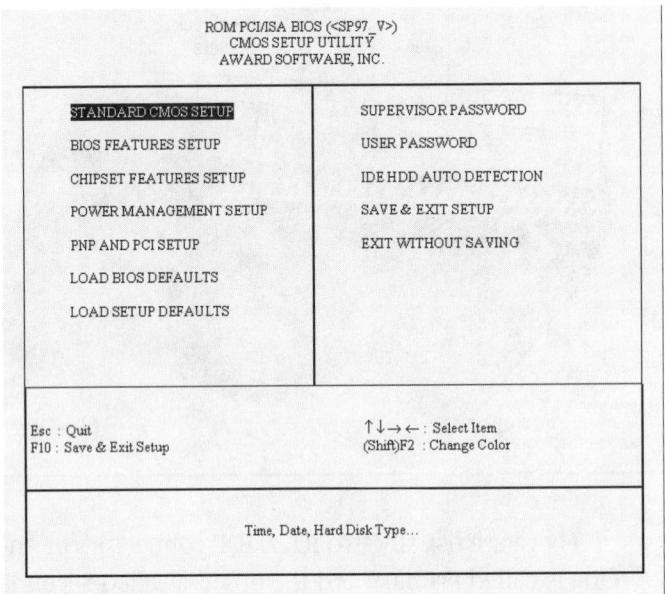

ROM PCI/ISA BIOS (<SP97_V>)
CMOS SETUP UTILITY
AWARD SOFTWARE, INC.

STANDARD CMOS SETUP	SUPERVISOR PASSWORD
BIOS FEATURES SETUP	USER PASSWORD
CHIPSET FEATURES SETUP	IDE HDD AUTO DETECTION
POWER MANAGEMENT SETUP	SAVE & EXIT SETUP
PNP AND PCI SETUP	EXIT WITHOUT SAVING
LOAD BIOS DEFAULTS	
LOAD SETUP DEFAULTS	

Esc : Quit   ↑ ↓ → ← : Select Item
F10 : Save & Exit Setup   (Shift)F2 : Change Color

Time, Date, Hard Disk Type...

Figure 32.15

The main BIOS setup screen

If you're like me, you're probably thinking that there are way too many options in the BIOS. But don't let it intimidate you. The first screen is just a table of contents. Every listing in the table of contents takes you to another page of options in the BIOS. Once you get into it, you'll find changing the BIOS options pretty easy.

In fact, some people get so comfortable with the BIOS setup that they start to change things they don't understand. *Don't do this.* If you don't know what you're doing, making changes to the BIOS can get you into more trouble than you even want to think about. Fortunately, there really aren't that many things that you'll need to do in the BIOS under normal circumstances. So let's move on to the things you need to do.

Setting the Time, the Date, and a Few Other Essentials

The settings you program into the BIOS will be saved by CMOS memory so the computer will know how to boot up each time you start it. The BIOS contains information on your hard drive, your built-in peripheral controllers like the floppy, COM ports, and so on.

If you're using an AMI BIOS like the one pictured in Figure 32.15, the first place you should go is to the Standard CMOS Setup page. To do this, just highlight it with the up or down arrow on the keyboard and press Enter. The Standard CMOS Setup screen is shown in Figure 32.16.

Figure 32.16

The Standard CMOS Setup screen

Take a look at the bottom of the screen. There you'll find the basic controls for the BIOS setup. Since it's text-based, you'll need to press different keys to make changes. To move from one item to the next, use the arrow keys on the keyboard. This moves the highlight around the screen. Once the item you want to change is highlighted, press the Page Up or the Page Down key to change the value in the highlighted area. To get an idea of how it works, move the highlight to the month at the top of the screen and press Page Up.

One thing that you should be aware of as you set the time is that the computer uses military time. This means that 12:00 (twelve hundred hours) is noon and 0:00 is midnight. Hours between 0:01 and 11:59 are A.M. hours. Hours between 12:01 to 23:59 are P.M. hours.

Another thing you may notice is that many of the items in the list are already filled in for you. This computer is set up to automatically detect quite a few devices. It found the 1.44MB floppy drive, the VGA display, and the memory. What you may also notice is that the hard drive is not listed. The BIOS, however, can automatically detect the hard drive. You just need to tell it you want it to. Once you're satisfied with all of the other settings on this screen, exit by pressing the Esc key on your keyboard to go back to the main screen.

Now move the highlight to IDE HDD Auto Detect and press Enter. The computer will immediately begin to auto-detect your drives. Once it finds one, it will display the drive's parameters in the box near the bottom of the screen. Sometimes it will give you two or three options for how you may want the drive set up. Generally, it's best to just press the Enter key to accept the default settings.

Once the system has detected your drives, exit the auto-detection screen by pressing the Esc key and go back to Standard CMOS Setup to confirm that your drives match what you have in the system. Finally, check the time and date.

Other BIOS Settings

On most motherboards, you can leave all the other settings as they are and function pretty well. But in case you get curious, here are some of the other common settings you might find in your BIOS setup program:

ECC Specifies ECC or non-ECC memory, two different types of DIMMs. You'll have this option only on a motherboard that supports both types of memory. ECC stands for error-correction code. Non-ECC is usually the default.

L2 cache ECC support If enabled, allows error checking to occur on data accessed from the L2 cache. Disabled is the default.

Plug and Play OS The default is No. Specifies whether a Plug-and-Play operating system is being used. No lets the BIOS configure all the devices; Yes lets the operating system configure them. You don't have to set this to Yes in order to use a PnP operating system.

Reset configuration data When set to Yes, clears the Plug-and-Play BIOS configuration data on the next boot and then resets itself to No.

Peripheral configuration Opens a screen in which you can configure your parallel, serial, and USB ports.

DMI events logging Lets you log any startup error messages and view them through the BIOS program.

Resource configuration Lets you tweak the memory block usage for various system resources. Not recommended unless you know what you're doing.

There are many other specialty settings that have to do with RAM, caches, recover time, aperture size, and so on, but you should not change these unless you have a specific reason for doing so. Such settings are set by default to standard values that work in almost all cases.

Exiting the BIOS Setup

If everything checks out, press Esc to get back to the main menu, move your cursor over to the item that says Save & Exit Setup, and press Enter.

This will reboot the system. Of course, it won't be able to boot up unless you already have a system on your hard drive, and you don't. But you're still not quite ready to install Windows. Remember that Windows is generally supplied on a CD-ROM, and so far you don't have a CD-ROM drive in the system. So let's do that now.

Installing the CD-ROM or DVD Drive

Installing a CD-ROM or DVD is pretty much the same as installing a hard drive. In fact, it's almost identical. You set the control block to Master or Slave (in this case there's only one other IDE-type drive, so make it Slave), plug in the power and data cables (remember, red stripe nearest the power connector), and you're done. You'll install the little audio cable later when you put everything into the case. To help you visualize the whole thing, Figure 32.17 shows a picture of the back of a typical IDE DVD drive (CD-ROMs look essentially the same).

Figure 32.17

The connectors
on the back of a
DVD drive

Attaching the Keyboard and Mouse

Okay, there's one more thing you need to do before you fire up the
computer to install the operating system. You need to attach a keyboard and mouse. Plug the keyboard into the keyboard connector.
There are two types of keyboard connectors: AT (larger) and PS/2
(smaller). All you need to worry about is whether you have the right
keyboard connector type for the plug on the motherboard. If not,
you can use an adapter to change it to the right type of plug.

Most new systems today come with a PS/2 style mouse port,
which looks identical to a PS/2 style keyboard port, so you need to
check the motherboard documentation to determine which is which.
Some cheaper systems may not have a PS/2 mouse port; if that's the
case, you'll need to get a serial mouse and plug it into one of the
nine-pin serial ports. See Figure 32.18.

Figure 32.18

9-pin and 25-pin
serial ports

Now, turn on the PC, and see whether the lights on the various
drives you've installed come on briefly and then go off. If they do,

it's a sign that they're working. Then turn the PC off again and go on to the next step.

Step 6: Install the Operating System

Ready to install the operating system? If you choose Windows as your operating system (and just about everybody does these days), it'll take between 30 and 60 minutes . . . at least, that's what Microsoft claims. Of course, as fast as this system is, you should be able to cut off quite a bit of that time. For home or small business use, Windows 98 is your best bet; for corporate use, you'll want Windows 2000.

The best way to install Windows on a brand-new system is to boot from the CD. You may need to go back into the BIOS setup program and set the Boot Sequence setting so that it checks the CD-ROM drive for a bootable CD, but that's an easy matter to take care of. Then insert the CD into the CD-ROM drive, turn everything on, and follow the onscreen prompts. Installation is painless and for the most part self-explanatory, with very clear instructions and explanations onscreen.

If you can't boot from the CD for some reason, boot from a floppy disk, switch to the CD-ROM drive (by typing its drive letter and a colon and pressing Enter), and type **SETUP** to begin the install process. As part of its setup, Windows will partition and format the new drive as needed. See Chapter 13, "Partitioning and Formatting IDE and SCSI Drives," for more information about drive setup.

Some notes on the process:

▶ As part of the Windows setup process, you'll be presented with Microsoft's terms and copyright notice. You'll have to accept these to continue. If you like, you can even read them all. On the other hand, almost no one ever does read them. Boiled down, they're telling you that you're not allowed to make extra copies of the program and that you may not modify it and distribute it or transfer the copy you have without deleting it from all your systems. There are a few other details, but that's basically it.

▶ Once you've agreed to abide by Microsoft's copyright, you need to prove that you are the rightful owner of the program. To do this, you need to enter the excessively long product code that is on the original sleeve or on a sheet of paper that came with the CD.

▶ The setup program asks you where you want to put the Windows files. It offers you the opportunity to put them into a subdirectory called Windows. Personally, I recommend you use that one. All of the programs you get for the system will expect it to be there.

▶ Some versions of Windows prompt you to create a boot disk as part of the install. You'll use this to boot up your system if, for some reason, you can't get your hard drive to cooperate some day. Think of it as a little insurance policy. It takes only a few minutes to make it, but it could really bail you out some day. For this step, you'll need a blank 3½-inch disk, labeled so that you'll remember what it is.

▶ After Windows installs itself, it goes through your system, searching for any Plug and Play devices. Of course, many of the things that you'll be adding are still lying on the table a few feet from the system, so it won't detect those. Don't worry, it'll notice them when you put them in later. For now, just relax and let it do its thing and reboot itself.

At the end of all this installation fervor, you'll end up with a basic system that can boot from the hard drive and load Windows. At that point, it's time to shut it all down again and add in the rest of your hardware. Onward to step 7!

Step 7: Install the Sound Card

For this system, you're using the Creative Labs' Sound Blaster Live! sound card. It provides 3D sound and 64 voices—it can play up to 64 sounds at once and can handle up to eight speakers!

Note

If you chose a motherboard with built-in sound support, you won't go through this step, of course, because the sound is already there.

It's a PCI board, so it needs to go into one of the PCI slots. This, by the way, is very important. It's actually possible to plug a PCI board into an ISA slot, but do not do this! You can fry both the board and/or the entire system, motherboard and all, if you are unlucky.

The PCI plugs are short and they are white or light colored. The ISA slots are much longer and are generally black or a dark color.

Now plug the sound card into one of the PCI sockets and plug in at least one set of powered speakers. These are speakers that have a built-in amplifier. They're necessary because the output from the Sound Blaster Live! card is not amplified. If you tried to play it through unpowered speakers, you would have a hard time hearing anything.

Note

Notice that when you plug in a card, there's a stem that goes down below the edge of the motherboard. This would normally engage in the bottom of the computer case to help secure the card. Here, however, if you've got the motherboard up on a box or book, as I suggested at the beginning of this chapter, it won't get in the way.

Turn on the computer and wait for it to start Windows. This time you'll probably get a lot of messages as you boot up, telling you that Windows has detected motherboard resources, the video card, and your sound card. It will also ask you for the disk(s) or CDs that came with the boards. Go ahead and install the drivers by putting in the disks it asks for, and let it continue booting up.

Once the system has finished booting, you should hear the Microsoft sound. If you don't, open the Control Panel by selecting it under Settings in the Start menu. Then double-click the Sounds icon and you'll get a window.

This window has a large area near the top labeled Events. This is a list of the different things that can trigger a sound in Windows. Next to the events that have sounds associated with them are little yellow speaker icons (see Figure 32.19). If you click one of the little speakers, the name of the sound associated to it will appear in the text window below the Events window.

Figure 32.19

The Sounds Properties window

Once you've selected one of the events, you can hear the sound it'll make by clicking the right arrow button to the right of the Preview window. Do that now.

Did you hear a sound?

If you did, the sound card is working correctly. Now, make sure the CD that came with the sound card is in its drive and run the setup program that came with it. This will install some additional drivers and a number of sound applications on your hard drive.

Step 8: Install the Rest of the Boards

Now you can pat yourself on the back and heave a deep sigh of pleasure—you're almost halfway through building the ultimate computer! There are only a few more things to install and test, and so let's get to those right now.

Installing the Modem

If you haven't already done it, power down the computer and plug in the modem. It also goes into a PCI slot.

Now power up the computer again and wait for the system to detect your modem and request the driver disk. Insert the disk into the floppy drive and press Enter. This will install the drivers for your modem and prepare it for connection to the Internet.

Installing the DVD Decoder Board

Shut down the system again and plug in the DVD decoder card. To understand what this card does, it's important to understand how movies are digitized and put onto a disc. Moving video images produce huge data files and, to make matters worse, they must be read at an incredibly fast rate to provide smooth full motion video on the screen.

As big as they are, DVD discs would not be large enough for a full two-hour movie if the video data were not compressed. DVD movies are compressed using a method called MPEG (Moving Picture Experts Group, the folks who created this method of compression). This compressed data is then stored on the disc and must be decompressed (also called decoded) before it can be viewed.

The computer has two methods of decoding the MPEG data, hardware and software decoding. The DVD decoder card you're installing will do hardware decoding, which produces an image that is much sharper than that produced by software decoding.

The DVD decoder card works in conjunction with the video card. To install the DVD decoder card, plug the card into another open PCI slot. A special video feed-through cable is included in the package with the video card. Connect the mini-DIN connector at one end of the feed-through cable to the DVD decoder card (shown in Figure 32.20). Then connect the other end of the feed-through cable (the end that has a 15-pin D-connector) to the video output of the video card (you'll need to remove the monitor's cable first). Finally, connect the monitor to the video output on the back of the DVD decoder board.

Figure 32.20

The DVD decoder card and its cable connections

Power up the computer one more time. This time the system should recognize the new DVD decoder board. Install the software that came with the board and then, as a final check, insert a DVD movie into the DVD drive and check it to make sure the video plays correctly.

Step 9: Put It All Together

Now it's finally time to put all of the pieces into the computer case. Take the system apart, put all of the cards, cables, and connectors aside, and get ready to put it all into the case, piece by piece. The first thing you should put in the case is the motherboard. It's easiest to do this when the case is empty.

Installing the Motherboard

The motherboard is held in the case by a couple of small brass nuts and screws and small white plastic standoffs like the one pictured in Figure 32.21.

Cross-sectional view

Motherboard

Standoff

Figure 32.21

A motherboard
standoff

One thing you may notice is that there are more metal clip locations than there are holes in the motherboard. This is so that one case design can accommodate a number of different board designs.

Holding the motherboard at an angle, make note of the locations of the clips and holes in the case that line up with holes in the motherboard. Some of the locations on the motherboard that line up will correspond to threaded holes in the case bottom. Screw the nuts into those holes (usually only one or two per case).

Tip

Use a nut driver to make sure the nuts are tight, but do not tighten them so much that you strip their threads or break them off.

Next, insert the white standoffs into the clips that aligned with holes in the motherboard. Then, very carefully, put the motherboard over the standoffs, making sure they all are showing through their respective holes, and gently press the motherboard down onto the standoffs. They should all snap into place.

Once the motherboard has been clipped to the standoffs, get a couple of the smaller screws and screw them into the nut(s) you installed earlier.

Most bags of screws that come with a case include several rust-colored paper washers. Install these between the motherboard and each screw to help prevent electrical shorting. This is not a problem in high-quality motherboards because the boards are manufactured with plenty of blank space around each screw hole, but on a cheaper board it can be a problem. Some people also put the paper washers *under* the motherboard around each screw hole, though it can be very awkward to do.

Installing the Power Supply

Once the motherboard is in, you can reinstall the power supply. The box itself goes in the same bracket it came out of near the top of the case, and, depending on the model, the power switch may need to be reinstalled in the front of the case. You'll probably need to take the plastic front piece off first so you can get to the screws that hold the switch on. This is all illustrated in Figure 32.22.

Figure 32.22

Installing the power supply

Attaching the Add-on Boards

If you look at the rear of the computer case, you'll see that there are a number of metal covers that line up with the various slot positions of the motherboard. You need to remove the covers that line up with the places you'll be installing boards into the motherboard.

Tip

When you unscrew the covers, be sure to put the little screws that come out in the container you set aside for them so that you can use them to attach the new boards you'll be installing.

There are three kinds of board connectors on the motherboard: AGP (for your video card), PCI (for all the other boards), and ISA (which you won't need now, but it can be used to add legacy boards later if you want).

Note

Ideally, the boards should fit straight down into the connector in the motherboard. Some, however, will be tight. There are a few tricks you can use to get these boards to cooperate. First, try rocking the board back and forth along its length as shown in Figure 32.23. *Never* rock it across its length; that could break the connector (see Figure 32.24).

Side to side motion

RIGHT

Figure 32.23

The right way to rock an expansion card

Front to back motion

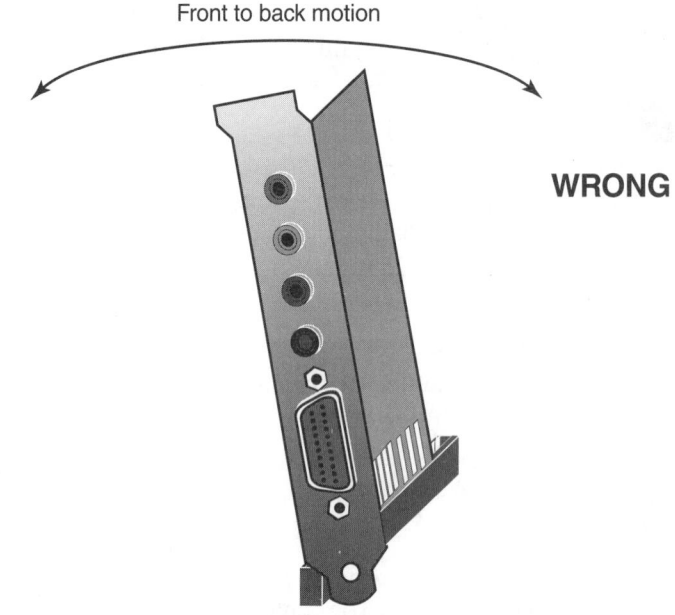

WRONG

Figure 32.24

The wrong way to
rock an expansion
card

Install the video card into the AGP slot (it's the one that's a bit
behind the other slots). Be sure to line up the metal tab at the bottom of the bracket so that it goes between the motherboard and the
case. Then, using one of the screws that came out of one of the
cover plates, secure the board into the computer case.

The one rule you should never break when you're installing
boards is ***don't force it!*** If it doesn't go in easily, look around. You'll
eventually find the culprit. Once I was installing a board and didn't
know about the "don't force it" rule. So I leaned into the board to
make it go in. Two things happened: (1) The connector cracked (this
is not a replaceable part). (2) I cut the wire that was under the board,
between the board and the connector—but not before jamming the
board and wire into the connector so tightly that I couldn't get
the board out of the connector without a pair of pliers. Needless to
say, I had no choice but to buy a new board and start all over again.

Once you've installed the video card, plug the power connectors
into the motherboard. I know I've said this before, but I think it's
important to remind you, just in case you've forgotten—be sure
you're plugging connectors into the correct spots.

Since there are two plugs on an AT power supply, it's possible to plug them into the wrong places. So remember this rule: the black wires go together near the center of the two connectors, as shown in Figure 32.25.

Power supply

Figure 32.25

Plugging the AT
power connectors
into the motherboard

Motherboard ⟶

Motherboard connectors ⟶

Okay, now it's time to test the system again. Plug in the mouse and keyboard. If you have a serial mouse, you'll need to plug in the serial adapter before you can attach the mouse. Don't worry about mounting the adapter in the case, just plug it into the motherboard for now.

Now plug in the power cord and monitor and switch on the system. After a few seconds you should see some activity on the display. If you do, you're ready to put in the rest of the boards and the drives.

Installing the Drives

Although there are several different arrangements you can use for the drives, I usually suggest that you put the DVD or CD-ROM in the topmost position in the case. This makes it easy to see and easy to reach over and put in CDs, since there's nothing on top of it. Next item down should be the Zip case, then the floppy drive, and finally, the hard drive.

Whichever drive arrangement you choose, be sure to reattach the smaller drive frame before you install any of the drives. Then grab the CD drive. Since the space at the top of most tower cases is a bit cramped, I suggest you plug the data and audio cables into the drive while it is still outside of the case. Then feed the loose ends of the cables through the front opening of the drive bay, followed by the drive itself (as shown in Figure 32.26).

Figure 32.26

Installing the CD drive

Once the CD drive is in the case, plug its power connector into its power receptacle, plug the end connector on the data cable into the motherboard, and screw the drive into the mounting. Make sure that the audio cable is routed into the computer so you can plug it into the sound card later.

The next drive to install is the Zip drive. The Zip drive is a 3½-inch drive, so you can put it into the top 3½-inch drive bay, or you can put it into a 5¼-inch bay using mounting rails and put it under the CD drive, as shown in Figure 32.27.

Figure 32.27

The Zip drive can go in the location shown or in the bay above (shown with floppy drive)

In this case, you'll put it in the 3½-inch bay. It should be installed just like the CD drive was. First, set the Master/Slave jumper to Master (it'll be the first drive on the secondary IDE connector). Then connect the data cable to the drive while it's still outside the case and feed the data cable through the open bay. Slide the drive in behind it, push the drive most of the way in, and attach the power cable to its connector. Then push it in the rest of the way and screw the drive into the side frames like you did with the CD drive. Oh, and don't forget to plug the other end of the data cable into the Secondary IDE connector on your motherboard. Also, check to make sure that pin 1 (the side of the data cable with the red stripe) is connected to pin 1 on both the drive and the motherboard connectors.

Now get the floppy drive and attach the twisted end of its data cable to the back of the floppy drive. Since there won't be a second floppy drive in this system, the second connector will be empty. Feed its cable through the open floppy bay and plug the far end of the floppy cable into the floppy connector on the motherboard just as you did with the Zip drive.

Installing the hard drive is similar to installing the other drives, but there is one small difference: it's installed from the inside of the computer. It doesn't show on the front of the system.

Unlike with the other drives, do not install the data cable yet. You'll be installing the connector in the center of the cable you used to connect the CD drive. Put the drive into the lowest position in the drive bay and push it forward into position, as shown in Figure 32.28.

Figure 32.28

Installing the hard drive

Next, find the middle connector of the data cable you used to connect the CD drive. Plug it into the data connector of the hard drive, aligning pin 1 on the drive with the red stripe on the data cable. Then plug the power connector into the hard drive and screw the drive into the drive frame.

Another System Check

Before you go any further, it's a good idea to test out the system again. This will confirm that you installed all of the drives correctly. So make sure the video cable is plugged into the monitor, your mouse and keyboard are connected, and your power plug is in. Then turn on the system.

The computer should boot up, read the hard drive, and go right into Windows. When it's finished booting, double-click My Computer and make sure that all of your drives appear in the window.

Note

If your system won't boot after putting the motherboard in the case, but it was working fine before, check to make sure there is no metal (besides the brass pieces) connecting the motherboard to the case. An errant screw is all it takes to create a short and make everything stop working. Check also to make sure there are paper washers around each of the screws holding the motherboard into the case.

Install the Rest of the Boards

Once you know that the system works with the drives, you can install the remaining boards. Insert them, one at a time, and then screw them down.

After you've installed all the boards, you should see one or more little wires dangling down from the back of the CD drive. This is the audio cable that feeds sound from the audio portion of the CD drive to the sound card, so you can play audio CDs and the sound from games that use audio tracks (like Diablo II and Age of Empires II).

Parallel and Serial Port Connectors

Getting tired of connecting wires? Well, hang on, you're almost done. Remember the serial and parallel cables? On an AT system, they're usually attached to one of those metal mounting brackets like the ones at the edge of the add-in boards. Get a small nut driver and remove the two cables from the mounting bracket. Now take a look at the back of the case. Notice the D-shaped recesses. These are mostly already cut out from the case. All you need to do is get a pair of pliers and push them back and forth a few times. They should pop out easily after that. On an ATX system, they're built right into the motherboard and have been there from the start of the process.

But wait! Don't start popping yet. Notice how one of the cutouts is larger than the others? The larger one is for the parallel port and the smaller one is for the serial port. I've had a few overzealous students pop out two large or two small cutouts. Do this, and you'll find yourself taping a cutout back into the case.

Front Panel Lights and Speaker

Okay, that's it! Only one more, tiny task left: connecting the LEDs and the system speaker. The front panel LEDs tell you if the system has power, when the hard drive is reading or writing, and so on. And the speaker beeps at you when the computer wants your attention. You may have connected a few of these earlier, when you were connecting the power switch and/or the system speaker for testing purposes.

The LED and speaker connections on the motherboard are all labeled—in tiny, almost unreadable letters. Unfortunately, there's always stuff around them that makes them hard to read. And of course, it's dark down in there. And to keep things interesting, the motherboard manufacturers change the positions of the connectors periodically, just to keep us on our feet (so to speak). Fortunately, there is often a chart in the motherboard manual that tells you what's what.

So get out your flashlight and magnifying lens, pull up close to the motherboard, and let's dive in.

In most cases, the bundle of little black connectors is rubber-banded together near the front of the case. Take off the rubber band (if it's there) and look closely at the connectors. Most of the time they'll also have labels. The following list tells you what wires you should have and what they are labeled.

HDD This is the hard disk drive activity light. The circuit that runs the hard drive turns this on whenever it writes/reads to/from the hard drive.

TBLD This is the Turbo LED, a holdover from the old days when some systems had two speeds at which it could operate. This is not used today. Ignore it.

SPKR The speaker beeps once when you boot and many times if there's an error. It also provides the sound for some applications, although more and more programs use the real sound card found in most systems today.

KEYLOCK The keylock is not commonly used because it is so easy to overcome. The keylock prevents the keyboard from entering data if the key is not in and turned. Trouble is, all anyone needs to do is remove the cover and pull off this connector.

PWR This is often grouped together with the keylock connector. It lights when the system has more than five volts of power available.

How do you plug these in? Simple, just shove the appropriate connector onto the pins. There is, however one minor thing you need to look out for. Since they're LEDs, the connectors are polarized. That is, they need to go on one particular way. And the way is almost never labeled. So you may need to experiment until you get it right. You can sometimes tell from the chart in the motherboard manual. The little connectors usually have writing on one side and indents on the other, and they all go the same direction. So if you figure out one of them, just face all the others the same way and you're home free.

Well, that's it—you're finished building the ultimate computer! All you need to do now is put the cover on and secure it with screws. Be sure to hang onto all the documentation that came with your components, both for future reference and in case you need them for warranty service or replacement.

Troubleshooting Tips

The list of things that can go wrong when you build your own computer can be rather large since you're working with so many different components. However, if you find yourself in trouble try these suggestions:

▶ Make sure you've properly installed all the components.

▶ Check to see that all your data cables are seated correctly and the pins line up.

▶ Consult the documentation for all your components to make sure you're following their installation and setup instructions.

Aside from these general troubleshooting tips, you might find these additional suggestions helpful:

▶ Do your research. Read everything that comes with your hardware, and if you can, visit manufacturer Web sites for FAQs, helpful hints, and more.

▶ Take your time. Block an entire day (or more) if you've never done this before.

▶ Plan on things going wrong. All but the most experienced technicians usually make mistakes. If you do, back up and—if you have to—start over.

▶ Don't get too frustrated. When things don't work, relax and take a deep breath. You won't be very productive if all you can think about is throwing your computer out the nearest window. If you need to, put it away and come back when you've calmed down.

▶ Give yourself plenty of space. Don't try to build a computer on a very small or crowded desktop. Use a large table or workbench so you can spread all the pieces around and everything isn't in one large pile.

▶ Be organized. Use separate bins for your different component subassemblies, screws, and other parts. If you have to, label your bins so you don't get confused. You might also label your data and power cables so you know where you want them to go. Organization also helps you not lose parts.

Well, now that you've got the computer built, it's time to use it! In the next chapter we'll cover some basics about setting up your Windows application so that it works best for you.

33

Software Solutions: Using the Control Panel

One of the most useful features of Windows is the Control Panel. The Control Panel gives you access to utility programs that can make the difference between finishing an installation and total frustration. (Trust me; I've been there.) In this chapter, we'll take a short tour of the utility programs you'll find in the Control Panel. We'll look at what they do and how to use them.

To open the Control Panel, click the Start button, click Settings, and then click Control Panel. By the way, since there are some applications that produce their own icons in the Control Panel, yours may look a little different from the one in Figure 33.1. Don't worry about it. We'll look at the most common utilities you'll need (or at least find useful). This chapter focuses on the Windows 9*x* platform, but Windows NT/2000 is similar.

Figure 33.1

The Control Panel

The screen shots and content in this chapter were written based on Windows 98 Second Edition (SE), but the Control Panel is virtually unchanged in the new Windows Millennium Edition which should be released by the time this book goes to press. Most of the features discussed here are also available in Windows 95.

Using the Control Panel

Set Accessibility Options

1. From the Control Panel, double-click Accessibility Options.

2. Set keyboard accessibility features on the Keyboard tab:

   StickyKeys Makes Shift, Alt, and Ctrl function as toggles

   FilterKeys Ignores brief or repeated keystrokes

   ToggleKeys Plays sounds when Caps Lock, Num Lock, and Scroll Lock are pressed

3. Set Sound accessibility features on the Sound tab:

   SoundSentry Generates visual warnings when Windows makes a sound

   ShowSounds Displays captions (in compatible programs) for the sounds it makes

4. Choose a High Contrast display option on the Display tab.

5. Set up the mouse to be controlled by the keyboard on the Mouse tab.

6. Set general usage options on the General tab.

7. Choose OK.

Set Up New Hardware in Windows

1. Install the new hardware and start the computer. Windows may detect the new device automatically.

2. If Windows does not detect the new device, run the Add New Hardware Wizard from the Control Panel, which will attempt to detect new devices.

3. If the device cannot be found, perhaps there is a device conflict. If you can determine which device is conflicting with the new one, remove it from the system and restart.

4. Go to Device Manager (from the System icon in the Control Panel) and remove the old device you took out. Then restart the PC again with the new device installed. Windows should detect it.

5. After you get the new device up and running, reinstall the old device. Windows will probably assign it a different resource than it had used before to avoid conflict.

Add New Software

1. Insert the disk or CD in your PC. Some CDs have an AutoRun feature that starts the installation program automatically.

2. If the installation program does not start, choose Add/Remove Programs from the Control Panel and click the Install button on the Install/Uninstall tab.

3. Follow the prompts that appear.

Remove Software

1. Choose Add/Remove Programs from the Control Panel.

2. Select the program to uninstall from the list on the Install/Uninstall tab.

3. Choose Add/Remove.

4. Follow the prompts that appear.

Add or Remove Windows Components

1. Choose Add/Remove Programs from the Control Panel.

2. Choose the Windows Setup tab.

3. Double-click a category to see the programs in it.

4. Place or remove checkmarks beside the program names to install or uninstall them.

5. Choose OK. You may be prompted to insert your Windows CD.

6. Follow the prompts. You may be prompted to restart Windows.

Change the System Date and Time

1. Double-click Date and Time in the Control Panel, or double-click the clock in the system tray.

2. Change the date and/or time as needed.

3. Choose OK.

Choose a Different Video Driver

1. Double-click the Display icon in the Control Panel, or right-click the desktop and choose Properties.

2. On the Settings tab, click the Advanced button.

3. Click the Change button.

4. Work through the Update Device Driver Wizard to choose a different driver.

Change the Video Resolution or Color Depth

1. Double-click the Display icon in the Control Panel, or right-click the desktop and choose Properties.

2. On the Settings tab, choose a color depth from the Colors list.

3. Drag the Screen Area slider bar to choose a different resolution.

4. Choose OK.

Test a Modem

1. Double-click Modems from the Control Panel.

2. Choose the Diagnostics tab.

3. Click the modem to test.

4. Choose More Info.

Setting Accessibility Options

The Accessibility Options are a set of controls that can make it easier for people with special disabilities to use their computer. Double-click this icon and you'll see a window that looks like the one pictured in Figure 33.2.

Figure 33.2

Accessibility
Properties

This control window contains a number of pages that are accessible through the tabs along the top of the pages. Each tab is labeled according to the options it provides.

Note

In addition to the Accessibility Options, there are also Accessibility Tools. These include a magnifier, high-contrast mouse pointers, and a wizard for setting up the Accessibility Options. These Accessibility Tools are not installed by default in Windows; you must use Add/Remove Programs in the Control Panel to install additional Windows components such as these. See "Windows Setup" later in this chapter.

Keyboard Functions

Use the Keyboard tab of the Accessibility Options to manage the settings for keyboard functions. Keyboard functions let you control your interaction with the keyboard and its interaction with your computer.

StickyKeys

StickyKeys are keys that stay in effect until you press them again. This is useful for people who find it difficult to press two keys at once. For example, if you turn on StickyKeys and then press and release the Alt key, the system will behave as though you were holding down the Alt key until you press the Alt key again. The Alt key, in this case, is the modifier key, because it modifies the meaning of the other keys you press in conjunction with it. Other modifier keys you can use are Ctrl and Shift.

To enable the StickyKeys feature, select its check box in the Accessibility Properties box.

To use StickyKeys, press the desired modifier key twice in a row. To cancel the sticky key, just press the modifier key one more time.

To configure how StickyKeys works, choose the Settings button next to it in the Accessibility Options window. For example, you can specify whether or not StickyKeys will make a short tone when you turn on a modifier key and when you turn it off again. Another option, which is disabled by default, is Use Shortcut. If you turn this on, you can enable StickyKeys by pressing the Shift key five times in a row. There are quite a few options you can adjust in this window; they're pictured in Figure 33.3.

Figure 33.3

Settings for
StickyKeys

FilterKeys

Take a look at the FilterKeys option in Figure 33.2. Choose its Settings button to display the dialog box shown in Figure 33.4, in which you can set two functions. First, it can be programmed to ignore multiple keystrokes of the same key. This is useful if you tend to press some keys twice or more accidentally when you type.

Figure 33.4

Settings for FilterKeys

Second, FilterKeys can ignore quick keystrokes and slow down the keyboard's key repeat rate. This is an especially useful setting if you find that you often get several repeats of a character as you're typing when you intended to type only one.

You can even choose the repeat rate and the rate at which multiple keys are detected by clicking the Settings buttons in the Settings for FilterKeys box and setting the rate on the slider (Figure 33.5).

Figure 33.5

The FilterKeys control slider

Note

Once you've chosen a new rate, it's a good idea to test the repeat speed by typing in the Test Area below the slider.

As with all the other Accessibility Options, you can tell the system to beep or flash the screen (or both) when the computer activates the function by choosing that option under Notification in the Settings box for the selected option.

ToggleKeys

This simple function makes a sound whenever the Caps Lock, Num Lock, or Scroll Lock key is pressed. It's useful for beginning typists who may accidentally press one of these without realizing it. If you enable it, you can then use a shortcut to turn ToggleKeys on or off as you work.

To enable the function, choose Settings in the ToggleKeys section of the Accessibility Options box. Then mark the Use Shortcut check box in the dialog box that appears. Once the feature is enabled, you can turn on ToggleKeys by pressing and holding the Num Lock key for five seconds.

Sound

The Sound tab of the Accessibility Properties window contains options for controlling sounds (see Figure 33.6).

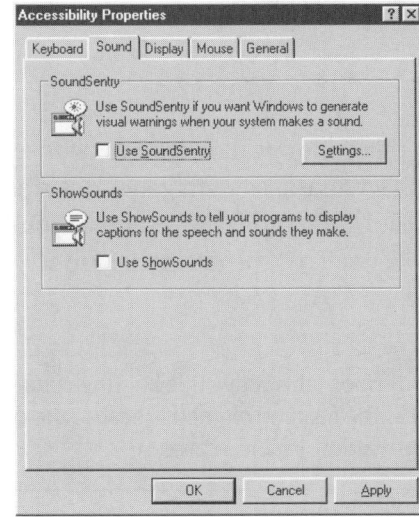

Figure 33.6

The Sound tab of the Accessibility Properties window includes the SoundSentry and ShowSounds options for controlling the sound of your computer.

SoundSentry

This feature is very useful for hearing-impaired users. It flashes parts of the screen when the computer would normally generate a sound. To set this, click the Settings button in the SoundSentry box, and it will open a window like the one in Figure 33.7.

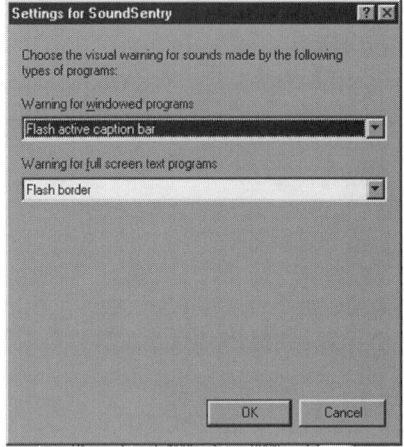

Figure 33.7

Settings for
SoundSentry

The controls in this window allow you to choose which part of the screen will flash when the system generates a sound. For windowed programs (those that aren't full screen) you can select the title bar, the window itself, or the entire desktop.

Note

In general, it's better to choose the active title bar (the colored bar across the top of the active window) as the flashing element because the desktop can be obscured by the active window in some cases.

ShowSounds

ShowSounds is an add-on function for SoundSentry that displays short text messages describing warnings that might have audio messages or signals.

Display

The Display tab of the Accessibility Options window contains options for controlling the display (see Figure 33.8).

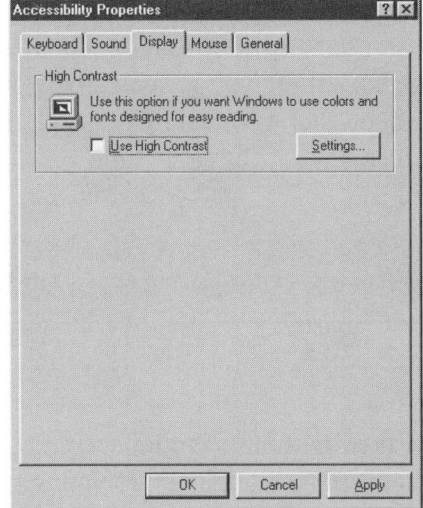

Figure 33.8

The Display tab of the Accessibility Properties window includes the Use High Contrast option for controlling the display of your computer.

This page has only one option: Use High Contrast. Actually, though, there's more to this setting than meets the eye (so to speak). Click on the Settings button to display the window in Figure 33.9, and you'll see what I mean.

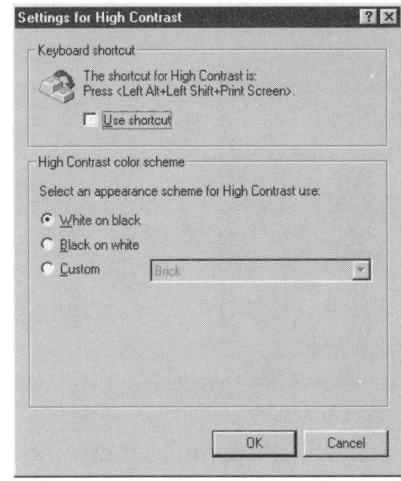

Figure 33.9

Select one of the High Contrast color schemes

If you use one of the two primary default color scheme options (White on Black or Black on White), you'll get a display that can be more easily seen by people with visual problems. Custom lets you choose any of the standard Windows color schemes. Marking the Use Shortcut check box allows you to switch between two color schemes (as your mood dictates) just by pressing the Left Alt, Left Shift, and Print Screen keys at the same time.

Note

In High Contrast mode, some system fonts may appear larger.

Mouse

The Mouse tab of the Accessibility Options window doesn't really control mouse functions. Instead, it allows you to control the mouse pointer with the keyboard (see Figure 33.10). It's designed to help people who have trouble with (or are unable to use) a mouse.

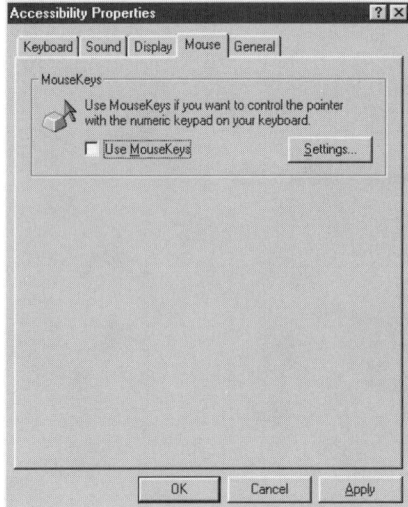

Figure 33.10

The Mouse tab of the Accessibility Properties window includes the MouseKeys option that allows you to control the mouse pointer using the keyboard.

Selecting this option will allow you to move the mouse pointer by pressing the arrow keys on the keyboard. Click the Settings button to get the window shown in Figure 33.11, and you can control the way the mouse behaves. The options let you control the speed and acceleration of the mouse pointer. You can also specify whether you want to be able to change the pointer speed on the fly by pressing the Ctrl key to speed up and the Shift key to slow down.

Figure 33.11

The MouseKeys settings window

General

The General tab of the Accessibility Options window has three functions: Automatic Reset, Notification, and SerialKey Devices (see Figure 33.12).

Figure 33.12

The General tab

Automatic Reset turns off the accessibility features if you don't use the computer for a while. The default time is 5 minutes, but it can be set to any time you like (in 5-minute increments) up to 30 minutes.

Notification gives you a warning message and/or sound when one of the accessibility features is turned on or off.

SerialKey allows you to use special add-on devices through one of your serial ports as an alternative interface to the mouse and keyboard. Because of his degenerative nerve disease, Dr. Stephen Hawking, the famous physicist, uses one of these controls (among other things) to control his computer.

Adding New Hardware

When you install a Plug-and-Play board in your system, Windows will generally detect it automatically and either install its drivers from those already in your system, or ask you to insert a driver disk from the manufacturer.

Some boards need a little help, however. You'll find that help in the Add New Hardware control. If you've installed a new board in your system and Windows didn't notice, double-click Add New Hardware and it'll open a wizard that will walk you through the process of getting it installed (Figure 33.13).

Figure 33.13

The Add New Hardware Wizard

Click the Next button to move through each step of the process, as Windows examines your system and detects first Plug-and-Play, then non-Plug-and-Play devices. Running this wizard can take a while, since the computer will check every possible hardware configuration. Once it's done, though, it will usually find any new devices that have been added.

But of course, there will always be exceptions. Sometimes the Add New Hardware Wizard will find the wrong things. And sometimes it won't find a new board because there is some kind of conflict. For example, if you have a new board that is designed to use IRQ15 and you already have a device using IRQ15, the wizard may be unable to find it.

Most modern devices are Plug-and-Play compatible, and can have their IRQs assigned on the fly by Windows when it first detects them. If a particular device requires one particular IRQ, you should install it first, let it have its persnickety pick of the IRQs, and then install more congenial devices afterward. That may mean removing some of your existing devices temporarily, then reinstalling them afterward.

To do this, first determine which existing device is conflicting with the new one. Check the new device's documentation to find out which IRQ it needs, and then use Device Manager to find out which device is using it.

To get to the Device Manager, double-click System in the Control Panel and the System Properties window (shown in Figure 33.14) will open. (You can also right-click the My Computer icon on the desktop and choose Properties to get to the same place.) This is another one of those windows that has a number of tabbed pages. The first page, called General, shows a brief list that describes the computer and lists your operating system version, owner's name, manufacturer, processor, and installed memory.

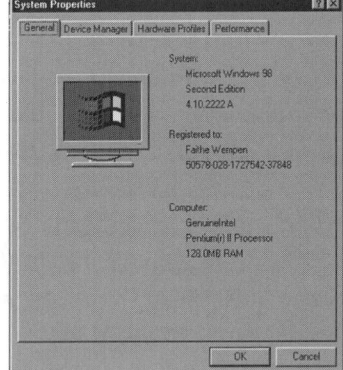

Figure 33.14

The General tab of the System Properties window

Click the Device Manager tab, and a list of installed devices appears. Double-click Computer at the top of the list. A box opens listing the system IRQs and telling what devices are assigned to them. (See Figure 33.15).

Figure 33.15

Check out IRQ allocation here.

Now return to the Device Manager tab (Figure 33.16). The Device Manager shows all of the devices that are installed in your computer. Since everyone's computer is a little different, chances are your list won't look exactly like this one. But it will have most of the same devices. The information in the list is organized like an outline, with main items and the items within them listed as subcategories below them.

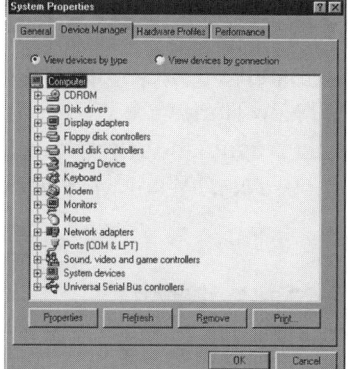

Figure 33.16

The Device
Manager tab

Under Computer, you'll find categories for your drives, controllers, keyboard, and so on. And under those categories you'll find the specific devices themselves. For example, under Modem, you might find US Robotics 56K V.90. To see the subcategories, click the plus sign beside the category.

We'll take a closer look at the Device Manager a little later on in this chapter in the section "System." Right now you're here to do one thing: delete the item from this list that corresponds to the removed hardware. Once it's gone from here, the computer can assign its resource to the uncooperative device you're trying to install. Let's say the conflicting device is a scanner. Go down the list until you find the scanner (hint: it's probably in the Imaging Device category), click it, then click the Remove button near the bottom of the window. Click OK to close the System Properties window.

Windows should ask if you wish to reboot, but if it doesn't, you need to shut down the system (choose Shut Down from the Start menu) and power the system down. Make sure the older device in the conflict is unhooked, removed, or turned off (so that Windows won't immediately redetect it at startup), and that the newer device is in, on, and ready to go. Now power up the system again. This time, the system should have little trouble installing the new board and its driver(s). Once the new board is installed, shut down the system again, plug in the old board, and let the system redetect it. It should find a new IRQ for it, and you'll have installed both boards.

Installing Boards that the System Can't Find

Sometimes you'll want to install a legacy board that the system just can't find at all. If the Add New Hardware Wizard is unable to detect the new device, try running it again, but this time, at the screen shown in Figure 33.17, choose No, I Want to Select the Hardware from a List.

Figure 33.17

Tell the Add New Hardware Wizard that you will select the device yourself.

Now when you click the Next button, you'll be asked to choose a hardware category. See Figure 33.18.

Figure 33.18

Select the device category.

Click Next again, and one of two things will happen, depending on the category you chose:

▶ You'll immediately see a list of manufacturers and models of that hardware type, from which you can select your model. Figure 33.19 shows an example for network cards.

▶ A specialized wizard runs for that type of hardware. Work through it, making one last-ditch effort at autodetection, before the list of manufacturers and models appears.

Figure 33.19

Select the make and model of your device.

Select your make and model, or, if you have a disk that came with the hardware, insert it and choose Have Disk to use the drivers from the disk instead. (You can also use Have Disk if you have downloaded drivers from the Internet, as described in the following section. Just point to the drive and folder on your system where you stored the download.)

If the manufacturer isn't listed and you don't have a driver disk, choose the top item, Standard Types, and click the item in the right-hand list box that most closely matches the device you're installing (good luck). This will install a driver that we hope will do an adequate job of running your device. Sometimes you'll get lucky and it'll work. Sometimes you won't be so lucky and . . . well, you may need to spend some time finding the right drivers.

Getting the Drivers Online

At one time, if you needed a driver and you didn't have it, you had only one recourse—call the manufacturer. Sometimes, if you were lucky, they would be able to send you the driver(s) you needed within a short period of time (a week or so). But all too often, it took longer . . . much longer. And you'd have to wait and wait to install your board. And sometimes, if you were really unlucky, the manufacturer was out of business or simply didn't support that board any more.

Today, things have improved a lot because of the Internet. If you need a driver, generally all you need to do is go to the manufacturer's Web site, find their support page, and download any drivers you need on the spot.

What's really amazing, though, is that not long ago, I needed a driver for a board that was made by a company that had gone out of business. In the old days, I'd have been out of luck. With the manufacturer gone, my chances of finding the driver were about zero.

But with the Internet, I was able to get the driver with almost the same ease I would have had if the company were still around. Once I found out that the company had disappeared, I went to a search engine (like Lycos, Alta Vista, or Yahoo), entered the name of the device I was looking for (I used its actual part number), and waited a few minutes.

I got about a thousand hits! (Hits, by the way are items that match your search criteria.) I looked down the list of hits and found a Web site that was operated by a users group that maintained a file of what they called "Obsolete Drivers."

They had exactly what I was looking for. Within minutes I had downloaded the driver and installed it in my system. Thanks, Internet!

Tip

One thing you should know when you are downloading anything from a Web site: it's a good idea to run a virus check on any file you download before you install it in your system. Even the best-intentioned Web site operators can inadvertently use files that have become infected.

Adding and Removing Programs

Like the Add/Remove Hardware feature in the Control Panel, the Add/Remove Programs feature has multiple tabbed pages (see Figure 33.20). The top page lists all of the programs that are currently in your Registry. The Registry is a file that contains a record of all the programs in your system that are Windows-compliant. These programs use an assortment of resources, and the Registry keeps track of them.

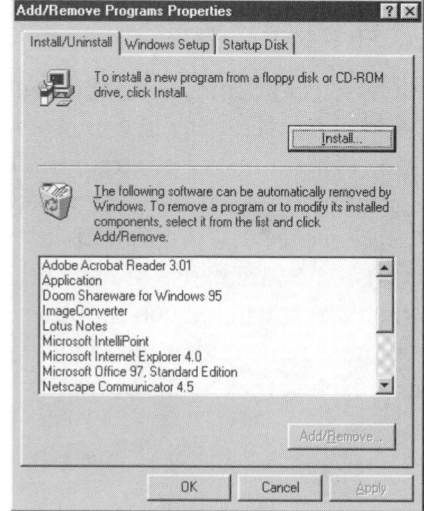

Figure 33.20

The Install/Uninstall tab of the Add/Remove Programs Properties window

Why have a Registry? Well, in the old days of computing, you just copied programs into your computer and it ran them. Some programs were a little large, so they might be broken into task-specific modules that made it easier to maintain them. Later, some programmers found that they could maintain a library of certain modules that did certain tasks that they could use over and over in different programs.

Eventually, this led to the concept of object-oriented programming where each object in a program had a set of qualities or capabilities that defined it. An object could have an image or an icon that was connected to it. It could use special kinds of windows and so on. These resources are maintained in different places. The Registry keeps track of all the pieces of your programs so it can find them when it needs them.

All this means that if you try to delete an installed program, you're very likely to wind up leaving a lot of the program behind to just take up space on your hard drive. By using the Add/Remove Programs utility, you can get rid of all the parts of a program when you delete it.

Removing (Uninstalling) a Program

To remove a program, select it from the list box on the Install/Uninstall tab and click Add/Remove. An Uninstall program will run that removes the program. (The Uninstall program will be different depending on the program; most programs come with their own.)

Sometimes there are pieces to a program that the Uninstall Wizard can't delete because they are in use or have other active components in them. In that case, it will tell you that there were pieces left behind and that you must remove them manually. To see which pieces were left behind, click the Details button.

Installing a Program

To install a program, insert the CD or disk containing the program and click the Install button on the Install/Uninstall page. It searches all your removable disk drives for programs to install and suggests an installation program to run, as shown in Figure 33.21. Choose Finish to run that program and install the software.

Note

Some CDs will AutoRun. This means that as soon as you put them into the drive, they are read and begin their installation process. If you insert a program CD and it offers to install itself, go ahead and let it.

Figure 33.21

The Run Installation window asks if this is the program you want to install

Windows Setup

Windows Setup lets you install additional Windows components that were not installed when you initially loaded Windows. When you select the Windows Setup tab, you'll get the page shown in Figure 33.22.

Figure 33.22

The Windows Setup tab

The list contains program categories. The ones with checkmarks in white boxes are fully installed (that is, all the programs in that category are installed). Those with checkmarks in gray boxes are partially installed (that is, some but not all of the programs in that category are installed). To see what programs are in a category, or to select individual programs from a category, double-click a category or click once and then click Details.

To install a program or an entire category, click its check box and click the OK button. (You can check more than one item before clicking OK.) To delete an item, uncheck its box by clicking it. The check will disappear and Windows Setup will remove those items when you click OK.

When you choose OK, you may be prompted for your Windows CD, so be prepared for that.

Startup Disk

The last tab in the Add/Remove Program Properties window opens the Startup Disk page (Figure 33.23). Creating a startup diskette is pretty simple—put a blank disk into your floppy drive and click the Create Disk button. You can use a startup disk to start the PC if it won't boot from the hard drive for some reason.

Figure 33.23

The Startup Disk tab is used to create a boot disk.

Date/Time

Clicking Date/Time in the Control Panel gives you the Date/Time Properties window, shown in Figure 33.24, which is used to adjust the time and date of your computer.

Figure 33.24

The Date/Time
Properties window

There's a calendar on the left and a clock on the right. To set the date, choose the month and year you want from the selection lists and click the day you want from the calendar. To change the time, click the item you want to change in the numeric list box and either type in a new time or click the up/down arrows to scroll to the correct time.

The Time Zone field tells your computer where it is so it can tell you the time and date of other countries accurately. To change time zones, just open the Time Zone drop-down list and choose one.

Display

The Display Properties windows has more options than we need to cover in an upgrade and maintenance book, but there are a few things that we should look at. Double-click the Display icon from the Control Panel and you'll see a window that looks like Figure 33.25. You can also see the same window by right-clicking the desktop and choosing Properties.

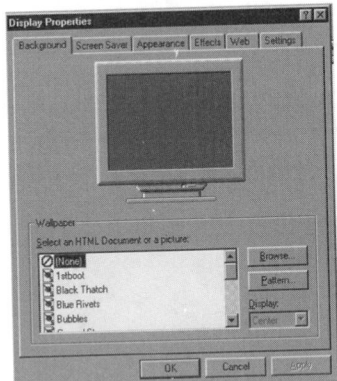

Figure 33.25

The Background tab of the Display Properties window

Display Properties lets you change your screen saver, background, and quite a few other items that can be fun, but the only thing that we'll need to look at is the Settings tab. This is where you can change the resolution of your screen, the number of colors displayed, and the type of display adapter and monitor you use (Figure 33.26).

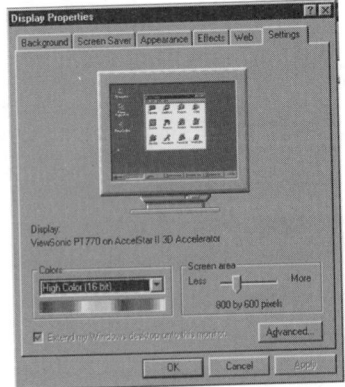

Figure 33.26

The Settings tab

Directly under the picture of a monitor, you'll find a description of the current display adapter and monitor. Below that are two areas that let you change the color depth and screen resolution. Depending upon the display adapter and monitor you're using, you'll be able to choose anything from 16-color to True Color, which may be either 24-bit or 32-bit, depending, once again, upon your display adapter and monitor.

To set other properties for the display, click the Advanced button. The tabs that appear in the resulting dialog box vary depending on your video card's driver (Figure 33.27 shows a typical one), but they all have at least these four tabs: General, Adapter, Monitor, and Performance. We'll look at only the four basic tabs, since there's no way I can guess what extra tabs you have.

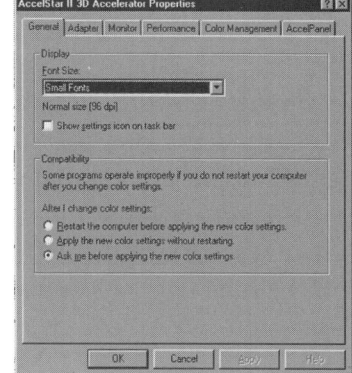

Figure 33.27

The General tab of the advanced Display Properties window

General

The General tab (Figure 33.27) lets you change the system font size and whether the system restarts after you change any of the display parameters.

Display (Font Size)

You can choose small, large, or custom font sizes. Large fonts are 125 percent the size of the Small (normal) fonts. If you select Other, a window like the one in Figure 33.28 will open.

Figure 33.28

The Custom Font Size window

You can change the font size by typing a percentage value in the text box at the top of the window or by dragging the ruler in the graphic below it to the left or the right. Dragging to the right makes the font larger and dragging it to the left makes it smaller. You can choose any size between 20-0 and 500-0.

Once you've chosen a size, a sample of the text size will appear in the graphic window below the ruler (Figure 33.29).

Note

Changing the font size can have a profound effect on the appearance of your computer display and the programs you run.

Figure 33.29

Viewing the new font size

Show Settings Icon on Taskbar

Select or deselect this check box to choose whether you want an icon in the system tray that provides quick access to the Display Properties dialog box.

Compatibility

When you change the color depth of the display (from the Color palette list on the Settings tab, as shown in Figure 30.26), Windows will prompt you to restart, or not, depending on what you choose here. If you do not restart after changing the color depth, some programs may not look quite right, or the icons on your desktop may appear in odd colors.

Adapter

The Adapter tab helps you control the settings for your video card.

Driver

To choose a different driver, click the Change button and work through the Update Device Drivers Wizard.

Just like when you install new hardware (as you learned earlier in the chapter), Windows may correctly detect your video card, or it may not. If it detects it as Standard VGA or some variant of that but you actually have a better card, you may need to tell it to look for drivers on disk, and then provide the driver disk that came with the video card. To do that, in the Update Device Drivers Wizard, choose Display a List of the Drivers in a Specific Location So You Can Select the Driver You Want as shown in Figure 33.30, and then choose Have Disk.

Figure 33.30

Choose to confine the search for drivers to a specific location.

Refresh Rate

The refresh rate is the frequency at which the display is repainted, or refreshed, on the monitor. This is limited to the highest rate that both the monitor and the video card can agree upon.

The default setting is Optimal, and that's what I recommend you leave it set at in most cases. However, if your monitor is not directly supported by Windows (see the following section), but you know that it can support a higher refresh rate than a generic monitor, you might want to choose a specific refresh rate.

After setting the refresh rate, Windows makes the change and gives you the opportunity to return to your previous settings. If you do not choose Yes to accept the new settings within a few seconds, it reverts automatically, so you are not stuck with an unusable setting. You can tell if the refresh rate is too high because the screen will look distorted, especially around the edges.

Monitor

On the Monitor tab (Figure 33.31), you can click the Change button to change the monitor that Windows thinks you have. This works just like changing the video card's driver, as in the preceding section.

You can also choose whether or not the monitor is Energy Star-compliant (a power savings standard), whether to automatically detect Plug-and-Play monitors (recommended, usually), and whether or not to reset the display when it resumes after being suspended (a Power Management thing).

Figure 33.31

Configure the settings for your monitor.

Performance

There is only one control on the Performance tab (Figure 33.32): a slider that sets the hardware acceleration. The higher the setting, the better video performance you get. You should leave this set to Full unless you are having problems with video compatibility with a specific program. (Games are usually the worst offenders here.) In that case, crank the Performance down one level and try the program again; keep doing this until you can run the program without errors.

I have found that video problems with running certain programs can be corrected in most cases by installing the most recent DirectX drivers for your video card. You can usually download these from the video card manufacturer's Web site, either separately or as part of a complete driver update.

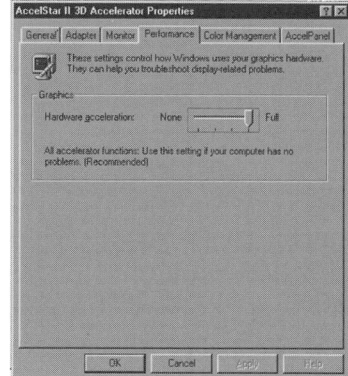

Figure 33.32

Use Full hardware acceleration unless you are experiencing problems.

Modems

Now skip to the Modems properties in the Control Panel. This is used to configure and test your modem. When you double-click this icon, you'll see the Modems Properties window as shown in Figure 33.33.

There are two tabbed pages in this control window, General and Diagnostics.

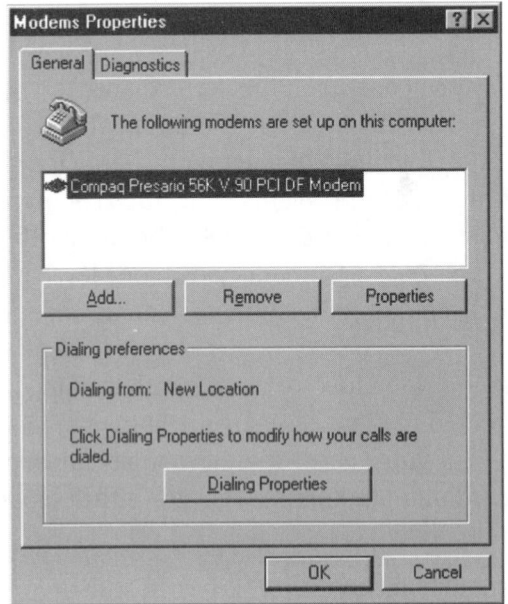

Figure 33.33

The Modems
Properties window

General

The first tabbed page, General, shows you the modems that are connected to your computer. Although most people never have more
than one, you can actually connect several if, for example, you
wanted to use your system as a dial-up e-mail server, or if you have
an ISDN modem for your Internet connection and a fax/modem for
sending faxes.

Dialing Properties

Click the Dialing Properties button at the bottom of the General tab to
open the Dialing Properties dialog box. From here you can configure
your location, including area code, number to dial for an outside line,
and so on. Incidentally, you can get to this same dialog box by choosing Telephony directly from the Control Panel. See Figure 33.34.

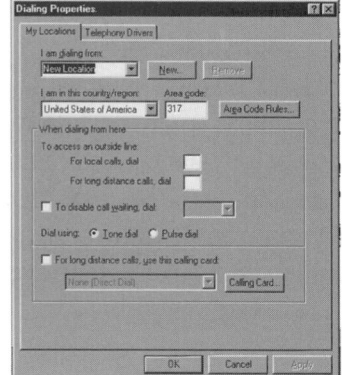

Figure 33.34

The Dialing Properties
dialog box

Adding or Removing Modems

Using the Add and Remove buttons in the Modems Properties window,
you can install or remove modems to or from your system. The Add
button runs the Add New Modem Wizard, which is a specialized version of the Add New Hardware Wizard you saw earlier in the chapter.

The Remove button removes a modem's driver from the system.
After you remove a modem's driver, you also need to physically
remove the modem from the PC (if it's an internal) or disconnect it
(if it's an external model). Otherwise, Windows may redetect it and
reinstall its driver the next time you start the PC.

Modem Properties

Choose a modem and then click the Properties button to open the
modem's Properties box. This box has two tabs, General and
Connection.

From the General tab, you can choose the modem's COM port,
adjust its speaker volume (if it has one), and set its maximum speed.

From the Connection tab, you can control the connection and call
preferences. Connection preferences control the number of data bits
transmitted, as well as the parity and stop bits. Of course, most

modem programs automatically set these parameters for you, so you'll rarely have to make any changes here.

Call preferences control how the modem dials. The default values (which you shouldn't change unless you really know what you're doing) are Wait for Dial Tone before Dialing and Cancel the Call If You Can't Get Connected within a Minute (60 Seconds). If you're ever in a foreign country that has a lot of trouble connecting, you might want to increase this value to give the modem a chance to eventually connect.

Diagnostics

The Diagnostics tab of the Modems Properties window lets you communicate with your modem and try a few of the standard commands to see if it will respond correctly. Although the test isn't conclusive, it does tell you if the modem is connected and can receive commands. Figure 33.35 shows the Diagnostics tab. Choose the modem and then click the More Info button. After a few seconds, a report appears. If at least some of the lines report "OK," then the modem is installed and working correctly.

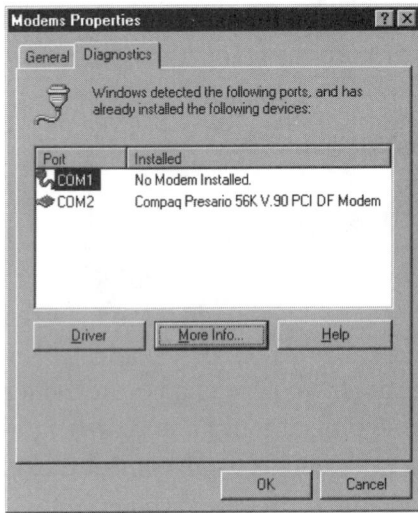

Figure 33.35

The Diagnostics tab

System

Although I mentioned the System feature of the Control Panel earlier, we really only touched on its capabilities. This is where you can look at and change any of the devices in your computer. Double-click the System icon and you'll see the System Properties window.

Device Manager

Click the Device Manager tab and you'll see the list of all your devices. Click any of the listed devices that have a plus sign beside it, and it will display a list of all the devices that are in that category. For example, double-click Ports. This displays all of the ports on your system, including your serial ports and parallel ports (see Figure 33.36). The serial ports are called Communications ports, and the parallel ports are called Printer ports.

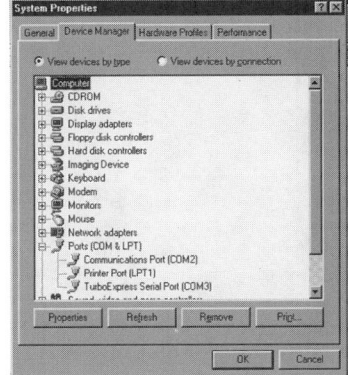

Figure 33.36

The Device Manager tab with the Ports list

There are two ways you can organize the devices in the Device Manager, by device type or by connection. Generally, it's easier to organize them by type because it organizes the devices by *what* they are, not *where* they are.

To look at the properties of a device, you can double-click the device or you can select it and then click the Properties button. If you do this, you'll open a window that shows the device specifications and the driver that's running it.

For some devices, you can look at and set which port, IRQ, and memory it uses. However, generally it's a bad idea to mess with those settings because it prevents Windows from reassigning resources should you decide to add or remove devices later. Sometimes you can choose an alternate IRQ and/or memory configuration for a device to resolve a resource conflict that otherwise has you stumped. For example, suppose you have two devices that both want to use IRQ11, and one of them isn't working because of it. You can display the properties for one of the devices by double-clicking it in Device Manager and displaying its Resources tab. At the bottom of the screen, it will report the conflict with the other device. To fix the conflict, deselect the Use Automatic Settings check box and choose a different configuration from the Settings Based On list. Make sure to choose a configuration that results in No Conflicts being reported in the Conflicting Device List. See Figure 33.37.

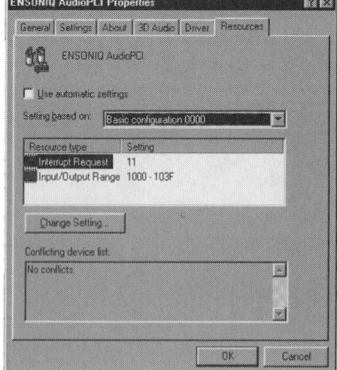

Figure 33.37

Choose an alternate set of resource settings for the device.

If there aren't any suitable configurations to choose from in the Settings Based On list, you can assign an IRQ or memory address manually. To do so, click the one you want (IRQ or Input/Output Range) and then click Change Setting. A box appears in which you can make your selection. See Figure 33.38.

If you see a message that the resource cannot be modified, try the other side of the equation—that is, try to change the resources for the other device involved in the conflict. (This process was covered in more detail in the section "Adding New Hardware.")

Figure 33.38

Manually assign
resources to a device
to eliminate a
conflict.

Troubleshooting Tips

If you're having problems with the software side of your computer—
that is, with Windows—try some of these ideas for fixing it up:

▶ If you don't have an Accessibility icon in your Control Panel, add
the Accessibility tools with Add/Remove Programs. Choose Accessibility from the list of categories on the Windows Setup tab.

▶ If Windows doesn't automatically detect your new hardware, use
the Add New Hardware icon in the Control Panel to detect it.

▶ If a device conflict prevents Windows from seeing the device, try
removing devices that are possibly competing with the new
device and adding them back in after the new device is working.

▶ Older devices may not be Plug-and-Play compatible; check older
circuit boards for jumpers or switches that set a particular I/O
address or IRQ.

▶ Sometimes removing a device from Device Manager and allowing
the system to redetect it will assign a different IRQ to the device
and avert a conflict.

▶ Use the Have Disk option to install an updated driver from a disk
or from a download.

▶ After removing a program from Windows, its folder may be left on the hard disk, along with a few stray files. You can manually delete these.

▶ If the settings choices on the Settings tab of the Display Properties dialog box are less than what you know your video card will support (for example, if it shows only 16 colors and only 640 × 480 standard VGA resolution when you have a better-than-VGA video card—that is, any video card made in the last eight years or so), perhaps the video driver being used is wrong. Windows may have incorrectly detected it as Standard VGA. In that case, choose Advanced. On the Adapter tab, choose Change to install a different video driver.

▶ If your modem isn't working but you don't know whether it is a problem with the modem itself or with the phone line, run a diagnostic check. Choose Modems from the Control Panel. On the Diagnostics tab, choose the modem and click More Info. If at least some of the lines in the resulting report say "OK," the modem itself is working.

Well, I hope you learned much and enjoyed reading this edition of *The Complete PC Upgrade & Maintenance Guide*. My goal with this book is to instruct not only how to remove and install new hardware and maintain your system, but to provide background information, in layperson's terms, of how computers and software actually work. It's this foundation that will help you understand the technologies of decades to come—how they work, how they fit into the big picture, and how they will affect older technologies. PC technology will continue to evolve, and as it does we'll find ourselves increasingly reliant on our PCs, both in the home and office environments. Knowing how to fix or diagnose a PC or make it perform better is, and will continue to be, a highly prized talent. And so I thank you for choosing the 11th edition of this book as your guide through the vast amounts of information, gotchas, real-world stories, and asides. Also, I'd like to add a hearty thanks to those of you who have been loyal readers throughout the years.

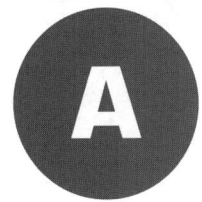

A Short Overview on Reading Hexadecimal

INTRODUCTION

Throughout this book, and in other technical publications, you see numbers expressed not in *decimal,* the numeric system that we're all accustomed to, but rather in *hexadecimal,* a somewhat different system. This appendix is a quick guide to what you need to know about hexadecimal.

The decimal system is based on the number 10 as we know it—the number of fingers on most people's hands. *Dec-,* a word root, permeates the language: *decathlon* refers to a contest with 10 sporting events, *decimate* literally means to kill every 10th man, and *December* is the name of what once was the 10th month. We write "ten" as "10," but that's really only correct if we base the numbering system on 10. Strictly speaking, the number that I wrote is "one zero," and it means different things in different number systems.

Look at the sequence of how we write the first 11 numbers: 0, 1, 2, 3, 4, 5, 6, 7, 8, 9, 10. Why is "ten" written with two digits, not with one digit, as all the numbers before are? Because the system is based on 10. So ten is written 10, pretty much by definition once you decide that you're using 10 as your number base. Next, look at 10 times 10, or 100: it is written 100—the first number with three digits. Ditto for the first number with four digits—1000, which is 10 times 10 times 10. Why'd we pick 10 as a basis for a number system? No one knows, but the obvious guess is that 10 is, again, the number of fingers that most people have.

For reasons that aren't really worth pursuing here, it's easiest to talk about numbers in a computer system (memory or I/O addresses, for example) not in a number system based on 10, but rather on 8 or 16. A base-8 system is called *octal,* and a base-16 system is called *hexadecimal,* or *hex* for short. PCs tend to use hex, so I'll discuss that here. You don't even have to know hex in its entirety, just a few salient points.

Counting in Hex

Recall that a base-10 system uses 10 single-digit numbers up to, but not including, the number 10 (0–9). A base-16 system, similarly, has 16 single-digit numbers up to, but not including, 16 (0–9 and A–F). You can see a base-16 system in Table B.1.

TABLE A.1 Hex Digits and Decimal Equivalents

Hex Digit	Decimal Value
0	0
1	1
2	2
3	3
4	4
5	5
6	6
7	7
8	8
9	9
A	10
B	11
C	12
D	13
E	14
F	15
10	16

As you can see, the next number after F is 10 (which is 16 in decimal). Next would come 11 (which is 17 in decimal). With any numbering system, you count from 0 to the highest number in the system and then go to 10. In decimal, the two-digit numbers increase up to 99, the last two-digit number. Hex goes up to FF. One hundred in hex is not 10 times 10, but 16 times 16—which is 100 in hex, 256 in decimal.

Reading Memory Hex Addresses

You will recall that the typical PC, when running DOS, can address 1MB of memory—640KB for user data and programs and 384KB of reserved area for video memory, ROMs, and buffers. Let's look at how to read memory addresses in hex.

First, understand that to a computer, 1MB is a binary number equivalent to decimal 1,048,576. It's composed of 16, 64KB (65,536 decimal) *segments.* Conveniently, 10000 in hex is equal to 64KB. And 640KB is 10, 64KB segments, so the low 640KB is the address range from 00000 to one short of A0000, or 9FFFF. All of the addresses in 64KB increments are shown in Table B.2.

TABLE A.2 Memory Addresses in Decimal and Hex

Decimal Address	Hexadecimal Address	Preceding Hex Address
0KB	00000	N/A
64KB	10000	0FFFF
128KB	20000	1FFFF
192KB	30000	2FFFF
256KB	40000	3FFFF
320KB	50000	4FFFF
384KB	60000	5FFFF
448KB	70000	6FFFF
512KB	80000	7FFFF
576KB	90000	8FFFF
640KB	A0000	9FFFF
704KB	B0000	AFFFF
768KB	C0000	BFFFF
832KB	D0000	CFFFF
896KB	E0000	DFFFF
960KB	F0000	EFFFF
1024KB	100000	FFFFF

So when you see that a VGA display adapter puts memory in addresses A0000–BFFFF, you know that the board is using the addresses starting just above 640KB and going up to just short of 768KB. And when you see that the BIOS ROM is addressed from FC000 to FFFFF, you know that it's using addresses right up to the top of the first megabyte.

You've endured enough theory for the moment. Right now, let's put it to good use. Here are a couple of examples.

Example 1: Counting in Hex— Determining the Size of a Range

If COM1 uses I/O addresses 3F8 to 3FF, how many I/O addresses does that mean that it uses?

Count 'em up: 3F8, 3F9, 3FA (remember that A comes after 9), 3FB, 3FC, 3FD, 3FE, 3FF—eight addresses.

Example 2: Comparing Overlapping ROM Address Ranges

Let's look at a hypothetical example concerning the installation of a ScanJet interface card. When installing this card, you should be concerned that the address of the ROM on the ScanJet card doesn't conflict with the addresses of any other ROM in the system.

Now let's say that the only thing in the system with ROM is a VGA, but what is its ROM address? C0000–C5FFF. The scanner interface has a factory default of C4000–C7FFF. That would be okay for an EGA, as the EGA's ROM ends at C3FFF, just short of C4000. But the VGA's ROM goes all the way up to C5FFF, which tromps all over the range C4000–C7FFF.

You may have had some trouble following that, so let's review exactly what the quandary is.

1. The factory default address for the scanner is C4000–C7FFF. Note that this is a range of values: C4001, C4002 . . . C7FFF, and there are lots of them—16KB of addresses, in fact.

2. The address range of the EGA ROM (if there were an EGA in the system) is C0000–C3FFF, and that range does not conflict with the ScanJet's range. The last value in the EGA range is C3FFF. C4000 comes after C3FFF in hex. You compare numbers in hex just as you do in decimal. If they've got the same number of digits, just compare the leftmost one. In this case, they've both got hex digits "C" in the leftmost position, so there's no difference. If the leftmost digits are the same, look immediately to the right. The number 4 comes after 3, so C4000 is after C3FFF.

3. The address range of the VGA ROM is C0000–C5FFF, and that conflicts with the ScanJet ROM range of C4000–C7FFF. The top of the VGA ROM range is C5FFF. The bottom of the ScanJet ROM range is C4000, which is below C5FFF. Again, how do you know? Compare them: The C in the leftmost position is the same, the 4 and 5 are different. The C5FFF, then, is above C4000—the starting point for the ScanJet ROM—and so the VGA range overlaps the ScanJet ROM range.

So we've briefly looked at how to use hex when looking at I/O address ranges and memory address ranges. If you'd like to get into the nitty-gritty details, like actually converting hex to decimal and back, read on. But you don't need to know any more.

Converting Hex to Decimal

This isn't tough, but you may live your whole life without having to know how to do it, if you prefer. This is especially true because the Windows calculator can do the conversions for you if you're in a hurry. But for those of you pioneers who want to know how it's done, here's what you do.

First, look back at Table B.1. Use it to convert each of the hex digits to decimal. For example, F in hex is 15 decimal, 8 in hex is 8 decimal, and so on. For this example we'll use the hex number C801F—how do you convert it to decimal?

1. **Write the hex number on a piece of paper. Create a column labeled "Subtotal" on your paper. Put a zero in it.** Work from left to right, crossing out hex digits as you convert them. Subtotal is where you'll accumulate the decimal value. So write down C801F, and put a zero under Subtotal.

2. **Examine the hex number.** If there are no digits left, stop. Subtotal contains your converted decimal value. Otherwise, remove the leftmost digit from what remains of the hex number, convert it to decimal, and add it to the subtotal. So remove the C and convert it to decimal—12, in this case—and add it to the subtotal. The subtotal becomes 12 for the moment. Cross out the C in the hex number, and you've got 801F left.

3. **Go back to step 2.** Step 2 says to first see if there are any hex digits left. There are, so continue: Multiply the subtotal (12) by 16 so it becomes 192. Take the leftmost digit—8—from the hex number, convert it to decimal (8 hex is equal to 8 decimal), and add it to the subtotal (192 + 8 = 200). Cross out the 8 in the hex number, leaving 01F.

4. Hex digits remain, so it's back to step 2 again. Subtotal times 16 makes the subtotal equal to 3200 (200×16). The next hex digit is 0; subtotal plus zero leaves it unchanged. Cross out the 0 in the hex number, leaving 1F.

5. The subtotal times 16 is 51,200 (3200×16). The next hex digit is 1, which is equal to 1 decimal. Add it to the subtotal, making the subtotal 51,201. Cross 1 from the hex number, leaving F.

6. Subtotal (51,201) times 16 is 819,216. The next hex digit is F, which is equal to 15 decimal. Add it to the subtotal (819,216 + 15), and you get 819,231. Cross out F from the hex number, leaving nothing.

7. There's nothing left in the hex number, so the subtotal is the desired result. C801F hex is equal to 819,231.

For those of you who prefer a simpler approach, open the Windows Calculator (choose Start ➢ Programs ➢ Accessories ➢ Calculator).

Then choose Scientific from the View menu. Make sure the Hex (hexa-decimal) button is selected and enter the number you want to convert. Then click the Dec (decimal) button, and the calculator will display the converted number.

Converting Decimal to Hex

This involves just about the reverse process. Let's convert 75,000 from decimal to hex.

1. **Divide the decimal number by 16. Convert the remainder to a hex digit and make that the *rightmost hex digit.*** That's the first digit in the subtotal. The number 75,000 divided by 16 yields a quotient of 4687 and a remainder of 8. Because 8 decimal is just 8 hex, the rightmost hex digit is 8.

2. **Divide the quotient by 16. Make the remainder the next hex digit—put it to the left of the subtotal.** Dividing 4687 by 16 yields a new quotient of 292 and a remainder of 15. As 15 decimal is F hex, the next hex digit is F, so the subtotal is now F8.

3. **If the new quotient is zero, stop.** Otherwise, just keep dividing the quotient by 16 and putting the hex remainder to the left of the subtotal. Dividing 292 by 16 yields a new quotient of 18 and a remainder of 4, so 4 goes in the subtotal. It's now 4F8.

4. **Divide 18 by 16** and you get a quotient of 1 with remainder 2, so the subtotal becomes 24F8.

5. **Finally, divide 1 by 16** and you get quotient 0, remainder 1, so the subtotal is now the final total—124F8. 124F8 hex equals 75,000 decimal.

To convert decimal to hex using the Windows Calculator, open the Scientific Calculator again. This time, make sure the Dec (decimal) button is selected and enter the number you want to convert. Then click the Hex (hexadecimal) button, and the calculator will display the converted new number.

Glossary

Numbers and Symbols

*
See asterisk.

/
See slash.

//
See double slash.

:
See colon.

?
See question mark.

@
See at symbol.

****
See backslash.

¼-inch cartridge
See quarter-inch cartridge.

10/100
A term used to indicate that a device can support both Ethernet (at a data transfer rate of 10Mbps) and Fast Ethernet (at a data transfer rate of 100Mbps).

10Base-T
A version of the Ethernet networking standard that uses unshielded twisted-pair cable and RJ-45 connectors.

10Base-T cable

A popular Ethernet cable that uses unshielded twisted-pair wiring and RJ-45 connectors at each end. You should use Category 3 10Base-T cable with 10Mbps Ethernet networks.

10Base-TX cable

A popular Ethernet cable that uses unshielded twisted-pair wiring and RJ-45 connectors at each end. You should use Category 5 10Base-TX cable with 100Mbps Ethernet networks.

10Mbps

An abbreviation for 10 megabits per second, the standard Ethernet network data rate.

100Mbps

An abbreviation for 100 megabits per second, the standard Fast Ethernet network data rate.

1394

See IEEE 1394.

23B+D

Common abbreviation for Primary Rate ISDN, which has 23 B or bearer channels, and one D or data channel.

24/7

Abbreviation for round-the-clock availability, implying that the service is available 24 hours a day for seven days per week.

24-bit color

A color display in which the level of each of the primary colors is represented by 8 bits of information. A 24-bit color image can contain over 16 million separate colors.

2B+D

Common abbreviation for Basic Rate ISDN, which has 2 B or bearer channels, and one D or data channel.

A

a-b box

A switching box that allows a peripheral device such as a printer to be shared between two or more computers. It can be switched manually or through software.

AC adapter

A small external power supply that converts main electrical power to the low-voltage DC required for a laptop or notebook computer or other device needing its own power supply.

Accelerated Graphics Port

Abbreviated AGP. A specification developed by Intel to support high-speed, high-resolution 3 D graphics and video images.

AGP uses a dedicated point-to-point connection between main memory and the graphics controller so that images can be displayed faster and more smoothly than when they have to travel across the main system bus. AGP runs at 66MHz and supports data transfer rates of up to 533Mbps.

accelerator board

An add-in, printed circuit board that replaces or augments the main processor with a higher-performance processor. Using an accelerator board can reduce upgrading costs substantially because you won't need to replace the monitor, case, keyboard, and so on. However, the main processor is not the only component that affects the overall performance of your system. Other factors, such as disk-access time and video speed, contribute to a system's performance.

access

To use, write to, or read from a file, or to log in to a computer system or network.

access time

The period of time that elapses between a request for information from disk or memory and the arrival of that information at the requesting device.

Memory-access time refers to the time it takes to transfer a character between memory and the processor. Disk-access time refers to the time it takes to place the read/write heads over the requested data. RAM (random-access memory) may have an access time of 80ns or less, while hard disk–access time would be less than 10ms.

ACPI

See Advanced Configuration and Power Interface.

active hub

A device that amplifies transmission signals in a network, allowing signals to be sent over a much greater distance than is possible with a passive hub.

An active hub may have ports for coaxial, twisted-pair, or fiber optic cable connections, as well as LEDs to show that each port is operating correctly.

active-matrix display

A high-quality liquid-crystal display used in laptop and notebook computers with a wide viewing angle and very narrow depth. Also known as thin-film transistor (TFT) display.

active termination

A technique used to terminate a Small Computer System Interface (SCSI). Active termination reduces electrical interference in a long string of SCSI devices.

adapter

A printed circuit board that plugs into a computer's expansion bus to provide added capabilities.

Common adapters include video adapters, joystick controllers, and input/output (I/O) adapters, as well as other devices, such as internal modems, CD-ROMs, and network interface cards (NICs). One adapter can often support several different devices. Some modern PC designs incorporate many of the functions previously performed by these individual adapters on the motherboard.

address

1. The precise location in memory or on disk where a piece of information is stored. Each byte in memory and each sector on a disk has its own unique address.
2. The unique identifier for a specific node on a network. An address may be a physical address specified by switches or jumpers on the network interface card hardware or a logical address established by the network operating system.
3. To reference or manage a storage location.
4. Information used by a network or the Internet to specify a specific location in the form `username@hostname`, where `username` is your user name, logon name, or account name or number, and `hostname` is the name of the Internet Service Provider (ISP) or computer system you use. The hostname

may consist of several different parts, each separated from the next by a period.

address bus

The electronic channel, usually from 20 to 64 lines wide, used to transmit the signals that specify locations in memory.

The number of lines in the address bus determines the number of memory locations that the processor can access because each line carries one bit of the address. A 20-line address bus (used in early Intel 8086/8088 processors) can access 1 MB of memory, a 24-line address bus can access 16MB, and a 32-line address bus can access more than 4 GB. A 64-line address bus can access 16 EB.

ADSL

See asymmetric digital subscriber line.

Advanced Configuration and Power Interface

Abbreviated ACPI. An interface specification developed by Intel, Microsoft, and Toshiba for controlling power use on the PC and all other devices attached to the system. A BIOS-level hardware specification, ACPI is dependent on specific hardware that allows the operating system to direct power management and system configuration.

Advanced Power Management

Abbreviated APM. An API specification from Microsoft and Intel intended to monitor and extend battery life on a laptop computer by shutting down certain system components after a period of inactivity.

Advanced SCSI Programming Interface

Abbreviated ASPI. A programming standard that defines how Small Computer System Interface (SCSI) devices work together and with the other components that make up the PC.

Advanced Technology Attachment

Abbreviated ATA. The ANSI X3T10 term for the disk drive interface standard known as Integrated Drive Electronics (IDE).

Advanced Technology Attachment Packet Interface

Abbreviated ATAPI. An interface standard used to connect a CD-ROM drive to an Enhanced IDE adapter.

aftermarket

The market for related hardware, software, and peripheral devices created by the sale of a large number of computers of a specific type.

alphanumeric

Consisting of letters, numbers, and sometimes special control characters, spaces, and other punctuation characters.

AGP

See Accelerated Graphics Port.

American Standard Code for Information Interchange

Abbreviated ASCII, pronounced "as-kee." A standard coding scheme that assigns numeric values to letters, numbers, punctuation characters, and control characters to achieve compatibility among different computers and peripheral devices. In ASCII, each character is represented by a unique integer value, from 0 to 255.

analog

Describes any device that represents changing values by a continuously variable physical property, such as a voltage in a circuit. Analog often refers to transmission methods developed to transmit voice signals rather than high-speed digital signals.

anonymous FTP

A method used to access an Internet computer with FTP that does not require you to have an account on the target computer system. Simply log on to the Internet computer with the username *anonymous* and use your e-mail address as your password. This access method was originally provided as a courtesy so that system administrators could see who had logged on to their system, but now it is often required to gain access to an Internet computer that has FTP service.

You cannot use anonymous FTP with every computer on the Internet; only with those systems set up to offer the service. The system administrator decides which files and directories will be open to public access, and the rest of the system is considered to be off limits and cannot be accessed by anonymous FTP users. Some sites only allow you to download from them; as a security precaution, you are not allowed to upload files to them.

antistatic device

Any device designed to minimize electrical shocks caused by a build-up of static electricity, including special floor mats, wrist bands, even sprays and lotions.

antivirus program

A program that detects or eliminates a computer virus. Some antivirus programs can detect suspicious activity on your computer as it happens; others must be run periodically as part of your normal housekeeping activities.

An antivirus program locates and identifies a virus by looking for characteristic patterns or suspicious activity in the system, such as unexpected disk access or EXE files changing in some unusual way. It recognizes the virus by comparing information from the system against a database of known viruses, which is kept on disk.

API

See *Application Programming Interface.*

APM

See *Advanced Power Management.*

Application Programming Interface

Abbreviated API. The complete set of all operating system functions that an application can use to perform such tasks as managing files and displaying information.

An API provides a standard way to write an application, and it also describes how the application should use the functions it provides. Using an API is quicker and easier than developing functions from scratch and helps to ensure some level of consistency among all the applications developed for a specific operating system.

In operating systems that support a graphical user interface, the API also defines functions to support windows, icons, pull-down menus, and other components of the interface. In network operating systems, an

API defines a standard method that applications can use to take advantage of all the network features.

application-specific integrated circuit

Abbreviated ASIC. A computer chip developed for a specific purpose, designed by incorporating standard cells from a library rather than created from scratch. Also known as a gate array, ASICs are found in all sorts of appliances, including modems, security systems, digital cameras, even microwave ovens and automobiles.

architecture

1. The overall design and construction of all or part of a computer, particularly the processor hardware and the size and ordering sequence of its bytes.
2. The overall design of software, including interfaces to other software, the operating system, and the network.

archive

1. To transfer files to some form of long-term storage, such as magnetic tape or large-capacity disk, when the files are no longer needed on a regular basis but must be maintained for periodic reference.
2. On the Internet, a site containing a collection of files available via anonymous FTP.
3. A compressed file.

archive file

A single file that contains one or more files or directories that may have been compressed to save space. Archives are often used as a way to transport large numbers of related files across the Internet.

arrow keys

Any of the four keys labeled with arrows pointing down, up, left, and right, which are used to move the onscreen cursor.

ASCII

See *American Standard Code for Information Interchange.*

ASCII extended character set

The second group of characters, from 128 to 255, in the ASCII character set. The extended ASCII character set used in the PC includes mathematical symbols and characters from the PC line-drawing set.

ASCII file

A file that contains only text characters from the ASCII character set. An ASCII file can include letters, numbers, and punctuation symbols but does not contain any hidden text-formatting codes. Also known as a text file or an ASCII text file.

ASCII standard character set

A character set that consists of the first 128 (from 0 to 127) ASCII characters. The values 0 to 31 are used for nonprinting control codes, and the range from 32 to 127 is used to represent the letters of the alphabet and common punctuation symbols. The entire set from 0 to 127 is referred to as the standard ASCII character set. All computers that use ASCII can understand the standard ASCII character set.

ASIC

See *application-specific integrated circuit.*

ASPI

See *Advanced SCSI Programming Interface.*

assembly language

A low-level programming language in which each program statement must correspond to a single machine language instruction that the processor can execute.

Assembly languages are specific to a given microprocessor or microprocessor family and, as such, are not portable; programs written for one type of processor must be rewritten before they can be used on another type of processor.

asterisk

You can use the asterisk (*) as a wildcard character to represent one or more unknown characters in a filename or filename extension.

asymmetric digital subscriber line

Abbreviated ADSL. A high-speed data transmission technology originally developed by Bellcore and now standardized by ANSI as T1.413 that delivers high bandwidth over existing twisted-pair copper telephone lines. Also called asymmetric digital subscriber loop.

ADSL supports speeds in the range of 1.5 to 9Mbps in the downstream direction (from the network to the customer), and upstream speeds in the range of 16 to 640Kbps; hence the term asymmetric.

Asynchronous Transfer Mode

Abbreviated ATM. A method used for transmitting voice, video, and data over high-speed LANs and WANs. ATM uses continuous bursts of fixed-length packets called cells to transmit data. The basic packet consists of 53 bytes, 5 of which are used for control functions and 48 for data.

ATM is a connection-oriented protocol, and two kinds of connection are possible: permanent virtual circuits (PVCs), in which connections are created manually, and switched virtual circuits (SVCs), in which connections are made automatically. Speeds of up to 2.488Gbps have been achieved in testing.

ATM will find wide acceptance in the LAN and WAN arenas as a solution to integrating disparate networks over large geographical distances. Also known as cell relay.

asynchronous transmission

A method of data transmission that uses start bits and stop bits to coordinate the flow of data so the time intervals between individual characters do not need to be equal. Parity may also be used to check the accuracy of the data received.

ATA

See *Advanced Technology Attachment*.

ATAPI

See *Advanced Technology Attachment Packet Interface*.

at symbol

The separating character (@) between account name and domain name in an Internet e-mail address.

attenuation

The decrease in power of a signal with increasing distance. Attenuation is measured in decibels, and it increases as the power of the signal decreases. The best cables (those exhibiting the least attenuation) are fiber optic lines, and the worst cables are unshielded, untwisted-pair lines, such as the silver, flat-satin cables used in short-run telephone and modem lines.

In a LAN, attenuation can become a problem when cable lengths exceed the stated network specification; however, the useful length of a cable may be extended by the use of a repeater.

ATM

See Asynchronous Transfer Mode.

attribute

1. A file attribute is a technique for describing access to and properties of files and directories within a file system. You may see the term attribute used interchangeably with the term property.
2. A screen attribute controls a character's background and foreground colors, as well as other characteristics, such as underlining, reverse video, and blinking.
3. In operating systems, a characteristic that indicates whether a file is a read-only file, a hidden file, a system file, or has changed in some way since it was last backed up.

auto-answer

A feature of a modem that allows it to answer incoming calls automatically.

auto-dial

A feature of a modem that allows it to open a telephone line and start a call. To auto-dial, the modem sends a series of pulses or tones that represents a stored telephone number.

B

backslash

1. Used to separate directory or subdirectory names in a path statement or when changing to another directory from a command prompt.
2. A shorthand name for the root directory. Sometimes called the reverse slash or backslant. It goes from the upper left to the lower right (\ ).

backup

An up-to-date copy of all your files. There are several reasons to make a backup:

▶ Insurance against possible hard disk or file-server failure. Hard disks often fail completely, taking all your work with them. If this failure occurs, you can reload your files and directories from the backup copy. A backup is your insurance against disk failure affecting the thousands or possibly tens of thousands of files you might have on your file server.

▶ Protection against accidental deletion of files or directories. Again, if you mistakenly delete a file or directory, you can retrieve a copy from your last backup.

▶ Protection against the new version of software you are about to install not working to your expectations; make a backup before installing new software.

▶ As an archive at the end of a project, when a person leaves your company, or at the end of a financial period such as year-end close.

Your decision when or how often to make a backup depends on how frequently important data on your system changes. If you rely on certain files always being available on your system, it is crucial that you make regular, consistent backups.

backward compatibility

Full compatibility with earlier versions of the same application or computer system.

bad sector

An area on a hard disk or floppy disk that cannot be used to store data because of a manufacturing defect or accidental damage.

Some operating systems will find, mark, and isolate bad sectors. Almost all hard disks have some bad sectors, often listed in the bad track table. Usually, bad sectors are a result of the manufacturing process and not a concern; the operating system will mark them as bad, and you will never even know they are there.

bad track table

A list of the defective areas on a hard disk, usually determined during final testing of the disk at the factory. Some disk-preparation programs ask you to enter information from this list to reduce the time that a low-level format takes to prepare the disk for use by the operating system.

bandwidth

1. In communications, the difference between the highest and lowest frequencies available for transmission in any given range.
2. In networking, the transmission capacity of a computer or a communications channel, stated in megabits per second (Mbps).

Basic Rate ISDN

Abbreviated BRI. An ISDN (Integrated Services Digital Network) service that offers two 64Kbps B channels used for data transfer and one 16Kbps D channel used for signaling and control information.

Each B channel can carry a single digital voice call or can be used as a data channel; the B channels can also be combined into a single 128Kbps data channel.

baud rate

In communications equipment, a measurement of the number of state changes (from 0 to 1 or vice versa) per second on an asynchronous communications channel.

Baud rate is often assumed to correspond to the number of bits transmitted per second, but baud rate and bits per second (bps) are not always the same. In modern high-speed digital communications systems, one state change can be made to represent more than one data bit.

BEDO DRAM

See Burst Extended Data Out DRAM.

binary

Any scheme that uses two different states, components, conditions, or conclusions. In mathematics, the binary or base-2 numbering system uses combinations of the digits 0 and 1 to represent all values. The more familiar decimal system has a base of 10 (0–9).

Unlike computers, people find binary numbers that consist of long strings of zeros and ones difficult to read, so most programmers use hexadecimal (base-16) or octal (base-8) numbers instead.

Binary also refers to an executable file containing a program.

BIOS

Acronym for basic input/output system, pronounced "bye-ose." In the PC, the BIOS is a set of instructions that tests the hardware when the computer is first turned on, starts to load the operating system, and lets the computer's hardware and operating system communicate with applications and peripheral devices, such as hard disks, printers, and video adapters. These instructions are stored in ROM (read-only memory) as a permanent part of the computer.

As new hardware is developed, new BIOS routines must be created to service those devices. For example, BIOS support has been added for power management and for ever-larger hard disks.

If you are experiencing problems accessing such devices after adding them to an existing system, your computer's BIOS may be out of date. Contact your computer supplier for information about BIOS updates.

bit

Contraction of binary digit. A bit is the basic unit of information in the binary numbering system, representing either 0 (off) or 1 (on). Bits can be grouped to form larger storage units; the most common grouping is the eight bits called a byte.

bit rate

The rate at which bits are transmitted over a communications channel, described in terms of bits per second (bps).

bits per inch

Abbreviated bpi. The number of bits that a tape or tape cartridge can store per inch of length.

bits per second

Abbreviated bps. The number of binary digits, or bits, transmitted every second during a data transfer procedure. Bits per second is a measurement of the speed of operation of equipment, such as a computer's data bus or a modem that connects a computer to a communications circuit.

BNC connector

A small connector with a half-turn locking shell for coaxial cable, used with thin Ethernet and RG-62 cabling.

boot

To load an operating system into memory, usually from a hard disk, although occasionally from a floppy disk. Booting is generally an automatic procedure that begins when you turn on or reset your computer.

A set of instructions contained in ROM (read-only memory) begins executing. The instructions run a series of Power-On Self Tests (POSTs) to check that devices such as hard disks are in working order, then locate and load the operating system, and finally pass control over to that operating system.

boot sector virus

A virus that infects the master boot record of a computer by overwriting the original boot code with infected boot code. This kind of virus is usually spread to a hard disk by using an infected floppy disk as a boot disk.

bootable disk

Any disk capable of loading and starting the operating system. Bootable floppy disks are becoming less common because operating systems are growing larger. In some cases, all the files needed to start the operating system will not fit on even the largest-capacity floppy disk, which makes it impossible to boot from a floppy disk.

bpi

See bits per inch.

bps

See bits per second.

brain damaged

An expression used to describe any poorly designed program or piece of hardware that does not include those features most users would consider essential. The implication is that the designer should have known better than to leave those features out of the product.

breakout box

A small device that can be connected into a multicore cable for testing the signals in a transmission. Small LEDs in the breakout box indicate when a signal is transmitted over one of the lines. Switches or short jumper cables can be used to reroute these signals to other pins as required for troubleshooting.

BRI

See Basic Rate ISDN.

brownout

A short period of low voltage, often the result of an unusually heavy demand for power, that may cause your computer to crash. If your area experiences frequent brownouts, consider using a UPS (uninterruptible power supply) as a battery backup system.

buffer

An area of memory set aside for temporary storage of data. Often, the data remains in the buffer until some external event finishes. A buffer can compensate for the differences in transmission or processing speed between two devices or between a computer and a peripheral device, such as a printer or modem.

Buffers are implemented in a variety of different ways, including first-in-first-out (FIFO) used for pipes and last-in-last-out used for stacks and circular buffers such as event logs.

bug

A logical or programming error in hardware or software that causes a malfunction of some sort. If the problem is in software, it can be fixed by changes to the program. If the fault is in hardware, new circuits must be designed and constructed. Some bugs are fatal and may cause a program to stop responding or cause data loss; others are just annoying, and many are not even noticeable.

burned-in address

The hardware address on a network interface card. This address is assigned by the manufacturer of the interface card, which ensures that every card has a unique address.

Burst Extended Data Out DRAM

Abbreviated BEDO DRAM. A type of EDO dynamic RAM that manages data in bursts of four items at a time to increase speed. This approach takes advantage of the fact that memory requests usually refer to a series of sequential addresses.

bus

An electronic pathway along which signals are sent from one part of a computer to another. A PC contains several buses, each used for a different purpose:

▶ The address bus allocates memory addresses.

- The data bus carries data between the processor and memory.
- The control bus carries signals from the control unit.

bus mastering

A technique that allows certain advanced bus architectures to delegate control of data transfers between the central processing unit (CPU) and associated peripheral devices to an add-in board. This technique gives greater system bus access and higher data transfer speeds.

In the PC, bus mastering is supported by all of the common architectures except for the older Industry Standard Architecture (ISA).

byte

Contraction of binary digit eight. A group of bits. In computer storage terms, a byte usually holds a single character, such as a number, letter, or symbol. A byte usually contains 8 bits, but on some older computer systems a byte may only have 7 bits or may have as many as 11.

Because bytes represent a very small amount of storage, they are usually grouped into kilobytes (1024 bytes), megabytes (1,048,576 bytes), and gigabytes (1,073,741,824 bytes) for convenience when describing hard disk capacity or computer memory size.

C

cable modem

A modem that sends and receives signals through a coaxial cable connected to a cable television system, rather than through conventional telephone lines.

Cable modems, with speeds of up to 500Kbps, are faster than current conventional modems but are subject to performance changes as system load increases. Theoretical data rates are much higher than those achieved with conventional modems; downstream rates of up to 36Mbps are possible, with 3Mbps to 10Mbps likely, and upstream rates up to 10Mbps.

cache

Pronounced "cash." A special area of memory, managed by a cache controller, which improves performance by storing the contents of frequently accessed memory locations and their addresses.

A memory cache and a disk cache are not the same. This entry describes a memory cache, which is implemented in hardware and speeds up access to memory. A disk cache is software that improves hard disk performance.

When the processor references a memory address, the cache checks to see if it holds that address. If it does, the information is passed directly to the processor, so random-access memory (RAM) access is not necessary. A cache can speed up operations in a computer whose RAM access is slow compared with its processor speed, because cache memory is always faster than normal RAM.

There are several different types of cache:

Direct-mapped cache A location in the cache corresponds to several specific locations in memory, so when the processor calls for certain data, the cache can locate it quickly. However, since several blocks in RAM correspond to that same location in the cache, the cache may spend its time refreshing itself and calling main memory.

Fully associative cache Information from RAM may be placed in any free blocks in the cache, so that the most recently accessed data is usually present; however, the search to find that information may be slow because the cache has to index the data in order to find it.

Set-associative cache Information from RAM is kept in sets, and these sets may have multiple locations, each holding a block of data; each block may be in any of the sets, but it will only be in one location within that set. Search time is shortened, and it is less likely that frequently used data will be overwritten. A set-associative cache may use two, four, or eight sets.

cache memory

Pronounced "cash memory." A relatively small section of very fast memory (often static RAM) reserved for the temporary storage of the data or instructions likely to be needed next by the processor.

Cache memory integrated directly onto the microprocessor is called primary cache or L1 cache, while cache memory located in an external circuit is known as secondary cache or L2 cache.

carrier signal

A signal of chosen frequency generated to carry data, often used for long-distance transmissions. A carrier signal does not convey any information until the data is added to the signal by modulation and then decoded on the receiving end by demodulation.

cascading

A technique used to connect two Ethernet hubs together when expanding the network; sometimes called daisy chaining. Cascading usually requires a special cable.

Category 1–5

The Telecommunications Industry Association and Electronics Industry Association (TIA/EIA) 586 cabling standards, sometimes abbreviated Cat 1–5, as follows:

Category 1 For unshielded twisted-pair (UTP) telephone cable. This cable may be used for voice but is not suitable for data transmissions.

Category 2 For UTP cable for use at speeds up to 4Mbps. Category 2 cable is similar to IBM Cabling System Type 3 cable.

Category 3 For UTP cable for use at speeds up to 10Mbps. Category 3 cable is the minimum requirement for 10Base-T and is required for token ring. This cable has four pairs of conductors and three twists per foot.

Category 4 For the lowest acceptable grade of UTP cable for use with 16Mbps token ring.

Category 5 For 100-ohm, four-wire twisted-pair copper cable for use at speeds up to 100Mbps with Ethernet or ATM. This cable is low-capacitance and shows low crosstalk when installed according to specifications.

CAV

See constant angular velocity.

CCD

See charge-coupled device.

CD-I

See Compact Disc-Interactive.

CD-R

See CD recordable.

CD-recordable

Abbreviated CD-R. Using CD-R, you can write to the disc just once; after that, the disc can only be read from and not written to.

From a functional point of view, a CD-R and a CD-ROM are identical; you can read CD-R discs using almost any CD-ROM drive, although the processes that create the discs are slightly different. Low-cost CD-R drives are available from several manufacturers including Kao, Kodak, Mitsui, Phillips, Ricoh, Sony, TDK, 3M, and Verbatim.

CD-rewritable

Abbreviated CD-RW. A CD format that can be written to and erased up to 1,000 times.

From a functional point of view, a CD-RW and a CD-ROM are identical, but not all CD-ROM drives can read CD-RW discs. Low-cost CD-RW drives are available from several manufacturers including Kodak, Mitsui, Phillips, and Sony.

CD-ROM

Acronym for Compact Disc Read-Only Memory. A high-capacity, optical storage device that uses the same technology used to make ordinary music discs to store large amounts of information. A single 4.72-inch disc can hold up to 650 megabytes.

CD-ROMs are important components of multimedia applications. They are also used to store encyclopedias, dictionaries, and other large reference works, as well as libraries of fonts and clip art for desktop publishing. CD-ROMs have replaced floppy disks as the distribution mechanism for software packages, including network operating systems and large applications, so you can load the whole package from a single compact disc and an operating system from a set of discs.

A CD-ROM uses the constant linear velocity data-encoding scheme to store information in a single, spiral track, divided into many equal-length segments. To read data, the CD-ROM disk drive must increase the rotational speed as the read head gets closer to the center of the disk and decrease as the head moves back out.

CD-ROM disk drive

A disk device that uses compact disc technology for information storage. Many CD-ROM disk drives also have headphone jacks, external speaker jacks, and a volume control. CD-ROM disk drives designed for computer use are more expensive than audio CD players are, because CD-ROM disk drives are manufactured to much higher tolerances. If a CD player misreads a small amount of data, the human ear probably will not detect the difference; if a CD-ROM disk drive misreads a few bytes of a program, the program will not run.

The two most popular CD-ROM drive interface cards are SCSI (Small Computer System Interface) and ATAPI (Advanced Technology Attachment Packet Interface). ATAPI is part of the Enhanced IDE specification introduced by Western Digital in 1994.

CD-ROM Extended Architecture

Abbreviated CD-ROM/XA. An extension to the CD-ROM format developed by Microsoft, Phillips, and Sony that allows for the storage of audio and visual information on compact disc, so you can play the audio at the same time you view the visual data.

CD-ROM/XA is compatible with the High Sierra specification, also known as ISO standard 9660.

CD-ROM/XA

See CD-ROM Extended Architecture.

CD-RW

See CD-rewritable.

Celeron

A low-cost version of Intel's Pentium II microprocessor. The Celeron includes an integrated 128KB L2 cache, supports Intel's MMX technology, and is available in a wide range of speeds.

charge-coupled device

Abbreviated CCD. A device in which the semiconductor elements are connected so that the electrical output from one provides the input to the next. CCDs are used in the light-detection circuitry in digital and video cameras.

chassis

The metal frame into which the PC's components, including power supply, printed circuit boards, and fan, are mounted.

checksum

A method of providing information for error detection, usually calculated by summing a set of values.

The checksum is usually appended to the end of the data that it is calculated from, so that they can be compared. A checksum cannot detect all possible errors and cannot be used to correct an error in the data.

chip

A slang expression for integrated circuit.

chip set

Sometimes chipset. A group of integrated circuits designed to perform as a unit.

CISC

See complex instruction set computing.

Class A certification

An FCC certification for computer equipment, including mainframe computers and minicomputers destined for industrial, commercial, or office use, rather than for personal use at home. The Class A commercial certification is less restrictive than the Class B certification for residential use because it assumes that most residential areas are more than 30 feet away from any commercial computer equipment.

Class B certification

An FCC certification for computer equipment, including PCs, laptops, and portables destined for use in the home rather than in a commercial setting. Class B levels of radio frequency interference (RFI) must be low enough so that they do not interfere with radio or television reception when there is more than one wall and 30 feet separating the computer from the receiver. Class B certification is more restrictive than the commercial Class A certification.

Clear To Send

Abbreviated CTS. A hardware signal defined by the RS-232-C standard that indicates that the transmission can proceed.

clock

An electronic circuit that generates regularly spaced timing pulses at speeds up to millions of cycles per second. These pulses are used to synchronize the flow of information through the computer's internal communications channels.

clock speed

The internal speed of a computer or processor, normally expressed in megahertz (MHz) or gigahertz (GHz). Also known as clock rate.

The faster the clock speed, the faster the computer will perform a specific operation (assuming the other components in the system, such as disk drives, can keep up with the increased speed).

The Intel 8088 processor used in the original IBM PC had a clock speed of 4.77MHz—painfully slow when compared with speeds used by modern processors, which can run at clock speeds of a gigahertz or more.

clone

A computer that contains all the same hardware elements as a name-brand system but which is usually cheaper.

cluster

The basic unit of data storage recorded onto a hard or floppy disk during a low-level format. Usually contains two or more sectors.

clustering

In networking, the grouping of several servers in a way that allows them to appear to be one server from the point of view of network clients. Clustering improves data security, increases network capacity, and provides live backup in the event a server fails.

CLV

See constant linear velocity.

CMOS

See Complementary Metal-Oxide Semiconductor.

coaxial cable

A high-capacity cable used in networking that contains a solid inner copper core surrounded by plastic insulation and an outer braided copper or foil sheath. Depending on the diameter of the cable, it may be known as thinnet (thin Ethernet, used for office installations) or thicknet (thick Ethernet, used for facility-wide applications).

codec

1. Acronym for coder/decoder. A device that converts analog signals (such as voice or video) into a digital bit stream suitable for transmission, and then converts those digital signals back into analog signals at the receiving end.
2. Acronym for compression/decompression. An overall term to describe the hardware and software used in processing animation, digital video, and stereo-quality audio.

cold boot

The computer startup process that begins when you turn on power to the computer. You are doing a cold boot when you first turn on your computer. A cold boot might also be necessary if a program or the operating system crashes and freezes entirely. If your keyboard is operational, a warm boot may suffice.

collision

An attempt by two computers on the network to send a message at exactly the same instant; Ethernet automatically resends both messages, but with altered timing so they do not collide and are received properly.

colon

The symbol used after the protocol name in a Universal Resource Locator (URL).

command line

An interface between the user and the command processor that allows you to enter commands from the keyboard for execution by the operating system.

command processor

The part of the operating system that displays the command prompt on the screen, interprets and executes all the commands and filenames that you enter, and displays error messages when appropriate. Also called the command interpreter. The command processor also contains the system environment.

command prompt

A symbol (character or group of characters) on the screen that lets you know that the operating system is available and ready to receive input.

command-line argument

A parameter that alters the default mode of a command. In many operating systems, a command-line argument is one or more letters or numbers preceded by the slash (/)

character. With some commands, you can group several arguments together. Sometimes called a command-line switch.

communications parameters

Any of several settings required to allow computers to communicate successfully. In asynchronous transmissions, commonly used in modem communications, the settings for baud rate, number of data bits, number of stop bits, and parity parameters must all be correct.

communications protocol

1. A standard way of communicating between computers or between computers and terminals. Communications protocols vary in complexity, ranging from Xmodem, a simple file-transfer protocol used to transfer files from one PC to another, to the seven-layer OSI reference model used as the theoretical basis for many large, complex computer networks.
2. A hardware interface standard, such as RS-232-C.

compact disc

Abbreviated CD. A nonmagnetic, polished, optical disk used to store large amounts of digital information. A CD can store approximately 650MB of information, equivalent to more than 450 floppy disks. This storage capacity translates into approximately 300,000 pages of text or 72 minutes of music, all on a single 4.72-inch disc.

Digital information is stored on the compact disc as a series of microscopic pits and smooth areas that have different reflective properties. A beam of laser light shines on the disc so that the reflections can be detected and converted into digital data.

compatibility

The extent to which a given piece of hardware or software conforms to an accepted standard, regardless of the original manufacturer.

In hardware, compatibility is often expressed in terms of widely accepted models—this designation implies that the device will perform in the same way as the standard device.

In software, compatibility is usually described as the ability to read data file formats created by another vendor's software, or the ability to work together and share data.

Complementary Metal-Oxide Semiconductor

Abbreviated CMOS, pronounced "see-moss." A type of integrated circuit used in processors and for memory.

CMOS devices operate at very high speeds and use little power, so they generate little heat. In the PC, battery-backed CMOS memory is used to store operating parameters, such as the hard disk type and the date and time, when the computer is switched off. CMOS is easily damaged by static electricity, so take appropriate precautions.

complex instruction set computing

Abbreviated CISC, pronounced "sisk." A processor that can recognize and execute more than one hundred different assembly-language, or low-level, instructions. CISC processors can be powerful, but the instructions take a high number of clock cycles to execute.

This complexity is in contrast to the simplicity of reduced instruction set computing (RISC) processors, in which the number of available instructions has been cut to a minimum. RISC processors are common in workstations and can be designed to run up to 70 percent faster than CISC processors.

COM port

The device name used for a serial communications port.

compressed file

A file that has been processed by a special utility so that it occupies as little hard disk space as possible. When the file is needed, the same program decompresses the file back into its original form so that it can be read by the computer.

Popular compression techniques include schemes that replace commonly occurring sequences of characters by tokens that take up less space. Some utilities use Huffman coding to shrink a file, while others use adaptive Lempel-Ziv coding.

connection speed

The speed of a data communications circuit. Some circuits are symmetrical and can maintain the same speed in both directions, while others are asymmetrical and use a faster speed in one direction, usually the downstream side.

constant angular velocity

Abbreviated CAV. An unchanging speed of rotation. Hard disks use a CAV encoding scheme. The constant rate of rotation means that sectors on the disk are at the maximum density along the inside track of the disk. As the read/write heads move outward, the sectors must spread out to cover the increased track circumference, and therefore the data transfer rate falls off.

constant linear velocity

Abbreviated CLV. A changing speed of rotation. CD-ROM disk drives use a CLV encoding scheme to make sure that the data density remains constant. Information on a compact disc is stored in a single, spiral track, divided into many equal-length segments. To read the data, the CD-ROM disk drive must increase the rotational speed as the read head gets closer to the center of the disc and decrease as the head moves back out.

control character

A nonprinting character with a special meaning.

Control characters, such as Carriage Return, Line Feed, Bell, or Escape, perform a specific operation on a terminal, printer, or communications line. They are grouped together as the first 32 characters in the ASCII character set.

You can type a control character from the keyboard by pressing and holding the Ctrl key while you simultaneously press another key. For example, if you press and hold the Ctrl key and then press C, you generate Ctrl+C.

corona wire

In a laser printer, the wire that applies an electrostatic charge to the paper.

crash

1. An unexpected program halt, sometimes due to a hardware failure but most often due to a software error, from which there is no recovery. You usually need to reboot the computer to recover after a crash.

2. A disk drive failure, sometimes called a head crash, which leaves the hard disk unusable.

CRC

See *cyclical redundancy check.*

cross-linked clusters

Clusters on a hard or floppy disk allocated to more than one file due to a storage error.

crosstalk

In computer communications, any interference from a physically adjacent channel that corrupts the signal and causes transmission errors.

Ctrl+Alt+Del

A three-key combination used to reset the machine and reload the operating system. By pressing Ctrl+Alt+Del, you initiate a warm boot, which restarts the computer without going through the Power-On Self Tests (POSTs) normally run when the computer goes through a cold boot.

In Windows 98/2000, the sequence opens a dialog box from which you can either end a task or shut down the computer. Sometimes called the three-finger salute.

Ctrl key

A key on the keyboard that, when pressed at the same time as another key, generates a nonprinting control character.

CTS

See *Clear To Send.*

cursor

A special character displayed on a monitor to indicate where the next character will appear when it is typed. In text or character mode, the cursor is usually a blinking rectangle or underline. In a graphical user interface, the mouse cursor can take many shapes, depending on the current operation and its screen location.

cursor-movement keys

The keys on the keyboard that move the cursor, also called cursor-control keys. These keys include the four arrow keys and the Home, Page Up, End, and Page Down keys.

On full-sized keyboards, cursor-movement keys are often found on the numeric keypad; laptops and notebooks often have separate cursor-movement keys.

cut through

A technique used by some Ethernet hardware to speed up packet forwarding. Only the first few bytes of the packet are examined before it is forwarded or filtered. This process is much faster than looking at the whole packet, but it does allow some bad packets to be forwarded.

cyclical redundancy check

Abbreviated CRC. A complex calculation method used to check the accuracy of a digital transmission over a communications link or to ensure the integrity of a file stored on a hard disk.

The sending computer uses one of several formulas to calculate a value from the information contained in the data, and this value is appended to the message block before it is sent. The receiving computer performs the same calculation on the same data and compares this number with the received CRC. If the two CRCs do not match, indicating a

transmission error occurred, the receiving computer asks the sending computer to retransmit the data.

This procedure is known as a redundancy check because each transmission includes extra or redundant error-checking values as well as the data itself.

As a security check, a CRC may be used to compare the current size of an executable file against the original size to determine if the file has been tampered with or changed in some way.

D

daisy chaining

See cascading.

DAT

See Digital Audio Tape.

data bits

In asynchronous transmissions, the bits that actually make up the data. Usually, seven or eight data bits are grouped together. Each group of data bits in a transmission is preceded by a start bit and followed by an optional parity bit as well as one or more stop bits.

Data Carrier Detected

Abbreviated DCD. A hardware signal defined by the RS-232-C standard that indicates the modem is ready to transmit.

data compression

Any method of encoding data so that it occupies less space than it did in its original form, thus allowing that data to be stored, backed up, retrieved, or transmitted more efficiently.

Data compression is used in fax and many other forms of data transmission, CD-ROM publishing, and in still- and video-image manipulation.

Data Set Ready

Abbreviated DSR. A hardware signal defined by the RS-232-C standard that indicates the device is ready to operate.

DB connector

Any of several types of cable connectors used for parallel or serial cables. The number following the letters DB (for data bus) indicates the number of pins that the connector usually has; a DB25 connector can have up to 25 pins, and a DB9 connector can have up to 9. In practice, not all the pins (and not all the lines in the cable) may be present in the larger connectors. If your situation demands that all the lines be present, make sure you buy the right cable. Common DB connectors include the following:

DB9 Defined by the RS-449 standard as well as the ISO (International Organization for Standardization).

DB25 A standard connector used with RS-232-C wiring, with 25 pins (13 on the top row and 12 on the bottom).

DB37 Defined as the RS-449 primary channel connector.

DB15, DB19, and DB50 connectors are also available.

DCD

See Data Carrier Detected.

D channel

The data channel in ISDN (Integrated Services Digital Network), used for control signals and customer data. In the Base Rate ISDN (BRI), the D channel operates at 16Kbps; in the Primary Rate ISDN (PRI), it operates at 64Kbps.

decibel

Abbreviated dB. One tenth of a bel, a unit of measurement common in electronics that quantifies the loudness or strength of a signal. A decibel is a relative measurement derived by comparing a measured level against a known reference.

decimal

The base-10 numbering system that uses the familiar numbers 0–9; also known as the base-10 radix, or the decimal radix.

defragmentation

The process of reorganizing and rewriting files so that they occupy one large area on a hard disk rather than several smaller areas.

When a file on a hard disk is updated, it may be written into different areas all over the disk. This outcome is particularly likely when the hard disk is continuously updated over a long period of time. This file fragmentation can lead to significant delays in loading files, but its effect can easily be reversed by reorganizing and rewriting the file.

defragmenter

Any utility that rewrites all the parts of a fragmented file into contiguous areas on a hard disk. A defragmenter (such as the Microsoft Windows utility Disk Defragmenter) can restore performance lost because of file fragmentation.

demand paging

A common form of virtual memory management, in which pages of information are read into memory from disk only when required by the program.

demodulation

In communications, the process of retrieving the data from a modulated carrier signal; the reverse of modulation.

Desktop Management Interface

Abbreviated DMI. A standard API for identifying desktop workstation hardware components automatically, without intervention from the user.

At a minimum, DMI identifies the manufacturer, component name, version, serial number (if appropriate), and installation time and date of any component installed in a networked workstation. This information is designed to help network administrators resolve configuration problems quickly and easily and to indicate when and where system upgrades should be applied. PCs, Macintosh computers, and Unix systems are all covered by DMI.

DMI is backed by Digital Equipment Corporation (DEC), IBM, Intel, Microsoft, Novell, Sun, and more than 300 other vendors.

desktop video

The combination of video capture hardware and application software that controls the display of video or television pictures on a desktop PC.

Desktop video is becoming increasingly important with the sharp increase in video-conferencing applications now available.

device

A general term used to describe any computer peripheral or hardware element that can send or receive data.

Some examples are modems, printers, serial ports, disk drives, cameras, and game ports. Some devices require special software, or device drivers, to control or manage them; others have built-in intelligence.

device dependence

The requirement that a specific hardware component be present for a program to work. Device-dependent software is often difficult to move or port to another computer because of its reliance on specific hardware.

device driver

A small program that allows a computer to communicate with and control a device. Each operating system contains a standard set of device drivers for the keyboard, the monitor, and so on. When you add specialized peripheral devices, such as a network interface card, you must install the appropriate device driver so that the operating system knows how to manage the device.

device independence

The ability to produce similar results in a wide variety of environments without requiring the presence of specific hardware.

The Java programming language and the PostScript page-description language are examples of device independence. Java runs on a wide range of computers, from the PC to a Cray; PostScript is used by many different printer manufacturers.

diagnostic program

A program that tests computer hardware and peripheral devices for correct operation. Some faults, known as hard faults, are relatively easy to find, and the diagnostic program will diagnose them correctly every time. Other faults, called soft faults, can be difficult to find, because they occur under specific circumstances rather than every time the memory location is tested.

Most computers run a simple set of system checks when the computer is first turned on. The PC tests are stored in read-only memory (ROM) and are known as Power-On Self Tests (POSTs). If a POST detects an error condition, the computer will stop and display an error message on the screen.

differential backup

A backup of a hard disk that includes only the information that has changed since the last complete backup was made.

A differential backup assumes that a full backup already exists, and in the event of an accident, this complete backup will be restored before the differential backup is reloaded.

differential SCSI

A Small Computer System Interface (SCSI) bus wiring scheme that uses two wires for each signal on the bus. One wire carries the signal, while the other carries its inverse. Differential SCSI minimizes the effects of external interference, and so allows longer SCSI cable lengths to be used.

digital

Describes any device that represents values in the form of binary digits or bits.

Digital Audio Tape

Abbreviated DAT. A method of recording information in digital form on a small audio tape cassette, originally developed by Sony and Hewlett-Packard. The most common format is a four-millimeter, helical-scan drive, which can hold more than three gigabytes of information. DATs can be used as backup media; however, like all tape devices, they are relatively slow.

Digital Signal Processing

Abbreviated DSP. An integrated circuit used in high-speed data manipulation. You will find DSP chips integrated into sound cards, modems, and video conferencing hardware where they are used in communications, image manipulation, and other data-acquisition applications.

digital subscriber line

Abbreviated DSL. A high-speed data transmission technology originally developed by Bellcore that delivers high bandwidth over existing twisted-pair copper telephone lines.

There are several different DSL services, providing data rates from 16Kbps to 52Mbps. The services can be symmetrical, with the same data rate in both upstream and downstream directions, or asymmetrical, with the downstream capacity greater than the upstream capacity. Asymmetric services are particularly suitable for Internet users, because more information is downloaded than is uploaded.

As DSL data rates increase, the distance over which the service is provided decreases; certain users who are located too far from the telephone company's central office may not be able to obtain the higher speeds, or in some cases, may not be able to receive the service at all.

digital versatile disc
See digital video disc.

digital video disc
Abbreviated DVD; sometimes called digital versatile disc. A compact disc format. A standard single-layer single-sided disc can currently store 4.7GB of information; a two-layer standard increases this to 8.5GB, and eventually double-sided discs are expected to store 17GB per disc. DVD drives can also read conventional compact discs.

digital video disc-erasable
Abbreviated DVD-E. An extension to the digital video disc format to allow multiple rerecordings.

digital video disc-recordable
Abbreviated DVD-R. An extension to the digital video disc format to allow one-time recording.

digital video disc-ROM
Abbreviated DVD-ROM. A computer-readable form of digital video disc with either 4.7 or 8.5GB of storage per side.

DIMM
See Dual Inline Memory Module.

DIP
See Dual Inline Package.

DIP switch
A small switch used to select the operating mode of a device, mounted as a dual inline package. DIP switches can be either sliding or rocker switches, and they are often grouped together for convenience. They are used in printed circuit boards, printers, modems, and many other peripheral devices.

direct-mapped cache
See cache.

direct memory access
Abbreviated DMA. A method of transferring information directly from a mass-storage device, such as a hard disk, into memory without the information passing through the processor. Because the processor is not involved in the transfer, DMA is fast. An alternative data transfer method known as programmed input/output moves data between a hard disk and memory via the processor, and so is much slower.

directory
In a hierarchical file system, a convenient way of organizing and grouping files and other directories on a disk. Sometimes called a folder.

The beginning directory is known as the root directory, from which all other directories must branch. Directories inside another directory are called subdirectories.

You can list the files in a directory in a variety of different ways: by name, by creation date and time, by file size, or by icon.

disk cache
Pronounced "disk cash." An area of computer memory where data is temporarily stored on its way to or from a disk.

When an application asks for information from the hard disk, the cache program first checks to see if that data is already in the cache memory. If it is, the disk cache program loads the information from the cache memory rather than from the hard disk. If the information is not in memory, the cache program reads the data from the disk, copies it into the cache memory for future reference, and then passes the data to the requesting application.

disk controller

The electronic circuitry that controls and manages the operation of floppy and hard disks.

A single disk controller may manage more than one hard disk. Many disk controllers also manage floppy disks and compatible tape drives. In the PC, the disk controller may be a printed circuit board inserted into the expansion bus, or it may be part of the hard disk drive itself.

disk drive

A peripheral storage device that reads and writes magnetic or optical disks. When more than one disk drive is installed on a computer, the operating system assigns each drive (or logical drive) a unique name.

Several types of disk drive are in common use: floppy disk drives, hard disk drives, compact disc drives, digital video disc drives, Zip drives, and magneto-optical disc drives.

disk optimizer

A utility that rearranges files and directories on a disk for optimum performance. By reducing or eliminating file fragmentation (storage in pieces in different locations on the hard disk), a disk optimizer can restore the original level of performance of your disk system. Also, it is usually easier to undelete, or recover, an unfragmented file than a fragmented one.

Many disk optimizers will not only rewrite files as contiguous files, but will also place specific unchanging files in particular locations on the disk, optimize directories, even place specific applications on the disk so they load more quickly.

DLL

See dynamic-link library.

DMA

See direct memory access.

DMI

See Desktop Management Interface.

docking station

A hardware system into which a portable computer fits so that it can be used as a full-fledged desktop computer.

Docking stations vary from simple port replicators that allow you access to parallel and serial ports and a mouse to complete systems that give you access to network connections, CD-ROMs, and even a tape backup system. The portable computer and docking station are designed as two parts of the same system; you cannot swap computers and docking stations from different manufacturers or even from different models from the same manufacturer.

double slash

Notation used with a colon to separate the communications protocol from the host computer name in a Universal Resource Locator (URL) as in `http://www.sybex.com`.

download

1. In communications, to transfer a file or files from one computer to another over a network or using a modem.
2. To send information, such as font information or a PostScript file, from a computer to a printer.

DRAM

See dynamic RAM.

drive letter

A designation used to specify a PC disk drive. For example, the first floppy disk drive is usually referred to as drive A: and the first hard disk drive is usually referred to as drive C:.

DSL

See digital subscriber line.

DSP

See digital signal processing.

DSR

See Data Set Ready.

Dual Inline Memory Module

Abbreviated DIMM. A group of memory chips mounted on a small circuit board. DIMMs have two sets of connectors that connect to different circuits, and they have a 64-bit data path.

Dual Inline Package

Abbreviated DIP. A standard housing constructed of hard plastic commonly used to hold an integrated circuit. The circuit's leads are connected to two parallel rows of pins designed to fit snugly into a socket; these pins may also be soldered directly to a printed circuit board.

duplex

In asynchronous transmissions, the ability to transmit and receive on the same channel at the same time; also referred to as full duplex. Half-duplex channels can transmit only or receive only.

DVD

See digital video disc.

DVD-E

See digital video disc-erasable.

DVD-R

See digital video disc-recordable.

DVD-ROM

See digital video disc-ROM.

dynamic-link library

Abbreviated DLL. A program module that contains executable code and data that can be used by applications, or even by other DLLs in performing a specific task.

DLLs are used extensively throughout the family of Microsoft Windows products. DLLs may have filename extensions of DLL, DRV, or FON.

The DLL is linked into the application only when the program runs, and it is unloaded again when no longer needed. If two DLL applications are running at the same time and both perform a particular function, only one copy of the code for that function is loaded, for more efficient use of limited memory.

Another benefit of using dynamic linking is that the EXE files are not as large as they would be without DLLs, because frequently used routines can be put into a DLL rather than repeated in each EXE file that uses them. A smaller EXE file means saved disk space and faster program loading.

dynamic RAM

Abbreviated DRAM, pronounced "dee-ram." A common type of computer memory that uses capacitors and transistors storing electrical charges to represent memory states. These capacitors lose their electrical charge, so they need to be refreshed every millisecond, during which time they cannot be read by the processor.

DRAM chips are small, simple, cheap, easy to make, and hold approximately four times as much information as a static RAM (SRAM) chip of similar complexity. However, they are slower than SRAM.

E

E

See exa-.

EB

See exabyte.

ECP

See Extended Capabilities Port.

EDO RAM

Abbreviation for Extended Data Out RAM. A type of random access memory (RAM) that keeps data available to the processor while the next memory access is being initialized, thus speeding up overall access times. EDO RAM is significantly faster than conventional dynamic RAM.

EIDE

See Enhanced IDE.

EISA

See Extended Industry Standard Architecture.

electromagnetic interference

Abbreviated EMI. Any electromagnetic radiation released by an electronic device that disrupts the operation or performance of another device.

EMI is produced by many sources commonly found in an office environment, including fluorescent lights, photocopiers, and motors such as those used in elevators. EMI is also produced by natural atmospheric or solar activity.

electrostatic

A term used to describe an electrical charge that is not flowing along a conductor. Electrostatic charges are used in laser printers and in copiers to attach particles of toner to a photoconducting drum as a part of the printing process.

electrostatic discharge

Abbreviated ESD. A discharge of static electricity, often from human hands, onto an integrated circuit, which usually results in severe damage to the integrated circuit.

ELF

See extremely low-frequency emission.

EMI

See electromagnetic interference.

encode

1. To compress a video file using a codec so that the file can be transmitted in the shortest possible time.

2. To convert a binary file into a form suitable for data transmission.

Enhanced IDE

Abbreviated EIDE, contraction of enhanced and Integrated Drive Electronics (IDE). An extension to the IDE standard, EIDE supports larger hard disks, allows you to connect four drives to your PC rather than just two, allows data transfer rates of up to 13.3MBps, and also supports the ATAPI interface, which connects CD-ROM drives, optical disks, and tape drives.

enhanced parallel port

Abbreviated EPP. A parallel port specification, developed by Microsoft and Hewlett-Packard, that allows for high-speed, two-way communication between the computer and a peripheral other than a printer or scanner. ECP is used with external drives, is a part of the IEEE 1284 standard for advanced parallel ports, and can provide data rates in excess of 1Mbps.

EPP

See enhanced parallel port.

error

The difference between the expected and the actual.

In computing, the way that the operating system reports unexpected, unusual, impossible, or illegal events is by displaying an error number or error message. Errors range from trivial, such as an attempt to write a file to a disk drive that does not contain a disk, to fatal, such as when a serious operating system bug renders the system useless.

In communications, errors are often caused by line noise and signal distortion.

Parity or cyclical redundancy check (CRC) information is often added as overhead to the data stream, and techniques such as error detection and correction are employed to detect and correct as many errors as possible.

error detection and correction

A mechanism used to determine whether transmission errors have occurred and, if so, to correct those errors.

Some programs or transmission protocols simply request a retransmission of the affected block of data if an error is detected. More complex protocols attempt to both detect and determine at the receiving end what the correct transmission should have been.

error handling

The way that a program copes with errors or exceptions that occur as the program is running.

Good error handling manages unexpected events or wrongly entered data gracefully, usually by opening a dialog box to prompt the user to take the appropriate action or enter the correct information. Badly written programs may simply stop running when the wrong data is entered or when an unanticipated disk error occurs.

error message

A message from the program or the operating system that contains information about a condition that requires some human intervention to solve.

Error messages can indicate relatively trivial problems, such as a disk drive that does not contain a disk, as well as fatal problems, such as when a serious operating system bug renders the system useless and requires a system reboot.

error rate

In communications, the ratio between the number of bits received incorrectly and the total number of bits in the transmission, also known as bit error rate (BER).

Some methods for determining error rate use larger or logical units, such as blocks, packets, or frames. In these cases, the measurement of error rate is expressed in terms of the number of units found to be in error out of the total number of units transmitted.

ESD

See electrostatic discharge.

Ethernet

A popular network protocol and cabling scheme with a transfer rate of 10Mbps, originally developed by Xerox in 1970 by Dr. Robert Metcalf. Ethernet uses a bus topology, and network nodes are connected by either thick or thin coaxial cable, fiber optic cable, or twisted-pair cable.

Ethernet uses CSMA/CD (Carrier Sense Multiple Access/Collision Detection) to prevent network failures or collisions when two devices try to access the network at exactly the same time.

The original DIX (Digital Equipment, Intel, Xerox), or Blue Book, standard has evolved into the slightly more complex IEEE 802.3 standard, and the ISO's 8802.3 specification.

The advantages of Ethernet include:

▶ It's easy to install at a moderate cost.
▶ Technology is available from many sources and is very well known.
▶ It offers a variety of cabling options.

▶ It works very well in networks with only occasional heavy traffic.
And the disadvantages include:
▶ Heavy traffic can slow down the network.
▶ A break in the main cable can bring down large parts of the network.
▶ Troubleshooting a bus topology can prove difficult.

Ethernet address

The address assigned to a network interface card by the original manufacturer, or by the network administrator if the card is configurable.

This address identifies the local device address to the rest of the network, and allows messages to reach the correct destination. Also known as the Media Access Control (MAC) or hardware address.

Ethernet packet

A variable-length unit in which information is transmitted on an Ethernet network.

An Ethernet packet consists of a synchronization preamble, a destination address, a source address, a type code indicator, a data field that can vary from 46 to 1500 bytes, and a cyclical redundancy check (CRC) that provides a statistically derived value used to confirm the accuracy of the data.

exa-

Abbreviated E. A prefix meaning one quintillion or 10^{18}. In computing, the prefix means 1,152,921,504,606,846,976, or the power of 2 closest to one quintillion (2^{60}).

exabyte

Abbreviated EB. 1 quintillion bytes, or 1,152,921,504,606,846,976 bytes.

extended capabilities port

Abbreviated ECP. A parallel port specification, developed by Microsoft and Hewlett-Packard, that allows for high-speed, two-way communication between the computer and the peripheral attached to the port, usually a printer or scanner. ECP is a part of the IEEE 1284 standard for advanced parallel ports.

Extended Industry Standard Architecture

Abbreviated EISA. A 32-bit bus standard introduced in 1988, now mostly eclipsed by the PCI bus.

extremely low-frequency emission

Abbreviated ELF. Radiation emitted by a computer monitor and other common electrical appliances.

ELF emissions fall into the range of 5 to 2000Hz and decline with the square of the distance from the source. Emissions are not constant around a monitor; they are higher from the sides and rear and weakest from the front of the screen. Low-emission models are available, and laptop computers with an LCD display do not emit any ELF fields.

F

fading

In both electrical and wireless systems, a decrease in a signal's strength.

Fading may be due to physical obstructions of the transmitter or receiver, distance from the source of the transmission, or some form of external interference from other signals or from atmospheric conditions.

fall back

A technique used by modems to adjust their data rate in response to changing line conditions.

far-end crosstalk

Abbreviated FEXT. Interference that occurs when signals on one twisted-pair are coupled with another pair as they arrive at the far end of a multipair cable system.

FEXT becomes a problem on short loops supporting high-bandwidth services such as very high-bit-rate digital subscriber line (VDSL) because of the high carrier frequencies used.

fast page-mode RAM

See page-mode RAM.

Fast Ethernet

A term applied to the IEEE 802.3 Higher Speed Ethernet Study Group proposals, which were originally developed by Grand Junction Networks, 3Com, SynOptics, Intel, and others. Also known as 100Base-T.

Fast Ethernet modifies the existing Ethernet standard to allow speeds of 10 or 100Mbps, or both, and uses CSMA/CD access method.

The official standard defines three specifications for different cabling types:

▶ 100Base-TX for two-pair Category 5 unshielded twisted-pair.

▶ 100Base-T4 for four-pair Category 3, 4, or 5 unshielded twisted-pair.

▶ 100Base-FX for fiber optic cable.

Fast IR

A 4Mbps extension to the Serial Infrared Data Link Standard that provides wireless data transmission between IrDA-compliant devices.

Fast SCSI

A version of the SCSI-2 interface that can transfer data eight bits at a time at data rates of up to 10MBps. The Fast SCSI connector has 50 pins.

Fast/Wide SCSI

A version of the SCSI-2 interface that can transfer data 16 bits at a time at data rates of up to 20MBps. The Fast/Wide SCSI connector has 68 pins.

FAT

See file allocation table.

FAT16

In Microsoft Windows, a file allocation table that uses a 16-bit cluster addressing scheme which restricts the maximum hard disk size to 2.6GB. Also, FAT16 is inefficient in disk-space utilization as the default cluster size can be as large as 32KB.

FAT32

In Microsoft Windows 95 (release 2) and later versions of Windows, a file allocation table that uses a 32-bit cluster addressing scheme to support hard disks larger than 2.6GB, as well as a default cluster size of as small as 4KB. FAT32 can support hard disks of up to 2 terabytes in size.

fax modem

An adapter that fits into a PC expansion slot providing many of the capabilities of a full-sized fax machine but at a fraction of the cost.

The advantages of a fax modem include ease of use and convenience; the main disadvantage is that the material you want to fax must be present in digital form in the computer. Unless you have access to a scanner, you cannot fax handwritten notes, line art, or certain kinds of graphics. Most faxes sent directly from a PC using a fax modem are text files.

FCC certification

Approval by the FCC (Federal Communications Commission) that a specific computer model meets its standards for radio frequency interference (RFI) emissions.

There are two levels of certification:

▶ Class A certification, which is for computers used in commercial settings, such as mainframes and minicomputers.

▶ The more stringent Class B certification, for computers used in the home and in home offices, such as PCs, laptops, and portables.

FDDI

See Fiber Distributed Data Interface.

female connector

Any cable connector with receptacles designed to receive the pins on the male connector.

Fiber Distributed Data Interface

Abbreviated FDDI. The ANSI X3T9.5 specification for fiber optic networks transmitting at a speed of up to 100Mbps over a dual, counter rotating, token ring topology.

FDDI's 100Mbps speed is close to the internal speed of most computers, which makes it a good choice to serve as a super backbone linking two or more LANs, or as a fiber optic bus connecting high-performance engineering workstations. FDDI is suited to systems that require the transfer of large amounts of information, such as medical imaging, three-dimensional seismic processing, and oil reservoir simulation.

The FDDI-II version of the standard is designed for networks transmitting real-time full-motion video (or other information that cannot tolerate any delays) and requires that all nodes on the network use FDDI-II; otherwise the network automatically reverts to FDDI.

An FDDI network using multimode fiber optic cable can include as many as 500 stations up to 2 kilometers (1.25 miles) apart; with single-mode fiber, run length increases up to 60 kilometers (37.2 miles) between stations. This type of network can also run over shielded and unshielded twisted-pair cabling (when it is known as CDDI, or Copper Distributed Data Interface) for shorter distances.

fiber optic cable

A transmission technology that sends pulses of light along specially manufactured optical fibers.

Each fiber consists of a core, thinner than a human hair, surrounded by a sheath with a much lower refractive index. Light signals introduced at one end of the cable are conducted along the cable as the signals are reflected from the sheath.

Fiber optic cable is lighter and smaller than traditional copper cable, is immune to electrical interference, offers better security, and has better signal-transmitting qualities. However, it is more expensive than traditional cables and is more difficult to repair.

file

A named collection of information that appears to the user as a single entity and is stored on disk.

A file can contain a program or part of a program, just data, or a user-created document. Files may actually be fragmented or stored in many different places across the disk. The operating system manages the task of locating all the pieces when a request is made to read the file.

file allocation table

Abbreviated FAT, pronounced "fat." A table, maintained by the operating systems, that lists all the blocks of disk space available on a disk.

The FAT includes the location of each block, as well as whether it is in use, available for use, or damaged in some way and therefore unavailable. Because files are not necessarily stored in consecutive blocks on a disk, the FAT also keeps track of which pieces belong to which file.

file compression

A technique that shrinks program or data files so that they occupy less disk space. The file must then be extracted or decompressed before use. Some types of files, such as word processor documents, can be compressed by 50 percent or more. Recompressing an already compressed file usually makes the file slightly larger because of the compression overhead.

File compression can be automatic and performed by the operating system, or it can be manual and be performed by a file-compression program.

file format

A file structure that defines the way information is stored in the file and how the file appears on the screen or on the printer.

The simplest file format is a plain ASCII file. Some of the more complex formats are DCA (Document Content Architecture) and RTF (Rich Text Format), which include control information for use by a printer; TIFF (Tagged Image File Format) and EPS (Encapsulated PostScript), which hold graphics information; and DBF (Xbase database file) and DB (Paradox file), which are database formats. Word processing programs, such as Microsoft Word, also create files in special formats.

file fragmentation

Storage of files in pieces scattered on a disk. As files grow on a hard disk, they can be divided into several small pieces. By fragmenting files, the operating system makes reasonable use of the disk space available.

The problem with file fragmentation is that the disk heads must move to different locations on the disk to read or write to a fragmented file. This process takes more time than reading the file as a single piece. To speed up file operations, you can use a disk optimizer or defragmenter.

file-infecting virus

Any virus that infects files on disk, usually executable files with filename extension of COM, EXE, and OVL. An unexpected change in the file size may indicate an infection. In certain cases, the original program is replaced with a new file containing an infected program.

filename

The name of a file on a disk used so that both you and the operating system can find the file again. Every file in a directory must have a unique name, but files in different directories can share the same name.

file transfer protocol

Abbreviated FTP. The TCP/IP Internet protocol used when transferring single or multiple files from one computer system to another.

FTP uses a client/server model, in which a small client program runs on your computer and accesses a larger FTP server running on an Internet host. FTP provides all the tools needed to look at directories and files, change to other directories, and transfer text and binary files from one system to another.

FireWire

See IEEE 1394.

firmware

Any software stored in a form of read-only memory (ROM), erasable programmable read-only memory (EPROM), or electrically erasable programmable read-only memory (EEPROM) that maintains its contents when power is removed.

flat panel display

A thin video display that does not use CRT technology. Flat panel displays were originally used in laptop and other portable computers, but now they are available as desktop units.

flash memory

A special form of read-only memory (ROM) that can be erased at signal levels commonly found inside the PC.

This ability allows the contents to be reprogrammed without removing the chips from the computer. Also, once flash memory has been programmed, you can remove the expansion board it is mounted on and plug it into another computer without loss of the new information.

flow control

1. In communications, control of the rate at which information is exchanged between two computers over a transmission channel. Flow control is needed when one of the devices cannot receive the information at the same rate as it can be sent, usually because some processing is required on the receiving end before the next transmission unit can be accepted. Flow control can be implemented either in hardware or in software.
2. In networking, control of the flow of data throughout the network, ensuring that network segments are not congested. A router controls data flow by routing around any trouble spots.

FM synthesis

Abbreviation for frequency modulation synthesis. A method used by a sound board to simulate musical instruments. FM synthesis is cheaper than wavetable synthesis but is also of lower quality.

footprint

The amount of desktop space or floor space occupied by a computer, printer, or monitor.

forced perfect termination

A technique used to terminate a Small Computer System Interface (SCSI). Forced perfect termination actively monitors the bus to ensure that no signal reflection occurs.

formatting

The process of initializing a new, blank floppy disk or hard disk so that it can be used to store information.

forward error correction

A technique used to control errors that insert extra or redundant bits into the data stream. The receiving device uses the redundant bits to detect and, if possible, correct the errors in the data.

four-wire circuit

A transmission system in which two half-duplex circuits, consisting of two wires each, are combined to create one full-duplex circuit.

fps

See frames per second.

frame

1. A block of data suitable for transmission as a single unit, also referred to as a packet or block. Some media can support multiple frame formats.
2. In digital video, one screen of information, including both text and graphics.

frames per second

Abbreviated fps. The number of video frames displayed each second. While 24fps is considered the slowest frame rate that provides convincing motion to the human eye, most Internet video runs at between 5 and 15fps.

free memory

Any area of memory not currently in use. Often refers to the memory space remaining for applications to use after the operating system and the system device drivers have been loaded.

fried

A slang expression for burned-out hardware, especially hardware that has suffered from a power surge. Also applied to people, as in "My brain is fried; I haven't slept since last weekend."

FTP

See file transfer protocol.

ftp

A command used to transfer files to and from remote computers using the file transfer protocol. You can use ftp to log in to an Internet computer and transfer text and binary files.

When you use ftp, you start a client program on your computer that connects to a server program on the Internet computer. The commands that you give to ftp are translated into instructions that the server program executes for you.

The original ftp program started life as a Unix utility, but versions are now available for all popular operating systems; ftp is also built into all the major Web browsers.

full backup

A backup that includes all files on a hard disk or set of hard disks. A network administrator must decide how often to perform a full backup, balancing the need for security against the time taken for the backup.

full-duplex

Abbreviated FDX. The capability for simultaneous transmission in two directions, so that devices can be sending and receiving data at the same time.

fully associative cache

See cache.

full-page display

Any monitor capable of displaying a whole page of text. Full-page displays are useful for graphical art and desktop publishing applications, as well as medical applications.

function keys

The set of programmable keys on the keyboard that can perform special tasks assigned by the current application.

Most keyboards have 10 or 12 function keys (F1 to F10 or F1 to F12), some of which are used by an application as shortcut keys. For example, many programs use F1 to gain access to the Help system. In some programs, the use of function keys is so complex that special plastic key overlays are provided as guides for users.

G

G

See giga-.

gauge

A measurement of the physical size of a cable. Under the American Wire Gauge (AWG) standards, higher numbers indicate thinner cable.

GB

See gigabyte.

gender changer

A special intermediary connector for use with two cables that each have only male connectors or only female connectors.

giga-

A prefix meaning 1 billion, or 10^9.

gigabit

Abbreviated Gb or Gbit. Usually 1,073, 741,824 binary digits or bits of data. Sometimes used as equivalent to one billion bits.

Gigabit Ethernet

A 1Gbps (1000Mbps) extension of the IEEE 802.3 Ethernet standard, also known as 1000Base-X.

This standard has been developed by the IEEE 802.3z Task Group and a number of interested companies collectively known as the Gigabit Ethernet Alliance. Gigabit Ethernet runs over multimode fiber optic cable and is intended for use as a backbone and a way to connect high-speed routers, switches, and hubs.

gigabyte

Abbreviated GB. Strictly speaking, one billion bytes; however, in computing, in which bytes are most often counted in powers of 2, a gigabyte becomes 2^{30}, or 1,073,741,824 bytes.

H

H.323

A videoconferencing standard defined by the International Telecommunication Union (ITU) that defines videoconferencing from the desktop over LANs, intranets, and the Internet.

H.323 specifies techniques for compressing and transmitting real-time voice, video, and data between a pair of videoconferencing workstations. It also describes signaling protocols for managing audio and video streams, as well as procedures for breaking data into packets and synchronizing transmissions across communications channels.

half-duplex

Abbreviated HDX. In asynchronous transmissions, the ability to transmit on the same channel in two directions, but only in one direction at a time.

handshaking

The exchange of control codes or particular characters to maintain and coordinate data flow between two devices, so that data is only transmitted when the receiving device is ready to accept the data.

Handshaking can be implemented in either hardware or software, and it occurs between a variety of devices. For example, the data flow might be from one computer to another computer, or from a computer to a peripheral device, such as a modem or printer.

hang

1. When a program waits for an event that never occurs, as in, "The program hangs waiting for a character from the keyboard."
2. A slang expression used when attaching a new piece of hardware to a system, usually an external device attached by one or more cables, as in, "I'm going to hang a new tape drive on the server this afternoon."

hard disk

That part of a hard disk drive that stores data, rather than the mechanism for reading and writing to it. Sometimes called a platter.

hard disk controller

The circuitry used to control and coordinate a hard disk drive.

Many hard disk controllers are capable of managing more than one hard disk, as well as floppy disks and tape drives. On some PCs, the hard disk controller is built into the motherboard, and in others, the controlling circuitry is mounted on the drive itself, eliminating the need for a separate controller.

hard disk drive

A storage device that uses a set of rotating, magnetically coated disks called platters to store data or programs. In everyday use, the terms hard disk, hard disk drive, and hard drive are used interchangeably, because the disk and the drive mechanism are a single unit.

A typical hard disk platter rotates at several thousand revolutions per minute, and the read/write heads float on a cushion of air from 10 to 25 millionths of an inch thick, so that the heads never come into contact with the recording surface. The whole unit is hermetically sealed to prevent airborne contaminants from entering and interfering with these close tolerances.

Hard disks range in storage capacity from a few tens of megabytes to several terabytes. The more storage space on the disk, the more important your backup strategy becomes. Hard disks are reliable, but they do fail, and usually at the most inconvenient moment.

hard disk interface

A standard way of accessing the data stored on a hard disk. Several different hard disk interface standards have evolved over time, including the ST506 Interface, Enhanced Small Device Interface (ESDI), Integrated Drive Electronics Interface (IDE), and SCSI (Small Computer System Interface).

hard disk type

A number stored in a PC's CMOS RAM memory area that defines certain hard disk characteristics, such as the number of read/write heads and the number of cylinders on the disk. This number is not accessible directly from the operating system. Some PCs require a special configuration program to access the hard disk type; others permit access via the computer's built-in ROM BIOS setup program.

hard reset

A system reset made by pressing the computer's reset button, or by turning the power off and then on again. A hard reset is used only when the system has crashed so badly that pressing Ctrl+Alt+Del to reboot does not work.

hardware

All the physical electronic components of a computer system, including peripheral devices, printed-circuit boards, displays, and printers. If you can stub your toe on it, it must be hardware.

hardware address

The address assigned to a network interface card by the original manufacturer, or if the interface card is configurable, by the network administrator.

This address identifies the local device address to the rest of the network and allows messages to find the correct destination. Also known as the physical address, Media Access Control (MAC) address, or Ethernet address.

hardware compatibility list

A list of all the hardware devices supported by Microsoft Windows NT and Windows 2000. Items on this list have actually been tested and verified to work properly with Windows.

hardware-dependent

The requirement that a specific hardware component be present for a program to work. Hardware-dependent software is often difficult to move or port to another computer.

hardware-independent

The ability to produce similar results in a wide variety of environments, without requiring the presence of specific hardware. The Java programming language and the PostScript page-description language are both examples of hardware independence. Java runs on a wide range of computers, from the PC to a mainframe; PostScript is used by many printer manufacturers.

hardware interrupt

An interrupt or request for service generated by a hardware device, such as a keystroke from the keyboard or a tick from the clock. Because the processor may receive several such signals simultaneously, hardware interrupts are usually assigned a priority level and processed according to that priority.

HDSL

See high-bit-rate digital subscriber line.

hertz

Abbreviated Hz. A unit of frequency measurement; 1Hz equals one cycle per second.

hexadecimal

Abbreviated hex. The base-16 numbering system that uses the digits 0 to 9, followed by the letters A to F, which are equivalent to the decimal numbers 10 through 15.

Hex is a convenient way to represent the binary numbers computers use internally, because it fits neatly into the 8-bit byte. All the 16 hex digits 0 to F can be represented in four bits, and two hex digits (one digit for each set of four bits) can be stored in a single byte. This means that one byte can contain any one of 256 different hex numbers, from 0 through FF.

hidden file

Any file that has the hidden attribute set, which indicates to the operating system that information about the file should not appear in normal directory listings. There may also be further restrictions on a hidden file, and you may not be able to delete, copy, or display the contents of such a file.

high-bit-rate digital subscriber line

Abbreviated HDSL. A high-speed data transmission technology originally developed by Bellcore that delivers high bandwidth over existing twisted-pair copper telephone lines.

HDSL is the most common digital subscriber line (DSL) service and provides T1 data rates of 1.544Mbps over lines of up to 3.6 kilometers (12,000 feet) in length. HDSL is symmetric, providing the same data rate in each direction.

The service is not intended for residential purposes but is used in the telephone company's own private data networks, Internet servers, and interexchange connections.

High Sierra specification

A specification for CD-ROM data that served as the basis for the ISO (International Organization for Standardization) 9660 standard. It is called High Sierra because it was defined at a meeting held near Lake Tahoe in November 1985.

hooked vector

An intercepted interrupt vector that now points to a replacement interrupt service routine (ISR) rather than to the original service routine.

hub

A device used to extend a network so that additional workstations can be attached. There are two main types of hub:

- Active hubs amplify transmission signals to extend cable length and ports.
- Passive hubs split the transmission signal, allowing additional workstations to be added, usually at a loss of distance.

In some star networks, a hub is the central controlling device.

Huffman coding

In data compression, a method of encoding data on the basis of the relative frequency of the individual elements. Huffman coding is often used with text files, where the coding is based on the frequency of occurrence of each letter, because it is a lossless compression method. Huffman coding is used in fax transmissions.

Hz

See hertz.

I

IC

See integrated circuit.

IDE

See Integrated Drive Electronics.

IEEE 1394

An IEEE standard for a digital Plug-and-Play bus, originally conceived by Apple Computer in 1986. IEEE 1394 supports up to 63 nodes per bus and up to 1023 buses.

Three speeds for device connections are w available:

- 100Mbps
- 200Mbps
- 400Mbps

All devices are hot pluggable, and both self-powered and bus-powered devices can be attached to the same bus. Also known as FireWire, IEEE 1394 uses six-pair shielded twisted-pair cable and is intended for high-end applications such as digitized video.

impedance

An electrical property of a cable that combines capacitance (the ability to store an electrical charge), inductance (the ability to store energy in the form of a magnetic field), and resistance (the ability to impede or resist the flow of electric current), measured in ohms.

Impedance can be described as the apparent resistance to the flow of alternating current at a given frequency. Mismatches in impedance along a cable cause distortions and reflections. Each transmission protocol and network topology specifies its own standards for impedance.

incremental backup

A backup of a hard disk that consists of only those files created or modified since the last backup was performed.

infection

The presence of a virus or Trojan Horse, which may be active in memory or which may be present on the hard disk.

An infection may remain hidden from the user for a considerable time. Some viruses are triggered by specific dates or by particular events on the system. Many macro viruses act immediately when you open the e-mail attachment containing the virus.

Infrared Data Association

Abbreviated IrDA. A trade association of over 150 computer and telecommunications hardware and software suppliers, including Hewlett-Packard, Apple Computer, AST, Compaq, Dell, IBM, Intel, Motorola, Novell, and others.

IrDA is concerned with standards definitions for products that use wireless communications.

infrared transmission

A method of wireless transmission that uses part of the infrared spectrum to transmit and receive signals.

Infrared transmissions take advantage of a frequency range just below that of visible light, and they usually require a line of sight connection between transmitter and receiver.

Infrared transmission can be used to send documents from portable computers to printers, to transmit data between portable computers, to exchange information between computers and cellular telephones and faxes, and to connect to home entertainment systems. Almost every manufacturer of portable devices is implementing infrared communications at some level.

inkjet printer

A nonimpact printer that sprays a mist of liquid ink through tiny jets in the print head to form characters or graphics on the page.

inoculate

To protect a file against attack from a virus by recording characteristic information about it and then monitoring any changes.

input/output

Abbreviated I/O. The transfer of data between the computer and its peripheral devices, disk drives, terminals, and printers.

input/output bound

Abbreviated I/O bound. A condition in which the speed of operation of the input/output port limits the speed of program execution. Getting the data into and out of the computer is more time-consuming than actually processing that same data.

install

To configure and prepare hardware or software for operation.

Many application packages have their own installation programs, which copy all the required files from the original distribution disks into appropriate directories on your hard disk and then help to configure the program to your own operating requirements. Microsoft Windows programs are installed by a program called Setup.

instruction set

The set of machine-language instructions that a processor recognizes and can execute.

An instruction set for reduced instruction set computing (RISC) may only contain a few instructions; a computer that uses complex instruction set computing (CISC) may be able to recognize several hundred instructions.

integrated circuit

Abbreviated IC, also known as a chip. A small semiconductor circuit that contains many electronic components.

Integrated Drive Electronics

Abbreviated IDE. A hard disk interface that removes the need for a separate disk controller card by integrating the required circuitry onto the drive itself or onto the motherboard; no expansion slot is needed.

Integrated Services Digital Network

Abbreviated ISDN. A standard for a worldwide digital communications network originally designed to replace all current systems with a completely digital, synchronous, full-duplex transmission system.

Computers and other devices connect to ISDN via simple, standardized interfaces. They can transmit voice, video, and data, all on the same line.

interface

The point at which a connection is made between two hardware devices, between a user and a program or operating system, or between two applications.

In hardware, an interface describes the logical and physical connections used, as in RS-232-C, and is often considered to be synonymous with the term port.

A user interface consists of the means by which a program communicates with the user, including a command line, menus, dialog boxes, online help systems, and so on.

Software interfaces are Application Program Interfaces (APIs) and consist of the codes and messages used by programs to communicate behind the scenes.

interleaved memory

A method of speeding up access by dividing dynamic RAM (DRAM) into two (or more) separate banks.

DRAM requires that its contents be updated at least every thousandth of a second, and while this update is taking place, it cannot be read by the processor. Interleaved memory divides available memory into banks so that the processor can read from one bank while the other is cycling, and so does not have to wait.

internal modem

A modem that plugs into the expansion bus of a personal computer, or into the PC Card connector of a laptop computer.

Internet

The world's largest computer network, consisting of millions of computers supporting tens of millions of users in hundreds of different countries. The Internet is growing at such a phenomenal rate that any size estimates are quickly out-of-date.

The Internet was originally established to meet the research needs of the U.S. Defense industry, but it has grown into a huge global network serving universities, academic researchers, commercial interests, government agencies, and private individuals, in the U.S. and the rest of the world.

The Internet uses TCP/IP protocols, and Internet computers run many different operating systems, including many variations of Unix, VMS, and Microsoft Windows 2000.

No government agency, single person, or corporate entity controls the Internet; there is no Internet Corporation working behind the scenes. All decisions on methods and standards are made by committees based on input from users.

Internet use falls into several major areas, including:

E-mail Well over 80 percent of the people who use the Internet on a regular basis use it for e-mail. You can send e-mail to recipients in over 150 countries on the Internet, as well as to subscribers of commercial online services such as America Online.

IRC chat A service that connects large numbers of users in real-time group discussions.

Mailing lists Private discussion groups accessed by e-mail.

Usenet newsgroups Larger public discussion groups that focus on a specific subject. Posts and threads in newsgroups are accessed using a newsreader.

World Wide Web A hypertext-based system for finding and accessing Internet resources; the World Wide Web is one of the fastest growing and most exciting of all Internet applications.

Other Internet applications such as Gopher, ftp and anonymous ftp, and Telnet have either been overshadowed by the growth of the World Wide Web, or have seen their function absorbed into the popular Web browsers.

The sheer volume of information available through the Internet is staggering; however, due to the fact that the Internet is a casual grouping of many networks, there is often no easy way to determine the location of specific information. This has led to the emergence of several prominent portal sites and a number of popular search engines.

Internet access can be via a permanent network connection or by dial-up through one of the many Internet Service Providers (ISPs).

internet

Abbreviation for internetwork. Two or more networks using different networking protocols, connected by means of a router. Users on an internetwork can access the resources of all connected networks.

Internet address

An address on the Internet. An Internet address usually takes the form $some-one@abc.def.xyz$, where $someone$ is a user's name or part of a user's name, $@abc$ is the network computer of the user, and def is the name of the host organization. The last three letters denote the kind of institution the user belongs to: edu for educational, com for commercial, gov for government, mil for the military, org for nonprofit organizations, and net for Internet administrative organizations.

Internet Protocol

Abbreviated IP, IP version 4, and IPv4. The protocol that regulates packet forwarding by tracking addresses, routing outgoing messages, and recognizing incoming messages in TCP/IP networks and the Internet.

Internet Service Provider

Abbreviated ISP. A company that provides commercial or residential customers access to the Internet via dedicated or dial-up connections. An ISP will normally have several servers and a high-speed connection to an Internet backbone. Some ISPs also offer Web site hosting services and free e-mail to their subscribers.

Internetwork Packet Exchange

Abbreviated IPX. Part of Novell NetWare's native protocol stack, used to transfer data between the server and workstations on the network. IPX packets are encapsulated and carried by the packets used in Ethernet and the frames used in Token Ring networks.

interprocess communication

Abbreviated IPC. A term that describes all the methods used to pass information between two programs running on the same computer in a multitasking operating system, or between two programs running on a network, including pipes, shared memory, message queues, sockets, semaphores, and Object Linking and Embedding (OLE).

interrupt

A signal to the processor generated by a device under its control, such as the system clock, that interrupts normal processing.

An interrupt indicates that an event requiring the processor's attention has occurred, causing the processor to suspend and save its current activity and then branch to an interrupt service routine (ISR).

In the PC, interrupts are often divided into three classes:

▶ Internal hardware
▶ External hardware
▶ Software

The Intel family of processors supports 256 prioritized interrupts, of which the first 64 are reserved for use by the system hardware or by the operating system.

interrupt handler

Special software located in the operating system kernel that manages and processes system interrupts. Also known as an interrupt service routine.

When an interrupt occurs, the processor suspends and saves its current activity and then branches to the interrupt handler. This routine processes the interrupt, whether it was generated by the system clock, a keystroke, or a mouse click. When the ISR is complete, it returns control to the suspended process.

Each type of interrupt is processed by its own specific interrupt handler. A table, called the interrupt vector table, maintains a list of addresses for these specific interrupt handlers.

interrupt request

Abbreviated IRQ. Hardware lines that carry a signal from a device to the processor.

A hardware interrupt signals that an event has taken place that requires the processor's attention. The interrupt may come from the keyboard, the network interface card, or the system's disk drives.

interrupt vector table

A list of addresses, maintained by the operating system kernel, for specific software routines known as interrupt handlers.

intranet

A private corporate network that uses Internet software and TCP/IP networking protocol standards.

Many companies use intranets for tasks as simple as distributing a company newsletter and for tasks as complex as posting and updating technical support bulletins to service personnel worldwide. An intranet does not always include a permanent connection to the Internet.

I/O

See *input/output.*

I/O bound

See *input/output bound.*

IP

See *Internet Protocol.*

IP address

The unique 32-bit number that identifies a computer on the Internet or other Internet Protocol network.

An IP address is usually written (in decimal) as four numbers separated by dots or periods, and can be divided into two parts. The network address is made up from the high-order bits in the address, and the host address comprises the rest. In addition, the host part of the address can be further subdivided to allow for a subnet address.

These numbers are very difficult for most people to remember, so humans tend to refer to computers by their domain names instead.

IPX

See *Internetwork Packet Exchange.*

IrDA

See *Infrared Data Association.*

IRQ

See *interrupt request.*

ISDN

See *Integrated Services Digital Network.*

ISR

See *interrupt service routine.*

J

Joint Photographic Experts Group

Abbreviated JPEG. An image-compression standard and file format that defines a set of compression methods for high-quality images such as photographs, single video frames, or scanned pictures; JPEG does not work very well when compressing text, line art, or vector graphics.

JPEG uses lossy compression methods that result in some loss of the original data; when you decompress the original image, you don't get exactly the same image that you started with, although JPEG was specifically designed to discard information not easily detected by the human eye.

JPEG can store 24-bit color images in as many as 16 million colors; files in Graphics Interchange Format (GIF) form can only store 256 colors.

JPEG
See *Joint Photographic Experts Group*.

jumper
A small plastic and metal connector that completes a circuit, usually to select one option from a set of several user-definable options. Jumpers are often used to select one particular hardware configuration from a choice of configurations.

K

K
See *kilo-*.

Kb
See *kilobit*.

KB
See *kilobyte*.

Kbit
See *kilobit*.

Kbps
See *kilobits per second*.

Kbyte
See *kilobyte*.

kernel
The most fundamental part of an operating system. The kernel stays resident in memory at all times, often hidden from the user, and manages system memory, the file system, and disk operations.

The kernel also runs processes and provides interprocess communications between those processes, including synchronization of events, scheduling, message passing,

management of input and output routines, and memory management.

keystroke
The action of pressing and then releasing a key on the keyboard to initiate some action or enter a character.

kilo-
A prefix indicating 1000 in the metric system. Because computing is based on powers of 2, kilo usually means 2^{10}, or 1024. To differentiate between these two uses, a lowercase k is used to indicate 1000 (as in kHz), and an uppercase K is used to indicate 1024 (as in KB).

kilobit
Abbreviated Kb or Kbit. 1024 bits (binary digits).

kilobits per second
Abbreviated Kbps. The number of bits, or binary digits, transmitted every second, measured in multiples of 1024bps. Used as an indicator of communications transmission rates.

kilobyte
Abbreviated K, KB, or Kbyte. 1024 bytes.

L

L1 cache
See *level 1 cache*.

L2 cache
See *level 2 cache*.

LAN
See *local area network*.

laptop computer
See notebook computer.

laser printer
A printer that is based on the same technology as that used by photocopiers.

A laser and rotating mirror create an image of the page on a rotating photosensitive drum. This image is converted into an electrostatic charge that attracts and holds the toner. Electrostatically charged paper is rolled against the drum, and the toner is transferred to the paper and fused to the paper using heat. The last step is to remove the electrostatic charge from the drum and collect any excess toner.

latency
The time it takes for the area of a hard disk containing the required information to rotate to a position under the read/write head. The faster the hard disk platter rotates, the lower the latency.

LBA
See logical block addressing.

LCC
See leadless chip carrier.

leadless chip carrier
Abbreviated LCC. A method used to mount integrated circuits onto a board. Although similar in appearance to the cheaper plastic leadless chip carrier (PLCC), LCCs are made from a ceramic material and the two chip carriers are incompatible.

level 1 cache
Abbreviated L1 cache. A primary cache built into microprocessors to increase speed. The L1 cache can be read in a single clock cycle, so it is always tried first. The Intel Pentium contains two separate 512 KB L1 caches, one each for data and instructions. Also called a primary cache.

level 2 cache
Abbreviated L2 cache. A secondary cache located between the L1 or primary cache and the rest of the system. A level 2 cache is often larger than the primary cache, and it is usually slower. Also called a secondary cache.

line analyzer
Any device that monitors and displays information about a transmission on a communications channel. A line analyzer is used for troubleshooting and load monitoring.

local area network
Abbreviated LAN. A group of computers and associated peripheral devices connected by a communications channel, capable of sharing files and other resources between several users.

logical block addressing
Abbreviated LBA. An element of the Enhanced IDE standard that allows a hard disk to store more than 8.4GB of information.

logical drive
The internal division of a large hard disk into smaller units. One single physical drive may be organized into several logical drives for convenience, with each one appearing to the user to be a separate drive.

logic bomb

A sabotage attack on a system timed to go off some time in the future; essentially a Trojan Horse with a fuse.

A logic bomb goes off at a certain time or when triggered by a certain event, and then performs some operation. It might release a virus, delete files, or send comments to a terminal. An unhappy programmer may plant a logic bomb on a system timed to go off long after they have left the company so as to avoid suspicion.

logical unit number

Abbreviated LUN. The logical address of a Small Computer System Interface (SCSI) device when several devices are attached to a single SCSI device ID. The LUN is usually set to zero, unless the SCSI adapter supports multiple LUNs on a single SCSI device ID.

loopback

A troubleshooting test in which a signal is transmitted from a source to a destination and then back to the source again so that the signal can be measured and evaluated or the data contained in the signal can be examined for accuracy and completeness.

lossless compression

Any data compression method that compresses a file by rearranging or recoding the data that it contains in a more compact fashion.

With lossless compression, there is no loss of original data when the file is decompressed. Lossless compression methods are used on program files and on images such as medical X-rays, when data loss cannot be tolerated, and can typically reduce a file to 40 percent of its original size.

Many lossless compression programs use a method known as the Lempel-Ziv-Welch (LZW) algorithm, which searches a file for redundant strings of data and converts them to smaller tokens. When the compressed file is decompressed, this process is reversed.

lossy compression

Any data compression method that compresses a file by discarding any data that the compression mechanism decides is not needed.

Original data is lost when the file is decompressed. Lossy compression methods may be used for shrinking audio or image files when absolute accuracy is not required and the loss of data will not be noticed; however, this technique is unsuitable for more critical applications in which data loss cannot be tolerated, such as with medical images or program files. Lossy compression can typically reduce a file to as little as 5 percent of its original size.

LPT ports

The device name used to denote a parallel communications port, often used with a printer.

LUN

See logical unit number.

M

M

See mega-.

m

See milli-.

machine language

The native binary language used internally by the computer; also known as machine code.

Machine language is difficult for humans to read and understand. Programmers create applications using high-level languages, which are translated into a form that the computer can understand by an assembler, a compiler, or an interpreter. Whichever method is used, the result is machine language.

macro virus

An executable program that attaches itself to a document created in Microsoft Word or Excel, or to an e-mail created in Outlook. When you open the attachment and execute the macro, the virus runs and does whatever damage it was programmed to do. Both the Melissa and ILOVEYOU viruses were Visual Basic programs distributed as an e-mail attachment.

male connector

Any cable connector with pins designed to engage the sockets on the female connector.

map

1. To direct a request for a file or service to an alternative resource. For example, in a virtual memory system, an operating system can translate or map a virtual memory address into a physical address; in a network, drive letters are assigned to specific volumes and directories.
2. An expression of the structure of an object. For example, a memory map describes the use and layout of physical memory.

mask

A binary number that is used to remove bits from another binary number by use of one of the logical operators (AND, OR, NOT, XOR) to combine the binary number and the mask. Masks are used in IP addresses and file permissions.

MB

See megabyte.

Mb

See megabit.

Mbps

See megabits per second.

mean time between failures

Abbreviated MTBF. The statistically derived average length of time for which a system component operates before failing. MTBF is expressed in thousands or tens of thousands of hours, also called power-on hours or POH.

mean time to repair

Abbreviated MTTR. The statistically derived average length of time that it takes to repair a component.

meg

A common abbreviation for megabyte.

mega-

Abbreviated M. A prefix meaning one million in the metric system. Because computing is based on powers of 2, mega usually means 2^{20} or 1,048,576; the power of 2 closest to one million.

megabit

Abbreviated Mb or Mbit. Usually 1,048,576 binary digits or bits of data. Often used as equivalent to 1 million bits.

megabits per second

Abbreviated Mbps. A measurement of the amount of information moving across a network or communications link in one second, measured in multiples of 1,048,576 bits.

megabyte

Abbreviated MB. Usually 1,048,576 bytes. Megabytes are a common unit of measurement for computer memory or hard disk capacity.

megahertz

Abbreviated MHz. One million cycles per second. A processor's clock speed is often expressed in megahertz.

The original IBM PC operated an Intel 8088 processor running at 4.77MHz; a Pentium processor runs at 800MHz; and modern systems are capable of running at more than 1000MHz or 1GHz.

memory

The primary physical RAM (random-access memory) installed in the computer. The operating system copies applications from disk into memory, where all program execution and data processing takes place, and then writes the results back to disk. The amount of memory installed in the computer can determine the size and number of programs that it can run, as well as the size of the largest data file.

memory address

The exact location in memory that stores a particular data item or program instruction.

memory board

A printed circuit board containing memory chips. When all the sockets on a memory board are filled and the board contains the maximum amount of memory that it can manage, it is said to be "fully populated."

memory cache

An area of high-speed memory on the processor that stores commonly used code or data obtained from slower memory, eliminating the need to access the system's main memory to fetch instructions.

The Intel Pentium contains two separate 512KB L1 or primary caches, one each for data and instructions.

memory chip

A chip that holds data or program instructions. A memory chip may hold its contents temporarily, as in the case of RAM (random-access memory), or permanently, as in the case of ROM (read-only memory).

memory leak

A programming error that causes a program to request new areas of computer memory rather than reusing the memory already assigned to it. This causes the amount of memory in use by the program to increase as time goes on. In a worst case, the application may consume all available memory and stop the computer.

memory management

The way in which the operating system handles the use of memory, usually as a combination of physical memory and virtual memory.

When applications are loaded, they are assigned space in which to run and store data. As they are removed, the memory space they occupied is released for use by the next program to run.

memory management unit

Abbreviated MMU. The part of the processor that manages the mapping of virtual memory addresses to actual physical addresses.

In some systems, such as those based on early Intel or Motorola processors, the MMU was a separate chip; however, in most modern systems, the MMU is integrated into the processor itself.

memory map

The organization and allocation of memory in a computer. A memory map will give an indication of the amount of memory used by the operating system, as well as the amount remaining for use by applications.

memory-resident

Always located in the computer's memory and available for use; not swapped out.

MHz

See megahertz.

microcode

Low-level instructions that define how a particular microprocessor works by specifying what the processor does when it executes a machine-language instruction.

micron

A unit of measurement. One millionth of a meter, corresponding to approximately 1/25,000 of an inch. The core diameter of fiber optic cable for networks is often specified in terms of microns; 62.5 microns is a common size.

microprocessor

A central processor unit on a single chip, often referred to as the processor. The first microprocessor was developed by Intel in 1969.

MIDI

See Musical Instrument Digital Interface.

milli-

Abbreviated m. A prefix meaning one thousandth in the metric system, often expressed as 10^{-3}.

millisecond

Abbreviated ms or msec. A unit of measurement equal to one thousandth of a second. In computing, hard disk and CD-ROM drive access times are often described in terms of milliseconds; the higher the number, the slower the disk system.

millivolt

Abbreviated mv. A unit of measurement equal to one thousandth of a volt.

mirroring

The process of duplicating stored information in real time to protect vital data from unexpected hardware failures.

MJ

See modular jack.

MMU

See memory management unit.

mobile computing

1. The everyday use of a portable computer as a normal part of the workday.
2. Techniques used to establish links to a network by employees who move from one remote location to another, such as members of a sales staff or telecommuters who work from home. Once the connection is made, users log in and access network resources as easily as if they were working from a computer in the corporate office.

modem

Contraction of modulator/demodulator, a device that allows a computer to transmit information over a telephone line.

The modem translates between the digital signals that the computer uses and analog signals suitable for transmission over telephone lines. When transmitting, the modem modulates the digital data onto a carrier signal on the telephone line. When receiving, the modem performs the reverse process to demodulate the data from the carrier signal.

modular jack

Abbreviated MJ. The jack used to connect telephone cables to a wall-mounted face plate.

modulation

In communications, the process used by a modem to add the digital signal onto the carrier signal, so that the signal can be transmitted over a telephone line. The frequency, amplitude, or phase of a signal may be modulated to represent a digital or analog signal.

Moore's Law

Moore's Law states that the number of transistors on a chip of a given size doubles approximately every 18 months. Named for Intel's Gordon Moore, who first made this statement in 1965.

motherboard

The main printed circuit board in a computer, containing the central processing unit, appropriate coprocessor and support chips, device controllers, and memory. It may also include expansion slots to give access to the computer's internal bus.

Motion Picture Experts Group

Abbreviated MPEG. A set of image-compression standards and file formats that defines a compression method for desktop audio, animation, and video.

MPEG is a lossy compression method that results in some data loss when a video clip is compressed. The following standards are available:

MPEG-1 The original MPEG standard, designed for CD-ROM use, with a bandwidth of 1.5Mbps, two audio channels, and noninterlaced video.

MPEG-2 An extension to MPEG-1 designed for broadcast television, including HDTV (High-Definition Television), with a bandwidth of up to 40Mbps, five audio channels, interlaced video, and a wider range of frame sizes.

MPEG-3 A standard designed for HDTV until it was discovered that MPEG-2 covered HDTV. This standard is no longer used.

MPEG-4 A standard designed for video phones and multimedia applications, with a bandwidth of up to 64Kbps.

mouse

A small input device with one or more buttons used with graphical user interfaces. As the mouse moves, an onscreen mouse cursor follows; all movements are relative. Once the pointer is in the correct position on the screen, you press one of the mouse buttons to initiate an action or operation.

MPEG

See Motion Picture Experts Group.

ms

See millisecond.

MTBF

See mean time between failures.

MTTR

See mean time to repair.

multimedia

A computer technology that displays information using a combination of full-motion video, animation, sound, graphics, and text, with a high degree of user interaction.

multimode fiber

A fiber optic cable with a wide core that provides multiple routes for light waves to travel.

Its wider diameter of between 25 to 200 microns prevents multimode fiber from carrying signals as far as single-mode fiber due to modal dispersion.

multipart virus

A form of virus that infects both the boot sector of a hard disk and executable files. Multipart viruses are difficult to detect as they use stealth and polymorphic techniques to avoid detection.

multiple zone recording

Abbreviated MZR. A method of increasing the storage capacity of a hard disk by using constant angular velocity (CAV) techniques. CAV allows for the storage of additional data on the disk's outer edges, which would otherwise not be filled to their full capacity.

Musical Instrument Digital Interface

Abbreviated MIDI. A serial interface standard and communications protocol that defines the connections between a computer and a synthesizer. MIDI devices can be used to create, record, and play back music.

mv

See millivolt.

MZR

See multiple zone recording.

N

n

See nano-.

name resolution

The process of translating the appropriate numerical IP address, which is required by a computer, into a name that is more easily understood and remembered by a person.

In the TCP/IP environment, names such as `www.sybex.com` are translated into their IP equivalents by the Domain Name System (DNS). In a Microsoft Windows

NT/2000 Server environment, NetBIOS names are resolved into IP addresses by Windows Internet Naming Service (WINS).

nano-

Abbreviated n. A prefix meaning one billionth in the American numbering scheme, and one thousand millionth in the British system.

nanosecond

Abbreviated ns. One billionth of a second. The speed of computer memory and logic chips is measured in nanoseconds.

narrow SCSI

A Small Computer System Interface (SCSI) or SCSI-2 interface capable of transferring only 8 bits of data at a time

NAT

See Network Address Translation.

National Television Standards Committee

Abbreviated NTSC. The standards-setting body for television and video in the United States. Most European and Asian countries use a different standard known as PAL (phase alteration line). The two standards are incompatible.

near-end crosstalk

Abbreviated NEXT. Any interference that occurs close to a connector at either end of a cable. NEXT is usually measured near the source of the test signal.

NetBEUI

Abbreviation for NetBIOS Extended User Interface, pronounced "net-boo-ee." A net-work device driver supplied with Microsoft's LAN Manager, Windows for Workgroups, Windows NT, Windows 98, and Windows 2000. NetBEUI communicates with the network interface card via the NDIS (Network Driver Interface Specification).

NetBEUI is a small protocol with no networking layer and therefore no routing capability. It is suitable only for small networks; you cannot build internetworks using NetBEUI, and so it is often replaced with TCP/IP.

Microsoft has added extensions to NetBEUI in Windows NT to remove the limitation of 254 sessions per node, and calls this extended NetBEUI the NetBIOS Frame (NBF).

NetBIOS

Acronym for network basic input/output system, pronounced "net-bye-ose." A session-layer network protocol, originally developed in 1984 by IBM and Sytek, to manage data exchange and network access.

NetBIOS provides an API with a consistent set of commands for requesting lower-level network services to transmit information from node to node, thus separating applications from the underlying network operating system. Many vendors provide either their own version of NetBIOS or an emulation of its communications services in their own products.

netiquette

A contraction of network etiquette. The set of unwritten rules governing the use of e-mail and other computer and network services.

Like any culture, the online world has its own rules and conventions, and if you understand and observe these conventions, you can take your place in the online community without problems. Here are a few tips:

- ▶ Remember that the people reading your post are human; if you wouldn't say it to their face, don't post it in your e-mail.
- ▶ Lurk before you leap. Spend a few days reading the posts in a newsgroup or mailing list before you post anything of your own.
- ▶ If you use a signature file to close your e-mail, remember to keep it short; people don't want to read lots of cute stuff every time you post.
- ▶ Don't post messages in uppercase as it is the e-mail equivalent of YELLING; to add emphasis, place an asterisk before and after a word.
- ▶ Don't flame or mount personal attacks on other users.
- ▶ Check your grammar and spelling before you post.
- ▶ Don't be shy; if you are an expert, share your knowledge with others.

network

A group of computers and associated peripheral devices connected by a communications channel capable of sharing files and other resources between several users.

A network can range from a peer-to-peer network connecting a small number of users in an office or department, to a LAN connecting many users over permanently installed cables and dial-up lines, to a metropolitan area network (MAN) or WAN connecting users on several different networks spread over a wide geographic area.

network adapter

See network interface card.

Network Address Translation

Abbreviated NAT. A term used to describe the process of converting between IP addresses on an intranet or other private network and Internet IP addresses.

network device driver

Software that controls the physical function of a network interface card, coordinating between the card and the other workstation hardware and software.

Network Driver Interface Specification

Abbreviated NDIS. A device-driver specification, originally developed by Microsoft and 3Com in 1990, that is independent of both the underlying network interface card hardware and the protocol being used. NDIS also allows multiple protocol stacks to be used at the same time in the same computer.

network interface card

Abbreviated NIC. In networking, the PC expansion board that plugs into a personal computer or server and works with the network operating system and the appropriate device drivers to control the flow of information over the network. Novell NetWare documentation uses the term network board, and some Microsoft documentation uses network adapter.

The network interface card is connected to the network media (twisted-pair, coaxial, or fiber optic cable), and is designed for a specific type of network such as Ethernet, token ring, FDDI, or ARCnet.

network operating system

Abbreviated NOS. In typical client/server architecture LANs, the NOS consists of two parts. The largest and most complex part is the system software running on the file server. This system software coordinates many functions, including user accounts and network access information, security, resource sharing, administrative functions, UPS and power monitoring, data protection, and error detection and control. A much smaller component of the NOS runs on each of the networked PCs or workstations attached to the network.

In peer-to-peer networks, a part of the NOS is installed on each PC or workstation attached to the network and runs on top of or as a part of the PC operating system. In some cases, the NOS may be installed on one PC designated as a file server, but this PC is not dedicated to the file server function; it is also available to run applications.

network printer

A printer attached to and accessible from the network. A network printer may be attached to a file server, a printer server, or may have its own direct connection to the network.

network protocol

A formal specification that defines the procedures to follow when transmitting and receiving data over the network. Protocols define the format, timing, sequence, and error checking used on the network. TCP/IP, NetBEUI, and IPX/SPX are three of the most common protocols in use.

newsgroup

A Usenet e-mail discussion group devoted to a single topic. Subscribers to a newsgroup post articles that can be read by all the other subscribers.

Newsgroup names fit into a formal structure in which each component of the name is separated from the next by a period. The leftmost portion of the name represents the category of the newsgroup, and the name gets more specific from left to right.

The major top-level newsgroup categories are

alt Newsgroups outside the main structure outlined below.

comp Computer science and related topics, including information about operating systems and hardware, as well as more advanced topics such as graphics and robotics.

misc Anything that does not fit into any of the other categories.

news Information on Usenet and newsgroups.

rec Recreational activities, such as hobbies, the arts, movies, and books.

sci Discussion groups on scientific topics, including math, physics, and biology.

soc Groups that address social and cultural issues.

talk Groups that concentrate on controversial subjects.

Private newsgroups are often available on corporate intranets, where organization, structure, and subject matter are decided by the system administrator.

newsreader

An application used to read articles posted to Usenet newsgroups. Newsreaders are of two kinds: *threaded* newsreaders group the posts into threads of related articles; *unthreaded* newsreaders present articles in their original order of posting without regard for the subject. Of the two, threaded newsreaders are much easier to use and are available in most popular Web browsers.

NEXT

See near-end crosstalk.

NIC

See network interface card.

noise

In communications, extraneous signals on a transmission channel that degrade the quality or performance of the channel. Noise is often caused by interference from nearby power lines, electrical equipment, or spikes in the AC line voltage.

nominal velocity of propagation

The speed at which a signal moves through a cable, expressed as a percentage or fraction of the speed of light in a vacuum. Some cable testers use this speed, along with the time it takes for a signal to return to the testing device, to calculate cable lengths.

notebook computer

A small, portable computer that is light enough to carry comfortably, with a flat screen and keyboard that fold together.

Advances in battery technology allow notebook computers to run for many hours between charges. Some models can mate with a docking station to perform as a full-sized desktop system back at the office, and many portable computers allow direct connection to the network via a network interface card (NIC).

ns

See nanosecond.

NTSC

See National Television Standards Committee.

null

A character that has all the binary digits set to zero (ASCII 0), and therefore has no value. In programming, a null character is used for several special purposes, including padding fields or serving as delimiter characters. In the C programming language, for example, a null character indicates the end of a character string.

null modem

A short serial cable that connects two personal computers so that they can communicate without the use of modems.

The cable connects the two computers' serial ports, and certain lines in the cable are crossed over so that the wires used for sending by one computer are used for receiving data by the other computer.

O

OCR

See optical character recognition.

octet

The Internet's own term for a unit of data containing exactly eight bits. Some of the computer systems attached to the Internet have bytes with more than eight bits, hence the need for this term.

OEM

See original equipment manufacturer.

offline

Describes a printer or other peripheral device that is not in ready mode and is therefore unavailable for use.

online

1. Most broadly, any work done on a computer instead of by more traditional manual means.
2. Any function available directly on a computer, such as an application's help system.
3. Describes a peripheral device, such as a printer or modem, when it is directly connected to a computer and ready to operate.
4. In communications, describes a computer connected to a remote computer over a network or a modem link.

online service

A service that provides an online connection via modem for access to various services. Online services fall into these main groups:

Commercial services MSServices such as America Online charge a monthly membership fee for access to online forums, e-mail services, software libraries, and online conferences.

Internet MSThe Internet is a worldwide network of computer systems and is not always easy to use, but the wealth of information available is staggering. The main problem for casual users is that there is no central listing of everything that is available.

Specialist databases MSSpecific databases aimed at researchers can be accessed through online services such as Dow Jones News/Retrieval for business news and Lexis and Nexis for the legal information and news archives.

operating system

Abbreviated OS. That software responsible for allocating system resources, including memory, processor time, disk space, and peripheral devices such as printers, modems, and monitors. All applications use the operating system to gain access to these resources as necessary. The operating system is loaded into the computer as it boots, and it remains in memory until the computer is turned off.

optical character recognition

Abbreviated OCR. The computer recognition of printed or typed characters. OCR is usually performed using a standard optical scanner and special software, although some systems use special readers. The text is reproduced just as though it had been typed. Certain advanced systems can even resolve neatly handwritten characters.

optical mouse

A mouse that must be used on a mouse pad containing a special grid. The mouse shines a small beam of light on the grid that conveys mouse movements back to the computer.

original equipment manufacturer

Abbreviated OEM. The original manufacturer of a hardware subsystem or component. For example, Canon makes the print engine used in many laser printers, including those from Hewlett-Packard (HP); in this case, Canon is the OEM and HP is a value-added reseller (VAR).

output

Computer-generated information that is displayed on the screen, printed, written to disk or tape, or sent over a communications link to another computer.

P

P

See peta-.

page-mode RAM

A memory-management technique used to speed up the performance of dynamic RAM (DRAM).

In a page-mode memory system, the memory is divided into pages by specialized DRAM chips. Consecutive accesses to memory addresses in the same page result in a page-mode cycle that takes about half the time of a regular DRAM cycle.

paged memory management unit

Abbreviated PMMU. A specialized chip designed to manage virtual memory. High-end processors, such as the Motorola 68040 and the Intel Pentium, have all the functions of a PMMU built into the chip itself.

Palm

The hand-held computer from 3Com Corporation, which has proved to be extremely popular, with over one million units sold to date.

parallel communications

The transmission of information from computer to computer, or from computer to peripheral device, in which all the bits that make up the character are transmitted at the same time over a multiline cable.

parallel port

An input/output (I/O) port that manages information 8 bits at a time, often used to connect a parallel printer.

parity

In communications, a simple form of error checking that uses an extra or redundant bit after the data bits but before the stop bit or bits. Parity may be set as follows:

Odd parity Indicates that the sum of all the 1 bits in the byte plus the parity bit must be odd. If the total is already odd, the parity bit is set to zero; if it is even, the parity bit is set to one.

Even parity If the sum of all the 1 bits is even, the parity bit must be set to zero; if it is odd, the parity bit must be set to one.

Mark parity The parity bit is always set to one and is used as the eighth bit.

Space parity The parity bit is set to zero and is used as the eighth bit.

None If parity is set to none, there is no parity bit, and no parity checking is performed.

The parity settings used by both communicating computers must match. Most online services, such as America Online, use no parity and an eight-bit data word.

parity bit

An extra or redundant bit used to detect data transmission errors.

parity checking

A check mechanism applied to a character or series of characters that uses the addition of extra or redundant parity bits.

Parity checking is useful for a variety of purposes, including asynchronous communications and computer memory coordination.

parity error

A mismatch in parity bits that indicates an error in transmitted data.

partition

A portion of a hard disk that the operating system treats as if it were a separate drive. In Windows, a hard disk can be divided into several partitions. A primary partition, generally assigned the drive letter C:, might contain files that start the computer running. You could also set up a non-Windows partition to be used by a different operating system.

partition table

An area of storage on a hard disk that contains information about the partitions the disk contains. This information is usually recorded during the initial preparation of the hard disk before it is formatted.

passive termination

A method used to terminate a Small Computer Systems Interface (SCSI) chain of devices. Passive termination is a simple termination method that works best with four or fewer devices on a SCSI daisy chain.

password

A security method that identifies a specific authorized user of a computer system or network by a unique string of characters.

In general, passwords should be a mixture of upper- and lowercase letters and numbers and should be longer than six characters.

Passwords should be kept secret and changed frequently. The worst passwords are the obvious ones: people's names or initials, place names, phone numbers, birth dates, and anything to do with computers or *Star Trek*. There are a limited number of words in the English language, and it is easy for a computer to try them all relatively quickly.

PB

See petabyte.

PC Card

A term that describes plug-in cards that conform to the PCMCIA (Personal Computer Memory Card International Association) standard. A PC Card is about the size of a credit card and uses a 68-pin connector with longer power and ground pins that will always engage before the signal pins engage. Several versions of the standard have been approved by PCMCIA:

Type I The thinnest PC Card, only 3.3 millimeters (0.13 inch) thick, used for memory enhancements, including dynamic RAM, static RAM, and flash memory.

Type II A card used for modems or network interface cards, 5 millimeters (0.2 inch) thick; may also hold a Type I card.

Type III A 10.5-millimeter (0.4 inch) card, used for mini-hard disks and other devices that need more space, including wireless network interface cards; may also hold two Type I or Type II cards.

In theory, each PC Card adapter can support 16 PC Card sockets (if there is enough space), and up to 255 adapters can be installed in a PC that follows the PCMCIA standard; in other words, PCMCIA allows up to 4080 PC Cards on one computer.

The majority of PC Card devices are modems, Ethernet and Token Ring network adapters, dynamic RAM, and flash memory cards, although mini-hard disks, wireless LAN adapters, and SCSI adapters are also available.

PC Card slot

An opening in the case of a portable computer, intended to receive a PC Card; also known as a PCMCIA slot.

PC Memory Card International Association

Abbreviated PCMCIA. A nonprofit association, formed in 1989, with more than 320 members in the computer and electronics industries, that developed a standard for credit card–sized plug-in adapters designed for portable computers.

PCI local bus

Abbreviation for Peripheral Component Interconnect local bus. A specification introduced by Intel in 1992 for a local bus that allows up to 10 PCI-compliant expansion cards to be plugged into the computer. One of these expansion cards must be the PCI controller card, but the others can include a video card, network interface card, SCSI interface, or any other basic function.

The PCI controller exchanges information with the computer's processor, either 32 or 64 bits at a time, and allows intelligent PCI adapters to perform certain tasks concur-

rently with the main processor by using bus-mastering techniques.

PCI is compatible with ISA, EISA, and MCA expansion buses for backward compatibility with older technologies. PCI can operate at a bus speed of 32MHz and can manage a maximum throughput of 132MBps with a 32-bit data path, or a rate of 264MBps with a 64-bit data path. PCI also supports Plug-and-Play.

PCI-X

A revision to the PCI standard proposed by IBM, Hewlett-Packard, and Compaq, that increases the bus width to 64 bits, the bus speed to 133MHz and the maximum throughput to 1GBps. Several vendors also offer hot-plug PCI slots that allow you to replace a failed component without a system reboot.

PCMCIA

See PC Memory Card International Association.

PCMCIA slot

See PC Card slot.

PDA

See personal digital assistant.

peer-to-peer

A network architecture in which two or more PCs can communicate with each other directly without the need for any intermediary devices. In a peer-to-peer system, a PC can be both a client and a server.

peer-to-peer network

A LAN in which drives, files, and printers on each PC can be available to every other PC on the network, eliminating the need for a dedicated file server. Each PC can still run local applications.

Peer-to-peer networks introduce their own system management problems, including administration and responsibility for system backup, reliability, and security. Peer-to-peer systems are often used in relatively small networks, with two to ten users.

Pentium

A family of microprocessors introduced by Intel in 1993. The Pentium represents the continuing evolution of the 80486 family of microprocessors and adds several notable features, including instruction code and data caches and a built-in floating-point processor and memory management unit. It also has a superscalar design and dual pipelining, which allows the Pentium to execute more than one instruction per clock cycle, a 32-bit address bus and a 64-bit data bus. The Pentium is equivalent to 3.1 million transistors, more than twice that of the 80486.

Pentium II

A family of microprocessors from Intel. The Pentium II includes several notable features, including integrated L1/L2 caches of up to 2MB, which can be accessed at the full clock speed, and a built-in floating-point processor and memory management unit. It also has a superscalar design and dual pipelining, which allows the Pentium II to execute more than one instruction per clock cycle.

Available in a whole range of clock speeds, the Pentium II can use a 100MHz system bus, and is equivalent to 7.5 million transistors, more than twice that of the Pentium.

Pentium III

A family of microprocessors introduced by Intel in 1999. The Pentium III includes 50 new floating-point instructions and eight new registers to speed up floating-point calculations in scientific and engineering calculation, along with 12 new multimedia instructions to increase MPEG-2 performance and speech recognition. The most controversial feature is the processor serial number, designed to increase network and online shopping security but feared by many as a threat to privacy.

Available in a whole range of clock speeds, the Pentium III can use the Pentium II 100MHz system bus and is equivalent to 9.5 million transistors.

Pentium Pro

A family of microprocessors introduced by Intel in 1995. The Pentium Pro is optimized for the execution of 32-bit software and is available with clock speeds from 150 to 200MHz. With a 32-bit data bus running at 60 or 66MHz, it supports superscalar architecture and pipelines and contains the equivalent of 5.5 million transistors.

Dynamic execution (a combination of branch prediction and speculative execution) allows the processor to anticipate and schedule the next instructions for execution. Pentium Pro offers up to 1MB of level 2 cache that runs at the same speed as the processor.

period

The . character; pronounced "dot." Used to indicate the name of the current directory in a pathname and used to separate the different elements in a domain name, as in `www.sybex.com`.

Peripheral Component Interconnect

See PCI local bus.

permanent swap file

A swap file that, once created, is used over and over again. This file is used in virtual memory operations, where hard disk space is used in place of RAM.

personal digital assistant

Abbreviated PDA. A tiny, pen-based, battery-powered computer that combines personal organization software with fax and e-mail facilities into a unit that fits into your pocket. PDAs are available from several manufacturers, including 3Com, Casio, Tandy, Toshiba, Motorola, Sharp, Sony, GRiD, and AT&T.

peta-

Abbreviated P. A metric system prefix for one quadrillion, or 10^{15}. In computing, based on the binary system, peta has the value of 1,125,899,906,842,624, or the power of 2 (2^{50}) closest to 1 quadrillion.

petabyte

Abbreviated PB. Usually 1,125,899,906,842,624 bytes (2^{50}), but may also refer to 1 quadrillion bytes (10^{15}).

PGA

See pin grid array.

PhotoCD

A standard for storing 35mm photographs taken with an ordinary (nondigital) camera onto CD-ROM.

physical device

An item of hardware, such as a disk drive or a tape drive, which is physically separate from other devices.

physical drive

A real device in the computer that you can see or touch, as opposed to a conceptual or logical drive. One physical drive may be divided into several logical drives, which are parts of the hard disk that function as if they were separate disk drives.

pin grid array

Abbreviated PGA. A method of mounting integrated circuits onto boards. PGA is often used with integrated circuits that have a very large number of pins.

pinouts

The configuration and purpose of each pin in a multipin connector.

PIO

See programmed input/output.

pipeline burst cache

A secondary or L2 cache associated with a microprocessor that allows fast data transfer rates. Pipeline burst cache requires RAM chips that can synchronize with the microprocessor's clock.

pipelining

In processor architecture, a method of fetching and decoding instructions that ensures that the processor never needs to wait; as soon as one instruction is executed, the next one is ready.

pipeline stall

A microprocessor design error that leads to delays in the processing of an instruction.

plastic leadless chip carrier

Abbreviated PLCC. A method used to mount integrated circuits onto a board. Although similar in appearance to the more expensive leadless chip carrier (LCC), which is made from a ceramic material, the two chip carriers are incompatible.

PLCC

See plastic leadless chip carrier.

Plug and Play

Abbreviated PnP. A standard from Compaq, Microsoft, Intel, and Phoenix that defines techniques designed to make PC configuration simple and automatic. A user can plug in a new device and the operating system will recognize it and configure it automatically when the system is next started.

PnP adapters contain configuration information stored in nonvolatile memory, which includes vendor information, serial number, and checksum information. The PnP chip set allows each adapter to be isolated, one at a time, until all cards have been properly identified by the operating system.

The PnP-compatible BIOS isolates and identifies PnP cards at boot time, and when you insert a new card, the BIOS performs an auto-configuration sequence enabling the new card with appropriate settings.

PMMU

See paged memory management unit.

PnP

See Plug and Play.

Point-to-Point Protocol

Abbreviated PPP. A TCP/IP protocol used to transmit data over serial lines and dial-up telephone point-to-point connections.

PPP allows a PC to establish a temporary direct connection to the Internet via modem and appear to the host system as if it were an Ethernet port on the host's network.

PPP provides an automatic method of assigning an IP (Internet Protocol) address so that mobile users can connect to the network at any point.

polymorphic virus

A form of virus that can change its appearance to avoid detection. The virus encrypts itself using a special formula each time an infection occurs. Virus detecting software uses special scanning techniques to find and remove polymorphic viruses.

POP

See Post Office Protocol.

port

1. The point at which a communications circuit terminates at a network, serial, or parallel interface card, usually identified by a specific port number or name.
2. A number used to identify a connection point to a specific Internet protocol.

port number

The default identifier for a TCP/IP or Internet process.

For example, ftp, HTML, and Telnet are all available at preassigned unique port numbers so that the computer knows how to respond when it is contacted on a specific port; Web servers use port 80, and SMTP e-mail is always delivered to port 25. You can override these defaults by specifying different values in a URL, but whether they will work or not depends on the configuration on the target system.

port replicator

A device containing standard computer ports used to avoid constantly connecting and disconnecting peripherals from a portable computer.

A port replicator duplicates your computer's ports and may even add a Small Computer Systems Interface (SCSI) port or a second Universal Serial Bus port. The external monitor, full-sized keyboard, and mouse you use in the office are connected to the port replicator; when it is time to take the portable computer on the road, you just unplug the port replicator, leaving everything attached to the replicator for your return.

portal

A large Web site that acts as a gateway to the Internet and may also offer search facilities, free e-mail, online chat, and instant messaging, as well as other services including hard news, sports, and personal finance. Many portals make money by selling advertising space.

POST

See Power-On Self Test.

post

An individual article or e-mail message sent to a Usenet newsgroup or mailing list, rather than a message sent to an individual.

Post Office Protocol

Abbreviated POP. An Internet mail server protocol that also provides an incoming mail storage mechanism.

POP works with Simple Mail Transfer Protocol (SMTP), which actually moves the e-mail from one system to another, and the latest version of the standard is POP3.

When a client connects to a POP3 server, all the messages addressed to that client are downloaded; there is no ability to download messages selectively. Once the messages are downloaded, the user can delete or modify messages without further interaction with the server

In some locations, POP3 is being replaced by another standard, Internet Mail Access Protocol (IMAP) version 4.

PostScript

A page-description language from Adobe Systems that offers flexible fonts and high-quality graphics. PostScript uses Englishlike commands for page layout and to scale fonts and is used with high-quality printers.

power conditioning

The use of protective and conditioning devices to filter out power surges and spikes and ensure clean power. There are three main types of power conditioning devices:

Suppression device Protects against sudden destructive transient voltages.

Regulation device Modifies the power waveform back to a clean sine wave. A UPS (uninterruptible power supply) is a common form of voltage regulator. It may be online, actively modifying the power, or offline, available only after the line voltage drops below a certain level.

Isolation device Protects against noise. These types of devices are often expensive.

Because power conditioning is expensive, usually just the servers or hosts in a network are protected.

Power-On Self Test

Abbreviated POST. A set of diagnostic programs loaded from ROM (read-only memory) before any attempt is made to load the operating system, designed to ensure that the major system components are present and operating. If a problem is found, the POST firmware writes an error message in the screen, sometimes with a diagnostic code number indicating the type of fault located.

power supply

A part of the computer that converts the power from a wall outlet into the lower voltages, typically 5 to 12 volts DC (direct current), required internally in the computer. PC power supplies are usually rated in watts, ranging from 90 to 300 watts. If the power supply in a computer fails, nothing works— not even the fan.

power surge

A sudden, brief, and often destructive increase in line voltage. A power surge may be caused by an electrical appliance, such as a photocopier or elevator, or by power being reapplied after an outage.

PPP

See Point-to-Point Protocol.

primary cache

See L1 cache.

Primary Rate ISDN

Abbreviated PRI. An ISDN (Integrated Services Digital Network) service that provides 23 B (bearer channels), capable of speeds of 64Kbps, and one D (data channel), also capable of 64Kbps. The combined capacity of 1.544Mbps is equivalent to one T1 channel.

printer emulation

The ability of a printer to change modes so that it behaves like a printer from another manufacturer. For example, many dot matrix printers offer an Epson printer emulation in addition to their own native mode. Most laser printers offer a Hewlett-Packard Laser-Jet emulation.

programmed input/output

Abbreviated PIO. A method of moving data between a hard disk and memory via the processor. An alternative data transfer method known as direct memory access (DMA) bypasses the processor and moves data directly between the hard disk and memory.

protocol stack

The several layers of software that define the computer-to-computer or computer-to-network protocol.

Several companies have developed important proprietary protocol stacks, including Novell NetWare's IPX/SPX, but the trend these days is moving toward more open systems such as TCP/IP.

Q

QIC

See quarter-inch cartridge.

quarter-inch cartridge

Abbreviated QIC. A set of tape standards defined by the Quarter-Inch Cartridge Drive Standards Association, a trade association established in 1987. Several standards are in use today.

question mark

A wildcard character (?) used in many operating systems to represent a single character in a filename or filename extension.

R

radio frequency interference

Abbreviated RFI. Many electronic devices, including radios, televisions, computers, and peripherals, can interfere with other signals in the radio frequency range by producing electromagnetic radiation. The use of radio frequencies is generally regulated by government agencies.

RAID

See Redundant Array of Inexpensive Disks.

RAM

See random-access memory.

RAM chip

A semiconductor storage device, either dynamic RAM or static RAM.

random access

Describes the ability of a storage device to go directly to the required memory address without needing to read from the beginning every time data is requested.

In a random-access device, the information can be read directly by accessing the appropriate memory address. There is

nothing random or haphazard about random access; a more precise term is direct access.

random-access memory

Abbreviated RAM. The main system memory in a computer, used for the operating system, applications, and data.

rate-adaptive digital subscriber line

Abbreviated RADSL. An asymmetric digital subscriber line (ADSL) service with a provision for testing the line length and quality before starting the service and adjusting the line speed accordingly.

read-after-write verification

A method of checking that data is written to a hard disk correctly. Data is written to the disk and then read back and compared with the original data still held in memory. If the data read from the disk matches, the data in memory is released. If the data does not match, that block on the disk is marked as bad, and another attempt is made to write the data elsewhere on the disk.

README file

A plain text file containing information about the software, placed on the distribution disks by the manufacturer.

The filename may vary slightly; it might be READ.ME, README.1ST, README.TXT, or README.DOC, for example. README files may contain last minute, important information that is not in the program manuals or online help system.

You should always look for a README file when installing a new program on your system; it may contain information pertinent to your specific configuration. You can open a

README file in any word processor or text editor because the file does not contain embedded formatting commands or program-specific characters.

read-only

Describes a file or other collection of information that may only be read; it may not be updated in any way or deleted.

Certain important operating system files are designated as read-only files to prevent accidental deletion. Also, certain types of ROM and some devices such as archive backup tapes and CD-ROMs can be read from but not changed.

read-only memory

Abbreviated ROM. A semiconductor-based memory system that stores information permanently, retaining its contents when power is switched off. ROMs are used for firmware, such as the BIOS used in the PC. In some portable computers, applications and even the operating system are stored in ROM.

reboot

To restart the computer and reload the operating system, usually after a crash.

In some cases, you may be able to restart the computer from the keyboard; in more severe crashes, you may have to turn the computer off and then back on again.

reduced instruction set computing

Abbreviated RISC, pronounced "risk." A processor that recognizes only a limited number of assembly-language instructions.

RISC chips are relatively cheap to produce and debug, because they usually contain fewer than 128 different instructions. RISC processors are commonly used in

workstations, and they can be designed to run up to 70 percent faster than processors that use complex instruction set computing (CISC).

Redundant Array of Inexpensive Disks

Abbreviated RAID. In networking and mission-critical applications, a method of using several hard disk drives (often SCSI or Integrated Drive Electronics [IDE] drives) in an array to provide fault tolerance in the event that one or more than one drive fails.

Each of the different levels of RAID is designed for a specific use:

RAID 0 Data is striped over one or more drives, but there is no redundant drive. RAID 0 provides no fault tolerance because the loss of a hard disk means a complete loss of data. Some classification schemes omit RAID 0 for this reason.

RAID 1 Two hard disks of equal capacity duplicate or mirror each other's contents. One disk continuously and automatically backs up the other disk. This method is also known as disk mirroring or disk duplexing, depending on whether one or two independent hard disk controllers are used.

RAID 2 Bit-interleaved data is written across several drives and then parity and error-correction information is written to additional separate drives. The specific number of error-correction drives depends on the allocation algorithm in use.

RAID 3 Bit-interleaved data is written across several drives, but only one parity drive is used. If an error is detected, the data is reread to resolve the problem. The fact that data is reread in the event of an error may add a small performance penalty.

RAID 4 Data is written across drives by sectors rather than at the bit level, and a separate drive is used as a parity drive for error detection. Reads and writes occur independently.

RAID 5 Data is written across drives in sectors, and parity information is added as another sector, just as if it were ordinary data. This level of RAID can provide faster performance as the parity information is written across all the drives, rather than to a single parity drive.

There is not much difference in speed or quality among these levels. The appropriate level of RAID for any particular installation depends on network usage. RAID levels 1, 3, and 5 are available commercially, and levels 3 and 5 are proving popular for networks.

Registry

In the Microsoft Windows family of operating systems, a system database containing configuration information.

The operating system continually references the Registry database for information on users and groups, the applications installed on the system and the types of document each can create, what hardware is available and which ports are in use, and property sheets for folders and application icons.

Changes to the Registry are usually made automatically as configuration information is changed using Control Panel applications or the Administrative Tools; however, knowl-

edgeable users can make changes directly using the application regedit or regedt32.

restore

To copy files from a backup or archival storage to their normal location, especially when the files are being copied to replace files lost by accident.

retensioning

A maintenance operation required by certain tape drives to ensure correct tape tension; retensioning fast forwards and then rewinds the entire tape or tape cartridge.

RFI

See *radio frequency interference.*

RISC

See *reduced instruction set computing.*

RJ-11

A commonly used modular telephone connector. RJ-11 is a four-wire (two-pair) connector most often used for voice communications.

RJ-45

A commonly used modular telephone connector. RJ-45 is an eight-wire (four-pair) connector used for data transmission over unshielded twisted-pair cable (UTP) and leased telephone line connections.

ROM

See *read-only memory.*

RS-232-C

A recommended standard interface established by the Telecommunications Industry Association and the Electronic Industries

Association (TIA/EIA). Also known as TIA/EIA-232.

The standard defines the specific electrical, functional, and mechanical characteristics used in asynchronous transmissions between a computer (data terminal equipment, or DTE) and a peripheral device (data communications equipment, or DCE). RS is the abbreviation for recommended standard, and the C denotes the third revision of that standard. RS-232-C is compatible with the CCITT V.24 and V.28 standards, as well as ISO IS2110.

RS-232-C uses a 25-pin or 9-pin DB connector and is used for serial communications between a computer and a peripheral device, such as a printer, modem, or mouse. The maximum cable limit of 15.25 meters (50 feet) can be extended by using high-quality cable, line drivers to boost the signal, or short-haul modems.

S

sag

A short-term drop in line voltage to between 70 and 90 percent of the nominal voltage.

SAN

See Storage Area Network.

SCSI

Acronym for Small Computer System Interface, pronounced "scuzzy."

A high-speed parallel interface defined by the ANSI X3T9.2 committee. SCSI is used to connect a computer to peripheral devices using just one port. Devices connected in this way are said to be "daisy-chained" together, and each device must have a unique identifier or priority number.

SCSI is often used to connect hard disks, tape drives, CD-ROM drives, and other mass storage media, as well as scanners and printers.

Features of the SCSI definition include:

▶ The bus can manage simultaneous reads and writes.

▶ The original standard supports up to seven devices on a single host adapter; new standards support up to 16 devices and a bus length of up to 25 meters (80 feet).

▶ SCSI devices have their own control circuitry and can disconnect from the host adapter to process tasks on their own, freeing up the bus for other purposes.

SCSI-1

A commonly used name for the first Small Computer System Interface (SCSI) definition, published in 1986 with an eight-bit parallel interface and a maximum data transfer rate of 5MBps.

SCSI-2

A 1994 extension to the Small Computer System Interface (SCSI) definition.

This standard broadened the 8-bit data bus to 16 or 32 bits (also known as Wide SCSI), doubling the data transfer rate to 10 or 20Mbps (also known as Fast SCSI). Wide SCSI and Fast SCSI can be combined to give Fast-Wide SCSI, with a 16-bit data bus and a maximum data transfer rate of 20Mbps. SCSI-2 is backward compatible with SCSI-1, but for maximum benefit, you should use SCSI-2 devices with a SCSI-2 controller.

SCSI-2 also adds new commands, and although the connector is physically smaller, it uses 68 pins rather than the 50 in SCSI-1.

Higher data transfer rates are achieved by using synchronous rather than asynchronous transfers.

SCSI-3

An extension to the Small Computer System Interface (SCSI) standard.

This definition increased the number of connected peripherals from 7 to 16, increased cable lengths, added support for a variety of interfaces including a serial interface, a Fibre Channel interface, an IEEE 1394 interface and support for Serial Storage Architecture and several packet interfaces.

Data transfer rates depend on the hardware implementation, but data rates in excess of 160Mbps are possible.

SCSI bus

Another name for the Small Computer System Interface (SCSI) interface and communications protocol.

SCSI terminator

The Small Computer System Interface (SCSI) interface must be correctly terminated to prevent signals echoing on the bus.

Many SCSI devices have built-in terminators that engage when they are needed. With some older SCSI devices, you must add an external SCSI terminator that plugs into the device's SCSI connector.

SDRAM

See synchronous DRAM.

SDSL

See single-line digital subscriber line.

search engine

A special Web site that lets you perform keyword searches to locate interesting Web pages.

To use a search engine, you enter one or more keywords or, in some cases, a more complex search string such as a Boolean expression. The search engine returns a list of matching Web pages, newsgroups, and FTP archives taken from its database, usually ranked in some way, containing the expression you are looking for, along with a brief text description of the material.

Searching this database is much faster than actually searching the Internet, but the accuracy and relevance of the information it contains depends on how often the data is updated and what proportion of the Web is actually searched for new content.

seek time

The time it takes to move a disk drive's read/write head to a specific location on the disk.

secondary cache

See L2 cache.

sector

A portion of one of the concentric tracks recorded on a hard or floppy disk during a low-level format, usually capable of storing 512 bytes of information.

Sequenced Packet Exchange

Abbreviated SPX. A set of Novell NetWare protocols implemented on top of IPX to form a transport-layer interface.

SPX provides additional capabilities over IPX. For example, it guarantees packet delivery by having the destination node verify that the data was received correctly. If no response is received within a specified time, SPX retransmits the packet. If several retransmissions fail to return an acknowledgment, SPX assumes that the connection has failed and informs the operator. All packets in the transmission are sent in sequence, and they all take the same path to their destination node.

sequential access
An access method used by some storage devices, such as tapes, that requires them to start at the beginning to find a specific storage location. If the information you are looking for is toward the end of the tape, access can take a long time.

serial communications
The transmission of information from computer to computer, or from computer to peripheral device, one bit at a time.

Serial communications can be synchronous and controlled by a clock, or asynchronous and coordinated by start and stop bits embedded in the data stream. The sending and receiving devices must both use the same baud rate, parity setting, and other communication parameters.

Serial Line Internet Protocol
Abbreviated SLIP. A protocol used to run Internet Protocol over serial lines or telephone connections using modems.

SLIP allows a computer to establish a temporary direct connection to the Internet via modem and appear to the host system as if it were a port on the host's network.

SLIP is being replaced by PPP (Point-to-Point Protocol).

serial port
A port on the computer that supports serial communications, in which information is processed one bit at a time.

RS-232-C is a common protocol used on serial ports when communicating with modems, printers, mice, and other peripherals; USB (Universal Serial Bus) is replacing RS-232-C.

set-associative cache
See cache.

SGRAM
See Synchronous Graphics RAM.

shielded cable
Cable protected against electromagnetic and radio frequency interference (RFI) by metal-backed Mylar foil and plastic or PVC.

shielded twisted-pair cable
Abbreviated STP. Cable with a foil shield and copper braid surrounding the pairs of wires.

The wires have a minimum number of twists per foot of cable length; the greater the number of twists, the lower the cross talk. STP offers high-speed transmission for useful distances, and it is often associated with Token Ring networks, but its bulk quickly fills up wiring conduits.

short circuit
Often abbreviated to short. A circuit that is accidentally completed at a point too close to its origin to allow normal or complete operation. In cabling, a short circuit often occurs when two stripped wires touch.

SIMM
See Single Inline Memory Module.

Simple Mail Transfer Protocol

Abbreviated SMTP. The TCP/IP protocol that provides a simple e-mail service and is responsible for moving e-mail messages from one e-mail server to another. SMTP provides a direct end-to-end mail delivery, which is rather unusual; most mail systems use store-and-forward protocols.

The e-mail servers run either Post Office Protocol (POP) or Internet Mail Access Protocol (IMAP) to distribute e-mail messages to users.

Single Inline Memory Module

Abbreviated SIMM. A group of memory chips mounted on a small circuit board. SIMMs have one set of connectors, and they have a 32-bit data path.

Single Large Expensive Disk

Abbreviated SLED. The traditional alternative to RAID (Redundant Array of Inexpensive Disks), used by most networks.

single-line digital subscriber line

Abbreviated SDSL; sometimes called symmetrical digital subscriber line. A symmetrical, bidirectional digital subscriber line service that operates on one twisted-pair wire.

SDSL can provide data rates of up to the T1 rate of 1.544Mbps over a cable length of up to 1,000 feet and, because it operates above the voice frequency, voice and data can be carried on the same connection at the same time.

single-mode fiber

Narrow diameter fiber optic cable in which lasers rather than LEDs are used to transmit signals through the cable.

Single-mode fiber allows only one route for a light wave to pass through, and it can transmit signals over considerable distances. For this reason, it is often used in telephone networks rather than in LANs.

slash

The / character. Used to separate command-line switches that alter the default settings for an operating system command.

SLED

See Single Large Expensive Disk.

SLIP

See Serial Line Internet Protocol.

Small Computer System Interface

See SCSI.

SMTP

See Simple Mail Transfer Protocol.

spike

A short, transient electrical signal, often of very high amplitude.

SPX

See Sequenced Packet Exchange.

SRAM

See static RAM.

start bit

In asynchronous transmissions, a start bit is transmitted to indicate the beginning of a new data word.

static RAM

Abbreviated SRAM, pronounced "ess-ram." A type of computer memory that retains its contents as long as power is applied; it does not need constant refreshment, as required by dynamic RAM (DRAM) chips.

An SRAM chip can store only about one-fourth of the information that a DRAM chip of the same complexity can hold. However, SRAM is much faster than DRAM and is often used in caches.

stealth virus

A form of virus that attempts to hide from antivirus software and from the operating system by remaining in memory.

stop bit

In asynchronous transmissions, a stop bit is transmitted to indicate the end of the current data word. Depending on the convention in use, one or two stop bits are used.

store-and-forward

A method that temporarily stores messages at intermediate nodes before forwarding them to the next destination. This technique allows routing over networks that are not available at all times and lets users take advantage of off-peak rates when traffic and costs might be lower.

Storage Area Network

Abbreviated SAN. A method used to physically separate the storage function of the network from the data processing function.

SAN provides a separate network devoted to storage, and so helps to reduce network traffic by isolating large data transfers such as backups. Most of the SAN vendors, including StorageTek and Compaq, use a Fibre Channel–based SAN system, although IBM has proposed a proprietary architecture.

STP

See shielded twisted-pair cable.

straight-tip connector

Abbreviated ST. A fiber optic cable connector that maintains the perfect alignment of the ends of the connected fibers, required for efficient light transmission.

streaming tape

A high-speed tape backup system designed to optimize throughput; the tape is not stopped during a backup. To use streaming tape, the computer and backup software must be fast enough to keep up with the tape drive.

stripe set

A single volume created across multiple hard disk drives and accessed in parallel to optimize disk-access time.

subdirectory

A directory contained within another directory. The root directory is the top-level directory, from which all other directories must branch. In common use, subdirectory is synonymous with directory or folder.

subnet

A logical network created from a single IP address. A mask is used to identify bits from the host portion of the address to be used for subnet addresses.

subnet address

The subnet portion of an IP address. In a subnetted network, the host part of the IP address is divided into a subnet portion and a host portion by a subnet mask.

subnet mask

A number, or more correctly, a bit pattern, that identifies which parts of an IP address correspond to the network, subnet, and host portions of the address. Also referred to as an address mask.

superpipelining

A preprocessing technique used by some microprocessors in which two or more execution stages (such as fetch, decode, execute, or write back) are divided into two or more pipelined stages, giving considerably higher performance.

superscalar

A microprocessor architecture that contains more than one execution unit, or pipeline, allowing the processor to execute more than one instruction per clock cycle.

For example, the Pentium processor is superscalar, with two side-by-side pipelines for integer instructions. The processor determines whether an instruction can be executed in parallel with the next instruction in line. If it does not detect any dependencies, the two instructions are executed.

surge

A short, sudden, and often destructive increase in line voltage. A voltage-regulating device, known as a surge suppressor, can protect computer equipment against surges.

surge suppressor

A voltage-regulating device placed between the computer and the AC line connection that protects the computer system from power surges; also known as a surge protector.

swap

To temporarily move a process from memory to disk, so that another process can use that memory space. When space becomes available again, the process is swapped back into memory. This allows more processes to be loaded than there is physical memory space to run them simultaneously.

swap file

On a hard disk, a file used to store parts of running programs that have been swapped out of memory temporarily to make room for other running programs.

A swap file may be permanent, always occupying the same amount of hard disk space even though the application that created it may not be running, or temporary, created as and when needed.

In Windows 2000 documentation, the swap file is called the paging file.

swapping

The process of exchanging one item for another. In a virtual memory system, swapping occurs when a program requests a virtual memory location that is not currently in memory. Swapping may also refer to changing floppy or compact disks as needed when using a single disk drive.

symmetrical digital subscriber line

See *single-line digital subscriber line*.

synchronous DRAM

Abbreviated SDRAM or syncDRAM. A high-speed memory technology, faster than EDO RAM, used in high-end systems and servers. SDRAM runs at higher speeds than conventional DRAM by using a technique that attempts to predict the location of the next memory address to be accessed.

Synchronous Graphics RAM

Abbreviated SGRAM. A type of high-speed dynamic RAM used in video adapters.

T

T

See tera-.

T.120

A group of communications and applications protocols that support real-time, multipoint data communications over LANs, ISDN, dial-up, and Internet connections. T.120 became well known after Microsoft incorporated it into the NetMeeting package.

tape cartridge

A self-contained tape storage module, containing tape much like that in a video cassette. Tape cartridges are primarily used to back up hard disk systems.

tape drive

A computer peripheral device that reads from and writes to magnetic tape.

The drive may use tape on an open reel or from an enclosed tape cartridge. Because tape management software must search from the beginning of the tape every time it wants to find a file (a process called sequential access), tape is too slow to use as a primary storage system; however, tapes are frequently used to back up hard disks.

TB

See terabyte.

TCP

See Transmission Control Protocol.

TCP ports

In a TCP/IP network when a computer connects with another computer to access a specific service, an end-to-end connection is established and a socket is set up at each end of the connection. This socket is created at a particular port number, depending on the application in use.

TCP/IP

See Transmission Control Protocol/Internet Protocol.

Telnet

A terminal emulation protocol, part of the TCP/IP suite of protocols, that provides remote terminal-connection services.

The most common terminal emulations are for Digital Equipment Corporation (DEC) VT-52, VT-100, and VT-220 terminals, although many companies offer additional add-in emulations.

temporary swap file

A swap space that is created every time it is needed. A temporary swap file can consist of several discontinuous pieces of hard disk space. A temporary swap file does not occupy hard disk space if the application that created it is not running.

tera-

Abbreviated T. A prefix meaning 10^{12} in the metric system, 1,000,000,000,000; commonly referred to as one trillion in the American numbering system, and one million million in the British numbering system.

terabyte
Abbreviated TB. In computing, usually 2^{40}, or 1,099,511,627,776 bytes. Terabytes are used to represent extremely large hard disk capacities.

terminal emulation
A method of operation or software that makes a PC act like a terminal attached to a mainframe, usually for the purpose of telecommunications. Communications programs often include popular emulations, such as ANSI, VT-52, VT-100, VT-200, and TTY.

terminator
A device attached to the last peripheral device in a series, or the last node on a network.

For example, the last device on a SCSI bus must terminate the bus; otherwise, the bus will not perform properly. A 50-ohm resistor is placed at both ends of an Ethernet cable to prevent signals reflecting and interfering with the transmission.

text mode
A mode in which the computer displays characters on the screen using the built-in character set but does not show any graphics characters or a mouse pointer. Also known as character mode.

TFT display
See active-matrix display.

thick Ethernet
Connecting coaxial cable used on an Ethernet network; also known as thicknet.

The cable is one centimeter (0.4 inch) thick, almost as thick as your thumb, and can be used to connect network nodes up to a distance of approximately 1006 meters (3300 feet). Thick Ethernet is primarily used for facility-wide installations.

thicknet
See thick Ethernet.

thin Ethernet
Connecting coaxial cable used on an Ethernet network; also known as thinnet.

The cable is five millimeters (0.2 inch) thick, about as thick as your little finger, and can be used to connect network nodes up to a distance of approximately 165 meters (500 feet). Thin Ethernet is primarily used for office installations.

thin film transistor display
See active-matrix display.

thinnet
See thin Ethernet.

thrashing
An excessive amount of disk activity that causes a virtual memory system to spend all its time swapping pages in and out of memory and no time executing the application.

Thrashing can be caused when poor system configuration creates a swap file that is too small or when insufficient memory is installed in the computer. Increasing the size of the swap file or adding memory are often the best ways to reduce thrashing.

thread
1. A concurrent process that is part of a larger process or program. In a multitasking operating system, a single program may contain several threads, all

running at the same time. For example, one part of a program can be making a calculation while another part is drawing a graph or chart.

2. A connected set of postings to a Usenet newsgroup. Many newsreaders present postings as threads rather than in strict chronological order.

throughput

A measure of the data transfer rate through a complex communications or networking scheme.

Throughput is considered to be an indication of the overall performance of the system. For example, the throughput of a server depends on the processor type, operating system in use, hard disk capacity, network interface card in use, and the size of the data transfer buffer.

In communications, throughput is usually measured as the number of bits or packets processed each second.

TIA/EIA 586

A standard, jointly defined by the Telecommunications Industry Association and the Electronic Industries Association (TIA/EIA), for telecommunications wiring used in commercial buildings.

The standard is designed to:

▶ Specify a generic wiring system for all commercial buildings.

▶ Define media types, as well as connections and terminations.

▶ Provide a basis for interoperation between competing products and services in wiring, design, installation, and management.

▶ Allow for the wiring of a building before the definition of the products that will use

that wiring, and allow for elegant future expansion.

TIA/EIA 586 applies to all unshielded twisted-pair wiring that works with Ethernet, Token Ring, ISDN, and other networking systems.

TIA/EIA structured cabling standards

Standards specified by the Telecommunications Industries Association and the Electronics Industry Association (TIA/EIA), including:

▶ ANSI/TIA/EIA-568-1991 Commercial Building Telecommunications Wiring.

▶ TIA/EIA TSB-36 Additional Cable Specifications for UTP Cables. 1991.

▶ TIA/EIA TSB-40 Telecommunications Systems Bulletin—Additional Transmission Specifications for UTP Connecting Hardware. 1992.

▶ ANSI/TIA/EIA-568A 1995. Revises the original 568 document and adds material from TSB-36 and TSB-40.

▶ ANSI/TIA/EIA-569-1990 Commercial Building Standard for Telecommunications Pathways and Spaces.

▶ ANSI/TIA/EIA-570-1991 Residential and Light Commercial Telecommunications Wiring Standard.

▶ ANSI/TIA/EIA-606-1993 Administration Standard for the Telecommunications Infrastructure of Commercial Buildings.

▶ ANSI/TIA/EIA-607-1994 Commercial Building Grounding and Bonding Requirements for Telecommunications.

Local codes and standards may impose additional requirements.

Token Ring network

IBM's implementation of the token-ring network architecture, which uses a token-passing protocol transmitting at 4 or 16Mbps.

Using standard telephone wiring, a Token Ring network can connect up to 72 devices; with shielded twisted-pair (STP) wiring, each ring can support up to 256 nodes. Although it is based on a closed-loop ring structure, a Token Ring network uses a star-shaped cluster of up to eight nodes, all attached to the same wiring concentrator or multistation access unit (MAU). The MAUs are then connected to the main ring circuit.

A Token Ring network can include personal computers, minicomputers, and mainframes. The IEEE 802.5 standard defines token ring networks.

token ring network

A LAN with a ring structure that uses token passing to regulate traffic on the network and avoid collisions.

On a token ring network, the controlling network interface card generates a token that controls the right to transmit. This token is continuously passed from one node to the next around the network.

When a node has information to transmit, it captures the token, sets its status to busy, and adds the message and the destination address. All other nodes continuously read the token to determine if they are the recipient of a message. If they are, they collect the token, extract the message, and return the token to the sender. The sender then removes the message and sets the token status to free, indicating that it can be used by the next node in sequence.

top-level domains

On the Internet, the highest category of host name, which either signifies the type of institution or the country of its origin.

In the United States, the most common top-level domains include:

com A commercial organization. Most companies end up in this category.

edu An educational establishment such as a university.

gov A branch of the United States government.

int An international organization such as NATO or the United Nations.

mil A branch of the United States military.

net A network organization.

org A nonprofit organization.

Most countries also have unique domains named after their international abbreviations; for example, ca represents Canada, uk represents Great Britain, and jp represents Japan.

topology

The map of a network. Physical topology describes where the cables are run and where the workstations, nodes, routers, and gateways are located. Networks are usually configured in bus, ring, star, or mesh topologies. Logical topology refers to the paths that messages take to get from one user on the network to another.

TP

See twisted-pair cable.

track

One of the concentric data areas recorded onto a hard or floppy disk during a low-level format.

trackball

A device used for pointing, designed as a space-saving alternative to the mouse.

A trackball contains a movable ball that you rotate with your fingers to move the cursor on the screen. Because it does not need the area of flat space that a mouse needs, trackballs are popular with users of portable computers; Microsoft has released a small trackball that clips onto the side of a laptop computer, and IBM has developed a dual-button, touch-sensitive pointing stick called the TrackPoint.

Transmission Control Protocol

Abbreviated TCP. The transport-level protocol used in the TCP/IP suite of protocols. It works above IP in the protocol stack, and provides reliable data delivery over connection-oriented links.

TCP adds a header to the datagram that contains the information needed to get the datagram to its destination. The source port number and the destination port number allow data to be sent back and forth to the correct processes running on each computer. A sequence number allows the datagrams to be rebuilt in the correct order in the receiving computer, and a checksum verifies that the data received is the same as the data sent.

Transmission Control Protocol/Internet Protocol

Abbreviated TCP/IP. A set of communications protocols first developed by the Defense Advanced Research Projects Agency (DARPA) in the late 1970s. The set of TCP/IP protocols encompasses media access, packet transport, session communications, file transfer, e-mail, and terminal emulation.

TCP/IP is a widely published open standard and, while completely independent of any specific hardware or software company, it is supported by a huge number of vendors and is available on many different computers, from PCs to mainframes, running many different operating systems. Many corporations, universities, and government agencies use TCP/IP, and it is also the basis of the Internet.

TCP/IP is separated from the network hardware and will run over Ethernet, token ring, X.25 networks, and dial-up connections. It is a routable protocol, so datagrams can be sent over specific routes, and it has reliable and efficient data-delivery mechanisms. TCP/IP uses a common expandable addressing scheme, so any system can address any other system, even in a network as large as the Internet, and new networks can be added without service disruptions.

The popularity that the TCP/IP family of protocols enjoys today did not arise just because the protocols were available or even because the United States government mandated their use. They are popular because they are robust, solid protocols that solve many of the most difficult networking problems and do so in an elegant and efficient way.

transmission medium

The physical cabling used to carry network information, such as fiber optic, coaxial, shielded twisted-pair (STP), or unshielded twisted-pair (UTP) cabling.

Trojan Horse

A type of computer virus that pretends to be a useful program, such as a game or a utility program, to entice you to use it, when in reality it contains special code that will intentionally damage any system onto which it is loaded.

twisted-pair cable

Abbreviated TP. Cable that comprises two or more pairs of insulated wires twisted together, at six twists per inch.

In twisted-pair cable, one wire carries the signal and the other is grounded. The cable may be shielded or unshielded. Telephone wire installed in modern buildings is often twisted-pair wiring.

Type 1–9 cable

IBM Cabling System specifications, as follows:

Type 1 cable Shielded, twisted, dual-pair cable with 22-gauge solid conductors and a braided shield. Used with Token Ring networks.

Type 2 cable Two-pair, shielded cable with solid conductors and a braided shield. Type 2 also includes four pairs of unshielded voice-grade lines, giving a total of six pairs in the same sheath.

Type 3 cable Four unshielded, solid, twisted pairs, used for voice or data. IBM's variant of twisted-pair telephone wire.

Type 4 cable No published specification.

Type 5 cable Dual 100/140-micron fiber optic cable; IBM now recommends 125-micron fiber optic cable, which is the current industry standard for fiber optic cable.

Type 6 cable Shielded, two-pair, braided cable used for patch cables. Type 6 is more flexible than Type 1 cable.

Type 7 cable No published specification.

Type 8 cable Shielded, dual-pair cable with no twists, housed in a flat jacket; commonly used under carpets.

Type 9 cable Shielded, dual-pair, plenum cable with solid or braided conductors and a fire-resistant outer coating, for use between floors in a building.

U

UART

See Universal Asynchronous Receiver/ Transmitter.

UDP

See User Datagram Protocol.

Ultra SCSI

An extension of the SCSI-2 standard that increases the data transfer rate to 20Mbps independent of the bus width. Ultra SCSI supports four to eight devices depending on cable type and length.

Ultra2 SCSI

An extension of the SCSI-2 standard that increases the data transfer rate to 40Mbps over an eight-bit bus. Ultra2 SCSI supports up to eight devices.

Ultra Wide SCSI

An extension of the SCSI-2 standard that increases the data transfer rate to 80Mbps over a 16-bit bus. Ultra2 SCSI supports up to 16 devices.

uncompress

The process of restoring a compressed file to its original form.

Uniform Resource Locator

Abbreviated URL. An address for a resource on the Internet.

URLs are used as a linking mechanism between Web pages and as an access method for Web browsers to access Web pages.

A URL specifies the protocol to be used to access the resource (such as HTTP or FTP), the name of the server where the resource is located (as in `www.sybex.com`), the path to that resource (as in `/catalog`), and the name of the document to open (`/index.html`).

uninterruptible power supply

Abbreviated UPS, pronounced "you-pea-ess." An alternative power source, usually consisting of a set of batteries, used to power a computer system if the normal power service is interrupted or falls below acceptable levels.

A UPS system is usually applied only to the most critical devices on the network, such as servers, routers, gateways, and independent hard disks. They are of two main types:

- An online UPS continuously monitors and modifies the power flowing through the unit. If an outage occurs, the UPS continues to provide regulated power.
- A standby UPS monitors the AC level, but only switches in when the power drops below a preset level; it contains circuitry capable of switching to backup power in 5ms or less.

Universal Asynchronous Receiver/Transmitter

Abbreviated UART; pronounced "you-art." An electronic module that combines the transmitting and receiving circuitry needed for asynchronous communications over a serial line.

Universal Serial Bus

Abbreviated USB. A standard from Intel and Microsoft for a high-speed peripheral bus designed to remove the need for almost all the connectors on the back of a personal computer.

USB defines the ports and bus characteristics with data transfer rates of up to 12Mbps over a single cable of up to five meters (16 feet) long. USB is capable of supporting up to 63 devices, such as external CD-ROM drives, printers, external modems, mice, and the keyboard, without rebooting the system, and also supplies power to some devices so there is no need for separate power cords or batteries. Most personal computers will have two USB ports.

unshielded cable

Any cable not protected from electromagnetic interference or radio frequency interference (RFI) by an outer foil shield.

unshielded twisted-pair cable

Abbreviated UTP. Cable that contains two or more pairs of twisted copper wires.

The greater the number of twists, the lower the crosstalk. UTP is offered in both voice grade and data grade. The advantages of UTP include ease of installation and low cost of materials. Its drawbacks are limited signaling speeds and shorter maximum cable-segment lengths.

UPS

See uninterruptible power supply.

UPS monitoring

The process that a server uses to make sure that an attached UPS (uninterruptible power supply) system is functioning properly.

URL

See Uniform Resource Locator.

USB

See Universal Serial Bus.

Usenet newsgroups

The individual discussion groups within Usenet.

Usenet newsgroups contain articles posted by Internet and Usenet subscribers; very few of them actually contain hard news.

Most newsgroups are concerned with a single subject, and the range of subjects throughout Usenet is simply phenomenal; if people are interested in a topic, you will find a newsgroup for that topic.

User Datagram Protocol

Abbreviated UDP. The connectionless, transport-level protocol used in the TCP/IP suite of protocols, usually bundled with IP-layer software. Because UDP does not add overhead, as does connection-oriented TCP, UDP is often used with SNMP (Simple Network Management Protocol) applications.

Multicast applications such as Mbone and the Real-time Transport Protocol that deliver audio and video streams use UDP as their delivery mechanism because the acknowledgment and retransmission services offered by TCP are not needed and add too much overhead. If a packet of audio data is lost, retransmission is neither practical nor desirable.

UTP

See unshielded twisted-pair cable.

V

V.90

A modem standard; also known as the 56K modem standard. V.90 describes an asymmetric connection, with theoretical speeds of up to 56Kbps downstream and an upstream connection rate of up to 33.6Kbps.

V.90 modems attain their high speed by assuming the circuit is a digital circuit and reducing the number of analog-to-digital conversions they perform, except for the conversion that takes place for outbound traffic at your modem.

Whether you actually achieve these rates depends on the quality of the phone line and the distance to the local telephone company central office. If the other end of the connection is not digital, the modem switches into full analog mode at 28.8 or 33.6Kbps.

In order to reduce crosstalk between adjacent lines, the FCC has placed restrictions on maximum signal strength levels and so 54Kbps is the theoretical maximum data rate.

vaccine

A utility program designed to protect files from viruses. By adding a small amount of code to an existing file, the vaccine program causes an alert to be generated if a virus does attack.

VBScript

A version of Microsoft Visual Basic used as a scripting language in Microsoft Internet Explorer Web browser.

very high-bit-rate digital subscriber line

Abbreviated VDSL. A higher-speed version of asymmetrical digital subscriber line (ADSL).

VDSL is asymmetrical with a higher downstream data transfer rate than its upstream rate. Upstream rates can be from 1.6Mbps to 2.3Mbps, while downstream rates range from 12.96Mbps to 51.84Mbps, depending on the distance involved.

very low-frequency emission

Abbreviated VLF. Radiation emitted by a computer monitor and other common household electrical appliances, such as televisions, hair dryers, electric blankets, and food processors.

VLF emissions range from 2 to 400kHz and decline with the square of the distance from the source. Emissions are not constant around a computer monitor; they are higher from the sides and rear and weakest from the front of the screen.

Sweden is the only country to have defined a set of standards for monitor emissions. In 1990, Mat Oct Provadet (MPR), the Swedish National Board for Meterology and Testing, revised its guidelines for acceptable VLF emissions as less than or equal to 25 nanoTesla (nT). A nanoTesla is a unit of measurement for small magnetic fields.

video adapter

An adapter that provides the text and graphics output to the monitor. Some video adapters, such as the SVGA, are included in the circuitry on the motherboard rather than as separate plug-in boards.

video conferencing

A method used to allow people at remote locations to join in a conference and share information. Originally done with analog video and expensive satellite links, video conferencing is now performed with compressed digital video transmitted over a LAN or the Internet.

From an application standpoint, video conferencing has gone way beyond looking at a picture of a person; users can look at and update charts, make drawings or sketches on a chalkboard, update spreadsheets, and so on, all online.

video RAM

Abbreviated VRAM, pronounced "vee-ram."
Special-purpose RAM with two data paths for
access (conventional RAM has just one).
These two paths let a VRAM board manage
two functions at once: refreshing the display
and communicating with the processor.
VRAM does not require the system to complete one function before starting the other,
so it allows faster operation for the whole
video system.

virtual memory

A memory-management technique that
allows information in physical memory to be
swapped out to a hard disk if necessary.

This technique provides applications with
more memory space than is actually available in the computer. True virtual-memory
management requires specialized hardware
in the processor for the operating system to
use; it is not just a matter of writing information out to a swap area on the hard disk at
the application level.

In a virtual memory system, programs
and their data are divided into smaller pieces
called *pages*. When more memory is needed,
the operating system decides which pages
are least likely to be needed soon (using an
algorithm based on frequency of use, most
recent use, and program priority), and it
writes these pages out to disk. The memory
space that they used is now available to the
rest of the system for other applications.
When these pages are needed again, they are
loaded back into real memory, displacing
other pages.

virus

A program intended to damage a computer
system without the user's knowledge or
permission.

A virus clones itself from disk to disk, or
from system to system over a network. Numbers are hard to come by, but certain authorities claim that there are approximately
30,000 known viruses, with 400 new ones
appearing each month.

A virus may attach itself to another program or to the partition table or boot track
on a hard disk. When a certain event occurs,
a date passes, or a specific program executes, the virus is triggered into action. Others, including the ILOVEYOU virus, take
advantage of the trusting relationship that
exists between Microsoft Office applications
and run as scripts as soon as an e-mail
attachment is opened.

VLF

See very low-frequency emission.

VRAM

See video RAM.

W

wait state

A clock cycle during which no instructions
are executed because the processor is waiting for data from memory.

Static RAM chips and paged-mode RAM
chips can store information without being
constantly refreshed by the processor, thus
eliminating the wait state. A computer that
can process information without wait states
is known as a zero-wait-state computer.

WAN

See wide area network.

warm boot

A reboot performed after the operating system has been running for some period of time, by pressing Ctrl+Alt+Del rather than cycling the power to the computer.

wavetable synthesis

A method used by a sound board to simulate musical instruments. Wavetable synthesis uses digitized samples of real orchestral instruments, which are edited and mixed to produce music. FM synthesis is cheaper than wavetable synthesis but is also of much lower quality.

Web browser

A client application that lets you look at hypertext documents, follow links to other HTML documents, and download files on the Internet or on a corporate intranet.

When you find something that interests you as you browse through a hypertext document, you can click on that object, and the system automatically takes care of accessing the Internet host that holds the document you requested; you don't need to know the IP address, the name of the host system, or any other details. A Web browser will also display the graphics in a Web page, play audio and video clips, and execute small Java or ActiveX programs called applets.

Netscape Navigator and Microsoft Internet Explorer are examples of popular Web browsers.

Webcam

A low-cost video camera used to capture live images for display on a Web site. Webcams are used to display traffic information, activity inside a person's apartment, fish tanks, scenic views, and street scenes.

Web page

Information placed on a Web server for viewing with a Web browser. A Web page may contain text, graphics, audio or video clips, and links to other Web pages.

Web server

A hardware and software package that provides services to client computers running Web browsers.

Clients make requests in the form of HTTP messages; the server responds to these messages, returning Web pages or other requested documents to the client. Most Web servers run one of the versions of Unix, or Microsoft Windows 2000 Server.

Web site

A group of HTML documents and associated scripts supported by a Web server on the World Wide Web.

Most Web sites have a home page used as a starting point or index into the site, with other Web pages or even other Web sites connected by links. To connect to a Web site, you need an Internet connection and a Web browser.

wide area network

Abbreviated WAN. A network that connects users across large distances, often crossing the geographical boundaries of cities or states.

Wide SCSI

A version of the SCSI-2 standard that provides data transfer rates of up to 20MBps over a 16-bit data bus.

Wide Ultra SCSI

A version of the SCSI-2 standard that provides data transfer rates of up to 40MBps over a 16-bit data bus.

Wide Ultra2 SCSI

A version of the SCSI-2 standard that provides data transfer rates of up to 80MBps over a 16-bit data bus.

wildcard character

A character that represents one or more unknown characters. In many operating systems, a question mark (?) represents a single unknown character in a filename or filename extension, and an asterisk (*) represents any number of unknown characters.

Windows Internet Naming Service

Abbreviated WINS. A Microsoft Windows NT Server and Windows 2000 Server service that maps NetBIOS computer names used in Windows networks to IP addresses used in TCP/IP-based networks. WINS is almost completely automated; it builds its own database and manages updates to the database.

WINS

See Windows Internet Naming Service.

Wintel

A contraction of Windows and Intel. Referring to an Intel-based computer that runs Microsoft Windows.

wireless communications

A method of connecting a node or a group of nodes into the main network using a technology other than conventional cabling.

The following methods are in use:

Infrared line of sight High-frequency light waves are used to transmit data between nodes up to 24.4 meters (80 feet) apart using an unobstructed path; infrared beams cannot pass through masonry walls. Data rates are relatively high, in the tens of megabits per second range.

High-frequency radio High-frequency radio signals transmit data to nodes from 12.2 to 39.6 meters (40 to 130 feet) apart, depending on the nature of obstructions separating them; the signal can penetrate thin walls but not supporting masonry. Data rates are usually less than 1Mbps.

Spread-spectrum radio A small set of frequencies is available for wireless LANs without FCC approval. The 902 to 928MHz band is known as the Industrial, Scientific, Medical (ISM) band and is not regulated. The 2.4 to 2.483GHz band is regulated and requires an FCC license for use. Spread-spectrum nodes can be up to 243.8 meters (800 feet) apart in an open environment, and these radio waves can pass through masonry walls. However, in an environment with fully enclosed offices, distances are limited to 33.5 meters (110 feet). Data rates are usually less than 1Mbps.

Wireless LANs are not always completely wireless. They may be used to replace the cabling on certain network segments or to connect groups of networks that use conventional cabling.

World Wide Web

Abbreviated WWW, W3, or simply the Web. A huge collection of hypertext pages on the Internet.

World Wide Web concepts were developed in Switzerland by the European Laboratory for Particle Physics (known as CERN), but the Web is not just a tool for scientists; it is one of the most flexible and exciting tools in existence.

Hypertext links connect pieces of information (text, graphics, animation, audio, and video) in separate HTML pages located at the same or at different Internet sites, and you explore these pages and links using a Web browser such as Netscape Navigator or Microsoft Internet Explorer.

You can also access a Web resource directly if you specify the appropriate URL (Uniform Resource Locator).

World Wide Web traffic is growing faster than most other Internet services, and the reason for this becomes obvious once you try a capable Web browser; it is very easy and a lot of fun to access World Wide Web information.

write-back cache

A technique used in cache design for writing information back into main memory.

In a write-back cache, the cache stores the changed block of data but only updates main memory under certain conditions, such as when the whole block must be overwritten because a newer block must be loaded into the cache, or when the controlling algorithm determines that too much time has elapsed since the last update. This method is rather complex to implement, but is much faster than other designs.

write-through cache

A technique used in cache design for writing information back into main memory.

In a write-through cache, each time the processor returns a changed bit of data to the cache, the cache updates that information in both the cache and in main memory. This method is simple to implement but is not as fast as other designs; delays can be introduced when the processor must wait to complete write operations to slower main memory.

WWW

See World Wide Web.

X

XON/XOFF

In asynchronous transmissions between two PCs, a simple method of flow control.

The receiving PC sends an XOFF control character (ASCII 19, Ctrl+S) to pause the transmission of data when the receive buffer is full, and then sends an XON character

(ASCII 17, Ctrl+Q) when it is ready to continue the transmission.

Z

ZBR

See Zone Bit Recording.

zero insertion force socket

Abbreviated ZIF socket. A specially designed chip socket that makes replacing a chip easier and safer.

To change a chip in a ZIF socket, you raise a lever beside the socket to free the original chip's pins from the socket. Then slide the old chip out and slide in the replacement chip, taking care to align the pins and holes. Finally, lower the lever again. A ZIF socket minimizes damage to the delicate pins that connect the chip to the rest of the system.

ZIF socket

See zero insertion force socket.

Zip drive

A popular removable storage device from Iomega Corporation, capable of 100MB or 250MB of storage on relatively cheap, portable, 3½-inch disks.

Zip drives have emerged as the de facto standard personal computer backup device.

ZIP file

A file whose contents have been compressed by one of the popular file-compression utilities, such as PKZIP, WinZip, or other comparable program; the filename extension is ZIP.

A ZIP file can contain a single compressed file, or a whole collection of archives. A file compressed in this way is said to have been zipped.

To uncompress a ZIP file, use the same utility that compressed it originally. Some ZIP files are self-extracting and can uncompress themselves when you click their icon.

Zone Bit Recording

Abbreviated ZBR. A Seagate Technologies term for multiple zone recording.

APPENDIX

Sample A+ Core Module Exam Questions

The A+ Certification testing program is sponsored by the Computer Technology Industry Association (CompTIA) and backed by major computer hardware and software vendors, retailers, and distributors. The A+ Certification provides employers with a benchmark for evaluating employees' knowledge.

In order to attain A+ Certification, candidates must pass two exams: the Core Module and the DOS/Windows Module. The Core Module exam is designed to test an applicant's knowledge of basic PC troubleshooting and repair techniques. This appendix contains a sample of the type of questions you can expect to find on the A+ Core Module exam.

While many of the topics included in the Core Module exam are covered in this book, I recommend it only as supplemental A+ study material. Sybex also publishes comprehensive study guides for the A+ certification. Check out your local bookstores or online booksellers for *A+ Complete Study Guide* written by David Groth and published by Sybex, 1999.

For detailed information about the A+ Certification program, visit the CompTIA Web site at `www.comptia.org`.

Sample A+ Core Module Exam Questions

1. Which of the following is *not* a consideration when upgrading the RAM on a common PC?

   A. Number of pins

   B. Parity

   C. Speed

   D. Number of clusters

2. What primary precaution should you take when replacing a keyboard?

   A. Completely power down the system

   B. Turn off the keyboard

   C. Wear an ESD strap

   D. Use a screwdriver

3. What is the standard I/O address for COM2?

   A. 2F8–2FF

   B. 3F8–3FF

   C. 2E8–2EF

   D. 3E8–3EF

4. What is the standard I/O address for COM3?

   A. 2F8

   B. 3F8

   C. 2E8

   D. 3E8

5. What is the standard I/O address for COM4?

   A. 2F8

   B. 3F8

   C. 2E8

   D. 3E8

6. Where is IDE hard disk drive configuration information kept?

   A. Hard disk controller

   B. CMOS

   C. `CONFIG.SYS`

   D. `AUTOEXEC.BAT`

7. Which of the following is an invalid DMA channel in a machine that contains an ISA bus?

   A. 0

   B. 1

   C. 5

   D. 8

8. What is IRQ6 used for in most PCs?

   A. Hard disk controller

   B. PS/2 mouse

   C. Floppy controller

   D. LPT1

9. How many pins does a standard serial port contain?

   A. 9

   B. 15

    C. 20

    D. 40

10. An IDE hard disk drive cable has how many pins?

    A. 10

    B. 34

    C. 40

    D. 50

11. Standard bidirectional parallel ports use which standard?

    A. RS-232C

    B. RS-241

    C. RJ-45

    D. IEEE 1284

12. Where are ROM BIOS routines stored?

    A. Hard disk 0

    B. Floppy disk

    C. CMOS

    D. Hard disk controller

13. Which component is activated first in a normal boot sequence?

    A. CPU

    B. Floppy disk

    C. Hard disk

    D. Memory

14. On ISA buses, which IRQ gets cascaded to IRQ9 to provide additional IRQ addresses?

    A. 1

    B. 2

    C. 3

    D. 4

15. A 25-pin D-shell connector is most often used for:

    A. Serial port

    B. Parallel port

    C. SCSI port

    D. Mouse port

16. A 15-pin, 2-row D-shell connector is most often used for:

    A. Parallel port

    B. Serial port

    C. Video port

    D. Game port

17. What may have to be upgraded when installing an EIDE drive?

    A. Memory

    B. BIOS

    C. Case

    D. Monitor

18. ATAPI provides which major benefit?

    A. Attaches up to four devices

    B. Adds a larger monitor

C. Adds a MIDI component

D. Compresses data

19. Each device on a wide SCSI bus must have its own unique SCSI ID.

A. True

B. False

20. What is the maximum bus length of a SCSI-2 Fast/Wide SCSI bus?

A. 1 meter

B. 2 meters

C. 3 meters

D. 4 meters

21. You have just installed a sound card. You now notice both your printer and your new sound card don't work. What is the most likely source of the problem?

A. Your printer is broken.

B. You've damaged the sound card during installation.

C. Your motherboard is faulty.

D. The sound card is set to the same IRQ as the printer port.

22. Your computer was accidentally shut off during the boot process. After turning it back on, you receive an error: "Bad or Missing Operating System." What is the most likely cause of the error?

A. Corrupt master boot record (MBR)

B. Power failure

C. Bad RAM

D. Bad monitor

23. You are trying to figure out what is wrong with your computer. When you turn on the computer, no video appears on the monitor, and the hard disk isn't making any noise. The only noise you hear is the power supply fan. Which of the following could be eliminated as a possible cause?

    A. Keyboard unplugged

    B. Power supply unplugged

    C. Monitor unplugged

    D. Hard disk failed

24. What voltage range should your multimeter be set to when measuring household AC voltage?

    A. 50

    B. 100

    C. 200

    D. 500

25. Which AT command will cause a modem to hang up?

    A. ATDT

    B. ATH

    C. ATDP

    D. AT

26. After downloading a new game from the Internet, your computer experiences strange, nonreproducible errors. What is the most likely cause?

    A. A virus

    B. Modem failure

C. Motherboard failure

D. Monitor failure

27. You are on the phone with a user who is trying to get a CD-ROM to work. They just finished installing it. What should you ask them first?

A. Is the cardboard insert still in the drive?

B. Can you change the IRQ to 5?

C. What did you mess up?

D. How much RAM do you have?

28. What should you use to clean a computer's case?

A. Emery cloth

B. Contact cleaning solution

C. Jeweler's cloth

D. Silicon carbide

29. What can you install to protect your computer against power spikes?

A. Power supply

B. Surge suppressor

C. Lightning rod

D. SPS

30. Store laser printer OPC drums in what kind of environment?

A. Warm, light

B. Warm, dark

C. Cool, light

D. Cool, dark

31. You should always wear an ESD grounding strap, except under what conditions?

    A. When servicing a printer

    B. When servicing a monitor

    C. When servicing a PC

    D. When servicing electronic equipment of any kind

32. What component is installed in an ESD strap to prevent shock?

    A. Resistor

    B. Capacitor

    C. Wire

    D. SIMM

33. What conditions promote ESD?

    A. Cool, dry

    B. Cool, wet

    C. Warm, dry

    D. Warm, wet

34. Memory locations are called ports.

    A. True

    B. False

35. Which of the following is a feature of EDO RAM?

    A. Intelligent data recovery

    B. Faster data transfer

    C. Support for more processor types

    D. Permanent storage

36. Which of the following is *not* a common PC bus expansion type?

    A. ISA

    B. OSB

    C. VLB

    D. PCI

37. Which of the following is *not* stored in the CMOS?

    A. Disk geometry

    B. Time

    C. Modem speed

    D. Memory configuration

38. A system that keeps losing the time and date is most likely caused by:

    A. System battery going dead

    B. Clock going bad

    C. Motherboard failing

    D. Bad sectors on the hard disk

39. Where is the boot sequence changed?

    A. BOOTCFG.EXE

    B. CMOS setup

    C. MSD

    D. ESD

40. Which EP printer component moves toner from the EP drum to the paper?

    A. Pickup roller

    B. Fuser roller

    C. Print head

    D. Corona wire

41. You just bought a new inkjet printer. After unpacking it, installing the ink cartridge, and installing the printer driver, the printer only produces blank pages. What is the *most likely* cause of the problem?

    A. The ink cartridge is plugged.

    B. You are using the wrong paper.

    C. You forgot to remove the sealing tape from the ink cartridge.

    D. The printer isn't plugged in.

42. A laser printer is printing all black pages. What is the *most likely* cause of the problem?

    A. Primary (charging) corona wire is broken or malfunctioning.

    B. Transfer corona is broken or malfunctioning.

    C. Laser is broken or malfunctioning.

    D. Fuser is broken or malfunctioning.

43. Which PC Card type is most often used for hard disks?

    A. Type I

    B. Type II

    C. Type III

    D. Type IV

44. To use resources on a network, you need:

    A. A print server

    B. Rights

    C. A file server

    D. A hard disk

45. Rules used to govern network communications are called:

    A. IEEE

    B. Laws

    C. Standards

    D. Protocols

46. To override PnP and configure an expansion card manually, which of the following must you disable?

    A. RJ-45

    B. IRQ6

    C. Plug and Play

    D. DMA

Answers

1. D	24. C
2. A	25. B
3. A	26. A
4. B	27. A
5. C	28. C
6. B	29. B
7. D	30. D
8. C	31. D
9. A	32. A
10. C	33. C
11. D	34. B
12. C	35. B
13. A	36. B
14. B	37. C
15. B	38. A
16. D	39. B
17. B	40. D
18. A	41. C
19. A	42. A
20. C	43. C
21. D	44. B
22. A	45. D
23. A	46. C

Credits

Figure 1.2 SOUND BLASTER is a trademark of Creative Technology Ltd. (www.soundblaster.com and www.creative.com).

Figure 2.4 provided by JDR Microdevices (www.jdr.com).

Figure 2.9 provided by PC Cables and Parts (www.pccables.com).

Figure 3.3 © Photopia.

Figure 3.4 Intel® Pentium® III Processor 600 MHz is a trademark of Intel. © 2000 Intel Corporation. All Rights Reserved. (www.intel.com)

Figure 3.9 © Photopia.

Figures 3.10 Rambus RIMM © 2000 Reprinted by permission of Kingston Technology Company, Inc. All Rights Reserved.

Figures 3.20, 3.21, and 3.22 © Photopia.

Figure 3.25 © Photopia.

Figure 3.27 RS-232 Reproduced courtesy of International Business Machines Corporation. Unauthorized use not permitted.

Figure 3.28 and 3.29 © Photopia.

Figures 3.31, 3.32, and 3.33 © Photopia.

Figure 4.1 110 Alert Heat Alarm manufactured by PC Power & Cooling, Inc. (www.pcpowercooling.com)

Figure 9.4 © Photopia.

Figure 9.5 © Photopia.

Figures 22.1 and 22.2 © Photopia.

Figure 29.1 Xircom 100. (www.xircom.com) © 2000 Xircom, Inc. All Rights Reserved.

Figure 29.3 © 2000 Palm Inc. All Rights Reserved. Palm™ handhelds and the Palm logo are registered trademarks of Palm Inc. or its subsidiaries.

Figures 31.2 and 31.3 provided by Intel Corporation (www.intel.com).

Index

Numbers

"0 hard disk(s) found" message, 732
2.1GB barrier, 535
2B+D abbreviation, 1402
3D video boards, **939–940**
3Dfx chip sets, 939–940
3DNow! Technology instructions, 135
4.2GB barrier, 535
5-bit error correction, 527
6x86 CPU, **133–134**
8-bit boards
    vs. 16-bit, **381–382**
    conflicts with, **381–382**
    slots for, 176–177, 179
    180–181
    sound cards, 964–965
8 mm format, 991
8.4GB barrier, 535
10/100 devices, 1401
10Base-2 networks, 235
10Base-5 networks, 241

10Base-T cable, 1402
10Base-T networks, 235,
    240, 241, 1401
10Base-TX cable, 1402
10Mbps, 1402
11-bit error correction, 527
16-bit applications, system
    file backups for,
    688–689
16-bit boards
    conflicts with, **381–382**
    slots for, **178–184**
    180–181
    sound cards, 964–965
23B+D abbreviation, 1402
24/7 availability, 1402
24-bit color, 1402
30-pin memory chips, 139,
    140, 430, *430*
32-bit boards
    slots for, **184–185**
    sound cards, 964–965
32GB barrier, 535

50-ohm cable terminators,
    1088
"55" error message, **830–831**
64-bit bus, **190–194**, *191*
64-bit computers, memory
    banks on, **432–433**
64-bit sound cards, 964–965
70-bit error correction, 527
72-Hz video, 938
72-pin memory chips, 139,
    140, **430–431**, *430*
75-ohm cable terminators,
    1088
76-bit error correction, 703
80-Hz video, 938
100Mbps, 1402
101-key keyboard, 899–900
110 Alert product, 254
120-Hz video, 938
"162" message, 305
386 extension, 151
528MB barrier, 534
"1701" message, 732

process for, **629–630**
quick steps in,
613–614
third-party tools for,
631
troubleshooting, **632**
for frame captures, **1015**
future of, **491**
in generic computers,
1152
hardware structure of,
497–504, *501–503*
heat damage to, **680–683**
heat from, 250
identifying, 227
installing. *See* installing
interfaces for, **492–497**,
1437
interleave factor for,
518–525, *520–524*
IRQs for, 355
logical, 617–618
cluster size in,
618–621
partitioning, 624–626
structure of, **649–651**,
649–651
logical block addressing
for, **508–510**, **537**
with lost clusters,
715–719, *716*, *718*
master/slave jumpers in,
551–556
media errors on, **724–728**
media tests for, **699–703**
motors in, 256
mounting, **1186**
in notebooks, **1174–1175**,
1184–1195
for old computer data,
1273–1274, *1273*
operating system limita-
tions for, **537–538**
parking heads in, 512
partitioning. *See* partitioning hard disk drives

for PC Card bus, 198,
1194–1195
PIO transfer in, **538–539**
and power surges, 269
preventive maintenance
for, **679**
protecting data. *See* data
protection; viruses
recovering data. *See*
recovering hard disk
data
rotational latency period
of, **515–517**
searching for text on,
711–712
sector translation in,
506–508
seek time of, **514–515**
size limitations in,
531–537
stepper motors for,
512–513
terms for, **492–494**
testing, **1191–1192**
timeouts with, **407**
tracing failures in,
729–730, *730*
type information for,
683–684, 1437
for ultimate computer,
1306–1307
unfragmenting files on,
703–705, *703*, *705*
for upgrading, 1158
in video capture, 1009
viruses on. *See* viruses
voice coils for, **511–512**,
511
hard errors on hard drives,
630–631
hard resets, 1437
hard rubber, triboelectric
value of, 273
hardware
in boot process, **402**
compatibility in, **8–9**
Control Panel for

not found by system,
1372–1374, *1372*
quick steps for,
1355–1356
wizard for, **1368–1371**,
1368
controllers for, **206–208**
defined, 1437
newsgroups for,
1252–1254
in reading MBR, **731–736**
software faults from, **305**
hardware addresses,
1437–1438
hardware compatibility list,
1438
hardware decoders for DVD
drives, 1309
hardware-dependence, 1438
hardware-independence,
1438
hardware interrupts, 1438
Hare virus, 666
Hawking, Stephen, 1368
Hayes modems, 865–866
HD manufacturer code, 416
"HDD Configuration Error"
message, 1191
HDD label, 1350
HDSL (high-bit-rate digital
subscriber line)
characteristics of, 880
defined, 1438–1439
frequency bands in, 881
HDX (half-duplex)
defined, 1436
and echo, 888
head gaps, 681
heads
disk, 497–498, *498*
for absolute sectors,
637–640, *637*
cleaning, **751–752**
and cylinder skew,
525–526
in disk drive geometry,
506

SYBEX BOOKS ON THE WEB

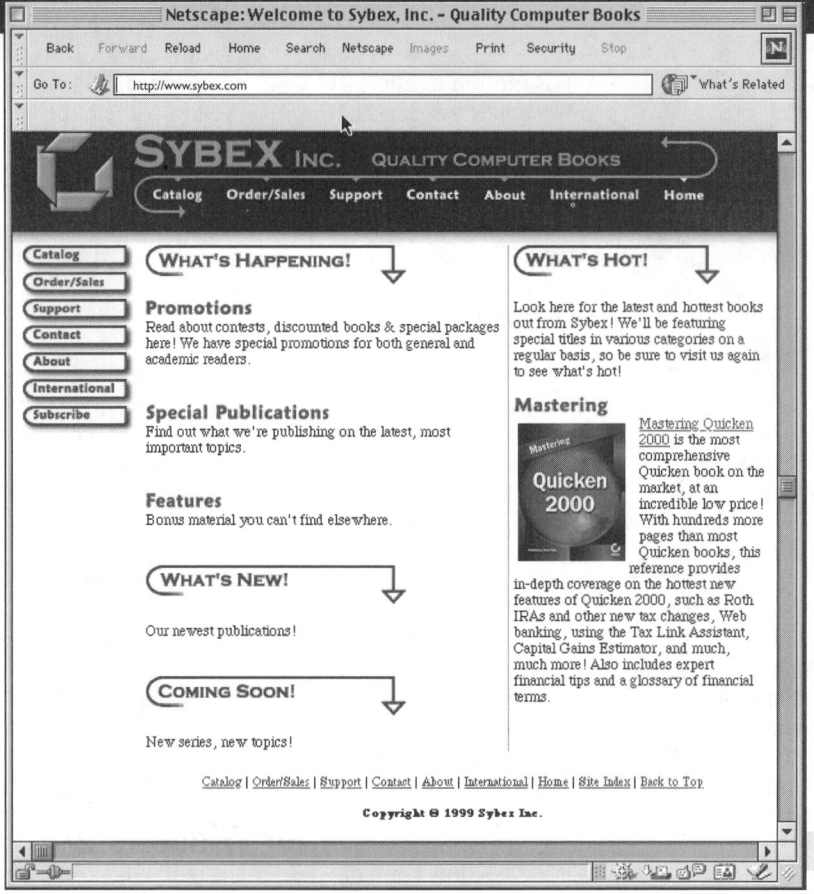

A t the dynamic and informative Sybex Web site, you can:

- · view our complete online catalog
- · preview a book you're interested in
- · access special book content

- · order books online at special discount prices
- · learn about Sybex

www.sybex.com

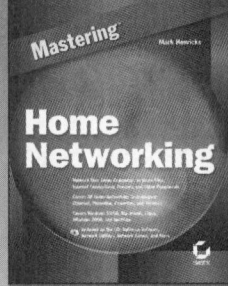

A+™ TEST PREPARATION FROM THE EXPERTS

Sybex presents the most comprehensive study guides
for CompTIA's A+ exams for PC technicians.

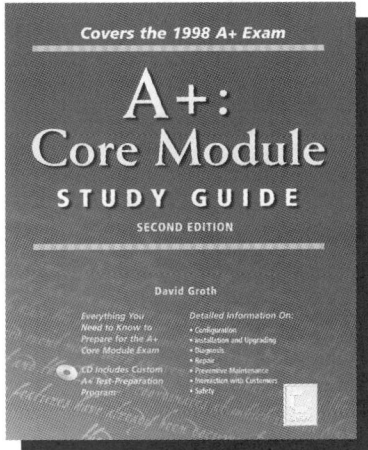

ISBN 0-7821-2344-9
800 pp. 7½" x 9" $49.99
Hardcover

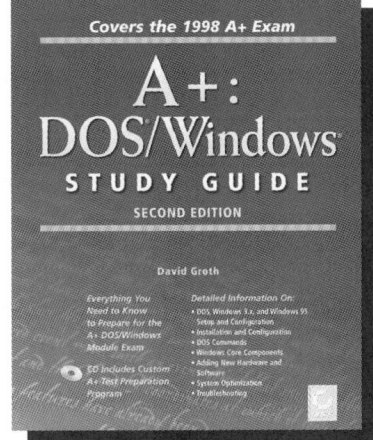

ISBN 0-7821-2351-1
688 pp. 7½" x 9" $49.99
Hardcover

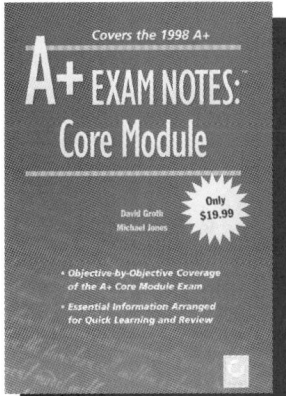

ISBN 0-7821-2345-7
304 pp. 5⅞" x 8¼" $19.99
Softcover

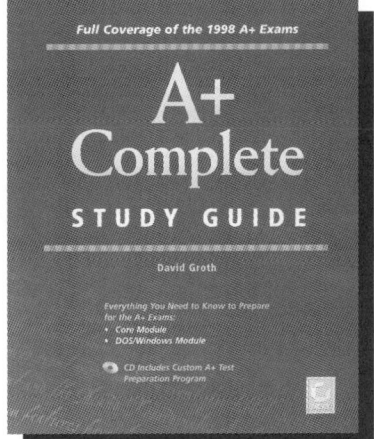

ISBN 0-7821-2490-9
1104 pp. 7½" x 9" $49.99
Softcover

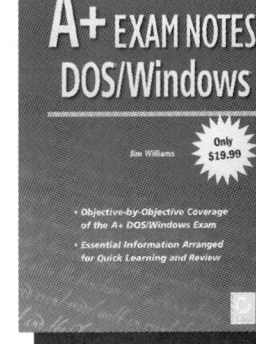

ISBN 0-7821-2346-5
304 pp. 5⅞" x 8¼" $19.99
Softcover

Visual JumpStart Books from Sybex

The Fast and Easy Way to Learn!

AutoCAD 2000 — 0-7821-2777-0 · $19.99

Home Networking — 0-7821-2795-9 · $19.99

Dreamweaver Fireworks — Available soon

Photoshop — Available soon

Visual JumpStart
The FAST and Easy Way to
Get Up and Running...

Are you tired of wading through an ocean of text when you want to learn new software? If so, why not try *Visual JumpStart* books from Sybex? Just look at these features:

- **Clear step-by-step explanations**

- **Concise coverage of essential features and tasks**

- **Easy-to-read screen shots reinforce your understanding**

- **Eye-pleasing illustrations to guide you through each task**

- **Real-world insights from expert trainers**

www.sybex.com

SYBEX®

CD #1
Mark Minasi PC Upgrading Videos

The CD in the front of the book contains approximately 60 minutes of video created exclusively by Sybex and Mark Minasi in July, 1999. These videos explore the essential upgrades that users generally make to their PCs and follow the format used in Mark Minasi's $800 Upgrading and Maintenance seminars.

No other PC book contains this much, or such up-to-date videos.

The contents include:

→ **The Central Processing Unit** Examine the new Pentium cartridges and learn how to install them.

→ **Motherboards** Take a tour of all of the components on today's typical motherboard.

→ **Power Supply** Learn how to replace a power supply in a matter of minutes.

→ **Computer Memory** Learn about types of memory and memory boards, and see how to install and uninstall SDRAM cards.

→ **Installing a DVD drive** Watch Mark install a DVD decoder card and the DVD drive itself; learn how to make all the right connections—without making any mistakes.

→ **Installing a Hard Drive** See how to install a drive, set the master/slave switches, connect all of the data and power cables—whether this is your first hard drive in your PC or your second or third.

→ **Circuit Boards** Learn tips and tricks about installing most circuit boards in your PC—from video cards to modems.

→ **Installing Sound Cards** Watch Mark install a sound card and connect it to a CD player.

The CD also provides Apple QuickTime 4, which you can use to view the files. QuickTime and the QuickTime logo are trademarks used under license. QuickTime is registered in the U.S. and other countries.

NOTE To view the files you'll need a Pentium 120 and a 4x CD-ROM drive although a Pentium 166 or better is recommended.

→ CD #2
The Upgrader's Toolbox

The CD at the back of the book contains A+ Preparation Software, useful utilities, and a bonus appendix that lists hard drives available on the market today.

A+ Preparation Software

Direct from David Groth's best-selling *A+ Complete Study Guide* are two test engines designed to get you up to speed for CompTIA's challenging A+ certification tests.

→ 199 Core Module practice questions   → 175 DOS/Windows practice questions

Utilities

The CD includes several valuable utilities that will assist you in your day-to-day computer activities, including

→ **Adobe Acrobat Reader**, from Adobe Systems, allows you to view portable document files (.PDF) created in Adobe Acrobat.

→ **AEF Disk**, from Nagy Daniel, creates disk partitions. AEF Disk is a utility that system administrators, schools, and computer store employees should not overlook.

→ **Internet Service Assistant**, from HL Lab Software, helps you check your connectivity problems, detects your connection speed, and can even detect who is working with your Internet Channel.

→ **MemWatcher**, from Matrix Software, is a small, system-tray utility that monitors your PC's memory, CPU, and resource usage.

→ **PartitionMagic**, from PowerQuest Corporation, allows you to create, resize, and merge partitions on your hard drive without destroying data.

→ **Registry Medic**, from easydesksoftware.com, is a System utility for repairing Registry Errors. It works on all versions of Windows 95 and Windows 98.

→ **Security Administrator**, from Ixis Ltd., restricts access to your computer. This password-protected security utility enables you to impose a variety of access restrictions to protect your privacy and stop others from tampering with your desktop. Security Administrator works with Windows 95 and Windows 98.

→ **Super System Info**, from Robert Nall/SC Productions, is a small system information program used to gather specific details from the computer and operating system. It displays information about the CPU such as which type of file extensions are registered on the user's computer system.

→ **System Mechanic**, from Iolo Technologies, keeps your PC running faster, cleaner, and error free. System Mechanic contains 12 powerful tools built for Windows.

→ **Tool Pro**, from Peter Pearson, is a tray program with many miscellaneous tools and utilities, including: POP3 Client, SMTP Client, DNS Lookup, Check Mail, Keep Alive, Download Files, Web Site Update Checker, Hotkey Support, etc.

→ **Windows Rescue Kit**, from Super Win Softare, gives you three Utilities in one: Crash fixer, File Backup, and Troubleshooter.

→ **WinXFiles**, from PEPSOFT, is an image encryption application that transforms your image files from public view to for-your-eyes-only.

●●●How Do I?●●